D1611338

VALUATION

MEASURING AND MANAGING THE VALUE OF COMPANIES

VALUATION

MEASURING AND MANAGING THE VALUE OF COMPANIES

SEVENTH EDITION

McKinsey & Company

Tim Koller
Marc Goedhart
David Wessels

WILEY

Published by John Wiley & Sons, Inc., Hoboken, New Jersey.
Published simultaneously in Canada.

For general information on our other products and services or for technical support, please contact our Customer Care Department within the United States at (800) 762-2974, outside the United States at (317) 572-3993 or fax (317) 572-4002.

Wiley publishes in a variety of print and electronic formats and by print-on-demand. Some material included with standard print versions of this book may not be included in e-books or in print-on-demand. If this book refers to media such as a CD or DVD that is not included in the version you purchased, you may download this material at http://booksupport.wiley.com. For more information about Wiley products, visit www.wiley.com.

Library of Congress Cataloging-in-Publication Data

Names: McKinsey and Company. | Koller, Tim, author. | Goedhart, Marc H., author. | Wessels, David, author.
Title: Valuation : measuring and managing the value of companies / McKinsey & Company, Tim Koller, Marc Goedhart, David Wessels.
Description: Seventh edition. | Hoboken, New Jersey: Wiley, [2020] | Series: Wiley finance | First edition entered under: Copeland, Thomas E.
Identifiers: LCCN 2020013692 (print) | LCCN 2020013693 (ebook) | ISBN 978-1-119-61088-5 (Hardcover) | ISBN 978-1-119-61087-8 (ePDF) | ISBN 978-1-119-61092-2 (ePub) | ISBN 978-1-119-61186-8 (University Edition) | ISBN 978-1-119-61246-9 (Cloth edition with DCF Model Download) | ISBN 978-1-119-61181-3 (Workbook) | ISBN 978-1-119-61086-1 (DCF Model Download)
Subjects: LCSH: Corporations—Valuation—Handbooks, manuals, etc.
Classification: LCC HG4028.V3 C67 2020 (print) | LCC HG4028.V3 (ebook) | DDC 658.15—dc23
LC record available at https://lccn.loc.gov/2020013692
LC ebook record available at https://lccn.loc.gov/2020013693

Printed in the United States of America

SKY10037861_110722

Contents

About the Authors

The authors are all current or former consultants of McKinsey & Company's Strategy & Corporate Finance Practice. Together they have more than 85 years of experience in consulting and financial education.

* * *

Tim Koller is a partner in McKinsey's Stamford, Connecticut, office, where he is a founder of McKinsey's Strategy and Corporate Finance Insights team, a global group of corporate-finance expert consultants. In his 35 years in consulting, Tim has served clients globally on corporate strategy and capital markets, mergers and acquisitions transactions, and strategic planning and resource allocation. He leads the firm's research activities in valuation and capital markets. Before joining McKinsey, he worked with Stern Stewart & Company and with Mobil Corporation. He received his MBA from the University of Chicago.

* * *

Marc Goedhart is a senior expert in McKinsey's Amsterdam office and an endowed professor of corporate valuation at Rotterdam School of Management, Erasmus University (RSM). Over the past 25 years, Marc has served clients across Europe on portfolio restructuring, M&A transactions, and performance management. He received his PhD in finance from Erasmus University.

* * *

David Wessels is an adjunct professor of finance at the Wharton School of the University of Pennsylvania. Named by *Bloomberg Businessweek* as one of America's top business school instructors, he teaches courses on corporate valuation and private equity at the MBA and executive MBA levels. David is also a director in Wharton's executive education group, serving on the executive development faculties of several Fortune 500 companies. A former consultant with McKinsey, he received his PhD from the University of California at Los Angeles.

* * *

McKinsey & Company is a global management consulting firm committed to helping organizations create change that matters. In more than 130 cities and 65 countries, teams help clients across the private, public, and social sectors shape bold strategies and transform the way they work, embed technology where it unlocks value, and build capabilities to sustain the change. Not just any change, but change that matters—for their organizations, their people, and, in turn, society at large.

Preface

The first edition of this book appeared in 1990, and we are encouraged that it continues to attract readers around the world. We believe the book appeals to readers everywhere because the approach it advocates is grounded in universal economic principles. While we continue to improve, update, and expand the text as our experience grows and as business and finance continue to evolve, those universal principles do not change.

The 30 years since that first edition have been a remarkable period in business history, and managers and investors continue to face opportunities and challenges emerging from it. The events of the economic crisis that began in 2007, as well as the Internet boom and its fallout almost a decade earlier, have strengthened our conviction that the core principles of value creation are general economic rules that continue to apply in all market circumstances. Thus, the extraordinarily high anticipated profits represented by stock prices during the Internet bubble never materialized, because there was no "new economy." Similarly, the extraordinarily high profits seen in the financial sector for the two years preceding the start of the 2007–2009 financial crisis were overstated, as subsequent losses demonstrated. The laws of competition should have alerted investors that those extraordinary profits couldn't last and might not be real.

Over time, we have also seen confirmed that for some companies, some of the time, the stock market may not be a reliable indicator of value. Knowing that value signals from the stock market may occasionally be unreliable makes us even more certain that managers need at all times to understand the underlying, intrinsic value of their company and how it can create more value. In our view, clear thinking about valuation and skill in using valuation to guide business decisions are prerequisites for company success.

Today, calls mount for changes in the nature of shareholder capitalism. As we explain in Chapter 1, we believe this criticism derives largely from a misguided focus by corporate leaders on short-term performance that is inconsistent with the value-creation principles we describe in this book. Creating value for shareholders does not mean pumping up today's share price. It means creating value for the collective of current and future shareholders by applying the techniques explained in this book.

WHY THIS BOOK

Not all CEOs, business managers, and financial managers possess a deep understanding of value, although they need to understand it fully if they are to do their jobs well and fulfill their responsibilities. This book offers them the necessary understanding, and its practical intent reflects its origin as a handbook for McKinsey consultants. We publish it for the benefit of current and future managers who want their companies to create value, and also for their investors. It aims to demystify the field of valuation and to clarify the linkages between strategy and finance. So while it draws on leading-edge academic thinking, it is primarily a how-to book and one we hope you will use again and again. This is no coffee-table tome: if we have done our job well, it will soon be full of underlining, margin notations, and highlighting.

The book's messages are simple: Companies thrive when they create real economic value for their shareholders. Companies create value by investing capital at rates of return that exceed their cost of capital. These two truths apply across time and geography. The book explains why these core principles of value creation are genuine and how companies can increase value by applying them.

The technical chapters of the book aim to explain, step-by-step, how to do valuation well. We spell out valuation frameworks that we use in our consulting work, and we illustrate them with detailed case studies that highlight the practical judgments involved in developing and using valuations. Just as important, the management chapters discuss how to use valuation to make good decisions about courses of action for a company. Specifically, they will help business managers understand how to:

- Decide among alternative business strategies by estimating the value of each strategic choice.
- Develop a corporate portfolio strategy, based on understanding which business units a corporate parent is best positioned to own and which might perform better under someone else's ownership.
- Assess major transactions, including acquisitions, divestitures, and restructurings.

- Improve a company's strategic planning and performance management systems to align the organization's various parts behind improved execution of strategic priorities and create value.
- Communicate effectively with investors, including whom to talk with and how.
- Design an effective capital structure to support the corporation's strategy and minimize the risk of financial distress.

STRUCTURE OF THE BOOK

In this seventh edition, we continue to expand the practical application of finance to real business problems, reflecting the economic events of the past decade, new developments in academic finance, and the authors' own experiences. The edition is organized into five parts, each with a distinct focus.

Part One, "Foundations of Value," provides an overview of value creation. We make the case that managers should focus on long-term value creation for current and future shareholders, not just some of today's shareholders looking for an immediate pop in the share price. We explain the two core principles of value creation: (1) the idea that return on invested capital and growth drive cash flow, which in turn drives value, and (2) the conservation of value principle, which says that anything that doesn't increase cash flow doesn't create value (unless it reduces risk). We devote a chapter each to return on invested capital and to growth, including strategic principles and empirical insights.

Part Two, "Core Valuation Techniques," is a self-contained handbook for using discounted cash flow (DCF) to value a company. The reader will learn how to analyze historical performance, forecast free cash flows, estimate the appropriate opportunity cost of capital, identify sources of value, and interpret results. We also show how to use multiples of comparable companies to supplement DCF valuations.

Part Three, "Advanced Valuation Techniques," explains how to analyze and incorporate in your valuation such complex issues as taxes, pensions, reserves, capital-light business models, inflation, and foreign currency. It also discusses alternative return-on-capital measures and applications.

Part Four, "Managing for Value," applies the value-creation principles to practical decisions that managers face. It explains how to design a portfolio of businesses; how to run effective strategic-planning and performance management processes; how to create value through mergers, acquisitions, and divestitures; how to construct an appropriate capital structure and payout policy; and how companies can improve their communications with the financial markets.

Part Five, "Special Situations," is devoted to valuation in more complex contexts. It explores the challenges of valuing high-growth companies, companies in emerging markets, cyclical companies, and banks. In addition, it shows how uncertainty and flexibility affect value and how to apply option-pricing theory and decision trees in valuations.

Finally, our nine appendixes provide a full accounting of our methodology in this book. They provide theoretical proofs, mathematical formulas, and underlying calculations for chapters where additional detail might be helpful in the practical application of our approach. Appendix H, in particular, pulls into one place the spreadsheets for the comprehensive valuation case study of Costco featured in this edition.

VALUATION SPREADSHEET

An Excel spreadsheet valuation model is available via Web download. This valuation model is similar to the model we use in practice. Practitioners will find the model easy to use in a variety of situations: mergers and acquisitions, valuing business units for restructuring or value-based management, or testing the implications of major strategic decisions on the value of your company. We accept no responsibility for any decisions based on your inputs to the model. If you would like to purchase the model (ISBN 978-1-118-61090-8 or ISBN 978-1-118-61246-9), please call (800) 225-5945, or visit www.wileyvaluation.com.

Acknowledgments

No book is solely the effort of its authors. This book is certainly no exception, especially since it grew out of the collective work of McKinsey's Strategy & Corporate Finance Practice and the experiences of its consultants throughout the world.

Most important, we would like to thank Tom Copeland and Jack Murrin, two of the coauthors of the first three editions of this book. We are deeply indebted to them for establishing the book's early success, for mentoring the current authors, and for their hard work in providing the foundations on which this edition builds.

Ennius Bergsma deserves our special thanks. Ennius initiated the development of McKinsey's Strategy & Corporate Finance Practice in the mid-1980s. He inspired the original internal McKinsey valuation handbook and mustered the support and sponsorship to turn that handbook into a real book for an external audience.

Bill Javetski, our lead editor, ensured that our ideas were expressed clearly and concisely. Dennis Swinford edited and oversaw the production of more than 390 exhibits, ensuring that they were carefully aligned with the text. Karen Schenkenfelder provided careful editing and feedback throughout the process. We are indebted to her excellent eye for detail.

Tim and Marc are founders of McKinsey's Strategy & Corporate Finance Insights team, a group of dedicated corporate-finance experts who influence our thinking every day. A special thank-you to Bernie Ferrari, who initiated the group and nurtured its development. The team is currently overseen by Werner Rehm and Chris Mulligan. Other leaders we are indebted to include Haripreet Batra, Matt Bereman, Alok Bothra, Josue Calderon, Susan Nolen Foushee, Andre Gaeta, Prateek Gakhar, Abhishek Goel, Baris Guener, Paulo Guimaraes, Anuj Gupta, Chetan Gupta, Peeyush Karnani, David Kohn, Tarun Khurana, Bharat Lakhwani, Ankit Mittal, Siddharth Periwal, Katherine Peters,

Abhishek Saxena, João Lopes Sousa, Ram Sekar, Anurag Srivastava, and Zane Williams.

We've made extensive use of McKinsey's Corporate Performance Analytics (CPAnalytics), led by Peter Stumpner, which provided data for the analyses in this book. We extend thanks also to the R+I Insights Team, led by Josue Calderon and Anuj Gupta. The team, which prepared much of the analyses for us, includes Rafael Araya, Roerich Bansal, Martin Barboza, Abhranil Das, Carlo Eyzaguirre, Jyotsna Goel, Dilpreet Kaur, Kumari Monika, Carolina Oreamuno, Victor Rojas, and Sapna Sharma. Dick Foster, a former McKinsey colleague and mentor, inspired the development of CPAnalytics.

Michael Cichello, professor of finance at Georgetown University, expertly prepared many of the teaching materials that accompany this book, including the end-of-chapter problems and answers for the university edition and exam questions and answers. These teaching materials are an essential supplement for professors and students using this book for finance courses. Thank you to our Costa Rica research team for their help in preparing and answering questions for these materials.

Concurrent with the fifth edition, McKinsey published a shorter book, titled *Value: The Four Cornerstones of Corporate Finance*, which explains the principles of value and their implications for managers and investors without going into the technical detail of this how-to guide. We've greatly benefited from the ideas of that book's coauthors, Richard Dobbs and Bill Huyett.

The intellectual origins of this book lie in the present-value method of capital budgeting and in the valuation approach developed by Nobel laureates Merton Miller and Franco Modigliani in their 1961 *Journal of Business* article titled "Dividend Policy, Growth, and the Valuation of Shares." Others have gone far to popularize their approach. In particular, Professor Alfred Rappaport (Northwestern University, Professor Emeritus) and the late Joel Stern (Stern Stewart & Co.) were among the first to extend the Miller-Modigliani enterprise valuation formula to real-world applications. In addition to these founders of the discipline, we would also like to acknowledge those who have personally shaped our knowledge of valuation, corporate finance, and strategy. For their support, teachings, and inspiration, we thank Buford Alexander, Tony Bernardo, Richard Dobbs, the late Mikel Dodd, Bernie Ferrari, Dick Foster, Bob Holthausen, Bill Huyett, Rob Kazanjian, Ofer Nemirovsky, Eduardo Schwartz, Chandan Sengupta, Jaap Spronk, the late Joel Stern, Bennett Stewart, Sunil Wahal, and Ivo Welch.

A number of colleagues worked closely with us on the seventh edition, providing support that was essential to its completion. In Part One, "Foundations of Value," David Schwartz, Bill Javetski, and Allen Webb helped with the always-difficult task of writing the first chapter to position the book properly. The discussion of valuation and ESG in Chapter 6 was based on an article coauthored by Witold Henisz and Robin Nuttall. The discussion of valuing digital initiatives in the same chapter benefited from collaboration with Liz Ericsson.

Over the years, we have valued many companies in Parts Two and Three. We would like to thank Wharton graduates Caleb Carter and Daniel Romeu for the extensive analysis they have conducted to underpin these sections.

Part Four, "Managing for Value," adds substantial new insights on how companies can improve the translation of their strategies into action and aligned resource allocation. We are indebted to Chris Bradley, Dan Lovallo, Robert Uhlaner, Loek Zonnenberg, and a host of others for this new material. Matt Gage and Steve Santulli provided analysis for the M&A chapter. The investor communications chapter benefits greatly from the work of Rob Palter and Werner Rehm. In Part Five, "Special Situations," Marco de Heer's dissertation formed the basis for the chapter on valuing cyclical companies.

Of course, we could not have devoted the time and energy to this book without the support and encouragement of McKinsey's Strategy & Corporate Finance Practice leadership—in particular, Martin Hirt and Robert Uhlaner. Lucia Rahilly and Rik Kirkland ensured that we received superior editorial support from McKinsey's external publishing team.

We would like to thank again all those who contributed to the first six editions. We owe a special debt to Dave Furer for help and late nights developing the original drafts of this book more than 30 years ago. Others not yet mentioned and to whom we owe our thanks for their contributions to the sixth edition include Ashish Kumar Agarwal, Andre Annema, Bing Cao, Bas Deelder, Ritesh Jain, Mimi James, Mauricio Jaramillo, Bin Jiang, Mary Beth Joyce, Jean-Hugues Monier, Rishi Raj, Eileen Kelly Rinaudo, Ram Sekar, Saravanan Subramanian, Zane Williams, and Angela Zhang.

The first five editions and this edition drew upon work, ideas, and analyses from Carlos Abad, Paul Adam, Buford Alexander, Petri Allas, Alexandre Amson, André Annema, the late Pat Anslinger, Vladimir Antikarov, Ali Asghar, Bill Barnett, Dan Bergman, Olivier Berlage, Peter Bisson, the late Joel Bleeke, Nidhi Chadda, Carrie Chen, Steve Coley, Kevin Coyne, Johan Depraetere, the late Mikel Dodd, Lee Dranikoff, Will Draper, Christian von Drathen, David Ernst, Bill Fallon, George Fenn, Susan Nolen Foushee, Russ Fradin, Gabriel Garcia, Richard Gerards, Alo Ghosh, Irina Grigorenko, Fredrik Gustavsson, Marco de Heer, Keiko Honda, Alice Hu, Régis Huc, Mimi James, Bin Jiang, Chris Jones, William Jones, Phil Keenan, Phil Kholos, David Krieger, Shyanjaw Kuo, Michael Kuritzky, Bill Lewis, Kurt Losert, Harry Markl, Yuri Maslov, Perry Moilinoff, Fabienne Moimaux, Mike Murray, Terence Nahar, Rafic Naja, Juan Ocampo, Martijn Olthof, Neha Patel, Vijen Patel, John Patience, Bill Pursche, S. R. Rajan, Werner Rehm, Frank Richter, David Rothschild, Michael Rudolf, Yasser Salem, Antoon Schneider, Ram Sekar, Meg Smoot, Silvia Stefini, Konrad Stiglbrunner, Ahmed Taha, Bill Trent, David Twiddy, Valerie Udale,

Sandeep Vaswani, Kim Vogel, Jon Weiner, Jack Welch, Gustavo Wigman, David Willensky, Marijn de Wit, Pieter de Wit, Jonathan Witter, David Wright, and Yan Yang.

For help in coordinating the flow of paper, e-mail, and phone calls, we owe our thanks to our assistants, Sue Cohen and Laura Waters.

We also extend thanks to the team at John Wiley & Sons, including Bill Falloon, Meg Freeborn, Purvi Patel, Carly Hounsome, and Kimberly Monroe-Hill.

Finally, thank you to Melissa Koller, Monique Donders, Kate Wessels, and our children: Katherine, Emily, and Juliana Koller; Max, Julia, and Sarah Goedhart; and Adin, Jacob, Lillia, and Nathaniel Wessels. Our wives and families are our true inspirations. This book would not have been possible without their encouragement, support, and sacrifice.

Part One

Foundations of Value

1

Why Value Value?

The guiding principle of business value creation is a refreshingly simple construct: companies that grow and earn a return on capital that exceeds their cost of capital create value. Articulated as early as 1890 by Alfred Marshall,[1] the concept has proven to be both enduring in its validity and elusive in its application.

Nevertheless, managers, boards of directors, and investors sometimes ignore the foundations of value in the heat of competition or the exuberance of market euphoria. The tulip mania of the early 1600s, the dot-coms that soared spectacularly with the Internet bubble, only then to crash, and the mid-2000's real estate frenzy whose implosion touched off the financial crisis of 2007–2008 can all to some extent be traced to a misunderstanding or misapplication of this guiding principle.

At other moments, the system in which value creation takes place comes under fire. That happened at the turn of the twentieth century in the United States, when fears about the growing power of business combinations raised questions that led to more rigorous enforcement of antitrust laws. The Great Depression of the 1930s was another such moment, when prolonged unemployment undermined confidence in the ability of the capitalist system to mobilize resources, leading to a range of new policies in democracies around the world.

Today many people are again questioning the foundations of capitalism, especially shareholder-oriented capitalism. Challenges such as globalization, climate change, income inequality, and the growing power of technology titans have shaken public confidence in large corporations.[2] Politicians and commentators push for more regulation and fundamental changes in corporate

---

[1] A. Marshall, *Principles of Economics* (New York: Macmillan, 1890), 1:142.
[2] An annual Gallup poll in the United States showed that the percentage of respondents with little or no confidence in big business increased from 27 percent in 1997 to 34 percent in 2019, and those with "a great deal" or "quite a lot" of confidence in big business decreased by five percentage points over that period, from 28 percent to 23 percent. Conversely, those with "a great deal" or "quite a lot" of confidence in small business *increased* by five percentage points over the same period (from 63 percent in 1997 to 68 percent in 2019). For more, see Gallup, "Confidence in Institutions," www.gallup.com.

3

governance. Some have gone so far as to argue that "capitalism is destroying the earth."[3]

Many business leaders share the view that change is needed to answer society's call. In August 2019, Business Roundtable, an association of chief executives of leading U.S. corporations, released its Statement on the Purpose of a Corporation. The document's 181 signers declared "a fundamental commitment to <u>all</u>[4] of our stakeholders."[5] The executives affirmed that their companies have a responsibility to customers, employees, suppliers, communities (including the physical environment), and shareholders. "We commit to deliver value to all of them," the statement concludes, "for the future success of our companies, our communities and our country."

The statement's focus on the future is no accident: issues such as climate change have raised concerns that today's global economic system is short-changing the future. It is a fair critique of today's capitalism. Managers too often fall victim to short-termism, adopting a focus on meeting short-term performance metrics rather than creating value over the long term. There also is evidence, including the median scores of companies tracked by McKinsey's Corporate Horizon Index from 1999 to 2017, that this trend is on the rise. The roots of short-termism are deep and intertwined, so a collective commitment of business leaders to the long-term future is encouraging.

As business leaders wrestle with that challenge, not to mention broader questions about purpose and how best to manage the coalescing and colliding interests of myriad owners and stakeholders in a modern corporation, they will need a large dose of humility and tolerance for ambiguity. They'll also need crystal clarity about the problems their communities are trying to solve. Otherwise, confusion about objectives could inadvertently undermine capitalism's ability to catalyze progress as it has in the past, whether lifting millions of people out of poverty, contributing to higher literacy rates, or fostering innovations that improve quality of life and lengthen life expectancy.

As business leaders strive to resolve all of those weighty trade-offs, we hope this book will contribute by clarifying the distinction between creating shareholder value and maximizing short-term profits. Companies that conflate the two often put both shareholder value *and* stakeholder interests at risk. In the first decade of this century, banks that acted as if maximizing short-term profits would maximize value precipitated a financial crisis that ultimately destroyed billions of dollars of shareholder value. Similarly, companies whose short-term focus leads to environmental disasters destroy shareholder value by incurring cleanup costs and fines, as well as via lingering reputational damage. The best managers don't skimp on safety, don't make value-destroying decisions just

---

[3] G. Monbiot, "Capitalism Is Destroying the Earth; We Need a New Human Right for Future Generations," *Guardian*, March 15, 2019, www.guardian.com.

[4] Emphasis added by Business Roundtable.

[5] Kevin Sneader, the global managing partner of McKinsey & Company, is a signatory of the statement.

because their peers are doing so, and don't use accounting or financial gimmicks to boost short-term profits. Such actions undermine the interests of all
stakeholders, including shareholders. They are the antithesis of value creation.

To dispel such misguided notions, this chapter begins by describing what value
creation *does* mean. We then contrast the value creation perspective with short-
termism and acknowledge some of the difficulties of value creation. We offer guidance on reconciling competing interests and adhering to principles that promote
value creation. The chapter closes with an overview of the book's remaining topics.

WHAT DOES IT MEAN TO CREATE SHAREHOLDER VALUE?

Particularly at this time of reflection on the virtues and vices of capitalism, it's
critical that managers and board directors have a clear understanding of what
value creation means. For value-minded executives, creating value cannot be
limited to simply maximizing today's share price. Rather, the evidence points
to a better objective: maximizing a company's collective value to its shareholders, now and in the future.

If investors knew as much about a company as its managers do, maximizing its current share price might be equivalent to maximizing its value over
time. But in the real world, investors have only a company's published financial results and their own assessment of the quality and integrity of its management team. For large companies, it's difficult even for insiders to know
how financial results are generated. Investors in most companies don't know
what's really going on inside a company or what decisions managers are making. They can't know, for example, whether the company is improving its
margins by finding more efficient ways to work or by skimping on product
development, resource management, maintenance, or marketing.

Since investors don't have complete information, companies can easily
pump up their share price in the short term or even longer. One global consumer products company consistently generated annual growth in earnings
per share (EPS) between 11 percent and 16 percent for seven years. Managers
attributed the company's success to improved efficiency. Impressed, investors
pushed the company's share price above those of its peers—unaware that the
company was shortchanging its investment in product development and brand
building to inflate short-term profits, even as revenue growth declined. Finally,
managers had to admit what they'd done. Not surprisingly, the company went
through a painful period of rebuilding. Its stock price took years to recover.

It would be a mistake, however, to conclude that the stock market is not
"efficient" in the academic sense that it incorporates all public information.
Markets do a great job with public information, but markets are not omni-
scient. Markets cannot price information they don't have. Think about the
analogy of selling an older house. The seller may know that the boiler makes
a weird sound every once in a while or that some of the windows are a bit

drafty. Unless the seller discloses those facts, a potential buyer may have great difficulty detecting them, even with the help of a professional house inspector.

Despite such challenges, the evidence strongly suggests that companies with a long strategic horizon create more value than those run with a short-term mindset. Banks that had the insight and courage to forgo short-term profits during the last decade's real-estate bubble, for example, earned much better total shareholder returns (TSR) over the longer term. In fact, when we studied the patterns of investment, growth, earnings quality, and earnings management of hundreds of companies across multiple industries between 2001 and 2014, we found that companies whose focus was more on the long term generated superior TSR, with a 50 percent greater likelihood of being in the top decile or top quartile by the end of that 14-year period.[6] In separate research, we've found that long-term revenue growth—particularly organic revenue growth—is the most important driver of shareholder returns for companies with high returns on capital.[7] What's more, investments in research and development (R&D) correlate powerfully with long-term TSR.[8]

Managers who create value for the long term do not take actions to increase today's share price if those actions will damage the company down the road. For example, they don't shortchange product development, reduce product quality, or skimp on safety. When considering investments, they take into account likely future changes in regulation or consumer behavior, especially with regard to environmental and health issues. Today's managers face volatile markets, rapid executive turnover, and intense performance pressures, so making long-term value-creating decisions requires courage. But the fundamental task of management and the board is to demonstrate that courage, despite the short-term consequences, in the name of value creation for the collective interests of shareholders, now and in the future.

SHORT-TERMISM RUNS DEEP

Despite overwhelming evidence linking intrinsic investor preferences to long-term value creation,[9] too many managers continue to plan and execute strategy—and then report their performance—against shorter-term measures, particularly earnings per share (EPS).

---

[6] *Measuring the Economic Impact of Short-Termism,* McKinsey Global Institute, February 2017, www.mckinsey.com.

[7] B. Jiang and T. Koller, "How to Choose between Growth and ROIC," *McKinsey on Finance,* no. 25 (Autumn 2007): 19–22, www.mckinsey.com. However, we didn't find the same relationship for companies with low returns on capital.

[8] We've performed the same analyses for 15 and 20 years and with different start and end dates, and we've always found similar results.

[9] R. N. Palter, W. Rehm, and J. Shih, "Communicating with the Right Investors," *McKinsey Quarterly* (April 2008), www.mckinsey.com. Chapter 34 of this book also examines the behaviors of intrinsic and other investor types.

As a result of their focus on short-term EPS, major companies often pass up long-term value-creating opportunities. For example, a relatively new CFO of one very large company has instituted a standing rule: every business unit is expected to increase its profits faster than its revenues, every year. Some of the units currently have profit margins above 30 percent and returns on capital of 50 percent or more. That's a terrific outcome if your horizon is the next annual report. But for units to meet that performance bar right now, they are forgoing growth opportunities that have 25 percent profit margins in the years to come. Nor is this an isolated case. In a survey of 400 chief financial officers, two Duke University professors found that fully 80 percent of the CFOs said they would reduce discretionary spending on potentially value-creating activities such as marketing and R&D in order to meet their short-term earnings targets.[10] In addition, 39 percent said they would give discounts to customers to make purchases this quarter rather than next, in order to hit quarterly EPS targets. That's no way to run a railroad—or any other business.

As an illustration of how executives get caught up in a short-term EPS focus, consider our experience with companies analyzing a prospective acquisition. The most frequent question managers ask is whether the transaction will dilute EPS over the first year or two. Given the popularity of EPS as a yardstick for company decisions, you might think that a predicted improvement in EPS would be an important indication of an acquisition's potential to create value. However, there is no empirical evidence linking increased EPS with the value created by a transaction.[11] Deals that strengthen EPS and deals that dilute EPS are equally likely to create or destroy value.

If such fallacies have no impact on value, why do they prevail? The impetus for a short-term view varies. Some executives argue that investors won't let them focus on the long term; others fault the rise of activist shareholders in particular. Yet our research shows that even if short-term investors cause day-to-day fluctuations in a company's share price and dominate quarterly earnings calls, longer-term investors are the ones who align market prices with intrinsic value.[12] Moreover, the evidence shows that, on average, activist investors strengthen the long-term health of the companies they pursue—for example, challenging existing compensation structures that encourage short-termism.[13] Instead, we often find that executives themselves or their boards are the source of short-termism. In one relatively recent survey of more than 1,000 executives and board members, most cited their own executive teams

---

[10] J. R. Graham, C. R. Harvey, and S. Rajgopal, "Value Destruction and Financial Reporting Decisions," *Financial Analysts Journal* 62, no. 6 (2006): 27–39.

[11] R. Dobbs, B. Nand, and W. Rehm, "Merger Valuation: Time to Jettison EPS," *McKinsey Quarterly* (March 2005), www.mckinsey.com.

[12] Palter et al., "Communicating with the Right Investors."

[13] J. Cyriac, R. De Backer, and J. Sanders, "Preparing for Bigger, Bolder Shareholder Activists," *McKinsey on Finance* (March 2014), www.mckinsey.com.

and boards (rather than investors, analysts, and others outside the company) as the greatest sources of pressure for short-term performance.[14]

The results can defy logic. At a company pursuing a major acquisition, we participated in a discussion about whether the deal's likely earnings dilution was important. One of the company's bankers said he knew any impact on EPS would be irrelevant to value, but he used it as a simple way to communicate with boards of directors. Elsewhere, we've heard company executives acknowledge that they, too, doubt the importance of impact on EPS but use it anyway, "for the benefit of Wall Street analysts." Investors also tell us that a deal's short-term impact on EPS is not that important. Apparently, everyone knows that a transaction's short-term impact on EPS doesn't matter. Yet they all pay attention to it.

The pressure to show strong short-term results often builds when businesses start to mature and see their growth begin to moderate. Investors continue to bay for high profit growth. Managers are tempted to find ways to keep profits rising in the short term while they try to stimulate longer-term growth. However, any short-term efforts to massage earnings that undercut productive investment make achieving long-term growth even more difficult, spawning a vicious circle.

Some analysts and some short-term-oriented investors will always clamor for short-term results. However, even though a company bent on growing long-term value will not be able to meet their demands all the time, this continuous pressure has the virtue of keeping managers on their toes. Sorting out the trade-offs between short-term earnings and long-term value creation is part of a manager's job, just as having the courage to make the right call is a critical personal quality. Perhaps even more important, it is up to corporate boards to investigate and understand the economics of the businesses in their portfolio well enough to judge when managers are making the right trade-offs and, above all, to protect managers when they choose to build long-term value at the expense of short-term profits.

Improving a company's corporate governance proposition might help. In a 2019 McKinsey survey, an overwhelming majority of executives (83 percent) reported that they would be willing to pay about a 10 percent median premium to acquire a company with a positive reputation for environmental, regulatory, and governance (ESG) issues over one with a negative reputation.

---

[14] Commissioned by McKinsey & Company and by the Canada Pension Plan Investment Board, the online survey, "Looking toward the Long Term," was in the field from April 30 to May 10, 2013, and garnered responses from 1,038 executives representing the full range of industries and company sizes globally. Of these respondents, 722 identified themselves as C-level executives and answered questions in the context of that role, and 316 identified themselves as board directors and answered accordingly. To adjust for differences in response rates, the data are weighted by the contribution of each respondent's nation to global gross domestic product (GDP). For more, see J. Bailey, V. Bérubé, J. Godsall, and C. Kehoe, "Short-termism: Insights from Business Leaders," FCLTGlobal, January 2014, https://www.fcltglobal.org.

Investors seem to agree; one recent report found that global sustainable investment topped $30 trillion in 2018, rising 34 percent over the previous two years.[15]

Board members might also benefit from spending more time on their board activities, so they have a better understanding of the economics of the companies they oversee and the strategic and short-term decisions managers are making. In a survey of 20 UK board members who had served on the boards of both exchange-listed companies and companies owned by private-equity firms, 15 of 20 respondents said that private-equity boards clearly added more value. Their answers suggested two key differences. First, private-equity directors spend on average nearly three times as many days on their roles as do those at listed companies. Second, listed-company directors are more focused on risk avoidance than value creation.[16]

Changes in CEO evaluation and compensation might help as well. The compensation of many CEOs and senior executives is still skewed to short-term accounting profits, often by formula. Given the complexity of managing a large multinational company, we find it odd that so much weight is given to a single number.

SHAREHOLDER CAPITALISM CANNOT SOLVE EVERY CHALLENGE

Short-termism is a critical affliction, but it isn't the only source of today's crisis of trust in corporate capitalism. Imagine that short-termism were magically cured. Would other foundational problems suddenly disappear as well? Of course not. Managers struggle to make many trade-offs for which neither a shareholder nor a stakeholder approach offers a clear path forward. This is especially true when it comes to issues affecting people who aren't immediately involved with the company—for example, a company's carbon emissions affecting parties that may be far away and not even know what the company is doing. These so-called externalities can be extremely challenging for corporate decision making, because there is no objective basis for making trade-offs among parties.

Consider how this applies to climate change. One natural place to look for a solution is to reduce coal production used to make electricity, among the largest human-made sources of carbon emissions.[17] How might the managers of a coal-mining company assess the trade-offs needed to begin solving environmental problems? If a long-term shareholder focus led them to anticipate

[15] *2018 Global Sustainable Investment Review*, Global Sustainable Investment Alliance, 2018, www.gsi-alliance.org.

[16] V. Acharya, C. Kehoe, and M. Reyner, "The Voice of Experience: Public versus Private Equity," *McKinsey on Finance* (Spring 2009): 16–21.

[17] In 2011, coal accounted for 44 percent of the global CO_2 emissions from energy production. CO_2 Emissions from Fuel Combustion online data service, International Energy Agency, 2013, www.iea.org.

potential regulatory changes, they would modify their investment strategies accordingly; they might not want to open new mines, for example.

With perfect knowledge a decade or even five years ago, a coal company could have reduced production dramatically or even closed mines in accordance with the decline in demand from U.S. coal-fired power plants. But perfect information is a scarce resource indeed, sometimes even in hindsight, and the timing of production changes and, especially, mine closures, would inevitably be abrupt. Further, closures would result in significant consequences even if the choice is the "right" one.

In the case of mine closures, not only would the company's shareholders lose their entire investment, but so would its bondholders, who are often pension funds. All the company's employees would be out of work, with magnifying effects on the entire local community. Second-order effects would be unpredictable. Without concerted action among all coal producers, another supplier could step up to meet demand. Even with concerted action, power plants might be unable to produce electricity, idling workers and causing electricity shortages that undermine the economy. What objective criteria would any individual company use to weigh the economic and environmental trade-offs of such decisions—whether they're privileging shareholders or stakeholders?

That's not to say that business leaders should just dismiss externalities as unsolvable or a problem to solve on a distant day. Putting off such critical decisions is the essence of short-termism. With respect to the climate, some of the world's largest energy companies, including BP and Shell, are taking bold measures right now toward carbon reduction, including tying executive compensation to emissions targets.

Still, the obvious complexity of striving to manage global threats like climate change that affect so many people, now and in the future, places bigger demands on governments. Trading off different economic interests and time horizons is precisely what people charge their governments to do. In the case of climate change, governments can create regulations and tax and other incentives that encourage migration away from polluting sources of energy. Ideally, such approaches would work in harmony with market-oriented approaches, allowing creative destruction to replace aging technologies and systems with cleaner and more efficient sources of power. Failure by governments to price or control the impact of externalities will lead to a misallocation of resources that can stress and divide shareholders and other stakeholders alike.

Institutional investors such as pension funds, as stewards of the millions of men and women whose financial futures are often at stake, can play a critical supporting role. Already, longer-term investors concerned with environmental issues such as carbon emissions, water scarcity, and land degradation are connecting value and long-term sustainability. In 2014, heirs to the Rockefeller Standard Oil fortune decided to join Stanford University's board of trustees in a campaign to divest shares in coal and other fossil fuel companies.

Long-term-oriented companies must be attuned to long-term changes that investors and governments will demand. This enables executives to adjust their strategies over a 5-, 10-, or 20-year time horizon and reduce the risk of holding still-productive assets that can't be used because of environmental or other issues. For value-minded executives, what bears remembering is that a delicate chemistry will always exist between government policy and long-term investors, and between shareholder value creation and the impact of externalities.

CAN STAKEHOLDER INTERESTS BE RECONCILED?

Much recent criticism of shareholder-oriented capitalism has called on companies to focus on a broader set of stakeholders beyond just its shareholders. It's a view that has long been influential in continental Europe, where it is frequently embedded in corporate governance structures. It's gaining traction in the United States as well, with the rise of public-benefit corporations, which explicitly empower directors to consider the interests of constituencies other than shareholders.

For most companies anywhere in the world, pursuing the creation of long-term shareholder value requires satisfying other stakeholders as well. You can't create long-term value by ignoring the needs of your customers, suppliers, and employees. Investing for sustainable growth should and often does result in stronger economies, higher living standards, and more opportunities for individuals.

Many corporate social-responsibility initiatives also create shareholder value.[18] Consider Alphabet's free suite of tools for education, including Google Classroom, which equips teachers with resources to make their work easier and more productive. As the suite meets that societal need, it also familiarizes students around the world with Google applications—especially in underserved communities, where people might otherwise not have access to meaningful computer science education at all. Nor is Alphabet reticent about choosing *not* to do business in instances the company deems harmful to vulnerable populations; the Google Play app store now prohibits apps for personal loans with an annual percentage rate of 36 percent or higher, an all too common feature of predatory payday loans.[19]

Similarly, Lego's mission to "play well"—to use the power of play to inspire "the builders of tomorrow, their environment and communities"—has led to a program that unites children in rural China with their working parents.

---

[18] S. Bonini, T. Koller, and P. H. Mirvis, "Valuing Social Responsibility Programs," *McKinsey Quarterly* (July 2009), www.mckinsey.com.
[19] Y. Hayashi, "Google Shuts Out Payday Loans with App-Store Ban," *Wall Street Journal*, October 13, 2019, www.wsj.com.

Programs such as these no doubt play a role in burnishing Lego's brand throughout communities and within company walls, where it reports that employee motivation and satisfaction levels beat 2018 targets by 50 percent. Or take Sodexo's efforts to encourage gender balance among managers. Sodexo says the program has not only increased employee retention by 8 percent, but also increased client retention by 9 percent and boosted operating margins by 8 percent.

Inevitably, though, there will be times when the interests of a company's stakeholders are not entirely complementary. Strategic decisions involve trade-offs, and the interests of different groups can be at odds with one another. Implicit in the Business Roundtable's 2019 statement of purpose is concern that business leaders have skewed some of their decisions too much toward the interests of shareholders. As a starting point, we'd encourage leaders, when trade-offs must be made, to prioritize long-term value creation, given the advantages it holds for resource allocation and economic health.

Consider employee stakeholders. A company that tries to boost profits by providing a shabby work environment, underpaying employees, or skimping on benefits will have trouble attracting and retaining high-quality employees. Lower-quality employees can mean lower-quality products, reduced demand, and damage to the brand reputation. More injury and illness can invite regulatory scrutiny and step up friction with workers. Higher turnover will inevitably increase training costs. With today's mobile and educated workforce, such a company would struggle in the long term against competitors offering more attractive environments.

If the company earns more than its cost of capital, it might afford to pay above-market wages and still prosper; treating employees well can be good business. But how well is well enough? A focus on long-term value creation suggests paying wages that are sufficient to attract quality employees and keep them happy and productive, pairing those wages with a range of non-monetary benefits and rewards. Even companies that have shifted manufacturing of products like clothing and textiles to low-cost countries with weak labor protection have found that they need to monitor the working conditions of their suppliers or face a consumer backlash.

Similarly, consider pricing decisions. A long-term approach would weigh price, volume, and customer satisfaction to determine a price that creates sustainable value. That price would have to entice consumers to buy the products not just once, but multiple times, for different generations of products. Any adjustments to the price would need to weigh the value of a lower price to buyers against the value of a higher price to shareholders and perhaps other stakeholders. A premium price that signals prestige for a luxury good can contribute long-term value. An obvious instance of going too far—or more accurately, not looking far enough ahead—is Turing Pharmaceuticals. In 2015, the company acquired the rights to a medication commonly used to treat

EXHIBIT 1.1 **Correlation between Total Shareholder Returns and Employment Growth**

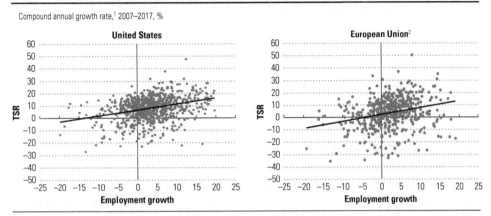

Compound annual growth rate,[1] 2007–2017, %

[1] Samples include companies with real revenues greater than $500 million and excludes outliers with more than 20% employment growth.
[2] Sample includes companies in the core 15 EU member states.

AIDS-related illnesses and then raised the price per pill by more than 5,000 percent. The tactic prompted outrage and a wave of government investigations. The CEO was even derided as "the most hated man in America."[20]

But far more often, the lines between creating and destroying value are gray. Companies in mature, competitive industries, for example, grapple with whether they should keep open high-cost plants that lose money, just to keep employees working and prevent suppliers from going bankrupt. To do so in a globalizing industry would distort the allocation of resources in the economy, notwithstanding the significant short-term local costs associated with plant closures.[21] At the same time, politicians pressure companies to keep failing plants open. The government may even be a major customer of the company's products or services.

In our experience, not only do managers carefully weigh bottom-line impact, they agonize over decisions that have pronounced consequences on workers' lives and community well-being. But consumers benefit when goods are produced at the lowest possible cost, and the economy benefits when operations that become a drain on public resources are closed and employees move to new jobs with more competitive companies. And while it's true that employees often can't just pick up and relocate, it's also true that value-creating companies create more jobs. When examining employment, we found that the U.S. and European companies that created the most shareholder value from

---

[20] Z. Thomas and T. Swift, "Who Is Martin Shkreli—'the Most Hated Man in America'?" BBC News, August 4, 2017, www.bbc.com.
[21] Some argue that well-functioning markets also need well-functioning governments to provide the safety nets and retraining support to make essential restructuring processes more equitable.

2007 to 2017—measured as total shareholder returns—have shown stronger employment growth (see Exhibit 1.1).[22]

CONSEQUENCES OF FORGETTING VALUE-CREATION PRINCIPLES

When companies forget the simple value-creation principles, the negative consequences to the economy can be huge. Two recent examples of many executives failing in their duty to focus on true value creation are the Internet bubble of the 1990s and the financial crisis of 2008.

During the Internet bubble, managers and investors lost sight of what drives return on invested capital (ROIC); indeed, many forgot the importance of this ratio entirely. Multiple executives and investors either forgot or threw out fundamental rules of economics in the rarefied air of the Internet revolution. The notion of "winner take all" led companies and investors to believe that all that mattered was getting big fast, on the assumption that they could wait until later to worry about creating an effective business model. The logic of achieving ever-increasing returns was also mistakenly applied to online pet supplies and grocery delivery services, even though these firms had to invest (unsustainably, eventually) in more drivers, trucks, warehouses, and inventory when their customer base grew. When the laws of economics prevailed, as they always do, it was clear that many Internet businesses did not have the unassailable competitive advantages required to earn even modest returns on invested capital. The Internet has revolutionized the economy, as have other innovations, but it did not and could not render obsolete the rules of economics, competition, and value creation.

Shortsighted focus can breed dishonorable dealing, and sometimes the consequences can shake confidence in capitalism to its foundations. In 2008, too many financial institutions ignored core principles. Banks lent money to individuals and speculators at low teaser rates on the assumption that housing prices would only increase. Banks packaged these high-risk debts into long-term securities and sold them to investors who used short-term debt to finance the purchase, thus creating a long-term risk for whoever lent them the money. When the home buyers could no longer afford the payments, the real estate market crashed, pushing the values of many homes below the values of the loans taken out to buy them. At that point, homeowners could neither make the required payments nor sell their homes. Seeing this, the banks that had issued short-term loans to investors in securities backed by mortgages became unwilling to roll over those loans, prompting the investors to sell all such securities at once. The value of the securities plummeted. Finally, many of the large banks themselves owned these securities, which they, of course, had also financed with short-term debt they could no longer roll over.

---

[22] We've performed the same analyses for 15 and 20 years and with different start and end dates, and we've always found similar results.

THIS BOOK

This book is a guide to how to measure and manage the value of a company. The faster companies can increase their revenues and deploy more capital at attractive rates of return, the more value they create. The combination of growth and return on invested capital (ROIC), relative to its cost, is what drives cash flow and value. Anything that doesn't increase ROIC or growth at an attractive ROIC doesn't create value. This category can include steps that change the ownership of claims to cash flows, and accounting techniques that may change the timing of profits without actually changing cash flows.

This guiding principle of value creation links directly to competitive advantage, the core concept of business strategy. Only if companies have a well-defined competitive advantage can they sustain strong growth and high returns on invested capital. To the core principles, we add the empirical observation that creating sustainable value is a long-term endeavor, one that needs to take into account wider social, environmental, technological, and regulatory trends.

Competition tends to erode competitive advantages and, with them, returns on invested capital. Therefore, companies must continually seek and exploit new sources of competitive advantage if they are to create long-term value. To that end, managers must resist short-term pressure to take actions that create illusory value quickly at the expense of the real thing in the long term. Creating value is not the same as, for example, meeting the analysts' consensus earnings forecast for the next quarter. Nor is it ignoring the effects of decisions made today that may create greater costs down the road, from environmental cleanup to retrofitting plants to meet future pollution regulations. It means balancing near-term financial performance against what it takes to develop a healthy company that can create value for decades ahead—a demanding challenge.

This book explains both the economics of value creation (for instance, how competitive advantage enables some companies to earn higher returns on invested capital than others) and the process of measuring value (for example, how to calculate return on invested capital from a company's accounting statements). With this knowledge, companies can make wiser strategic and operating decisions, such as what businesses to own and how to make trade-offs between growth and return on invested capital. Equally, this knowledge will enable investors to calculate the risks and returns of their investments with greater confidence.

Applying the principles of value creation sometimes means going against the crowd. It means accepting that there are no free lunches. It means relying on data, thoughtful analysis, a deep understanding of the competitive dynamics of your industry, and a broad, well-informed perspective on how society continually affects and is affected by your business. We hope this book provides readers with the knowledge to help them throughout their careers to make and defend decisions that will create value for investors and for society at large.

2

Finance in a Nutshell

Companies create value when they earn a return on invested capital (ROIC) greater than their opportunity cost of capital.[1] If the ROIC is at or below the cost of capital, growth may not create value. Companies should aim to find the combination of growth and ROIC that drives the highest discounted value of their cash flows. In so doing, they should consider that performance in the stock market may differ from intrinsic value creation, generally as a result of changes in investors' expectations.

To illustrate how value creation works, this chapter uses a simple story. Our heroes are Lily and Nate, who start out as the owners of a small chain of trendy clothing stores. Success follows. Over time, their business goes through a remarkable transformation. They develop the idea of Lily's Emporium and convert their stores to the new concept. To expand, they take their company public to raise additional capital. Encouraged by the resulting gains, they develop more retail concepts, including Lily's Furniture and Lily's Garden Supplies. In the end, Lily and Nate are faced with the complexity of managing a multibusiness retail enterprise.

THE EARLY YEARS

When we first met Lily and Nate, their business had grown from a tiny boutique into a small chain of trendy, midpriced clothing stores called Lily's Dresses. They met with us to find out how they could know if they were achieving attractive financial results. We told them they should measure their business's return on invested capital: after-tax operating profits divided by the capital invested in working capital and property, plant, and equipment.

---

[1] A simple definition of return on invested capital is after-tax operating profit divided by invested capital (working capital plus fixed assets). ROIC's calculation from a company's financial statements is explained in detail in Chapters 10 and 11.

Then they could compare the ROIC with what they could earn if they invested their capital elsewhere—for example, in the stock market.

Lily and Nate had invested $10 million in their business, and in 2020 they earned about $1.8 million after taxes, with no debt. So they calculated their return on invested capital as 18 percent. They asked what a reasonable guess would be for the rate they could earn in the stock market, and we suggested they use 10 percent. They easily saw that their money was earning 8 percent more than what we were assuming they could earn by investing elsewhere, so they were pleased with their business's performance.

We commented that growth is also important to consider in measuring financial performance. Lily told us that the business was growing at about 5 percent per year. Nate added that they discovered growth can be expensive; to achieve that growth, they had to invest in new stores, fixtures, and inventory. To grow at 5 percent and earn 18 percent ROIC on their growth, they reinvested about 28 percent of their profits back into the business each year. The remaining 72 percent of profits was available to withdraw from the business. In 2020, then, they generated cash flow of about $1.30 million.

Lily and Nate were satisfied with 5 percent growth and 18 percent ROIC until Lily's cousin Logan told them about his aggressive expansion plans for his own retail business, Logan's Stores. Based on what Logan had said, Lily and Nate compared the expected faster growth in operating profit for Logan's Stores with their own company's 5 percent growth, as graphed in Exhibit 2.1. Lily and Nate were concerned that Logan's faster-growing profits signaled a defect in their own vision or management.

"Wait a minute," we said. "How is Logan getting all that growth? What about his ROIC?" Lily and Nate checked and returned with the data shown in Exhibit 2.2. As we had suspected, Logan was achieving his growth by

EXHIBIT 2.1 **Expected Profit Growth at Logan's Stores Outpacing Lily's Dresses**

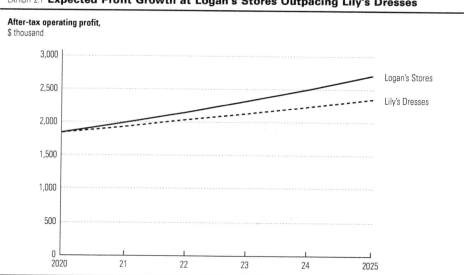

After-tax operating profit,
$ thousand

EXHIBIT 2.2 **Lily's Dresses Outperforming in Return on Invested Capital (ROIC) and Cash Flow**

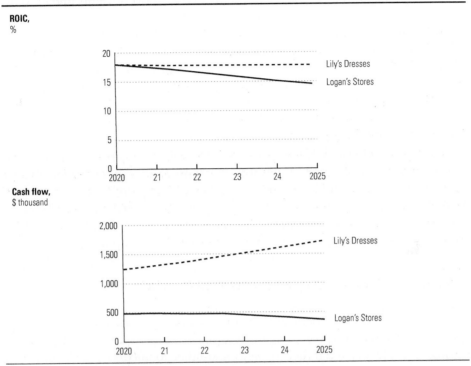

investing heavily. Despite all the growth in operating profit, his company's ROIC was declining significantly, so cash flow was slipping downward.

We asked the two why they thought their stores earned higher returns on capital than Logan's. Nate said one reason was that their products were unique and cutting-edge fashion, so their customers were willing to pay higher prices for their dresses than for the products at many other dress shops. Lily added that each of their stores attracted more customers, so their sales per square foot (a proxy for fixed costs) were greater than Logan's. As they saw it, Logan's products were not much different from those of his competitors, so he had to match his prices to theirs and had less customer traffic in his stores. This discussion helped Nate and Lily appreciate that it was beneficial to consider ROIC along with growth.

A NEW CONCEPT

Several years later, Lily and Nate called us with a great idea. They wanted to develop a new concept, which they called Lily's Emporium. Lily's Emporium would operate larger stores carrying a wider assortment of clothes and accessories that their talented designers were working on. But when they looked at the projected results (they now had a financial-analysis department), they found that all the new capital investment to convert their stores would reduce ROIC and cash flow for four years, even though revenue and profits would be growing faster, as shown in Exhibit 2.3. After four years, cash flow would be greater, but they didn't know how to trade off the short-term decline in ROIC and cash flow against the long-term improvement.

We affirmed that these were the right questions and explained that answering them would require more sophisticated financial tools. We advised them to use discounted cash flow (DCF), a measure that is also known as present value. DCF is a way of collapsing the future performance of the company into a single number. Lily and Nate needed to forecast the future cash flow of the company and discount it back to the present at the same opportunity cost of capital we had used for our earlier comparisons.

We helped Lily and Nate apply DCF to their new concept, discounting the projected cash flows at 10 percent. We showed them that the DCF value of their company would be $53 million if they did not adopt the new concept. With the new concept, the DCF value would be greater: $62 million. (Actually, on our spreadsheet, we rounded to the nearest thousand: $61,911,000.) These numbers gave them confidence in their idea for Lily's Emporium.

SHOULD LILY AND NATE TRY TO MAXIMIZE ROIC?

As they saw how these financial measures could help them build a more valuable business, Lily and Nate began to formulate more questions about measuring value. Lily asked if their strategy should be to maximize their return on

EXHIBIT 2.3 **Expansion's Impact on ROIC and Cash Flow**

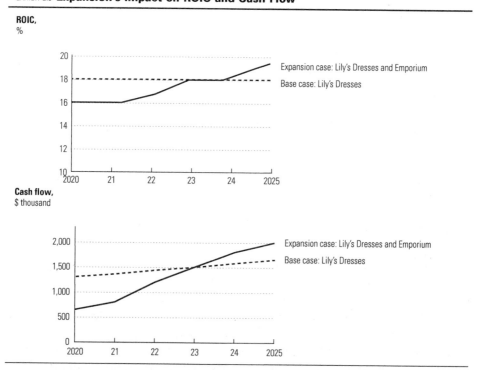

EXHIBIT 2.4 **Economic Profit Is Higher with Lower-Performing Stores in the Mix**

	ROIC, %	Cost of capital, %	Spread, %	Invested capital, $ thousand	Economic profit, $ thousand
Entire company	18	10	8	12,000	960
Without lower-performing stores	19	10	9	9,500	855

invested capital. She pointed to the fact that some stores outperformed others. For example, some were earning an ROIC of only 14 percent. If the business closed those lower-performing stores, they could increase their average return on invested capital.

Our advice was to focus not on the ROIC itself, but on the combination of ROIC (versus cost of capital) and the amount of capital. A tool for doing that is called economic profit. We showed them how economic profit applies to their business, using the measures in Exhibit 2.4.

We defined economic profit as the spread between ROIC and cost of capital multiplied by the amount of invested capital. In Lily and Nate's case, their economic profit forecast for 2024 would be the 8 percent spread by $12 million in invested capital, or $960,000. If they closed their low-returning stores, their average ROIC would increase to 19 percent, but their economic profit would decline to $855,000. This is because even though some stores earn a lower ROIC than others do, the lower-earning stores are still earning more than the cost of capital. Using this example, we made the case that Lily and Nate should seek to maximize economic profit, not ROIC, over the long term.

For Nate, though, this analysis raised a practical concern. With different methods available, it wasn't obvious which one to use. He asked, "When do we use economic profit, and when do we use DCF?"

"Good question," we said. "In fact, they're the same." We prepared Exhibit 2.5 to show Nate and Lily a comparison, using the DCF we had previously estimated for their business: $61,911,000. To apply the economic-profit method, we discounted the future economic profit at the same cost of capital we had used with the DCF. Then we added the discounted economic profit to the amount of capital invested today. The results for the two approaches are the same—exactly, to the penny.[2]

GOING PUBLIC

Now Lily and Nate had a way to make important strategic decisions over multiple time periods. Lily's Emporium was successful, and the next time they called us, they talked excitedly about new ambitions. "We need more

---

[2] See Chapter 10 for a detailed discussion of these two valuation approaches.

EXHIBIT 2.5 **Identical Results from DCF and Economic-Profit Valuation**

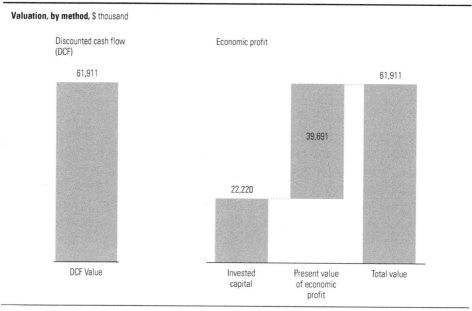

capital to build more stores more quickly," Nate said. "Besides, we want to provide an opportunity for some of our employees to become owners. So we've decided to go public." They asked us to help them understand how going public would affect their financial decision making.

"Well," we said, "now's the time to learn what the distinction is between financial markets and real markets and how they are related to each other. You'll want to understand that good performance in one market does not necessarily mean good performance in another."

Up until now, we'd been talking with Lily and Nate about the real market. How much profit and cash flow were they earning relative to the investments they were making? Were they maximizing their economic profit and cash flow over time? In the real market, the decision rule is simple: choose strategies or make operational decisions that maximize the present value of future cash flow or future economic profit.

When a company enters the capital market, the decision rules for the real market remain essentially unchanged. But life gets more complicated, because management must simultaneously deal with the financial market.

When a company goes public and sells shares to a wide range of investors who can trade those shares in an organized market, the interaction (or trading activity) between investors and even market speculators sets a price for those shares. The price of the shares is based on what investors think those shares are worth. Each investor decides what he or she thinks the value of the shares should be and makes trades based on whether the current price is above or below that estimate of the intrinsic value.

This intrinsic value is based on the future cash flows or earnings power of the company. This means, essentially, that investors are paying for the performance they expect the company to achieve in the future, not what the company has done in the past (and certainly not the cost of the company's assets).

Lily asked us how much their company's shares would be worth. "Let's assume," we said, "that the market's overall assessment of your company's future performance is similar to what you think your company will do. The first step is to forecast your company's performance and discount the future expected cash flows. Based on this analysis, the intrinsic value of your shares is $20 per share."

"That's interesting," said Nate, "because the amount of capital we've invested is only $7 per share." We told them that this difference meant the market should be willing to pay their company a premium of $13 over the invested capital for the future economic profit the company would earn.

"But," Lily asked, "if they pay us this premium up front, how will the investors make any money?"

"They may not," we said. "Let's see what will happen if your company performs exactly as you and the market expect. Let's value your company five years into the future. If you perform exactly as expected over the next five years and if expectations beyond five years don't change, your company's value will be $32 per share. Let's assume that you have not paid any dividends. An investor who bought a share for $20 per share today could sell the share for $32 in five years. The annualized return on the investment would be 10 percent, the same as the discount rate we used to discount your future performance. The interesting thing is that as long as you perform as expected, the return for your shareholders will be just their opportunity cost. But if you do better than expected, your shareholders will earn more than 10 percent. And if you do worse than expected, your shareholders will earn less than 10 percent."

"So," said Lily, "the return that investors earn is driven not by the performance of our company, but by its performance relative to expectations."

"Exactly!" we said.

Lily paused and reflected on the discussion. "That means we must manage our company's performance in the real markets and the financial markets at the same time."

We agreed and explained that if they were to create a great deal of value in the real market—say, by earning more than their cost of capital and growing fast—but didn't do as well as investors expected, the investors would be disappointed. Managers have a dual task: to maximize the intrinsic value of the company and to properly manage the expectations of the financial market.

"Managing market expectations is tricky," we added. "You don't want investor expectations to be too high or too low. We've seen companies convince the market that they will deliver great performance and then not deliver on those promises. Not only does the share price drop when the market realizes that the company won't be able to deliver, but regaining credibility may take years. Conversely, if the market's expectations are too low and you have a low share price relative to the opportunities the company faces, you may be subject to a hostile takeover."

After exploring these issues, Lily and Nate felt prepared to take their company public. They went forward with an initial public offering and raised the capital they needed.

EXPANSION INTO RELATED FORMATS

Lily and Nate's business was successful, growing quickly and regularly beating the expectations of the market, so their share price was a top performer. They were comfortable that their management team would be able to achieve high growth in their Emporium stores, so they decided next to try some new concepts they had been thinking about: Lily's Furniture and Lily's Garden Supplies. But they grew concerned about managing the business as it became more and more complex. They had always had a good feel for the business, but as it expanded and they had to delegate more decision making, they were less confident that things would be managed well.

They met with us again and told us that their financial people had put in place a planning and control system to closely monitor the revenue growth, ROIC, and economic profit of every store and each division overall. Their team set revenue and economic-profit targets annually for the next three years, monitored progress monthly, and tied managers' compensation to economic profit against these targets. Yet they told us they weren't sure the company was on track for the long-term performance that they and the market expected.

"You need a planning and control system that incorporates forward-looking measures besides looking backward at financial measures," we told them.

"Tell us more," Nate said.

"As you've pointed out," we said, "the problem with any financial measure is that it cannot tell you how your managers are doing at building the business for the future. For example, in the short term, managers could improve their financial results by cutting back on customer service, such as by reducing the number of employees available in the store to help customers, by cutting into employee training, or by deferring maintenance costs or brand-building expenditures. You need to make sure that you build in measures related to customer satisfaction or brand awareness—measures that let you know what the future will look like, not just what the current performance is."

Lily and Nate both nodded, satisfied. The lessons they so quickly absorbed and applied have placed their company on a solid foundation. The two of them still come to see us from time to time, but only for social visits. Sometimes they bring flowers from their garden supplies center.

SOME LESSONS

While we have simplified the story of Lily and Nate's business, it highlights the core ideas around value creation and its measurement:

1. In the real market, you create value by earning a return on your invested capital greater than the opportunity cost of capital.

2. The more you can invest at returns above the cost of capital, the more value you create. That is, growth creates more value as long as the return on invested capital exceeds the cost of capital.

3. You should select strategies that maximize the present value of future expected cash flows or economic profit. The answer is the same regardless of which approach you choose.

4. The value of a company's shares in the stock market equals the intrinsic value based on the market's expectations of future performance, but the market's expectations of future performance may not be same as the company's.

5. The returns that shareholders earn depend on changes in expectations as much as on the actual performance of the company.

In the next chapter, we develop a more formal framework for understanding and measuring value creation.

3

Fundamental Principles of Value Creation

Companies create value for their owners by investing cash now to generate more cash in the future. The amount of value they create is the difference between cash inflows and the cost of the investments made, adjusted to reflect the fact that tomorrow's cash flows are worth less than today's because of the time value of money and the riskiness of future cash flows. As we illustrated in Chapter 2, the conversion of revenues into cash flows—and earnings—is a function of a company's return on invested capital (ROIC) and its revenue growth. That means the amount of value a company creates is governed ultimately by its ROIC, revenue growth, and ability to sustain both over time. Keep in mind that a company will create value only if its ROIC is greater than its cost of capital.[1] Moreover, only if ROIC exceeds the cost of capital will growth increase a company's value. Growth at lower returns actually reduces a company's value. Exhibit 3.1 illustrates this core principle of value creation.[2]

Following these principles helps managers decide which strategies and investments will create the most value for shareholders in the long term. The principles also help investors assess the potential value of companies they might consider investing in. This chapter explains the relationships that tie together

---

[1] The cost of capital is an opportunity cost for the company's investors, not a cash cost. See Chapter 4 for a more detailed explanation.

[2] In its purest form, *value* is the sum of the present values of future expected cash flows—a point-in-time measure. *Value creation* is the change in value due to company performance (changes in growth and ROIC). Sometimes we refer to value and value creation based on explicit projections of future growth, ROIC, and cash flows. At other times, we use the market price of a company's shares as a proxy for value, and total shareholder returns (share price appreciation plus dividends) as a proxy for value creation.

EXHIBIT 3.1 **Growth and ROIC Drive Value**

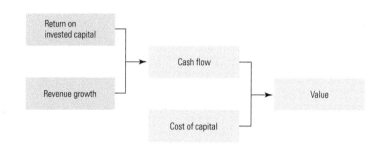

growth, ROIC, cash flows, and value, and it introduces the way managers can use these relationships to decide among different investments or strategies. For example, we will show that high-ROIC companies typically create more value by focusing on growth, while lower-ROIC companies create more value by increasing ROIC. We'll also explore the principle, often forgotten by executives, that anything that doesn't increase cash flows, such as noncash accounting charges or changes in accounting methods, won't create value. And we'll introduce a simple equation that captures the essence of valuation in practice.

One might expect universal agreement on a notion as fundamental as value, but this isn't the case: many executives, boards, and financial media still treat accounting earnings and value as one and the same and focus almost obsessively on improving earnings. However, while earnings and cash flow are often correlated, earnings don't tell the whole story of value creation. Focusing too much on earnings or earnings growth often leads companies to stray from a value-creating path.

For example, earnings growth alone can't explain why investors in discount retailer Costco, the fourth-largest retailer in the United States, with sales of $126 billion in 2017, and Brown-Forman, the producer of Jack Daniels and other alcoholic beverages, with sales of $4 billion the same year, earned similar shareholder returns (dividends plus appreciation in the share price) between 1996 and 2017. These two successful companies had very different growth rates. During the period, after-tax operating profits for Costco grew 11 percent per year, while those of Brown-Forman grew 7 percent annually. This means that profits for Costco in 2017 were nine times larger than in 1996, while profits at Brown-Forman were only four times larger. Costco was one of the fastest-growing companies in the United States during this time; its average annual shareholder returns were 15 percent. Brown-Forman was growing much more slowly, yet its annual shareholder returns were also 15 percent. The reason Brown-Forman could create the same value as Costco, despite much slower growth, was that Brown-Forman earned a 29 percent ROIC (excluding the impact of acquisitions), while Costco's ROIC was 13 percent.

To be fair, if all companies in an industry earned the same ROIC, then earnings growth *would* be the differentiating metric, because then only growth and not ROIC would determine differences in companies' cash flow. For reasons of simplicity, analysts and academics have sometimes made this assumption. But as Chapter 8 demonstrates, returns on invested capital can vary considerably, not only across industries but also between companies within the same industry and across time.

THE RELATIONSHIP OF GROWTH, ROIC, AND CASH FLOW

Disaggregating cash flow into revenue growth and ROIC helps illuminate the underlying elements that power a company's performance. Say a company's cash flow was $100 last year and will be $115 next year. This doesn't tell us much about its economic performance, since the $15 increase in cash flow could come from many sources, including revenue growth, a reduction in capital spending, or a reduction in marketing expenditures. But if we told you that the company was generating revenue growth of 7 percent per year and would earn a return on invested capital of 15 percent, then you would be able to evaluate its performance. You could, for instance, compare the company's growth rate with the growth rate of its industry or the economy, and you could analyze its ROIC relative to peers, its cost of capital, and its own historical performance.

Growth, ROIC, and cash flow are mathematically linked. To see how, consider two companies, Value Inc. and Volume Inc., whose projected earnings, investment, and resulting cash flows are displayed in Exhibit 3.2. Earnings, in this illustration, are expressed as net operating profit after taxes (NOPAT), a term we use throughout the book. Both companies earned NOPAT of $100 million in year 1 and are expected to increase their revenues and earnings at 5 percent per year, so their projected earnings are identical. If the popular view that value depends only on earnings were true, the two companies' values also would be the same. But this simple example demonstrates how wrong that view can be.

EXHIBIT 3.2 **Tale of Two Companies: Same Earnings, Different Cash Flows**

$ million

Value Inc.	Year 1	Year 2	Year 3	Year 4	Year 5
NOPAT[1]	100	105	110	116	122
Investment	(25)	(26)	(28)	(29)	(31)
Cash flow	75	79	82	87	91

Volume Inc.	Year 1	Year 2	Year 3	Year 4	Year 5
NOPAT[1]	100	105	110	116	122
Investment	(50)	(53)	(55)	(58)	(61)
Cash flow	50	52	55	58	61

[1] Net operating profit after taxes.

Almost all companies need to invest in plant, equipment, or working capital to grow. Free cash flow is what's left over for investors once investments have been subtracted from earnings. Value Inc. generates higher free cash flows with the same earnings because it invests only 25 percent of its profits—its investment rate—to achieve the same profit growth as Volume Inc., which invests 50 percent of its profits. Value Inc.'s lower investment rate results in 50 percent higher cash flows each year than Volume Inc. sees while generating the same level of profits.

We can value the two companies by discounting their future free cash flows at a discount rate that reflects what investors expect to earn from investing in the companies—that is, their cost of capital. For both companies, we assumed their growth and investment rates were perpetual, and we discounted each year's cash flow to the present at a 10 percent cost of capital. So, for example, Value Inc.'s year 1 cash flow of $75 million has a present value of $68 million today (see Exhibit 3.3). We summed each year's results to derive a total present value of all future cash flows: $1,500 million for Value Inc. and $1,000 million for Volume Inc.

The companies' values can also be expressed as price-to-earnings ratios (P/Es). Divide each company's value by its first-year earnings of $100 million. Value Inc.'s P/E is 15, while Volume Inc.'s is only 10. Despite identical earnings and growth rates, the companies have different earnings multiples because their cash flows are so different. Value Inc. generates higher cash flows because it doesn't have to invest as much as Volume Inc. does.

Differences in ROIC—defined here as the incremental NOPAT earned each year relative to the prior year's investment—are what drives difference in investment rates. In this case, Value Inc. invested $25 million in year

EXHIBIT 3.3 **Value Inc.: DCF Valuation**

$ million

| | Value Inc. | | | | | | |
	Year 1	Year 2	Year 3	Year 4	Year 5	Year X	Sum
NOPAT[1]	100	105	110	116	122	...	
Investment	(25)	(26)	(28)	(29)	(31)	...	
Cash flow	75	79	82	87	91	...	
Value today	68	65	62	59	56	...	1,500

Present value of 75 discounted at 10% for 1 year

Present value of 87 discounted at 10% for 4 years

[1] Net operating profit after taxes.

1 to increase its profits by $5 million in year 2. Its return on new capital is 20 percent ($5 million of additional profits divided by $25 million of investment).[3] In contrast, Volume Inc.'s return on invested capital is 10 percent ($5 million in additional profits in year 2 divided by an investment of $50 million).

Growth, ROIC, and cash flow (as represented by the investment rate) are tied together mathematically in the following relationship:

$$\text{Growth} = \text{ROIC} \times \text{Investment Rate}$$

Applying the formula to Value Inc.:

$$5\% = 20\% \times 25\%$$

Applying it to Volume Inc.:

$$5\% = 10\% \times 50\%$$

As you can see, Volume Inc. needs a higher investment rate to achieve the same growth.

Another way to look at this comparison is in terms of cash flow:

$$\text{Cash Flow} = \text{Earnings} \times (1 - \text{Investment Rate})$$

In this equation, the investment rate is equal to growth divided by ROIC:

$$\text{Cash Flow} = \text{Earnings} \times (1 - \text{Growth}/\text{ROIC})$$

For Value Inc.:

$$\$75 = \$100 \times (1 - 5\% / 20\%)$$
$$= \$100 \times (1 - 25\%)$$

For Volume Inc.:

$$\$50 = \$100 \times (1 - 5\% / 10\%)$$
$$= \$100 \times (1 - 50\%)$$

Since the three variables are tied together mathematically, you can describe a company's performance with any two variables. We generally describe a company's performance in terms of growth and ROIC because, as mentioned earlier, you can analyze growth and ROIC across time and versus peers.

---

[3] We assumed that all of the increase in profits is due to the new investment, with the return on Value Inc.'s existing capital remaining unchanged.

EXHIBIT 3.4 **Translating Growth and ROIC into Cash Flow Available for Distribution**

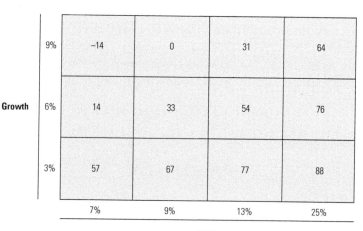

% of NOPAT

Growth		ROIC			
		7%	9%	13%	25%
	9%	−14	0	31	64
	6%	14	33	54	76
	3%	57	67	77	88

Exhibit 3.4 shows how different combinations of growth and ROIC generate different levels of cash flow that can be paid out to investors. The numbers in the boxes represent cash flow as a percentage of NOPAT, which represents the profits available for distribution to investors. You can see that as growth slows at any level of ROIC, the cash generated per dollar of NOPAT increases. That explains why even maturing companies experiencing slowing growth can pay out much larger amounts of their earnings to investors. Note also that companies with high ROIC tend to generate lots of cash flow as long as they are growing modestly. This explains why mature tech and pharma companies with high returns on capital pay out so much of their earnings to investors. They don't really have a choice, because they typically generate much more cash flow than they can reinvest at attractive returns on capital.

Note that near-term cash flow by itself may not be a meaningful performance indicator. Consider what would happen if Value Inc. were to find more investment opportunities at a 25 percent ROIC and be able to increase its growth to 8 percent per year. Exhibit 3.5 shows the projected NOPAT and cash flow. Because it would be growing faster, Value Inc. would need to invest more of its earnings each year, so its cash flow at 8 percent growth would be lower than at 5 percent growth until year 9. However, its value, which at 5 percent growth would be $1.5 billion, would double at 8 percent growth to $3 billion, because its cash flows would be higher in the long term.

EXHIBIT 3.5 **Value Inc.: Lower Initial Cash Flow at Higher Growth Rate**

$ million

5% growth

	Year 1	Year 2	Year 3	Year 4	Year 5	Year 6	Year 7	Year 8	Year 9	Year 10	Year 11	Year 12
NOPAT	100	105	110	116	122	128	138	141	148	155	163	171
Net investment	(25)	(26)	(28)	(29)	(30)	(32)	(34)	(35)	(37)	(39)	(41)	(43)
Cash flow	75	79	83	87	91	96	101	106	111	116	122	128

8% growth

	Year 1	Year 2	Year 3	Year 4	Year 5	Year 6	Year 7	Year 8	Year 9	Year 10	Year 11	Year 12
NOPAT	100	108	117	126	136	147	159	171	185	200	216	233
Net investment	(40)	(43)	(47)	(50)	(54)	(59)	(63)	(69)	(74)	(80)	(86)	(93)
Cash flow	60	65	70	76	82	88	95	103	111	120	130	140

Higher growth rate initially generates less cash flow

If you simplify some assumptions—for example, that a company grows at a constant rate and maintains a constant ROIC—you can reduce the discounted cash flow to a simple formula. We call this the value driver formula. Here, NOPAT represents the net operating profit after taxes, g is the growth rate of the company, and WACC is the cost of capital.

$$\text{Value} = \frac{\text{NOPAT}_{t=1}\left(1 - \dfrac{g}{\text{ROIC}}\right)}{\text{WACC} - g}$$

Using this equation, you can see that value is driven by growth, ROIC, and the cost of capital, just as we described in the example. In practice, we rarely use this formula by itself, because of its assumption of constant growth and ROIC forever. Still, we find it useful as a reminder of the elements that drive value. Note that improving ROIC, for any level of growth, always increases value because it reduces the investment required for growth. The impact of growth, however, is ambiguous, as it appears in both the numerator and the denominator. In the next section, we'll show that faster growth increases value only when a company's ROIC is greater than its cost of capital. At the end of this chapter, we'll also show how this equation is derived.

BALANCING ROIC AND GROWTH TO CREATE VALUE

It is possible to create a matrix that shows how different combinations of growth and ROIC translate into value (Exhibit 3.6). Each cell in the matrix represents the present value of future cash flows under each of the assumptions of growth and ROIC, discounted at the company's cost of capital. This case assumes a 9 percent cost of capital and a company that earns $100 in the first year.[4]

Observe that for any level of growth, value increases with improvements in ROIC. In other words, when all else is equal, a higher ROIC is always good, because it means that the company doesn't have to invest as much to achieve a given level of growth. The same can't be said of growth. When ROIC is high, faster growth increases value. But when ROIC is lower than the company's cost of capital, faster growth destroys value. When return on capital is lower than the cost of capital, growing faster means investing more at a value-destroying return. Where ROIC equals the cost of capital, we can draw the dividing line between creating and destroying value through growth. On that line, value is neither created nor destroyed, regardless of how fast the company grows. It's as if management were on a treadmill. They're working hard, but after their workout, they are right where they started.

From the exhibit, you can also see that a company with high ROIC and low growth may have a similar or higher valuation multiple than a company with

EXHIBIT 3.6 **Translating Growth and ROIC into Value**

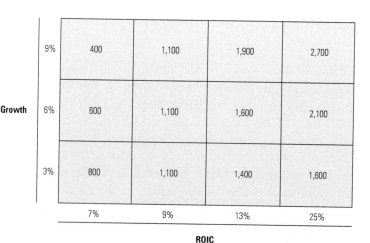

Value,[1] $

Growth		ROIC			
		7%	9%	13%	25%
	9%	400	1,100	1,900	2,700
	6%	600	1,100	1,600	2,100
	3%	800	1,100	1,400	1,600

[1] Present value of future cash flows, assuming year 1 earnings of $100 and a 9% cost of capital. After 15 years, all scenarios grow at 4.5%.

[4] We made explicit cash flow forecasts for the first 15 years and assumed that growth after that point converges on 4.5 percent in all scenarios. If a company grew faster than the economy forever, it would eventually overtake the entire world economy.

higher growth but low ROIC. For example, at the end of 2017, Brown-Forman and Costco were both valued with a ratio of enterprise value to pretax operating profits in the range of 19 to 20 times. Yet Costco had been growing at 7 percent per year over the prior three years, while Brown-Forman had grown at less than 2 percent per year. Again, Brown-Forman made up for its lower growth with a higher ROIC of 30 percent in 2017, versus 15 percent for Costco (which is good for a capital-intensive, low-margin retailer).

We sometimes hear the argument that even low-ROIC companies should strive for growth. The logic is that if a company grows, its ROIC will naturally increase. However, we find this is true only for young, start-up businesses. Most often in mature companies, a low ROIC indicates a flawed business model or unattractive industry structure. Don't fall for the trap that growth will lead to scale economies that automatically increase a company's return on capital. It almost never happens for mature businesses.

SOME EXAMPLES

The logic laid out in this section reflects the way companies perform in the stock market. Recall the earlier explanation of why shareholder returns for Costco and Brown-Forman were the same even though earnings for Costco grew much faster. Another example of the relative impact of growth and ROIC on value is Rockwell Automation, which provides integrated systems to monitor and control automation in factories. Rockwell's total shareholder returns (TSR) from 1995 to 2018 were 19 percent per year, placing it in the top quartile of industrial companies. During this period, Rockwell's revenues actually shrank from $13 billion in 1995 to $7 billion in 2018 as it divested its aviation and power systems divisions. The major factor behind its high TSR was its success in increasing ROIC, from about 12 percent in the mid-1990s to about 35 percent in 2018 (including goodwill). After spinning off its aviation business (now known as Rockwell Collins) in 2001, Rockwell focused on its core industrial-automation business and improved ROIC significantly. While this was partially accomplished by divesting lower-margin ancillary businesses, the majority of the improvement came from operational improvement in industrial automation. The company publicly reiterated its focus on cost and capital productivity many times during the period.

Clearly, the core valuation principle applies at the company level. We have found that it applies at the sector level, too. Consider companies as a whole in the consumer packaged-goods sector. Even though well-known names in the sector such as Procter & Gamble and Colgate-Palmolive aren't high-growth companies, the market values them at average or higher earnings multiples because of their high returns on invested capital.

The typical large packaged-goods company increased its revenues 1.2 percent a year from 2014 to 2019, slower than the median of about 4.5 percent for all Standard & Poor's (S&P) 500 companies, excluding financial institutions. Yet at the end of 2018, the median P/E of consumer packaged-goods companies was about 15, almost exactly the same as the median S&P 500 company. The valuations of companies in this sector rested on their high ROICs—in aggregate above 40 percent, compared with an aggregate ROIC of 22 percent for the S&P 500 in 2018.

To test whether the core valuation principle also applies at the level of countries and the aggregate economy, we compared large companies based in Europe and the United States. The median trailing P/E ratio for large U.S. companies was 15.5 times, versus 12.8 for large European companies. The difference in valuation relative to invested capital is even more extreme. The median enterprise value to invested capital for U.S. companies was 5.4, versus 3.2 for European companies. Some executives assume the reason is that investors are simply willing to pay higher prices for shares of U.S. companies (an assumption that has prompted some non-U.S. companies to consider moving their share listings to the New York Stock Exchange in an attempt to increase their value). But the real reason U.S. companies trade at higher multiples is that they typically earn higher returns on invested capital. The median large U.S. company earned a 30 percent ROIC (before goodwill and intangibles) in 2018, while the median large European company earned 19 percent. A large part of the difference is a different industry mix; the United States has many more high-ROIC pharmaceutical, medical-device, and technology companies. These broad comparisons also hide the fact that some European companies—for example, Robert Bosch in auto parts and Reckitt Benckiser in consumer packaged goods—outperform many of their U.S. counterparts.

More evidence showing that ROIC and growth drive value appears in Chapter 7.

IMPLICATIONS FOR MANAGERS

We'll dive deeper into the managerial dimensions of ROIC and growth in Chapters 8 and 9, respectively. For now, we outline several lessons managers should learn for strategic decision making.

Start by referring back to Exhibit 3.6, because it contains the most important strategic insights for managers concerning the relative impact that changes in ROIC and growth can have on a company's value. In general, companies already earning a high ROIC can generate more additional value by increasing their rate of growth, rather than their ROIC. For their part, low-ROIC companies will generate relatively more value by focusing on increasing their ROIC.

For example, Exhibit 3.7 shows that a typical high-ROIC company, such as a branded consumer packaged–goods company, can increase its value by

EXHIBIT 3.7 **Increasing Value: Impact of Higher Growth and ROIC**

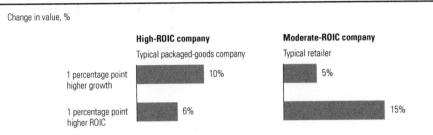

Change in value, %

	High-ROIC company	**Moderate-ROIC company**
	Typical packaged-goods company	Typical retailer
1 percentage point higher growth	10%	5%
1 percentage point higher ROIC	6%	15%

10 percent if it increases its growth rate by one percentage point, while a typical moderate-ROIC company, such as the average retailer, will increase its value by only 5 percent for the same increase in growth. In contrast, the moderate-ROIC company gets a 15 percent bump in value from increasing its return on invested capital by one percentage point, while the high-ROIC company gets only a 6 percent bump from the same increase in return on invested capital.

The general lesson is that high-ROIC companies should focus on growth, while low-ROIC companies should focus on improving returns before growing. Of course, this analysis assumes that achieving a one-percentage-point increase in growth is as easy as achieving a one-percentage-point increase in ROIC, everything else being constant. In reality, achieving either type of increase poses different degrees of difficulty for different companies in different industries, and the impact of a change in growth and ROIC will also vary between companies. However, every company needs to conduct the analysis to set its strategic priorities.

Until now, we have assumed that all growth earns the same ROIC and therefore generates the same value, but this is clearly unrealistic: different types of growth earn different returns on capital, so not all growth is equally value-creating. Each company must understand the pecking order of growth-related value creation that applies to its industry and company type.

Exhibit 3.8 shows the value created from different types of growth for a typical consumer products company.[5] These results are based on cases with which we are familiar, not on a comprehensive analysis. Still, we believe they reflect the broader reality.[6] The results are expressed in terms of value created for $1.00 of incremental revenue. For example, $1.00 of additional revenue from a new product creates $1.75 to $2.00 of value. The most important implication of this chart is the rank order. New products typically create more value for shareholders, while acquisitions typically create the least. The key to the difference between these extremes is differences in returns on capital for the different types of growth.

[5] This exhibit will look different for different industries.
[6] We identified examples for each type of growth and estimated their impact on value creation. For instance, we obtained several examples of the margins and capital requirements for new products.

EXHIBIT 3.8 **Value Creation by Type of Growth**

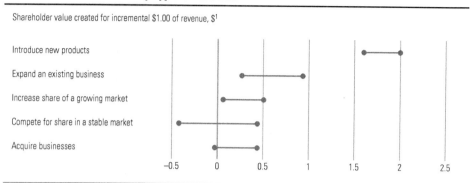

Shareholder value created for incremental $1.00 of revenue, $[1]

[1] Value for a typical consumer packaged goods company.

Growth strategies based on organic new-product development frequently have the highest returns because they don't require much new capital; companies can add new products to their existing factory lines and distribution systems. Furthermore, the investments to produce new products are not all required at once. If preliminary results are not promising, future investments can be scaled back or canceled.

Acquisitions, by contrast, require that the entire investment be made up front. The amount of up-front payment reflects the expected cash flows from the target plus a premium to stave off other bidders. So even if the buyer can improve the target enough to generate an attractive ROIC, the rate of return is typically only a small amount higher than its cost of capital.

To be fair, this analysis doesn't reflect the risk of failure. Most product ideas fail before reaching the market, and the cost of failed ideas is not reflected in the numbers. By contrast, acquisitions typically bring existing revenues and cash flows that limit the downside risk to the acquirer. But including the risk of failure would not change the pecking order of investments from a value-creation viewpoint.

The interaction between growth and ROIC is a key factor to consider when assessing the likely impact of a particular investment on a company's overall ROIC. For example, we've found that some very successful, high-ROIC companies in the United States are reluctant to invest in growth if it will reduce their returns on capital. One technology company had a 30 percent operating margin and ROIC of more than 50 percent, so it didn't want to invest in projects that might earn only 25 percent returns, fearing this would dilute its average returns. But as the first principle of value creation would lead you to expect, even an opportunity with a 25 percent return would still create value as long as the cost of capital was lower, despite the resulting decline in average ROIC.

The evidence backs this up. We examined the performance of 157 companies with high (greater than 20 percent) ROIC over two time periods: 1996–2005

EXHIBIT 3.9 **Impact of Growth and ROIC on High- and Low-ROIC Companies**

Median annualized TSR vs. S&P 500, 1996–2005 and 2010–2017, %

Drivers of performance		Performance, by high vs. low ROIC	
Growth	Change in ROIC	Companies with ROIC over 20%	Companies with ROIC of 6%–9%
Above average	Increased	6	4
Above average	Decreased	2	−2
Below average	Increased	0	3
Below average	Decreased	−3	−7

Source: B. Jiang and T. Koller, "How to Choose between Growth and ROIC," *McKinsey on Finance*, no. 25 (Autumn 2007): 19–22. Updated to include 2010–2017 data by the authors of this book.

and 2010–2017.[7] Not surprisingly, the companies that created the most value, measured by total shareholder returns, were those that grew fastest and maintained their high ROICs (see Exhibit 3.9). But the second-highest value creators within this group were those that grew fastest even though they experienced moderate declines in their ROICs. They created more value than companies that increased their ROICs but grew slowly.

We've also seen companies with low returns pursue growth on the assumption that this will also improve their profit margins and returns, reasoning that growth will increase ROIC by spreading fixed costs across more revenues. As mentioned earlier in this chapter, however, except at small start-up companies, faster growth rarely fixes a company's ROIC problem. Low returns usually indicate a poor industry structure (as is the case with airlines in Europe and Asia),[8] a flawed business model, or weak execution. If a company has a problem with ROIC, the company shouldn't grow until the problem is fixed.

The evidence backs this up as well. We examined the performance of 110 low-ROIC companies (the right column in Exhibit 3.9). The companies that

[7] B. Jiang and T. Koller, "How to Choose between Growth and ROIC," *McKinsey on Finance*, no. 25 (Autumn 2007): 19–22. Updated to include 2010–2017 data by the authors of this book.
[8] Airlines have traditionally suffered from overcapacity and lack of differentiation, leading to price competition and low returns. Recently, U.S. airlines, after a wave of consolidation, have been disciplined about adding capacity and creating ways to charge for services, like checking bags, with the result that returns on capital are higher than in the past.

EXHIBIT 3.10 **Impact on Value of Improving Margin vs. Capital Productivity**

| | Increase in value from improving ROIC by 1 percentage point[1] | | |
| | % change | | |
ROIC, %	Through margin improvement	Through capital productivity	Ratio of margin impact to capital productivity impact
10	20.0	13.5	1.2x
20	6.7	2.9	2.3x
30	4.0	1.2	3.4x
40	2.9	0.6	4.6x

[1] For a company with a 9% cost of capital.

had low growth but increased their ROICs outperformed the faster-growing companies that did not improve their ROICs.

One final factor for management to consider is the method by which it chooses to improve ROIC. A company can increase ROIC by either improving profit margins or improving capital productivity. With respect to future growth, it doesn't matter which of these paths a company emphasizes. But for current operations, at moderate ROIC levels, a one-percentage-point increase in ROIC through margin improvement will have a moderately higher impact on value relative to improving capital productivity. At high levels of ROIC, though, improving ROIC by increasing margins will create much more value than an equivalent ROIC increase by improving capital productivity. Exhibit 3.10 shows how this works for a company that has a 9 percent cost of capital.

The reason for this relationship is best explained by an example. Consider a company with zero growth, $1,000 of revenues, $100 of profits, and $500 of invested capital (translating to a 10 percent margin, a 50 percent ratio of invested capital to revenues, and ROIC of 20 percent). One way to increase ROIC by one percentage point is to increase the profit margin to 10.5 percent, increasing profits by $5. Since the company is not growing, the $5 of extra profits translates to $5 of cash flow each year going forward. Discounting at a 10 percent cost of capital, this represents a $50 increase in value. The company could also increase ROIC by reducing working capital. If it reduced working capital by $24, ROIC would increase to 21 percent ($100 divided by $476). The company's value would increase only by the $24 one-time cash inflow from reducing working capital. Future cash flows would not be affected.

ECONOMIC PROFIT COMBINES ROIC AND SIZE

You can also measure a company's value creation using economic profit, a measure that combines ROIC and size into a currency metric (here we use the

U.S. dollar). Economic profit measures the value created by a company in a single period and is defined as follows:

$$\text{Economic Profit} = \text{Invested Capital} \times (\text{ROIC} - \text{Cost of Capital})$$

In other words, economic profit is the spread between the return on invested capital and the cost of capital times the amount of invested capital. Value Inc.'s economic profit for year 1 is $50 (Value Inc. must have $500 of starting capital if it earns $100 at a 20 percent return in year 1):

$$\text{Economic Profit} = \$500 \times (20\% - 10\%)$$
$$= \$500 \times 10\%$$
$$= \$50$$

Volume Inc.'s economic profit in year 1 is zero (Volume Inc. must have $1,000 of starting capital if it earns $100 at a 10 percent return in year 1):

$$\text{Economic Profit} = \$1,000 \times (10\% - 10\%)$$
$$= \$1,000 \times 0\%$$
$$= \$0$$

You can also value a company by discounting its projected economic profit at the cost of capital and adding the starting invested capital. Value Inc. starts with $500 of invested capital. Its economic profit in year 1 is $50, which grows at 5 percent. Discounting the growing economic profit at a 10 percent discount rate gives a present value of economic profit of $1,000.[9] Use these amounts to solve for value:

$$\text{Value} = \text{Starting Invested Capital} + \text{PV(Projected Economic Profit)}$$
$$= \$500 + \$1,000$$
$$= \$1,500$$

The value of Value Inc. using the economic-profit approach is $1,500, exactly the same as with the discounted-cash-flow (DCF) approach.

Economic profit is also useful for comparing the value creation of different companies or business units. Consider Value Inc.'s economic profit of $50. Suppose Big Inc. had $5,000 in invested capital but earned only a 15 percent return on capital (and assume it doesn't have investment opportunities with

---

[9] The present value of economic profit for a growing perpetuity is economic profit in year 1 divided by the cost of capital minus the growth rate. For Value Inc., the present value of economic profit is therefore $50/(10% − 5%).

higher returns on capital). Its economic profit would be $250. Clearly, creating $250 of economic profit is preferable to creating $50.

Finally, measuring performance in terms of economic profit encourages a company to undertake investments that earn more than their cost of capital, even if their return is lower than the current average return. Suppose Value Inc. had the opportunity to invest an extra $200 at a 15 percent return. Its average ROIC would decline from 20 percent to 18.6 percent, but its economic profit would increase from $50 to $60.

CONSERVATION OF VALUE

A corollary of the principle that discounted cash flow (DCF) drives value is the conservation of value: anything that doesn't increase cash flows doesn't create value. That means value is conserved, or unchanged, when a company changes the ownership of claims to its cash flows but doesn't change the total available cash flows—for example, when it substitutes debt for equity or issues debt to repurchase shares. Similarly, changing the appearance of the cash flows without actually changing the cash flows—say, by changing accounting techniques—doesn't change the value of a company.[10] While the validity of this principle is obvious, it is worth emphasizing because executives, investors, and pundits so often forget it, as when they hope that one accounting treatment will lead to a higher value than another or that some fancy financial structure will turn a mediocre deal into a winner.

The battle over how companies should account for executive stock options illustrates the extent to which executives continue to believe (erroneously) that the stock market is unaware of the conservation of value. Even though there is no cash effect when executive stock options are issued, they reduce the cash flow available to existing shareholders by diluting their ownership when the options are exercised. Under accounting rules dating back to the 1970s, companies could exclude the implicit cost of executive stock options from their income statements. In the early 1990s, as options became more material, the Financial Accounting Standards Board (FASB) proposed a change to the accounting rules, requiring companies to record an expense for the value of options when they are issued. A large group of executives and venture capitalists thought investors would be spooked if options were brought onto the income statement. Some claimed that the entire venture capital industry would be decimated because young start-up companies that provide much of their compensation through options would show low or negative profits.

The FASB issued its new rules in 2004,[11] more than a decade after taking up the issue and only after the bursting of the dot-com bubble. Despite dire

---

[10] In some cases, a company can increase its value by reducing its cost of capital by using more debt in its capital structure. However, even in this case, the underlying change is to reduce taxes, but the overall pretax cost of capital doesn't change. See Chapter 33 for further discussion.

[11] Financial Accounting Standard 123R, released in December 2004, effective for periods beginning after June 15, 2005.

predictions, the stock prices of companies didn't change when the new accounting rules were implemented, because the market already reflected the cost of the options in its valuations of companies.[12] One respected analyst told us, "I don't care whether they are recorded as an expense or simply disclosed in the footnotes. I know what to do with the information."

In this case, the conservation of value principle explains why executives didn't need to worry about any effects that changes in stock option accounting would have on their share price. The same applies to questions such as whether an acquisition creates value simply because reported earnings increase, whether a company should return cash to shareholders through share repurchases instead of dividends, or whether financial engineering creates value. In every circumstance, executives should focus on increasing cash flows rather than finding gimmicks that merely redistribute value among investors or make reported results look better. Executives should also be wary of proposals that claim to create value unless they're clear about how their actions will materially increase the size of the pie. If you can't pinpoint the tangible source of value creation, you're probably looking at an illusion, and you can be sure that's what the market will think, too.

Conserving Value: A Brief History

The value conservation principle is described in the seminal textbook *Principles of Corporate Finance*, by Richard Brealey, Stewart Myers, and Franklin Allen.[13] One of the earliest applications of the principle can be found in the pioneering work of Nobel Prize winners Franco Modigliani and Merton Miller, financial economists who in the late 1950s and early 1960s questioned whether managers could use changes in capital structure to increase share prices. In 1958, they showed that the value of a company shouldn't be affected by changing the structure of the debt and equity ownership unless the overall cash flows generated by the company also change.[14]

Imagine a company that has no debt and generates $100 of cash flow each year before paying shareholders. Suppose the company is valued at $1,000. Now suppose the company borrows $200 and pays it out to the shareholders. Our knowledge of the core valuation principle and the value conservation principle tells us that the company would still be worth $1,000, with $200 for the creditors and $800 for the shareholders, because its cash flow available to pay the shareholders and creditors is still $100.

---

[12] D. Aboody, M. Barth, and R. Kasznik, "Firms' Voluntary Recognition of Stock-Based Compensation Expense," *Journal of Accounting Research* 42, no. 2 (December 2004): 251–275; D. Aboody, M. Barth, and R. Kasznik, "SFAS No. 123 Stock-Based Compensation Expense and Equity Market Values," *Accounting Review* 79, no. 2 (2004): 251–275; M. Semerdzhian, "The Effects of Expensing Stock Options and a New Approach to the Valuation Problem" (working paper, May 2004, SSRN).

[13] R. Brealey, S. Myers, and F. Allen, *Principles of Corporate Finance*, 12th ed. (New York: McGraw-Hill/Irwin, 2017).

[14] F. Modigliani and M. H. Miller, "The Cost of Capital, Corporation Finance and the Theory of Investment," *American Economic Review* 48, no. 3 (1958): 261–297.

In most countries, however, borrowing money does change cash flows because interest payments are tax deductible. The total taxes paid by the company are lower, thereby increasing the cash flow available to pay both shareholders and creditors. In addition, having debt may induce managers to be more diligent (because they must have cash available to repay the debt on time) and, therefore, increase the company's cash flow. On the downside, having debt could make it more difficult for managers to raise capital for attractive investment opportunities, thereby reducing cash flow. The point is that what matters isn't the substitution of debt for equity in and of itself; it matters only if the substitution changes the company's cash flows through tax reductions or if associated changes in management decisions change cash flows.

In a similar vein, finance academics in the 1960s developed the idea of efficient markets. While the meaning and validity of efficient markets are subjects of continuing debate, especially after the bursting of the dot-com and real estate bubbles, one implication of efficient-market theory remains: the stock market isn't easily fooled when companies undertake actions to increase reported accounting profit without increasing cash flows. One example is the market's reaction to changes in accounting for employee stock options, as described in the previous section of this chapter. And when the FASB eliminated goodwill amortization effective in 2002 and the International Accounting Standards Board (IASB) did the same in 2005, many companies reported increased profits, but their underlying values and stock prices didn't change, because the accounting change didn't affect cash flows. The evidence is overwhelming that the market isn't fooled by actions that don't affect cash flow, as we will show in Chapter 7.

A Tool for Managers

The conservation of value principle is so useful because it tells us what to look for when analyzing whether some action will create value: the cash flow impact and nothing else. This principle applies across a wide range of important business decisions, such as accounting policy, acquisitions (Chapter 31), corporate portfolio decisions (Chapter 28), dividend payout policy (Chapter 33), and capital structure (also Chapter 33).

This section provides three examples where applying the conservation of value principle can be useful: share repurchases, acquisitions, and financial engineering.

Share Repurchases   Share repurchases have become a popular way for companies to return cash to investors (see Chapter 33 for more detail). Until the early 1980s, more than 90 percent of the total distributions by large U.S. companies to shareholders were dividends, and less than 10 percent were share repurchases. But since 1998, about 50 percent of total distributions have been share repurchases.[15]

While buying back shares is often a good thing for management to do, a common fallacy is that share repurchases create value simply because they increase earnings per share (EPS).[16] For example, assume that a company with $700 of earnings and 1,000 shares outstanding borrows $1,000 to repurchase 10 percent of its shares. For every $1,000 of shares repurchased, the company will pay, say, 5 percent interest on its new debt. After tax savings of 25 percent, its total earnings would decline by $37.50, or 5.4%. However, the number of shares has declined by 10 percent, so earnings per share (EPS) would increase by about 5 percent.

A 5 percent increase in EPS without working very hard sounds like a great deal. Assuming the company's P/E ratio doesn't change, its market value per share also will increase by 5 percent. In other words, you can get something for nothing: higher EPS with a constant P/E.

Unfortunately, this doesn't square with the conservation of value, because the total cash flow of the business has not increased. While EPS has increased by 5 percent, the company's debt has increased as well. With higher leverage, the company's equity cash flows will be more volatile, and investors will demand a higher return. This will bring down the company's P/E, offsetting the increase in EPS.

Moreover, you must consider where the company could have invested the cash rather than returning it to shareholders. If the return on capital from the investment exceeded the company's cost of capital, it's likely that the longer-term EPS would be higher from the investment than from the share repurchases. Share repurchases increase EPS immediately, but possibly at the expense of lower long-term earnings.[17]

However, even if cash flow isn't increased by a buyback, some have rightly argued that repurchasing shares can reduce the likelihood that management will invest the cash at low returns. If this is true and it is likely that management would otherwise have invested the money unwisely, then you have a legitimate source of value creation, because the operating cash flows of the company would increase. Said another way, when the likelihood of investing cash at low returns is high, share repurchases make sense as a tactic for avoiding value destruction. But they don't in themselves create value.

Some argue that management should repurchase shares when the company's shares are undervalued. Suppose management believes that the current

[15] T. Koller, "Are Share Buybacks Jeopardizing Future Growth?," *McKinsey on Finance*, no. 56 (October 2015), www.mckinsey.com.
[16] O. Ezekoye, T. Koller, and A. Mittal, "How Share Repurchases Boost Earnings without Improving Returns," *McKinsey on Finance*, no. 58 (April 2016), www.mckinsey.com.
[17] Ibid.

share price of the company doesn't reflect its underlying potential, so it buys back shares today. One year later, the market price adjusts to reflect management's expectations. Has value been created? Once again, the answer is no, value has not been created; it has only been shifted from one set of shareholders (those who sold) to the shareholders who did not sell. So while the holding shareholders may have benefited, the shareholders as a whole were not affected. Buying back shares when they are undervalued may be good for the shareholders who don't sell, but studies of share repurchases have shown that companies aren't very good at timing share repurchases, often buying when their share prices are high, not low.[18]

Executives as a rule need to exercise caution when presented with transactions like share repurchases that appear to create value by boosting EPS. Always ask, "Where is the source of the value creation?" Some research and development (R&D)–intensive companies, for example, have searched for ways to capitalize R&D spending through complex joint ventures, hoping to lower expenses that reduce EPS. But does the joint venture create value by increasing short-term EPS? No, and in fact it may destroy value because the company now transfers upside potential—and risk, of course—to its partners.

Acquisitions   Chapter 31 covers acquisitions in more detail, but for now we can say that acquisitions create value only when the combined cash flows of the two companies increase due to cost reductions, accelerated revenue growth, or better use of fixed and working capital.

To give you a sense of how a good transaction might work, we'll use the example of United Rentals' purchase of RSC (another equipment rental company) for $1.9 billion in 2011. Within several years, they had achieved more than $250 million of annual cost savings. We conservatively estimated that the cost savings were worth over $1.5 billion in present value. That's equivalent to about 80 percent of the purchase price.

A revenue acceleration example comes from Johnson & Johnson, which in 1994 acquired Neutrogena, a maker of skin-care products, for $924 million. Over the next eight years, management introduced 20 new products within existing product categories and launched an entire line of men's care products. It also accelerated the brand's presence outside the United States. As a result, J&J increased Neutrogena's sales from $281 million to $778 million by 2002.

---

[18] B. Jiang and T. Koller, "The Savvy Executive's Guide to Buying Back Shares," *McKinsey on Finance*, no. 41 (Autumn 2011): 14–17. The results here are counter to academic studies that were based on earlier samples and included many small companies. Our study included only companies in the S&P 500. When share buybacks were rare, announcements were made with great fanfare and often provided strong signals of management's concern for capital discipline. Most of the fanfare has faded, as companies regularly repurchase shares, so announcements aren't a surprise to the market anymore.

The common element of both these acquisitions was radical performance improvement, not marginal change. But sometimes we have seen acquisitions justified by what could only be called magic.

Assume, for example, that Company A is worth $100 and Company B is worth $50, based on their respective expected cash flows. Company A buys Company B for $50, issuing its own shares. For simplicity, assume that the combined cash flows are not expected to increase. What is the new Company AB worth?

Immediately after the acquisition, the two companies are the same as they were before, with the same expected cash flows, and the original shareholders of the two companies still own the shares of the combined company. So Company AB should be worth $150, and the original A shareholders' shares of AB should be worth $100, while the original B shareholders' shares of AB should be worth $50.

As simple as this seems, some executives and financial professionals will still see some extra value in the transaction. Assume that Company A is expected to earn $5 next year, so its P/E is 20 times. Company B is expected to earn $3 next year, so its P/E is 16.7 times. What then will be the P/E of Company AB? A straightforward approach suggests that the value of Company AB should remain $150. Its earnings will be $8, so its P/E will be about 18.8, between A's and B's P/Es. But here's where the magic happens. Many executives and bankers believe that once A buys B, the stock market will apply A's P/E of 20 to B's earnings. In other words, B's earnings are worth more once they are owned by A. By this thinking, the value of Company AB would be $160, a $10 increase in the combined value.

There are even terms for this: *multiple expansion* in the United States and *rerating* in the United Kingdom. The notion is that the multiple of Company B's earnings expands to the level of Company A's because the market doesn't recognize that perhaps the new earnings added to A are not as valuable. This must be so, because B's earnings will now be all mixed up with A's, and the market won't be able to tell the difference.

Another version of the multiple-expansion illusion works the other way around. Now suppose Company B purchases Company A. We've heard the argument that since a company with a lower price-to-earnings (P/E) ratio is buying a higher-P/E company, it must be getting into higher-growth businesses. Higher growth is generally good, so another theory postulates that because B is accelerating its growth, its P/E will increase.

If multiple expansion were true, all acquisitions would create value because the P/E on the lower-P/E company's earnings would rise to that of the company with the higher P/E, regardless of which was the buyer or seller. But no data exist that support this fallacy. Multiple expansion may sound great, but it is an entirely unsound way of justifying an acquisition that doesn't have tangible benefits.

Every corporate leader must know this. So why are we discussing such obvious fallacies? The answer is that companies often do justify acquisitions using this flawed logic. Our alternative approach is simple: if you can't point to specific sources of increased cash flow, the stock market won't be fooled.

Financial Engineering   Another area where the value conservation principle is important is financial engineering, which unfortunately has no standard definition. For our purposes, we define financial engineering as the use of financial instruments or structures other than straight debt and equity to manage a company's capital structure and risk profile.

Financial engineering can include the use of derivatives, structured debt, securitization, and off-balance-sheet financing. While some of these activities can create real value, most don't. Even so, the motivation to engage in non-value-added financial engineering remains strong because of its short-term, illusory impact.

Consider that many of the largest hotel companies in the United States don't own most of the hotels they operate. Instead, the hotels themselves are owned by other companies, often structured as partnerships or real estate investment trusts (REITs). Unlike corporations, partnerships and REITs don't pay U.S. income taxes; only their owners do. Therefore, an entire layer of taxation is eliminated by placing hotels in partnerships and REITs in the United States. This method of separating ownership and operations lowers total income taxes paid to the government, so investors in the ownership and operating companies are better off as a group, because their aggregate cash flows are higher. This is an example of financial engineering that adds real value by increasing cash flows.

In contrast, sale-leaseback transactions rarely create value for investment-grade companies.[19] In a sale-leaseback transaction, a company sells an asset that it owns but wants to continue to use, such as an office building, to a buyer who then leases it back to the company. Often, the company structures the lease so that it is treated as a sale for accounting purposes, and then removes the asset from the company's balance sheet. It can also use the sale proceeds to pay down debt. Now it appears that the company has fewer assets and less debt. Rental expense replaces future depreciation and interest expense (though rental expense is typically higher than the sum of depreciation and interest expense).

For larger investment-grade companies, the implied interest rate on the lease is often higher than the company's regular borrowing rate, because the lessor uses the creditworthiness of the lessee to finance its purchase. In addition, the company buying the asset must cover its cost of equity and its operating costs.

---

[19] Both the FASB and IASB changed the lease accounting rules effective for the 2019 calendar year. Under the new rules, all leases greater than one year must be capitalized.

If the company intends to use the asset for its remaining life (by renewing the lease as it expires), then it has created no value, even though the company appears to be less capital-intensive and to have lower debt. In fact, it has destroyed value because the cost of the lease is higher than the cost of borrowing. The company also incurs its own transaction costs and may have to pay taxes on any gain from the sale of the asset. What's more, other creditors and rating agencies will often treat the lease as a debt equivalent anyway.

The transaction may create value if the company wants the ability to stop using the asset before its remaining life expires and wants to eliminate the risk that the value of the asset will be lower when it decides to stop using the asset.

Sale-leaseback transactions may also create value if the lessor is better able to use the tax benefits associated with owning the asset, such as accelerated depreciation. This does not violate the conservation of value principle, because the total cash flows to the companies involved have increased—at the expense of the government.

THE MATH OF VALUE CREATION

Earlier in this chapter, we introduced the value driver formula, a simple equation that captures the essence of valuation. For readers interested in the technical math of valuation, this section will show how we derive the formula. Let's begin with some terminology that we will use throughout the book (Part Two defines the terms in detail):

- *Net operating profit after taxes (NOPAT)* represents the profits generated from the company's core operations after subtracting the income taxes related to those core operations.
- *Invested capital* represents the cumulative amount the business has invested in its core operations—primarily property, plant, and equipment and working capital.
- *Net investment* is the increase in invested capital from one year to the next:

$$\text{Net Investment} = \text{Invested Capital}_{t+1} - \text{Invested Capital}_t$$

- *Free cash flow (FCF)* is the cash flow generated by the core operations of the business after deducting investments in new capital:

$$\text{FCF} = \text{NOPAT} - \text{Net Investment}$$

- *Return on invested capital (ROIC)* is the return the company earns on each dollar invested in the business:

$$\text{ROIC} = \frac{\text{NOPAT}}{\text{Invested Capital}}$$

ROIC can be defined in two ways: as the return on all capital or as the return on new, or incremental, capital. For now, we assume that both returns are the same.

- *Investment rate (IR)* is the portion of NOPAT invested back into the business:

$$IR = \frac{\text{Net Investment}}{\text{NOPAT}}$$

- *Weighted average cost of capital (WACC)* is the rate of return that investors expect to earn from investing in the company and therefore the appropriate discount rate for the free cash flow. WACC is defined in detail in Chapter 15.
- *Growth (g)* is the rate at which the company's NOPAT and cash flow grow each year.

Assume that the company's revenues and NOPAT grow at a constant rate and the company invests the same proportion of its NOPAT in its business each year. Investing the same proportion of NOPAT each year also means that the company's free cash flow will grow at a constant rate.

Since the company's cash flows are growing at a constant rate, we can begin by valuing a company using the well-known cash-flow perpetuity formula:

$$\text{Value} = \frac{FCF_{t=1}}{WACC - g}$$

This formula is well established in the finance and mathematics literature.[20]

Next, define free cash flow in terms of NOPAT and the investment rate:

$$FCF = \text{NOPAT} - \text{Net Investment}$$
$$= \text{NOPAT} - (\text{NOPAT} \times IR)$$
$$= \text{NOPAT}(1 - IR)$$

Earlier, we developed the relationship between the investment rate (IR), the company's projected growth in NOPAT (g), and the return on investment (ROIC):[21]

$$g = \text{ROIC} \times IR$$

---

[20] For the derivation, see T. E. Copeland and J. Fred Weston, *Financial Theory and Corporate Policy*, 3rd ed. (Reading, MA: Addison-Wesley, 1988), Appendix A.

[21] Technically, we should use the return on new, or incremental, capital, but for simplicity we assume that the ROIC and incremental ROIC are equal.

Solving for IR, rather than g, leads to:

$$IR = \frac{g}{ROIC}$$

Now build this into the definition of free cash flow:

$$FCF = NOPAT\left(1 - \frac{g}{ROIC}\right)$$

Substituting for free cash flow in the cash-flow perpetuity formula gives the key value driver formula:[22]

$$Value = \frac{NOPAT_{t=1}\left(1 - \frac{g}{ROIC}\right)}{WACC - g}$$

This formula underpins the discounted-cash-flow (DCF) approach to valuation, and a variant of the equation lies behind the economic-profit approach. Chapter 10 describes in depth these two mathematically equivalent valuation techniques. You might go so far as to say that this formula represents all there is to valuation. Everything else is mere detail.

Substituting the forecast assumptions given for Value Inc. and Volume Inc. in Exhibit 3.2 into the key value driver formula results in the same values we came up with when we discounted their cash flows:

Company	NOPAT$_{t=1}$, \$	Growth, %	ROIC, %	WACC, %	Value, \$
Value Inc.	100	5	20	10	1,500
Volume Inc.	100	5	10	10	1,000

In most cases, we do not use this formula in practice. The reason is that in most situations, the model is overly restrictive, as it assumes a constant ROIC and growth rate going forward. For companies whose key value drivers are expected to change, we need a model that is more flexible in its forecasts. Nevertheless, while we do not use this formula in practice, it is extremely useful as a means to maintain focus on what drives value.

Until now, we have concentrated on how ROIC and growth drive the DCF valuation. It is also possible to use the key value driver formula to show that ROIC and growth determine the multiples commonly used to analyze company

---

[22] Technically, this formula should use the return on new invested capital (RONIC), not the company's return on all invested capital (ROIC). For convenience throughout this book, we frequently use ROIC to denote both the return on all capital and the return on new invested capital.

valuation, such as price-to-earnings and market-to-book ratios. To see this, divide both sides of the key value driver formula by NOPAT:

$$\frac{Value}{NOPAT_{t=1}} = \frac{\left(1 - \dfrac{g}{ROIC}\right)}{WACC - g}$$

As the formula shows, a company's earnings multiple is driven by both its expected growth and its return on invested capital.

You can also turn the formula into a value-to-invested-capital formula. Start with the identity:

$$NOPAT = Invested\ Capital \times ROIC$$

Substitute this definition of NOPAT into the key value driver formula:

$$Value = \frac{Invested\ Capital \times ROIC \times \left(1 - \dfrac{g}{ROIC}\right)}{WACC - g}$$

Divide both sides by invested capital:[23]

$$\frac{Value}{Invested\ Capital} = ROIC \left(\frac{1 - \dfrac{g}{ROIC}}{WACC - g}\right)$$

Now that we have explained the logic behind the DCF approach to valuation, you may wonder why analysts' reports and investment-banking pitches so often use earnings multiples, rather than valuations based on DCF analysis. The answer is partly that earnings multiples are a useful shorthand for communicating values to a wider public. A leading sell-side analyst told us that he uses discounted cash flow to analyze and value companies but typically communicates his findings in terms of implied multiples. For example, an analyst might say Company X deserves a higher multiple than Company Y because it is expected to grow faster, earn higher margins, or generate more cash flow. Earnings multiples are also a useful sanity check for your valuation. In practice, we always compare a company's implied multiple based on our valuation with those of its peers to see if we can explain why its multiple is higher or lower in terms of its ROIC or growth rates. See Chapter 18 for a discussion of how to analyze earnings multiples.

---

[23] If total ROIC and incremental ROIC are not the same, then this equation becomes:

$$\frac{Value}{Invested\ Capital} = ROIC \left(\frac{1 - \dfrac{g}{RONIC}}{WACC - g}\right)$$

where ROIC equals the return on the company's current capital and RONIC equals the return on new invested capital.

SUMMARY

This chapter has explored how expected cash flows, discounted at a cost of capital, drive value. Cash flow, in turn, is driven by expected returns on invested capital and revenue growth. Companies create value only when ROIC exceeds their cost of capital. Further, higher-ROIC companies should typically prioritize growth over further improving ROIC, as growth is a more powerful value driver for them. In contrast, lower-ROIC companies should prioritize improving ROIC, as it is a stronger value driver for them.

A corollary of this is the conservation of value: anything that doesn't increase cash flows doesn't create value. So changing the appearance of a company's performance through, say, accounting changes or write-ups or write-downs, without changing cash flows, won't change a company's value. Risk enters into valuation both through the company's cost of capital and in the uncertainty of future cash flows. Because investors can diversify their portfolios, the only risk that affects the cost of capital is the risk that investors cannot diversify, a topic we take up in Chapters 4 and 15.

4

Risk and the Cost
of Capital

In valuing companies or projects, the subjects of risk and the cost of capital are essential, inseparable, and fraught with misconceptions. These misconceptions can lead to damaging strategic mistakes. For example, when a company borrows money to finance an acquisition and applies only the cost of debt to the target's cash flows, it might easily overestimate by two times the target's value. Conversely, when a company adds an arbitrary risk premium to a target's cost of capital in an emerging market, it could underestimate the value of the target by half.

A company's cost of capital is critical for determining value creation and for evaluating strategic decisions. It is the rate at which you discount future cash flows for a company or project. It is also the rate you compare with the return on invested capital to determine if the company is creating value. The cost of capital incorporates both the time value of money and the risk of investment in a company, business unit, or project.

In this chapter, we'll explain why the cost of capital is *not* a cash cost, but an opportunity cost. The opportunity cost is based on what investors could earn by investing their money elsewhere at the same level of risk. This is always an option for publicly listed companies.[1] Only certain types of risks—those that cannot be diversified—affect a company's cost of capital. Other risks, which can be diversified, should only be reflected in the cash flow forecast using multiple cash flow scenarios.

We'll also discuss how much cash flow risk to take on. Companies should take on all investments that have a positive expected value,[2] regardless of

---

[1] As a reminder from Chapter 2, the amount of value that companies create is the amount they earn above their cost of capital. That is, companies create value only when they can invest funds at higher returns than their investors can earn themselves.

[2] This is often referred to as net present value (NPV); we prefer the term *expected value* because it emphasizes the riskiness of underlying cash flows.

their risk profile, unless the projects are so large that failure would threaten the viability of the entire company. Most executives are reluctant to take on smaller risky projects even if the returns are very high. By aggregating projects into portfolios, rather than assessing them individually, executives can often overcome excessive loss aversion.

Our focus in this chapter will be on key principles. Chapter 15 provides detail on how to measure the cost of capital.

COST OF CAPITAL IS AN OPPORTUNITY COST

The cost of capital is not a cash cost. It is an opportunity cost. To illustrate, when one company acquires another company, the alternative might have been to return that cash to shareholders, who could then reinvest it in other companies. So the cost of capital for the acquiring company is the price investors charge for bearing risk—what they could have earned by reinvesting the proceeds in other investments with similar risk.[3] Similarly, when valuing individual business units or projects for strategic decision making, the correct cost of capital is what a company's investors could expect to earn in other similarly risky projects, not necessarily the whole company. The core principle is that the cost of capital is driven by investors' opportunity cost, because the executives leading the company are the investors' agents and have a fiduciary responsibility to the company's investors.[4] That's why the cost of capital is also referred to as the investors' required return or expected return. The meaning of these terms may differ in academia, but for the most part you can use cost of capital, required return, and expected return interchangeably.

Chapter 15 describes in detail how to estimate a company's opportunity cost of capital. Most practitioners use a weighted average cost of capital (WACC), meaning the weighted average of the cost of equity capital and the cost of debt capital.[5] For now, it's enough to say that a company's cost of equity capital is what investors could earn by investing in a broad portfolio of

---

[3] To be more precise, the cost of capital is the return investors can earn from investing in a well-diversified, "efficient" portfolio of investments with similar risk.

[4] In some countries, executives also have a duty to the "company," but that concept is typically vaguely defined and does not provide executives with much guidance. For the most part, even in those countries, the opportunity cost for investors is the best calculation to make. In the United States, a recent innovation is the "benefit" corporation, whose charter includes additional objectives that executives can weigh against the interest of shareholders, including positive impact on society, workers, communities, and the environment. The concept is relatively new; not many large listed companies are benefit corporations, the conversion to which requires a shareholder vote.

[5] The use of WACC is a practical solution. In theory, the opportunity cost of capital is independent of capital structure (a company's amount of debt versus equity) except for the tax benefit of debt. An alternative is to estimate the opportunity cost of capital as the company's cost of equity (what equity investors expect to earn) if it had no debt, adjusted directly for the tax benefit of debt. In theory, the two approaches should yield the same result.

companies (say, the S&P 500), adjusted for the riskiness of the company relative to the average of all companies.

Within a company, individual business units can have different costs of capital if their risk profiles differ. The company's overall cost of capital is simply a weighted average of its business units' costs of capital. In banking, for example, risky trading operations carry much higher costs of capital than more stable retail banking units.

Executives often fail to adequately incorporate the idea of opportunity cost in thinking about their cost of capital. Sometimes they mix up the opportunity cost of capital by associating different funding streams with different investments. For example, when one company acquires another, the buyer might raise enough debt to pay for the entire company. It is tempting to say that the cost of capital for the acquisition is the cost of the debt. But this would be a mistake, because the risk of the target's free cash flows does not equal the risk of the bondholders' cash flows.

To illustrate, say Company A is considering buying Company B. Both operate in the same product area with similar risk. Company A has no debt and an opportunity cost of capital of 8 percent. Suppose Company A can borrow at 4 percent after taxes. For a target company growing at 3 percent with $1 billion in earnings and a 15 percent return on capital, the value of the target would be $80 billion at a 4 percent cost of capital and $20 billion at an 8 percent cost of capital. To get a sense of how absurd it would be to use the 4 percent cost of capital, consider that the implied price-to-earnings ratio (P/E) at 4 percent is 80, compared with 20 at an 8 percent cost of capital. Companies growing at 3 percent don't trade at a P/E of 80.

In addition, if you apply the cost of debt to the acquisition, you end up with a perverse situation: Company A's existing businesses are assigned an 8 percent cost of capital, and the acquired business is assigned a 4 percent cost of capital. In addition, the only reason Company A can borrow 100 percent of the cost of the acquisition is that it has unused debt capacity in its existing businesses. And don't forget, the cost of capital is determined by the acquired company's riskiness, not that of the parent company (although their risk profiles are likely to be the same if they are in the same industry).

COMPANIES HAVE LITTLE CONTROL OVER THEIR COST OF CAPITAL

It might be surprising to learn that the cost of capital for a company with steady revenues, like Procter & Gamble, isn't that different from a company like LyondellBasell, a chemical company in an industry known for having more variable earnings and cash flows. In 2019, most large companies' WACC fell in the range of 7 to 9 percent. The range is small because investors purposely avoid putting all their eggs in one basket. The ability of investors to diversify their portfolios means that only nondiversifiable risk affects the cost

EXHIBIT 4.1 **Volatility of Portfolio Return Declines with Diversification**

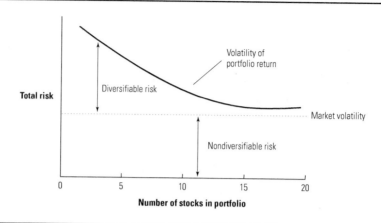

of capital. Furthermore, because nondiversifiable risk also generally affects all companies in the same industry in the same way, a company's industry is what primarily drives its cost of capital. Companies in the same industry will have similar costs of capital.

Stock market investors, especially institutional investors, may hold hundreds of different stocks in their portfolios. Even the most concentrated investors have at least 50. As a result, their exposure to any single company is limited. It is possible to show how the total risk of a portfolio of stocks declines as more shares are added to the portfolio (Exhibit 4.1). The risk declines because companies' cash flows are not perfectly correlated. Over any period of time, some will increase while others decline.

One of the durable tenets of academic finance concerns the effect of diversification on the cost of capital. If diversification reduces risk to investors and it is not costly to diversify, then investors will not demand a higher return for any risks that can be eliminated through diversification. They require compensation only for risks they cannot diversify away.

The risks they cannot diversify away are those that affect all companies—for example, exposure to economic cycles. However, since most of the risks that companies face are, in fact, diversifiable, most risks don't affect a company's cost of capital. One way to see this in practice is to note the relatively narrow range of P/Es for large companies. Most large companies have P/Es between 12 and 20. If the cost of capital varied from 5 to 15 percent instead of 7 to 9 percent, many more companies would have P/Es below 8 and above 25.

Whether a company's cost of capital is 7 percent or 9 percent or somewhere in between is a question of great dispute (as we explore in Chapter 15). For decades, the standard model for measuring differences in costs of capital has been the capital asset pricing model (CAPM). The CAPM has been challenged by academics and practitioners, but so far, no practical competing model has emerged.[6] At any rate, when returns on capital across companies vary from less than 5 percent to more than 30 percent (sometimes even within the same sector), a one-percentage-point difference in the cost of capital seems hardly worth arguing about.

The unique risks that any company faces—say, product obsolescence and new competition—are not priced into the cost of capital. That does not mean a company's value is immune to these risks; they do affect expected cash flows and therefore expected value. Companies certainly do need to worry about the effects of such risks, as we discuss later in this chapter.

It is a common misconception that the cost of capital is company-specific, rather than a function of the industries in which a company operates and the specific investments it makes. For the most part, companies have scant influence over the cost of capital of their individual business units or their company as a whole. There are some theoretical examples of how companies could reduce their cost of capital. For example, a company could outsource production to lower fixed costs and therefore reduce the volatility of cash flows. If you can achieve lower volatility than your peers', your cost of capital will be slightly lower. But it's unlikely that the change in the cost of capital will be large enough relative to other strategic considerations of outsourcing manufacturing. Some companies have shortened the duration of their debt to try to reduce their cost of capital. What these companies fail to recognize is that this increases their risk because of the possibility that interest rates will be higher when the shorter-term debt is rolled over or that the company may have difficulty refinancing the debt at all.

CREATE BETTER FORECASTS, NOT AD HOC RISK PREMIUMS

Certain projects carry what many investors see as high risk.[7] These include large capital projects in politically unstable countries (common among companies in the mining and oil and gas sectors), speculative R&D projects in

---

[6] Many in the academic community use the Fama-French three-factor model, but mostly for capital market research rather than business valuation. With this model, a stock's excess returns are regressed on excess market returns (like the CAPM), the excess returns of small stocks minus big stocks (SMB), and the excess returns of high book-to-market stocks minus low book-to-market stocks (HML). In 2015, the authors expanded the model to five factors, adding operating profitability and investment. See E. Fama and K. French, "The Cross-Section of Expected Stock Returns," *Journal of Finance* (June 1992): 427–465; E. Fama and K. French, "Common Risk Factors in the Returns on Stocks and Bonds," *Journal of Financial Economics* 33 (1993): 3–56; and E. Fama and K. French, "A Five-Factor Asset Pricing Model," *Journal of Financial Economics* 116 (2015): 1–22.

[7] This section is adapted from R. Davies, M. Goedhart, and T. Koller, "Avoiding a Risk Premium That Unnecessarily Kills Your Project," *McKinsey on Finance*, no. 44 (Summer 2012).

high tech and pharmaceuticals, and acquisitions of unproven technologies or businesses in a wide range of industries. The potential returns for such investments are alluring, but what if the projects or companies fail? The answer is not to ignore these risks, but to explicitly include them in cash flow forecasts, not the cost of capital. The preferred way is to develop multiple cash flow scenarios.

It's not unusual for companies to bump up the assumed cost of capital to reflect the uncertainty of risky projects. In doing so, however, they often unwittingly set these rates at levels that even substantial underlying risks would not justify—and end up rejecting good investment opportunities as a result.[8] What many don't realize is that assumptions of discount rates that are only three to five percentage points higher than the cost of capital can significantly reduce estimates of expected value. Adding just three percentage points to an 8 percent cost of capital for an acquisition, for example, can reduce its present value by 30 to 40 percent.

Moreover, increasing the discount rate embeds into the valuation process opaque risk assumptions that are often based on little more than a gut sense that the risk is higher. The problem arises because companies take shortcuts when they estimate cash flows. To calculate expected value, project analysts should discount the expected cash flows at an appropriate cost of capital. In many cases, though, they use only estimates of cash flow that assume everything goes well. Managers, realizing this, increase the discount rate to compensate for the possibility that cash flows are overstated.

A better approach for determining the expected value of a project is to develop multiple cash flow scenarios, value them at the unadjusted cost of capital, and then apply probabilities for the value of each scenario to estimate the expected value of the project or company. Exhibit 4.2 provides an example. For simplicity, we assume just two scenarios, one with a present value of $1,000 and the other with a present value of $1,667, based on each scenario's expected cash flow. Assuming a 50 percent probability for each scenario leads to an expected value of $1,333.

EXHIBIT 4.2 **Scenario Approach to Incorporating Nondiversifiable Risk**

Expected net present value (NPV), $	Probability of scenario	NPV at 8% WACC, $	Cash flows, $			
			Year 1	Year 2	Year 3	...
1,333 ◄	Base case: 50%	1,667	100	102	104	
	Downside case: 50%	1,000	60	61	62	

---

[8] M. Goedhart and P. Haden, "Are Emerging Markets as Risky as You Think?" *McKinsey on Finance*, no. 7 (Spring 2003).

Using scenarios has several advantages:

- It provides decision makers with more information. Rather than looking at a project with a single-point estimate of expected value (say, $100 million), decision makers know that there is a 20 percent chance that the project's value is –$20 million and an 80 percent chance it is $120 million. Making implicit risk assumptions explicit encourages dialogue about the risk of the project.
- It encourages managers to develop strategies to mitigate specific risks, because it explicitly highlights the impact of failure or less than complete success. For example, executives might build more flexibility into a project by providing options for stepwise investments—scaling up in case of success and scaling down in case of failure. Creating such options can significantly increase the value of projects.
- It acknowledges the full range of possible outcomes. When project advocates submit a single scenario, they need it to reflect enough upside to secure approval but also be realistic enough that they can commit to its performance targets. These requirements often produce a poor compromise. If advocates present multiple scenarios, they can show a project's full upside potential and realistic project targets they can truly commit to while also fully disclosing a project's potential downside risk.

Managers applying the scenario approach should be wary of overly simplistic assumptions—say, a 10 percent increase or decrease to the cash flows. A good scenario analysis will often lead to a highly successful case that is many multiples of the typical base case. It will often also include a scenario with a negative value. In addition, there may not be a traditional base case. For many projects, there is only big success or failure, with low likelihood that a project will just barely earn more than the cost of capital.

Consider an extreme example. Project A requires an up-front investment of $2,000. If everything goes well with the project, the company earns $1,000 per year forever. If not, the company gets zero. (Such all-or-nothing projects are not unusual.) To value project A, finance theory directs you to discount the expected cash flow at the cost of capital. But what is the expected cash flow in this case? If there is a 60 percent chance of everything going well, the expected cash flows would be $600 per year. At a 10 percent cost of capital, the project would be worth $6,000 once completed. Subtracting the $2,000 investment, the net value of the project before the investment is made is $4,000.

But the project will never generate $600 per year. It will generate annual cash flows of either $1,000 or zero. That means the present value of the discounted cash flows will be either $10,000 or nothing, making the project net of the initial investment worth either $8,000 or –$2,000. The probability of it being worth the expected value of $4,000 (that is, $6,000 less the investment) is zero. Rather than trying to identify the expected value, managers would be better off knowing that the project carries a 60 percent chance of being worth $8,000 and a 40 percent risk of losing $2,000. Managers can then examine the scenarios under which each outcome prevails and decide whether the upside compensates for the downside, whether the company can comfortably absorb the potential loss, and whether they can take actions to reduce the magnitude or risk of loss. The theoretical approach of focusing on expected values, while mathematically correct, hides some important information about the range and exclusivity of particular outcomes.

Moreover, some companies don't apply the expected-value approach correctly. Few companies discuss multiple scenarios, preferring a single-point forecast on which to base a yes-or-no decision. Most companies would simply represent the expected cash flows from this project as being $1,000 per year, the amount if everything goes well, and allow for uncertainty in the cash flow by arbitrarily increasing the discount rate. While you can get to the right answer with this approach, it has two flaws. First, there is no easy way to determine the cost of capital that gives the correct value. In this case, using a 16.7 percent cost of capital instead of 10 percent results in a project value of $6,000 before the investment and $4,000 after the investment. But the only way to know that this is the correct value would be to conduct a thorough scenario analysis. Companies sometimes arbitrarily add a risk premium to the cost of capital, but there is no way for them to know whether the amount they add is even reasonably accurate. Second, the decision makers evaluating a project with cash flows of $1,000 per year and a 16.7 percent cost of capital are still not thinking through the 40 percent risk that it might generate no cash at all.

If for some reason you must use a single cash flow scenario, you can analytically estimate the equivalent risk premium for different probability levels of failure, as in Exhibit 4.3. The exhibit shows the amounts by which you would increase the cost of capital instead of using cash flow scenarios for different combinations of the probability of failure, as represented on the vertical axis, and the size of loss relative to the base case, as represented by the horizontal axis. For example, if there was a 50 percent chance of failure in which case the project would be worth 40 percent less than expected, the equivalent risk premium would be 1.5 percent. Notice in this exhibit that the risk premiums are small relative to what most people expect. To get close to a 3 percent risk premium, for example, you'd have to believe there was a 50 percent chance of failure and a 60 percent reduction in cash flows associated with failure. To get to a 5 percent risk premium, you'd have to believe there is a 50 percent chance of failure and more than an 80 percent reduction in cash flows.[9]

Adding ad hoc risk premiums is a crude way to include project-specific uncertainty in a valuation. Scenario-based approaches have the dual appeal of better answers and more transparency on the assumptions embedded within them.

---

[9] Note that the risk premium will be determined not just by the probability and magnitude of loss, but also by the duration of the project or company and pattern of cash flows.

EXHIBIT 4.3 **Example of Equivalent Risk Premiums for Different Probability Levels of Failure**

Risk premium, %

		Size of cash flow reduction, %				
		20	40	60	80	100
	10	0.1	0.2	0.4	0.5	0.7
	20	0.2	0.5	0.8	1.1	1.5
Probability of lower cash flow, %	30	0.4	0.8	1.3	1.9	2.6
	40	0.5	1.1	1.9	2.8	4.0
	50	0.7	1.5	2.6	4.0	6.0

A 1.5% risk premium is required, assuming even odds that an investment will lose 40% of its value

Note: This particular example is for a company with an indefinite life, assuming a smooth cash flow profile, 8% weighted average cost of capital, and 2% terminal growth. The cost of capital adjustments would be larger for a project with a short life.

Source: R. Davis, M. Goedhart, and T. Koller, "Avoiding a Risk Premium That Unnecessarily Kills Your Project," *McKinsey Quarterly* (August 2012).

DECIDE HOW MUCH CASH FLOW RISK TO TAKE ON

Now let's turn to cash flow risk. When we talk about total cash flow risk, we mean the uncertainty that a company faces about its future cash flows, whether for the company as a whole, a business unit, or a single project. Finance theory provides guidance on pricing the nondiversifiable part of cash flow risk in the cost of capital. In theory, a company should take on all projects or growth opportunities that have positive expected values even if there is high likelihood of failure, as long as the project is small enough that failure will not put the company in financial distress. In practice, we've found that companies overweight the impact of losses from smaller projects, thereby missing value creation opportunities.

For instance, how should a company think through whether to undertake a project—let's call it project A—with a 60 percent chance of earning $8,000, a 40 percent chance of losing $2,000, and an expected value of $4,000? Theory says to take on all projects with a positive expected value, regardless of the upside-versus-downside risk. A company is likely to have many small projects like this example, so for small projects, it should take on all projects with positive expected value, regardless of risk.

But what if the company instead has one large project where the downside possibility would bankrupt the company? Consider an electric power company with the opportunity to build a nuclear power facility for $15 billion (a realistic amount for a facility with two reactors). Suppose the company has $25 billion in existing debt and $25 billion in equity market capitalization. If the plant is successfully constructed and brought on line, there is an 80 percent chance it will be worth $28 billion, for a net value of $13 billion. But there is a 20 percent chance it will fail to receive regulatory approval and be worth zero, leading to a loss of $15 billion. The expected value is $7 billion net of investment.[10] Failure will bankrupt the company, because the cash flow from the company's existing plants would be insufficient to cover its existing debt plus the debt on the failed plant. In this case, the economics of the nuclear plant spill over onto the value of the rest of the company. Failure would wipe out all the equity of the company, not just the $15 billion invested in the plant.

The implication is that a company should not take on a risk that will put the rest of the company in danger. In other words, don't do anything that has large negative spillover effects on the rest of the company. This caveat would be enough to guide managers in the earlier example of deciding whether to go ahead with project A. If a $2,000 loss would endanger the company as a whole, management should forgo the project, despite its 60 percent likelihood of success. But by the same token, companies should not avoid risks that don't threaten their ability to operate normally.

Executives making decisions for their companies should think about the company's risk profile, not their own.[11] After all, that's the job of corporations; they are designed to take risks and overcome the natural loss aversion of individuals. The earliest corporations were the British and Dutch East India shipping companies. With those, if a ship sank, all shareholders would lose a tolerable amount instead of having one ship owner lose his entire fortune.

Professors Daniel Kahneman and Amos Tversky have demonstrated that most people place greater weight on the potential economic losses from their decisions than on the potential equivalent gains. In a McKinsey survey of 1,500 global executives across many industries,[12] we presented the executives with the following scenario: You are considering making a $10 million investment that has some chance of returning, in present value, $40 million over three years, with some chance of losing the entire investment in the first year. What is the highest loss you would tolerate and still proceed with the investment?

A risk-neutral executive would be willing to accept a 75 percent chance of loss and a 25 percent chance of gain. One-quarter of $40 million is $10 million, which is the initial investment, so a 25 percent chance of gain creates an expected risk-neutral value of zero. But most survey respondents demonstrated extreme loss aversion; they were willing to accept only a 19 percent chance of loss to make this investment, nowhere near the risk-neutral answer of 75 percent. In fact, only 9 percent of respondents were willing to accept a 40 percent

[10] The calculation is ($13 billion × 80%) + (−$15 billion × 20%).
[11] "The remainder of this section is adapted from D. Lovallo, T. Koller, R. Uhlaner, and D. Kahneman, "Your Company Is Too Risk-Averse," *Harvard Business Review* (March–April 2020), hbr.org.
[12] T. Koller, D. Lovallo, and Z. Williams, "Overcoming a Bias against Risk," McKinsey & Company (August 2012), https://www.mckinsey.com/business-functions/strategy-and-corporate-finance/our-insights/overcoming-a-bias-against-risk.

EXHIBIT 4.4 **Aggregating Projects Reduces Risk While Achieving High Expected Returns**

Projects	Return, ratio of present value to investment	Risk, standard deviation of expected return, %	Expected net present value, $ million
Portfolio of selected projects A–Q	4.5	15	8,100
A	15.4	64	200
B	12.4	104	500
C	7.5	66	50
D	4.7	22	5
E	4.7	150	200
F	4.4	52	500
G	3.7	37	30
H	3.7	29	400
I	2.7	58	900
J	2.6	31	400
K	2.5	150	300
L	2.3	20	220
M	1.9	18	520
N	1.5	20	300
O	1.1	13	850
P	0.9	5	2,000
Q	0.3	5	850

or greater chance of loss. Informally, we've asked groups of executives the same question at even lower levels of investment and found similar results. Our findings echo those from Professor Ralph O. Swalm, going back to 1966.[13]

This phenomenon has serious consequences for hierarchical organizations. Executives are just as loss-averse when the bets are small as they are when the gambles are large, even though small gambles do not raise the same issues of survival or ruin that provide a rationale for aversion to large risks. What's more, small gambles offer opportunities for the risk-reducing effects of aggregation.

To overcome loss aversion and make better investment decisions, individuals and organizations must learn to frame choices in the context of the entire company's success, not the individual project's performance. In practice, this means looking at projects as a portfolio by aggregating them, rather than focusing on the risk of individual projects.

One technology company successfully used a portfolio approach to assess its projects. First, executives estimated the expected return of each project proposal (measured as expected present value divided by investment) and the risks associated with each (measured as the standard deviation of projected returns). Executives then built portfolios of projects and identified combinations that would deliver the best balance between return and risk. When they viewed portfolios of projects in the aggregate (Exhibit 4.4), executives could

[13] These results build on a 1966 *Harvard Business Review* article, "Utility Theory: Insights into Risk Taking," by Ralph O. Swalm. He studied executives with varying levels of spending authority and found that risk-preference profiles were very similar for executives at different levels of the organization.

see that portfolios of projects had higher returns than most of the individual projects and much lower risk compared with most of the individual projects.

It's worth pointing out that even though a portfolio of projects has lower risk, the use of portfolios does not lower a company's cost of capital. That's because the portfolio, by definition, cannot reduce the nondiversifiable risk, which is the risk embedded in the cost of capital.

DECIDE WHICH TYPES OF RISK TO HEDGE

There are also risks that investors are eager for companies to take. For example, investors in gold-mining companies and oil production companies buy those stocks to gain exposure to often-volatile gold or oil prices. If gold and oil companies attempt to hedge their revenues, that effort merely complicates life for their investors, who then must guess how much price risk is being hedged and how and whether management will change its policy in the future. Moreover, hedging may lock in today's prices for two years, the time horizon within which it is possible to hedge those commodities, but a company's present value includes the cash flows from subsequent years at fluctuating market prices. So while hedging may reduce the short-term cash flow volatility, it will have little effect on the company's valuation based on long-term cash flows.

Some risks, like the commodity price risk in this example, can be managed by shareholders themselves. Other, similar-looking risks—for example, some forms of currency risk—are harder for shareholders to manage. The general rule is to avoid hedging the first type of risk but hedge the second if possible.

Consider the effect of U.S. dollar currency risk on Heineken, the global brewer. For the U.S. market, Heineken produces its flagship brand, Heineken, in the Netherlands, and ships it to America. In most other markets, it produces and sells in the same country. So, for most markets, an exchange rate change affects only the translation of local profits into their reporting currency. For example, for most markets, a 1 percent change in the value of the local currency relative to the euro translates into a 1 percent change in revenues and a 1 percent change in profits as well. Note that the effect on revenues and profits is the same, because all the revenues and costs are in the same currency. There is no change in operating margin.

The U.S. market is different. When the dollar/euro exchange rate changes, Heineken's revenues in euros are affected, but its costs are not. If the dollar declines by 1 percent, Heineken's euro revenues also decline by 1 percent. But since its costs are in euros, those don't change. Assuming a 10 percent margin to begin with, a 1 percent decline in the dollar will reduce Heineken's margin to 9 percent, and its profits reported in euros will decline by a whopping 10 percent.

Because Heineken's production facilities are in a different country and it is unable to pass on cost increases because it is competing with locally produced products, its currency risk is larger for its U.S. business than for its other markets. Hedging might be much more important for Heineken's U.S. business than for other markets, because a rise or fall in the dollar/euro exchange rate has a much greater impact on its business.

SUMMARY

To avoid unfavorable strategic decisions, executives must understand well the dynamic relationship between the cost of capital and risk. Risk enters valuation both through the company's cost of capital (an opportunity cost) and through the uncertainty surrounding future cash flows. Because investors can diversify their portfolios, a company's cost of capital is for the most part determined by the industry in which it operates.

Valuations that use multiple cash flow scenarios better reflect diversifiable risks than those that adjust the cost of capital. Executives tend to shy away from risky projects even if the potential return is high. This excessive loss aversion can be overcome by examining portfolios of projects, rather than individual ones.

5

The Alchemy of Stock
Market Performance

A commonly used measure for evaluating the performance of a company and its management is total shareholder returns (TSR), defined as the percent increase in share price plus the dividend yield over a period of time.[1] In fact, in the United States, the Securities and Exchange Commission requires that companies publish in their annual reports their TSR relative to a set of peers over the last five years. That sounds like a good idea: if managers focus on improving TSR to win performance bonuses, then their interests and the interests of their shareholders should be aligned. The evidence shows that this is indeed true over long periods—at a minimum, 10 to 15 years. But TSR measured over shorter periods may not reflect the actual performance of a company, because TSR is heavily influenced by changes in investors' expectations, not just the company's performance.

Earning a high TSR is much harder for managers leading an already-successful company than for those leading a company with substantial room for improvement. That's because a company performing above its peers will attract investors expecting more of the same, pushing up the share price. Managers then must pull off herculean feats of real performance improvement to exceed those expectations and outperform on TSR. We call their predicament the "expectations treadmill." For high-performing companies, TSR in isolation can unfairly penalize their high performance. Another drawback is that using TSR by itself, without understanding its components, doesn't help executives or their boards understand how much of the TSR comes from operating performance, nonoperating items, and changes in expectations.

---

[1] Later in this chapter, we'll show that we also need to consider the impact of share repurchases as a significant source of cash distributions.

The widespread use of TSR over short periods as a measure of management performance can create perverse incentives. Managers running full tilt on the expectations treadmill may be tempted to pursue ideas that give an immediate bump to their TSR at the expense of longer-term investments that will create more value for shareholders over a longer horizon. In addition, TSR may rise or fall across the board for all companies because of external factors beyond managers' control, such as changing inflation rates. Strictly speaking, such factors should play no part in managers' compensation.

This chapter starts by explaining the expectations treadmill. It then shows an approach to analyzing TSR that isolates how much TSR comes from revenue growth and improvements in return on invested capital (ROIC)—the factors that drive long-term value creation—versus changes in expectations and nonoperating items. Managers, boards of directors, and investors can learn much more about company performance from this granular breakdown of TSR.

WHY SHAREHOLDER EXPECTATIONS BECOME A TREADMILL

As we described in Chapter 2, the return on capital that a company earns is not the same as the return earned by every shareholder. Suppose a company can invest $1,000 in a factory and earn $200 a year, which it pays out in dividends to its shareholders. The first investors in the company pay $1,000 in total for their shares, and if they hold the shares, they will earn 20 percent per year ($200 divided by $1,000).

Suppose that after one year, all the investors decide to sell their shares, and they find buyers who pay $2,000 for the lot. The buyers will earn only 10 percent per year on their investment ($200 divided by $2,000). The first investors will earn a 120 percent return ($200 dividends plus $1,000 gain on their shares versus their initial investment of $1,000). The company's return on capital is 20 percent, while one group of investors earns 120 percent, and the other group earns 10 percent. All the investors collectively will earn, on a time-weighted average, the same return as the company. But individual groups of investors will earn very different returns, because they pay different prices for the shares, based on their expectations of future performance.

One way of understanding the effects of this dynamic is through the analogy of a treadmill, the speed of which represents the expectations built into a company's share price. If the company beats expectations, and if the market believes the improvement is sustainable, the company's stock price goes up, in essence capitalizing the future value of this incremental improvement. But it also means that managers must run even faster just to maintain the new stock price,[2] let alone improve it further: the speed of the treadmill quickens as performance improves. So a company with low expectations of success among shareholders at the beginning of a period may have an easier time outperforming the stock market simply because low expectations are easier to beat.

The treadmill analogy is useful because it describes the difficulty of continuing to outperform the stock market. At some point, it becomes almost impossible for management to deliver on accelerating expectations without faltering, just as anyone would eventually stumble on a treadmill that keeps moving faster.

Consider the case of Terry Turnaround, a fictional character based on the experience of many CEOs. Terry has just been hired as the CEO of Prospectus, a company with below-average returns on capital and growth relative to competitors. Because of this past performance, the market doesn't expect much, so the value of Prospectus is low relative to competitors. Terry hires a top-notch team and gets to work. After two years, Prospectus is gaining ground on its peers in margins and return on capital, and its market share is rising. Prospectus's stock price rises twice as fast as its peers' because the market wasn't expecting the company's turnaround.

Terry and her team continue their hard work. After two more years, Prospectus has become the industry leader in operating performance, with the highest return on capital. Because of its low starting point, the company's share price has risen at four times the rate of the industry average. Given Prospectus's new trajectory and consistent performance, the market expects continued above-average returns on capital and revenue growth.

As time goes by, Prospectus maintains its high return on capital and leading market share. But two years later, Terry notes with frustration that her company's shares are now doing no better than those of its peers, even though the company has outperformed rivals. At this point, Terry is trapped on the expectations treadmill: she and her team have done such a good job that the expectation of continued high performance is already incorporated into the company's share price. As long as Prospectus delivers results in line with the market's expectations, its share price performance will be no better or worse than average.

This explains why extraordinary managers may deliver only ordinary TSR: even for the extraordinary manager, it can be extremely difficult to keep beating high expectations. It also explains why managers of companies with low performance expectations might easily earn a high TSR, at

---

[2] Theoretically, if a company's performance exactly matches expectations, its TSR will equal the cost of equity. In practice, however, with continual changes in interest rates, inflation, and economic activity, comparison to the broader market is sometimes preferable.

least for a short time. They can create a higher TSR by delivering performance that raises shareholder expectations to the level of expectations for their peers in the sector.

The danger for companies whose shareholders already have high expectations is that in their quest to achieve above-peer TSR, they may resort to misguided actions, such as pushing for unrealistic earnings growth or pursuing big, risky acquisitions. Consider the electric power boom at the end of the 1990s and in the early 2000s. Deregulation led to high hopes for power-generation companies, so deregulated energy producers were spun off from their regulated parents at extremely high valuations. Mirant, for instance, was spun off from Southern Company in October 2000 with a combined equity and debt capitalization of almost $18 billion, a multiple of about 30 times earnings before interest, taxes, and amortization (EBITA)—quite extraordinary for a power-generation company. To justify its value, Mirant expanded aggressively, as did similar companies, investing in power plants in the Bahamas, Brazil, Chile, the United Kingdom, Germany, China, and the Philippines, as well as 14 U.S. states. The debt burden from these investments quickly became too much for Mirant to handle, and the company filed for bankruptcy in July 2003. The expectations treadmill pushed Mirant into taking enormous risks to justify its share price, and it paid the ultimate price.

The expectations treadmill is the dynamic behind the adage that a good company and a good investment may not be the same. In the short term, good companies may not be good investments, because future great performance might already be built into the share price. Smart investors may prefer weaker-performing companies, because they have more upside potential, as the expectations expressed in their lower share prices are easier to beat.

THE TREADMILL'S REAL-WORLD EFFECTS

Tyson Foods and J&J Snack Foods are two U.S. branded-food processors. Tyson is one of the largest in the world, with brands such as Hillshire Farm and Sara Lee. Its revenues in 2017 were $40 billion. J&J Snack Foods is smaller, at just over $1 billion of revenues in 2017, with brands such as Icee and Auntie Anne's. Not surprisingly, given its smaller size and more snack-oriented products, J&J grew its revenues faster, at 6 percent per year from 2013 to 2017, while Tyson grew only 3 percent (Exhibit 5.1). J&J also outperformed on ROIC, with after-tax ROIC (before goodwill and intangibles) averaging about 24 percent over the period, compared with Tyson's 19 percent. Yet Tyson's shareholders earned almost twice the TSR: 27 percent versus 14 percent annualized.

EXHIBIT 5.1 **Tyson Foods vs. J&J Snack Foods: Growth, Return on Invested Capital (ROIC), and Total Shareholder Returns (TSR)**

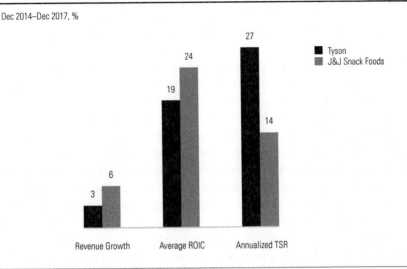

Dec 2014–Dec 2017, %

The expectations treadmill explains the mismatch between TSR and the underlying value created by the two companies. Using the ratio of enterprise value (EV) to net operating profit after taxes (NOPAT) as a proxy for market expectations, J&J's EV/NOPAT started the period at 23 times, while Tyson started at 13 times. This means that J&J's treadmill was already running fast, with high expectations already built into the share price. Tyson's EV/NOPAT was below average, reflecting modest performance expectations. The EV/NOPAT for both companies increased during the period—J&J from 23 times to 29 times, and Tyson from 13 times to 17 times.

Another source of the difference in TSR was changes in ROIC, driven primarily by changes in margins. Tyson's adjusted EBITA/revenues increased from 4 percent to 9 percent, while J&J's remained flat at about 12 percent. Similarly, Tyson's ROIC (excluding goodwill) increased from 12 percent to 22 percent, while J&J's declined from 25 percent to 21 percent.[3]

Which company did a better job? You can make arguments for either one: Tyson succeeded in outperforming its expectations, and J&J Snack Foods succeeded in delivering against high expectations. TSR might have been a fair measure of the performance of Tyson's managers, but it would not have reflected what a great job the J&J team did. For TSR to provide deeper insight into a company's true performance, we need a finer-grained look inside this measure.

[3] J&J Snack Foods' ROIC declined while its EBITA margin went up because it used more capital (working capital and net property, plant, and equipment) to generate each dollar of revenues in 2017 versus 2013.

DECOMPOSING TSR

We recommend analyzing TSR by decomposing it and quantifying its components in the manner outlined in this section. The effort serves two purposes. First, when managers, boards of directors, and investors understand the sources of TSR, they are better able to evaluate management. For example, it's important to know that J&J's TSR, though lower than Tyson's, reflects strong underlying performance against high expectations. Second, decomposing TSR can help with setting future targets. For example, it may be challenging for Tyson's managers to repeat their high TSR, because that would probably require raising profit margins and earnings multiples much higher.

The traditional approach to analyzing total shareholder returns is mathematically correct, but it does not link TSR to the true underlying sources of value creation. The decomposition we recommend gives managers a clearer understanding of the elements of TSR they can change, those that are beyond their control, and the speed at which their particular expectations treadmill is running. This information helps managers focus on creating lasting value and communicate to investors and other stakeholders how their plans are likely to affect TSR in the short and long terms.

Decomposition of TSR begins with its definition as the percent change in a company's market value plus its dividend yield (for simplicity, we assume the company has no debt and distributes all its excess cash flow as dividends each year):

$$\text{TSR} = \text{Percent Change in Market Value} + \text{Dividend Yield}$$

The change in market value is the change in net income plus the change in a company's price-to-earnings ratio (P/E).[4] Adding the dividend yield gives the following equation for TSR:

$$\text{TSR} = \text{Percent Change in Net Income} + \text{Percent Change in P/E}$$
$$+ \text{Dividend Yield}$$

This equation expresses what we refer to as the "traditional" approach to analyzing TSR. While technically correct, however, this expression of TSR misses some important factors. For example, a manager might assume that all forms of net-income growth create an equal amount of value. Yet we know from Chapter 3 that different sources of earnings growth may create different amounts of value, because they are associated with different returns on capital and therefore generate different cash flows. For example, growth from acquisitions may reduce future dividend growth because of the large investments required.

---

[4] Technically, there is an additional cross-term, which reflects the interaction of the share price change and the P/E change, but it is generally small, so we ignore it here.

EXHIBIT 5.2 **TSR Driven by Revenue Growth, Margin, ROIC, and Changes in Expectations**

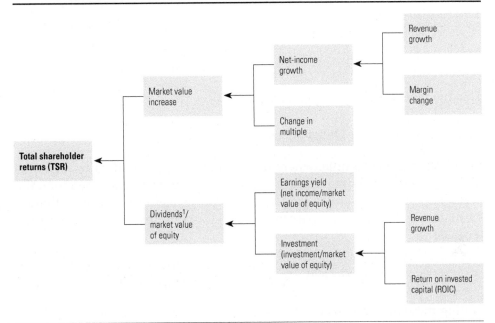

Note: Assumes company has no debt and no share repurchases.
[1]Dividends = Net Income − Investment

A second problem is that this approach assumes that the dividend yield can be increased without affecting future earnings and dividends, as if dividends themselves create value. But dividends are merely a residual. For example, if a company pays a higher dividend today by taking on more debt, that simply means future dividends must be lower because future interest expense and debt repayments will be higher. Similarly, if a company manages to pay a higher dividend by forgoing attractive investment opportunities, then future dividends will suffer, as future cash flows from operations will be lower.

Finally, the traditional expression of TSR fails to account for the impact of financial leverage: two companies that create underlying value equally well could generate very different TSR, simply because of the differences in their debt-to-equity ratios and the resulting differences in the risk to their investors.

To avoid these problems, we can decompose the traditional TSR components into ones that provide better insight into understanding the underlying sources of value creation. Exhibit 5.2 shows this graphically.

The derivation works as follows. Assume a company with no debt pays out all its cash flow as dividends. Start with the traditional definition:

$$\text{TSR} = \text{Percent Change in Net Income} + \text{Percent Change in P/E} + \text{Dividend Yield}$$

The percent increase in earnings can be decomposed into the increase in revenues and the change in profit margin:[5]

$$\text{Percent Change in Net Income} = \text{Percent Increase in Revenues} \\ + \text{Impact of Increase in Profit} \\ \text{Margin on Net Income}$$

The dividend yield also can be decomposed:

$$\text{Dividend Yield} = \frac{\text{Dividends}}{\text{Market Value}}$$

In this simplified example, where the company pays out all its cash flow as dividends, dividends will equal net income less investment. Therefore, the dividend yield can be expressed as the earnings yield (net income divided by market value) less the percent of market value invested back into the business:

$$\text{Dividend Yield} = \frac{\text{Net Income}}{\text{Market Value}} - \frac{\text{Investment}}{\text{Market Value}}$$

Putting these components together gives the following expression for TSR:

$$\text{TSR} = \text{Percent Change in Revenue} - \frac{\text{Investment}}{\text{Market Value}} \\ + \text{Impact of Change in Profit Margin} \\ + \frac{\text{Net Income}}{\text{Market Value}} + \text{Percent Change in P/E}$$

To summarize, TSR is driven by these five factors:

1. Revenue growth
2. Investment required to achieve that revenue growth
3. Impact of a change in margin on net income growth
4. Starting ratio of net income to market value (which is the inverse of the P/E ratio)
5. Change in P/E ratio

The investment required for growth is a function of growth and ROIC, as described in Chapter 3:

$$\text{Investment} = \text{Net Income} \times \text{Growth} / \text{ROIC}$$

[5] To be precise, there is an additional cross-term that reflects the interaction of these two effects, which we have omitted to focus on the key points.

EXHIBIT 5.3 **Traditional vs. Enhanced TSR Decomposition**

Company A financials				Decomposition of TSR		
$ million	Base year	1 year later		%	Traditional	Enhanced
Invested capital	100.0	107.0		Growth	7.0	7.0
Earnings	12.5	13.4		Required investment	–	(5.6)
				TSR from performance	7.0	1.4
P/E (multiple)	10.0	10.3				
Equity value	125.0	137.5		Earnings yield	–	10.0
Dividends	5.0	5.5		Change in P/E	3.0	3.0
				Dividend yield	4.4	–
TSR, %		14.4		TSR, %	14.4	14.4

The percent of market value invested therefore equals

$$\frac{\text{Investment}}{\text{Market Value}} = \frac{\text{Net Income} \times \text{Growth}/\text{ROIC}}{\text{Market Value}}$$

$$= \frac{\text{Net Income}}{\text{Market Value}} \times \frac{\text{Growth}}{\text{ROIC}}$$

The ratio of net income to market value is just the inverse of the P/E ratio; therefore,

$$\frac{\text{Investment}}{\text{Market Value}} = \frac{1}{\text{P}/\text{E}} \times \text{Growth}/\text{ROIC}$$

Now we can see how TSR is driven by growth and ROIC, adjusted by the beginning P/E.

Exhibit 5.3 uses the financials of hypothetical Company A to compare the traditional method of TSR decomposition with our enhanced approach.[6] Looking at the two decomposition approaches on the right side of the exhibit, the traditional approach indicates that Company A has a 14.4 percent TSR, based on 7 percent earnings growth, a 3 percent change in the company's P/E (a proxy for changed expectations), and a 4.4 percent dividend yield. The enhanced approach breaks down the TSR of Company A into three of the four parts of our full process of decomposition (for simplicity, in this example, Company A does not increase its margins). This shows that not much of the 14.4 percent TSR reflects the creation of new value. First, the reinvestment required to achieve 7 percent growth in earnings consumed most of the earnings growth itself, leaving TSR arising from performance at only 1.4 percent. Another 3 percent of TSR comes from a change in shareholder expectations (reflected in the P/E multiple increase), rather than performance, and the

---

[6] The example assumes no changes in profit margins for both companies, so that earnings growth can arise only from investments.

EXHIBIT 5.4 **Earnings Yield: TSR with Zero Growth**

	Company H		Company L	
	Year 0	Year 1	Year 0	Year 1
Earnings, $	100	100	100	100
P/E	20	20	15	15
Value, $	2,000	2,000	1,500	1,500
Dividends (equals earnings), $		100		100
Value plus dividends, $		2,100		1,600
TSR, %		5.0		6.7
Inverse of P/E, %		5.0		6.7

remaining 10 percent is simply the earnings yield, reflecting what the TSR would have been with zero growth and if investors had not changed their expectations.

We have found that many people struggle with the earnings yield (zero-growth return) part of this decomposition. Here's a simple example of how this works. Suppose you have two companies, H and L, each with $100 of earnings and zero growth. Since the companies aren't growing, they don't need to invest, so dividends to shareholders would equal earnings. Company H has a P/E of 20, and Company L has a P/E of 15. Exhibit 5.4 shows why the inverse of the P/E, the earnings yield, is the return the companies would earn if they didn't grow and their P/Es didn't change.

In the example, you can see that the TSR of Company H is 5.0 percent, exactly equal to the inverse of the P/E, the earnings yield. Similarly, Company L's TSR of 6.7 percent equals the inverse of its P/E. Note also that Company H, with the higher P/E, has the lower earnings yield (or zero-growth TSR). This demonstrates that companies with higher P/Es must achieve greater growth or improvements in ROIC to outperform the TSR of companies with lower P/Es.

The next example shows the impact of debt financing on the TSR decomposition. Suppose you own a house worth $500,000 and you've borrowed $200,000 against the house. If the house increases in value to $550,000, your equity value would increase from $300,000 to $350,000. A 10 percent increase in the value of the house leads to a 17 percent return on your equity.

The same concept applies to companies. Consider Company B, which is identical to Company A (our simpler example in Exhibit 5.3) except for its debt financing. As detailed in Exhibit 5.5, the difference in financing means Company B generated a higher TSR of 18 percent. The traditional approach to decomposing TSR suggests that Company B's shareholders benefited from a higher dividend yield and a stronger increase in expectations. However, our more fundamental decomposition of Company B, based on earnings yield (zero-growth TSR) and changed expectations measured by the unlevered P/E

EXHIBIT 5.5 **Enhancing TSR Decomposition to Uncover Effects of Leverage**

Company B financials			Decomposition of TSR		
$ million	Base year	1 year later	%	Traditional	Enhanced
Enterprise value	125.0	137.5	Growth	7.0	7.0
Debt[1]	(25.0)	(25.0)	Required investment	–	(5.6)
Equity value	100.0	112.5	TSR from performance	7.0	1.4
Dividends		5.5	Earnings yield	–	10.0
			Change in P/E[2]	5.5	3.0
P/E (multiple)	8.0	8.4	Impact of financial leverage	–	3.6
			Dividend yield	5.5	–
TSR, %		18.0	TSR, %	18.0	18.0

[1] Assumes, for illustrative purposes, that debt carries no interest.

[2] Change in P/E multiple for traditional approach vs. change in unlevered P/E multiple in enhanced approach (enterprise value/earnings).

(ratio of enterprise value to earnings), shows that the first three parts of the company's decomposed TSR are in fact identical to those of Company A. The additional 3.6 percent TSR for Company B arises from the higher proportion of debt in its capital, rather than any newly created value. Adjusting for the higher financial risk associated with higher debt shows that Company B did not in fact create more value than Company A—an important fact for investors and the companies' executives.

We can apply this approach to our earlier comparison of Tyson and J&J Snack Foods. Exhibit 5.6 shows the TSR decomposition for the two companies. While Tyson's 27 percent annual TSR for 2013–2017 was higher than J&J's14 percent, J&J outperformed Tyson on the TSR derived from growth: growth, net of investments, contributed 3 percent to TSR, versus a negative amount for Tyson, which made significant acquisitions that outweighed its modest revenue growth.

Tyson benefited from a much larger increase in operating profit margin: a TSR effect of 22 percent by increasing its margin from 4 percent to 9 percent, while J&J's margin was flat, at about 12 percent. Note that even though Tyson's

EXHIBIT 5.6 **Tyson Foods vs. J&J Snack Foods: TSR Decomposition, 2013–2017**

% Annualized

	Tyson Foods	J&J Snack Foods	Difference
Revenue growth	3	6	(3)
Investment for growth	(22)	(3)	(19)
Net impact of growth	(19)	3	(22)
Change in margin	22	0	22
TSR from performance	3	3	0
Earnings yield (zero growth return)	7	4	3
Change in earnings multiple	8	7	1
Impact of financial leverage	6	(1)	7
Nonoperating cash flows	3	1	2
TSR	27	14	13

margin increased more, J&J still earned a higher margin. Interestingly, both companies earned similar ROIC in 2017, about 22 percent, because Tyson had higher capital productivity.

While the impact of increasing expectations (the change in multiple) was similar at the two companies, J&J's multiple remained at a much higher level. Tyson's EV/NOPAT multiple increased from 13 times to 17 times, while J&J's increased from 23 times to 29 times.

Tyson had a further seven-percentage-point advantage in TSR due to higher financial leverage. The impact of leverage on J&J's TSR was actually negative, because it had more cash than debt. In contrast, Tyson's debt added six percentage points to its TSR.

UNDERSTANDING EXPECTATIONS

As the examples in this chapter have shown, investors' expectations at the beginning and end of the measurement period have a big effect on TSR. A crucial issue for investors and executives to understand, however, is that a company whose TSR has consistently outperformed the market will reach a point where the company will no longer be able to satisfy expectations reflected in its share price. From that point, TSR will be lower than it was in the past, even though the company may still be creating huge amounts of value. Managers need to realize and communicate to their boards and to investors that a small decline in TSR is better for shareholders in the long run at this juncture than a desperate attempt to maintain TSR through ill-advised acquisitions or new ventures.

This was arguably the point that Home Depot had reached in 1999. Earlier, we used earnings multiples to express expectations, but you can also translate those multiples into the revenue growth rate and ROIC required to satisfy current shareholder expectations by reverse engineering the share price. Such an exercise can also help managers assess their performance plans and spot any gaps between their likely outcome and the market's expectations. At the end of 1999, Home Depot had a market value of $132 billion, with an earnings multiple of 47. Using a discounted-cash-flow model that assumes constant margins and return on capital, Home Depot would have had to increase revenues by 26 percent per year over the next 15 years to maintain its 1999 share price. Home Depot's actual revenue growth through 2006 averaged a very healthy 13 percent per year, an impressive number for such a large company but far below the growth required to justify its share price in 1999. It's no surprise, therefore, that Home Depot's shares underperformed the S&P 500 by 8 percent per year over the period. Since then, Home Depot's revenues increased from $90 billion in 2006 to $108 billion in 2018, an annualized increase of 2 percent per year. A large part of the slow growth was due to the weakness in the housing market, with revenue dropping to $66 billion in 2010 before recovering to the current level.

What should Home Depot's board of directors have done immediately after 1999, given the company's high market value? Celebrating is definitely not the answer. Some companies would try to justify their high share prices by considering all sorts of risky strategies. But given Home Depot's size, the chances of finding enough high-ROIC growth opportunities to justify its 1999 share price were virtually nil.

Realistically, there wasn't much Home Depot could have done except prepare for an inevitable decline in share price: Home Depot's market value dropped from $130 billion in December 1999 to $80 billion in December 2006 (it increased to over $200 billion by mid-2019). Some companies can take advantage of their high share prices to make acquisitions. But that probably wasn't a good idea for Home Depot because of its high growth—a large-enough management challenge to maintain—even without considering that the retail industry doesn't have a track record of making large acquisitions successfully.

Home Depot's situation in 1999 was unusual. Most companies, most of the time, will not have much trouble satisfying the shareholder expectations expressed in their current share price simply by performing as well as the rest of their industry. We have reverse engineered hundreds of companies' share prices over the years using discounted cash flows. With the exception of the Internet bubble era (1999–2000), at least 80 percent of the companies have had performance expectations built into their share prices that are in line with industry growth expectations and returns on capital. TSR for a company among these 80 percent is unlikely to be much different from the industry average unless the company performs significantly better or worse than expected, relative to its industry peers. The other 20 percent, however, should brace themselves for a significantly faster or slower ride on the treadmill. Managers who reverse engineer their share prices to understand expectations of their ROIC and growth can benefit from seeing on which side of this 80/20 divide they fall.

IMPLICATIONS FOR MANAGERS

The expectations treadmill makes it difficult to use TSR as a performance measurement tool. As we saw in the example of Tyson and J&J Snack Foods, the sizable differences in TSR for the two companies from 2013 to 2017 masked the big difference in expectations at the beginning of the measurement period. In Home Depot's case, living up to the expectations was virtually impossible, as no company can run that fast for very long.

As a result of the expectations treadmill, many executive compensation systems tied to TSR do not reward managers for their performance as managers, since the majority of a company's short-term TSR is driven by movements in its industry and the broader market. That was the case for the many executives who became wealthy from stock options in the 1980s and 1990s, a time when share prices increased primarily because of falling inflation and interest rates, rather than anything those managers did. Conversely, many stock option gains were wiped out during the 2008 financial crisis. Again, the causes of these gains and losses were largely disconnected from anything managers did or didn't do (except for managers in financial institutions).

Instead of focusing primarily on a company's TSR over a given period, effective compensation systems should focus on growth, ROIC, and TSR performance relative to peers. That would eliminate much of the TSR that is not driven by company-specific performance.

In addition to fixing compensation systems, executives need to become much more sophisticated in their interpretation of TSR, especially short-term TSR. If executives and boards understand what expectations are built into their own and their peers' share prices, they can better anticipate how their actions might affect their own share prices when the market finds out about them. For example, if you're executing a great strategy that will create significant value, but the market already expects you to succeed, you can't expect to outperform on TSR. The management team and board need to know this, so the board will take a long-term view and continue to support management's value-creating priorities, even if these do not immediately strengthen the share price.

Executives also need to give up incessantly monitoring their stock prices. It's a bad habit. TSR is largely meaningless over short periods. In a typical three-month time frame, more than 40 percent of companies experience a share price increase or decrease of over 10 percent,[7] movements that are nothing more than random. Therefore, executives shouldn't even try to understand daily share price changes unless prices move over 2 percent more than the peer average in a single day or 10 percent more in a quarter.

Finally, be careful what you wish for. All executives and investors like to see their company's share price increase. But once your share price rises, it's hard to keep it rising faster than the market average. The expectations treadmill is virtually impossible to escape, and we don't know any easy way to manage expectations down.

---

[7] Share price movement relative to the S&P 500 index for a sample of nonfinancial companies with greater than $1 billion market capitalization, measured during 2004–2007.

6

Valuation of ESG and Digital Initiatives

As we write this book at the beginning of 2020, two items on any executive's agenda are noteworthy for their emerging importance in creating value and their slipperiness when it comes to valuing them. One is managing the intertwined elements of environmental, social, and governance (ESG) concerns. The other is grappling with the myriad manifestations of technological improvement or transformation commonly referred to as "digital."

The principles of corporate valuation do not include simple prescriptions for assigning values to various approaches to ESG or individual digital assets or strategies. Today, for even the most proficient analyst seeking a corporate valuation, there is only so much that can be done with these elusive elements. Many services publish various ESG ratings, for example, but researchers have found that the ratings are uncorrelated across different services, because work is still in progress on how to identify robust metrics of their success.

This chapter offers instead a way to think about how to value strategies and decisions related to ESG and digital initiatives. Our view is that companies should focus on the few areas that make a difference in their industry—for example, water consumption for beverage makers, supply chain management for apparel companies, or carbon emissions for many industries. It's also important, particularly at times of rapid technological change, to fix a gimlet eye on the risks of embracing—or ignoring—trends big and small. In each case, we recommend trying out the basic principles of valuation to establish a foundation for measuring outcomes, combined with gathering data to improve their application in the future.

A COMMON FRAMEWORK

Before we dive into the details of ESG and digital valuation, it's worth pointing out that valuing these strategies or projects follows the same principles that apply to all investment decisions: use discounted cash flows, and compare scenario cash flows with a base case. Often, what is most critical for this analysis is the definition of the base case.

Sometimes executives argue that hard-to-quantify investments are necessary because they are "strategic," or that their benefits can't be measured. This is rarely the case. The logic error is often in defining the base case. Take the decision by a bank to invest in a mobile-banking app. How would you quantify the value of this investment? The key is the base case. If all of a bank's competitors have mobile apps and the bank doesn't invest in one, its market share will likely fall over time as it loses customers (or fails to attract new ones). Therefore, the base case would be a decline in profits and cash flows, not stable profits and cash flows.

Companies are often reluctant to create business-as-usual projections that show declines in profits and cash flows. Yet such declines are what will most often happen when companies avoid change. Companies must become comfortable with declining-base cases; if they don't, they will have difficulty quantifying the value of many investments in ESG and digital. Quantifying the value is essential to making smart choices. It allows you to compare these initiatives against other investments that may be competing for scarce resources. And as in the example of the mobile-banking app, it may cause you to think about how much to invest in particular initiatives. It's not good enough to look at advancing technology or increasing demand for sustainability and act blindly, based on an uninformed sense of obligation to keep up with outside forces.

ENVIRONMENTAL, SOCIAL, AND GOVERNANCE (ESG) CONCERNS

Every business is deeply intertwined with environmental, social, and governance (ESG) concerns:[1]

- Environmental criteria include the energy a company takes in and the waste it discharges, the resources it needs, and the consequences for living beings as a result. Some of the most significant measures are carbon emissions and climate change.

---

[1] This section on ESG is an adaptation of an article coauthored by one of this book's authors: W. Henisz, T. Koller, and R. Nuttall, "Five Ways That ESG Creates Value," *McKinsey Quarterly* (November 2019), www.mckinsey.com.

- Social criteria address the relationships a company has and the reputation it fosters with people and institutions in the communities in which it does business. Important criteria include labor relations, diversity, and inclusion.
- Governance is the internal system of practices, controls, and procedures a company adopts in order to govern itself, make effective decisions, comply with the law, and meet the needs of external stakeholders.

These individual elements are themselves intertwined. For example, social criteria overlap with environmental criteria and governance when companies seek to comply with environmental laws and broader societal concerns about sustainability.

The combining of these reputation and business risks and benefits has more executives thinking and acting on ESG in a proactive way. As we discussed in Chapter 1, the U.S. Business Roundtable in August 2019 issued a statement strongly affirming businesses' connection with a broad range of stakeholders, including customers, employees, suppliers, communities, and shareholders.[2] Investors are becoming more interested in a company's ESG performance, and ESG-oriented investing is on the rise. ESG-related investment funds now top $30 trillion—up 68 percent since 2014 and tenfold since 2004.[3] The acceleration has been driven by heightened social, governmental, and consumer attention to the broader impact of corporations, as well as by the investors and executives who realize that a strong ESG proposition can safeguard a company's long-term success.

The weight of accumulated research finds that companies that pay attention to environmental, social, and governance concerns do not experience a drag on value creation.[4] Better performance in ESG also corresponds with a

---

[2] The stakeholder-minded approach is elaborated upon in Witold J. Henisz, *Corporate Diplomacy: Why Firms Need to Build Ties with External Stakeholders* (New York: Routledge, 2016); J. Browne, R. Nuttall, and T. Stadlen, *Connect: How Companies Succeed by Engaging Radically with Society* (New York: PublicAffairs, 2016); and C. Mayer, *Prosperity: Better Business Makes the Greater Good* (Oxford: Oxford University Press, 2019).

[3] *Global Sustainable Investment Review 2018*, Global Sustainable Investment Alliance, 2018, www.gsi-alliance.org.

[4] W. J. Henisz and J. McGlinch, "ESG, Material Credit Events, and Credit Risk," *Journal of Applied Corporate Finance* 31 (July 2019): 105–117; M. Khan, G. Serafeim, and A. Yoon, "Corporate Sustainability: First Evidence on Materiality," *Accounting Review* 91, no. 6 (November 2016): 1697–1724; and Z. Nagy, A. Kassam, and L.-E. Lee, "Can ESG Add Alpha? An Analysis of ESG Tilt and Momentum Strategies," white paper, MSCI, June 2015, msci.com.

within various sectors. They found a significant correlation between resource efficiency and financial performance. The study also identified companies across sectors that did particularly well in terms of resource efficiency and financial performance—precisely the companies that had taken their sustainability strategies the furthest.

As with each of the five links to ESG value creation, the first step to realizing value begins with recognizing the opportunity. Consider 3M, which has long understood that being proactive about environmental risk can be a source of competitive advantage. The company has a program called "pollution prevention pays," which aims to prevent rather than clean up pollution; efforts have included reformulating products, improving manufacturing processes, redesigning equipment, and recycling and reusing waste from production. Since introducing the program in 1975, 3M has saved $2.2 billion. Another enterprise, a major water utility, achieved cost savings of almost $180 million per year through lean initiatives aimed at improving preventive maintenance, refining spare-parts inventory management, and tackling energy consumption and recovery from sludge. FedEx, for its part, aims to convert its entire 35,000-vehicle fleet to electric or hybrid engines. To date, 20 percent have been converted, which has already reduced fuel consumption by more than 50 million gallons.[9]

Reduced Regulatory and Legal Interventions

A stronger external-value proposition can enable companies to achieve greater strategic freedom, easing regulatory pressure. In case after case, across sectors and geographies, we've seen that strength in ESG helps reduce companies' risk of adverse government action. It can also engender government support.

The value at stake may be higher than you think. Typically one-third of corporate profits are at risk from state intervention.[10] Regulation's impact, of course, varies by industry. For pharmaceuticals and health care, the profits at stake are about 25 to 30 percent. In banking, where provisions on capital requirements, "too big to fail" regulations, and consumer protection are so critical, the value at stake is typically 50 to 60 percent. For the automotive, aerospace and defense, and tech sectors, where government subsidies (among other forms of intervention) are prevalent, the value at stake can reach 60 percent as well.

---

[9] W. J. Henisz, "The Costs and Benefits of Calculating the Net Present Value of Corporate Diplomacy," *Field Actions Science Reports*, special issue 14 (2016), https://journals.openedition.org/factsreports/4109.
[10] See Henisz et al., "Five Ways That ESG Creates Value."

Employee Productivity Uplift

A strong ESG proposition can help companies attract and retain quality employees, enhance employee motivation by instilling a sense of purpose, and increase productivity overall. Employee satisfaction is positively correlated with shareholder returns.[11] For example, the London Business School's Alex Edmans found that the companies that made *Fortune*'s list of the 100 Best Companies to Work For in America generated 2.3 to 3.8 percent higher stock returns per year than their peers, measured over a period of more than 25 years.[12] Moreover, it has long been observed that employees who report feeling not just satisfied but also connected perform better. The stronger an employee's perception of impact on the beneficiaries of their work, the greater the employee's motivation to act in a "prosocial" way.[13]

Recent studies have also shown that positive social impact correlates with higher job satisfaction, and field experiments suggest that when companies "give back," employees react with enthusiasm. For instance, randomly selected employees at one Australian bank who received bonuses in the form of company payments to local charities reported greater and more immediate job satisfaction than their colleagues who were not selected for the donation program.[14]

Just as a sense of higher purpose can inspire employees to perform better, a weaker ESG proposition can drag productivity down. The most glaring examples are strikes, worker slowdowns, and other labor actions within an organization. But it's worth remembering that productivity constraints can also manifest outside of a company's four walls, across the supply chain.[15] Primary suppliers often subcontract portions of large orders to other firms or rely on purchasing agents, and subcontractors are typically managed loosely, sometimes with little oversight regarding workers' health and safety.

---

[11] A. Edmans, "Does the Stock Market Fully Value Intangibles? Employee Satisfaction and Equity Prices," *Journal of Financial Economics* 101, no. 3 (September 2011): 621–640.

[12] A. Edmans, "The Link between Job Satisfaction and Firm Value, with Implications for Corporate Social Responsibility," *Academy of Management Perspectives* 26, no. 4 (November 2012): 1–19.

[13] A. M. Grant, "Does Intrinsic Motivation Fuel the Prosocial Fire? Motivational Synergy in Predicting Persistence, Performance, and Productivity," *Journal of Applied Psychology* 93, no. 1 (2008): 48–58; A. M. Grant, "Relational Job Design and the Motivation to Make a Prosocial Difference," *Academy of Management Review* 32, no. 2 (April 2007): 393–417; and J. S. Bunderson and J. A. Thompson, "Violations of Principle: Ideological Currency in the Psychological Contract," *Academy of Management Review* 28, no. 4 (2003): 571–586.

[14] J.-E. De Neve et al., "Work and Well-Being: A Global Perspective," in *Global Happiness Policy Report*, ed. Global Council for Happiness and Wellbeing (New York: Sustainable Development Solutions Network, 2018).

[15] A.-T. Bové and S. Swartz, "Starting at the Source: Sustainability in Supply Chains," McKinsey & Co., November 2016, www.mckinsey.com.

Farsighted companies pay heed. Consider General Mills, which works to ensure that its ESG principles apply "from farm to fork to landfill." Walmart, for its part, tracks the work conditions of its suppliers, including those with extensive factory floors in China, according to a proprietary company score-card. And Mars seeks opportunities where it can deliver what it calls "win-win-wins" for the company, its suppliers, and the environment. Mars has developed model farms that not only introduce new technological initiatives to farmers in its supply chains, but also increase farmers' access to capital so they are able to obtain a financial stake in those initiatives.[16]

Investment and Asset Optimization

A strong ESG proposition can enhance investment returns by allocating capi-tal to more promising and more sustainable opportunities (for example, re-newables, waste reduction, and scrubbers). It can also help companies avoid stranded investments that may not pay off because of longer-term environ-mental issues (such as massive write-downs in the value of oil tankers). Re-member, taking proper account of investment returns requires that you start from the proper baseline. When it comes to ESG, it's important to bear in mind that a do-nothing approach is usually an eroding line, not a straight one. Continuing to rely on energy-hungry plants and equipment, for example, can drain cash going forward. While the investments required to update opera-tions may be substantial, choosing to wait it out can be the most expensive option of all.

The rules of the game are shifting: regulatory responses to emissions will likely add to energy costs and could especially affect balance sheets in carbon-intense industries. And bans or limitations on such things as single-use plas-tics or diesel-fueled cars in city centers will introduce new constraints on an immense number of businesses, many of which could find themselves having to play catch-up. One way to get ahead of the future curve is to consider re-purposing assets right now—for instance, converting failing parking garages into uses with higher demand, such as residences or day-care facilities, a trend we're beginning to see in reviving cities.

Foresight flows to the bottom line, and riding sustainability's tailwinds presents new opportunities to enhance investment returns. "Consider China, for example. The country's imperative to combat air pollution is forecast to create more than $3 trillion in investment opportunities through 2030, ranging across industries from air-quality monitoring to indoor air purification and even cement mixing.

---

[16] K. Askew, "'Extended Supply Chains Are Broken': Why Mars Thinks the Commodities Era Is Over," *Food Navigator*, June 6, 2018, www.foodnavigator.com.

DIGITAL INITIATIVES

The definition of *digital* is fuzzy. Some view it as simply the upgraded term for what their IT function does. Others focus on digital marketing and sales, providing digital services to customers, or connecting devices. The applications of digital technology in organizations involve all of these and probably ideas that haven't been thought of yet. Several of our colleagues examined a typical consumer packaged-goods company to see how many ways digitization and digital applications could be used to improve performance. They identified at least 33 possibilities, including digital marketing, optimizing trade spending, improving sales force coverage, predictive maintenance, supply chain planning, and robotic process automation in the back office.

Given the wide scope of potential digital initiatives, it is no surprise that most companies are launching them. In a 2018 survey of 1,733 managers, about eight in ten said their organizations had begun a digital transformation. However, just 14 percent said their efforts had made and sustained performance improvements. What's more, only 3 percent reported complete success at sustaining their change.[17] Evidently, digital is an area where management discipline is much needed.

Measuring the Value of Digitization

It's not surprising that companies struggle with how to evaluate the myriad "digital" initiatives being proposed. Yet the fundamental principle still applies: evaluate digital projects based on the cash flow they are expected to generate. While it sounds simple, getting it right requires some thoughtful strategic analysis.

Ideally, all investment decisions should be analyzed against an alternative course of action. For digital projects, the alternative may be to do nothing. But the do-nothing case doesn't mean zero cash flows. In fact, the do-nothing or business-as-usual case is often the key to evaluating digital projects.

Banks have faced this challenge several times over the past 40 years. In the 1970s and 1980s, banks introduced automated teller machines. In the 2000s, banks set up online banking. In the 2010s, banks developed mobile-banking apps. It seems obvious that banks needed to introduce all these innovations. But these innovations probably didn't generate new revenues, because customers expected them. Thus, although a mobile-banking app makes strategic sense, it appears to create a negative present value due to its additional costs with no added revenues.

[17] J. Deakin, L. LaBerge, and B. O'Beirne, "Five Moves to Make During a Digital Transformation," McKinsey & Company, April 2019.

Here's where the importance of the base case comes in. If the bank doesn't build a mobile app, it will likely lose market share and revenues over time. In this case, the cash inflows are the avoidance of lost revenues, which could be substantial. So this project likely does have a positive present value.

Ideally, the bank would estimate the timing of market-share loss to decide on the best time to build the app. Perhaps delaying a year or two might maximize value if the bank's customer base isn't clamoring for it yet. The bank should also consider alternative features for the app and ways to build it. Should it start with something simple and low cost to roll out and then improve it over time? Or should it spend more up front on a more feature-laden product? As you can see, there are many different cash flow scenarios to analyze when making this decision.

Paths to Improved Performance

Digital initiatives can improve a company's performance in numerous ways. To analyze the potential impact of digital, it helps to frame the discussion as two opportunities or threats. The first—and the highest-profile manifestation of digital in the business press—is an application of digital tools that fundamentally disrupts an industry, requiring a major revamp of a company's business model.

The second kind of impact, less dramatic but also important, occurs when companies use digital to simply do the things they already do, only better. Digital strategies can be applied in more mundane but also important ways including cost reduction, improved customer experience, new revenue sources, and better decision making. The line between the two applications can blur, such as when clothing retailers integrate their physical and online sales. The retailer is still selling clothes, but the customer's experience has changed, and the retailer must substantially retool its business.

New Business Models   In some cases, digital disruption upends entire business models or creates entirely new businesses. The Internet changed the way consumers research and purchase airline tickets and hotel rooms, disintermediating many traditional travel agents. The introduction of video-streaming services has disrupted the economics of traditional broadcast and cable TV channels. In some cases, digital has created enormous new businesses. Cloud computing services generated between $80 billion and $100 billion of revenues in 2019, up from less than $10 billion ten years earlier. The rise of cloud computing disrupted two other industries. First, the standardization of servers by leading players disrupted the manufacturers of mainframe and server computers. Second, it disrupted the IT services business that ran companies' data centers.

To value these new businesses, use the standard DCF approach. The fact that these businesses are often growing fast and don't earn profits early on does not affect the valuation approach. Eventually, they will need to generate profits and cash flow and earn an attractive ROIC. In Chapter 36, we describe how to value high-growth companies. The key point is that with high-growth companies, you must start in the future to estimate revenues when the market begins to stabilize, based on the market's potential size. You should estimate ROIC based on an assessment of the fundamental economics of the business.

An important consideration in estimating the potential size and ROIC of a new digital business is whether or not it will have *network effects*, also called increasing returns to scale. The basic idea is this: in certain situations, as companies grow, they can earn higher margins and return on capital because their product becomes more valuable with each new customer. In most industries, competition forces returns back to reasonable levels. But in industries with network effects, competition is kept at bay by the low and decreasing unit costs of the market leader (hence the tag "winner take all" for this kind of industry).

Take Microsoft's Office software, a product that provides word processing, spreadsheets, and graphics. Office has long been the standard used by most companies and other users. Early on, as the installed base of Office users expanded, it became ever more attractive for new customers to use Office for these tasks, because they could share documents, calculations, and images with so many others. As the customer base grew, margins were very high, because the incremental cost of providing software through DVD or download was so low. Office is one of the most profitable products of all time. That said, even such a successful product may be threatened by competition as more computing moves to the cloud.

Such network effects are not the usual case. The history of innovation shows how difficult it is to earn monopoly-size returns on capital for any length of time except in very special circumstances. Many companies and investors didn't realize how rare this was during the dot-com bubble of 1999–2000. More recently, investors again may have gone overboard with the number of "unicorns," typically defined as start-up companies with values above $1 billion (usually still private) and negative profits. In 2019, as some unicorns went public or tried to, there was a renewed realization that not all these companies could earn extraordinary returns from network effects, and values fell considerably. It's unlikely that companies offering analytics services, selling e-cigarettes, or renting out short-term office space will achieve long-term network effects.

Cost Reduction   Many digital initiatives can help companies reduce their operating costs. Predictive maintenance on factory equipment reduces both maintenance costs and lost production from downtime. Another example is the grandly named robotic process automation (RBA). This doesn't refer to physical robots, but rather to software that automates processes like accounts-payable processing. As these robots become more sophisticated, they can take on even more difficult tasks, handling exceptions in addition to plain-vanilla accounts payable.

Some examples show great progress for this kind of cost reduction. One mining company saved over $360 million per year from process automation in the field that gave managers more insight into what exactly was happening, enabling managers to make adjustments and anticipate needed ones. Fossil-fuel power generators have improved a plant's heat rate (how efficiently the plant uses fuel) by up to 3 percent by using sensors and actuators for remote monitoring and automated operations, as well as employing smart valves that self-report and repair leakages. They've also used automated work-order generation, remote expert support using virtual-reality devices, and automated warehouses to reduce operating costs by 5 to 20 percent. At the same time, they have improved safety by using robots for tasks in confined spaces, as well as advanced analytics to prevent accidents due to fatigue or distraction.[18]

Understanding the economics of cost reduction is not as straightforward as it may seem. You might be tempted to estimate the present value by simply discounting the expected savings and subtracting the investments required. But you also must examine the second-order effects. Are your competitors pursuing the same initiatives? In a competitive industry like the chemicals business, those cost reductions might simply be passed through to customers as price reductions. Chemical companies typically find ways to reduce costs by around 2 percent per year, but their margins don't increase, because industry players pass the savings on to customers.

In a situation like this, where the present value of cost reduction efforts is zero because the savings are passed on to customers, the alternative case becomes important. If your competitors are pursuing digital initiatives to reduce costs and you are not, you'll still have to reduce your prices in line with your competitors'. The alternative to the digital initiative would be a decline in cash flows due to lower prices without reduced costs. So the present value of the initiative may turn positive again, once you compare your initiative to the right base case. In practice, whether the savings are passed on to customers will vary by industry, but it's critical to think carefully through the alternative case.

Improved Customer Experience   Consumers have benefited tremendously from the digital actions of companies serving them. Many retailers have become "omnichannel," giving consumers a high degree of flexibility. Consumers can

---

[18] G. Guzman, A. Prasanna, P. Safarik, and P. Tanwar, "Unlocking the Value of Digital Operations in Electric-Power Generation," McKinsey & Company, October 2019, www.mckinsey.com.

purchase an item of clothing in a store or online, to be shipped to the buyer's home or to a local store. If the local store doesn't have the right size for an in-store shopper, the customer can order it on the spot and have it delivered to the customer's home. A customer who decides to return an item can return it to any store or mail it back, regardless of how it was purchased. Consumers can also track in real time the progress of shipments heading their way.

Using digitization to improve customer experience can add value to the business in a variety of ways. One leading manufacturer of agricultural products was struggling with low customer satisfaction scores and an erosion of its customer base. Using digital solutions, the company created a seamless online process for ordering, tracking, and query management. This increased the company's customer satisfaction score by 24 percentage points and improved throughput by 20 percent.[19] In some cases, improved customer service also reduces costs. An electricity distribution company fully redesigned its customer interfaces in a "digital-first" way that made a priority of the customer's online interaction. Customer satisfaction rose 25 percentage points, employee satisfaction increased by 10 percentage points, and customer service costs fell 40 percent.

As is the case with applying digital solutions to reduce costs, it's critical to think through the competitive effects of investing in digital to gain a superior customer experience. Recall our earlier example of the mobile-banking app. The value proposition boils down to cash flow, but special considerations emerge. Does the improved customer service lead to higher market share because your customer service is better than that of your competitors? Or does it maintain your market share or avoid losing market share because your competitors are doing the same thing?

In many situations, customers have come to expect an improved customer experience and are unwilling to pay extra for it. In the case of omnichannel retailers, today's customers routinely expect seamless transactions across channels from many retailers, but for the retailers, providing omnichannel services is expensive. The cost to ship online orders often makes these sales unprofitable, while in-store sales may be declining, leading to lower margins, as some costs are fixed. Even so, retailers have no choice but to provide the omnichannel services despite lower profitability. If they don't, they'll lose even more revenues and profits.

New Revenue Sources   Some companies have been able to create new revenue sources through digital initiatives. In these cases, the economic analysis versus the base case is more straightforward, because at least for a while, you (and maybe your competitors) are making the pie bigger for the whole

---

[19] J. Boringer, B. Grehan, D. Kiewell, S. Lehmitz, and P. Moser, "Four Pathways to Digital Growth That Work for B2B Companies," McKinsey & Company, October 2019.

industry. However, genuinely new revenue sources can be hard to find and difficult to convince customers to pay for.

Imagine you are sitting at home with an urge for some ice cream but don't want to go out to the local convenience store. Ben & Jerry's in the United Kingdom has set up centralized ice-cream freezers where a delivery company picks up the ice cream and delivers it to the customer within a short time period. These centralized freezers generate ten times the volume of convenience store freezers—mostly additional sales, because without the convenient delivery, many customers would simply skip the ice cream.

Or consider farm equipment manufacturer John Deere's introduction of precision farming services. The company has created a data-driven service business that collects soil samples and analyzes weather patterns to help farmers optimize crop yields. Sensors in tractors and other machinery provide data for predictive maintenance, automated sprinkler systems synchronize with weather data, and an open-software platform lets third parties build new service apps.[20]

Then there's one transportation company's digital solution to help its customers improve fleet maintenance. That solution helped generate more than $10 million of additional revenue through software subscriptions and after-market parts sales.[21]

These new revenue sources can create value because they don't involve just keeping up with the competition. In two of the examples, digital innovations created an overall increase in the revenue pool for the industry. In Ben & Jerry's case, the overall consumption of ice cream increased. In John Deere's case, a new product offering also increased overall demand.

Better Decision Making   Finally, some executives are pairing the trove of data being generated and new advanced analytics techniques to enable managers to make better decisions about a broad range of activities, including how they fund marketing, utilize assets, and retain customers.

Consider two examples. A maker of high-tech hardware implemented a partially automated solution to improve pricing for thousands of product configurations. Key features included configuration-based price benchmarking, analysis of price trends, and automated pricing recommendations with weekly updates of up to 200,000 price points for up to 20,000 products. A consumer products company used advanced analytics to improve the design of its planograms. A planogram is a model of how a consumer packaged-goods company allocates its limited space on retail shelves. It describes which products will be included and how to display them. Analytics showed decision

[20] J. Bughin, T. Catlin, M. Hirt, and P. Willmott, "Why Digital Strategies Fail," *McKinsey Quarterly* (January 2018), www.mckinsey.com.
[21] M. Banholzer, M. Berger-de Leon, S. Narayanan, and M. Patel, "How Industrial Incumbents Create New Businesses," McKinsey & Company (September 2019), www.mckinsey.com.

makers at the company that they could dramatically improve effectiveness. At the same time, they reduced the number of people required to design planograms from ten to just two.

Advanced analytics to improve decision making can generate additional revenues, reduce costs, or both. In the planogram example, the improvement can increase total customer spending by getting customers to upgrade to more profitable products. In this case, because the change involves only choices within the company's product mix, the improvement can create value without necessarily inviting a competitive response. In other cases, the benefits may be diluted because competitors take similar actions, but the investment in analytics still may create value by maintaining competitive parity.

CLOSING THOUGHTS

As executives and investors alike grapple with understanding the impact on business value of emerging environmental, social, and governance issues, as well as the competitive implications of digital technologies in all their forms, it bears remembering that these topics and the management responses to them will likely be fluid for some time to come. Still, as new as these topics may seem, existing valuation principles can help with framing initial responses and surfacing techniques for dealing with such challenges as they evolve. Companies will also do well if they concentrate on the specific areas that will have the greatest impact on the factors that create value.

7

The Stock Market Is Smarter Than You Think

The stock market's volatility and the sometimes-erratic pricing of companies' shares have always raised questions about the link between stock prices and economic fundamentals. Some experts have at times even posited that stock markets seem to lead lives of their own. In 2017 the level of market valuations led Nobel laureate Richard Thaler to comment, "We seem to be living in the riskiest moment of our lives, and yet the stock market seems to be napping. . . . I admit to not understanding it."[1] Several years earlier, another Nobel Prize–winning economist, Robert Shiller, wrote, "Fundamentally, stock markets are driven by popular narratives, which don't need basis in solid facts."[2] American investor Bill Gross claimed in 2012 that the last 100 years of U.S. stock returns "belied a commonsensical flaw much like that of a chain letter or yes—a Ponzi scheme."[3]

Does it make sense to view the stock market as an arena where emotions rule supreme? We think not. Certainly, irrational behavior can drive prices for some stocks in some sectors in the short term. And for shorter periods of time, even the market overall can lose touch with economic fundamentals. But in the long term, the facts clearly show that individual stocks and the market as a whole track return on invested capital (ROIC) and growth. For this reason, managers should continue to make decisions based on these fundamental drivers of value. By doing so, managers can also detect and perhaps exploit any irrational market deviations if and when they occur.

In this chapter, we'll explain how a market with different types of investors can lead to rational prices most of the time, even if some of the investors don't

---

[1] J. Smialek, "Nobel Economist Thaler Says He's Nervous about Stock Market," *Bloomberg News*, October 10, 2017, www.bloomberg.com.
[2] R. Shiller, "When a Stock Market Is Contagious," *New York Times*, October 18, 2014, www.nytimes.com.
[3] W. H. Gross, "Cult Figures," *Investment Outlook* (PIMCO), August 2012, www.pimco.com.

make decisions based on economic fundamentals. Then we'll show the empirical evidence that growth and return on invested capital (ROIC) are, in fact, the key drivers of value. Finally, we'll explode the myths behind some commonly accepted beliefs that are at odds with the fundamental principles of valuation.

MARKETS AND FUNDAMENTALS: A MODEL

We use a straightforward model to illustrate how market trading by both fundamental, or informed, investors and nonfundamental investors (what we call "noise traders") will produce prices that are generally in line with intrinsic value but can still be volatile.[4] These prices may even deviate significantly from intrinsic value under certain, albeit rare, conditions.

Assume a basic market where trading is limited to one company's stock and, for comparison, a risk-free asset. Two types of investors trade in this market. Informed investors develop a point of view about the intrinsic value of the company's shares based on its underlying fundamentals, such as return on capital and growth. They base their buy and sell decisions on this informed point of view. They may not all agree on the intrinsic value. Some may believe the company's shares are worth $40, others $50, and others $60. Because of transaction costs and uncertainty about the intrinsic value, they will trade only if the stock price deviates by more than 10 percent from their value estimates.

The other investors in this market are the noise traders. These traders may be news oriented, trading on any event they believe will move the share price in the near term, without having a point of view on the company's intrinsic value. Noise traders can also trade on momentum, basing their trades only on price trends: when shares are going up, they buy, assuming the price will continue to increase, and when prices are going down, they sell.[5]

Say trading starts when the price of a single share in the market is $30. Informed investors start buying shares because they believe the shares should be worth $40 to $60; such buying drives up the share price. Some noise traders notice the rising share price and begin to purchase as well. This accelerates the share price increase, attracting more and more noise traders. As the share price increases, the informed investors gradually slow their purchases. At $44, the most pessimistic begin to sell. Once the price passes $66, all informed investors are selling. Momentum declines, which some of the noise traders sense, so they begin to sell as well. The selling pressure builds, and the stock

---

[4] Nonfundamental investors could be called "irrational" because they don't make decisions based on an economic analysis of a company. We call them nonfundamental, because their strategies might be rational and sophisticated even though not based on fundamentals.

[5] Our two investor groups are similar to feedback traders and smart-money investors, as in W. N. Goetzmann and M. Massa, "Daily Momentum and Contrarian Behavior of Index Fund Investors," *Journal of Financial and Quantitative Analysis* 37, no. 3 (September 2002): 375–389.

EXHIBIT 7.1 **Model of Share Price Trading Boundaries**

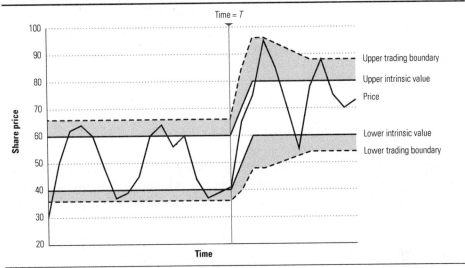

price begins to fall. The noise investors accelerate the fall, but this slows as more and more informed investors begin to buy until, at $36, all informed investors are buying again, and the fall is reversed.

The pattern continues, with the share price oscillating within a band whose boundaries are set by the informed investors, as shown in Exhibit 7.1. If the noise traders act not only on price movements but also on random, insignificant events, there will also be price oscillations within the band. The band itself can change over time, depending on the uncertainty among informed investors about the company's intrinsic value. For example, product launches or successes in research and development can lead informed investors to increase their value estimates as well as their trading bandwidth. As a result, price volatility will be temporarily higher while investors are absorbing the new information, as shown in the period after time T in Exhibit 7.1.

In this model, prices will move within the bandwidth if there is enough informed capital. This mechanism can break down, but only in rare situations. For example, when fundamental investors are vastly outnumbered by noise traders, their sales of stocks might not be able to stop a price rally. Such circumstances are unlikely, given the amounts of capital managed by sophisticated, professional—that is to say, fundamental—investors today.[6] Nevertheless, once they have sold all the overvalued stock, some fundamental investors can be reluctant to engage in short sales for fear of losing significant amounts before prices revert to lower levels. Others can face institutional or regulatory

[6] This is also what the academic literature predicts: informed investors outweigh and ultimately survive noise traders. See, for example, L. Blume and D. Easley, "Market Selection and Asset Pricing," in *Handbook of Financial Markets: Dynamics and Evolution*, ed. T. Hens and K. Hoppe (Amsterdam: Elsevier, 2009); and J. De Long, A. Shleifer, L. Summers, and R. Waldman, "The Survival of Noise Traders in Financial Markets," *Journal of Business* 64, no. 1 (1991): 1–19.

restrictions. As a result, the price rally might continue. But noise traders cannot push share prices above their intrinsic levels for prolonged periods; at some point, fundamentals prevail in setting prices in the stock market. In extreme cases, such as the technology bubble of the 1990s, this could take a few years, but the stock market always corrects itself to align with the underlying fundamental economics.

MARKETS AND FUNDAMENTALS: THE EVIDENCE

In general, the empirical evidence supports the idea that growth and ROIC are the key drivers of value. That means the evidence tends not to support beliefs that value is shaped as much by other measures. Even some of the most conventional beliefs about the stock market are not supported by the facts. For example, most growth and value indexes, like those of Standard & Poor's, categorize companies as either "value" or "growth" based on a combination of factors, including market-to-book ratios and price-to-earnings ratios (P/Es). Typically, companies with high market-to-book ratios and high P/Es end up in the growth category, while the others fall in the value category. However, growth is only one factor driving differences in market-to-book ratios and P/Es. ROIC also is important. In fact, we have found no difference in the distribution of growth rates between so-called value and growth stocks (see Exhibit 7.2). We did, however, find that so-called growth stocks tend to have high ROIC, and value stocks have lower ROIC. The median return on capital for so-called value companies was 15 percent, compared with 35 percent for the growth companies. So the companies classified as growth did not grow faster on average, but they did have higher returns on capital. That's

EXHIBIT 7.2 **Distribution of Growth Rates for Growth and Value Stocks**

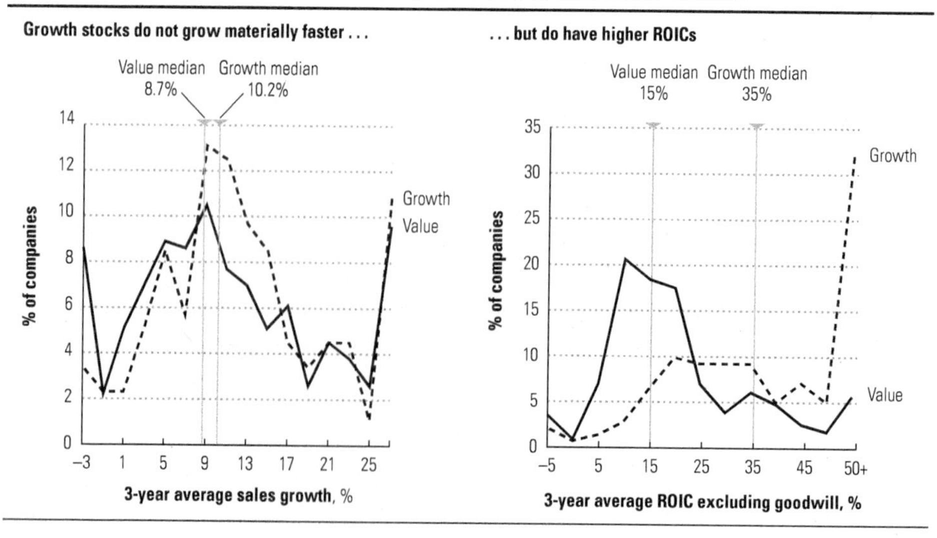

EXHIBIT 7.3 **Stock Performance against Bonds in the Long Run, 1801–2018**

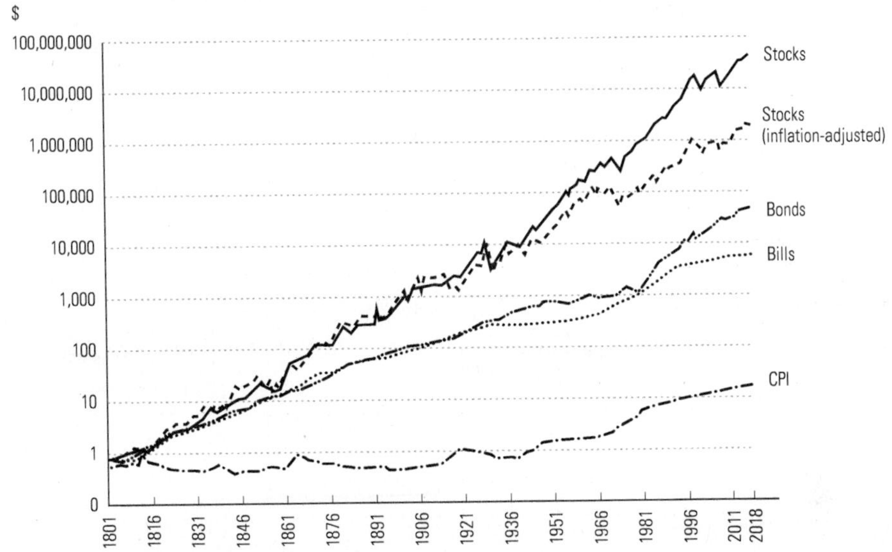

Source: J. J. Siegel, *Stocks for the Long Run: The Definitive Guide to Financial Market Returns and Long-Term Investment Strategies* (New York: McGraw-Hill, 2014); R. G. Ibbotson, 2019 SBBI Yearbook (Duff & Phelps).

why a modestly growing company, like the high-ROIC consumer packaged goods company Clorox, ends up on the growth-stock list.

Decades of Consistent Returns

Similarly, market bubbles and crises have always captured public attention, fueling the belief that the stock market moves in chaotic ways, detached from economic fundamentals. The 2008 financial crisis, the technology bubble of the 1990s, the Black Monday crash of October 1987, the leveraged-buyout (LBO) craze of the 1980s, and, of course, the Wall Street crash of 1929 appear to confirm such ideas. But the facts tell a different story. Despite these occurrences, U.S. equities over the past 200 years have delivered decade after decade of consistent returns to shareholders of about 6.75 percent annually, adjusted for inflation. Over the long term, the stock market has been far from chaotic (Exhibit 7.3).

The origins of this 6.75 percent total shareholder return (TSR) lie in the fundamental performance of companies and the long-term cost of equity. TSR is simply the sum of the relative share price appreciation plus the cash yield (see Exhibit 7.4). Over the past 70 years, corporate profits in the United States have grown about 3 to 3.5 percent per year in real terms, and the median P/E has hovered around a level of about 15 to 17.[7] If P/Es revert to a normal level over time, share price appreciation should therefore amount to around 3 to 3.5 percent per year. Moreover, corporate America typically reinvests about

---

[7] Note that the P/E is stable if long-term growth rates, returns on capital, and costs of equity are stable.

EXHIBIT 7.4 **Economic Fundamentals Explain Long-Term Total Shareholder Returns**

Range of annual performance over past 70 years

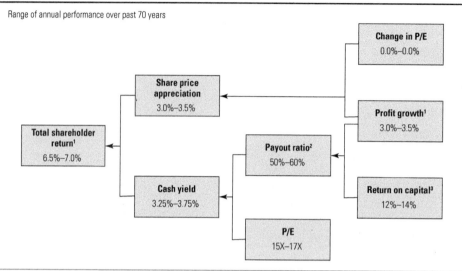

[1] Measured in real terms.

[2] Estimated as (1 – growth/return on capital), where growth is real-terms profit growth plus inflation at 2.0%–2.5%.

[3] Long-term average ROIC—recent years have been above average levels.

40 to 50 percent of profits every year to achieve this profit growth, leaving the remainder to be paid to shareholders as dividends and share repurchases. The resulting 50 to 60 percent payout ratio is not a coincidence: it follows from a typical 12 to 14 percent return on equity for U.S. companies, combined with 3 to 3.5 percent growth in real terms, or 5 to 6 percent including inflation. It translates to a cash yield to shareholders (that is, the inverse of the P/E times the payout ratio) of around 3.5 percent at the long-term average P/E of 15 to 17. Adding the cash yield to the annual 3 to 3.5 percent share price appreciation results in total real shareholder returns of about 6.5 to 7 percent per year.

P/E Fundamentals

Some analysts miss an important element of stock returns: the gains are driven by both share price appreciation and cash yields. In the view of these analysts share prices cannot increase faster than corporate profits. But this perspective erroneously misses the cash distributions entirely. Other experts have been too pessimistic about the share price appreciation component when they've predicted convergence of the P/E toward long-term average levels. Their estimates for the long-term average level are too low because they incorporate the 1970s and 1980s, when P/Es were severely depressed because of exceptionally high inflation levels.[8]

[8] In addition, Robert Shiller's measure of the current P/E is overestimated because it does not exclude extraordinary losses such as goodwill impairments. See J. Siegel, "Don't Put Faith in Cape Crusaders," *Financial Times*, August 20, 2013; "Siegel vs. Shiller: Is the Stock Market Overvalued?," Knowledge@Wharton, September 18, 2018, knowledge.wharton.upenn.edu/article/siegel-shiller-stock-market/.

EXHIBIT 7.5 **Estimating Fundamental Market Valuation Levels**

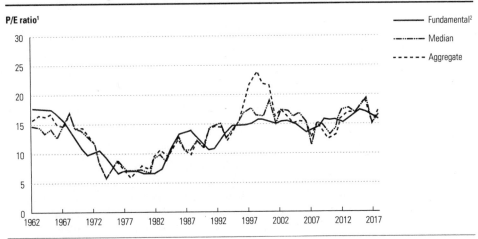

P/E ratio[1]

Fundamental[2]
Median
Aggregate

[1] Price-to-earnings ratio on 12-month forward-looking earnings for S&P 500.

[2] Moving average over three years.

The fundamental performance of companies and of the economy also explains the level of the stock market over shorter periods of time. We estimated a fundamental P/E for the U.S. stock market for each year from 1962 to 2019, using the simplest equity discounted-cash-flow (DCF) valuation model, following the value driver formula first presented in Chapter 2. We estimated what the price-to-earnings ratios would have been for the U.S. stock market for each year, had they been based on these fundamental economic factors. Exhibit 7.5 shows how well even a simple fundamental valuation model fits the stock market's actual P/E levels over the past decades, despite periods of extremely high economic growth in the 1960s and 1990s, as well as periods of low growth and high inflation in the 1970s and 1980s. By and large, the U.S. stock market has been fairly priced and in general has oscillated around its fundamental P/Es. We conducted a similar analysis of the European stock markets and obtained similar results.

Note that both the fundamental and actual P/Es have shown an upward trend over the past 35 years, rising toward 17 in 2019. To a large extent, this pattern is driven by steadily increasing margins and returns on capital.[9] Excess cash balances held by large companies form another factor. Cash has a high implied P/E because it carries little after-tax interest. Correcting for the excess cash balance in corporate P/Es lowers the 2017 ratio for the market as a whole by a full point, from 19 to 18.[10]

[9] See also Chapter 8 and R. Jain, B. Jiang, and T. Koller, "What's behind This Year's Buoyant Market," *McKinsey on Finance*, no. 52 (Autumn 2014): 27–31.

[10] See R. Gupta, B. Jiang, and T. Koller, "Looking behind the Numbers for US Stock Indexes," *McKinsey on Finance*, no. 65 (January 2018): 11–15.

EXHIBIT 7.6 **Market Value vs. ROIC and Growth across Selected Industry Sectors**

Global companies with real revenues > $1 billlion, 2018 median

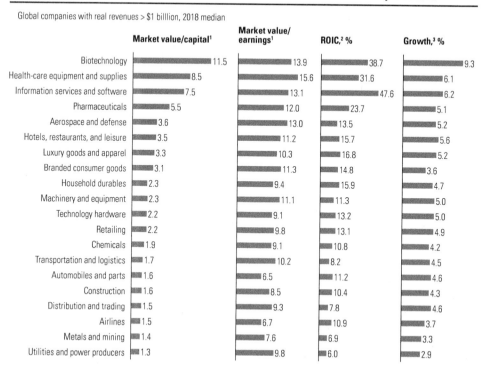

	Market value/capital[1]	Market value/earnings[1]	ROIC,[2] %	Growth,[3] %
Biotechnology	11.5	13.9	38.7	9.3
Health-care equipment and supplies	8.5	15.6	31.6	6.1
Information services and software	7.5	13.1	47.6	6.2
Pharmaceuticals	5.5	12.0	23.7	5.1
Aerospace and defense	3.6	13.0	13.5	5.2
Hotels, restaurants, and leisure	3.5	11.2	15.7	5.6
Luxury goods and apparel	3.3	10.3	16.8	5.2
Branded consumer goods	3.1	11.3	14.8	3.6
Household durables	2.3	9.4	15.9	4.7
Machinery and equipment	2.3	11.1	11.3	5.0
Technology hardware	2.2	9.1	13.2	5.0
Retailing	2.2	9.8	13.1	4.9
Chemicals	1.9	9.1	10.8	4.2
Transportation and logistics	1.7	10.2	8.2	4.5
Automobiles and parts	1.6	6.5	11.2	4.6
Construction	1.6	8.5	10.4	4.3
Distribution and trading	1.5	9.3	7.8	4.6
Airlines	1.5	6.7	10.9	3.7
Metals and mining	1.4	7.6	6.9	3.3
Utilities and power producers	1.3	9.8	6.0	2.9

[1] Market value is enterprise value, capital is invested capital excluding goodwill, and earnings is earnings before interest, taxes, depreciation, and amortization (EBITDA).

[2] Average return on invested capital excluding goodwill over 2015–2017.

[3] Analyst consensus forecast of annual revenue growth from 2018 to 2020.

Source: Corporate Performance Analytics by McKinsey.

Higher Returns, Higher Value

What holds for the stock market as a whole also holds across industries. For the largest listed companies in the world grouped by industry in 2018,[11] we took their average ROIC for the previous three years as a proxy for expected future returns and used the analysts' consensus estimate of their three-year growth outlook as the proxy for long-term expected growth (see Exhibit 7.6). Industries with higher ratios of market value to capital or market value to earnings also have higher growth and/or higher ROIC driven by better sales margins and capital turnover. Life science and technology companies had the highest valuation levels, thanks to having the highest ROIC combined with superior growth. Other companies, like those in the hotels and restaurants or luxury-goods sectors, receive high valuations from strong growth at average

[11] This sample comprises all listed companies (excluding financial institutions) with revenues exceeding $1 billion from the United States, Europe, Australia, New Zealand, and Japan.

EXHIBIT 7.7 **Market Value, ROIC, and Growth: Empirical Relationship**

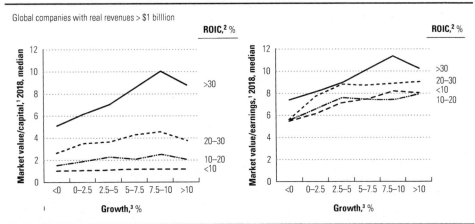

Global companies with real revenues > $1 billlion

[1] Market value is enterprise value, capital is invested capital excluding goodwill, and earnings is earnings before interest, taxes, depreciation, and amortization (EBITDA).

[2] Average return on invested capital excluding goodwill over 2016–2017.

[3] Analyst consensus forecast of annual earnings growth from 2018 to 2020.

Source: Corporate Performance Analytics by McKinsey.

levels of ROIC. Utilities and companies in metals and mining were valued at low market-value-to-capital multiples because of their low returns on capital and low expected growth. Note that the ratios of market value to earnings show less variation across sectors, reflecting investor expectations of converging earnings growth in the long term.

The same principles apply to individual companies. We compared the ratios of market value to capital of all the companies in the same sample versus their expected ROIC and growth. Exhibit 7.7 shows that, for a given level of growth, higher rates of ROIC generally lead to higher market values, and above a given level of ROIC, higher growth also leads to higher value. Although the empirical results do not fit the theoretical model perfectly, they still clearly demonstrate that the market values companies based on growth and ROIC.

For example, consider the fact that valuation multiples in the United States tend to be higher than in most other countries. That fact has even made some European companies consider relisting their stocks in the U.S. stock market in the hope of obtaining a higher valuation. As we discuss later in this chapter, however, such hope is false. U.S. investors do not pay more than European investors for the same stock. The difference in valuation multiples can be explained by underlying fundamentals. First, there is a marked difference in sector composition between the U.S and European economies. The technology and life science sectors, which have high valuation multiples, carry far more weight in the U.S. economy. Second, we find that U.S. companies typically generate higher returns on capital than European companies in the same sector.

EXHIBIT 7.8 **U.S. and European Equity Markets in High-Tech and Credit Bubbles**

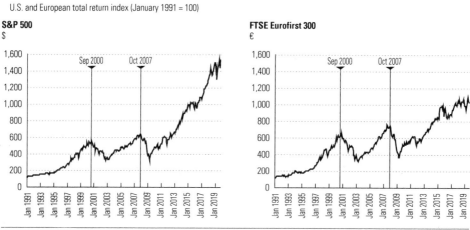

Source: S&P Capital IQ.

Deviations from Fundamentals

Nevertheless, there have been periods when deviations from economic fundamentals were so significant and widespread that they affected the stock market as a whole. Two examples are the technology bubble that burst in 2000 and the credit bubble that collapsed in 2007 (see Exhibit 7.8).

The technology market boom is a classic example of a valuation bubble, in which stocks are priced at earnings multiples that underlying fundamentals cannot justify. When Netscape Communications became a public company in 1995, it saw its market capitalization soar to $6 billion on an annual revenue base of just $85 million. As investors quickly became convinced that the Internet would change the world, they sent the Standard & Poor's (S&P) 500 index to a new peak in 2000. By 2003, the index had tumbled back to half that level.

Although the valuation of the market overall was affected, the technology bubble was concentrated in technology stocks and certain very large stocks (so-called megacaps) in other sectors. Before and after the bubble, the P/Es of the 30 largest companies were about the same on average as those of the other 470 companies in the index (see Exhibit 7.9). However, in 1999, the average

EXHIBIT 7.9 **Impact of Largest Stocks on Overall Market Valuation**

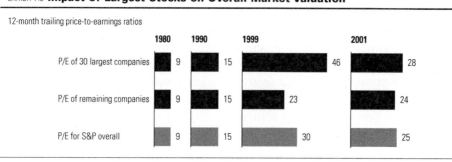

Source: Compustat.

top-30 company had a P/E of 46 times, compared with an average of 23 times for the other 470 companies. As a result, the weighted average P/E for the market overall reached 30 times.

Most of the large-capitalization companies with high P/Es were clustered in just three sectors: technology, media, and telecommunications (TMT). Of course, some of the companies born in this era (including Amazon and eBay) have created substantial economic value. But for every solid, innovative new business idea, there were dozens of companies that forgot or purposely threw out fundamental rules of economics.

By 2007, stock markets around the world had more than recovered from the technology bubble fallout, and the S&P 500 reached a new peak value (see Exhibit 7.8). The largest property boom and credit expansion in U.S. and European history drove corporate earnings to exceptional levels that ultimately proved unsustainable. Although all companies were affected, this bubble too was mainly driven by a few sectors. The financial, energy, utilities, and materials sectors showed sharply inflated earnings, from 41 percent of total S&P earnings in 1997 to 51 percent in 2006. But in 2007, a chain reaction of collapsing funding structures for mortgages and other forms of credit brought financial institutions across the world into distress. U.S. and European stock markets lost more than half of their value as the world's economy experienced the steepest downturn since the 1930s.

After 2009, U.S. stock markets quickly regained momentum and reached new record levels, this time fueled by strong increases in returns on capital and revenue growth, especially in the life science and technology sectors (see also Chapter 8). The megacap phenomenon emerged again, although on a far more modest scale than in the high-tech bubble. As of 2018, just four megacap companies—Alphabet (Google), Amazon, Facebook, and Microsoft—accounted for 10 percent of the S&P 500 index.[12] European stock markets took much longer to regain pre-crisis levels, due to weaker underlying return on capital and growth. The 2010 sovereign debt crisis caused a prolonged slowdown of economic activity across the largest European countries. In addition, European countries did not experience the emergence and ongoing growth of a strong technology sector, as the United States did.

Paradoxically, the fact that market deviations do occur from time to time makes it even more important for corporate managers and investors to understand the true, intrinsic value of their companies; otherwise, they will be unsure how to exploit any market deviations, if and when they occur. For instance, they might use shares to pay for acquisitions when those shares are overvalued by the market, or they might divest particular businesses at times when trading and transaction multiples in those sectors are higher than underlying fundamentals can justify.

---

[12] See Gupta et al., "Looking behind the Numbers for US Stock Indexes."

MYTHS ABOUT EARNINGS

So far, we've made the positive case for managers to focus their energy on growth at an attractive ROIC. Yet some companies go to great lengths to achieve a certain earnings per share (EPS) number or to smooth out their earnings. This is wasted energy. The evidence shows that these efforts aren't worth it, and they may actually hurt the company.

We're not saying that EPS doesn't matter. Companies that create value often have attractive earnings growth, and earnings will equal cash flow over the life span of the company. But not all earnings growth creates value. Consider the three most important drivers of EPS growth: revenue growth, margin improvement, and share repurchases. As we've pointed out, revenue growth (especially organic growth) is a powerful driver of value if it generates a return on invested capital exceeding the cost of capital. Margin improvements that are coming purely from cost cutting are not sustainable in the long term and might even hurt a company's future growth and value creation if investments in research or marketing are cut back. Share repurchases typically increase EPS but also increase a company's debt or reduce its cash. In either case, this leads to a decline in a company's P/E, which affects the increase in EPS so that value per share does not change. Consider Microsoft, with around $130 billion in liquid assets in 2019. The liquid assets are low risk and low return, so they have a high P/E (higher than for Microsoft's operating assets). Paying out the liquid assets would reduce the proportion of high-P/E assets relative to lower-P/E assets, reducing the overall (weighted-average) P/E for Microsoft as a whole.

In this section, we'll show that the sophisticated investors who drive stock market values dig beneath a company's accounting information to understand the underlying economic fundamentals. A classic example is the share price reaction to changes in inventory accounting by U.S. companies in the 1960s and 1970s. Because of rising price levels in these years, changing from first-in-first-out (FIFO) to last-in-first-out (LIFO) accounting decreased reported profits as well as taxable income. But the investor reaction reflected by the share price was typically positive, because investors understood that free cash flows would be higher as a result of lower taxes.[13]

Sometimes investors have difficulty detecting the true economic situation behind accounting information. For example, investors found it hard to assess the true risks and returns on capital of many financial institutions prior to the 2008 credit crisis because the financial reports were so opaque. Some companies, including Enron and WorldCom, misled stock markets by purposely manipulating their financial statements. But all managers should understand that markets can be mistaken or fooled for only so long. Sooner or later, share prices need to be justified by cash flows rather than accounting earnings.

---

[13] G. Biddle and F. Lindahl, "Stock Price Reactions to LIFO Adoptions: The Association between Excess Returns and LIFO Tax Savings," *Journal of Accounting Research* 20, no. 2 (1982): 551–588.

EXHIBIT 7.10 **Relationship between Share Repurchases and Shareholder Returns**

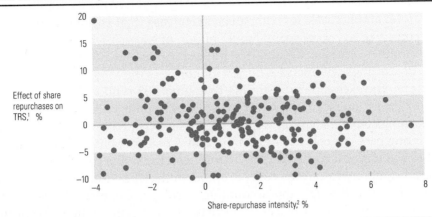

Based on a sample set of more than 250 nonfinancial S&P 500 companies.

[1] Effect of share repurchases on TRS is measured by residuals of multivariate regression. Variables are share-repurchase intensity and economic-profit growth. Economic-profit growth is a measure that combines earnings growth and return on capital (relative to cost of capital). This regression shows that the effect of share-repurchase intensity is not statistically significant.

[2] Difference between EPS growth and net income growth used as proxy for degree of share-repurchase intensity.

Source: Corporate Performance Analytics by McKinsey.

EPS Growth from Share Repurchases

Even though EPS is not a reliable indicator of value creation, many companies still use it as a key measure of financial performance and an important input for executive compensation. Not surprisingly, we find that executives pursue share repurchase programs mainly because they believe the resulting EPS growth creates value for shareholders. But savvy markets see through such moves with a gimlet eye. One company managed to create strong growth in EPS while its net income was falling, simply by retiring its shares even faster.[14] When investors understood that business results were declining, the company's share price dropped by 40 percent relative to the overall market change.

The empirical evidence is clear. At face value, there appears to be a correlation between shareholder value creation and the intensity of a company's share repurchase program. But that is simply because companies with higher returns on capital and growth also tend to pay out more cash to shareholders. After we control for differences in growth and return on capital, no relationship is left between share repurchases and shareholder value creation (see Exhibit 7.10).[15]

[14] See O. Ezekoye, T. Koller, and A. Mittal, "How Share Repurchases Boost Earnings without Improving Returns," *McKinsey on Finance*, no. 58 (2016): 15–24.

[15] If companies could time share repurchases when share prices are truly low, they could create value for shareholders who do not sell. However, as we discuss in Chapter 33, most companies do not time repurchases effectively.

Earnings from Mergers and Acquisitions

There is yet another way for companies to increase their earnings: buying another company. Say a company has $1 billion of excess cash. It uses the cash to buy another company earning $50 million per year at a P/E multiple of 20 times. Its earnings will increase by $50 million, less the forgone interest it was earning on the excess cash; assuming that equals $5 million (at a 0.5 percent after-tax return on cash), the net increase is $45 million. Though the company's earnings have increased, we can't tell whether it has created value. At a 20 P/E purchase price, it will be earning only 5 percent on its invested capital. If it has a 10 percent cost of capital, it will need to double the earnings of the acquired company to earn its cost of capital on the $1 billion it just invested.

Investors see through the accounting earnings. Chapter 31 shows that whether an acquisition increases or decreases earnings in the first year or two after the acquisition has no correlation with the stock market's reaction to the transaction.

Investors also see through the illusion of "multiple expansion," as we discussed in Chapter 3. There is no empirical evidence or economic logic that the stock market will value an acquired business at the earnings multiple of the acquiring business. The earnings multiple of two combined businesses will simply equal the weighted average of the individual earnings multiples. Any value increase must come from additional cash flows over and above those of the individual businesses.

Write-Downs

Executives are often reluctant to take the earnings hit from writing down the value of assets, assuming that investors will react negatively. But investors don't respond mechanically to write-downs. Rather, they assess what information the write-down conveys about the future performance of the company.

We looked at 99 companies in the United States that had written off at least $2 billion of impaired goodwill against their profits from 2007 to 2011.[16] There was no statistically significant drop in share prices on the day a write-off was announced. The markets had already anticipated the lower benefits from past acquisitions and reduced the share prices long before the write-off announcements. For example, prices jumped nearly 10 percent when Boston Scientific announced a $2.7 billion write-down associated with its 2006 acquisition of Guidant. Prices rose almost 8 percent when U.S. Steel announced a goodwill impairment charge of $1.8 billion with its third-quarter earnings in 2013. We found a similar pattern for the 15 largest goodwill impairments by European companies from 2010 to 2012. The pattern is consistent over many

---

[16] See B. Cao, M. Goedhart, and T. Koller, "Goodwill Shunting: How to Better Manage Write-Downs," *McKinsey on Finance*, no. 50 (Spring 2014): 13–15.

EXHIBIT 7.11 **No Market Reaction to Announcement of Goodwill Impairment**

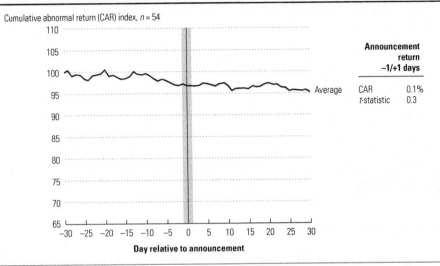

Cumulative abnormal return (CAR) index, $n = 54$

Source: SEC filings, Datastream, Bloomberg.

years. Likewise, Exhibit 7.11 shows there was no statistically significant drop in share prices on the announcement of goodwill impairments in an earlier sample of 54 companies in the United States and Europe from 2002 to 2004.[17]

Stock markets clearly look at the underlying cash flows and business fundamentals rather than reported earnings and goodwill impairments. In the 2010 to 2012 sample of European write-offs, in fact, only one analyst report issued after one announcement even commented on the size of the impairment. Analysts did, however, comment strongly on indications of how the company would move forward. Changes in signals or explicit guidance about future operating earnings, the outlook for the market and business units, and any management actions or plans to address changing conditions are important.

Employee Stock Options

In the early 2000s, proposed new accounting rules requiring employee stock options to be expensed in the income statement caused much concern. Some executives and venture capitalists claimed that expensing stock options would reduce the earnings of small high-growth companies so much that they would not be able to take the companies public.

Of course, there was no need for concern, because stock prices are driven by cash flows, not reported earnings. Academic research has shown that the stock market already took account of employee options in its valuation of

[17] The sample comprises selected U.S. and European companies with a market capitalization of at least $500 million and an impairment charge of at least 2 percent of market capitalization.

companies that give full information about their options schemes—even when the option values are not explicitly expensed in the companies' income statements.[18] In fact, companies that voluntarily expensed their employee options before doing so became mandatory experienced no decrease in share price, despite the negative implications for reported earnings.[19]

We came to a similar conclusion after examining 120 U.S. companies that began expensing their stock options between July 2002 and May 2004. Furthermore, we found no relationship between the size of the earnings decrease due to option expensing and any abnormal returns during the days surrounding the new policy's announcement. The market already had the relevant information on the option plans and was not confused by a change in reporting policy.

Different Accounting Standards

Share price data for companies that report different accounting results in different stock markets provide additional evidence that stock markets do not take reported earnings at face value. Prior to 2008, non-U.S. companies that had securities listed in the United States and did not report under U.S. Generally Accepted Accounting Principles (GAAP) or International Financial Reporting Standards (IFRS), for example, were required to report equity and net profit under U.S. GAAP.[20] These could have provided results that differed significantly from the equity and net profit reported under their domestic accounting standards. We analyzed a sample of 50 European companies that began reporting reconciliations of equity and profit to U.S. GAAP after obtaining U.S. listings between 1997 and 2004. The differences between net income and equity under U.S. and local accounting standards were often quite large; in more than half the cases, the gap exceeded 30 percent.

Many executives probably worried that lower earnings under U.S. GAAP would translate directly into a lower share price. But this was not the case. Even though two-thirds of the companies in our sample reported lower earnings following U.S. disclosure, the stock market reaction to their disclosure was positive, as shown in Exhibit 7.12. At that time, following U.S. GAAP standards also generally meant disclosing more information than required by local standards. Evidently, improved disclosure outweighed any artificial accounting effects.

---

[18] D. Aboody, M. Barth, and R. Kasznik, "SFAS No. 123 Stock-Based Compensation Expense and Equity Market Values," *Accounting Review* 79, no. 2 (2004): 251–275.

[19] D. Aboody, M. Barth, and R. Kasznik, "Firms' Voluntary Recognition of Stock-Based Compensation Expense," *Journal of Accounting Research* 42, no. 2 (December 2004): 251–275.

[20] Since March 2008, non-U.S. companies reporting under IFRS are no longer required to reconcile financial statements to U.S. GAAP in their Securities and Exchange Commission (SEC) filings.

EXHIBIT 7.12 **No Clear Impact of U.S. GAAP Reconciliation**

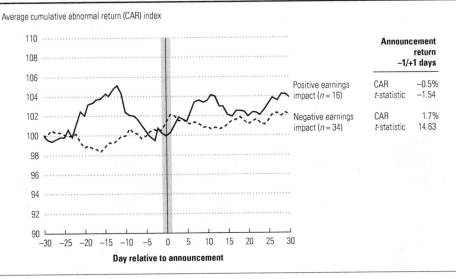

Average cumulative abnormal return (CAR) index

Source: SEC filings, Datastream, Bloomberg.

MYTHS ABOUT EARNINGS MANAGEMENT

On July 17, 2019, Internet entertainment service company Netflix reported second-quarter earnings of $0.56 per share, just four cents short of the $0.60 analyst consensus expectations. In addition, it had generated $4.92 billion in revenues, 25 percent higher than for the same quarter the year before, but missed analyst revenue targets by $10 million. On the same day, its share price dropped by more than 10 percent. The trigger for the price decline was not the company's missing its earnings or revenue targets. Rather, investors were concerned about the company's long-term outlook because of a decline in U.S. subscribers when an increase was expected, as well as significantly lower growth in international subscribers. Still, events such as this have led many managers to believe that stock markets are increasingly sensitive to short-term earnings that undershoot analysts' expectations or to volatility in earnings generally. As we'll show, events like these are not driven by the earnings announcement itself, but by other information that accompanies the earnings, such as the underlying subscriber base growth in the case of Netflix. Furthermore, investors are not much concerned by earnings volatility and offer no rewards for predictable earnings or earnings guidance.

Earnings Volatility

Some managers believe investors will pay a premium for steady earnings growth. Indeed, executives regularly cite stabilizing earnings growth as a reason for strategic actions. For example, the CEO of Conoco once justified a

EXHIBIT 7.13 **Earnings Growth of Least Volatile Companies: Not So Smooth**

Earnings growth,[1] %

	Home Depot	3M	McDonald's	Automatic Data Processing	Costco
2009	13	−8	9	18	−15
2010	30	26	11	−9	19
2011	23	6	15	5	13
2012	22	6	1	12	18
2013	25	7	3	−1	19
2014	25	12	−13	11	0
2015	16	1	−1	−7	15
2016	18	8	14	12	−1
2017	13	−3	17	18	14
2018	34	12	18	−5	17

[1] Earnings is net income before extraordinary items, adjusted for goodwill impairment.
Source: S&P Capital IQ.

pending merger with Phillips Petroleum in part by asserting that the merger would offer greater earnings stability over the commodity price cycle.[21]

In contrast, academic research finds that earnings variability has either limited or no impact on market value and shareholder returns. Ratios of market value to capital are diminished by cash flow volatility, but not by earnings volatility. Investors see through earnings smoothing that is unconnected to cash flow.[22] In 30 years of U.S. profit data, there is no correlation between variability in EPS and a company's market value.[23] Some researchers find a statistically significant, but practically negligible, relationship between the two: between the 1 percent of companies with the lowest earnings volatility and the 1 percent with the highest lies a difference in market-to-book ratios of less than 10 percent.[24]

Part of the explanation for the results is that smooth earnings growth is a myth. Almost no companies demonstrate smooth earnings growth. Exhibit 7.13 shows the earnings growth of the five firms among the 10 percent of large listed U.S. companies that had the least volatile earnings growth from 2008 to 2018.[25] Of the companies examined, Home Depot was the only one with ten years of steady earnings growth. Only a handful had earnings growth that was steady for four or

[21] Analyst teleconference, November 19, 2001.
[22] See B. Rountree, J. Weston, and G. Allayannis, "Do Investors Value Smooth Performance?" *Journal of Financial Economics* 90, no. 3 (December 2008): 237–251.
[23] J. McInnis, "Earnings Smoothness, Average Returns, and Implied Cost of Equity Capital," *Accounting Review* (January 2010).
[24] R. Barnes, "Earnings Volatility and Market Valuation: An Empirical Investigation" (LBS Accounting Subject Area Working Paper ACCT 019, 2003). The difference was 0.2, and the average market-to-book ratio for the entire sample was around 2.
[25] These were all listed nonfinancial U.S. companies with revenues of more than $1 billion in 2018.

more years. Most companies with relatively stable earnings growth follow a pattern similar to the four companies other than Home Depot in Exhibit 7.13: several years of steady growth interrupted by a sudden decline in earnings.

Meeting Consensus Earnings Estimates

When a high-profile company misses an earnings target, it certainly makes headlines, but the impact of short-term earnings on share prices should not be overstated. For example, empirical research has shown that earnings surprises explain less than 2 percent of share price volatility in the four weeks surrounding the announcements.[26] Investors place far more importance on a company's economic fundamentals than on reported earnings. Sometimes, however, short-term earnings are the only data investors have on which to base their judgment of fundamental corporate performance. In these cases, investors may interpret a missed EPS target as an omen of a decline in long-term performance and management credibility, so they lower the company's share price accordingly. As we describe in more detail in Chapter 34, the announcement of lower-than-expected earnings only drives share prices down in case of downward revisions of long-term fundamental prospects.

Similarly, share prices do not rise if the market believes a positive earnings surprise is simply the result of some imaginative accounting, such as deliberate timing of book gains from asset divestments or acceleration of sales from deep discounts to customers. For such accruals-dependent earnings increases, subsequent shareholder returns are poor, relative to peers.[27] And investors are wise to be wary when accruals contribute substantially to earnings, because this typically indicates that a company has reached a turning point and will post lower earnings in the future.

Earnings Guidance

Many companies believe that providing guidance on their expected earnings for the upcoming quarter or year can lead to higher valuations, lower share price volatility, and greater market liquidity for their shares at what they perceive to be limited costs. Unfortunately, there is no evidence that guidance delivers any of these benefits. As we discuss in Chapter 34, we find that whether companies issue guidance does not affect their earnings multiples, returns to shareholders, or share price volatility. The impact of guidance on a stock's liquidity, if any, typically disappears in the following year, making it practically irrelevant from a shareholder's perspective.[28]

---

[26] W. Kinney, D. Burgstahler, and R. Martin, "Earnings Surprise 'Materiality' as Measured by Stock Returns," *Journal of Accounting Research* 40, no. 5 (December 2002): 1297–1329.

[27] K. Chan, L. Chan, N. Jegadeesh, and J. Lakonishok, "Earnings Quality and Stock Returns," *Journal of Business* 79, no. 3 (2006): 1041–1082.

[28] See T. Koller, B. Jiang, and R. Raj, "Three Common Misconceptions about Markets," *Journal of Applied Corporate Finance* 25, no. 3 (2006): 32–38.

However, earnings guidance could lead to significant but hidden costs. Companies at risk of missing their own forecasts could be tempted to artificially improve their short-term earnings. As described previously, that is not likely to convince the market and could come at the expense of long-term value creation. When providing guidance at all, companies are therefore better off if they present ranges rather than point estimates and if they present these for underlying operational performance (for example, targets for volume and revenue, operating margins, and initiatives to reduce costs) rather than for earnings per share.

MYTHS ABOUT DIVERSIFICATION

Diversification is intrinsically neither good nor bad; it all depends on whether the parent company is the best owner of the businesses in its portfolio. Some executives believe that diversification brings benefits, such as more stable aggregate cash flows, tax benefits from higher debt capacity, and better timing of investments across business cycles. However, as we discuss in Chapter 28, there is no evidence of such advantages in developed economies. Yet the evidence does point to *costs* of diversification: the business units of diversified companies often underperform their focused peers because of added complexity and bureaucracy.

Another misconception about diversification is that it leads to so-called conglomerate discounts to the fair value of the business. According to this viewpoint, spin-offs and other forms of divestment are effective instruments to unlock these conglomerate discounts. Those who hold this view note that share price reactions to divestment announcements are typically positive, which is taken as evidence that such transactions are an easy solution to low valuations.

Typically, this misunderstanding is based on a misleading sum-of-the-parts calculation, in which analysts estimate the value of each of a company's businesses based on the earnings multiples of each business's industry peers. If the value of the sum of the businesses exceeds the company's current market value, the analysts assume the market value includes a conglomerate discount. However, as we discuss in Chapter 19, the analyses are often based on industry peers that are not actually comparable in terms of performance or sector. When the analysis uses true industry peers, the conglomerate discount disappears.

Positive share price reactions to divestment announcements therefore do not represent any correction of undervaluation or oversight by investors. The reactions simply reflect investor expectations that performance will improve at both the parent company and the divested business once each has the freedom to change its strategies, people, and organization. As a large body of empirical evidence shows, investors are right in anticipating performance step-ups.[29] For example, we found that for 85 major spin-offs since 1992, both the divested businesses and the parent companies delivered significant improvements in operating profit margins over five years following the transaction (see Chapter 32).

MYTHS ABOUT COMPANY SIZE

Many executives are tempted by the illusion that the absolute size or scale of a company brings benefits in the form of either higher share prices in the stock market or higher ROIC and growth in the businesses. Academics and practitioners have claimed that larger companies are in higher demand by investors because they get more coverage from equity analysts and media. Or they say the cost of capital is lower because large companies are less risky and their stocks more liquid. Higher demand and lower cost of capital should lead to higher valuation in the market.

However, there is no evidence that size matters once companies have reached a certain size. The cutoff point probably lies in the range of a market capitalization of $250 million to $500 million.[30] Only below that range is there some indication of higher cost of capital, for example. Whether a company has a market capitalization of $1 billion, $5 billion, or more does not matter for its relative valuation in the market.

The same holds for any positive effect of a company's size on its ROIC and growth. In most businesses, economies of scale make a difference only up to a certain size of the business. Large (and medium-size) companies have typically already extracted maximum benefits from such economies of scale. For example, it is tempting to believe that package-delivery companies such as FedEx or UPS can easily process more packages at limited additional costs (the planes and trucks are already in place). But the networks of these companies are finely tuned and optimized for minimum unused capacity. Increasing volume by 10 percent might in fact require 10 percent more planes and trucks.

For most companies, increases in size alone no longer automatically bring further improvements in performance but just generate more complexity.

[29] See, for example, J. Miles and J. Rosenfeld, "The Effect of Voluntary Spin-Off Announcements on Shareholder Wealth," *Journal of Finance* 38 (1983): 1597–1606; K. Schipper and A. Smith, "A Comparison of Equity Carve-Outs and Seasoned Equity Offerings: Share Price Effects and Corporate Restructuring," *Journal of Financial Economics* 15 (1986): 153–186; K. Schipper and A. Smith, "Effects of Recontracting on Shareholder Wealth: The Case of Voluntary Spin-Offs," *Journal of Financial Economics* 12 (1983): 437–468; J. Allen and J. McConnell, "Equity Carve-Outs and Managerial Discretion," *Journal of Finance* 53 (1998): 163–186; and R. Michaely and W. Shaw, "The Choice of Going Public: Spin-Offs vs. Carve-Outs," *Financial Management* 24 (1995): 5–21.
[30] See R. McNish and M. Palys, "Does Scale Matter to Capital Markets?" *McKinsey on Finance* (Summer 2005): 21–23.

Growth often means adding more business units and expanding geographically, which lengthen the chain of command and involve more people in every decision. Smaller, nimbler companies can well end up with lower costs. Whether size helps or hurts, whether it creates scale economies or diseconomies, depends on the unique circumstances of each company.

MYTHS ABOUT MARKET MECHANICS

Conventional wisdom has long held that companies can capture benefits for their shareholders without any improvements to underlying cash flows by having their stock included in a key market index, listing it in multiple markets, or splitting their stocks. True, a company from an emerging market in Asia securing a U.S. listing or a little-known European company joining a leading global stock index might secure some appreciable uplift. But well-functioning capital markets are entirely focused on the fundamentals of cash flow and revenue growth.

Index Membership

Becoming a member of a leading stock market index such as the S&P 500 or FTSE 100 appeals to managers because many large institutional investors track these indexes. Managers believe that when institutional investors rebalance their portfolios to reflect the change of index membership, demand will shift dramatically, boosting the share price. Anecdotal evidence appears to confirm this view. In 2001, Nortel, Shell, Unilever, and four other companies based outside the United States were removed from the S&P 500 index and replaced with the same number of U.S. corporations. The departing companies lost, on average, nearly 7.5 percent of their value in the three days after the announcement. The stock prices of the new entrants—including eBay, Goldman Sachs, and UPS—increased by more than 3 percent in the same period.

But empirical evidence shows that such changes are typically short-lived. On average, share prices of companies excluded from a major stock index do indeed decrease after the announcement. But this fall is fully reversed within one or two months.[31] Surprisingly, the evidence on the impact of index inclusions appears less conclusive; several publications report that price increases occurring immediately after an inclusion are only partly reversed over time.[32] We analyzed the effect

---

[31] H. Chen, G. Noronha, and V. Singal, "The Price Response to S&P 500 Index Additions and Deletions: Evidence of Asymmetry and a New Explanation," *Journal of Finance* 59, no. 4 (August 2004): 1901–1929.
[32] See also, for example, L. Harris and E. Gurel, "Price and Volume Effects Associated with Changes in the S&P 500: New Evidence for the Existence of Price Pressures," *Journal of Finance* 41 (1986): 815–830; and R. A. Brealey, "Stock Prices, Stock Indexes, and Index Funds," *Bank of England Quarterly Bulletin* (2000): 61–68.

EXHIBIT 7.14 **Effects of Inclusion Disappear after 45 Days**

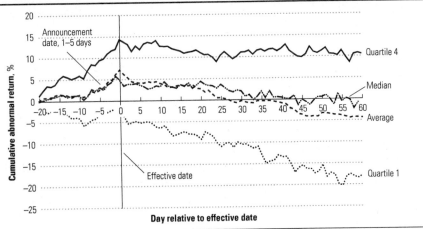

on share price of 103 inclusions and 41 exclusions from the S&P 500 between December 1999 and March 2004.[33] As Exhibit 7.14 shows, new entrants to the index experienced only a short-lived increase in share price: statistically significant positive returns disappeared after only 20 days, and all effects largely disappeared after 45 days. As investors adjust their portfolios to changes in the index, share prices of new entrants initially increase but then revert to normal once portfolios are rebalanced. For 41 companies ejected from the S&P 500 over the same period, we found similar patterns of temporary price change. The pressure on their prices following exclusion from the index lifted after two to three weeks.

Cross-Listing

For years, many academics, executives, and analysts believed companies cross-listing their shares on exchanges in the United States, London, and Tokyo could realize a higher share price and a lower cost of capital.[34] Cross-listed shares would benefit from more analyst coverage, a broader shareholder base, improved liquidity, higher governance standards, and better access to capital.

But our analysis does not find any significant impact on shareholder value from cross-listings for companies in the developed markets of North America, Western Europe, Japan, and Australia.[35] We found no decline in share price when companies announced a delisting from U.S. and UK stock exchanges

[33] For further details, see M. Goedhart and R. Huc, "What Is Stock Membership Worth?" *McKinsey on Finance*, no. 10 (Winter 2004): 14–16.

[34] See, for example, C. Doidge, A. Karolyi, and R. Stulz, "Why Are Foreign Firms That List in the U.S. Worth More?" *Journal of Financial Economics* 71, no. 2 (2004): 205–238; and M. King and U. Mittoo, "What Companies Need to Know about International Cross-Listing," *Journal of Applied Corporate Finance* 19, no. 4 (Fall 2007): 60–74.

[35] For further details, see R. Dobbs and M. Goedhart, "Why Cross-Listing Shares Doesn't Create Value," *McKinsey on Finance*, no. 29 (Autumn 2008): 18–23.

EXHIBIT 7.15 **Delisting from U.S./UK Exchanges: No Value Impact on Companies from Developed Markets**

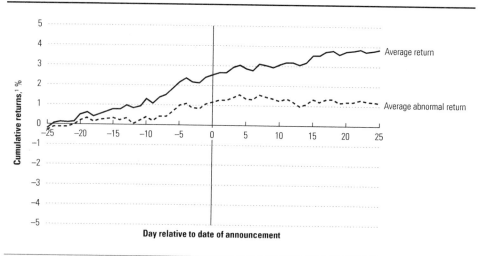

¹ Sample of 229 delistings from New York Stock Exchange, NASDAQ, or London International Main Market. Announcement dates between December 31, 2002, and December 31, 2007.

Source: Reuters; Bloomberg; Datastream.

(Exhibit 7.15).[36] In fact, most announcements in our sample produced hardly any reaction from analysts and investors. Neither did we find any valuation premium for companies with cross-listings in New York or London relative to companies without any cross-listing, once we corrected for differences in return on invested capital (Exhibit 7.16).

In fact, we did not find evidence for any of the deemed benefits from cross-listings. After correcting for size, cross-listed European companies have only marginally more analyst coverage than those not cross-listed.[37] Institutional investors from the United States do not require the foreign companies in which they want to invest to be listed in the United States.[38] There is no impact on liquidity, as cross-listed shares of European companies in the United States—American depositary receipts (ADRs)—typically account for less than 3 percent of these companies' total trading volumes. Corporate governance standards across the developed world have converged with those in the United States and the United Kingdom. There is hardly any benefit from better access to capital, given that three-quarters of the U.S. cross-listings of companies from the European Union have never involved raising any new capital in the United States.[39]

[36] We analyzed the stock market reactions to 229 voluntary delistings between 2002 and 2008.
[37] See, for example, M. Lang, K. Lins, and D. Miller, "ADRs, Analysts, and Accuracy: Does Cross Listing in the U.S. Improve a Firm's Information Environment and Increase Market Value?" *Journal of Accounting Research* 41, no. 2 (May 2003): 317–345.
[38] For example, CalPERS, a large U.S. investor, has an international equity portfolio of around 2,400 companies, but less than 10 percent of them have a U.S. cross-listing.
[39] Based on 420 depositary receipt issues on the New York Stock Exchange, NASDAQ, and American Stock Exchange from January 1970 to May 2008. Data from the Bank of New York Mellon Corporation, www.adrbnymellon.com.

EXHIBIT 7.16 **U.S. Cross-Listing: No Impact on Valuation of Developed-Market Companies**

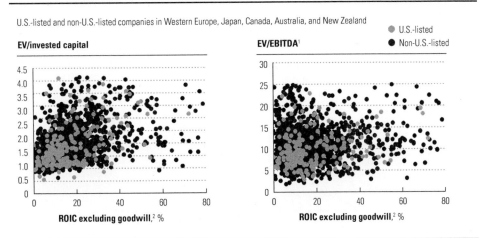

U.S.-listed and non-U.S.-listed companies in Western Europe, Japan, Canada, Australia, and New Zealand

● U.S.-listed
● Non-U.S.-listed

EV/invested capital

EV/EBITDA[1]

ROIC excluding goodwill,[2] %

ROIC excluding goodwill,[2] %

[1] Enterprise value at year-end 2006 divided by 2006 EBITDA.

[2] Average ROIC for 2004–2006.

Source: New York Stock Exchange, NASDAQ, Bloomberg, Datastream, Corporate Performance Analytics by McKinsey.

For companies from the emerging world, however, the story might be different. These companies might benefit from access to new equity and more stringent corporate governance requirements through cross-listings in U.S. or UK equity markets.[40]

Stock Splits

Although their numbers have come down significantly over the past decade, each year some listed companies in the United States increase their number of shares through a stock split to bring a company's share price back into the "optimal trading range."[41] But fundamentally, stock splits can't create value, because the size of the pie available to shareholders does not change. For example, after a two-for-one stock split, a shareholder who owned two shares worth $5 apiece ends up with four shares, each worth $2.50. But some managers and academics claim that the lower price should make the stock more attractive for capital-constrained investors, thereby increasing demand, improving liquidity, and leading to higher returns for shareholders.[42]

[40] See R. Newell and G. Wilson, "A Premium for Good Governance," *McKinsey Quarterly*, no. 3 (2002): 20–23.

[41] R. D. Boehme and B. R. Danielsen report over 6,000 stock splits between 1950 and 2000: "Stock-Split Post-Announcement Returns: Underreaction or Market Friction?" *Financial Review* 42 (2007): 485–506. D. Ikenberry and S. Ramnath report over 3,000 stock splits between 1988 and 1998: "Underreaction to Self-Selected News Events: The Case of Stock Splits," *Review of Financial Studies* 15 (2002): 489–526.

[42] There is ample evidence to show that this is not the case: after a split, trading volumes typically decline, and brokerage fees and bid-ask spreads increase, indicating lower liquidity, if anything. See T. Copeland, "Liquidity Changes Following Stock Splits," *Journal of Finance* 34, no. 1 (March 1979): 115–141.

EXHIBIT 7.17 **Cumulative Average Abnormal Returns around Stock Splits**

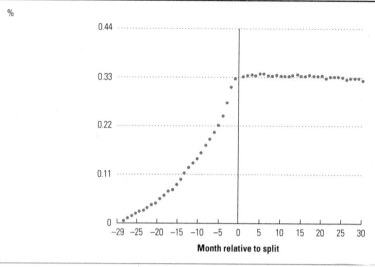

Source: E. Fama, L. Fisher, M. Jensen, and R. Roll, "The Adjustment of Stock Prices to New Information," *International Economic Review* 10 (1969): 1–21.

In many cases, a stock split is indeed accompanied by positive abnormal returns to shareholders in the months prior to the split (see Exhibit 7.17).[43] The abnormal returns have nothing to do with the split as such but are simply a function of self-selection and signaling. Self-selection is the tendency of companies to split their stocks into lower denominations because of a prolonged rise in their share price.

More insightful is the abnormal return for the three days around the date of the stock split announcement, at about 3 percent.[44] When managers announce a stock split, they are also signaling that they expect further improvement in economic fundamentals. Indeed, two-thirds of companies reported higher-than-expected earnings and dividends in the year following a stock split. When performance improvements followed the split, the stock market did not react, indicating that investors had already factored them into their decisions at the time of the stock split announcement. Consistent with this pattern, companies that did not improve performance as expected in the year after a stock split saw their share prices fall.[45]

[43] E. Fama, L. Fisher, M. Jensen, and R. Roll, "The Adjustment of Stock Prices to New Information," *International Economic Review* 10 (1969): 1–21.

[44] Some researchers have reported positive abnormal returns not only in the days around but in the entire year following a split announcement. They conclude that the market is inefficient by underreacting to stock splits; see Ikenberry and Ramnath, "Underreaction to Self-Selected News Events." Others find that these abnormal returns do not lead to any arbitrage opportunities and that the market is efficient; see Boehme and Danielsen, "Stock-Split Post-Announcement Returns"; and J. Conrad and G. Kaul, "Long-Term Market Overreaction or Biases in Computed Returns?" *Journal of Finance* 48 (1993): 39–63.

[45] See Fama et al., "Adjustment of Stock Prices."

MYTHS ABOUT VALUE DISTRIBUTION

Another common misconception among executives is that share repurchases and dividends create value for shareholders. This view is often reinforced by both private and public demands from investors for companies to return more cash to shareholders, particularly as share repurchases. If you dig deeper into understanding investor demands, though, you will typically find that investors want more cash distributed not because the cash distribution itself creates value, but because investors are concerned that companies will squander excess cash and debt capacity on value-destroying investments. They view cash distributions as a way to impose discipline on the company's use of its cash.[46]

More important, companies create value when they generate cash flows. Distributing those cash flows to shareholders cannot create additional value. That would be double-counting and akin to violating principles like the conservation of matter in physics.

So why do companies' share prices often increase on the announcement of share repurchases or dividend increases? In some cases, investors interpret dividend increases as a sign that management is confident enough about future cash flow generation to commit to a higher dividend level. In other cases, investors are relieved that management is less likely to squander cash on value-destroying investments. The result is that investors raise their expectations of future cash flows. If these expectations are not met, the companies' share prices will decline later.

Dividends and share repurchases are merely instruments for distributing cash generated by the company's operations. Furthermore, as we discuss in Chapter 33, decisions about cash distributions should not drive a company's investment decisions; they should be an integral part of a company's capital allocation that matches its investment needs, financing opportunities, and desired level of risk.

SUMMARY

Dramatic swings in share prices sometimes lead finance practitioners to suggest that established valuation theories are irrelevant and that stock markets lead lives of their own, detached from the realities of economic growth and business profitability. We disagree. There is compelling evidence that valuation levels for individual companies and the stock market as a whole clearly reflect the underlying fundamental performance in terms of return on capital and growth. Yes, there are times when valuations deviate from fundamentals, but these typically do not last long. Evidence also shows that some widespread

---

[46] See, for example, M. Goedhart and T. Koller, "How to Attract Long-Term Investors: An Interview with M&G's Aled Smith," *McKinsey on Finance* 46 (Spring 2013): 8–13.

beliefs espoused by managers and finance professionals are inconsistent with the fundamental principles of valuation and are erroneous.

We also find that executives are often overly focused on earnings and earnings growth. Earnings don't drive value in their own right; only cash flows do. Companies with attractive growth and returns on invested capital will also generate good earnings. The market sees through earnings that aren't backed up by solid fundamentals, such as earnings increases from share repurchases or from mergers and acquisitions that don't earn adequate returns on capital. Managers should also not be concerned about noneconomic events that reduce earnings, such as asset write-downs or the effects of changes in accounting rules. Nor should they be concerned about delivering smooth earnings or meeting short-term consensus earnings forecasts.

Finally, myriad myths have grown up about how the market values companies based on measures unrelated to the companies' economic performance. None stand up to scrutiny. There is no value premium from diversification, from cross-listing, or from size for size's sake. Conversely, there is no conglomerate discount, only a performance discount for many diversified companies. Dividends and share repurchases don't create value, but markets react positively when management signals it will be disciplined about future investments.

8

Return on Invested Capital

As Chapter 3 explains, the higher a company can raise its return on invested capital (ROIC), and the longer it can earn a rate of return on that capital greater than its cost of capital, the more value it will create. So it is critical to every strategic and investment decision to be able to understand and predict what drives and sustains ROIC.

Why do some companies develop and sustain much higher returns on capital than others? Consider a classic example from the days of the tech boom at the turn of the millennium. Two newcomers at the height of the boom in 2000 were the companies eBay and Webvan. In November 1999, eBay's market capitalization was $23 billion, while Webvan's was $8 billion. Over the years that followed, eBay continued to prosper, reaching a market capitalization of more than $70 billion in 2015, when it spun off its subsidiary PayPal. By mid-2018, the combined market capitalization of eBay and PayPal was more than $160 billion. Webvan, in contrast, disappeared into bankruptcy and liquidation after just a few years. To understand why, we can look at what these companies' underlying strategies meant for their respective returns on invested capital.

The core business of eBay is an online marketplace that collects a small amount of money for each transaction between a buyer and a seller. The business needs no inventories or accounts receivable, and it requires little invested capital. Once the service started and a growing number of buyers used eBay, more sellers were attracted to it, in turn drawing in still more buyers. Moreover, the marginal cost of each additional buyer or seller is close to zero. Economists say that a business in a situation like eBay's exhibits *increasing returns to scale*. In such a business, the first competitor to grow big can generate a very high ROIC and will usually create the bulk of value in its market. If, as in eBay's case, the business easily expands across borders, the potential for value creation becomes even greater.

Webvan was an online grocery-delivery business based in California. In contrast to eBay, it had a capital-intensive business model involving substantial warehouses, trucks, and inventory. In addition, Webvan was competing with local grocery stores in selling products at very thin margins. The complexity and costs of making physical deliveries to customers within precise time frames more than offset Webvan's savings from not having physical stores. Finally, Webvan's business did not enjoy increasing returns to scale; as demand increased, it needed more food pickers, trucks, and drivers to serve customers.

From the outset, it was clear that eBay's business model had a sound and sustainable competitive advantage that permitted high returns. Webvan had no such advantage over its grocery store competitors. Whereas eBay's strategy was primed for success, Webvan's foreshadowed doom. In general, success in the online grocery business has since proven to be far more elusive than in other forms of online retail. For example, Amazon Fresh has faced challenges expanding beyond the most densely populated metropolitan areas. Amazon's 2017 acquisition of Whole Foods was one signal that in grocery, competition from traditional stores is hard to overcome.

The importance of ROIC is universal: it applies to companies as well as to businesses within companies. For example, within its retail business model, Amazon creates substantial revenues from third-party sellers using its online platform. Platform sales by third parties generate increasing returns to scale, more so than Amazon's direct sales. Platform sales require little invested capital, and Amazon's marginal cost of additional transactions is minimal. As a result, platform sales have become an important driver of Amazon's overall value creation.

This chapter explores how rates of return on invested capital depend on competitive advantage. We examine how strategy drives competitive advantage, which when properly fitted to industry structure and competitive behavior can produce and sustain a superior ROIC. This explains why some companies earn only a 10 percent ROIC while others earn 50 percent. The final part of the chapter presents 55 years of ROIC data by industry over time. This analysis shows how ROIC varies by industry and how rates of ROIC fluctuate or remain stable over time.

WHAT DRIVES ROIC?

To understand how strategy, competitive advantage, and return on invested capital are linked, consider the following representation of ROIC:

$$\text{ROIC} = (1 - \text{Tax Rate})\frac{\text{Price per Unit} - \text{Cost per Unit}}{\text{Invested Capital per Unit}}$$

This version of ROIC simply translates the typical formula of net operating profit after taxes (NOPAT) divided by invested capital into a per unit calculation: price per unit, cost per unit, and invested capital per unit.[1] To earn a higher ROIC, a company needs a competitive advantage that enables it to charge a price premium or produce its products more efficiently (at lower cost, lower capital per unit, or both). A company's competitive advantage depends on its chosen strategy and the industry in which it operates.

The strategy model that underlies our thinking about what drives competitive advantage and ROIC is the structure-conduct-performance (SCP) framework. According to this framework, the structure of an industry influences the conduct of the competitors, which in turn drives the performance of the companies in the industry. Originally developed in the 1930s by Edward Mason, this framework was not widely influential in business until Michael Porter published *Competitive Strategy* (Free Press, 1980), applying the model to company strategy. While there have been extensions and variations of the SCP model, such as the resource-based approach,[2] Porter's framework is probably still the most widely used for thinking about strategy.

According to Porter, the intensity of competition in an industry is determined by five forces: the threat of new entry, pressure from substitute products, the bargaining power of buyers, that of suppliers, and the degree of rivalry among existing competitors. Companies need to choose strategies that build competitive advantages to mitigate or change the pressure of these forces and achieve superior profitability. Because the five forces differ by industry, and because companies within the same industry can pursue different strategies, there can be significant variation in ROIC across and within industries.

Exhibit 8.1 underlines the importance of industry structure to ROIC. It compares the median return on invested capital over more than 20 years in two sectors: branded consumer goods and extraction industries (such as mining and oil and gas). Consumer goods have earned consistently higher ROICs than extraction companies. In addition, the returns of extraction-based companies have been highly volatile.

The reason for this difference in the industries' performances lies mainly in differences between their competitive structures. In the branded-consumer-goods industry, companies such as Nestlé, Procter & Gamble, and Unilever developed long-lasting brands with high consumer loyalty that made it difficult for new competitors to gain a foothold. Building on these advantages, these companies were able to increase their returns on capital from around 20 percent in the mid-1990s to roughly 30 percent two decades later, despite challenges to traditional brands from new market entrants. One example is

---

[1] We introduce *units* to encourage discussion regarding price, cost, and volume. The formula, however, is not specific to manufacturing. Units can represent the number of hours billed, patients seen, transactions processed, and so on.

[2] See, for example, J. Barney, "Resource-Based Theories of Competitive Advantage: A Ten-Year Retrospective on the Resource-Based View," *Journal of Management* 27 (2001): 643–650.

EXHIBIT 8.1 **Company Profitability: Industry Matters**

Industry median ROIC excluding goodwill, %

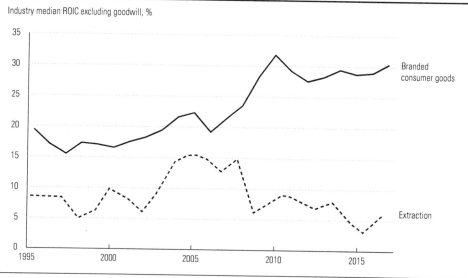

Source: Corporate Performance Analytics by McKinsey.

the competition faced by Procter & Gamble's Gillette shaving business from challengers such as Harry's and Dollar Shave Club.[3]

In extraction industries, one company's products are the same as another's (iron ore is iron ore, with minor quality differences), so prices are the same across the industry at any point in time. In addition, the companies use the same capital-intensive processes to extract their products. As a result, the median company in the industry doesn't have a competitive advantage, and returns are low, averaging only 9 percent during this 20-year period. It is worth noting that imbalances in supply and demand can lead to cycles in product price and ROIC, as was the case with a long run-up in commodity prices in the years leading up to 2005. In the end, though, competition leads to low ROIC on average.

Industry structure is by no means the only determinant of ROIC, as the significant variation among companies within industries shows. Consider the global automotive industry, which has been plagued by overcapacity for years. Still, the industry's low returns do not deter new entrants, whether from different geographies (such as South Korean automakers' entry into the U.S. and European markets) or due to the emergence of new technologies (such as electric-vehicle producers, including Tesla). Add in the difficulties that some manufacturers encounter in trying to close unionized plants, and it's easy to see how overcapacity keeps returns across the sector low. Only a few manufacturers, such as BMW, can parlay their premium brands and higher quality into higher prices and superior returns on capital compared with other

---

[3] Unilever acquired Dollar Shave Club in 2016.

manufacturers. Or consider the highly competitive European airline industry, where most players typically generate returns very close to their cost of capital—and occasionally below it. Nevertheless, Ryanair earns superior returns, thanks to its strategy of strictly point-to-point connections between predominantly secondary airports at the lowest cost in the industry.

Finally, industry structure and competitive behavior aren't fixed; they're subject to shocks from technological innovation, changes in government regulation, and competitive entry—any or all of which can affect individual companies or an entire industry. We show in this chapter's final section that the software and pharmaceutical industries, for example, consistently earn high returns. However, the leading companies may not be the same in 20 years, just as many of today's leaders were not major players or didn't even exist 20 years ago.

COMPETITIVE ADVANTAGE

Competitive advantage derives from some combination of ten sources, defined in Exhibit 8.2. Of these, five allow companies to charge a price premium, four contribute to cost and capital efficiency, and one (often referred to as "network economies") combines price and cost advantages to produce increasing returns to scale. It is important to understand that competitive advantage drawn from these sources is enjoyed not by entire companies but by particular business units and product lines. This is the only level of competition at which the concept of competitive advantage affords you any real traction in strategic thinking; even if a company sells soup or dog food exclusively, it may still have individual businesses and product lines with very different degrees of competitive advantage and therefore different returns on invested capital.

EXHIBIT 8.2 **Sources of Competitive Advantage**

Price premium	Cost and capital efficiency
Innovative products: Difficult-to-copy or patented products, services, or technologies	**Innovative business method**: Difficult-to-copy business method that contrasts with established industry practice
Quality: Customers willing to pay a premium for a real or perceived difference in quality over and above competing products or services	**Unique resources**: Advantage resulting from inherent geological characteristics or unique access to raw material(s)
Brand: Customers willing to pay a premium based on brand, even if there is no clear quality difference	**Economies of scale**: Efficient scale or size for the relevant market
Customer lock-in: Customers unwilling or unable to replace a product or service they use with a competing product or service	**Scalable product/process**: Ability to add customers and capacity at negligible marginal cost
Rational price discipline: Lower bound on prices established by large industry leaders through price signaling or capacity management	

Increasing returns to scale: Scalable products that offer increasing value to customers with scale

On balance, price premiums offer any business the greatest scope for achieving an attractive ROIC, but they are usually more difficult to achieve than cost efficiencies. Also, the businesses or products with the highest returns are often those that weave together more than one advantage.

Price Premium Advantages

In commodity markets, companies are typically price takers, meaning they must sell at the market price to generate sales, because the products are hard to differentiate. To sell its products at a price premium, a company must find a way to differentiate its products from those of competitors. We distinguish five sources of price premiums: innovative products, quality, brand, customer lock-in, and rational price discipline.

Innovative Products   Innovative goods and services yield high returns on capital if they are protected by patents, are difficult to copy, or both. Absent these protections, even an innovative product won't do much to generate high returns.

Pharmaceutical companies earn high returns because they produce innovative products that, although often easy to copy, are protected by patents for up to 20 years. The business can charge a price premium during the protected period, after which generics will enter the market and drive the price down. Even after the patent expires, the holder may enjoy some price "stickiness."

An example of an innovative product line that is not patent protected but still difficult to copy was Apple's series of iPod MP3 players. MP3 players had been on the market for several years before Apple introduced the iPod, and the core technology was the same for all competitors. The iPod was more successful, however, because of its appealing design and ease of use afforded by its user interface and integration with iTunes. Apple followed a similar approach with the iPhone and iPad; once again, the design and user interface were core drivers of the price premium. Although not patent protected, good design can be difficult to copy.

Quality   A term used as broadly as *quality* requires definition. In the context of competitive advantage and ROIC, quality means a real or perceived difference between one product or service and another for which consumers are willing to pay a higher price. In the car business, for example, BMW enjoys a price premium because customers perceive that its cars handle and drive better than comparable automobiles that cost less. The cost of providing the extra quality is less than the price premium. Hence, BMW has often been able to earn higher returns than many other carmakers. Appliance makers such as Weber can price their products at a premium over those of their competitors because customers perceive their reliability and durability to be superior.

Sometimes the perception of quality lasts significantly longer than any actual difference in quality. This has been the case with Honda and Toyota, relative to many automakers (at least until Toyota had to make product recalls in 2009). While American and Japanese cars have been comparable in terms of quantifiable quality measures, such as the J.D. Power survey, Japanese companies have enjoyed a price premium for their products. Even when American and Japanese sticker prices on comparable vehicles were the same, American manufacturers were often forced to sell at a $2,000 to $3,000 discount, whereas Japanese cars sold for nearer the asking price.

Brand   Price premiums based on brand are sometimes hard to distinguish from price premiums based on quality, and the two are highly correlated (as in the example of BMW). While the quality of a product may matter more than its established branding, sometimes the brand itself is what matters more—especially when the brand has lasted a very long time, as in the cases of Heineken, Coca-Cola, Perrier, and Mercedes-Benz.

Packaged food, beverages, and durable consumer goods are good examples of sectors where brands earn price premiums for some but not all products. In some categories, such as bottled water and breakfast cereals, customers are loyal to brands like Perrier and Cheerios despite the availability of high-quality branded and private-label alternatives. In other categories, including meat, branding has not been successful. Because of their strong brands, beverage and cereal companies can earn returns on capital of around 30 percent, while meat processors earn returns of around 15 percent.

Customer Lock-In   When replacing one company's product or service with another's is relatively costly (relative to the price of the product) for customers, the incumbent company can charge a price premium—if not for the initial sale, then at least for additional units or for subsequent generations and iterations of the original product. Gillette's shaving products offer a classic example: the manufacturer realizes its margin not on the starter pack but on replacement razor blades. In consumer electronics, wireless-audio product manufacturers such as Sonos also create a form of lock-in: once customers have one or more loudspeakers installed, they are not likely to switch to other brands when replacing or adding units, as these would lack compatibility with their existing Sonos units.

High switching costs, relative to the price of the product or service, create the strongest customer lock-in. Medical devices, such as artificial joints, can lock in the doctors who purchase them, because doctors need time to train and become proficient in the procedures for using and/or implanting those devices. Once doctors are up to speed on a device, they won't switch to a competing product unless there is a compelling reason to invest the necessary effort. Similarly, bankers and traders who have invested considerable time in learning how to work with particular brands of financial terminals are often reluctant to learn another system. An installed base can be a powerful driver of competitive advantage.

Rational Price Discipline   In commodity industries with many competitors, the laws of supply and demand will drive down prices and ROIC. This applies not just to obvious commodities—say, chemicals and paper—but also to more recently commoditized products and services, such as airline seats. It would take a net increase of only 5 to 10 percent in airline ticket prices to turn the industry's aggregate loss to an aggregate profit. But each competitor is tempted to get an edge in filling seats by keeping prices low, even when fuel prices and other costs rise for all competitors. In the past several years, the airline sector in the United States has rapidly consolidated and become more cautious about adding seat capacity. That has allowed U.S. airlines to operate at more attractive price levels and earn healthy returns on capital. In contrast, most European airlines still face strong price competition and are rarely able to earn returns on capital above their cost of capital.

Occasionally, we find an example such as the U.S. airline industry that manages to overcome the forces of competition and set its prices at a level that earns its companies reasonable returns on capital (though rarely more than 15 percent) without breaking competition law. For example, for many years, almost all real estate agents in the United States charged a 6 percent commission on the price of each home they sold. In other cases, government sanctions disciplined pricing in an industry through regulatory structures. Until the late 1990s, airline fares in Europe were high because in most national markets, foreign competitors faced restrictions when competing with domestic airlines. Prices collapsed when the European airline markets were fully deregulated in 1997.

Rational, legitimate pricing discipline typically works when one competitor acts as the leader and others quickly replicate its price moves. In addition, there must be barriers to new entrants, and each competitor must be large enough that a price war will surely reduce the profit on its existing volume by more than any extra profit gained from new sales. If there are smaller competitors with more to gain from extra volume than they would lose from lower prices, then price discipline will be very difficult to maintain.

Most attempts by industry players to maintain a floor price fail. Take the paper industry, for example. Its ROIC averaged less than 10 percent from 1990 to 2013. The industry created this problem for itself because the companies all tended to expand at once, after demand and prices had risen. As a result, a large chunk of new capacity came on line at the same time, upsetting the balance of supply and demand and forcing down prices and returns.

Even cartels (which are illegal in most of the world) find it difficult to maintain price levels, because each cartel member has a great incentive to lower prices and attract more sales. This so-called free-rider issue makes it difficult to maintain price levels over long periods, even for the Organization of Petroleum Exporting Countries (OPEC), the world's largest and most prominent cartel.

Cost and Capital Efficiency Advantages

Theoretically, cost and capital efficiency are two separate competitive advantages. Cost efficiency is the ability to deliver products and services at a lower cost than the competition. Capital efficiency is about delivering more products per dollar of invested capital than competitors. In practice, both tend to share common drivers and are hard to separate. (Is a company's outsourcing of manufacturing to Asia a source of cost efficiency or capital efficiency?) Consequently, we treat the following four sources of competitive advantage as deriving from both the cost and capital efficiencies they achieve.

Innovative Business Method   A company's business method is the combination of its production, logistics, and pattern of interaction with customers. Most production methods can be copied, but some are difficult to copy at some times. For example, early in its life, Dell developed a new way of making and distributing personal computers. Dell sold directly to its customers, made its machines to order with almost no inventory (by assembling machines with standardized parts that could be purchased from different suppliers at different times at very low cost), and received payments from customers as soon as products shipped. In contrast, Hewlett-Packard and Compaq, Dell's dominant competitors at that time, were producing in large batches and selling through retailers. Dell's cost and capital efficiency enabled the company initially to generate a much higher ROIC than its competitors, who couldn't switch quickly to a direct-sales model without angering their retailers and reengineering their production processes.

Notably, Dell's success formula eroded over time as its sales shifted from desktop to notebook computers. Notebook computers are built to much tighter part specifications, often using parts from vendors made expressly for Dell. Since everything must fit together just right, Dell needed more support from its vendors and saw its leverage over them diminished.

Sweden's IKEA provides another example of advantage gleaned from an innovative business method. IKEA transformed the home furniture business around the world, driving innovations in all steps of the business chain from design to manufacturing and distribution to sales. Its concept of self-assembly furniture reduces production and storage costs. Close collaboration in design and manufacturing minimizes product development costs and time. Manufacturing costs are kept low by using a limited range of raw materials. Its automated distribution centers are highly efficient because its product meets standard packaging requirements. Its retail stores are highly standardized and operate at low labor costs because customers pick up their furniture, still in packages, directly from storage. By making sure all these steps in the chain also stay carefully aligned with customer preferences, IKEA has become the largest furniture retailer in the world, operating more than 400 stores in more than 50 markets as of 2018.

Unique Resources   Sometimes a company has access to a unique resource that cannot be replicated. This provides a significant competitive advantage. For example, in general, gold miners in North America earn higher returns than those in South Africa because the northern ore is closer to the surface, so extracting it is easier and costs less. These lower extraction costs are a primary driver of higher returns from North American mines (though partially offset by higher investment costs).

Another example is Nornickel's nickel mine in northern Siberia. The content of precious metals (e.g., palladium) in the mine's nickel ore is significantly higher than in the ore from Canadian and Indonesian mines. In other words, Nornickel extracts not only nickel from its ore but also some high-priced palladium. As a result, Siberian mines earn higher returns than other nickel mines.

Geography often plays a role in gaining advantage from unique resources. Obviously, most leading seaports and airports owe their success to their specific location. The Port of Rotterdam Authority operates the largest seaport of Europe, benefiting from a location that connects the Rhine River (Europe's busiest waterway) and the continent's largest economy (Germany) to the North Sea and global shipping routes. But geography is important not only for infrastructure companies. In general, whenever the cost of shipping a product is high relative to the value of the product, producers near their customers have a unique advantage. China is the largest consumer of iron ore. South American mines, therefore, face a distinct transportation cost disadvantage compared with Australian iron mines, and this contributes to the South American mines' lower returns compared with Australian competitors.

Economies of Scale   The notion of economies of scale is often misunderstood to mean that there are automatic economies that come with size. Scale can indeed be important to value, but usually only at the regional or even local level, not in the national or global market. For example, for many retail businesses in dry cleaning, funeral services, or workspace rentals, it's much more important to be large in one city than large across the entire country, because local costs for facilities and advertising are either lumpy or fixed. Buying advertising airtime and space in Chicago is the same whether you have one store or a dozen. Likewise, a key element that determines the profitability of health insurers in the United States is their ability to negotiate prices with providers (hospitals and doctors), who tend to operate locally rather than nationally. The insurer with the highest market share in a local market will be in a position to negotiate the lowest prices, regardless of its national market share. In other words, it's better to have the number-one market share in ten states than to be number one nationwide but number four in every state.

Another aspect of scale economies is that a company derives benefit only if competitors cannot easily achieve similar scale. Sometimes the required investments are large enough to deter competitors. Anyone who wants to compete with United Parcel Service (UPS), for instance, must first pay the enormous fixed expense of installing an international network and then operate at a loss for quite some time while drawing customers away from the incumbent. Even though UPS continually must add new costs for planes, trucks, and drivers, these costs are variable—in contrast to the fixed cost of building the international network—and are incurred in stepwise fashion. That does not mean the industry is completely safe from competition. Over the past few years, Amazon has been building its own shipping network. Scale is less effective as a barrier to entry for Amazon: the company can rapidly reach sufficient scale thanks to its internal demand, and it has shown itself prepared and able to incur significant upfront investments.

Scalable Product or Process   Having products or processes that are scalable means the cost of supplying or serving additional customers is very low at almost any level of scale. Businesses with this advantage usually deliver their products and services using information technology (IT). Consider a company that provides standardized software (in other words, a product that requires little customization). Once the software is developed, it can be sold to many customers with no incremental development costs. So the gross margin on incremental sales could be as high as 100 percent. As sales rise the only costs that increase are typically for selling, marketing, and administration.

For scalable software businesses, the upfront investments are not the only hurdle that competitors must deal with. Customers face costs of switching to other software providers, so competitors cannot easily achieve a similar scale as the incumbent player. That does not mean such competitive advantages last indefinitely, however; ongoing technological innovations in IT create opportunities for new competitors. For example, in financial and payments services, new entrants such as PayPal or Ayden have secured leading positions by starting new business models built on innovative technology platforms. Incumbent players, strapped with heritage organizations, systems, and processes, have found it difficult to copy the innovations.

Other examples of scalable businesses include media companies that make and distribute movies or TV shows. Making the movie or show requires an initial outlay for the crew, sets, actors, and so on. But those costs are fixed regardless of how many people end up viewing and paying for the show. There may be some incremental advertising costs and very small costs associated with putting the movie on DVD or streaming it. But overall, costs do not rise as customer numbers increase. In this case, it is the access to unique resources—namely, media content—that holds off competitors from capturing similar scale economies.

Most IT-based or IT-enabled businesses offer some form of scalability, especially given recent developments in cloud-based computing. But what counts is whether all critical elements of a business system are scalable. Take, for example, online food delivery businesses. These businesses can easily scale up in terms of number of registered restaurants, customers, and orders, but they still incur incremental costs for each individual order delivery, if only for transportation. Such costs still mount with the number of clients, which presents some limits on scalability and reduction of costs to serve as the business grows.

Network Economies

Some scalable businesses models provide extraordinarily high returns on capital because they exhibit network economies that lead to increasing returns to scale. As the business gains customers and grows, the cost of offering the products decreases, and their value to customers increases. The eBay example we related at the beginning of this chapter illustrates this. Other examples are online lodging and travel platforms such as Airbnb and Booking.com. These models feature scalable products where the marginal cost of additional transactions is minimal. In addition, with scale, these platform services also become more valuable to both end customers and lodging providers. As a result, Airbnb and Booking.com can realize competitive advantages both in price and in cost and capital efficiencies.

Such sources of competitive advantage become even more powerful when customers face high switching costs. Consider a company like Microsoft. Its Office software benefits from scalable operations on the cost side because it can supply online products and services at extremely low marginal cost. Office has also become more valuable as the customer base has expanded over time. Microsoft has been able to lock in customers who want to easily exchange documents with other Office users and who are not keen to spend time and effort switching to alternative software. Some social-media business models, such as Facebook's, offer similar customer lock-in combined with increasing returns on scale.

Although many new digital business models for social media, digital marketplaces, and e-commerce like to claim such increasing returns to scale, they occur in rare circumstances only. Economists Carl Shapiro and Hal Varian popularized this concept in their 1998 book *Information Rules*.[4]

---

[4] C. Shapiro and H. Varian, *Information Rules: A Strategic Guide to the Network Economy* (Boston: Harvard Business School Press, 1998).

The management implication of this insight was that in a business with in-creasing returns, it is important to get big faster than anyone else. Shapiro and Varian also explained the rare conditions under which it is possible to increase returns to scale. Sadly, executives who ignored that part of the book and pursued "network effects" faced disaster. For example, many U.S. electric-power producers tried to get big fast by buying up everything they could. Most collapsed, because there are no increasing returns from scaling electric-power production. Perhaps more important, such scale effects lead to superior lasting returns only if a company can prevent competitors from achieving similar scale.

SUSTAINING RETURN ON INVESTED CAPITAL

The longer a company can sustain a high ROIC, the more value management will create. In a perfectly competitive economy, ROIC higher than the cost of capital get competed away. Whether a company can sustain a given level of ROIC depends on the length of the life cycles of its businesses and products, the length of time its competitive advantages can persist, and its potential for renewing businesses and products.

Length of Product Life Cycle

The longer the life cycle of a company's businesses and products, the better its chances of sustaining its ROIC. To illustrate, while the products of companies such as Coca-Cola or Mars may not seem as exciting as the latest flashy elec-tronics items, culturally entrenched, branded soft drinks and snacks are likely to have a market for far longer than many new gadgets. Similarly, a unique resource (like palladium-rich nickel ore) can be a durable source of advantage if it is related to a long product life cycle but will be less so if it isn't (this ap-pears to be the case for lignite and coal today).

A business model that locks customers into a product with a short life cycle is far less valuable than one that locks customers in for a long time. Once users of Microsoft's Windows have become well versed in the plat-form, they are unlikely to switch to a new competitor. Even Linux, a low-cost alternative to Windows, has struggled to gain market share as system administrators and end users remain wary of learning a new way of com-puting. Microsoft's success in extending the life cycle of Windows has been a huge source of value to the company. Contrast this with a company like BlackBerry, which had an impressive customer base until the life cycle of its early smartphones was cut short by the introduction of the iPhone and other next-generation devices.

Persistence of Competitive Advantage

If a company cannot prevent competition from duplicating its business, high ROIC will be short-lived, and the company's value will diminish. Consider two major cost improvements that airlines implemented over the past decade. The self-service kiosk and, more recently, the smartphone app allow passengers to purchase a ticket and to print or download a boarding pass from anywhere in the world without waiting in line. From the airlines' perspective, fewer ground personnel and equipment are needed to handle even more passengers. So why has this cost improvement not translated into high ROIC for the airlines?[5] Since every company has access to the technology, any cost improvements are passed directly to the consumer in the form of lower prices. A similar example comes from robotic automation's ongoing effect on productivity improvements in automotive manufacturing: all players adopt the new technology and pass on the cost reductions to customers. In general, advantages that arise from brand and quality on the price side and scalability on the cost side tend to have more staying power than those arising from more temporary sources of advantage, such as an innovation that will tend to be superseded by subsequent innovations.

Potential for Product Renewal

Few businesses or products have life cycles as long as Coca-Cola's. Most companies need to find renewal businesses and products where they can leverage existing advantages or build new ones. This is an area where brands prove their value. Consumer goods companies excel at using their brands to launch new products: think of Apple's success with the iPhone, Bulgari moving into fragrances, Mars entering the ice cream business, Netflix switching from DVD rentals by mail to video streaming online, John Deere offering information services to farmers, and Signify (the former Philips Lighting) developing connected lighting solutions such as Hue. Being good at innovation also helps companies renew products and businesses. Thus, pharmaceutical companies exist because they can discover new drugs, and semiconductor technology players such as ASML and Intel rely on their technology innovation to launch new products and stay ahead of competitors.

Some companies, such as Procter & Gamble and Alphabet's Google subsidiary, are able to maintain their primary product lines while simultaneously expanding into new markets. Google built new advertising and subscription businesses around, for example, YouTube and G Suite (which comprises Gmail, Calendar, and Google+) to complement the original advertising business that its search engine powers. Procter & Gamble has a strong record of

[5] Although ROIC in the U.S. airline industry has increased over recent years, credit for this improvement goes not to cost reduction from new technology but to earnings gains from ongoing consolidation and lower fuel prices.

continuing to introduce successful new products, including Swiffer, Febreze, and Crest Whitestrips. It also anticipated the strong growth in beauty products in the early 2000s with a number of acquisitions that increased its revenues in the category from $7.3 billion to $20 billion from 1999 to 2013. Product development and renewal have enabled the company to advance from owning just a single billion-dollar brand (by sales) in 1999 to 23 such brands in 2013. Underlining its competitive strength in managing very large brands, Procter & Gamble announced in 2014 that it would discontinue or divest 90 to 100 smaller brands from a total of 180 brands in its portfolio.

As the next section of this chapter indicates, empirical studies show that over the past five decades, companies have been generally successful in sustaining their rates of ROIC. It appears that when companies have found a strategy that creates competitive advantages, they are often able to sustain and renew these advantages over many years. This also holds for the relatively new digital business models with which Amazon, Google, Microsoft, and others have retained and renewed their competitive advantages for two decades and more. While competition clearly plays a major role in driving down ROIC, managers can sustain a high rate of return by anticipating and responding to changes in the environment better than their competitors do.

AN EMPIRICAL ANALYSIS OF RETURNS ON INVESTED CAPITAL

Several key findings concerning ROIC emerge from a study of 1963–2017 returns on invested capital at U.S.-based nonfinancial companies with (inflation-adjusted) revenues greater than $1 billion:[6]

- The median ROIC was stable at about 10 percent until the turn of the century and then increased to 17 percent after 2010, where it has remained since. Important drivers of this effect were a general increase in profitability across sectors, combined with a shift in the mix of U.S.-based companies to higher-returning sectors in life sciences and technology. These sectors not only significantly increased their ROIC, but also grew faster.

- Returns on invested capital differ by industry. Industries such as pharmaceuticals and branded consumer goods that rely on patents and brands for their sustainable competitive advantages tend to have high median ROIC, whereas companies in basic industries, such as oil and gas, mining, and utilities, tend to earn low ROIC.

---

[6] The results come from Corporate Performance Analytics by McKinsey, which relies on financial data provided by Standard & Poor's Compustat and Capital IQ. The number of companies in the sample varies from year to year and excludes financial institutions and industrial companies with significant financial businesses. In 2017, the sample included 1,095 companies.

- There are large variations in rates of ROIC within industries. Some companies earn attractive returns in industries where the median return is low (e.g., Walmart), and vice versa.
- Relative rates of ROIC across industries are generally stable, especially compared with rates of growth (discussed in the next chapter). Industry rankings by median ROIC do not change much over time, with only a few industries making a clear aggregate shift upward or downward. These shifts typically reflect structural changes, such as the widespread consolidation in the defense and airline industries over the past two decades and the maturing of the biotech industry. Individual company returns gradually tend toward their industry medians over time but are generally persistent. Even the 2008 financial crisis did not upset this trend.

ROIC Trends and Drivers

Relatively stable ROIC levels from the early 1960s to the early 2000s are evident in Exhibit 8.3, which plots median ROIC between 1963 and 2017 for U.S.-based nonfinancial companies.[7] In that exhibit, the measure of ROIC excludes goodwill and acquired intangibles, which allows us to focus on the underlying economics of companies without the distortion of premiums paid for acquisitions (discussed later in the chapter).

EXHIBIT 8.3 **ROIC of U.S.-Based Nonfinancial Companies, 1963–2017**

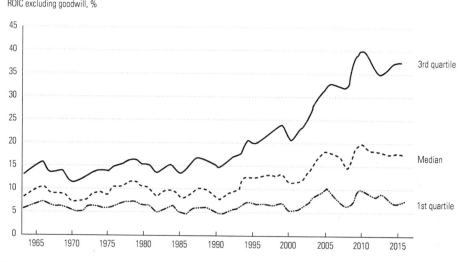

Source: Corporate Performance Analytics by McKinsey.

[7] The numbers in this section are based on U.S. companies because longer-term data for non-U.S. companies are not readily available.

Until the 2000s, the median ROIC without goodwill was about 10 percent. Furthermore, annual medians oscillated in a tight range, with higher returns in high-GDP-growth years and lower returns in low-growth years. Since the 2000s, however, median ROIC without goodwill has increased to what appears to be a new level of about 17 percent in 2010 and beyond. Notice also that the spread between the first and third quartiles has widened. The first-quartile company earned around 5 to 7 percent during the entire period, while the third-quartile company's return has increased from the midteens to over 35 percent.

In fact, the entire distribution of ROIC has widened as more and more companies earn high returns on capital. Exhibit 8.4 shows the distribution of ROICs over different eras. In the 1965–1967 period, only 14 percent of companies earned more than a 20 percent ROIC, compared with 45 percent in 2015–2017. At the same time, the share of companies earning less than 10 percent has declined from 53 percent to 30 percent.

One factor powering the shift in the median ROIC is the steady increase of operating margins across sectors since the mid-1990s. As shown in Exhibit 8.5, the median operating margin (NOPAT over sales) has risen by two percentage points. When higher margins combine with improved capital productivity (lower invested capital over sales), returns on capital rise. The U.S. economy's changing industry mix serves as an even more powerful driver and helps to explain the widening dispersion of returns. Among U.S.-based nonfinancial companies, the share of operating profits from companies in the life science and technology sectors increased from 19 percent of total operating profits in 1995 to 38 percent in 2017.[8] This impressive increase has been driven by the

EXHIBIT 8.4 **Distribution of ROIC**

% of companies with given annual ROIC excluding goodwill, by time period

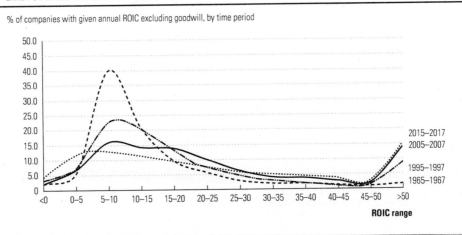

Source: Corporate Performance Analytics by McKinsey.

[8] We defined life science and technology sectors to comprise pharmaceuticals, biotechnology, healthcare equipment and supplies, information services and software, and technology hardware, storage, and peripherals.

faster growth of these sectors relative to the rest of the economy, these sectors' generally higher margins and returns on capital, and increases in these sectors' margins and returns on capital. As a result, the life science and technology sectors generate six percentage points of the total 16 percent return on capital for the U.S. economy as a whole, compared with only two percentage points of a 12 percent overall return in 1995 (see Exhibit 8.6).[9]

ROIC by Industry

To see how differences in ROIC across industries and companies relate to likely differences in drivers of competitive advantage, we examined variations in ROIC by industry over the past two decades. Our findings are in line with results from prior editions of this book, in which we tracked profitability going back to the 1960s. Exhibit 8.7 shows the median returns on invested

EXHIBIT 8.5 **Disaggregating ROIC of U.S.-Based Nonfinancial Companies, 1995–2017**

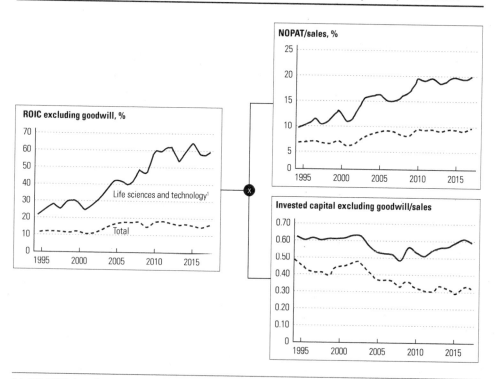

Note: ROIC, NOPAT/sales, and invested capital/sales are aggregate metrics.

[1] Life sciences and techonology sectors comprise pharmaceuticals, biotechnology, health-care equipment and supplies, information services and software, and technology hardware, storage, and peripherals.

Source: Corporate Performance Analytics by McKinsey.

[9] The ROIC contribution is calculated as the total NOPAT of the life science and technology sectors divided by the invested capital of all sectors. Note that the aggregate ROIC for the total sample is close to the median ROIC of 12.4% in 1995, 16.7% in 2005, and 17.4% in 2017.

EXHIBIT 8.6 **Contribution of Life Sciences and Technology Industries to the Broader Economy, 1995–2017**

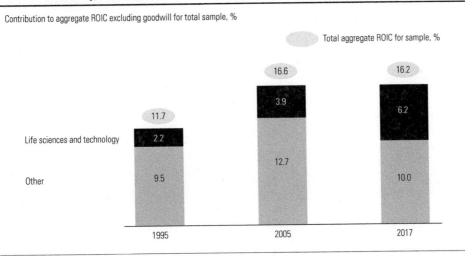

Contribution to aggregate ROIC excluding goodwill for total sample, %

Total aggregate ROIC for sample, %

Life sciences and technology

Other

	1995	2005	2017
Total aggregate ROIC	11.7	16.6	16.2
Life sciences and technology	2.2	3.9	6.2
Other	9.5	12.7	10.0

Source: Corporate Performance Analytics by McKinsey.

capital for a range of industries during the periods 1995–1999 and 2013–2017. The exhibit reveals large differences in median ROIC across industries. Not surprisingly, industries with the highest returns, such as pharmaceuticals, health-care equipment, and technology-related businesses, are those with sustainable competitive advantages. In the case of pharmaceuticals and health-care equipment, this is due to patent-protected innovation. In technology-related businesses, advantage typically flows from increasing returns to scale and customer lock-in. The branded consumer goods and luxury goods sectors have high returns thanks to customer loyalty based on brand strength. The industries at the bottom of the chart tend to be those where it is difficult to achieve a price premium or cost advantage—often commodity-based industries, including oil, gas, metals, and mining.

Industries typically recognized for having higher returns have often been the ones that also deliver the clearest improvements in ROIC over time. The reasons vary by sector. For example, leading aerospace and defense companies tend to focus on government contracts that include advance payments. This keeps the companies' invested capital at low levels relative to revenues. The biotechnology sector matured over the past 20 years with large companies such as Amgen and Gilead generating outstanding returns from the successful development and marketing of innovative blockbuster drugs. Finally, technology players benefited from growth and innovation in hardware (via semiconductors, servers, and smartphones) and in software and services. As markets became increasingly global, the shift to more scalable online software and information services also contributed to higher margins and returns; consider Facebook's and YouTube's growth in social media or Microsoft and Oracle in software. One outlier from this high-return club: the airline sector, which has

EXHIBIT 8.7 **ROIC by Industry, 1995–2017**

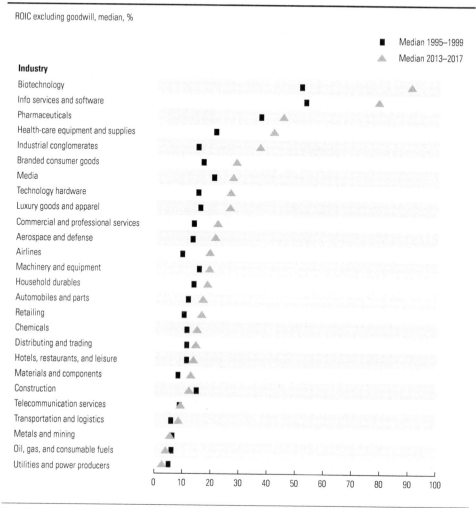

ROIC excluding goodwill, median, %

■ Median 1995–1999
▲ Median 2013–2017

Industry	
Biotechnology	
Info services and software	
Pharmaceuticals	
Health-care equipment and supplies	
Industrial conglomerates	
Branded consumer goods	
Media	
Technology hardware	
Luxury goods and apparel	
Commercial and professional services	
Aerospace and defense	
Airlines	
Machinery and equipment	
Household durables	
Automobiles and parts	
Retailing	
Chemicals	
Distributing and trading	
Hotels, restaurants, and leisure	
Materials and components	
Construction	
Telecommunication services	
Transportation and logistics	
Metals and mining	
Oil, gas, and consumable fuels	
Utilities and power producers	

Source: Corporate Performance Analytics by McKinsey.

delivered low ROIC historically but managed to increase returns in recent years, thanks to ongoing consolidation in the United States and significantly lower fuel prices.

To some extent, the increases in ROIC reflect a trend across industries to lower capital intensity, as we observed in Exhibit 8.5. This could be interpreted as U.S. companies simply reducing their capital base—for example, by outsourcing operations without necessarily creating value.[10] This is not the case, however. Total economic profit for our sample of the largest U.S. companies increased from $31 billion in 1995 to $560 billion in 2017. Moreover, economic profit increased for most sectors over the same period, with similar patterns as for ROIC.

[10] A ROIC increase from a reduction in invested capital from outsourcing does not necessarily indicate value creation. As Chapter 24 notes, the change in economic profit provides a reliable indication.

Differences in ROIC within industries can be considerable. Exhibit 8.8 shows the variation between the first and third quartiles for the same industries. Note the wide range of returns in information services and software. Some of the companies in the sector earn low returns because they are capital intensive, and low margins because their business model is not scalable, as in the case of running data centers. Other companies provide services that are based on standardized and scalable software, where the incremental cost to serve a new customer is small, leading to high ROIC. In some industries, the largest players also generate the highest returns, and median ROIC does not reflect the aggregated ROIC for the sector as a whole (defined as NOPAT for the sector divided by its total invested capital). An example is the technology hardware sector, where players like Apple drive the aggregate ROIC to almost 70 percent, versus a median of 27 percent in 2015–2017.

EXHIBIT 8.8 **Variation in ROIC within Industries, 2015–2017**

ROIC,[1] excluding goodwill, %

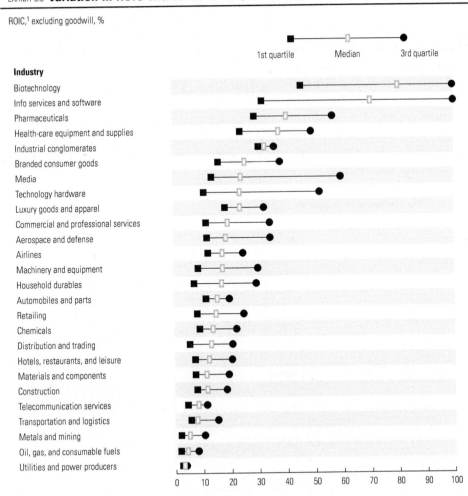

This chart also shows that the best performers in a weaker or mediocre industry may outperform the median performer in a stronger industry. Consider, for example, retailing, shown in the bottom half of the chart. The stronger retailers (like Walmart) outperform the weaker companies in the media industry, which appears in the top half of the chart.

Stability of ROIC

While industries often exhibit variations in their respective ROIC, many industries tend to remain fairly stable over time. We can see this by grouping the industry-level returns on invested capital according to whether they are relatively high, medium, or low. As shown in Exhibit 8.9, most industries stayed in the same group over the period we studied, starting in the early 1960s. In addition, some industries are cyclical, having high and low returns at different points in the cycle but demonstrating no clear trend up or down over time.

Persistently high-return industries included household and personal products, beverages, pharmaceuticals, and information services and software. These industries have consistently high returns because they are scalable or are protected by brands or patents. Persistently low returns characterize paper and forest products, railroads, and utilities. These are industries in which price premiums are difficult to achieve because of, for example, low barriers to entry, commodity products, or regulated returns. Perhaps surprisingly, this group also includes department stores. Like commodity industries, department stores can achieve little price differentiation, so as a rule, they realize persistently low returns.

EXHIBIT 8.9 **Persistence of Industry ROIC**

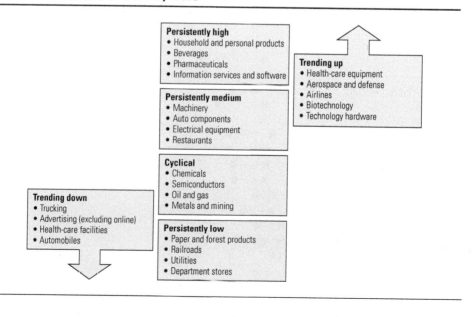

Persistently high
- Household and personal products
- Beverages
- Pharmaceuticals
- Information services and software

Trending up
- Health-care equipment
- Aerospace and defense
- Airlines
- Biotechnology
- Technology hardware

Persistently medium
- Machinery
- Auto components
- Electrical equipment
- Restaurants

Cyclical
- Chemicals
- Semiconductors
- Oil and gas
- Metals and mining

Trending down
- Trucking
- Advertising (excluding online)
- Health-care facilities
- Automobiles

Persistently low
- Paper and forest products
- Railroads
- Utilities
- Department stores

In several industries, there was a clear downward trend in returns. These included trucking, health care facilities, and automobiles. Competition in trucking, advertising, and automobiles has increased substantially over the past five decades. Health-care facilities have had their prices squeezed by the government, insurers, and competition with nonprofits.

Industries where returns on invested capital clearly are trending up are rare. Examples are health-care equipment, airlines, and aerospace and defense. Innovation in health-care equipment has enabled the industry to produce higher-value-added, differentiated products such as artificial joints, as well as more commoditized products, including syringes and forceps. As mentioned earlier, the U.S. airlines industry benefited from consolidation, and companies in aerospace and defense reduced their capital intensity as governments provided up-front funding for many more contracts.

There is similar evidence of sustained rates of return at the company level. We measured the sustainability of company ROIC in our database of nonfinancial corporations by ranking companies based on their ROIC in each year and dividing the group into quintiles. We treated each quintile as a portfolio and tracked the median ROIC for the portfolio over the following 15 years, as shown in Exhibit 8.10. The results indicate some mean reversion: companies earning high returns tended to see their ROIC fall gradually over the succeeding 15 years, and companies earning low returns tended to see them rise over time. Only in the portfolio containing companies generating returns between 5 and 10 percent (mostly regulated companies) do rates of return

EXHIBIT 8.10 **ROIC Decay Analysis**

Median ROIC of portfolios (without goodwill), by quintile,[1] %

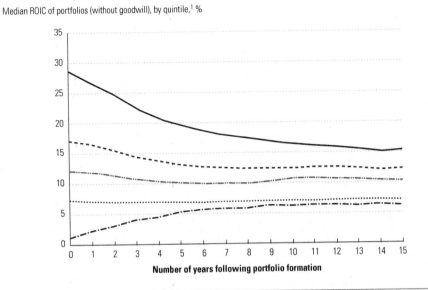

Number of years following portfolio formation

[1] At year 0, companies are grouped into one of five portfolios, based on ROIC.

Source: Corporate Performance Analytics by McKinsey.

remain constant. However, an important phenomenon is the persistence of superior performance beyond ten years. The returns of the best-performing companies do *not* decline all the way to the aggregate median over 15 years. High-performing companies are in general remarkably capable of sustaining a competitive advantage in their businesses and/or finding new business where they continue or rebuild such advantages. The pattern is stable over time—even over the most recent 15 years, which included the 2008 credit crisis (see Exhibit 8.11).

Since a company's continuing value is highly dependent on long-run forecasts of ROIC and growth, this result has important implications for corporate valuation. Basing a continuing value on the economic concept that ROIC will approach the weighted average cost of capital (WACC) is overly conservative for the *typical* company generating high ROIC. (Continuing value is the focus of Chapter 14.)

Keeping this range of performance in mind, it is important when benchmarking the historical decay of company ROIC to segment results by industry, especially if industry is a proxy for sustainability of competitive advantage. As an example, Exhibit 8.12 plots the ROIC decay rates for branded consumer goods, again sorting the companies into five portfolios based on their starting ROICs. Here, the top-performing companies don't show much reversion to the mean. Even after 15 years, the original class of best performers still outperforms the bottom quintile by more than 13 percentage points.

EXHIBIT 8.11 **ROIC Decay through Economic Crisis and Recovery**

Median ROIC of portfolios (excluding goodwill), by 2003 quartile,[1] %

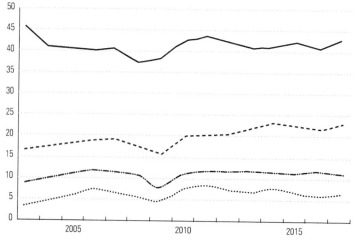

[1] As of 2003, companies are grouped into quartiles, based on ROIC.
Source: Corporate Performance Analytics by McKinsey.

EXHIBIT 8.12 **ROIC Decay for Branded Consumer Goods**

Median ROIC of portfolios (without goodwill), by quintile,[1] %

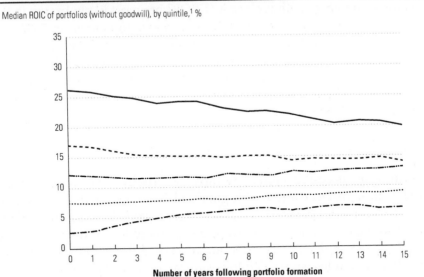

Number of years following portfolio formation

[1] At year 0, companies are grouped into one of five portfolios, based on ROIC.

Source: Corporate Performance Analytics by McKinsey.

Although decay rates examine the *rate* of regression toward the mean, they present only aggregate results and tell us nothing about the spread of potential future performance. Does every company generating returns greater than 20 percent eventually migrate to 15 percent, or do some companies actually go on to generate higher returns? Conversely, do some top performers become poor performers? To address this question, we measured the probability that a company will migrate from one ROIC grouping to another in ten years. The results are presented in Exhibit 8.13. Read each row from left to right.

EXHIBIT 8.13 **ROIC Transition Probability**

Probability of achieving ROIC in 2017, %

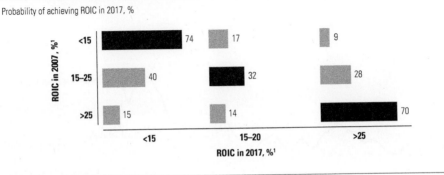

[1] ROIC excluding goodwill.

Source: Corporate Performance Analytics by McKinsey.

Both high and low performers demonstrate significant stability in their performance. Companies with high or low ROIC are most likely to stay in the same grouping. A company whose ROIC was below 15 percent in 2007 had a 74 percent chance of earning less than 15 percent in 2017. For companies with a ROIC above 25 percent, the probability of maintaining that high performance was 70 percent. Among companies whose ROIC was between 15 and 25 percent in 2007, there was no clear tendency for companies to increase or decrease their ROIC ten years later.

Effect of Acquisitions on ROIC

While returns on invested capital without goodwill have been increasing, returns on invested capital with goodwill have been flat, as shown in Exhibit 8.14. Companies paid high prices for their acquisitions, so much of the value the deals created was transferred to the shareholders of the target company. (Acquisitions and value creation are discussed in Chapter 31.) It does not mean that companies have failed to create value from acquisitions: returns on capital including goodwill above the cost of capital, combined with ongoing growth, indicate that they have created value above and beyond the price paid for these acquisitions. Increasing returns without goodwill indicates that companies have captured significant synergies to improve the performance of the acquired businesses.

For some industries, the differences in return with and without goodwill are even bigger than shown here. For the life science and technology sectors, for example, returns on capital including goodwill were around 25 percent, versus 65 percent without goodwill. Companies in this sector have created more value than any other sector, but shareholders of acquired companies captured much of it.

EXHIBIT 8.14 **ROIC Including and Excluding Goodwill, 1995–2017**

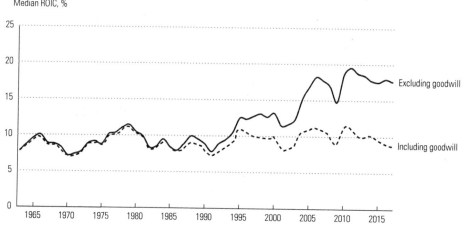

SUMMARY

There is much to learn about returns on invested capital. First, these returns are driven by competitive advantages that enable companies to realize price premiums, cost and capital efficiencies, or some combination of these. Second, industry structure is an important—but not an exclusive—determinant of ROIC. Certain industries are more likely to earn either high, medium, or low returns, but there is still significant variation in the rates of return for individual companies within each industry. Third, and most important, if a company finds a formula or strategy that earns an attractive ROIC, there is a good chance it can sustain that attractive return over time and through changing economic, industry, and company conditions, especially in the case of industries that enjoy relatively long product life cycles. Of course, the converse also is true: if a company earns a low ROIC, that is likely to persist as well.

9

Growth

Growth and its pursuit grip the business world. The popular view is that a company must grow to survive and prosper. There is certainly some truth to this. Slow-growing companies present fewer interesting opportunities for managers and so may have difficulty attracting and retaining talent. They are also much more likely to be acquired than faster-growing firms. Over the past 25 years, most of the companies that have disappeared from the S&P 500 index were acquired by larger companies or went private.

However, as discussed in Chapters 2 and 3, growth creates value only when a company's new customers, projects, or acquisitions generate returns on invested capital (ROIC) greater than its cost of capital. And as companies grow larger and their industries become ever more competitive, finding good, high-value-creating projects becomes increasingly difficult. Striking the right balance between growth and return on invested capital is critically important to value creation. Our research shows that for companies with a high ROIC, shareholder returns are affected more by an increase in revenues than an increase in ROIC.[1] Indeed, we have found that if such companies let their ROIC drop a bit (though not too much) to achieve higher growth, their returns to shareholders are higher than for companies that maintain or improve their high ROIC but grow more slowly. Conversely, for companies with a low ROIC, increasing it will create more value than growing the company will.

The previous chapter explored why executives need to understand whether their strategies will lead to high returns on invested capital. Similarly, they also need to know which growth opportunities will create the most value. This chapter discusses the principal strategies for driving revenue growth, the ways in which growth creates value, and the challenges of sustaining growth. It ends by analyzing the data on corporate growth patterns over the past 55 years.

---

[1] See T. Koller and B. Jiang, "How to Choose between Growth and ROIC," *McKinsey on Finance*, no. 25 (Autumn 2007): 19–22.

DRIVERS OF REVENUE GROWTH

When executives plan for growth, a good starting point is for them to disaggregate revenue growth into its three main components:[2]

1. *Portfolio momentum.* This is the organic revenue growth a company enjoys because of overall expansion in the market segments represented in its portfolio.
2. *Market share performance.* This is the organic revenue growth (or reduction) a company earns by gaining or losing share in any particular market.
3. *Mergers and acquisitions (M&A).* This represents the inorganic growth a company achieves when it buys or sells revenues through acquisitions or divestments.

Baghai, Smit, and Viguerie showed that for large companies, the most important source of growth by far was portfolio momentum.[3] In other words, being in fast-growing markets was the largest driver of growth. Least important was market share growth. Yet managers tend to focus most of their attention on gaining share in their existing product markets. While it's necessary to maintain and sometimes increase market share, changing a company's exposure to growing and shrinking market segments should be a major focus.

To see the effect of portfolio momentum, consider how the median growth from 2008 to 2017 differs by industry (Exhibit 9.1). Not surprisingly, the fastest-growing sector over this period was biotechnology, which in 2008 was still a small industry that fueled impressive growth from a wave of innovative, blockbuster drugs. Makers of traditional pharmaceuticals delivered the second-highest growth, but mostly driven by consolidation rather than innovation, as many of the highest-selling drugs from the 1990s came off patent. For the same reason, airlines stand high on the list, with some of largest U.S. players having merged in the past decade. Compared with the prior decade, oil and gas companies dropped to a spot near the bottom of the list, primarily because of significant oil price decreases since 2014. These underlined the industry's cyclicality in terms of growth as well as ROIC, as discussed in the prior chapter. Note how a sector with high volume growth, such as technology hardware, nonetheless fails to beat many other sectors in terms of revenue growth (in contrast to other technology sectors, such as information services and software). Despite tremendous increases in volume, lower prices have kept total revenue growth relatively modest.

---

[2] This section draws on P. Viguerie, S. Smit, and M. Baghai, *The Granularity of Growth* (Hoboken, NJ: John Wiley & Sons, 2008).
[3] M. Baghai, S. Smit, and P. Viguerie, "The Granularity of Growth," *McKinsey on Finance*, no. 24 (Summer 2007): 25–30.

EXHIBIT 9.1 **Variation in Revenue Growth by Industry**

Annual revenue growth rate, adjusted for inflation, %

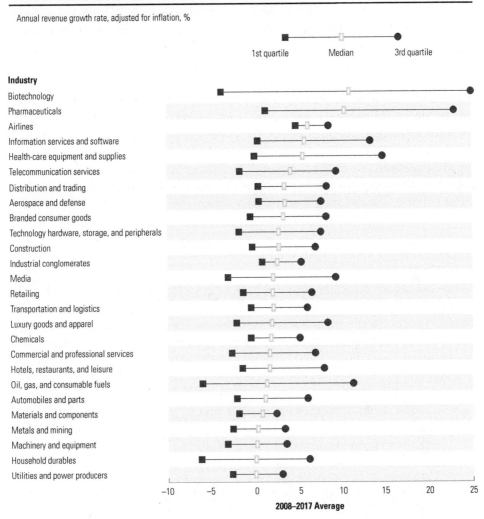

Source: Compustat; Corporate Performance Analytics by McKinsey.

Exhibit 9.1 also shows widely varied growth within industries. For some sectors, such as pharmaceuticals and airlines, part of the variation can be explained by growth from mergers and acquisitions. In this instance, some players benefited, but not all. But for many other sectors, M&A cannot explain the wide variation in growth. If a company's growth depends mainly on the dynamics of the sector markets in which it operates, why should there be such big differences in growth among different companies operating in the same sector? The most important reason is that the median growth rate of companies competing in any sector masks big differences in growth across the sector's market segments and subsegments.

To understand markets in this fine-grained way and the differences in companies' revenue growth, Baghai, Smit, and Viguerie analyzed market growth at the level of individual product and geographical segments with around $50 million to $200 million in sales, rather than at the company, divisional, or business unit level.[4] Their example of a large European manufacturer of personal-care products shows why such analysis is revealing. The company has three divisions with apparently low prospective growth rates ranging from 1.6 percent to 7.5 percent a year. However, the range of forecast growth rates for individual product lines within the divisions is much wider. For instance, the division with the lowest expected growth rate has one product line growing at 24 percent, one of the company's best growth opportunities. At the same time, the division with the highest growth rate has several product lines that are shrinking fast and may warrant divestment.

GROWTH AND VALUE CREATION

While managers typically strive for high growth, the highest growth will not necessarily create the most value. The reason is that the three drivers of growth (portfolio momentum, acquisitions, and market share gains) do not all create value in equal measure. To understand why not, consider who loses under alternative scenarios for revenue growth and how effectively losers can retaliate:

- Growth from increases in market share, particularly in slow- and moderate-growth markets, rarely creates much value for long, because established competitors typically retaliate to protect their market shares. Lasting value creation could only occur in situations where smaller competitors are pushed out of the market entirely or where the company introduces differentiated products or services that are hard for competitors to copy.

- Growth driven by price increases comes at the expense of customers, who are likely to react by reducing consumption and seeking substitute products, so new value created by price increases may not last long either.

- Growth driven by general market expansion comes at the expense of companies in other industries, which may not even know to whom they are losing market share. This category of victim is the least able to retaliate, which makes product market growth the driver likely to create the most value.

---

[4] See M. Baghai, S. Smit, and P. Viguerie, "Is Your Growth Strategy Flying Blind?" *Harvard Business Review* (May 2009): 86–96.

EXHIBIT 9.2 **Value Creation from Organic Growth Higher Than from Acquisitions**

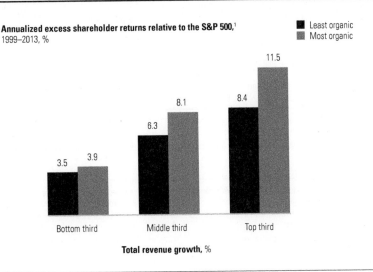

Annualized excess shareholder returns relative to the S&P 500,[1]
1999–2013, %

■ Least organic
■ Most organic

[1] Excludes banks, insurance companies, extraction companies, and cyclical commodities.

- The value of growth from acquisitions is harder to characterize, because it depends so much on the price of the acquisition (as discussed in Chapter 31). However, as shown in Exhibit 9.2, a sample of 550 U.S. and European companies reveals that, in general, growth from acquisitions creates less value than organic growth.[5] The main reason is that companies don't have to invest as much up front for organic growth. In growing through acquisitions, companies typically must pay for the stand-alone value of an acquired business plus a takeover premium. This results in a lower return on invested capital and lower value creation compared with growing organically.

A Hierarchy of Growth Scenarios

It is possible to rank different growth scenarios that fall within the three overall growth strategies according to their potential for creating value (see Exhibit 9.3). This ranking may not be exactly the same for all industries, but it works well as a starting point. The scenarios with the highest potential to create value are all variations on entering fast-growing product markets that take revenues from distant companies, rather than from direct competitors or customers via price increases.

[5] See M. Goedhart and T. Koller, "The Value Premium of Organic Growth," *McKinsey on Finance*, no. 61 (Autumn 2017): 14–15.

EXHIBIT 9.3 **Value of Major Types of Growth**

Value created[1]	Type of growth	Rationale
↑ Above average **↓**	• Create new markets through new products • Convince existing customers to buy more of a product • Attract new customers to the market	• No established competitors; diverts customer spending • All competitors benefit; low risk of retaliation • All competitors benefit; low risk of retaliation
↑ Average **↓**	• Gain market share in fast-growing market • Make bolt-on acquisitions to accelerate product growth	• Competitors can still grow despite losing share; moderate risk of retaliation • Modest acquisition premium relative to upside potential
↑ Below average **↓**	• Gain share from rivals through incremental innovation • Gain share from rivals through product promotion and pricing • Make large acquisitions • Increase prices	• Competitors can replicate and take back customers • Competitors can retaliate quickly • High premium to pay; most value diverted to selling shareholders • Unless demand has low price elasticity; customers likely to reduce or divert consumption

[1] Per dollar of revenue.

Developing *new products* or services that are so innovative as to create entirely new product categories has the highest value-creating potential. The stronger the competitive advantage a company can establish in the new-product category, the higher will be its ROIC and the value created. For example, the coronary stent commercialized in the early 1990s reduced the need for heart surgery, lowering both the risk and cost of treating cardiac problems. Owing to this innovation's overwhelming competitive advantage over traditional treatments, as well as over subsequent products entering the market,[6] neither type of competitor could retaliate, so the innovators created large amounts of value. (As the stent market became highly competitive over the past decade, however, returns on capital have declined considerably.) Similarly, traditional music retailers have been all but competed away, first by online music sales giants such as iTunes and Amazon, and more recently as consumers have taken up online streaming services for mobile devices offered by Spotify, Amazon Music, Apple Music, and others. However, competition in the new digital-entertainment category is itself fierce, so the value created per dollar of revenue in this sector is unlikely to reach the levels that coronary stents once generated.

Next in the pecking order of value-creating growth tactics comes *persuading existing customers to buy more* of a product or related products. For example, if Procter & Gamble convinces customers to wash their hands more frequently,

---

[6] Products that entered the market at a later stage were less successful because of high switching costs for customers (see Chapter 8).

the market for hand soap will grow faster. Similarly, if antivirus software provider McAfee convinces computer owners that they need better protection against hackers and viruses, total demand for antivirus software and services will grow faster. Direct competitors will not respond, because they benefit as well. The ROIC associated with the additional revenue is likely to be high, because the companies' manufacturing and distribution systems can typically produce the additional products at little additional cost. Clearly, the benefit will not be as large if the company has to increase costs substantially to secure those sales. For example, offering bank customers insurance products requires the expense of an entirely new sales force, because the products are too complex to add to the list of products the bankers are already selling.

Attracting new customers to a market also can create substantial value. Consumer packaged-goods company Beiersdorf accelerated growth in sales of skin-care products by convincing men to use its Nivea products. Once again, competitors didn't retaliate because they also gained from the category expansion. Men's skin-care products aren't much different from women's, so much of the research and development, manufacturing, and distribution cost could be shared. The major incremental cost was for marketing and advertising.

The value a company can create from increasing market share depends on both the market's rate of growth and the way the company goes about gaining share. There are three main ways to grow market share, and these don't fall next to each other in our pecking order shown in Exhibit 9.3. When a company *gains market share in a fast-growing market*, the absolute revenues of its competitors may still be growing strongly, too, so the competitors may not retaliate. However, gaining share in a mature market is more likely to provoke retaliation by competitors.

Gaining share from *incremental innovation*—for example, through incremental technology improvements that neither fundamentally change a product nor create an entirely new category and that are possible to copy—won't create much value or maintain the advantage for long. From a customer's viewpoint, hybrid and electric vehicles aren't fundamentally different from gas or diesel vehicles, so they cannot command much of a price premium to offset their higher costs. The total number of vehicles sold will not increase, and if one company gains market share for a while, competitors will try to take it back, as competitors can copy each other's innovations before the innovator has been able to extract much value, if any. All in all, auto companies, whether new or incumbent, may not create much value from hybrid or electric vehicles; competition will likely transfer most benefits to consumers.

Gaining share through *product pricing and promotion* in a mature market rarely creates much value, if any. Huggies and Pampers dominate the disposable-diaper market and are financially strong, and each can easily respond if the other tries to gain share. Therefore, any growth arising from, say, an intense campaign to reduce prices that hits directly at the other competitor will provoke a response. And as Amazon continued expanding into the U.S.

consumer electronics retail market in 2009, Walmart reduced prices on key products such as top-selling video games and game consoles, even though Amazon's $20 billion in sales in 2008 were a fraction of Walmart's $406 billion sales in the same year. Although Walmart's competitive reaction could not stop Amazon from surpassing Walmart as the largest U.S. electronics retailer by 2014, it drove down margins across the segment and rewrote the competitive dynamics of the electronics category.

In concentrated markets, share battles often lead to a cycle of market share give-and-take but rarely to a permanent share gain for any one competitor, unless that competitor changes the product or its delivery enough to create what is effectively a new product. The possible exception, as with the Amazon example in the preceding paragraph, is stronger companies gaining share from smaller, weaker competitors and forcing the weaker players out of the market entirely.

Price increases, over and above cost increases, can create value as long as any resulting decline in sales volume is small. However, they tend not to be repeatable: if a company or several competitors get away with a price increase one year, they are unlikely to have the same good fortune the next. Furthermore, the first increase could be eroded fairly quickly. Otherwise, you would see some companies increasing their profit margins year after year, while in reality, long-term increases in profit margins are rare. There was an exception among packaged-goods companies in the mid-1990s. They passed on increases in commodity costs to customers but did not lower prices when their commodity costs subsequently declined. But the prospect of higher margins made it more attractive for retailers to enter the packaged-goods segments with offerings of private-label brands, sometimes via online sales channels.

There are two main approaches to growing through acquisitions. Growth through *bolt-on acquisitions* can create value if the premium paid for the target is not too high. Bolt-on acquisitions make incremental changes to a business model—for example, by completing or extending a company's product offering or filling gaps in its distribution system. In the 2000s, IBM was very successful in bolting on smaller software companies and subsequently marketing their applications through its existing global sales and distribution system, which could absorb the additional sales without too much extra investment. Because such acquisitions are relatively small, they boosted IBM's growth but added little cost and complexity.

In contrast, creating growth through *large acquisitions*—say, one-third the size or more of the acquiring company—tends to create less value. Large acquisitions typically occur when a market has begun to mature and the industry has excess capacity. While the acquiring company shows revenue growth, the combined revenues often do not increase, and sometimes they decrease because customers prefer to have multiple suppliers. Any new value comes primarily from cost cutting, not from growth. Furthermore, integrating the two companies requires significant investments and involves far more complexity and risk than integrating small, bolt-on acquisitions.

Choosing a Growth Strategy

The logic explaining why growth from product market expansion creates greater and more sustainable value than growth from taking share is compelling. Nevertheless, the dividing line between the two types of growth can be fuzzy. For instance, some innovations prevent existing competitors from retaliating, even though the innovator's products and services may not appear to be that new. Walmart's innovative approach to retailing in the 1960s and 1970s offered an entirely new shopping experience to its customers, who flocked to the company's stores. One could argue that Walmart was merely taking share away from small local stores. But the fact that its competitors could not retaliate suggests that Walmart's approach constituted a truly innovative product. However, if Walmart were to grow by winning customers from Target, that would count as market share gain, because Target and Walmart offer their retailing product in a similar fashion. Notably, over the past decade, Walmart itself has been facing competition from innovative offerings in direct and platform sales by Amazon, which has taken significant market share from Walmart in many retail categories.

In general, underlying product market growth tends to create the most value. Companies should aim to be in the fastest-growing product markets, so they can achieve growth that consistently creates value. If a company is in the wrong markets and can't easily get into the right ones, it may do better by sustaining growth at the same level as its competitors while finding ways to improve and sustain its ROIC.

WHY SUSTAINING GROWTH IS HARD

Sustaining high growth is much more difficult than sustaining ROIC, especially for larger companies. The math is simple. Suppose your core product markets are growing at the rate of the gross domestic product (GDP)—say, 5 percent nominal growth—and you currently have $10 billion in revenues. Ten years from now, assuming you grow at 5 percent a year, your revenues will be $16.3 billion. Assume you aspire to grow organically at 8 percent a year. In ten years, your revenues will need to be $21.6 billion. Therefore, you will need to find new sources of revenues that can grow to more than $5.3 billion per year by the tenth year. Adjusting for inflation of 1 to 2 percent, you need an extra $4.3 billion to $4.8 billion per year in today's dollars. Another way to think of it is that to find such revenues, you would need to reinvent a

EXHIBIT 9.4 **Variation in Growth over Product Life Cycle**

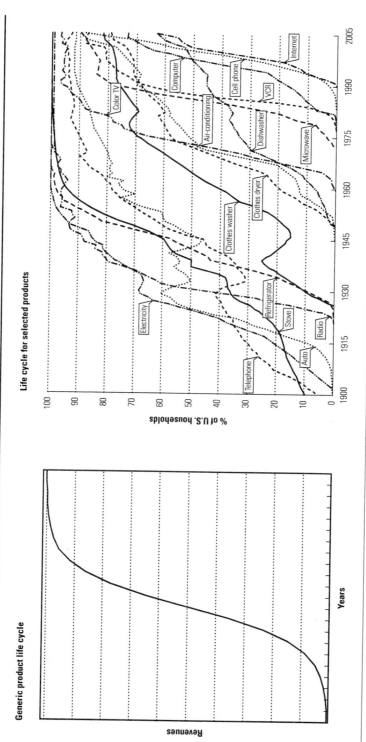

Generic product life cycle

Revenues

Years

Life cycle for selected products

% of U.S. households

100
90
80
70
60
50
40
30
20
10
0

1900   1915   1930   1945   1960   1975   1990   2005

Telephone
Electricity
Auto
Refrigerator
Stove
Radio
Clothes washer
Clothes dryer
Color TV
Air-conditioning
Computer
Dishwasher
Cell phone
VCR
Microwave
Internet

Source: W. Cox and R. Alm, "You Are What You Spend," *New York Times*, February 10, 2008.

EXHIBIT 9.5 **Walmart and eBay: Growth Trajectories**

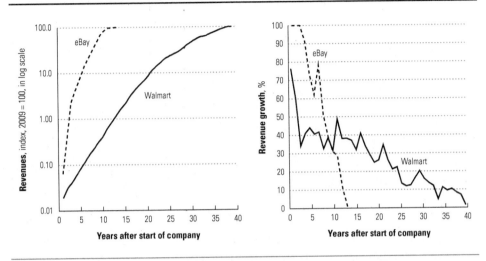

business almost half your current size and close to a Fortune 500 company.[7] If your product markets are growing at only 5 percent, how can you possibly achieve that magnitude of growth?

Given this difficulty, the growth targets that some companies embrace are simply unrealistic. One with sales already in excess of $5 billion announced organic growth targets of more than 20 percent a year for the next 20 years. Since annual world economic growth is typically less than 4 percent in real terms and many companies are competing for a share of that growth, such growth targets are hardly achievable.

Sustaining growth is difficult because most product markets have natural life cycles. The market for a product—which means the market for a narrow product category sold to a specific customer segment in a specific geography —typically follows an S-curve over its life cycle until maturity, as shown on the left side of Exhibit 9.4. The right side shows the growth curves for various real products, scaled to their relative penetration of U.S. households. First, a product has to prove itself with early adopters. Growth then accelerates as more people want to buy the product, until it reaches its point of maximum penetration. After this point of maturity, and depending on the nature of the product, either sales growth falls back to the same rate of growth as the population or the economy, or sales may start to shrink. To illustrate, autos and packaged snacks have continued to grow in line with economic growth for half a century or more, while videocassette recorders (VCRs) lasted less than 20 years before they started to decline and then disappeared.

While the pattern of growth is usually the same for every product and service, the amount and pace of growth will vary for each one. Exhibit 9.5

[7] The cutoff point for the Fortune 500 in terms of revenues was around $5.5 billion in 2018.

EXHIBIT 9.6 **The Challenge of Sustaining High Growth**

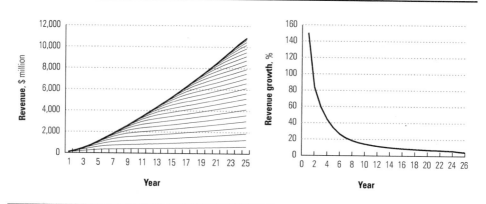

compares Walmart and eBay. While both have some activities outside their core business, they are largely one-product companies. Walmart's growth did not dip below 10 percent until the end of the 1990s, some 35 years after it was founded. In contrast, eBay saw its growth fall to below 10 percent after only 12 years, having grown very rapidly to reach maturity early. Because eBay is an Internet-based auction house, it doesn't need to add many more staff members in order to grow. In contrast, Walmart, as a physical retailer, has to add people as quickly as it adds stores and sales. The speed at which Walmart can hire and train people limits its rate of growth relative to eBay. But Walmart's core market is much larger than eBay's. In 2018, Walmart generated $500 billion of revenues, mostly from its core discount and supercenter stores, whereas eBay generated only about $10 billion of revenues because its core addressable market is so much smaller.[8]

Sustaining high growth presents major challenges to companies. Given the natural life cycle of products, the only way to achieve consistently high growth is to consistently find new product markets and enter them successfully in time to enjoy their more profitable high-growth phase. Exhibit 9.6 illustrates this by showing the cumulative sales for a company that introduces one new product in one market (geographic or customer segment) in each year. All products are identical in terms of sales volume and growth; their growth rates are very high in the beginning and eventually slow to 3 percent once the market is fully penetrated. Although the company continues to launch new products that are just as successful as their predecessors, aggregate sales growth slows down rapidly as the company gets bigger. In the long term, growth approaches 3 percent, equal to the long-term growth rate of the markets for the company's products. Ultimately, a company's growth and size are constrained by the growth and size of its product markets and the number of product markets in which it competes.

---

[8] The comparison is somewhat distorted: eBay spun off its subsidiary PayPal in 2012, reducing its revenues by $6 billion from $14 billion at that time.

To sustain high growth, companies need to overcome this "portfolio treadmill" effect: for each product that matures and declines in revenues, the company needs to find a similar-size replacement product to stay level in revenues—and even more to continue growing. Think of the pharmaceutical industry, which showed unprecedented growth from the mid-1990s, thanks to so-called blockbuster drugs such as Lipitor and Celebrex. Then growth plummeted as these drugs came off patent and the next generation of drugs didn't deliver the same outsize sales as the blockbusters. Finding sizable new sources of growth requires more experimentation and a longer time horizon than many companies are willing to invest in. Royal Philips's health technology business was a small corporate division in 1998, when it generated around 7 percent of total company revenues. It took 15 years of ongoing investments and acquisitions to become Philips's largest business unit, generating half of its total revenues. After the carve-out of its lighting business and other divestitures, health technology has now become Philips's core business.

EMPIRICAL ANALYSIS OF CORPORATE GROWTH

The empirical research backs up the principles we have been discussing. This section presents our findings on the level and persistence of corporate growth for U.S.-based nonfinancial companies with revenues greater than $1 billion (inflation-adjusted) from 1963 to 2017. (The sample size for each year is different but amounts to 1,095 companies in 2017.) The analysis of their revenue growth follows the same procedure as the analysis of ROIC data in Chapter 8, except here we use three-year rolling averages to moderate distortions caused by currency fluctuations and M&A activity. We also use real, rather than nominal, data to analyze all corporate growth results, because even mature companies saw a dramatic increase in revenues during the 1970s as inflation increased prices. Ideally, we would report statistics on *organic* revenue growth, but current reporting standards do not require companies to disclose the effects of currencies and M&A on their revenues.

The overall findings concerning revenue growth are as follows:

- The median rate of revenue growth between 1965 and 2017 was 4.9 percent in real (inflation-adjusted) terms. Real revenue growth fluctuated significantly, ranging from around 0 percent to 9 percent, with significant cyclicality.
- High growth rates decayed very quickly. Companies growing faster than 20 percent in real terms typically grew at only 8 percent within five years and at 5 percent within ten years.

EXHIBIT 9.7 **Long-Term Revenue Growth for Nonfinancial Companies, 1965–2017**

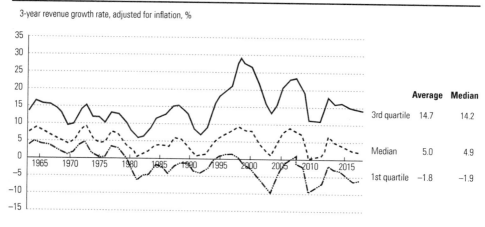

3-year revenue growth rate, adjusted for inflation, %

	Average	Median
3rd quartile	14.7	14.2
Median	5.0	4.9
1st quartile	−1.8	−1.9

Source: Compustat; Corporate Performance Analytics by McKinsey.

Growth Trends

Let's begin by examining aggregate levels and trends of corporate growth. Exhibit 9.7 presents median revenue growth rates in real terms between 1965 and 2017. The average median revenue growth rate for that period equals 4.9 percent per year and oscillates between roughly 0 percent and 9 percent. Median revenue growth demonstrates no trend over time, but over the past five years, growth rates declined to around 2 percent in real terms.

Real revenue growth of 4.9 percent is quite high when compared with real GDP growth in the United States, which was at 3.0 percent during the same period. Why the difference? Possible explanations abound. The first is self-selection: companies with good growth opportunities need capital to grow. Since public markets are large and liquid, high-growth companies are more likely to be publicly traded than privately held ones. We measure only publicly traded companies, so these growth results are likely to be higher.

Second, as companies become increasingly specialized and outsource more services, firms providing services will grow and develop quickly without affecting the GDP figures. Consider Jabil Circuit, a contract electronics manufacturer. When a company like Apple or IBM has Jabil manufacture products or components on its behalf, GDP, which measures aggregate output, will not change. Yet Jabil's growth will influence our sample.

A third explanation is global expansion. Many of the companies in the sample create products and generate revenue outside the United States, so they can grow faster than U.S. GDP without gaining sales in the United States. Finally, although we use rolling averages and medians, these cannot eliminate but only dampen the effects of M&A and currency fluctuations, which do not reflect organic growth.

EXHIBIT 9.8 **Distribution of Growth Rates**

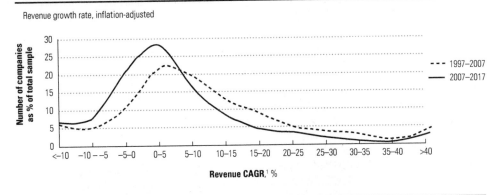

Revenue growth rate, inflation-adjusted

Revenue CAGR,[1] %

1997–2007
2007–2017

[1] Compound annual growth rate.

Source: Compustat; Corporate Performance Analytics by McKinsey.

In addition to mapping median growth, Exhibit 9.7 also reveals that from the mid-1970s to 2017, at least one-quarter of all companies shrank in real terms almost every year. Thus, although most companies project healthy growth over the next years in their public communications or even analyst guidance, the reality is that many mature firms will shrink. This underlines the need to exercise caution before projecting strong growth for a valuation, especially for large companies in mature sectors.

Exhibit 9.8 shows the distribution of three-year real revenue growth for two periods, 1997–2007 (before the 2008 financial crisis) and 2007–2017. Not surprisingly, the distribution became wider and shifted to the left in the latter period. From 2007 to 2017, almost two-thirds of companies in the sample grew at an annual real rate of less than 5 percent. Only 21 percent grew faster than 10 percent. (This includes the effect of acquisitions, so fewer companies grew faster than 10 percent just through organic growth.)

Growth across Industries

As Exhibit 9.1 illustrated, growth rates vary widely across and within industries. In addition—unlike ROIC, where the industry ranking tends to be stable—the industry growth ranking varies significantly over time, as shown in Exhibit 9.9 for the decades 1997–2007 and 2007–2017. Some of the variation is explained by structural factors, such as the saturation of markets (the declining growth in hotels and restaurants and in chemicals) or the effect of technological innovation in creating entirely new markets (the strong growth in biotechnology and information services). In other cases, growth is more cyclical. Growth in the oil and gas sector varied from more than 10 percent in the first decade to just 1 percent over the past ten years, as oil prices plummeted after 2014. Similarly, the construction industry is subject to cycles, with growth

EXHIBIT 9.9 **Volatile Growth by Industry**

10-year revenue growth rate,[1] industry median adjusted for inflation, %

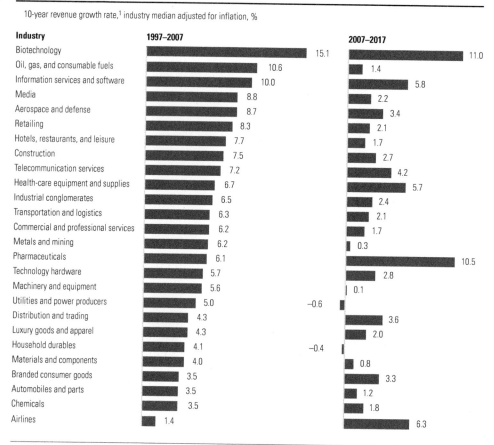

Industry	1997–2007	2007–2017
Biotechnology	15.1	11.0
Oil, gas, and consumable fuels	10.6	1.4
Information services and software	10.0	5.8
Media	8.8	2.2
Aerospace and defense	8.7	3.4
Retailing	8.3	2.1
Hotels, restaurants, and leisure	7.7	1.7
Construction	7.5	2.7
Telecommunication services	7.2	4.2
Health-care equipment and supplies	6.7	5.7
Industrial conglomerates	6.5	2.4
Transportation and logistics	6.3	2.1
Commercial and professional services	6.2	1.7
Metals and mining	6.2	0.3
Pharmaceuticals	6.1	10.5
Technology hardware	5.7	2.8
Machinery and equipment	5.6	0.1
Utilities and power producers	5.0	−0.6
Distribution and trading	4.3	3.6
Luxury goods and apparel	4.3	2.0
Household durables	4.1	−0.4
Materials and components	4.0	0.8
Branded consumer goods	3.5	3.3
Automobiles and parts	3.5	1.2
Chemicals	3.5	1.8
Airlines	1.4	6.3

[1] Compound annual growth rate.
Source: Compustat; Corporate Performance Analytics by McKinsey.

at much lower levels since the 2008 credit crisis. Telecommunications service providers enjoyed a burst of growth in the 2000s, when mobile phones became ubiquitous. But revenue growth rates over the past decade ended significantly lower due to strong price pressure.

Despite this high degree of variation, some sectors have consistently been among the fastest growing, not only during the 30 years covered in this sample, but also for earlier periods. These include life sciences and technology, such as information services and software, technology hardware, pharmaceuticals, biotechnology, and health care, where demand has remained strong for three decades. Others, such as automobile parts, chemicals, and branded consumer goods, have consistently registered lower growth rates, as their markets had already reached maturity well before the 1990s.

EXHIBIT 9.10 **Revenue Growth Decay Analysis**

Median growth of portfolios, by quintile,[1] %

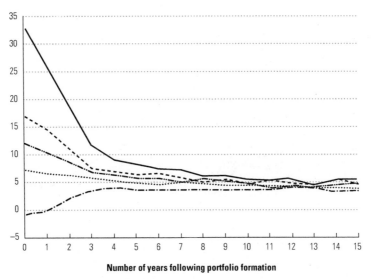

Number of years following portfolio formation

[1] At year 0, companies are grouped into one of five portfolios, based on revenue growth.

Source: Compustat; Corporate Performance Analytics by McKinsey.

Sustaining Growth

Understanding a company's potential for growing revenues in the future is critical to valuation and strategy assessment. Yet developing reasonable projections is a challenge, especially given the upward bias in growth expectations demonstrated by equity research analysts and the media. Research shows that analyst forecasts of one-year-out aggregate earnings growth for the S&P 500 are systematically overoptimistic, exceeding actual earnings growth by five percentage points or more.[9]

To put long-term corporate growth rates in their proper perspective, we analyzed historical rates of growth decay since 1963. Companies were segmented into five portfolios, depending on their growth rate in the year the portfolio was formed. Exhibit 9.10 plots how each portfolio's median company grows over time. As the exhibit shows, growth decays very quickly; high growth is not sustainable for the typical company. Within three years, the difference across portfolios narrows considerably, and by year 5, the highest-growth portfolio outperforms the lowest-growth portfolio by less than five percentage points. Within ten years, this difference drops to less than two percentage points.

[9] See, for example, M. Goedhart, B. Raj, and A. Saxena, "Equity Analysts: Still Too Bullish," *McKinsey on Finance*, no. 35 (Spring 2010): 14–17.

EXHIBIT 9.11 **Revenue Growth Decay through Economic Crisis and Recovery**

Median growth of portfolios,[1] %

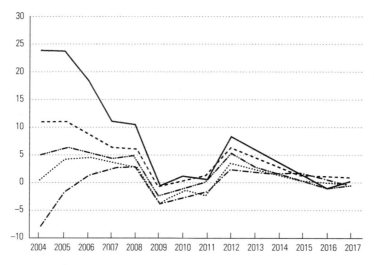

[1] As of 2002, companies are grouped into one of five portfolios, based on their 2002–2004 revenue growth.

Source: Compustat; Corporate Performance Analytics by McKinsey.

We also analyzed the decay rates for the most recent 15 years and found similar patterns of rapid convergence to 5 percent and lower (Exhibit 9.11). Note how the 2008 credit crisis caused a temporary decline of growth rates overall but without changing the typical decay pattern from the long-term data in Exhibit 9.10. Comparing the decay of growth to that of ROIC shown in the previous chapter, it is possible to see that although companies' rates of return on invested capital generally remain fairly stable over time—top companies still outperform bottom companies by more than ten percentage points after 15 years—rates of growth do not.

As discussed earlier in this chapter, companies struggle to maintain high growth because product life cycles are finite and growing becomes more difficult as companies get bigger. Do any companies counter this norm? The short answer: very few. Exhibit 9.12 shows what happened to the growth rates of companies grouped by their 2004–2007 growth rates. Reading across each row, the percentages indicate the share of companies in each group that fell into each of the growth categories one decade later. Clearly, maintaining high growth is much less common than being stuck with slow growth. Of the companies reporting less than 5 percent revenue growth from 2004 to 2007, 68 percent continued to report growth below 5 percent ten years later. In contrast, only 21 percent of high-growth companies maintained better than 15 percent real growth ten years later. Even more concerning for high-growth companies, 58 percent of the companies that grew faster than 15 percent from 2004 to 2007 were growing at real rates below 5 percent a decade later. Sustaining high growth is very difficult—much more difficult than sustaining high ROIC.

EXHIBIT 9.12 **Revenue Growth Transition Probability**

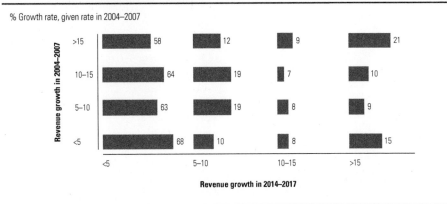

% Growth rate, given rate in 2004–2007

Revenue growth in 2004–2007

	<5	5–10	10–15	>15
>15	58	12	9	21
10–15	64	19	7	10
5–10	63	19	8	9
<5	68	10	8	15

Revenue growth in 2014–2017

SUMMARY

To maximize value for their shareholders, companies should understand what drives growth and how it creates value. For large companies, the growth of the markets in which they operate largely drives long-term revenue growth. Although gains in market share contribute to revenues in the short term, these gains are far less important for long-term growth.

Revenue growth is not all that matters for creating value; the value created per dollar of additional revenues is the crucial point. In general, this depends on how easily competitors can respond to a company's growth strategy. The growth strategy with the highest potential in this respect is true product innovation, because entirely new product categories by definition have no established competition. Attracting new customers to an existing product or persuading existing customers to buy more of it also can create substantial value, because direct competitors in the same market tend to benefit as well. Growth through bolt-on acquisitions can add value, because such acquisitions can boost revenue growth at little additional cost and complexity. Typically, revenue growth from market share gains is much less attractive, because it comes at the expense of established direct competitors, who are likely to retaliate, especially in maturing markets.

Sustaining high growth is no less a challenge than initiating it. Because most products have natural life cycles, the only way to achieve lasting high growth is to continue introducing new products at an increasing rate—which is nearly impossible. Not surprisingly, growth rates for large companies decay much faster than do returns on invested capital; growth rates for even the fastest-growing companies tend to fall below 5 percent within ten years.

Core Valuation Techniques

10

Frameworks for Valuation

In Part One, we built a conceptual framework to show what drives the creation of value for investors. A company's value stems from its ability to earn a healthy return on invested capital (ROIC) and its ability to grow. Healthy rates of return and growth produce future cash flows, the ultimate source of value.

Part Two offers a step-by-step guide for analyzing and valuing a company in practice, including technical details for properly measuring and interpreting the drivers of value. Among the many ways to value a company (see Exhibit 10.1 for an overview), we focus particularly on two: enterprise discounted cash flow (DCF) and discounted economic profit. When applied correctly, both valuation methods yield the same results; however, each model has certain benefits in practice. Enterprise DCF remains a favorite of practitioners and academics because it relies on the flow of cash in and out of the company, rather than on accounting-based earnings. For its part, the discounted economic-profit valuation model can be quite insightful because of its close link to economic theory and competitive strategy. Economic profit highlights whether a company is earning its cost of capital and quantifies the amount of value created each year. Given that the two methods yield identical results and have different but complementary benefits, we recommend creating *both* enterprise DCF and economic-profit models when valuing a company.

Both the enterprise DCF and economic-profit models rely on the weighted average cost of capital (WACC). WACC-based models work best when a company maintains a relatively stable debt-to-value ratio. If a company's debt-to-value ratio is expected to change, WACC-based models can still yield accurate results but are more difficult to implement correctly. In such cases, we recommend an alternative to WACC-based models: adjusted present value (APV). APV discounts the same free cash flows as the enterprise DCF model but uses the unlevered cost of equity as the discount rate (without the tax benefit of debt).

EXHIBIT 10.1 **Frameworks for DCF-Based Valuation**

Model	Measure	Discount factor	Assessment
Enterprise discounted cash flow	Free cash flow	Weighted average cost of capital	Works best for projects, business units, and companies that manage their capital structure to a target level.
Discounted economic profit	Economic profit	Weighted average cost of capital	Explicitly highlights when a company creates value.
Adjusted present value	Free cash flow	Unlevered cost of equity	Incorporates changing capital structure more easily than WACC-based models.
Capital cash flow	Capital cash flow	Unlevered cost of equity	Combines free cash flow and the interest tax shield in one number, making it difficult to compare operating performance among companies and over time.
Equity cash flow	Cash flow to equity	Levered cost of equity	Difficult to implement correctly because capital structure is embedded within the cash flow. Best used when valuing financial institutions.

It then values the tax benefits associated with debt and adds them to the all-equity value to determine the total enterprise value.[1] When applied properly, the APV model results in the same value as the enterprise DCF value.

This chapter also includes a brief discussion of capital cash flow and equity cash flow valuation models. Properly implemented, these models will yield the same results as enterprise DCF. However, given that they mix operating performance and capital structure in cash flow, we believe implementation errors occur more easily. For this reason, we avoid capital cash flow and equity cash flow valuation models, except when valuing banks and other financial institutions, where capital structure is an inextricable part of operations (for how to value banks, see Chapter 38).

ENTERPRISE DISCOUNTED CASH FLOW MODEL

The enterprise DCF model discounts free cash flow (FCF), meaning the cash flow available to all investors—equity holders, debt holders, and any other investors—at the weighted average cost of capital, meaning the blended cost of capital for all investor capital. The company's debt and other nonequity claims on cash flow are subtracted from enterprise value to determine equity value.[2] Equity valuation models, in contrast, value directly the equity holders' cash flows. Exhibit 10.2 demonstrates the relationship between enterprise value and equity value. For this example, it is possible to calculate equity holders'

---

[1] Leveraged buyouts conducted by private-equity companies often use substantial leverage to finance the acquisition. In these situations, discount free cash flow at the unlevered cost of equity and evaluate the benefits of financial structure separately.

[2] Throughout this chapter, we refer to debt and other nonequity claims. Other nonequity claims arise when stakeholders other than shareholders have a claim against the company's future cash flow but do not hold traditional interest-bearing debt or common stock. Nonequity claims include debt equivalents (e.g., operating leases and unfunded pension liabilities) and hybrid securities (e.g., convertible debt and employee options).

EXHIBIT 10.2 **Enterprise Valuation of a Single-Business Company**

$ million

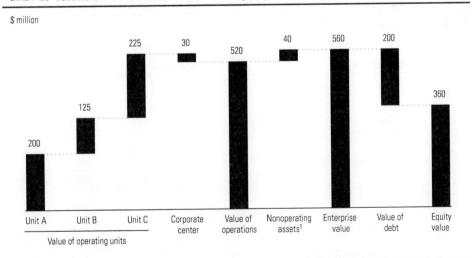

Free cash flow

Enterprise value
427.5

110
70
65
20
15

After-tax cash flow to debt holders

180
140
110   100   120

Discount free cash flow by
the weighted average
cost of capital.

90   70   85   55   70

Cash flow to equity holders

427.5

Debt value[1]
200.0

Equity value
227.5

[1] Debt value equals discounted after-tax cash flow to debt holders plus the present value of interest tax shield.

value either directly at $227.5 million or by estimating enterprise value ($427.5 million) and subtracting the value of debt ($200.0 million).

The enterprise DCF method is especially useful when applied to a multibusiness company. As Exhibit 10.3 shows, the enterprise value equals the summed value of the individual operating units less the present value of the corporate-center costs, plus the value of nonoperating assets.[3] You can use the enterprise DCF model to value individual projects, business units, and even the entire company with a consistent methodology.

EXHIBIT 10.3 **Valuation of a Multibusiness Company**

$ million

225   30   520   40   560   200

125   360

200

Unit A   Unit B   Unit C   Corporate   Value of   Nonoperating   Enterprise   Value of   Equity
center   operations   assets[1]   value   debt   value

Value of operating units

[1] Including excess cash and marketable securities.

[3] Many investment professionals define enterprise value as interest-bearing debt plus the market value of equity minus cash, whereas we define enterprise value as the value of operations plus nonoperating assets. The investment banker's definition of enterprise value resembles our definition of the value of operations, but only for companies that do not own nonoperating assets (e.g., nonconsolidated subsidiaries) or owe debt equivalents (e.g., unfunded pension liabilities). For companies with significant nonoperating assets or debt equivalents, the banking version of enterprise value can lead to distortions in analysis.

Valuing a company's equity using enterprise DCF is a four-step process:

1. Value the company's operations by discounting free cash flow at the weighted average cost of capital.
2. Identify and value nonoperating assets, such as excess cash and marketable securities, nonconsolidated subsidiaries, and other nonoperating assets not incorporated into free cash flow. Summing the value of operations and nonoperating assets gives enterprise value.[4]
3. Identify and value all debt and other nonequity claims against the enterprise value. Debt and other nonequity claims include fixed-rate and floating-rate debt, debt equivalents such as unfunded pension liabilities and restructuring provisions, employee options, and preferred stock, which are discussed in Chapter 16.
4. Subtract the value of debt and other nonequity claims from enterprise value to determine the value of common equity. To estimate value per share, divide equity value by the number of current shares outstanding.

Exhibit 10.4 presents the results of an enterprise DCF valuation for GlobalCo, an imaginary international logistics company. GlobalCo is used throughout the chapter to compare valuation methods. GlobalCo is a simplified example that ignores the complexities of modern companies. In Appendix H, we present a complete valuation of the global retailer Costco Wholesale.

EXHIBIT 10.4 **GlobalCo: Enterprise DCF Valuation**

$ million, except where noted

Forecast year	Free cash flow (FCF)	Discount factor at 7.8%	Present value of FCF
Year 1	(2.0)	0.928	(1.9)
Year 2	22.5	0.861	19.4
Year 3	54.6	0.798	43.6
Continuing value	1,176.2	0.798	938.9
Value of operations			1,000.0
Value of nonoperating assets			–
Enterprise value			1,000.0
Less: Value of debt			(250.0)
Less: Debt equivalents and noncontrolling interests			–
Equity value			750.0
Shares outstanding, million			12.5
Equity value per share, $			60.00

[4] Many investment professionals do not include excess cash when estimating enterprise value and instead net excess cash directly against debt.

We use Costco throughout Part Two to demonstrate in greater detail various parts of the valuation process.

To value GlobalCo, we forecast three years of cash flow. Cash flows generated beyond year 3 are valued using the key value driver formula and reported as continuing value. Next, discount each year's projected free cash flow and the continuing value by the company's weighted average cost of capital.[5] Sum the present values of the annual cash flows and discounted continuing value to determine the present value of operations.

For simplicity, the first year's projected cash flow is discounted by one full year, the second by two full years, and so on. For the purpose of clear exposition, we assume cash flows occur in lump sums. In actuality, cash flows occur throughout the year, not as a lump sum. Therefore, adjust the discount rate as necessary to better match the timing of cash flows.[6] The resulting present value is known as the value of operations, which equals $1 billion for GlobalCo.

To the value of operations, add nonoperating assets, such as excess cash and noncontrolling interests in other companies. Since GlobalCo has no nonoperating assets, the value of operations equals enterprise value. To determine equity value, subtract the value of debt and other nonequity claims. GlobalCo has $110 million in short-term debt and $140 million in long-term debt, for a total debt of $250 million. The company has no unfunded pension obligations or noncontrolling interests held by other companies, but if it did, their value would be subtracted as well.[7] Divide the resulting equity value of $750 million by the number of shares outstanding (12.5 million) to estimate a per-share intrinsic value of $60.

Over the course of the next few sections, we dig deeper into the inputs and the valuation process. Although this chapter presents the enterprise DCF valuation sequentially, valuation is an iterative process.

Valuing Operations

The value of operations equals the discounted value of future free cash flow. Free cash flow equals the cash flow generated by the company's operations, less any reinvestment back into the business. As defined at the beginning of this section, free cash flow is the cash flow available to all investors—equity holders, debt holders, and any other investors—so it is independent of how

---

[5] To generate identical results across valuation methods, we have not adjusted figures to eliminate rounding errors. Rounding errors occur in most exhibits.

[6] If cash flow occurs smoothly throughout the year, lower each discount factor by half a year. If cash flow is heavily weighted toward the year end, as in retail, a smaller adjustment to the discount factor is required. For more on this issue and how to value a company in between fiscal years, see Chapter 16.

[7] A noncontrolling interest arises when an outside investor owns a minority share of a subsidiary. Since this outside investor has a claim on cash flows, the claim's value must be deducted from enterprise value to compute equity value.

EXHIBIT 10.5 **GlobalCo: Income and Shareholders' Equity Statements**

$ million

	Historical	Year 1	Year 2	Year 3	Continuing value
			Forecast		
Revenue	200.0	250.0	287.5	301.9	308.5
Operating costs	(120.0)	(150.0)	(172.5)	(181.1)	(185.1)
Depreciation	(20.0)	(25.0)	(28.8)	(30.2)	(30.9)
Operating profit	60.0	75.0	86.3	90.6	92.6
Interest expense	(9.0)	(10.0)	(10.8)	(11.4)	(11.8)
Earnings before taxes	51.0	65.0	75.5	79.1	80.8
Income taxes	(10.2)	(13.0)	(15.1)	(15.8)	(16.2)
Net income	40.8	52.0	60.4	63.3	64.6
Statement of shareholders' equity					
Equity, beginning of year	65.0	98.0	140.0	171.1	
Net income	40.8	52.0	60.4	63.3	
Dividends	(7.8)	(10.0)	(14.3)	(24.1)	
Share issuances (repurchases)	–	–	(15.0)	(30.0)	
Equity, end of year	98.0	140.0	171.1	180.3	

the company is financed. Consistent with this definition, free cash flow must be discounted using the weighted average cost of capital, because the WACC represents rates of return required by the company's debt and equity holders blended together. It is the company's opportunity cost of funds.

Reorganizing the Financial Statements   To begin the valuation process, collect the company's historical financial statements. In Exhibit 10.5, we present the income statement and statement of shareholders' equity for GlobalCo. Exhibit 10.6 presents the company's balance sheet. For ease of exposition, we present only one historical year of financial statements. In practice, collect multiple years in order to better assess the long-run performance and future potential of the company.

Although ROIC and free cash flow (FCF) are central to the valuation process, the two measures cannot be computed easily from a company's financial statements, which commingle operating performance and capital structure. Therefore, to calculate ROIC and FCF, first reorganize the accounting financial statements into new statements that clearly separate operating items, nonoperating items, and sources of financing.

This reorganization leads to two new terms: invested capital and net operating profit after taxes (NOPAT). Invested capital represents the investor capital required to fund operations, without distinguishing how the capital is financed. NOPAT represents the total after-tax operating income generated by the company's invested capital, available to all investors. We briefly summarize the reorganization process next, but for a more detailed discussion using Costco, see Chapter 11.

EXHIBIT 10.6 **GlobalCo: Balance Sheet**

$ million

		Forecast		
	Historical	Year 1	Year 2	Year 3
Cash	4.0	5.0	5.8	6.0
Accounts receivable	20.0	25.0	28.8	30.2
Inventories	40.0	50.0	57.5	60.4
Current assets	64.0	80.0	92.0	96.6
Property and equipment	200.0	250.0	287.5	301.9
Goodwill and acquired intangibles	100.0	100.0	100.0	100.0
Total assets	364.0	430.0	479.5	498.5
Liabilities and equity				
Short-term debt	110.0	110.0	125.4	134.0
Accounts payable	16.0	20.0	23.0	24.2
Current liabilities	126.0	130.0	148.4	158.2
Long-term debt	140.0	160.0	160.0	160.0
Shareholders' equity	98.0	140.0	171.1	180.3
Total liabilities and equity	364.0	430.0	479.5	498.5

In Exhibit 10.7, we reorganize the income statement into NOPAT. To estimate NOPAT, deduct only operating costs and depreciation from revenue. Do
not deduct interest expense or add nonoperating income; they will be analyzed and valued separately as part of nonoperating assets and debt, respectively. Operating taxes are computed on operating profit and represent the
level of taxes that would be paid if the firm were financed entirely by equity
and held only operating assets. A robust valuation will reconcile net income

EXHIBIT 10.7 **GlobalCo: Net Operating Profit after Taxes (NOPAT)**

$ million

		Forecast			
	Historical	Year 1	Year 2	Year 3	Continuing value
Revenue	200.0	250.0	287.5	301.9	308.5
Operating costs	(120.0)	(150.0)	(172.5)	(181.1)	(185.1)
Depreciation	(20.0)	(25.0)	(28.8)	(30.2)	(30.9)
Operating profit	60.0	75.0	86.3	90.6	92.6
Operating taxes	(12.0)	(15.0)	(17.3)	(18.1)	(18.5)
NOPAT	48.0	60.0	69.0	72.5	74.0
Reconciliation to net income					
Net income	40.8	52.0	60.4	63.3	64.6
Interest expense	9.0	10.0	10.8	11.4	11.8
Interest tax shield	(1.8)	(2.0)	(2.2)	(2.3)	(2.4)
NOPAT	48.0	60.0	69.0	72.5	74.0

EXHIBIT 10.8 **GlobalCo: Invested Capital and Total Funds Invested**

$ million

		Forecast		
	Historical	Year 1	Year 2	Year 3
Working capital	48.0	60.0	69.0	72.5
Property, plant, and equipment, net	200.0	250.0	287.5	301.9
Invested capital, excluding goodwill	248.0	310.0	356.5	374.3
Goodwill and acquired intangibles	100.0	100.0	100.0	100.0
Invested capital, including goodwill	348.0	410.0	456.5	474.3
Nonoperating assets	–	–	–	–
Total funds invested	348.0	410.0	456.5	474.3
Reconciliation of total funds invested				
Short-term debt	110.0	110.0	125.4	134.0
Long-term debt	140.0	160.0	160.0	160.0
Debt and debt equivalents	250.0	270.0	285.4	294.0
Shareholders' equity	98.0	140.0	171.1	180.3
Total funds invested	348.0	410.0	456.5	474.3

to NOPAT. The reconciliation will prevent unintended errors and force explicit choices about how each piece of data will be incorporated in the valuation.

In Exhibit 10.8, we reorganize the balance sheet into invested capital and total funds invested. Invested capital includes working capital, property, plant, equipment, and other operating assets, net of other operating liabilities. Measure invested capital both including and excluding goodwill and acquired intangibles. By analyzing invested capital with and without goodwill, we can assess the impact of acquisitions on past performance. A company with robust margins and lean operations can have low ROIC with goodwill because of the high prices it paid for acquisitions.

GlobalCo holds only operating assets, so invested capital equals total funds invested. Since nonoperating assets are typically valued using methods other than DCF, we explicitly distinguish them from operating assets and operating liabilities. Next, reconcile total funds invested with sources of capital: debt, equity, and their equivalents. Examples of debt equivalents include unfunded pension obligations and environmental-remediation liabilities. Examples of equity equivalents include deferred taxes.

To calculate ROIC in year 1, divide NOPAT by the prior-year invested capital.[8] In year 1, ROIC excluding goodwill equals 24.2 percent ($60/$248), and ROIC including goodwill equals 17.2 percent ($60/$348). Because ROIC

[8] In this calculation, we estimate ROIC using prior-year invested capital (that is, measured at the beginning of the year) to link our enterprise DCF valuation with an economic profit valuation presented later in this chapter. When benchmarking performance, use a two-year average of invested capital.

is greater than the cost of capital of 7.8 percent, the company is creating value, both with and without the effect of acquisition premiums.

Analyzing Historical Performance   Once the company's financial statements are reorganized into NOPAT and invested capital, analyze the company's historical financial performance. By thoroughly analyzing the past, we can understand whether the company has created value, how fast it has grown, and how it compares with its competitors. A good analysis will focus on the key drivers of value: return on invested capital, revenue growth, and free cash flow. Understanding how these drivers behaved in the past will help you make more reliable estimates of future cash flow.

Exhibit 10.9 presents a historical analysis of organic revenue growth and ROIC. GlobalCo has been performing well, with organic growth rates and

EXHIBIT 10.9 **GlobalCo: Forecast Revenue Growth and ROIC**

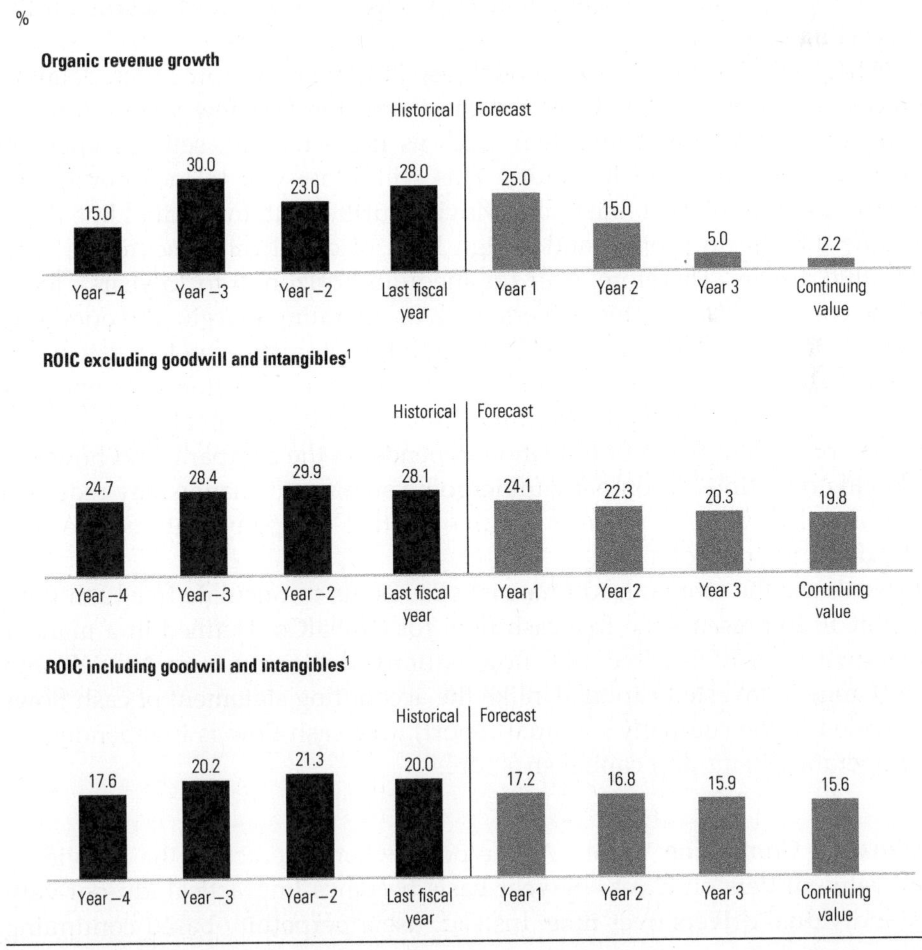

[1] Measured using beginning-of-year capital to match economic-profit models presented later in the chapter.

ROICs without goodwill both above 20 percent. A good analysis will assess many years—even decades—of past performance. While analysis from long ago may be outdated, understanding how the company performs in different phases of the economic cycle will better inform your forecasts. For an in-depth discussion of financial analysis using reorganized financial statements, see Chapter 12.

Projecting Revenue Growth, ROIC, and Free Cash Flow   Based on insights from your historical analysis, as well as forecasts of economic and industry trends, create a set of integrated financial statements going forward. In Exhibits 10.5 and 10.6, we present line-by-line forecasts of the income statement, statement of shareholders' equity, and balance sheet. The three statements should be integrated in that net income should flow through the statement of equity, which should match the corresponding account in the balance sheet. Use excess cash, debt, dividends, or a combination thereof to ensure that the balance sheet balances. Chapter 13 provides details on the forecasting process.

When building the forecast model, use judgment on how much detail to forecast at various points. Over the short run (the first few years), forecast each financial-statement line item, such as gross margin, selling expenses, accounts receivable, and inventory. This will allow you to incorporate visible trends in individual line items. Moving further out, individual line items become difficult to project, and a high level of detail can obscure the critical value drivers. Therefore, over the medium horizon (5 to 15 years), focus on the company's key value drivers, such as operating margin, the operating tax rate, and capital efficiency. At some point, projecting even key drivers on a year-by-year basis becomes impractical. To value cash flows beyond this point, use a continuing-value formula, often called the terminal value. Choosing an appropriate point of transition depends on the company and how it is changing over time. A company undergoing significant change may require a long, detailed window, whereas a stable, mature company may require very little detail in your forecasts.

Next, use the reorganized financial statements to calculate free cash flow. Exhibit 10.10 presents the free cash flow for GlobalCo. Defined in a manner consistent with ROIC, free cash flow is derived directly from NOPAT and the change in invested capital. Unlike the accounting statement of cash flows (provided in the company's annual report), free cash flow is independent of nonoperating items and capital structure.

Estimating Continuing Value   At the point where predicting the individual key value drivers on a year-by-year basis becomes impractical, do not vary the individual drivers over time. Instead, use a perpetuity-based continuing value, such that:

EXHIBIT 10.10 **GlobalCo: Projected Free Cash Flow**

$ million

	Year 1	Year 2	Year 3
NOPAT	60.0	69.0	72.5
Depreciation	20.0	25.0	28.8
Gross cash flow	80.0	94.0	101.2
Decrease (increase) in operating working capital	(12.0)	(9.0)	(3.4)
Capital expenditures, net of disposals	(70.0)	(62.5)	(43.1)
Free cash flow	(2.0)	22.5	54.6
Reconciliation of free cash flow			
Interest expense	10.0	10.8	11.4
Interest tax shield	(2.0)	(2.2)	(2.3)
Decrease (Increase) in short-term debt	0.0	(15.4)	(8.6)
Decrease (Increase) in long-term debt	(20.0)	–	–
Flows to (from) debt holders	(12.0)	(6.8)	0.5
Cash dividends	10.0	14.3	24.1
Repurchased (issued) shares	–	15.0	30.0
Flows to (from) equity holders	10.0	29.3	54.1
Free cash flow	(2.0)	22.5	54.6

$$\text{Value of Operations} = \begin{array}{c} \text{Present Value of Free Cash Flow} \\ \text{during Explicit Forecast Period} \\ + \\ \text{Present Value of Free Cash Flow} \\ \text{after Explicit Forecast Period} \end{array}$$

Although many continuing-value models exist, we prefer the key value driver formula presented in Chapter 3. The key value driver formula is superior to alternative methodologies because it is based on cash flow and it links cash flow directly to growth and ROIC. The key value driver formula is expressed as follows:

$$\text{Continuing Value}_t = \frac{\text{NOPAT}_{t+1}\left(1 - \dfrac{g}{\text{RONIC}}\right)}{\text{WACC} - g}$$

The formula requires a forecast of NOPAT in the year following the explicit forecast period, the long-run forecast for return on new invested capital (RONIC) purchased during the continuing value period, the WACC, and long-run growth (g) in NOPAT.

Exhibit 10.11 presents an estimate for GlobalCo's continuing value. Based on a final-year estimate of NOPAT from Exhibit 10.7 of $74.0 million, RONIC excluding goodwill from Exhibit 10.9 of 19.8 percent, and a long-term growth

EXHIBIT 10.11 **GlobalCo: Continuing Value**

$ million

Key inputs[1]		
Projected NOPAT in final forecast year	74.0	
NOPAT growth rate in perpetuity (g)	2.2%	
Return on new invested capital (RONIC)	19.8%	
Weighted average cost of capital (WACC)	7.8%	

$$\text{Continuing value}_t = \frac{\text{NOPAT}_{t+1}\left(1 - \frac{g}{\text{RONIC}}\right)}{\text{WACC} - g}$$

$$= 1{,}176.2^1$$

[1] $1,176.2 is calculated from unrounded data. Rounded inputs calculate to $1,174.6 million.

rate from Exhibit 10.9 of 2.2 percent, the continuing value is estimated at
$1,176.2 million. The valuation model presented in Exhibit 10.4 discounts this
value into today's dollars and adds it to the value from the explicit forecast
period to determine GlobalCo's operating value.

Alternative methods and additional details for estimating continuing
value are provided in Chapter 14.

Discounting Free Cash Flow at the Weighted Average Cost of Capital   In
an enterprise valuation, free cash flows are available to all investors. Consequently, the discount factor for free cash flow must represent the risk faced by
all investors. The WACC blends the rates of return required by debt holders
(k_d) and equity holders (k_e). For a company financed solely with debt and equity, the WACC is defined as follows:

$$\text{WACC} = \frac{D}{D+E}k_d(1-T_m) + \frac{E}{D+E}k_e$$

where debt (D) and equity (E) are measured using market values. Note how
the cost of debt has been reduced by the marginal tax rate (T_m). The reason for
doing this is that the tax shield attributable to interest has been excluded from
free cash flow. Since the interest tax shield (ITS) has value to the shareholder,
it must be incorporated in the valuation. Enterprise DCF values the tax shield
by reducing the weighted average cost of capital.

Why move interest tax shields from free cash flow to the cost of capital?
By calculating free cash flow as if the company were financed entirely with
equity, one can compare operating performance across companies and over
time without regard to capital structure. By focusing solely on operations, it is
possible to develop a clearer picture of historical performance, and this leads
to better performance measurement and forecasting.

Although applying the WACC is intuitive and relatively straightforward,
it has some drawbacks. If you discount all future cash flows with a constant
cost of capital, as most analysts do, you are implicitly assuming the company
keeps its capital structure constant at a target ratio of debt to equity. But if
a company plans, say, to increase (or decrease) its debt-to-value ratio, the

EXHIBIT 10.12 **GlobalCo: Weighted Average Cost of Capital**

%

Source of capital	Proportion of total capital	Cost of capital	Marginal tax rate	After-tax cost of capital	Contribution to weighted average
Debt	25.0	4.0	20.0	3.2	0.8
Equity	75.0	9.3		9.3	7.0
WACC	100.0				7.8

current cost of capital will understate (or overstate) the expected tax shields. The WACC can be adjusted to accommodate a changing capital structure. However, the process is complicated, and in these situations, we recommend an alternative method such as adjusted present value (APV).

The weighted average cost of capital for GlobalCo is presented in Exhibit 10.12. GlobalCo's 7.8 percent WACC is based on a cost of equity of 9.3 percent, pretax cost of debt of 4.0 percent, and a debt-to-value ratio of 25 percent.

Identifying and Valuing Nonoperating Assets

Many companies own assets that have value but whose cash flows are not included in accounting revenue or operating profit. As a result, the cash generated by these assets is not part of free cash flow and must be valued separately.

For example, consider equity investments, known outside the United States as nonconsolidated subsidiaries. When a company owns a minority stake in another company, it will not record the company's revenue or costs as part of its own. Instead, the company will record only its proportion of the other company's net income as a separate line item.[9] Including net income from nonconsolidated subsidiaries as part of the parent's operating profit will distort margins, since only the subsidiaries' profit is recognized and not the corresponding revenues. Consequently, nonconsolidated subsidiaries are best analyzed and valued separately.

Other nonoperating assets include excess cash, tradable securities, and customer-financing business units. A detailed process for identifying and valuing nonoperating assets appears in Chapter 16.

Identifying and Valuing Debt and Other Nonequity Claims

To convert enterprise value into equity value, subtract debt and other nonequity claims, such as unfunded retirement liabilities, capitalized operat-

[9] For stakes between 20 percent and 50 percent, the parent company will recognize its proportion of the subsidiary's income. A parent that owns less than a 20 percent stake in another company records only dividends paid as part of its own income. This makes valuation of stakes of less than 20 percent in privately held companies extremely challenging.

ing leases, and outstanding employee options. Common equity is a residual claimant, receiving cash flows only *after* the company has fulfilled its other contractual claims. Careful analysis of all potential claims against cash flows is therefore critical.

Nonequity claims on a company's cash flow are not always easy to spot. Many of the accounting scandals that led to the Sarbanes-Oxley legislation in the United States involved undisclosed or carefully hidden liabilities. Even more than a decade later, hidden liabilities remain an issue for investors. For instance, Netflix was accused in 2012 of failing to disclose $3.7 billion in contractual promises to production companies.[10] In this case, these promises were operating related and would already be incorporated into projections of free cash flow. Nonetheless, these promises are a priority claim on the company's assets and need to be assessed accordingly.

Although a comprehensive list of nonequity claims is impractical, here are the most common:

- *Debt.* If available, use the market value of all outstanding debt, including fixed- and floating-rate debt. If that information is unavailable, the book value of debt is a reasonable proxy, unless the probability of default is high or interest rates have changed dramatically since the debt was originally issued. Any valuation of debt, however, should be consistent with your estimates of enterprise value. (See Chapter 16 for more details.)

- *Leases.* Rather than purchase assets outright, many companies lease certain assets for a fixed period. Any lease payments recorded as interest expense and not rental expense must be valued separately and deducted from enterprise value.

- *Unfunded retirement liabilities.* Companies with defined-benefit pension plans and promised retiree medical benefits may have unfunded obligations that should be treated like debt.

- *Preferred stock.* For large stable companies, preferred stock more closely resembles unsecured debt. For small start-ups, preferred stock contains valuable options. In both situations, value preferred stocks separately from common stock.

- *Employee options.* Many companies offer their employees compensation in the form of options. Since options give the employee the right to buy company stock at a discounted price, they can have great value and must also be factored into equity value.

- *Noncontrolling interests.* When a company has majority control of a subsidiary but does not own 100 percent, the entire subsidiary must be consolidated on the parent company's balance sheet. The funding other investors provide for this subsidiary is recognized on the parent

[10] Cory Johnson, "The Scary $3B Bomb Not on Netflix's Balance Sheet," Bloomberg TV, July 5, 2012, www .bloomberg.com.

company's balance sheet as noncontrolling interests (formerly called minority interest). When valuing noncontrolling interests, it is important to realize that the minority interest holder does not have a claim on the company's assets, but rather a claim on the subsidiary's assets.

The identification and valuation of nonequity claims are covered in detail in Chapter 16. A detailed discussion of how to analyze leases is presented in Chapter 22. Additional detail on retirement obligations can be found in Chapter 23.

A common mistake made when valuing companies is to double-count nonequity claims already deducted from cash flow. Consider a company with a pension shortfall. You have been told the company will make extra payments to eliminate the liability. If you deduct the present value of the liability from enterprise value, do not model the extra payments within free cash flow; that would mean double-counting the shortfall (once in cash flow and once as a debtlike claim), leading to an underestimate of equity value.

Valuing Equity

Once you have identified and valued all nonequity claims, subtract the value of these claims from enterprise value to determine equity value. In Exhibit 10.4, we subtract $250 million in debt, both short-term and long-term debt, from $1 billion in enterprise value. Since GlobalCo has no debt equivalents, this leads to an intrinsic equity value of $750 million.

To determine GlobalCo's share price, divide the intrinsic equity value by the number of *undiluted* shares outstanding. Do not use diluted shares. Convertible debt, convertible preferred stock, and employee stock options should be valued separately. If you were to subtract the value of these claims and use diluted shares, you would double-count the options' value. At the time of GlobalCo's valuation, the company had 12.5 million shares outstanding. Dividing the equity estimate of $750 million by 12.5 million shares generates an estimated value of $60 per share.

Although it appears the valuation is complete, the job is not done. Compare the intrinsic value with market prices. If the two values differ, and they probably will, search for the cause, such as overly optimistic forecasts or missing liabilities. Next, use the model to test the sensitivity of various inputs on the valuation. Determine which inputs lead to the biggest changes, and which lead to negligible differences. Use this analysis to identify opportunities, prioritize operating activities, and identify risks.

ECONOMIC PROFIT-BASED VALUATION MODELS

The enterprise DCF model is a favorite of academics and practitioners because it relies solely on how cash flows in and out of the company. Complex accounting can be replaced with a simple question: Does cash change hands? One shortfall of enterprise DCF, however, is that each year's cash flow provides little insight into the company's competitive position and economic performance. Declining free cash flow can signal either poor performance or investment for the future. The economic-profit model highlights how and when the company creates value, yet properly implemented, it leads to a valuation that is identical to that of enterprise DCF.

Economic profit measures the value created by the company in a single period and is defined as follows:

$$\text{Economic Profit} = \text{Invested Capital} \times (\text{ROIC} - \text{WACC})$$

Since ROIC equals NOPAT divided by invested capital, we can rewrite the equation as follows:

$$\text{Economic Profit} = \text{NOPAT} - (\text{Invested Capital} \times \text{WACC})$$

Exhibit 10.13 presents economic-profit calculations for GlobalCo using both methods. Not surprisingly, with an ROIC more than double its cost of capital, GlobalCo generates significant economic profits.

To demonstrate how economic profit can be used to value a company—and to demonstrate its equivalence to enterprise DCF—consider a stream of growing cash flows valued using the growing-perpetuity formula:

$$\text{Value}_0 = \frac{\text{FCF}_1}{\text{WACC} - g}$$

In Chapter 3, we transformed this cash flow perpetuity into the key value driver model. The key value driver model is superior to the simple cash flow perpetuity model, because it explicitly models the relationship between growth and required investment. Using a few additional algebraic steps (detailed in Appendix A) and the assumption that the company's ROIC on new projects equals the ROIC on existing capital, it is possible to transform the cash flow perpetuity into a key value driver model based on economic profits:

$$\text{Value}_0 = \text{Invested Capital}_0 + \frac{\text{Invested Capital}_0 \times (\text{ROIC}_1 - \text{WACC})}{\text{WACC} - g}$$

Finally, we substitute the definition of economic profit:

$$\text{Value}_0 = \text{Invested Capital}_0 + \frac{\text{Economic Profit}_1}{\text{WACC} - g}$$

As can be seen in the economic-profit-based key value driver model, the operating value of a company equals its book value of invested capital plus the present value of all future value created. In this case, the future economic

EXHIBIT 10.13 **GlobalCo: Economic-Profit Summary**

$ million, except where noted

	Year 1	Year 2	Year 3
Method 1			
Return on invested capital,[1] %	24.2	22.3	20.3
Weighted average cost of capital, %	(7.8)	(7.8)	(7.8)
Economic spread, %	16.4	14.5	12.5
× Invested capital[1]	248.0	310.0	356.5
= Economic profit	40.7	44.8	44.6
Method 2			
Invested capital[1]	248	310	357
× Weighted average cost of capital, %	7.8	7.8	7.8
= Capital charge	19.3	24.2	27.8
NOPAT	60.0	69.0	72.5
Capital charge	(19.3)	(24.2)	(27.8)
Economic profit	40.7	44.8	44.6
Including goodwill			
Economic profit including goodwill	32.9	37.0	36.8

[1] Invested capital measured at the beginning of the year, excluding goodwill and acquired intangibles.

profits are valued using a growing perpetuity, because the company's economic profits are increasing at a constant rate over time. The formula also demonstrates that when economic profit is expected to be zero, the value of operations will equal invested capital. If a company's value of operations exceeds its invested capital, be sure to identify the sources of competitive advantage that allows the company to maintain superior financial performance.

More generally, economic profit can be valued as follows:

$$\text{Value}_0 = \text{Invested Capital}_0 + \sum_{t=1}^{\infty} \frac{\text{Economic Profit}_t}{(1+\text{WACC})^t}$$

Since the economic-profit valuation was derived directly from the free cash flow model (see Appendix A for a general proof of equivalence), any valuation based on discounted economic profits will be identical to enterprise DCF. To assure equivalence, however, it is necessary to do the following:

- Use beginning-of-year invested capital (i.e., last year's value) instead of average or current-year invested capital, which is common to competitive benchmarking.
- Define invested capital for both economic profit and ROIC using the same value. For example, ROIC can be measured either with or without

goodwill. If you measure ROIC without goodwill, you must also measure invested capital without goodwill. All told, it doesn't matter how you define invested capital, as long as you are consistent.

- Use a constant cost of capital to discount projections.

Exhibit 10.14 presents the valuation results for GlobalCo using discounted economic profit. Economic profits are explicitly forecast for three years; the remaining years are valued using an economic-profit continuing-value formula.[11] Comparing the equity value from Exhibit 10.4 with that of Exhibit 10.14, we see that the estimate of GlobalCo's DCF value is the same, regardless of the method.

The benefits of economic profit become apparent when we examine the drivers of economic profit, ROIC and WACC, on a year-by-year basis in Exhibit 10.14. Note that the valuation is contingent on returns that exceed the

EXHIBIT 10.14 **GlobalCo: Valuation Using Discounted Economic Profit**

$ million, except where noted

Year	Invested capital[1]	ROIC,[1] %	WACC, %	Economic profit	Discount factor at 7.8%	Present value of economic profit
Year 1	348.0	17.2	(7.8)	32.9	0.928	30.5
Year 2	410.0	16.8	(7.8)	37.0	0.861	31.9
Year 3	456.5	15.9	(7.8)	36.8	0.798	29.4
Continuing value				701.8	0.798	560.3
Present value of economic profit						652.0
Invested capital including goodwill[1]						348.0
Value of operations						1,000.0
Nonoperating assets						—
Enterprise value						1,000.0
Less: Value of debt						(250.0)
Less: Value of noncontrolling interest						—
Equity value						750.0

[1] Invested capital measured at the beginning of the year with goodwill and acquired intangibles.

[11] To calculate continuing value, you can use the economic-profit-based key value driver formula, but only if RONIC equals ROIC in the continuing-value year. If RONIC going forward differs from the final year's ROIC, then the equation must be separated into current and future economic profits:

$$\text{Value}_t = IC_t + \underbrace{\frac{IC_t(ROIC_{t+1} - WACC)}{WACC}}_{\text{Current Economic Profits}} + \underbrace{\frac{PV(\text{Economic Profit}_{t+2})}{WACC - g}}_{\text{Future Economic Profits}}$$

such that:

$$PV(\text{Economic Profit}_{t+2}) = \frac{NOPAT_{t+1}\left(\dfrac{g}{RONIC}\right)(RONIC - WACC)}{WACC}$$

For more on these and other continuing value formulas, see Chapter 14.

cost of capital but drop over time as new competitors enter and put pressure on operating margins. Explicitly modeling ROIC as a primary driver of economic profit prominently displays expectations of value creation. Conversely, the FCF model fails to highlight when a company creates and destroys value. Free cash flow combines ROIC and growth, two critical but very different value drivers.

Also note how GlobalCo's high ROIC—double its cost of capital—leads to an operating value that exceeds the book value of its invested capital ($1 billion versus $348 million). When investors believe a company will create value, enterprise value will be greater than invested capital.

ADJUSTED-PRESENT-VALUE MODEL

When building an enterprise DCF or economic-profit valuation, most investment professionals discount all future flows at a constant WACC. Using a constant WACC, however, assumes the company manages its capital structure to a target debt-to-value ratio.

In most situations, debt grows with company value. But suppose the company planned to change its capital structure significantly, as in a leveraged buyout. Indeed, companies with a high proportion of debt often pay it down as cash flow improves, thus lowering their future debt-to-value ratios. In these cases, a valuation based on a constant WACC would overstate the value of the tax shields. Although the WACC can be adjusted yearly to handle a changing capital structure, the process is complex. Therefore, we turn to the most flexible of valuation models: adjusted present value (APV).

The APV model separates the value of operations into two components: the value of operations as if the company were all-equity financed and the value of tax shields that arise from debt financing:[12]

$$\text{Adjusted Present Value} = \text{Enterprise Value as if the Company Were All-Equity Financed} + \text{Present Value of Tax Shields}$$

The APV valuation model follows directly from the teachings of economists Franco Modigliani and Merton Miller, who proposed that in a market with no taxes (among other things), a company's choice of financial structure will not affect the value of its economic assets. Only market imperfections, such as taxes and distress costs, affect enterprise value.

When building a valuation model, it is easy to forget these teachings. To see this, imagine a company (in a world with no taxes) that has a 50/50 mix

---

[12] This book focuses on the tax shields generated by interest expense. On a more general basis, the APV values any cash flows associated with capital structure, such as tax shields, issuance costs, and distress costs. Distress costs include direct costs, such as court-related fees, and indirect costs, such as the loss of wary customers and suppliers.

of debt and equity. If the company's debt has an expected return of 5 percent and the company's equity has an expected return of 15 percent, its weighted average cost of capital would be 10 percent. Suppose the company decides to issue more debt, using the proceeds to repurchase shares. Since the cost of debt is lower than the cost of equity, it would appear that issuing debt to retire equity should lower the WACC, raising the company's value.

This line of thinking is flawed, however. In a world without taxes, a change in capital structure would not change the cash flow generated by operations, nor the risk of those cash flows. Therefore, neither the company's enterprise value nor its cost of capital would change. So why would we think it would? When adding debt, we adjusted the weights, but we failed to properly increase the cost of equity. Since debt payments have priority over cash flows to equity, adding leverage increases the risk to equity holders. When leverage rises, they demand a higher return. Modigliani and Miller postulated that this increase would perfectly offset the change in weights.

In reality, taxes play a role in determining capital structure. Since interest is tax deductible, profitable companies can lower taxes by raising debt. But if the company relies too heavily on debt, the company's customers and suppliers may fear financial distress and be reluctant to do business with the company, reducing future cash flow (academics call this distress costs or deadweight costs). Rather than model the effect of capital-structure changes in the weighted average cost of capital, APV explicitly measures and values the cash flow effects of financing separately.

To build an APV valuation, value the company as if it were all-equity financed. Do this by discounting free cash flow by the unlevered cost of equity (what the cost of equity would be if the company had no debt).[13] To this value, add any value created by the company's use of debt. Exhibit 10.15 values GlobalCo using adjusted present value.

Since we assume (for expositional purposes) that GlobalCo will manage its capital structure to a target debt-to-value level of 25 percent, the APV-based valuation leads to the same value for equity as did enterprise DCF (see Exhibit 10.4) and economic profit (see Exhibit 10.14). A simplified proof of equivalence between enterprise DCF and adjusted present value can be found in Appendix B. The following subsections explain adjusted present value in detail.

Valuing Free Cash Flow at Unlevered Cost of Equity

When valuing a company using the APV, explicitly separate the unlevered value of operations (V_u) from any value created by financing, such as tax

---

[13] Free cash flow projections in the APV model are identical to those presented in Exhibit 10.4. Continuing value is computed using the key value driver formula. Only the cost of capital is used for discounting changes.

EXHIBIT 10.15 **GlobalCo: Valuation Using Adjusted Present Value**

$ million, except where noted

Year	Free cash flow (FCF)	Interest tax shield (ITS)	Discount factor at 8.0%	Present value of FCF	Present value of ITS
Year 1	(2.0)	2.0	0.926	(1.9)	1.9
Year 2	22.5	2.2	0.857	19.3	1.9
Year 3	54.6	2.3	0.794	43.4	1.8
Continuing value	1,135.6	40.6	0.794	901.5	32.2
Present value				962.3	37.7
Present value of free cash flow					962.3
Present value of interest tax shield					37.7
Value of operations					1,000.0

shields (V_{txa}). For a company with debt (D) and equity (E), this relationship is as follows:

$$V_u + V_{txa} = D + E \qquad (10.1)$$

A second result of Modigliani and Miller's work is that the total risk of the company's assets, real and financial, must equal the total risk of the financial claims against those assets. Thus, in equilibrium, the blended cost of capital for operating assets (k_u), which we call the unlevered cost of equity) and financial assets (k_{txa}) must equal the blended cost of capital for debt (k_d) and equity (k_e):

$$\frac{V_u}{V} k_u + \frac{V_{txa}}{V} k_{txa} = \frac{D}{V} k_d + \frac{E}{V} k_e \qquad (10.2)$$

In the corporate-finance literature, academics combine Modigliani and Miller's two equations to solve for the cost of equity (k_e) in order to demonstrate the relationship between leverage and the cost of equity. Appendix C algebraically rearranges Equation 10.2 to solve for the most flexible version of the levered cost of equity:

$$k_e = k_u + \frac{D}{E}(k_u - k_d) - \frac{V_{txa}}{E}(k_u - k_{txa}) \qquad (10.3)$$

As this equation indicates, the cost of equity depends on the unlevered cost of equity, or the cost of equity when the company has no debt, plus a premium for leverage, less a reduction for the tax deductibility of debt. Note that when a company has no debt ($D = 0$) and subsequently no tax shields ($V_{txa} = 0$), k_e equals k_u. This is why k_u is referred to as the unlevered cost of equity.

Unfortunately, k_u cannot be observed directly. In fact, none of the variables on the left side of Equation 10.2 can be observed directly. Only the values on the right—that is, those related to debt and equity—can be estimated using market data. Because there are so many unknowns and only one equation, we must impose additional restrictions to build a usable relationship between the levered (k_e) and unlevered (k_u) cost of equity.

If you believe the company will manage its debt-to-value ratio to a target level (the company's debt will grow with the business), then the value of the tax shields will track the value of the operating assets. Thus, the risk of tax shields will mirror the risk of operating assets ($k_{txa} = k_u$). Setting k_{txa} equal to k_u, Equation 10.3 can be simplified as follows:

$$k_e = k_u + \frac{D}{E}(k_u - k_d)$$ (10.4)

The unlevered cost of equity can now be reverse engineered using the observed cost of equity, the cost of debt, and the market debt-to-equity ratio. (Appendix C shows some alternative versions for deriving k_u from k_e.)

Valuing Tax Shields and Other Capital Structure Effects

To complete an APV valuation, forecast and discount capital structure side effects such as tax shields, security issuance costs, and distress costs. Since GlobalCo has only a small probability of default, we estimated the company's future interest tax shields using the company's expected interest payments and marginal tax rate (see Exhibit 10.16). To calculate the expected interest payment in year 1, multiply the prior year's debt of $250 million by the interest rate of 4.0 percent. This results in an expected interest payment of $10 million. Next, multiply the expected interest payment by the marginal tax rate of 20 percent, for an expected interest tax shield of $2 million in year 1. To determine the continuing value of interest tax shields beyond year 3, use a growth perpetuity based on interest tax shields in the continuing-value year, the unlevered cost of capital, and growth in NOPAT.

A company with significant leverage may not be able to fully use the tax shields (it may not have enough profits to shield). If there is a significant

EXHIBIT 10.16 **GlobalCo: Forecast of Interest Tax Shields**

$ million

Forecast year	Prior-year net debt[1]	Interest rate, %	Expected interest payment	Marginal tax rate, %	Interest tax shield
Year 1	250.0	4.0	10.0	20.0	2.0
Year 2	270.0	4.0	10.8	20.0	2.2
Year 3	285.4	4.0	11.4	20.0	2.3
Continuing-value forecast	294.0	4.0	11.8	20.0	2.4

[1] Total debt net of excess cash.

probability of default, you must model *expected* tax shields, rather than the calculated tax shields based on promised interest payments.[14] To do this, reduce each promised tax shield by the cumulative probability of default.

CAPITAL CASH FLOW MODEL

When a company actively manages its capital structure to a target debt-to-value level, both free cash flow (FCF) and the interest tax shield (ITS) should be discounted at the unlevered cost of equity, k_u, such that enterprise value equals the sum of discounted cash flows plus the sum of discounted interest tax shields:

$$V = \sum_{t=1}^{\infty} \frac{FCF_t}{(1+k_u)^t} + \sum_{t=1}^{\infty} \frac{ITS_t}{(1+k_u)^t}$$

In 2002, Richard Ruback of the Harvard Business School argued that there is no need to separate free cash flow from tax shields when both flows are discounted by the same cost of capital.[15] He combined the two flows and named the resulting cash flow (i.e., FCF plus interest tax shields) capital cash flow (CCF):

$$V = PV\left(\text{Capital Cash Flow}\right) = \sum_{t=1}^{\infty} \frac{FCF_t + ITS_t}{(1+k_u)^t}$$

Given that Ruback's assumptions match those of the weighted average cost of capital, the capital cash flow and WACC-based valuations will lead to identical results. In fact, we have now detailed three distinct but identical valuation methods created solely around how they treat tax shields: WACC (tax shield valued in the cost of capital), APV (tax shield valued separately), and CCF (tax shield valued in the cash flow).

Although free cash flow and capital cash flow lead to the same result when debt is proportional to value, we believe FCF models are superior to CCF models. By keeping NOPAT and FCF independent of leverage, it is easier to evaluate the company's operating performance over time and against competitors. A clean measure of historical operating performance leads to better forecasts.

---

[14] The Tax Cuts and Jobs Act of 2017 placed additional restrictions on the deductibility of interest, even for profitable companies. Only value interest tax shields if they meet deductibility guidelines.

[15] R. S. Ruback, "Capital Cash Flows: A Simple Approach to Valuing Risky Cash Flows," *Financial Management* (Summer 2002): 85–103.

CASH-FLOW-TO-EQUITY VALUATION MODEL

Each of the preceding valuation models determined the value of equity indirectly by subtracting debt and other nonequity claims from enterprise value. The equity cash flow model values equity directly by discounting cash flows to equity (CFE) at the cost of equity, rather than at the weighted average cost of capital.[16]

Exhibit 10.17 details the cash flow to equity for GlobalCo. Cash flow to equity starts with net income. To this, add back noncash expenses to determine gross cash flow. Next, subtract investments in working capital, fixed assets, and nonoperating assets. Finally, add any increases in debt and other nonequity claims, and subtract decreases in debt and other nonequity claims. Unlike free cash flow, cash flow to equity includes operating, nonoperating, and financing items in the calculation. Alternatively, you can compute cash flow to equity as dividends plus share repurchases minus new equity issues. The two methods generate identical results.[17]

To value GlobalCo using cash flow to equity holders, discount projected equity cash flows at the cost of equity (see Exhibit 10.18). Unlike enterprise-based models, this method makes no adjustments to the DCF value for nonoperating assets or debt. Rather, they are embedded as part of the equity cash flow.

EXHIBIT 10.17 **GlobalCo: Equity Cash Flow Summary**

$ million

	Forecast		
	Year 1	Year 2	Year 3
Net income	52.0	60.4	63.3
Depreciation	20.0	25.0	28.8
Gross cash flow	72.0	85.4	92.1
Decrease (increase) in operating working capital	(12.0)	(9.0)	(3.4)
Capital expenditures, net of disposals	(70.0)	(62.5)	(43.1)
Increase (decrease) in short-term debt	–	15.4	8.6
Increase (decrease) in long-term debt	20.0	–	–
Cash flow to equity holders	10.0	29.3	54.1
Reconciliation of cash flow to equity			
Cash dividends	10.0	14.3	24.1
Repurchased (issued) shares	–	15.0	30.0
Cash flow to equity holders	10.0	29.3	54.1

[16] The equity method can be difficult to implement correctly, because capital structure is embedded in the cash flow, so forecasting is difficult. For companies whose operations are related to financing, such as financial institutions, the equity method is appropriate. Chapter 38 discusses valuing financial institutions.
[17] Calculate the continuing value using an equity-based variant of the key value driver formula:

$$V_e = \frac{\text{Net Income}\left(1 - \dfrac{g}{\text{ROE}}\right)}{k_e - g}$$

EXHIBIT 10.18 **GlobalCo: Valuation Using Cash Flow to Equity**

$ million, except where noted

Forecast year	Cash flow to equity (CFE)	Discount factor at 8.9%	Present value of CFE
2014	10.0	0.915	9.1
2015	29.3	0.837	24.5
2016	54.1	0.765	41.4
Continuing value	882.1	0.765	675.0
Present value of equity cash flows			750.0
Less: Value of noncontrolling interest			–
Equity value			750.0

Once again, note how the valuation, derived using equity cash flows, matches each of the prior valuations. This occurs because we have carefully modeled GlobalCo's debt-to-value ratio at a constant level. If leverage is expected to change, the cost of equity must be appropriately adjusted to reflect the change in risk imposed on equity holders. Although formulas exist to adjust the cost of equity (as done in the APV section earlier in this chapter), many of the best-known formulas are built under restrictions that may be inconsistent with the way you are implicitly forecasting the company's capital structure via the cash flows. This will cause a mismatch between cash flows and the cost of equity, resulting in an incorrect valuation.

It is quite easy to change the company's capital structure without realizing it when using the cash-flow-to-equity model—and that is what makes implementing the equity model so risky. Suppose you plan to value a company whose debt-to-value ratio is 25 percent. You believe the company will pay extra dividends, so you increase debt to raise the dividend payout ratio. Presto! Increased dividends lead to higher equity cash flows and a higher valuation. Even though operating performance has not changed, the equity value has mistakenly increased. What is happening? Using new debt to pay dividends causes a rise in the debt-to-value ratio. Unless you adjust the cost of equity, the valuation will rise incorrectly.

A second major shortcoming of the equity cash flow model is how it values nonoperating assets. Imagine a company that holds a significant amount of low-risk, low-return excess cash. Since operating and nonoperating cash flows are combined in cash flows to equity, they will both be discounted at the same rate, the cost of equity. Since the cost of equity exceeds the rate of return on cash, it appears as if the nonoperating asset is destroying value, and the asset will be incorrectly valued below its book value, even if the asset in actuality is earning a fair rate of return.

A third shortcoming of the cash-flow-to-equity model emerges when valuing a company by business unit. The direct equity approach requires allocating debt and interest expense to each unit. This creates extra work yet provides few additional insights.

One situation where the equity cash flow model leads to the simplest implementation is the analysis and valuation of financial institutions. Since capital structure is a critical part of operations in a financial institution, using enterprise DCF to separate operations and capital structure requires unnecessary assumptions. This is why Chapter 38 uses the cash-flow-to-equity model to value banks and other financial institutions.

PROBLEMATIC MODIFICATIONS TO DISCOUNTED CASH FLOW

In this chapter, we valued GlobalCo by discounting nominal cash flows at a nominal cost of capital. An alternative is to value companies by projecting cash flow in real terms, ignoring the rise in prices, and discounting this cash flow at a real discount rate (the nominal rate less expected inflation). But most managers think in terms of nominal rather than real measures, so nominal measures are often easier to communicate. In addition, interest rates are generally quoted nominally rather than in real terms, excluding expected inflation.

A second difficulty occurs when calculating and interpreting ROIC. The historical statements are nominal, so historical returns on invested capital are nominal. But if the projections for the company use real rather than nominal forecasts, returns on new capital are also real. Projected returns on total capital—new and old—are a combination of nominal and real, so they are impossible to interpret. The only way around this is to restate historical performance on a real basis, which is a complex and time-consuming task. The extra insights gained rarely equal the effort, except in extremely high-inflation environments, described in Chapter 26.

A second alternative to the enterprise DCF method outlined earlier is to discount pretax cash flows at a pretax hurdle rate (the market-based cost of capital multiplied by 1 plus the marginal tax rate) to determine a pretax value. This method, however, leads to three fundamental inconsistencies. First, the government calculates taxes on profits after depreciation, not on cash flow after capital expenditures. By discounting pretax cash flow at the pretax cost of capital, you implicitly assume capital investments are tax deductible when made, not as they are depreciated. Furthermore, working-capital investments, such as accounts receivable and inventory, are never tax deductible. Selling a product at a profit, rather than holding inventory, is what leads to incremental taxes. By discounting pretax cash flow at the pretax cost of capital, you incorrectly assume that investments in operating working capital are tax deductible. Finally, it can be shown that even when net investment equals depreciation, the result will be downward biased—and the larger the cost of capital, the larger the bias. This bias occurs because the method is only an approximation, not a formal mathematical relationship. Because of these inconsistencies, we recommend against discounting pretax cash flows at a pretax hurdle rate.

ALTERNATIVES TO DISCOUNTED CASH FLOW

To this point, we've focused solely on discounted cash flow models. Two additional valuation techniques are using the multiples of comparable companies and real options.

Multiples

One simple way that investors and executives value companies is to value a company in relation to the value of other companies, akin to the way a real estate agent values a house by comparing it with similar houses that have recently sold. To do this, first calculate how similar companies are valued as a multiple of a relevant metric, such as earnings, invested capital, or an operating metric like barrels of oil reserves. You can then apply that multiple to the company you are valuing. For example, assume the company's NOPAT equals $100 million and the typical enterprise-value-to-NOPAT multiple for companies in the industry with similar growth and ROIC prospects is 13 times. Multiplying 13 by $100 million leads to an estimated value of $1.3 billion.

Multiples can be a great check on your DCF valuation if done properly. Suppose the value estimated by multiples is $1.3 billion, but your DCF value is $2.7 billion. This might be a clue that there is something wrong with your DCF valuation model. Alternatively, it could be that the company you are valuing is expected to perform differently than the comparable companies. Finally, it could be that investors have a different outlook for the entire industry than you do (in which case the multiples of all the comparable companies would be out of line with their DCF value). Of course, it could just be that your multiples valuation wasn't performed properly. Because of their broad use and potential for error, we devote Chapter 18 to valuation using multiples.

In a nutshell, to use multiples properly, you need to carefully choose the multiple and the comparable companies. In the case of earnings multiples, we recommend using ratios of enterprise value to NOPAT rather than price to earnings or enterprise value to earnings before interest, taxes, depreciation, and amortization (EBITDA). We also urge you to be careful when choosing the comparable companies. The comparable companies not only should be in the same industry, but also should have similar performance, as measured by ROIC and growth.

Real Options and Replicating Portfolios

In 1997, Robert Merton and Myron Scholes won the Nobel Prize in economics for developing an ingenious method to value derivatives that avoids the need to estimate either cash flows or the cost of capital.[18] Their model relies

---

[18] Fischer Black would have been named as a third recipient, but the Nobel Prize is not awarded posthumously.

on what today's economists call a "replicating portfolio." They argued that if a portfolio exists of traded securities whose future cash flows perfectly mimic the security you are attempting to value, the portfolio and security must have the same price. This is known as the law of one price. As long as you can find a suitable replicating portfolio, you need not discount future cash flows.

Given the model's power in valuing derivatives like stock options, there have been many recent attempts to translate the concepts of replicating portfolios to corporate valuation. This valuation technique, commonly known as real options, is especially useful in situations of great uncertainty. Unlike those for financial options, however, replicating portfolios for companies and their projects are difficult to create. Therefore, although option-pricing models may teach powerful lessons, today's applications are limited. Chapter 39 covers valuation using options-based models.

SUMMARY

Our exploration of the most common DCF valuation models has put a particular focus on the enterprise DCF model and the economic-profit model. Each model has its own rationale, and each has an important place in corporate valuation. The remaining chapters in Part Two describe a step-by-step approach to valuing a company. These chapters explain the technical details of valuation, including how to reorganize the financial statements, analyze return on invested capital and revenue growth, forecast free cash flow, compute the cost of capital, and estimate an appropriate terminal value.

11

Reorganizing the Financial Statements

Traditional financial statements—the income statement, balance sheet, and statement of cash flows—do not provide easy insights into operating performance and value. They simply aren't organized that way. The balance sheet mixes together operating assets, nonoperating assets, and sources of financing. The income statement similarly combines operating profits, interest expense, and other nonoperating items.

To prepare the financial statements for analyzing economic performance, you should reorganize each financial statement into three categories: operating items, nonoperating items, and sources of financing. This often requires searching through the notes to separate accounts that aggregate operating and nonoperating items. This task may seem mundane, but it is crucial for avoiding the common traps of double-counting, omitting cash flows, and hiding leverage that distorts performance metrics, such as return on equity and cash flow from operations.

Since reorganizing the financial statements is complex, this chapter breaks down the process into three sections. The first section presents a simple example demonstrating how to build invested capital, net operating profit after taxes (NOPAT), and free cash flow. The second section applies this method to the financial statements for Costco Wholesale, with comments on some of the intricacies of implementation. Finally, we provide a brief summary of advanced analytical topics, including how to adjust for restructuring charges, operating leases, pensions, and capitalized expenses. An in-depth analysis of each of these topics can be found in the chapters of Part Three.

REORGANIZING THE ACCOUNTING STATEMENTS: KEY CONCEPTS

To calculate return on invested capital (ROIC) and free cash flow (FCF), it is necessary to reorganize the balance sheet to estimate invested capital, as well as to likewise reorganize the income statement to estimate NOPAT. Invested capital represents the investor capital required to fund operations, without regard to how the capital is financed. NOPAT represents the after-tax operating profit (generated by the company's invested capital) that is available to all investors.

ROIC and FCF are both derived from NOPAT and invested capital. ROIC is defined as

$$ROIC = \frac{NOPAT}{Invested\ Capital}$$

and free cash flow is defined as

$$FCF = NOPAT + Noncash\ Operating\ Expenses - Investment\ in$$
$$Invested\ Capital$$

By combining noncash operating expenses, such as depreciation, with investment in invested capital, it is also possible to express FCF as

$$FCF = NOPAT - Increase\ in\ Invested\ Capital$$

Invested Capital: Key Concepts

To build an economic balance sheet that separates a company's operating assets from its nonoperating assets and financial structure, we start with the traditional balance sheet. The accounting balance sheet is bound by the most fundamental rule of accounting:

$$Assets = Liabilities + Equity$$

The traditional balance sheet equation, however, mixes operating liabilities and sources of financing on the right side of the equation.

Assume a company has only operating assets (OA), such as accounts receivable, inventory, and property, plant, and equipment (PP&E); operating liabilities (OL), such as accounts payable and accrued salaries; interest-bearing debt (D); and equity (E). Using this more explicit breakdown of assets, liabilities, and equity leads to an expanded version of the balance sheet relationship:

$$OA = OL + D + E$$

Moving operating liabilities to the left side of the equation leads to invested capital:

$$OA - OL = Invested\ Capital = D + E$$

This new equation rearranges the balance sheet to reflect more accurately capital used for operations and the financing provided by investors to fund those operations. Note how invested capital can be calculated using either the operating method (that is, operating assets minus operating liabilities) or the financing method (debt plus equity).

For many companies, the previous equation is too simple. Assets consist of not only operating assets, but also nonoperating assets (NOA), such as marketable securities, prepaid pension assets, nonconsolidated subsidiaries, and other long-term investments. Liabilities consist of not only operating liabilities and interest-bearing debt, but also debt equivalents (DE), such as unfunded retirement liabilities, and equity equivalents (EE), such as deferred taxes and income-smoothing provisions. (We explain debt and equity equivalents in detail later in the chapter.) We can expand our original balance sheet equation to show these:

$$\underset{\substack{\text{(operating} \\ \text{assets)}}}{\text{OA}} + \underset{\substack{\text{(nonoperating} \\ \text{assets)}}}{\text{NOA}} = \underset{\substack{\text{(operating} \\ \text{liabilities)}}}{\text{OL}} + \underset{\substack{\text{(debt and its} \\ \text{equivalents)}}}{\text{D}+\text{DE}} + \underset{\substack{\text{(equity and its} \\ \text{equivalents)}}}{\text{E}+\text{EE}}$$

Rearranging leads to total funds invested:

$$\underset{\substack{\text{(invested} \\ \text{capital)}}}{\text{OA} - \text{OL} +} \underset{\substack{\text{(nonoperating} \\ \text{assets)}}}{\text{NOA}} = \underset{\text{Invested}}{\text{Total Funds} =} \underset{\substack{\text{(debt and its} \\ \text{equivalents)}}}{\text{D}+\text{DE}} + \underset{\substack{\text{(equity and its} \\ \text{equivalents)}}}{\text{E}+\text{EE}}$$

For a company with debt and equity equivalents, invested capital no longer equals debt plus equity. It equals operating assets minus operating liabilities. From an investing perspective, total funds invested equals invested capital plus nonoperating assets. From the financing perspective, total funds invested equals debt and its equivalents plus equity and its equivalents. Exhibit 11.1

EXHIBIT 11.1 **An Example of Invested Capital**

$ million

Accountant's balance sheet

Assets	Prior year	Current year
Cash	5	15
Inventory	200	225
Net PP&E	300	350
Equity investments	15	25
Total assets	520	615

Liabilities and equity		
Accounts payable	125	150
Interest-bearing debt	225	200
Shareholders' equity	170	265
Total liabilities and equity	520	615

Invested capital

	Prior year	Current year	
Cash	5	15	
Inventory	200	225	Operating liabilities
Accounts payable	(125)	(150)	are netted against
Operating working capital	80	90	operating assets
Net PP&E	300	350	
Invested capital	380	440	
Equity investments	15	25	Nonoperating assets are not included in
Total funds invested	395	465	invested capital

Reconciliation of total funds invested

	Prior year	Current year
Interest-bearing debt	225	200
Shareholders' equity	170	265
Total funds invested	395	465

rearranges the balance sheet into invested capital for a simple hypothetical company with only a few line items. The reconciliation at the lower right shows how the amount of total funds invested is identical regardless of the method used.

Net Operating Profit after Taxes: Key Concepts

NOPAT is the after-tax profit generated from core operations, excluding any income from nonoperating assets or financing expenses, such as interest. Whereas net income is the profit available to equity holders only, NOPAT is the profit available to *all* investors, including providers of debt, equity, and any other types of investor financing. It is critical to define NOPAT consistently with your definition of invested capital and to include only those profits generated by invested capital.

To calculate NOPAT, we reorganize the accounting income statement in three ways (see Exhibit 11.2). First, interest is not subtracted from operating income, because interest is compensation for the company's debt investors, not an operating expense. By reclassifying interest as a financing item, we make NOPAT independent of the company's capital structure.

Second, when calculating NOPAT, exclude income generated from assets that were excluded from invested capital. Mistakenly including nonoperating income in NOPAT without including the associated assets in invested capital

EXHIBIT 11.2 **An Example of NOPAT**

$ million

Accountant's income statement	Current year		NOPAT	Current year	
Revenues	1,000		Revenues	1,000	
Operating costs	(700)		Operating costs	(700)	
Depreciation	(20)		Depreciation	(20)	
Operating profit	280		EBITA	280	
Interest expense	(20)		Operating taxes[1]	(70)	Taxes are calculated on operating profits
Income from equity investments	4		NOPAT	210	
Earnings before taxes (EBT)	264				
			Income from equity investments	4	Do not include income from any asset excluded from invested capital as part of NOPAT
Income taxes	(66)		Tax shield on nonoperating items[2]	4	
Net income	198		Income available to investors	218	
			Reconciliation with net income		
			Net income	198	Treat interest as a financial payout to investors, not an operating expense
			Interest expense	20	
			Income available to investors	218	

[1] Assumes a marginal tax of 25% on all income.

[2] Interest tax shield less taxes on equity income.

will lead to an inconsistent definition of ROIC; the numerator and denominator will include unrelated elements. If one-time items such as a major litigation settlement are reported, exclude them from NOPAT as well. One-time items are important to analyze, but make trends in core performance difficult to identify.

Finally, since reported taxes are calculated after interest and nonoperating income, they are a function of nonoperating items and capital structure. Keeping NOPAT focused solely on ongoing operations requires that the effects of interest expense and nonoperating income also be removed from taxes. To calculate operating taxes, start with reported taxes, add back the tax shield from interest expense, and remove the taxes paid on nonoperating income. The resulting operating taxes should equal the hypothetical taxes that would be paid by an all-equity, pure operating company. Nonoperating taxes, the difference between operating taxes and reported taxes, are not included in NOPAT, but instead as part of income available to investors.

Free Cash Flow: Key Concepts

To value a company's operations, we discount projected free cash flow at a company's weighted average cost of capital. Free cash flow is the after-tax cash flow available to all investors: debt holders and equity holders. Unlike "cash flow from operations" reported in a company's annual report, free cash flow is independent of financing flows and nonoperating items. It can be thought of as the after-tax cash flow that would be generated if the company held only core operating assets and financed the business entirely with equity. Free cash flow is defined as:

$$FCF = NOPAT + Noncash\ Operating\ Expenses - Investments\ in$$
$$Invested\ Capital$$

As shown in Exhibit 11.3, free cash flow excludes nonoperating flows and items related to capital structure. Unlike the accounting cash flow statement, the free cash flow statement starts with NOPAT (instead of net income). As discussed earlier, NOPAT excludes nonoperating income and interest expense. Instead, interest is classified as a financing cash flow.

Changes in nonoperating assets and the gains, losses, and income associated with these nonoperating assets are not included in free cash flow. Instead, nonoperating cash flows should be analyzed and valued separately. Combining free cash flow and nonoperating cash flow leads to cash flow available to investors. As is true with total funds invested and NOPAT, cash flow available to investors can be calculated using two methodologies: one focuses on how the cash flow is generated, and the other focuses on the recipients of free cash flow. Although the two methods seem redundant,

EXHIBIT 11.3 **An Example of Free Cash Flow**

$ million

Accountant's cash flow statement	Current year	Free cash flow	Current year	
Net income	198	NOPAT	210	
Depreciation	20	Depreciation	20	
Decrease (increase) in inventory	(25)	Gross cash flow	230	
Increase (decrease) in accounts payable	25			
Cash flow from operations	218	Decrease (increase) in operating cash	(10)	Subtract investments
		Decrease (increase) in inventory	(25)	in operating items from
Capital expenditures	(70)	Increase (decrease) in accounts payable	25	gross cash
Decrease (increase) in equity investments	(10)	Capital expenditures	(70)	flow
Cash flow from investing	(80)	Free cash flow	150	
				Evaluate cash
Increase (decrease) in interest-bearing debt	(25)	Nonoperating income	4	flow from nonoperating
Dividends	(103)	Nonoperating taxes	4	assets
Cash flow from financing	(128)	Decrease (increase) in equity investments	(10)	separately from free
		Cash flow available to investors	148	cash flow
Starting cash	5			
Cash flow from operations	218			
Cash flow from investing	(80)	**Reconciliation of cash flow available to investors**		Treat interest
Cash flow from financing	(128)			as a financial
Ending cash	15	Interest expense	20	payout to
		Increase (decrease) in interest-bearing debt	25	investors, not
		Dividends	103	an expense
		Cash flow available to investors	148	

checking that both give the same result can help avoid line item omissions and classification pitfalls.

REORGANIZING THE ACCOUNTING STATEMENTS: IN PRACTICE

Reorganizing a company's financial statements can be difficult, even for the savviest analyst. Which assets are operating assets? Which are nonoperating? Which liabilities should be treated as debt? Which count as equity?

In the following pages, we examine reorganization in practice using Costco Wholesale. (A complete valuation of Costco with commentary is presented in Appendix H.) Costco, the fourth-largest retailer in the world, is well known for selling everyday items in bulk. It has stores in Australia, Canada, Iceland, Japan, Mexico, South Korea, the United Kingdom, and the United States. The company entered China in 2019. We set the stage for analyzing Costco's financial performance by first reorganizing its financial statements into operating, nonoperating, and financial items.

EXHIBIT 11.4 **Costco: Balance Sheet**

$ million

Assets	2015	2016	2017	2018	2019
Cash and cash equivalents[1]	6,419	4,729	5,779	7,259	9,444
Receivables, net	1,224	1,252	1,432	1,669	1,535
Merchandise inventories	8,908	8,969	9,834	11,040	11,395
Deferred income taxes[2]	521	—	—	—	—
Other current assets	227	268	272	321	1,111
Total current assets	17,299	15,218	17,317	20,289	23,485
Property, plant, and equipment	15,401	17,043	18,161	19,681	20,890
Deferred income taxes[2]	109	202	254	316	398
Other assets	631	700	615	544	627
Total assets	33,440	33,163	36,347	40,830	45,400
Liabilities and shareholders' equity					
Accounts payable	9,011	7,612	9,608	11,237	11,679
Accrued salaries and benefits	2,468	2,629	2,703	2,994	3,176
Accrued member awards	813	869	961	1,057	1,180
Deferred membership fees	1,269	1,362	1,498	1,624	1,711
Current portion of long-term debt	1,283	1,100	86	90	1,699
Current portion of capital leases[3]	10	10	7	7	26
Other current liabilities	1,686	1,993	2,632	2,917	3,766
Total current liabilities	16,540	15,575	17,495	19,926	23,237
Long-term debt	4,864	4,061	6,573	6,487	5,124
Capital leases[3]	286	364	373	390	395
Deferred income taxes[2]	462	297	312	317	543
Other liabilities	445	534	515	607	517
Total liabilities	22,597	20,831	25,268	27,727	29,816
Costco shareholders' equity	10,617	12,079	10,778	12,799	15,243
Noncontrolling interests	226	253	301	304	341
Total shareholders' equity	10,843	12,332	11,079	13,103	15,584
Liabilities and shareholders' equity	33,440	33,163	36,347	40,830	45,400

Note: Costco's fiscal year ends on the Sunday nearest August 31. For example, FY 2019 ended on September 1, 2019.

[1] Includes short-term investments.

[2] Deferred taxes are aggregated in other current assets, other assets, and other liabilities in original filings.

[3] Capital leases are aggregated in other current liabilities and other liabilities in original filings.

Invested Capital: In Practice

To compute invested capital, we reorganize the company's balance sheet. Exhibit 11.4 presents historical balance sheets for Costco, whose fiscal year ends on the Sunday nearest August 31. The version presented is slightly more detailed than the balance sheets reported in Costco's annual reports, because we have searched the notes in each annual report for information about accounts that mix operating and nonoperating items. For instance, the notes in

Costco's 2019 annual report reveal that the company aggregates capital leases in other liabilities. Since capital leases are a form of debt and must be treated as such, the balance sheet in its original form would be unusable for valuation purposes.

Invested capital combines operating working capital (current operating assets minus current operating liabilities), fixed assets (net property, plant, and equipment), net other long-term operating assets (net of long-term operating liabilities), and when appropriate, intangible assets (goodwill, acquired intangibles, and capitalized software). Exhibit 11.5 demonstrates this line-by-line aggregation for Costco. In the following subsections, we examine each element in detail.

Operating Working Capital   Operating working capital represents operating current assets minus operating current liabilities. Operating current assets comprise all current assets necessary for the operation of the business, including working cash balances, trade accounts receivable, inventory, and prepaid expenses. Specifically *excluded* are excess cash and marketable securities—that is, cash greater than the operating needs of the business.[1] Excess cash generally represents temporary imbalances in the company's cash position. We discuss this later in this section.[2]

Operating current liabilities include those liabilities that are related to the ongoing operations of the firm. The most common operating liabilities are those related to suppliers (accounts payable), employees (accrued salaries), customers (as either prepayments or, in the case of Costco, deferred membership fees), and the government (income taxes payable).[3] If a liability is deemed operating rather than financial, it should be netted from operating assets to determine invested capital and consequently incorporated into free cash flow. Interest-bearing liabilities are nonoperating and should *not* be netted from operating assets, but rather valued separately (the related interest expense is classified as a nonoperating expense).

Some argue that operating liabilities, such as accounts payable, are a form of financing and should be treated no differently than debt. However, this

---

[1] Analyze excess cash separately from operating working capital for two reasons. First, excess cash is more accurately valued using a market value rather than as part of free cash flow. Second, excess cash will have a much lower risk–return profile than operating capital. Commingling assets with different risk profiles can distort your perception of performance.

[2] In a company's financial statements, accountants often distinguish between cash and marketable securities, but not between working cash and excess cash. We provide guidance on distinguishing working cash from excess cash later in this chapter.

[3] When analyzing Costco, we treat accrued member rewards as an operating-related current liability and thus part of working capital. While we believe accrued member rewards are no different from other customer prepayments, the member is not paying cash specifically for the reward. One alternative is to use cash accounting for accrued member rewards, treating the liability as an equity equivalent. To convert to cash, add the increase in accrued member rewards to EBITA. Since taxes will not change, compute taxes using original EBITA.

EXHIBIT 11.5 **Costco: Invested Capital and Total Funds Invested**

$ million

	2015	2016	2017	2018	2019
Operating cash[1]	2,324	2,374	2,581	2,832	3,054
Receivables, net	1,224	1,252	1,432	1,669	1,535
Merchandise Inventories	8,908	8,969	9,834	11,040	11,395
Other current assets	227	268	272	321	1,111
Operating current assets	12,683	12,863	14,119	15,862	17,095
Accounts payable	(9,011)	(7,612)	(9,608)	(11,237)	(11,679)
Accrued salaries and benefits	(2,468)	(2,629)	(2,703)	(2,994)	(3,176)
Accrued member awards	(813)	(869)	(961)	(1,057)	(1,180)
Deferred membership fees	(1,269)	(1,362)	(1,498)	(1,624)	(1,711)
Other current liabilities	(1,686)	(1,993)	(2,632)	(2,917)	(3,766)
Operating current liabilities	(15,247)	(14,465)	(17,402)	(19,829)	(21,512)
Operating working capital	(2,564)	(1,602)	(3,284)	(3,967)	(4,417)
Property, plant, and equipment	15,401	17,043	18,161	19,681	20,890
Capitalized operating leases[2]	2,230	2,320	2,528	2,500	2,414
Other assets[3]	631	700	615	544	627
Other liabilities[3]	(445)	(534)	(515)	(607)	(517)
Invested capital	15,253	17,928	17,506	18,151	18,997
Excess cash[1]	4,095	2,355	3,199	4,427	6,390
Foreign tax credit carryforward[4]	—	—	—	—	65
Total funds invested	19,348	20,282	20,704	22,578	25,452
Reconciliation of total funds invested					
Long-term debt and capital leases[5]	6,443	5,535	7,039	6,974	7,244
Capitalized operating leases[2]	2,230	2,320	2,528	2,500	2,414
Debt and debt equivalents	8,673	7,855	9,567	9,474	9,658
Deferred income taxes, operating[4]	(61)	158	76	(39)	120
Deferred income taxes, nonoperating[4]	(107)	(63)	(18)	40	90
Noncontrolling interests	226	253	301	304	341
Costco shareholders' equity	10,617	12,079	10,778	12,799	15,243
Equity and equity equivalents	10,675	12,427	11,137	13,104	15,794
Total funds invested	19,348	20,282	20,704	22,578	25,452

[1] Operating cash estimated at 2% of revenues. Remaining cash is treated as excess cash.

[2] Capitalized operating leases are estimated for 2019 in Exhibit 22.10.

[3] Other assets and liabilities are classified as operating because no description is provided by the company.

[4] Foreign tax credit carryforward and other deferred taxes are reported in Exhibit 11.7.

[5] Includes current portion.

would lead to a definition of NOPAT that is inconsistent with invested capital. NOPAT is the income available to both debt and equity holders, so when you are determining ROIC, you should divide NOPAT by debt plus equity. Although a supplier may charge customers implicit interest for the right to pay in 30 days, the charge is an indistinguishable part of the price, and hence an indistinguishable and inseparable part of the cost of goods sold. Since cost of goods sold is subtracted from revenue to determine NOPAT, operating liabilities must be subtracted from operating assets to determine invested capital. A theoretical but cumbersome alternative would be to treat accounts payable as debt and adjust NOPAT for the implicit interest cost.

Property, Plant, Equipment, and Other Capitalized Investments   Include the book value of property, plant, and equipment net of accumulated depreciation in operating assets. Book value measures the company's ability to create value on past investments. Use market value or replacement cost only when evaluating the sale or replacement of a specific asset.

Some companies, including IBM and UPS, have significant investments in software they have developed for internal use. Under certain restrictions, these investments can be capitalized on the balance sheet rather than immediately expensed. Although it is labeled as an intangible asset, treat capitalized software no differently than property and equipment; treat amortization as if it were depreciation; and treat investments in capitalized software as if they were capital expenditures. (The cash flow statement in the IBM annual report separates investment in software from investment in PP&E. In contrast, UPS combines the two accounts within capital expenditures. In this case, attributing reported capitalized expenditures entirely to PP&E would overstate the actual investment.) Only internally generated intangible assets, and not acquired intangibles, should be treated in this manner. Acquired intangibles require special care and are discussed in a later subsection in this chapter.

Other Operating Assets, Net of Liabilities   If other long-term assets and liabilities are small—and not detailed by the company—we typically assume they are operating. To determine net other long-term operating assets, subtract other long-term liabilities from other long-term assets. This figure should be included as part of invested capital. If, however, other long-term assets and liabilities are relatively large, you will need to disaggregate each account into its operating and nonoperating components before you can calculate other long-term operating assets, net of other liabilities.

For instance, a relatively large other long-term assets account might include nonoperating items such as deferred-tax assets, prepaid pension assets, nonconsolidated subsidiaries, or other equity investments. Nonoperating items should not be included in invested capital. Classifying assets as operating or nonoperating requires judgment, especially for obscure accounts. For instance, we treat restricted cash as operating when cash must be set aside to secure third-party guarantees, as is the case with distressed airlines that accept credit card payments with payment insurance. As a helpful guidepost, operating assets typically scale with revenues.

Long-term liabilities might similarly include operating and nonoperating items. Operating liabilities are liabilities that result directly from an ongoing operating activity. For instance, one manufacturer records long-term customer advances within other liabilities. In general, however, most long-term liabilities are not operating liabilities, but rather what we deem debt and equity equivalents. These include unfunded pension liabilities, unfunded postretirement medical costs, restructuring reserves, and deferred taxes.

Where can you find a breakdown of other assets and other liabilities in the annual report? In some cases, companies provide a comprehensive table in the footnotes. Most of the time, however, you must work through the footnotes, note by note, searching for items aggregated within other assets and liabilities.

Goodwill and Acquired Intangibles   In Chapter 12, return on invested capital is analyzed both with and without goodwill and acquired intangibles. ROIC with goodwill and acquired intangibles measures a company's ability to create value after paying acquisition premiums. ROIC without goodwill and acquired intangibles measures the competitiveness of the underlying business. For example, our colleagues studied the return on capital for large consumer packaged-goods companies from 1963 through 2009. What they found was intriguing. From the 1960s through the mid-1980s, the median ROIC without goodwill of these companies was consistently in the mid-teens. ROIC with goodwill was only slightly lower. Then, beginning in the mid-1980s, the companies were able to use the power of their brands to increase their ROIC without goodwill to a median of almost 35 percent. At the same time, they also stepped up their acquisition activity. Their median ROIC including goodwill remained in the mid to high teens. By 2009, the gap between the ROIC with goodwill and ROIC without goodwill was 17 percentage points. When you are analyzing the performance of a company, it's critical to understand ROIC with and without goodwill.

To evaluate the effect of goodwill and acquired intangibles properly, you should make two adjustments. First, subtract deferred-tax liabilities related to the amortization of acquired intangibles.[4] Why? When amortization is not tax deductible, accountants create a deferred-tax liability at the time of the acquisition that is drawn down over the amortization period (since reported taxes will be lower than actual taxes). To counterbalance the liability, acquired intangibles are artificially increased by a corresponding amount, even though no cash is laid out. Subtracting deferred taxes related to acquired intangibles eliminates this distortion. For companies with significant acquired intangibles—for example, Coca-Cola—the adjustment can be substantial.

Second, add back cumulative amortization and impairment. Unlike other fixed assets, goodwill and acquired intangibles do not wear out, nor are they replaceable. Therefore, you need to adjust reported goodwill and acquired

---

[4] Since goodwill is tested regularly for impairment and cannot be amortized, this issue relates only to acquired intangibles.

intangibles upward to recapture historical impairments of goodwill and amortization of intangibles. (To maintain consistency, do not deduct impairments of goodwill or amortization of acquired intangibles from revenues to determine NOPAT. This is why NOPAT starts with EBITA.)

Consider FedEx, which wrote down approximately $900 million in goodwill and acquired intangibles when it converted the acquired brand name Kinko's to FedEx Office. Failing to add back this impairment would have caused a large artificial jump in return on invested capital following the write-down. The money spent on an acquisition is real and needs to be accounted for, even when the investment loses value.

Computing Total Funds Invested

Invested capital represents the capital necessary to operate a company's core business. In addition to invested capital, companies can also own nonoperating assets. The combination of invested capital and nonoperating assets leads to total funds invested. Nonoperating assets include excess cash and marketable securities, receivables from financial subsidiaries (for example, credit card receivables), nonconsolidated subsidiaries, overfunded pension assets, and tax loss carry-forwards. Costco has two nonoperating assets: excess cash and foreign tax credit carryforwards.

There are two reasons to diligently separate operating and nonoperating assets. First, nonoperating assets can distort performance measures for both economic and accounting reasons. For example, many nonoperating assets generate income, but companies do not report the income unless certain ownership thresholds are met. Including an asset without its corresponding income distorts performance measurements. Second, there are better methods than discounted cash flow to value nonoperating assets. You would never discount interest income to value excess cash. For this asset, the book value suffices.

Now let's examine the most common nonoperating assets.

Excess Cash and Marketable Securities   Do not include excess cash in invested capital. By its definition, excess cash is unnecessary for core operations. Rather than mix excess cash with core operations, analyze and value excess cash separately. Given its liquidity and low risk, excess cash will earn very small returns. Failing to separate excess cash from core operations will incorrectly depress the company's apparent ROIC.

Companies do not disclose how much cash they deem necessary for operations. Nor does the accounting definition of cash versus marketable securities distinguish working cash from excess cash. Based on past analysis, companies with the smallest cash balances held cash just below 2 percent of sales. If this is a good proxy for working cash, any cash above 2 percent should be considered excess.[5] In 2019, Costco held just under $9.5 billion in cash and marketable securities on $152.7 billion in revenue. At 2 percent of revenue, operating cash equals $3.1 billion. The remaining cash of $6.4 billion is treated as excess. Exhibit 11.5 separates operating cash from excess cash. Excess cash is not included in invested capital, but rather is treated as a non-operating asset.

Nonconsolidated Subsidiaries and Equity Investments Nonconsolidated subsidiaries, also referred to as investments in associates, investments in affiliated companies, and equity investments, should be measured and valued separately from invested capital. When a company owns a minority stake in another company, it will record the investment as a single line item on the balance sheet and will not record the individual assets owned by the subsidiary. On the income statement, only the net income from the subsidiary will be recorded on the parent's income statement, not the subsidiary's revenues or costs. Since only net income—not revenue—is recorded, including nonconsolidated subsidiaries as part of operations will distort margins and capital turnover. Therefore, we recommend separating nonconsolidated subsidiaries from invested capital and analyzing and valuing nonconsolidated subsidiaries separately from core operations.

Financial Subsidiaries Some companies, including General Motors and Siemens, have financing subsidiaries that finance customer purchases. Because these subsidiaries charge interest on financing for purchases, they resemble banks. Since bank economics are quite different from those of manufacturing and service companies, you should separate line items related to the financial subsidiary from the line items for the manufacturing business. Then evaluate the return on capital for each type of business separately. Otherwise, significant distortions of performance will make a meaningful comparison with competitors impossible. For more on how to analyze and assess financial subsidiaries, see Chapter 19.

Overfunded Pension Assets If a company runs a defined-benefit pension plan for its employees, it must fund the plan each year. And if a company funds its plan faster than its pension expenses dictate or assets grow faster than expected, under U.S. Generally Accepted Accounting Principles (GAAP) and International Accounting/Financial Reporting Standards (IAS/IFRS) the

---

[5] This aggregate figure, however, is not a rule. Required cash holdings vary by industry. For instance, one study found that companies in industries with higher cash flow volatility hold higher cash balances. To assess the minimum cash needed to support operations, look for a minimum clustering of cash to revenue across the industry. To better understand the reason behind significant cash holdings in a historical context, see J. Graham and M. Leary, "The Evolution of Corporate Cash," SSRN working paper (May 25, 2018).

company can recognize a portion of the excess assets on the balance sheet. Pension assets are considered a nonoperating asset and not part of invested capital. Their value is important to the equity holder, so they will be valued later, but separately from core operations. Chapter 23 examines pension assets in detail.

Tax Loss Carryforwards   Unless they are small and grow consistently with revenue, do not include tax loss carryforwards—also known as net operating losses (NOLs)—as part of invested capital. Depending on the type of deferred-tax asset, it will be valued either separately or as part of operating cash taxes. Given the complexity of reorganizing deferred taxes, we discuss them in more detail later in this chapter, in the subsection titled "Equity Equivalents Such as Deferred Taxes."

Other Nonoperating Assets   Other nonoperating assets, such as derivatives, excess real estate, and discontinued operations, also should be excluded from invested capital. For Costco, derivatives were disclosed in the footnotes but were immaterial, so no adjustments were made to the balance sheet accounts.

Reconciling Total Funds Invested

Total funds invested can be calculated as invested capital plus nonoperating assets, as in the previous section, or as the sum of debt, equity, and their equivalents. The totals produced by the two approaches should reconcile. A summary of sources of financing appears in Exhibit 11.6. We next examine each of these sources of capital contributing to total funds invested.

EXHIBIT 11.6 **Sources of Financing**

Source of capital	Description
Debt	Interest-bearing debt from banks and public capital markets
Debt equivalents	Off-balance-sheet debt and one-time debts owed to others that are not part of ongoing operations (e.g., severance payments as part of a restructuring, an unfunded pension liability, or expected environmental remediation following a plant closure)
Equity	Common stock, additional paid-in capital, retained earnings, and accumulated other comprehensive income
Equity equivalents	Balance sheet accounts that arise because of noncash adjustments to retained earnings; similar to debt equivalents but not deducted from enterprise value to determine equity value (e.g., most deferred-tax accounts and income-smoothing provisions)
Hybrid securities	Claims that have equity characteristics but are not yet part of owners' equity (e.g., convertible debt and employee options)
Noncontrolling interest by other companies	External shareholders' minority position in any of the company's consolidated subsidiaries

Debt   Debt includes all short-term or long-term interest-bearing liabilities. Short-term debt includes commercial paper, notes payable, and the current portion of long-term debt. Long-term debt includes fixed debt, floating debt, and convertible debt with maturities of more than a year.

Debt Equivalents Such as Retirement Liabilities and Restructuring Reserves   If a company's defined-benefit plan is underfunded, it must recognize the underfunding as a liability. The amount of underfunding is not an operating liability. Rather, treat unfunded pension liabilities and unfunded postretirement medical liabilities as a debt equivalent (and treat the net interest expense associated with these liabilities as nonoperating). It is as if the company must borrow money to fund the plan. As an example, UPS announced in 2012 that it would withdraw from a multiemployer pension fund. To be released from its obligations to the fund, UPS promised to pay $43 million per year for 50 years. This fixed repayment promise, an obligation with seniority to equity claims, is no different from traditional debt.

We discuss other debt equivalents, such as reserves for plant decommissioning and restructuring reserves, in Chapter 21.

Equity   Equity includes original investor funds, such as common stock and additional paid-in capital, as well as investor funds reinvested into the company, such as retained earnings and accumulated other comprehensive income (OCI). In the United States, accumulated OCI consists primarily of currency adjustments, aggregate unrealized gains and losses from liquid assets whose value has changed but that have not yet been sold, and pension plan fluctuations within a certain band. IFRS also includes accumulated OCI within shareholders' equity but reports each reserve separately. Any stock repurchased and held in the treasury should be deducted from total equity. In Exhibit 11.5, we consolidate these accounts into a single account titled shareholders' equity.

Equity Equivalents Such as Deferred Taxes   Equity equivalents are balance sheet accounts that arise because of noncash adjustments to retained earnings. Equity equivalents are like debt equivalents; they differ only in that they are not deducted from enterprise value to determine equity value.

The most common equity equivalent, deferred taxes, arises from differences in how businesses and the government account for taxes. For instance, the government typically uses accelerated depreciation to determine a company's taxes, whereas the accounting statements are prepared using straight-line depreciation. This leads to cash taxes that are lower than reported taxes during the early years of an asset's life. For growing companies, this difference will cause reported taxes consistently to overstate the company's actual tax payments. To avoid this bias, use cash-based (versus accrual) taxes to determine NOPAT. Since reported taxes will now match cash taxes on the income statement, the

EXHIBIT 11.7 **Costco: Reorganized Deferred Taxes**

$ million

	As reported				Reorganized		
	2017	2018	2019		2017	2018	2019
Deferred-tax assets				**Operating deferred-tax assets, net of liabilities**			
Equity compensation	109	72	74	Equity compensation	109	72	74
Deferred income/membership fees	167	136	180	Deferred income/membership fees	167	136	180
Foreign tax credit carryforward	—	—	65	Accrued liabilities and reserves	647	484	566
Accrued liabilities and reserves	647	484	566	Property and equipment	(747)	(478)	(677)
Other	18	—	—	Merchanise inventories	(252)	(175)	(187)
Total deferred-tax assets	941	692	885	Valuation allowance	—	—	(76)
				Operating deferred-tax assets, net of liabilities	(76)	39	(120)
Valuation allowance	—	—	(76)				
Total net deferred-tax assets	941	692	809	**Nonoperating deferred-tax assets, net of liabilities**			
				Other assets	18	—	—
Deferred-tax liabilities				Foreign branch deferreds	—	—	(69)
Propery and equipment	(747)	(478)	(677)	Other liabilities	—	(40)	(21)
Merchandise inventories	(252)	(175)	(187)	Nonoperating deferred-tax assets, net of liabilities	18	(40)	(90)
Foreign branch deferreds	—	—	(69)				
Other	—	(40)	(21)	**Tax loss carryforwards**			
Total deferred-tax liabilities	(999)	(693)	(954)	Foreign tax credit carryforward	—	—	65
Deferred-tax assets, net of liabilities	(58)	(1)	(145)	Deferred-tax assets, net of liabilities	(58)	(1)	(145)

deferred-tax account—in this case related to accelerated depreciation—is no longer necessary. This is why the deferred-tax account is referred to as an equity equivalent. It represents the adjustment to retained earnings that would be made if the company reported cash taxes to investors instead of accrual taxes.

Not every deferred-tax account is operating. Although both operating and nonoperating deferred-tax accounts are equity equivalents, incorporate only deferred-tax accounts associated with ongoing operations into operating cash taxes.[6] In contrast, value nonoperating deferred taxes as part of the corresponding account.[7] For instance, when valuing an underfunded pension, do not use the book value of deferred taxes to value potential tax savings. Instead, reduce the underfunding by the projected taxes likely to be saved when the plan is funded.

Exhibit 11.7 converts deferred-tax assets and liabilities for Costco into operating, nonoperating, and tax loss carryforwards, using the tax footnote in the company's annual report. Although individual operating-related accounts, such as accrued liabilities and reserves, are large, the net amount is close to zero. For this reason, operating cash taxes for Costco will not differ significantly from accrual-based taxes.

[6] Separating deferred taxes into operating and nonoperating items can be challenging and often requires advanced knowledge of accounting conventions. For an in-depth discussion of deferred taxes, see Chapter 20.

[7] As discussed earlier, deferred-tax assets related to past losses should be classified as a nonoperating asset and valued separately. Deferred-tax liabilities related to amortization of acquired intangibles should be netted against acquired intangibles. These accounts are not equity equivalents.

Hybrid Securities and Noncontrolling Interests   Some sources of financing resist easy classification as debt or equity. These include hybrid securities and noncontrolling interests. Unlike debt, these accounts do not have fixed interest payments. Unlike equity, they are not the residual claim on cash flows. Therefore, these accounts should be valued separately and deducted from enterprise value to determine equity value.

- *Hybrid securities.* The three most common hybrid securities are convertible debt, preferred stock, and employee options. Since hybrid securities contain embedded options, they cannot be treated as common stock. Instead, use the market price or, if necessary, option-pricing models to value these claims separately. Failing to do so can undervalue the hybrid security and overstate the value of common stock. This is especially important for venture-capital-backed preferred stock and long-dated employee options.
- *Noncontrolling interests.* A noncontrolling interest occurs when a third party owns a minority holding in one of the company's consolidated subsidiaries. If a noncontrolling interest exists, treat the balance sheet amount as a source of financing. Treat the earnings attributable to any noncontrolling interest as a financing cash flow similar to dividends. If data are available, value the subsidiary separately, and deduct the noncontrolling interest from the company's enterprise value to determine equity value. If data for the subsidiary are available, discount earnings related to the noncontrolling interest at an appropriate cost of equity. Chapter 16 presents various valuation methodologies for noncontrolling interests.

Correctly classifying balance sheet items can be a daunting task. But fret not: perfect classification is not required. You need only to assure that each account is included as part of free cash flow or valued separately.

Calculating NOPAT

To determine NOPAT for Costco, we turn to the income statement (see Exhibit 11.8) and convert it into NOPAT, as shown in Exhibit 11.9.

Net Operating Profit (EBITA)   NOPAT starts with earnings before interest, taxes, and amortization (EBITA) of acquired intangibles, which equals revenue minus operating expenses, such as cost of goods sold, selling costs, general and administrative costs, and depreciation.

Why use EBITA and not EBITDA? When a company purchases a physical asset such as equipment, it capitalizes the asset on the balance sheet and depreciates the asset over its lifetime. Since the asset wears out over time,

EXHIBIT 11.8 **Costco: Income Statement**

$ million

	2015	2016	2017	2018	2019
Merchandise sales	113,666	116,073	126,172	138,434	149,351
Membership fees	2,533	2,646	2,853	3,142	3,352
Revenues	116,199	118,719	129,025	141,576	152,703
Merchandise costs	(101,065)	(102,901)	(111,882)	(123,152)	(132,886)
Selling, general, and administrative	(10,318)	(10,813)	(11,580)	(12,439)	(13,502)
Depreciation[1]	(1,127)	(1,255)	(1,370)	(1,437)	(1,492)
Preopening expenses	(65)	(78)	(82)	(68)	(86)
Operating income	3,624	3,672	4,111	4,480	4,737
Interest expense	(124)	(133)	(134)	(159)	(150)
Interest income	50	41	50	75	126
Other income	54	39	12	46	52
Earnings before taxes	3,604	3,619	4,039	4,442	4,765
Provision for income taxes	(1,195)	(1,243)	(1,325)	(1,263)	(1,061)
Net income, consolidated	2,409	2,376	2,714	3,179	3,704
Net income, noncontrolling interests	(32)	(26)	(35)	(45)	(45)
Net income, Costco	2,377	2,350	2,679	3,134	3,659

[1] Aggregated in selling, general, and administrative expenses in original filings.

any measure of profit (and return) must recognize this loss in value. While depreciation does not match the periodic loss in value perfectly, it is a suitable proxy.

Why use EBITA and not EBIT? After all, the same argument could be made for the amortization of acquired intangibles: they, too, have fixed lives and lose value over time. But the accounting for intangibles differs from the accounting for physical assets. Unlike capital expenditures, internally created intangible assets such as new customer lists and product brands are *expensed* and not capitalized. Thus, when the acquired intangible loses value and is replaced through additional investment internally, the reinvestment is *already* expensed, and the company is penalized twice in the same time period: once through amortization and a second time through reinvestment. Although not perfect, using EBITA is consistent with existing accounting rules.

Choosing which line items to include as operating expenses requires judgment. As a guiding principle, include ongoing expenses related to the company's core operations. One company we recently analyzed included rationalizations as part of operating expenses. Since rationalizations had been a consistent part of the company's expense structure and are likely to continue as the industry continues to mature, we kept them as operating expenses. Had they been a one-time expense, we would not have included them in EBITA.

EXHIBIT 11.9 **Costco: NOPAT and Its Reconciliation to Net Income**

$ million

	2015	2016	2017	2018	2019
Revenue	116,199	118,719	129,025	141,576	152,703
Merchandise costs	(101,065)	(102,901)	(111,882)	(123,152)	(132,886)
Selling, general, and administrative	(10,318)	(10,813)	(11,580)	(12,439)	(13,502)
Depreciation	(1,127)	(1,255)	(1,370)	(1,437)	(1,492)
Preopening expenses	(65)	(78)	(82)	(68)	(86)
EBITA, unadjusted[1]	3,624	3,672	4,111	4,480	4,737
Operating lease interest[2]	73	75	57	74	91
EBITA, adjusted	3,697	3,747	4,168	4,554	4,828
Operating cash taxes[3]	(1,184)	(1,149)	(1,493)	(1,455)	(1,009)
NOPAT	2,513	2,598	2,675	3,098	3,818
Reconciliation to net income					
Net income, consolidated	2,409	2,376	2,714	3,179	3,704
Operating taxes deferred[3]	7	219	(82)	(115)	159
Adjusted net income	2,416	2,595	2,632	3,064	3,863
Interest expense	124	133	134	159	150
Operating lease interest[2]	73	75	57	74	91
Interest income	(50)	(41)	(50)	(75)	(126)
Other income[4]	(54)	(39)	(12)	(46)	(52)
Taxes related to nonoperating accounts[5]	(35)	(48)	(49)	(32)	(15)
Other nonoperating taxes[3]	39	(77)	(37)	(45)	(92)
NOPAT	2,513	2,598	2,675	3,098	3,818

[1] Earnings before interest, taxes, and amortization.

[2] Operating lease interest is estimated in Exhibit 11.15.

[3] Operating cash taxes and other nonoperating taxes are detailed in Exhibit 11.11.

[4] Other income consists primarily of foreign-currency transaction gains and treated as nonoperating for simplicity of exposition.

[5] Estimated by multiplying the statutory tax rate by the sum of interest and operating lease interest expense, less the sum of interest and other income. The statutory tax rate is reported in Exhibit 11.10.

Adjustments to EBITA   In many companies, nonoperating items are embedded within operating expenses. To ensure that your EBITA calculation flows solely from operations, dig through the notes to weed out nonoperating items from operating expenses. The most common nonoperating items are related to pensions, embedded interest expenses from operating leases, and one-time restructuring charges hidden in the cost of sales.

In Exhibit 11.9, we adjust operating profit for operating lease interest. Since Costco does not offer defined-benefit retirement plans, no adjustment was made for the nonoperating portion of pension expense. The comprehensive processes for operating leases and pensions are addressed at the end of this chapter and in Part Three of this book, which covers advanced valuation issues.

No other adjustments were required, as Costco did not embed material one-time items in operating expenses. Although not common, it can happen.

EXHIBIT 11.10 **Costco: Tax Reconciliation Table**

$ million

	2015	2016	2017	2018	2019
Federal taxes at statutory rate	1,262	1,267	1,414	1,136	1,001
State taxes, net	85	91	116	154	171
Foreign taxes, net	(125)	(21)	(64)	32	(1)
Employee stock ownership plan (ESOP)	(66)	(17)	(104)	(14)	(18)
2017 tax act	—	—	—	19	(123)
Other	39	(77)	(37)	(64)	31
U.S. and foreign tax expense (benefit)	1,195	1,243	1,325	1,263	1,061
Tax rates[1]					
Federal income tax rate, %	35.0	35.0	35.0	25.6	21.0
State income tax rate, %	2.4	2.5	2.9	3.5	3.6
Statutory tax rate, %	37.4	37.5	37.9	29.0	24.6

[1] To determine each tax rate, divide each tax amount by earnings before taxes. Earnings before taxes are reported in Exhibit 11.8.

Source: Reported in Costco's annual report, note 8: Income Taxes.

UPS's decision to withdraw from a multiemployer pension plan in 2012 caused its compensation and benefits expense to spike that year. Since the withdrawal was a one-time event, it is better evaluated separately as a nonoperating expense and not embedded in operating income. Choosing whether an expense is one-time or ongoing requires judgment. Separating one-time items from ongoing expenses, however, highlights trends and opens the valuation discussion to future risks.

Operating Cash Taxes   Since many nonoperating items affect income taxes, they also must be adjusted to an all-equity operating level. The process for adjusting taxes is the most complicated part of reorganizing the financial statements. Chapter 20 goes into more detail about the specifics of the process, the reasoning behind it, and alternative ways to implement it. For now, we summarize the process.

To determine operating taxes, you will need the tax reconciliation table from the company's notes. Some companies report the tax reconciliation table in percent; others report the table in currency. In Chapter 20, we present how to estimate operating taxes using both reporting styles. Exhibit 11.10 presents the tax reconciliation table for Costco.

To estimate operating cash taxes, proceed in three steps:

1. Using the tax reconciliation table, determine the statutory tax rate. The statutory tax rate equals the government tax rate paid on income. Multiply the statutory tax rate by adjusted EBITA to determine statutory taxes on adjusted EBITA.

2. Increase (or decrease) statutory taxes on EBITA by other operating taxes (or credits). To estimate other operating taxes, search the tax reconciliation table for ongoing, operating-related taxes other than statutory taxes. The most

EXHIBIT 11.11 **Costco: Taxes**

$ million

	2015	2016	2017	2018	2019
EBITA	3,697	3,747	4,168	4,554	4,828
× Statutory tax rate[1]	37.4%	37.5%	37.9%	29.0%	24.6%
Statutory taxes on EBITA	1,382	1,406	1,579	1,322	1,187
Foreign taxes, net[2]	(125)	(21)	(64)	32	(1)
Employee stock ownership plan (ESOP)[2]	(66)	(17)	(104)	(14)	(18)
Operating taxes	1,191	1,368	1,411	1,340	1,168
Operating taxes deferred[3]	(7)	(219)	82	115	(159)
Operating cash taxes	1,184	1,149	1,493	1,455	1,009
Reported taxes					
Operating taxes	1,191	1,368	1,411	1,340	1,168
Taxes related to nonoperating accounts[4]	(35)	(48)	(49)	(32)	(15)
Other nonoperating taxes[5]	39	(77)	(37)	(45)	(92)
Income taxes, reported	1,195	1,243	1,325	1,263	1,061

[1] Estimated by dividing federal plus state income taxes by earnings before taxes.

[2] Reported in the tax reconciliation table presented in Exhibit 11.10.

[3] Computed as the increase (decrease) in operating deferred tax assets, net of liabilities. Operating deferred taxes are reported in Exhibit 11.7.

[4] Estimated in Exhibit 11.9.

[5] Other nonoperating taxes include taxes related to the 2017 tax act and other taxes, reported in Exhibit 11.10.

common operating tax is the difference between domestic and foreign tax rates. Sum the other rates deemed operating, and if the table is presented in percent, multiply the resulting summation of by earnings before taxes (EBT). Multiplying the percentages by EBT (not EBITA) converts the percentages found in the tax reconciliation table into a dollar-based adjustment.[8]

3. Convert accrual-based taxes into operating cash taxes. For companies that systematically defer taxes, accrual-based taxes will not properly represent cash taxes actually paid. The simplest way to calculate operating cash taxes is to subtract the increase in operating deferred-tax liabilities (net of assets) from operating taxes. While the notes provide information on taxes that have been deferred, they do not separate operating from nonoperating deferred taxes, making the disclosure unusable. Not every company discloses enough information to separate operating deferred taxes, such as accelerated depreciation, from nonoperating deferred taxes, such as those related to prepaid pension assets. When this information is unavailable, we recommend using operating taxes without a cash adjustment.

To demonstrate the three-step process, we construct operating cash taxes for Costco in Exhibit 11.11. In 2019, the statutory tax rate for Costco was 24.6

---

[8] When adjusting statutory taxes on EBITA for other operating items, we prefer to use dollar adjustments rather than percentage adjustments. This is because artificially low earnings before taxes can distort the percentages in a significant way. For instance, when UPS withdrew from the multistate pension plan in 2012, adjustment percentages related to foreign tax savings were uncharacteristically large because of the smaller-than-usual EBT.

percent. This value includes both federal taxes (21.0 percent) and state taxes (3.6 percent). To determine statutory taxes on EBITA, multiply the statutory tax rate (24.6 percent) by EBITA ($4,828 million), which was estimated in Exhibit 11.9. In 2019, statutory taxes on EBITA were $1,187 million.

Next, search the tax reconciliation table for other operating taxes. We classify foreign income taxed at rates different from the U.S. statutory rate ($1 million) and tax savings from the employee stock ownership plan ($18 million) as operating. In contrast, taxes related to the substantial change in U.S. corporate tax rates brought about by the 2017 Tax Cuts and Jobs Act are a one-time event. Therefore, treat them as nonoperating. To determine other operating taxes, sum across operating-related tax adjustments. In 2019, other operating taxes decreased Costco's taxes on EBITA by $19 million. Summing statutory taxes on EBITA ($1,187 million) and other operating taxes (–$19 million) leads to $1,168 million in operating taxes.

To convert operating taxes into operating cash taxes, add (subtract) the increase in *operating* deferred-tax assets (liabilities). As discussed in the section on invested capital, do not incorporate the change in nonoperating deferred taxes into cash taxes. Instead, value nonoperating deferred taxes as part of your valuation of the corresponding nonoperating account. For instance, future taxes on pension shortfalls should be computed using projected contributions, not on the historical deferred-tax account.

Exhibit 11.7 separates Costco's operating and nonoperating deferred taxes. Since operating deferred-tax assets net of liabilities decreased in 2019, Costco is paying less in cash taxes than reported using accrual accounting. In 2019, operating deferred-tax assets net of liabilities fell by $159 million. Therefore, operating taxes of $1,168 million is reduced by $159 million to estimate operating cash taxes at $1,009 million.[9]

Like other balance sheet accounts, operating deferred-tax accounts rise and fall for reasons other than deferrals, such as acquisitions, divestitures, and revaluations. However, only organic changes in deferred taxes should be included in operating cash taxes, not one-time changes resulting from revaluation or consolidation. For instance, most American companies revalued their 2018 deferred-tax accounts to reflect the 2017 Tax Cuts and Jobs Act. To estimate the organic change in deferred-tax assets and liabilities, estimate what the change would have been if tax rates had remained unchanged. In the case of Costco, the effect was immaterial.

For many companies, a clean measure of operating cash taxes may be impossible to calculate. When this is the case, use operating taxes without converting to cash.

---

[9] In Appendix H, we forecast the operating cash tax rate as part of our valuation of Costco. Since the percentage of Costco's taxes that are deferred is volatile, we use a five-year average to estimate the percentage of operating taxes that are likely to be deferred.

Reconciliation of Reported Taxes   To reconcile NOPAT to net income, it is helpful to first reconcile operating taxes to reported taxes. At the bottom of Exhibit 11.11, we present a reconciliation of reported taxes. The reconciliation includes the taxes related to nonoperating accounts and other nonoperating taxes. Although the two accounts sound similar, they are estimated differently.

The taxes related to nonoperating accounts, which equal –$15 million in 2019, is calculated by multiplying the marginal tax rate by the sum of non-operating accounts reported in the reconciliation of NOPAT to net income presented in Exhibit 11.9. For Costco, nonoperating accounts include interest expense, operating lease interest, interest income, and other income. To determine other nonoperating taxes, search the tax reconciliation table presented in Exhibit 11.10 for nonoperating items, such as one-time audits and write-offs. In the previous section, we classified taxes related to the 2017 Tax Cuts and Jobs Act (–$123 million) and the "other" account ($31 million) as nonoperating. Summing the two equals –$92 million.

Note how the reconciliation ties to the reported income taxes on the income statement presented in Exhibit 11.8. Although reconciliation can be time-consuming, it assures that the modeling has been carried out correctly.

Reconciliation to Net Income

To ensure that the reorganization is accurate, we recommend reconciling net income to NOPAT (see the lower half of Exhibit 11.9). To reconcile NOPAT, start with net income available to both common shareholders and noncontrolling interests, and add back the increase (or subtract the decrease) in operating deferred-tax liabilities. We label this amount adjusted net income.

Next, add any nonoperating charges (or subtract any income) reported by the company, such as interest expense and other nonoperating expenses. After this, include any adjustments that have been made, like adjustments for operating lease interest and, if required, the nonoperating portion of the pension expense. Finally, subtract tax shields on the nonoperating expenses calculated previously and add any nonoperating taxes from the tax reconciliation table. Whether NOPAT is estimated using revenues less expenses or alternatively as net income plus nonoperating items and other adjustments, the result should be identical.

Free Cash Flow: In Practice

This subsection details how to build free cash flow from the reorganized financial statements. For estimating free cash flow, the income statement and balance sheet will not suffice; the statement of shareholders' equity also is required. Exhibit 11.12 presents the statement of shareholders' equity for Costco. This statement reconciles the income statement with the balance sheet and

EXHIBIT 11.12 **Costco: Statement of Shareholders' Equity**

$ million

	2015	2016	2017	2018	2019
Equity, beginning of year	12,303	10,617	12,079	10,778	12,799
Net income	2,377	2,350	2,679	3,134	3,659
Foreign-currency translation adjustment	(1,045)	22	85	(185)	(237)
Comprehensive income	1,332	2,372	2,764	2,949	3,422
Stock-based compensation	394	459	518	547	598
Stock options exercised	69	—	—	—	—
Release of vested restricted stock units	(122)	(146)	(165)	(217)	(272)
Repurchases of common stock	(494)	(477)	(473)	(322)	(247)
Cash dividends declared	(2,865)	(746)	(3,945)	(936)	(1,057)
Equity, end of year	10,617	12,079	10,778	12,799	15,243

presents additional information required to estimate free cash flow and cash flow available to investors. Free cash flow is defined as:

$$FCF = NOPAT + Noncash\ Operating\ Expenses - Investments\ in\ Invested\ Capital$$

Exhibit 11.13 presents the free cash flow calculation for Costco and reconciles free cash flow to cash flow available to investors. To create free cash flow, start with NOPAT and add back noncash expenses, such as depreciation and depletion. From gross cash flow, subtract investments in working capital, capital expenditures, and investments in other long-term assets net of liabilities.

Gross Cash Flow   Gross cash flow represents the cash operating profits that the company generates. It represents the cash available for investment and investor payout without the company having to sell nonoperating assets, such as excess cash, or to raise additional capital. Gross cash flow has two components:

1. *NOPAT.* As previously defined, net operating profit after taxes is the after-tax operating profit available to all investors.
2. *Noncash operating expenses.* Some expenses embedded in NOPAT are noncash and represent the economic decay of past investments. To convert NOPAT into cash flow, add back depreciation, depletion, and amortization of capitalized assets. Only add back amortization deducted from revenues to compute NOPAT, such as the amortization of capitalized software or purchased customer contracts. Do not add back the amortization from acquired intangibles and impairments to NOPAT;

EXHIBIT 11.13 **Costco: Free Cash Flow and Cash Flow to Investors**

$ million

	2016	2017	2018	2019
NOPAT	2,598	2,675	3,098	3,818
Depreciation	1,255	1,370	1,437	1,492
Gross cash flow	3,853	4,045	4,535	5,310
Decrease (increase) in working capital	(962)	1,682	684	449
Less: Capital expenditures[1]	(2,649)	(2,502)	(2,969)	(2,998)
Decrease (increase) in capitalized operating leases	(91)	(208)	28	86
Decrease (increase) in other assets, net of liabilities	20	6	163	(173)
Free cash flow	**171**	**3,083**	**2,441**	**2,675**
Interest income	41	50	75	126
Other income	39	12	46	52
Taxes related to nonoperating accounts	48	49	32	15
Other nonoperating taxes	77	37	45	92
Decrease (increase) in excess cash	1,740	(844)	(1,229)	(1,962)
Decrease (increase) in tax credit carryforward	—	—	—	(65)
Unexplained foreign-currency translation[2]	(226)	99	(173)	60
Cash flow to investors	1,890	2,486	1,238	993
Reconciliation of cash flow to investors				
Interest expense	133	134	159	150
Operating lease interest	75	57	74	91
Decrease (increase) in long-term debt and capital leases	908	(1,504)	65	(270)
Decrease (increase) in capitalized operating leases	(91)	(208)	28	86
Cash flow to debt and debt equivalents	1,025	(1,521)	326	57
Nonoperating deferred income taxes	(44)	(45)	(58)	(50)
Shares issued for stock-based compensation, net[3]	(313)	(353)	(330)	(326)
Repurchases of common stock	477	473	322	247
Dividends	746	3,945	936	1,057
Payments to (investments in) noncontrolling interests[4]	(1)	(13)	42	8
Cash flow to equity and equity equivalents	865	4,007	912	936
Cash flow to investors	1,890	2,486	1,238	993

[1] Capital expenditures are reported on the statement of cash flows.

[2] Foreign-currency translation adjustment, less the portion allocated to the change of property, plant, and equipment; detailed in Exhibit 11.14.

[3] Includes stock-based compensation, stock options exercised, net of the release of vested restricted stock units.

[4] Equals net income to nonconsolidated interests minus (plus) the increase (decrease) in noncontrolling interests.

they were not subtracted from revenue in calculating NOPAT. Another major noncash expense is share-based employee compensation. Do not add back share-based compensation to NOPAT to determine gross cash flow. Since employees have a new claim on cash flows, this claim must be incorporated into the valuation, either as part of cash flow or as a separate calculation. (Share-based employee compensation is discussed in Chapter 16.)

Investments in Invested Capital   To maintain and grow their operations, companies must reinvest a portion of their gross cash flow back into the business. To determine free cash flow, subtract gross investment from gross cash flow. We segment gross investment into five primary areas:

1. *Change in operating working capital.* Growing a business requires investment in operating cash, inventory, and other components of working capital. Operating working capital excludes nonoperating assets, such as excess cash, and financing items, such as short-term debt and dividends payable.

2. *Capital expenditures, net of disposals.* Capital expenditures represent investments in property, plant, and equipment (PP&E), less the book value of any PP&E sold. One way to estimate net capital expenditures is to add depreciation to the increase in net PP&E.[10] Do not estimate capital expenditures by taking the change in gross PP&E. Since gross PP&E drops when companies retire assets, the change in gross PP&E will often understate the actual amount of capital expenditures.

3. *Change in capitalized operating leases.* To keep the definitions of NOPAT, invested capital, ROIC, and free cash flow consistent, include investments in capitalized operating leases in gross investment. Capitalized operating leases are discussed later in the chapter.

4. *Investment in goodwill and acquired intangibles.* For acquired intangible assets, where cumulative amortization has been added back, you can estimate investment by computing the change in net goodwill and acquired intangibles. For intangible assets that are being amortized, use the same method as for determining net capital expenditures (by adding amortization to the increase in net intangibles).

5. *Change in other long-term operating assets, net of long-term liabilities.* Subtract investments in other net operating assets. As with invested capital, do not confuse other long-term operating assets with other long-term nonoperating assets, such as equity investments and excess pension assets. Changes in nonoperating assets need to be evaluated—but should be analyzed separately.

For most assets and liabilities, the year-to-year change in a balance sheet account will suitably approximate net investment. This will not always be the case. Currency translations, acquisitions, write-offs, and accounting changes

---

[10] If possible, use capital expenditures reported in the accounting statement of cash flows, but only after reconciling reported capital expenditures with the change of net PP&E plus depreciation. Capital expenditures can differ from net PP&E plus depreciation because of currency translations (discussed later in this section), acquisitions, and impairments. Acquisitions should be analyzed separately, and impairments should be treated as a nonoperating noncash expense in the income statement.

EXHIBIT 11.14 **Costco: Changes in Property, Plant, and Equipment**

$ million

	2015	2016	2017	2018	2019
Property, plant, and equipment, beginning of year	14,830	15,401	17,043	18,161	19,681
Capital expenditures[1]	2,393	2,649	2,502	2,969	2,998
Depreciation[1]	(1,127)	(1,255)	(1,370)	(1,437)	(1,492)
Currency and unexplained changes[2]	(695)	248	(14)	(12)	(297)
Property, plant, and equipment, end of year	15,401	17,043	18,161	19,681	20,890

[1] Reported in the statement of cash flows.

[2] Calculated as the unexplained difference between beginning and end of year.

also can affect the change in accounts. For example, companies translate for-eign balance sheets into their home currencies, so changes in accounts will capture both true investments (which involve cash) and currency-based re-statements (which are merely accounting adjustments and not the flow of cash into or out of the company). If a particular account is a significant part of cash flow, use the cash flow statement and notes from the annual report to better understand the year-to-year change in the account.

Exhibit 11.14 deconstructs the change in property, plant, and equipment for Costco. Capital expenditures and asset dispositions are reported in the accountant's cash flow statement. To estimate deprecation, start with depre-ciation and amortization from the cash flow statement and, if amortization of acquired intangibles exists, subtract it (it is often found in the note on goodwill and intangible assets). The remaining line items are found in the management discussion and analysis, or when not disclosed, they have been estimated.

It is not always possible to eliminate the currency effects for each line item on the balance sheet. If this is the case, adjust aggregate free cash flow for currency effects using the balance sheet account titled foreign-currency translation, which under U.S. GAAP and IFRS is found within the statement of accumulated other comprehensive income. Unfortunately, the balance sheet account reports the aggregate effect across *all* foreign as-sets and liabilities, not just operating items. If you believe most currency adjustments are related to operating items, add the increase in the cur-rency translation account to determine free cash flow. Consider the situa-tion where inventory is rising on the balance sheet due to currency changes and not investment. To balance the balance sheet, the company increases the currency translation account within equity. Since the increase in in-ventory overstates actual investment in inventory, adding the increase in foreign-currency translation back to free cash flow undoes the negative cash flow caused by currency translation. For Costco, since we adjusted critical accounts one by one, we classify the unexplained currency transla-tions as nonoperating.

Cash Flow Available to Investors

Although not included in free cash flow, cash flows related to nonoperating assets are valuable in their own right. They must be evaluated and valued separately and then added to free cash flow to give the total cash flow available to investors:

$$
\begin{array}{ccc}
\text{Present Value} & \text{Value of} & \text{Total Value} \\
\text{of Company's} \quad + & \text{Nonoperating} \quad = & \text{of} \\
\text{Free Cash Flow} & \text{Assets} & \text{Enterprise}
\end{array}
$$

To reconcile free cash flow with total cash flow available to investors, include the following nonoperating cash flows:

- *Nonoperating income and expenses.* Unless you can net the account against a change in a corresponding asset or liability (because it is noncash), include nonoperating income and expenses in total cash flow available to investors, not in free cash flow.

- *Nonoperating taxes.* Include nonoperating taxes in total cash flow available to investors. Nonoperating taxes include tax shields on nonoperating items and other nonoperating taxes disclosed in the tax reconciliation table.

- *Cash flow related to excess cash and marketable securities.* Subtract the increase (or add the decrease) in excess cash and marketable securities to compute total cash flow available to investors. If the company reports unrecognized gains and losses related to marketable securities in its statement of other comprehensive income, net the gain or loss against the change computed previously.

- *Cash flow from other nonoperating assets.* Repeat the process used for excess cash and marketable securities for other nonoperating assets. When possible, combine nonoperating gains and losses from a particular asset with changes in that nonoperating asset.

Reconciling Cash Flow Available to Investors

Cash flow available to investors should be identical to the company's total financing flow. By modeling cash flow to and from investors, you will catch mistakes otherwise missed. Financial flows include flows related to debt, debt equivalents, and equity:

- *Interest expenses.* Interest from both traditional debt and operating leases should be treated as a financing flow.

- *Debt issues and repayments.* The change in debt represents the net borrowing or repayment on all the company's interest-bearing debt, including short-term debt, long-term debt, and capitalized operating leases. All changes in debt should be included in the reconciliation of total funds invested, not in free cash flow.

- *Change in debt equivalents.* Since accrued pension liabilities and accrued postretirement medical liabilities are considered debt equivalents (see Chapter 23 for more on issues related to pensions and other postretirement benefits), their changes should be treated as a financing flow.[11]

- *Dividends.* Dividends include all cash dividends on common and preferred shares. Dividends paid in stock have no cash effects and should be ignored.

- *Share issues and repurchases.* When new equity is issued or shares are repurchased, four accounts will be affected: common stock, additional paid-in capital, treasury shares, and retained earnings (for shares that are retired). Although different transactions will have varying effects on the individual accounts, only the aggregate matters, not how the individual accounts are affected. Exhibit 11.13 refers to the aggregate change as "Repurchases of common stock."

- *Outflows to nonconsolidated subsidiaries.* Income attributable to nonconsolidated subsidiaries, found at the bottom of the income statement, is a financing flow, similar to dividends.

ADVANCED ISSUES

In this section, we summarize a set of the most common advanced topics in reorganizing a company's financial statements, including nonoperating charges and restructuring reserves, operating leases, pensions, and capitalized research and development (R&D). We provide only a brief summary of these topics here, as each one is discussed in depth in the chapters of Part Three, "Advanced Valuation Techniques."

Nonoperating Charges and Restructuring Reserves   Provisions are noncash expenses that reflect future costs or expected losses. Companies record provisions by reducing current income and setting up a corresponding reserve as a liability (or deducting the amount from the relevant asset).

For the purpose of analyzing and valuing a company, we categorize provisions into one of four types: ongoing operating provisions, long-term operating provisions, nonoperating restructuring provisions, and provisions created for the purpose of smoothing income (transferring income from one period to

---

[11] Pensions will affect many accounts, including the pension expense on the income statement, pension assets, pension liabilities, and deferred taxes. Exhibit 11.16, shown later in this chapter, aggregates each of the pension accounts into a single number for the cash flow statement.

another). Based on the characteristics of each provision, adjust the financial statements to reflect the company's true operating performance:

- *Ongoing operating provisions.* Operating provisions such as product warranties are part of operations. Therefore, deduct the provision from revenue to determine NOPAT, and deduct the corresponding reserve from net operating assets to determine invested capital.
- *Long-term operating provisions.* For certain liabilities, such as expected plant decommissioning costs, deduct the operating portion from revenue to determine NOPAT, and treat the interest portion as nonoperating. Treat the corresponding reserve as a debt equivalent.
- *Nonoperating provisions.* Unless deemed as ongoing, provisions such as one-time restructuring charges related to severance are nonoperating. Treat the expense as nonoperating and the corresponding reserve as a debt equivalent.
- *Income-smoothing provisions.* Classify any provisions identified for the purpose of income smoothing as nonoperating, and their corresponding reserve as an equity equivalent. Since income-smoothing provisions are noncash, they do not affect value.

The process for classifying and properly adjusting for provisions is explained in more detail in Chapter 21.

Operating Leases

Starting in 2019, companies that report under U.S. Generally Accepted Accounting Principles (GAAP) or International Financial Reporting Standards (IFRS) are required to capitalize nearly all asset leases, including short-term ones known as operating leases.[12] Under both standards, the present value of operating lease payments will be recorded on the balance sheet. On the income statement, IFRS allocates operating lease payments to depreciation and interest expense as appropriate, so no adjustment is necessary. For companies using GAAP, the entire lease expense, including embedded interest, is incorporated into other operating expenses like cost of sales. If this is the case, reclassify embedded interest in the lease expense as an interest expense.

Since past statements will not be restated, make sure to adjust them for operating leases to create a like-for-like analysis. To estimate the present value of operating leases prior to adoption of the new standard, search the notes for future rental commitments. Costco reports rental commitments in its note on

---

[12] The International Accounting Standards Board (IASB) published IFRS 16, "Leases," in January 2016, and the Financial Accounting Standards Board (FASB) issued Accounting Standards Update (ASU) 2016-02, "Leases" (Topic 842), in February 2016.

EXHIBIT 11.15 **Costco: Impact of Capitalizing Operating Leases on ROIC**

$ million

	2015	2016	2017	2018	2019
EBITA					
EBITA, using rental expense	3,624	3,672	4,111	4,480	4,737
Implied interest expense[1]	73	75	57	74	91
EBITA, adjusted for operating leases	3,967	3,747	4,168	4,554	4,828
Yield-to-maturity on 10-year AA-rated debt	3.19%	3.36%	2.44%	2.91%	3.63%
Operating cash taxes					
Operating cash taxes, using rental expense	1,156	1,121	1,471	1,434	987
Tax shield on implied interest expense[2]	27	28	21	21	22
Operating cash taxes, adjusted for operating leases	1,184	1,149	1,493	1,455	1,009
NOPAT					
NOPAT, using rental expense	2,468	2,551	2,640	3,046	3,750
After-tax implied interest expense	46	47	35	52	68
NOPAT, adjusted for operating leases	2,513	2,598	2,675	3,098	3,818
Invested capital					
Invested capital, without operating leases	13,023	15,607	14,978	15,651	16,583
Capitalized operating leases[3]	2,230	2,320	2,528	2,500	2,414
Invested capital, including capitalized operating leases	15,253	17,928	17,506	18,151	18,997
ROIC, using beginning-of-year capital					
ROIC, using rental expenses	19.5%	19.6%	16.9%	20.3%	24.0%
ROIC, adjusted for operating leases	16.8%	17.0%	14.9%	17.7%	21.0%

[1] Implied interest is calculated by multiplying the yield-to-maturity of 10-year AA-rated debt by the beginning-of-year capitalized operating leases.

[2] The tax shield on implied interest expense is calculated by multiplying implied interest expense by the statutory tax rate. The statutory tax rate is reported in Exhibit 11.10.

[3] Capitalized operating leases are estimated for 2019 in Exhibit 22.10.

leases. Discount each future rental commitment by an interest rate on low-risk debt to determine the present value of operating leases. Since companies report only five years of payments and aggregate the remaining payments into a single number, use an annuity to value remaining payments beyond the first year.

Exhibit 11.15 presents the adjustment for operating leases for Costco's historical statements.[13] The present value of lease payments for Costco in 2018 equals $2.5 billion. To determine interest embedded in 2019 EBITA, multiply 2018 capitalized operating leases by the rate of secured debt. (Given the ease of repossessing capital for operating leases, use an AA interest rate for

---

[13] Because Costco's fiscal year ends prior to December 15, the company will not adopt the new leasing standard until 2020. Therefore, the value of operating leases must be estimated for historical years prior to 2020. For companies whose fiscal years end after December 15, no adjustment is required for 2019.

discounting and estimating embedded interest.) Next, adjust operating taxes to eliminate the tax shield related to implied interest. Subtract adjusted operating taxes from adjusted EBITA to determine NOPAT, adjusted for leases. Note how capitalizing operating leases increases both NOPAT and invested capital. The increase is not symmetric, causing ROIC to fall for Costco. This is because operating leases are a form of debt. For companies earning a return greater than their cost of debt, leverage artificially increases returns.

While capitalizing operating leases improves the quality of benchmarking, whether or not you capitalize will not affect intrinsic value as long as it is incorporated correctly in free cash flow, the cost of capital, and debt equivalents. Chapter 22 demonstrates how to incorporate operating leases throughout the valuation. The chapter also discusses alternative models to value operating leases.

Retirement Obligations Such as Pensions

Following the passage of FASB Statement 158 under U.S. GAAP in 2006, companies now report the present value of pension shortfalls (and excess pension assets) on their balance sheets.[14] Since excess pension assets do not generate operating profits, nor do pension shortfalls fund operations, pension accounts should not be included in invested capital. Instead, pension assets should be treated as nonoperating assets, and pension shortfalls as a debt equivalent (and both should be valued separately from operations). If pension accounts are not explicitly detailed on the company's balance sheet, search the pension footnote to determine where they are embedded. Often excess pension assets are embedded in other assets, and unfunded pension liabilities are in other liabilities.

Reporting rules under IFRS (IAS 19) differ slightly in that companies can postpone recognition of their unfunded pension obligations resulting from changes in actuarial assumptions, but only as long as the cumulative unrecognized gain or loss does not exceed 10 percent of the obligations. For companies reporting under IFRS, search the notes for the current value of obligations.

On the income statement, new GAAP accounting for pensions in 2018 dictates that only service cost—the new benefits promised to employees for service rendered in a given year—be included in operating expenses like cost of goods sold.[15] The remaining items, such as expected return on assets and interest cost on the liabilities, are now included as nonoperating income or expense. For years prior to 2018, an adjustment is still required.

---

[14] From December 2006, FASB Statement 158 eliminated pension smoothing on the balance sheet. Companies are now required to report excess pension assets and unfunded pension obligations on the balance sheet at their current values, not as smoothed values as in the past.

[15] The FASB published ASU 2017-07, "Compensation—Retirement Benefits (Topic 715): Improving the Presentation of Net Periodic Pension Cost and Net Periodic Postretirement Benefit Cost," on March 10, 2017. IFRS already separates service cost from financial performance in pensions.

Since Costco does not provide pension benefits to employees, we do not adjust the company's historical statements. Chapter 23 provides details on how to adjust NOPAT for pensions and how to factor under- or overfunded pensions into a company's value.

Capitalized Research and Development

In line with the conservative principles of accounting, accountants expense R&D, advertising, and certain other costs in their entirety in the period when they are incurred, even when economic benefits resulting from such expenses continue beyond the current reporting period.[16] This practice can dramatically understate invested capital and overstate return on capital for some companies. Therefore, you should consider whether it would be effective to capitalize and amortize R&D and other quasi investments in a manner like that used for capital expenditures. Equity should be adjusted correspondingly to balance the invested-capital equation.

If you decide to capitalize R&D, do *not* deduct the reported R&D expense from revenue to calculate operating profit. Instead, deduct the amortization associated with past R&D investments, using a reasonable amortization schedule. Since amortization is based on past investments (versus expense, which is based on current outlays), this approach will prevent reductions in R&D from driving short-term improvements in ROIC.

Whether or not you capitalize certain expenses will not affect computed value; it will affect only the timing of ROIC and economic profit. Chapter 24 analyzes the complete valuation process for R&D-intensive companies, including adjustments to free cash flow and value.

Other Advanced Adjustments

Some companies may have industry-specific items that require adjustment. These adjustments arise from an uncommon line item on the income statement or balance sheet and, given their rarity, require thoughtful judgment based on the economic principles of this book.

Consider an example from FedEx. In 2013, the company sold aircraft to another company and leased the aircraft back. This transaction is commonly known as a sale-leaseback. If a gain arises from the sale, the company cannot recognize the gain as income, but instead must lower the annual rental expense over the life of the contract. Since cash increases but retained earnings do not rise, a liability for deferred gains is recognized.

---

[16] One exception to this conservatism is the development of software. Although software is an intangible asset, both GAAP and IFRS accounting allow for certain software investments to be capitalized and amortized over the life of the asset.

Should the liability for deferred gains be treated as operating and deducted from operating assets to determine invested capital? Or perhaps classified as a debt or equity equivalent? From a valuation perspective, it doesn't matter how to classify the item, as long as it is treated consistently. It will, however, have an impact on our perceptions about return on invested capital and ultimately value creation. Accounting rules prevent the one-year spike in income caused by a financial transaction, but we believe the downward distortion in future rental expense is worse, since this lower rental expense is noncash and could distort the perceived cost of new leases. Therefore, undo the transaction entirely and recognize the account as an equity equivalent.

Not every advanced issue will lead to material differences in ROIC, growth, and free cash flow. Before collecting extra data and estimating required unknowns, decide whether the adjustment will further your understanding of a company and its industry. An unnecessarily complex model can sometimes obscure the underlying economics that would be obvious in a simple model. Remember, the goal of financial analysis is to provide a strong context for good financial decision making and robust forecasting, not to create an overly engineered model that deftly handles unimportant adjustments.

12

Analyzing Performance

Understanding a company's past is essential to forecasting its future, so a thorough analysis of historical performance is a critical component of valuation. Always begin with the core elements of value creation: return on invested capital (ROIC) and revenue growth. Examine trends in the company's long-run performance and its performance relative to that of its peers, so you can base your forecasts of future cash flows on reasonable assumptions about the company's key value drivers.

Start by analyzing ROIC, both with and without goodwill. ROIC with goodwill measures the company's ability to create value over and above premiums paid for acquisitions. ROIC without goodwill is a better measure of the company's underlying operating performance compared with that of its peers. Then drill down into the components of ROIC to build an integrated view of the company's operating performance and understand which aspects of the business are responsible for its overall performance. Next, examine what drives revenue growth. Does revenue growth stem, for instance, more from organic growth or from currency effects, which are largely beyond management control and probably not sustainable? Finally, assess the company's financial health to determine whether it has the financial resources to conduct business and make investments for growth.

ANALYZING RETURNS ON INVESTED CAPITAL

Chapter 11 reorganized the income statement into net operating profit after taxes (NOPAT) and the balance sheet into invested capital. ROIC measures the ratio of NOPAT to invested capital:

$$ROIC = \frac{NOPAT}{Invested\ Capital}$$

Companies that report ROIC in their annual reports may compute it using starting invested capital, ending capital, or the average of the two. Since profit is measured over an entire year, whereas capital is measured only at one point in time, we recommend that you average starting and ending invested capital. If the business is highly seasonal, such that capital is changing substantially at the company's fiscal close, consider using quarterly averages.

ROIC is a better analytical tool than return on equity (ROE) or return on assets (ROA) for understanding the company's performance because it focuses solely on a company's operations. ROE mixes operating performance with capital structure, making peer-group analysis and trend analysis less insightful. ROA—even when calculated on a pre-interest basis—is an inadequate measure of performance because it includes nonoperating assets and ignores the benefits of accounts payable and other operating liabilities that together reduce the amount of capital required from investors.

As an example of using ROIC to analyze performance, Exhibit 12.1 plots ROIC for Costco and the median of its peers from 2015 to 2019, based on the NOPAT and invested-capital calculations presented in Chapter 11.[1] Costco has consistently earned higher returns on invested capital than its peers, and

EXHIBIT 12.1 **Costco versus Peer Group: Return on Invested Capital**

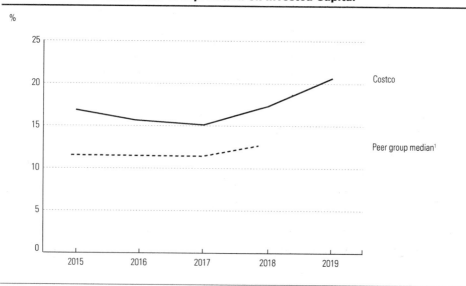

[1] ROIC measured on average capital without goodwill and acquired intangibles.

[2] For peers, 2019 results were not available at the time of this writing. Costco's fiscal year ended September 1, 2019, versus December 2019 to January 2020 for peers.

[1] Costco's fiscal year ends on the Sunday closest to August 31, so its 2019 fiscal year ended September 1, 2019. Its peers end their fiscal years in December or January, and their 2019 results were not available at the time of this writing.

showed significant increases in 2018 and 2019. As we will show later, Costco's higher ROIC can be traced to its lower operating profit margin offset by strong capital productivity.

Analyzing ROIC with and without Goodwill and Acquired Intangibles

Goodwill and acquired intangibles are intangible assets purchased in an acquisition. ROIC should be computed both with and without goodwill and acquired intangibles. In our analysis, we treat goodwill identically to acquired intangibles.[2] Therefore, we will often shorten the expression *goodwill and acquired intangibles* to simply *goodwill.*

The reason to compute ROIC with and without goodwill is that each ratio analyzes different things. ROIC with goodwill measures whether the company has earned adequate returns for shareholders, factoring in the price paid for acquisitions. ROIC excluding goodwill measures the underlying operating performance of a company. It tells you whether the underlying economics generate ROIC above the cost of capital. It can be used to compare a company's performance against that of peers and to analyze trends. It is not affected by the price premiums paid for acquisitions. ROIC without goodwill is also more relevant for projecting future cash flows and setting strategy. A company does not need to spend more on acquisitions to grow organically, so ROIC without goodwill is a more relevant baseline for forecasting cash flows. Finally, companies that have a high ROIC without goodwill will likely create more value from growth, while companies that have low ROIC without goodwill will likely create more value by improving ROIC.

Costco doesn't have any goodwill, having grown entirely organically, but for companies that make significant acquisitions, the difference between ROIC with and without goodwill can be large. Exhibit 12.2 presents ROIC with and without goodwill for the U.S. luxury-goods maker Tapestry, formerly known as Coach. In 2017, the company purchased Kate Spade, a luxury fashion design house, for $2.4 billion in cash. Since the two companies had quite similar returns on capital, Tapestry's ROIC without goodwill remained fairly constant before and after the acquisition. In contrast, ROIC with goodwill after the acquisition fell from 24 percent to 12 percent in 2017. Does the decline in ROIC when measured with goodwill imply that the acquisition destroyed value? Not necessarily: cost savings and cross-selling opportunities take time to realize, and Tapestry's access to new customers, especially millennials, may accelerate growth in its own product lines.

[2] To be classified as an acquired intangible, the asset must be separable and identifiable, as in the case of patents. Goodwill describes assets that are not separable or identifiable. Acquired intangibles are amortized over the life of the asset, whereas goodwill is impaired if value falls below book value. Since we analyze the two accounts in the same manner, we do not make a distinction.

EXHIBIT 12.2 **Tapestry: Return on Invested Capital**

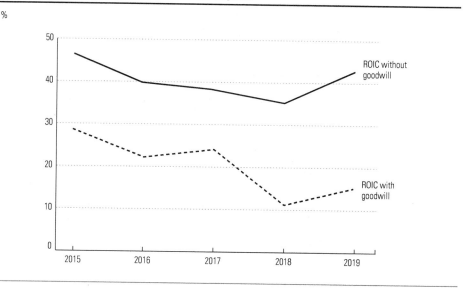

Accurately evaluating ROIC with goodwill leads to a second challenge: ROIC may increase even without improvements to the underlying business. We've seen situations where a business unit submitted a new strategic plan saying it expected to improve its ROIC over time. On the surface, its forecast looked impressive, but we then discovered that the ROIC included goodwill, and the expected improvement in ROIC would be caused solely by goodwill remaining constant as the business grew profits organically. The management team would earn accolades for improving ROIC purely as a result of the accounting for goodwill, not an underlying improvement to the business.

Decomposing ROIC to Develop an Integrated Perspective of Company Economics

To show how we analyze a company's economics based on decomposition of its ROIC, we return to the example of Costco and its peers. Costco has consistently earned a higher ROIC than its peers. But what caused this difference in performance? To understand which elements of a company's business are driving the company's ROIC, split apart the ratio as follows:

$$\text{ROIC} = (1 - \text{Operating Cash Tax Rate}) \times \frac{\text{EBITA}}{\text{Revenues}} \times \frac{\text{Revenues}}{\text{Invested Capital}}$$

The preceding equation is one of the most powerful equations in financial analysis. It demonstrates the extent to which a company's ROIC is driven by

EXHIBIT 12.3 **Costco versus Peer Group: ROIC Tree, 2018**

%

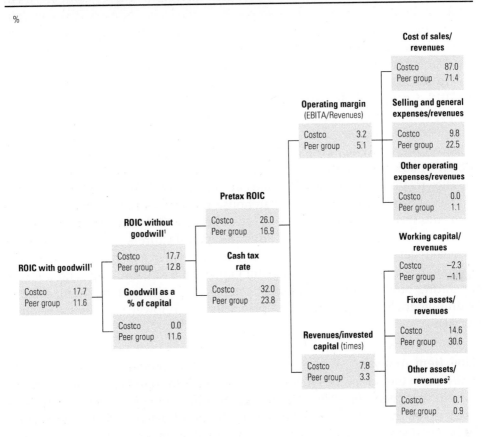

[1] To match economic-profit valuation, invested capital is measured at beginning of year.

[2] Other assets, net other liabilities.

its ability to maximize profitability (EBITA divided by revenues, or the operating margin), optimize capital turnover (measured by revenues over invested capital), or minimize operating taxes.

Each of these components can be further disaggregated, so that each expense and capital item can be analyzed, line item by line item. Exhibit 12.3 shows how the components can be organized into a tree. On the right side of the tree are operational financial ratios, the drivers of value over which managers have control. Reading from right to left, each subsequent box is a function of the boxes to its right. For example, operating margin equals 100 percent less the ratios of cost of sales to revenues, selling and general expenses to revenues, and other operating expenses to revenues. Pretax ROIC equals operating margin times capital turnover (revenues divided by invested capital), and so on.

Once you have calculated the historical drivers of ROIC, compare them with the ROIC drivers of other companies in the same industry. You can then weigh this perspective against your analysis of the industry structure (opportunities for differentiation, barriers to entry or exit, etc.) and a qualitative assessment of the company's strengths and weaknesses.

To illustrate, let's examine the difference between Costco and its peers. In 2018, Costco's ROIC with goodwill equaled 17.7 percent, compared with its peers' median of 11.6 percent. The difference is somewhat smaller without goodwill, because Costco had no goodwill. You might ask what drives Costco's higher ROIC. Costco has an unusual business model for a retailer. It doesn't mark up its costs as much as other retailers, leading to a higher cost of sales relative to revenues. It makes up for that with lower selling and general expenses. For example, its warehouse format has much lower depreciation, and its cost to stock shelves is lower because it doesn't put items on the shelves individually but instead uses the manufacturers' containers. Costco also sells larger sizes of its products with a smaller assortment to manage. Despite the lower selling and general expenses, it still ends up with a lower operating profit margin (3.2 percent, versus 5.1 percent). It makes up for this with higher capital productivity—primarily much lower fixed assets relative to sales.

Line Item Analysis   A comprehensive valuation model will convert every line item in the company's financial statements into some type of ratio. For the income statement, most items are taken as a percentage of sales. (Exceptions exist: operating cash taxes, for instance, should be calculated as a percentage of pretax operating profits, not as a percentage of sales.)

For the balance sheet, each line item can also be taken as a percentage of revenues (or as a percentage of cost of goods sold for inventories and payables, to avoid distortion caused by changing prices). For operating current assets and liabilities, you can also convert each line item into days, using the following formula:

$$\text{Days} = 365 \times \frac{\text{Balance Sheet Item}}{\text{Revenues}}$$

If the business is seasonal, operating ratios such as inventories should be calculated using quarterly data. The differences can be quite substantial.

The use of days lends itself to a simple operational interpretation. How much cash is tied up in the business, and for how long? As Exhibit 12.4 demonstrates, Costco and its peers have negative working capital, with Costco's somewhat lower. Costco's product selection and business model results in lower levels of inventory and accounts payable. In 2018, it had only 30.9 days of inventory, versus 52.7 for its peers. In other words, goods don't stay on Costco's shelves

EXHIBIT 12.4 **Costco versus Peer Group: Working Capital in Days on Hand**

Number of days of revenues or cost of sales[1]

	Costco			Peer Group		
	2016	2017	2018	2016	2017	2018
Operating cash	7.2	7.0	7.0	6.7	6.1	6.1
Accounts receivable, net	3.8	3.8	4.0	4.2	4.2	4.6
Inventory	31.7	30.7	30.9	54.3	52.3	52.7
Other current assets	0.8	0.8	0.8	1.5	1.4	1.6
Operating current assets[2]	39.3	38.2	38.6	49.6	50.1	51.7
Accounts payable	29.5	28.1	30.9	48.2	50.6	54.4
Accrued salaries and benefits	7.8	7.5	7.3	4.8	5.3	5.7
Other current liabilities[3]	12.3	13.2	13.8	12.8	12.1	11.8
Operating current liabilities[2]	45.7	45.1	48.0	51.7	57.1	57.7
Working capital	(6.4)	(6.9)	(9.3)	(2.1)	(7.0)	(6.0)

[1] Days in inventory and accounts payable computed using cost of sales. Everything else computed using revenues. Measured using beginning- and end-of-year working capital account.

[2] Operating current assets and operating current liabilities do not equal the sum of individual accounts. Instead they are denoted in days of revenue.

[3] Other current liabilities for Costco include accrued member rewards and deferred membership fees.

as long as they do at its peers'. Costco also has lower accounts payable days (30.9 versus 54.4 in 2018). This means it pays its suppliers faster, perhaps to get better prices.

Operating Analysis Using Nonfinancial Drivers In an external analysis, ratios are often confined to financial performance. If you are working from inside a company, however, or if the company releases operating data, link operating drivers directly to return on invested capital. By evaluating the operating drivers, you can better assess whether any differences in financial performance between competitors are sustainable.

Consider airlines, which are required for safety reasons to release a tremendous amount of operating data. Exhibit 12.5 details financial and operating data for two U.S. carriers we'll refer to as Airline A and Airline B between 2016 and 2018. Operating statistics include the number of employees, measured using full-time equivalents, and available seat-miles (ASMs), the common measurement of capacity for U.S. airlines.

Exhibit 12.6 transforms the data presented in Exhibit 12.5 into the operating-margin branch on the ROIC tree. Operating margin (operating profit divided by revenues) equals 9.1 percent for Airline A and 9.4 percent for Airline B. For airlines, operating margin is driven by three primary accounts: aircraft fuel, labor expenses, and other expenses. At first glance, it appears that Airlines A and B have similar labor costs. Labor expenses as a percentage of revenues average 27.7 percent for Airline A and 26.7 percent for Airline B. But

EXHIBIT 12.5 **Airline A and Airline B: Financial and Operating Statistics**

$ million

	Airline A			Airline B		
	2016	2017	2018	2016	2017	2018
Revenues	25,591	26,449	28,912	4,609	4,908	5,361
Aircraft fuel and related taxes	(4,069)	(4,839)	(6,515)	(752)	(954)	(1,329)
Salaries and related costs	(7,123)	(7,659)	(8,021)	(1,189)	(1,321)	(1,431)
Other operating expenses	(10,836)	(11,258)	(11,731)	(1,786)	(1,938)	(2,094)
Operating profit	3,562	2,693	2,645	882	695	506
Operating statistics						
Employees, full-time equivalent	64,400	62,860	61,600	11,190	12,197	12,787
Available seat-miles, millions	177,513	183,670	192,683	37,534	39,205	41,917

this statistic is misleading. To see why, disaggregate the ratio of labor expenses to revenues using available seat-miles (ASMs):

$$\frac{\text{Labor Expenses}}{\text{Revenues}} = \left(\frac{\text{Labor Expenses}}{\text{ASMs}}\right) \div \left(\frac{\text{Revenues}}{\text{ASMs}}\right)$$

The ratio of labor expenses to revenues is a function of labor expenses per ASM and revenues per ASM. Labor expenses per ASM are the labor costs required to fly one ASM, and revenues per ASM represent the average price charged per ASM. Although Airlines A and B have similar ratios of labor expenses to revenues, they have different operating models. Airline B has an 18 percent advantage in labor cost per ASM ($34.1 per thousand ASMs versus $41.6 for Airline A). But what Airline A loses in labor costs, it recovers with higher prices. Because of its locations and reach, especially internationally, Airline A can charge an average price 17 percent higher than Airline B ($150.0 per thousand ASMs versus $127.9 per thousand ASMs).

But what is driving this differential in labor expenses per ASM? Are Airline B's employees more productive? Or are they paid less? To answer these questions, disaggregate labor expenses to ASMs, using the following equation:

$$\frac{\text{Labor Expenses}}{\text{ASM}} = \left(\frac{\text{Labor Expenses}}{\text{Employees}}\right) \div \left(\frac{\text{ASMs}}{\text{Employees}}\right)$$

Two elements drive labor expenses per ASM: the first term represents the average salary per full-time employee; the second measures the productivity of each full-time employee (millions of ASMs flown per employee). The boxes on the right side of Exhibit 12.6 report the calculations for this equation. The

EXHIBIT 12.6 **Operating Drivers of Labor Expenses to Revenues, 2018**

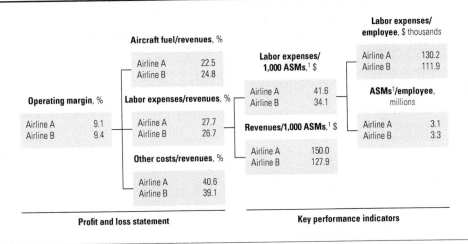

| | Profit and loss statement | | Key performance indicators | |

[1] Available seat-miles (ASMs) are the standard unit of measure for the U.S. airline industry.

average salary is 16.4 percent higher for Airline A, while productivity per mile is 4.6 percent lower. Although the salary differential appears significant, it is quite small in 2018 compared with the early 2000s, when average salaries differed by a factor of almost 2. Furthermore, the differences in productivity can be driven by different route structures and the level of service provided.

Analyzing performance using operating drivers gives additional insight into the competitive differences among airlines. But the analysis is far from done. In fact, a thoughtful analysis will often raise more questions than it answers. For instance, can the salary difference between Airline A and Airline B be explained by the mix of employees (pilots are more expensive than gate personnel) or the location of the employees (the East and West coasts are more expensive than the Midwest)? Each of these analyses will provide additional insight into each carrier type's ability to survive and prosper.

ANALYZING REVENUE GROWTH

Chapter 3 showed that ROIC, cost of capital, and growth in cash flows drive a company's value. By analyzing historical revenue growth, you can assess the potential for growth in the future.

The calculation of year-to-year revenue growth is straightforward, but the results can be misleading. Three prime culprits distort revenue growth: the effects of changes in currency values, mergers and acquisitions, and changes in

EXHIBIT 12.7 **Compass and Sodexo: Revenue Growth Analysis**

%

	Compass			Sodexo		
	2016	2017	2018	2016	2017	2018
Persistent revenue	5.0	4.0	5.5	2.0	2.5	2.0
Rugby World Cup	–	–	–	0.5	(0.6)	–
Organic revenue growth	5.0	4.0	5.5	2.5	1.9	2.0
Currency effects	5.4	11.3	(4.6)	(0.4)	(0.8)	(5.9)
53-week year in United States	–	–	–	–	0.7	(0.4)
Acquisitions and divestitures	1.1	(0.2)	0.9	0.1	0.4	2.9
Reported revenue growth	11.5	15.1	1.8	2.2	2.2	(1.4)

accounting policies. Strip out any distortions created by these effects to arrive at a better forecast of organic revenue growth.

Exhibit 12.7 demonstrates how misleading raw year-to-year revenue growth figures can be. Compass (based in the United Kingdom) and Sodexo (based in France) are global providers of canteen services in businesses, health systems, schools, and sporting venues. As shown in the bottom line of the exhibit for 2017, total revenues at Compass grew by 15.1 percent, and revenues at Sodexo grew by just 2.2 percent. The difference in growth rates appears dramatic but is driven primarily by changes in currency values (pounds sterling versus euros), not by long-term stable organic revenue growth. When we strip out these and other distortions, we see that like-for-like organic revenue growth at Compass (4.0 percent) still exceeded Sodexo's revenue growth (1.9 percent), but by a much smaller amount.

In general, for large multinationals, swings in currency values and changes in corporate portfolios can make historical revenue growth extremely volatile, so benchmarking is difficult. At Compass, reported revenue growth fell from a high of 15.1 percent in 2017 to just 1.8 percent in 2018. This stands in stark contrast to the company's relatively stable organic revenue growth: between 4.0 and 5.5 percent over the same time period.

The next three sections discuss in detail each of the major sources of distortions— changes in currency values, mergers and acquisitions, and changes in accounting policies. For each, we consider its effect on performance measurement, forecasting, and, ultimately, valuation.

Currency Effects

Multinational companies conduct business in many currencies. At the end of each reporting period, these revenues are converted to the home currency of the reporting company. If foreign currencies are rising in value relative to the company's home currency, this translation at better rates will lead to higher revenue numbers. Thus, a rise in revenue may not reflect increased pricing power or greater quantities sold, but simply depreciation in the company's home currency.

Compass and Sodexo are two companies exposed to foreign currency. The companies have similar geographic mixes, with nearly half of each company's revenues coming from North America. Since each company translates U.S. dollars into a different currency for its consolidated financial statements, however, exchange rates will affect each company quite differently.

Compass translates U.S. dollars from its North American business into pounds. Given the weakening of the pound against the U.S. dollar ($1.51 per pound in 2015 versus $1.30 per pound by 2017), Compass reported an increase in revenues of 5.4 percent in 2016 and 11.3 percent in 2017 attributable to the weakening pound, shown as "currency effects" in Exhibit 12.7. For Sodexo, exchange rates had the opposite effect. As the euro strengthened slightly against the dollar, Sodexo translated revenue from North America into fewer euros, leading to a 0.4 percent drop in euro-denominated revenues in 2016 and a 0.8 percent drop in 2017. Note how movements that helped Compass in 2016 and 2017 reversed themselves in 2018. Failing to acknowledge these currency movements can lead to a critical misunderstanding of a global company's ability to grow organically.

Mergers and Acquisitions

Growth through acquisition may have very different effects on value creation than internal growth does because of the sizable premiums a company must pay to acquire another company. Therefore, it is important to understand how companies have been generating historical revenue growth: through organic means or through acquisition.

Many large companies provide data tables such as the ones for Compass and Sodexo in Exhibit 12.7. Without voluntary disclosure, stripping the effect of acquisitions from reported revenues can be difficult. Unless an acquisition is deemed material by the company's accountants, company filings do not need to detail or even report the acquisition. For larger acquisitions, a company will report pro forma statements that recast historical financials as though the acquisition were completed at the beginning of the fiscal year. Organic revenue growth, then, should be calculated using the pro forma revenue numbers.[3] If the target company publicly reports

---

[3] For example, Sodexo purchased Centerplate in November 2017. Since 2018 includes a full year of revenue from the Centerplate acquisition and 2017 does not, the company's consolidated revenue cannot be compared with the prior year's revenue without adjustment.

EXHIBIT 12.8 **Effect of Acquisitions on Revenue Growth**

$ million

	Year				
	1	**2**	**3**	**4**	**5**
Revenue by company					
Acquiring company	100.0	110.0	121.0	133.1	146.4
Target company	20.0	22.0	24.2	26.6	29.3
Consolidated revenues					
Revenue of acquirer	100.0	110.0	121.0	133.1	146.4
Revenue from target			14.1	26.6	29.3
Consolidated revenues[1]	100.0	110.0	135.1	159.7	175.7
Growth rates of acquirer, %					
Reported growth[1]		10.0	22.8	18.2	10.0
Organic growth		10.0	10.0	10.0	10.0

[1] Only consolidated revenues are reported in a company's annual report.

its own financial data, you can construct pro forma statements manually by combining revenue of the acquirer and target for the prior year. But beware: the bidder will include partial-year revenues from the target for the period after the acquisition is completed. To remain consistent from year to year, reconstructed prior years also must include only partial-year revenue.

Exhibit 12.8 presents the hypothetical purchase of a target company in the seventh month of year 3. Both the parent company and the target are growing organically at 10 percent per year. Whereas the individual companies are growing organically at 10 percent, consolidated revenue growth is reported at 22.8 percent in year 3 and 18.2 percent in year 4.

To create an internally consistent comparison for years 3 and 4, adjust the prior year's consolidated revenues to match the current year's composition. To do this, add seven months of the target's year 2 revenue ($7/12 \times \$22$ million = $12.8 million) to the parent's year 2 revenue ($110.0 million). This leads to adjusted year 2 revenues of $122.8 million, which matches the composition of year 3. To compute an organic growth rate, divide year 3 revenues ($135.1 million) by adjusted year 2 revenues ($122.8 million) to get the correct 10 percent organic growth of the two companies.

Even though the acquisition occurs in year 3, the revenue growth rate for year 4 also will be affected by the acquisition. Year 4 contains a full year of revenues from the target. Therefore, to estimate year 4 organic growth, you must increase year 3 revenue by five months of target revenue ($5/12 \times \$24.2$ million = $10.1 million).

Accounting Changes and Irregularities

Each year, the Financial Accounting Standards Board (FASB) in the United States and the International Accounting Standards Board (IASB) make recommendations concerning the financial treatment of certain business transactions through either formal standards or topic notes issued by assigned task forces. Changes in a company's revenue recognition policy can significantly affect revenues during the year of adoption, distorting the one-year growth rate.[4] You therefore need to eliminate their effects in order to understand real historical revenue trends.

Consider the new revenue recognition standards that replaced existing IFRS and GAAP revenue rules in 2017.[5] These standards introduced a requirement that companies follow a five-step process to determine the allocation of revenue over the life of a contract, implied or written. In some cases, initiating this process caused revenues to be delayed to later in the contract, causing a one-time drop in like-for-like revenues. For example, automobile companies that provide free maintenance saw a one-time drop as revenues were delayed. Other industries, including cell phone providers, experienced a one-time increase in revenue as cell phone equipment sales can now be recognized immediately, rather than over the life of the contract.[6]

If an accounting change is material, a company will document the change in its section on management discussion and analysis (MD&A). For instance, as shown in Exhibit 12.7, Sodexo specifically called attention to an unusual 53-week year in 2017. The longer time period in 2017 artificially raised 2017 growth rates while lowering 2018 growth rates.

Decomposing Revenue Growth to Develop an Integrated Perspective of Growth Drivers

Once you have removed the effects of mergers and acquisitions, currency translations, and accounting changes from the year-to-year revenue growth numbers, analyze organic revenue growth from an operational perspective. The most standard breakdown is:

$$\text{Revenues} = \frac{\text{Revenues}}{\text{Units}} \times \text{Units}$$

---

[4] Revenue recognition changes can also affect margins and capital turnover ratios. They will not, however, affect free cash flow.
[5] ASC 606 and IFRS 15, "Revenue from Contracts with Customers," was issued jointly by the FASB and IASB on May 28, 2014. Implementation began in 2017.
[6] F. Norris, "New Standards for Companies' Revenue Accounting Will Begin in 2017," *New York Times*, May 28, 2014.

Using this formula, determine whether prices or quantities are driving growth. Do not, however, confuse revenue per unit with price; they can be different. If revenue per unit is rising, the change could be due to rising prices, or the company could be shifting its product mix from low-price to high-price items.

The operating statistics that companies choose to report (if any) depend on the industry's norms and competitors' practices. For instance, most retailers provide information on the number of stores they operate, the number of square feet in those stores, and the number of transactions they conduct annually. By relating different operating statistics to total revenues, it is possible to build a deeper understanding of the business.

Consider this retailing standard:

$$\text{Revenues} = \frac{\text{Revenues}}{\text{Stores}} \times \text{Stores}$$

Exhibit 12.9 reports disguised operating statistics for two big-box retailers we'll call Delta and Gamma. Using the operating statistics reported in Exhibit 12.9, we discover that Delta has more stores than Gamma and generates more revenue per store ($47 million per store for Delta in 2018 versus $37 million for Gamma). Using the three operating statistics, it is possible to build ratios on revenues per store, transactions per store, square feet per store, dollars per transaction, and number of transactions per square foot.

Although operating ratios are powerful in their own right, what can really change one's thinking about performance is how the ratios change over time. Exhibit 12.10 organizes each ratio based on Exhibit 12.9 into a tree. Rather than report a calculated ratio, such as revenues per store, however, we report the growth in the ratio over the period analyzed and relate this back to the growth in revenue.

EXHIBIT 12.9 **Hypothetical Retailers: Operating Statistics**

	Delta			Gamma		
Reported	**2016**	**2017**	**2018**	**2016**	**2017**	**2018**
Revenues, $ million	51,081	54,488	58,430	35,109	37,054	38,507
Average number of stores	1,229	1,232	1,234	1,076	1,070	1,050
Number of transactions, millions	834	853	875	510	515	511
Average square footage, millions	90	90	90	85	86	85
Derived						
Revenues per store, $ million	42	44	47	33	35	37
Transactions per store, thousands	678	692	709	474	481	487
Revenues per transaction, $	61	64	67	69	72	75

EXHIBIT 12.10 **Hypothetical Retailers: Organic Revenue Growth Analysis, 2018**

Growth rates, %

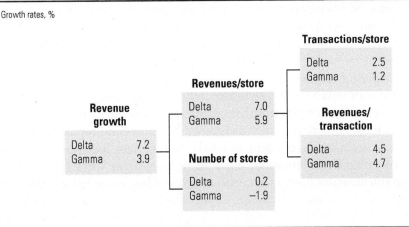

As the exhibit demonstrates, Delta grew faster than Gamma, because Gamma closed stores while Delta slightly increased the number of stores, and Delta grew revenues per store faster than Gamma. Growth in revenues per store is the key driver for these two companies, because the category is near full penetration. This growth in same-store sales is extremely important, to the point that financial analysts have a special name for growth in revenue per store: *comps*, shorthand for comparables, or year-to-year same-store sales.[7] Why is this revenue growth important? First, the number of stores to open is an investment choice, whereas same-store sales growth reflects each store's ability to compete effectively in its local market. Second, new stores require large capital investments, whereas growth in comps requires little incremental capital. Hence, same-store sales growth comes with higher capital turnover, higher ROIC, and greater value creation.

Moving farther right in the tree, we gain additional insight into what has been driving same-store sales for each company. Delta also generated more foot traffic, increasing transactions per store at 2.5 percent versus Gamma's 1.2 percent. Revenues per transaction grew at the same rate for the two stores.

CREDIT HEALTH AND CAPITAL STRUCTURE

To this point, we have focused on the operating performance of the company and its ability to create value. We have examined the primary drivers of

[7] In Exhibit 12.10, we present the change in revenues per store. This value differs from comparable-store sales reported by each company, which includes only stores that were open for at least 13 months.

value: a company's return on invested capital and organic revenue growth. In the final step of historical analysis, we focus on how the company has financed its operations. What proportion of invested capital comes from creditors instead of from equity investors? Is this capital structure sustainable? Can the company survive an industry downturn? How much cash, if any, has been distributed to shareholders?

To assess a company's capital structure, conduct four analyses. First, examine liquidity using coverage ratios. Liquidity measures the company's ability to meet short-term obligations, such as interest expenses and rental payments. Next, evaluate leverage using debt to EBITDA and debt to value. Leverage measures the company's ability to meet obligations over the long term. To evaluate equity, measure the payout ratio and operating value to EBITDA. The payout ratio measures the percentage of income being sent to shareholders. Operating value to EBITDA measures shareholders' future expectations of financial performance.

This section introduces the tools for evaluating a company's capital structure. Chapter 33 examines how capital structure decisions must be an integral part of a company's operating strategy and its plan for how it will return cash to shareholders.

Measuring Liquidity Using Coverage Ratios

To estimate the company's ability to meet short-term obligations, analysts use ratios that incorporate three measures of earnings:

1. Earnings before interest, taxes, and amortization (EBITA)
2. Earnings before interest, taxes, depreciation, and amortization (EBITDA)
3. Earnings before interest, taxes, depreciation, amortization, and rental expense (EBITDAR)

With the first two earnings measures, you can calculate interest coverage. To do this, divide either EBITA or EBITDA by interest. The first coverage ratio, EBITA to interest, measures the company's ability to pay interest using profits without cutting capital expenditures intended to replace depreciating equipment. The second ratio, EBITDA to interest, measures the company's ability to meet short-term financial commitments using both current profits and the depreciation dollars earmarked for replacement capital. Although EBITDA provides a good measure of the short-term ability to meet interest payments, most companies cannot compete effectively without replacing worn assets.

An alternative is to divide EBITDAR by the sum of interest expense and rental expense. Like the interest coverage ratio, the EBITDAR ratio measures the company's ability to meet its known future obligations, including the effect of operating leases. For many companies, especially retailers and airlines,

EXHIBIT 12.11 **Costco versus Peer Group: Measuring Coverage**

$ million

	Costco			Peer Group		
	2016	2017	2018	2016	2017	2018
EBITA	4,111	4,480	4,737			
EBITDA	5,481	5,917	6,229			
EBITDAR[1]	5,739	6,182	6,497			
Interest	134	159	150			
Rental expense	258	265	268			
Interest plus rental expense	392	424	418			
Coverage ratios						
EBITA/interest	30.7	28.2	31.6	9.0	8.3	15.3
EBITDA/interest	40.9	37.2	41.5	13.1	12.7	19.8
EBITDAR/interest plus rental expense	14.6	14.6	15.5	5.2	4.7	4.8
Debt multiples						
Debt to EBITA	1.71	1.56	1.53	2.21	2.35	2.40
Debt to EBITDA	1.28	1.18	1.16	1.53	1.53	1.67
Debt plus leases to EBITDAR	1.67	1.53	1.49	2.55	2.63	2.72

[1] Earnings before interest, taxes, depreciation, amortization, and rental expense.

including rental expenses is a critical part of understanding the financial health of the business.

Returning to our previous example of Costco and its peers, Exhibit 12.11 presents their financial data and coverage ratios. For 2018, Costco's coverage ratio of EBITA to interest equaled 31.6 times, whereas its peers had a ratio of 15.3 times. By most standards, Costco has very little debt, which is reflected in its extremely high AA– rating by Standard & Poor's. Costco's peers also have small amounts of leverage and high debt ratings, but to a lesser degree.

Measuring Leverage

Over the past decade, interest rates have dropped to unprecedented lows, making interest coverage ratios uncharacteristically high. To evaluate leverage in this low-interest-rate environment, many analysts are now measuring and evaluating debt multiples such as debt to EBITDA or debt to EBITA. Given its much larger denominator, debt to EBITDA tends to be more stable, making assessments over time much clearer. The ratio also does a better job of teasing out companies that are exposed to rollover risk and widening default spreads, neither of which is captured when interest rates are extremely low.

A second reason the debt-to-EBITDA measure has gained in popularity involves the increased use of convertible securities. Many convertibles compensate through the potential conversion to equity rather than interest, making interest coverage ratios artificially high. By using the debt-to-EBITDA ratio, one can build a more comprehensive picture of the risk of leverage.

A variation of these debt multiples is the multiple of debt plus leases to EBITDAR. This multiple works best for companies with extensive operating leases, such as airlines and retailers.

To better understand the power—and danger—of leverage, consider the relationship between return on equity (ROE) and return on invested capital (ROIC):

$$ROE = ROIC + [ROIC - (1 - T)k_d]\frac{D}{E}$$

As the formula demonstrates, a company's ROE is a direct function of its ROIC, its spread of ROIC over its after-tax cost of debt (k_d), and its book-based debt-to-equity ratio (D/E). Consider a company that is earning an ROIC of 10 percent and has an after-tax cost of debt of 5 percent. To raise its ROE, the company can either increase its ROIC (through operating improvements) or increase its debt-to-equity ratio (by swapping debt for equity). Although each strategy can lead to an identical change in ROE, increasing the debt-to-equity ratio makes the company's ROE more sensitive to changes in operating performance (ROIC). Thus, while increasing the debt-to-equity ratio can increase ROE, it does so by increasing the risks faced by shareholders.

To assess leverage, measure the company's (market) debt-to-equity ratio over time and against peers. Does the leverage ratio compare favorably with the industry? How much risk is the company taking? Chapter 33 offers in-depth answers to these and other questions about the use of debt to finance operations.

Payout Ratio

The dividend payout ratio equals total common dividends divided by net income available to common shareholders. We can better understand the company's financial situation by analyzing the payout ratio in relation to its cash flow reinvestment ratio:

- If the company has a high dividend payout ratio and a reinvestment ratio greater than 1, then it must be borrowing money to fund negative free cash flow, to pay interest, or to pay dividends. But is this sustainable?
- A company with positive free cash flow and low dividend payout is probably paying down debt (or accumulating excess cash). In this situation, is the company passing up the valuable tax benefits of debt or hoarding cash unnecessarily?

Applying these questions to Costco, we find that from 2015 to 2019, Costco generated $14.7 billion in NOPAT, paid $1.1 billion in interest, and returned $9.5 billion to shareholders in dividends.

Valuation Metrics

To conclude your assessment of capital structure, measure the shareholders' perception of future performance by calculating a market multiple. To build a market multiple, divide core operating value (defined in Chapter 10 as enterprise value less the market value of nonoperating assets, such as excess cash and nonconsolidated subsidiaries) by a normalizing factor, such as revenue, EBITA, or the book value of invested capital. By comparing the multiple of one company versus another, you can examine how the market perceives the company's future relative to other companies.

Exhibit 12.12 presents the operating-value-to-EBITDA multiples for Costco and its peers between 2005 and 2019. Although Costco traded in line with its peers from 2005 to 2011, its multiple has since increased substantially, while the multiple for its peers remained the same. We infer that Costco's higher multiple is driven by its stronger revenue growth and enduring higher ROIC.

While operating value to EBITDA is the most common measure of valuation, other measures, including operating value to EBITA and operating value to NOPAT, often provide helpful insights as well. For more on how to create and interpret valuation multiples, see Chapter 18.

EXHIBIT 12.12 **Costco versus Peer Group: Operating Value to EBITDA**

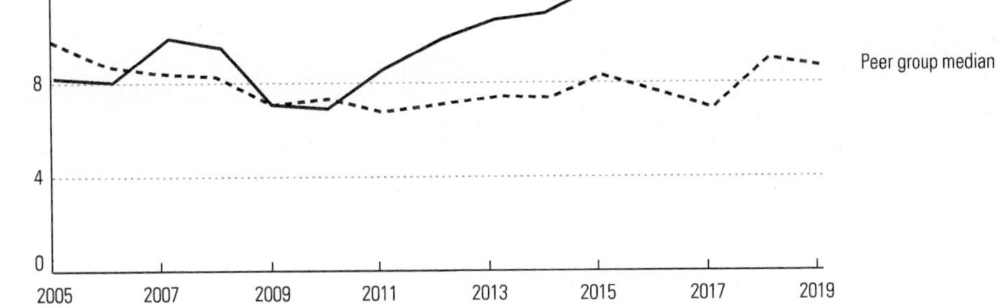

Note: Operating value equals enterprise value less the book value of nonoperating assets.

GENERAL CONSIDERATIONS

Although it is impossible to provide a comprehensive checklist for analyzing a company's historical financial performance, here are some guidelines to keep in mind:

- Look back as far as possible (at least ten years). Long time horizons will allow you to determine whether the company and industry tend to revert to some normal level of performance and whether short-term trends are likely to be permanent.
- Disaggregate value drivers—both ROIC and revenue growth—as far as possible. If possible, link operational performance measures with each key value driver.
- If there are any radical changes in performance, identify the source. Determine whether the change is temporary, permanent, or merely an accounting effect.
- If possible, perform your analysis on a fine-grained level, not just on the company as a whole. Real insight comes from analysis of individual business units, product lines, and, if the data exist, even customers.

With historical analysis complete, we now have the appropriate context to build a robust set of forecasts, a critical ingredient of any valuation.

13

Forecasting Performance

This chapter focuses on the *mechanics* of forecasting—specifically, how to develop an integrated set of financial forecasts. We'll explore how to build a well-structured spreadsheet model: one that separates raw inputs from computations, flows from one worksheet to the next, and is flexible enough to handle multiple scenarios. Then we'll discuss the process of forecasting.

To arrive at future cash flow, we forecast the income statement, balance sheet, and statement of changes in equity. The forecast financial statements provide the information necessary to compute net operating profit after taxes (NOPAT), invested capital, return on invested capital (ROIC), and, ultimately, free cash flow (FCF).

While you are building a forecast, it is easy to become engrossed in the details of individual line items. But we stress the importance of placing your aggregate results in the proper context. You can do much more to improve your valuation through a careful analysis of whether your forecast of future ROIC is consistent with the company's ability to generate value than you can by precisely (but perhaps inaccurately) forecasting an immaterial line item ten years out.

DETERMINE THE FORECAST'S LENGTH AND DETAIL

Before you begin forecasting individual line items on the financial statements, decide how many years to forecast and how detailed your forecast should be. The typical solution, described in Chapter 10, is to develop an explicit year-by-year forecast for a set period and then to value the remaining years by using a perpetuity formula, such as the key value driver formula introduced in Chapter 3. Whatever perpetuity formula you choose, all the continuing-value approaches assume steady-state performance. Thus, the explicit forecast period must be long enough for the company to reach a steady state, defined by the following characteristics:

- The company grows at a constant rate by reinvesting a constant proportion of its operating profits into the business each year.
- The company earns a constant rate of return on both existing capital and new capital invested.

As a result, free cash flow for a steady-state company will grow at a constant rate and can be valued using a growth perpetuity. The explicit forecast period should be long enough that the company's growth rate is less than or equal to that of the economy. Higher growth rates would eventually make companies unrealistically large relative to the aggregate economy.

In general, we recommend using an explicit forecast period of 10 to 15 years—perhaps longer for cyclical companies or those experiencing very rapid growth. Using a short explicit forecast period, such as five years, typically results in a significant undervaluation of a company or requires heroic long-term growth assumptions in the continuing value. Even so, a long forecast period raises its own issues—namely, the difficulty of forecasting individual line items 10 to 15 years into the future.

To simplify the model and avoid the error of false precision, we often split the explicit forecast into two periods:

1. A detailed five-year to seven-year forecast, which develops complete balance sheets and income statements with as many links as possible to real variables such as unit volumes and cost per unit
2. A simplified forecast for the remaining years, focusing on a few important variables, such as revenue growth, margins, and capital turnover

Using a simplified intermediate forecast forces you to focus on the business's long-term economics, rather than become engrossed in too much detail.

COMPONENTS OF A GOOD MODEL

If you combine 15 years of financial forecasts with 10 years of historical analysis, even the simplest valuation spreadsheet becomes complex. Therefore, you should carefully design and structure your model before starting to forecast. In Exhibit 13.1, we structure a valuation model with seven distinct worksheets:

1. *Raw historical data.* Collect raw data from the company's financial statements, footnotes, and external reports in one place.[1] By keeping the data

---

[1] For large, established companies, the amount of collected data can be substantial. To analyze Costco in Chapter 11 and Appendix H, we created separate worksheets for the company's financial statements, statutory tax table, and note on deferred taxes.

EXHIBIT 13.1 **Sample Workbook**

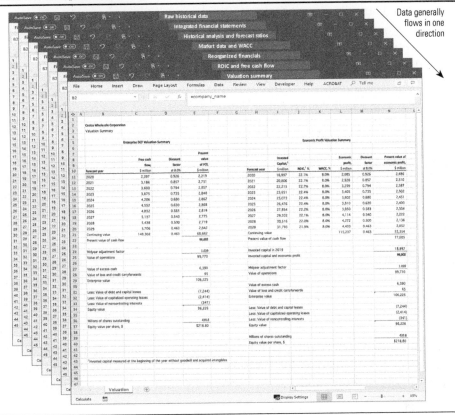

together, you can verify information as needed and update data year by year. Report the raw data in their original form.

2. *Integrated financial statements.* Using figures from the raw-data worksheet, create a set of historical financials that find the right level of detail. As a general rule, operating and nonoperating items should not be aggregated within the same line item. The income statement should be linked with the balance sheet through retained earnings. This worksheet will contain historical and forecast financial statements.

3. *Historical analysis and forecast ratios.* For each line item in the financial statements, build historical ratios, as well as forecasts of future ratios. These ratios will generate the forecast financial statements contained on the previous sheet.

4. *Market data and weighted average cost of capital (WACC).* Collect all financial market data on one worksheet. This worksheet will contain estimates of beta, the cost of equity, the cost of debt, and the weighted average cost of capital, as well as historical market values and trading multiples for the company.

5. *Reorganized financial statements.* Once you have built a complete set of financial statements (both historical and forecast), reorganize the financial

statements to calculate NOPAT, its reconciliation to net income, invested capital, and its reconciliation to total funds invested.

6. *ROIC and FCF.* Use the reorganized financials to build return on invested capital, economic profit, and free cash flow. Future free cash flow will be the basis of your enterprise valuation.

7. *Valuation summary.* Create a summary worksheet that sums discounted cash flows and converts the value of operations into equity value. The valuation summary includes the value of operations, value of nonoperating assets, value of nonequity claims, and resulting equity value.

Well-built valuation models have certain characteristics. First, original data and user input are collected in only a few places. For instance, limit original data and user input to just three worksheets: raw data (worksheet 1), forecasts (worksheet 3), and market data (worksheet 4). To provide additional clarity, denote raw data and user input in a different color from calculations. Second, whenever possible, a given worksheet should feed into the next worksheet. Formulas should not bounce from sheet to sheet without clear direction.[2] Raw data should feed into integrated financials, which in turn should feed into ROIC and FCF. Third, unless specified as data input, numbers should never be hard-coded into a formula. Hard-coded numbers are easily forgotten as the spreadsheet grows in complexity. Finally, use formulas that come built into the spreadsheet software sparingly, such as the net present value (NPV) formula. Built-in formulas can obscure the model's logic and make auditing results difficult.

MECHANICS OF FORECASTING

The enterprise discounted-cash-flow (DCF) valuation model relies on a forecast of free cash flow (FCF). However, as noted at the beginning of this chapter, FCF forecasts should be created indirectly by first forecasting the income statement, balance sheet, and statement of retained earnings. Compute forecasts of free cash flow in the same way as when analyzing historical performance. (A well-built spreadsheet will use the same formulas for historical and forecast ROIC and FCF without any modification.)

We break the forecasting process into six steps:

1. *Prepare and analyze historical financials.* Before forecasting future financials, you must build and analyze historical financials. A robust analysis will place your forecasts in the appropriate context.

2. *Build the revenue forecast.* Almost every line item will rely directly or indirectly on revenues. Estimate future revenues by using either a top-down

---

[2] Data should always flow in one direction and never loop back to create a circular reference. Circular references will prevent your spreadsheet from calculating results accurately.

(market-based) or a bottom-up (customer-based) approach. Forecasts should be consistent with evidence on growth.

3. *Forecast the income statement.* Use the appropriate economic drivers to forecast operating expenses, depreciation, nonoperating income, interest expense, and reported taxes.

4. *Forecast the balance sheet: invested capital and nonoperating assets.* On the balance sheet, forecast operating working capital, net property, plant, and equipment, goodwill, and nonoperating assets.

5. *Reconcile the balance sheet with investor funds.* Complete the balance sheet by computing retained earnings and forecasting other equity accounts. Use excess cash and/or new debt to balance the balance sheet.

6. *Calculate ROIC and FCF.* Calculate ROIC on future financial statements to ensure your forecasts are consistent with economic principles, industry dynamics, and the company's ability to compete. To complete the forecast, calculate free cash flow as the basis for valuation. Future FCF should be calculated the same way as historical FCF.

Give extra emphasis to your revenue forecast. Almost every line item in the spreadsheet will be either directly or indirectly driven by revenues, so you should devote enough time to arrive at a good revenue forecast, especially for rapidly growing businesses.

Step 1: Prepare and Analyze Historical Financials

Before starting to build a forecast, input the company's historical financials into a spreadsheet. To do this, you can rely on data from a professional service, such as Bloomberg, Capital IQ, Compustat, or Thomson ONE, or you can use financial statements directly from the company's filings.

Professional services offer the benefit of standardized data (i.e., financial data formatted into a set number of categories). Since data items do not change across companies, a single spreadsheet can quickly analyze any company. However, using a standardized data set carries a cost. Many of the specified categories aggregate important items, hiding critical information. For instance, Compustat groups "advances to sales staff" (an operating asset) and "pension and other special funds" (a nonoperating asset) into a single category titled "other assets." Because of this, models based solely on preformatted data can lead to meaningful errors in the estimation of value drivers, and hence to poor valuations.

Alternatively, you can build a model using financials from the company's annual report. To use raw data, however, you must dig. Often, companies aggregate critical information to simplify their financial statements. Consider, for instance, the financial data for Honeywell presented in Exhibit 13.2. On Honeywell's reported balance sheet, the company consolidates many items into the account titled "accrued liabilities." In the notes that follow the company's

EXHIBIT 13.2 **Honeywell: Current Liabilities in Balance Sheet**

$ million

Balance Sheet	2017	2018
Accounts payable	6,584	5,607
Commercial paper and other short-term borrowings	3,958	3,586
Current maturities of long-term debt	1,351	2,872
Accrued liabilities	6,968	6,859
Total current liabilities	18,861	18,924
Note 12: Accrued liabilities		
Customer advances and deferred income	2,198	2,403
Compensation, benefit, and other employee-related costs	1,420	1,469
Asbestos-related liabilities	350	245
Repositioning	508	566
Product warranties and performance guarantees	307	243
Environmental costs	226	175
Income taxes	134	166
Accrued interest	94	94
Other taxes	277	234
Insurance	199	170
Other (primary operating expenses)	1,255	1,094
Accrued liabilities	6,968	6,859

Source: Honeywell International annual report, 2018.

financial statements, note 12 details this line item. Some of the components (such as compensation, benefit, and other employee-related costs) are operating liabilities, and others are debt equivalents (such as environmental costs). Since the valuation of each of these items requires different treatment, the items must be separated on the expanded balance sheet.

We prefer to collect raw data on a separate worksheet. On the raw-data sheet, record financial data as originally reported, and never combine multiple data into a single cell. Once you have collected raw data from the reported financials and notes, use the data to build a set of expanded (or simplified) financial statements: the income statement, balance sheet, statement of equity, and statement of accumulated other comprehensive income. Although the statement of equity appears redundant, it will be critical for error checking during the forecasting process, because it connects the income statement to the balance sheet. If available, accumulated other comprehensive income will be necessary to complete the free cash flow statement.

As you build the integrated financials, you must decide whether to aggregate immaterial line items. Analyzing and forecasting too many line items can lead to confusion, introduce errors, and cause the model to become unwieldy. Returning to the Honeywell example presented in Exhibit 13.2, the income taxes payable account amounts to under 0.1 percent of Honeywell's revenues.[3] Therefore, you might simplify a valuation of Honeywell by combining income

[3] Contrast this to accrued compensation and employee benefit costs; that account is nearly 15 times as large as taxes payable. Given its size, accrued compensation and employee benefit costs should not be aggregated with other accrued liabilities.

taxes payable with the "other" account. When aggregating, however, make sure never to combine operating and nonoperating accounts into a single category. If operating and nonoperating accounts are combined, you cannot calculate ROIC and FCF properly.

Step 2: Build the Revenue Forecast

To build a revenue forecast, you can use a *top-down* forecast, in which you estimate revenues by sizing the total market, determining market share, and forecasting prices. Alternatively, with the *bottom-up* approach, you can use the company's own forecasts of demand from existing customers, customer turnover, and the potential for new customers. When possible, use both methods to establish bounds for the forecast.

The top-down approach can be applied to any company. For companies in mature industries, the aggregate market grows slowly and is closely tied to economic growth and other long-term trends, such as changing consumer preferences. In these situations, you can rely on third-party forecasts of the aggregate market and focus your own efforts on forecasting market share by competitor.[4] To do this, you must determine which companies have the capabilities and resources to compete effectively and capture share. A good place to start, of course, is with historical financial analysis. But more importantly, make sure to address how the company is positioned for the future. Does it have the required products and services to capture share? Do other competitors have products and services that will displace the company's market position? A good forecast will address each of these issues.

Over the short term, top-down forecasts should build on the company's announced intentions and capabilities for growth. For instance, retailers like Costco have well-mapped plans for new store openings, which are their primary driver of revenue growth. Oil companies like BP have proven reserves and relatively fixed amounts of refining capacity. And pharmaceutical companies like Merck have a fixed set of drugs under patent and in clinical trials.

To value Costco in Appendix H, we relied on forecasts from the sell-side analyst community to project company revenue. Exhibit 13.3 presents one analyst's forecasts for Costco. The forecast is split into domestic revenues, international revenues, membership fees, and ancillary businesses. The ancillary-businesses segment includes gas stations and pharmacies. Using a geographically segmented forecast for Costco is important because revenue per square foot and square feet per store differ between domestic and international stores. Details such as these will vary depending on the company and industry. Some analysts will provide their corporate clients with forecasts of the number of transactions, average revenue per transaction, and other

---

[4] Examples of third-party forecasts include EvaluatePharma for drug-by-drug revenue forecasts, McCoy Power Reports for power generation equipment, and RBR for point-of-sale systems.

EXHIBIT 13.3 **Costco: Sample Revenue Forecast**[1]

$ million

	Historical			Forecast					
	2017	**2018**	**2019**	**2020**	**2021**	**2022**	**2023**	**2024**	**2025**
U.S. revenues									
Revenue per square foot, $	1,007	1,054	1,100	1,144	1,172	1,202	1,226	1,250	1,275
× Square footage per store, thousands	147	147	147	147	148	148	148	148	148
× Number of stores	514	527	543	558	566	574	582	590	598
= U.S. revenues	76,087	81,652	87,803	93,838	98,176	102,112	105,603	109,150	112,843
International stores									
Revenue per square foot, $	904	958	968	997	1,027	1,058	1,089	1,122	1,156
× Square footage per store, thousands	142	142	144	144	144	144	144	144	144
× Number of stores	225	233	236	244	252	260	268	276	284
= International revenues	28,883	31,696	32,897	35,031	37,268	39,612	42,027	44,593	47,276
Membership fees									
Average fee per member	32	33	34	35	35	36	37	38	38
× Number of members, millions	90	94	99	102	104	108	110	114	116
= Membership fees	2,853	3,140	3,349	3,539	3,682	3,899	4,048	4,286	4,443
Ancillary businesses[2]	21,400	24,900	28,600	30,900	33,400	36,100	39,000	42,100	45,500
Total revenues	129,223	141,389	152,649	163,308	172,525	181,723	190,677	200,129	210,061

[1] For better comparability across companies, data are presented on a calendar basis. Costco's fiscal year-end is August 31.

[2] Ancillary businesses include gas stations, pharmacies, optical dispensing centers, food courts, and hearing-aid centers.

Source: Trefis, "Costco," November 2019.

revenue drivers. Taking a fine-grained look at a company's sources of growth will make clear what drives the company's valuation.

In new-product markets, the top-down approach is especially helpful but often requires more work than for established markets. For instance, consider the recent launch of June Life, a maker of web-enabled ovens. The company's smart oven is marketed as many appliances in one, including a toaster, dehydrator, and slow cooker. The accompanying smartphone app allows the user to control the oven remotely, check on remaining time, and even view the product cooking.

Given the lack of history for the company's products, how do you estimate the potential size and speed of penetration of this new product? You could start by sizing the more traditional products of Black & Decker and Cuisinart. Analyze whether the new smart ovens, given their greater functionality, will be adopted by even more users than traditional ovens—or perhaps by fewer, because of their higher price. Next, forecast how quickly web-enabled products might penetrate the market. To do this, look at the speed of migration for other electronics that have gone through a similar transition, such as the voice-only cell phone to the smartphone. Determine the characteristics that drive conversion in other markets; this helps you place your forecast in context. Next, assess the price point and resulting operating margin for the company's products. How many companies are developing the product, and how competitive will the market be? As you can see, there are more questions than answers. The key is structuring the analysis and applying historical evidence from comparable markets to help bound forecasts whenever possible.

Whereas a top-down approach starts with the aggregate market and predicts penetration rates, price changes, and market shares, a bottom-up approach relies on projections of customer demand. In some industries, a company's customers will have projected their own revenue forecasts and can give their suppliers a rough estimate of their own purchase projections. By aggregating across customers, you can determine short-term forecasts of revenues from the current customer base. Next, estimate the rate of customer turnover. If customer turnover is significant, you must eliminate a portion of estimated revenues. As a final step, project how many new customers the company will attract and how much revenue those customers will contribute. The resulting bottom-up forecast combines new customers with revenues from existing customers.[5]

Regardless of the method, forecasting revenues over long time periods is imprecise. Customer preferences, technologies, and corporate strategies change. These often-unpredictable changes can profoundly influence the winners and losers in the marketplace. Therefore, you must constantly reevaluate whether the current forecast is consistent with industry dynamics, competitive positioning, and the historical evidence on corporate growth. If you lack confidence in your revenue forecast, use multiple scenarios to model uncertainty. Doing this not only will bound the forecast, but also will help company management make better decisions. A discussion of scenario analysis can be found in Chapter 16.

Step 3: Forecast the Income Statement

With a revenue forecast in place, forecast individual line items related to the income statement. To forecast a line item, use a three-step process:

1. *Decide what economic relationships drive the line item.* For most line items, forecasts will be tied directly to revenues. Some line items will be economically tied to a specific asset or liability. For instance, interest income is usually generated by cash and marketable securities; if this is the case, forecasts of interest income should be tied to cash and marketable securities.

2. *Estimate the forecast ratio.* For each line item on the income statement, compute historical values for each ratio, followed by estimates for each of the forecast periods. To get the model working properly, initially set the forecast ratio equal to the previous year's value. Your forecasts are

---

[5] For more on company valuation using customer acquisition and retention statistics, see Daniel McCarthy, Peter Fader, and Bruce Hardie, "Valuing Subscription-Based Businesses Using Publicly Disclosed Customer Data," *Journal of Marketing* 81, no. 1 (2018): 17–35.

EXHIBIT 13.4 **Partial Forecast of the Income Statement**

Forecast worksheet

%	2019	Forecast 2020
Revenue growth	20.0	20.0
Cost of goods sold/revenues	37.5	37.5
Selling and general expenses/revenues	18.8	
Depreciation$_t$/net PP&E$_{t-1}$[1]	9.5	

Step 1: Choose a forecast driver, and compute historic ratios.

Step 2: Estimate the forecast ratio.

Income statement

$ million	2019	Forecast 2020
Revenues	240.0	288.0
Cost of goods sold	(90.0)	(108.0)
Selling and general expenses	(45.0)	
Depreciation	(19.0)	
EBITA	86.0	
Interest expense	(15.0)	
Interest income	2.0	
Nonoperating income	4.0	
Earnings before taxes (EBT)	77.0	
Provision for income taxes	(18.0)	
Net income	59.0	

Step 3: Multiply the forecast ratio by next year's estimate of revenues (or appropriate forecast driver).

[1] Net PP&E = net property, plant, and equipment.

likely to change as you learn about the company, so at this point, a working model should be your priority. Once the entire model is complete, return to the forecast page and enter your best estimates.

3. *Multiply the forecast ratio by an estimate of its driver.* Since most line items are driven by revenues, most forecast ratios, such as cost of goods sold (COGS) to revenues, should be applied to estimates of future revenues. This is why a good revenue forecast is critical. Any error in the revenue forecast will be carried through the entire model. Ratios dependent on other drivers should be multiplied by their respective drivers.

Exhibit 13.4 presents the historical income statement and partially completed forecast for a hypothetical company. To demonstrate the three-step process, we forecast cost of goods sold. In the first step, calculate historical COGS as a function of revenues, which equals 37.5 percent. To start the model, initially set next year's ratio equal to 37.5 percent as well. Finally, multiply the forecast ratio by an estimate of next year's revenues: 37.5 percent × $288 million = $108 million.

Note that we did not forecast COGS by increasing the previous year's costs by 20 percent (the same growth rate as revenues). Although this process leads to the same *initial* answer, it reduces flexibility. By using a forecast ratio rather than a growth rate, we can either vary estimates of revenues (and COGS will change in step) or vary the forecast ratio (for instance, to value a potential improvement). If we had increased the COGS directly, however, we could only vary the COGS growth rate.

EXHIBIT 13.5 **Typical Forecast Drivers for the Income Statement**

	Line item	Typical forecast driver	Typical forecast ratio
Operating	Cost of goods sold (COGS)	Revenue	COGS/revenue
	Selling, general, and administrative (SG&A)	Revenue	SG&A/revenue
	Depreciation	Prior-year net PP&E	$\text{Depreciation}_t / \text{net PP\&E}_{t-1}$
Nonoperating	Nonoperating income	Appropriate nonoperating asset, if any	Nonoperating income/nonoperating asset or growth in nonoperating income
	Interest expense	Prior-year total debt	$\text{Interest expense}_t / \text{total debt}_{t-1}$
	Interest income	Prior-year excess cash	$\text{Interest income}_t / \text{excess cash}_{t-1}$

Exhibit 13.5 presents typical forecast drivers and forecast ratios for the most common line items on financial statements. The appropriate choice for a forecast driver, however, depends on the company and the industry in which it competes.

Most valuation models, especially those of public companies, rely on ratios created directly from the company's financial statements. If you have access to other data that improves your forecast, incorporate it. For instance, the external valuation of a delivery company such as UPS will tie fuel costs directly to revenue. A more sophisticated model might tie fuel costs to the price of fuel and the number of packages delivered. Be mindful about incorporating new data, however. While additional data often improves the realism of your model, it will also increase its complexity. A talented modeler carefully balances realism with simplicity.

Operating Expenses   For each operating expense on the income statement—such as cost of goods sold; selling, general, and administrative expenses; and research and development—we recommend generating forecasts based on revenues. In most cases, the process for operating expenses is straightforward. However, as outlined in Chapter 11, the income statement sometimes embeds certain nonoperating items in operating expenses. Before you begin the forecasting process, reformat the income statement to properly separate ongoing expenses from one-time charges.

Depreciation   To forecast depreciation, you have three options. You can forecast depreciation as either a percentage of revenues or a percentage of property, plant, and equipment (PP&E), or—if you are working inside the company—you can also generate depreciation forecasts based on specific equipment purchases and depreciation schedules.

Although one can link depreciation to revenue, you will get better forecasts if you use PP&E as the forecast driver. To illustrate this, consider a company that makes a large capital expenditure every few years. Since depreciation is directly tied to a particular asset, it should increase only following an expenditure.

If you tie depreciation to sales, it will incorrectly grow as revenues grow, even when capital expenditures haven't been made.

When using PP&E as the forecast driver, forecast depreciation as a percentage of net PP&E, rather than gross PP&E. Ideally, depreciation would be linked to gross PP&E, since depreciation for a given asset's life (assuming straight-line depreciation) equals gross PP&E divided by its expected life. But linking depreciation to gross PP&E requires modeling asset life and retiring the asset when it becomes fully depreciated. Implementing this correctly is tricky. If you forget to model asset retirements, for example, you would overestimate depreciation (and consequently its tax shield) in the later years.

If you have access to detailed, internal information about the company's assets, you can build formal depreciation tables. For each asset, project depreciation using an appropriate depreciation schedule, asset life, and salvage value. To determine company-wide depreciation, combine the annual depreciation of each asset.

Exhibit 13.6 presents a forecast of depreciation, as well as the remaining line items on the income statement.

Nonoperating Income   Nonoperating income is generated by nonoperating assets, such as customer loans, nonconsolidated subsidiaries, and other equity investments. Since nonoperating income is typically excluded from free cash flow and the corresponding nonoperating asset is valued separately from core operations, the forecast will not affect the value of core operations. Instead, the primary purposes of nonoperating-income forecasts are cash flow planning and estimating earnings per share.

EXHIBIT 13.6 **Completed Forecast of the Income Statement**

Forecast worksheet			Income statement		
%	2019	Forecast 2020	$ million	2019	Forecast 2020
Revenue growth	20.0	20.0	Revenues	240.0	288.0
Cost of goods sold/revenues	37.5	37.5	Cost of goods sold	(90.0)	(108.0)
Selling and general expenses/revenues	18.8	18.8	Selling and general expenses	(45.0)	(54.0)
Depreciation$_t$/net PP&E$_{t-1}$	9.5	9.5	Depreciation	(19.0)	(23.8)
			EBITA	86.0	102.3
Interest rates			Interest expense	(15.0)	(13.8)
Interest expense	5.4	5.4	Interest income	2.0	1.2
Interest income	2.0	2.0	Nonoperating income	4.0	5.3
			Earnings before taxes (EBT)	77.0	95.0
Nonoperating items					
Nonoperating-income growth	33.3	33.3	Provision for income taxes	(18.0)	(22.2)
			Net income	59.0	72.7
Taxes					
Operating tax rate	23.4	23.4			
Statutory tax rate	24.0	24.0			
Effective tax rate	23.4	23.4			

For nonconsolidated subsidiaries and other equity investments, the forecast methodology depends on how much information is available. For illiquid investments in which the parent company owns less than 20 percent, the company records income only when dividends are received or assets are sold at a gain or loss. For these investments, you cannot use traditional drivers to forecast cash flows; instead, estimate future nonoperating income by examining historical growth in nonoperating income or by examining the revenue and profit forecasts of publicly traded companies that are comparable to the equity investment.

For nonconsolidated subsidiaries with greater than 20 percent ownership, the parent company records income even when it is not paid out. Also, the recorded asset grows as the investment's retained earnings grow. Thus, you can estimate future income from the nonconsolidated investment either by forecasting a nonoperating-income growth rate or by forecasting a return on equity (nonoperating income as a percentage of the appropriate nonoperating asset) consistent with the industry dynamics and competitive position of the subsidiary.

Interest Expense and Interest Income   Interest expense (or income) should be tied directly to the liability (or asset) that generates the expense (or income). The appropriate driver for interest expense is total debt. To simplify implementation, use *prior-year* debt to drive interest expense, rather than same year-end debt. To see why, consider a rise in operating costs. If the company uses debt to fund short-term needs, total debt will rise to cover the financing gap caused by lower profits. This increased debt load will cause interest expense to rise, dropping profits even further. The reduced level of profits, once again, requires more debt. To avoid the complexity of this feedback effect, compute interest expense as a function of the prior year's total debt. This shortcut will simplify the model and avoid circularity.[6]

A forecast of interest expense requires data from the income statement and the balance sheet. The balance sheet for our hypothetical company is presented in Exhibit 13.7. From the income statement presented in Exhibit 13.6, start with the 2019 interest expense of $15 million, and divide by 2018's total debt of $280 million (from the balance sheet, the sum of $200 million in short-term debt plus $80 million in long-term debt). This ratio equals 5.4 percent. To estimate the 2020 interest expense, multiply the estimated forecast ratio (5.35 percent) by 2019's total debt ($258 million), which leads to a forecast of $13.8 million. In this example, interest expense is falling even while revenues rise, because total debt is shrinking as the company generates cash from operations.

Using historical interest rates to forecast interest expense is a simple, straightforward estimation method. And since interest expense is not part of free cash flow, the choice of how to forecast interest expense will not affect the

---

[6] If you are using last year's debt multiplied by current interest rates to forecast interest expense, the forecast error will be greatest when year-to-year changes in debt are significant.

EXHIBIT 13.7 **Historical Balance Sheet**

$ million

Assets	2018	2019	Liabilities and shareholders' equity	2018	2019
Operating cash	5.0	5.0	Accounts payable	15.0	20.0
Excess cash	100.0	60.0	Short-term debt	200.0	178.0
Inventory	35.0	45.0	Current liabilities	215.0	198.0
Current assets	140.0	110.0			
			Long-term debt	80.0	80.0
Net PP&E	200.0	250.0	Shareholders' equity	145.0	182.0
Equity investments	100.0	100.0	Total liabilities and equity	440.0	460.0
Total assets	440.0	460.0			

company's valuation (only free cash flow drives valuation; the cost of debt is modeled as part of the weighted average cost of capital).[7] When a company's financial structure is a critical part of the forecast, however, split debt into two categories: existing debt and new debt. Until repaid, existing debt should generate interest expense consistent with contractual rates reported in the company's financial notes. Interest expense based on new debt, in contrast, should be paid at current market rates, available from a financial data service. Projected interest expense should be calculated using a yield to maturity for comparably rated debt at a similar duration.

Estimate *interest income* the same way, with forecasts based on the asset generating the income. Be careful: interest income can be generated by multiple investments, including excess cash, short-term investments, customer loans, and other long-term investments. If a footnote details the historical relationship between interest income and the assets that generate the income (and the relationship is material), develop a separate calculation for each asset.

Income Taxes Do not forecast the provision for income taxes as a percentage of earnings before taxes. If you do, ROIC and FCF in forecast years will inadvertently change as leverage and nonoperating income change. Instead, start with a forecast of operating taxes on EBITA, and adjust for taxes related to nonoperating accounts, such as interest expense. Use this combined number to generate taxes on the income statement.

Exhibit 13.8 presents the forecast process for income taxes. To forecast operating taxes for 2020, multiply earnings before interest, taxes, and amortization (EBITA) by the *operating* tax rate (23.4 percent). Earlier, we estimated EBITA equal to $102.3 million for 2020. Do not use the statutory tax rate to forecast operating taxes. Many companies pay taxes at rates below their local statutory rate because

---

[7] In a WACC-based valuation model, the cost of debt and its associated tax shields are fully incorporated in the cost of capital. In an adjusted present value (APV) model, the interest tax shield is valued separately using a forecast of interest expense.

EXHIBIT 13.8 **Forecast of Reported Taxes**

$ million

	2019	Forecast 2020
Operating taxes		
EBITA	86.0	102.3
× Operating tax rate	23.4%	23.4%
= Operating taxes	20.2	24.0
Taxes on nonoperating accounts		
Interest expense	(15.0)	(13.8)
Interest income	2.0	1.2
Nonoperating income	4.0	5.3
Nonoperating income (expenses), net	(9.0)	(7.3)
× Marginal tax rate	24.0%	24.0%
= Nonoperating taxes	(2.2)	(1.8)
Provision for income taxes[1]	18.0	22.2

[1] The provision for income taxes equals the sum of operating and nonoperating taxes.

of low foreign rates and operating tax credits.[8] Failure to recognize operating credits can cause errors in forecasts and an incorrect valuation. Also, if you use historical tax rates to forecast future tax rates, you implicitly assume that these special incentives will grow in line with EBITA. If this is not the case, EBITA should be taxed at the marginal rate, and tax credits should be forecast one by one.

Next, forecast the taxes related to nonoperating accounts. Although such taxes are not part of free cash flow, a robust forecast of them will provide insights about future net income and cash needs. For each line item between EBITA and earnings before taxes, compute the marginal taxes related to that item. If the company does not report each item's marginal tax rate, use the country's statutory rate. In Exhibit 13.8, the cumulative net nonoperating expense ($7.3 million in 2020) was multiplied by the marginal tax rate of 24 percent. It is possible to do this because each item's marginal income tax rate is the same. When marginal tax rates differ across nonoperating items, forecast nonoperating taxes line by line.

To determine the 2020 provision for income taxes, sum operating taxes ($24.0 million) and taxes related to nonoperating accounts (–$1.8 million). You now have a forecast of $22.2 million for reported taxes, calculated such that future values of FCF and ROIC will not change with leverage.

Step 4: Forecast the Balance Sheet: Invested Capital and Nonoperating Assets

To forecast the balance sheet, start with items related to invested capital and nonoperating assets. Do not forecast excess cash or sources of financing (such as debt and equity). Excess cash and sources of financing require special treatment and will be handled in step 5.

[8] For an in-depth discussion on the difference between statutory, effective, and operating tax rates, see Chapter 20.

EXHIBIT 13.9 **Stock-versus-Flow Example**

	Year 1	Year 2	Year 3	Year 4
Revenues, $	1,000	1,100	1,200	1,300
Accounts receivable, $	100	105	121	120
Stock method				
Accounts receivable as a % of revenues	10.0	9.5	10.1	9.2
Flow method				
Change in accounts receivable as a % of change in revenues		5.0	16.0	(1.0)

When forecasting the balance sheet, one of the first issues you face is whether to forecast the line items in the balance sheet directly (in stocks) or indirectly by forecasting the year-to-year changes in accounts (in flows). For example, the stock approach forecasts end-of-year receivables as a function of revenues, while the flow approach forecasts the *change* in receivables as a function of the growth in revenues. We favor the stock approach. The relationship between the balance sheet accounts and revenues (or other volume measures) is more stable than that between balance sheet changes and changes in revenues. Consider the example presented in Exhibit 13.9. The ratio of accounts receivable to revenues remains within a tight band between 9.2 percent and 10.1 percent, while the ratio of changes in accounts receivable to changes in revenues ranges from –1 percent to 16 percent, too volatile to be insightful.

Exhibit 13.10 summarizes forecast drivers and forecast ratios for the most common line items on the balance sheet. The three primary operating line items are operating working capital, long-term capital such as net PP&E, and intangible

EXHIBIT 13.10 **Typical Forecast Drivers and Ratios for the Balance Sheet**

	Line item	Typical forecast driver	Typical forecast ratio
Operating line items	Operating working capital		
	Accounts receivable	Revenues	Accounts receivable/revenues
	Inventories	Cost of goods sold	Inventories/COGS
	Accounts payable	Cost of goods sold	Accounts payable/COGS
	Accrued expenses	Revenues	Accrued expenses/revenue
	Net PP&E	Revenues or units sold	Net PP&E/revenues
	Goodwill and acquired intangibles	Acquired revenues	Goodwill and acquired intangibles/acquired revenues
Nonoperating line items	Nonoperating assets	None	Growth in nonoperating assets
	Pension assets or liabilities	None	Trend toward zero
	Deferred taxes	Operating taxes or corresponding balance sheet item	Change in operating deferred taxes/operating taxes, or deferred taxes/corresponding balance sheet item

EXHIBIT 13.11 **Partial Forecast of the Balance Sheet**

Forecast worksheet

Forecast ratio	2019	Forecast 2020
Working capital		
Operating cash, days' sales	7.6	7.6
Inventory, days' COGS	182.5	182.5
Accounts payable, days' sales	81.1	81.1
Fixed assets		
Net PP&E/revenues, %	104.2	104.2
Nonoperating assets		
Growth in equity investments, %	0.0	0.0

Balance sheet

$ million	2018	2019	Forecast 2020
Assets			
Operating cash	5.0	5.0	6.0
Excess cash	100.0	60.0	
Inventory	35.0	45.0	54.0
Current assets	140.0	110.0	
Net PP&E	200.0	250.0	300.0
Equity investments	100.0	100.0	100.0
Total assets	440.0	460.0	
Liabilities and equity			
Accounts payable	15.0	20.0	24.0
Short-term debt	200.0	178.0	
Current liabilities	215.0	198.0	
Long-term debt	80.0	80.0	
Shareholders' equity	145.0	182.0	
Total liabilities and equity	440.0	460.0	

assets related to acquisitions. Nonoperating line items include nonoperating assets, pensions, and deferred taxes, among others. We discuss each category next.

Operating Working Capital   To start the balance sheet, forecast items within operating working capital, such as accounts receivable, inventories, accounts payable, and accrued expenses. Remember, operating working capital excludes any nonoperating assets (such as excess cash) and financing items (such as short-term debt and dividends payable).

When forecasting operating working capital, estimate most line items as a percentage of revenues or in days' sales.[9] Possible exceptions are inventories and accounts payable. Since these two accounts are economically tied to input prices, estimate them instead as a percentage of cost of goods sold (which is also tied to input prices).[10] Look for other links between the income statement and balance sheet that may exist. For instance, accrued wages can be calculated as a percent of compensation and benefits.

Exhibit 13.11 presents a partially completed forecast of our hypothetical company's balance sheet, in particular its operating working capital, long-term operating assets, and nonoperating assets (investor funds will be detailed later). All working-capital items are forecast in days, most of which are computed

---

[9] To compute a ratio in days' sales, multiply the percent-of-revenue ratio by 365. For instance, if accounts receivable equal 10 percent of revenues, this translates to accounts receivable at 36.5 days' sales. This implies that, on average, the company collects its receivables in 36.5 days.

[10] As a practical matter, we sometimes simplify the forecast model by projecting each working-capital item using revenues. The distinction is material only when price is expected to deviate significantly from cost per unit.

using revenues. Working cash is estimated at 7.6 days' sales, inventory at 182.5 days' COGS, and accounts payable at 81.1 days' COGS. We forecast in days for the added benefit of tying forecasts more closely to the velocity of operating activities. For instance, if management announces its intention to reduce its inventory holding period from 180 days to 120 days, it is possible to compute changes in value by adjusting the forecast directly.

Property, Plant, and Equipment   Consistent with our earlier argument concerning stocks and flows, net PP&E should be forecast as a percentage of revenues.[11] A common alternative is to forecast capital expenditures as a percentage of revenues. However, this method too easily leads to unintended increases or decreases in capital turnover (the ratio of PP&E to revenues). Over long periods, companies' ratios of net PP&E to revenues tend to be quite stable, so we favor the following three-step approach for PP&E:

1. Forecast net PP&E as a percentage of revenues.
2. Forecast depreciation, typically as a percentage of gross or net PP&E.
3. Calculate capital expenditures by summing the projected increase in net PP&E plus depreciation.

To continue our example, we use the forecasts presented in Exhibit 13.11 to estimate expected capital expenditures. In 2019, net PP&E equaled 104.2 percent of revenues. If this ratio is held constant for 2020, the forecast of net PP&E equals $300 million. To estimate capital expenditures, compute the increase in net PP&E from 2019 to 2020, and add 2020 depreciation from Exhibit 13.6.

$$\text{Capital Expenditures} = \text{Net PP\&E}_{2020} - \text{Net PP\&E}_{2019} + \text{Depreciation}_{2020}$$
$$= \$300.0 \text{ million} - \$250.0 \text{ million} + \$23.8 \text{ million}$$
$$= \$73.8 \text{ million}$$

For companies with low growth rates and projected improvements in capital efficiency, this methodology may lead to negative capital expenditures (implying asset sales). Although positive cash flows generated by equipment sales are possible, they are unlikely. In these cases, make sure to assess the resulting cash flow carefully.

Goodwill and Acquired Intangibles   A company records goodwill and acquired intangibles when the price it pays for an acquisition exceeds the target's book value.[12] For most companies, we choose not to model potential

---

[11] Some companies, such as oil refiners, will report number of units. In these cases, consider using number of units instead of revenue to forecast equipment purchases.

[12] This section refers to acquired intangibles only. Forecast internal investments in intangibles, such as capitalized software and purchased sales contracts, with the methodology used for capital expenditures and PP&E.

acquisitions explicitly, so we set revenue growth from new acquisitions equal to zero and hold goodwill and acquired intangibles constant at their current level. We prefer this approach because of the empirical literature documenting how the typical acquisition fails to create value (any synergies are transferred to the target through high premiums). Since adding a zero-NPV investment will not increase the company's value, forecasting acquisitions is unnecessary. In fact, by forecasting acquired growth in combination with the company's current financial results, you make implicit (and often hidden) assumptions about the present value of acquisitions. For instance, if the forecast ratio of goodwill to acquired revenues implies positive NPV for acquired growth, increasing the growth rate from acquired revenues can dramatically increase the resulting valuation, even when good deals are hard to find.

If you decide to forecast acquisitions, first assess what proportion of future revenue growth they are likely to provide. For example, consider a company that generates $100 million in revenues and has announced an intention to grow by 10 percent annually—5 percent organically and 5 percent through acquisitions. In this case, measure historical ratios of goodwill and acquired intangibles to acquired revenues, and apply those ratios to acquired revenues. For instance, assume the company historically adds $3 in goodwill and intangibles for every $1 of acquired revenues. Multiplying the expected $5 million of acquired growth by 3, you obtain an expected increase of $15 million in goodwill and acquired intangibles. Make sure, however, to perform a reality check on your results by varying acquired growth and observing the resulting changes in company value. Confirm that your results are consistent with the company's past performance related to acquisitions and the challenges of creating value through acquisition.

Nonoperating Assets, Unfunded Pensions, and Deferred Taxes Next, forecast nonoperating assets (such as nonconsolidated subsidiaries), debt equivalents (such as pension liabilities), and equity equivalents (such as deferred taxes). Because many nonoperating items are valued using methods other than discounted cash flow (see Chapter 16), any forecasts of these items are primarily for the purpose of financial planning and cash management, not enterprise valuation. For instance, consider unfunded pension liabilities. Assume management announces its intention to reduce unfunded pensions by 50 percent over the next five years. To value unfunded pensions, do not discount the projected outflows over the next five years. Instead, use the current actuarial assessments of the shortfall, which appear in the note on pensions. The rate of reduction will have no valuation implications but will affect the ability to pay dividends or may require additional financing. To this end, model a reasonable time frame for eliminating pension shortfalls.

We are extremely cautious about forecasting (and valuing) nonconsolidated subsidiaries and other equity investments. Valuations should be based on assessing the investments currently owned, not on discounting the forecast changes in their book values and/or their corresponding income. If a forecast is necessary for planning, keep in mind that income from associates is often noncash, and nonoperating assets often grow in a lumpy fashion unrelated to a company's revenues. To forecast equity investments, rely on historical precedent to determine the appropriate level of growth.

Regarding deferred-tax assets and liabilities, those used to occur primarily through differences in depreciation schedules (investor and tax authorities use different depreciation schedules to determine taxable income). Today, deferred taxes arise for many reasons, including tax adjustments for pensions, stock-based compensation, acquired-intangibles amortization, and deferred revenues (see Chapter 20 for an in-depth discussion of deferred taxes).

For sophisticated valuations that require extremely detailed forecasts, forecast deferred taxes line by line, tying each tax to its appropriate driver. In most situations, forecasting operating deferred taxes by computing the aggregate proportion of taxes likely to be deferred will lead to reasonable results. For instance, if operating taxes are estimated at 23.4 percent of EBITA and the company historically could defer one-fifth of operating taxes paid, we often assume it can defer one-fifth of 23.4 percent going forward. Operating-related deferred-tax liabilities will then increase by the amount deferred.

Step 5: Reconcile the Balance Sheet with Investor Funds

To complete the balance sheet, forecast the company's sources of financing. To do this, rely on the rules of accounting. First, use the principle of clean surplus accounting:

$$\text{Equity}_{2020} = \text{Equity}_{2019} + \text{Net Income}_{2020}$$
$$- \text{Dividends}_{2020} + \text{Net Equity Issued}_{2020}$$

Applying this to our earlier example, Exhibit 13.12 presents the statement of shareholders' equity. To estimate equity in 2020, start with 2019 equity of $182 million from Exhibit 13.11. To this value, add the 2020 forecast

EXHIBIT 13.12 **Statement of Shareholders' Equity**

$ million

	2018	2019	Forecast 2020
Shareholders' equity, beginning of year	120.8	145.0	182.0
Net income	40.2	59.0	72.7
Dividends	(16.0)	(22.0)	(27.1)
Issuance (repurchase) of common stock	–	–	–
Shareholders' equity, end of year	145.0	182.0	227.6
Dividends/net income, %	39.8	37.3	37.3

EXHIBIT 13.13 **Forecast Balance Sheet: Sources of Financing**

$ million

	2018	2019	Preliminary 2020F	Completed 2020F	
Assets					
Operating cash	5.0	5.0	6.0	6.0	**Step 1:** Determine retained earnings using the clean surplus relation, forecast existing debt using contractual terms, and keep common stock constant.
Excess cash	100.0	60.0		49.6	
Inventory	35.0	45.0	54.0	54.0	
Current assets	140.0	110.0	60.0	109.6	
Net PP&E	200.0	250.0	300.0	300.0	
Equity investments	100.0	100.0	100.0	100.0	**Step 2:** Test which is higher: (a) assets excluding excess cash or (b) liabilities and equity, excluding newly issued debt.
Total assets	440.0	460.0	460.0	509.6	
Liabilities and equity					
Accounts payable	15.0	20.0	24.0	24.0	**Step 3:** If assets excluding excess cash are higher, set excess cash equal to zero, and plug the difference with the newly issued debt. Otherwise, plug with excess cash.
Short-term debt	200.0	178.0	178.0	178.0	
Current liabilities	215.0	198.0	202.0	202.0	
Long-term debt	80.0	80.0	80.0	80.0	
Newly issued debt	–	–		–	
Shareholders' equity	145.0	182.0	227.6	227.6	
Total liabilities and equity	440.0	460.0	509.6	509.6	

of net income: $72.7 million from the income statement in Exhibit 13.6. Next, estimate the dividend payout. In 2019, the company paid out 37.3 percent of net income in the form of dividends. Applying a 37.3 percent payout ratio to estimated net income leads to $27.1 million in expected dividends. Finally, add new equity issued net of equity repurchased, which in this example is zero. Using the clean surplus relationship, we estimate 2020 equity at $227.6 million.

At this point, four line items on the balance sheet remain: excess cash, short-term debt, long-term debt, and a new account titled "newly issued debt." Some combination of these line items must make the balance sheet balance. For this reason, these items are often referred to as "the plug." In simple models, existing debt either remains constant or is retired on schedule, according to contractual terms.[13] To complete the balance sheet, set one of the remaining two items (excess cash or newly issued debt) equal to zero. Then use the primary accounting identity—assets equal liabilities plus shareholders' equity—to determine the remaining item.

Exhibit 13.13 presents the elements of this process for our example. First, hold short-term debt, long-term debt, and common stock constant. Next, sum total assets, excluding excess cash: cash ($6 million), inventory ($54 million), net PP&E ($300 million), and equity investments ($100 million) total $460 million. Then sum total liabilities and equity, excluding newly

[13] Given the importance of debt in a leveraged buyout, buyout models often contain a separate worksheet detailing interest and principal repayment by year for each debt contract.

issued debt: accounts payable ($24 million), short-term debt ($178 million), long-term debt ($80 million), and shareholders' equity ($227.6 million) total $509.6 million. Because liabilities and equity (excluding newly issued debt) are greater than assets (excluding excess cash), newly issued debt is set to zero. Now total liabilities and equity equal $509.6 million. To ensure that the balance sheet balances, we set the only remaining item, excess cash, equal to $49.6 million. This increases total assets to $509.6 million, and the balance sheet is complete.

To implement this procedure in a spreadsheet, use the spreadsheet's prebuilt If function. Set up the function so it sets excess cash to zero when assets (excluding excess cash) exceed liabilities and equity (excluding newly issued debt). Conversely, if assets are less than liabilities and equity, the function should set short-term debt equal to zero and excess cash equal to the difference.

The Link Between Capital Structure Forecasts and Valuation   When using excess cash and newly issued debt to complete the balance sheet, you will likely encounter one common side effect: as growth drops, newly issued debt will drop to zero, and excess cash will become very large.[14] But what if a drop in leverage is inconsistent with your long-term assessments concerning capital structure? In an enterprise DCF valuation that uses the weighted average cost of capital for discounting, this side effect does not matter. Excess cash and debt are not included as part of free cash flow, so they do not affect the enterprise valuation. Capital structure affects enterprise DCF only through the weighted average cost of capital.[15] Thus, only an adjustment to WACC will lead to a change in valuation.

To bring the capital structure on the balance sheet in line with the capital structure implied by WACC, adjust the dividend payout ratio or amount of net share repurchases. For instance, as the dividend payout is increased, retained earnings will drop, and this should cause excess cash to drop as well. By varying the payout ratio (both dividends and share repurchases), you can also test how robust your FCF model is. Specifically, ROIC and FCF, and hence value, should not change when the dividend rate or amount of share repurchases is adjusted.

How you choose to model the payout ratio depends on the requirements of the model. In most situations, you can adjust the dividend payout ratio

---

[14] Whenever ROIC is greater than revenue growth, a company will generate operating cash flow; that is, the investment rate will be negative. If dividends or share repurchases are not increased to disgorge cash, debt will drop, and/or excess cash will accumulate.

[15] In the APV model, your forecast of debt will affect valuation. Interest tax shields are computed year by year based on the amount of debt, the interest rate, and the tax rate. Models that discount with a constant WACC implicitly assume debt-to-value never changes, such that balance sheet forecasts are ignored.

or amount of repurchases by hand when needed (remember, the ratio does not affect value but rather brings excess cash and newly issued debt closer to reality). For more complex models, determine net debt (total debt less excess cash) by applying the target net-debt-to-value ratio modeled in the WACC at each point in time. Next, using the target debt-to-value ratio, solve for the required payout. To do this, however, you must perform a valuation in each forecast year and iterate backward—a time-consuming process for a feature that will not affect the final valuation.[16]

Step 6: Calculate ROIC and FCF

Once you have completed your income statement and balance sheet forecasts, calculate ROIC and FCF for each forecast year. This process should be straightforward if you have already computed ROIC and FCF historically. Since a full set of forecast financials is now available, merely copy the two calculations from historical financials to projected financials.

For companies that are creating value, future ROICs should fit one of three general patterns: ROIC should either remain near current levels (when the company has a distinguishable sustainable advantage), trend toward an industry or economic median, or trend to the cost of capital. Think through the economics of the business to decide what is appropriate. For more on long-term trends of ROIC, refer to Chapter 8.

ADVANCED FORECASTING

The preceding sections detailed the process for creating a comprehensive set of financial forecasts. When forecasting, you are likely to come across three advanced issues: forecasting using nonfinancial operating drivers, forecasting using fixed and variable costs, and handling the impact of inflation.

Nonfinancial Operating Drivers

Until now, the chapter has created forecasts that rely solely on financial drivers. In industries where prices are changing or technology is advancing, forecasts should incorporate nonfinancial ratios, such as volume and productivity.

Consider the turmoil in the airline industry during the early 2000s. Fares requiring Saturday-night stays and advance purchases disappeared as

---

[16] To value Costco in Appendix H, we modeled a constant leverage ratio year by year and iterated backward. While iteration is not necessary to value a company more generally, it is required to ensure that the enterprise DCF valuation ties to other valuation methodologies, such as cash-flow-to-equity models.

competition from low-cost carriers intensified. Network carriers could no longer distinguish business travelers, their primary source of profit, from leisure travelers. As the average price dropped, costs rose as a percentage of sales. But were airlines truly becoming higher-cost?[17] And how would this trend continue? To forecast changes more accurately, it is necessary to separate price from volume (as measured by seat-miles). Then, instead of forecasting costs as a percentage of revenues, forecast costs as a function of expected quantity—in this case, seat-miles.

The same concept applies to advances in technology. For instance, rather than estimate labor as a percentage of revenues, you could forecast units per employee and average salary per employee. Separating these two drivers of labor costs allows you to model a direct relationship between productivity improvements from new technology and estimated changes in units per employee.

Fixed versus Variable Costs

When you are valuing a small project, it is important to distinguish fixed costs (incurred once to create a basic infrastructure) from variable costs (correlated with volume). When you are valuing an individual project, only variable costs should be increased as revenues grow.

At the scale of most publicly traded companies, however, the distinction between fixed and variable costs is often immaterial, because nearly every cost is variable. For instance, consider a mobile-phone company that transmits calls using radio-frequency towers. In spite of the common perception that the tower is a fixed cost, this is true for only a given number of subscribers. As subscribers increase beyond a certain limit, new towers must be added, even in an area with preexisting coverage. (A small company adding 1,000 customers can leverage economies of scale more than a large company adding 100,000 customers.) What is a fixed cost in the short run for small increases in activity becomes variable over the long run even at reasonable growth rates (10 percent annual growth doubles the size of a company in about seven years). Since corporate valuation is about long-run profitability and growth, nearly every cost should be treated as variable.

When an asset, such as computer software or a mobile app, is truly scalable, its development cost should be treated as a fixed cost. Be careful, however. Many technologies, such as computer software, quickly become obsolete, requiring new incremental expenditures for the company to remain competitive. In this case, a cost deemed fixed actually requires repeated cash outflows, just not in traditional ways.

---

[17] For example, Spirit Airlines dedicates a higher percentage of revenue to labor than American Airlines does. In terms of cost per seat-mile, however, American is the higher-cost airline of the two.

Incorporating Inflation

In Chapter 10, we recommended that financial-statement forecasts and the cost of capital be estimated in nominal currency units (with inflation), rather than real currency units (without inflation). To remain consistent, the nominally based financial forecast and the nominally based cost of capital must reflect the same expected general inflation rate. This means the inflation rate built into the forecast must be derived from an inflation rate implicit in the cost of capital.[18]

When possible, derive the expected inflation rate from the term structure of government bond rates. The nominal interest rate on government bonds reflects investor demand for a real return plus a premium for expected inflation. Estimate expected inflation as the nominal rate of interest less an estimate of the real rate of interest, using the following formula:

$$\text{Expected Inflation} = \frac{(1+\text{Nominal Rate})}{(1+\text{Real Rate})} - 1$$

To estimate expected inflation, start by calculating the nominal yield to maturity on a ten-year government bond. But how do you find the real rate? Many countries, such as the United States, United Kingdom, and Japan, issue inflation-linked bonds (ILBs). An ILB is a bond that protects against inflation by growing the bond's coupons and principal at the consumer price index (CPI). Consequently, the yield to maturity on an ILB is the market's expectation of the real interest rate over the life of the bond. In March 2019, the yield on a ten-year U.S. Treasury bond equaled 2.57 percent, and the yield on a U.S. Treasury inflation-protected security (TIPS) bond equaled 0.66 percent.[19] Unlike previous decades, when the real rate hovered around 2 percent, the real rate has been volatile during the last ten years, even dropping below zero in 2012. To determine expected inflation, apply the previous formula to the data:

$$\text{Expected Inflation} = \frac{1.0257}{1.0066} - 1 = 0.0190$$

Expected inflation, as measured by the difference in nominal and real bonds, equals 1.90 percent annually over the next ten years.

---

[18] Individual line items may have inflation rates that are higher or lower than the general rate, but they should still derive from the general rate. For example, the revenue forecast should reflect the growth in units sold and the expected increase in unit prices. The increase in unit prices, in turn, should reflect the generally expected level of inflation in the economy plus or minus an inflation rate differential for that specific industry. Suppose general inflation is expected to be 4 percent and unit prices for the company's products are expected to increase at one percentage point less than general inflation. Overall, the company's prices would be expected to increase at 3 percent per year. If we assume a 3 percent annual increase in units sold, we would forecast 6.1 percent annual revenue growth (1.03 × 1.03 − 1).
[19] 10-Year Treasury Constant Maturity Rate (DGS10) and 10-Year Treasury Inflation-Indexed Security, Constant Maturity (FII10), Federal Reserve Bank of St. Louis.

EXHIBIT 13.14 **Expected Inflation versus Growth in the Consumer Price Index**

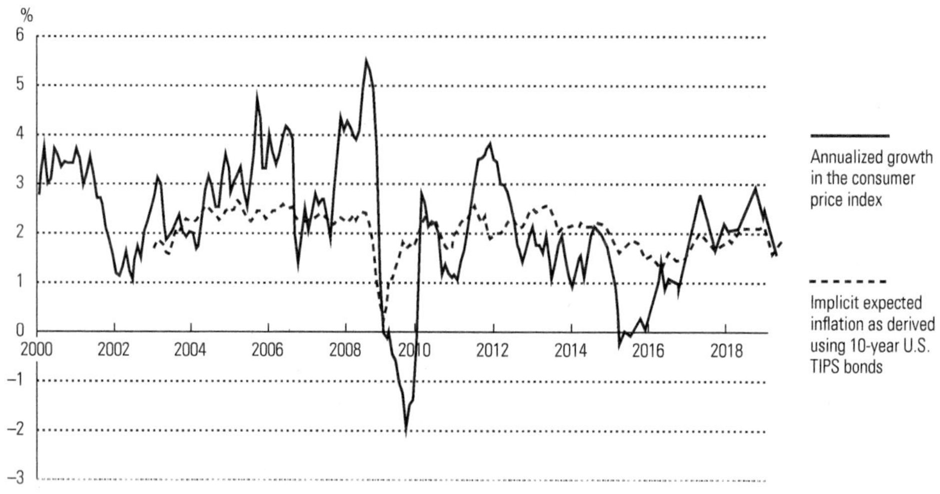

Source: Federal Reseve Bank of St. Louis.

Exhibit 13.14 presents annualized growth in the U.S. consumer price index (CPI) versus expected ten-year inflation implied by traditional U.S. Treasury bonds and U.S. TIPS bonds. Since the ten-year TIPS bond is based on long-term inflation, the implied inflation rate is much more stable than the one-year change in CPI (in mid-2008, CPI grew at more than 5 percent when crude oil spiked, only to crater after the recession as companies cut prices to generate demand). Since 2000, actual and implied inflation have both hovered around 2 percent annually.

Inflation can distort historical analysis, especially when it exceeds 5 percent annually. In these situations, historical financials should be adjusted to reflect operating performance independent of inflation. We discuss the impact of high inflation rates in Chapter 26.

CONCLUDING THOUGHTS

In this chapter, we provided a detailed line-by-line process to create a set of financial forecasts. While it is important that the model reflect the complexities of the business you are analyzing, always keep a close eye on the bigger picture. Make sure resulting value drivers, such as ROIC and growth, are consistent with the past performance of the business and the industry's economics. When the model is complete, use the model to test the importance of various inputs. A sensitivity table can provide insight on not only the valuation but also on the actions management must undertake to capture it.

14

Estimating
Continuing Value

A thoughtful estimate of continuing value is essential to any company valuation. It serves as a useful method for simplifying the valuation process while still incorporating solid economic principles. To estimate a company's value, separate the forecast of expected cash flow into two periods and define the company's value as follows:

$$\text{Value} = \frac{\text{Present Value of Cash Flow}}{\text{during Explicit Forecast Period}} + \frac{\text{Present Value of Cash Flow}}{\text{after Explicit Forecast Period}}$$

The second term is the continuing value: the value of the company's expected cash flow beyond an explicit forecast period. By deliberately making some simple assumptions about the company's performance during this second period—for example, assuming a constant rate of growth and return on capital—you can estimate continuing value by using formulas instead of explicitly forecasting and discounting cash flows over an extended period.

Continuing value often accounts for a large percentage of a company's total value. Exhibit 14.1 shows continuing value as a percentage of total value for companies in four industries, given an eight-year explicit forecast. In these examples, continuing value accounts for 56 percent to 125 percent of total value. These large percentages do not necessarily mean that most of a company's value will be created in the continuing-value period. Often, continuing value is large because profits and other inflows in the early years are offset by outflows for capital spending and working-capital investment—investments that should generate higher cash flow in later years. We discuss the interpretation of continuing value in more detail later in this chapter.

The continuing-value formulas developed over the next few pages are consistent with the principles of value creation and discounted cash flow (DCF). This

EXHIBIT 14.1 **Continuing Value as a Percentage of Total Value**

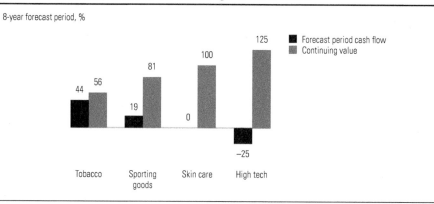

8-year forecast period, %

is important, because many investment professionals ignore the economics that underpin their estimate of continuing value. For example, we have seen acquirers estimate the continuing value for a target company by applying the same multiple of earnings five years in the future as the multiple they are currently paying for the acquisition target.[1] By doing this, they are implicitly assuming that someone would be willing to pay the same multiple five years from now, regardless of changes in prospects for growth and return on invested capital over that period. This type of circular reasoning leads to inaccurate valuations that are often overly optimistic. Instead, acquirers should estimate what the multiple will be at the end of the forecast period, given the company's potential at that time.

This chapter begins with the recommended continuing-value formulas for DCF and economic-profit valuation models. It then discusses concerns that arise out of common misinterpretations of continuing value, explaining how proper measurement addresses these concerns. Then we identify common pitfalls in estimation and offer best practices for avoiding these. Finally, we compare the recommended formulas with other common techniques, such as multiples and liquidation values.

RECOMMENDED FORMULA FOR DCF VALUATION

If you are using the enterprise DCF model, you should estimate continuing value by using the value driver formula derived in Chapter 3:

$$\text{Continuing Value}_t = \frac{\text{NOPAT}_{t+1}\left(1 - \dfrac{g}{\text{RONIC}}\right)}{\text{WACC} - g}$$

---

[1] Typical multiples include enterprise value-to-EBITA, where EBITA equals earnings before interest, taxes, and amortization, and enterprise value-to-EBITDA, where EBITDA equals earnings before interest, taxes, depreciation, and amortization.

where NOPAT_{t+1} = net operating profit after taxes in the first year after the
explicit forecast period
g = expected growth rate in NOPAT in perpetuity
RONIC = expected rate of return on new invested capital
WACC = weighted average cost of capital

A simple example demonstrates that the value driver formula does, in fact, replicate the process of projecting the cash flows and discounting them to the present. Begin with the following cash flow projections:

	Year 1	Year 2	Year 3	Year 4	Year 5
NOPAT	$10.0	$10.6	$11.2	$11.9	$12.6
Net investment	5.0	5.3	5.6	6.0	6.3
Free cash flow	$ 5.0	$ 5.3	$ 5.6	$ 6.0	$ 6.3

Beyond year 5, the company continues to reinvest half its after-tax operating profit at a 12 percent rate of return, driving continued growth at 6 percent. The weighted average cost of capital (WACC) is assumed to be 11 percent.

To compare the methods of computing continuing value, first discount a long forecast—say, 100 years:

$$CV = \frac{\$5.0}{1.11} + \frac{\$5.3}{(1.11)^2} + \frac{\$5.6}{(1.11)^3} + \ldots + \frac{\$50(1.06)^{99}}{(1.11)^{100}}$$

$$CV = \$99$$

Next, use the growth perpetuity formula:

$$CV = \frac{\$5.0}{0.11 - 0.06}$$

$$CV = \$100$$

Finally, use the value driver formula:

$$CV = \frac{\$10\left(1 - \dfrac{0.06}{0.12}\right)}{0.11 - 0.06}$$

$$CV = \$100$$

All three approaches yield virtually the same result. If we had carried out the discounted cash flow beyond 150 years, the result would have been nearly identical.[2]

---

[2] The sum of discounted cash flow will approach the perpetuity value as the forecast period is extended. In this example, a 75-year forecast period will capture 96.9 percent of the perpetuity value, whereas a 150-year forecast period will capture 99.9 percent. This is only true, however, when growth is substantially less than the cost of capital. If the two variables are of near-equal value, an infinitely lived perpetuity will overstate the value of a company with a limited life. In these situations, either incorporate a probability of failure into your perpetuity, or approximate continuing value with a growth annuity.

Although the value driver formula and the cash-flow-based growth perpetuity formula are technically equivalent, applying the growth perpetuity formula is tricky, and it is easy to make the common error of ignoring the interdependence between free cash flow and growth. More specifically, if growth in the continuing-value period is forecast to be lower than the growth at the end of the explicit forecast period (as is normally the case), then required reinvestment is likely to be less, leading to higher free cash flow. If the perpetuity's free cash flow is computed using cash flow from the higher-growth explicit forecast period, this cash flow will be too low, and the calculation will underestimate the continuing value. Later in this chapter, an example illustrates what can go wrong when using the cash flow perpetuity formula rather than the key value driver formula.

Because perpetuity-based formulas rely on parameters that never change, use a continuing-value formula only when the company has reached a steady state, with low revenue growth and stable operating margins. Chapters 8 and 9 provide guidance for thinking about return on capital and long-term growth. In addition, when estimating the continuing-value parameters, keep in mind the following technical considerations:

- *NOPAT.* The level of NOPAT should be based on a normalized level of revenues, sustainable margin, and return on invested capital (ROIC). This is especially important in a cyclical business; revenues and operating margins should reflect the midpoint of the company's business cycle, not its peak or trough.

- *RONIC.* The expected rate of return on new invested capital (RONIC) should be consistent with expected competitive conditions beyond the explicit forecast period. Economic theory suggests that competition will eventually eliminate abnormal returns, so for companies in competitive industries, set RONIC equal to WACC. However, for companies with sustainable competitive advantages, such as brands and patents, you might set RONIC equal to the return the company is forecast to earn during later years of the explicit forecast period. Chapter 8 contains data on the long-term returns on capital for companies in different industries.

- *Growth rate.* A company's growth rate typically reverts to industry growth rates very quickly, and few companies can be expected to grow faster than the economy for long periods. The best estimate is probably the expected long-term rate of consumption growth for the industry's products, plus inflation. Sensitivity analyses are useful for understanding how the growth rate affects continuing-value estimates. Chapter 9 provides empirical evidence on historical corporate growth rates.

- *WACC.* The weighted average cost of capital should incorporate a sustainable capital structure and an underlying estimate of business risk consistent with expected industry conditions.

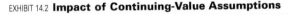

EXHIBIT 14.2 **Impact of Continuing-Value Assumptions**

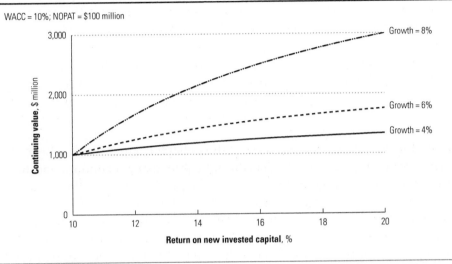

Exhibit 14.2 shows how continuing value, calculated using the value driver formula, is affected by various combinations of growth rate and RONIC. The example assumes a $100 million base level of NOPAT and a 10 percent WACC. For RONIC near the cost of capital, there is little change in value as the growth changes. This is because the company is taking on projects whose net present value is close to zero. At an expected RONIC of 14 percent, however, changing the growth rate from 6 percent to 8 percent increases the continuing value by 50 percent, from about $1.4 billion to about $2.1 billion. The higher the RONIC, the more sensitive the continuing value is to changing growth rates.

Two-Stage Continuing-Value Models

For high-growth companies or companies undergoing long-term structural changes, we recommend extending the explicit forecast period until the company reaches a steady state. If the resulting model is too cumbersome, use a multistage continuing value that aggregates multiple years into a single formula. In a two-stage model, the continuing value is split into a growth annuity followed by a growth perpetuity. This allows for distinct returns on capital and growth rates for different stages of the company's life, without the burden of year-by-year forecasts. We provide two-stage continuing-value formulas for discounted cash flow and economic-profit models in Appendix I.

CONTINUING VALUE USING ECONOMIC PROFIT

To estimate continuing value in an economic-profit valuation, we again rely on perpetuity-based formulas. With the economic-profit approach, however, the continuing value does not equal the value of the company following the explicit forecast period, as it does for discounted free cash flow. Instead, it is the incremental value over the company's invested capital at the end of the explicit forecast period. Today's value of the company is as follows:

$$\text{Value}_0 \quad = \quad \begin{array}{c} \text{Invested} \\ \text{capital}_0 \end{array} \quad + \quad \begin{array}{c} \text{Present value of} \\ \text{forecast economic} \\ \text{profit } during \text{ explicit} \\ \text{forecast period} \end{array} \quad + \quad \begin{array}{c} \text{Present value of} \\ \text{forecast economic} \\ \text{profit } after \text{ explicit} \\ \text{forecast period} \end{array}$$

The continuing value is the last term in the preceding equation.

The formula to estimate continuing value using economic profit is more complicated than that for discounted cash flow. Unlike the key value driver formula used in an enterprise DCF model, the continuing value for economic profit contains two terms. The first term represents the present value of economic profits on capital in place at the end of the forecast period. The second term represents the present value of economic profits for annual investments beyond the explicit forecast period. The formula is as follows:

$$CV_t = \frac{IC_t \left(ROIC_{t+1} - WACC \right)}{WACC} + \frac{PV \left(\text{Economic Profit}_{t+2} \right)}{WACC - g}$$

where

$$PV \left(\text{Economic Profit}_{t+2} \right) = \frac{NOPAT_{t+1} \left(\dfrac{g}{RONIC} \right) \left(RONIC - WACC \right)}{WACC}$$

where

IC_t = invested capital at the end of the explicit forecast period
$ROIC_t$ = ROIC on existing capital at the end of the explicit forecast period, measured as $NOPAT_{t+1}/IC_t$
$WACC$ = weighted average cost of capital
g = expected growth rate in NOPAT in perpetuity
$RONIC$ = expected rate of return on new invested capital after the explicit forecast period

According to the formula, total economic profit following the explicit forecast period equals the present value of economic profit in the first year after the explicit forecast in perpetuity plus any incremental economic profit after that year. Incremental economic profit is created by additional growth at returns exceeding the cost of capital. If expected RONIC equals WACC, the third term (economic profits beyond year 1) equals zero, and the continuing economic-profit value is the value of just the first year's economic profit in perpetuity.

MISUNDERSTANDINGS ABOUT CONTINUING VALUE

Properly applied, continuing value can simplify your valuation while incorporating robust economic principles. In practice, however, proper application often requires correcting three common misunderstandings about continuing value. The first is the perception that the length of the explicit forecast affects the company's value. As we show in this section, only the *split* of value is changing, not the total value. Second, people incorrectly believe that value creation stops at the end of the explicit forecast period, when return on *new* invested capital is set equal to WACC in the continuing-value formula. As we demonstrate, since returns from *existing* capital carry into the continuing-value period, aggregate ROIC will only gradually approach the cost of capital. Finally, some investment professionals incorrectly infer that a large continuing value relative to the company's total value means that value creation occurs primarily after the explicit forecast period. This makes them uneasy about using enterprise DCF. In this section, we show why these concerns are not necessarily justified and why continuing value is more robust than often perceived.

Why Forecast Length Doesn't Affect a Company's Value

While the length of the explicit forecast period you choose is important, it does not affect the value of the company; it affects only the distribution of the company's value between the explicit forecast period and the years that follow. In Exhibit 14.3, the value of the company is $893 million, regardless of how long the forecast period is. With a forecast horizon of five years, the continuing value accounts for 79 percent of total value. With an eight-year horizon, the continuing value accounts for only 67 percent of total value. As the explicit forecast horizon grows longer, value shifts from the continuing value to the explicit forecast period, but the total value always remains the same.

EXHIBIT 14.3 **Comparison of Total-Value Estimates Using Different Forecast Horizons**

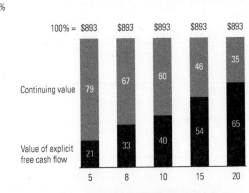

Length of explicit forecast period, years

EXHIBIT 14.4 **Valuation Using Five-Year Explicit Forecast Period**

$ million

	Year 1	Year 2	Year 3	Year 4	Year 5	Base for CV
NOPAT	100.0	109.0	118.8	129.5	141.2	149.6
Depreciation	20.0	21.8	23.8	25.9	28.2	
Gross cash flow	120.0	130.8	142.6	155.4	169.4	
Gross investment	(76.3)	(83.1)	(90.6)	(98.7)	(107.6)	
Free cash flow (FCF)	43.8	47.7	52.0	56.7	61.8	
× Discount factor	0.893	0.797	0.712	0.636	0.567	
Present value of FCF	39.1	38.0	37.0	36.0	35.0	

Present value of FCF$_{1-5}$	185.1
Continuing value	707.5
Total value	892.6

Calculation of continuing value (CV)

$$CV_5 = \frac{NOPAT_{cv}\left(1 - \frac{g}{RONIC}\right)}{WACC - g} = \frac{\$149.6\left(1 - \frac{0.06}{0.12}\right)}{0.12 - 0.06} = \$1,246.9$$

$$CV_0 = \frac{CV_5}{(1 + WACC)^5} = \frac{\$1,246.9}{(1.12)^5} = \$707.5$$

To see how the value shift works, compare Exhibits 14.4 and 14.5. The former details the calculations for the valuation model using a five-year explicit forecast period, whereas the latter repeats the analysis with an eight-year period.

In Exhibit 14.4, NOPAT starts at $100 million. During the first five years, NOPAT grows at 9 percent per year. Following year 5, NOPAT growth slows to 6 percent. Using the definition of free cash flow derived in Chapter 10,

EXHIBIT 14.5 **Valuation Using Eight-Year Explicit Forecast Period**

$ million

	Year 1	Year 2	Year 3	Year 4	Year 5	Year 6	Year 7	Year 8	Base for CV
NOPAT	100.0	109.0	118.8	129.5	141.2	149.6	158.6	168.1	178.2
Depreciation	20.0	21.8	23.8	25.9	28.2	29.9	31.7	33.6	
Gross cash flow	120.0	130.8	142.6	155.4	169.4	179.6	190.3	201.7	
Gross investment	(76.3)	(83.1)	(90.6)	(98.7)	(107.6)	(104.7)	(111.0)	(117.7)	
Free cash flow (FCF)	43.8	47.7	52.0	56.7	61.8	74.8	79.3	84.1	
× Discount factor	0.893	0.797	0.712	0.636	0.567	0.507	0.452	0.404	
Present value of FCF	39.1	38.0	37.0	36.0	35.0	37.9	35.9	34.0	

Present value of FCF$_{1-8}$	292.9
Continuing value	599.8
Total value	892.6

Calculation of continuing value (CV)

$$CV_8 = \frac{NOPAT_{cv}\left(1 - \frac{g}{RONIC}\right)}{WACC - g} = \frac{\$178.2\left(1 - \frac{0.06}{0.12}\right)}{0.12 - 0.06} = \$1,485.1$$

$$CV_0 = \frac{CV_8}{(1 + WACC)^8} = \frac{\$1,485.1}{(1.12)^8} = \$599.8$$

we compute gross cash flow by adding depreciation to NOPAT. Free cash flow equals gross cash flow minus gross investment. To compute the company's gross investment, multiply NOPAT by the reinvestment rate, where the reinvestment rate equals the ratio of growth to ROIC (9 percent divided by 16 percent), plus depreciation. To determine the present value of the company, sum the present value of the explicit forecast period cash flows plus the present value of continuing value. (Since the continuing value is measured as of year 5, the continuing value of $1,246.9 million is discounted by five years, not by six, a common mistake.) The total value equals $892.6 million.

Exhibit 14.5 details the calculations for a valuation model that uses an eight-year explicit forecast period and a continuing value that starts in year 9. The structure and forecast inputs of the model are identical to those of Exhibit 14.4. In the first five years, growth is 9 percent, and ROIC equals 16 percent. After five years, growth drops to 6 percent, and ROIC drops to 14 percent. This leads to an explicit forecast value of $292.9 million, which is higher than under the shorter five-year window. Since NOPAT in the continuing value is higher, continuing value also is higher, but since it occurs three years later, its discounted value is lower.

You can see that the amounts under the two valuation methods are identical. Since the underlying value drivers are the same in both valuations, the results will be the same. The length of your forecast horizon should affect only the proportion of total value allocated between the explicit forecast period and continuing value, not the total value.

The choice of forecast horizon will indirectly affect value if it is associated with changes in the economic assumptions underlying the continuing-value estimate. You can unknowingly change the amount of value creation when you change your forecast horizon. Many forecasters assume the company will generate returns above the cost of capital during the explicit forecast period, and they set return on new capital equal to WACC in the continuing value. By extending the explicit forecast period, you increase the number of years the company is creating value. Extending the forecast period indirectly raises the value, even when that is not intended.

So how do you choose the appropriate length of the explicit forecast period? The period should be long enough that the business will have reached a steady state by the end of it. Suppose you expect the company's margins to decline as its customers consolidate. Margins are currently 14 percent, and you forecast they will fall to 9 percent over the next seven years. In this case, the explicit forecast period must be at least seven years, because continuing-value approaches cannot account for the declining margin (at least not without complex computations). The business must be operating at an equilibrium level for the continuing-value approaches to be useful. If the explicit forecast period is more than seven years, there will be no effect on the company's total value.

Why Continuing Value Doesn't Mark the End of Competitive Advantage

A related but subtle issue is the concept of the competitive-advantage period, or that period during which a company earns supernormal returns above the cost of capital. Although counterintuitive, setting RONIC equal to WACC in the continuing-value formula does not imply that the competitive-advantage period will conclude at the end of the explicit forecast period.

Remember, the key value driver formula is based on the return for new capital invested, not company-wide average ROIC. If you set RONIC in the continuing-value period equal to the cost of capital, you are *not* assuming that the return on total capital (old and new) will equal the cost of capital. The *original* capital (prior to the continuing-value period) will continue to earn the returns projected in the last forecast period. In other words, the company's competitive-advantage period has not come to an end once the continuing-value period is reached. Existing capital will continue to earn supernormal returns in perpetuity. For example, imagine a retailer that opens its initial stores in high-traffic, high-growth, extremely profitable areas. These stores earn a superior rate of return and fund ongoing expansion. But as the company grows, new locations become difficult to find, and the ROIC related to expansion starts to drop. Eventually, the ROIC on the newest store will approach the cost of capital. But does this imply that ROIC on early stores will drop to the cost of capital as well? Probably not. A great location is hard to beat.

Exhibit 14.6 shows the average ROIC, based on continuing-value growth of 5 percent, the return on base capital is 18 percent, return on new capital is 10 percent, and WACC is 10 percent. Note how the average return on aggregate capital declines only gradually. From its starting point at 18 percent, it declines to 14 percent (the halfway point to RONIC) after 10 years in the continuing-value period. It reaches 12 percent after 21 years, and 11 percent after 37 years. How quickly this decay occurs from ROIC in the forecast period to RONIC in the continuing value depends on the growth rate in the continuing value. The higher the growth rate, the more capital there is to be deployed at lower returns, and the faster the drop.

EXHIBIT 14.6 **Gradual Decline in Average ROIC According to Continuing-Value Formula**

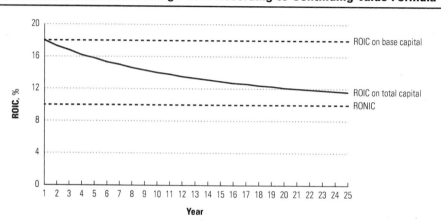

EXHIBIT 14.7 **Innovation Inc.: Free Cash Flow Forecast and Valuation**

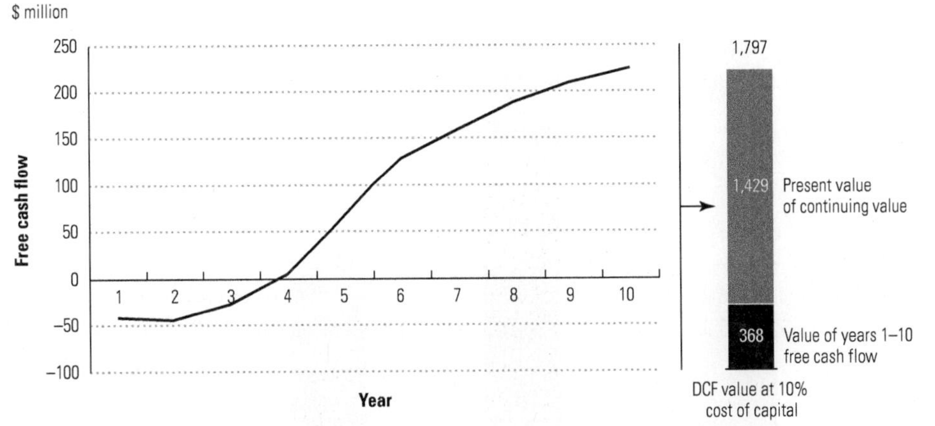

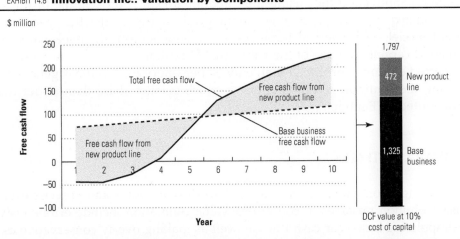

Why Value Isn't Just from Continuing Value

"All the value is in the continuing value" is a comment we've often heard from dismayed executives. Exhibit 14.7 illustrates the problem for a hypothetical company, Innovation Inc. Based on discounted free cash flow, it appears that 80 percent of Innovation's value comes from the continuing value. But there are other interesting ways to interpret the source of value.

Exhibit 14.8 suggests an alternative: a business components approach. Innovation Inc. has a base business that earns a steady 20 percent return on capital and is growing at 5 percent per year. It also has developed a new product line that will require several years of negative cash flow for development of a new sales channel, which management hopes will lead to organic growth. As shown in Exhibit 14.8, the base business has a value of $1,326 million,

EXHIBIT 14.8 **Innovation Inc.: Valuation by Components**

EXHIBIT 14.9 **Innovation Inc.: Comparison of Continuing-Value Approaches**

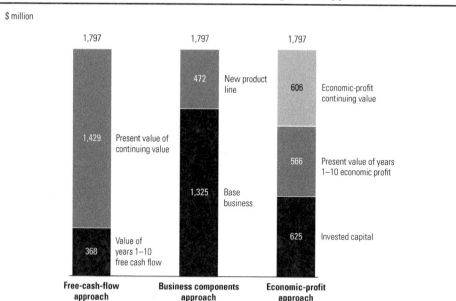

or 74 percent of Innovation's total value. In other words, 74 percent of the company's value comes from operations that are currently generating stable, predictable cash flow. Only 26 percent of total value can be attributed to the unpredictable growth business. When the situation is viewed this way, uncertainty plays only a small role in the total value of the company.

It is possible to use the economic-profit model to generate another interpretation of continuing value. Exhibit 14.9 compares the components of value for Innovation Inc., using the discounted-FCF approach, the business components approach, and an economic-profit model. Under the economic-profit model, 35 percent of Innovation's value is simply the book value of invested capital. The rest of the value, $1,172 million, is the present value of projected economic profit. Of that, only 34 percent of total value is generated during the continuing-value period—a much smaller share than under the discounted-FCF model.

COMMON PITFALLS

Estimating a company's performance 10 to 15 years out is an imprecise exercise. Common mistakes in continuing value estimation include erroneously extrapolating base-year cash flow, as well as making overly conservative assumptions on capital returns, both naively and purposely.

EXHIBIT 14.10 **Correct and Incorrect Methods of Forecasting Base FCF**

$ million

	Year 9	Year 10	Year 11, 5% growth Incorrect	Year 11, 5% growth Correct
Revenues	1,000	1,100	1,155	1,155
Operating expenses	(850)	(935)	(982)	(982)
EBITA	150	165	173	173
Operating taxes	(60)	(66)	(69)	(69)
NOPAT	90	99	104	104
Depreciation	27	30	32	32
Gross cash flow	117	129	136	136
Capital expenditures	(30)	(33)	(35)	(35)
Increase in working capital	(27)	(30)	(32)	(17)
Gross investment	(57)	(63)	(67)	(52)
Free cash flow	60	66	69	84
Supplemental calculations				
Working capital, year-end	300	330	362	347
Working capital/revenues, %	30.0	30.0	31.3	30.0

Erroneous Base-Year Extrapolation

Exhibit 14.10 illustrates a common error in forecasting the base level of free cash flow: assuming that the investment rate is constant, so that NOPAT, investment, and FCF all grow at the same rate. From year 9 to year 10 (the last forecast year), the company's earnings and cash flow grow by 10 percent. It is believed that revenue growth in the continuing-value period will be 5 percent per year. A common, yet incorrect, forecast for year 11 (the continuing-value base year) simply increases every line item from year 10 by 5 percent, as shown in the third column. This forecast is wrong because the increase in working capital is far too large, given the smaller increase in sales. Since revenues are growing more slowly, the proportion of gross cash flow devoted to working capital requirements should decline significantly, as shown in the last column. In the final column, the increase in working capital should be the amount necessary to maintain the year-end working capital at a constant percentage of revenues.

The erroneous approach continually increases working capital as a percentage of revenues (5 percent) and will significantly understate the value of the company. Note that in the third column, free cash flow is 18 percent lower than it should be. The same problem applies to capital expenditures. To keep the example simple, we limited it to working capital.

To avoid making an error in estimating final-year cash flow, we highly recommend using the value driver formula instead of the cash flow perpetuity model. The value driver model implicitly computes the required investment based on expectations of growth and ROIC.

Naive Overconservatism

Many investment professionals routinely assume that the incremental return on capital during the continuing-value period will equal the cost of capital. This practice relieves them of having to forecast a growth rate, since growth in this case neither adds nor destroys value. For some businesses, this assumption is too conservative. For example, both Coca-Cola's and PepsiCo's soft-drink businesses earn high returns on invested capital, and their returns are unlikely to fall substantially as they continue to grow, due to the strength of their brands, high barriers to entry, and limited competition.[3] For these businesses, an assumption that RONIC equals WACC would understate their values.[4] This problem applies equally to almost any business selling a product or service that is unlikely to be duplicated, including many pharmaceutical companies, numerous consumer products companies, and some software companies.

However, even if RONIC remains high, growth will drop as the market matures. Therefore, any assumption that RONIC is greater than WACC should be coupled with an economically reasonable growth rate.

Purposeful Overconservatism

Some investment professionals are overly conservative because of the uncertainty and size of the continuing value. But if continuing value is to be estimated properly, the uncertainty should cut both ways: the results are just as likely to be higher than an unbiased estimate as they are to be lower. So conservatism overcompensates for uncertainty. Uncertainty matters, but it should be modeled using scenarios, not through conservatism regarding ROIC or growth in the continuing-value formula.

OTHER APPROACHES TO CONTINUING VALUE

Several alternative approaches to estimating continuing value are used in practice. A few approaches are acceptable if applied carefully, but in general, these alternatives often produce misleading results. We prefer the methods

---

[3] Even the strongest brands face pressure from new technologies and changing customer preferences. For instance, Coca-Cola and PepsiCo have looked to new businesses as consumers have shifted away from soft drinks to bottled water and flavored teas.

[4] In this example, RONIC equaling WACC is unlikely because of economic reasons. RONIC may also permanently exceed the cost of capital because capital is systematically understated. Under current accounting standards, only physical (or contractual) investment is capitalized on the balance sheet. Companies that have valuable brands, distribution, and intellectual property do not recognize their investment on the balance sheet unless acquired. For more on how to compute invested capital for companies with large intangible assets, see Chapter 24.

EXHIBIT 14.11 **Continuing-Value Estimates for a Sporting Goods Company**

$ million

Technique	Assumptions	Continuing value
Other DCF approaches		
Perpetuity based on final year's NOPAT	Normalized NOPAT growing at inflation rate	582
Perpetuity based on final year's cash flow	Normalized FCF growing at inflation rate	428
Multiples (comparables)		
Price-to-earnings ratio	Industry average of 15 times earnings	624
Market-to-book ratio	Industry average of 1.4 times book	375
Asset-based valuations		
Liquidation value	80% of working capital	186
	70% of net fixed assets	
Replacement cost	Book value adjusted for inflation	275

explored earlier in this chapter, because they explicitly rely on the underlying economic assumptions embodied in the company analysis. Other approaches tend to obscure the underlying economic assumptions. Using the example of a sporting goods company, Exhibit 14.11 illustrates the wide dispersion of continuing-value estimates arrived at by different techniques.

The most common techniques fall into three categories: other DCF approaches, multiples, and asset-based valuations. This section describes techniques in these categories and explains why we prefer the approaches we recommended earlier.

Other DCF Approaches

The recommended DCF formulas can be modified to create additional continuing-value formulas with more restrictive (and sometimes unreasonable) assumptions.

One variation is the *convergence* formula. For companies in competitive industries, many expect that the return on net new investment will eventually converge to the cost of capital as all the excess profits are competed away. This assumption allows a simpler version of the value driver formula, as follows:

$$CV = \frac{NOPAT_{t+1}}{WACC}$$

The derivation begins with the value driver formula:

$$CV = \frac{NOPAT_{t+1}\left(1 - \dfrac{g}{RONIC}\right)}{WACC - g}$$

Assume that RONIC = WACC (that is, the return on incremental invested capital equals the cost of capital):

$$CV = \frac{NOPAT_{t+1}\left(1 - \dfrac{g}{WACC}\right)}{WACC - g}$$

$$= \frac{NOPAT_{t+1}\left(\dfrac{WACC - g}{WACC}\right)}{WACC - g}$$

Canceling the term $WACC - g$ leaves a simple formula:

$$CV = \frac{NOPAT_{t+1}}{WACC}$$

The fact that the growth term has disappeared from the equation does *not* mean that the nominal growth in NOPAT will be zero. The growth term drops out because new growth adds nothing to value, as the RONIC associated with growth equals the cost of capital. This formula is sometimes interpreted as implying zero growth (not even with inflation), but this is not an accurate interpretation.

Misinterpretation of the convergence formula has led to another variant: the *aggressive-growth* formula. This formula assumes that earnings in the continuing-value period will grow at some rate, most often the inflation rate. Some investment professionals then conclude that earnings should be discounted at the real WACC rather than at the nominal WACC. The resulting formula is:

$$CV = \frac{NOPAT_{t+1}}{WACC - g}$$

Here, g is the inflation rate. This formula can substantially overstate continuing value, because it assumes that NOPAT can grow without any incremental capital investment. This is unlikely, or impossible, because any growth will probably require additional working capital and fixed assets.

To see the critical assumption hidden in the preceding formula, we analyze the key value driver formula as RONIC approaches infinity:

$$CV = \frac{NOPAT_{t+1}\left(1 - \dfrac{g}{RONIC}\right)}{WACC - g}$$

$$RONIC \to \infty; \text{ therefore, } \frac{g}{RONIC} \to 0$$

$$CV = \frac{NOPAT_{t+1}(1 - 0)}{WACC - g}$$

$$= \frac{NOPAT_{t+1}}{WACC - g}$$

EXHIBIT 14.12 **Rates of Return Implied by Alternative Continuing-Value Formulas**

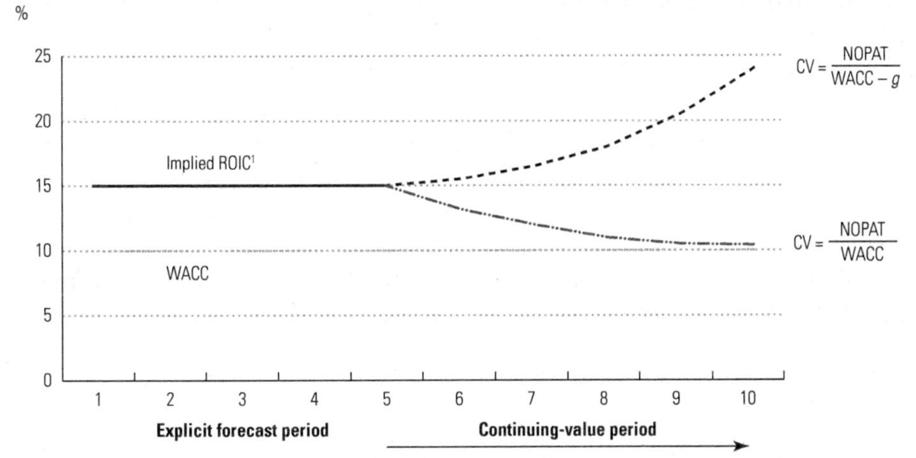

$$CV = \frac{NOPAT}{WACC - g}$$

$$CV = \frac{NOPAT}{WACC}$$

[1] Implied ROIC equals the return on both new and existing capital.

Exhibit 14.12 compares the two variations of the key value driver formula, showing how the average return on invested capital (both existing and new investment) behaves under the two assumptions. In the aggressive-growth case, NOPAT grows without any new investment, so the return on invested capital eventually approaches infinity. In the convergence case, the average return on invested capital moves toward the weighted average cost of capital as new capital becomes a larger portion of the total capital base.

Multiples

Multiples, also known as comparables, assume that a company will be worth some multiple of future earnings or book value in the continuing period. But how do you estimate an appropriate future multiple?

A common approach is to assume that the company will be worth a multiple of earnings or book value based on the multiple for the company today. Suppose we choose today's industry average enterprise-value-to-EBITDA ratio. This ratio reflects the economic prospects of the industry during the explicit forecast period as well as the continuing-value period. In maturing industries, however, prospects at the end of the explicit forecast period are likely to be very different from today's. Therefore, a different EV-to-EBITDA is needed; one that reflects the company's prospects at the end of the forecast period. What factors will determine that ratio? As discussed in Chapter 3, the primary determinants are the company's expected growth, the rate of return on new capital, and the cost of capital. The same factors are in the key value driver formula. Unless you are comfortable using an arbitrary multiple, you are much better off with the value driver formula.

When valuing an acquisition, companies sometimes fall into the circular reasoning that the multiple for the continuing value should equal the multiple paid for the acquisition. In other words, if I pay 15 times EBITDA today, I should be able to sell the business for 15 times EBITDA at the end of the explicit forecast period. In most cases, the reason a company is willing to pay a particular multiple for an acquisition is that it plans to improve the target's profitability. So the effective EBITDA multiple it is paying on the improved level of EBITDA will be much less than 15. Once the improvements are in place and earnings are higher, buyers will not be willing to pay the same multiple unless they can make *additional* improvements beyond those already made. Chapter 18 describes other common mistakes made when using multiples.

Asset-Based Valuations

Unlike the previous methods, which rely on future cash flow or earnings, estimating continuing value using replacement cost or liquidation value is known as an asset-based approach. Since these approaches ignore the future potential of the company, use them only in situations where ongoing operations are in jeopardy.

The liquidation value approach sets the continuing value equal to the estimated proceeds from the sale of the assets, after paying off liabilities at the end of the explicit forecast period. Liquidation value is often far different from the value of the company as a going concern. In a growing, profitable industry, a company's liquidation value is probably well below the going-concern value. In a dying industry, liquidation value may exceed going-concern value. Do not use this approach unless liquidation is likely at the end of the forecast period.

The replacement cost approach sets the continuing value equal to the expected cost to replace the company's assets. This approach has at least two drawbacks. First, not all tangible assets are replaceable. The company's organizational capital can be valued only on the basis of the cash flow the company generates. The replacement cost of just the company's tangible assets may greatly understate the value of the company. Second, not all the company's assets will ever be replaced. Consider a machine used by a particular company. As long as it generates a positive cash flow, the asset is valuable to the ongoing business of the company. But the replacement cost of the asset may be so high that replacing it is not economical. Here, the replacement cost may exceed the value of the business as an ongoing entity.

CLOSING THOUGHTS

The future is inherently unknowable, so it is understandable why many professionals are skeptical about enterprise DCF models that rely on a continuing-value formula. This skepticism may be warranted in some cases, but for many valuations, disaggregating the continuing value into its economic components can show why these concerns are overstated. Remember, the value of a company is merely its invested capital plus the economic profits it generates on that capital. If most of the value creation occurs during the explicit forecast period, then the continuing value plays a much smaller role than the free cash flow would lead you to believe.

When estimating continuing value, remember to follow a few simple guidelines for successful valuation. First, use the key value driver formula to estimate continuing value. Unlike the free-cash-flow model, the value driver formula implicitly models the correct investment required for growth. Second, carefully assess the value drivers at the time of continuing value. The value drivers should be consistent with the company's potential in the future, rather than today's performance or economic environment. We believe a thoughtful analysis will lead to insights not available with other models.

15

Estimating the Cost of Capital

To value a company using enterprise discounted cash flow (DCF), discount your forecast of free cash flow (FCF) at the weighted average cost of capital (WACC). The WACC represents the returns that all investors in a company—equity and debt—expect to earn for investing their funds in one particular business instead of others with similar risk. The investment return they are forgoing is also referred to as their opportunity cost of capital. Since a company's investors will earn the cost of capital if the company meets expectations, the cost of capital is used interchangeably with expected return.

The WACC has three primary components: the cost of equity, the after-tax cost of debt, and the company's target capital structure. Estimating WACC with precision is difficult because there is no way to directly measure an investor's opportunity cost of capital, especially the cost of equity. Furthermore, many of the traditional approaches that worked for years have been complicated by recent monetary policies that have led to unusually low interest rates on government bonds. To estimate the cost of capital, we employ various models and approximations that are grounded in corporate-finance theory and build on empirical observations about the market value of companies. These models estimate the expected return on alternative investments with similar risk.

This chapter begins with a brief summary of the WACC calculation and then presents detailed sections on how to estimate its components: the cost of equity, the after-tax cost of debt, and the target capital structure, which is used to weight the first two components. The chapter concludes with a discussion of WACC estimation for companies whose capital structure is more complex than just traditional debt and common stock.

CALCULATING THE WEIGHTED AVERAGE COST OF CAPITAL

In its simplest form, the weighted average cost of capital equals the weighted average of the after-tax cost of debt and cost of equity:

$$\text{WACC} = \frac{D}{V} k_d \left(1 - T_m\right) + \frac{E}{V} k_e$$

where
$\quad D/V$ = target level of debt to value using market-based values
$\quad E/V$ = target level of equity to value using market-based values
$\quad k_d$ = cost of debt
$\quad k_e$ = cost of equity
$\quad T_m$ = company's marginal tax rate on income

For companies with other securities, such as preferred stock, additional terms must be added to the cost of capital, representing each security's expected rate of return and percentage of total enterprise value. The cost of capital does not include expected returns of operating liabilities, such as accounts payable. Required compensation for capital provided by customers, suppliers, and employees is embedded in operating expenses, so it is already incorporated in free cash flow.

The cost of equity is determined by estimating the expected return on the market portfolio, adjusted for the risk of the company being valued. In this book, we estimate risk by using the capital asset pricing model (CAPM). The CAPM adjusts for company-specific risk using beta, which measures how a company's stock price responds to movements in the overall market. Stocks with high betas have expected returns that exceed the market return; the converse is true for low-beta stocks. Only beta risk is priced. Any remaining risk, which academics call idiosyncratic risk, can be diversified away by holding multiple securities, as explained in Chapter 4. In practice, measurements of individual company betas are highly imprecise. Therefore, use a set of peer company betas to estimate an industry beta.

To approximate the after-tax cost of debt for an investment-grade firm, use the company's after-tax yield to maturity on its long-term debt.[1] For companies whose debt trades infrequently or for nontraded debt, use the company's debt rating to estimate the yield to maturity. Since free cash flow is measured without interest tax shields, use the after-tax cost of debt to incorporate the interest tax shield into the WACC.

Finally, predict the target capital structure, and use the target levels to weight the after-tax cost of debt and cost of equity. For stable companies, the target capital structure is often approximated by the company's current debt-to-value ratio, using market values of debt and equity. As we'll explain later in this chapter, do not use book values.

---

[1] The yield to maturity is not a good proxy for the cost of debt when a company has significant leverage. We discuss alternative methods to estimate the cost of debt for highly leveraged companies later in this chapter.

EXHIBIT 15.1 **Costco: Weighted Average Cost of Capital (WACC)**

%

Source of capital	Target proportion of total capital	Cost of capital	Marginal tax rate	After-tax cost of capital	Contribution to weighted average
Debt	10.4	4.9	24.6	3.7	0.4
Equity	89.6	8.5		8.5	7.6
WACC	100.0				8.0

For an example of the WACC calculation, see Exhibit 15.1, which presents the calculation for Costco. We estimate the company's cost of equity at 8.5 percent using the CAPM. To estimate Costco's pretax cost of debt, we add the default premium on Costco debt to a forecast of the risk-free rate, which leads to a cost of debt of 4.9 percent. In Chapter 11, we estimated Costco's marginal tax rate at 24.6 percent, so the company's after-tax cost of debt equals 3.7 percent. To weight the after-tax cost of debt and cost of equity, we set the target capital structure equal to the company's current-debt-to-value, excluding excess cash. Normally, we net excess cash against gross debt to determine the cost of capital, but since Costco has little net debt compared with its peer group, we assume the company will disgorge excess cash to increase leverage. Adding together the weighted contributions from debt and equity, WACC equals 8.0 percent.

Always estimate the WACC in a manner consistent with the principles of free cash flow. For example, since free cash flow is the cash flow available to all financial investors, the company's WACC must also include the expected return for each class of investor. In general, the cost of capital must meet the following criteria:

- It must include the cost of capital for all investors—debt, preferred stock, common stock, and so on—since free cash flow is available to all investors, who expect compensation for the risks they take.
- Any financing-related benefits or costs, such as interest tax shields, not included in free cash flow must be incorporated into the cost of capital or valued separately using adjusted present value.[2]
- WACC must be computed after corporate income taxes (since free cash flow is calculated in after-tax terms).
- It must be based on the same expectations of inflation as those embedded in forecasts of free cash flow.
- The duration of the securities used to estimate the cost of capital must match the duration of the cash flows.

[2] For most companies, discounting forecast free cash flow at a constant WACC is a simple, accurate, and robust method of arriving at a corporate valuation. If, however, the company's target capital structure is expected to change significantly—for instance, in a leveraged buyout—WACC can overstate (or understate) the impact of interest tax shields. In this situation, you should discount free cash flow at the unlevered cost of equity and value tax shields and other financing effects separately (as described in Chapter 10).

ESTIMATING THE COST OF EQUITY

The cost of equity is the central building block of the cost of capital. Unfortunately, it is also extremely difficult to measure. Academics and practitioners have proposed numerous models to estimate the cost of equity, but none have been reliable, especially at the company level. Even if a model could be agreed upon, accurately measuring the required inputs has also proven elusive. Consequently, deriving the cost of equity is far more difficult in practice than many core finance texts imply. With these hurdles in mind, we estimate the cost of equity in two steps:

1. *Estimate market return.* First, we estimate the expected return on the entire stock market. Although a particular company will not necessarily have the same cost of capital as the market as a whole, the market return provides a critical benchmark for judging how reasonable estimates of cost of equity for individual companies are.
2. *Adjust for risk.* We next adjust for company risk using one of two well-known models, the capital asset pricing model (CAPM) and the Fama-French three-factor model. Each model measures company risk by measuring the correlation of its stock price to market changes, known as beta. Since estimates of beta are at best imprecise, we rely on peer group betas, rather than individual company betas.

Estimating the Market Return

Every day, thousands of investors attempt to estimate the market's expected return. Since the future is unobservable, many practitioners use one of two approaches to estimate it.

The first method calculates the cost of equity implied by the relationship between current share prices and future financial performance. By valuing a large sample of companies like the Standard & Poor's (S&P) 500 index, we can reverse engineer the embedded cost of equity. Although the method requires a forecast of future performance, it is quite powerful, since it incorporates up-to-date market prices.

The second method looks backward using historical market returns. However, given that past market returns are heavily influenced by the rate of inflation prevalent at the time, a simple average of past returns isn't helpful in predicting today's market return. Instead, we add a historical market risk premium (stocks minus bonds) to today's interest rate, which incorporates today's expected inflation, rather than past inflation rates.

Using Market Prices to Estimate the Cost of Equity   Our first approach—estimating the aggregate cost of equity based on current share prices and expected corporate performance (earnings, return on invested capital [ROIC], and growth expectations) of a large sample of companies—generates striking results. After inflation is stripped out, the expected market return (*not* excess return) is remarkably constant, averaging 7 percent between 1962 and 2018.

To reverse engineer the expected market return, we start with the value driver formula described in Chapter 3. In this case, we've expressed it in terms of equity value rather than enterprise value (substituting the cost of equity for the weighted average cost of capital, return on equity for ROIC, etc.):

$$\text{Equity Value} = \frac{\text{Earnings}\left(1 - \dfrac{g}{\text{ROE}}\right)}{k_e - g}$$

where

$$\text{Earnings} = \text{equity earnings}$$
$$g = \text{expected growth in earnings}$$
$$\text{ROE} = \text{expected return on equity}$$
$$k_e = \text{cost of equity}$$

Solving for the cost of equity gives the following equation:

$$k_e = \frac{\text{Earnings}\left(1 - \dfrac{g}{\text{ROE}}\right)}{\text{Equity Value}} + g$$

Earnings divided by the equity value is the inverse of the price-to-earnings ratio (P/E), so it is possible to further reduce the equation:

$$k_e = \left(\frac{1}{\text{P/E}}\right)\left(1 - \frac{g}{\text{ROE}}\right) + g$$

We apply this formula to the S&P 500 index, using the long-run return on equity of 14.5 percent and the long-run growth in real gross domestic product (GDP) of 3.5 percent to convert a given year's S&P 500 median P/E into the cost of equity.[3] Implementing the model is slightly more complex than implied by the formula, because we also strip out the effects of inflation to arrive at a real cost of equity. Exhibit 15.2 plots the real expected market returns between 1962 and 2018. As the exhibit demonstrates, the nominal return changes substantially over time, but the real expected return hovers quite close to 7 percent. For the United Kingdom, the real market return is slightly more volatile and averages 6 percent.

Techniques similar to this date back to Charles Dow in the 1920s, and many authors have tested the concept.[4] Two studies used analyst forecasts

[3] R. Dobbs, T. Koller, and S. Lund, "What Effect Has Quantitative Easing Had on Your Share Price?" *McKinsey on Finance*, no. 49 (Winter 2014): 15–18; and M. H. Goedhart, T. M. Koller, and Z. D. Williams, "The Real Cost of Equity," *McKinsey on Finance*, no. 5 (Autumn 2002): 13–15.

[4] E. Fama and K. French, "Dividend Yields and Expected Stock Returns," *Journal of Financial Economics* 22, no. 1 (1988): 3–25; R. F. Stambaugh, "Predictive Regressions," *Journal of Financial Economics* 54, no. 3 (1999): 375–421; and J. Lewellen, "Predicting Returns with Financial Ratios," *Journal of Financial Economics* 74, no. 2 (2004): 209–235.

EXHIBIT 15.2 **S&P 500 Real and Nominal Expected Returns, 1962–2018**

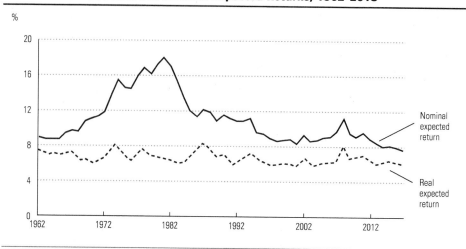

to estimate growth,[5] but many argue that analyst forecasts focus on the short term and are upward biased. In 2003, Eugene Fama and Kenneth French used long-term dividend growth rates as a proxy for future growth, but they focus on dividend yields, not on available cash flow.[6] Therefore, we believe this implementation is best.

To convert the real expected return into a nominal return appropriate for discounting, add an estimate of future inflation that is consistent with your cash flow projections. In the United States, the Federal Reserve Bank of Philadelphia provides a long-run forecast of expected inflation.[7] In December 2018, this equaled 2.3 percent. Alternatively, you can estimate expected long-term inflation using the spread between the yield on inflation-protected bonds and regular government bonds. In 2018, this spread was approximately 1.7 percent. When you add inflation in the range of 1.7 to 2.3 percent to a real return of 7 percent, you get an expected market return of 8.7 to 9.3 percent.

Later in this chapter, we use the CAPM to adjust the market return for company risk. The CAPM requires an estimate of the market risk premium, measured as the difference between stock returns and the return on risk-free bonds. Using data from 1962 to 2018, we estimate the average inflation-adjusted stock market return at 7 percent and the average inflation-adjusted U.S. Treasury return at 2 percent. The difference represents a market risk premium of 5 percent.

---

[5] J. Claus and J. Thomas, "Equity Premia as Low as Three Percent? Evidence from Analysts' Earnings Forecasts for Domestic and International Stocks," *Journal of Finance* 56, no. 5 (October 2001): 1629–1666; and W. R. Gebhardt, C. M. C. Lee, and B. Swaminathan, "Toward an Implied Cost of Capital," *Journal of Accounting Research* 39, no. 1 (2001): 135–176.

[6] E. F. Fama and K. R. French, "The Equity Premium," *Journal of Finance* 57, no. 2 (April 2002): 637–659.

[7] See Federal Reserve Bank of Philadelphia, Survey of Professional Forecasters, www.philadelphiafed .org.

Alternatively, if we expect the market to earn 7 percent in real terms going forward and subtract the December 2018 inflation-adjusted interest rate of 1 percent, this implies a market risk premium going forward of 6 percent. While we are not averse to this larger-than-normal risk premium, our statistical tests do not provide confirming evidence that risk premiums have risen. If this were the case, low-risk stocks should increase in value relative to high-risk stocks, because as the price of risk rises, high-risk stocks require greater returns and consequently have lower valuations. When we examined the trend of P/Es for low-risk stocks versus high-risk stocks, we did not observe any widening of the spread as real interest rates fell, even to historical lows.

Historical Estimates of the Market Risk Premium   A second method to estimate the expected market return starts with a historical estimate of the market risk premium and then adds this estimate to today's long-term government bond rate. We add today's rates so the estimate of the expected market return incorporates current interest rates, rather than those in the past.

Estimating the historical risk premium properly requires some statistical sophistication. A full description of the most relevant issues is available in Appendix F; we offer only a summary here. First, use as long a time period as possible. Our work relies on research by Elroy Dimson, Paul Marsh, and Mike Staunton, who provide market returns dating back to 1900.[8] Although some argue that market risk premiums have dropped over time, a simple regression analysis does not support this. Therefore, we believe more data improve the quality of estimation. Second, neither the arithmetic average nor a geometric average of past returns will estimate multiyear discount rates well. The best value falls somewhere between the two averages. While the arithmetic average is best for estimating a one-period return, compounding the average return also compounds any estimation error, causing the compounded number to be too high. To counter this bias, Marshall Blume created an estimator using a combination of the two averages.[9]

Exhibit 15.3 presents the average cumulative returns of the U.S. stock market, the U.S. bond market, and excess returns (stocks minus bonds) between 1900 and 2018. Using five- to ten-year holding periods, the average annual excess return is 5.5 to 5.7 percent. Blume's estimator for longer-date cash flows is slightly higher, at just above 6 percent. Even with the best statistical techniques, however, this number is probably too high, because the observable sample includes only countries with strong historical returns.[10] Statisticians

[8] E. Dimson, P. Marsh, and M. Staunton, "The Worldwide Equity Premium: A Smaller Puzzle," in *Handbook of Investments: Equity Risk Premium*, ed. R. Mehra (Amsterdam: Elsevier Science, 2007).

[9] D. C. Indro and W. Y. Lee, "Biases in Arithmetic and Geometric Averages as Estimates of Long-Run Expected Returns and Risk Premia," *Financial Management* 26, no. 4 (Winter 1997): 81–90; and M. E. Blume, "Unbiased Estimators of Long-Run Expected Rates of Return," *Journal of the American Statistical Association* 69, no. 347 (September 1974): 634–638.

[10] S. Brown, W. Goetzmann, and S. Ross, "Survivorship Bias," *Journal of Finance* (July 1995): 853–873.

EXHIBIT 15.3 **Cumulative Returns for Various Intervals, 1900–2018**

Arithmetic mean, %

Holding period	Average cumulative returns			Annualized returns	
	U.S. stocks	U.S. government bonds	U.S. excess returns[1]	U.S. excess returns	Blume estimate of market risk premium
1 year	11.3	5.4	6.3	6.3	6.3
2 years	23.8	11.0	12.6	6.1	6.3
4 years	51.2	23.3	25.0	5.7	6.3
5 years	67.4	30.2	32.2	5.7	6.2
10 years	172.6	72.1	71.3	5.5	6.2

[1] Measured by averaging year-by-year excess returns, not as the difference between cumulative stock and bond returns.

Source: Data for 1900–2002 from E. Dimson, P. Marsh, and M. Staunton, "The Worldwide Equity Premium: A Smaller Puzzle," in *Handbook of Investments: Equity Risk Premium*, ed. R. Mehra (Amsterdam: Elsevier Science, 2007); data for 2003–2017 from R. G. Ibbotson, *2018 SBBI Yearbook: Stocks, Bonds, Bills, and Inflation* (New York: Duff & Phelps, 2018); data from 2018 from Bloomberg.

refer to this phenomenon as survivorship bias. Zvi Bodie writes, "There were 36 active stock markets in 1900, so why do we only look at two [the UK and U.S. markets]? I can tell you—because many of the others don't have a 100-year history, for a variety of reasons."[11]

Since it is unlikely that the U.S. stock market will replicate its performance over the next century, we adjust downward the historical market risk premium. Dimson, Marsh, and Staunton find that the U.S. arithmetic annual return exceeded a 17-country composite return by 0.8 percent in real terms.[12] If we subtract a 0.8 percent survivorship premium from our range of 5.5 percent to 6.2 percent U.S. excess returns reported in Exhibit 15.2, the difference implies that the U.S. market risk premium, as measured by excess returns, is in the range of 4.7 to 5.4 percent, which we round to 5 percent. It's interesting that this number matches the average risk premium measured by reverse engineering the expected market return using the key value driver formula.

Estimating the Risk-Free Rate

With an estimate of the historical market risk premium in hand, it is now possible to estimate the expected market return by adding the market risk premium to the current risk-free rate. Adding the historical risk premium to the current Treasury yield worked well until the financial crisis of 2007–2009. With interest rates at unprecedented lows, however, further analysis is required.

To combat the financial crisis, the U.S. Federal Reserve reduced short-term rates to almost zero, pulling down long-term rates as a by-product. It also began a policy of repurchasing bonds in the open market (known as quantitative easing), further pushing up prices and driving down yields. At the same time, U.S. government bonds became a haven for investors around the world, leading to high prices and lower yields for government bonds. As the crisis and

[11] Z. Bodie, "Longer Time Horizon 'Does Not Reduce Risk,'" *Financial Times*, January 26, 2002.
[12] Dimson, Marsh, and Staunton, "The Worldwide Equity Premium."

subsequent recession unfolded, the yield on ten-year government bonds began a long and volatile decline, reaching an all-time low of 1.5 percent in July 2016. (Just prior to this book going to press, the U.S. Federal Reserve reduced interest rates in response to the global Coronavirus outbreak. As a result, in March 2020, the 10-year government bond fell below 1 percent for the first time.)

In the period following July 2016, many practitioners realized that valuation models based on these historically low interest rates didn't lead to sensible results. With government bonds at 1.5 percent, a 5 percent market risk premium implies an expected market return of just 6.5 percent. Compared with pre-crisis expected returns, this should have caused a dramatic rise in the market's price relative to earnings. Mathematically, every 1 percent decrease in the cost of equity for the S&P 500 index should increase the P/E of the index by roughly 20 to 25 percent. So a 3 percent drop in cost of equity would have increased the P/E from a typical trading range of 15 times to over 25 times. Yet no rise occurred. Instead, the P/E for the S&P 500 index has recovered to pre-crisis levels of approximately 20 times.

To overcome the inconsistency between low interest rates and the market values of equities, we recommend using a synthetic risk-free rate in both the estimate of the expected market return and for use in the CAPM. To build a synthetic risk-free rate, add the expected inflation rate of 1.7 to 2.3 percent presented in the previous section to the long-run average real interest rate of 2 percent, which leads to a synthetic risk-free rate of between 3.7 and 4.3 percent.[13]

Adding the 5 percent market risk premium estimated earlier leads to an expected market return of 8.7 to 9.3 percent. If market prices eventually rise to incorporate ultralow interest rates (or if interest rates rise to better match market prices), make sure to reevaluate your perspective.

Matching Cash Flow Duration   In the preceding analysis, we focused on returns from ten-year bonds. But why ten years and not something longer or shorter? The most theoretically sound approach is to discount a given year's cash flow at a cost of capital that matches the maturity of the cash flow. In other words, year 1 cash flows would be discounted at a cost of capital based on a one-year risk-free rate, while year 10 cash flows would be discounted at a cost of capital based on a ten-year discount rate. To do this, use zero-coupon bonds (known as STRIPS),[14] rather than Treasury bonds that make interim

---

[13] For ease of implementation, we use a single cost of equity to discount all cash flows. More advanced models split cash flows into two periods: an explicit forecast period and a continuing value. When using two periods, discount the first set of cash flows at observed yields, and create the perpetuity using a synthetic risk-free rate. Although a two-period model uses short-term market data more effectively, the valuation differences between one- and two-period models are relatively small, especially for short forecast windows.

[14] Introduced by the U.S. Treasury in 1985, STRIPS stands for "separate trading of registered interest and principal of securities." The STRIPS program enables investors to hold and trade the individual components of Treasury notes and bonds as separate securities.

payments. The interim payments cause their effective maturity to be much shorter than their stated maturity.

Using multiple discount rates is quite cumbersome. Therefore, few practitioners discount each cash flow using its matched bond maturity. Instead, most choose a single rate that best matches the cash flow stream being valued. For U.S.-based corporate valuations, we recommend ten-year government STRIPS (longer-dated bonds such as the 30-year Treasury bond might match the cash flow stream better, but they may not be liquid enough to correctly represent the risk-free rate). When valuing European companies, use ten-year German government bonds, because they trade more frequently and have lower credit risk than bonds of other European countries. Always use government bond yields denominated in the same currency as the company's cash flow to estimate the risk-free rate. Also, make sure the inflation rate embedded in your cash flows is consistent with the inflation rate embedded in the government bond rate you are using.

Do *not* use a short-term Treasury bill to determine the risk-free rate. When introductory finance textbooks calculate the CAPM, they typically use a short-term Treasury rate because they are estimating expected returns for the next *month*. Use longer-term bonds; they will be better in line with the time horizon of corporate cash flows.

Closing Thoughts on Expected Market Returns   Although many in the finance profession disagree about how to measure the market risk premium, we believe a number around 5 percent is appropriate. Historical estimates found in various textbooks (and locked in the minds of many), which often report numbers near 8 percent, are too high for valuation purposes, because they compare the market risk premium versus Treasury bills (very-short-term bonds) and are biased by the historical strength of the U.S. market.

Adjust for Industry/Company Risk

Once you've estimated the cost of equity for the market as a whole, adjust it for differences in risk across companies. Keep in mind the discussion from Chapter 4 about the difference between diversifiable and nondiversifiable risk. Only the nondiversifiable risk that investors cannot eliminate by holding a portfolio of stocks is incorporated into the cost of equity.

The most common model used to adjust the cost of equity for differences in risk is the capital asset pricing model (CAPM). Other models include the Fama-French three-factor model and the arbitrage pricing theory (APT). The three models differ primarily in which factors are used to estimate the effect of compensated risk. Despite extensive criticism of the CAPM, we believe that it remains the best model to adjust for risk. Even so, significant judgment is required. A blind application of historical data may result in a cost of equity that is unrealistic.

Capital Asset Pricing Model   Because the CAPM is discussed at length in modern finance textbooks,[15] we focus only on the key ideas. The CAPM postulates that the expected rate of return on any security equals the risk-free rate plus the security's beta times the market risk premium:

$$E(R_i) = r_f + \beta_i[E(R_m) - r_f]$$

where

$E(R_i)$ = expected return of security i
r_f = risk-free rate
β_i = security i's sensitivity to the market portfolio
$E(R_m)$ = expected return of the market portfolio

In the CAPM, the risk-free rate and the market risk premium, which is defined as the difference between $E(R_m)$ and r_f, are common to all companies; only beta varies across companies. Beta represents a stock's incremental risk to a diversified investor, where risk is defined as the extent to which the stock moves up and down in conjunction with the aggregate stock market.

Consider General Mills, a manufacturer of cereals and snack foods, and Micron Technology, a semiconductor manufacturer that produces memory chips. Basic consumer foods purchases are relatively independent of the stock market's value, so the beta for General Mills is low; we estimated it at 0.64.[16] Based on a risk-free rate of 4.3 percent and a market risk premium of 5 percent, the cost of equity for General Mills equals 7.5 percent (see Exhibit 15.4). In contrast, technology companies tend to have high betas. When the economy struggles, the stock market drops, and companies stop purchasing new technology. Thus, the value of Micron Technology is highly correlated with the market's value, and its beta is high. Based on a beta of 1.68, Micron's expected rate of return equals 12.7 percent. Since General Mills offers greater protection against market downturns than Micron Technology does, investors are willing to pay a premium for the stock, driving down the stock's expected return. Conversely, since Micron offers little diversification in relation to the market portfolio, the company must earn a higher return to entice investors.

To apply the CAPM in practice, you must estimate each component. The core question for a particular company's cost of equity is its risk relative to the aggregate market and, consequently, beta. Keep in mind that when you are valuing a company, your objective is not to precisely measure the company's historical beta. Rather, it is to estimate its future beta. Therefore, you must use judgment and common sense, not a purely mechanical approach.

[15] For example, R. Brealey, S. Myers, and F. Allen, *Principles of Corporate Finance*, 11th ed. (New York: McGraw-Hill, 2014); and T. Copeland, F. Weston, and K. Shastri, *Financial Theory and Corporate Policy* (Boston: Pearson Education, 2013).
[16] For the purpose of simple exposition, we regress 60 months of General Mills stock returns on the Morgan Stanley Capital International (MSCI) World Index to determine beta. Later, we use peer groups to estimate industry betas.

EXHIBIT 15.4 **Cost of Equity Using the Capital Asset Pricing Model (CAPM)**

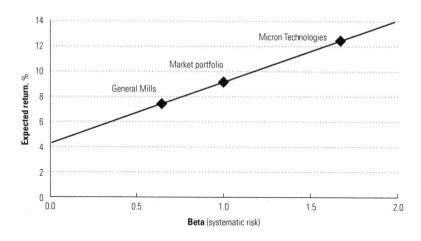

Source: Refinitiv Thomson One.

We find that individual company betas can be heavily influenced by nonrepeatable events, so we recommend using an industry peer median rather than the historically measured beta for the company in question. Betas can also be affected by unusual events in the stock market, such as the dot-com bubble of the early 2000s or the financial crisis of 2007–2009. By examining how industry betas have changed over time, you can apply judgment about whether betas will revert to their long-term level if they are currently not there.

The remainder of this section describes how to estimate a company's beta step-by-step. First, use regression to estimate the beta for each company in the peer group. Then convert each company's observed beta into an unlevered beta—that is, what the beta would be if the company had no debt. Once you have a collection of betas, examine the sample for a representative beta, such as the median beta. To ensure that the current beta is representative of risk and not an artifact of unusual data, do not rely on a point estimate. Instead, examine the trend over time. We discuss each step next.

Estimating Beta for Each Company in the Industry Sample Set   To develop an industry beta, you first need the betas of the company's peer set. Since beta cannot be observed directly, you must *estimate* its value. The most common regression used to estimate a company's raw beta is the market model:

$$R_i = \alpha + \beta R_m + \varepsilon$$

In the market model, the stock's return (R_i), not price, is regressed against the market's return.

Exhibit 15.5 plots 60 months of Costco stock returns versus Morgan Stanley Capital International (MSCI) World Index returns between September 2015

EXHIBIT 15.5 **Costco: Stock Returns, 2015–2019**

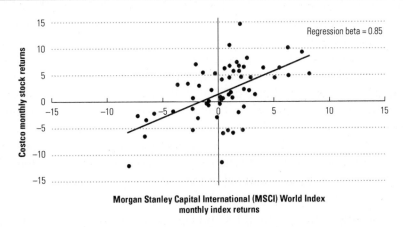

Morgan Stanley Capital International (MSCI) World Index
monthly index returns

Source: Refinitiv Thomson One.

and August 2019. The solid line represents the "best fit" relationship between Costco's stock returns and the stock market. The slope of this line is commonly denoted as beta. For Costco, the company's raw regression beta (slope) is 0.85.

But why did we choose to measure Costco returns in months? Why did we use five years of data? And how precise is this measurement? The CAPM is a one-period model and provides little guidance on how to use it for valuation. Yet following certain market characteristics and the results of a variety of empirical tests leads to several guiding conclusions:

- The measurement period for raw regressions should include at least 60 data points (e.g., five years of monthly returns). Rolling betas should be graphed to search for any patterns or systematic changes in a stock's risk.
- Raw regressions should be based on monthly returns. Using more frequent return periods, such as daily and weekly returns, leads to systematic biases.[17]
- Company stock returns should be regressed against a value-weighted, well-diversified market portfolio, such as the MSCI World Index, bearing in mind that this portfolio's value may be distorted if measured during a market bubble.

In the CAPM, the market portfolio equals the portfolio of all assets, both traded (such as stocks and bonds) and untraded (such as private companies and human capital). Since the true market portfolio is unobservable, a proxy is necessary. For U.S. stocks, the most common proxy is the S&P 500, a value-weighted

[17] Using daily or even weekly returns is especially problematic when the stock is rarely traded. An illiquid stock will have many reported returns equal to zero, not because the stock's value is constant but because it hasn't traded (only the last trade is recorded). Consequently, estimates of beta on illiquid stocks are biased downward. Using longer-dated returns, such as monthly returns, lessens this effect.

index of large U.S. companies. Outside the United States, financial analysts rely on either a regional index like the MSCI Europe Index or the MSCI World Index, a value-weighted index comprising large stocks from 23 developed countries, including the United States.

Most well-diversified indexes, such as the S&P 500 and MSCI World Index, are highly correlated (the two indexes had a 97 percent correlation between 2000 and 2018). Thus, the choice of index will have only a small effect on beta. Do *not*, however, use a local market index, which some data services provide. Most countries are heavily weighted in only a few industries and, in some cases, a few companies. Consequently, when measuring beta versus a local index, you are not measuring market-wide systematic risk, but often a company's sensitivity to a particular set of industries.

Beta Smoothing Many academics and beta services also adjust a company's raw beta closer to the mean of all companies, a process called smoothing. Smoothing moves the point estimate of beta toward the overall average. Consider the simple smoothing process used by Bloomberg:

$$\text{Adjusted Beta} = 0.33 + 0.67 (\text{Raw Beta})$$

This formula smooths raw regression estimates toward 1. For instance, a raw beta of 0.5 leads to an adjusted beta of 0.67, while a raw beta of 1.5 leads to an adjusted beta of 1.34.

Bloomberg's smoothing mechanism dates to Marshall Blume's observation that betas revert to the mean.[18] Today, more advanced smoothing techniques exist.[19] Although the proof is beyond the scope of this book, the following adjustment will reduce beta estimation error:

$$\beta_{adj} = \left(\frac{\sigma_\varepsilon^2}{\sigma_\varepsilon^2 + \sigma_b^2} \right) 1 + \left(1 - \frac{\sigma_\varepsilon^2}{\sigma_\varepsilon^2 + \sigma_b^2} \right) \beta_{raw}$$

where

σ_ε = standard error of the regression beta
σ_b = cross-sectional standard deviation of all betas

The raw regression beta receives the most weight when the standard error of beta from the regression (σ_ε) is smallest. In fact, when beta is measured perfectly ($\sigma_\varepsilon = 0$), the raw beta receives all the weight. Conversely, if the regression provides no meaningful results (σ_ε is very large), you should set beta equal to 1.0.

Since we are using an industry peer beta for Costco, we did not smooth regression results.

---

[18] M. Blume, "Betas and Their Regression Tendencies," *Journal of Finance* 30 (1975): 1–10.
[19] For instance, see P. Jorion, "Bayes-Stein Estimation for Portfolio Analysis," *Journal of Financial and Quantitative Analysis* 21 (1986): 279–292.

Creating an Industry Beta   Estimating beta is an imprecise process. We used historical regression to estimate Costco's beta at 0.85. But the regression's *R*-squared was only 30 percent, and the standard error of the beta estimate was 0.17. Using two standard errors as a guide, a statistician would feel confident Costco's true beta lies between 0.5 and 1.18—hardly a tight range.

To reduce the noise around beta estimates, use industry, rather than company-specific, betas. Companies in the same industry face similar *operating* risks, so they should have similar operating betas. If estimation errors across companies are uncorrelated, overestimates and underestimates of individual betas will tend to cancel, and an industry median (or average) beta will produce a superior estimate.

Consider two similarly skilled companies competing for a large customer contract. Depending on which company wins the contract, one company's stock price will rise; the other company's stock price will fall. If the market rises during this period, the winning company will have a higher measured beta, and the losing company will have a lower measured beta, even though the contract selection had nothing to do with market performance. Using an industry beta to proxy for company risk lessens the effect of random shocks.

Simply using the median of an industry's raw regression betas overlooks a second important factor: leverage. A company's beta is a function of not only its operating risk, but also the financial risk it takes. Shareholders of a company with more debt face greater risks, and this increase is reflected in beta. Therefore, to compare companies with similar operating risks, you must first strip out the effect of leverage. Only then can you compare betas across an industry.

To undo the effect of leverage (and its tax shield), we rely on the theories of Franco Modigliani and Merton Miller, introduced in Chapter 10. According to Modigliani and Miller, the weighted average risk of a company's financial claims equals the weighted average risk of a company's economic assets. In Appendix C, we present this concept algebraically and rearrange the equation to isolate the risk of equity, as measured by beta. The general equation for the beta of equity is as follows:

$$\beta_e = \beta_u + \frac{D}{E}(\beta_u - \beta_d) - \frac{V_{txa}}{E}(\beta_u - \beta_{txa})$$

where

β_u = beta of the company's operating assets
β_d = beta of the company's debt
β_{txa} = beta of the company's interest tax shields
D = market value of the company's debt
E = market value of the company's equity
V_{txa} = present value of the company's interest tax shields

To simplify the formula further, if the company maintains a constant ratio of debt to equity, the value of tax shields will fluctuate with the value of operating assets, and the beta of the tax shields (β_{txa}) will equal the beta of the unlevered company (β_u). Setting β_{txa} equal to β_u eliminates the final term:[20]

$$\beta_e = \beta_u + \frac{D}{E}(\beta_u - \beta_d)$$

Some people further simplify by assuming that the beta of debt is zero. Others use a beta of 0.15 for the debt of investment-grade companies, which is the implied beta based on the spread between investment-grade corporate debt and government debt.

Thus, a company's equity beta equals the company's operating beta (also known as the unlevered beta) times a leverage factor. As leverage rises, so will the company's equity beta. Using this relationship, we can convert equity betas into unlevered betas. Since unlevered betas focus solely on operating risk, they can be averaged across an industry, assuming industry competitors have similar operating characteristics.

To calculate an industry beta, follow these steps. First, calculate the beta for each company in your peer set and unlever each beta at each company's debt-to-equity ratio. Remove any outliers, that is, companies where the beta is unusually far away from those of the other companies; these are typically driven by anomalous events and are unlikely to recur. Calculate a median beta and an average beta of the sample set. Statistically speaking, the sample average will have the smallest estimation error. However, because small-sample averages are heavily influenced by outliers, we prefer the median beta. The final step is to plot the median industry beta over a long period. Look to see if the beta is changing in a predictable way and whether the current beta is the best predictor of future beta for the industry.

Examining the Long-Term Trend   To determine the cost of equity for Costco, we create an industry peer beta from a set of discount retailers. We start by estimating the beta for each company using regression analysis (as shown in Exhibit 15.5) and then unlever the results using each company's respective debt-to-equity ratio. Rather than using beta from a single point in time, we look for trends. Unless there is a discernible trend or dramatic change in the industry, we believe the long-run unlevered beta provides a better estimate of future beta than a single point estimate. Therefore, use the long-run mean when relevering the industry beta to the company's target capital structure.

Exhibit 15.6 presents estimates of levered betas for a selection of industries, including retailers. For Costco, we use an unlevered beta of 0.8, at the low end of the historical range. We use this value because discount retailers have been trading recently at a beta well below 1. To estimate the cost of equity for Costco, we relever the unlevered beta to a peer group debt-to-equity ratio. To lever beta, we use the same capital structure that was used to weight debt and equity in the WACC. The levered beta for Costco equals 0.88 (in practice, we often round

---

[20] See Appendix C for a comprehensive set of equations with different assumptions for the proportion of debt to equity, the beta of debt, and the beta of the tax shields.

EXHIBIT 15.6 **Unlevered Beta Estimates by Industry**

Industry	Beta range
Electric utilities	0.5–0.7
Healthcare providers	0.7–0.8
Integrated oil and gas	0.7–0.8
Airlines	0.7–0.9
Consumer packaged goods	0.8–0.9
Pharmaceuticals	0.8–1.0
Retail	0.8–1.0
Telecom	0.8–1.0
Mining	0.9–1.0
Automotive and assemblers	0.9–1.1
Chemicals	0.9–1.1
IT services, hardware	0.9–1.1
Software	0.9–1.1
Banking	1.0–1.1
Insurance	1.0–1.1
Semiconductors	1.0–1.3

to one decimal to avoid misleading precision). Using a 4.1 percent risk-free rate and a 5 percent market risk premium, this leads to a cost of equity of 8.5 percent.

In some cases, examining the long-term trend will reveal important insight about beta and market prices. During the dot-com boom of the late 1990s, equity markets rose dramatically, but this increase was confined primarily to extremely-large-capitalization stocks and stocks in the telecommunications, media, and technology (commonly known as TMT) sectors. Historically, TMT stocks contribute approximately 15 percent of the market value of the S&P 500. Between 1998 and 2000, this percentage rose to 40 percent. And as the market portfolio changed, so too did industry betas. Exhibit 15.7 presents the median beta over time for stocks outside TMT, such as food companies, airlines, and pharmaceuticals.[21] The median beta dropped from 1.0 to 0.6 as TMT became a dominant part of the overall market portfolio.

EXHIBIT 15.7 **Effect of the Dot-Com Bubble on Beta**

[1] TMT = telecommunications, media, and technology.

With the collapse of the TMT sector in 2001, TMT stocks returned to their original proportion of the overall market. Since beta is computed using 60 months of historical data, however, non-TMT betas still reflected the TMT-heavy market composition. Thus, to value future cash flows after 2001, a more appropriate beta than the 2001 beta would be the one from 1997, when the market composition last matched the post-2001 composition. Remember, the end goal is not to measure beta historically, but rather to use the historical estimate as a predictor of future value. In this case, recent history isn't very useful, so the important lesson is not to overweight it.

Alternatives to CAPM: Fama-French Three-Factor Model   In 1992, Eugene Fama and Kenneth French published a paper in the *Journal of Finance* that received a great deal of attention for its authors' conclusion: "In short, our tests do not support the most basic prediction of the SLB [Sharpe-Lintner-Black] Capital Asset Pricing Model that average stock returns are positively related to market betas."[22] Based on prior research and their own comprehensive regressions, Fama and French concluded that equity returns are inversely related to the size of a company (as measured by market capitalization) and positively related to the ratio of a company's book value to its market value of equity.

Given the strength of Fama and French's empirical results, the academic community now measures risk with a model commonly known as the Fama-French three-factor model. With this model, a stock's excess returns are regressed on excess market returns (similar to the CAPM), the excess returns of small stocks over big stocks (commonly referred to as SMB for "small minus big"), and the excess returns of high-book-to-market stocks over low-book-to-market stocks (known as HML for "high minus low").[23] Because the risk premium is determined by a regression on the SMB and HML stock portfolios, a company does not receive a premium for being small. Instead, the company receives a risk premium if its stock returns are correlated with those of small stocks or high-book-to-market companies. The SMB and HML portfolios are meant to replicate unobservable risk factors, factors that cause small companies with high book-to-market values to outperform their CAPM expected returns.

We use the Fama-French three-factor model to estimate Costco's cost of equity in Exhibit 15.8. To determine the company's three betas, we regress Costco's monthly stock returns against the excess market portfolio, SMB, and HML. As the exhibit indicates, the Costco beta on the market portfolio is

---

[21] A. Annema and M. Goedhart, "Better Betas," *McKinsey on Finance*, no. 6 (Winter 2003): 10–13; and A. Annema and M. Goedhart, "Betas: Back to Normal," *McKinsey on Finance*, no. 20 (Summer 2006): 14–16.

[22] E. Fama and K. French, "The Cross-Section of Expected Stock Returns," *Journal of Finance* (June 1992): 427–465.

[23] For a complete description of the factor returns, see E. Fama and K. French, "Common Risk Factors in the Returns on Stocks and Bonds," *Journal of Financial Economics* 33 (1993): 3–56.

EXHIBIT 15.8 **Costco: Cost of Equity Using the Fama-French Model, August 2019**

Factor	Average monthly premium,[1] %	Average annual premium, %	Regression coefficient[2]	Contribution to expected return, %
Market portfolio		5.0	0.90	4.5
Small-minus-big (SMB) portfolio	0.20	2.4	(0.33)	(0.8)
High-minus-low (HML) portfolio	0.35	4.3	(0.54)	(2.3)
Premium over risk-free rate[3]				1.4
			Risk-free rate	4.1
			Cost of equity	5.5

[1] SMB and HML premiums based on average monthly returns data, 1926–2019.

[2] Based on monthly returns data, 2014–2019.

[3] Summation rounded to one decimal point.

slightly higher in the Fama-French regression than in the market regression presented in Exhibit 15.5, but its levered cost of equity is much lower because Costco is negatively correlated with small companies (remember, small companies outperform big companies on average) and companies with a high book-to-market ratio (high-book-to-market companies outperform low-book-to-market companies on average).

While the Fama-French model outperforms the CAPM in predicting future returns, it is important to use caution when relying on regression results for one company at a point in time. As we discussed earlier in this chapter, regression results for a single company are quite imprecise. To best implement the CAPM, for instance, we recommend using a peer group beta, rather than raw regression results. In the Fama-French model, three beta coefficients exist, and their estimation depends on one another. A set of industry betas cannot be created cleanly. Consequently, the Fama-French model works well for controlling the risk of large historical data sets but may not be appropriate for measuring a single company's cost of equity.

The bottom line? It takes a better theory to kill an existing theory, and we have yet to see the better theory. Therefore, we continue to use the CAPM while keeping a watchful eye on new research in the area.

Alternatives to CAPM: Arbitrage Pricing Theory   Another proposed alternative to the CAPM, the arbitrage pricing theory (APT), resembles a generalized version of the Fama-French three-factor model. In the APT, a security's actual returns are generated by k factors and random noise:

$$R_i = \alpha + \beta_1 F_1 + \beta_2 F_2 + \dots + \beta_k F_k + \varepsilon$$

where F_i = return on factor i.

Since investors can hold well-diversified factor portfolios, epsilon risk will disappear. In this case, a security's expected return must equal the risk-free rate plus the cumulative sum of its exposure to each factor times the factor's risk premium (λ):[24]

$$E(R_t) = r_f + \beta_1 \lambda + \beta_2 \lambda + ... + \beta_k \lambda_k$$

Otherwise, arbitrage (positive return with zero risk) is possible.

On paper, the theory is extremely powerful. Any deviations from the model result in unlimited returns with no risk. In practice, implementation of the model has been tricky, as there is little agreement about how many factors there are, what they represent, and how to measure them. For this reason, use of the APT resides primarily in the classroom.

ESTIMATING THE AFTER-TAX COST OF DEBT

The weighted average cost of capital blends the cost of equity with the after-tax cost of debt. To estimate the cost of debt for investment-grade companies, use the yield to maturity of the company's long-term, option-free bonds. Multiply your estimate of the cost of debt by 1 minus the marginal tax rate to determine the cost of debt on an after-tax basis.

Technically speaking, yield to maturity is only a proxy for expected return, because the yield is a *promised* rate of return on a company's debt; it assumes all coupon payments are made on time and the debt is paid in full. An enterprise valuation based on the yield to maturity is therefore theoretically inconsistent, as expected free cash flows should be discounted by an expected return, not a promised yield. For companies with investment-grade debt (debt rated at BBB or better), the probability of default is so low that we believe this inconsistency is immaterial, especially when compared with the estimation error surrounding the cost of equity. Thus, for estimating the cost of debt for a company with investment-grade debt, yield to maturity is a suitable proxy.

For companies with below-investment-grade debt, we recommend one of two methods. If the debt-to-value ratio is uncharacteristically high, estimate the cost of debt using a target capital structure that better reflects the long-term dynamics of the industry. If the company's strategy includes substantial leverage, value the company using adjusted present value (APV) discounted at the unlevered cost of equity, rather than the WACC.

Yield to Maturity as a Proxy

To solve for yield to maturity (YTM), reverse engineer the discount rate required to set the present value of the bond's promised cash flows equal to its price:

$$\text{Price} = \frac{\text{Coupon}}{(1+\text{YTM})} + \frac{\text{Coupon}}{(1+\text{YTM})^2} + ... + \frac{\text{Face} + \text{Coupon}}{(1+\text{YTM})^N}$$

---

[24] For a thorough discussion of the arbitrage pricing theory, see M. Grinblatt and S. Titman, *Financial Markets and Corporate Strategy*, 2nd ed. (New York: McGraw-Hill, 2001).

EXHIBIT 15.9 **Costco: Trading Data on Corporate Debt, August 2019**

Bond: 3% due May 15, 2027

Trade	Trade date	Trade time	Trade volume, thousands	Bond price, $	Yield, %
1	8/30/19	15:48	250.0	106.8	2.01 ←
2	8/30/19	15:48	250.0	106.8	2.01
3	8/30/19	15:35	26.0	107.0	1.98
4	8/30/19	15:35	26.0	107.0	1.98
5	8/30/19	15:35	26.0	107.0	1.98
6	8/30/19	15:17	5.0	106.7	2.03
7	8/30/19	15:17	5.0	106.7	2.03
8	8/30/19	14:40	200.0	106.9	2.00
9	8/30/19	14:40	200.0	106.9	2.00
10	8/30/19	10:39	14.0	106.7	2.03

Costco bond yield	2.0
7-year U.S. Treasury yield	(1.4)
Costco default premium	0.6

Source: Financial Industry Regulatory Authority's Trade Reporting and Compliance Engine (TRACE).

Ideally, yield to maturity should be calculated on liquid, option-free, long-term debt. As discussed earlier in this chapter, short-term bonds do not match the duration of the company's free cash flow. If the bond is rarely traded, the bond price will be outdated, or "stale." Using stale prices will lead to an out-dated yield to maturity. Yield to maturity can also be distorted when corporate bonds have attached options, such as callability or convertibility at a fixed price, as their value will affect the bond's price but not its promised cash flows.

In the United States, you can download the yield to maturity for corporate debt free of charge by using the TRACE pricing database.[25] Exhibit 15.9 displays TRACE data for Costco's 3 percent bonds due in May 2027 (the longest duration bond in Costco's capital structure). TRACE reports four data items: when the trade occurred, the size of the trade, the bond price, and the implied yield to maturity. When measuring the yield to maturity, use the largest trades available, as smaller trades are unreliable. The largest trade for Costco's 2027 bond on August 30, 2019, was consummated at 2.01 percent (0.6 percent above the yield for a seven-year U.S. Treasury bond).

For companies with only short-term bonds or bonds that rarely trade, do not use market prices. Instead, use credit ratings to determine yield to maturity. First, determine the company's credit rating on unsecured long-term debt. Next, examine the average yield to maturity on a portfolio of long-term bonds with the same credit rating. Use this yield as a proxy for the company's implied yield on long-term debt.

---

[25] The Financial Industry Regulatory Authority (FINRA) introduced TRACE (Trade Reporting and Compliance Engine) in July 2002. The system captures and disseminates transactions in investment-grade, high-yield, and convertible corporate debt, representing all over-the-counter market activity in these bonds.

EXHIBIT 15.10 **Yield Spread over U.S. Treasuries by Bond Rating, August 2019**

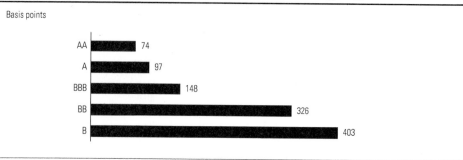

Source: Bloomberg bond portfolio with 10-year maturity.

To determine a company's bond rating, a rating agency like S&P or Moody's will examine the company's most recent financial ratios, analyze the company's competitive environment, and interview senior management. Corporate bond ratings are freely available to the public and can be downloaded from rating-agency websites. For instance, Costco was rated A+ in September 2019 by S&P and Aa3 by Moody's. Once you have a rating, convert the rating into a yield to maturity. Exhibit 15.10 presents the difference in yields between U.S. corporate bonds and U.S. Treasury bonds. The difference is referred to as the yield spread. All quotes are presented in basis points (hundredths of 1 percent).

Because the duration of Costco's longest-maturity debt was less than ten years, we use Costco's rating to determine the cost of debt. To do this, we add the default premium for an A+/Aa3 bond (0.8 percent) to our estimate of the risk-free rate (4.1 percent), discussed in the previous section. This leads to a pretax cost of debt of 4.9 percent.

Using the company's bond ratings to determine the yield to maturity is a good alternative to calculating the yield to maturity directly from bond prices. Never, however, approximate the yield to maturity using a bond's coupon rate. Coupon rates are set by the company at time of issuance and approximate the yield only if the bond trades near its par value. When valuing a company, you must estimate expected returns relative to *today's* comparable investments. Thus, when you measure the cost of debt, estimate what a comparable investment would earn if bought or sold today.

Cost of Below-Investment-Grade Debt

In practice, few financial analysts distinguish between expected and promised returns. But for debt below investment grade, rated BB or below, using the yield to maturity as a proxy for the cost of debt can significantly overestimate the cost of debt.

To understand the difference between expected returns and yield to maturity, consider the following example. You have been asked to value a one-year zero-coupon bond whose face value is $100. The bond is risky; there is a 25 percent chance the bond will default and you will recover only half the final payment. Finally, the cost of debt (not yield to maturity), estimated using the CAPM, equals 6 percent.[26]

Based on this information, you estimate the bond's price by discounting *expected* cash flows by the cost of debt:

$$\text{Price} = \frac{E(\text{Cash Flows})}{1+k_d} = \frac{(.75)(\$100)+(.25)(\$50)}{1.06} = \$82.55$$

Next, to determine the bond's yield to maturity, place promised cash flows, rather than expected cash flows, into the numerator. Then solve for the yield to maturity:

$$\text{Price} = \frac{\text{Promised Cash Flows}}{1+\text{YTM}} = \frac{\$100}{1+\text{YTM}} = \$82.55$$

Solving for YTM, the $82.55 price leads to a 21.1 percent yield to maturity—much higher than the 6 percent cost of debt.

Why the large difference between the cost of debt and yield to maturity? Three factors drive the yield to maturity: the cost of debt, the probability of default, and the recovery rate after default. When the probability of default is high and the recovery rate is low, the yield to maturity will deviate significantly from the cost of debt. Thus, for companies with high default risk and low ratings, the yield to maturity is a poor proxy for the cost of debt.

When a company is not investment-grade, start by assessing the company's financial strategy related to capital structure. If the company has uncharacteristically high levels of debt relative to its peers, use the company's stated target or a peer-based capital structure to determine the WACC. Estimate the debt rating your company is likely to generate based on this target capital structure.

If the company purposely maintains a debt rating below investment grade, we do not recommend using the weighted average cost of capital to value the company. Instead, use adjusted present value. The APV model discounts projected free cash flow at the company's industry-based unlevered cost of equity and adds the present value of tax shields. For more on APV valuation, see Chapter 10.

Incorporating the Interest Tax Shield

To calculate free cash flow (using techniques detailed in Chapters 10 and 11), we compute taxes as if the company were entirely financed by equity. By using all-equity taxes, it is possible to make comparisons across companies and over time, without regard to capital structure. Yet since the tax shield has value, it

[26] The CAPM applies to any security, not just equities. In practice, the cost of debt is rarely estimated using the CAPM, because infrequent trading makes estimation of beta impossible.

must be accounted for. In an enterprise DCF using the WACC, the tax shield is valued as part of the cost of capital. To value the tax shield, reduce the cost of debt by the marginal tax rate:

$$\text{After-Tax Cost of Debt} = \text{Cost of Debt} \times (1 - T_m)$$

Chapters 10 and 11 detail how to calculate the marginal tax rate for historical analysis. For use in the cost of capital, calculate the marginal tax rate in a consistent manner, with one potential modification. Multinational companies often borrow money in high-tax countries to lower their tax burden in those countries. Check the annual report for the location of corporate debt, and, if necessary, use the marginal tax rate where the debt was raised, not the statutory tax rate of the company's home country.

For companies with either low or volatile earnings, the statutory tax rate may overstate the marginal tax rate in future years. According to research by John Graham, the statutory marginal tax rate overstates the *future* marginal tax rate because of rules related to tax loss carryforwards, tax loss carrybacks, investment tax credits, and alternative minimum taxes.[27] Graham uses simulation to estimate the realizable marginal tax rate on a company-by-company basis. Graham estimates that the marginal tax rate is on average five percentage points below the statutory rate, primarily driven by smaller, less profitable companies.

FORECASTING TARGET CAPITAL STRUCTURE TO WEIGHT WACC COMPONENTS

With our estimates of the cost of equity and after-tax cost of debt in hand, it is now possible to blend the two expected returns to estimate the WACC. To do this, use the target weights of debt (net of excess cash) and equity to enterprise value (net of excess cash) on a market basis:

$$\text{WACC} = \frac{D}{V} k_d (1 - T_m) + \frac{E}{V} k_e$$

Using market values rather than book values to weight expected returns follows directly from the formula's algebraic derivation (see Appendix B for a derivation of free cash flow and WACC). But consider a more intuitive explanation: the WACC represents the expected return on a *different* investment with identical risk. Rather than reinvest in the company, management could return capital to investors, who could reinvest elsewhere. To return capital without changing the capital structure, management can repay debt and

---

[27] J. Graham and L. Mills, "Using Tax Return Data to Simulate Corporate Marginal Tax Rates," *Journal of Accounting and Economics* 46 (2009): 366–388; and J. Graham, "Proxies for the Corporate Marginal Tax Rate," *Journal of Financial Economics* 42 (1996): 187–221.

repurchase shares but must do so at their *market* value. Conversely, book value represents a sunk cost, so it is no longer relevant.

The cost of capital should rely on a forecast of target weights, rather than current weights, because at any point a company's current capital structure may not reflect the level expected to prevail over the life of the business. The current capital structure may merely reflect a short-term swing in the company's stock price, a swing that has yet to be rebalanced by management. Thus, using today's capital structure may cause you to overestimate (or underestimate) the value of tax shields for companies whose leverage is expected to drop (or rise).

Many companies are already near their target capital structure. If the company you are valuing is not, decide how quickly the company will achieve the target. In the simplest scenario, the company will rebalance immediately and maintain the new capital structure. In this case, using the target weights and a constant WACC (for all future years) will lead to a reasonable valuation. If you expect the rebalancing to happen over a long period of time, then use a different cost of capital each year, reflecting the capital structure at the time. In practice, this procedure is complex; you must correctly model the weights, as well as the changes in the cost of debt and equity (because of increased default risk and higher betas). For extreme changes in capital structure, modeling enterprise DCF using a constant WACC can lead to a substantially erroneous valuation. In this case, do not use WACC. Instead, value the company using adjusted present value.

To estimate the target capital structure from an external perspective, first estimate the company's current market-value-based capital structure. Next, review the capital structure of comparable companies. Finally, examine management's implicit or explicit approach to financing and its implications for the target capital structure. We discuss each step next.

Current Capital Structure

To determine the company's current capital structure, measure the market value of all claims against enterprise value. For most companies, the claims will consist primarily of traditional debt and equity (this chapter's final section addresses more complex securities). If a company's debt and equity are publicly traded, simply multiply the quantity of each security by its most recent price. Most difficulties arise when securities are not traded and prices cannot be readily observed.

Debt and Debt Equivalents, Net of Excess Cash   To value debt and debt equivalents, sum short-term debt, long-term debt, and debt equivalents like unfunded retirement obligations. From this total, subtract excess cash to determine net debt. Debt will be recorded on the balance sheet at book value, which may differ from market value. Therefore, use a data service to determine market value when possible. In the case of debt equivalents, the valuation method will depend on the account. We discuss the valuation of debt and debt equivalents next.

Market prices for U.S. corporate debt are reported on the Financial Industry Regulatory Authority (FINRA) TRACE system. As previously shown in Exhibit 15.9, Costco's 2027 bond traded at $106.8, or 106.8 percent of par value, on August 30, 2019. To determine the market value of the bond, multiply 106.8 percent by the bond's book value of $1 billion (found in the Costco annual report); the result is $1.068 billion. Since a bond's price depends on the bond's coupon rate versus its yield, not every Costco bond trades at the same price. For instance, the Costco bond maturing in 2024 closed at 104.0 percent of par on the same day. Consequently, each debt security needs to be valued separately.

If an observable market value is not readily available, value debt securities at book value (referred to as carrying value), or use discounted cash flow. In most cases, the book value reported on the balance sheet reasonably approximates the current market value. This will not be the case, however, if interest rates have changed since the company's last valuation or if the company has entered into financial distress. In these two situations, the current price will differ from carrying value because either expected cash flows have changed or the discount rate has changed from its last valuation.[28] In these situations, value each bond separately by discounting promised cash flows at the appropriate yield to maturity. The size and timing of coupons will be disclosed in the notes of a company's annual report. Determine the appropriate yield to maturity by examining the yields from comparably rated debt with similar maturities.

Next, value debt equivalents, such as operating leases and unfunded retirement obligations. In Chapters 22 and 23, we describe in detail the accounting for operating leases and pensions, including the required adjustments to free cash flow and cost of capital. Consistency between free cash flow and the cost of capital is paramount. Starting in December 2019, the value of operating leases is to be presented directly on the balance sheet; estimation is no longer necessary. To find the value of unfunded retirement obligations, search the pension note for the most recent market value. Although accounting authorities require disclosure of unfunded retirement obligations on the balance sheet, it is often embedded in other accounts.

Equity   If the company's common stock is publicly traded, multiply the market price by the number of shares *outstanding*. The market value of equity should be based on shares outstanding in the capital market. Do not use shares issued, as they may include shares repurchased by the company but not retired. For European companies in particular, you need to be careful in

---

[28] For floating-rate bonds, changes in Treasury rates won't affect value, since coupons float with Treasury yields. Changes in market-based default premiums, however, will affect the market value of floating-rate bonds, since bonds are priced at a fixed spread above Treasury yields.

EXHIBIT 15.11 **Median Debt to Value by Industry, 2018**

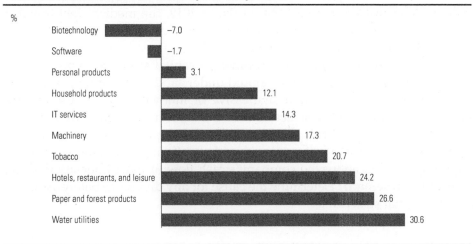

%

Biotechnology	−7.0
Software	−1.7
Personal products	3.1
Household products	12.1
IT services	14.3
Machinery	17.3
Tobacco	20.7
Hotels, restaurants, and leisure	24.2
Paper and forest products	26.6
Water utilities	30.6

Note: Calculated using S&P 1500 classified by GICS industry. Market values used when available.

determining the correct amount of shares outstanding because of the way companies sometimes account for treasury shares.

At this point, you may be wondering why you are valuing the company if you are going to rely on the market's value of equity in the cost of capital. Shouldn't you be using the estimated equity value? No. Remember, you are only estimating today's market value to frame management's philosophy concerning capital structure. To value the company, use forward-looking *target* weights.

For privately held companies, the equity value is unobservable. In this case, you must determine equity value (for the cost of capital) either using a multiples approach or through DCF iteratively. To perform an iterative valuation, assume a reasonable capital structure, and value the enterprise using DCF. Using the estimate of debt-to-enterprise value, repeat the valuation. Continue this process until the valuation no longer materially changes.

Capital Structure of Peer Companies

To place the company's current capital structure in the proper context, compare its capital structure with those of similar companies. Exhibit 15.11 presents the median debt-to-value levels for ten industries. As the exhibit shows, high-growth industries like software and IT services, especially those with intangible investments, tend to use very little debt. In fact, many companies hold more excess cash than debt, causing the net debt ratio to be negative.[29]

[29] Over the past 15 years, cash balances have grown substantially because companies must pay taxes in their home country on any repatriated earnings. For companies whose home country's tax rate is relatively high, cash will become trapped abroad. Following the change in U.S. tax code in 2017, the cash balance at American companies is expected to drop as companies repatriate foreign earnings at new, lower tax rates.

Industries with heavy fixed investment in tangible assets, like mining and utilities, tend to have higher debt levels. In 2018, the median debt-to-value ratio for S&P 1500 nonfinancial companies was 17.6 percent, and the median debt-to-equity ratio was 21.4 percent.

It is perfectly acceptable for a company's capital structure to be different from that of its industry. But you should understand why. For instance, is the company philosophically more aggressive or innovative in the use of debt financing, or is the capital structure only a temporary deviation from a more conservative target? Often, companies finance acquisitions with debt they plan to retire quickly or refinance with a stock offering. Alternatively, is there anything different about the company's cash flow or asset intensity that can explain the difference? Determine the cause for any difference before applying a target capital structure.

Management's Financing Philosophy

As a final step, review management's historical financing philosophy. Even better, question management outright, if possible. Has the current team been actively managing the company's capital structure? Is the management team aggressive in its use of debt? Or is it overly conservative? Consider Garmin, the personal-technology company that makes GPS devices. Although cash flow is strong and stable, the company rarely issues debt. From a financing perspective, it doesn't need to issue additional securities; investments can be funded with current profits.

ESTIMATING WACC FOR COMPLEX CAPITAL STRUCTURES

The weighted average cost of capital is determined by weighting each security's expected return by its proportional contribution to total value. For a complex security, such as convertible debt, measuring expected return is challenging. Is a convertible bond similar enough to straight debt, enabling us to use the yield to maturity? Or is it like equity, enabling us to use the CAPM? In actuality, it is neither, so we recommend an alternative method.

If the treatment of hybrid securities will make a material difference in valuation results,[30] we recommend using adjusted present value (APV). In the APV model, enterprise value is determined by discounting free cash flow at the industry-based unlevered cost of equity. The value of incremental cash flows related to financing, such as interest tax shields, is then computed separately.

---

[30] If the hybrid security is out-of-the-money and unlikely to be converted, it can be treated as traditional debt. Conversely, if the hybrid security is well in-the-money, it should be treated as traditional equity. In these situations, errors are likely to be small, and a WACC-based valuation remains appropriate.

In some situations, you may still desire an accurate representation of the WACC. In these cases, split hybrid securities into their individual components. For instance, you can replicate a convertible bond by combining a traditional bond with a call option on the company's stock. You can further disaggregate a call option into a portfolio consisting of a risk-free bond and the company's stock. By converting a complex security into a portfolio of debt and equity, you once again have the components required for the traditional cost of capital. The process of using replicating portfolios to value options is discussed in Chapter 39.

CLOSING THOUGHTS

The cost of capital is one of the most hotly debated topics in the field of finance. While robust statistical techniques have improved our understanding of the issues, a practical measurement of the cost of capital remains elusive. Nonetheless, we believe the steps outlined in this chapter, combined with a healthy perspective of long-term trends, will lead to a cost of capital that is reliable and reasonable. Even so, do not let a lack of precision overwhelm you. A company creates value when ROIC exceeds the cost of capital, and for many of our clients, the variation in ROIC across projects greatly exceeds any variation in the cost of capital. Smart selection of strategies and their corresponding investments based on forward-looking ROIC, not a precise measurement of the cost of capital, often generates most of the impact in day-to-day decision making.

16

Moving from Enterprise Value to Value per Share

When you have completed the valuation of core operations, as described in Chapter 10, you are ready to estimate enterprise value, equity value, and value per share. Enterprise value represents the value of the entire company, while equity value represents the portion owned by shareholders.

To determine enterprise value, add nonoperating assets to the value of core operations. The most common nonoperating assets are excess cash, investments in nonconsolidated companies, and tax loss carryforwards.[1] To estimate equity value, subtract all nonequity claims from enterprise value. Nonequity claims include short-term and long-term debt, debt equivalents like unfunded pension liabilities, and hybrid securities like convertible securities and employee stock options. Finally, to estimate the intrinsic value per share, divide the resulting equity value by the most recent number of shares outstanding.

While nonoperating assets and nonequity claims may feel like an afterthought, this is not the case. Many sophisticated investors have discovered substantial value hidden in nonoperating assets, especially in privately held conglomerates. In contrast, other investors have been burned by not accurately identifying and valuing all nonequity claims against enterprise value, as happened in the well-publicized case of Enron. It is critical to know who has a claim on cash flow before equity holders do.

This chapter lays out the process for converting core operating value into enterprise value and subsequently into equity value. The chapter goes

---

[1] Throughout the book, we define enterprise value as the value of core operations plus nonoperating assets. Many bankers define enterprise value as debt plus equity minus cash. For a company whose only nonoperating asset is excess cash and owes only traditional debt, this definition is equivalent to our definition of the value of core operations. This simple definition of enterprise value, however, fails to account for other nonoperating assets and debt equivalents, which can lead to errors in valuation.

335

step-by-step through the process of identifying and valuing the most common nonoperating assets, debt and debt equivalents, hybrid securities, and noncontrolling interests, ending with the final step in valuation—estimating the intrinsic value per share.[2]

THE VALUATION BUILDUP PROCESS

The valuation buildup begins with a company's core operating value, based on discounted cash flow (DCF)—the top line of the example shown in Exhibit 16.1. This amount plus nonoperating assets equals enterprise value. The equity value—the bottom line in the exhibit—is the value that remains after subtracting from the enterprise value all the nonequity claims, which include interest-bearing debt, debt equivalents, and hybrid claims. We use the term *nonequity claim* because there are many financial claims against a company's cash flows other than traditional fixed-coupon debt and shareholders' equity.

EXHIBIT 16.1 **Sample Comprehensive Valuation Buildup**

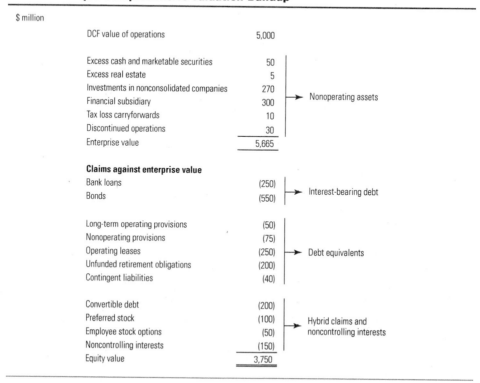

$ million		
DCF value of operations	5,000	
Excess cash and marketable securities	50	
Excess real estate	5	
Investments in nonconsolidated companies	270	Nonoperating assets
Financial subsidiary	300	
Tax loss carryforwards	10	
Discontinued operations	30	
Enterprise value	5,665	
Claims against enterprise value		
Bank loans	(250)	Interest-bearing debt
Bonds	(550)	
Long-term operating provisions	(50)	
Nonoperating provisions	(75)	
Operating leases	(250)	Debt equivalents
Unfunded retirement obligations	(200)	
Contingent liabilities	(40)	
Convertible debt	(200)	
Preferred stock	(100)	Hybrid claims and
Employee stock options	(50)	noncontrolling interests
Noncontrolling interests	(150)	
Equity value	3,750	

[2] Estimating the value per share completes the technical aspect of the valuation, yet the job is not complete. It is then time to revisit the valuation with a comprehensive look at its implications. We examine this process in Chapter 17.

In general, a nonoperating asset is any asset that you have not incorporated as part of free cash flow. Common nonoperating assets are excess cash, one-time receivables, investments in nonconsolidated companies (also known as equity investments and by other names), excess pension assets, discontinued operations, and financial subsidiaries. Take extra care not to classify an asset required for ongoing operations as nonoperating. For instance, some analysts who follow retailers add the value of real estate to the value of core operations. Since the real estate is required to conduct business, its benefits are already embedded in the value of operations. The value of real estate can only be added to core operations if the company is charged a market-based rent in free cash flow. Otherwise, including the value of real estate will lead to an overestimate of value.

Nonequity claims are financial claims against enterprise value whose expenses are not included in EBITA and consequently are excluded from free cash flow. Traditional debt contracts like bank debt and corporate bonds are the most common nonequity claims. Other debt-like claims, known as debt equivalents, include the present value of operating leases, unfunded pension and other retirement liabilities, and environmental remediation liabilities, among others. Because these claims do not scale with revenue or can affect the cost of capital, they are best valued separately from free cash flow.

Nonequity claims also include hybrid securities, such as preferred stock, convertible securities, and employee options, which have characteristics of both debt and equity. Such hybrids require special care: their valuations are highly dependent on enterprise value, so you should value them using option-pricing models rather than book value.[3] Finally, if other shareholders have noncontrolling interests against certain consolidated subsidiaries, deduct the value of the noncontrolling interests to determine equity value. Like hybrid securities, noncontrolling interests will correlate with enterprise value, so extra care is required.

VALUING NONOPERATING ASSETS

Although not included in free cash flow, nonoperating assets still represent value to the shareholder. Thus, to arrive at enterprise value, you must estimate the market value of each nonoperating asset separately and add the resulting value to the DCF value of operations. If necessary, adjust for circumstances that could affect shareholders' ability to capture the full value of these assets. For example, if the company has announced it will sell off a nonoperating asset in the near term, deduct the estimated capital gains taxes (if any) on the asset from its market value. If ownership of the asset is shared with another company, include only your company's portion of the value.

---

[3] For investment-grade companies, the value of debt is driven mostly by interest rates. In this case, there will be little interdependence between enterprise value and debt. For distressed companies, default risk also drives the value of debt. In this case, interdependence will be high and must be modeled. We discuss highly levered companies later in the chapter.

This section identifies the most common nonoperating assets and describes how to handle each of them in the valuation.

Excess Cash and Marketable Securities

As discussed in Chapter 11, companies often hold more cash and marketable securities than they need to run the business. Companies hold excess cash for a number of reasons, parking it in short-term securities until they can invest it or return it to shareholders. Prior to the change in American tax laws in 2018, American companies held significant amounts of excess cash when they had substantial earnings outside the United States. They were reluctant to repatriate cash because they were required to pay any difference in taxes upon repatriation. With a drop in the corporate tax rate from 35 percent to 21 percent, many companies have committed to repatriating cash. How they deploy this cash will unfold over time, but it will probably consist of new investment, increased dividends, and significant share repurchases.[4]

You should make an estimate of how much the business needs for operations. The remaining cash and marketable securities are treated as nonoperating. As a rule of thumb, we often assume that a company requires about 2 percent of revenues in cash to operate the business. The remaining cash and marketable securities are considered excess.

Cash and marketable securities are reported on a company's balance sheet at fair market value. You can use these assets' book value in your valuation, unless you have reason to believe they have significantly changed in value since the reporting date (as in the limited case of volatile equity holdings).

Investments in Nonconsolidated Companies

Companies often invest in other companies without taking control, and hence they do not consolidate the investment's financial statements into their own. Investments in nonconsolidated companies can be found on the balance sheet under many names. For instance, Philips reports its investments in nonconsolidated companies as investments in associates, Intel reports them as equity investments, and PPG Industries reports them as investment in equity affiliates.

Because the parent company does not have control over these subsidiaries, their financials are not consolidated, so these investments must be valued separately from operations. Under U.S. Generally Accepted Accounting Principles (GAAP) and International Financial Reporting Standards (IFRS),

---

[4] For examples of repatriation and redeployment, see A. Balakrishnan, "Apple Announces Plans to Repatriate Billions in Overseas Cash, Says It Will Contribute $350 Billion to the US Economy over the Next 5 Years," CNBC, January 17, 2018, www.cnbc.com. For more on share buybacks, see K. Rooney, "Share Buybacks Soar to Record $806 Billion—Bigger Than a Facebook or Exxon Mobil," CNBC, March 25, 2019, www.cnbc.com.

there are two ways in which nonconsolidated subsidiaries can appear in the parent company's accounts:

1. For equity stakes in which the parent company exerts "significant influence" but lacks control (often between 20 and 50 percent ownership), the equity holding in the subsidiary is reported on the parent's balance sheet at the investment's historical cost plus any reinvested income. The parent company's portion of the subsidiary's profits is shown on the parent's income statement as other income, unless specifically disclosed. Accountants refer to this as the equity method.

2. For equity stakes below 20 percent, the parent company is often assumed to have no influence. The equity holdings are shown at historical cost on the parent's balance sheet. The parent's portion of the subsidiary's *dividends* is included in other income on the income statement.

In response to the accounting and financial scandals of the early 2000s, global accounting moved away from absolute thresholds to consolidation methods that rely on the parent's influence around key activities and exposure to gains and losses. Implementation has been complex, and companies can report under multiple standards. Always investigate the notes to determine which investments contribute to EBITA and which do not.

Investments in Publicly Traded Companies   If an investment in another company is publicly listed, use the market value to determine the value of the parent company's equity stake. Verify that the market value is indeed a good indicator of intrinsic value. In some cases, these listed subsidiaries have very limited free float and/or very low liquidity, so the share price may not properly reflect current information.

Exhibit 16.2 presents the equity investments held by Coca-Cola. Since Coca-Cola does not control these companies, their revenue, income, and assets are not consolidated on Coca-Cola's financial statements. Therefore, each investment must be valued separately and added to Coca-Cola's value of operations to determine enterprise value.

In the management discussion and analysis section of its 2018 annual report, Coca-Cola reports both book value and fair value for its equity investments.[5] Therefore, if you are valuing Coca-Cola near its fiscal-year close, the valuation from the annual report will suffice. As the year progresses, however, these data become stale, and each investment must be revalued. For example, consider Coca-Cola Amatil, Coca-Cola's bottler in Australia. To value this

---

[5] Companies will disclose how fair value is determined for each security, using a system of levels. Level 1 inputs are quoted prices of identical securities in liquid markets. Level 2 inputs are quoted prices of identical securities in illiquid markets or similar securities in liquid markets. Level 3 inputs are not observed and are estimated using financial models.

EXHIBIT 16.2 **Coca-Cola Company: Publicly Traded Equity Investments, December 2018**

$ million

	Book value	Fair value	Valuation of Coca-Cola Amatil Limited (ASX: CCL)	
Monster Beverage Corporation	3,573	5,026	Share price, AU $	8.19
Coca-Cola European Partners plc	3,551	4,033	× Shares outstanding, million	724
Coca-Cola FEMSA, S.A.B. de C.V.	1,714	3,401	= Market capitalization, AU $ million	5,930
Coca-Cola HBC AG	1,260	2,681		
Coca-Cola Amatil Limited	656	1,325	× Percent ownership	30.8%
Coca-Cola Bottlers Japan Holdings Inc.	1,142	978	= Ownership stake, AU $ million	1,826
Embotelladora Andina S.A.	263	497		
Coca-Cola Consolidated, Inc.	138	440	× Currency conversion, US $/AU $	0.73
Coca-Cola İçecek A.Ş.	174	299	= Ownership stake	1,325
Total	12,471	18,680		

Source: Coca-Cola Company annual report, 2018; Coca-Cola Amatil annual report, 2018; Yahoo Finance.

equity stake, multiply the enterprise value for Coca-Cola Amatil (AU $5,930 million) by Coca-Cola's ownership percentage (30.8 percent). The resulting ownership stake equals AU $1,826 million. Since Coca-Cola reports in U.S. dollars, the stake must be converted into U.S. dollars at the prevailing exchange rate. Multiplying AU $1,826 million by 0.73 equals the value of Coca-Cola's ownership of Coca-Cola Amatil ($1,325 million).

Although this valuation was accurate as of December 31, 2018, any change in one of the inputs will require an update to the valuation. For instance, during the first quarter of 2019, Amatil's stock price rose by approximately 3 percent. This rise in value was reflected in Coca-Cola's next quarterly report but not during the interim.

Investments in Privately Held Companies   If the subsidiary is not listed but you have access to its financial statements (for instance, through a public bond offering or private disclosure), perform a separate DCF valuation of the equity stake. Discount the cash flows at the appropriate cost of capital (which may be different than the parent company's weighted average cost of capital). Also, when completing the parent valuation, include only the value of the parent's equity stake and not the subsidiary's entire enterprise value or equity value.

If the parent company's accounts are the only source of financial information for the subsidiary, we suggest the following alternatives to DCF:

- *Simplified cash-flow-to-equity valuation.* This is a feasible approach when the parent has a 20 to 50 percent equity stake, because the subsidiary's net income and book equity are disclosed in the parent's accounts.[6]

---

[6] The book value of the subsidiary equals the historical acquisition cost plus retained profits, which is a reasonable approximation of book equity. If goodwill is included in the book value of the subsidiary, this should be deducted.

Build forecasts for how the equity-based key value drivers (net income growth and return on equity) will develop, so you can project cash flows to equity. Discount these cash flows at the *cost of equity* for the subsidiary in question and not at the parent company's cost of capital.

- *Multiples valuation.* As a second alternative, estimate the partial stake using a price-to-earnings and/or market-to-book multiple. If the company owns 20 to 50 percent of the subsidiary, apply an appropriate multiple to reported income.

- *Tracking portfolio.* For parent equity stakes below 20 percent, you may have no information beyond the investment's original cost—that is, the book value shown in the parent's balance sheet and often only disclosed in the notes. Even applying a multiple is difficult, because neither net income nor the current book value of equity is reported. If you know when the stake was acquired (or last valued), you can approximate its current market value by applying the relative price change for a portfolio of comparable stocks over the same holding period.

You should triangulate your results as much as possible, given the lack of precision for these valuation approaches.

Loans to Other Companies

For loans to nonconsolidated subsidiaries and other companies, use the reported book value. This is a reasonable approximation of market value if the loans were given at fair market terms and if the borrower's credit risk and general interest rates have not changed significantly since issuance. If this is not the case and the investment is substantial, you should perform a separate DCF valuation of the promised interest and principal payments at the yield to maturity for corporate bonds with similar risk and maturity.

Finance Subsidiaries

To make their products more accessible, some companies operate customer financing businesses.[7] Because financial subsidiaries differ greatly from manufacturing and services businesses, it is critical to separate revenues, expenses, and balance sheet accounts associated with the subsidiary from core operations. Failing to do so will distort return on invested capital, free cash flow, and ultimately your perspective on the company's valuation.

Once the finance subsidiary is separated from operations, use the reorganized financial statements to value the subsidiary as if it were a financial

---

[7] Companies that sell expensive products typically offer financing of purchases. Significant customer financing subsidiaries exist at IBM and Textron, among others.

institution. Add this value to the value of core operations to determine enterprise value. Since the finance subsidiary's debt will already be incorporated into your valuation of the finance subsidiary, do not subtract total debt from the parent company's enterprise value to determine equity value. Subtract only general obligation debt unrelated to the finance subsidiary.

We present the valuation of a company with a finance subsidiary in Chapter 19, and we cover bank valuation in Chapter 38.

Discontinued Operations

Discontinued operations are businesses being sold or closed. The earnings from discontinued operations are explicitly shown in the income statement, and the associated net asset position is disclosed on the balance sheet. Because discontinued operations are no longer part of a company's operations, their value should not be modeled as part of free cash flow or included in the DCF value of operations. Under U.S. GAAP and IFRS, the assets and liabilities associated with the discontinued operations are written down to their fair value and disclosed as a net asset on the balance sheet, so the most recent book value is usually a reasonable approximation.[8]

Excess Real Estate

Excess real estate and other unutilized assets are assets no longer required for the company's operations. As a result, any cash flows that the assets generate are excluded from the free-cash-flow projection, and the assets are not included in the DCF value of operations. Identifying these assets in an outside-in valuation is nearly impossible unless they are specifically disclosed in the company's footnotes. For that reason, only internal valuations are likely to include their value separately as a nonoperating asset. For excess real estate, use the most recent appraisal value when it is available. Alternatively, estimate the real estate value either by using a multiple, such as value per square meter, or by discounting expected future cash flows from rentals at the appropriate cost of capital. Of course, be careful to exclude any operating real estate from these figures, because that value is implicitly included in the free-cash-flow projections and value of operations.

We do not recommend a separate valuation for unutilized operating assets unless they are expected to be sold in the near term. If the financial projections for the company reflect growth, the value of any underutilized assets should instead be captured in lower future capital expenditures.

---

[8] Any upward adjustment to the current book value of assets and liabilities is limited to the cumulative historical impairments on the assets. Thus, the fair market value of discontinued operations could be higher than the net asset value disclosed in the balance sheet.

Excess Pension Assets

Surpluses in a company's pension funds show up as net pension assets on the balance sheet and typically reported at market value.[9] (Small amounts are typically embedded within other assets.) On an after-tax basis, the pension's value depends on management's plans. If pensions are expected to be dissolved soon, subtract liquidation taxes—typically set higher than the statutory tax rate—from the market value of excess pension assets. Otherwise, subtract taxes at the statutory rate, which reflects the need for lower future contributions. For details on pension accounting and valuation, see Chapter 23.

Tax Loss Carryforwards

When a company generates a loss in a given year, it can accumulate those losses and net them against future income, thereby reducing future taxes.[10] This is known as a tax loss carryforward. Since tax savings will increase future cash flows, estimate their value using discounted cash flow, and add your result to the company's value of operations.

The potential tax loss carryforward is recorded on the balance sheet as a deferred-tax asset.[11] Use the deferred-tax asset as a starting point to value the tax loss carryforwards. If the company is unlikely to use the tax loss carryforward, the company will record a valuation allowance against the deferred-tax asset. Both numbers can be found in the note on taxes that accompanies the company's financial statements. The company's valuation allowance will reflect its current expectations of future profitability, which may be different from your projections, so use caution in adopting the company's calculation. If you develop multiple scenarios to value operations, estimate your own allowance against the deferred-tax asset based on the probability of the asset being realized under each scenario.

Because tax savings are recorded on an undiscounted basis, apply discounted cash flow to estimate their value as of today. Ideally, you would discount tax savings at a cost of capital that perfectly matches their risk. In practice, use the weighted average cost of capital. This will appropriately counter the value of operating taxes embedded in your value of operations.

To estimate the present value, forecast the year-by-year tax savings based on your projected earnings for the company. Unless income by geography is

---

[9] Under IFRS, companies can still report excess pension assets at book value. If pensions are not marked to market, search the company's pension footnote for the value of excess pension assets.

[10] Tax policy varies widely across countries. Check local tax policy to determine if, how, and when you can net past losses against future income.

[11] As detailed in Chapter 11, we classify deferred taxes into tax loss carryforwards, operating deferred taxes, and nonoperating deferred taxes. Only tax loss carryforwards should be valued separately. The other two accounts are either incorporated into free cash flow via cash operating taxes or valued as part of the account that generated the deferral.

available, year-by-year tax savings will be difficult to assess because tax loss carryforwards must be matched in the country in which they are generated. A pragmatic approach is to assume the tax benefits will be realized over an arbitrary period—say, five years. If your valuation of tax loss carryforwards affects share price in a meaningful way, ask management for additional disclosures regarding the location and timing of tax credits.

Finally, be careful not to double-count future tax savings by also incorporating them into the projected free cash flow. Since we value tax loss carryforwards separately, the tax loss carryforward is classified as a nonoperating asset and not included as part of either net operating profit after taxes (NOPAT) or invested capital.

VALUING INTEREST-BEARING DEBT

With enterprise value in hand, subtract the value of nonequity claims to determine equity value. Nonequity claims are found in the liability and equity sections of the balance sheet. Nonequity claims include traditional interest-bearing debt, debt equivalents such as unfunded retirement obligations, and hybrid securities that have characteristics of both debt and equity. In this section, we discuss traditional interest-bearing debt.

Traditional debt comes in many forms: commercial paper, notes payable, fixed and floating bank loans, corporate bonds, and capitalized leases. For companies with investment-grade debt, the value of debt will be independent of the value of operations. Consequently, each security's value can be estimated separately. For highly levered companies and companies in distress, this is not the case. In these situations, the value of debt will be linked to value of core operations, and both values must be determined concurrently.

Investment-Grade Debt If the debt is relatively secure and actively traded, use the market value of debt.[12] Market prices for U.S. corporate debt are reported on the Financial Industry Regulatory Authority (FINRA) Trade Reporting and Compliance Engine (TRACE) system.[13] If the debt instrument is not traded, estimate current value by discounting the promised interest payments and the principal repayment at a yield to maturity that reflects the riskiness

---

[12] When a bond's yield is below its coupon rate, the bond will trade above its face value. Intuition dictates that, at most, the bond's face value should be deducted from enterprise value. Yet since enterprise value is computed using the cost of debt (via the weighted average of cost of capital) and not the coupon rate, subtracting face value is inconsistent with how enterprise value is computed. In cases where bonds are callable at face value, market prices will rarely exceed face value.

[13] Developed by FINRA, the TRACE system facilitates the mandatory reporting of over-the-counter market transactions for eligible debt securities in the United States. It is available to the public via FINRA's website. At the time of publication, FINRA provided an online bond search tool on its home page.

of the debt—typically based on the company's bond rating. The book value of debt is a reasonable approximation for fixed-rate debt if interest rates and default risk have not significantly changed since the debt issuance. For floating-rate debt, value is not sensitive to interest rates, and book value is a reasonable approximation if the company's risk of default has been generally stable.

If you are using your valuation model to test changes in operating performance (for instance, a new initiative that will improve operating margins), the value of debt under your new assumptions may differ from its current market value. Always check leverage ratios, such as the interest coverage ratio, to test whether the company's bond rating will change under the new forecasts; often it will not. A change in bond rating can be translated into a new yield to maturity for debt, which in turn will allow you to revalue the debt. For more on debt ratings and interest rates, see Chapter 33.

Highly Levered Companies   For companies with significant debt or companies in financial distress, valuing debt requires careful analysis. For distressed companies, the intrinsic value of the debt will be at a significant discount to its book value and will fluctuate with the value of the enterprise. Essentially, the debt has become like equity: its value will depend directly on your estimate for the enterprise value.

To value debt in these situations, apply an integrated-scenario approach. Exhibit 16.3 presents a simple two-scenario example for a company with significant debt. In scenario A, the company's management can implement improvements in operating margin, inventory turns, and so on. In scenario B, changes are unsuccessful, and performance remains at its current level.

For each scenario, estimate the enterprise value conditional on your financial forecasts.[14] Next, deduct the *full value* of the debt and other nonequity claims from enterprise value. The full value is not the market value, but rather the value of debt if the company were default free.[15] If the full value of debt is greater than enterprise value, set the equity value to zero. To complete the valuation, weight each scenario's resulting equity value by its probability of occurrence. For the company in Exhibit 16.3, scenario A leads to an equity valuation of $300 million, whereas the equity value in scenario B is zero. If the probability of each scenario is 50 percent, the value of equity is $150 million.

The scenario valuation approach treats equity like a call option on enterprise value. A more comprehensive model would estimate the entire distribution of potential enterprise values and use an option-pricing model, such as the Black-Scholes model, to value equity.[16] Using an option-pricing model

[14] All nonequity claims need to be included in the scenario approach for distressed companies. The order in which nonequity claims are paid upon liquidation will make a difference for the value of each nonequity claim but not for the equity value.
[15] If the coupon rate does not equal the yield on comparable bonds, the value of debt will not equal the book value, even if the debt is default free.
[16] Chapter 39 describes option-pricing models.

EXHIBIT 16.3 **Valuation of Equity Using Scenario Analysis**

$ million

	Enterprise value	Face value of debt	Equity value[1]	Probability of occurrence	Weighted equity value
Scenario A					
New owner successfully implements value improvements.	1,500	1,200	300	50%	150
Scenario B					
Company maintains current performance.	900	1,200	–	50%	–
				Equity value:	150

[1]Equity value equals enterprise value less the face value of debt, or zero, whichever is greater.

rather than scenario analysis to value equity, however, has practical drawbacks. First, to model the distribution of enterprise values, you must forecast the expected change and volatility for each source of uncertainty, such as revenue growth and gross margin. This too easily becomes a mechanical exercise that replaces a thoughtful analysis of the underlying economics of potential scenarios. Second, most options models treat each source of uncertainty as independent of the others. This can lead to outcomes that are economically unrealistic. For these reasons, we believe a thoughtful scenario analysis will lead to a better-informed and more accurate valuation than an advanced options model will.

VALUING DEBT EQUIVALENTS

Debt equivalents have the characteristics of debt but are not formal loan contracts or traded securities. They include operating provisions such as plant decommissioning, nonoperating provisions such as restructuring charges, operating leases, and contingent liabilities such as pending lawsuits. We discuss the most common debt equivalents next.

Provisions

Certain provisions other than retirement-related liabilities must be deducted as debt equivalents. We distinguish four types of provisions (as introduced in Chapter 11 and discussed in detail in Chapter 21) and value them as follows:

1. Ongoing operating provisions (such as for warranties and product returns) are already accounted for in the free cash flows and therefore *should not be deducted* from enterprise value.

2. Long-term operating provisions (e.g., plant-decommissioning costs) *should be deducted* from enterprise value as debt equivalents. Because these provisions cover cash expenses that are payable in the long term, they are recorded at the discounted value in the balance sheet. In this case, there is no need to perform a separate DCF analysis, and you can *use the book value of the liability* in your valuation.[17]

3. Nonoperating provisions (in cases such as restructuring charges resulting from layoffs) *should be deducted* from enterprise value as a debt equivalent. Although a discounted value would be ideal, the book value from the balance sheet is often a reasonable approximation. These provisions are recorded on the financial statements at a nondiscounted value, because outlays are usually made in the near term.

4. Income-smoothing provisions should be eliminated from NOPAT. Consequently, they *should not be deducted* from enterprise value. For an example of income smoothing, see the sale-leaseback example for FedEx presented at the end of Chapter 11.

Leases

Starting in 2019, companies are required to recognize nearly all leases, including operating leases, on the balance sheet. For companies that report using IFRS, lease-related interest is recorded as a financial expense, and lease-related liabilities are incorporated within debt. Therefore, no adjustment is required.

For companies that report using U.S. GAAP, there are two types of leases: finance leases and operating leases. The treatment of finance leases is identical to IFRS, so no adjustment to enterprise value is required. In contrast, operating leases require special care. To determine equity value, remove embedded interest from operating expense, include the year-to-year change in "right-to-use" assets in free cash flow, and deduct the operating-lease liability from enterprise value to determine equity value.[18] To value equity consistently, all three actions are required. If you choose not to adjust for embedded interest or include the change of "right-to-use" assets on free cash flow, do *not* subtract the value of operating leases.

Chapter 22 details the new accounting rules, required adjustments, and valuation of leases.

Unfunded Retirement Obligations

Unfunded retirement obligations, such as unfunded pensions and post-retirement medical benefits, should be treated as debt equivalents and

[17] The company will also recognize a decommissioning asset at the time of initial investment. The decommissioning asset is already incorporated into free cash flow, so no adjustment for the asset is required.

[18] For a more comprehensive summary, see the Operating Leases section of Chapter 11.

reported on the balance sheet below their principal value, at $181.2 million and $718.5 million, respectively.[24]

The first column in Exhibit 16.4 values Square's equity using the fair value of convertible debt reported in the company's 10-K. The second column presents the year-end closing price collected from the TRACE database. Compared with the book value reported on the balance sheet, the company's convertible debt trades at a significant premium. For instance, the convertible debt due in 2023 was valued by Square at $901.5 million in December 2018 versus $718.5 million in book value.

The significant premium to book value can be traced to the value of the conversion feature. According to Square's annual report, the bonds maturing in 2022 are convertible at $22.95 per share.[25] At this conversion price, $211.7 million in outstanding principal is convertible into 9.23 million shares. With Square's stock trading at $56.09 in December 2018, the bonds can be converted into the equivalent of $517.5 million in equity. The bond trades at a market price ($523.2 million), which is slightly higher than the bond's conversion value ($517.5 million), given the upside potential and downside protection the bond offers.

EXHIBIT 16.4 **Square Convertible Debt, December 2018**

$ million

Capital structure	Fair value[1]	Market price[2]	Black-Scholes value[3]	Conversion value	Carrying value	Principal outstanding
Enterprise value	26,300.0	26,300.0	26,300.0	26,300.0		
Convertible debt at 0.375% due 2022	(515.7)	(523.2)	(534.8)	–	181.2	211.7
Convertible debt at 0.5% due 2023	(901.5)	(899.2)	(917.9)	–	718.5	862.5
Convertible note hedge	230.9	230.9	230.9	–		
Employee options	(1,543.8)	(1,543.8)	(1,543.8)	(1,543.8)		
Equity value	23,570.0	23,564.8	23,534.5	24,756.2		
Number of shares, millions						
Number of nondiluted shares	419.7	419.7	419.7	419.7		
New shares issued	–	–	–	20.3		
Number of diluted shares	419.7	419.7	419.7	440.0		
Value per share, $	56.1	56.1	56.0	56.3		

[1] Value of convertible bonds reported in 2018 10-K in note 5, "Fair Value of Financial Instruments," under "Fair Value (Level 2)."

[2] Market price reported by the FINRA TRACE database as of December 31, 2018.

[3] Value estimated using Black-Scholes option-pricing model and company-disclosed inputs.

[24] When a company issues convertible debt at a coupon rate below the yield on similar nonconvertible debt, it will be recorded on the balance sheet at a discount but may not trade at a discount. This is because the conversion feature has value. The value of the conversion feature, however, is not recorded as part of debt, but rather as shareholders' equity. Since the book value of equity is not used in DCF valuation, this can lead to a significant underestimation of the convertible's value. For more on the accounting related to convertible debt, see Accounting Principles Board (APB) 14-1, "Accounting for Convertible Debt Instruments That May Be Settled in Cash upon Conversion (Including Partial Cash Settlement)." Financial Accounting Standards Board, May 9, 2008, www.fasb.org.

[25] Reported in Square's 2018 annual report, note 12, "Indebtedness."

If improvements to operations increase enterprise value, it becomes necessary to revalue Square's convertibles using an option-pricing model. To model the value of Square's convertible debt, disaggregate the value of convertible debt into underlying straight debt and the option value to convert. For the bond maturing in 2022, the value of straight debt equals the net present value of a 0.375 percent coupon bond yielding 2.48 percent (the yield on comparable bonds without conversion features), maturing in 3.25 years (the remaining life). Without conversion, this bond is valued at 93.45 percent of $211.7 million in outstanding principal, or $197.9 million.

To determine the option to convert's value, you need six inputs: the underlying asset value, the strike price, the volatility of the underlying asset, the risk-free rate, the time to maturity, and the dividend rate on the underlying asset. For the option embedded in Square's 2022 convertible bond, the underlying asset is 9.23 million shares of Square stock, whose current value equals $517.5 million. The strike price, which represents what the investor must pay to receive the shares, equals the current value of straight debt, currently valued at $197.9 million. The volatility of Square shares (30.9 percent) is reported in the company's 10-K. The bond's time to maturity is 3.25 years, and the current risk-free rate is 2.48 percent.[26] Square does not pay dividends, so the dividend yield is set at zero.

Plugging the data into a Black-Scholes estimator leads to an option value of $336.9 million. Thus, as illustrated in the third data column of Exhibit 16.4, the Black-Scholes value of the convertible debt equals $534.8 million ($197.9 in straight debt plus $336.9 in option value). This result is contingent on stability of the Black-Scholes inputs, especially volatility. If volatility is expected to drop as the company matures, the historical estimate of volatility will overestimate the option value. The errant valuation is largest for long-dated options, which is often the case for convertible debt.

An alternative to option pricing is the conversion value approach, shown in the fourth data column of Exhibit 16.4. The method is easier to implement than Black-Scholes but ignores optionality. Under the conversion value approach, convertible bonds are converted immediately into equity. Since Square's bonds are convertible into 20.3 million shares (9.2 million shares from the convertible debt due in 2022 and 11.1 million shares from the convertible debt due in 2023), non-diluted shares are increased from 419.7 million to 440.0 million. This approach zeroes out convertible debt and divides the equity value by diluted shares.

In this case, each approach leads to a similar value because the value of conversion is much higher than the value of traditional debt (known as being in the money). For bonds out of the money, the conversion approach will lead to an underestimation of the bonds' value. Therefore, we recommend using an option valuation model, such as Black-Scholes.

---

[26] Square's convertible debt is not callable, so the remaining maturity can be used in the options valuation. If the debt is callable, this must be incorporated into the bond's valuation.

Convertible Bond Hedges   When a company issues a convertible bond, the bond is sometimes accompanied by a complex derivative transaction to effectively increase the strike price.[27] For example, Square, Etsy, and Twitter have all issued convertible debt with accompanying hedges. Investors prefer strike prices close to the current share price. Issuers, concerned about dilution from conversion into equity, prefer a higher strike price that lowers the odds of conversion.

In its annual report, Square reports, "The Company entered into convertible note hedge transactions . . . to effectively increase the overall conversion price from approximately $22.95 per share to approximately $31.18 per share." To account for the value of the hedge, we use Black-Scholes to revalue the convertible bond at the higher strike price. The convertible note hedge reported in Exhibit 16.4 equals the difference between the original and synthetic bond price.

Although Square does not report the value of the hedge on the balance sheet or in the notes, the company does disclose that "the convertible note hedge and warrant transactions may affect the value of our Class A common stock." Even with the recent improvements in accounting transparency, a diligent analysis of the notes continues to be critical!

Employee Stock Options

Many companies offer their employees stock options as part of their compensation. Options give the holder the right, but not the obligation, to buy company stock at a specified price, known as the exercise price. Since employee stock options have long maturities and the company's stock price could eventually rise above the exercise price, options can have great value.

Employee stock options affect a company valuation in two ways. First, the value of options that will be *granted in the future* needs to be captured in the free-cash-flow projections or in a separate DCF valuation, following the guidelines in Chapter 11. If captured in the free-cash-flow projections, the value of future options grants is included in the value of operations and should not be treated as a nonequity claim. Second, the value of options *currently outstanding* must be subtracted from enterprise value as a nonequity claim. Note, however, that the value of the options will depend on your estimate of enterprise value. Your option valuation should reflect this.

The following approaches can be used for valuing employee options:

- *Company-disclosed fair value.* Start by searching the annual report for the company's assessment of fair value. For instance, Square reports the "aggregate intrinsic value" of employee options at $1.544 billion in the note on stockholders' equity.

[27] In the transaction, the company purchases a call option on its own shares at the original share price and writes a second call option at the preferred conversion price.

- *Option-pricing model.* If the company's enterprise value has changed since the last financial filing, estimate the value using option valuation models such as Black-Scholes or more advanced binomial (lattice) models. Under U.S. GAAP and IFRS, the notes to the balance sheet report the total value of all employee stock options outstanding, as estimated by such option-pricing models. Note that the balance sheet value is a good approximation only if your estimate of share price is close to the one underlying the option values in the annual report. Otherwise, you need to create a new valuation using an option-pricing model.[28] The notes disclose the information required for valuation.

- *Exercise value approach.* The exercise value approach provides only a lower bound for the value of employee options, the smallest value that would round up to the estimated value. It assumes that all options are exercised immediately and thereby ignores the time value of the options. The resulting valuation error increases as options have longer time to maturity, the company's stock has higher volatility, and the company's share price is closer to the exercise price. Given that a more accurate valuation is already disclosed in the annual report, we do not recommend this method. However, it is still quite common among practitioners.

Exhibit 16.5 provides an example of the three valuation methods. The first data column is based on the fair value reported by the company, which it calls "aggregate intrinsic value." The second and third data columns use the Black-Scholes option-pricing model to value first the outstanding options and second the options that can be currently exercised. The value of outstanding options will be less than that of options that can be exercised, because outstanding options include some options that will be lost if the employee leaves the company.

To estimate the value of employee stock options, you need six inputs: the current stock price, the average strike price, the stock's volatility, the risk-free rate, the time to maturity, and the stock's dividend rate. Square's current share price equals $56.09. The other inputs are disclosed in Square's 10-K for both outstanding and exercisable options. For outstanding options, the weighted average strike price equals $9.52, the volatility of Square's shares equals 30.9 percent, and the average time to maturity is reported at 5.45 years. The current risk-free rate over five years is 2.51 percent, and the expected dividend rate is zero. The Black-Scholes estimator prices the average option at $47.81.[29]

---

[28] For more on the valuation of employee stock options, see, for example, J. Hull and A. White, "How to Value Employee Stock Options," *Financial Analysts Journal* 60, no. 1 (January/February 2004): 114–119.
[29] Using Black-Scholes to determine the value of a single option on an average strike price will undervalue a portfolio of options with a spread of strike prices. Unless you know the spread of strike prices, you cannot measure the bias.

EXHIBIT 16.5 **Square Employee Options, December 2018**

$ million

| Capital structure | Aggregate intrinsic value[1] | Using Black-Scholes[2] | | Exercise value approach |
		Value of outstanding options	Value of exercisable options	
Enterprise value	26,300.0	26,300.0	26,300.0	26,300.0
Convertible debt at 0.375% due 2022	(515.7)	(515.7)	(515.7)	(515.7)
Convertible debt at 0.5% due 2023	(901.5)	(901.5)	(901.5)	(901.5)
Convertible note hedge	230.9	230.9	230.9	230.9
→ Employee options: value	(1,543.8)	(1,584.9)	(1,507.9)	–
→ Employee options: exercise proceeds	–	–	–	315.6
Equity value	23,570.0	23,528.9	23,605.8	25,429.4
Number of shares, millions				
Number of nondiluted shares	419.7	419.7	419.7	419.7
→ New shares issued	–	–	–	33.2
Number of diluted shares	419.7	419.7	419.7	452.8
Value per share, $	56.1	56.0	56.2	56.1

[1] Value of options reported in 2018 10-K in note 15, "Shareholder's Equity," under "Aggregate Intrinsic Value."

[2] Value estimated using Black-Scholes option-pricing model and company-disclosed inputs.

With 33.2 million options outstanding, the aggregate value of options is valued at $1.58 billion. To estimate share price, deduct the aggregate value from enterprise value, and divide by the number of undiluted shares. Since some outstanding options will go unclaimed, repeat the process for just the options that can be exercised. The actual value will fall somewhere between the two.

Under the exercise value approach, employee options are assumed to be exercised immediately. According to Square's 2018 10-K, 33,152,881 shares can be exercised at an average strike price of $9.52, for total proceeds of $315.6 million. Exercise of employee options generates cash for the company and increases shares outstanding from 419.7 million to 452.8 million. Dividing equity value by diluted shares leads to a value of $56.1, slightly lower than the value under the Black-Scholes method.

Noncontrolling Interests by Other Companies

When a company controls a subsidiary but does not fully own it, the subsidiary's financial statements must be fully consolidated in the group accounts. The subsidiary's assets and liabilities will be indistinguishable from the parent company's accounts, but the portion of the subsidiary's equity not owned by the parent company will be separated from other equity accounts as noncontrolling interest.[30] Since the full value of the subsidiary will be incorporated

[30] For example, Berkshire Hathaway reported $3.8 billion in noncontrolling interests in 2018. This amount can be found on the company's balance sheet under shareholders' equity.

into the value of operations, a valuation adjustment must be made for the portion of the subsidiary not owned by the parent company being valued.

Because noncontrolling interests by other companies are to a certain extent the mirror image of nonconsolidated assets, the recommended valuation approach for noncontrolling interests is similar to that of nonconsolidated assets, described earlier in this chapter. In the case of a minority carve-out (in which the consolidated but not fully owned subsidiary is publicly traded), deduct the proportional market value owned by outsiders from enterprise value to determine equity value. Alternatively, you can perform a separate valuation using a DCF approach, multiples, or a tracking portfolio, depending on the amount of information available. Remember, however, that a noncontrolling interest is a claim on a subsidiary, not the entire company. Thus, any valuation should be directly related to the subsidiary and not to the company as a whole.

ESTIMATING VALUE PER SHARE

The final step in a valuation is to calculate the value per share. Assuming that you have used an option-based valuation approach for convertible bonds and employee options, divide the total equity value by the number of *undiluted* shares outstanding. Use the undiluted (rather than diluted) number of shares because the full values of convertible debt and stock options have already been deducted from the enterprise value as nonequity claims. Also, use the most recent number of undiluted shares outstanding. Do not use the weighted average of shares outstanding; it is reported in the financial statements to determine average earnings per share.

The number of shares outstanding is the gross number of shares issued, less the number of shares held in treasury. Most U.S. and European companies report the number of shares issued and those held in treasury under shareholders' equity. However, some companies report treasury shares as an investment asset, which is incorrect from an economic perspective. Treat them instead as a reduction in the number of shares outstanding.

If you used the conversion and exercise value approach to account for employee options and convertible debt and stock options, divide by the diluted number of shares.

With intrinsic value per share in hand, you have completed the mechanics of your valuation. But the job is not done. The next two chapters discuss how to stress-test your valuation using integrated scenarios and trading multiples.

17

Analyzing the Results

Now that the valuation model is complete, we are ready to put it to work. Start by testing its validity. Even a carefully planned model can have mechanical errors or flaws in economic logic. To help you avoid such troubles, this chapter presents a set of systematic checks and other tricks of the trade that test the model's sturdiness. During this verification, you should also ensure that key ratios like return on invested capital are consistent with the economics of the industry.

Once you are comfortable that the model works, learn the ins and outs of your valuation by changing each forecast input one at a time. Examine how each part of your model changes, and determine which inputs have the largest effect on the company's valuation and which have little or no impact. Since forecast inputs are likely to change in concert, build a sensitivity analysis that tests multiple changes at a time. Use this analysis to set priorities for strategic actions.

Next, use scenario analysis to deepen the understanding that your valuation provides. Start by determining the key uncertainties that affect the company's future and use these to construct multiple forecasts. Uncertainty can take the form of a simple question (will a product launch be successful?) or a complex one (which technology will dominate the market?). Construct a comprehensive forecast consistent with each scenario, and weight the resulting equity valuations by their probability of occurring. Scenario analysis will not only guide your valuation range but also inform your thinking about strategic actions and resource allocation under alternative situations.

VALIDATING THE MODEL

Once you have a workable valuation model, perform several checks to test the logic of your results, minimize the possibility of errors, and ensure that you understand the forces driving the valuation. Start by making sure that the model is technically robust—for example, by checking that the balance sheet balances in each forecast year. Second, test whether results are consistent with industry economics. For instance, do key value drivers, such as return on invested capital (ROIC), change in a way that is consistent with the intensity of competition? Next, compare the model's output with the current share price and trading multiples. Can differences be explained by economics, or is an error possible? We address each of these tasks next.

Is the Model Technically Robust?

Ensure that all checks and balances in your model are in place. Your model should reflect the following fundamental equilibrium relationships:

- In the unadjusted financial statements, the balance sheet should balance every year, both historically and in forecast years. Check that net income flows correctly through shareholders' equity.
- In the rearranged financial statements, check that the sum of invested capital plus nonoperating assets equals the cumulative sources of financing. Is net operating profit after taxes (NOPAT) identical when calculated top down from sales and bottom up from net income? Does net income correctly link to retained earnings, dividends, and share issues or repurchases in changes to equity?
- Does the change in excess cash and debt line up with the cash flow statement?

A good model will automatically compute each check as part of the model. A technical change to the model that breaks a check can then be clearly noted. To stress-test the model, change a few key inputs in an extreme manner. For instance, if gross margin is increased to 99 percent or lowered to 1 percent, does the balance sheet still balance?

As a final consistency check, adjust the dividend payout ratio. Since payout will change funding requirements, the company's capital structure will change. Because NOPAT, invested capital, and free cash flow are independent of capital structure, these values should not change with variations in the payout ratio. If they do, the model has a mechanical flaw.

Is the Model Economically Consistent?

The next step is to check that your results reflect appropriate value driver economics. If the projected returns on invested capital are above the weighted average cost of capital (WACC), the value of operations should be above the book value of invested capital. Moreover, if revenue growth is high, the value of operations should be considerably above book value. If not, a computational error has probably occurred. Compare your valuation results with a back-of-the-envelope value estimate based on the key value driver formula, using long-term average revenue growth and return on invested capital as key inputs.

Make sure that patterns of key financial and operating ratios are consistent with economic logic:

- *Are the patterns intended?* For example, does invested-capital turnover increase over time for sound economic reasons (economies of scale) or simply because you modeled future capital expenditures as a fixed percentage of revenues? Are future cash tax rates changing dramatically because you forecast deferred-tax assets as a percentage of revenues or operating profit?

- *Are the patterns reasonable?* Avoid large step changes in key assumptions from one year to the next, because these will distort key ratios and could lead to false interpretations. For example, a large single-year improvement in capital efficiency could make capital expenditures in that year negative (the sale of fixed equipment for cash at book value is unlikely), leading to an unrealistically high cash flow.

- *Are the patterns consistent with industry dynamics?* In certain cases, reasonable changes in key inputs can lead to unintended consequences. Exhibit 17.1 presents price and cost data for a hypothetical company in a competitive industry. To keep pace with inflation, you decide to forecast the company's prices to increase by 3 percent per year. Because of cost efficiencies, operating costs are expected to drop by 2 percent per year. In isolation, each rate appears innocuous. Computing ROIC reveals a significant trend. Between year 1 and year 10, ROIC grows from 9.3 to 39.2 percent—unlikely in a competitive industry. Since cost advantages are difficult to protect, competitors are likely to mimic production and lower prices to capture share. A good model will highlight this economic inconsistency.

EXHIBIT 17.1 **ROIC Impact of Small Changes: Sample Price and Cost Trends**

$

	Year 1	Year 2	Year 3	Year 4	Year 5	...	Year 10	Growth, %
Price	50.0	51.5	53.0	54.6	56.3	...	65.2	3.0
Number of units	100.0	103.0	106.1	109.3	112.6	...	130.5	
Revenue	5,000.0	5,304.5	5,627.5	5,970.3	6,333.9	...	8,512.2	
Cost per unit	43.0	42.1	41.3	40.5	39.7	...	35.9	−2.0
Number of units	100.0	103.0	106.1	109.3	112.6	...	130.5	
Cost	4,300.0	4,340.4	4,381.2	4,422.4	4,464.0	...	4,677.8	
Operating profit	700.0	964.1	1,246.3	1,547.9	1,869.9	...	3,834.4	
Invested capital	7,500.0	7,725.0	7,956.8	8,195.5	8,441.3	...	9,785.8	
Pretax ROIC, %	9.3	12.5	15.7	18.9	22.2	...	39.2	

- *Is the company in a steady state by the end of the explicit forecasting period?*
  Following the explicit forecasting period, when you apply a continuing-value formula, the company's margins, returns on invested capital, and growth should be stable. If this is not the case, extend the explicit forecast period until a steady state is reached.

Are the Results Plausible?

Once you are confident that the model is technically sound and economically consistent, test whether the model's valuation results are plausible. If the company is publicly listed, compare your results with the market value. If your estimate is far from the market value, do not jump to the conclusion that the market price is wrong. If a difference exists, search for the cause. For instance, perhaps not all relevant information has been incorporated in the share price—say, due to a small free float or paucity of trading in the stock.

Also perform a sound multiples analysis. Calculate the implied forward-looking valuation multiples of the operating value over, for example, earnings before interest, taxes, and amortization (EBITA). Compare these with equivalently defined multiples of traded peer-group companies. Chapter 18 describes how to do a proper multiples analysis. Make sure you can explain any significant differences with peer-group companies in terms of the companies' value drivers and underlying business characteristics or strategies.

SENSITIVITY ANALYSIS

With a robust model in hand, test how the company's value responds to changes in key inputs. Senior management can use sensitivity analysis to prioritize the actions most likely to affect value materially. From the investor's perspective, sensitivity analysis can focus on which inputs to investigate further and monitor more closely. Sensitivity analysis also helps bound the valuation range when there is uncertainty about the inputs.

Assessing the Impact of Individual Drivers

Start by testing each input one at a time to see which has the largest impact on the company's valuation. Exhibit 17.2 presents a sample sensitivity analysis. Among the alternatives presented, a permanent one-percentage-point reduction in selling expenses has the greatest effect on the company's valuation.[1]

---

[1] Some analysts test the impact of both positive and negative changes to each driver and then plot the results from largest to smallest variation. Given its shape, the resulting chart is commonly known as a tornado chart.

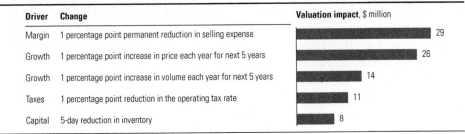

EXHIBIT 17.2 **Sample Sensitivity Analysis**

Driver	Change	Valuation impact, $ million
Margin	1 percentage point permanent reduction in selling expense	29
Growth	1 percentage point increase in price each year for next 5 years	26
Growth	1 percentage point increase in volume each year for next 5 years	14
Taxes	1 percentage point reduction in the operating tax rate	11
Capital	5-day reduction in inventory	8

The analysis will also show which drivers have a minimal impact on value. Too often, we find our clients focusing on actions that are easy to measure but fail to increase value by very much.

Although an input-by-input sensitivity analysis will increase your knowledge about which inputs drive the valuation, its use is limited. First, inputs rarely change in isolation. For instance, an increase in selling expenses should, if managed well, increase revenue growth. Second, when two inputs are changed simultaneously, interactions can cause the combined effect to differ from the sum of the individual effects. Therefore, you cannot compare a one-percentage-point increase in selling expenses with a one-percentage-point increase in growth. If there are interactions in the movements of inputs, the one-by-one analysis would miss them. To capture possible interactions between inputs, analyze trade-offs.

Analyzing Trade-Offs

Strategic choices typically involve trade-offs between inputs into your valuation model. For instance, raising prices leads to fewer purchases, lowering inventory results in more missed sales, and entering new markets often affects both growth and margin. Exhibit 17.3 presents an analysis that measures the impact on a valuation when two inputs are changed simultaneously. Based on

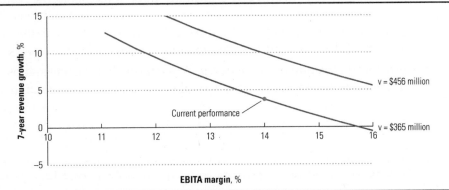

EXHIBIT 17.3 **Valuation Isocurves by Growth and Margin**

an EBITA margin of 14 percent and revenue growth of 3 percent (among other forecasts), the company is currently valued at $365 million. The curve drawn through this point represents all the possible combinations of EBITA margin and revenue growth that lead to the same valuation. (Economists call this an isocurve.) To increase the valuation by 25 percent, from $365 million to $456 million, the organization needs to move northeast to the next isocurve. Using this information, management can set performance targets that are consistent with the company's valuation aspirations and competitive environment.

When performing sensitivity analysis, do not limit yourself to changes in financial variables. Check how changes in sector-specific operational value drivers affect the final valuation. This is where the model's real power lies. For example, if you increase customer churn rates for a telecommunications company, does company value decrease? Can you explain with back-of-the-envelope estimates why the change is so large or small?

CREATING SCENARIOS

Valuation requires a forecast, but the future can take many paths. A government might pass legislation affecting the entire industry. A new discovery could revolutionize a competitor's product portfolio. Since the future is never knowable, consider making financial projections under multiple scenarios.[2] The scenarios should reflect different assumptions regarding future macroeconomic, industry, or business developments, as well as the corresponding strategic responses by industry players. Collectively, the scenarios should capture the future states of the world that would have the most impact on value creation over time and a reasonable chance of occurrence. Assess how likely it is that the key assumptions underlying each scenario will change and assign to each scenario a probability of occurrence.

When analyzing the scenarios, critically review your assumptions concerning the following variables:

- *Broad economic conditions.* How critical are these forecasts to the results? Some industries are more dependent on basic economic conditions than others are. Home building, for example, is highly correlated with the overall health of the economy. Branded food processing, in contrast, is less so.

- *Competitive structure of the industry.* A scenario that assumes substantial increases in market share is less likely in a highly competitive and

---

[2] Overconfidence is a well-known behavioral bias. Embracing uncertainty through the use of scenario analysis helps mitigate overconfidence. For more on overconfidence and valuation, see J. Lambert, V. Bessiere, and G. N'Goala, "Does Expertise Influence the Impact of Overconfidence on Judgment, Valuation and Investment Decision?" *Journal of Economic Psychology* 33, no. 6 (December 2012): 1115–1128.

concentrated market than in an industry with fragmented and inefficient competition.

- *Operating capabilities of the company.* Focus on capabilities that are necessary to achieve the business results predicted in the scenario. Can the
  company develop its products on time and manufacture them within
  the expected range of costs?
- *Financing capabilities of the company.* Financing capabilities are often implicit in the valuation. If debt or excess marketable securities are excessive relative to the company's targets, how will the company resolve
  the imbalance? Should the company raise equity if too much debt is
  projected? Should the company be willing to raise equity at its current
  market price?

Complete the alternative scenarios suggested by the preceding analyses.
The process of examining initial results may well uncover unanticipated questions that are best resolved by creating additional scenarios. In this way, the
valuation process is inherently circular. Performing a valuation often provides
insights that lead to additional scenarios and analyses.

Exhibits 17.4 and 17.5 provide a simplified example of a scenario approach to
discounted-cash-flow (DCF) valuation. The company being valued faces great
uncertainty because of a new-product launch for which it has spent considerable time and money on research and development (think of a major launch
such as when Tesla introduced its economically priced Model 3 in 2019). If the
new product is a top seller, revenue growth will more than double over the
next few years. Returns on invested capital will peak at above 20 percent and
remain above 12 percent in perpetuity. If the product launch fails, however,
growth will continue to erode as the company's current products become obsolete. Lower average selling prices will cause operating margins to fall. The
company's returns on invested capital will decline to levels below the cost of
capital, and the company will struggle to earn its cost of capital in the long
term. Exhibit 17.4 presents forecasts on growth, operating margin, and capital
efficiency that are consistent with each of these two scenarios.

Next, build a separate free cash flow model for each set of forecasts. Although not presented here, the resulting cash flow models are based on the
DCF methodology outlined in Chapter 10. Exhibit 17.5 presents the valuation
results. In the case of a successful product launch, the DCF value of operations
equals $5,044 million. The nonoperating assets consist primarily of noncon-
solidated subsidiaries, and given their own reliance on the product launch,
they are valued at the implied NOPAT multiple for the parent company, $672
million. A comprehensive scenario will examine all items, including nonoperating items, to make sure they are consistent with the scenario's underlying
premise. Next, deduct the face value of the debt outstanding at $2,800 million

EXHIBIT 17.4 **Key Value Drivers by Scenario**

%

				Financial forecasts					
	2019A	2020	2021	2022	2023	2024	2025	Continuing value	Scenario assessment
Scenario 1: New product is a top seller									
Revenue growth	5.0	12.0	15.0	14.0	12.0	10.0	5.0	3.5	New-product introduction leads to spike in revenue growth.
After-tax operating margin	7.5	9.0	11.0	14.0	14.0	12.0	10.0	8.0	Margins improve to best in class as consumers pay a price premium for product.
× Capital turnover, times	1.5	1.4	1.3	1.4	1.5	1.6	1.6	1.6	Capital turnover drops slightly during product launch as company builds inventory to meet expected demand.
Return on invested capital	11.3	12.6	14.3	19.6	21.0	19.2	16.0	12.8	
Scenario 2: Product launch fails									
Revenue growth	5.0	3.0	(1.0)	(1.0)	1.5	1.5	1.5	1.5	Revenue growth drops as competitors steal share.
After-tax operating margin	7.5	7.0	6.5	6.0	5.5	5.5	6.5	6.5	Lower prices put pressure on margins; cost reductions cannot keep pace.
× Capital turnover, times	1.5	1.4	1.4	1.4	1.3	1.3	1.3	1.3	Capital efficiency falls as price pressure reduces revenue; inventory reductions mitigate fall.
Return on invested capital	11.3	9.8	9.1	8.4	7.2	7.2	8.5	8.5	

EXHIBIT 17.5 **Example of a Scenario Approach to DCF Valuation**

$ million

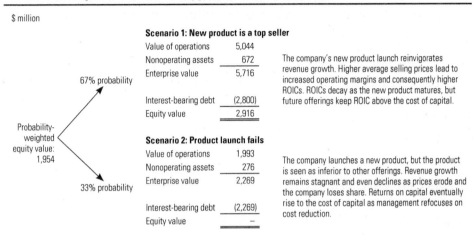

Scenario 1: New product is a top seller

Value of operations	5,044
Nonoperating assets	672
Enterprise value	5,716
Interest-bearing debt	(2,800)
Equity value	2,916

67% probability

The company's new product launch reinvigorates revenue growth. Higher average selling prices lead to increased operating margins and consequently higher ROICs. ROICs decay as the new product matures, but future offerings keep ROIC above the cost of capital.

Probability-weighted equity value: 1,954

Scenario 2: Product launch fails

Value of operations	1,993
Nonoperating assets	276
Enterprise value	2,269
Interest-bearing debt	(2,269)
Equity value	–

33% probability

The company launches a new product, but the product is seen as inferior to other offerings. Revenue growth remains stagnant and even declines as prices erode and the company loses share. Returns on capital eventually rise to the cost of capital as management refocuses on cost reduction.

(assuming interest rates have not changed, so the market value of debt equals the face value). The resulting equity value is $2,916 million.

If the product launch fails, the DCF value of operations is only $1,993 million. In this scenario, the value of the subsidiaries is much lower ($276 million), as their business outlook has deteriorated due to the failure of the new product. The value of the debt is no longer $2,800 million in this scenario. Instead, the debt holders would end up with $2,269 million by seizing control of the enterprise. In scenario 2, the common equity would have no value.

Given a two-thirds probability of success for the product, the probability-weighted equity value across both scenarios amounts to $1,954 million. Since estimates of scenario probabilities are likely to be rough at best, determine the range of probabilities that point to a particular strategic action. For instance, if this company were an acquisition target available for $1.5 billion, any probability of a successful launch above 50 percent would lead to value creation. Whether the probability is 67 percent or 72 percent does not affect the decision outcome.

When using the scenario approach, make sure to generate a complete valuation buildup from value of operations to equity value. Do not shortcut the process by deducting the face value of debt from the scenario-weighted value of operations. Doing this would seriously underestimate the equity value, because the value of debt is different in each scenario. In this case, the equity value would be undervalued by $175 million ($2,800 million face value minus $2,625 million probability-weighted value of debt).[3] A similar argument holds for nonoperating assets.

[3] Although this approach is typically recommended, deducting the market value of debt from enterprise value will lead to an inconsistent estimate of equity value if your estimate of default does not match market expectations. For more on how to correctly incorporate debt into the valuation, see Chapter 16.

Creating scenarios also helps you understand the company's key priorities. In our example, reducing costs or cutting capital expenditures in the downside scenario will not meaningfully affect value. Any improvements in the downside scenario whose value is less than $531 million ($2,800 million in face value less $2,269 million in market value) will accrue primarily to the debt holders. In contrast, increasing the odds of a successful launch has a much greater impact on shareholder value. Increasing the success probability from two-thirds to three-fourths would boost shareholder value by more than 10 percent.

THE ART OF VALUATION

Valuation can be highly sensitive to small changes in assumptions about the future. Take a look at the sensitivity of a typical company with a forward-looking price-to-earnings ratio of 15 to 16. Increasing the cost of capital for this company by half a percentage point will decrease the value by approximately 10 percent. Changing the growth rate for the next 15 years by one percentage point annually will change the value by about 6 percent. For high-growth companies, the sensitivity is even greater. Considering this, it shouldn't be surprising that the market value of a company fluctuates over time. Historical volatilities for a typical stock over the past several years have been around 25 percent per annum. Taking this as an estimate for future volatility, the market value of a typical company could well fluctuate around its expected value by 15 percent over the next month.[4]

We typically aim for a valuation range of plus or minus 15 percent, which is similar to the range used by many investment bankers. Even the best professionals cannot generate exact estimates. In other words, keep your aspirations for precision in check.

---

[4] Based on a 95 percent confidence interval for the end-of-month price of a stock with an expected return of 9 percent per year.

18

Using Multiples

While discounted cash flow (DCF) is the most accurate and flexible method for valuing companies, using a relative valuation approach, such as juxtaposing the earnings multiples of comparable companies, can provide insights and help you summarize and test your valuation. In practice, however, multiples are often used in a superficial way that leads to erroneous conclusions. This chapter explains how to use multiples correctly. Most of the focus will be on earnings multiples, the most commonly used variety. At the end, we'll also touch on some other multiples.

The basic idea behind using multiples for valuation is that similar assets should sell for similar prices, whether they are houses or shares of stock. In the case of a share of stock, the typical benchmark is some measure of earnings, most popularly the price-to-earnings (P/E) multiple, which is simply the equity value of the company divided by its net income. Multiples can be used to value nontraded companies or divisions of traded companies and to see how a listed company is valued relative to peers. Companies in the same industry and with similar performance should trade at the same multiple.

Valuing a company by using multiples may seem straightforward, but arriving at useful insights requires careful analysis. Exhibit 18.1 illustrates what happens if you don't go deep enough in your multiples analysis. The managers of Company A, a producer of packaged foods, looked only at P/Es and were concerned that their company was trading at a P/E of 7.3 times while most of their peers were trading at a P/E of about 14, a discount of 50 percent. The management team believed the market didn't understand Company A's strategy or performance. In fact, management didn't understand the math of multiples. If the managers had looked at the more instructive multiple shown in the exhibit—net enterprise value to earnings before interest, taxes, and amortization (EV/EBITA)—they would have seen that the company was

EXHIBIT 18.1 **Multiples for Packaged Foods Companies**

$ billion

Company	Market value of equity	Enterprise value (equity + debt)	Net income (1 year forward)	EBITA (1 year forward)	Multiples Price/ earnings	Multiples Enterprise value/EBITA
A	2,783	9,940	381	929	7.3	10.7
B	13,186	16,279	856	1,428	15.4	11.4
C	8,973	11,217	665	1,089	13.5	10.3
D	14,851	22,501	1,053	2,009	14.1	11.2
Mean					12.6	10.9
Median					13.8	11.0
Mean (excluding A)					14.3	11.0
Median (excluding A)					14.1	11.2

trading right in line with its peers. The reason for the difference was that their company had much more debt relative to equity than the other companies. We estimated that if the company had had the same relative debt as its peers, its P/E also would have been 14. Except for very-high-growth companies, a company with higher debt relative to peers will have a lower P/E because more debt translates to higher risk for shareholders and a higher cost of equity. Therefore, each dollar of earnings (and cash flow to shareholders) will be worth less to an investor.[1]

To use earnings multiples properly, you should dig into the accounting statements to make sure you are comparing companies on an apples-to-apples basis. You also must choose the right companies to compare. Keep in mind these five principles for correctly using earnings multiples:

1. *Value multibusiness companies as a sum of their parts.* Even companies that appear to be in a single industry will often compete in subindustries or product areas with widely varying return on invested capital (ROIC) and growth, leading to substantial variations in multiples.

2. *Use forward estimates of earnings.* Multiples using forward earnings estimates typically have much lower variation across peers, leading to a narrower range of uncertainty of value. They also embed future expectations better than multiples based on historical data.

3. *Use the right multiple, usually net enterprise value to EBITA or net enterprise value to NOPAT.* Although the P/E is widely used, it is distorted by capital structure and nonoperating gains and losses. (In this book, when we

[1] The P/E multiple is a function of return on capital, cost of capital, and growth. For very-high-growth companies, whose enterprise multiples are greater than the multiple for debt, the multiple will actually increase with leverage. See also Appendix D.

refer to the enterprise value multiple, including abbreviations such as EV/EBITA, we use "enterprise value" as shorthand for net enterprise value, equal to the value of operations.)

4. *Adjust the multiple for nonoperating items.* Nonoperating items embedded in reported EBITA, as well as balance sheet items like excess cash and pension items, can lead to large distortions of multiples.

5. *Use the right peer group, not a broad industry average.* A good peer group consists of companies that not only operate in the same industry but also have similar prospects for ROIC and growth.

VALUE MULTIBUSINESS COMPANIES AS A SUM OF THEIR PARTS

Most large companies, even if they operate in a single industry, have business units that are in subindustries with different competitive dynamics and therefore differ widely in ROIC and growth. For example, many analysts would classify Johnson & Johnson as a health-care company, but its three major units (pharmaceuticals, medical devices, and consumer health products) have widely varying economic characteristics in terms of growth and return on capital. Each of the units will therefore have different valuation multiples. For such multibusiness companies, a valuation using multiples requires a sum-of-parts approach, which values each business unit with a multiple appropriate to its peers and performance.

Even companies in more narrowly defined sectors often have units with different economics. For example, oil and gas services companies provide oil and gas companies with equipment and services that might include bottom hole assemblies, drill pipes, pressure-control services, intervention services, pressure pumping, fluid handling, subsea construction, and even temporary housing for workers. Some of these product areas, including bottom hole assemblies and drill pipes, tend to earn much higher returns on capital than pressure-control services and intervention services. Ideally, you would value units by using as fine-grained an approach as possible, comparing them with companies that have similar units and economics.

For an example of a good sum-of-parts valuation, see Exhibit 18.2. For each unit of this disguised company, we apply a different multiple to its earnings based on different peers. Then we sum the values of the units to estimate net enterprise value. To estimate equity value, we add nonoperating assets and subtract debt and debt equivalents.

Note that the business unit multiples range from the midteens to below ten. Without the sum-of-parts approach, it would be impossible to value this company accurately. We also used ranges for the value of each unit, reflecting the imprecision of valuing any business based on the valuation of peers at a single point in time.

EXHIBIT 18.2 **Sample Sum-of-Parts Valuation**

	NOPAT, 2014, $ million	EV/NOPAT, times		Value, $ million	
		High	Low	High	Low
Business Unit 1	410	16.0	14.5	6,568	5,952
Business Unit 2	299	13.9	12.5	4,165	3,749
Business Unit 3	504	13.1	12.5	6,597	6,306
Business Unit 4	587	9.7	9.4	5,681	5,533
Business Unit 5	596	9.0	8.0	5,365	4,769
Business Unit 6	116	8.0	7.0	931	814
Corporate	(542)	8.0	9.1	(4,339)	(4,917)
Net Enterprise Value	1,971	12.7	11.3	24,968	22,207

	After-tax net income, 2013, $ million	Book value, $ million	Earnings multiple, 2013 times	Market value/ book value, times	Value, $ million	
					High	Low
Joint ventures	157	675	12.0	2.5	1,879	1,688
Other investments		1,525			1,525	1,525
Cash and marketable securities		2,879			2,879	2,879
Gross enterprise value					31,251	28,298
Debt		(10,776)			(10,776)	(10,776)
Unfunded retirement liabilities		(2,907)			(2,907)	(2,907)
Noncontrolling interest	(45)	(296)	12.0	2.5	(540)	(739)
Other		(1,940)			(1,940)	(1,940)
Equity value					15,088	11,937
Shares outstanding, millions					500	500
Equity value per share					$30.18	$23.87

USE FORWARD EARNINGS ESTIMATES

When you are building multiples, the denominator should be a forecast of profits, preferably normalized for unusual items, rather than historical profits. Unlike backward-looking multiples, forward-looking multiples are consistent with the principles of valuation—in particular, that a company's value equals the present value of future cash flows, not sunk costs. When companies have recently acquired or divested significant parts of their operations, historical profits are even less meaningful. Normalized earnings estimates better reflect long-term cash flows by avoiding one-time items. For example, Warren Buffett and other disciples of value-investing guru Benjamin Graham don't use reported earnings. Rather, they rely on a sustainable level of earnings that they refer to as "earnings power."[2]

Forward-looking multiples generally also have lower variation across peer companies. A particularly striking example is the stock market valuation of the 20 largest pharmaceutical companies worldwide in 2019. The

[2] B. C. N. Greenwald, J. Kahn, P. D. Sonkin, and M. van Biema, *Value Investing: From Graham to Buffett and Beyond* (Hoboken, NJ: John Wiley & Sons, 2001).

EXHIBIT 18.3 **Pharmaceuticals: Backward- and Forward-Looking Multiples, September 2019**

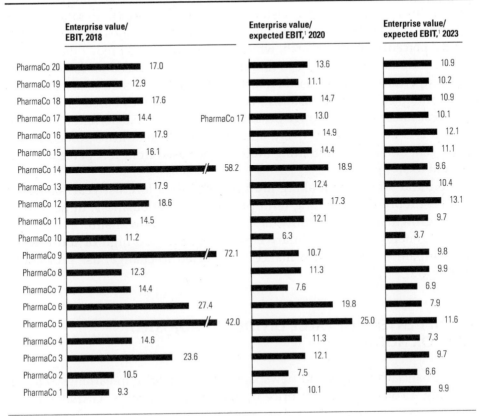

	Enterprise value/ EBIT, 2018	Enterprise value/ expected EBIT,[1] 2020	Enterprise value/ expected EBIT,[1] 2023
PharmaCo 20	17.0	13.6	10.9
PharmaCo 19	12.9	11.1	10.2
PharmaCo 18	17.6	14.7	10.9
PharmaCo 17	14.4	13.0	10.1
PharmaCo 16	17.9	14.9	12.1
PharmaCo 15	16.1	14.4	11.1
PharmaCo 14	58.2	18.9	9.6
PharmaCo 13	17.9	12.4	10.4
PharmaCo 12	18.6	17.3	13.1
PharmaCo 11	14.5	12.1	9.7
PharmaCo 10	11.2	6.3	3.7
PharmaCo 9	72.1	10.7	9.8
PharmaCo 8	12.3	11.3	9.9
PharmaCo 7	14.4	7.6	6.9
PharmaCo 6	27.4	19.8	7.9
PharmaCo 5	42.0	25.0	11.6
PharmaCo 4	14.6	11.3	7.3
PharmaCo 3	23.6	12.1	9.7
PharmaCo 2	10.5	7.5	6.6
PharmaCo 1	9.3	10.1	9.9

[1] Consensus analyst forecast.

backward-looking ratio of enterprise value of last year's EBIT ranged from about 10 to more than 70 times (see Exhibit 18.3). The ratio of enterprise value to the next year's expected EBIT, based on equity analyst estimates, also showed significant variation, ranging from about 6 to 25 times. But when we extended the forecast window to four years, the variation across companies was significantly lower, with multiples for all but one company between about 7 and 12 times.

The convergence of multiples four years out in the pharmaceuticals industry is extreme. This is most likely due to the market's ability to project near-term earnings well, because drug introductions and patent expirations are well known. By contrast, it is difficult to differentiate long-term success across companies because it depends on an individual company's ability to discover or develop new drugs. No one has figured out a good way to do that.

Empirical evidence shows that forward-looking multiples are indeed more accurate predictors of value than historical multiples are. One empirical study examined the characteristics and performance of historical multiples versus forward industry multiples for a large sample of companies trading on U.S. exchanges.[3] When multiples for individual companies were compared with their industry multiples, their historical earnings-to-price (E/P) ratios had 1.6 times the standard deviation of one-year-forward E/P ratios (6.0 percent versus 3.7 percent). Other research, which used multiples to predict the prices of 142 initial public offerings, also found that multiples based on forecast earnings outperformed those based on historical earnings.[4] As the analysis moved from multiples based on historical earnings to multiples based on one- and two-year forecasts, the average pricing error fell from 55.0 percent to 43.7 percent to 28.5 percent, respectively, and the percentage of firms valued within 15 percent of their actual trading multiple increased from 15.4 percent to 18.9 percent to 36.4 percent.

To build a forward-looking multiple, choose a forecast year for EBITA that best represents the long-term prospects of the business. In periods of stable growth and profitability, next year's estimate will suffice. For companies generating extraordinary earnings (either too high or too low) or for companies whose performance is expected to change, use projections further out.

USE NET ENTERPRISE VALUE DIVIDED BY ADJUSTED EBITA OR NOPAT

Most financial websites and newspapers quote a price-to-earnings ratio by dividing a company's share price by the prior 12 months' GAAP-reported earnings per share. Yet these days, sophisticated investors and bankers use what we call forward-looking multiples of net enterprise value to EBITA (or NOPAT). They find that these multiples provide a more apples-to-apples comparison of company values.

The reasons for using forward earnings are the same as the ones discussed in the previous section. Using net enterprise value to EBITA (or NOPAT) rather than a P/E eliminates the distorting effect of different capital structures, nonoperating assets, and nonoperating income statement items, such as the nonoperating portion of pension expense. Any item that isn't a helpful indicator of a company's future cash-generating ability should be excluded from your calculation of the multiple. For example, one-time gains or losses and nonoperating expenses, such as the amortization of intangibles, have no direct relevance to future cash flows; including them in the multiple would distort comparisons with other companies.

---

[3] J. Liu, D. Nissim, and J. Thomas, "Equity Valuation Using Multiples," *Journal of Accounting Research* 40 (2002): 135–172.

[4] M. Kim and J. R. Ritter, "Valuing IPOs," *Journal of Financial Economics* 53, no. 3 (1999): 409–437.

Sometimes analysts use an alternative multiple: enterprise value to earnings before interest, taxes, depreciation, and amortization (EBITDA). Later in this section, we'll explain the logic of using EBITA or NOPAT instead of EBITDA.

Why Not Price to Earnings?

This book has focused throughout on the drivers of operating performance—ROIC, growth, and free cash flow—because the traditional metrics, such as return on assets (ROA) and return on equity (ROE), mix the effects of operations and capital structure. The same logic holds for multiples. Since the price-to-earnings ratio mixes capital structure and nonoperating items with expectations of operating performance, a comparison of P/Es is a less reliable guide to companies' relative value than a comparison of enterprise value (EV) to EBITA or NOPAT.

To show how capital structure distorts the P/E, Exhibit 18.4 presents financial data for four companies, named A through D. Companies A and B trade at 10 times enterprise value to EBITA, and Companies C and D trade at 25 times enterprise value to EBITA. In each pair, the companies have different P/Es. Companies A and B differ only in how their business is financed, not in their operating performance. The same is true for Companies C and D.

Since Companies A and B trade at typical enterprise value multiples, the P/E drops for the company with higher leverage. This is because the EV-to-EBITA ratio ($1,000 million/$100 million = 10 times) is lower than the ratio of debt value to interest expense ($400 million/$20 million = 20 times).

EXHIBIT 18.4 **P/E Multiple Distorted by Capital Structure**

$ million

	Company A	Company B	Company C	Company D
Income statement				
EBITA	100	100	100	100
Interest expense	–	(20)	–	(25)
Earnings before taxes	100	80	100	75
Taxes	(40)	(32)	(40)	(30)
Net income	60	48	60	45
Market values				
Debt	–	400	–	500
Equity	1,000	600	2,500	2,000
Enterprise value (EV)	1,000	1,000	2,500	2,500
Multiples, times				
EV/EBITA	10.0	10.0	25.0	25.0
Price/earnings	16.7	12.5	41.7	44.4

Since the blend of debt at 20 times and pretax equity must equal the enterprise value at 10 times, the pretax equity multiple must drop below 10 times to offset the greater weight placed on high-multiple debt.[5] The opposite is true when enterprise value to EBITA exceeds the ratio of debt to interest expense (less common, given today's low interest rates). Company D has a higher P/E than Company C because Company D uses more leverage than Company C. In this case, a high pretax P/E (greater than 25 times) must be blended with the debt multiple (20 times) to generate an EV-to-EBITA multiple of 25 times.

Why Not EV to EBIT?

It's clear that shifting to enterprise-value multiples provides better insights and comparisons across peer companies. The next question is what measure of operating profits to use in the denominator—EBIT, EBITDA, EBITA (adjusted), or NOPAT? We recommend EBITA or NOPAT.

The difference between EBIT and EBITA is amortization of intangible assets. Most often, the bulk of amortization is related to acquired intangible assets, such as customer lists or brand names. Chapter 11 explained why we exclude amortization of acquired intangibles from the calculation of ROIC and free cash flow. It is noncash, and, unlike depreciation of physical assets, the replacement of these intangible assets is already incorporated in EBITA through line items such as marketing and selling expenses. So using EBITA is preferred, both from a logical perspective and because it leads to more comparable multiples across peers.

To illustrate the distortion caused by amortization of acquired intangible assets, we compare two companies with the same size and underlying operating profitability. The difference is that Company A achieved its current size by acquiring Company B, whereas Company C grew organically. Exhibit 18.5 compares these companies before and after A's acquisition of B.

Concerned that its smaller size might lead to a competitive disadvantage, Company A purchased Company B. Assuming no synergies, the combined financial statements of Companies A and B are identical to Company C's with two exceptions: acquired intangibles and amortization. Acquired intangibles are recognized when a company is purchased for more than its book value. In this case, Company A purchased Company B for $1,000 million, which is $750 million greater than its book value. If these acquired intangibles are separable and identifiable, such as patents, Company A + B must amortize them over the estimated life of the asset. Assuming an asset life of ten years, Company A + B will record $75 million in amortization each year.

---

[5] Appendix D derives the explicit relationship between a company's actual P/E and its unlevered P/E, that is, the P/E as if the company were entirely financed with equity. For companies with large unlevered P/Es (i.e., companies with significant opportunities for future value creation), P/E systematically increases with leverage. Conversely, companies with small unlevered P/Es would exhibit a drop in P/E as leverage rises.

EXHIBIT 18.5 **Enterprise-Value-to-EBIT Multiple Distorted by Acquisition Accounting**

$ million

| | Before acquisition | | | After A acquires B | |
	Company A	Company B	Company C	Company A + B	Company C
EBIT					
Revenues	375	125	500	500	500
Cost of sales	(150)	(50)	(200)	(200)	(200)
Depreciation	(75)	(25)	(100)	(100)	(100)
EBITA	150	50	200	200	200
Amortization	–	–	–	(75)	–
EBIT	150	50	200	125	200
Invested capital					
Organic capital	750	250	1,000	1,000	1,000
Acquired intangibles	–	–	–	750	–
Invested capital	750	250	1,000	1,750	1,000
Enterprise value	1,500	500	2,000	2,000	2,000
Multiples, times					
EV/EBITA	10.0	10.0	10.0	10.0	10.0
EV/EBIT	10.0	10.0	10.0	16.0	10.0

The bottom of Exhibit 18.5 reports enterprise value multiples using EBITA and EBIT, both before and after the acquisition. Since all three companies generated the same level of operating performance, they traded at identical multiples before the acquisition, 10 times EBIT (and EBITA). After the acquisition, the combined Company A + B should continue to trade at a multiple of 10 times EBITA, because its performance is identical to that of Company C. However, amortization expense causes EBIT to drop for the combined company, so its EV-to-EBIT multiple increases to 16 times. This rise in the multiple does not reflect a premium, however (remember, no synergies were created). It is merely an accounting artifact. Companies that acquire other companies must recognize amortization, whereas companies that grow organically have none to recognize. To avoid forming a distorted picture of their relative operating performance, use EV-to-EBITA multiples.

In limited cases, companies will capitalize organic investments in intangible assets. For example, telecommunication service providers capitalize the purchase costs for spectrum licenses and then amortize them over their useful life. In a similar way, development costs for software that is to be sold or licensed to third parties can be capitalized and amortized under IFRS and U.S. GAAP if certain conditions are met. In such cases, the amortization charges are operating costs and should be separated from acquisition amortization. Just like depreciation charges, operating amortization should be included in adjusted EBITA.

EXHIBIT 18.6 **Enterprise-Value-to-EBITDA Multiple Distorted by Capital Investment**

$ million

	Company A	Company B		Company A	Company B
Income statement			**Free cash flow**		
Revenues	1,000	1,000	NOPAT	210	210
Raw materials	(100)	(250)	Depreciation	200	50
Operating costs	(400)	(400)	Gross cash flow	410	260
EBITDA	500	350			
			Investment in working capital	(60)	(60)
Depreciation	(200)	(50)	Capital expenditures	(200)	(50)
EBITA	300	300	Free cash flow	150	150
Operating taxes	(90)	(90)	Enterprise value	3,000	3,000
NOPAT	210	210			
Multiples, times					
EV/EBITA	10.0	10.0			
EV/EBITDA	6.0	8.6			

Choosing between EBITA and EBITDA

A common alternative to the EBITA multiple is the EBITDA multiple. Many practitioners use EBITDA multiples because depreciation is, strictly speaking, a noncash expense, reflecting sunk costs, not future investment. This logic, however, does not apply uniformly. For many industries, depreciation of existing assets is the accounting equivalent of setting aside the future capital expenditure that will be required to replace the assets. Subtracting depreciation from the earnings of such companies therefore better represents future cash flow and consequently the company's valuation.

To see this, consider two companies that differ in only one aspect: in-house versus outsourced production. Company A manufactures its products using its own equipment, whereas Company B outsources manufacturing to a supplier. Exhibit 18.6 provides financial data for each company. Since Company A owns its equipment, it recognizes significant annual depreciation—in this case, $200 million. Company B has less equipment, so its depreciation is only $50 million. However, Company B's supplier will include its own depreciation costs in its price, and Company B will consequently pay more for its raw materials. Because of this difference, Company B generates EBITDA of only $350 million, versus $500 million for Company A. This difference in EBITDA will lead to differing multiples: 6.0 times for Company A versus 8.6 times for Company B. Does this mean Company B trades at a valuation premium? No, when Company A's depreciation is deducted from its earnings, both companies trade at 10.0 times EBITA.

EXHIBIT 18.7 **Company M Peer Multiples Comparison**

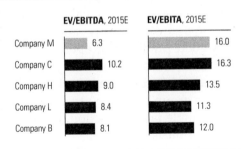

When computing the EV-to-EBITDA multiple in the previous example, we failed to recognize that Company A (the company that owns its equipment) will have to expend cash to replace aging equipment: $200 million for Company A versus $50 million for Company B (see the right side of Exhibit 18.6). Since capital expenditures are recorded in free cash flow and not NOPAT, the EBITDA multiple is distorted.

We came across an interesting example in a processing industry, as shown in Exhibit 18.7. On an EV-to-EBITDA basis, Company M trades at a multiple of 6.3 times, far below its peers' multiples of 8.1 to 10.2 times. However, on an EV-to-EBITA basis, it actually trades at the high end of its peers. In this industry, companies have to replace depreciated assets constantly, so the EBITA multiple provides a better comparison of valuation levels. In Company H's case, its low cash margins also contribute to the larger gap between EBITA and EBITDA.

In some situations, EBITDA scales a company's valuation better than EBITA. These occur when current depreciation is not an accurate predictor of future capital expenditures. For instance, consider two companies, each of which owns a machine that produces identical products. Both machines have the same cash-based operating costs, and each company's products sell for the same price. If one company paid more for its equipment (for whatever reason—perhaps poor negotiation), it will have higher depreciation and, thus, lower EBITA. Valuation, however, is based on future discounted cash flow, not past profits. And since both companies have identical cash flow, they should have identical values.[6] We would therefore expect the two companies to have identical multiples. Yet, because EBITA differs across the two companies, their multiples will differ as well.

---

[6] Since depreciation is tax deductible, a company with higher depreciation will have a smaller tax burden. Lower taxes lead to higher cash flows and a higher valuation. Therefore, even companies with identical EBITDAs will have different EBITDA multiples. The distortion, however, is less pronounced.

NOPAT vs. EBITA

Analysts and investors often use enterprise value to EBITA instead of NOPAT because there is no need to figure out the operating taxes on EBITA. (Reported taxes are not usually a good predictor of operating taxes, because they include nonoperating items. Therefore, most analysts ignore taxes altogether.) We often use EBITA because it's common practice and works well when all the companies in the peer group have the same operating tax rate, as when they all operate within a single tax jurisdiction. However, when tax rates are different, NOPAT is a better measure to use.

U.S. oil and gas pipeline companies provide a classic example. Until the mid-2010s, many pipeline companies were organized as master limited partnerships (MLPs), which eliminated an entire layer of taxation compared with pipeline companies organized as regular corporations, called C corporations in the U.S. tax code. Unlike C corporations, MLPs pay no corporate income taxes; rather, investors pay taxes on their share of the profits. Exhibit 18.8 shows that the stock market clearly reflected these tax differences when valuing companies in these industries. NOPAT multiples across all the companies are in a narrow range of 19 to 25 times. The EBITA multiples, however, show a clear delineation between the regular corporations and the MLPs. While the EBITA multiples for the MLPs remain the same, at 19 to 25 times, the multiples for regular corporations drop to 13 to 14 times. Clearly, the NOPAT multiples are superior in this case.

EXHIBIT 18.8 **Enterprise Value to EBITA vs. Enterprise Value to NOPAT**

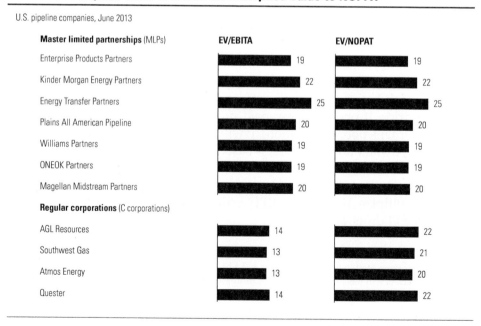

U.S. pipeline companies, June 2013

	EV/EBITA	EV/NOPAT
Master limited partnerships (MLPs)		
Enterprise Products Partners	19	19
Kinder Morgan Energy Partners	22	22
Energy Transfer Partners	25	25
Plains All American Pipeline	20	20
Williams Partners	19	19
ONEOK Partners	19	19
Magellan Midstream Partners	20	20
Regular corporations (C corporations)		
AGL Resources	14	22
Southwest Gas	13	21
Atmos Energy	13	20
Quester	14	22

The stock market recognizes differences in tax rates not only for pipeline companies but across all sectors. The difference between a company's post- and pretax earnings valuation multiple simply follows from the company's tax rate. If the stock market correctly reflects taxation in company valuations, we would expect that for companies with higher tax rates, the difference between their pre- and posttax earnings multiples also would be bigger. This is indeed the pattern that we found when examining the market valuations of the largest U.S. companies between 2013 and 2017 (before the Tax Cuts and Jobs Act of 2017). Exhibit 18.9 shows the average difference in pretax earnings multiples (EV/EBIT) and posttax earnings multiples (P/E) over the five-year period for companies categorized according to their income tax rates. As predicted, the difference between the multiples steadily increases with the tax rate that a company pays. Differences in tax rates clearly matter for market valuation. Thus, when companies face different tax rates, they should not be valued at the same EBITA multiple (or any other pretax earnings multiple).

This is an important consideration for international comparisons, because corporate tax rates vary widely from country to country. For example, as of 2019, the Irish corporate tax rate is one of the lowest, at 12.5 percent, the U.S. tax rate is at 21.0 percent, and the French tax rate is one of the highest, at 34.4 percent. Because of such variations, companies in the same industry with a different geographic mix of operations can have different tax rates, which must be factored into their valuation using multiples. If the tax rates are different across peers, use net enterprise value to NOPAT rather than net enterprise value to EBITA.

EXHIBIT 18.9 **Difference between Pre- and Posttax Earnings Multiples for U.S. Stock Market**

2013–2017, average

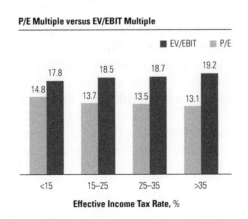

P/E Multiple versus EV/EBIT Multiple

Effective Income Tax Rate, %

Source: S&P CapitaliQ

ADJUST FOR NONOPERATING ITEMS

In a presentation to a group of professional investors, we provided the audience with financial data on two companies. We then asked the audience which company traded at a higher EV multiple. The results were surprising. Upon polling the group, we discovered that there was no common agreement on how to compute the EV multiple. A group of 100 professionals generated nearly a dozen different comparisons. Further investigation revealed that the primary cause of this divergence was inconsistency in defining enterprise value.

Only one approach to building an EV-to-EBITA multiple is theoretically consistent. Enterprise value should include *only* the portion of value attributable to assets and liabilities that generate (adjusted) EBITA. Strictly speaking, it should be referred to as "net" enterprise value, meaning net of nonoperating assets. Including value, such as the value of joint ventures, in the numerator without including its corresponding income or loss in the denominator will systematically distort the multiple upward. Conversely, failing to recognize a component of enterprise value will understate the numerator and bias the multiple downward. This occurs, for example, when the value of noncontrolling interest is not added to the value of common equity.

Oracle offers an example of a biased multiple. At the end of September 2019, Oracle had $38 billion of cash and marketable securities. With total debt, pensions, and debt equivalents of $76 billion, as well as equity of $177 billion, it had a gross enterprise value of $253 billion. Subtracting nonoperating cash gives a net enterprise value of $216 billion. With expected EBITA of $19 billion, its gross enterprise value to EBITA would be 13.3 times, while its net enterprise value to EBITA would be 11.3 times, or 15 percent lower.[7]

A way to think about the difference is to think of Oracle as a portfolio with two components: one is an operating business that sells software and services, and the other is a pile of cash. The operating business is valued at 11.3 times EBITA, while if the cash earned 1.0 percent pretax, it would be valued at 100 times (the inverse of the earnings yield). The company as a whole is valued at the weighted average of the two multiples, 13.3 times. Since the 13.3 times is a weighted average of two very different numbers, it doesn't provide any insight into how to think about Oracle's value.

To see how the math provides additional clarity, Exhibit 18.10 presents three companies—A, B, and C—with identical EV-to-EBITA multiples. Company A holds only core operating assets and is financed by traditional debt and equity. Its combined market value of debt and equity equals $900 million. Dividing $900 million by $100 million in EBITA leads to an EV multiple of 9 times.

---

[7] Even if we adjusted EBITA to include income on the cash (say, 1 percent after taxes), its gross enterprise value multiple would have been roughly the same.

EXHIBIT 18.10 **Enterprise Value Multiples and Complex Ownership**

$ million

	Company A	Company B	Company C
Partial income statement			
EBITA	100	100	100
Interest income	–	4	–
Interest expense	(18)	(18)	(18)
Earnings before taxes	82	86	82
Gross enterprise value			
Value of core operations	900	900	900
Excess cash	–	100	–
Nonconsolidated subsidiaries	–	200	–
Gross enterprise value	900	1,200	900
Debt	300	300	300
Noncontrolling interest	–	–	100
Market value of equity	600	900	500
Gross enterprise value	900	1,200	900
Multiples, times			
Net EV/EBITA	9.0	9.0	9.0
Debt plus equity minus cash/EBITA	9.0	11.0	8.0
Debt plus equity/EBITA	9.0	12.0	8.0

Company B operates a similar business to Company A but also owns $100 million in excess cash and a minority stake in a nonconsolidated subsidiary, valued at $200 million. Since excess cash and nonconsolidated subsidiaries do not contribute to EBITA, do not include them in the numerator of an EV-to-EBITA multiple. To compute a net enterprise value consistent with EBITA, sum the market value of debt and equity ($1,200 million), and subtract the market value of nonoperating assets ($300 million).[8] Divide the resulting net enterprise value ($900 million) by EBITA ($100 million). The result is an EV-to-EBITA multiple of 9, which matches that of Company A. Failing to subtract the market value of nonoperating assets will lead to a multiple that is too high. For instance, if you divide debt plus equity by EBITA for Company B, the resulting multiple is 12 times, three points higher than the correct value.

Similar adjustments are necessary for financial claims other than debt and equity. To calculate enterprise value consistently with EBITA, you must include the market value of all financial claims, not just debt and equity. For Company C, outside investors hold a noncontrolling interest in a consolidated subsidiary. Since the noncontrolling stake's value is supported by EBITA, you

---

[8] Alternatively, we could adjust the denominator rather than the numerator by adding interest income to EBITA. This definition of EV to EBITA is consistent but is biased upward. This is because the multiple for excess cash typically exceeds that of core operations. The greater the proportion of cash to overall value, the higher the resulting multiple.

must include it in the enterprise value calculation. Otherwise, the EV-to-EBITA multiple will be biased downward. For instance, when only debt plus equity is divided by EBITA for Company C, the resulting multiple is only 8 times.

As a general rule, any nonoperating asset that does not contribute to EBITA should be removed from enterprise value. This includes not only the market value of excess cash and nonconsolidated subsidiaries, as just mentioned, but also excess real estate, other investments, and the market value of prepaid pension assets. Financial claims include debt and equity, but also minority interest, the value of unfunded pension liabilities, and the value of employee grants outstanding. A detailed discussion of nonoperating assets and financial claims is presented in Chapter 16.

A trickier adjustment is needed for pensions and other retirement benefits, as explained in Chapter 23. Treat the unfunded liabilities as debt or the excess assets as a nonoperating asset. In addition, exclude the nonoperating parts of pension expense from EBITA.

USE THE RIGHT PEER GROUP

Selecting the right peer group is critical to coming up with a reasonable valuation using multiples. Common practice is to select a group of 8 to 15 peers and take the average of the multiples of the peers. Getting a reasonable valuation, though, requires judgment about which companies and their multiples are truly relevant for the valuation.

A common approach to identifying peers is to use the Standard Industrial Classification (SIC) codes or the newer Global Industry Classification Standard (GICS) system developed by Standard & Poor's and Morgan Stanley.[9] These may be a good starting point, but they are usually too broad for a good valuation analysis. For example, United Parcel Service (UPS) is included in the air freight and logistics GICS code, which includes dozens of companies, most of which do not compete with UPS in its core business of delivering small parcels. Another approach is to use peers provided by the company being valued. However, companies often provide aspirational peers rather than companies that truly compete head-to-head. It is better to have a smaller number of peers of companies that truly compete in the same markets with similar products and services.

Even if you find companies that compete head-to-head, differences in performance may justify differences in multiples. Remember the value driver formula expressed as a multiple:

---

[9] Beginning in 1997, SIC codes were replaced by a major revision called the North American Industry Classification System (NAICS). The NAICS six-digit code not only provides for newer industries but also reorganizes the categories on a production/process-oriented basis. The Securities and Exchange Commission (SEC), however, still lists companies by SIC code.

$$\frac{\text{Value}}{\text{EBITA}} = \frac{(1-T)\left(1 - \dfrac{g}{\text{ROIC}}\right)}{\text{WACC} - g}$$

or

$$\frac{\text{Value}}{\text{NOPAT}} = \frac{\left(1 - \dfrac{g}{\text{ROIC}}\right)}{\text{WACC} - g}$$

As both versions of the formula indicate, a company's EBITA or NOPAT valuation multiple is driven by growth (g), ROIC, and the weighted average cost of capital (WACC). While most peers will have similar costs of capital, the other variables may be different, leading to differences in expected multiples.

A common flaw is to compare a particular company's multiple with an average multiple of other companies in the same industry, regardless of differences in their performance. Better to use a smaller subsample of peers with similar performance. Exhibit 18.11 shows the multiples of nine disguised companies that manufacture equipment and provide services for oil and gas drilling. The EV-to-NOPAT multiples range from approximately 10 times to almost 17 times. The company being evaluated, Swallow, had a multiple of 12 times, at the lower end of the range. Does this mean the company is undervalued? Probably not. When you examine the performance of the companies, you can see that they neatly divide into three groups: a top group with multiples of about 15 to 17 times, a middle group with multiples of about 12 times, and a low group with multiples of about 10 times. Note that the ROIC and growth

EXHIBIT 18.11 **Peer Groups by ROIC and Growth**

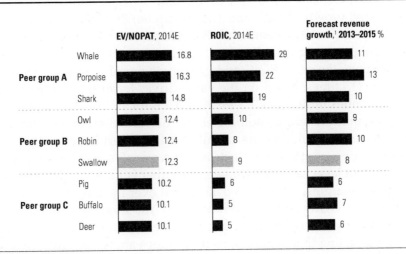

		EV/NOPAT, 2014E	ROIC, 2014E	Forecast revenue growth,[1] 2013–2015 %
Peer group A	Whale	16.8	29	11
	Porpoise	16.3	22	13
	Shark	14.8	19	10
Peer group B	Owl	12.4	10	9
	Robin	12.4	8	10
	Swallow	12.3	9	8
Peer group C	Pig	10.2	6	6
	Buffalo	10.1	5	7
	Deer	10.1	5	6

[1] Compound annual growth rate.

rates line up with the ranges of multiples. Swallow, with a multiple of 12 times, is valued right in line with the other two companies (Owl and Robin) that have similar ROIC and growth. If you didn't know Swallow's multiple, your best estimate would be the average of Owl and Robin, 12 times, not the average of the entire sample or some other sample.

Once you have collected a list of peers and measured their multiples properly, the digging begins. You must answer a series of questions: Why are the multiples different across the peer group? Do certain companies in the group have superior products, better access to customers, recurring revenues, or economies of scale? If these strategic advantages translate to superior ROIC and growth rates, better-positioned companies should trade at higher multiples.

ALTERNATIVE MULTIPLES

Although we have so far focused on enterprise value multiples based on EBITA or NOPAT, other multiples can prove helpful in certain situations. The EV-to-revenues multiple can be useful in bounding valuations with volatile EBITA. The P/E-to-growth (PEG) ratio somewhat controls for different growth rates across companies. Nonfinancial multiples can be useful for young companies where current financial information is not relevant. This section discusses each of these alternative multiples.

Enterprise Value to Revenues

In most cases, value-to-revenues multiples are not particularly useful for explaining company valuations, except in industries with unstable or negative profits. We'll use a simple example to illustrate. Companies A and B have the same expected growth, ROIC, and cost of capital; the only difference is that A's EBITA margin is 10 percent, while B's is 20 percent (B is more capital intensive, so its higher margin is offset by its greater invested capital). Because the companies have the same ROIC and growth, their value-to-EBIT ratios must be the same (13 times, based on the value driver formula). But the resulting value-to-revenues multiple is 1.3 for A and 2.6 for B. In this case, the value-to-revenues multiple tells us nothing about the valuations of the companies.

EV-to-revenues multiples are useful as a last resort in several situations. One is in the case of start-up industries, where profits are negative or a sustainable margin level can't be estimated. Another is in industries with highly volatile profit margins, where you believe that over the long term the companies will have roughly similar profit margins. You might also find situations where a company is periodically spending more on research and development (R&D) or marketing than its peers, so its earnings are temporarily depressed.

If investors are confident about the return to profit margins similar to those of peers, an EV-to-revenues multiple in line with peers might prove more relevant than an EV-to-EBITA multiple that is out of line with peers. Finally, a revenue multiple can provide a quick understanding of the potential value a company could generate if it were able to achieve the same levels of growth, operating margins, and capital efficiency as its peer group.

PEG Ratio

Some analysts and investors use a P/E-to-growth (PEG) ratio to assess the value of a company. For example, a company with a P/E of 15 and expected growth of 4 percent would have a PEG ratio of 3.75:

$$\text{PEG ratio} = \frac{\text{P/E}}{\text{Growth} \times 100} = \frac{15}{4\% \times 100} = 3.75$$

The PEG ratio is seriously deficient, however, because it doesn't take into consideration ROIC, which, as seen earlier, has a significant impact on a company's valuation.

While the concept of relating P/E to growth is relevant, there is no mathematical derivation that says you can simply divide one by the other and produce a significant result. Furthermore, there is no standardized approach for PEG ratios, particularly the choice of time horizon for growth. Should it be one year, five years, or a decade? The choice of horizon can make a big difference, as growth tends to flatten out over time. A company with 6 percent expected growth over five years may have only 4 percent expected growth over ten years. Shifting the growth horizon, in this case, would increase a company's PEG ratio by 50 percent. Finally, as you increase the time frame, growth rates in an industry will converge, so you will end up with differences in the PEG ratios just reflecting differences in P/Es.

The bigger problem, though, is ignoring ROIC. Exhibit 18.12 shows a DCF valuation we conducted for two companies. Company A has a higher ROIC (30 percent, versus 14 percent for B), while Company B has higher expected

EXHIBIT 18.12 **PEG Ratios Distorted by ROIC Differences**

	Company A	Company B
ROIC, %	30	14
Expected growth years 1–10, %	5	10
Expected growth after year 10, %	3	3
WACC, %	9	9
P/E = EV/NOPAT, times	17.0	17.0
PEG ratio, times	3.4	1.7

growth over the first ten years (10 percent, versus 5 percent for A). The DCF valuations of both companies at a 9 percent cost of capital and no debt lead to the same earnings multiple: 17 times. But Company A's PEG ratio is 3.4, while Company B's is 1.7. The common interpretation is that Company A is overvalued relative to Company B because its PEG ratio is higher. Yet it's clear that both companies are valued the same when both growth and ROIC are taken into account.

Multiples of Invested Capital

In some industries, multiples based on invested capital can provide better insights than earnings multiples. One example comes from the banking industry. In the years after the 2008 credit crisis, there was tremendous uncertainty about what levels of return on equity banks would be able to earn.[10] Furthermore, earnings forecasts one to three years out were not reliable and were often negative. Most investors resorted to using multiples of book equity. Banks with higher expected long-term returns on equity, based on their mix of businesses and the underlying economics of those businesses, tended to have higher multiples than banks in lower-return businesses. For example, banks whose portfolios emphasized wealth management and transaction processing, which are stable and earn high returns, were valued at higher multiples to equity than banks focused on more volatile and lower-return investment banking and retail banking.

Regulated industries provide another application of invested capital multiples. Under some regulatory regimes, profits are capped by the allowed return on a company's so-called regulatory asset base (RAB). The RAB is separately reported and represents the invested capital as calculated following certain rules that the regulator sets for qualified capital expenditures. If regulators were to not allow any excess returns above the cost of capital, the enterprise value-to-RAB multiple of a regulated company should be (close to) 1. In practice, the multiples end up at higher levels because regulators often provide various efficiency incentives allowing companies to generate excess returns. In addition, most companies have growth opportunities; they can expand their RAB by new, approved investment projects. For companies under similar regulatory regimes, many investors and analysts use RAB multiples for comparison and valuation.

Multiples Based on Operating Metrics

Sometimes company valuations are based on multiples of operating metrics. For example, values of oil and gas companies can be expressed as value per

---

[10] As explained in Chapter 38, we use return on equity, rather than return on capital, for banks.

barrel of oil reserves. Clearly, the amount of oil reserves in the ground the company has access to will drive the company's value. While the value of each barrel once the oil is extracted and sold is roughly the same, the costs to extract those barrels will vary widely and affect profit per barrel, depending on the geology of those reserves and the techniques needed to extract them. When estimating the value of an oil and gas company based on a valuation multiple of the amount of reserves it holds, you therefore have to make adjustments for any differences in the costs of extraction and distribution relative to the companies for which the multiple was estimated.

In other cases, investors and analysts resort to operating multiples when valuing young, fast-growing companies, because of the great uncertainty surrounding potential market size, profitability, and required investments. Financial multiples that normally provide a benchmark for valuation are often useless, as profitability (measured in any form) is often negative. A way to overcome this shortcoming is to apply nonfinancial multiples, comparing enterprise value with operating statistics such as website hits, unique visitors, or number of users or subscribers. This happened, for example, in the late 1990s, when numerous Internet companies went public with meager sales and negative profits. In 2000, *Fortune* reported market-value-to-customer multiples for a series of Internet companies.[11] *Fortune* determined that Yahoo was trading at $2,038 per customer, Amazon.com at $1,400 per customer, and NetZero at $1,140 per customer.

Today, similar multiples are sometimes used to analyze and compare the valuation of fast-growing companies with digital user–based or subscription-based business models. For example, the market value of audio- and video-streaming companies Netflix, Spotify, and Sirius XM can be expressed per paying user or subscriber. As of July 2019, Netflix was trading at about $1,200 per subscriber, Spotify at about $200 per subscriber, and Sirius XM at $900 per subscriber.[12] The question is whether such multiples offer real insights.

Effective use of a nonfinancial multiple requires that the nonfinancial metric be a reasonable predictor of future value creation and thus somehow tied to ROIC and growth. Simply taking the average of the customer or subscriber multiples for a set of apparently similar businesses provides little, if any, insight. Netflix, Spotify, and Sirius XM differ in terms of the underlying drivers of revenues and costs per user, because they operate with distinct business models. Netflix streams TV series, films, and documentaries on demand, and

---

[11] E. Schonfeld, "How Much Are Your Eyeballs Worth?" *Fortune*, February 21, 2000, 197–200.

[12] As of mid-2019, Netflix had an enterprise value of about $180 billion and about 150 million paying users, Spotify had a value of about $23 billion and 110 million paying users, and Sirius XM had a value of about $32 billion and 35 million paying users.

Spotify offers music streaming on demand. Sirius XM combines on-demand and radio-format music streaming (via its 2019 Pandora acquisition) with its original business of satellite radio broadcasting. All three generate revenues from user subscriptions, but Spotify and Sirius XM also generate advertising income. For Netflix, the cost of streamed content is largely independent of the number of users; it produces an increasing portion of the content itself and does not pay per view to its content suppliers. Spotify, in contrast, does not produce content and pays an amount per song-play to the content owners (record companies and artists). Sirius XM develops part of its content (for example, its radio shows) and buys music from third parties—also paying per song-play, but at lower rates for radio broadcasting than for on-demand streaming. In addition, the companies' user growth rates for 2019 varied widely: about 30 percent for Spotify, 20 percent for Netflix, and 3 percent for Sirius XM (with Sirius active in the United States only and Netflix and Spotify in many countries). Because of these differences in user economics and growth, an average of the value per user of Netflix, Spotify, and Sirius XM is not very meaningful for valuing another online music or video-streaming business. You would need to analyze the underlying business model in detail to understand which of the three is the most comparable business.

In the end, what matters is the underlying value creation, not the number of users, website hits, or unique visitors. In the late-1990s Internet examples from *Fortune*, Yahoo traded at a higher multiple than Amazon.com because investors expected that Yahoo's profit per user would be higher than Amazon's. Academic studies have demonstrated for these valuations that the number of unique visitors to a website or the number of pages on a site viewed per visit was directly correlated to a company's stock price, even after controlling for the company's current financial performance.[13] The power of a given nonfinancial metric, however, depended on the company. For portal and content companies such as Yahoo, page views and unique visitors were both correlated to a company's market value. For online retailers such as Amazon.com, only the page views per visit were correlated with value. Evidently, the market believed that merely stopping by would not translate to future cash flow for online retailers.

Research has also shown that as an industry matures, financial metrics such as gross profit and R&D spending become increasingly predictive, whereas nonfinancial data tend to lose power.[14] This indicates a return to traditional valuation metrics for new industries as they mature and once financial metrics became meaningful.

---

[13] B. Trueman, M. H. F. Wong, and X. J. Zhang, "The Eyeballs Have It: Searching for the Value in Internet Stocks," *Journal of Accounting Research* 38 (2000): 137–162.

[14] P. Jorion and E. Talmor, "Value Relevance of Financial and Non Financial Information in Emerging Industries: The Changing Role of Web Traffic Data" (working paper no. 021, London Business School Accounting Subject Area, 2001).

A problem with all multiples is that they are relative valuation tools. They measure one company's valuation relative to another's, normalized by some measure of size, be it size of earnings, revenues, or number of customers. They do not measure absolute valuation levels. For multiples based on operating metrics, there is an additional challenge of interpretation, because you can only compare them across a very limited number of companies that have a very similar operating model. Financial multiples are easier to interpret and compare. Take the example of an EV-to-EBITA multiple of 20 times for a mature industrial company. Basic understanding of underlying value drivers can readily lead you to a first conclusion: this multiple reflects high expectations for ROIC and growth (at a reasonable cost of capital). But it is much harder to come to such a conclusion when you observe an EV multiple of $1,200 per customer.

SUMMARY

Of the available valuation tools, discounted cash flow continues to deliver the best results. However, a thoughtful comparison of selected multiples for the company you are valuing with multiples from a carefully selected group of peers merits a place in your tool kit as well. When that comparative analysis is careful and well reasoned, it not only serves as a useful check of your DCF forecasts, but also provides critical insights into what drives value in a given industry. The distinction between operating and nonoperating results, capital, and cash flows should follow the exact same logic as applied in DCF valuation. The most insightful multiples are those that compare operating value to operating results. Operating metrics such as mineral reserve size or number of subscribers can be used when these are clearly related to value creation. In all cases, be sure that you analyze the underlying reasons that multiples differ from company to company, and never view multiples as a shortcut to valuation. Instead, approach your multiples analysis with as much care as you bring to your DCF analysis.

19

Valuation by Parts

Up to this point, our analysis has focused on single-business companies. But many large companies have multiple business units, each competing in segments with different economic characteristics. For instance, Anglo-Dutch Unilever competes in food and refreshments, personal products, and home-care products. Even so-called pure-play companies, such as Vodafone (mobile telecommunication services) and Amazon (online retail), often have a wide variety of underlying geographical and category segments. This is not just the case for large companies: consider the local bicycle shop that also has an online sales channel.

If the economics of a company's segments are different, you will generate more insights by valuing each segment and adding them up to estimate the value of the entire company. Trying to value the entire company as a single enterprise will not provide much understanding, and your final valuation may be way off the mark. Consider a simple case where a faster-growing segment has lower returns on capital than a slower-growing segment. If both segments maintain their return on invested capital (ROIC), the corporate ROIC would decline as the weights of the different segments change, while the corporate growth rate would steadily increase.

Valuing by parts generates better valuation estimates and deeper insights into where and how the company is generating value. That is why it is standard practice in industry-leading companies and among sophisticated investors. This chapter explains four critical steps for valuing a company by its parts:

1. Understanding the mechanics of and insights from valuing a company by the sum of its parts
2. Building financial statements by business unit—based on incomplete information, if necessary

3. Estimating the weighted average cost of capital (WACC) by business unit

4. Testing the value based on multiples of peers

THE MECHANICS OF VALUING BY PARTS

The most effective way to explore the mechanics of valuing by parts and the insights that can result is to work through a valuation. Exhibit 19.1 details the key financials, value drivers, valuation results, and multiples for each part of ConsumerCo, a hypothetical business. Its parts are four business units, a financial subsidiary, and a nonconsolidated joint venture. To simplify, we kept all future returns and growth rates constant at 2020 levels for each business unit.

All of ConsumerCo's businesses sell products for personal care, but their economics differ widely. The key financials and value drivers in Exhibit 19.1 make this clear. The company's primary business unit, branded consumer products, sells well-known brands in personal care (mainly skin creams, shaving creams, and toothpaste). It generates $2.0 billion in revenues at returns well above its 8.6 percent cost of capital, but mainly in slow-growth, mature markets. Private label, the next-largest business at $1.5 billion in revenues, produces for large discount chains selling products under their own names. This unit is growing faster than the branded-products business, but at far lower returns on capital that barely meet its cost of capital.

The devices business, with $1.25 billion in revenues, sells electronic devices for personal care, such as sun beds, shavers, and toothbrushes, at a very healthy 18.1 percent return on capital, paired with high growth rates. The newly developed organic-products business has $750 million in revenues in premium products made with natural materials. It generates both the highest returns and the highest growth. The $83 million in annual costs for running the corporate center are shown as a separate business unit. Finally, internal revenues, earnings before interest, taxes, and amortization (EBITA), and invested capital are eliminated in the consolidation of ConsumerCo's financials, as the branded-products business buys components from the private-label business unit.

The discounted-cash-flow (DCF) valuation results and multiples in Exhibit 19.1 reflect these differences in size, growth, and ROIC across the businesses. Not surprisingly, the high returns and large scale in branded products lead to the largest valuation ($5,188 million), and the implied multiple of enterprise value (EV) to net operating profit after taxes (NOPAT) is 16.0 times. The private-label business generates almost a third of the company's revenues but contributes only around 10 percent of value ($1,128 million) because of its low returns on capital. Despite its higher growth rate, its

EXHIBIT 19.1 **ConsumerCo: Valuation Summary, January 2020**

	Key financials $ million			Value drivers %												WACC	Valuation $ million	Multiples	
			Invested capital	Revenue growth				Operating margin				ROIC						EV/	EV/
	Revenue	EBITA	capital														DCF value	NOPAT	NOPAT
	2020	2020	2020	2018	2019	2020	2020–25	2018	2019	2020	2020–25	2018	2019	2020	2020–25				Peers
Branded products	2,000	500	1,600	1.5	2.5	3.0	3.0	23.0	24.3	25.0	25.0	19.7	19.9	20.3	20.3	8.6	5,188	16.0	15.6
Private label	1,500	143	900	4.6	4.7	5.0	5.0	7.7	8.5	9.5	9.5	8.5	9.3	10.3	10.3	9.1	1,128	12.2	11.7
Devices	1,250	156	563	7.1	7.3	7.5	7.5	11.2	12.0	12.5	12.5	15.8	17.1	18.1	18.1	10.1	1,474	14.5	14.0
Organic products	750	206	488	9.3	9.5	10.0	10.0	27.6	27.3	27.5	27.5	27.6	27.5	27.5	27.5	8.6	3,440	25.7	24.5
Corporate center	–	(83)	806	4.4	5.0	5.4	5.6[1]									9.1	(1,123)	20.9	–
Eliminations	(500)	(2)	(50)													–	–	–
Total operations	5,000	920	4,306	4.5	5.1	5.5	5.7	17.7	18.4	18.4	18.3	12.6	13.2	13.9	14.7		10,107	16.9	–
Customer finance																10.5[2]	150[3]	12.1[2]	12.0[2]
Cosmetics joint venture																9.1	609[4]	17.6	17.0
Excess cash																	250		
Gross enterprise value																	11,117		
Debt																	(1,941)[5]		
Equity value																	9,175		

[1] For HQ, growth of HQ costs
[2] For customer finance: P/E cost of equity.
[3] At equity value, net of debt, in customer finance.
[4] Equity value of minority stake in cosmetics joint venture.
[5] Excluding debt in customer finance: $1,038 million.

EV/NOPAT multiple of 12.2 is lower than that of the branded-products unit. The devices business, with returns well above cost of capital and growth rates exceeding those of private-label products, is valued at $1,474 million and has a multiple of 14.5 times NOPAT. The organic-products business combines high returns with high growth, achieving a value of $3,440 million, second highest after branded products, but at a much higher implied multiple of 25.7 times NOPAT. With headquarters DCF at a negative $1,123 million and no impact on value from eliminations (see later in this chapter), the value of operations for ConsumerCo totals $10,107 million, corresponding to a weighted average multiple of 16.9 times NOPAT.

ConsumerCo's customer-finance subsidiary provides loans for about a quarter of device revenues. It is valued at $150 million (net of $1,038 million of debt), using cash flow to equity discounted at its cost of equity of 10.5 percent (see the next section). The cosmetics joint venture is valued using an enterprise DCF valuation, but only ConsumerCo's 45 percent stake of the equity, valued at $609 million, is included in ConsumerCo's value.

The combined total of ConsumerCo's businesses, including the finance subsidiary, the cosmetics joint venture, and $250 million of excess cash, is $11,117 million. Subtracting $1,941 million of debt (excluding the portion allocated to the finance subsidiary from the company's total debt of $2,980 million) leads to an equity value of $9,175 million.

ConsumerCo's results illustrate why valuation by parts leads to better results. For example, even while all business units are at constant (but different) growth rates and returns on capital, ConsumerCo's overall growth and return continue to change between 2020 and 2025 as the weight of organic products in the portfolio steadily increases. When the economics of business segments differ greatly, it becomes difficult via a purely top-down approach to understand historical patterns and to project future trajectories for a company's returns and growth. If you had conducted a top-down DCF valuation of ConsumerCo as a single business at a constant 2020 ROIC of 13.9 percent and an ongoing growth rate of 5.5 percent, the resulting value would have been 10 percent too low. Also note how large the differences in multiples are across the businesses (from 12.2 to 25.7 times NOPAT) and how the aggregate multiple for the operating enterprise value matches none of the underlying businesses.

The equity value buildup in Exhibit 19.2 illustrates that branded and organic products generate the bulk of the company's value. They also stand out for their market value added—the difference between DCF value and book value of invested capital. For each dollar of invested capital, value creation is the highest in these two business units.

A valuation-by-parts approach offers insights into the sources and drivers of a company's value creation that a purely top-down view cannot reveal. Exhibit 19.3 shows how additional growth or ROIC affects the value of each of the business units. Given the high returns on capital for the organic-products unit, growth through additional investments in that business would create

EXHIBIT 19.2 **ConsumerCo: Equity Value Buildup, January 2020**

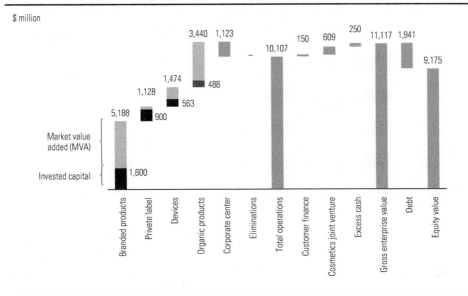

EXHIBIT 19.3 **ConsumerCo: How Changes in ROIC and Growth Affect Value**

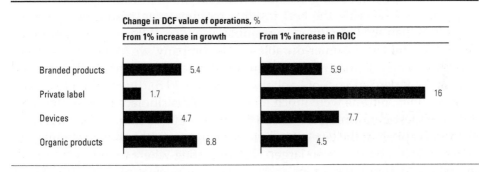

more value for the company than investments in other units. In contrast, the private-label unit creates the least amount of value, due to its low returns on capital. Improving returns is the best way to generate more value from this segment. To maximize value creation, ConsumerCo's management should differentiate priorities for growth and return across its segments, rather than set company-wide targets.

Many companies, ConsumerCo among them, struggle with such differentiation. As the investment map in Exhibit 19.4 shows, ConsumerCo's capital expenditures over the five years from 2015 to 2020 have been more in line with the size of each business than with their returns or growth. Investments

EXHIBIT 19.4 **ConsumerCo: Historical Investments, 2015–2020**

	Cumulative net investments,[1] $ million	Cumulative revenues, $ million	Average ROIC, %	Revenue growth, CAGR, %
Organic products	205	3,620	27.4	9.6
Devices	214	6,343	16.3	7.1
Private Label	240	8,070	9.0	4.2
Branded products	334	11,373	20.1	1.8

[1] Capital expenditures plus investments in net working capital minus depreciation.

were largest in the private-label and branded-products businesses, and lowest in organic products. In the typical annual budgeting process, many companies routinely allocate their capital, research and development (R&D), and marketing budgets to the same activities year after year, regardless of their relative contribution to value creation. The cost is high, since companies that more actively reallocate resources generate, on average, 30 percent higher total shareholder returns (TSR).[1] A valuation by parts can highlight whether a company's capital spending is aligned with its value-creation opportunities.

Sometimes securing the best insights requires even more finely grained valuations than the ConsumerCo example provides. When we analyzed four divisions within a consumer-durable-goods company, we found that all were generating fairly similar returns, between 12 and 18 percent, well above the company's 9 percent cost of capital (see Exhibit 19.5). But at the next level, business units, returns were much more widely distributed. Even in the company's highest-performing division, a business unit was earning returns below its cost of capital. At the level of individual activities within business units, the return distribution was even larger. Differentiating where to invest in growth and where to improve margins at such granular levels can trigger significant improvements in value creation for the company as a whole.[2]

BUILDING BUSINESS UNIT FINANCIAL STATEMENTS

To value a company's individual business units, you need income statements, balance sheets, and cash flow statements. Ideally, these financial statements should approximate what the business units would look like if they

[1] S. Hall, D. Lovallo, and R. Musters, "How to Put Your Money Where Your Strategy Is," *McKinsey Quarterly* (March 2012).

[2] M. Goedhart, S. Smit, and A. Veldhuijzen, "Unearthing the Source of Value Hiding in Your Corporate Portfolio," *McKinsey on Finance* (Fall 2013).

EXHIBIT 19.5 **Breakdown of Return on Invested Capital at Each Level of Analysis**

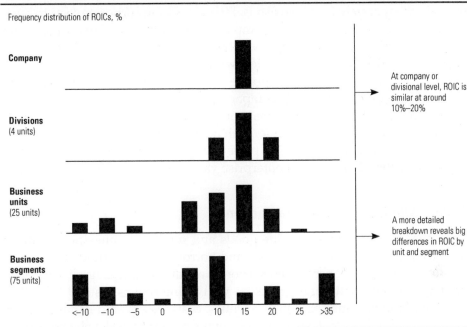

were stand-alone companies. Creating financial statements for business units requires consideration of several issues:

- Allocating corporate overhead costs
- Dealing with intercompany transactions
- Understanding financial subsidiaries
- Navigating incomplete public information

We will illustrate each of these issues by extending the ConsumerCo example.

Allocating Corporate Overhead Costs

Most multibusiness companies have shared services and corporate overhead, so you need to decide which costs should be allocated to the businesses and which retained at the corporate level. For services that the corporate center provides, such as payroll, human resources, and accounting, allocate the costs by cost drivers. For example, the aggregate cost of human resources services provided by the corporate parent can be allocated by the number of employees in each business unit.

When costs are incurred only because the units are part of a larger company (for example, the CEO's compensation or the corporate art collection), do not allocate the costs. They should be retained as a corporate cost center and valued separately for two reasons. First, allocating corporate costs to business units reduces your ability to compare them with pure-play business unit peers that don't incur such costs (most business units already have their own chief executives, CFOs, and controllers who are comparable to pure-play competitors). Second, keeping the corporate center as a separate unit reveals how much of a drag it creates on the company's value.

For ConsumerCo, the unallocated corporate costs are estimated at $83 million, around 1.7 percent of revenue, with a present value amounting to about 10 percent of enterprise value. The present value of corporate costs is often in the range of 10 to 20 percent of enterprise value for multibusiness companies.

Dealing with Intercompany Transactions

Sometimes business units provide goods and services to one another, incur intragroup payables and receivables, and borrow and lend funds to a group treasury. To arrive at consolidated corporate results, accountants eliminate the internal revenues, costs, and profits, as well as internal assets and liabilities, to prevent double-counting. Only revenues, costs, assets, and liabilities from transactions with external parties remain at the consolidated level. Exhibit 19.6 shows how the 2020 reorganized financials for ConsumerCo's businesses are consolidated with the accounts of the parent company, ConsumerCo Corporation. In this example, ConsumerCo Corporation has no business activities and only holds the equity stakes in the business subsidiaries and most of the group's debt.

Intercompany Sales and Profits ConsumerCo's private-label segment sells partially finished products to the open market but also to the branded-products unit, generating $500 million of internal sales in 2020 (in Exhibit 19.6, see the first line under Eliminations I). If the branded-products unit would process and resell all transferred materials in the same year, $500 million of internal revenues and internal costs could simply be eliminated in the consolidation. Since one unit's revenues are another unit's costs, overall earnings are unaffected.[3]

But, as is often the case for intercompany sales, ConsumerCo's branded-products unit typically does not process and resell all of the private-label deliveries in the same year. Because of the resulting inventory changes of internally

---

[3] The cumulative value of business units will equal the aggregate value, but the value split depends on the level of transfer pricing between the two units. The higher the transfer price, the more aggregate value is transferred to the private-label business. To value each business unit accurately, record intercompany transfers at the value that would be transacted with third parties. Otherwise, the relative value of the business units will be distorted.

EXHIBIT 19.6 **ConsumerCo: Eliminations and Consolidation, 2020**

$ million

	Subsidiary companies						ConsumerCo parent company	Eliminations I	Eliminations II	ConsumerCo consolidated
	Branded products	Private label	Devices	Organic products	Corporate center	Customer finance				
NOPAT										
Revenues	2,000	1,500	1,250	750	–	–	–	(500)	–	5,000
Operating costs	(1,500)	(1,358)	(1,094)	(544)	(83)	–	–	498	–	(4,080)
EBITA	500	143	156	206	(83)	–	–	(2)	–	920
Taxes on EBITA	(175)	(50)	(55)	(72)	29	–	–	–	–	(323)
NOPAT	325	93	102	134	(54)	–	–	(2)	–	597
Income from associates and joint ventures	–	–	–	–	–	–	972	–	(942)	30
Interest income	–	–	–	–	–	77	16	–	–	93
Interest expense	–	–	–	–	–	(58)	(118)	–	–	(177)
Taxes on nonoperating items	–	–	–	–	–	(7)	(304)	–	330	19
Net income	325	93	102	134	(54)	12	565	(2)	(612)	563
Invested capital										
Accounts receivable	240	105	25	75	–	–	–	–	–	445
Accounts payable	(216)	(74)	(18)	(5)	–	–	–	–	–	(312)
Inventory	700	375	500	150	–	–	–	(50)	–	1,675
Net PP&E	876	494	55	268	806	–	–	–	–	2,498
Invested capital	1,600	900	563	488	806	–	–	(50)	–	4,306
Excess cash	–	–	–	–	–	–	250	–	–	250
Intercompany receivables	300	–	450	–	–	–	200	–	(950)	–
Loans	–	–	–	–	–	1,154	–	–	–	1,154
Investments in associates and joint ventures	–	–	–	–	–	–	5,097	–	(5,021)	76
Total funds invested	1,900	900	1,013	488	806	1,154	5,547	(50)	(5,971)	5,785
Intercompany payables	–	200	–	–	–	–	750	–	(950)	–
Debt and debt equivalents	–	–	–	–	–	1,038	1,941	–	–	2,980
Adjusted equity	1,900	700	1,013	488	806	115	2,856	(50)	(5,021)	2,806
Total funds invested	1,900	900	1,013	488	806	1,154	5,547	(50)	(5,971)	5,785

supplied materials, one unit's revenues are no longer another unit's costs, and some earnings and inventory now must be eliminated in the consolidation as well. ConsumerCo's consolidated financials eliminate $2 million in earnings and $50 million in inventory (see the Eliminations I column of Exhibit 19.6).[4] As in most situations, the earnings impact is small because it is driven by the change in inventory, not the final inventory. Note that in any case, the eliminations cannot affect ConsumerCo's aggregate free cash flow and enterprise DCF valuation, because consolidation adjustments to inventory always offset the changes in NOPAT.

When you build and forecast the financial statements for the business units, treat each unit as if it were a stand-alone company, using total sales (external plus internal). Otherwise, margins and comparisons over time and with peers will be distorted. Prepare separate projections of the consolidation eliminations, similar to the corporate center. The growth rate of intercompany sales can be estimated from the details of how and why these items arise. It is simplest to assume that the eliminations grow at the same rate as the entire group or as the receiving businesses. Remember, however, that the eliminations are used only to reconcile business unit forecasts to the consolidated-enterprise forecasts. They do not affect the value of the company or the individual business units.

Intercompany Financial Receivables and Payables Multibusiness companies typically manage cash and debt centrally for all business units, which can lead to intercompany receivables from, and payables to, the corporate parent. Sometimes these intercompany accounts are driven by tax considerations. For example, one business unit might lend directly to another unit so that funds don't flow through the parent company, which could trigger additional taxes. Sometimes the accounts have no economic purpose but are simply an artifact of the company's accounting system. Regardless of their purpose, intercompany receivables and payables should not be treated as part of operating working capital but as intercompany equity in the calculation of invested capital.

The Eliminations II column of Exhibit 19.6 shows how this occurs for ConsumerCo. The parent company has $5,097 million of equity investments in its subsidiaries, of which $700 million is in the private-label unit, for example, as reflected in the equity of the subsidiary accounts. This accounting treatment is for internal reports only; since ConsumerCo Corporation owns the private-label business in its entirety, its financial statements are consolidated for external reports, eliminating the $700 million of equity investment. The same holds for the other businesses shown. This leads to the elimination of $5,021

---

[4] There is no impact on cash taxes or free cash flow from the accounting consolidation. We abstract from any impact of tax consolidation (fiscal grouping) in this example.

million of equity investments in consolidation, leaving only the $76 million stake in the minority-owned cosmetics joint venture as equity investment in the consolidated accounts.

In addition, ConsumerCo Corporation has lent $200 million to the private-label unit, which shows up as an intercompany receivable for the parent company and an intercompany payable for the private-label unit. For the parent company, it represents a nonoperating asset that does not generate operating profits and hence should not be included in its operating working capital. For private label, it represents a financial infusion that is similar to equity. In the consolidated financials, the amounts are eliminated. Similarly, the intercompany receivables for the branded-products and devices businesses are treated as nonoperating assets that are eliminated in the consolidated financials against the $750 million of parent intercompany payables. Failure to handle the intercompany receivables and payables correctly can generate seriously misleading results. In the ConsumerCo example, if the intercompany accounts had been treated as working capital instead of equity, the private-label business's invested capital would have been understated by more than 20 percent, leading to an overstatement of ROIC by roughly the same percentage.

Understanding Financial Subsidiaries

Some firms have financial subsidiaries that provide financing for customers (for example, John Deere Financial and practically all automotive manufacturers). If these subsidiaries are majority owned, they are fully consolidated in the company financial statements. But balance sheets of financial businesses are structured differently from those of industrial or service businesses. The assets tend to be financial rather than physical (largely receivables or loans) and are usually highly leveraged. As detailed in Chapter 38, financial businesses should be valued using cash flow to equity, discounted at the cost of equity. Most companies with significant financial subsidiaries provide a separate balance sheet and income statement for those subsidiaries; the information can be used to analyze and value the financial subsidiaries separately.

Exhibit 19.6 shows that in 2020, ConsumerCo's customer-finance unit has $1,154 million in outstanding customer loans. We estimated the ratio of debt to customer loans required to maintain its current BBB credit rating at 90 percent, so that its funding consists of $1,038 million of debt (0.90 × $1,154 million) and $115 million of equity. The loans generate $77 million in annual interest income. After deducting $58 million of interest expenses on debt and taxes of $7 million, after-tax net income of $12 million remains. The return on equity for the customer-finance unit is 10.8 percent ($12 million of net income divided by $115 million of equity), just above its 10.5 percent cost of equity (see also Exhibit 19.1). These loans, debt, and financial income streams need to be valued separately from ConsumerCo's business operations. Looking ahead, the

EXHIBIT 19.7 **ConsumerCo: Public Information for Business Segments, 2020**

Reported financials, $ million	Branded products	Private label	Devices	Organic products	Corporate center	Intersegment eliminations	Consolidated
Revenues	2,000	1,500	1,250	750	–	(500)	5,000
Operating profit	500	143	156	206	(83)	(2)	920
Depreciation[1]	150	59	57	31	42		338
Capital expenditures	208	107	90	79	42		526
Assets	1,872	882	596	531	830	(50)	4,662
Invested capital: Estimate vs. actual							
Assets/total assets, %	40	19	13	11	18		99
Invested capital estimate, $ million	1,711	806	545	486	759		4,306
Invested capital actual, $ million	1,600	900	563	488	806		4,306
Estimation error, %	6.9	(10.4)	(3.1)	(0.4)	(5.9)		

[1] Included in operating profit.

customer-finance unit's loans are assumed to grow in line with the revenues of the devices business (for which it provides the customer loans). Keeping interest rates and the ratio of debt to customer loans stable at 90 percent, the cash-flow-to-equity DCF value is estimated at $150 million (see Exhibit 19.1).

Be careful not to double-count the debt of the financial subsidiary in the overall valuation of the company. The equity value of the customer-finance subsidiary is already net of its $1,038 million debt, so when we subtracted debt from ConsumerCo's total enterprise value to arrive at the consolidated company's equity value in Exhibit 19.1, we subtracted only the $1,941 million debt associated with business operations.

Navigating Public Information

For our ConsumerCo example, we have the benefit of complete financial statements by business unit. But that will typically not be the case if you are valuing a multibusiness company from the outside in. Exhibit 19.7 shows the disclosure of financial information typical of U.S. Generally Accepted Accounting Principles (GAAP) and International Financial Reporting Standards (IFRS) for a company like ConsumerCo. Companies disclose revenues, operating profit (or something similar, such as EBITA), depreciation, capital expenditures, and assets by segment. You must convert these items to NOPAT and invested capital.

NOPAT   To estimate NOPAT, start with reported operating earnings by business unit.[5] Next, allocate operating taxes, any pension adjustment (to

[5] Companies use different names, such as operating profit, underlying profit, or simply earnings before interest and taxes (EBIT), for business unit results.

eliminate the nonoperating effect of pension expense), and operating lease adjustment (eliminating interest expense embedded in rental expense before new accounting standards were introduced in 2019) to each of the business units. (For more information on these adjustments, see Chapter 11.) Use the overall operating tax rate for all business units unless you have information to estimate each unit's tax rate—for example, if units are in different tax jurisdictions. For the ConsumerCo example, this would have resulted in exactly the right NOPAT per business unit, because no pension, lease, or other adjustments are needed on reported EBITA, though this is not typically the case.

After estimating NOPAT, reconcile the sum of all business unit NOPATs to consolidated net income. This step ensures that all adjustments have been properly made.

Invested Capital   To estimate invested capital, you can use an incremental approach or a proportional approach, depending on the information available. When possible, use both approaches to triangulate your estimates.

In the *incremental* approach, start with total assets by business unit, and subtract estimates for nonoperating assets and non-interest-bearing operating liabilities. (Note that many companies will hold nonoperating assets at the corporate level, not the unit level. In that case, no adjustment is necessary.) Nonoperating assets include excess cash, investments in nonconsolidated subsidiaries, pension assets, and deferred tax assets. Non-interest-bearing operating liabilities include accounts payable, taxes payable, and accrued expenses. They can be allocated to the business units by either revenue or total assets. As discussed in the earlier section on intercompany payables and receivables, do not treat intercompany loans and debt as an operating liability.

Then allocate the invested capital for the consolidated entity to all of its business units by the amount of total assets minus nonoperating assets and non-interest-bearing liabilities for each business unit. To measure invested capital excluding goodwill,[6] subtract allocated goodwill by business unit. If goodwill is not reported by business unit, you can try to make an estimate from past transactions if these can be aligned with individual business units.

Using the *proportional* approach for ConsumerCo, you could have allocated its total operating invested capital (excluding the customer loans and joint venture, of course) to each of the business units by each unit's proportion of total assets as reported before intersegment eliminations. Note that this would have resulted in some estimation errors, such as allocating $1,711 million invested capital (calculated as $1,872/$4,712 × $4,306 million) to branded products when its true invested capital is $1,600 million.

---

[6] By goodwill, we mean both goodwill and acquired intangibles.

Once you have estimated invested capital for the business units and corporate center, reconcile these estimates with the total invested capital derived from the consolidated statements.

COST OF CAPITAL

Each business segment should be valued at its own cost of capital, because the systematic risk (beta) of operating cash flows and their ability to support debt—that is, the implied capital structure—will differ by business. To determine an operational business unit's weighted average cost of capital (WACC), you need the unit's target capital structure, its cost of equity (as determined by its levered beta), and its cost of borrowing. For a financial business, you simply need the cost of equity following from its equity beta. (For details on estimating the cost of equity and WACC, see Chapter 15.) The results for ConsumerCo's segments are summarized in Exhibit 19.8.

First, estimate the target capital structure in terms of the debt-to-equity (D/E) ratio for each of ConsumerCo's business units. We recommend using the median capital structure of publicly traded peers, especially if most peers have similar capital structures. Next, determine the levered beta, cost of equity, and WACC. To determine a business unit's beta, first estimate an unlevered median beta for its peer group (be thoughtful about which companies to include, especially outliers). Relever the beta, using the same business unit's

EXHIBIT 19.8 **ConsumerCo: WACC Estimates, January 2020**

Business	Debt/ equity[1]	Cost of debt,[2] %	Beta, unlevered	Beta, levered	Cost of equity,[3] %	WACC,[4] %	DCF value, $ million	Implied debt, $ million
Branded products	0.30	5.5	0.9	1.1	10.1	8.6	5,188	1,197
Private label	0.30	5.5	1.0	1.2	10.7	9.1	1,128	260
Devices	0.25	5.5	1.2	1.5	11.8	10.1	1,474	295
Organic products	0.25	5.5	0.9	1.1	9.9	8.6	3,440	688
Corporate center	0.30					9.4	(1,123)	(259)
Eliminations							–	–
Total operations							10,107	2,181
Customer finance								1,038
Total ConsumerCo: Net debt, implied								3,220
Excess cash, actual								(250)
Debt, actual in operations								1,941
Debt, actual in customer finance								1,038
Total ConsumerCo: Net debt, actual								2,730

[1] At targeted BBB credit rating.
[2] Beta of debt equals 0.2 and risk-free rate of interest equals 4.5%.
[3] Assuming market risk premium of 5.0%.
[4] Tax rate set at 35%.

target capital structure, and estimate its WACC. For the corporate headquarters cash flows, use a weighted average of the business units' costs of capital. Most of ConsumerCo's businesses have similar betas in a range of 1.1 to 1.2, with resulting WACC estimates between 8.6 and 9.1 percent. An exception is the devices business, which is more cyclical at a beta of around 1.5 and a cost of capital of 10.1 percent. For ConsumerCo's customer-finance subsidiary, we directly estimated the equity beta of its peers in retail banking at 1.2, leading to an estimated cost of equity of 10.5 percent.

Finally, using the debt levels based on industry medians, aggregate the business unit debt to see how the total compares with the company's total target debt level.[7] Set the headquarters target D/E at a weighted average of the business units' D/Es, as its negative cash flow is reducing the company's overall debt capacity. If the sum of business unit target debt differs from the consolidated company's actual debt, we typically record the difference as a corporate item, valuing its tax shield separately (or its tax cost when the company is more conservatively financed). Remember that the business units' valuations are based on target, not actual, capital structure.

In ConsumerCo's case, the resulting aggregate target debt level for its business units and finance subsidiary is $3,220 million. That amount is above its total current net debt of $2,730 million, or $2,980 million debt, net of $250 million excess cash (see Exhibit 19.8). If ConsumerCo held on to its current leverage, it would realize a loss in value relative to the value of its parts. To estimate this loss, project the lost tax shields from the company's current below-peer-level leverage into perpetuity at the overall revenue growth rate, and discount these at the unlevered cost of equity.[8]

When you value a company by summing the business unit values, there is no need to estimate a corporate-wide cost of capital or to reconcile the business unit betas with the corporate beta. The individual business unit betas are more relevant than the corporate beta, which is subject to significant estimation

---

[7] The allocation of debt among business units for legal or internal corporate purposes is generally irrelevant to the economic analysis of the business units. The legal or internal debt is generally driven by tax purposes or is an accident of history (cash-consuming units have lots of debt). These allocations rarely are economically meaningful and should be ignored.

[8] Recall from Chapter 15 that using the cost of debt to discount tax shields significantly overestimates their value. In theory, a company's unlevered cost of equity is a complex average of the unlevered cost of equity of its underlying businesses that changes over time. You can use a simple average of the unlevered costs of equity of the underlying businesses as an approximation, as any associated error has very small impact on value. Assuming a tax rate of 35 percent and an interest rate of 6 percent, the tax shields lost from $490 million in debt below target are $10.3 million for 2020. Assuming future tax shield losses would roughly grow in line with overall revenues, and discounting at ConsumerCo's unlevered cost of equity of around 9.5 percent, the loss in value would amount to around $190 million.

EXHIBIT 19.9 **ConsumerCo: Multiples for Peer Branded-Product Companies, January 2020**

Company		ROIC 2020, %	Growth, 2020–2025, %	EV/EBITA	EV/NOPAT	
Peer	1	31.0	4.7	16.5	22.0	
Peer	2	29.6	4.4	15.8	22.6	Top-peer average: 21.0
Peer	3	28.5	4.5	14.3	20.4	
Peer	4	27.1	3.9	12.8	19.1	
Peer	5	22.0	3.0	12.0	16.0	
Peer	6	21.1	2.8	10.5	15.7	Close-peer average: 15.6
Peer	7	19.7	2.4	11.0	15.7	
Peer	8	19.0	2.1	10.0	15.4	
Peer	9	18.5	2.2	9.5	15.1	
Peer	10	18.3	4.0	20	26.7	Outliers
Peer	11	9.0	3.4	32	45.7	
Overall average					18.0	Excluding outliers
					21.3	Including outliers

error and is likely to change over time as the weights of the underlying businesses in the company portfolio change.[9]

TESTING THE VALUE BASED ON MULTIPLES OF PEERS

Whenever possible, triangulate the discounted cash flow results with valuation multiples, following the recommendations made in Chapter 18. For each of the company's segments, carefully select a group of companies that are comparable not only in terms of sector but also in terms of return on capital and growth. Do not simply take an average or median of the peer group multiples. Instead, always eliminate outliers with multiples that are out of line with their underlying economics, and where possible, estimate a median of close peers with similar returns and growth. Furthermore, we recommend using NOPAT-based instead of EBITA-based multiples, as the latter can be distorted by tax differences across companies.

Exhibit 19.9 shows the EV-to-earnings multiples and underlying ROIC and growth for the competitors of ConsumerCo's branded-products business. Eliminated from the sample are two outliers with valuation multiples that are far above all other peers and not justified by their growth and return on capital. Note how the spread in the EBITA multiples is larger than that of the NOPAT multiples because of different company tax rates. NOPAT multiples are therefore a more reliable basis for the valuation.

[9] The implied cost of capital for ConsumerCo as a whole for each future year is around 8.8 percent. It can be derived by backing it out from the sum of the underlying business units' free cash flows and the sum of the discounted values of these free cash flows.

The overall average NOPAT multiple across the entire peer group is 18.0 times, which would suggest a significantly higher value than the DCF estimate (which has an implied NOPAT multiple of 16.0). But the peers in this group appear to be clustered in two groups with very different underlying returns and growth rates, making the overall average less meaningful. There is a group of leading players with outstanding returns and growth rates that are valued in the stock market at an average of 21.0 times NOPAT. Based on the multiple for this top peer group, ConsumerCo's branded-products business would be valued at $6,883 million, which would be a clear overestimation, given its actual performance and growth (see Exhibit 19.10). At best, it could represent what ConsumerCo's business would be worth if it were able to attain the economics of these leading players in the sector. In contrast, the players in the peer group with returns and growth rates closer to ConsumerCo's business have an average multiple of 15.6 times NOPAT, leading to a value estimate of $5,060 million, which is much closer to the DCF results.

Adopting the same approach of using close-peer multiples to value all of ConsumerCo's other segments, including ConsumerCo finance and the cosmetics joint venture, the estimated equity value is $8,774 million (Exhibit 19.10). Note that by using top-peer multiples for the valuation, ConsumerCo's value would be estimated some 30 percent higher than its DCF value, at $11,956 million. Showing the range of value estimates for close-peer and top-peer multiples helps to triangulate the DCF valuation results. In our experience, close-peer multiples typically lead to valuation results within

EXHIBIT 19.10 **ConsumerCo: Valuation with Multiples, January 2020**

		EV/NOPAT		Multiples-based value				
Business	NOPAT, $ million	Close peers	Top peers	Close peers, $ million	Delta to DCF, %	Top peers, $ million	Delta to DCF, %	DCF value, $ million
Branded products	325	15.6	21.0	5,060	-2	6,833	32	5,188
Private label	93	11.7	16.0	1,084	-4	1,482	31	1,128
Devices	102	14.0	19.5	1,422	-4	1,980	34	1,474
Organic products	134	24.5	26.5	3,285	-5	3,553	3	3,440
Corporate center	(54)			(1,123)		(1,123)		(1,123)
Eliminations	(2)	–	–	–		–		–
Total operations	597			9,727	-4	12,726	26	10,107
Customer finance	12[1]	12.0[1]	12.0[1]	149	0	149	0	150[2]
Cosmetics joint venture	81	17.0	22.0	589	-3	772	27	609[3]
Excess cash				250		250		250
Gross enterprise value				10,716	-4	13,897	25	11,117
Debt				(1,941)		(1,941)		(1,941)
Equity value				8,774	-4	11,956	30	9,175

[1] For customer finance, P/E and net income are shown.

[2] At equity value, net of debt in customer finance.

[3] At equity value of minority stake in cosmetics joint venture.

10 to 15 percent of the DCF outcomes—in other words, within the normal margin of error for any valuation.

However, many analysts and other practitioners often base their valuations on top-peer multiples. The valuation by parts then easily leads to a conclusion that a company suffers from a so-called conglomerate discount and a recommendation that it should be broken up into parts to unlock the valuation gap versus its peers.

The conclusion is as wrong as the recommendation. The discount simply reflects the fact that compared with its top peers, the company is at a lower valuation level because of lower performance. Splitting up the company does not automatically fix that performance gap (and might not even be needed).

Over the years, practitioners and academics have debated whether a conglomerate or diversification discount exists. In other words, does the market value conglomerates at less than the sum of their parts? Unfortunately, the results are incomplete. There is no consensus about whether diversified firms are valued at a discount relative to a portfolio of pure plays in similar businesses.[10] Some argue that they may even trade at a premium. Among studies that claim a discount, there is no consensus about whether the discount results from the weaker performance of diversified firms relative to more focused firms, or whether the market values diversified firms lower than focused firms.[11] In our experience, however, whenever we have examined a company valued at less than pure-play peers, the company's business units had lower growth and/or returns on capital relative to those peers. In other words, there was a performance discount, not a diversification or conglomerate discount.

SUMMARY

Many large companies have multiple business units, each competing in segments with different economic characteristics. Valuing such companies by their individual parts is standard practice in industry-leading companies and among sophisticated investors. Not only does it generate better valuation results, but it also produces deeper insights into where and how the company is generating value.

To value a company by its parts, you need statements of NOPAT, invested capital, and free cash flow that approximate what the business units would look like if they were stand-alone companies. In preparing such statements,

---

[10] P. Berger and E. Ofek, "Diversification's Effect on Firm Value," *Journal of Financial Economics* 37 (1995): 39–65; and B. Villalonga, "Diversification Discount or Premium? New Evidence from Business Information Tracking Series," *Journal of Finance* 59, no. 2 (April 2004): 479–506.

[11] A. Schoar, "Effects of Corporate Diversification on Productivity," *Journal of Finance* 57, no. 6 (2002): 2379–2403; and J. Chevalier, "What Do We Know about Cross-Subsidization? Evidence from the Investment Policies of Merging Firms" (working paper, University of Chicago, July 1999).

you likely have to separate out corporate center costs, deal with intercompany transactions, and make a separate equity-cash-flow valuation of any financial subsidiaries. Estimate the weighted average cost of capital for each business unit separately, based on the leverage and the betas of its most relevant peer companies.

To triangulate your DCF estimate, make a multiples-based valuation estimate for each individual unit. Make sure to use a peer group that closely matches the unit's return on capital and growth. In our experience, conclusions that a corporate group suffers from a so-called conglomerate discount are often the result of selecting a peer group with significantly higher returns on capital and growth.

Part Three

Advanced Valuation Techniques

20

Taxes

A good valuation begins with good housekeeping. Reorganize the company's income statement and balance sheet into three categories: operating, nonoperating, and financing items. The reorganized statements can then be used to estimate return on invested capital (ROIC) and free cash flow (FCF), which in turn drive the company's valuation.

One line item that incorporates all three categories is taxes. In this chapter, we explore the role of operating taxes in valuation and discuss how to use the notes in the annual report to estimate operating taxes and the operating tax rate. Since some companies can defer a portion of their reported taxes over long periods, we'll also go through the steps for converting operating taxes to operating cash taxes and, as a result, how to incorporate deferred taxes into a valuation.

ESTIMATING OPERATING TAXES

The operating tax rate is the tax rate a company would pay if the company generated only operating income and was financed entirely with equity. It is the best tax rate for estimating net operating profit after taxes (NOPAT), a key component of free cash flow. The operating tax rate is better suited than two well-known alternatives, the *statutory* tax rate and the *effective* tax rate. The statutory tax rate, which equals the domestic tax rate on a dollar of income, fails to account for differences in foreign tax rates and ongoing, operating-related tax credits. For a company that actively manages its tax burden, the statutory tax rate will often overestimate the taxes paid. In contrast, the effective tax rate, which equals income taxes divided by pretax income, includes too many nonoperating items, such as one-time audit resolutions. Because of these one-time nonoperating items, the effective tax rate can be quite volatile, making accurate tax forecasts challenging.

To determine operating taxes, it is necessary to remove the effects of non-operating and financing items from taxes reported on the income statement. This can be challenging because of the complexity of tax accounting and the need for data not often disclosed. We'll introduce a hypothetical company to show several ways to estimate operating taxes, as each approach requires assumptions to fill in gaps left by public financial statements.

To illuminate these trade-offs, we begin by estimating operating taxes when you have complete information, including information that is not typically disclosed to the public. Exhibit 20.1 presents the internal financial statements of a hypothetical global company, TaxCo, for a single year. TaxCo generated $2.2 billion in domestic earnings before interest, taxes, and amortization (EBITA) and $600 million in EBITA from foreign operations. TaxCo amortizes domestically held intangible assets of $400 million per year. The company finances operations with debt raised in its home country and deducts interest of $600 million on its domestic statements. It recently sold an asset held in a foreign country and recorded a gain of $100 million in that country. TaxCo pays a statutory tax rate of 25 percent on earnings before taxes at home and 15 percent on foreign operations.

TaxCo generates $40 million in *ongoing* research and development (R&D) tax credits (credits determined by the amount and location of the company's R&D activities), which are expected to grow as the company grows. It also has $24 million in *one-time* tax credits—in this case, a tax rebate from the successful resolution of a historical tax dispute. All told, TaxCo paid an effective tax rate on pretax profits of 17.9 percent, well below its statutory domestic rate of 25 percent.

EXHIBIT 20.1 **TaxCo: Income Statement by Geography**

$ million

	Domestic subsidiary	Foreign subsidiary	R&D tax credits	Resolution of tax dispute	Consolidated
EBITA[1]	2,200	600	–	–	2,800
Amortization	(400)	–	–	–	(400)
EBIT[1]	1,800	600	–	–	2,400
Interest expense	(600)	–			(600)
Gains on asset sales	–	100	–	–	100
Pretax profit	1,200	700	–	–	1,900
Income taxes	(300)	(105)	40	24	(341)
Net income	900	595	40	24	1,559
Tax rates, %					
Statutory tax rate	25.0	15.0			
Effective tax rate					17.9

[1] EBITA is earnings before interest, taxes, and amortization; EBIT is earnings before interest and taxes.

EXHIBIT 20.2 **TaxCo: Operating Taxes and NOPAT by Geography**

$ million

	Domestic subsidiary	Foreign subsidiary	R&D tax credits	Resolution of tax dispute	Consolidated
EBITA	2,200	600	–	–	2,800
Operating taxes	(550)	(90)	40	–	(600)
NOPAT[1]	1,650	510	–	–	2,160
Tax rates, %					
Statutory tax rate	25.0	15.0			
Operating tax rate					21.4

[1] Net operating profit after taxes.

As noted earlier, operating taxes are the taxes that would be paid by a company with only operating income and financed entirely with equity. Exhibit 20.2 calculates operating taxes and NOPAT for TaxCo. To determine operating taxes, apply the appropriate statutory tax rate to each jurisdiction's EBITA. (Although the interest tax shield is valuable, it is typically valued not as part of income, but as part of the weighted average cost of capital or valued separately in adjusted present value. And since amortization is typically nondeductible for tax purposes, it has no value. This is the rationale for the calculation being a function of EBITA.) In this case, multiply 25 percent by domestic EBITA of $2.2 billion and 15 percent by $600 million in foreign EBITA, which equals statutory taxes of $640 million. Since the $40 million in research and development (R&D) credits are related to operations and are expected to grow as the company grows, they are treated as operating. As a result, the company pays $600 million in operating taxes. To find the operating tax rate, divide operating taxes by global EBITA of $2.8 billion, for a rate of 21.4 percent.

Note how the statutory, effective, and operating taxes differ. The statutory tax rate on domestic income is 25.0 percent, the effective tax rate (shown in Exhibit 20.1) equals 17.9 percent, and the operating tax rate is 21.4 percent. The operating tax rate is the best tax rate for converting EBITA to NOPAT.

Using Public Statements to Estimate Operating Taxes

In practice, companies do not publicly disclose income by country. Instead, you must rely on a company-wide income statement and a tax reconciliation table. The tax reconciliation table can be found in the notes that accompany the financial statements. It explains why a company's reported taxes do not equal the product of pretax profit times the statutory rate. At the company's discretion, the table can express amounts in percentages or in the company's reporting currency.

EXHIBIT 20.3 **TaxCo: Operating Taxes Using a Tax Table Reported in Percent**

Tax reconciliation table		Operating taxes $ million	
Statutory tax rate	25.0%	EBITA	2,800
Foreign-income adjustment	(3.7%)	× Statutory tax rate	25.0%
R&D tax credits	(2.1%)	= Statutory taxes on EBITA	700
Resolution of tax dispute	(1.3%)		
Effective tax rate	17.9%	Foreign-income adjustment	(3.7%)
		R&D tax credit	(2.1%)
		Cumulative adjustments	(5.8%)
		× Pretax profit	1,900
		= Operating adjustments	(110)
		Operating taxes	590

To illustrate how such a table denoted in percentages explains the difference between statutory and effective rates, the left side of Exhibit 20.3 presents the tax reconciliation table for TaxCo. Because foreign income was taxed at 15 percent, TaxCo paid $70 million less in taxes than if it had been taxed at the domestic rate of 25 percent (i.e., it paid $105 million in taxes at 15 percent, rather than $175 million at 25 percent). To report this difference as a percent of pretax profit, the tax reconciliation table divides the $70 million by pretax profit of $1.9 billion to obtain 3.7 percent of pretax income. Each of the adjustments is divided by pretax profit to determine the corresponding percentages in the reconciliation table.

The right side of Exhibit 20.3 shows how to use the tax reconciliation table to estimate operating taxes in millions of dollars. Start by calculating statutory taxes on EBITA. Next, work through the table looking for line items that are ongoing and related to operations. Finally, add the statutory taxes on EBITA to the operating-related adjustments. The following paragraphs take a closer look at these steps.

To calculate statutory taxes on EBITA for TaxCo, multiply EBITA by the statutory tax rate: 25 percent times $2.8 billion equals $700 million.

Next, search the tax reconciliation table for tax adjustments that are ongoing and related to operations. The most common operating adjustments are state and foreign taxes. To determine if other adjustments are operating, look for consistency over time, and use the account description. Some account descriptions are cryptic, so an online search may shed light on the adjustment. For TaxCo, we classify R&D tax credits as operating and the resolution of past tax disputes as nonoperating.

To calculate cumulative operating adjustments for TaxCo, sum the foreign-income adjustment (3.7 percent) and the R&D tax credit (2.1 percent), and multiply the results by pretax profit, not EBITA. Use pretax profit because the company creates the tax reconciliation table using pretax profit, not EBITA.

EXHIBIT 20.4 **TaxCo: Operating Taxes Using a Tax Table Reported in Dollars**

$ million

Tax reconciliation table		Operating taxes	
Pretax profits at the statutory rate	475	Pretax profits at the statutory rate	475
Foreign-income adjustment	(70)	/ Pretax profit	1,900
R&D tax credits	(40)	= Statutory tax rate on EBITA	25.0%
Resolution of tax dispute	(24)		
Income taxes	341	× EBITA	2,800
		= Statutory taxes on EBITA	700
		Foreign-income adjustment	(70)
		R&D tax credit	(40)
		Estimated operating taxes	590

For TaxCo, operating adjustments equal $110 million. Subtracting $110 million from $700 million produces operating taxes of $590 million.[1]

While this method is effective, it is only an estimate. In our example, the calculation of $590 million using public reports does not match the internal results of $600 million generated in Exhibit 20.2. The difference is explained by the $100 million in gains that were taxed at 15 percent, not at the statutory rate of 25 percent. Had gains been taxed at 25 percent, the methodology in Exhibit 20.3 would have estimated operating taxes without error. Without access to internal financial statements, however, our analysis is limited.

If a company denotes the tax reconciliation table in its home currency, the process for calculating operating taxes follows the same principles, but differs slightly in implementation. The left side of Exhibit 20.4 presents the tax reconciliation table for TaxCo in millions of dollars. The first line item represents what the company would pay if pretax profit were taxed at the statutory tax rate. Often the company's statutory tax rate is reported in the text accompanying the table. However, if it is not, divide the line item by pretax profit to estimate the statutory tax rate.

With the statutory tax rate in hand, multiply EBITA by the statutory tax rate to determine statutory taxes on EBITA (see the right side of Exhibit 20.4). Next, work through the tax table for other operating adjustments. Since operating adjustments are already denoted in dollars, they can be transferred directly to the calculation of operating taxes. The process may vary, but our estimate of operating taxes remains unchanged.

---

[1] To estimate operating taxes, some professionals add the percentage-based operating adjustments directly to the statutory tax rate. While this method works in simple situations, it is not reliable. When a company has a large nonoperating expense such as an asset write-off, this will depress pretax profit, causing the percentage-based tax reconciliation items to spike. These spikes make historical analysis challenging and forecasting unreliable. As a result, we recommend adjusting statutory taxes using currency-based adjustments.

EXHIBIT 20.5 **Walmart: Tax Reconciliation Table**

%

	2016	2017	2018
U.S. statutory tax rate[1]	35.0	33.8	21.0
U.S. state income taxes	1.7	1.8	3.3
Impact of 2017 tax act			
One-time transition tax	—	12.3	3.6
Deferred tax effects	—	(14.1)	(0.7)
Income taxed outside the United States	(4.5)	(6.3)	(3.5)
Disposition of Walmart Brazil	—	—	6.7
Valuation allowance	—	2.1	6.4
Repatriated international earnings	(1.0)	(0.1)	0.8
Federal tax credits	(0.6)	(0.9)	(1.2)
Other, net	(0.3)	1.8	1.0
Effective income tax rate	30.3	30.4	37.4

[1] Walmart ends its fiscal year on January 31. Therefore, 2017 includes 11 months at a 35% statutory tax rate and 1 month at 21%.

Operating Taxes at Walmart   To provide a real-world example, Exhibit 20.5 presents the tax reconciliation table for the discount retailer Walmart. In its tax reconciliation table, Walmart expresses its adjustments to the statutory tax rate as percentages. As is the case for all American companies during this period, Walmart's tax reconciliation table includes several adjustments related to recent tax law changes in the United States. The 2017 Tax Cuts and Jobs Act (TCJA) reduced the U.S. corporate income tax rate from 35 percent to 21 percent in 2018.[2] Since Walmart ends its fiscal year on January 31 of the following year, the 2017 fiscal year includes one month of profit at the new tax rate.

In Exhibit 20.6, we use the tax reconciliation table to estimate operating taxes for Walmart using the process described earlier in this section. We do not present the company's income statement but use EBITA and pretax profit as needed. The following paragraphs detail these steps.

To begin, multiply the statutory tax rate by EBITA. In 2018, for example, statutory taxes on EBITA equaled $4,611 million for Walmart. Next, adjust statutory taxes for other operating items. The first two operating adjustments in this step are state and foreign income taxes. While we could have netted these two percentages directly against the statutory rate for simplicity, we instead convert them to dollar amounts, using pretax profit. We do this because the 2018 write-off of Brazilian operations depressed pretax profit, causing the adjustment for state taxes to spike in percentage terms (see Exhibit 20.5). We also treat federal tax credits as operating. While Walmart does not disclose the nature of these credits, they appear with consistency, so we consider them ongoing.

[2] The TCJA includes many changes to U.S. corporate tax law. Some deductions, such as the domestic production activities deduction (known as DPAD), were eliminated. New minimum tax thresholds, such as the global intangible low-tax income (GILTI), were introduced.

EXHIBIT 20.6 **Walmart: Operating Taxes**

$ million

	2016	2017	2018
Statutory tax rate	35.0%	33.8%	21.0%
× EBITA	22,764	20,437	21,957
= Statutory taxes on EBITA	7,967	6,908	4,611
U.S. state income taxes	1.7%	1.8%	3.3%
Income taxed outside the United States	(4.5%)	(6.3%)	(3.5%)
Federal tax credits	(0.6%)	(0.9%)	(1.2%)
Other operating taxes	(3.4%)	(5.4%)	(1.4%)
× Earnings before taxes (EBT)	20,497	15,123	11,460
= Other operating taxes	(697)	(817)	(160)
Operating taxes	7,271	6,091	4,451
Operating tax rate[1]	31.9%	29.8%	20.3%

[1] Operating taxes divided by EBITA.

We treat the remaining adjustments in Exhibit 20.5 as nonoperating. These include one-time taxes related to the reduction in the U.S. tax rate, the disposition in Brazil, and repatriation of past earnings. Because they are nonoperating, they do not factor into the calculation of operating taxes and the operating tax rate in Exhibit 20.6.

On an aggregate basis, the three adjustments included in Exhibit 20.6 lower statutory taxes on EBITA by 1.4 percentage points in 2018. Multiplying this percentage by earnings before taxes gives us a negative adjustment of $160 million, resulting in operating taxes of $4,451 million. Dividing the amount of operating taxes by EBITA of $21,957 million leads to an operating tax rate of 20.3 percent in 2018, slightly below the statutory rate of 21 percent.

CONVERTING OPERATING TAXES TO OPERATING CASH TAXES

In the previous section, we estimated operating taxes on an accrual basis. For most companies, especially growing companies, the taxes reported on the income statement will not reflect the actual cash taxes paid, because of differences in accounting rules versus tax rules. For instance, tax rules allow for accelerated depreciation of physical assets, whereas financial accounting typically uses straight-line depreciation. With higher expenses and lower pretax profits on its tax books, companies can significantly delay or perhaps even perpetually postpone paying accrual-based taxes. For companies that consistently defer or prepay taxes, we recommend using cash-based operating taxes, which we call operating cash taxes. (In the case of low-growth companies, deferred-tax accounts may rise and fall unpredictably. If the operating

EXHIBIT 20.7 **Walmart: Deferred-Tax Assets and Liabilities**

$ million

	2017	2018
Deferred-tax assets		
Loss and tax credit carryforwards	1,989	2,964
Accrued liabilities	2,482	2,135
Share-based compensation	217	245
Other	1,251	1,131
Total deferred-tax assets	5,939	6,475
Valuation allowances	(1,843)	(2,448)
Deferred-tax assets, net of allowances	4,096	4,027
Deferred-tax liabilities		
Accelerated depreciation[1]	(3,954)	(4,175)
Acquired intangibles	(401)	(2,099)
Inventory	(1,153)	(1,354)
Other	(540)	(899)
Total deferred-tax liabilities	(6,048)	(8,527)
Deferred-tax assets, net of liabilities	(1,952)	(4,500)

[1] Reported as property and equipment in the annual report.

cash tax rate is volatile, do not adjust for deferrals in order to benchmark historical performance. Instead, use the operating tax rate on an accrual basis.)

To convert operating taxes to operating cash taxes, start with operating taxes and add the increase (or subtract the decrease) in *operating-related* deferred-tax assets net of deferred-tax liabilities.[3] Since deferred taxes on the balance sheet include both operating and nonoperating items, we need to separate them. To do this, search the notes for a detailed listing of deferred taxes.

Exhibit 20.7 presents the deferred-tax table for Walmart, found in note 9 of the company's annual report. Deferred-tax assets (DTAs) are presented in the upper portion of the table. Walmart recognizes a valuation allowance against tax assets because some tax assets are unlikely to be realized. In the lower portion of the table are deferred-tax liabilities (DTLs). The table concludes by netting deferred-tax liabilities against deferred-tax assets.

Exhibit 20.8 reorganizes deferred-tax assets and liabilities into operating and nonoperating items. Walmart has four deferred-tax accounts related to operations: accrued liabilities, share-based compensation, accelerated depreciation, and inventory. One of these, accrued liabilities, includes things like membership fees, which are collected from the customer upfront but recorded as income over the life of the membership. The government recognizes income when the cash is collected, but the accounting statements recognize income over

[3] Given the complexity of today's deferred-tax accounting, adjusting taxes by the change in aggregate deferred taxes is insufficient for calculating free cash flow. For Coca-Cola in 2018, 85 percent of the increase in deferred tax assets was attributable to a restatement of their value due to an accounting change, rather than the actual prepayment of taxes.

EXHIBIT 20.8 **Walmart: Reorganization of Deferred-Tax Accounts**

$ million

	2017	2018
Operating deferred-tax assets (DTAs), net of liabilities (DTLs)		
Accrued liabilities	2,482	2,135
Share-based compensation	217	245
Accelerated depreciation	(3,954)	(4,175)
Inventory	(1,153)	(1,354)
Operating DTAs, net of DTLs	(2,408)	(3,149)
Nonoperating deferred-tax assets (DTAs), net of liabilities (DTLs)		
Loss and tax credit carryforwards	1,989	2,964
Valuation allowances	(1,843)	(2,448)
Loss carryforwards, net of allowances	146	516
Acquired intangibles	(401)	(2,099)
Other assets net of liabilities	711	232
Nonoperating DTAs, net of DTLs	456	(1,351)
DTAs, net of DTLs	(1,952)	(4,500)

time, so a deferred-tax asset is created. As a result, for Walmart and for other growing companies in this situation, cash taxes are higher than reported on the income statement.

Another operating item, accelerated depreciation, is a deferred-tax liability. It is a liability as a result of Walmart using straight-line depreciation for its financial statements and accelerated depreciation for its tax returns (because larger depreciation expenses lead to lower pretax income and hence smaller taxes). For a growing company, accelerated depreciation is typically larger than straight-line depreciation, so accrual-based taxes typically overstate the actual cash taxes paid.

As shown in Exhibit 20.8, operating-related deferred-tax liabilities (such as those associated with accelerated depreciation) should be netted against deferred-tax assets (such as those related to accrued liabilities). This reorganization will make the components of operating taxes, the reorganized balance sheet, and ultimately the final valuation more transparent and less prone to error.

The remaining items in Exhibit 20.8 are classified as nonoperating. Walmart has three nonoperating deferred-tax accounts:

1. *Loss carryforwards net of allowances.* When a company loses money, it does not receive a cash reimbursement from the government (as negative taxes in the income statement would imply), but rather an offset toward future taxes. Given that these offsets are unrelated to current profitability, they should be analyzed and valued separately from operations. Because most of the offsets are trapped in a particular tax jurisdiction and unlikely to be realized, we net the valuation allowance against the loss carryforwards.

2. *Acquired intangibles.* When a company buys another company, such as Walmart's purchase of Flipkart in 2018, it recognizes intangible assets on its balance sheet for items such as patents and customer lists.[4] Since these assets are amortized on the income statement but are not deductible for tax purposes, the company will record a deferred tax liability during the year of the acquisition and then draw down the liability as the intangible amortizes. Since operating taxes (computed in Exhibit 20.6) already exclude the amortization tax benefit in calculating NOPAT, no adjustment is required for deferrals related to these intangible assets. Instead, treat deferred taxes related to amortization of intangibles as nonoperating.

3. *Other nonoperating assets net of liabilities.* Other examples of nonoperating deferred taxes are deferred taxes related to pensions or convertible debt. Without further disclosure, classifying other accounts is tricky. Since we did not see a consistent pattern in other deferred taxes, we treat them as nonoperating.

To convert accrual-based operating taxes into operating cash taxes, add the increase in operating DTAs net of operating DTLs to operating taxes. In most cases, DTLs will exceed DTAs, so this is equivalent to subtracting the increase in operating DTLs net of operating DTAs. For Walmart, net operating DTLs grow from $2,408 million in 2017 to $3,149 million in 2018, an increase of $741 million (see Exhibit 20.8). Subtracting the $741 million from 2018 operating taxes of $4,451 million (computed in Exhibit 20.6) gives $3,710 million of operating cash taxes:

$ million	2018
Operating taxes	4,451
Decrease (increase) in net operating DTLs	(741)
Operating cash taxes	3,710

The operating cash tax rate for 2018 equals operating cash taxes of $3,710 million divided by EBITA of $21,957 million (given in Exhibit 20.6), which equals 16.9 percent. Because of the operating deferrals, operating cash taxes are approximately 17 percent lower than operating taxes on an accrual basis. The operating cash tax rate can be applied to forecasts of EBITA when projecting future free cash flow.

Once the estimation of cash taxes is complete, analyze the results. For instance, a significant portion of the change in operating-related deferred taxes for Walmart was driven by a decline in the accrued liabilities DTA. Ask

[4] Under current accounting standards, the premium paid in an acquisition is split between goodwill and other intangible assets (acquired intangibles). Acquired intangibles include identifiable and separable assets like patents, copyrights, product formulas, and customer lists. Unlike goodwill, acquired intangibles are amortized over their estimated lives.

yourself if the decline is sustainable or perhaps the result of a one-time reduction in benefits, such as new limitations on accrued vacation. Include only ongoing, operating-related differences in your forecast cash taxes and ultimately free cash flow.

DEFERRED TAXES ON THE REORGANIZED BALANCE SHEET

One critical component of a well-structured valuation model is a properly reorganized balance sheet. As outlined in Chapter 11, the accounting balance sheet is reorganized into invested capital, nonoperating items, and sources of financing. Since operating DTAs and DTLs flow through NOPAT via cash taxes, they are considered equity equivalents. Why equity? When we convert accrual taxes to cash taxes, income is adjusted, and the difference becomes part of retained earnings, making it an equity equivalent. As discussed in Chapter 11, equity equivalents are not part of invested capital. If operating DTAs and DTLs were mistakenly included as part of invested capital, they could be double-counted in free cash flow: once in NOPAT via cash taxes and again when taking the change in invested capital.

Exhibit 20.9 presents a reorganized balance sheet that includes the deferred-tax items from Exhibit 20.8. Equity equivalents, which appear in the equity section of total funds invested (the right side of Exhibit 20.9), include all deferred-tax accounts, except for loss carryforwards and nondeductible intangibles, which appear elsewhere. In 2018, Walmart's equity equivalents equaled $2,917 million. This amount consists of negative $3,149 million in operating DTAs net of DTLs, plus $232 million from other DTAs net of other DTLs. Because we record the result in the equity section (and not as an asset), we reverse the sign.

EXHIBIT 20.9 **Walmart: Treatment of Deferred Taxes on the Reorganized Balance Sheet**

$ million

Total funds invested: Uses	2017	2018	Total funds invested: Sources	2017	2018
Working capital	(9,195)	(7,750)	Short-term borrowing	5,257	5,225
Property, plant, and equipment	114,818	111,395	Debt due within one year	4,405	2,605
Other assets, net of liabilities	5,396	7,341	Long-term debt	36,825	50,203
Invested capital, excluding intangibles	111,019	110,986	Debt and debt equivalents	46,487	58,033
Acquired intangibles	18,242	31,181	➤ Deferred-tax liabilities, net[1]	1,697	2,917
➤ Less: Nondeductible intangibles	(401)	(2,099)	Noncontrolling interest	2,953	7,138
Acquired intangibles, net of gross-up	17,841	29,082	Walmart shareholders' equity	77,869	72,496
			Equity and equity equivalents	82,519	82,551
Invested capital, including intangibles	128,860	140,068			
➤ Tax loss carryforwards	146	516	Total funds invested	129,006	140,584
Total funds invested	129,006	140,584			

[1] Deferred-tax liabilities (net of assets), excluding tax loss carryforwards and deferred taxes related to acquired intangibles.

Two nonoperating deferred-tax accounts will not be classified as equity equivalents: tax loss carryforwards and deferred taxes related to acquired intangibles. The DTA for tax loss carryforwards ($516 million in 2018) shows up as a nonoperating asset and should be valued separately. The deferred-tax liability related to the acquired intangibles ($2,099 million) is treated as an offset to the intangible asset itself, since the asset was grossed up for nondeductible amortization when the asset was created.

Why deduct deferred taxes for intangible assets from acquired intangibles? When a company buys another company, it typically recognizes as intangible assets those intangibles that are separable and identifiable (such as patents). These intangible assets are amortized over their estimated life on the GAAP income statement. But since, in most countries, the amortization is not deductible for tax purposes, a mismatch will occur. As a result, the company creates a deferred-tax liability when it makes the acquisition. To keep the balance sheet balanced, the company also increases intangible assets (known in accounting as "grossing up") by the size of the new DTL. Since the grossed-up intangible and DTL are purely accounting conventions and do not reflect cash transactions, they should be eliminated from the analysis of intangible assets and deferred taxes.

To apply this offset for 2018 in Exhibit 20.9, we subtract the deferred-tax liability of $2,099 million from acquired intangibles of $31,181 million. As shown with the uses of funds on the left side the exhibit, this results in adjusted intangibles of $29,082 million. By calculating taxes on EBITA and subtracting the DTL from acquired intangibles, we have essentially converted accrual taxes to the cash taxes actually paid.

Finding Deferred Taxes on the Balance Sheet

One practical difficulty with DTAs and DTLs is finding them. Sometimes they are explicitly listed on the balance sheet, but often they are embedded within other assets and other liabilities. Check the tax footnote for embedded items. For instance, in the notes to its 2018 annual report, Walmart discloses that it embeds $1,796 million in deferred-tax assets in "other long-term assets."

VALUING DEFERRED TAXES

As noted in the previous section, any deferred-tax assets and liabilities classified as operating are incorporated into operating cash taxes. As such, they flow through NOPAT and free cash flow, so they are already embedded in the value of operations. In contrast, the valuation process for nonoperating deferred taxes depends on the particulars of the account.

The valuation of tax loss carryforwards depends on the information provided. If details are elusive, apply the reported valuation allowance against the loss carryforward. If information allows, apply past losses against projections of future income to estimate the timing of tax savings. Discount these cash flows at an appropriate cost of capital, such as the unlevered cost of equity. Be careful to check with local tax experts, since the statutes governing tax loss carryforwards are complex. Also keep in mind that tax loss carryforwards are country specific. A company with tax loss carryforwards in one country cannot use the benefit against profits in another country. For more on tax loss carryforwards and how to value them, see Chapter 16.

Deferred-tax liabilities related to acquired intangibles are netted against intangible assets and ignored. As described in the previous section, amortization is noncash and, in many countries, nondeductible. Thus, amortization and its corresponding deferred-tax liability have no effect on cash flow.[5]

To value the remaining deferred-tax accounts, including pensions and convertible debt, turn to their corresponding accounts. How you will do this depends on the nuances of the account. As an example, deferred taxes related to pensions arise when pension expense differs from the cash contribution. But the deferred-tax account recognized on the balance sheet reflects accumulated *historical* differences, not future tax savings. Therefore, to value the tax shield associated with unfunded pensions, multiply the current unfunded liability by the marginal tax rate (that is, the expected tax savings attributable to funding the shortfall). We can do this because under U.S. law, cash contributions to close gaps in funding are tax deductible.

Regardless of the deferred-tax account, never use the book value of the account to approximate value. Deferred-tax accounts reflect past differences between accounting and tax statements. They reflect neither future cash flows nor the present value of those flows.

CLOSING THOUGHTS

Accounting for taxes is complex and can be daunting for even the most seasoned professional. However, given the number of companies whose operating tax rates consistently differ from both the statutory tax rate and the effective tax rate, a careful assessment of the operating tax rate is critical to an accurate valuation.

If you are confused about a particular line item in the tax reconciliation table, rely on the general principles of this book by asking two questions: First,

---

[5] Some treat the deferred-tax liability as operating and embed it in free cash flow using the following logic. First, operating taxes are calculated on EBIT, not EBITA. If amortization is not deductible, the resulting estimate for taxes is too low. As the deferred-tax liability declines, this implies a negative cash flow. This decline offsets the amortization tax shield generated by using EBIT. However, since we compute operating taxes on EBITA, we ignore the amortization tax shield and consequently do not apply the offset.

is the item ongoing and related to core operations? Second, does the item materially change your perception of the company's performance or valuation? Finally, when converting from operating taxes to cash operating taxes, always assess whether the deferral rate is reasonable and can be continued. Perhaps an acquisition is causing an artificial jump in a deferred-tax account, making the deferral rate uncharacteristically high. If so, use long-term trends to forecast future deferral rates.

21

Nonoperating Items, Provisions, and Reserves

To project free cash flow, you would typically focus on operating expenses, such as cost of sales, distribution expenses, selling expenses, and administrative expenses. But what about nonoperating expenses, such as business realignment expenses, goodwill impairment, and extraordinary items?

Nonoperating expenses are infrequent or unusual charges that are indirectly related to the company's typical activities and not expected to recur. The conventional wisdom is that discounted-cash-flow (DCF) calculations should ignore nonoperating expenses as backward-looking, one-time costs. Yet research shows that the type and accounting treatment of nonoperating expenses can affect future cash flow and in certain situations must be incorporated into your valuation.

This chapter analyzes the most common nonoperating expenses. These include the amortization of acquired intangibles, restructuring charges, unusual charges such as litigation expenses, asset write-offs, and goodwill impairments. Since noncash expenses will be accompanied by a corresponding provision, we create a classification system of various provisions and describe the process for reorganizing the income statement and balance sheet to reflect the true effect of such provisions, if any, on company value. We show how to treat provisions in free cash flow and equity valuation.

NONOPERATING EXPENSES AND ONE-TIME CHARGES

Given their infrequent nature, nonoperating expenses and one-time charges can distort a company's historical financial performance and consequently distort our view of the future. It is therefore critical to separate one-time nonoperating expenses from ongoing operating expenses. The idea sounds simple, but implementing it can be tricky. Nonoperating expenses are often spread across the income statement, and some are hidden within other accounts and can be discovered only by searching the company's notes. Even after you've properly identified nonoperating expenses, the job is not done. Each nonoperating expense must be carefully analyzed to determine its impact on future cash flow, and if necessary, forecasts must be adjusted to reflect any information embedded in the expense.

To assess the impact of nonoperating expenses and incorporate their information in cash flow forecasts, we recommend a three-step process:

1. *Separate operating from nonoperating items.* This process requires judgment. As a general rule, treat items that grow in line with revenues and are related to running the core business as operating. For line items that are lumpy but only tangentially related to core operations, test the impact of each line item on long-term ROIC.

2. *Search the notes for embedded one-time items.* Not every one-time charge will be separately disclosed on the income statement. Sometimes the management discussion and analysis section of the annual report will disclose additional information on one-time items.

3. *Analyze each nonoperating item for its impact on future operations.* Line items not included in earnings before interest, taxes, and amortization (EBITA) will not be included in free cash flow (FCF), so they are not part of core operating value. Therefore, it is critical to analyze each nonoperating line item separately and determine whether the charge is likely to continue in the future, in which case it should be incorporated into FCF projections.

Separating Operating from Nonoperating Expenses

Many companies include a line item on their income statement that reads "Operating income (loss)" or "Operating profit/loss." For example, in Exhibit 21.1, the income statement for Boston Scientific shows that in 2018 the company reported an operating profit of $1.5 billion. But is this profit an accurate reflection of the company's long-run earnings potential? The accounting definition of operating profit differs from our definition of EBITA, in that the accounting standards for classifying items as nonoperating (i.e., to be recorded below operating profit or loss) are extremely strict. To benchmark core operations effectively, EBITA and net operating profit after taxes (NOPAT) should include only items related to the ongoing core business, regardless of their classification by accounting standards.

EXHIBIT 21.1 **Boston Scientific: Income Statement**

$ million

Accounting income statement[1]	2016	2017	2018	Reorganized income statement	2016	2017	2018
Net sales	8,386	9,048	9,823	Net sales	8,386	9,048	9,823
Cost of products sold	(2,424)	(2,593)	(2,813)	Cost of products sold	(2,424)	(2,593)	(2,813)
Gross profit	5,962	6,455	7,010	Gross profit	5,962	6,455	7,010
SG&A expense	(3,099)	(3,294)	(3,569)	SG&A expense	(3,099)	(3,294)	(3,569)
R&D expense	(920)	(997)	(1,113)	R&D expense	(920)	(997)	(1,113)
Royalty expense	(79)	(68)	(70)	Royalty expense	(79)	(68)	(70)
Amortization expense	(545)	(565)	(599)	EBITA	1,864	2,096	2,258
Intangible-asset impairment charges	(11)	(4)	(35)				
Contingent consideration benefit	(29)	80	21				
Restructuring charges	(28)	(37)	(36)				
Litigation-related charges	(804)	(285)	(103)				
Operating income (loss)	447	1,285	1,506				

[1] As reported in the Boston Scientific 2018 annual report.

Boston Scientific reports several so-called operating expenses that are in fact nonoperating. Amortization of intangibles ($599 million in 2018) and intangible-asset impairment charges ($35 million) are all noncash reductions in the value of intangible assets; they differ only in their timing and regularity. Other nonoperating expenses include contingent consideration benefit ($21 million), restructuring charges ($36 million), and litigation-related charges ($103 million). For valuation purposes, such nonoperating expenses should not be deducted from revenue to determine EBITA.

The right side of Exhibit 21.1 presents the calculation of EBITA for Boston Scientific. Only operating expenses that grow in line with revenue— such as cost of products sold; selling, general, and administrative (SG&A) expense; research and development (R&D) expense; and royalty expense—are included in the calculation of EBITA. Note how the accounting definition of operating income grows dramatically, while the growth in EBITA is much more measured.

As noted earlier, judgment is called for in classifying items as operating or nonoperating. Operating expenses tend to be ongoing and tied to revenue, so a long-term perspective is critical. For instance, treat a plant closure that occurs once in ten years as nonoperating. Conversely, for a retailer with hundreds of stores, treat expenses related to closing stores each year as operating.

For Boston Scientific, we classify royalty payments as operating because royalties are a fundamental part of the medical-devices industry and grow in line with revenue. In contrast, litigation expenses are sporadic and come in waves. Exhibit 21.2 presents litigation expenses for Boston Scientific between 2004 and 2018. While litigation expenses have been declining over the last three years, this trend does not capture the long-term levels. We could treat the litigation expenses as operating, but this would depress ROIC during

EXHIBIT 21.2 **Boston Scientific: Litigation Expenses by Year**

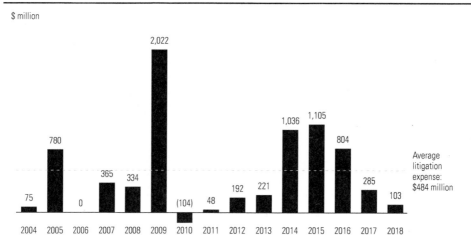

\$ million

Source: Boston Scientific annual reports.

periods when the expenses were recognized, rather than in the years when the corresponding benefits were reaped. At the same time, litigation expenses are real, so a valuation of Boston Scientific must incorporate them. Although time-consuming, an analysis of the company's current exposure to litigation and an analysis of average litigation expenses across all medical-technology companies could provide valuable insights.

When classification is unclear, measure ROIC with and without the expense. If the expense is lumpy, smooth the expense over the period in which the expense was generated.

Searching the Notes for Hidden One-Time Items

The income statement does not explicitly report every nonoperating expense or one-time charge. These can also be embedded in cost of sales or selling expenses. To find embedded expenses, read the management discussion and analysis section in the company's annual report. The section details the changes in cost of sales and other expenses from year to year and will sometimes report unusual items. In 2011, Boston Scientific reported such an expense:

During the first quarter of 2011, we reversed \$20 million of previously established allowances for doubtful accounts against long-outstanding receivables in Greece. During the first quarter of 2011, the Greek government converted these receivables into bonds, which we were able to monetize, reducing our allowance for doubtful accounts as a credit to selling, general and administrative expenses.

Whether you make an adjustment to NOPAT for such an expense depends on whether the charge is large enough to affect perceptions of performance. If it is not, don't bother. An adjustment could make your analysis overly complex and time-consuming.

Analyzing Each Nonoperating Item for Impact on Future Operations

In Kimberly-Clark's 2018 annual report, the company writes, "The 2018 Global Restructuring Program will reduce our structural cost base by streamlining and simplifying our manufacturing supply chain and overhead organization. The restructuring is expected to generate annual pre-tax cost savings of $500 to $550 [million] by the end of 2021." If credible, such projections should be incorporated into your forecast of future cash flow.

More broadly, academic researchers have been examining the predictive component of special items and one-time charges. Early research pointed to the low persistence of special items, indicating that they are in fact transitory and should not be incorporated into forecasts. However, this research examined persistence only on a year-to-year basis. In 2009, researchers extended the window to multiple years and found persistence in special items for companies with strong core profits.[1] In other words, a highly profitable company that reports a series of, say, restructuring charges is likely to continue with similar charges in the future. Persistence was low for companies with little operating profit.

One reason special items may persist year after year for profitable companies is that management may be shifting ongoing operating costs into special items to meet certain earnings targets, as many academic researchers believe they do. This belief also appears common among research analysts, as they decrease their earnings forecasts following the disclosure of a special item.[2] Although the research showing that special items are used to manage earnings is persuasive, it remains unclear how to relate the research results to an individual company. Judgment is required: pay close attention to companies disclosing special items. If the special items seem likely to recur, especially in a challenging economy, adjust your forecasts accordingly.

A comprehensive list of nonoperating items and one-time charges is impractical, but the following items are the most common: amortization of acquired intangibles; asset write-offs, including write-offs of goodwill and purchased R&D; restructuring charges; litigation charges; and gains and losses on asset sales. Since each of these nonoperating items requires a particular adjustment, we will work through them one by one.

---

[1] P. M. Fairfield, K. A. Kitching, and V. W. Tang, "Are Special Items Informative about Future Profit Margins?" *Review of Accounting Studies* 14, nos. 2–3 (2009): 204–236.
[2] N. Li, H. Su, W. Dong, and K. Zhu, "The Effect of Non-recurring Items on Analysts' Earnings Forecasts," *China Journal of Accounting Research* 11, no. 1 (2018): 21–31.

Amortization of Acquired Intangibles Although accounting standards require amortization of acquired intangibles, in most circumstances you should *not* deduct amortization from operating profit to determine NOPAT. As an alternative to expensing amortization, use EBITA (not EBIT) to determine operating profits. Since amortization is excluded from operating profit, remember to include the cumulative excluded amortization in your total for intangible assets on the balance sheet. A corresponding entry should be made to equity (titled "cumulative amortization") to balance total funds invested.

Why not amortize intangibles, particularly since we include depreciation in our calculation of ROIC? The idea of recognizing an intangible asset and then amortizing its use over a useful life is a good one. Yet current accounting standards do not allow companies to take this approach consistently across all intangibles. Today, only *acquired* intangibles are capitalized and amortized, while *internally generated* intangible assets, such as brand and distribution networks, are expensed when they are created. Thus, the EBIT of a company that acquires an intangible asset and then replenishes the asset through internal investment will be penalized twice on its financial statements, once through SG&A expenses and again through amortization. In fact, expensing the creation of new intangible assets while amortizing old intangibles would be tantamount to including both capital expenditures and depreciation on the income statement, a clearly undesirable characteristic. For valuation purposes, avoid mixing amortization and expensing by maintaining goodwill and acquired intangibles at their original values. To do this, compute operating profit before amortization, and add cumulative amortization to the current value of goodwill and intangible assets.

Exhibit 21.3 demonstrates the effect of amortizing acquired intangibles on margins for three companies in the pharmaceuticals industry. Based on EBIT margin, it appears as if the three companies have nearly identical performance. The amortization of acquired intangibles, however, is distorting our perspective. Pfizer has been extremely active in acquiring companies and

EXHIBIT 21.3 **EBIT and EBITA Margins in the Pharmaceuticals Industry, 2018**

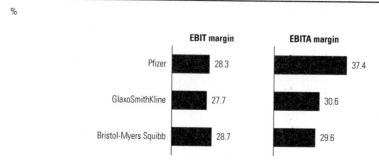

products, including the 2016 purchases of Medivation and Anacor. Stripping out amortization from these and other acquisitions reveals that Pfizer outperformed these peers by roughly seven percentage points.

One situation in which it is appropriate to deduct amortization is when intangibles can be capitalized (versus expensed) consistently. Consider a company that has no sales force and instead purchases customer contacts from a third party. Since sales outlays are never expensed via SG&A, they should be amortized to arrive at a meaningful measure of operating profitability. Otherwise, the income statement would not accurately reflect the cost of selling. Another example is the purchase of frequency rights by telecom companies. Since these assets can be capitalized and amortized without exception, treat them no differently than fixed equipment and depreciation.

Asset Write-Offs   If the value of an asset falls below its book value, accounting standards dictate that the asset should be written down (sometimes entirely) to its fair value. Although write-downs and write-offs give lenders insight into the diminished value of their collateral, the resulting balance sheet value understates the historical investment made by shareholders. Thus, ROIC can artificially rise following a write-down. To counteract this effect, treat asset write-downs and write-offs as nonoperating, and *add* cumulative write-downs to invested capital. To balance total funds invested, create a corresponding equity equivalent.

Two categories of asset write-offs are common:

1. *Asset write-offs.* In general, treat an asset write-off as nonoperating. In the rare cases when they occur systematically, treat them as operating. Add back write-downs to the asset, except when you are estimating capital turnover to project future capital needs. In this case, compute the ratio in a manner that best reflects future capital needs.

2. *Goodwill and intangibles impairments.* Treat goodwill and other intangibles impairments as nonoperating and add back cumulative impairments to goodwill on the balance sheet. Since the purpose of computing ROIC with goodwill is to measure historical performance *including* all past acquisition premiums, goodwill should remain at its original level.

Restructuring Charges   As business changes, companies must adapt. Major changes often require plant closures, employee layoffs, inventory write-downs, asset write-offs, and other restructuring charges. If a restructuring charge is unlikely to recur, treat the charge as nonoperating. If, however, a pattern of ongoing restructuring charges emerges, further analysis is required. Exhibit 21.4 presents the restructuring charges for Boston Scientific between 2009 and 2018. During this period, Boston Scientific's restructuring charges averaged

EXHIBIT 21.4 **Boston Scientific: EBITA and Restructuring Charges**

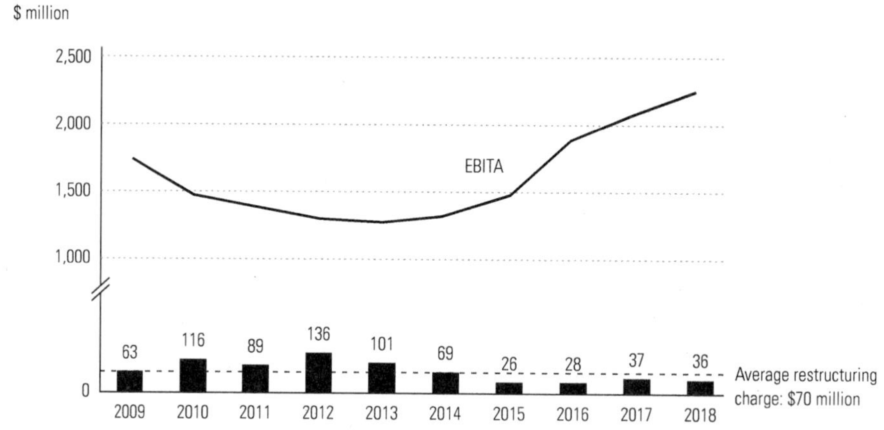

Source: Boston Scientific annual reports.

$70 million per year, or 0.9 percent of revenues. These expenses are reported separately from cost of sales and SG&A.

Given their persistence, Boston Scientific's restructuring charges should be analyzed to determine what portion of them represents cash (such as severance payments), whether any cash restructuring charges are likely to continue, and for how long. To this end, a careful reading of the company's notes reveals the following:

> In November 2018, the Board of Directors approved, and we committed to, a new global restructuring program (the 2019 Restructuring Plan). The 2019 Restructuring Plan is expected to result in total pre-tax charges of approximately $200 million to $300 million and reduce gross annual pre-tax operating expenses by approximately $100 million to $150 million by the end of 2022 as program benefits are realized.

Many restructuring charges are recorded before any cash is spent. If this is the case, a corresponding reserve will be recorded in the liabilities section of the balance sheet. In the next main section, we consider treatment of various reserves, including those related to restructuring charges.

Litigation Charges When there is likely to be a legal judgment against a company, the company will recognize a litigation charge. If the litigation charge recurs frequently and grows with revenue, treat the charge as operating. For instance, hospital systems frequently defend themselves against malpractice lawsuits. Since these lawsuits are a cost of doing business, the litigation costs should be treated as operating costs for valuation and projected forward. However, if a litigation cost is truly a one-time expense, treat it as nonoperating, and value any claims against the company separately from core operations.

Gains and Losses on Asset Sales   When an asset's sale price differs from its book value, the company will recognize a gain or loss. Since current gains and losses are backward-looking (value has been created or destroyed in the past), treat them as nonoperating. Additionally, double-check to make sure projected free cash flow does not incorporate the asset recently sold. For instance, make sure future depreciation reflects only the remaining assets.

Although gains and losses should not be included in operating profit, past asset sales may provide insight about the level of cash to be generated by future asset sales. Again, be careful to value future asset sales (and their corresponding gains and losses) only when the assets are not incorporated in free cash flow. Otherwise, the resulting double-counting will overstate the company's value.

PROVISIONS AND THEIR CORRESPONDING RESERVES

Provisions are noncash expenses that reflect future costs or expected losses. Companies take provisions by reducing current income and setting up a corresponding reserve as a liability (or deducting the amount from the relevant asset).

For the purpose of analyzing and valuing a company, we categorize provisions into one of four types: ongoing operating provisions, long-term operating provisions, nonoperating provisions like restructuring provisions, or provisions created for the purpose of smoothing income (transferring income from one period to another). Based on the characteristics of each provision, adjust the financial statements to reflect the company's true operating performance. For example, ongoing operating provisions are treated the same way as any other operating expense, whereas restructuring provisions are converted from an accrual to a cash basis and treated as nonoperating. Exhibit 21.5 summarizes the four types of provisions and how to treat them in NOPAT, invested capital, and valuation.

We believe our classification system of reserves leads to better analysis, but the way you adjust the financial statements should not affect the company's valuation. The valuation depends solely on how and when cash flows through the business, not on accrual-based accounting.

Adjustments for the Provisions

In Exhibit 21.6, we present the abbreviated financial statements for a hypothetical company that recognizes four provisions: an environmental provision

EXHIBIT 21.5 **Treatment of Provisions and Reserves**

Classification	Examples	Treatment in NOPAT[1]	Treatment in invested capital	Treatment in valuation
Ongoing operating provisions	Product returns and warranties	Deduct provisions from revenue to determine NOPAT.	Deduct reserve from operating assets to determine invested capital.	Provision is part of free cash flow.
Long-term operating provisions	Plant decommissioning costs and unfunded retirement plans	Deduct operating portion from revenue to determine NOPAT, and treat interest portion as nonoperating.	Treat reserve as a debt equivalent.	Deduct reserve's present value from the value of operations.
Nonoperating provisions	Restructuring charges, such as expected severance due to layoffs	Convert accrual provision into cash provision, and treat as nonoperating.	Treat reserve as a debt equivalent.	Deduct reserve's present value from the value of operations.
Income-smoothing provisions	Provisions for the sole purpose of income smoothing	Eliminate provision by converting accrual provision into cash provision.	Treat reserve as an equity equivalent.	Since income-smoothing provisions are noncash, there is no effect.

[1] Net operating profit after taxes.

EXHIBIT 21.6 **Provisions and Reserves in the Financial Statements**

$ million

	Today	Year 1	Year 2	Year 3	Year 4
Income statement					
Revenue		1,000.0	1,200.0	1,400.0	1,600.0
Operating costs		(750.0)	(900.0)	(1,190.0)	(1,200.0)
Decommissioning asset, depreciation[1]		(7.7)	(7.7)	(7.7)	–
Decommissioning reserve, accretion[2]		(15.0)	(16.5)	(18.2)	–
Provision for product defects[2]		(100.0)	(120.0)	(140.0)	(160.0)
Income-smoothing provision[2]		(40.0)	(40.0)	80.0	–
Operating profit, as reported		87.3	115.8	124.1	240.0
Provision for restructuring		–	(30.0)	–	–
Net income		87.3	85.8	124.1	240.0
Balance sheet					
Decommissioning asset, gross	77.1	77.1	77.1	77.1	–
Accumulated depreciation	(54.0)	(61.7)	(69.4)	(77.1)	–
Decommissioning asset, net	23.1	15.4	7.7	–	–
Other operating assets	700.0	840.0	980.0	1,120.0	–
Total assets	723.1	855.4	987.7	1,120.0	–
Reserve for decommissioning	150.3	165.3	181.8	–	–
Reserve for product defects	100.0	120.0	140.0	160.0	–
Reserve for restructuring	–	–	30.0	–	–
Reserve for income smoothing	–	40.0	80.0	–	–
Equity	472.9	530.1	555.9	960.0	–
Total liabilities and equity	723.1	855.4	987.7	1,120.0	–

[1] Typically embedded in depreciation and amortization.

[2] Typically embedded in operating costs, such as cost of sales.

EXHIBIT 21.7 **ROIC with Provisions and Reserves**

$ million

	Today	Year 1	Year 2	Year 3	Year 4
NOPAT					
Operating profit, as reported		87.3	115.8	124.1	240.0
Decommissioning reserve, accretion		15.0	16.5	18.2	–
Increase (decrease) in income-smoothing reserve		40.0	40.0	(80.0)	–
NOPAT		142.3	172.3	62.3	240.0
Reconciliation to net income					
Net income		87.3	85.8	124.1	240.0
Decommissioning reserve, accretion		15.0	16.5	18.2	–
Increase (decrease) in income-smoothing reserve		40.0	40.0	(80.0)	–
Provision for restructuring		–	30.0	–	–
NOPAT		142.3	172.3	62.3	240.0
Invested capital					
Plant decommissioning, net	23.1	15.4	7.7	–	–
Other operating assets	700.0	840.0	980.0	1,120.0	–
Reserve for product defects	(100.0)	(120.0)	(140.0)	(160.0)	–
Invested capital	623.1	735.4	847.7	960.0	–
Reconciliation of invested capital					
Reserve for plant decommissioning	150.3	165.3	181.8	–	–
Reserve for restructuring	–	–	30.0	–	–
Reserve for income smoothing	–	40.0	80.0	–	–
Equity	472.9	530.1	555.9	960.0	–
Invested capital	623.1	735.4	847.7	960.0	–
ROIC on beginning-of-year capital, %		22.8	23.4	7.3	25.0

for decommissioning the company's plant, an operating provision for future product defects, a provision for smoothing income, and a restructuring provision for future severance payments. In this example, we reorganize forecast statements, rather than historical statements, to demonstrate how each type of provision would be treated from a valuation perspective. (Historical statements should be adjusted in the same way as forecast statements.) For simplicity, we assume the company pays no taxes and has no debt.

The process for adjusting the financial statements depends on the type of provision. Exhibit 21.7 shows how to reorganize the income statement and balance sheet for each provision for our hypothetical company. In the following discussion of this example, all numbers in parentheses refer to the year 1 reorganized financial statements.

Provisions Related to Ongoing Operations When a company warranties a product, expects that some products will be returned, or self-insures a service, it must create a corresponding liability when that product or service is sold. If the reserve is related to the ongoing operations, the reserve should be treated the same way as other non-interest-bearing liabilities (e.g., accounts payable and wages payable). Specifically, the provision should be deducted from revenues to determine EBITA. The corresponding reserve ($100 million) should be netted against operating assets ($723.1 million) to measure invested capital ($623.1 million). Since the provision and reserve are treated as operating items, they appear as part of free cash flow and should not be valued separately.

Long-Term Operating Provisions   Sometimes, when a company decommissions a plant, it must pay for cleanup and other costs. Assume our hypothetical company owns a plant that will operate for ten years and requires $200 million in decommissioning costs. Rather than expense the cash outflow in a lump sum at the time of decommissioning, a company will instead record the present value of the cost as both an asset and a liability at the time of investment.[3] In this case, the ten-year present value of $200 million at 10 percent equals $77.1 million.[4] It's as if the company borrowed $77.1 million and holds the money in restricted cash to fund the future decommissioning outlay.

Once the decommissioning asset and reserve are recognized, the decommissioning asset is depreciated (similar to the way restricted cash is paid into an outside fund set aside for cleanup), and the reserve is grown (as if the debt accumulates unpaid interest charges). As a result, the decommissioning cost is recognized over the life of the asset, instead of a lump sum at closing.

If the decommissioning costs are substantial, as with a nuclear power plant or a mine, the costs will be presented in the company's footnotes. We show a sample note in Exhibit 21.8. In Panel A of Exhibit 21.8, the decommissioning asset declines by $7.7 million each year. This expense is computed using straight-line depreciation on the original decommissioning asset. In Panel B, the decommissioning reserve grows each year by an ever-increasing amount, computed at 10 percent of the prior year's ending reserve. This expense, which mimics interest, is known as accretion. In year 1, the current-year reserve of $150.3 million grows by $15.0 million in accretion. The income statement presented in Exhibit 21.6 reports both depreciation and accretion as operating items, often embedded within depreciation and operating costs, respectively.

To estimate NOPAT, invested capital, ROIC, and FCF, apply the guiding principles presented in Chapter 11. When reorganizing the income statement,

[3] In the United States, asset retirement obligations (AROs) are governed by SFAS 143. Entities covered by IFRS use IAS 37, where the AROs are called "provisions."
[4] In Exhibit 21.6, the current year represents the seventh year of the plant's expected ten-year life. Consequently, the decommissioning asset and the decommissioning reserve no longer equal their initial value of $77.1 million. Instead, the decommissioning asset has been depreciated seven years to $23.1 million, using straight-line depreciation. Conversely, the decommission reserve grows annually at the discount rate. As a result, the current year reserve equals $77.1 million $\times (1.10)^7$, which equals $150.3 million.

EXHIBIT 21.8 **Provisions and Reserves in the Notes**

$ million

	Today	Year 1	Year 2	Year 3
Panel A: Change in the asset account				
Decommissioning asset, starting	30.8	23.1	15.4	7.7
Depreciation	(7.7)	(7.7)	(7.7)	(7.7)
Decommissioning asset, ending	23.1	15.4	7.7	–
Panel B: Change in the liability account				
Decommissioning reserve, starting	136.6	150.3	165.3	181.8
Accretion expense at 10%	13.7	15.0	16.5	18.2
Payout	–	–	–	(200.0)
Decommissioning reserve, ending	150.3	165.3	181.8	–
Panel C: Income statement				
Decommissioning asset, depreciation	7.7	7.7	7.7	–
Decommissioning reserve, accretion	15.0	16.5	18.2	–
Decommissioning expense	22.7	24.2	25.9	–

treat depreciation as an operating item. Conversely, since accretion mimics interest, do not include accretion in NOPAT; instead, include it in the reconciliation to net income, next to interest expense. NOPAT and the reconciliation to net income are computed in the top portion of Exhibit 21.7. To reorganize the balance sheet, classify the decommissioning asset (which is comparable to restricted cash) as part of invested capital and the reserve as a debt equivalent. Invested capital and its reconciliation are presented in the bottom half of Exhibit 21.7. To compute free cash flow, start with NOPAT, add back depreciation of the decommissioning asset (since it is noncash), and subtract investments in invested capital. Free cash flow is presented in Exhibit 21.9.

When you treat the plant closure reserve as a debt equivalent, the interest expense and reserve drawdown will not flow through free cash flow. Therefore, subtract the current reported reserve ($150.3 million as of today) from the value of operations ($858.9 million) to determine equity value. The value of operations, which includes this and other deductions, is converted into equity value in Exhibit 21.10.

One-Time Restructuring Provisions   When management decides to restructure a company, it will often recognize certain future expenses (e.g., severance payments) immediately. We recommend treating one-time provisions as nonoperating and treating the corresponding reserve as a debt equivalent. In year 2, our hypothetical company declared a $30 million restructuring provision, which will be paid in year 3 (see Exhibit 21.6). Since the restructuring is nonoperating, it is not deducted from revenues to determine NOPAT. Rather, it is included in the reconciliation to net income (see Exhibit 21.7). Because we plan to value the provision on a cash basis, the noncash reserve is treated as a debt

EXHIBIT 21.9 **Free Cash Flow with Provisions and Reserves**

$ million

	Year 1	Year 2	Year 3	Year 4	
NOPAT	142.3	172.3	62.3	240.0	
Depreciation	7.7	7.7	7.7	–	
Gross cash flow	150.0	180.0	70.0	240.0	
Investment in invested capital	(120.0)	(120.0)	(120.0)	960.0	Present value at 10% = 858.9
Free cash flow	30.0	60.0	(50.0)	1,200.0	
Reconciliation of free cash flow					
Provision for restructuring	–	30.0	–	–	
(Increase) decrease in restructuring reserve	–	(30.0)	30.0	–	
Cash-based restructuring provision	–	–	30.0	–	Present value at 10% = 22.5
Decommissioning reserve, accretion	15.0	16.5	18.2	–	
(Increase) decrease in decommissioning reserve	(15.0)	(16.5)	181.8	–	
Dividends	40.0	70.0	–	1,120.0	
Equity repurchases (issues)	(10.0)	(10.0)	(280.0)	80.0	
Free cash flow	30.0	60.0	(50.0)	1,200.0	

equivalent and therefore is not netted against operating assets to determine invested capital.

Since nonoperating income and expenses do not flow through free cash flow, the restructuring expense must be valued separately on a cash basis. To convert accrual-based restructuring expenses to cash, start with the restructuring expense, and subtract the increase in the restructuring reserve. This leads to a cash-based restructuring provision of $0 in year 2 and $30 million in year 3 (free cash flow and its reconciliation are presented in Exhibit 21.9). The present value of the nonoperating cash flow stream equals $22.5 million, which must be deducted from the value of operations to determine equity value, as shown in Exhibit 21.10.

Income-Smoothing Provisions   Except for limited circumstances, provisions to smooth earnings are not allowed under International Financial Reporting Standards or U.S. Generally Accepted Accounting Principles (GAAP). To

EXHIBIT 21.10 **Enterprise DCF with Provisions and Reserves**

$ million

Valuation		Methodology
Value of operations	858.9	Summation of discounted cash flow
Value of restructuring provision	(22.5)	Present value at 10% (debt equivalent)
Reserve for plant decommissioning	(150.3)	Reported on balance sheet (debt equivalent)
Equity value	686.1	

prevent earnings manipulation or even the perception of it, many companies use a third party to estimate key provisions. In some situations, companies can use provisions to smooth earnings. For instance, defense contractors will use income smoothing when they believe a long-term contract's value has changed.

In Exhibit 21.6, our hypothetical company was able to show a smooth growth in reported EBITA and net income by using a smoothing provision. We choose a straightforward title for the account, "Income-smoothing provision," but actual companies typically use subtler wording, such as "Other provisions." For our hypothetical company, a provision was recorded in years 1 and 2 and was reversed in year 3. By using an income-smoothing provision, the company hid its year 3 decline in operating performance (operating costs rose from 75 percent to 85 percent of sales).

To evaluate the company's performance properly, eliminate any income-smoothing provisions. Do this by adding the income-smoothing provision back to reported EBITA (essentially undoing the income-smoothing provision). In this way, we are converting the provision to cash, rather than accounting for it as an accrual, and subsequently need to treat the reserve as an equity equivalent (using a process identical to the one for deferred taxes). Since income-smoothing provisions are entirely noncash, they don't affect free cash flow or valuation.

Provisions and Taxes

In most situations, provisions are tax deductible only when cash is disbursed, not when the provision is reported. Thus, most provisions will give rise to deferred-tax assets. For example, a $30 million noncash restructuring charge would lead to a $30 million restructuring reserve. If the restructuring charge is tax deductible on the GAAP income statement, retained earnings would drop by only $21 million (assuming a 30 percent tax rate). Since the increase in the restructuring reserve does not match the drop in retained earnings, the balance sheet will not balance. To eliminate the difference, a deferred-tax asset is recognized for $9 million.

For operating-related provisions, we recommend using cash, rather than accrual taxes. For nonoperating provisions, estimate the tax impact of the corresponding provision. Do not use book values, as they reflect past accounting and not necessarily future cash flow. For an in-depth discussion of deferred taxes, see Chapter 20.

CLOSING THOUGHTS

The accounting definition of nonoperating expense is narrow and limited to interest expense and a few other items. Therefore, the accounting definition of operating profits will inappropriately include many one-time and other nonoperating items. Always start your financial analysis by separating operating from nonoperating items on the income statement. This will create a better picture of the company's performance and its potential for generating future cash flow. In some cases, the proper classification of a particular expense will be unclear. But don't let this distract you from the task at hand. A proper valuation will not depend on how the item is treated, as long as you include it somewhere and treat it consistently.

22

Leases

Many companies, especially retailers and airlines, lease their assets from other companies rather than purchasing the assets outright. They do this for many reasons, including greater flexibility and to lower taxes.

In the past, clever use of accounting rules allowed companies to keep assets and debts off balance sheets. These included leased assets and their corresponding debts, securitized assets like receivables, and unfunded retirement obligations. In some cases, this helped companies manage cash flow or take advantage of alternative routes to raise funds. In other instances, off-balance-sheet items were used to artificially boost results such as earnings per share or return on assets.

In response, the International Accounting Standards Board (IASB) and the Financial Accounting Standards Board (FASB) made significant changes to their guidelines. As of 2019, companies are required to capitalize nearly all asset leases, including operating leases, on their balance sheet.[1] This stands in stark contrast to past guidelines, where a company could rent an asset, even for long periods, and recognize only the periodic rental expense.

The new accounting guidelines bring the treatment of operating leases closer to the underlying principles of this book. Implementation of the new guidelines, however, differs across accounting bodies, so incorporating operating leases into your valuation still requires special care.

This chapter begins with a review of the new accounting rules, how they differ across accounting bodies, and how they are presented on the financial statements. We then outline how to incorporate operating leases into an enterprise valuation. Since operating leases affect each part of the valuation, this chapter provides a review of the valuation principles outlined in Part Two. As companies will not revise their historical financial statements, we discuss how

---

[1] The International Accounting Standards Board (IASB) published IFRS 16, "Leases," in January 2016, and the Financial Accounting Standards Board (FASB) issued Accounting Standards Update (ASU) 2016-02, "Leases (Topic 842)" in February 2016.

to adjust past financial statements to assure consistent benchmarking over time. The chapter concludes with a discussion of an alternative method for lease valuation, which can be helpful when benchmarking across companies.

ACCOUNTING FOR OPERATING LEASES

Although both IASB and FASB now require capitalization of operating leases, there are differences in implementing the new standards. For companies that use International Financial Reporting Standards (IFRS), nearly all leases greater than one year are treated as "finance" leases, meaning that leased assets and their corresponding liabilities are capitalized on the balance sheet, and lease expense is appropriately split between depreciation and interest expense. The enterprise valuation methodology outlined in Part Two of this book will correctly incorporate leases under IFRS without further adjustment.

Capitalizing leases under U.S. Generally Accepted Accounting Principles (GAAP) is more complicated. Companies classify asset leases into either "finance" leases, similar to IFRS, or "operating" leases. A lease is classified as a finance lease if cumulative payments to the lessor exceed certain thresholds.[2] Finance leases are not typically visible on the financial statements, as each element is embedded within another financial statement account. The leased asset is included with property, plant, and equipment. The leased liability is included with short-term and long-term debt.

To better understand the impact of the new accounting guidelines, we analyze and value FlightCo, a hypothetical airline that uses operating leases. To avoid the unnecessary complexities of continuing value, we assume the company leases only one aircraft and plans to liquidate at the end of the third year. At that point, parts inventory is sold, general obligation debt is retired, and a liquidating dividend is paid. The lease is classified as an operating lease because the contract length is significantly shorter than the life of the underlying asset.

Exhibit 22.1 presents the valuation of FlightCo's operating lease using discounted cash flow. The lease has payments of $9 million, $9 million, and $12 million in years 1 through 3, respectively. Using discounted cash flow at a cost of debt of 5 percent, the lease has a present value of $27.1 million. Because the contract life is only three years, the present value of lease payments is significantly lower than the asset's actual value. Later in this chapter, under "An Alternative Method for Valuing Operating Leases," we present a valuation method for estimating the full value of leased assets using data in the annual report. This is helpful when benchmarking two companies that have different financing policies.

---

[2] A lease is classified as a finance if the lease term is greater than 75 percent of the useful life, if the present value of lease payments is greater than 90 percent of the original cost, if the asset is specialized and has no value to the lessor once returned, or if ownership of the asset is transferred to the lessee at the end of the lease.

EXHIBIT 22.1 **FlightCo: Valuation of Operating Lease**

$ million

	Lease payment	Discount factor	Discounted cash flow
Year 1	9.0	0.952	8.6
Year 2	9.0	0.907	8.2
Year 3	12.0	0.864	10.4
Present value of operating lease			27.1

Exhibit 22.2 presents the financial statement accounts related to leases for FlightCo and shows how the accounts evolve over time. Although the evolution is neither required for valuation nor disclosed in practice, it will be helpful for explaining the accounting behind leases.

On the income statement, U.S. GAAP requires the total lease payments of $30 million to be spread evenly over the life of the contract, even though the cash payments change over time.[3] The annual lease expense is recorded on the income statement at $10 million per year. The lease payment covers the depreciation of the asset, as well as financial compensation for the lessor.

On the balance sheet, the present value of lease payments is recorded as a "right-of-use" asset, and the corresponding liability is recorded as an "operating lease." Both accounts start at $27.1 million—the present value of the lease. While the two accounts will match when initially recorded, they will

EXHIBIT 22.2 **FlightCo: Financial Statement Accounts Related to Leases**

$ million

	Year 1	Year 2	Year 3
Income statement			
Lease expense	10.0	10.0	10.0
Assets: Right-of-use asset			
Right-of-use asset, start	27.1	18.5	9.4
Lease expense	(10.0)	(10.0)	(10.0)
Embedded interest[1]	1.4	1.0	0.6
Right-of-use asset, end	18.5	9.4	–
Liabilities: Operating lease			
Lease principal, start	27.1	19.5	11.4
Interest at 5%	1.4	1.0	0.6
Lease payment	(9.0)	(9.0)	(12.0)
Lease principal, end	19.5	11.4	–

[1] Under U.S. GAAP, the interest on the operating lease *liability* is netted against the lease expense to determine the annual reduction in the right-of-use asset.

[3] Some might think the expense accounting for operating leases mirrors that of finance leases; it does not. In a finance lease, the *present value* is straight-line amortized over the life of the lease. If FlightCo's lease were a finance lease, amortization expense would equal $9.03 million per year for three years. Lease amortization is included in the depreciation and amortization. Lease interest expense is calculated on the liability and included in interest expense.

not match over time if cash payments vary year to year. That is the case in our FlightCo example. The right-of-use asset will decline $8.6 million in the first year (from $27.1 to $18.5 million), equal to the lease expense of $10.0 million less interest of $1.4 million. (As if this were not confusing enough, interest is calculated on the operating lease *liability*, not the asset.) In the same year, the operating lease liability declines by $7.6 million (from $27.1 to $19.5 million), equal to the cash payment of $9.0 million less the interest of $1.4 million.

Because of the mismatch described in the previous paragraph, most companies report operating lease liabilities that differ from their corresponding right-of-use assets. Delta Airlines, for example, reported $6.0 billion in right-of-use assets in its 10-Q for the first quarter of 2019. In contrast, current maturities of operating leases equal $941 million, and noncurrent operating leases equal $5.8 billion, totaling $6.7 billion. In this reporting period, the corresponding values differ by more than 10 percent.

VALUING A COMPANY WITH OPERATING LEASES

Incorporating operating leases into an enterprise valuation follows the same process outlined in Part Two of this book. We use four steps to value FlightCo:

1. Reorganize the financial statements. During the reorganization, adjust earnings before interest, taxes, and amortization (EBITA) upward by removing the implicit interest in operating lease expense. Adjust operating taxes to determine adjusted net operating profit after tax (NOPAT).

2. Estimate free cash flow (FCF), using adjusted NOPAT and changes in the right-of-use asset. Liabilities classified as operating leases should be treated as debt and incorporated into the reconciliation of free cash flow.

3. Estimate a weighted average cost of capital (WACC) that includes the value of the operating lease liability as debt.

4. Value the enterprise by discounting free cash flow (based on the adjusted NOPAT) at the WACC, including operating leases. Subtract traditional debt and the value of operating lease liability from enterprise value to determine equity value.

As long as you treat right-of-use assets as purchased equipment and treat the operating lease liability as a form of debt, your results will be theoretically consistent. Only operating profit requires an upward adjustment for implicit lease interest. Failing to adjust operating profit will undervalue equity, because implicit interest would be double-counted: once as part of lease expense and again as part of lease value when subtracting the value of leases from enterprise value to get to equity value.

Reorganizing the Financial Statements

To start the valuation of FlightCo, first reorganize the financial statements. Exhibit 22.3 presents the income statement, balance sheet, and statement of equity for FlightCo.

Using the information from FlightCo's financial statements, Exhibit 22.4 presents a calculation of NOPAT and its reconciliation to net income. The process starts by adding back the implicit interest embedded in the operating lease expense. To estimate implicit interest, multiply the prior year's operating lease liability by the interest rate used to value the operating lease. (If the company does not disclose the discount rate for operating leases in the notes, use the yield to maturity on AA-rated debt.) For FlightCo, embedded interest equals the operating lease liability of $27.1 million multiplied by the interest rate of 5 percent. Estimate implicit interest using the operating lease liability and not the right-of-use asset.

EXHIBIT 22.3 **FlightCo: Financial Statements**

$ million

	Year 0	Year 1	Year 2	Year 3
Income statement				
Revenue		75.0	75.0	75.0
Operating expenses		(40.0)	(40.0)	(40.0)
Operating lease expense[1]		(10.0)	(10.0)	(10.0)
Operating profit, unadjusted		25.0	25.0	25.0
Interest expense, debt[2]		(0.4)	(0.3)	(0.3)
Earnings before taxes		24.6	24.7	24.7
Income taxes at 20%		(4.9)	(4.9)	(4.9)
Net income		19.7	19.7	19.8
Balance sheet				
Inventory	15.0	15.0	15.0	–
Right-of-use assets	27.1	18.5	9.4	–
Total assets	42.1	33.5	24.4	–
Operating leases	27.1	19.5	11.4	–
Debt	7.8	6.6	5.0	–
Equity	7.2	7.4	8.0	–
Liabilities and equity	42.1	33.5	24.4	–
Statement of equity				
Equity, start		7.2	7.4	8.0
Net income		19.7	19.7	19.8
Dividends and/or share repurchases		(19.5)	(19.1)	(27.8)
Equity, end		7.4	8.0	–

[1] Typically embedded in operating expenses, such as cost of sales.

[2] Interest equals 0.39, 0.33, and 0.25 in Year 1 through Year 3. As such, rounding errors affect earnings before taxes and net income.

EXHIBIT 22.4 **FlightCo: NOPAT and Reconciliation to Net Income**

$ million

	Year 1	Year 2	Year 3
EBITA,[1] unadjusted	25.0	25.0	25.0
Operating lease interest	1.4	1.0	0.6
EBITA, adjusted for lease interest	26.4	26.0	25.6
Operating taxes at 20%	(5.3)	(5.2)	(5.1)
NOPAT[2]	21.1	20.8	20.5
Reconciliation to net income			
Net income	19.7	19.7	19.8
Interest expense, debt	0.4	0.3	0.3
Operating lease interest	1.4	1.0	0.6
Interest tax shield at 20%	(0.3)	(0.3)	(0.2)
NOPAT	21.1	20.8	20.5

[1] Earnings before interest, taxes, and amortization.
[2] Net operating profit after taxes.

To calculate NOPAT, subtract operating taxes from adjusted operating profit. Operating taxes are estimated by multiplying operating profit by the operating tax rate. The resulting NOPAT for year 1 is $21.1 million. The tax shield for embedded interest will be incorporated into the cost of capital.

We do not present a reorganized balance sheet for FlightCo, as the simplified balance sheet already matches invested capital. In general, include the right-of-use asset as part of invested capital and the operating lease liability as a source of financing.

Estimating Free Cash Flow

Once the financial statements are reorganized, estimate free cash flow. Exhibit 22.5 presents the free cash flow statement and its reconciliation to cash flow to investors for FlightCo. Free cash flow starts with NOPAT. Since FlightCo does not own property or equipment, there is no add-back for depreciation.[4] From this value, subtract increases in working capital (inventory) and long-term assets (in this case, the right-of-use assets). Since both accounts are declining over time, they are positive numbers.

Note in Exhibit 22.5 how the summation of operating lease interest and the decrease in right-of-use assets equal the operating lease expense from Exhibit 22.3. Essentially, the valuation process eliminates the entire lease expense for existing assets from free cash flow. At the completion of the valuation, the lease of existing assets will not be valued as part of free cash flow, but rather as debt. Consistent with fundamental finance principles, this process separates investing flows from the manner in which they are financed.

[4] To determine free cash flow, we incorporate the change in the right-of-use asset, which for FlightCo is decreasing over time. The positive value generated by the decline mimics the depreciation add-back. Essentially, the cash flows from capitalizing a lease are identical to those from purchasing an asset financed with debt.

EXHIBIT 22.5 **FlightCo: Free Cash Flow and Its Reconciliation**

$ million

	Year 1	Year 2	Year 3
EBITA,[1] unadjusted	25.0	25.0	25.0
Operating lease interest	1.4	1.0	0.6
EBITA, adjusted for lease interest	26.4	26.0	25.6
Operating taxes at 20%	(5.3)	(5.2)	(5.1)
NOPAT[2]	21.1	20.8	20.5
Decrease (increase) in inventory	–	–	15.0
Decrease (increase) in right-of-use assets	8.6	9.0	9.4
Free cash flow	29.7	29.8	44.9
Interest tax shield at 20%	0.3	0.3	0.2
Cash flow available for investors	30.1	30.1	45.1
Reconciliation of free cash flow			
Interest, debt	0.4	0.3	0.3
Interest, operating leases	1.4	1.0	0.6
Decrease (increase) in debt	1.2	1.6	5.0
Decrease (increase) in operating leases	7.6	8.0	11.4
Flows to debt holders	10.6	10.9	17.3
Dividends	19.5	19.1	27.8
Cash flow to investors	30.1	30.1	45.1

[1] Earnings before interest, taxes, and amortization.

[2] Net operating profit after taxes.

When reconciling cash flow to investors, treat embedded interest on operating leases and the change in the operating lease liability as a flow to debt holders. Again, note in Exhibit 22.5 how the summation of these two accounts matches the *cash-based* lease payment. Financing and its associated taxes should not be part of free cash flow.

Incorporating Operating Leases into Financial Projections

To forecast right-of-use assets, use the forecasting process introduced in Chapter 13. Link right-of-use assets to sales or a quantity-based measure, such as the number of units sold. In the airline industry, units are represented by number of available seat-miles. Make sure the mix of purchased and leased assets is consistent with the amount of capacity necessary to conduct operations.

Set the operating lease liability as a percentage of the right-of-use asset. While this estimation method is far from precise, flows to and from financing do not affect an enterprise-based valuation. Instead, financing affects valuation only through the target capital structure set in the weighted average cost of capital. If helpful, you can model the combination of operating leases and debt to the target capital structure, but it is not required.

Estimating the Cost of Capital

To discount free cash flow, use the weighted average cost of capital inclusive of the value of operating leases. Exhibit 22.6 presents the weighted average cost of capital for FlightCo.

We assume the company will maintain its current capital structure of 40 percent adjusted debt to value. Total debt equals the sum of the operating lease liability of $27.1 million and traditional debt of $7.8 million, divided by enterprise value, estimated at $87.4 million. When estimating enterprise value, include operating leases as well. For FlightCo, the mix of operating leases and debt will change over time, but we set the combination to be stable at 40 percent of enterprise value. Since operating leases and interest expense are tax deductible, reduce the cost of capital for operating leases and debt by the company's marginal tax rate.

In the calculations for this example, the cost of equity is provided. In practice, the cost of equity must be estimated using beta. Following the principles of Chapter 15, start by estimating an industry unlevered beta. Unlever each company's beta using a debt-to-equity ratio adjusted for operating leases. Next, to determine the target company's beta, relever the unlevered beta to the target company's capital structure, again inclusive of leases.

Moving from Enterprise Value to Equity Value

To calculate enterprise value, discount free cash flow at the weighted average cost of capital, both inclusive of leases. Exhibit 22.7 shows the enterprise DCF valuation for FlightCo.

Since free cash flow excludes future payments related to existing operating leases, the value of operating leases must be deducted from enterprise value to determine intrinsic equity value. For FlightCo, enterprise value is estimated at $87.4 million. Deducting the present value of the operating lease liability ($27.1 million) and debt of $7.8 million leads to an equity value of $52.4 million.

EXHIBIT 22.6 **FlightCo: Weighted Average Cost of Capital (WACC)**

%

Source of capital	Value, $ million	Proportion of total capital	Cost of capital	Marginal tax rate	After-tax cost of capital	Contribution to weighted average
Operating leases[1]	27.1	31.0	5.0	20.0	4.0	1.2
Debt	7.8	9.0	5.0	20.0	4.0	0.4
Equity	52.4	60.0	12.0		12.0	7.2
WACC	87.4	100.0				8.8

[1] The present value of operating leases, found in the liabilities section of the balance sheet.

EXHIBIT 22.7 **FlightCo: Enterprise DCF Valuation**

$ million, except where noted

Forecast year	Free cash flow (FCF)	Discount factor at 8.8%	Present value of FCF
Year 1	29.7	0.919	27.3
Year 2	29.8	0.845	25.2
Year 3	44.9	0.776	34.9
Value of operations			87.4
Less: Operating leases[1]			(27.1)
Less: Debt			(7.8)
Equity value			52.4

[1] The present value of operating leases, found in the liabilities section of the balance sheet.

Valuation Using Cash Flow to Equity

In general, we do not recommend a valuation model based on cash flow to equity, because it mixes assets of different risks and commingles operating performance with the capital structure. If implemented properly, however, a cash-flow-to-equity valuation can confirm the accuracy of the enterprise DCF process described in this chapter. It can also provide insight into choices made during the capitalization process.

Exhibit 22.8 presents cash flow to equity for FlightCo. In this exhibit, each line item represents actual cash flowing into or out of the company, from the equity holder's perspective. In the equity model, do not capitalize lease expense. Instead, deduct the cash payments paid to the lessor when they occur. Since leases are expensed and not capitalized, do not include either the change in the right-of-use asset or the change in the operating lease liability. This stands in contrast to debt flows, where both interest expense and payoff of debt are included in the calculation, since they represent actual cash flows.

EXHIBIT 22.8 **FlightCo: Cash Flow to Equity Holders**

$ million

	Year 1	Year 2	Year 3
Revenue	75.0	75.0	75.0
Operating costs	(40.0)	(40.0)	(40.0)
Lease payments[1]	(9.0)	(9.0)	(12.0)
Interest expense, debt	(0.4)	(0.3)	(0.3)
Earnings before taxes	25.6	25.7	22.7
Income taxes	(4.9)	(4.9)	(4.9)
Earnings after taxes	20.7	20.7	17.8
Change in inventory	0.0	0.0	15.0
Increase (decrease) in debt	(1.2)	(1.6)	(5.0)
Cash flow to equity	19.5	19.1	27.8

[1] Cash-based lease payments.

EXHIBIT 22.9 **FlightCo: Valuation Using Cash Flow to Equity**

$ million, except where noted

Forecast year	Cash flow to equity (CFE)	Discount factor, at 12%	Present value of CFE
Year 1	19.5	0.893	17.4
Year 2	19.1	0.797	15.3
Year 3	27.8	0.712	19.8
Equity value			52.4

Exhibit 22.9 values cash flow to equity at the cost of equity. The cost of equity used to discount equity cash flows equals the cost of equity used to determine the weighted average cost of capital. One may think the cost of equity should fall, since the leverage associated with operating leases is being ignored. This is not the case, however. The underlying risk of equity has not changed when switching models, so the cost of equity should not change either.

Discounting cash flow to equity at a 12 percent cost of equity leads to an equity valuation of $52.4 million. This is the same valuation as we calculated by using the enterprise DCF model.

ADJUSTING HISTORICAL FINANCIAL STATEMENTS FOR OPERATING LEASES

As time progresses, distortions caused by operating leases will be forgotten in the same way most investors have forgotten the adjustments required for the long-defunct pooling of interests prior to 2000. Until then, it is important to recognize that historical financial statements will remain unadjusted. To assure consistency in historical analysis prior to 2019, adjust historical statements to match current accounting policy.

In the analysis of Costco presented in Chapter 11 and Appendix H, we used information from their annual report to value operating leases and adjust the historical financial statements accordingly. Exhibit 22.10 presents the valuation of operating leases for Costco in 2019, the year before Costco adopted the new standard.[5] To value operating leases, we discount future lease payments at the cost of AA-rated debt. Lease commitments are reported in note 5 of Costco's 2019 annual report. The company reports only the first five years of lease payments year by year. Lease payments beyond 2024 are lumped into a single undiscounted number. At the bottom of Exhibit 22.10, we value the lump sum using an annuity formula. In the formula, set the cash

---

[5] Companies whose fiscal year ends after December 15 had to implement the new leasing standard in 2019. Since Costco's fiscal year ended on September 1, 2019, it chose to adopt the new standard in 2020.

EXHIBIT 22.10 **Costco: Operating Lease Valuation, 2019**

$ million

Forecast year	Rental commitments	Discount factor at 3.6%[1]	Present value of payments
2020	239.0	0.965	230.6
2021	229.0	0.931	213.2
2022	202.0	0.898	181.5
2023	193.0	0.867	167.3
2024	181.0	0.837	151.4
Payments beyond 2024	1,757.1	0.837	1,470.0
Value of operating leases			2,414.0
Value beyond 2024			
Rental commitments beyond 2024	2,206.0		
/ Final year rental payment	181.0		
= Number of years	12.19		

Annuity value of $181.0 per year for 12.19 years = $1,757.1

[1] Yield-to-maturity on 10-year AA-rated debt.

Source: Costco 2019 annual report, note 5.

flow equal to the 2024 lease payment. To estimate the number of years, divide the undiscounted lump sum by the 2024 rental payment. For Costco, the annuity value equals almost $1.8 billion. Since the annuity values the lump-sum payments beyond 2024 as of 2024, make sure to discount the result back to 2019, as you would any other cash flow.

In general, when reorganizing the balance sheet, include the value of operating leases as part of invested capital. Incorporate the corresponding liability as a debt equivalent. For past statements, the asset will equal the liability.

In Chapter 11, we adjust Costco's reorganized financial statements for operating leases. Exhibit 11.5 presents invested capital inclusive of operating leases, and Exhibit 11.9 adjusts EBITA and NOPAT for implicit interest. To calculate implicit interest for 2019, multiply the cost of debt of 3.63 percent by the 2018 capitalized operating lease of $2.5 billion. The resulting adjustment to EBITA equals $91 million.

AN ALTERNATIVE METHOD FOR VALUING OPERATING LEASES

To capitalize operating leases on the balance sheet, the company discounts future lease commitments at the company's borrowing rate. For short-term leases, this methodology will understate the actual value of the asset, since it ignores the residual value of the asset being returned to the lessor. Consider FlightCo, which rented an aircraft for three years of the plane's 40-year life. A new aircraft may cost $125 million, but three years of rental expense will be far lower.

While using the present value of lease payments in place of the true asset value will not bias the valuation, it will understate the value of the assets being deployed to run operations. (The error will be largest for short-term leases on long-term assets. In the case of finance leases, the error will be small, since the lease life more closely matches the asset life.) When benchmarking two companies, one that purchases assets and one that rents them, the comparison will not be like-for-like, even under new accounting standards.[6] Distortions to ROIC and capital turnover will be largest when leased assets are a significant proportion of invested capital.

One way to create a like-for-like comparison for companies with different leasing policies is to estimate each company's asset value by using a perpetuity. To see how, let's examine the determinants of rental expense. To compensate the lessor properly, the rental expense includes compensation for the cost of financing the asset (at the cost of secured debt, denoted by k_d in the following equations) and the periodic depreciation of the asset (for which we assume straight-line depreciation). The following equation solves for periodic rental expense:

$$\text{Lease Expense}_t = \text{Asset Value}_{t-1} \left(k_d + \frac{1}{\text{Asset Life}} \right) \tag{22.1}$$

To estimate the asset's value, rearrange equation 22.1 as follows:

$$\text{Asset Value}_{t-1} = \frac{\text{Lease Expense}_t}{\left(k_d + \dfrac{1}{\text{Asset Life}} \right)} \tag{22.1}$$

Lease expense is disclosed in the notes, and the cost of debt can be estimated using AA-rated yields. This leaves only the asset life, which is often unreported. If this is the case, search the notes for the type of asset being leased, and estimate an asset life appropriate to the asset type. As an alternative, Lim, Mann, and Mihov propose using property, plant, and equipment (PP&E) divided by annual depreciation.[7] In their research, they examined 7,000 firms over 20 years and computed the median asset life at 10.9 years.

---

[6] In this section, we focus on the distortions to benchmarking caused by different leasing policies. Companies choose different leasing policies for many reasons, including flexibility and taxes.
[7] S. C. Lim, S. C. Mann, and V. T. Mihov, "Market Evaluation of Off–Balance Sheet Financing: You Can Run but You Can't Hide" (EFMA 2004 Basel Meetings paper, European Financial Management Association, December 1, 2003).

CLOSING THOUGHTS

Recent changes in lease accounting have brought financial reporting very close to the core principles of this book. Still, a proper valuation requires special care regarding operating leases. To inform better forecasts, adjust statements created prior to the accounting rules changes to incorporate operating leases. If you do not, apples-to-oranges comparisons may obscure crucial trends. For statements reported after the changes, remember to eliminate any interest embedded in operating expenses. Otherwise, you risk double-counting embedded interest, biasing your valuation downward. The task requires discipline and attention to detail, but with practice, the adjustments should become routine.

23

Retirement Obligations

To attract and retain talent, companies often offer retirement benefits to employees. These benefits include fixed pension payments, tax-advantaged savings plans, and promises to provide medical benefits when the employee retires. In some countries, companies are required to set up separate funds to pay these benefits, but inconsistencies are common because of differences in regulations and tax policy. For example, in the United States, companies must set up separate funds for pension promises (known as defined-benefit plans) but not for promises of retiree medical benefits. If the value of investments does not fully fund future promises, the company will have unfunded retirement obligations. Since the company is responsible for any shortfalls and these obligations take precedence over equity, any accurate valuation must account for them.

This chapter explores how to analyze and value a company with pension and other retirement obligations. Recent accounting changes have made the analysis easier, but careful thinking and reorganizing of financial statements are still required. The challenges include deciding which part of the pension expense is operating versus nonoperating, treating the balance sheet for unfunded or overfunded obligations, estimating the cost of capital for companies with pensions, and adjusting equity value to reflect unfunded (or overfunded) retirement obligations.

REORGANIZING THE FINANCIAL STATEMENTS WITH PENSIONS

In the past, accounting for pensions and other retirement obligations severely distorted operating profit, requiring adjustments to correctly measure the impact of retirement obligations on the company's value. In response, accounting policy has changed, gradually bringing the accounting for retirement obligations in line with the underlying doctrines of this text.

For companies that report under U.S. Generally Accepted Accounting Principles (GAAP), the changes occurred over many decades. Under original accounting principles, companies did not recognize unfunded pension liabilities on their balance sheets. The first changes involved recording unfunded retirement liabilities, albeit at a smoothed value intended to address the effects of short-term irregularities. In the 1980s, the rules were updated, and companies were required to record not only unfunded pension liabilities, but also other postretirement obligations, particularly promised medical benefits. Starting in 2006, companies were required to recognize the actual value of the unfunded (or overfunded) pension liability on the balance sheet.[1]

Although the balance sheet reflected the value of unfunded pension liabilities after 2006, the pension expense continued to include both operating and nonoperating items. It included not only new benefits granted to employees, but also interest on the liability, returns on plan assets, and adjustments for actuarial changes. In 2018, nonoperating items were removed from pension expense. (This change mirrored adjustments we'd recommended in earlier editions of this book.) Any new benefits granted to employees are now included in the appropriate operating expense, such as cost of sales or selling expenses. All other items, such as interest expense, actuarial changes, and earnings, are classified as "other" expense.

Because of these changes, you no longer need to make as many adjustments to the GAAP financial statements for pensions and retirement benefits for 2018 and forward. You must still adjust financial statements released before 2018. International Financial Reporting Standards (IFRS) have been updated as well, but under multiple revisions to existing standards, rather than by adopting an entirely new standard.

Throughout the chapter, we examine pension accounting using the American food manufacturer Kellogg. Kellogg is an interesting case because, even though its pension obligations are almost fully funded (about 95%, which is within the margin of year-to-year fluctuations), it's still necessary to dive into the details to make the right adjustments to estimate net operating profit after taxes (NOPAT) and invested capital. The information required to analyze pensions for Kellogg is in the footnotes to their financial statements, note 10, "Pension Benefits," and note 11, "Nonpension Postretirement and Postemployment Benefits."[2] In these two notes, the company provides information on projected benefit obligations, the fair value of plan assets, and a breakout of the annual pension expense.

Reorganizing the Balance Sheet

To start, find all the retirement-related assets and liabilities on the balance sheet. If these items are relatively small, companies may include prepaid pension

[1] Statement of Financial Accounting Standards (SFAS) 158 was passed by the Financial Accounting Standards Board (FASB) in September 2006. Accounting Standards Update (ASU) Number 2017-07 was passed by the FASB in March 2017.
[2] All the data related to Kellogg in this chapter appear in Kellogg's 2018 10-K filing.

EXHIBIT 23.1   **Kellogg: Pension Note in Annual Report, Funded Status**

$ million

	Pension benefits[1]	Other benefits[2]	Total benefits
Fair value of plan assets at end of year	4,677	1,140	5,817
Projected benefit obligation at end of year	(5,117)	(1,069)	(6,186)
Funded status	(440)	71	(369)
Amounts included in the consolidated balance sheet			
Other assets	228	107	335
Other current liabilities	(17)	(2)	(19)
Pension liability	(651)	–	(651)
Other liabilities	–	(34)	(34)
Net amount recognized	(440)	71	(369)

[1] Kellogg 2018 annual report, Note 10, "Pension Benefits."

[2] Kellogg 2018 annual report, Note 11, "Nonpension Postretirement and Postemployment Benefits."

assets in other long-term assets and unfunded pension liabilities as part of other long-term liabilities, but the details will be in the pension footnote.

Exhibit 23.1 reports the funded status of Kellogg's defined-benefit plans and the location of the company's underfunding on the balance sheet, as reported in the notes. In 2018, Kellogg had $369 million in unfunded pension and other postretirement liabilities. This amount does not appear as a single value on the balance sheet. Instead, the net underfunding is disaggregated across four accounts, including $335 million embedded in other assets, $19 million embedded in other current liabilities, a pension liability of $651 million, and $34 million embedded in other liabilities. A company can have both excess pension assets and unfunded pension liabilities, because companies may have multiple pension plans, and pension assets from one plan are not netted against underfunding from another.

Note that most companies don't fund their "other" retirement obligations, like promised medical benefits, so this will typically appear as showing zero assets and only the liability.

When reorganizing the balance sheet, separate operating assets from pension assets, and treat excess pension assets as nonoperating. Unfunded pension liabilities (on a gross basis) should be treated as a debt equivalent and, as such, should not be deducted from operating assets to determine invested capital. Instead, they will be valued separately during the transition from enterprise value to equity value.

Reorganizing the Income Statement

Pension accounting combines several items into a single expense, known as the pension expense. Some components are operating, while others are related to the performance of the plan assets. As such, pension expense must be

EXHIBIT 23.2 **Kellogg: Pension and Other Postretirement Expenses**

$ million

	2016	2017	2018		
Service cost	119	114	105	⟶	Operating expense
Amortization of prior service cost	4	–	(1)	⟶	Operating for historical benchmarking only
Interest cost	213	201	201		
Expected return on plan assets	(442)	(469)	(455)		
Recognized net (gain) loss	304	(126)	350	⟶	Nonoperating, related to plan performance
Settlements (curtailments)	1	(151)	(30)		
Net periodic (benefit) cost	199	(431)	170	⟶	Information recorded on income statement

Source: Kellogg 2016–2018 annual reports.

analyzed line by line. Exhibit 23.2 presents the pension expense for Kellogg. For ease of exposition, the exhibit combines pension expense with other post-retirement benefits, which Kellogg reports in two separate notes.

In Exhibit 23.2, you will find six accounts. Service cost and the amortization of prior service cost represent benefits granted to the employee in return for service to the company.[3] Interest cost on plan liabilities, expected return on plan assets, and recognized gains and losses represent the evolution of plan assets and liabilities over time.[4] If the change in plan assets matched the change in plan liabilities each year, these accounts would cancel. Since markets are volatile, this is not the case. As a result, the investment performance of plan assets contaminates pension expense. Curtailments represent changes to the pension plan that restrict benefits.

Prior to 2018, companies using GAAP reported the entire pension expense as part of operating expenses. Although not visible on the income statement, the expense was subtly embedded in cost of sales and in selling, general, and administrative (SG&A) expenses. This meant operating expenses and consequently operating profit were a function of the investment performance of plan assets, leading to distortions in competitive benchmarking.

To better understand potential distortions, examine the portion of pension expense titled "recognized net (gain) loss" in Exhibit 23.2. In 2016, Kellogg recognized $304 million in *losses* on plan assets. This increased pension expense relative to other years. In 2017, Kellogg reported recognized *gains* of $126 million. This caused pension expense to convert from a $199 million expense in 2016 to a $431 million benefit in 2017. Since pension expense is embedded within cost of sales, this caused

---

[3] Service cost represents the present value of retirement promises given to the company's employees in a particular year. Prior service costs are additional retroactive benefits given to employees from an amendment to the pension plan. Prior service costs are not expensed immediately. Instead, they are amortized over the expected lifetimes of employees. For more on pension accounting, see D. Kieso, J. Weygandt, and T. Warfield, *Intermediate Accounting*, 17th ed. (Hoboken, NJ: John Wiley & Sons, 2019), chap. 20.

[4] Interest cost represents the present value of service cost growing into the actual retiree payout. Expected return on plan assets equals the expected return based on asset mix. Recognized gains and losses represent the gradual recognition of past gains and losses of the pension fund.

EXHIBIT 23.3   **Kellogg: EBITA Adjusted for Pensions**

$ million

	2016	2017	2018
Operating profits, unadjusted			
Revenues	13,014	12,923	13,547
Operating costs	(11,619)	(10,977)	(11,841)
EBITA, unadjusted	1,395	1,946	1,706
Operating profits, adjusted			
Revenues	13,014	12,923	13,547
Operating costs	(11,619)	(10,977)	(11,841)
Add: Net periodic (benefit) cost	199	(431)	–
Less: Service cost	(119)	(114)	–
EBITA, adjusted	1,475	1,401	1,706
Operating margin, %			
Operating margin, unadjusted	10.7	15.1	12.6
Operating margin, adjusted	11.3	10.8	12.6

Source: Kellog 2016–2018 annual reports.

operating profit to rise in 2017. As a result, the unadjusted operating margin rose from 10.7 percent to 15.1 percent in 2017, even though adjusted margins—that is, those that only include service expense—fell from 11.3 percent to 10.8 percent.

To eliminate plan performance from past operating expenses, remove the pension expense—in Kellogg's case, a $431 million gain in 2017—and replace it with the service cost of $114 million. These adjustments are shown in the middle section of Exhibit 23.3. If benchmarking across companies, one can also include the amortization of prior service costs as an operating expense. While these prior service costs represent real benefits given to employees, they are noncash and represent past changes. Therefore, they should not be incorporated into free cash flow. These service costs are also often small and unlikely to change our perception of historical performance; for simplicity's sake we usually treat them as nonoperating.

Under new accounting standards, the pension expense is no longer treated as operating. Instead, service cost is allocated to the appropriate operating expense account (cost of goods sold or SG&A), and the nonoperating portion of pension expense is treated as "other income or expenses," as is the case for Kellogg in 2018. Since other income or expenses usually accumulates nonoperating items, this makes reorganizing simple.

Given that accounting guidelines across countries may differ, always check the notes for the location of various elements and adjust accordingly.

Expected Return and Earnings Manipulation

To avoid volatility in the income statement, accounting standards allow companies to include an "expected return" on pension plan assets as part of pension expense, rather than actual returns. For example, Exhibit 23.2 shows that Kellogg recorded $455 million in expected return on plan assets in 2018, even

EXHIBIT 23.4   **Capital Structures of Three ConsumerProducts Companies, 2018**

$ million

	Kellogg	General Mills	Mondelēz
Projected benefit obligations[1]	6,186	7,415	11,089
Value of plan assets[1]	(5,817)	(6,904)	(9,975)
Unfunded pension liabilities	369	511	1,114
Debt, net of cash	9,221	16,225	19,826
Debt and debt equivalents	9,590	16,736	20,940
Market value of equity	19,784	25,073	58,197
Enterprise value	29,374	41,809	79,137

[1] Includes domestic pensions, foreign pensions, and other retirement obligations.

Source: Kellogg, General Mills, and Mondelēz 2018 annual reports.

though the plan assets lost $350 million that same year. This enables companies to smooth pension returns from year to year, avoiding volatility in net income.

Since expected return must be estimated, company management has discretion over the rate used—a license that management may sometimes use to manipulate accounting profitability. Bergstresser, Desai, and Rauh found that management increases expected rates of return to increase profitability immediately before acquiring other firms and before exercising stock options.[5] They also found that companies with the weakest shareholder protections tend to use the highest estimates for expected return. With nonoperating items now incorporated into other income and expenses, cost of sales and operating profit are no longer affected by expected-return choices. Even so, net income remains susceptible, which is just one of many reasons why NOPAT, and not earnings per share (EPS), remains a critical measure of accurate benchmarking and financial forecasting.

PENSIONS AND THE COST OF CAPITAL

A key component of valuation is the cost of equity, which is typically estimated using the capital asset pricing model (CAPM) and beta. As discussed in Chapter 15, it is difficult to accurately measure the beta of a single company. Therefore, we recommend using an industry beta derived from multiple companies in similar lines of business.

To isolate the economic risk each company faces, it is important to remove the effect of leverage and, if meaningful, the effect of pensions from beta. In Exhibit 23.4, we present the pension details, debt, and equity of three consumer

---

[5] D. B. Bergstresser, M. A. Desai, and J. Rauh, "Earnings Manipulation, Pension Assumptions, and Managerial Investment Decisions," *Quarterly Journal of Economics* 121, no. 1 (February 2006): 157–195. For more on shareholder protection indexes, see P. Gompers, J. Ishii, and A. Metrick, "Corporate Governance and Equity Prices," *Quarterly Journal of Economics* 118, no. 1 (2003): 107–155.

products companies, including Kellogg. The data include pension plans and other retiree benefits, such as health care. Each company's plan is well funded, with pension shortfalls at or below 10 percent of projected benefit obligations.

There are two ways to incorporate pensions into the unlevering process. In the first method, we assume the pension fund manager has successfully matched the beta risk of plan assets to the beta risk of projected benefits. In this case, the funded portion will net out, and only the unfunded portion will affect the equity beta. In the second method, we relax the assumption of matched beta. While the second method is more flexible than the first, it requires an estimate of the beta risk for plan assets. Since the estimate requires data found only in the notes (versus a professional data provider), as well as a few assumptions regarding asset composition, its use should be limited to situations where pensions play a critical role in company valuation.

In the first method, we assume that only the unfunded pension liability affects the equity beta. Since the unfunded pension liability mirrors debt, we can use the equation for unlevering beta presented in Chapter 15:

$$b_u = \frac{D}{V}b_d + \frac{E}{V}b_e \qquad (1)$$

where b_u equals the unlevered beta, b_d equals the beta of debt, b_e equals the beta of equity, and E equals the market value of equity. The unfunded pension liability is a debt equivalent. Therefore, D equals traditional debt *plus* unfunded pension liabilities less excess cash.

In Exhibit 23.5, we estimate the unlevered beta for Kellogg and two other companies. We present the results with and without pensions for the purpose of comparison. In the analysis, we assume a debt beta of 0.17. Many assume that the debt beta equals zero, but we use a positive beta to assess the various methodologies in a consistent manner. The beta of equity for Kellogg, measured using five years of monthly stock returns, equals 0.64. The debt-to-value

EXHIBIT 23.5   **Unlevered Betas for Three Consumer Products Companies**

	Kellogg	General Mills	Mondelēz	
Beta of debt	0.17	0.17	0.17	
Beta of equity[1]	0.64	0.75	0.83	
Beta of plan assets[2]	0.66	0.75	0.42	
Debt-to-value, excluding pensions, %	31.8	39.3	25.4	
Debt-to-value, including pensions, %	32.6	40.0	26.5	
Unlevered beta				**Average**
Unlevered beta, unadjusted for pensions	0.49	0.52	0.66	0.59
Method 1: Treat unfunded pension as debt equivalent	0.48	0.52	0.66	0.59
Method 2: Allow plan asset beta to differ from obligations beta	0.39	0.42	0.63	0.52

[1] Beta of equity from ThomsonOne, July 2019.

[2] Assumes the beta of debt investments equals 0.17 and the beta of all remaining investments equals 1.0.

ratio equals 31.8 percent without unfunded pensions and 32.6 percent with unfunded pensions. The resulting unlevered betas with and without unfunded pensions are nearly identical because Kellogg's unfunded pension of $369 million is quite small compared with its debt of $9.2 billion. Not surprisingly, the equity beta is higher than the unlevered beta, because leverage increases risk.

To unlever beta when the risk is mismatched, we separate plan assets from pension liabilities and apply the teachings of economists Franco Modigliani and Merton Miller (see Chapter 10) to solve for the risk of operating assets. In Appendix C, we step through the algebraic derivation, leading to the following formula for unlevered beta:

$$b_u = \frac{D + V_{pbo}}{V} b_d + \frac{E}{V} b_e - \frac{V_{pa}}{V} b_{pa} \qquad (2)$$

where b_u represents unlevered beta, b_d represents the beta of debt, b_e represents the equity beta, b_{pa} represents the beta of plan assets, D equals the value of traditional debt net cash, V_{pbo} equals the projected benefit obligations, E equals the market value of equity, V_{pa} equals the market value of plan assets, and V equals enterprise value, as measured by the sum of debt, unfunded pension liabilities, and the market value of equity.

To measure the beta of plan assets, we use the target allocation reported in the pension footnote. Following the research of Jin, Merton, and Bodie, we assume debt securities have a beta of 0.17 and other investments have a beta of 1.0.[6] Using the data from Exhibit 23.4 and Exhibit 23.5, we solve for unlevered beta. For Kellogg, the resulting unlevered beta equals 0.39. Because the beta of plan assets exceeds that of projected benefits, the resulting estimate of unlevered beta is lower than we obtained using earlier methods. Had the betas for plan assets and plan liabilities been the same, the two methods would yield the same results.

While each method has its benefits, we believe Equation 1 inclusive of unfunded pension liabilities is the easiest and most reliable method for unlevering beta. An estimate of unfunded pension liabilities is already required for equity valuation, and the method does not require an extensive analysis of plan assets—a daunting task when there are many companies to analyze within an industry.

RELEVERING BETA TO ESTIMATE THE COST OF EQUITY

Once you have estimated the unlevered industry beta, relever the industry beta to the company's target capital structure and compute the company's cost of capital. To relever the industry beta, do *not* incorporate pensions. While

---

[6] L. Jin, R. Merton, and Z. Bodie, "Do a Firm's Equity Returns Reflect the Risk of Its Pension Plan?" *Journal of Financial Economics* 81, no. 1 (2006): 1–26.

this may seem inconsistent for a company with pensions, it is not. We have eliminated pensions from free cash flow and the cost of capital, and there is no reason to reintroduce pensions, or the risk associated with them, into the value of operations. Instead, value pensions separately, and sum the parts.

INCORPORATING PENSIONS INTO THE VALUE OF EQUITY

Pension plans and other obligations, such as promised medical benefits, will affect a company's value in two ways. First, service cost will be embedded within free cash flow. Since only cash contributions and not service costs are tax deductible, make sure to adjust taxes appropriately for companies that systematically underfund their obligations. Not every country provides tax relief on pension contributions, so check local tax law to determine the marginal tax rate for contributions. Second, past over- or underfunding must be incorporated into value as a nonoperating asset or debt equivalent.

For an ongoing enterprise, excess pension assets can be netted against unfunded liabilities to determine net assets (or liabilities) outstanding. If the company is being valued for liquidation or the pension plan is being terminated, net unfunded liabilities cannot be netted against excess pension assets, as most countries charge a significant penalty for withdrawing excess funds from pension plans. Instead, add after-tax excess pension assets at the penalty rate, and deduct after-tax unfunded pension liabilities at the marginal tax savings for pension contributions.

To value companies with net unfunded liabilities, reduce enterprise value by the product of (1 − marginal tax rate) times net pension liabilities. To incorporate pensions for a company with net excess assets, increase enterprise value by the product of (1 − marginal tax rate on pensions) times net pension assets, as excess pension assets will lead to fewer required contributions in the future.

In 2018, Kellogg recognized $440 million in unfunded pension liabilities and $71 million in prefunded other benefits (see Exhibit 23.1), for a net total liability of $369 million. Assuming a marginal tax rate of 24 percent, the after-tax liability equals $280 million. To determine equity value, deduct the after-tax liability from enterprise value.

CLOSING THOUGHTS

The International Accounting Standards Board and the U.S.-based Financial Accounting Standards Board have worked to eliminate the distortions caused by pension accounting. For most companies, the income statement now separates service cost from nonoperating pension expenses, and the balance sheet recognizes the market value of unfunded pension obligations. The result is better benchmarking, requiring fewer adjustments, and a valuation that is easier to carry out.

24

Measuring Performance in Capital-Light Businesses

In this book, our primary measure of return on capital is return on invested capital (ROIC). We define ROIC as net operating profit after taxes (NOPAT) divided by invested capital. We derive ROIC from items on a company's financial statements, with some adjustments, such as separating operations from financing and separating operating items from nonoperating items.[1] ROIC correctly reflects return on capital in most cases, but special circumstances require alternative measures. For example, a young biotech company could spend a billion dollars on research and development (R&D) before its product is launched. Since R&D is expensed, not capitalized, the company would show a negative ROIC in its early years and a very high ROIC once the product is launched. The actual economic return on capital over the life of the product would lie at some average level in between.

In this chapter, we show how to deal with such investments in R&D and in marketing and sales that are expensed when they are incurred. Creating pro forma financial statements that capitalize these expenses can provide more insight into the underlying economics of a business. In addition, we discuss businesses with very low capital requirements, where we recommend using economic profit or economic profit scaled by revenues to measure return on capital.

CAPITALIZING EXPENSED INVESTMENTS

When a company builds a plant or purchases equipment, it capitalizes the asset on the balance sheet and depreciates it over time. Conversely, when a company invests in intangible assets such as a new production technology, a brand name, or

---

[1] In Chapter 11, we explain why we use ROIC instead of other accounting-based metrics like return on equity (ROE) or return on assets (ROA).

a distribution network, the entire outlay must be expensed immediately. In sectors such as pharmaceuticals, high technology, and branded consumer goods, failure to recognize such expenses as investments can lead to significantly underestimating a company's invested capital and overstating its return on invested capital.

To get a more accurate measurement of ROIC,[2] it's best to capitalize outlays for intangible investments if they bring benefits over multiple years in the future rather than merely for the current year. Earnings in any given year are supported by not just that year's R&D or brand advertising expenses, but instead by many prior years of these expenses. It has taken companies such as Coca-Cola and PepsiCo many decades and billions of dollars to build their global brand names. Pharmaceutical companies such as Pfizer, and high-tech companies such as Intel and ASML, had to invest in technology development projects over many years to build and sustain their current product offerings.

The economics of investments in intangible assets are very similar to those of investments in tangible assets. Their treatment in ROIC should therefore also be the same to ensure that it adequately reflects the internal rate of return (IRR), or true return, of the underlying investments.[3] Failure to do so would lead to ROICs far above the true return of the business. Consider what would happen to ROIC if capital expenditures for net property, plant, and equipment (net PP&E) were not capitalized but were expensed instead.

In addition to improving the measurement of ROIC, capitalizing intangible investments can reduce the manipulation of short-term profits. Under traditional accounting, a manager looking to meet short-term earnings targets can simply reduce R&D spending. With R&D capitalized, however, amortization charges to earnings will remain almost unchanged in the short term. Capitalizing investments can also provide strategic insights. For example, many companies set R&D budgets at a fixed percentage of revenue. When combined with expensing R&D, this masks the change in performance resulting from any change in revenues, because the earnings margin remains unchanged. But when R&D is capitalized, amortization charges do not change with revenues, and the impact on performance is clearly reflected in earnings.

Example: Capitalizing R&D Expenses

As an illustration of capitalizing intangible investments and its impact on ROIC, Exhibit 24.1 presents the reorganized financial statements for PharmaCo. This fictional company has experienced rapid growth over the past 25 years, reaching around $1.2 billion in revenues by 2020. The after-tax earnings margin is 11 percent of sales. R&D expenses, to renew the product pipeline, are at around 20 percent of sales. ROIC is at 33 percent, with revenues at three times invested capital as

[2] The same applies to return on capital measures such as cash flow return on investment (CFROI), as discussed in the following chapter.
[3] To be truly "value based," the measure for return on capital should reflect the internal rate of return (IRR) of the underlying business from the time investments are made until all the cash flows from that investment have been collected (see also Chapter 25).

EXHIBIT 24.1 **PharmaCo: Reorganized Financial Statements**

$ million

Partial income statement	2015	2016	2017	2018	2019	2020	
Revenues	1,045	1,077	1,109	1,142	1,176	1,212	← Fixed at 60% of revenues
Cost of sales	(627)	(646)	(665)	(685)	(706)	(727)	
R&D expense	(229)	(235)	(242)	(248)	(255)	(262)	
Operating profit	189	195	202	208	215	222	
Taxes	(76)	(78)	(81)	(83)	(86)	(89)	
NOPAT[1]	113	117	121	125	129	133	

Partial balance sheet	2015	2016	2017	2018	2019	2020	
Invested capital	348	359	370	381	392	404	← Fixed at 3 times capital turnover
NOPAT/revenues, %	10.9	10.9	10.9	10.9	11.0	11.0	
ROIC, %	32.6	32.7	32.8	32.8	32.9	33.0	

[1] Net operating profit after taxes.

computed directly from the balance sheet. But this ROIC does not represent the company's true economic performance, because the invested capital includes only purchased capital and not the intellectual capital created internally from R&D.

To estimate ROIC with capitalized investments in R&D, use the following three-step process:

1. Capitalize and amortize the R&D asset, using an appropriate asset lifetime.
2. Adjust invested capital upward by the historical cost of the R&D asset, net of cumulative amortization.
3. Adjust NOPAT by replacing R&D expense with R&D amortization. (Do not adjust operating taxes.)

To capitalize the R&D asset, choose a starting year, and begin accumulating R&D expenses. Choose the earliest year feasible, as the model requires accumulated R&D to reach a steady state before the adjusted ROIC calculation becomes meaningful. Exhibit 24.2 starts in 1995, assuming straight-line amortization and an eight-year R&D asset life. PharmaCo spent $22 million on R&D in 1995, which we capitalize and add to invested capital and start to amortize in 1996. By adding R&D expenses to the prior year's net asset value and then deducting amortization charges in each year, we arrive at a capitalized R&D asset base of $1,666 million in 2020.[4]

To adjust invested capital for the intangible investments, add the capitalized R&D asset to invested capital. On this basis, PharmaCo's total capital amounts to $2,070 million in 2020, most of it in the form of capitalized R&D.[5]

---

[4] In this example, for illustration purposes, we approximate amortization at 10 percent of the preceding year's ending balance. Advanced models use straight-line amortization of actual R&D expense.
[5] If we add capitalized R&D to operating assets, total funds invested will no longer balance. To balance total funds invested, add capitalized R&D to equity equivalents. For more on total funds invested and their reconciliation, see Chapter 11.

EXHIBIT 24.2 **PharmaCo: Capitalization of R&D**

$ million

			Estimated R&D asset lifetime: 8 years				
Partial income statement	1995	1996	1997		2018	2019	2020
Revenues	10	22	43	...	1,142	1,176	1,212
R&D expense	(22)	(24)	(29)	...	(248)	(255)	(262)
Capitalized R&D asset							
Capitalized R&D, starting	–	22	44	...	1,477	1,541	1,604
R&D expense	22	24	29	...	248	255	262
Amortization	-	(3)	(5)	...	(185)	(193)	(200)
Capitalized R&D, ending	22	44	67	...	1,541	1,604	1,666
Partial balance sheet	1995	1996	1997		2018	2019	2020
Invested capital, unadjusted	3	7	14	...	381	392	404
Capitalized R&D	22	44	67	...	1,541	1,604	1,666
Invested capital, adjusted	25	51	81	...	1,922	1,996	2,070

Adjust NOPAT by replacing R&D expense ($262 million in 2020) with R&D amortization ($200 million), computed as outlined in Exhibit 24.3. Operating taxes remain unchanged, because capitalization and amortization of R&D expense does not change taxable income for fiscal purposes. For PharmaCo, replacing R&D expense with amortization raises NOPAT in 2020 from $133 million to $195 million. This is quite common for growth firms, as current R&D is typically higher than the amortization of historical R&D. As the company's growth rate tapers off, however, amortization will catch up with expense, and NOPAT adjustments will be small.

EXHIBIT 24.3 **PharmaCo: NOPAT Adjusted for R&D Capitalization**

$ million

	2016	2017	2018	2019	2020
Revenues	1,077	1,109	1,142	1,176	1,212
Cost of sales	(646)	(665)	(685)	(706)	(727)
R&D expense	(235)	(242)	(248)	(255)	(262)
Operating profit	195	202	208	215	222
Operating taxes	(78)	(81)	(83)	(86)	(89)
NOPAT	117	121	125	129	133
Add back: R&D expense	235	242	248	255	262
R&D amortization	(168)	(177)	(185)	(193)	(200)
Adjusted NOPAT	184	186	189	192	195
ROIC, %	32.7	32.8	32.8	32.9	33.0
ROIC adjusted for R&D capitalization, %	10.4	10.1	9.8	9.6	9.4

EXHIBIT 24.4 **PharmaCo: Free Cash Flow**

$ million

R&D expensed, unadjusted	2017	2018	2019	2020
NOPAT	121	125	129	133
Depreciation	37	38	39	40
Gross cash flow	158	163	168	174
Capital expenditures	(48)	(49)	(51)	(52)
Free cash flow	**110**	**114**	**118**	**122**

R&D capitalized	2017	2018	2019	2020
Adjusted NOPAT	186	189	192	195
Depreciation	37	38	39	40
⟶ Amortization of R&D	177	185	193	200
Gross cash flow	400	412	424	436
Capital expenditures	(48)	(49)	(51)	(52)
⟶ Investment in R&D	(242)	(248)	(255)	(262)
Free cash flow	**110**	**114**	**118**	**122**

Note that for PharmaCo's historical years, free cash flows cannot change when R&D expenses are capitalized (see Exhibit 24.4). The amortization is a noncash charge in NOPAT and is added back to calculate gross cash flow. This effectively moves R&D expenses from gross cash flow to investments, leaving free cash flow unchanged.

Based on the new measures for invested capital, with capitalized R&D investments and for NOPAT with R&D amortization instead of expenses, we derive an adjusted ROIC. The adjusted ROIC with R&D capitalized represents PharmaCo's return on capital, including intangible investments. It can be compared with an unadjusted ROIC with R&D expensed, as shown in Exhibit 24.5. Because the R&D asset lifetime was estimated at eight years, at least as many years of constant growth must elapse for capital and ROIC to reach a steady state and provide a meaningful indication of true economic returns. As Exhibit 24.5 shows, the adjusted ROIC computed on total capital stabilizes at around 9.5 percent, dramatically lower than the 33 percent ROIC derived from the unadjusted financial statements. As long as the R&D investments needed to support earnings remain unchanged, PharmaCo's adjusted ROIC is the better estimate of its true economic return and underlying performance.[6]

One of the key assumptions made in capitalizing intangible investments is the asset lifetime. Although it may be hard to come up with an accurate estimate, this should not keep you from capitalizing the R&D expenses. Asset lifetime has less impact on ROIC than you might expect. In the PharmaCo example, we

---

[6] That is, ROIC is the better estimate of the investments' value creation, as explained in Chapter 25.

EXHIBIT 24.5 **PharmaCo: ROIC, 1997–2020**

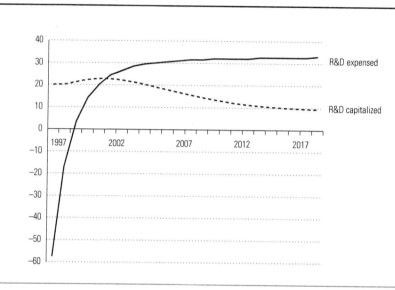

assumed an asset life of eight years. In Exhibit 24.6, we stress-test this assumption by varying asset life between two and 12 years. Even an asset life of just two years dramatically reduces PharmaCo's ROIC from 33 percent when R&D is expensed to 16 percent when it is capitalized. Increasing the asset life continues to lower ROIC, but by smaller amounts as asset life increases. So choosing an asset life of 12 rather than eight years (a reasonable range for the life of most R&D

EXHIBIT 24.6 **PharmaCo: ROIC at Different Estimates of R&D Asset Lifetime, 2020**

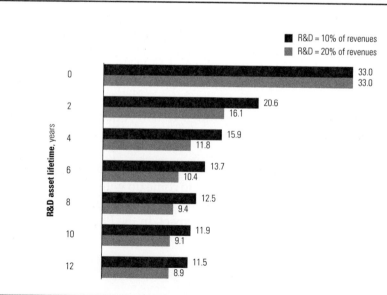

assets) does not materially affect perceptions of performance: for PharmaCo, ROIC would be 8.9 percent for a 12-year life, versus 9.4 percent for an eight-year life. This pattern remains unchanged when R&D spending is much lower—for example, at only 10 percent of revenues. Furthermore, when using ROIC to compare the performance of competing companies, what matters most is that asset lifetime estimates are consistent across all companies. Keep in mind that the lifetimes for tangible assets are also based on rough estimates and accounting conventions. Yet most managers and analysts are quite comfortable using tangible-asset book values and depreciation charges as the basis for return on capital and earnings.[7]

Interpreting Return on Capital, Including Capitalized Expenses

In general, capitalizing intangible investments will lead to lower ROIC. For mature companies with stable revenues and investment spending, the amortization charges for intangible assets are likely to be close to the amounts expensed. As a result, capitalizing the expenses may have little impact on NOPAT. But the capital base will always increase when the expenses are capitalized, leading to lower ROIC.

Although the capitalization can never change historical free cash flows, as discussed in the PharmaCo example, the resulting adjustments to capital turnover and ROIC can affect projections of future free cash flows. For PharmaCo, required investments in R&D to achieve growth of 10 percent per year would be estimated at $375 million in 2021, which is $113 million more than the $262 million spent in 2020. This follows from required growth of the net R&D asset base (10 percent, or $167 million) plus an annual amortization charge of $208 million (one-eighth of the 2020 ending balance). When R&D investments going forward would be modeled as expenses, the required additional R&D outlay in 2021 would be only 10 percent of the additional 2021 revenues, or $26 million. This is comparable to what happens to investment projections if capital expenditures for tangible assets are derived from a constant ratio to revenues or instead implied from a constant capital turnover (see Chapter 13).

If PharmaCo can increase its revenues by 10 percent as a result of increasing its R&D expenses by 10 percent, the unadjusted ROIC provides the best estimate of the IRR of future investments in its business. In contrast, if achieving that same revenue growth would require PharmaCo to increase its net R&D asset base, rather than its R&D expenses, by 10 percent, the adjusted ROIC is the better estimate. Of course, these R&D investment estimates for PharmaCo are not likely to apply from year to year. What matters is which R&D investments are required for growth over the long term.

More accurately reflecting the economics of intangible investments on ROIC can have major implications for investment decisions, performance

---

[7] Note also that for an alternative measure of ROIC, such as cash flow return on investment (CFROI) with or without resource capitalization, estimates of asset lifetimes are critical—not for book value or depreciation, but for estimating the CFROI itself (see Chapter 25).

assessments, resource allocation, and competitive behavior. For instance, if the cost of capital is 10 percent, PharmaCo is in fact destroying value, and management should question continued investment. Competitors should question the validity of entering the company's product markets. The margins may be high, but required investments in R&D are large.

To illustrate the impact of capitalizing intangibles on estimates of ROIC and perspectives on value creation, we analyzed past spending on research and advertising over a ten-year period for four global companies in branded consumer goods. After the estimated past expenses in R&D and advertising were capitalized and amortized, ROIC for all companies decreased significantly and also provided a very different ranking of performance, as shown in the top portion of Exhibit 24.7. A similar analysis of ROIC including capitalized

EXHIBIT 24.7 **Impact of Adjusting ROIC for Intangible Investments**

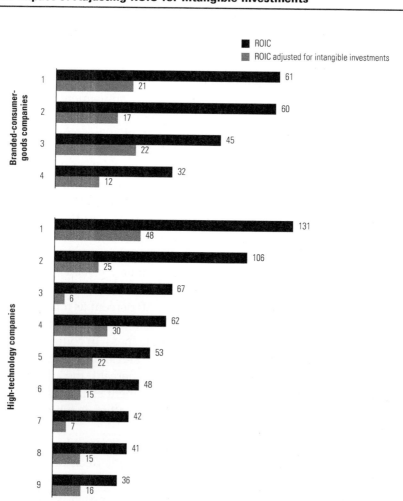

R&D expenses among high-tech hardware manufacturers provided similar shifts in perceived performance levels and rankings (see the bottom portion of Exhibit 24.7).

Capitalizing intangibles can provide a better financial perspective on competitive positions. Think of comparing current budgets on brand advertising between incumbents and new entrants in personal or household products. The comparison is not very useful if the incumbent brands have been built by many years of marketing efforts. Incumbents' current advertising budgets will then underestimate the investments required by new entrants to reach similar levels of brand awareness among customers. A capitalized investment base can provide a more accurate estimate.

While insights from capitalizing resources are valuable, companies must take care. Left unchecked, managers could have an incentive to classify all expenses as investments, even those with no long-term benefits, because this will maximize reported short-term performance. They could also be reluctant to write off investments that prove worthless after they have been capitalized. For instance, a distribution channel may be kept open merely to avoid a write-down on the manager's economic balance sheet.

WHEN BUSINESSES NEED LITTLE OR NO CAPITAL

Some businesses do not require significant amounts of capital—for example, those in the professional services sector, but also consumer electronics companies with outsourced manufacturing. Because of these companies' low or even negative capital base, ROIC can become less meaningful. In such cases, we recommend using economic profit as the key measure of value creation.

Capital-Light Business Models and ROIC

Examples of businesses with an inherently low need for capital include accounting, legal counseling and other professional services, and real estate and other forms of brokerage services. Businesses such as software development and services have limited fixed capital needs, and customer license prepayments and supplier financing often bring their overall invested capital close to zero. In these cases, capital is very low relative to earnings generated, and ROIC accordingly is high. Modest changes in an already small invested-capital base can lead to very large swings in ROIC, making ROIC in any particular year hard to use for performance management or financial planning and target setting.

Let's illustrate with a stylized example of TradeCo, whose financial statements are summarized in Exhibit 24.8. TradeCo is a trading company in plumbing supplies and tools. It has offices and a warehouse in a low-cost location. Inventories are kept to a minimum: except for those items with the

EXHIBIT 24.8 **TradeCo: Financial Statements**

$ million

NOPAT	2015	2016	2017	2018	2019	2020
Revenues	200.0	209.0	212.1	216.4	214.2	212.1
Cost of goods sold	(160.0)	(165.1)	(169.7)	(175.3)	(171.4)	(170.7)
SG&A	(20.0)	(20.9)	(21.2)	(21.6)	(21.4)	(21.2)
Operating taxes	(7.0)	(8.0)	(7.4)	(6.8)	(7.5)	(7.1)
NOPAT	13.0	14.9	13.8	12.7	13.9	13.1

Invested capital	2015	2016	2017	2018	2019	2020
Net working capital	(12.0)	(8.4)	(10.6)	(2.2)	(4.3)	(6.4)
Net PP&E	10.0	9.5	9.1	9.0	8.7	8.4
Invested capital	(2.0)	1.1	(1.5)	6.8	4.4	2.1

Free cash flow	2015	2016	2017	2018	2019	2020
NOPAT	13.0	14.9	13.8	12.7	13.9	13.1
Net investments	(2.0)	(3.1)	2.6	(8.3)	2.4	2.3
Free cash flow	11.0	11.9	16.3	4.4	16.3	15.4

Key value drivers, %	2015	2016	2017	2018	2019	2020
NOPAT/revenues	6.5	7.2	6.5	5.9	6.5	6.2
Invested capital/revenues	(1.0)	0.5	(0.7)	3.1	2.1	1.0
→ ROIC	N/M[1]	1,371	N/M	186	316	632

Economic profit	2015	2016	2017	2018	2019	2020
NOPAT	13.0	14.9	13.8	12.7	13.9	13.1
Capital charge[2]	0.2	(0.1)	0.1	(0.7)	(0.4)	(0.2)
→ Economic profit	13.2	14.8	13.9	12.0	13.5	12.9

[1] Not meaningful.
[2] Cost of capital equals 10%.

highest turnover, supplies and tools are purchased on customer order. Because TradeCo pays its suppliers after receiving payment on its own customer invoices, working capital is negative.

As Exhibit 24.8 shows, revenues, earnings, and free cash flow are fairly stable on a year-by-year basis. But as the graph in Exhibit 24.9 shows, ROIC fluctuates wildly and is even unmeasurable in some years, despite stable earnings margins and healthy cash flows. The reason is that TradeCo's invested capital is very small and sometimes even negative, mainly because of movements in working capital. ROIC is not meaningful in 2015 and 2017 because the company had negative invested capital. ROIC is numerically negative, but it lacks any economic interpretation.[8] Looking at the bottom of Exhibit 24.8, we see that economic profit was positive in 2017, clearly indicating value creation. The movements in ROIC could mislead your assessment of performance. For example, ROIC increased from 316 percent in 2019 to 632 percent

[8] Mathematically, ROIC still ties perfectly with cash flow and value, following the fundamental logic described in Chapter 3.

EXHIBIT 24.9 **TradeCo: ROIC and NOPAT Margin**

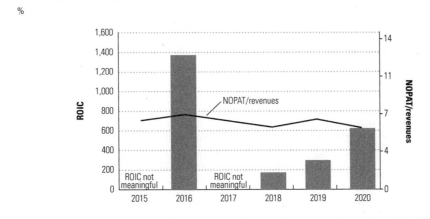

in 2020. Yet value creation declined, as the change in economic profit for the same period shows. The change in ROIC was driven by a decline in working capital. Earnings declined simultaneously and pushed down value creation.

Not all businesses with low capital are inherently capital light. Indeed, some capital-intensive businesses have adopted capital-light models by outsourcing their most capital-intensive processes—typically manufacturing and distribution. The high-tech electronics sector provides examples of this approach, including Apple, Fujitsu, Hewlett-Packard, and Sony. In the apparel sector, companies such as Nike have outsourced their manufacturing.

ROICs for businesses that have aggressively outsourced parts of their business chain can be very high and volatile. In addition, the capital reduction that comes with outsourcing can lead to confusion when ROIC is used to assess whether outsourcing creates any value to begin with. After outsourcing, many businesses end up with much higher ROICs. In some cases, managers even refer to the higher ROIC as one of the main benefits of outsourcing. But the ROIC increase does not necessarily mean that the company has created value for its shareholders.

Consider the companies InhouseCo and ContractCo in Exhibit 24.10. The companies are identical, with one exception: ContractCo has outsourced all of its production to a third party. It has no net PP&E and no depreciation charges, but it has higher operating costs compared with InhouseCo. Although ContractCo's earnings are lower than InhouseCo's, its ROIC is more than five times larger because it no longer needs PP&E. But ContractCo is not creating more value in its business than InhouseCo. In fact, as the measure of economic profit indicates, the two companies' value creation is identical. In this example, ContractCo has separated out its capital-intensive and low-ROIC production activities from its other activities without creating value. The ROIC for ContractCo goes up simply because it retains only the high-ROIC activities. But that does not say anything about the value creation from

EXHIBIT 24.10 **Impact of Production Outsourcing on ROIC**

$ million

	InhouseCo	ContractCo
NOPAT		
Revenues	100.0	100.0
Operating costs	(85.0)	(94.5)
Depreciation	(3.8)	–
Operating taxes	(3.9)	(1.9)
NOPAT	7.3	3.6
Invested capital		
Net working capital	5.0	5.0
Net PP&E	50.0	–
Invested capital	55.0	5.0
Key value drivers, %		
NOPAT/revenues	7.3	3.6
Invested capital/revenues	55.0	5.0
→ ROIC	13.3	71.2
Economic profit		
NOPAT	7.3	3.6
Capital charge[1]	(4.1)	(0.4)
→ Economic profit	3.2	3.2

[1] Cost of capital equals 7.5%.

outsourcing.[9] Managers should therefore not make decisions to outsource merely on the grounds that it raises ROIC. These decisions need to be supported by an analysis of economic profit or, equivalently, a DCF valuation.

Economic Profit as a Key Value Metric

Although there is no objective way to determine a cutoff point, we believe that ROICs above 50 percent need to be handled with caution when used as a measure of value creation. Special caution is required in businesses where high capital turnover, rather than high earnings margins, drives such ROIC levels.

In such cases, economic profit is a more solid performance measure that is always in line with value creation. (For more details on economic profit, see Chapter 3.) It can be defined in either of the following two equivalent ways:

$$\text{Economic Profit} = (\text{ROIC} - \text{WACC}) \times \text{Invested Capital} \qquad (24.1)$$

$$\text{Economic Profit} = \text{NOPAT} - \text{Capital Charge} \qquad (24.2)$$

In Equation 24.2, the capital charge equals WACC times invested capital.

[9] Of course, outsourcing in this example could still create real value if it enables ContractCo to realize higher growth because it needs less capital for its business.

EXHIBIT 24.11 **DiversiCo: Economic Profit Scaled by Revenues**

	Revenues	Invested capital	NOPAT	NOPAT/ revenues, %	ROIC, %	Economic profit[1]	Economic profit/ revenues,[1] %
Software	100	(5)	25	25	n/m[2]	25	25
Hardware services	250	10	44	18	438	43	17
Supplies	750	250	94	13	38	73	10
Hardware	2,500	1,000	188	8	19	103	4

[1] Cost of capital equals 8.5%.

[2] Not meaningful.

Because ROIC is multiplied by invested capital, economic profit automatically corrects for any distortion in ROIC for business models with extremely low capital intensity. The TradeCo example in Exhibit 24.8 illustrated this. ROIC shows very large fluctuations over the years, even becoming unmeasurable in some years. In contrast, economic profit is fairly stable, just as TradeCo's cash flows are stable and consistently positive over the years. Economic profit is a much better reflection of TradeCo's underlying business economics. It provides more accurate insights into its historical performance and a useful basis for predicting s future performance.

As economic profit is a measure of return on capital in absolute terms, it is very useful for understanding whether value creation in a particular business has increased from one year to the next. But it is harder to use for interpreting differences in economic profit generated by businesses of different sizes. Take, for example, DiversiCo in Exhibit 24.11. DiversiCo is a diversified industrial company with business units in software, hardware, hardware services, and supplies. The business units are very different in size and economics. Hardware, for example, has annual revenues of $2.5 billion, dwarfing the $100 million in revenues generated by software development. The software business has negative invested capital, thanks to customer prepayments, whereas hardware requires $1 billion in capital, mainly for manufacturing and distribution facilities and inventories. ROIC is meaningless for comparing performance across DiversiCo's businesses, because software and hardware services have little or negative capital. Economic profit provides an accurate picture of value creation, but comparisons among businesses of such different sizes are difficult. Economic profit is lowest for the software business (at $25 million), not so much because of the business's performance, but because of its size.

To better compare the value creation of DiversiCo's businesses, scale economic profit by revenues, turning it into a measure of value creation per dollar of sales.[10] As graphed in the final column of Exhibit 24.11, it now becomes clear that DiversiCo's software business generates the highest value per dollar

[10] See M. Dodd and W. Rehm, "Comparing Performance When Invested Capital Is Low," *McKinsey on Finance* (Autumn 2005): 17–20.

EXHIBIT 24.12 **Better Performance Comparison with Economic Profit over Revenues**

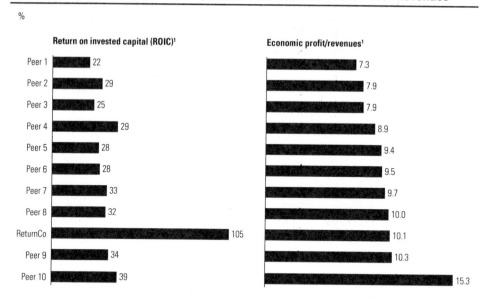

%

Return on invested capital (ROIC)[1]

Peer	ROIC
Peer 1	22
Peer 2	29
Peer 3	25
Peer 4	29
Peer 5	28
Peer 6	28
Peer 7	33
Peer 8	32
ReturnCo	105
Peer 9	34
Peer 10	39

Economic profit/revenues[1]

Peer 1	7.3
Peer 2	7.9
Peer 3	7.9
Peer 4	8.9
Peer 5	9.4
Peer 6	9.5
Peer 7	9.7
Peer 8	10.0
ReturnCo	10.1
Peer 9	10.3
Peer 10	15.3

[1] Excluding goodwill and acquired intangibles.

Source: Capital IQ, Corporate Performance Analytics by McKinsey.

of revenues, and its hardware business the lowest. Driving revenue growth in software development would therefore be most beneficial for shareholders.[11] Scaling economic profit in this way provides DiversiCo's management with a better yardstick for decisions on resource allocation and portfolio strategy.

In the same way, the ratio of economic profit over revenues can help in benchmarking performance with peers of different size and capital intensity. Consider the example of a branded-consumer-goods company, which we refer to as ReturnCo, in Exhibit 24.12. ReturnCo is generating a ROIC of 105 percent, far above its international peers' ROIC levels of around 30 to 40 percent. But this does not necessarily mean that ReturnCo creates more value and that it has some source of competitive advantage over its peers. Following our rule of thumb, ROICs above 50 percent should be interpreted with caution and carefully analyzed. In this case, it turns out that ReturnCo provides its customers with aggressive discounts for early payment. The discount pushes its earnings margins below peer levels, but the early payments make its net working capital negative and reduce its invested capital. The net result is an exceptionally high ROIC. Comparing its ROIC with those of its peers is pointless because of this difference in capital intensity, and absolute economic profit will of course differ with the size of the competitors. Instead, an analysis of

---

[11] Note how economic profit over revenues is almost identical to NOPAT margin for capital-light businesses, such as software and hardware services in this example. This is easily explained by examining Equation 24.2: when invested capital is 0, the capital charge is 0, and economic profit is equal to NOPAT.

economic profit over revenues best reveals how ReturnCo performs relative to its peers in terms of value creation. As the exhibit shows, the increased capital efficiency is roughly offset by the discount provided: ReturnCo's ratio of economic profit to revenues is very similar to those of its peers. At first sight, ReturnCo's ROIC appeared superior, but a closer look has revealed that its value creation is in line with that of its peers.

In general, when you are comparing the performance of businesses with very different capital intensity and size, using economic profit over revenues provides the best insights into performance and value creation.

SUMMARY

For most businesses, ROIC is a good measure of return on capital. However, for businesses that rely on significant investments in intangibles, such as R&D or brands, you should make some adjustments to ROIC to include the capitalized value of these resources. For businesses that use very little or no capital, economic profit is a better measure of value creation. To allow for comparison across businesses of different sizes, you can scale economic profit by revenues.

25

Alternative Ways to Measure Return on Capital

Valuations often assume that historical return on capital is a good starting point for projecting future returns as a company grows. But if historical return on capital is measured in a way that gives us no meaningful information about value creation, decisions about whether to continue investing in a business may be incorrect. To be truly value based, the measure for return on capital should reflect the internal rate of return (IRR) of the underlying business from the time investments are made until all the cash flows from that investment have been collected. That's not possible in practice, because we can't wait until the end of every project to assess a company's performance; a business is an accumulation of different investments made at different times. So we need a proxy that measures how much value a company has created in the recent past and that can help a company with the particularly important task of planning for the future.

Return on invested capital (ROIC), our primary measure of return on capital, correctly reflects value creation in most cases. But ROIC has some imperfections. For example, it doesn't account for the age of assets or the effect that inflation has on its measurement. Analysts have therefore proposed alternatives to overcome some of ROIC's weaknesses. One of these, cash flow return on investment (CFROI), is estimated from cash flows rather than from accounting measures. CFROI is the better measure of value creation in certain rare situations. This chapter explores the conditions under which ROIC accurately reflects the true economic return on capital and when to consider a more complex CFROI measure. We then look at some other alternatives and explain why they are flawed measures of value creation.

As we compare these measures, note that all of them apply this important principle: any measure of return on capital should be based on the amount invested, not the current market value of the company or its assets.

Take, for example, the case where the fair value of an asset is based on the intrinsic, discounted-cash-flow (DCF) value of its future cash flows. By definition, the return on capital for the asset at its fair value does not provide any indication of an investment's value creation in such assets. For a growing business, a return on capital measured against the DCF value will always be less than the cost of capital, because the DCF value reflects the value creation of future investments.

WHEN ROIC EQUALS IRR

The simplest approach to measuring return on capital, which works well in most cases, is the one we use throughout this book: ROIC, or operating earnings divided by the net book value of a company's operating capital (purchase cost less accumulated depreciation). To illustrate when ROIC accurately estimates the IRR of an asset and the business activities it supports, we will use a stylized example, shown in Exhibit 25.1. The initial investment is $100, and operating cash flows gradually decline over the asset's five-year lifetime. With linear depreciation charges of $20, the operating profit is proportional to the net invested capital in each year, declining from $15 in the first year to $3 in the last. We define ROIC in a particular year as the operating profit for that year divided by the invested capital at the beginning of the year, net of accumulated depreciation (ignoring taxes for simplicity). In this example, the asset's ROIC is constant over the asset's lifetime at 15 percent.

EXHIBIT 25.1   **Returns When Profits Are Proportional to Net Invested Capital**

$

		Individual asset						Business of five assets
		Year						
		0	1	2	3	4	5	
Operating cash flow		(100)	35	32	29	26	23	145
Depreciation			(20)	(20)	(20)	(20)	(20)	(100)
Operating profit			15	12	9	6	3	45
Gross invested capital[1]			100	100	100	100	100	500
Cumulative depreciation[1]			–	(20)	(40)	(60)	(80)	(200)
Net invested capital[1]			100	80	60	40	20	300
IRR, %		15.0						15.0
Cash return on gross invested capital, %			35.0	32.0	29.0	26.0	23.0	29.0
Cash return on net invested capital, %			35.0	40.0	48.3	65.0	115.0	48.3
ROIC, %			15.0	15.0	15.0	15.0	15.0	15.0
CFROI, %			22.1	18.0	13.8	9.4	4.8	13.8

ROIC is constant over asset lifetime.

CFROI decreases over asset lifetime.

ROIC = IRR

CFROI < IRR

[1] At beginning of year.

When ROIC is constant, the asset provides a constant return over the initial investment, net of recovering the initial investment itself. Therefore, this return must also equal the IRR of the cash flows for the asset, or 15 percent. More precisely, the investment's ROIC equals the IRR if the earnings generated from the investment are proportional to the invested capital, net of accumulated depreciation, in each year of the investment's lifetime.

It is possible to generalize the result for a business consisting of a portfolio of five of these individual assets, which have remaining lifetimes of one, two, three, four, and five years, respectively (see the rightmost column in Exhibit 25.1). For this business, the operating cash flow, profit, and invested capital are a straightforward sum of the operating cash flow, profit, and invested capital for each year of the individual asset's lifetime (for example, operating cash flows for the business equal $35 + $32 + $29 + $26 + $23 = $145). What holds for the assets will therefore also hold for the business as a whole, so its ROIC must equal an individual asset's ROIC and IRR of 15 percent. If this business wants to grow its earnings by, say, 10 percent, it will need to expand its net invested capital by 10 percent as well—requiring an investment outlay of $30 in this case. The IRR on that incremental investment for carbon-copy growth equals exactly the business's ROIC of 15 percent.

This means that the ROIC of a business (or company) is equal to the IRR of new investments if the operating earnings for the business are proportional to net invested capital.[1] In these conditions, ROIC is a value-based measure of return on capital, even though it is based on accounting measures of earnings and capital.

WHEN CFROI EQUALS IRR

CFROI is an alternative measure of return on capital based on cash flow rather than profit and book value.[2] For any given year, CFROI is defined as the discount rate for which the present value of that year's operating cash flow (as an N-year annuity) equals gross invested capital at the beginning of the year, where N is the lifetime of the underlying asset. The basic formula for calculating CFROI in a given year T is

$$\text{GIC}_T = \sum_{t=1}^{N} \frac{\text{OCF}_T}{(1 + \text{CFROI})^t}$$

where GIC_T = gross invested capital at the beginning of year T
OCF_T = operating cash flow in year T

---

[1] The same logic underlies the value driver formula introduced in Chapter 3, which showed that DCF value increases only for earnings growth at a ROIC above the cost of capital.

[2] For more information, see B. Madden, *CFROI Valuation: A Total System Approach to Valuing the Firm* (Oxford: Butterworth-Heinemann, 1999).

EXHIBIT 25.2 **Returns When Cash Flows Are Proportional to Gross Invested Capital**

$

		Individual asset						Business of five assets
		Year						
	0	1	2	3	4	5		
Operating cash flow	(100)	29	29	29	29	29		145
Depreciation		(20)	(20)	(20)	(20)	(20)		(100)
Operating profit		9	9	9	9	9		45
Gross invested capital[1]		100	100	100	100	100		500
Cumulative depreciation[1]		–	(20)	(40)	(60)	(80)		(200)
Net invested capital[1]		100	80	60	40	20		300
IRR, %	13.8							13.8
Cash return on gross invested capital, %		29.0	29.0	29.0	29.0	29.0		29.0
Cash return on net invested capital, %		29.0	36.3	48.3	72.5	145.0		48.3
ROIC, %		9.0	11.3	15.0	22.5	45.0		15.0
CFROI, %		13.8	13.8	13.8	13.8	13.8		13.8

ROIC increases over asset lifetime.   ROIC > IRR

CFROI is constant over asset lifetime.   CFROI = IRR

[1] At beginning of year.

Any residual value of the asset should be included as an additional cash flow for year N and discounted at CFROI.

We illustrate CFROI as an alternative measure of returns by showing financial projections for an asset whose economics are different from those of the prior example. In this case, shown in Exhibit 25.2, the operating cash flows are proportional to gross invested capital and constant over the asset's lifetime, at $29 per year. The IRR for the investment is 13.8 percent and exactly equals the CFROI, which is constant over the asset's lifetime. Take, for example, year 2. We estimate the asset's CFROI by solving the following equation:

$$\$100 = \frac{\$29}{(1+\text{CFROI})^1} + \ldots + \frac{\$29}{(1+\text{CFROI})^5} \Rightarrow \text{CFROI} = 13.8\%$$

In fact, when the operating cash flow is constant over an asset's lifetime, CFROI must be equal to the IRR, as follows from the preceding formula. We could also say that CFROI equals the IRR of an investment if the operating cash flows generated are proportional to the gross invested capital (before accumulated depreciation).

Let's generalize the results again to a business consisting of five such individual assets, with remaining lifetimes of one, two, three, four, and five years (the right column in Exhibit 25.2). As in the prior example, the business's overall cash flows, earnings, and invested capital derive from those of the underlying five assets. The business's CFROI and IRR therefore equal the CFROI and IRR of each individual asset. If this business wants to grow its cash flows by 10 percent, it must expand its gross invested capital by 10 percent as well—an investment outlay of $50. The IRR on that incremental investment is now equal to its CFROI of 13.8 percent. Note that the business ROIC of 15 percent overestimates the IRR in this case. In general, the business (or company) CFROI is exactly equal to the IRR of new investments if operating cash flows for the business are proportional to gross invested capital.

CHOOSING BETWEEN ROIC AND CFROI

To understand when to use ROIC and when to use CFROI, let's now compare the two examples in Exhibits 25.1 and 25.2 in more detail. Note that the businesses (not the assets) in both examples have identical ROIC, CFROI, earnings (operating profit), operating cash flow, and invested capital. Nevertheless, the underlying economics and value creation are quite different, as is the "right" measure for return on capital.[3]

For the example in Exhibit 25.1, ROIC is the right measure of return on capital for the asset and the business, equaling the IRR of 15 percent. The reason: the cash flow pattern over the lifetime of the asset leads to *earnings* that are proportional to *net* invested capital in each year. At the asset level, this results in a constant ROIC and a changing CFROI over the asset's lifetime. At the business level, it implies that aggregate earnings and net invested capital grow in line with each other (assuming that growth comes only from adding more assets to the business).[4]

For the example in Exhibit 25.2, CFROI is the right measure and equal to the IRR of 13.8 percent, because now the *operating cash flows* are proportional to *gross* invested capital. At the asset level, CFROI is constant over the asset's lifetime, and ROIC continues to increase as the capital base is depreciated. For the business, this means that aggregate operating cash flows and gross invested capital grow in line with each other.

These two examples illustrate that there is no single right measure of return on capital. Depending on the earnings and cash flow pattern of the investment projects underlying a business, ROIC or CFROI can be equal to IRR—in theory. The fact that CFROI is calculated based on cash components does not mean it is always superior to the accounting-based ROIC.

Theoretical Trade-Offs

Although the examples were stylized, it is possible to derive general insights about the theoretical trade-offs between ROIC and CFROI. CFROI is more

---

[3] Even though the cumulative cash flows over the lifetime of the underlying assets are equal, the assets shown in Exhibit 25.1 generate higher cash flows earlier in their lifetimes. As a result, the value creation is higher, as reflected in the assets' IRR of 15.0 percent, versus 13.8 percent for the assets in Exhibit 25.2.

[4] Note that this is in fact the economic model that we assumed in deriving the ROIC-growth value driver formula in Chapter 3.

appropriate in businesses where investments are very lumpy. As two extreme examples, think of infrastructure projects or hydroelectric power plants. These require very substantial up-front investments that generate relatively stable cash flows without significant investments in maintenance or overhauling over many years or even decades. Although accounting conventions may require that the assets be depreciated, their net capital base has little bearing on the capacity to generate cash flows. ROIC often rises to levels that are unrelated to the project's economic return (IRR), but CFROI will be much closer to the IRR because the operating cash flows are very stable.

In contrast, ROIC is likely to be a better estimate of the underlying IRR in businesses where investments occur in a more regular and smoother pattern because they are needed to support the earnings. As an example, think of retail supermarkets or a manufacturing company with many plants and pieces of equipment. These businesses require regular investments as management maintains, upgrades, and renews product lines and shop formats. In the periods between making such investments, pricing and earnings are likely to face pressure from competition with newer products or formats. As a result, the depreciated capital base is a reasonable approximation of the ability to generate earnings, making ROIC a better estimate of underlying IRR. In our experience, this is the case for most companies: maintenance and replacement investments are required on an ongoing basis to support the operating earnings.

Practical Considerations

Apart from these theoretical considerations, some practical trade-offs exist between ROIC and CFROI. First, it is easier to estimate ROIC and its components, such as operating earnings and book value of invested capital, from standard financial reporting statements with some reorganization and adjustments (as described in Chapter 11). Once you have the components, ROIC is a straightforward ratio that most managers are familiar with. In contrast, CFROI requires a far more complex, iterative calculation that is not transparent to many managers.[5]

Because of the way CFROI is defined and calculated, interpreting it also is less straightforward than in the case of ROIC. For example, it follows that to double the ROIC, managers would need to double their profit margin or double their capital turnover. With this logic, any reductions in inventory levels or costs of raw materials, for example, translate easily into ROIC improvements. In contrast, doubling capital turnover does not necessarily translate to doubling CFROI, because it is not a simple ratio. For the same reason, deriving

---

[5] For this reason, practitioners have developed approximations of CFROI that are based on less complex calculations. See, for example, A. Damodaran, *Investment Valuation*, 2nd ed. (New York: John Wiley & Sons, 2002), chap. 32.

the CFROI for a division or corporate group does not easily follow from the CFROI calculations of the underlying business units. A group's ROIC, however, is simply the capital-weighted average of the returns on invested capital of the underlying businesses.

An additional feature of CFROI is that, in its precise definition, it includes an adjustment for the effect of inflation on returns. The gross invested capital is indexed for inflation over the years dating to the initial purchase of the assets involved. For most economies in North America and Western Europe, this usually does not make a big difference. But the impact of the adjustment is significant when inflation is more than a couple of percentage points per year. In some cases, we found that this adjustment was the key source of difference between a company's CFROI and ROIC. However, adjustments for inflation can also be made when calculating ROIC. Basically, the adjustment involves using current-year dollars to express depreciation and property, plant, and equipment (PP&E). Adjusting ROIC for inflation and using CFROI with its inflation adjustment typically lead to similar results across widely different inflation rates and asset lifetimes, as illustrated for a range of stylized examples in Exhibit 25.3. (See Chapter 26 for more details about inflation's impact on ROIC and cash flows.)

Differences between ROIC and CFROI could be sizable for specific businesses, depending on their economics, as we saw in the preceding two examples. Nevertheless, when we analyzed 1,000 U.S. companies between 2003

EXHIBIT 25.3 **Returns under Inflation: ROIC vs. CFROI**

%

		Return after 20 years		
Inflation rate	Asset life, years	ROIC	CFROI[1]	Inflation-adjusted ROIC
0	5	15	14	15
2	5	17	13	12
4	5	19	13	11
6	5	22	13	10
8	5	24	12	10
10	5	26	12	10
0	10	15	13	15
2	10	19	12	11
4	10	23	12	10
6	10	27	11	10
8	10	31	11	10
10	10	35	11	10
0	20	17	12	17
2	20	21	12	15
4	20	25	12	14
6	20	30	12	13
8	20	35	11	13
10	20	39	11	13

[1] CFROI includes an inflation adjustment.

EXHIBIT 25.4   **Pretax ROIC and CFROI per Sector, 2003–2013**

10-year average of median ROIC and CFROI by sector,[1] %

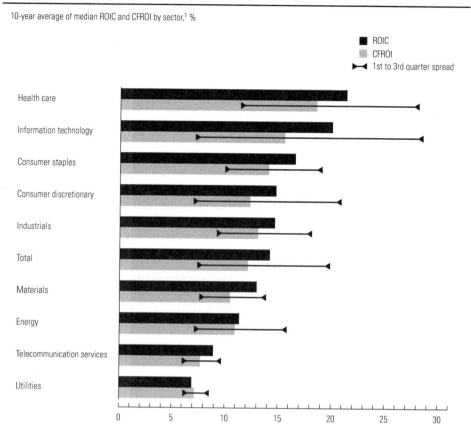

¹ For the 1,000 largest U.S. companies by market capitalization.

and 2013, we found that, on average, these differences were not very large (see Exhibit 25.4). For all but one of the ten nonfinancial sectors we considered, the spread between the average ROIC and CFROI was three percentage points or less when taking both ROIC and CFROI without inflation adjustments. The difference between the highest- and lowest-quartile ROIC in a sector was typically four times larger than this spread. Thus, your decision whether to measure a business's return on capital by using ROIC or CFROI is unlikely to make a difference in what the result tells you about the company's relative performance versus that of sector peers.

FLAWS OF OTHER CASH RETURNS ON CAPITAL

In practice, we see managers and analysts apply other measures of return on capital, not just ROIC and CFROI. Sometimes the only difference is in the name. For example, most definitions of return on capital employed (ROCE) are fairly similar to ROIC and calculated as operating earnings divided by operating capital employed—although the exact definition of earnings and capital varies across applications.

Another set of measures, based on cash return on capital, is fundamentally different. They appear under various names, such as cash return on capital invested (CROCI), cash return on gross investment (CROGI), and cash return on assets (CashROA). These cash returns are typically calculated as operating cash flow divided by invested capital:[6]

$$\text{Cash Return on Net Invested Capital} = \frac{\text{Operating Cash Flow}}{\text{Net Invested Capital}}$$

$$\text{Cash Return on Gross Invested Capital} = \frac{\text{Operating Cash Flow}}{\text{Gross Invested Capital}}$$

Unfortunately, such cash returns are flawed measures of value creation, as they do not equal the underlying IRR. In Exhibits 25.1 and 25.2, the cash returns on both gross and net invested capital overestimate the true underlying IRR. The main reason is that these cash returns on capital fail to account for the charge of depleting the underlying capital, because they ignore depreciation charges.[7] For the cash return on invested capital net of cumulative depreciation, the error is magnified, as the denominator becomes smaller over the lifetime of the asset. This makes the overestimation of IRR even worse, as indicated by the results for operating cash flow divided by net invested capital in Exhibits 25.1 and 25.2. Because of these variances from IRR, we advise against using cash returns on capital as measures of business performance.

SUMMARY

For most businesses, ROIC is a good measure of return on capital. It accurately reflects the economic return, as defined by the internal rate of return of the cash flows that the business generates. In addition, it is derived from information that is readily available from standard financial reports, and it is easy for managers to understand. For businesses with high up-front investments in capital that generate steady cash flows for many years, you can consider whether using CFROI justifies the additional effort and complexity relative to ROIC.

---

[6] See, for example, P. Costantini, *Cash Return on Capital Invested: Ten Years of Investment Analysis with the CROCI Economic Profit Model* (Amsterdam: Elsevier, 2006).

[7] CFROI is also based on operating cash flows, but it includes an implicit charge for the use of the underlying assets, because it is calculated as the IRR over the lifetime of the asset. The simple "cash return" discussed here equals CFROI if the lifetime of the asset is infinite.

26

Inflation

High-inflation environments make analyzing and forecasting companies' financial performance a challenge. Inflation distorts the financial statements, adding to the difficulty of year-to-year historical comparisons, ratio analyses, and performance forecasts.

When inflation is high, analysis and valuation depend on insights from both nominal- and real-terms approaches. Sometimes nominal indicators are not useful (e.g., for capital turnover). In other cases, real indicators are problematic (e.g., when determining corporate income taxes). But when properly applied, valuations in real and nominal terms should yield an identical value.

Although all the familiar tools described in Part Two still apply to periods of high inflation, such times cause particular complications. This chapter discusses the following issues:

- How inflation leads to lower value creation in companies, because it erodes real-terms free cash flow (FCF), as companies don't increase prices enough to overcome higher capital costs as well as operating costs
- How to evaluate a company's historical performance when inflation is high
- How to prepare financial projections of a company's performance in both nominal and real terms

INFLATION LEADS TO LOWER VALUE CREATION

Since the 1980s, inflation has generally been mild in the developed economies of Europe and North America, at levels around 2 to 3 percent per year. But this does not mean inflation has become irrelevant. As Exhibit 26.1 shows, the situation was quite different in the 1970s, when inflation hovered around

10 percent for the same economies. A return to such levels is unlikely, but some economists are warning of rising inflation in, for example, the United States as a result of rising wage levels, import tariffs, and government deficits.[1] And some of the largest economies in Latin America and Asia—such as, for example, Brazil, China, and India—as well as Russia have faced inflation at double-digit levels for intervals of many years. In stark contrast, Japan has experienced extremely low inflation and even deflation since the early 1990s.

Inflation often persists, stretching over several years as it did during the 1970s and 1980s, because suppressing it requires strict and unpopular government measures. For example, curbing inflation caused by overheating in the economy typically requires increasing interest rates and reducing public spending to dampen growth. In most cases, such measures are undertaken

EXHIBIT 26.1 **Historical Inflation Rate in Developed and Emerging Economies**

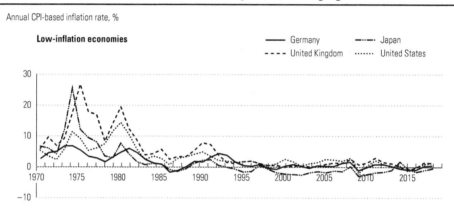

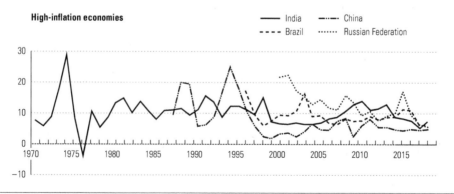

[1] See, for example, J. Lahart, "Get Ready to Worry about Inflation Again," *Wall Street Journal*, December 12, 2018; or M. Feldstein, "The Fed Must Reassure Markets on Inflation," *Financial Times*, June 28, 2009.

only when everything else has failed and when inflation has become too high to ignore—but even more difficult to fix.

It's necessary to take account of persistent inflation in analysis and valuation, because a large body of academic research clearly shows that inflation is negatively correlated with stock market returns.[2] To illustrate, as inflation increased from around 2 or 3 percent in the late 1960s to around 10 percent in the second half of the 1970s, the average price-to-earnings (P/E) ratio for companies in the United States declined from around 18 to below 10. When inflation finally came down, from 1985 onward, P/Es returned to their historical levels.

Inflation has obvious pernicious effects on value creation. Academic research has found evidence that investors often misjudge inflation, which pushes up the cost of capital in real terms and depresses market valuations.[3] Inflation creates a one-off loss in value for companies with so-called net monetary assets—that is, asset positions that are fixed in nominal terms.[4] For example, a balance of receivables loses 10 percent in value when inflation unexpectedly increases by 10 percent. The reverse holds for net monetary liabilities, such as fixed-rate debt. Depending on the relative size of a particular company's receivables, payables, and debt, the direct effect could be positive or negative. Companies also can end up paying higher taxes if their depreciation tax shields are not inflation adjusted for tax purposes—and this is typically the case.

Inflation's most value-destroying impact is not obvious. Though companies may increase prices, most cannot or do not increase them enough to cover both their higher operating costs (salaries and purchased goods) and the higher cost of future capital expenditures. As a result, they fail to maintain profitability in real terms.

To understand how significant the challenge of passing on cost increases can be, consider this simple example. Assume a company generates steady sales of $1,000 per year. Earnings before interest, taxes, and amortization (EBITA) are $100, and invested capital is $1,000. Assume the asset base is evenly spread across 15 groups with remaining lifetimes of 1 to 15 years. Gross property, plant, and equipment (PP&E) is $1,875, and annual capital expenditures equal depreciation charges at $125.[5] The company's key financials would

[2] See, for example, E. Fama and G. Schwert, "Asset Returns and Inflation," *Journal of Financial Economics* 5 (1977): 115–146; and J. Ritter and R. Warr, "The Decline of Inflation and the Bull Market of 1982–1999," *Journal of Financial and Quantitative Analysis* 37, no. 1 (2002): 29–61.

[3] See, for example, F. Modigliani and R. Cohn, "Inflation, Rational Valuation, and the Market," *Financial Analysts Journal* 35 (1979): 24–44; and Ritter and Warr, "The Decline of Inflation," who found that in times of high inflation, investors tend to capitalize real cash flows at nominal discount rates.

[4] See, for example, H. Hong, "Inflation and the Market Value of the Firm: Theory and Test," *Journal of Finance* 32, no. 4 (1977): 1031–1048.

[5] At the end of each year, after replacement of the asset group that is fully depreciated, the average remaining life of assets is exactly eight years. Annual depreciation is therefore $1,000 ÷ 8 = $125, and gross PP&E equals 15 × $125 = $1,875.

EXHIBIT 26.2 **Financial Projections without Inflation**

$

	Year 1	Year 2	Year 3	Year 4	Year 16	Year 17
Sales	1,000	1,000	1,000	1,000	1,000	1,000
EBITDA[1]	225	225	225	225	225	225
Depreciation	(125)	(125)	(125)	(125)	(125)	(125)
EBITA[2]	100	100	100	100	100	100
Gross property, plant, and equipment	1,875	1,875	1,875	1,875	1,875	1,875
Cumulative depreciation	(875)	(875)	(875)	(875)	(875)	(875)
Invested capital	1,000	1,000	1,000	1,000	1,000	1,000
EBITDA	225	225	225	225	225	225
Capital expenditures	(125)	(125)	(125)	(125)	(125)	(125)
Free cash flow (FCF)	100	100	100	100	100	100
EBITA growth, %	–	–	–	–	–	–
EBITA/sales, %	10.0	10.0	10.0	10.0	10.0	10.0
Return on invested capital, %	10.0	10.0	10.0	10.0	10.0	10.0
FCF growth, %	–	–	–	–	–	–

[1] Earnings before interest, taxes, depreciation, and amortization

[2] Earnings before interest, taxes, and amortization

be as shown in Exhibit 26.2. If the cost of capital is 8 percent, the discounted-cash-flow (DCF) value at the start of year 2—or any year—equals:

$$DCF = \frac{\$100}{(8\% - 0\%)} = \$1,250$$

Now assume that in year 2, inflation suddenly increases to 15 percent and stays at that level in perpetuity, affecting costs and capital expenditures equally. Let's assume the company increases prices enough that its EBITA grows with inflation and its sales margin (EBITA divided by sales) stays near 10 percent while keeping sales volume and physical production capacity constant. In the process, the company even succeeds in lifting its return on invested capital (ROIC) to almost 20 percent after 15 years (see Exhibit 26.3).

Although these results may be impressive at first sight, a closer inspection of the financial performance reveals significant value destruction. Even though EBITA grows at 15 percent per year, growth in earnings before interest, taxes, depreciation, and amortization (EBITDA) is at only 7 to 8 percent per year because depreciation is recorded at historical nominal cost. As a result, capital spending should exceed depreciation charges to keep physical capacity constant, leading to an actual decline in free cash flow (FCF) in the first few years. FCF growth only gradually rises to the rate of inflation in year 17.[6]

[6] Given our assumption of an asset lifetime of 15 years, FCF growth gradually increases from 0 to 15 percent until year 17, when a new steady state is reached if inflation remains constant.

EXHIBIT 26.3 **Financial Projections with Incomplete Inflation Pass-On**

$	Year 1	Year 2	Year 3	Year 4		Year 16	Year 17
Sales	1,000	1,131	1,283	1,460		7,516	8,644
EBITDA	225	240	259	281		1,210	1,392
Depreciation	(125)	(125)	(126)	(129)		(397)	(456)
EBITA	100	115	132	152		814	936
Gross property, plant, and equipment	1,875	1,894	1,934	1,999		6,840	7,866
Cumulative depreciation	(875)	(875)	(876)	(880)		(2,082)	(2,394)
Invested capital	1,000	1,019	1,058	1,119		4,758	5,472
EBITDA	225	240	259	281		1,210	1,392
Capital expenditures	(125)	(144)	(165)	(190)		(1,017)	(1,170)
Free cash flow (FCF)	100	96	93	91		193	222
EBITA growth, %	–	15.0	15.0	15.0		15.0	15.0
EBITA/sales, %	10.0	10.2	10.3	10.4		10.8	10.8
Return on invested capital, %	10.0	11.5	13.0	14.4		19.7	19.7
FCF growth, %	0.0	−3.7	−3.2	−2.4		14.3	15.0

Combine this with a cost of capital increase to 24 percent,[7] and the company's value plummets. An explicit DCF valuation with continuing value estimated as of year 17 would show the value at the start of year 2 being as low as $481.

EXHIBIT 26.4 **Financial Projections with Full Inflation Pass-On**

$	Year 1	Year 2	Year 3	Year 4		Year 16	Year 17
Sales	1,000	1,150	1,323	1,521		8,137	9,358
EBITDA	225	259	298	342		1,831	2,105
Depreciation	(125)	(125)	(126)	(129)		(397)	(456)
EBITA	100	134	171	213		1,434	1,649
Gross property, plant, and equipment	1,875	1,894	1,934	1,999		6,840	7,866
Cumulative depreciation	(875)	(875)	(876)	(880)		(2,082)	(2,394)
Invested capital	1,000	1,019	1,058	1,119		4,758	5,472
EBITDA	225	259	298	342		1,831	2,105
Capital expenditures	(125)	(144)	(165)	(190)		(1,017)	(1,170)
Free cash flow (FCF)	100	115	132	152		814	936
EBITA growth, %	–	33.7	28.1	24.5		15.1	15.0
EBITA/sales, %	10.0	11.6	13.0	14.0		17.6	17.6
Return on invested capital, %	10.0	13.4	16.8	20.2		34.7	34.7
FCF growth, %		15.0	15.0	15.0		15.0	15.0

[7] With inflation at 15 percent, the cost of capital increases from 8 percent to $(1 + 8\%) \times (1 + 15\%) - 1 = 24\%$.

To pass on inflation to customers in full without losing sales volume, the company must increase its *cash flows*, not its earnings, at 15 percent per year (see Exhibit 26.4). In this case, the DCF value at the start of year 2 is fully preserved:

$$DCF = \frac{\$115}{(24\% - 15\%)} = \$1,250$$

But having all cash flows grow with inflation means that earnings must increase much faster than inflation. As the summary financials show, EBITA growth is now more than 33 percent in year 2. In the same year, the sales margin increases from 10.0 percent to 11.6 percent, and ROIC increases from 10.0 percent to 13.4 percent. After 15 years of constant inflation, the sales margin and ROIC would end up at 17.6 percent and 34.7 percent, respectively. ROIC needs to rise this far to keep up with inflation and the higher cost of capital.[8]

Although this example is stylized, the conclusion applies to all companies: after each acceleration in inflation, we should expect reported earnings to outpace inflation, and reported sales margin and ROIC to increase—even though, in real terms, nothing has changed. Unfortunately, history shows that in periods of inflation, companies do not achieve such big improvements in reported return on invested capital. ROICs remained in the range of 7 to 12 percent in the United States during the 1970s and 1980s, when inflation was at 10 percent or more. If companies had succeeded in passing on inflation effects, they should have reported much higher ROICs in those years. Instead, they hardly managed to keep returns at preinflation levels.

One likely cause is that companies cannot pass on the cost increases to customers without losing volume, or they can pass on increases only with some time lag. Another reason could be that managers do not sufficiently adjust targets for growth of earnings and sales margin when faced with inflation. If a company keeps its sales margins and ROIC constant in times of inflation, cash flows and value are eroding in real terms. Maintaining EBITA growth in line with inflation is also insufficient to sustain a company's value; this is even more the case for a leveraged indicator such as earnings per share.

Whatever the exact reason, history shows that companies do not manage to pass on inflation in full. As a result, their cash flow in real terms declines. In addition, there is empirical evidence that in times of inflation, investors are likely to undervalue stocks as they misjudge inflation's effects.[9] Lower cash flow and higher cost of capital form a proven recipe for lower share prices, just as occurred in the 1970s and 1980s.

---

[8] The reason is that invested capital and depreciation do not grow with inflation immediately. For example, in year 2, annual capital expenditures increase by 15 percent, but this adds only $15\% \times \$125 = \$18.75$ to invested capital. Assets are acquired at the end of each year and depreciated for the first time in the next year. Annual depreciation changes in year 3 by only a small amount: $1/15 \times 19 = 1.25$. In each year, the company replaces only 1/15 of assets at inflated prices, so it takes 15 years of constant inflation to reach a steady state where capital and depreciation grow at the rate of inflation. As the example shows, sales margin and ROIC increase each year until the steady state in year 17.

[9] Modigliani and Cohn, "Inflation, Rational Valuation, and the Market"; Ritter and Warr, "The Decline of Inflation."

HISTORICAL ANALYSIS IN TIMES OF HIGH INFLATION

In countries experiencing extreme inflation (more than 25 percent per year), companies often report in year-end currency. In the income statement, items such as revenues and costs that were booked throughout the year are restated at year-end purchasing power. Otherwise, the addition of these items would have no relevance. The balance sheet usually has adjustments to fixed assets, inventory, and equity; the accounts payable and receivables are already in year-end terms.

In most countries, however, financial statements are not adjusted to reflect the effects of inflation. High inflation leads to distortions in the balance sheet and income statement. In the balance sheet, nonmonetary assets, such as inventories and PP&E, are shown at values far below current replacement value. In the income statement, depreciation charges are too low relative to current replacement costs. Sales and costs in December and January of the same year are typically added as if they represented the same purchasing power.

As a result, many financial indicators typically used in historical analyses can be distorted when calculated directly from the financial statements in high-inflation economies. In such circumstances, companies often index their internal management accounts to overcome these issues. If they do not, or if you are conducting an outside-in analysis, at least correct for the following distortions:

- Growth is overstated in times of inflation, so restate it in real terms by deflating with an annual inflation index if sales are evenly spread across the year. If sales are not spread evenly, use quarterly or monthly inflation indexes to deflate the sales in each corresponding interval.

- Capital turnover is typically overstated because operating assets are carried at historical costs. You can approximate the current costs of long-lived assets by adjusting their reported values with an inflation index for their estimated average lifetimes. Or consider developing ratios of real sales relative to physical-capacity indicators appropriate for the sector—for example, sales per square meter in consumer retail. Inventory levels also need restating if turnover is low and inflation is very high.

- Operating margins (operating profit divided by sales) can be overstated because depreciation is too low and slow-moving inventories make large nominal holding gains. Corrections for depreciation charges follow from adjustments to PP&E. You can estimate cash operating expenses at current-cost basis by inflating the reported costs for the average time held in inventory. Alternatively, use historical EBITDA-to-sales ratios to assess the company's performance relative to peers; these ratios at least do not suffer from any depreciation-induced bias.

- Credit ratios and other indicators of capital structure health become distorted and require cautious interpretation. Distortions are especially significant in solvency ratios such as debt to equity or total assets, because long-lived assets are understated relative to replacement costs, and floating-rate debt is expressed in current currency units. As Chapter 33 advises, use coverage ratios such as EBITDA to interest expense.[10] These are less exposed to accounting distortions, because depreciation has no impact on them and debt financing is mostly at floating rates or in foreign currency when inflation is persistent.

FINANCIAL PROJECTIONS IN REAL AND NOMINAL TERMS

When you make financial projections of income statements and balance sheets for a valuation in a high-inflation environment, keep in mind that accounting adjustments should not affect free cash flow. Projections are typically made in either nominal or real terms, but high-inflation environments require a hybrid approach because each single approach has different strengths, as Exhibit 26.5 shows. On the one hand, projecting in real terms makes it difficult to calculate taxes correctly, as tax charges are often based on nominal financial statements. Furthermore, you need to project explicitly the effects of working-capital changes on cash flow, because these do not automatically follow from the annual change in real-terms working capital. On the other hand, using nominal cash flows makes future capital expenditures difficult to project, because the typically stable relationship between revenues and fixed assets does not hold in times of high inflation. This means it will also be difficult to project depreciation charges and EBITA.

EXHIBIT 26.5 **Combining Real and Nominal Approaches to Financial Modeling**

✓✓ Preferred Application

Estimates	Modeling approach	
---	Real	Nominal
Operational performance		
Sales	✓✓	✓
EBITDA	✓✓	✓
EBITA	✓✓	–
Capital expenditures	✓✓	–
Investments in working capital	✓✓[1]	✓
Other		
Income taxes	–	✓✓
Financial statements	✓[2]	✓✓
Continuing value	✓✓[1]	✓✓

[1] If inflation impact on investments in working capital is explicitly included.

[2] If inflation corrections are separately modeled and included in income statement and balance sheet.

[10] Distortions occur in the ratio of EBITA to interest coverage if operating profit is overstated due to low depreciation charges and low costs of procured materials.

EXHIBIT 26.6 **DCF under Inflation: Operational and Financial Assumptions**

	Year 1	Forecasts					
		Year 2	Year 3	Year 4	Year 5	...	Year 25
Operational assumptions							
Real growth rate, %		2	2	2	2	...	2
Real revenues, $	1,000	1,020	1,040	1,061	1,082	...	1,608
Real EBITDA, $	300	306	312	318	325	...	483
Net working capital/revenues, %		20	20	20	20	...	20
Real net PP&E/real revenues, %		40	40	40	40	...	40
Lifetime of net PP&E, years	5						
Financial assumptions							
Inflation rate, %		20	10	10	10	...	10
Inflation index	1.00	1.20	1.32	1.45	1.60	...	10.75
Tax rate, %		35	35	35	35	...	35
Real WACC, %		8	8	8	8	...	8
Nominal WACC, %		29.6	18.8	18.8	18.8	...	18.8

To prepare consistent financial projections, you therefore need to use elements of both nominal and real forecasts. This section illustrates how to combine the two approaches in a DCF valuation. The example considers a company whose revenues grow at 2 percent in real terms while the annual inflation rate is 20 percent in the first forecast year and 10 percent thereafter (see Exhibit 26.6). To simplify, we assume that all cash flows occur at the end of the year.[11]

In practice, financial projections for high-inflation valuations raise many more issues than in this simplified example. Nevertheless, the example is useful for showing how to address some key issues when developing a cash flow forecast in periods of inflation. Using the following step-by-step approach leads to the real and nominal valuation results shown in Exhibit 26.7.

Step 1: Forecast Operating Performance in Real Terms

To the extent possible, convert historical nominal balance sheets and income statements into real terms (usually at the current year's currency value). At a minimum, make a real-terms approximation of the historical development of the key value drivers—growth and return on capital—and the underlying capital turnover and EBITA margin, so you can understand the true

---

[11] At extremely high, fluctuating levels of inflation, however, this assumption could distort financial projections, because the cash flows that accumulate throughout the year are subject to different inflation rates. In such cases, split the year into quarterly or even monthly intervals, project cash flows for each interval, and discount the cash flows at the appropriate discount rate for that interval.

EXHIBIT 26.7 **DCF under Inflation: Real and Nominal Models**

	Nominal projections						Real projections					
	Year 1	Year 2	Year 3	Year 4	Year 5	... Year 25	Year 1	Year 2	Year 3	Year 4	Year 5	... Year 25
NOPAT, $ million												
Revenues	1,000	1,224	1,373	1,541	1,729	17,283	1,000	1,020	1,040	1,061	1,082	1,608
EBITDA	300	367	412	462	519	5,185	300	306	312	318	325	483
Depreciation	(80)	(80)	(85)	(92)	(100)	(926)	(80)	(80)	(82)	(83)	(85)	(126)
EBIT	220	287	327	370	419	4,259	220	226	231	235	240	356
Taxes	(77)	(101)	(114)	(130)	(147)	(1,491)	(77)	(84)	(87)	(89)	(92)	(139)
NOPAT[1]	143	187	212	241	272	2,768	143	142	144	146	148	218
Free cash flow, $ million												
NOPAT	143	187	212	241	272	2,768	143	142	144	146	148	218
Depreciation	80	80	85	92	100	926	80	80	82	83	85	126
Capital expenditures	(80)	(106)	(118)	(133)	(149)	(1,491)	(80)	(88)	(90)	(92)	(93)	(139)
Investment in net working capital		(45)	(30)	(34)	(38)	(376)		(37)	(23)	(23)	(24)	(35)
Free cash flow		116	149	166	185	1,827		97	113	114	116	170
Invested capital, $ million												
Net PP&E (beginning of year)	400	400	426	459	500	4,631	400	400	408	416	424	631
Depreciation	(80)	(80)	(85)	(92)	(100)	(926)	(80)	(80)	(82)	(83)	(85)	(126)
Capital expenditures	80	106	118	133	149	1,491	80	88	90	92	93	139
Net PP&E (end of year)	400	426	459	500	549	5,196	400	408	416	424	433	643
Net working capital	200	245	275	308	346	3,457	200	204	208	212	216	322
Invested Capital	600	670	734	808	895	8,653	600	612	624	637	649	965
Ratios, %												
Net PP&E/revenues		35	33	32	32	30		40	40	40	40	40
Net working capital/revenues		20	20	20	20	20		20	20	20	20	20
ROIC		31	32	33	34	36		24	24	23	23	23
FCF growth rate			28	11	12	12			17	1	1	2
DCF valuation, $ million												
Free cash flow		116	149	166	185	1,827		97	113	114	116	170
Continuing value (Value driver formula)[2]						31,063						2,891
Continuing value (Cash flow perpetuity formula)						31,064						2,891
Present value factor	0.77	0.65	0.55	0.46	0.01		0.93	0.86	0.79	0.74	0.16	
DCF value, $ million	**1,795**						**1,795**					

[1] Net operating profit after taxes.

[2] Adjusted formula for real-terms continuing value.

economics of the business. With these approximations, forecast the operating performance of the business in real terms:

- Project future revenues and cash expenses to obtain EBITDA forecasts.[12]
- Estimate PP&E and capital expenditures from your assumptions for real-terms capital turnover.
- Working capital follows from projected revenues and assumptions about days of working capital required.
- From projected net PP&E and assumptions about the lifetime of the assets, derive the annual depreciation to estimate real-terms EBITA.

Step 2: Build Financial Statements in Nominal Terms

Nominal projections can be readily derived through the following steps, which convert the real operating projections into nominal terms:[13]

- Project nominal revenues, cash expenses, EBITDA, and capital expenditures by multiplying their real-terms equivalents by an estimated inflation index for the year.
- Estimate net PP&E on a year-by-year basis from the prior-year balance plus nominal capital expenditures minus nominal depreciation (which is estimated as a percentage of net PP&E according to the estimated asset lifetime).
- Project working capital by multiplying the real-terms amounts by the inflation index for the year (or derive from real-terms revenues and days of working capital required).
- Subtract the nominal depreciation charges from EBITDA to obtain nominal EBITA.
- Calculate income taxes on nominal EBITA without inflation corrections, unless tax laws allow for such corrections.

This example did not build a complete balance sheet and income statement. Complete financial statements would be needed for major decisions concerning, for example, dividend policy and capital structure, debt financing,

---

[12] This step assumes that all expenses included in EBITDA are cash costs.

[13] As noted, these projections are made for valuation purposes and not necessarily in accordance with local or international accounting standards prescribing any inflation or monetary corrections for particular groups of assets and liabilities under, for example, inflation accounting. Free cash flows would not be affected by such adjustments.

and share repurchase. Developing complete nominal financial statements would require the following additional steps:

- Forecast interest expense and other nonoperating income statement items in nominal terms (based on the previous year's balance sheet).
- Check that equity equals last year's equity plus earnings, less dividends, plus or minus any share issues or repurchases.
- Balance the balance sheet with debt or marketable securities.

Step 3: Build Financial Statements in Real Terms

Most of the operating items for the real-terms income statement and balance sheet were already estimated in step 1. Now include the real-terms taxes on EBITA by deflating the nominal taxes as estimated in step 2. For full financial statements, use the inflation index to convert debt, marketable securities, interest expense, income taxes, and nonoperating terms from the nominal statements into real terms. The real-terms equity account is a plug to balance the balance sheet. To make sure you have done this correctly, be sure the real equity account equals last year's equity plus earnings, less dividends, plus or minus share issues or repurchases, and plus or minus inflationary gains or losses on the monetary assets and liabilities (such as cash, receivables, payables, and debt).

Step 4: Forecast Free Cash Flows in Real and Nominal Terms

Forecast the future free cash flows in real and nominal terms from the projected income statements and balance sheets. Follow the general approach described in Chapter 10. The only difference is that the real-terms investment in net working capital (NWC^R) is equal to the increase in working capital plus a monetary loss due to inflation:[14]

$$\text{Investment in } NWC_t^R = \text{Increase in } NWC_t^R + NWC_{t-1}^R \left(\frac{i_t}{1+i_t} \right)$$

where i_t is the inflation rate in year t.

To check for consistency, use the inflation index to convert the free cash flows from the nominal projections to real terms. These should equal the free cash flows from the real-terms projections in each year.

---

[14] Even for assets held at constant levels in real-terms balance sheets, replacement investments are required at increasing prices in an inflationary environment. These replacement investments represent a cash outflow, also in real terms, but do not show up from real-terms balance sheet differences from year to year. In contrast, the nominal investment cash flow does follow from the nominal balance sheet differences from year to year.

Step 5: Estimate DCF Value in Real and Nominal Terms

When discounting real and nominal cash flows under high inflation, you must address three key issues:

1. Ensure that the weighted average cost of capital estimates in real terms ($WACC^R$) and nominal terms ($WACC^N$) are defined consistently with the assumptions for inflation (i) in each year:

$$1 + WACC_t^N = \left(1 + WACC_t^R\right)\left(1 + i_t\right)$$

2. Make sure the explicit forecast period is long enough for the model to reach a steady state with constant growth rates of free cash flow in the year when you apply the continuing-value formula. Because of the way inflation affects capital expenditures and depreciation, you need a much longer horizon than for valuations with no or low inflation.

3. The value driver formula as presented in Chapter 14 can be readily applied when estimating continuing value in nominal terms, but it should be adjusted when estimating in real terms in high-inflation environments. The return on capital in real-terms projections ($ROIC^R$) overestimates the economic returns in the case of positive net working capital. The free cash flow in real terms differs from the cash flow implied by the value driver formula by an amount equal to the annual monetary loss on net working capital:

$$FCF_t^R = \left(1 - \frac{g_t^R}{ROIC_t^R}\right) NOPAT_t^R - NWC_{t-1}^R \left(\frac{i_t}{1 + i_t}\right)$$

where g^R is growth rate in real terms, and $NOPAT^R$ is net operating profit after taxes in real terms. The real-terms value driver formula is adjusted for this monetary loss, reflecting the perpetuity assumptions for inflation (i) and the ratio of net working capital to invested capital (NWC^R/IC^R):

$$CV^R = \frac{\left(1 - \dfrac{G^R}{ROIC^R}\right) NOPAT^R}{WACC^R - g^R}$$

where

$$G^R = g^R + \left[\frac{NWC^R}{IC^R}\left(\frac{i}{1 + i}\right)\right]$$

The resulting continuing-value estimate is the same as that obtained from an FCF perpetuity growth formula. After indexing for inflation, it also equals the continuing-value estimates derived from nominal projections.

Of course, the DCF valuations in nominal and real terms should lead to exactly the same result. Combining both approaches not only provides additional insights into a company's economics under inflation but also is a useful cross-check on the validity of the valuation outcomes.

SUMMARY

High and persistent inflation destroys value because companies typically cannot increase prices enough to offset higher capital outlays. To analyze and value companies in the presence of such inflation, we use the same tools and approaches as introduced in Part Two. However, applying them can be somewhat different.

When analyzing a company's historical performance, you should be aware that persistent inflation can distort many familiar financial indicators, such as growth, capital turnover, operating margins, and solvency ratios. Ensure that you make appropriate adjustments to these ratios. When making financial projections, use a combined nominal- and real-terms approach, because real-terms and nominal-terms projections offer relevant insights and can be used for cross-checking your results. When discounting cash flows, use inflation assumptions in the weighted average cost of capital that are fully consistent with those underlying your cash flow projections.

27

Cross-Border Valuation

To value businesses, subsidiaries, or companies in foreign countries, follow the same principles and methods that we presented in Part Two. Fortunately, accounting issues in cross-border valuations have diminished. Most of the world's major economies have adopted either International Financial Reporting Standards (IFRS) or U.S. Generally Accepted Accounting Principles (GAAP), and these two standards are rapidly converging. Moreover, remember that if you follow Chapter 11's recommendations for rearranging financial statements, you will obtain identical results regardless of which accounting principles you follow in preparing the financial statements.

Nevertheless, the following issues arise in cross-border valuations and still require special attention:

- Forecasting cash flows, whether in foreign currency (the currency of the foreign entity to be valued) or domestic currency (the home currency of the person performing the valuation)
- Estimating the cost of capital
- Applying a domestic- or foreign-capital WACC
- Incorporating foreign-currency risk in valuations
- Using translated foreign-currency financial statements

This chapter highlights the steps involved in the special analyses required for each of these issues.

FORECASTING CASH FLOWS

A company or business unit valuation should always result in the same value regardless of the currency or mix of currencies in which cash flows are projected. To achieve this, you should use consistent monetary assumptions and one of the two following methods for forecasting and discounting cash flows denominated in foreign currency.

1. *Spot-rate method.* Project foreign cash flows in the foreign currency, and discount them at the foreign cost of capital. Then convert the present value of the cash flows into domestic currency, using the spot exchange rate.

2. *Forward-rate method.* Project foreign cash flows in the foreign currency, and convert these into the domestic currency, using the relevant forward exchange rates. Then discount the converted cash flows at the cost of capital in domestic currency.

Let's use a simple example to illustrate. Assume you want to estimate the value of a Swiss subsidiary for its German parent company as of January 2020. Exhibit 27.1 shows the cash flow projections for the subsidiary in the foreign currency (Swiss francs).

EXHIBIT 27.1   **Cash Flows Projected and Discounted under Consistent Monetary Assumptions**

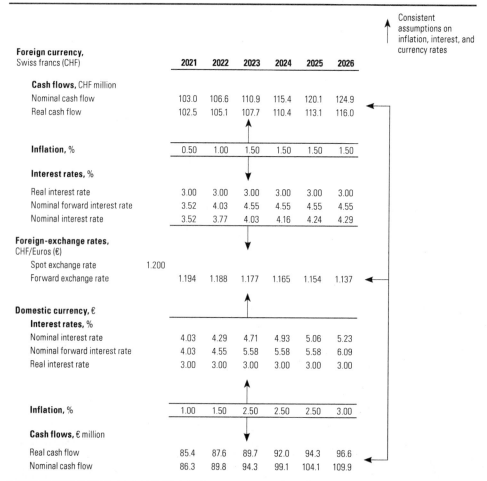

Foreign currency, Swiss francs (CHF)		2021	2022	2023	2024	2025	2026
Cash flows, CHF million							
Nominal cash flow		103.0	106.6	110.9	115.4	120.1	124.9
Real cash flow		102.5	105.1	107.7	110.4	113.1	116.0
Inflation, %		0.50	1.00	1.50	1.50	1.50	1.50
Interest rates, %							
Real interest rate		3.00	3.00	3.00	3.00	3.00	3.00
Nominal forward interest rate		3.52	4.03	4.55	4.55	4.55	4.55
Nominal interest rate		3.52	3.77	4.03	4.16	4.24	4.29
Foreign-exchange rates, CHF/Euros (€)							
Spot exchange rate	1.200						
Forward exchange rate		1.194	1.188	1.177	1.165	1.154	1.137
Domestic currency, €							
Interest rates, %							
Nominal interest rate		4.03	4.29	4.71	4.93	5.06	5.23
Nominal forward interest rate		4.03	4.55	5.58	5.58	5.58	6.09
Real interest rate		3.00	3.00	3.00	3.00	3.00	3.00
Inflation, %		1.00	1.50	2.50	2.50	2.50	3.00
Cash flows, € million							
Real cash flow		85.4	87.6	89.7	92.0	94.3	96.6
Nominal cash flow		86.3	89.8	94.3	99.1	104.1	109.9

Consistent assumptions on inflation, interest, and currency rates

To value the subsidiary using the spot-rate method, simply discount nominal cash flows in Swiss francs (CHF) at the Swiss nominal risk-free interest rates (we assume the subsidiary's beta is zero). The resulting present value is 589.9 Swiss francs. Converting this value at the spot exchange rate of 1.200 Swiss francs per euro results in a discounted-cash-flow (DCF) value of €491.6 million:

		Year				
	2021	2022	2023	2024	2025	2026
Spot-rate method						
Cash flow, CHF million	103.0	106.6	110.9	115.4	120.1	124.9
Discount factor	0.966	0.929	0.888	0.85	0.813	0.777
Present value of cash flow, CHF million	99.5	99.0	98.6	98.1	97.6	97.1
DCF value, CHF million	589.9					
DCF value, € million	491.6					

Note: Numbers may not sum due to rounding.

The forward-rate method for valuation is more elaborate. The projected nominal cash flows in Swiss francs are now converted to euros on a year-by-year basis, using forward exchange rates and then discounted at nominal euro interest rates. Estimate synthetic forward rates by using interest parity as described in the forward exchange rate section below. You could use market-based forward exchange rates, too, but check for interest-rate parity to ensure consistent valuation results across currencies. We obtain a present value of €491.6 million, exactly the same value as obtained under the spot-rate method:

		Year				
	2021	2022	2023	2024	2025	2026
Forward-rate method						
Cash flow at forward exchange rate, € million	86.3	89.8	94.3	99.1	104.1	109.9
Discount factor	0.961	0.919	0.871	0.825	0.781	0.737
Present value of cash flow, € million	82.9	82.5	82.1	81.7	81.3	80.9
DCF value, € million	491.6					

Note: Numbers may not sum due to rounding.

The results for the spot-rate and forward-rate valuations are identical because the domestic and foreign cash flows are projected and discounted under consistent monetary assumptions, as shown in Exhibit 27.1. As we explain in more detail in the two following sections, you cannot make independent assumptions for inflation, interest rates, and forward exchange rates across currencies:

- Inflation assumptions underlying cash flow projections in a specific currency must be consistent with inflation assumptions underlying interest rates in that currency.
- Forward exchange rates between two currencies must be consistent with inflation and interest rate differences between those currencies.
- Conversion of cash flow projections from one currency into another should be done at forward exchange rates.

Inflation and Interest Rates

Inflation and interest rates should be projected in accordance with the Fisher effect.[1] For each currency, the inflation rate i_t in each year should align with the nominal forward interest rate (f_t) and real interest rate (R_t) in that year:

$$(1+f_t) = (1+R_t) \times (1+i_t)$$

For example, in Exhibit 27.1, the Swiss forward interest rate in 2022 equals the real interest rate plus the expected inflation rate for that year:

$$4.03\% = (1+3.00\%)(1+1.00\%) - 1$$

The two-year interest rate as of 2020 is the geometric average of the first- and second-year nominal forward interest rates:

$$3.77\% = \left[(1+3.52\%)(1+4.03\%)\right]^{1/2} - 1$$

Forward Exchange Rates

Forward exchange rates should reflect inflation and interest rates following interest rate parity. For currencies with liquid forward markets, arbitrage

---

[1] See, for example, R. Brealey, S. Myers, and F. Allen, *Principles of Corporate Finance*, 13th ed. (Burr Ridge, IL: McGraw-Hill/Irwin, 2020), chap. 27.

trading drives forward rates to interest rate parity, but you should always verify that the rates are consistent with inflation and interest rates you are using in your cash flow projections and valuation. The forward foreign-exchange rate in year t, X_t, should equal the current spot rate, X_0, multiplied by the ratio of nominal interest rates in the two currencies over the forecast interval, t:

$$X_t = X_0 \left(\frac{1+r^F}{1+r^D} \right)^t$$

where r^F is the interest rate in foreign currency and r^D is the interest rate in domestic currency. In our example, the four-year nominal interest rate in Switzerland, r^F, is 4.16 percent as of January 2020, while the borrowing rate in euros, r^D, is 4.93 percent for the same period. As the spot exchange rate, X_0, is 1.200 Swiss francs per euro, the four-year forward rate, X_4, should be calculated as follows:[2]

$$X_4 = 1.200 \left(\frac{1+4.16\%}{1+4.93\%} \right)^4 = 1.165$$

The Fisher effect and interest rate parity imply that the ratio of the inflation rates for two currencies over a forecast interval t should also align with the forward exchange rate in year t, X_t, and the current spot rate, X_0:

$$X_t = X_0 \left[\frac{\left(1+i_1^F\right) \times \left(1+i_2^F\right) \times ... \times \left(1+i_t^F\right)}{\left(1+i_1^D\right) \times \left(1+i_2^D\right) \times ... \times \left(1+i_t^D\right)} \right]$$

where i_t^D = inflation rate in year t in domestic currency

           i_t^F = inflation rate in year t in foreign currency

In the example from Exhibit 27.1, the four-year forward rate ties not only with the euro and Swiss franc interest rates but also with the inflation rates:

$$X_4 = 1.200 \left[\frac{1.005 \times 1.010 \times 1.015 \times 1.015}{1.010 \times 1.015 \times 1.025 \times 1.025} \right] = 1.165$$

---

[2] Interest rate parity implies that whether a company borrows in Swiss francs or euros has no impact on value (unless there are any tax implications). You could borrow 1,200 Swiss francs today at 4.16 percent interest per year, totaling 1,412 Swiss francs to repay in 2024. At the four-year forward exchange rate, this amounts to €1,212 (1,412 ÷ 1.165). Alternatively, you could take up a €1,000 loan today at 4.93 percent annual interest in euros, accruing to a total payment of €1,212 in 2024.

Conversion of Cash Flows

Conversion of future cash flows should be done only at forward exchange rates that are consistent with the interest and inflation rates used in your valuation. Otherwise, valuation results are likely to differ depending on the currency used in the cash flow projections. Do not rely on "forecast" exchange rates for your projections, as these rates could induce a bias in your valuation if they are not consistent with your assumptions on inflation and discount rates.

ESTIMATING THE COST OF CAPITAL

As when you are forecasting cash flows in different currencies, the most important rule for estimating costs of capital for cross-border valuations is to have consistent monetary assumptions. The expected inflation that determines the foreign-currency cash flows should equal the expected inflation included in the foreign-currency weighted average cost of capital (WACC) through the risk-free rate. Then estimate the cost of capital, depending on the investor's position.

For investors and companies that face little or no restriction on investing outside their home markets, the cost of capital is best estimated following a global capital asset pricing model (CAPM) that applies equally to foreign and domestic investments.

For investors and companies in markets facing capital controls that prevent them from freely investing abroad, we recommend using a so-called local CAPM. Since they can invest in domestic assets only, they should estimate the cost of capital from a domestic perspective, measuring market risk premium and beta versus a (diversified) domestic portfolio.

Many practitioners make ad hoc adjustments to the discount rate to reflect political risk, foreign-investment risk, or foreign-currency risk. We don't recommend this. As the discussion of emerging markets explains in Chapter 35, political or country risk is diversifiable and best handled by using probability-weighted scenarios of future cash flows.

Finally, keep in mind that estimating a cost of capital is not a mechanical exercise with a precise outcome. You should pair the approach outlined in this chapter with sound judgment on long-term trends in interest rates and market risk premiums (see Chapter 15) to obtain a cost of capital estimate that is sufficiently robust for financial decision making. The following sections and Appendix G provide further background for our recommendations and practical guidelines for estimating the cost of capital in foreign currency.

Global CAPM

For investors and companies able to invest outside their home markets without restrictions, we recommend using a global CAPM. In a global CAPM, there is a single, real-terms risk-free rate, and the market risk premium and beta are measured against a global market portfolio:

$$E(r_j) = r_f + \beta_{j,G}[E(r_G) - r_f]$$

where r_j = return for asset j
   r_f = risk-free rate
   $\beta_{j,G}$ = beta of asset j versus global market portfolio G
   r_G = return for global market portfolio G

Effectively, this means applying the approach described in Chapter 15. The cost of capital for domestic and foreign assets is determined in exactly the same way. What matters is their beta, relative to the global market portfolio, and the market risk premium of that same portfolio, relative to the risk-free rate.

We recommend this approach because capital markets are global. A considerable share of all equity trades is international, and traders, primarily large institutional investors, draw their capital and invest it globally. For example, consider the consumer goods companies Procter & Gamble and Unilever. Both sell their household products around the world and have roughly the same geographic spread. The shares of both are traded in the United States and Europe. The primary difference is that Procter & Gamble is domiciled in the United States, and Unilever is domiciled in the United Kingdom and the Netherlands. With such similar business profiles and investor bases, it would be odd if the two companies had different costs of capital. In general, we find that the domicile of otherwise-comparable companies does not influence their valuation levels. For example, the valuation multiples of U.S. and European pharmaceutical companies are all in a very narrow range around 10 times enterprise value to EBIT, regardless of the company domicile.

As explained in Appendix G, the global CAPM technically holds only if purchasing power parity (PPP) holds, which is the case in the long run.[3] Although evidence on PPP has been mixed, academic research has converged around the conclusion that on average, deviations from PPP between currencies are reduced to half their value within three to five years. In other words, exchange rates ultimately adjust for differences in inflation between countries, although not immediately and perfectly.

Estimating Market Risk Premium in Global CAPM   In the absence of capital controls for investors, the global market risk premium should be based on a global index that includes most of the world's investment assets. As explained in Chapter 15, the market risk premium for an index can be estimated from its

---

[3] For an overview, see A. M. Taylor and M. P. Taylor, "The Purchasing Power Parity Debate," *Journal of Economic Perspectives* 18, no. 4 (Fall 2004): 135–158.

historical returns or from forward-looking models, which by and large lead to similar results. Global indexes rarely go far back in time, so long-term estimates of historical market risk premiums are not readily available. Therefore, we generally resort to specially compiled estimates for the global market or the well-diversified U.S. market as a basis for a global market risk premium. Correlation between the S&P 500 and global market indexes (such as the MSCI World Index) has, so far, been very high, making the S&P 500 a good proxy. Estimates from both sources are typically not far apart, falling in the range of 4.5 to 5.5 percent (also see Chapter 15).

Estimating Beta across Currencies in Global CAPM   Since we are using a global market risk premium, a global beta also should be used. Follow the guidelines from Chapter 15 on how to estimate beta. There is one special issue to consider when estimating betas for stocks in international markets: the currency in which returns are measured. For example, should a Swiss investor estimate the beta of IBM based on returns in U.S. dollars or Swiss francs? If you use total returns to estimate beta, the results will be different when returns are expressed in U.S. dollars or Swiss francs, because the dollar-to-franc exchange rate fluctuates over time. But a stock's beta should be the same in all currencies, as any difference would imply differences in the real-terms cost of capital across currencies. The solution is to use excess returns over the risk-free rate, rather than total returns.[4] Beta estimates are consistent across currencies when the stock's excess returns are regressed against the excess return of a global market portfolio, as follows for any period ending at time t:

$$\left(r_{j,t}^{A} - r_{f,t}^{A} \right) = \beta_{j} \left(r_{M,t}^{A} - r_{f,t}^{A} \right)$$

where $r_{j,t}^{A}$ = realized return for stock j in currency A

$r_{f,t}^{A}$ = risk-free rate in currency A

$r_{M,t}^{A}$ = realized return for global market portfolio in currency A

If the international Fisher effect and purchasing power parity would hold, differences in international interest rates would reflect differences in inflation across countries, and differences in inflation across countries would also be reflected in changes in exchange rates. In that case, the risk-free rate for each

---

[4] Most practitioners use the so-called market model, estimating beta from absolute returns instead of excess returns. This is an approximation that produces good results if the risk-free rate is relatively stable. When translating returns from another currency, the approximation no longer holds, as the nominal risk-free rate will fluctuate with exchange rates.

currency should equal the U.S. dollar risk-free return and the change in the exchange rate:

$$\left(1+r_{f,t}^{A}\right)=\left(1+r_{f,t}^{\$}\right)\frac{X_{t-1}}{X_{t}}$$

(27.1)

where $r_{f,t}^{\$}$ = risk-free rate in U.S. dollars

X_{t} = exchange rate at time t of currency A expressed in U.S. dollars

If risk-free rates across currencies are tied to changes in exchange rates in this way, beta estimates based on excess returns will be the same whether we use U.S. dollars, Swiss francs, or any other currency. In practice, the relations will not hold perfectly. To avoid any differences in beta estimates, we recommend using a synthetic risk-free rate for each currency when calculating a stock's excess returns, based on the U.S. risk-free rate and the U.S. dollar exchange rate as defined in Equation 27.1.

Local CAPM   We recommend using a local CAPM for investors and companies facing restrictions to investing abroad. In that case, the local market portfolio is the right reference to estimate the cost of capital. As a result, valuations in such restricted markets can be out of line with those in global markets—which is what we have encountered in the past for valuations in, for example, the Indian and some Asian stock markets. The local CAPM is similar to the model described in Chapter 15 but stated in terms of a local risk-free rate, a risk premium of the local market portfolio over that risk-free rate, and a local beta measured against that same local market portfolio:

$$E\left(r_{j}\right)=r_{f,L}+\beta_{j,L}\left[E\left(r_{L}\right)-r_{f,L}\right]$$

where r_j = return for asset j
$r_{f,L}$ = local risk-free rate
$\beta_{j,L}$ = local beta of asset j versus local market portfolio L
r_L = return for local market portfolio L

Some practitioners and academic researchers propose always using a local CAPM, regardless of any investment restrictions for investors and companies.[5] Interestingly enough, empirical research finds that the local and global CAPM generate similar results for well-integrated markets (which is in line

[5] See, for example, R. Stulz, "The Cost of Capital in Internationally Integrated Markets: The Case of Nestlé," *European Financial Management* 1, no. 1 (1995): 11–22.

with theoretical predictions, as explained in Appendix G). For the United States, United Kingdom, Germany, France, and smaller economies such as the Netherlands and Switzerland, cost of capital estimates from a local and a global CAPM are very close to each other.[6]

Nevertheless, we don't recommend the local CAPM approach for integrated markets, for several reasons. When applying the local CAPM for investments in different countries, you need to estimate the local market risk premium and beta for each of these countries instead of only the global market risk premium when applying the global CAPM. Using a local CAPM also means you cannot make a straightforward estimate of a company's beta based on the average of the estimated betas for a sample of industry peers. In Chapter 15, we recommend estimating an industry average beta to reduce its standard error, but if the peers are in different countries, their local betas are not directly comparable. Finally, local risk premiums are typically less stable over time than their aggregate, the global risk premium. See Appendix G for more detail.

APPLYING A DOMESTIC- OR FOREIGN-CAPITAL WACC

When cash flows and cost of capital are estimated in a consistent manner, the currency in which the cash flows are denominated will not affect the valuation. This holds regardless of whether you are using the enterprise DCF approach, the adjusted present value (APV) approach, or the cash-flow-to-equity approach.

But you should be aware of some implicit assumptions made when applying the enterprise DCF approach with a weighted average cost of capital (WACC) for cross-border valuations. As explained in Chapter 15, the WACC automatically accounts for the value of interest tax shields in your valuation of free cash flows. When you translate a WACC from one currency into another, you also translate the implied interest tax shields—and the underlying assumptions on debt financing and taxation.[7] As a result, there are two basic choices in applying WACC in cross-border valuations:

1. *Domestic-capital WACC.* Use a domestic-capital WACC if the cross-border business is financed and taxed at domestic interest and tax rates. As international companies tend to borrow in their parent country at parent company currencies, this is the most common approach.[8] To discount foreign cash flows, convert the domestic-capital WACC into a

---

[6] R. Harris, F. Marston, D. Mishra, and T. O'Brien, "Ex-Ante Cost of Equity Estimates of S&P 500 Firms: The Choice between Domestic and Global CAPM," *Financial Management* 32, no. 3 (2003): 51–66.

[7] This assumption concerns only the taxation of interest charges, not the foreign operating tax rate.

[8] As always, account for the riskiness of the cross-border business in the WACC via the unlevered beta.

foreign-currency equivalent WACC by adding the inflation-rate difference between the currencies in each year.[9] The valuation result can be converted at the spot rate to obtain a value in domestic currency.

2. *Foreign-capital WACC.* Use a foreign-capital WACC if cross-border businesses are financed and taxed at foreign rates. Discount the foreign cash flows directly at this WACC, and convert the result into domestic currency at the spot rate. Alternatively, you could convert the foreign-capital WACC and cash flows into domestic currency and value the business using the forward-rate approach, which leads to the same result.

Note that even when converted into the same currency, the domestic- and foreign-capital WACCs are not equal and therefore generate different valuation results. For example, consider a WACC estimate for the valuation of a Mexican subsidiary by its German parent company (Exhibit 27.2). For illustration purposes, we assume that the parent and subsidiary have identical business risk (k_u = 9.0 percent in euros), tax rates (33 percent), credit quality (k_d = 5.0 percent in euros), and target leverage (debt-to-value = 33 percent). The domestic-capital WACC for cash flows in euros is 8.5 percent. When we account for the seven-percentage-point inflation difference between the two currencies, the 8.5 percent WACC is equivalent to 16.0 percent in Mexican pesos. Applying this 16.0 percent WACC assumes that the debt financing and taxation of interest are taking place in euros.

EXHIBIT 27.2   **WACC Measures for Mexican Subsidiary of German Parent Company**

Cross-border DCF valuation example, %

	Domestic-capital WACC	Foreign-capital WACC	
Currency for measuring cash flows	Euros	Mexican pesos	
Cost of debt (k_d)	5.0	12.3	
Tax rate on interest	33.0	33.0	
Debt/(debt + equity)	33.0	33.0	Difference from tax
Weighted k_d after taxes	**1.1**	**2.7**	◄— deduction of interest in
			foreign versus domestic
Unlevered cost of equity (k_u)	9.0	16.6	currency
Debt/equity	49.3	49.3	
Cost of equity (k_e)	11.0	18.7	
Equity/(debt + equity)	67.0	67.0	
Weighted k_e	**7.3**	**12.5**	
WACC	**8.5**	**15.2**	
€ inflation	1.0	1.0	
Peso inflation	8.0	8.0	
Equivalent WACC[1]	(in Mex$) **16.0**	(in €) **7.7**	

[1] Equivalent WACC in the other currency after adjusting for the difference in inflation.

[9] That is, by adding to the domestic-capital WACC any forward inflation difference between the domestic and foreign currency, as explained in the first section of this chapter.

The foreign-capital WACC is derived by converting the euro-based cost of debt and unlevered cost of equity into pesos (k_d = 12.3 percent, and k_u = 16.6 percent). The foreign-capital WACC based on cash flow in pesos amounts to 15.2 percent, equivalent to 7.7 percent in euros. The difference from the domestic-capital WACC stems from the after-tax cost of debt: tax shields are larger when the debt is financed and taxed in a higher-inflation currency, everything else being equal.

In practice, financing choices for cross-border business operations are far from straightforward, because companies need to take into account many complicating factors. These include differences in international taxation, the cost of local versus international debt funding, the depth of alternative debt markets, the impact on foreign-currency exposure, and others. How to make such international financing choices is beyond the scope of this book. But you should be careful in properly reflecting the outcome of such financing choices via the cost of capital in cross-border valuations. In practice, a domestic-capital WACC is most common—but beware of exceptions.

INCORPORATING FOREIGN-CURRENCY RISK IN THE VALUATION

Many executives are concerned about the impact that currency fluctuations from foreign investments have on value creation in company results. The analyst community and investors may be wary of the resulting earnings volatility, even though it does not matter for value creation. As a result, many companies still add a premium for currency risk to the cost of capital for foreign investments. This is unnecessary. As we discuss in Appendix G, currency risk premiums in the cost of capital—if any—are likely to be small. There should be no difference between the cost of capital for investments in foreign currency and otherwise identical investments in domestic currency (when you apply consistent monetary assumptions). First, price fluctuations tend to mitigate currency fluctuations because of purchasing power parity. Second, currency risk is largely diversifiable for companies and shareholders. Any remaining risk from currency rate changes is best reflected in the cash flow projections for the investment.

Keep in mind that nominal currency risk is irrelevant if exchange rates immediately adjust to differences in inflation rates. The only relevant currency risk is therefore real currency risk as measured by changes in relative purchasing power. For example, if you held $100 million of Brazilian currency in 1994, by 2019 it would be worth about $25 million in U.S. dollars. Yet if you adjust for purchasing power, the value of the currency has fluctuated around the $100 million mark during the 25-year period. Exhibit 27.3 shows the estimated real effective (inflation-adjusted) exchange rate for the Brazilian currency, which has continued to hover around the 1994 level although the nominal exchange rate to the U.S. dollar plummeted.

EXHIBIT 27.3 **Brazilian Inflation-Adjusted Exchange Rate**

Real effective exchange rate (REER) index and U.S. $ nominal exchange rate index, 7/1/1994 = 100

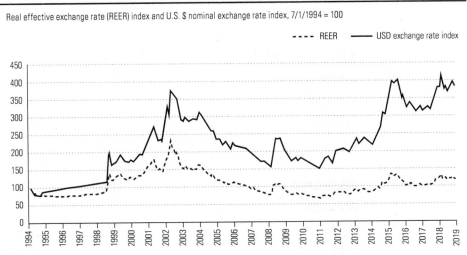

Source: Banco Central do Brasil.

Analysis of purchasing power parity (PPP) indicates that, in general, currencies indeed revert to parity levels following changes in relative rates of inflation, albeit not immediately.[10] Short-term deviations from exchange rates at purchasing power parity potentially leave corporations exposed to real-terms currency risk. However, shareholders are typically able to diversify this risk. To see how, consider Exhibit 27.4, which shows the monthly volatility of real exchange rates for a selection of Latin American and Asian currencies, as well as the British pound, and compares them with four currency portfolios. Although some of the currencies are highly volatile, holding a regional portfolio already eliminates a lot of the resulting real currency risk, as shown by the lower volatility of the regional portfolios. Combining a developing-markets portfolio with a British-pounds portfolio diversifies the real risk even further. If shareholders can disperse most real currency risk by diversifying, there is no need for a currency risk premium of any significance in the company's cost of capital.

Sometimes currency exchange rates move fast and far from PPP. As Exhibit 27.3 showed, during a period of just two weeks in 1999, Brazil's currency weakened by more than 50 percent relative to the U.S. dollar in nominal terms. When conducting a valuation in a currency that shows large deviations from PPP, you should account for the risk of a few weeks or even several years passing before the currency moves back toward PPP. Do not adjust the cost of capital, but instead use scenarios to account for this risk, as described in Chapter 4.

[10] See Taylor and Taylor, "The Purchasing Power Parity Debate."

EXHIBIT 27.4   **Diversification of Real Currency Risk**

10-year monthly real exchange rate[1] volatility, %

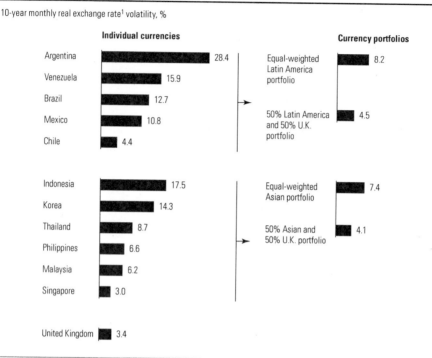

[1] Exchange rates to U.S. dollar.
Source: International Monetary Fund.

If the foreign business being valued has limited international purchases and sales, the impact of any exchange rate convergence toward PPP is likely to be limited as well. In this case, value the business's forecast cash flows using either the spot-rate or forward-rate approach to obtain a valuation in your domestic currency. Apply two different currency scenarios: one using spot and forward rates based on the actual exchange rate, and one based on a deemed convergence of the exchange rate toward PPP. The valuation results in the local currency of the foreign business will be identical for both scenarios. But that won't be the case for the result in your domestic currency, highlighting the exposure to a potential exchange-rate change.

If the business has significant cash flows in international currencies, such as an exporting oil company, exchange-rate adjustments toward PPP will affect cash flows in local currency. Prepare the local cash flow forecasts for the business based on two scenarios: one with convergence of the exchange rate toward PPP, and one without. Then value the cash flows for both currency scenarios using the spot-rate or forward-rate approach. Ensure that the spot and forward rates correctly reflect the assumptions on the convergence of the exchange rate made in your currency scenarios. The result will again be a valuation range in domestic currency, indicating the potential impact of an exchange-rate convergence to PPP.

USING TRANSLATED FOREIGN-CURRENCY FINANCIAL STATEMENTS

To conduct analysis of the historical performance of foreign businesses, it's best to use the foreign currency. But this is impossible if you are conducting your analysis on an outside-in basis and the business's statements in foreign currency have been translated into its parent company's domestic currency and consolidated in the parent's accounts.

For example, a British subsidiary of a European corporate group will always prepare financial statements in British pounds, and when the European parent company prepares its financial statements, it will translate the British pounds in the statements of the British subsidiary at the current euro–pound exchange rate. However, if the exchange rate fluctuates from year to year, the European parent company will report the same asset at a different euro amount each year, even if the asset's value in British pounds has not changed. This change in the value of the British asset in the parent's reporting currency would suggest a cash expenditure. But no cash has been spent, because the change is solely due to a change in the exchange rate. Therefore, following the guidelines from Chapter 11, you need to make a correction to the cash flow estimated from the financial statements that is equal to the gains or losses from the currency translation.

Three Approaches

Between them, U.S. GAAP and IFRS sanction three approaches to translating the financial statements of foreign subsidiaries into the parent company's currency: the current method, the temporal method, and the inflation-adjusted current method. Exhibit 27.5 shows the approach recommended by each standard for countries with moderate inflation and for those with hyperinflation.

EXHIBIT 27.5   **Currency Translation Approaches**

	U.S. GAAP	IFRS
Moderate inflation	Current method	Current method
Hyperinflation	Temporal method	Inflation-adjusted current method

Current Method For subsidiaries in moderate-inflation countries, translating the financial statements into the currency of the parent company is straightforward. Both U.S. GAAP and IFRS apply the current method, which requires translating all balance sheet items except equity at the year-end exchange rate. Translation gains and losses on the balance sheet are recognized in the equity account in other comprehensive income (OCI), so they do not affect net income. The average exchange rate for the period is used to translate the income statement.

For subsidiaries in countries with higher inflation rates, IFRS and U.S. GAAP differ in what they define as hyperinflation, whether to adjust statements for inflation, and what approach to use for translating the financial statements. U.S. GAAP defines hyperinflation as cumulative inflation over three years of approximately 100 percent or more. IFRS states that this is one indicator of hyperinflation but suggests considering other factors as well, such as the degree to which local investors prefer to keep wealth in nonmonetary assets or stable foreign currencies.

Temporal Method U.S. GAAP requires companies to use the temporal method for translating financial statements of subsidiaries in hyperinflation countries into the parent's currency. To use this method, you must translate all items in the financial statements at the exchange rate prevailing at the relevant transaction date. This means using historical exchange rates for items carried at historical cost, current exchange rates for monetary items, and year-average or other appropriate exchange rates for other balance sheet items and the income statement. Any resulting currency gains or losses are reported in the equity account of the parent in OCI.

Inflation-Adjusted Current Method The IFRS approach to currency translation for subsidiaries in hyperinflation countries is like that for moderate-inflation countries. The key difference? IFRS requires that the hyperinflation country statements be restated in current (foreign) currency units based on a general price index before they are translated into the parent company's currency. All except some monetary items need to be restated to account for the estimated impact of very high inflation on values over time. The restatement will result in a gain or loss on the subsidiary's income statement. Because the full statements are restated in current (year-end) foreign-currency units, the year-end exchange rate should be used to translate both the balance sheet and the income statement into the parent company's currency. Any translation gains or losses will be included in the equity account of the parent in OCI.

An Application of the Methods

Exhibit 27.6 shows an example for a U.S. parent company using all three approaches to currency translation. In this example, the exchange rate has changed from 0.95 at the beginning of the year to 0.85 at the end of the year, consistent with 14 percent inflation in the foreign country during the year and U.S. inflation of 2 percent. The average exchange rate for the year is 0.90. As the exhibit illustrates, the three approaches can result in significantly different amounts for net income and equity in the parent company's currency.

Of course, these differences should not affect your estimate of free cash flow for the subsidiary. As a general rule, you should ensure that translation adjustments in components of invested capital are excluded from the investment cash flows. Under IFRS, companies typically specify currency translation adjustments by category of fixed assets, so that you can identify the "cash" investments. Under U.S. GAAP, this information is usually not provided; you will have to add back the translation results to the change in invested capital. For the analysis of historical performance, ratios such as ROIC, operating margin, and capital turnover typically are not significantly distorted under the current method. You do have to adjust growth rates for currency translation effects (see also Chapter 12). For translated financial statements from hyper-inflation countries, we recommend you analyze performance based on the original statements or by reversing translations made for the key operating items (following the analysis recommendations found in Chapter 35).

EXHIBIT 27.6   **Currency Translation**

| | Local currency | Current method | | Temporal method | | Inflation-adjusted currency method | | |
		Foreign-exchange rate	U.S. $	Foreign-exchange rate	U.S. $	Adjusted	Foreign-exchange rate	U.S. $
Balance sheet								
Cash and receivables	100	0.85	85	0.85	85	100	0.85	85
Inventory	300	0.85	255	0.90	270	321	0.85	273
Net fixed assets	600	0.85	510	0.95	570	684	0.85	581
	1,000	–	850	–	925	1,105	–	939
Current liabilities	265	0.85	225	0.85	225	265	0.85	225
Long-term debt	600	0.85	510	0.85	510	684	0.85	581
Equity								
Common stock	100	0.95	95	0.95	95	100	0.95	95
Retained earnings	35	–	32	–	95	56	–	48
Foreign-currency adjustment	–	–	(12)	–	–	–	–	(10)
	1,000	–	850	–	925	1,105	–	939
Income statement								
Revenue	150	0.90	135	0.90	135	161	0.85	137
Cost of goods sold	(70)	0.90	(63)	0.93	(65)	(75)	0.85	(64)
Depreciation	(20)	0.90	(18)	0.95	(19)	(23)	0.85	(20)
Other expenses, net	(10)	0.90	(9)	0.90	(9)	(11)	0.85	(9)
Foreign-exchange gain/(loss)	–	–	–	–	66	20[1]	0.85	17
Income before taxes	50	–	45	–	108	72	–	61
Income taxes	(15)	0.90	(13)	0.90	(13)	(16)	0.85	(13)
Net income	35	–	32	–	95	56	–	48

[1] Gain from restatement.

SUMMARY

In principle, applying the DCF valuation approach to foreign businesses is the same as applying it to domestic companies. But there are some additional issues to consider. You'll want to reflect local accounting in your analysis, following the general guidelines from Chapter 11. Because IFRS and U.S. GAAP are now the dominant standards, accounting issues have become less of a burden.

You can project and discount cash flows for foreign businesses in foreign or domestic currency if you apply consistent assumptions for exchange rates, interest, and inflation and if you correctly apply the spot-rate or forward-rate method of valuation. The approach for estimating the cost of capital should be the same for any company anywhere in the world. With the global integration of capital markets in mind, we recommend using a single real-terms, risk-free rate and market risk premium for companies around the world. For investors and companies facing restrictions on investing abroad, we recommend estimating a local cost of capital. It is not necessary to add separate premiums to the cost of capital to address currency risks. These are best reflected in a scenario-based valuation.

Part Four

Managing for Value

28

Corporate Portfolio Strategy

A company's value depends greatly, though not entirely, on the actions of its managers. In 2018, colleagues of ours published the results of their global research on 2,393 companies, in which they identified the core drivers that helped some ascend to the top quintile of value creators.[1] These drivers of value included the industry and geography in which the company participated plus five strategic management actions: changing the business portfolio (through programmatic acquisitions and divestitures), allocating resources, spending capital, improving productivity, and innovating to differentiate products and services better.

Applying a management perspective to the science and art of value creation is the focus of the seven chapters that make up Part Four of this book. Specifically, we examine two critical top management decisions: What should executives decide to hold in the company's portfolio of businesses? And how should they allocate resources in support of decisions on capital expenditures, research and development (R&D), talent management, and more? We also explore managing the performance of the company's businesses through target setting, monitoring performance, and taking corrective action where necessary.

We begin in this chapter with the question of what businesses a company should be in, along with two related questions: What constitutes being the best owner of a company, and how might the best owner change over time? The chapter also discusses how a business portfolio evolves and how to manage

[1] C. Bradley, M. Hirt, and S. Smit, *Strategy Beyond the Hockey Stick* (Hoboken, NJ: John Wiley & Sons, 2018).

that portfolio throughout its evolution. We then explore why diversification's role in creating value is often misunderstood. The chapter concludes with a guide to systematic construction of a portfolio of businesses, using a case study of a company that applied the approaches we explain.

BET ON THE HORSE—OR THE JOCKEY?

Deciding what businesses to operate in is clearly one of the most important decisions executives make. As our colleagues' research showed, it is a critical determinant of a company's destiny. For example, a company that produces commodity chemicals is unlikely ever to earn as much return on capital as one that makes branded breakfast cereal can. That said, different owners and managers might be able to extract more or less value from the same business. So creation of the most value requires picking attractive businesses, combined with identifying the owner able to generate the greatest cash flows from each business.

In pointing out the importance of picking the right business, Kaplan, Sensoy, and Strömberg use the analogy of deciding at the racetrack whether to bet on the horse or the jockey.[2] These researchers analyzed small start-up companies financed by venture capital firms, tracking whether the start-ups eventually grew large and successful enough to go public. They found that it was better to have a competitive advantage (horse) than to have a good management team (jockey). With a competitive advantage, the venture capitalists could always replace a weak management team. But even the best management team might be unable to turn a nag into a sleek thoroughbred—a weak business into a winner. In other words, go with the horse, not the jockey. Warren Buffett made the same point in his own unique way: "When a management team with a reputation for brilliance joins a business with poor fundamental economics, it is the reputation of the business that remains intact."

Although even great managers may find it impossible to salvage a poor or declining business, for any given business, different owners or management teams may extract higher levels of performance than others can and thus be better owners of that business at that time. For many years, businesses making pharmaceuticals for animals were owned by companies that also made pharmaceuticals for people. Then, from 2009 to 2019, a massive restructuring transformed the animal health business. With different economics, sales, and distribution channels, five of the largest pharmaceutical companies—Bayer, Johnson & Johnson, Novartis, Pfizer, and Sanofi—sold or spun off their animal

---

[2] S. N. Kaplan, B. A. Sensoy, and P. Strömberg, "Should Investors Bet on the Jockey or the Horse? Evidence from the Evolution of Firms from Early Business Plans to Public Companies," *Journal of Finance* 64, no. 1 (February 2009): 75–115.

health businesses. Elanco, a division of Eli Lilly, bought six animal health companies during this period and in 2019 was itself spun off as an independent company. During the same period, many large pharmaceutical companies (including Johnson & Johnson, Merck, and Pfizer) sold off significant parts of their consumer businesses.

A classic example of the better-owner principle is General Mills' 2001 purchase of Pillsbury from Diageo. Shortly after buying Pillsbury for $10.4 billion, General Mills increased the business's pretax cash flows by more than $400 million per year, increasing Pillsbury's operating profits by roughly 70 percent. Diageo's core business is in alcoholic beverages, while General Mills and Pillsbury sell packaged foods. Under Diageo, Pillsbury was run entirely separately from Diageo's core business, because the two companies' manufacturing, distribution, and marketing operations rarely overlapped. In contrast, General Mills substantially reduced costs in Pillsbury's purchasing, manufacturing, and distribution, because the two companies' operations duplicated significant costs. On the revenue side, General Mills boosted Pillsbury's revenues by introducing Pillsbury products to schools in the United States, where General Mills already had a strong presence. The synergies worked both ways; for instance, Pillsbury's refrigerated trucks were used to distribute General Mills' new line of refrigerated meals.

Pillsbury represented value in at least two ways at the time of the sale: its value to General Mills and its value to Diageo. For General Mills to consider the deal attractive, Pillsbury's worth under General Mills' ownership had to be greater than the $10.4 billion purchase price. For Diageo to consider the deal attractive, General Mills' offer had to represent more than the value Diageo expected to create from Pillsbury in the future. From a value-creating perspective, General Mills was a better owner of Pillsbury than Diageo.

In practice, one can never pinpoint a company's ideal owner, but only the best among potential owners in the given circumstances. In the Pillsbury example, it is theoretically possible that some company could have generated even higher cash flows than General Mills as Pillsbury's owner. But the change in ownership to General Mills illustrates that a different owner can make a huge difference in a company's value: a 70 percent increase in this case.

Best ownership also helps the economy by redirecting resources to their highest-value use. Significant activities can be carried out at much lower cost, freeing up capital and human resources for other activities.

WHAT MAKES AN OWNER THE BEST?

To identify the best owner of a business in any given industry circumstances, you must first understand the sources of value that potential new owners might draw upon. Some owners add value by linking a new business with other activities in their portfolio—for example, by using existing sales channels to access additional customers or by sharing an existing manufacturing infrastructure. Others add value by applying distinctive skills such as operational or marketing excellence, by providing better governance and incentives for the management team, or by having better insight into how a market will develop. Still others add value by more effectively influencing a particular market's critical stakeholders—for instance, governments, regulators, or customers. Let's examine these sources of value one at a time, understanding that in some cases, the best owner may be able to draw on two or more sources at once.

Unique Links with Other Businesses

The most direct way that owners add value is by creating links between businesses within their portfolio, especially when only the parent company can make such links. Suppose a mining company has the rights to develop a coalfield in a remote location far from any rail lines or other infrastructure. Another mining company already operates a coal mine just ten miles away and has built the necessary infrastructure, including the rail line. The second mining company would be a better owner of the new mine because its incremental costs to develop the mine are much lower than anyone else's. It can afford to purchase the undeveloped mine at a higher price than any other firm in the market and still earn an attractive return on invested capital (ROIC).

Such unique links can be made across the value chain, from R&D to manufacturing to distribution to sales. For instance, a large pharmaceutical company with a sales force dedicated to oncology might be the best owner of a small pharmaceutical company with a promising new oncology drug but no sales force.

Distinctive Skills

Better owners may have distinctive functional or managerial skills from which the new business can benefit. Such skills may reside anywhere in the business system, including product development, manufacturing processes, and sales and marketing. But to make a difference, any such skill must be an important driver of success in the industry. For example, a company with great manufacturing skills probably wouldn't be a better owner of a consumer packaged-goods business, because the latter company's manufacturing costs aren't large enough to affect its competitive position.

In consumer packaged goods, distinctive skills in developing and marketing brands are more likely to make one company a better owner than another. Take Procter & Gamble (P&G), which in 2013 had 180 brands, including 23 billion-dollar brands in terms of net sales—almost all of which ranked first or second in their respective markets—and 14 half-billion-dollar brands. Its brands were spread across a range of product categories, including laundry detergent, beauty products, pet food, and diapers. As of 2013, some brands, including Tide and Crest, had been P&G brands for decades. The company added newer brands to its portfolio in different ways: for example, it acquired Gillette and Oral-B, while it developed Febreze and Swiffer from scratch. In 2014, P&G determined that its distinctive skills were best applied to very large brands. It announced that it would discontinue or divest 90 to 100 of its brands, focusing its energy on the brands that remained.

Another example of distinctive skills is Danaher, a diversified company with revenues of $19 billion. What makes Danaher successful is its well-known Danaher Business System. Danaher makes acquisitions only where it believes it can apply its management approach to substantially improve margins. By applying this strategy over the past 25 years, Danaher has consistently increased the margins of its acquired companies. These include Gilbarco Veeder-Root, a leader in point-of-sale solutions, and Videojet Technologies, which manufactures coding and marking equipment and software. Both companies' margins improved by more than 700 basis points after Danaher acquired them. As Danaher's activities grew in size and complexity, it also began to divest or spin off some of the businesses that were large enough to stand on their own. For example, in 2016, it spun off its professional instrumentation and industrial technologies businesses. Fortive, the spun-off company, included Gilbarco Veeder-Root and 21 other businesses that Danaher had acquired and whose performance it had improved. Danaher also announced the spin-off of its dental business in 2018 (the spin-off was not yet completed at the time of this writing).

Better Governance

Regardless of whether owners are running day-to-day operations, better owners can add value through their overall governance of a business. They provide better governance through the way they (or their representatives) interact with the management team to create maximum value in the long term. For example, the best private-equity firms don't just recapitalize companies with debt; they improve the companies' performance through better governance.

Two of our colleagues analyzed 60 successful investments by 11 leading private-equity firms. They found that in almost two-thirds of the transactions, the primary source of new value was improvement in the operating performance of the company, relative to peers, through fruitful interaction between the owners and the management team.[3] The use of financial leverage and clever timing of investments, often cited as private-equity firms' most important sources of success, were not as important as improved governance.

---

[3] C. Kehoe and J. Heel, "Why Some Private Equity Firms Do Better," *McKinsey Quarterly*, no. 1 (2005): 24–26.

Private-equity firms don't have the time or skills to run their portfolio companies from day to day, but the higher-performing private-equity firms do govern these companies very differently from the way exchange-listed companies are governed. This is a key source of their outperformance. Typically, the private-equity firms introduce a stronger performance culture and make quick management changes when necessary. They encourage managers to abandon any sacred cows, and they give managers leeway to focus on a longer horizon, say five years, rather than the typical one-year horizon for a listed company. Moreover, the boards of private-equity companies spend three times as many days on their roles as do those at public companies. Private-equity firms' boards spend most of their time on strategy and performance management, rather than compliance and risk avoidance, where boards of public companies typically focus.[4]

Better Insight and Foresight

Companies that act on their insight into how a market and industry will evolve to expand existing businesses or develop new ones can be better owners because they capitalize on innovative ideas. One example is Alibaba, China's leading online marketplace. Its leaders realized that lack of trust between buyers and sellers was a barrier to the growth of online marketplaces in China. So in 2004, five years after Alibaba's founding, the company launched Alipay, an escrow service to facilitate online transactions. A buyer deposits money with Alipay for the purchase of goods. Once the goods are shipped and are found acceptable, Alipay releases the funds to the seller. Alipay provides services not only to Alibaba's online businesses but also to thousands of other merchants. In 2011, Alipay was spun off into a stand-alone company.

Or consider Amazon Web Services (AWS). As the largest e-commerce company in the world, Amazon had developed unique skills running distributed computing systems. In 2006, Amazon officially launched AWS and, using its unique skills, sold cloud computing services to companies, governments, and individuals. By 2012, its revenues were estimated to be $1.8 billion (Amazon didn't disclose AWS's results as a separate unit until 2015). In 2018, AWS generated $25 billion of revenues and $7.3 billion of operating profits.

Distinctive Access to Critical Stakeholders

Distinctive access to talent, capital, government, suppliers, and customers primarily benefits companies in some Asian and emerging markets. Several factors complicate running companies in emerging markets: relatively small

---

[4] V. Acharya, C. Kehoe, and M. Reyner, "The Voice of Experience: Public versus Private Equity," *McKinsey on Finance* (Spring 2009): 16–20.

pools of managerial talent from which to hire, undeveloped capital markets, and governments that are heavily involved in business as customers, suppliers, and regulators.

In such markets, large-scale diversified conglomerates, such as Tata and Reliance in India and Samsung and Hyundai in South Korea, can be better owners of many businesses because they are more attractive employers, allowing them to skim off the best talent. Regarding capital, many emerging countries still need to build up their infrastructures; such projects typically require large amounts of capital that smaller companies can't raise. Companies also often need government approval to purchase land and to build factories, as well as government assurances that there will be sufficient infrastructure to get products to and from factories and sufficient electricity to keep them operating. Large conglomerates typically have the resources and relationships needed to navigate the maze of government regulations and to ensure relatively smooth operations.

In more developed markets, access to talent and capital is rarely an issue. In fact, in the United States, smaller, high-growth companies are often more attractive to talent than larger companies. Moreover, capital is readily available in these markets, even for small businesses. Finally, with some exceptions, clout with the government rarely provides an advantage, given the arm's-length government procurement processes more common in these countries.

THE BEST-OWNER LIFE CYCLE

The definition of *best owner* isn't static, and best owners themselves will change over time as a business's circumstances change. Thus, a business's best owner could at different times be a larger company, a private-equity firm, a government, a sovereign wealth fund, a family, the business's customers, its employees, or shareholders whenever a business becomes an independent public company listed on a stock exchange.

Furthermore, the parties vying to become best owners are continually evolving in different ways in different parts of the world. In the United States, most large companies are either listed or owned by private-equity funds. They tend to go public earlier than companies elsewhere, so they rarely involve the second generation of a founding family. In Europe, government ownership also plays an important role. In Asia and South America, large companies are often controlled for several generations by members of their founding families, and family relationships also create ownership links between different businesses. Capital markets in these regions aren't as well developed, so founders are more concerned about ensuring that their firms stay true to their legacy after the founders have retired.

Consider an example of how the best owner for a company might change with its circumstances. Naturally, a business's founders will almost always be its first best owners. The founders' entrepreneurial drive, passion, and tangible commitment to the business are essential to getting the company off the ground.

As a business grows, it will probably need more capital, so it may sell a stake to a venture capital fund that specializes in helping new companies to grow. At this point, it's not unusual for the fund to put in new managers who supplant or supplement the founders, bringing skills and experience better suited to managing the complexities and risks of a larger organization.

To provide even more capital, the venture capital firm may take the company public, selling shares to a range of investors and, in the process, enabling itself, the founders, and the managers to realize the value of the company they created. When the company goes public, control shifts to an independent board of directors (though the founders will still have important influence if they continue to own substantial stakes).

As the industry evolves, the company might find that it cannot compete with larger companies because, for instance, it needs distribution capability far beyond what it can build by itself in a reasonable time to challenge global competitors. Other external factors, such as regulatory or technological changes, also can create a need to change owners. In response to this limitation, the company may sell itself to a larger company that has the needed capability. In this way, it becomes a product line or business within a division of a multibusiness corporation. Now the original company will merge with the manufacturing, sales, distribution, and administrative functions of the division.

As the markets mature for the businesses in the division where the original company now operates, its corporate owner may decide to focus on other, faster-growing businesses. So the corporation may sell its division to a private-equity firm. Now that the division stands alone, the private-equity firm can see how it has amassed an amount of central overhead that is far higher than is needed for a slow-growth market. The response: the private-equity firm restructures the division to give it a leaner cost structure. Once the restructuring is done, the private-equity firm sells the division to a large company that specializes in running slow-growth brands.

At each stage of the company's life, each best owner took actions to increase the company's cash flows, thereby adding value. The founder came up with the idea for the business. The venture capital firm provided capital and professional management. Going public provided the early investors with a way to realize the value of the founders' groundwork and raised more cash. The large corporation accelerated the company's growth with a global distribution capability. The private-equity firm restructured the company's division when growth slowed. The company that became the final best owner applied its skills in managing slow-growth brands. All these changes of ownership made sense in terms of creating value.

DYNAMIC PORTFOLIO MANAGEMENT

Applying the best-owner sequence, executives must continually identify and develop or acquire companies where they could be the best owner and must divest businesses where they used to be the best owner but now have less to contribute than another potential owner. Since the best owner for a given business changes with time, a company needs to have a structured, regular corporate strategy process to review and renew its list of development ideas and acquisition targets, and to test whether any of its existing businesses have reached their sell-by date. Similarly, as demand falls off in a mature industry, long-standing companies are likely to have excess capacity. If they don't have the will or ability to shrink assets and people along with capacity, then they're not the best owner of the business anymore. At any time in a business's history, one group of managers may be better equipped to manage the business than another. At moments like these, acquisitions and divestitures are often the best or only way to allocate resources sensibly.

A McKinsey study of 200 large U.S. companies over a ten-year period showed that companies with a passive portfolio approach—those that didn't sell businesses or only sold poor businesses under pressure—underperformed companies with an active portfolio approach.[5] The best performers systematically divested and acquired companies. The process is natural and never ends. A divested unit may very well pursue further separations later in its lifetime, especially in dynamic industries undergoing rapid growth and technological change.

General Dynamics, the U.S. defense company, provides an interesting example of an active portfolio approach that created considerable value. At the beginning of the 1990s, General Dynamics faced an unattractive industry environment. According to forecasts at that time, U.S. defense spending would decline significantly, and this was expected to hurt General Dynamics, since it was a supplier of weapons systems. When CEO William A. Anders took control in 1991, he initiated a series of divestitures. Revenues were halved in a period of two years, but shareholder returns were extraordinary: an annualized rate of 58 percent between 1991 and 1995, more than double the shareholder returns of General Dynamics' major peers. Then, starting in 1995, Anders began acquiring companies in attractive subsectors. Over the next seven years, General Dynamics' annualized return exceeded 20 percent, again more than double the typical returns in the sector.

For acquisitions, applying the best-owner principle often leads potential acquirers toward targets that are very different from those produced by traditional screening approaches. Traditional approaches often focus on finding

---

[5] J. Brandimarte, W. Fallon, and R. McNish, "Trading the Corporate Portfolio," *McKinsey on Finance* (Fall 2001): 1–5.

536 CORPORATE PORTFOLIO STRATEGY

potential targets that perform well financially and are somehow related to the
parent's business lines. But through the best-owner lens, such characteristics
might be less important or irrelevant.

Potential acquirers might do better to seek a financially weak company
that has great potential for improvement, especially if the acquirer has proven
expertise in improving performance. Focusing attention on tangible opportunities to reduce costs or on identifying common customers may be more
rewarding in the long run than investigating a target for the vague reason that
it is somehow related to your company.

Companies following the best-owner philosophy are as active in divesting
as they are in acquiring; they sell and spin off companies regularly and for
good reasons. To illustrate, 50 years ago, many pharmaceutical and chemical
companies were combined because they required similar manufacturing processes and skills. But as the two industries matured, their research, manufacturing, and other skills diverged considerably, to the extent that they became
distant cousins rather than sister companies.

Today the keys to running a commodity chemicals company are scale, operating efficiency, and management of costs and capital expenditures. In contrast, the keys to running a pharmaceutical company are managing an R&D
pipeline, a sophisticated sales force, the regulatory approval process, and
relations with government in state-run health systems that buy prescription
drugs. So while it might once have made sense for the two types of business
to share a common owner, it no longer does. This is why nearly all formerly
combined chemical-pharmaceutical companies have split up. For instance, the
pharmaceutical company Zeneca was split from Imperial Chemical Industries
in 1993 and later merged with another pharmaceutical company to form As-
traZeneca. Similarly, pharmaceutical company Aventis was split off from the
chemical company Hoechst in 1999; it was later purchased by Sanofi Synthe-
labo to create Sanofi Aventis, forming a bigger pharma-only company.[6]

Dynamic portfolio management has also driven the creation of three of the
top four oil-refining companies in the United States, based on refining capacity. Marathon Petroleum, the largest U.S. refiner, was spun off from Marathon
Oil in 2011. Phillips 66, the fourth largest, came into being as a spin-off from
ConocoPhillips in 2012. Valero Energy, the number-two refiner, was originally
spun off from Coastal States Gas in 1980. Valero grew into its ranking through
major acquisitions in 2000, 2001, 2005, and 2011. Valero then spun off its gaso-
line retailing operations in 2013, to become a pure refining company. In 2019,
Marathon Petroleum also announced its intention to spin off its retailing operations.

Executives are often concerned that divestitures look like an admission of
failure, will make their company smaller, and will reduce their stock market
value. Yet the research shows that, on the contrary, the stock market consistently

---

[6] In 2011, Sanofi Aventis changed its name to Sanofi.

reacts positively to divestitures, both sales and spin-offs.[7] Research has also shown that spun-off businesses tend to increase their profit margins by one-third during the three years after the transactions are complete.[8] Thus, planned divestitures are a sign of successful value creation.

In recent years, prominent companies have decided that shrinking is a good thing. Notably, along with P&G's 2014 announcement that it would discontinue or divest 90 to 100 small brands, the company said it would sell its pet food businesses and spin off its Duracell battery business. This kind of thoughtful shrinking allows disparate businesses to focus on their unique needs and competitive situations.

In another example of purposely shrinking, Kraft in 2012 split into two businesses: Mondelez International and Kraft Foods Group. Mondelez is a global snack-food business selling cookies, crackers, and chocolate. Kraft is a largely North American–only grocery products company, focusing on cheese, meat products, sauces, and coffee. Although both companies are in branded foods, management believed that the challenges and opportunities of the two businesses were different enough that they would be better managed as separate companies.[9]

THE MYTH OF DIVERSIFICATION

A perennial question in corporate strategy is whether companies should hold a diversified portfolio of businesses. The idea seemed to be discredited in the 1970s, yet today some executives still say things like "It's the third leg of the stool that makes a company stable." Our perspective is that diversification is intrinsically neither good nor bad; which one it is depends on whether the parent company adds more value to the businesses it owns than any other potential owner could, making it the best owner of those businesses in the circumstances.

Smoothing Cash Flow Isn't the Key

Over the years, different ideas have been advanced to encourage or justify diversification, but these theories simply don't add up. Most rest on the idea that different businesses have different business cycles, so cash flows at the peak of one business's cycle will offset the lean cash years of other businesses, thereby stabilizing a company's consolidated cash flows. If cash flows and earnings are smoothed in this way, the reasoning goes, then investors will pay higher prices for the company's stock.

---

[7] J. Mulherin and A. Boone, "Comparing Acquisitions and Divestitures," *Journal of Corporate Finance* 6 (2000): 117–139.

[8] P. Cusatis, J. Miles, and J. Woolridge, "Some New Evidence That Spinoffs Create Value," *Journal of Applied Corporate Finance* 7 (1994): 100–107.

[9] In 2015, Kraft merged with Heinz to form Kraft Heinz Company.

The facts refute this argument. First, we haven't found any evidence that diversified companies actually generate smoother cash flows. We examined the 50 companies from the Standard & Poor's (S&P) 500 index with the lowest earnings volatility from 1997 to 2007. Fewer than ten could be considered diversified companies, in the sense of owning businesses in more than two distinct industries. Second, and just as important, there is no evidence that investors pay higher prices for less volatile companies (see Chapter 7). In our regular analyses of diversified companies for our clients, we almost never find that the value of the sum of a diversified company's business units is substantially different from the market value of the consolidated company.

Another argument is that diversified companies with more stable cash flows can safely take on more debt, thus getting a larger tax benefit from debt. While this may make sense in theory, however, we've never come across diversified companies that systematically used more debt than their peers.

A more nuanced argument is that diversified companies are better positioned to take advantage of different business cycles in different sectors. They can use cash flows from their businesses in sectors at the top of their cycle to invest in businesses in sectors at the bottom of their cycle (when their undiversified competitors cannot). Once again, we haven't found diversified companies that actually behave that way. In fact, we typically find the opposite: the senior executives at diversified companies don't understand their individual business units well enough to have the confidence to invest at the bottom of the cycle, when none of the competitors are investing. Diversified companies tend to respond to opportunities more slowly than less diversified companies.

Elusive Benefits, Real Costs

While any benefits from diversification are elusive, the costs are very real. Investors can diversify their investment portfolios at lower cost than companies can diversify their business portfolios, because they only have to buy and sell stocks, something they can do easily and relatively cheaply many times a year. In contrast, substantially changing the shape of a portfolio of real businesses involves considerable transaction costs and disruption, and it typically takes many years. Moreover, the business units of diversified companies often perform less well than those of more focused peers, partly because of added complexity and bureaucracy.

Today, many executives and boards in developed markets realize how difficult it is to add value to businesses that aren't connected to each other in some way. As a result, many pairings have largely disappeared. In the United States, for example, by the end of 2010, there were only 22 true conglomerates.[10] Since then, five have announced that they would split up or divest major businesses, too.

[10] J. Cyriac, T. Koller, and J. Thomsen, "Testing the Limits of Diversification," *McKinsey Quarterly* (February 2012). Conglomerates were defined as a company with three or more business units that do not have common customers, distribution systems, technologies, or manufacturing facilities.

We examined the performance of these conglomerates versus focused companies. The striking insight was not that average total shareholder returns (TSR) was lower for conglomerates, but that the top end of the distribution was chopped off. No conglomerate in our study exceeded a TSR above 20 percent, while the TSR of more focused companies topped out above 30 percent (see Exhibit 28.1). Upside gains are limited for conglomerates because it's unlikely that all of their diverse businesses will outperform at the same time. The returns of units that do are dwarfed by underperformers. Moreover, conglomerates are usually made up of relatively mature businesses, well beyond the point where they would be likely to generate unexpected high returns. But the downside isn't limited, because the performance of more mature businesses can fall a lot further than it can rise. Consider a simple mathematical example: if a business unit accounting for a third of a conglomerate's value earns a 20 percent TSR while other units earn 10 percent, the weighted average will be about 14 percent. But if that unit's TSR is –50 percent, the weighted average TSR will be dragged down to about 2 percent, even before other units are affected. In addition, the poor aggregate performance can affect the motivation of the entire company and the company's reputation with customers, suppliers, and prospective employees.

What Does Matter

What matters in a diversification strategy is whether managers have the skills to add value to businesses in unrelated industries. We found three ways high-performing conglomerates outperform. First, as discussed in greater depth

EXHIBIT 28.1 **Distribution of TSR by Levels of Diversification**

Distribution of S&P 500 companies by total shareholder returns (TSR), $n = 461$[1]

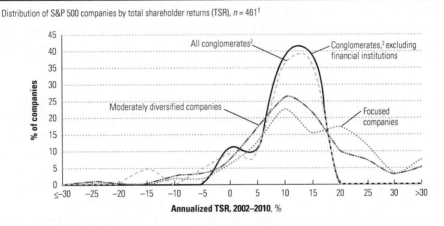

[1] Includes companies in 2010 S&P 500 that were also publicly listed on December 31, 2002.

[2] Defined as any company with three or more business units that do not have common customers, distribution systems, manufacturing facilities, or technologies.

in Chapter 31, "Mergers and Acquisitions," high-performing conglomerates continually rebalance their portfolios by purchasing companies whose performance they can improve.

Second, high-performing conglomerates aggressively manage capital allocation across units at the corporate level. All cash that exceeds what's needed for operating requirements is transferred to the parent company, which decides how to allocate it across current and new business or investment opportunities, based on their potential for growth and returns on invested capital. Berkshire Hathaway's business units, for example, are rationalized from a capital standpoint: excess capital is sent where it is most productive, and all investments pay for the capital they use.

Finally, high-performing conglomerates operate in much the same way as better private-equity firms: with a lean corporate center that restricts its involvement in the management of business units to selecting leaders, allocating capital, vetting strategy, setting performance targets, and monitoring performance. Just as important, these firms do not create extensive corporate-wide processes or large shared-service centers. For instance, you won't find corporate-wide programs to reduce working capital, because that may not be a priority for all parts of the company. At Illinois Tool Works, business units are primarily self-supporting, with broad authority to manage themselves as long as managers adhere to the company's 80/20 rule (80 percent of a company's revenue is derived from 20 percent of its customers) and innovation principles. The corporate center largely handles taxes, auditing, investor relations, and some centralized human resources functions.

Conglomerates in Emerging Markets

As mentioned earlier, the economic situation in emerging markets is distinct enough that we are cautious in applying insights gleaned from developed-world companies. Some preliminary, unpublished McKinsey research shows that more diversified companies in emerging markets outperform their less diversified peers. That is not the case in developed markets. While we expect the conglomerate structure to fade away eventually, the pace will vary from country to country and industry to industry.

We can already see the rough contours of change in the role that conglomerates play in emerging markets. Infrastructure and other capital-intensive businesses are likely to be parts of large conglomerates as long as access to capital and connections is important. In contrast, companies that rely less on access to capital and connections tend to focus on opportunities that differ from those of large conglomerates. These companies include export-oriented ones such as those in information technology (IT) services and pharmaceuticals.

The rise of IT services and pharmaceuticals in India and of Internet companies in China shows that the large conglomerates' edge in access to managerial talent has already fallen. As emerging markets open to more foreign investors, these companies' advantage in access to capital may also decline. That will leave access to government as their last remaining strength, further restricting their opportunities to industries where its influence remains important. Although the time could be decades away, conglomerates' large size and diversification will eventually become impediments rather than advantages.

CONSTRUCTING THE PORTFOLIO

Executives can apply the principles discussed in this chapter to construct a portfolio of businesses for their company. A typical large company already owns enterprises in a single business or has an existing collection of diverse businesses. While there's no single right way to think through this task, we've found over the past 30 years that a systematic approach to constructing a company's portfolio of businesses is helpful. This section describes that approach.

Assessment of Business Units

The process starts with analyzing the value creation characteristics of each business unit. The following questions can direct the analysis:

- Is the unit in an attractive market—specifically, a market with attractive ROIC and growth opportunities?
- Does the unit have a competitive advantage over peers, as evidenced by higher growth or ROIC? What are the sources of advantage? Are they sustainable?
- Why is the parent company a better owner of the unit? What advantages does it bring?
- Does the unit provide the company with the option of expansion?
- Are there inflection points ahead in the unit's product market (either positive or negative) that affect its value?

In addition, you should evaluate the following secondary factors:

- Does the unit have any risk impact on the rest of the company?
- On a net basis, does the unit provide or consume cash?
- Is the potential to create value large enough to have a meaningful impact on the entire company's value?
- Does the unit consume much more management time than others, relative to its value creation potential?

Once you have conducted these analyses, you could lay them out in summary form, as in Exhibit 28.2.

EXHIBIT 28.2 **Assessment of Business Units: Format with Sample Data**

Primary factor criteria	Unit A	Unit B	Unit C	Unit D	Unit E	Unit F	Unit G
ROIC, 2019, %	14%	33%	17%	12%	13%	22%	10%
Growth, 2019–2023, %	–4%	–4%	2%	4%	14%	7%	2%
ROIC vs. peers, 2019	Above	Above	Comparable	Comparable	n/a	Below	Comparable
Growth vs. peers, 2014–2019	Above	Above	Comparable	Comparable	n/a	Comparable	Comparable
Source of advantages	• Manufacturing process	• Manufacturing process	• Cost leadership • Technology leadership	• Market position	• Stakeholder relationships • R&D/patents	• Product quality • Brand	• None
Corporate value added	• Customer insight • Process excellence • Innovation leadership	• Customer insight • Process excellence • Innovation leadership	• Insights into industry's market • Process excellence • Supply chain expertise	• Process excellence	• Customer insight • Process excellence • Innovation leadership	• Capital to drive market consolidation	• None
Expansion scope	Low	Low	Low: Few other product applications	Low: Highly specialized skills/application	High: Wide range of product applications	Medium: Highly specialized skills/application	Low: Few other product applications
Inflection points	• Currency shifts • Changes in pricing and replacement cycle • Competitor capacity		• New competitor entry	• Product adoption • Regulatory changes	• User-friendly technology applications • New competitor entry	• Channel consolidation • R&D in emerging markets	• Anti-dumping suits • Regional market recovery
Secondary factor criteria							
Risk impact on company	High: Many factors outside control (e.g., currency)	High: Many factors outside control (e.g., currency)	Medium: Risk of new competitors and technologies	Low: Too small	High: Source of future growth; adoption unclear	Low: Too small	High: Market exposure
Cash flows, 2019 FCF, $ billion	0.90	0.60	–0.10	0.03	–0.20	0.20	0.20
Size, value estimate, $ billion	6.30	5.70	2.80	1.90	3.00	0.90	2.30
Management time vs. value potential	Adequate	Adequate	Adequate	Adequate	Adequate	Too high	Too high

Scenario Analysis

Next, estimate the value of each business unit under four scenarios:

1. A baseline or momentum DCF value that grows in line with its underlying product markets without any changes in performance relative to peers (which could be supplemented with a multiples valuation relative to peers to see if there is a gap that needs to be closed)
2. A DCF value based on potential or planned operating improvements, for example, by increasing margins, accelerating core revenue growth, and improving capital efficiency
3. Value to alternative owners if the unit were to be divested
4. Value with additional growth opportunities through innovation or acquisitions

We can demonstrate how a real company (we'll call it Hexa Corporation) applied this approach. Hexa is a $10.65 billion company with six operating businesses. Consumerco, which manufactures and markets branded consumer packaged goods, was earning a high return on invested capital (ROIC), but its growth had barely kept up with inflation. Nevertheless, because of its size and high ROIC, it accounted for about 72 percent of Hexa's total enterprise value. Foodco operates a contract food service business. Its earnings had been growing, but ROIC was low because of high capital-investment requirements in facilities. Woodco, a midsize furniture manufacturer, was formed through the acquisition of eight smaller companies, but their operations were still being consolidated. Woodco had suffered steadily declining returns. The other three businesses in the portfolio are a small newspaper (Newsco), a small property development company (Propco), and a small consumer finance company (Finco).

As shown in Exhibit 28.3, the discounted-cash-flow (DCF) value of Hexa based on a momentum cash flow scenario approximately matched its market value. A cash flow analysis showed that, while Hexa had been generating substantial discretionary (or free) cash flow in the Consumerco business, a large portion of that money had been sunk into Woodco and Foodco, and relatively little was reinvested in Consumerco. Moreover, little of the cash had found its way back to Hexa's shareholders. Over the previous five years, Hexa had, in effect, been borrowing to pay dividends to its shareholders.

The corporate-strategy team analyzed each business unit to find opportunities to improve operations or possibly divest the business. While Consumerco had built strong brand names and most of its product lines had enjoyed

EXHIBIT 28.3 **Hexa Corporation: Current Situation**

	Sales, $ million	EBITA, $ million	Revenue growth, %	ROIC, %	DCF value of momentum case, $ million
Consumerco	6,300	435	3	30	6,345
Foodco	1,500	120	15	9	825
Woodco	2,550	75	19	6	1,800
Newsco	300	45	6	20	600
Propco	–	15	–	–	450
Finco	–	9	–	–	105
Corporate overhead	–	–	–	–	(1,275)
Total	10,650	699			8,850
Debt					(900)
Equity value					7,950
Less: Stock market value					7,200
Value gap					750
% of stock market value					10

a leading market share, this analysis suggested that it had room to increase revenue significantly and earn even higher margins:

- Consumerco had been cutting back on R&D and advertising spending to generate cash for Hexa's efforts to diversify and to buffer poor performance in other parts of Hexa's portfolio. Boosting investments in R&D and advertising would likely lead to higher sales volumes in existing Consumerco products and encourage the introduction of additional high-margin products.

- Despite Consumerco's leading position in its market categories, its prices were lower than for less popular brands. The value created by price increases would more than offset any losses in volume.

- Consumerco's sales force was less than half as productive as sales forces at other companies selling through the same channels. Sales productivity could increase to near the level of Consumerco's peers.

- Consumerco had room to cut costs, particularly in purchasing and inventory management. In fact, the cost of sales could easily be reduced by one percentage point.

When the team factored in these possibilities, it found that Consumerco's value could be increased by at least 37 percent.

Similar analysis of Foodco showed that it was clearly a candidate for divestiture. Foodco's ROIC was less than its cost of capital, so its growth was destroying value. Its industry as a whole was extremely competitive, although a few large players were earning respectable returns. However, even their returns were starting to decline. The Consumerco brand, which Foodco used, was found to be of little value in building the business, and Foodco would be unable to develop significant scale economies, at least in the near future. To make matters worse, Foodco had a voracious appetite for capital to build facilities but was not generating a return on new investment sufficient to cover the cost of its capital. Last, Foodco was a particularly strong divestiture candidate because a new owner that was a larger, growing competitor could dramatically improve its performance.

Woodco, too, was in a position to improve on its performance dramatically as planned under Hexa's ownership, if it could achieve the same level of performance as other top furniture companies. This would likely require Woodco to focus less on growth and more on higher margins. To do this, Woodco would need to build better management information and control systems and would have to stick to its familiar mass-market products instead of striking out into new upmarket furnishings, as it had planned.

Although this analysis suggested that Woodco also might be sold (for instance, to a company that bought and improved smaller furniture firms), it would make little sense for Hexa to sell Woodco right away, midway through its consolidation, when potential buyers might be concerned that the business could fall apart. If the consolidation succeeded, Hexa could sell Woodco for a much higher price in 12 to 18 months, and Woodco's value could increase as a result by 33 percent.

Newsco and Propco were both subscale and could not attract top talent as part of Hexa. Furthermore, ready buyers existed for both, so divestiture was the clear choice.

The consumer finance sector had become so competitive that the spread between borrowing costs and the rates Finco earned on new loans did not cover the consumer finance company's operating costs. It turned out that the existing loan portfolio might be sold for more than the entire business was worth. In effect, each year's new business was dissipating some of the value inherent in the existing loan portfolio. The team recommended that the board liquidate the portfolio and shut down Finco.

Looking for further internal improvements, the team found that Hexa's corporate staff had grown with the increasing complexity of its portfolio to the point where the business units had been obliged to add staff simply to interact with the corporate staff. By simplifying the portfolio, Hexa would be able to cut corporate costs by 50 percent.

On the revenue side, Hexa had done little to take advantage of Consumerco's strong brands to incubate new businesses. A quick analysis showed that if Hexa could find new growth opportunities that generated $1.5 billion to $3 billion in sales, it could increase the market value of Consumerco by $2.4 billion or more. While restructuring was Hexa's priority, it decided to keep generating new growth ideas as well.

All told, the restructuring could increase Hexa's value by 48 percent without the extra growth initiatives and by as much as 78 percent with successful growth initiatives, although these might be hard to realize. Exhibit 28.4 summarizes Hexa's restructuring plan.

EXHIBIT 28.4 **Hexa Corporation: Value Created through Restructuring**

	DCF value of momentum case, $ million	New corporate strategy, $ million	Difference, %	Actions
Consumerco	6,345	8,700	37	Operating improvements
Foodco	825	1,050	27	Divest
Woodco	1,800	2,400	33	Consolidate and divest
Newsco	600	600	–	Divest
Propco	450	480	7	Divest
Finco	105	135	29	Liquidate
Corporate overhead	(1,275)	(675)	n/a	Streamline
Total	8,850	12,690	43	
Debt	(900)	(900)	–	
Equity value	7,950	11,790	48	
New growth opportunities	–	2,400+	–	
Equity value with new growth opportunities	7,950	14,190+	78	

SUMMARY

To construct a portfolio of value-creating businesses, managers should put the question of best ownership front and center in any analysis of a company's current business lineup. If another company would be a better owner for a business, then the business is a candidate for divestment. Conversely, if you identify businesses from which the company could create more value than their present owners can, those businesses are appropriate acquisition targets.

The owner that qualifies as best for a business may change over the course of the business's life cycle and can vary with geography. A company in the United States, for instance, is likely to start up owned by its founders and may end its days in the portfolio of a company that specializes in extracting cash from businesses in declining sectors. In between, the business may have passed through a whole range of owners.

The following chapters build on these ideas to continue our study of how managers can contribute to a company's value. Chapter 29 examines the analytical aspects of resource allocation and performance management; Chapter 30 explores related behavioral and social aspects. Chapters 31 and 32 cover acquisitions and divestitures as tools to change a company's portfolio of businesses. Chapter 33 explains a company's need to have its strategy supported by the right financial underpinnings, including policies for capital structure, dividends, and share repurchases. Finally, Chapter 34 discusses some core principles of communicating with investors.

29

Strategic Management: Analytics

The value that a company creates is the sum of the outcomes of innumerable business decisions that its managers and staff take at every level, from choosing when to open the door to customers to deciding whether to acquire a new business. Successful strategic management encompasses all the tasks a company undertakes to achieve its strategic goals and create long-term value.

At the company's senior-management level, the following tasks are particularly important for creating value:

- Overseeing and developing corporate and business unit strategies
- Setting long-term targets for strategic and financial outcomes
- Allocating resources across the business portfolio (including mergers, acquisitions, and divestitures) and setting budgets to achieve strategic targets
- Managing performance by reviewing business unit results and deciding when and how to intervene
- Managing talent—in particular, creating effective incentives for managers

As value-minded managers navigate these tasks, traps abound. Primary among them is finding the right balance between generating profits in the short term and investing for value creation in the long term. This is one of management's most difficult challenges. Especially in companies with many businesses, markets, and management layers, decisions tend to be biased toward short-term profit, because it is the most readily available and widely understood performance measure. Investors, equity analysts, supervisory directors, the press, and even internal reporting processes all contribute to this short-term bias.

Overcoming such obstacles in order to manage strategically requires fluency in two distinct yet interrelated disciplines. The first of these—and the subject of this chapter—is to apply an emphasis on strong analytics to ferret out sources of value and make the right decisions for value creation. The second is to establish and maintain effective strategic-management processes that orient the entire management team toward common goals. We take up the second discipline in Chapter 30.

The analytical discipline of strategic management should combine three processes. First, managers should adopt a fine-grained approach to setting targets and allocating resources, drilling down to the level of 20 to 50 or even more units or projects. Next, applying this granular approach, executives should rank investment opportunities and set priorities for them across the entire enterprise, using the lens of how each unit or project contributes to the company's overall success. Finally, in planning and monitoring performance, management should use not only financial performance metrics but also, and more importantly, approaches pegged to value drivers that combine long-term and short-term perspectives on value creation. These drivers can also include strategic, organizational, environmental, and social indicators.

ADOPTING A GRANULAR PERSPECTIVE

The larger the company and the more diversified its portfolio, the more likely executives are to allocate resources and manage performance using high-level metrics, such as corporate or divisional top-line growth, profit, and return on invested capital (ROIC).[1] Such metrics are understandable shorthand for comparing performance among multiple divisions and myriad business units. But like all averages, they tend to hide the outliers—the strongest and weakest performers, which are the ones most in need of promotion or correction. Exhibit 29.1 shows one example where the four divisions of a diversified industrial company each fell between 5 and 10 percent short of overall economic-profit goals, suggesting only modest underperformance. Yet a closer look found that two-thirds of the company's 150 business segments were underperforming on its economic-profit goals by as much as 40 percent, while the rest were outperforming enough to skew the averages. As a result, the opportunity for improvement turned out to be much larger than the executives had anticipated.

It's clear from this example that strategic management should take place at the level of business segments, so that senior management clearly sees where value is created, not at the corporate center. However, the management

---

[1] This section draws on M. Goedhart, S. Smit, and A. Veldhuijzen, "Unearthing the Sources of Value Hiding in Your Corporate Portfolio," *McKinsey on Finance*, no. 48 (Autumn 2013): 2–9.

EXHIBIT 29.1   **Improvement Opportunity at Different Levels of Review**

€ million

Review level	Economic profit vs. target,[1]
Company overall, 1 unit	−200
By division, 4 units	−200
By business unit, 26 units	−500 ‖ 300
By business segment, 150 units	−1,100 ‖ 900

Total improvement
opportunity

[1] Economic-profit target: €2,650 million

structure of division heads overseeing business units, business unit leaders supervising segment managers, and so on typically gets in the way of value-oriented decision making. Divisional managers like the "averaging" of business unit results, which enables them to achieve short-term targets for their division, possibly at the expense of long-term value creation.

In our experience, for a company earning $10 billion in revenue, strategic management by corporate executives should typically take place at the level of at least 20 to 50 or sometimes more units or projects.[2] One rule of thumb is to further dissect businesses as long as underlying subsegments show significant differences in terms of growth and return on capital and are material in value relative to the company as a whole. Wherever managers find that their companies lack the necessary financial data, such as revenue, operating earnings, and capital expenditures, they will probably also find that they rely too heavily on averages when setting strategic priorities, financial targets, and resource budgets.

The finer-grained perspective we recommend offers several important benefits. First, it reveals more value-creation opportunities, as it dissects average performance and growth across the portfolio. For example, executives at one global company considered a consumer goods business in Asia to be the most successful in the company's portfolio, because it consistently delivered double-digit top-line growth. But a more detailed analysis revealed that this business was losing market share because the relevant local markets were growing even faster—which would almost inevitably lead to lower value creation in the long term.

Second, taking a finer-grained perspective helps managers understand performance trends for business units that consist of several distinct product or market segments. While a higher number of segments might appear to complicate matters for executives and the corporate center, the reverse is often the case. For example, the aggregated growth rate and return on invested capital

---

[2] These segments are similar to what we have elsewhere called "value cells." See, e.g., M. Giordano and F. Wenger, "Organizing for Value," *McKinsey on Finance*, no. 28 (Summer 2008): 20–25.

for a business unit will continuously change over time if its underlying segments have different growth rates and returns on capital, even if these are stable for each segment. Unless you analyze performance at the segment level, it will be very difficult to understand and forecast the business unit performance.

Finally, a granular approach offers executives better information for direct and radical interventions at the level of individual units or projects, should stepping in become necessary. This can occur when a division-based structure leads to misaligned management incentives.[3] For example, in one global industrial company, whenever one of the business units needed to achieve its overall profit target it would cut its research investments in breakthrough renewable-energy technology, although the technology had excellent potential to create long-term value. To remedy the situation, management separated out the renewable-energy project as an independent unit reporting directly to the executive team. Detached from the original business unit's profit goals, the new unit increased and stabilized these value-creating research investments.

TAKING THE ENTERPRISE VIEW

In addition to taking a granular view of strategic management, companies need to examine all resource allocation decisions (including capital expenditures, research and development, talent, and sales and marketing) in the context of the entire enterprise, not as single, stand-alone decisions and not as a part of a division or business unit.[4]

Taking the enterprise view means evaluating resource investments from the perspective of how they affect the company as a whole. This approach provides several benefits:

- It ensures that resources are allocated to where they will create the greatest value for the company as a whole, regardless of which division or business unit receives the resources.

- It helps overcome the inertia that leads to resources being allocated to the same units from year to year. Research shows that the best predictor of how companies typically allocate resources is last year's allocation. Yet companies that more actively reallocate resources create more value, translating into 30 percent higher total shareholder returns, on average.[5]

- It mitigates the negative effects of loss aversion—the tendency to pass on high-risk, high-reward investments because individuals tend to

---

[3] Giordano and Wenger, "Organizing for Value."

[4] This section draws on D. Lovallo, T. Koller, R. Uhlaner, and D. Kahneman, "Your Company Is Too Risk-Averse," *Harvard Business Review* (March/April 2020), hbr.org.

[5] S. Hall, D. Lovallo, and R. Musters, "How to Put Your Money Where Your Strategy Is," *McKinsey Quarterly* (March 2012), www.mckinsey.com.

weight losses more heavily than gains. Mid- and lower-level managers are typically too risk averse, attaching much more importance to potential losses than gains from investments (see Chapter 4). This applies even when the amounts at stake are small and any losses could be easily absorbed by the organization as a whole.[6] Combining investment opportunities from different business units and segments typically generates diversification benefits, reducing the risk per dollar invested.[7]

Effective strategic management should aim to make allocation decisions for the entire company all at once or at least in groups, using some form of project ranking and prioritization across the company. Ideally, a company would apply a portfolio optimization model that incorporates risk correlations across potential investment projects. In Chapter 4 we discussed the example of a technology company that adopted this approach. Regardless of which division or business unit individual projects belong to, they are combined in alternative portfolios, and the portfolios are ranked by their aggregate return and risk.[8] With this approach, a company can find the portfolio of projects that would provide the best balance between risk and return. For example, it can derive what would be the least risky portfolio that achieves an overall target rate of return.

A Simpler Alternative

Following the same underlying logic, a less technical approach can generate similar insights without explicit estimates of project risk correlations. Consider the example of a company that operates three business units, each with ten projects seeking investment. In this approach, the business units submit all their project proposals to the teams responsible for overseeing financial planning and analysis, corporate strategy, and other functions. Each proposal includes a range of possible present-value outcomes and an assessment of the associated risks. The corporate staff then simply ranks all 30 projects across the company based on their expected return, ignoring risk for the moment. Given a certain investment budget and based on this ranking, the staff determines which projects should be selected to maximize overall value creation, regardless of which business they belong to (see Exhibit 29.2).

For this preliminary selection, the corporate staff assesses whether the overall risk profile is acceptable for the company as a whole. If the projects are largely uncorrelated, the aggregate risk per dollar invested for the selected

---

[6] See T. Koller, D. Lovallo, and Z. Williams, "Overcoming a Bias against Risk," McKinsey & Company, August 2012, www.mckinsey.com.

[7] As noted in Chapter 4, this does not mean that the company's cost of capital is lower. By definition, diversification cannot reduce a project's beta and cost of capital.

[8] We measure return as expected PV/I (that is, present value divided by investment) and risk as the standard deviation of return.

EXHIBIT 29.2 **Ranking of Investment Projects at Aggregate Portfolio Level**

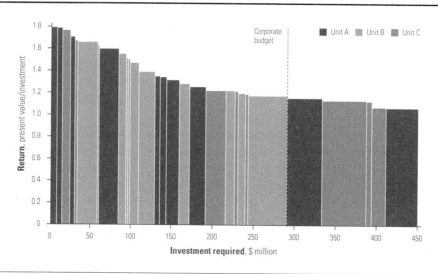

portfolio will be lower than for the individual projects. Of course, the risk reduction will be less for a portfolio of projects with returns that are positively correlated. Depending on the situation, the corporate staff could therefore exchange parts of the portfolio with less correlated projects from the next-best-ranked projects, to reduce aggregate portfolio risk, even though the reduction in risk will come at the expense of overall return.

The approach aims to create the best allocation from a corporate perspective, maximizing value creation with an acceptable risk profile for the company as whole. But it may well allocate investments unevenly from the viewpoint of the business units—for example, when one unit has very few proposals approved relative to others. If uneven allocations are the rule rather than the exception, that can be an important insight. Businesses that are unable to compete successfully for investment resources could be candidates for divestment to a better owner or should focus their strategy on cash generation rather than growth through investments.

Allocating resources through project ranking and prioritizing should be done annually at the very least, preferably more frequently, depending on the length of projects. Of course, doing this at the corporate rather than business level might hamper an organization's ability to react quickly to new opportunities or information. Each organization will have to find the right balance between flexibility and efficiency in resource allocation. For example, some companies set up investment reserves for unforeseen initiatives. Others assign investment funds to projects on a conditional basis, so that allocations can be changed during the year if projects don't meet predetermined milestones. One company we know devotes several weeks per year to discussion of resource allocation. Most of the company's investment decisions are made during these weeks, always in the context of the overall portfolio of projects. If certain investment decisions must be made outside this allocation cycle, their impact on the company's overall portfolio is analyzed separately.

When a company is faced with too many projects to assess individually, the approach can be easily modified. Instead of submitting all investment projects separately, the business units could propose tranches of logically grouped projects. For example, the units could submit a tranche of $50 million investments just to "keep the lights on," a second tranche of $100 million projects to maintain market share and growth with their market, and a third tranche that might provide $100 million for some new products or services or enhancements to customer service. The investment proposal for each tranche would include an estimated value and risk profile. Then the corporate staff would rank and prioritize the tranches (rather than the individual projects) across all business units, following the same logic as described earlier. Some units would receive all three tranches, others only one or two, as shown in Exhibit 29.3.

Sometimes business units need to consider projects that address critical threats or opportunities but also have significant investment needs and/or risks, even from a corporate perspective. In a hybrid approach, such projects could be classified as strategic if they exceed certain limits for investment and risk; the limits could be predetermined by, for example, the company's CEO

EXHIBIT 29.3 **Ranking by Tranches of Investment Opportunities**

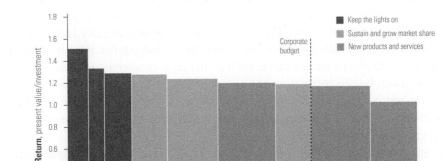

and CFO. The strategic projects are then included alongside the business unit tranches in the overall ranking. This approach ensures that critical strategic projects are highlighted for discussion and funding at the level of the company's executive leadership, rather than by business unit management.

APPLYING VALUE DRIVERS TO MONITOR PERFORMANCE

Analyzing business units and projects at a fine-grained level while allocating investment opportunities across the entire enterprise unveils the promise of managing strategically. In many companies, communication between management layers revolves entirely around missing or hitting profit targets for divisions, business units, and other groups. Strategic management, done well, helps an organization's various layers communicate frankly and effectively. Managers gain leeway to manage while assuring their bosses that agreed-upon levels of performance will be achieved. They can also carefully disaggregate such targets to business segments that can be individually monitored and managed. Attention shifts to the long-term, value-creating potential behind short-term profit targets and the adjustments needed to achieve long-term performance goals.

To plan and monitor progress, it is critical to understand what drives long-term performance. Think of a patient visiting the doctor. The patient may be feeling fine, in the sense of meeting requirements for weight, strength, and energy. But if the patient's cholesterol is above the target level that medical science has established as safe, the patient may need to take corrective action now to prevent future heart disease. Similarly, if a company shows strong growth and return on invested capital (ROIC), it still needs to know whether that performance is sustainable. Comparing readings of company health indicators against meaningful targets can tell us whether a company has achieved impressive past financial results at a cost to its long-term health, perhaps crippling its ability to create value in the future. Companies should look beyond the usual health indicators for business performance to also assess their health on environmental, social, and governance criteria, as these measures are sometimes even more important for sustaining value creation over the long term (see Chapter 6).

To see the difference between companies' recorded performance and their long-term health, consider the pharmaceutical industry. In the year after the patent on a drug expires, sales of that drug for the patent owner often decline by 50 to 75 percent or more, as producers of generics lower prices and steal market share. Investors know that future profits will suffer when a major product will be going off patent in a couple of years with no replacement on the horizon. In such a case, the company could have strong current performance but a poor performance outlook reflected in a low market value, because market values reflect long-term health, not just short-term profits. Or consider retail chains that sometimes maintain apparently impressive margins by scrimping on store refurbishment and brand building, to the detriment of their future competitive strength.

To effectively manage short-term and long-term performance, companies should identify and understand the underlying value drivers of their businesses. Based on these insights, they should develop a coherent set of actionable metrics that are tailored to their business and set appropriate targets against which to monitor results.

Identifying Value Drivers

We can gain insight into a company's health by examining what drives long-term growth and ROIC, the key drivers of value creation. A systematic method for analytically and visually linking a business's unique value drivers to financial metrics and shareholder value is the value driver tree. It breaks down each element of financial performance into value drivers.

The value driver tree in Exhibit 29.4 illustrates the basic kinds of value drivers. The left side of the exhibit shows the financial drivers of intrinsic value: revenue growth and ROIC.[9] Proceeding to the right, the exhibit calls out short-term value drivers, followed by medium- and long-term value drivers. The choice of a particular value driver, along with metrics and targets for testing and strengthening each one, should vary from company to company, reflecting each company's different sectors and aspirations.

Companies should choose their own set of value drivers and metrics, under the generic headings set out here, and tailor their choice to their industry and strategy. Such tailoring is critical for setting the right strategic priorities. For example, product innovation may be important to companies in one industry, while for companies in another, tight cost control and customer service may matter more. For companies in electric power generation, the growth of generation from renewable resources may well be critical over the next decade. The way executives set priorities for value drivers should reflect these differences. Similarly, an individual company will have different value drivers at different points in its life cycle.

Every company will need to develop its own appropriate value drivers and metrics. The generic categories of short-, medium-, and long-term drivers presented in Exhibit 29.4 offer a practical starting point for analysis. Using them will ensure that a company systematically explores all the important drivers.

---

[9] Cost of capital is also a driver of company value, but it is largely determined by the company's industry sector and is difficult for management to influence.

EXHIBIT 29.4 **Value Driver Tree with Three Horizons**

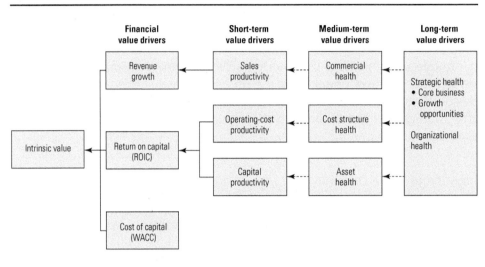

Short-Term Value Drivers   Short-term value drivers are the immediate drivers of ROIC and growth. They are typically the easiest to quantify and monitor frequently (monthly or quarterly). They are indicators of whether current growth and ROIC can be sustained, will improve, or will decline over the short term. They might include cost per unit for a manufacturing company or same-store sales growth for a retailer.

Following the growth and ROIC framework in Exhibit 29.4, short-term value drivers fall into three categories:

1. *Sales productivity* refers to drivers of recent sales growth, such as price and quantity sold, market share, the company's ability to charge higher prices relative to peers (or charge a premium for its product or services), sales force productivity, and for retailers, same-store sales growth versus new-store growth.

2. *Operating-cost productivity* includes drivers of unit costs, such as the component costs for building an automobile or delivering a package. UPS, for example, is well known for charting the optimal delivery path of its drivers to enhance their productivity and for developing well-defined standards on how to deliver packages.

3. *Capital productivity* measures how well a company uses its working capital (inventories, receivables, and payables) and its property, plant, and equipment. Dell revolutionized the personal-computer business in the 1990s by building to order so it could minimize inventories. Because the company kept inventory levels so low and had few receivables to boot, it could on occasion operate with negative working capital.

When assessing drivers of short-term corporate performance, separate the effects of forces outside management's control (both good and bad) from things management can influence. For instance, executives of upstream oil companies shouldn't get much credit for higher profits that result from higher oil prices, nor should real estate executives be credited for higher real estate prices (and the resulting higher commissions). Oil company performance should be evaluated with an emphasis on new reserves and production growth, exploration costs, and drilling costs. Real estate brokerages should be evaluated primarily on the number of sales, not whether housing prices are increasing or decreasing.

Medium-Term Value Drivers   Medium-term value drivers look forward to indicate whether a company can maintain and improve its growth and ROIC over the next one to five years (or longer for companies such as pharmaceutical manufacturers that have long product cycles). In most cases, there is no clear mathematical relation between these drivers and financial performance in terms of ROIC and growth. These drivers may also be harder to translate into metrics than short-term drivers and are more likely to be measured or assessed annually or over even longer periods.

The medium-term value drivers fall into three categories:

1. *Commercial health* indicates whether the company can sustain or improve its current revenue growth. Drivers in this category include the company's product pipeline quality (talent and technology to bring new products to market over the medium term), brand strength (investment in brand building), and customer satisfaction. Commercial-health metrics vary widely by industry and over time. In branded consumer product sectors, such as packaged food and personal products, minimizing the use of scarce resources and trading fairly with suppliers are becoming more relevant as health indicators of a company's product line in some categories. For a pharmaceutical company, the obvious priority is its product pipeline. For a telecom service provider, customer satisfaction and brand strength may be the most important components of medium-term commercial health. For a consumer electronics company, multiyear price trends for its individual products are an important indicator, as steadily declining prices often indicate lack of innovation compared with competitors.

2. *Cost structure health* is a company's ability to manage its costs relative to competitors over three to five years. For an automotive manufacturer, the number of shared platforms and components across its model range is an important driver. Insights in cost health drivers often follow from programs such as Six Sigma, a method to reduce costs continually and maintain a cost advantage relative to competitors across most of the company's businesses.

3. *Asset health* is how well a company maintains and develops its assets. For land transportation and logistics companies, the share of electric or hybrid vehicles in their fleets can indicate the extent of their exposure to potential tax increases on fossil fuels. For an airline, indicators may be the average lifetime of the current fleet and the resale or trade-in value of decommissioned aircraft. For a refining company, it could be the average time between plant turnarounds. For a hotel or restaurant chain, the average time between remodeling projects may be an important driver of asset health.

Long-Term Value Drivers Long-term value drivers reflect a company's ability to sustain its core business, capture new growth areas, and develop its talent, skills, and culture over the next decade and more. Assessing long-term value drivers often requires more qualitative milestones, such as progress in selecting partners for mergers or for entering a market.[10] In most cases, these drivers affect ROIC and growth through multiple categories of short- and medium-term value drivers. For example, a company's ability to attract and develop talented employees likely affects its future commercial and cost structure health, with higher sales and cost productivity as a result. In another instance, a track record of trading fairly with suppliers could improve a company's reputation with key stakeholders and enable it to charge a price premium for its products or attract more talented employees.

We distinguish two basic categories of long-term value drivers:

1. *Strategic health* consists of a company's ability to sustain its core business and to identify new growth opportunities. For example, the growth of market share captured by new entrants to the sector can be an insightful measure of strategic health for a company. New entrants often rely on radically different business models that incumbents may find hard to compete with. Even small current market shares for such attackers could translate into significant strategic threats over the longer term. Illustrations are found when looking back at the success of Ayden in the payments sector, Booking.com in the travel sector, or Dollar Shave Club and Harry's in razors and personal grooming. Besides guarding against threats, companies must continually watch for new growth opportunities, whether in related industries or in new geographies. A meaningful indicator can be the number of successful ventures or partnerships in new business areas. Examples are the successes of Alibaba and Apple in building new businesses outside their traditional core, such as Alipay and Apple Pay. In the automotive industry, the share of electric vehicle offerings in the development pipeline of a manufacturer could be a meaningful indicator of long-term growth in premium car categories.

---

[10] See Chapter 1 for a discussion of long-term value creation and the evolving context in which companies view their commitment to shareholders and broader stakeholders. Chapter 6 addresses the challenges of valuing companies' approaches to environmental, social, and governance (ESG) issues.

2. *Organizational health* reflects whether the company has the people, skills, and culture to sustain and improve its performance. Diagnostics of organizational health typically measure the skills and capabilities of a company, its ability to retain its employees and keep them satisfied, its culture and values, and the depth of its management talent. Again, what is important varies by a company's sector and life-cycle stage. E-commerce businesses need entrepreneurial and innovation capabilities in the start-up phase and require more managers and customer-service-oriented staff as they mature. Semiconductor and biotechnology companies need deep scientific innovation capabilities but relatively few managers. Retailers need lots of trained store managers, a few great merchandisers, and in most cases, store staff with a customer-service orientation.

Understanding Value Drivers Pays Benefits

Clearly understanding a business's value drivers has several advantages. If managers know the relative impact of their company's value drivers on long-term value creation, they can make explicit trade-offs between pursuing a critical driver and allowing performance against a less critical driver to deteriorate. This is particularly helpful for choosing between activities that deliver short-term performance and those that build the long-term health of the business. These trade-offs are material: increasing investment for the long term will cause short-term returns to decline, as management expenses some of the costs, such as R&D or advertising, in the year they occur rather than the year the investments achieve their benefits. Other costs are capitalized but will not earn a return before the project is commissioned, so they too will suppress overall returns in the short term. Understanding the long-term benefits of sacrificing short-term earnings in this way should help corporate boards support managers in making investments that build a business's long-term capability to create value.

Clarity about value drivers also enables the management team to set priorities so that activities expected to create substantially more value take precedence over others. Setting priorities encourages focus and often adds more to value than efforts to improve on multiple dimensions simultaneously. For example, reducing accounts receivable in telecom services creates value, but far less so than increases in customer retention levels. And improvements in customer retention might well require a company to refrain from cutting back on customer credit. Without an explicit discussion of such priorities and trade-offs, members of the management team could interpret and execute the business strategy in numerous and perhaps incompatible ways.

In general, distinctive strategic management promotes a common language and understanding of value drivers that shape the way top management and employees think about creating value at each level of the organization. For example, in a pharmaceutical company, distinctive strategic management would encourage discussion and coordinated action across the organization about specific steps to increase the speed of product launches, thus accelerating value creation. In contrast, strategic management in refining and other commodity-based process industries would focus on operational excellence in terms of capacity utilization and operational expenses.

Creating Actionable Metrics

As we saw in Exhibit 29.4, most value driver trees start on the left side with financial value drivers such as ROIC and growth, and each of these is disaggregated into more specific drivers of business value and operational value, moving from left to right. Where possible, managers and analysts should specify actionable metrics for the value drivers.

The more a value driver tree is tailored to the business, the more insight it yields about a company's key sources of value creation and how to influence them. Exhibit 29.5 shows a basic value driver tree developed for a manufacturing company. In this example, the key drivers for growth turn out to be sales force effectiveness and new-product pipeline, because of low market growth and strong competition. For return on capital, the key drivers of value are capacity utilization (measured as invested capital per unit) and the

EXHIBIT 29.5 **Basic Value Driver Tree: Manufacturing Company**

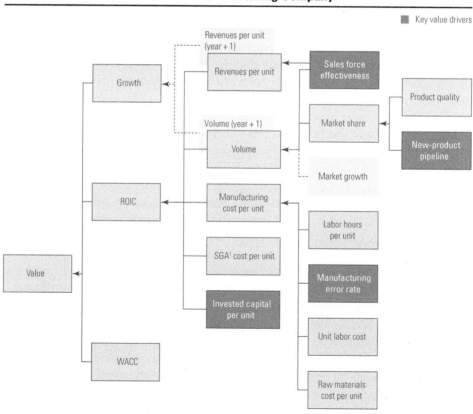

---

[1] Selling, general, and administrative.

EXHIBIT 29.6 **Basic Value Driver Tree: Grocery Retailer**

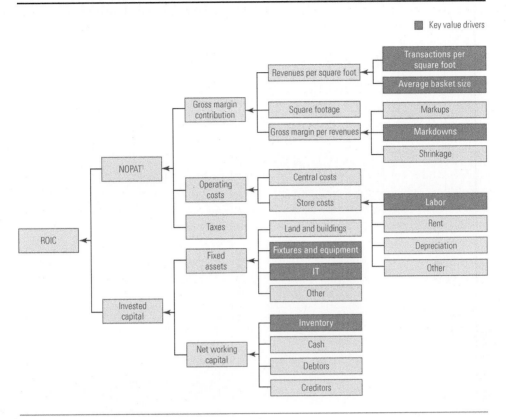

[1] Net operating profit after taxes.

manufacturing error rate. These are important because invested capital is fixed over the next several years, and labor and raw materials costs per unit are very high. In contrast, Exhibit 29.6 shows a value driver tree for a grocery retailer. In this very different example, the key value drivers for gross margin are the average basket size (the number of transactions per square foot is important but always has an upper limit) and the markdown percentage on product prices. For operating costs, labor productivity is key, as most other components are fixed in the near term. Similarly, within invested capital, inventory level is one of the key value drivers; again, most other components are fixed in the near term.

How do you tailor the tree to get such insights? Our experience has taught us that developing different initial versions of trees based on different hypotheses and business knowledge will stimulate the identification of unconventional sources of value. The information from these versions should then be integrated into one tree (or in some cases, a few trees) that best reflects the understanding of the business.

To illustrate this process, we apply it to a hypothetical company running a chain of bicycle repair shops. Exhibit 29.7 shows four different approaches

562

EXHIBIT 29.7 **Alternative Value Driver Trees for a Bicycle Repair Company**

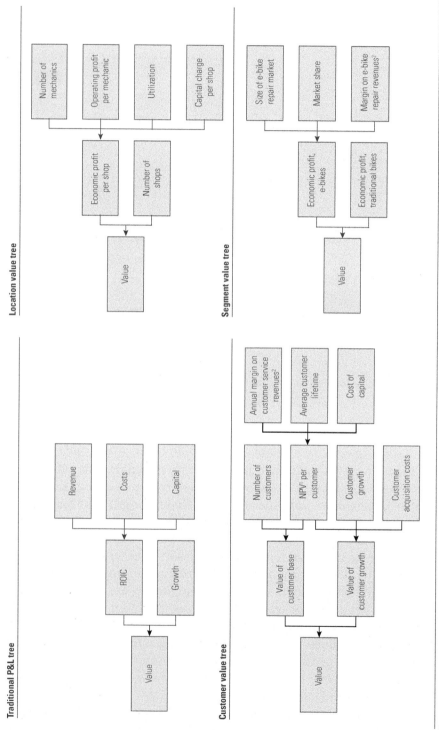

Traditional P&L tree

Location value tree

Customer value tree

Segment value tree

[1] Net present value.
[2] Including capital charge.

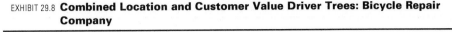

EXHIBIT 29.8 **Combined Location and Customer Value Driver Trees: Bicycle Repair Company**

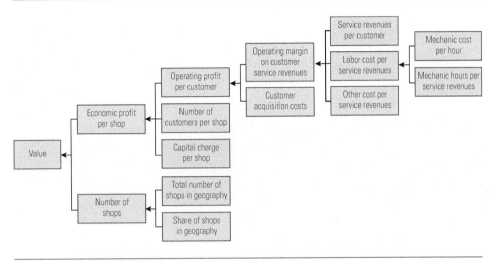

to developing the short-term portion of a value driver tree for this company. We used these trees to develop the summary short-term value driver tree shown in Exhibit 29.8. Adopting the most useful insights provided by the original four approaches, this tree combines the location and customer value driver trees.

Managers often expect that the most natural and easiest-to-complete tree is one based on a profit-and-loss (P&L) structure. Such a tree, however, is unlikely to provide the insight gained by looking at the business from the perspective of a customer, a shop location, or some other relevant vantage point. For example, in most parts of the world, fuel service stations create much more value per customer from selling food and beverage products than fuel. As a result, the conversion of station visits into food and beverage sales is an even more important value driver than the number of station visits itself.

When you develop value driver trees, pay particular attention to the drivers of growth, because of the lag time between investment in developing a growth opportunity and the eventual payoff. Lag times for opportunities will differ. Continuing the example of the bicycle repair company, Exhibit 29.9 illustrates a value tree created for developing business in a new geographic market. For this opportunity, important value drivers include those associated with building the customer base (such as market share, revenues per customer, customer acquisition costs, and number of shops per customer) and improving employee productivity in the new geography (the number of mechanic hours per dollar of revenues), both of which take time to achieve.

EXHIBIT 29.9 **Value Driver Tree for New Geography: Bicycle Repair Company**

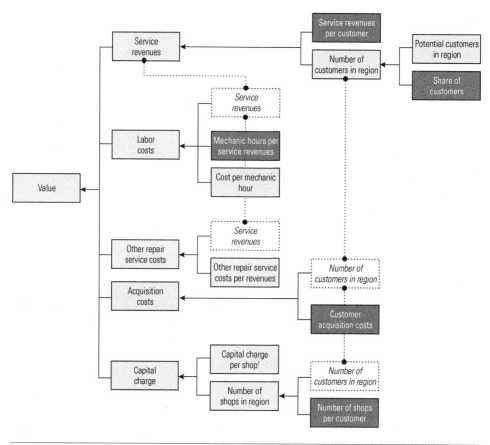

Carefully disaggregating value drivers helps managers identify and set priorities for operating initiatives to improve a company's performance. Exhibit 29.10 shows the value driver tree for a component-manufacturing company. Financial value drivers such as ROIC are cascaded to business value drivers such as gross manufacturing margin and to operating value drivers such as labor productivity and manufacturing error rates. Understanding what is most critical for value creation at the operating or work-floor level is important and can be expressed in a range of potential upside and downside for ROIC. Carefully aligning various operating initiatives with the value drivers affected enables a systematic comparison and can serve as a basis for deciding which initiatives matter most. For example, initiatives to improve employee effectiveness are linked to sales force effectiveness and thus to sales volume and earnings. Product redesign improves earnings via lowering materials, energy, and/or labor costs.

The tip of every branch of a value tree is a potential value driver, so a full disaggregation would result in many value drivers and metrics, more than

EXHIBIT 29.10 **Aligning Operating Initiatives and Value Drivers: Manufacturing Company**

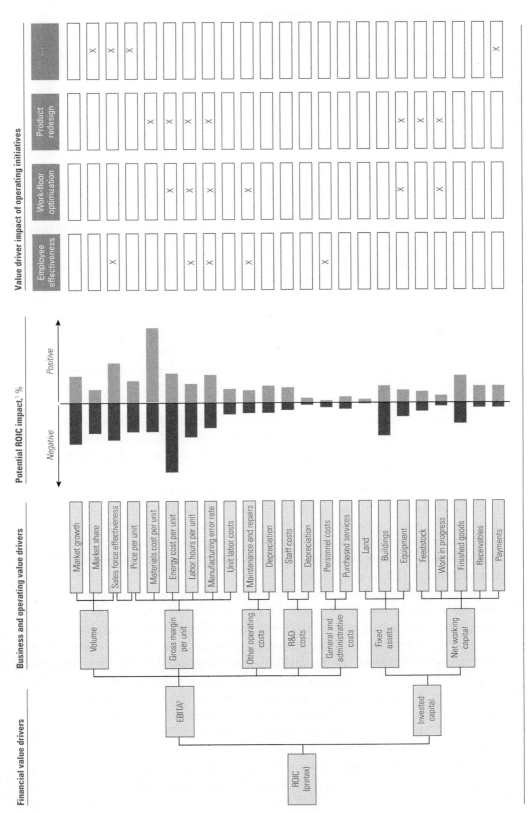

[1] Potential negative and positive ROIC impact, given the likely range of outcomes for underlying value driver.

[2] Earnings before interest, taxes, and amortization.

could possibly be helpful for running the company. To be sure that performance management remains practical and effective, managers need to decide at this stage which drivers are the most important for value creation and then should focus on these.

SETTING TARGETS

To make best use of their understanding of key value drivers and to safeguard their company's future health, managers need to agree on objectives for each driver. These targets should be both challenging and realistic enough that managers can take responsibility for meeting them.

Businesses can identify realistic opportunities and set targets by studying world-class competitors' performance on a particular value metric or milestone and comparing it with their own potential. Alternatively, executives can perform a similar analysis of high-performing firms operating in a different but similar sector. For instance, a petroleum company might benchmark product availability in its service station shops against a grocery retailer's equivalents. This is in part how lean manufacturing approaches developed by automakers have been successfully transplanted into many other industries, including retailing and services.

Businesses can also learn from internal benchmarks. This may involve measuring the performance of the same operation at different time periods, or from studying comparable operations in different businesses controlled by the same parent. These measures may be less challenging than external benchmarks, as they do not necessarily involve world-class players. However, the use of internal benchmarks delivers several benefits. The data are likely to be more readily available, since sharing the information poses no competitive or antitrust problems. Also, unearthing the causes of differences in performance is much easier, as the unit heads can visit the benchmark unit. Finally, these comparisons facilitate peer review.

After assessing the data, companies typically arrive at performance targets defined as single points, although ranges can be more helpful. Some companies set a range in terms of base and stretch targets. The base target is set by top management based on prior-year performance and the competitive environment. Managers should meet the base target under any circumstance. The stretch target is a statement of the aspiration for the business and is developed by the management team responsible for delivery. Those who meet their stretch targets are rewarded, but those who miss them are seldom penalized. Using base and stretch targets makes a performance management system much more complex, but it allows the managers of the business units to communicate what they aspire to deliver (and what it would take for them to achieve that goal) without committing themselves to delivery.

The setting of targets must shift at some organizational level below divisions or business units. At some point, accurately allocating key components of invested capital and costs may become impossible. When that occurs, performance targets are best set in terms of particular elements of sales, operating, or capital productivity metrics instead of return on capital itself (see Exhibit 29.4). For example, most consumer electronics companies have concentrated their manufacturing, R&D, and brand-advertising activities in a handful of locations. The invested capital and costs of these centralized activities are largely independent of what happens in individual product and market segments (say, single-serve coffee machines in Southern California). Although some companies allocate the centralized capital and costs to individual segments by their sales volumes or sales revenues, this has little economic relevance.[11] Furthermore, segment managers have little or no control over the efficiency of the centralized activities. In situations like these, it is more effective to set targets for underlying value drivers such as market share growth, gross margin, and inventory levels rather than return on capital. Of course, companies should ensure that the targets are consistent with driving aggregate return on invested capital of the business units and divisions encompassing the segments. At some point, expansion of market share and sales will require additional production capacity. Once that point is reached, the associated investments and operating costs need to be factored in for target setting in individual business segments.

Choosing the right performance metrics lays the groundwork for discovering new insights into how a company might improve its performance in the future. For instance, a hypothetical pharmaceutical company has the key value drivers shown in Exhibit 29.11. For each of these value drivers, the exhibit shows the company's current performance relative to best- and worst-in-class benchmarks, its targets for each driver, and the potential value impact from meeting its targets. The greatest value creation would come from three areas: accelerating the rate of release of new products from 0.5 to 0.8 per year, reducing from six years to four the time it takes for a new drug to reach 80 percent of peak sales, and cutting the cost of goods sold from 26 percent to 23 percent of sales. Some of the value drivers (such as new-drug development) are long-term, whereas others (such as reducing cost of goods sold) have a shorter-term focus.

MONITORING RESULTS

Focusing on the right performance metrics can reveal what may be driving underperformance. A consumer goods company we know illustrates the importance of having a tailored set of key value metrics. For several years, a

---

[11] For example, declining sales in one segment would imply increasing capital allocated to other segments even if their sales would be unchanged.

EXHIBIT 29.11 **Key Value Drivers: Pharmaceutical Company**

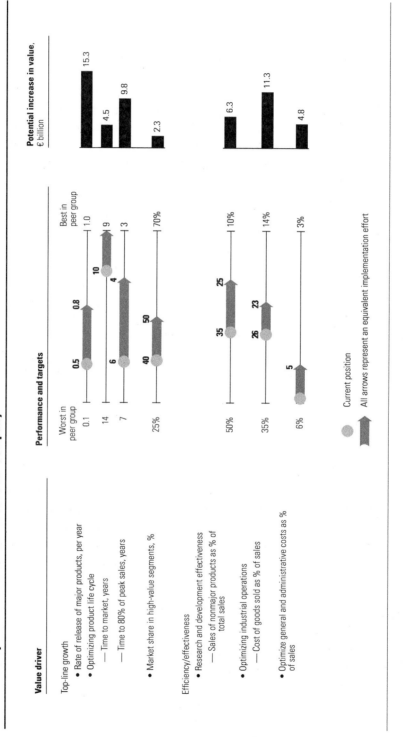

business unit showed consistent double-digit growth in economic profit. Since the financial results were consistently strong—in fact, the strongest across all the business units—corporate managers were pleased and did not ask many questions of the business unit. One year, the unit's economic profit unexpectedly began to decline. Corporate management began digging deeper into the unit's results and discovered that for the preceding three years, the unit had been increasing its profit by raising prices and cutting back on product promotion. That created the conditions for competitors to take away market share. The unit's strong short-term performance was coming at the expense of its long-term health. The company changed the unit's management team, but lower profits continued for several years as the unit recovered its position with consumers.

A well-defined and appropriately selected set of key value drivers ought to allow management to articulate how the organization's strategic, marketing, operating, or other initiatives create value. If it is impossible to represent some component of a strategic initiative using the key value drivers, or if some key value driver does not serve as a building block in the initiative, then managers should reexamine the value trees. Similarly, managers must regularly revisit the targets they set for each value driver. As their business environment changes, so will the limits of what they can achieve.

SUMMARY

Strategic management encompasses some of the most important decisions executives make for creating value in a company. One critical element of managing strategically is establishing the analytics to assess performance and investment opportunities. To establish the right analytical base, executives should adopt a fine-grained approach to planning and target setting at the level of individual business segments. Managers should use those granular insights to rank and set priorities for investment opportunities that contribute to value creation for the company as a whole. To monitor performance, managers should move beyond standard financial and operating metrics to apply an approach that identifies what drives both short- and long-term value.

Another critical element of strategic management is establishing processes to orient the organization toward achievement of long-term value creation. That is the subject of the next chapter.

30

Strategic Management: Mindsets and Behaviors

As we described at the beginning of Chapter 29, effective strategic management requires fluency in two distinct yet interrelated disciplines. One, strong analytics capabilities, was the subject of that chapter. This chapter focuses on the other discipline: the mindsets, behaviors, and processes that orient and motivate the entire management team toward its long-term common goals.

For all the time managers spend developing strategic plans, they are often ineffective at turning those plans into actions. Budgets and actual spending don't always reflect strategic priorities. In a 2016 survey of 1,271 executives, only 30 percent said their company's budgets for capital expenditures, research and development (R&D), and sales and marketing were closely aligned with their strategic plans.[1] Instead, companies frequently cut back R&D spending or sales and marketing expenditures to meet arbitrary short-term earnings targets. Similarly, managers responding to another survey indicated that their companies are too stingy, especially with investments expensed immediately through the income statement and not capitalized over the longer term.[2] About two-thirds of the respondents said their companies underinvest in product development, and more than half said their companies underinvest in sales and marketing and in new products or new markets (see Exhibit 30.1).

Durably tying strategy to effective action requires effort to change these practices. The greatest opportunity lies in enterprise-wide resource allocation. Mastering the art of resource allocation requires executives to escape the strictures of organizational silos and break them down to make allocation decisions across the entire enterprise, ranking all opportunities according

---

[1] T. Koller, D. Lovallo, and Z. Williams, "The Finer Points of Linking Resource Allocation to Value Creation," *McKinsey on Finance*, no. 62 (Spring 2017), www.mckinsey.com.
[2] T. Koller, D. Lovallo, and Z. Williams, "A Bias against Investment?" *McKinsey Quarterly*, September 2011, www.mckinsey.com.

EXHIBIT 30.1 **Where Executives Would Spend More to Maximize Value**

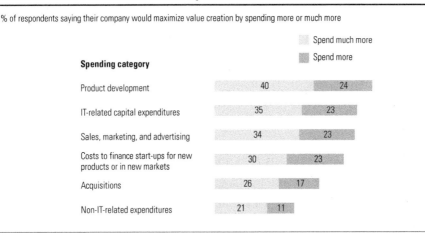

% of respondents saying their company would maximize value creation by spending more or much more

to their strategic importance. Too often, however, the chief executive officer (CEO) allocates large clumps of resources to division heads, who in turn allocate resources to business units in amounts that are smaller but still too large. This approach detaches resources from broad strategic priorities and makes the entire process vulnerable to the barriers and biases that skew effective resource allocation. In contrast, when executives rank all initiatives, they improve the chances that the most important ones will be fully funded, regardless of where they are within the company—even if, say, all five of a unit's projects receive funding, compared with only one out of five in another unit.

Making such decisions requires not only the analytics discussed in Chapter 29 but also a strong set of mindsets, behaviors, and processes to guide and support thinking, motivate managers and employees, and shape and reinforce a strategic management culture focused on long-term strategic goals. This chapter examines three elements that are particularly important:

1. *Strong governance.*[3] The CEO and top team must be fully committed to the company's long-term strategy and be willing to invest enough resources accordingly, regardless of short-term consequences. The CEO and top team must also have the support of an influential corporate staff that can challenge the business units' investment plans.

2. *Debiased decision making.* Most organizations are susceptible to a wide range of decision-making biases. Companies must make a systematic effort to overcome these biases in order to improve the quality of their decisions.

---

[3] The term *governance* takes many different forms in a corporate setting. In Chapter 6, we explored the all-encompassing system of processes and controls a company adopts to govern itself. In this chapter, our focus is internal decision making and the CEO's role in making and delegating important strategy decisions to pursue long-term value creation.

3. *Synchronized processes.* Companies must link together more explicitly their strategic planning, budgeting, and other processes to ensure that strategic initiatives are funded with a view to maximizing enterprise value. To support the development of such streamlined processes, companies also need to nurture excellent strategic skills throughout the organization.

STRONG GOVERNANCE

A company can have a very good strategy, but it won't succeed unless its top executives are committed to making the tough decisions required to carry out that strategy. For example, a technology company announced a thoughtful and ambitious strategy that was on target with emerging trends and technologies. However, the company's existing businesses were simultaneously under pressure from declining demand. To keep short-term profits growing, management held back on making serious investments in the new strategic areas. A competitor spotted the new opportunity and became the first to make the necessary investments to win in the market. As of 2019, that competitor was garnering five times the revenues from this new area than the first company was taking in.

Long-Term Vision

To commit to their company's strategy, executives must take a long-term view. Otherwise, the demands of short-term profit are likely to create a distraction, as they did at the tech company in the previous example. This is not to say that maintaining a long-term view is easy. In many cases, management and employee incentives are tied to short-term performance, and the company's board may observe only short-term measurable results, not progress toward long-term goals.

Ultimately, overcoming these obstacles requires some subjective behaviors. A commitment to a company's strategy can often depend on the courage of the CEO and executive team to pursue a long-term vision of value creation against the inclination of executives to give in to short-term pressures and incentives. Three approaches can indicate that governance links strategy to long-term value:

1. *Adequate investment where it counts.* Investment should be directed to prime prospects at a level sufficient to secure a leadership position. Executives need to avoid spreading investment thinly across too many strategies. The executive team should put enough resources and talent behind the most important initiatives, even if this causes a dip in short-term profits. The success stories of many companies include a period in which profitability pauses while investment in the next wave of growth takes root. Investing to win also means passing up some ideas in favor of those with bigger payouts. That also helps to keep the management team from fragmenting as it tries to oversee too many projects.

2. *The right incentives for top management.* Most management incentive plans suffer from short-term bias and are heavily weighted to a single year's accounting and earnings measures. Even those based on share price performance typically rely on earnings over a single year to determine how many shares an executive receives. Ideally, incentives should weight more to revenue growth and achieving strategic milestones, even if they are measured qualitatively.

3. *An engaged, supportive board of directors.* To be engaged and supportive, board members must understand and back up the strategy, enabling managers to avoid skimping on investment to meet short-term profit growth. To do this, they must be familiar with the details of the strategy and understand performance at a granular level. This equips them to ensure that managers are striking the right balance between investments and current financial performance.

The Right Decision Makers

Managing strategically requires the conviction to make difficult choices. A CEO's core activities in pursuit of value creation are setting targets and allocating resources, such as capital, R&D, and people. Yet targets and resource allocation often don't align with tough strategic choices, either because decisions are not made at the right level or because the CEO strives for consensus, which results in compromises that dilute strategic efforts.

One remedy is to create a kind of funnel effect in which broad debate about a company's investment options eventually narrows down to a subset of the executive team that makes the ultimate allocation decisions. For example, the CEO, chief operating officer (COO), and chief financial officer (CFO) might organize a broad discussion among division and business unit leaders and others to field strategy ideas and pitches for resources. Then the top three executives might meet separately to debate, narrow down options, and decide on final targets and resource allocation. This approach helps to overcome a common dynamic: business unit leaders maneuvering to secure maximum resources for their units, rather than having the allocation process sort out what's best for the company's overall strategy. Tough calls on final allocation decisions should also be easier to make when fewer people are in the room.

This kind of funnel effect helped the CEO of a financial technology company where resource allocation decisions had long been made by a group of more than 15 executives. The CEO preferred to build consensus but realized that consensus tended to make everyone a little bit happy at the cost of poorly aligning investment spending with strategic priorities. He soon realized that the only way to improve resource allocation was to make the decisions himself.

That said, modifications may be necessary, depending on the culture of the company or in countries where consensus is essential. For example, a CEO could shape her own proposed allocation plan and come back to the senior management team to gain consensus support for it.

Granular Decisions

Decisions also need to be made at the right level of granularity. Consider a large health-care company that was organized around three divisions, with each division having roughly 20 business units. The company had a culture of decentralized decision making, so executives allocated R&D and sales and marketing spending to the three divisions and let the division leaders decide how to allocate across their business units. The result: spending was aligned not with corporate priorities, but with the short-term incentives of the division heads. Even worse, if one business unit was having a difficult year, the division head would frequently ask other units to pull back funding from longer-term investments.

The solution in such a case is for the CEO, often with the CFO, to allocate resources and set performance targets at a much finer-grained level. As we discussed in Chapter 29, for a company with around $10 billion in annual revenues, resource allocation works well at a level of 20 to 50 units or projects, though some companies go further.

Allocating resources at a more granular level requires more CEO time. But we believe that careful allocation, as one of the CEO's most important decisions, is well worth the extra time and effort. In our discussions with companies, we've observed a dichotomy between companies where the CEO and CFO allocate at only a high level versus those that are much more detailed. More granular allocation is typically more effective at ensuring that spending is aligned with long-term priorities. One large company spent more than $10 billion per year in capital expenditures, but the top corporate executives spent only several hours per year in their final deliberations on how to allocate that spending. After working through a new process, they increased their time spent on resource allocation to two days. The result: a finer-grained capital spending plan more tightly linked to the company's overall strategic priorities.

Strong Staff

To make allocation decisions, CEOs and CFOs need effective staff support. This usually takes the form of a financial planning and analysis (FPA) team and/or a corporate-strategy team. Despite the importance of this role, many companies have in recent years cut the resources of their FPA teams to levels where they barely have time to coordinate the planning process and add up the numbers. This misguided gesture, aimed at setting an example of commitment to spending reductions, has left no capacity for thoughtful analysis or for challenges to business units' resource requests. In these situations, any challenges to business unit plans are left to the CEO or CFO, who often lacks sufficient knowledge to build a strong case.

In contrast, we've observed that companies with stronger FPA or corporate-strategy teams tend to draw valuable insight and influence from the teams. This appears to make a large difference in the effectiveness of their planning and resource allocation. Common indicators of a strong FPA capability include an FPA leader with real stature and influence inside the company, team members with extensive experience in different parts of the company beyond finance, and a team with time to do its own analysis of the current and potential performance and opportunities for different business units.

DEBIASED DECISION MAKING

When it comes to making decisions, human beings have built-in biases. So do companies and other organizations. In any number of ways, these biases can stall, skew, or deny the kind of clear-sighted decisions that are at the heart of strategic management. To put in place the right sets of behaviors and processes to tie strategy to value creation, management must make tangible efforts to overcome these biases. This section defines some of the most common behavioral biases that we have seen affecting important strategic-planning situations. By identifying and remedying the distorted thinking associated with these biases, executives can improve the quality of their company's decision making. The good news is that, in many cases, simply having strictly enforced rules and processes for managers and employees can reduce the incidence of biased thinking. A culture that promotes strong analytics also can help (see Chapter 29).

Inertia (Stability Bias)

Inertia, or stability bias, is the natural tendency of organizations to resist change. A study by colleagues of ours found, on average, a greater than 90 percent correlation of spending allocations across business units from year to year.[4] Furthermore, the correlation for fully one-third of the companies was 99 percent; that is, the allocation of spending to business units essentially never changed. The same study showed that companies that reallocated more resources—the top third of our sample over a 15-year period—earned, on average, 30 percent higher total shareholder returns (TSR) annually than companies in the bottom third of the sample.

The solution to inertia bias is relatively straightforward. Rank initiatives across the entire enterprise, as described in Chapter 29. In addition, ensure that the budget you are building is rooted in the current strategic plan, not last year's budget. The essential idea is to ignore as much as possible the influences of past allocations or budgets. In practice, you may not be able to shift resources as quickly or as much as this approach suggests. But trying to ignore the past as a starting point will help you minimize the inertia.

[4] S. Hall, D. Lovallo, and R. Musters, "How to Put Your Money Where Your Strategy Is," *McKinsey Quarterly* (March 2012), www.mckinsey.com.

Groupthink

Groups of decision makers have a tendency to engage in groupthink, a focus on harmony and consensus. This can get in the way of examining all the options objectively, leading to weaker—and sometimes disastrous—decisions. Consider the failed Bay of Pigs invasion of Cuba during U.S. president John F. Kennedy's administration. Arthur Schlesinger Jr., one of Kennedy's advisers, wrote this about his participation in the debate leading up to the humiliating defeat of U.S.-backed Cuban exiles trying to overthrow the regime of Cuban leader Fidel Castro: "In the months after the Bay of Pigs I bitterly reproached myself for having kept so silent in the Cabinet Room . . . . I can only explain my failure to do more than raise a few timid questions by reporting that one's impulse to blow the whistle on this nonsense was simply undone by the circumstance."[5]

A variation on this failing occurs when participants don't speak up because they feel the subject under discussion does not fall into their area of responsibility or expertise. At one global agriculture company, the members of the executive committee tended to speak up during strategy conversations only if their area of the business was being discussed. The tacit assumption was that colleagues wouldn't intrude on other colleagues' area of responsibility—an assumption that deprived the committee of their insights.

The weight of evidence strongly supports that decisions are better when there is rigorous debate. One research effort found that for big-bet decisions, high-quality debate led to decisions that were 2.3 times more likely to be successful.[6] Extensive study has explored the importance of vigorous debate in improving decision making.[7] There is a reason why some U.S. Supreme Court justices have hired clerks with different political views than their own: it helps to ensure that their own thinking remains rigorous.

Ideally, a company dedicated to pursuing long-term strategic success should have a culture of dissent, where rigorous debate is the norm. But most companies need to take more active steps to stimulate debate. The key ingredient is to depersonalize debate and make it socially acceptable to be a contrarian. Here are some useful techniques:

- *Assigning a devil's advocate.* At a strategy discussion, assign someone the task of taking an opposing point of view. Make sure this contrarian's contribution is more than just offering opinions. The focus should be

[5] A. Schlesinger Jr., *A Thousand Days: John F. Kennedy in the White House* (New York: Houghton Mifflin, 1965), 255.

[6] I. Aminov, A. De Smet, G. Jost, and D. Mendelsohn, "Decision Making in the Age of Urgency," McKinsey & Company, April 2019, www.mckinsey.com.

[7] See, for example, A. Duke, *Thinking in Bets: Making Smarter Decisions When You Don't Have All the Facts* (New York: Portfolio/Penguin, 2018).

on bringing out potential opposing scenarios of what could happen or highlighting missing information important to the debate.

- *Bringing a diverse group to the discussion.* More than 150 years ago, John Stuart Mill wrote in *On Liberty,* "The only way in which a human being can make some approach to knowing the whole of a subject is by hearing what can be said about it by persons of every variety of opinion." More recent research has proven his point.[8] Diversity means drawing on the opinions of people from different disciplines, roles, genders, and races in important discussions. Bring in more junior people with special expertise, create an environment where it is safe for them to speak up, and ask them for ideas.

- *Encouraging debate with secret ballots.* Use a secret ballot at the beginning of the debate, not the end. Once a proposal has been presented and before it is debated, ask participants to vote on the idea in secret. The request could be for a yes-or-no vote on a project or for a ranking of investment priorities. When the results are revealed, assuming participants discover at least one other person shares their views, the knowledge will likely make them more comfortable expressing their opinion.

- *Setting up a red-team/blue-team activity for large investments.* Arrange two teams to prepare arguments for opposing outcomes. While undertaking the preparatory work and analysis for this approach is expensive, it can make a difference for particularly large decisions with high uncertainty.

Confirmation Bias and Excessive Optimism

Confirmation bias and overoptimism are two distinct biases. However, the same set of techniques applies to both, so we discuss them together.

Confirmation bias is the tendency to look for evidence that supports your hypothesis or to interpret ambiguous data in a way that achieves the same result. For business decisions, this often takes the form of "I have a hunch that investing in x would create value. Therefore, let's look for some supporting facts that will back up our hunch." The universal foundation of the scientific approach to addressing a hypothesis is the opposite: you should look for disconfirming evidence.

Overoptimism is the tendency to assume that everything will go right with a project, even though past projects tell us that such smooth outcomes are rare. A classic example is the construction of the famous Sydney Opera House, whose schedule and budget were both overly optimistic. The project was completed ten years late and cost 14 times the original budget.

---

[8] Ibid.

Some of the techniques used to overcome groupthink, such as the use of opposing red and blue teams, can help here. The simplest approaches are to avoid developing hypotheses too early in the process and to actively look for contrary evidence. Other potential correctives for confirmation bias and over-optimism include the following two methods:

1. *Conducting a pre-mortem.* A "pre-mortem" is an exercise in which, after a project team has been briefed on a proposed plan, its members purposely imagine that the plan has failed. The very structure of a pre-mortem makes it safe to identify problems. Sometimes team members will compete to see who can raise the most worrisome issues.[9]

2. *Taking the outside view.* One way to make better forecasts is to take the outside view, which means building a statistical view of a project based on a reference class of similar projects. To understand how the outside view works, consider an experiment performed with a group at a private-equity company. The group was asked to build a forecast for an ongoing investment from the bottom up—tracing its path from beginning to end and noting the key steps, actions, and milestones required to meet proposed targets. The group's median expected rate of return on this investment was about 50 percent. The group was then asked to fill out a table comparing that ongoing investment with categories of similar investments, looking at factors such as relative quality of the investment and average return for an investment category. Using this outside view, the group saw that its median expected rate of return was more than double that of the most similar investments.[10]

Loss Aversion

We previously explored loss aversion in Chapter 4, via survey results showing that most executives are loss averse and unwilling to undertake risky projects with high estimated present values.[11] The primary solution to overcoming loss aversion is to view investment decisions based not on their individual risk but on the basis of their contribution to the risk of the enterprise as a whole (see Chapter 29).

---

[9] G. Klein, T. Koller, and D. Lovallo, "Pre-Mortems: Being Smart at the Start," *McKinsey Quarterly* (April 2019), www.mckinsey.com.

[10] T. Koller and D. Lovallo, "Bias Busters: Taking the 'Outside View,'" *McKinsey Quarterly*, September 2018, www.mckinsey.com.

[11] For more on overcoming loss aversion, see D. Lovallo, T. Koller, R. Uhlaner, and D. Kahneman, "Your Company Is Too Risk-Averse," *Harvard Business Review* (March–April 2020), hbr.org.

That's easy in theory, but executives are typically concerned about the risk of their own projects and the potential impact on their careers. That's why those decisions should be elevated to executives with a broader portfolio of projects whose risks cancel each other out. Often, the decisions must be pushed up to the CEO.

To be most effective, companies also must encourage middle-level managers and other employees to propose risky ideas. Companies can do this by eliminating risks to the employee. Many employees censor themselves because of concerns that their careers will suffer if their idea for a project fails. To overcome this concern, it's important to agree on the various risks up front with the top leadership and conduct post-mortems on projects, particularly to identify causes of failure. If a project fails because the decision to go ahead with the project turned out to be incorrect (which should happen frequently), that failure should not bear on the manager responsible for the project. The responsible manager should only be accountable for the quality of execution of the project.

Some companies have gone even further by demonstrating that failure, depending on the circumstances, does not damage one's career. For example, David Pottruck, former CEO of Charles Schwab, wrote about what he calls Noble Failures.[12] If a project was well planned, had contingencies, limited the negative fallout, and followed a policy of "no surprises," and if participants learned from their experience, even a failed effort might be considered "noble." Pottruck explained, "The Noble Failure concept is intended to encourage people to voice their opinions and ideas more freely because they know that even a failing effort will be tolerated, sometimes even celebrated, and never punished."

SYNCHRONIZED AND STREAMLINED PROCESSES

The typical company's planning and performance management process includes developing a corporate strategy, creating a three- to five-year strategic financial plan, converting that to an annual operating plan, and finally producing a detailed budget. During the year, the company needs to monitor performance for potential corrective action or adjustments and may need to adjust its resource allocation. Exploring each of these processes in detail is beyond the scope of the book. Instead, we'll focus on certain key elements that are essential to ensuring that the corporate strategy and its required enterprise resource allocation are implemented effectively.

---

[12] D. Pottruck, *Stacking the Deck: How to Lead Breakthrough Change against All Odds* (San Francisco: Jossey-Bass, 2015), 164.

Start with Strategy

Let's begin with the corporate strategy itself. The strategy should include the company's broad strategic direction, including high-level resource allocation across units, key strategic initiatives, and portfolio changes (for example, significant acquisitions and divestitures). The company's strategy need not be on the same rigid schedule as the rest of the planning and performance management process. In fact, some argue that the timing should be delinked so that the strategy can be refined and revised as circumstances change and new information becomes available.[13] This also provides more time for introspection and avoids the "all hands on deck" approach that consumes so much time. The CEO and top team, supported by a strong staff, should handle the strategy itself.

Build a Plan

Once a year, the strategy must be translated into specific plans.[14] Companies typically start with a three- to five-year strategic financial plan. Ideally, the plan should focus on resource allocation: where investment dollars (capital as well as expensed investments) will be allocated and how much will be invested overall. The plan should also consider whether the company has the right people in the right places to execute the investments effectively.

One mistake that companies often make in their three- to five-year strategic plan is putting the detail in the wrong places. A good strategic financial plan should be granular in terms of its number of business units and strategic initiatives to pursue but simplified when it comes to the number of line items per business. Companies often require detailed, line-by-line income statement and balance sheet projections. In our experience, a value driver approach (see Chapter 29) is better for streamlining the process and focusing on strategic issues. This approach focuses on the most important items for each unit—for instance, market growth, share growth, changes in costs per unit and pricing, overall general and administrative spending, and overall R&D spending. This approach also requires fewer people and simplifies iteration.

Shape Operations

After the three- to five-year financial plan is set, it's time to craft an annual operating plan (AOP), although some companies skip this step and go straight to preparing a detailed budget. The AOP is the opportunity for the company to finalize spending decisions and performance targets for the year.

---

[13] C. Bradley, M. Hirt, and S. Smit, *Strategy Beyond the Hockey Stick* (Hoboken, NJ: John Wiley & Sons, 2019), 175–177.
[14] While some companies use continuously updated budgets instead of an annual plan and budget, these are still limited to unique circumstances.

This is where linking strategy to action can go haywire. As we mentioned at the beginning of this chapter, only about 30 percent of surveyed executives reported that the ultimate budget allocation for capital expenditures and other investments at their company was "very similar" to the strategic financial plan. This means that for many companies, the process of shaping the first year of the strategic financial plan fails to translate into the AOP. Sometimes this occurs because the two processes are disconnected; the AOP builds off last year's spending rather than off the strategy. At other times, the desire to hit short-term targets derails the planning process, and the strategy is forgotten.

This disconnect can be repaired. Senior management should mandate that the AOP spending align with the first year of the strategic financial plan. Another helpful tweak is to shorten the time between development of the three- to five-year financial plan and creation of the budget. The longer the gap, the more likely the two will be misaligned. For some companies, the gap between these tasks can be two to three months. That's too long. It's better to move the strategic plan later in the process.

Strategic financial plans and AOPs can feel static, given that no action plan backs them up. Successful companies remedy that situation by ensuring that action plans support strategic initiatives and detail clear lines of responsibility. Only when these requirements are met should a company put together the detailed budget for every unit and department.

Review Performance, Repeat

The next step is managing performance during the year, which comprises a regular review of performance against AOP and budget targets. The major stumbling blocks to insightful performance management are a lack of good, timely data at a sufficient level of detail and the wrong kind of data. The best companies have automated and integrated systems that allow them to review results, typically monthly, shortly after the end of the month. Unfortunately, many companies still spend too much time generating and debating the performance numbers. Or they focus on just the accounting results, rather than the business drivers of performance. Only by understanding the business drivers can executives take action to improve performance. Is the market growing faster or slower than expected? Are we losing or gaining share? Are competitors behaving as expected? If the market is growing slower, should we try to gain share, or will a price war just exacerbate the problem? Should we cut discretionary costs because sales are not at target levels? If we do, won't that move hurt us next year?

It's impossible to know during the planning process what unexpected events will come up during the year. Companies need a process for adjusting their resource allocation during the year and sometimes adjusting performance targets as well.

In addition, once projects have gotten underway, companies tend to delay stopping them even if those projects aren't going to earn attractive returns. What's more, some companies don't even measure the expected return once the project has started. Several techniques can help here.

First, we've found that some companies provide flexibility by allocating less than their entire spending pool during the budgeting process. They'll hold back 5 or 10 percent at the corporate level for opportunities that may arise during the year. These may be from new ideas that shouldn't be delayed or in response to competitive actions and customer demands that have changed.

Second, companies should use a stage-gating process for releasing spending for projects. This flips on its head the common practice of not actively looking to stop projects once they've started. With stage gating, managers aren't allowed at the start to spend all that's allocated to a project; instead, they must obtain periodic approvals to continue moving forward. The benefit of stage gating is that projects unlikely to succeed can be killed earlier, thereby freeing up resources that can be allocated elsewhere. Similarly, some projects should be conditionally approved. Say a project is included in the budget for the year, but spending won't start until October. That project could be reviewed in, say, August or September to make sure its present value is still positive and aligned with strategy.

In hewing to the benefits of allocating resources at the most granular level possible, management should also require business units to ask for approval to shift spending from one project to another. At too many companies, once a budget has been approved, the business unit can move around money in ways that may not be aligned with longer-term strategic objectives.

One company successfully combined several of these tactics. Management set up monthly meetings of an investment committee to deal with in-year allocation issues. The committee did not review every project at each meeting, but it established an agenda for approving or denying a variety of allocation proposals. Proposals involved advancing stage-gated projects and provisionally approved projects, requests for funds for unbudgeted projects, and requests to shift spending within a business unit from one project to another.

Another common shortcoming of many companies lies in the quality of business cases advanced to support investments. Some companies' decision processes even lack business cases altogether. It's surprising how frequently CFOs complain about this situation. In some companies, many investment proposals don't even measure the value impact of the investment, on the grounds that the project either is deemed "strategic" or is related to safety or regulatory needs.

We believe that almost every project should have a business case with a quantified present value and risk assessment, even if the value is a rough estimate. At one company, managers argued that they couldn't quantify the value of projects to improve customer service, because the projects would serve only to maintain, not increase, revenues. Their fallacy was the improper definition of the base case as no change in revenue forecasts. But what would actually happen if they didn't improve customer service? Would revenues decline? How quickly? Would the customers they would lose be marginal ones or profitable ones? After they posed and answered these questions and incorporated the insights into their analysis, the managers could quantify the value impact of these projects and rank them against other projects.

CLOSING THOUGHTS

Executives squander good corporate strategy when they can't overcome the organizational barriers, behavioral biases, weak processes, and plain lack of courage needed to turn ideas into value-creating actions. Strategic management requires combining strong analytics capabilities with the mindsets, behaviors, and operating guidelines that link strategy to value and inform and motivate managers toward long-term value creation. A prime goal for forward-looking executives should be making a solid connection between strategic goals and resource allocation. The list of best practices is long and can be daunting, but executives can begin by focusing on those that are easiest and likely to have the biggest impact on their performance. Adding new refinements over time will move any company closer to the goal of managing strategically for the long term.

31

Mergers and Acquisitions

Mergers and acquisitions (M&A) are an important element of a dynamic economy. At different stages of an industry's or a company's life span, resource decisions that once made economic sense no longer do. For instance, the company that invented a groundbreaking innovation may not be best suited to exploit it. As demand falls off in a mature industry, companies are likely to have built excess capacity. At any time in a business's history, one group of managers may be better equipped to manage the business than another. At moments like these, acquisitions are often the best or only way to reallocate resources sensibly and rapidly.

Acquisitions that reduce excess capacity or put companies in the hands of better owners or managers typically create substantial value both for the economy generally and for investors. You can see this effect in the increase in the combined cash flows of the many companies involved in acquisitions. Even though acquisitions overall create value, however, the distribution of any value they create tends to be lopsided, with the selling companies' shareholders capturing the bulk. In fact, most empirical research shows that for large acquisitions, one-third or more of acquiring companies destroy value for their shareholders because they transfer all the benefits of the acquisition to the selling companies' shareholders.

For companies in growth mode, acquisitions can be an effective way to accelerate their expansion or fill in gaps in products, technologies, or geographies. Typically, numerous smaller acquisitions can help companies access markets faster or help smaller companies get their products to market faster.

The challenge for managers, therefore, is to ensure that their acquisitions are among those that *do* create value for their shareholders. To that end, this chapter provides a framework for analyzing how to create value from acquisitions and summarizes the empirical research. It discusses the archetypal approaches that are most likely to create value, as well as some other strategies that are often attempted but have longer odds of executing successfully. It provides practical advice on how to estimate and achieve operating improvements and whether to pay in cash or in stock. Finally, it reminds managers that stock markets respond to the expected impact of acquisitions on intrinsic value, not accounting results.

A FRAMEWORK FOR VALUE CREATION

Acquisitions create value when the cash flows of the combined companies are greater than they would have otherwise been. If the acquirer doesn't pay too much for the acquisition, some of that value will accrue to the acquirer's shareholders. Acquisitions are a good example of the conservation of value principle (explained in Chapter 3).

The value created for an acquirer's shareholders equals the difference between the value received by the acquirer and the price paid by the acquirer:

$$\text{Value Created for Acquirer} = \text{Value Received} - \text{Price Paid}$$

The value received by the acquirer equals the intrinsic value of the target company as a stand-alone company run by its former management team plus the present value of any performance improvements to be achieved after the acquisition, which will show up as improved cash flows for the target's business or the acquirer's business. The price paid is the market value of the target plus any premium required to convince the target's shareholders to sell their shares to the acquirer:

$$
\begin{aligned}
\text{Value Created for Acquirer} = {}& (\text{Stand-Alone Value of Target} \\
& + \text{Value of Performance Improvements}) \\
& - (\text{Market Value of Target} \\
& + \text{Acquisition Premium})
\end{aligned}
$$

Exhibit 31.1 uses this framework to illustrate a hypothetical acquisition. Company A buys Company B for $1.3 billion, which includes a 30 percent premium over its market value. Company A expects to increase the value of Company B by 40 percent through various operating improvements, so the

EXHIBIT 31.1 **Acquisition Evaluation Framework**

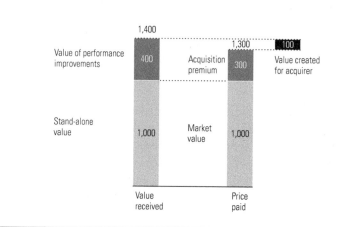

EXHIBIT 31.2 **Value Creation for Given Performance Improvements and Premium Paid**

Value creation as % of deal value

Premium paid, % of stand-alone target value	10	20	30	40	50
0	10	20	30	40	50
10	0	9	18	27	36
20	−8	0	8	17	25
30	−15	−8	0	8	15

Value of performance improvements, % of stand-alone target value

value of Company B to Company A is $1.4 billion. Subtracting the purchase price of $1.3 billion from the value received of $1.4 billion leaves $100 million of value created for Company A's shareholders.

In the case where the stand-alone value of the target equals its market value, value is created for the acquirer's shareholders only when the value of improvements is greater than the premium paid:

$$\text{Value Created} = \text{Value of Improvements} - \text{Acquisition Premium}$$

Examining this equation, it's easy to see why most of the value created from acquisitions goes to the seller's shareholders: if a company pays a 30 percent premium, then it must increase the value of the target by at least 30 percent to create any value.

Exhibit 31.2 shows the value created for the acquirer's shareholders relative to the amount invested in acquisitions at different levels of premiums and operating improvements. For example, Company A, from the example just considered, paid a 30 percent premium for Company B and improved Company B's value by 40 percent, so the value created for the acquirers' shareholders represents 8 percent of the amount Company A invested in the deal.

If we further assume that Company A was worth about three times Company B's worth at the time of the acquisition, this major acquisition would be expected to increase Company A's value by only about 3 percent: $100 million of value creation (see Exhibit 31.1) divided by Company A's value of $3 billion. As this example shows, it is difficult for an acquirer to create a substantial amount of value from acquisitions.

While a 40 percent performance improvement sounds steep, that's what better acquirers often achieve. Exhibit 31.3 presents estimates of the value

EXHIBIT 31.3 **Selected Acquisitions: Significant Improvements**

%

	Year	Value of improvements relative to target value[1]	Premium paid	Net value created relative to price[2]
Abbott Labs/Alere	2016	45–55	35	10–20
Tesoro/Western Refining	2016	45–55	35	10–20
RF Micro Devices/Triquint Semiconductor	2014	60–70	10	50–60
InBev/Anheuser-Busch	2008	35–45	20	15–25
Henkel/National Starch	2007	60–90	55	5–25
Kellogg/Keebler	2000	45–70	15	30–50
PepsiCo/Quaker Oats	2000	35–55	10	25–40
Clorox/First Brands	1998	70–105	60	5–25

[1] Present value of announced performance improvements divided by target value.

[2] Net value created from acquisition divided by purchase price.

created from a sample of deals over the past 20 years. To estimate the gross value creation, we discounted the announced actual performance improvements at the company's weighted average cost of capital (WACC). The performance improvements were substantial, typically exceeding 50 percent of the value of the target. In addition, Kellogg and PepsiCo paid unusually low premiums for their acquisitions, allowing them to capture more value.

EMPIRICAL RESULTS

Acquisitions and their effects on value creation are a perennial topic of interest to researchers. Empirical studies of acquisitions have yielded useful insights into when they occur, whether they create value, and for whom they create value.

When Do Acquisitions Take Place?

Acquisition activity tends to occur in waves, as shown in Exhibit 31.4. Several factors drive these waves. First, we tend to see more acquisitions when stock prices are rising and managers are optimistic (though to maximize the amount of value created, they should really make acquisitions when prices are low). Low interest rates also stimulate acquisitions, especially heavily leveraged acquisitions by private-equity firms. Finally, one large acquisition in an industry encourages others in the same industry to acquire something, too.

Do Acquisitions Create Value?

For decades, academics and other researchers have studied the question of whether acquisitions create value. Most studies have examined the stock price reaction to the announcement of acquisitions. One effect of this approach is

EXHIBIT 31.4 **Historical M&A Activity: U.S. and European Transactions**

Inflation-adjusted value of M&A transactions, 2018 $ billion

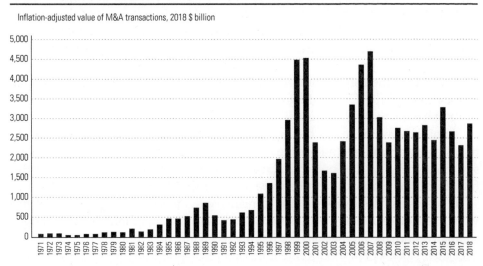

Source: Dealogic, Capital IG, Mergerstat, Thomson Reuters.

that large acquisitions (relative to the size of the acquirer) tend to dominate the results. The market's assessment of small acquisitions is hard to discern, yet 95 percent of acquisitions by large companies are of targets that are smaller than 5 percent of the acquirer's market capitalization.

Researchers have shown that acquisitions do create value for the collective shareholders of the acquirer and the acquired company. According to McKinsey research on 1,770 acquisitions from 1999 through 2013, the combined value of the acquirer and target increased by about 5.8 percent on average.[1] So we can conclude that acquisitions tend to create value for the economy, through some combination of cost and revenue synergies.

For Whom Do Acquisitions Create Value?

To see who benefits from acquisitions, we'll begin by reviewing the studies driven mostly by large acquisitions. While buying and selling shareholders collectively derive value from acquisitions, large acquisitions on average do not create any value for the acquiring company's shareholders. Empirical studies examining the reaction of capital markets to M&A announcements find that the value-weighted average large deals lower the acquirer's stock price between 1 and 3 percent.[2] Stock returns following the acquisition are no better. Mark Mitchell and Erik Stafford have found that acquirers underperform

[1] D. Cogman, "Global M&A: Fewer Deals, Better Quality," *McKinsey on Finance*, no. 50 (Spring 2014): 23–25.

[2] S. B. Moeller, F. P. Schlingemann, and R. M. Stulz, "Do Shareholders of Acquiring Firms Gain from Acquisitions?" (NBER Working Paper W9523, Ohio State University, 2003).

comparable companies on shareholder returns by 5 percent during the three years following the acquisitions.[3] The United Kingdom has new rules requiring a shareholder vote on larger acquisitions. Research by Marco Becht, Andrea Polo, and Stefano Rossi showed that in situations where shareholders voted, the stock price reaction of the acquirer was much more likely to be positive than when shareholders didn't vote. They also showed that in larger transactions in the United States, where shareholders don't vote, the stock price reactions were also more likely to be negative.[4]

Another way to look at the question is to estimate the percentage of deals that create any value at all for the acquiring company's shareholders. McKinsey research found that one-third created value, one-third did not, and for the final third, the empirical results were inconclusive.[5]

It comes as no surprise to find conclusive evidence that most or all of the value creation from large acquisitions accrues to the shareholders of the target company, since the target shareholders are receiving, on average, high premiums over their stock's preannouncement market price—typically about 30 percent.

Most of these studies examine the stock market reaction to an acquisition within a few days of its announcement. Many people have criticized using announcement effects to estimate value creation. The evidence on whether announcement effects persist is inconsistent. Sirower and Sahna have shown that the initial market reactions are persistent and indicate future performance for the next year.[6] Some of our colleagues, however, examined a different sample of larger transactions over a two-year period and found inconclusive evidence of persistence.[7]

Although studies of announcement effects give useful results for large samples, the same approach cannot be applied to individual transactions. While the market correctly assesses the results of transactions on average, that statistic does not mean its initial assessment of a single transaction will always be correct.

To overcome the large acquisition bias of the studies described, several of our colleagues looked at acquisition programs of companies rather than single acquisitions.[8] They examined 1,645 nonbanking companies from 2007 to 2017 and grouped them into four categories:

[3] M. L. Mitchell and E. Stafford, "Managerial Decisions and Long-Term Stock Price Performance," *Journal of Business* 73 (2000): 287–329.

[4] M. Becht, A. Polo, and S. Rossi, "Does Mandatory Shareholder Voting Prevent Bad Acquisitions? The Case of the United Kingdom," *Journal of Applied Corporate Finance* 31, no. 1 (Winter 2019): 42–61.

[5] W. Rehm and C. Sivertsen, "A Strong Foundation for M&A in 2010," *McKinsey on Finance*, no. 34 (Winter 2010): 17–22.

[6] M. Sirower and S. Sahna, "Avoiding the Synergy Trap: Practical Guidance on M&A Decisions for CEOs and Boards," *Journal of Applied Corporate Finance* 18, no. 3 (Summer 2006): 83–95.

[7] Rehm and Sivertsen, "A Strong Foundation for M&A in 2010." An unpublished update in 2018 showed similar results.

[8] Updated and expanded analysis of W. Rehm, R. Uhlaner, and A. West, "Taking a Longer-Term Look at M&A Value Creation," *McKinsey Quarterly* (January 2012), www.mckinsey.com.

EXHIBIT 31.5 **Success Rates of Observed Acquisition Strategies**

1,645 nonbanking companies, 2007–2017, %

● Median
— 25th to 75th percentile

Strategy	Median excess total shareholder returns (TSR),[1] December 1999–December 2012	Probability of excess return greater than 0
Programmatic	0.9	56
Selective	−0.1	49
Organic	−0.6	45
Large deal	−1.6	43

[1] Outperformance against global industry index for each company.

Source: Dealogic.

1. Programmatic acquirers[9] completed many acquisitions.
2. Large-deal companies completed at least one deal that was larger than 30 percent of the acquiring company's value.
3. Organic companies conducted almost no M&A.
4. Selective acquirers did not fit into the other three categories.

Exhibit 31.5 shows the results, including median total shareholder returns (TSRs) versus peers, along with the 25th and 75th percentiles, and the number of companies outperforming peers. Programmatic acquirers performed best, with a median outperformance of 0.9% TSR per year. The large-deal companies performed the worst, consistent with the studies of announcement effects.

That said, the medians conceal important details. Note that the band of 25th to 75th percentiles is very large and overlaps across the different acquisition strategies. Of all the categories, the distribution of the programmatic acquirers has the most positive skewing, and these acquirers also have the highest percentage of companies outperforming. Large deals skewed heavily negative. The case of organic companies is interesting for its very wide distribution of results. This is not surprising, since the sample includes fast-growing, younger companies with high TSRs that may think it too early to embark on much M&A, as well as declining or troubled companies focused on managing decline. We also found that the results varied by industry. For

[9] We define programmatic acquirers as companies that make more than two small or midsize deals in a year.

example, large acquisitions tended to be more successful in slower-growing, mature industries, where there is great value to reducing excess capacity. By contrast, large deals in faster-growing sectors underperformed significantly. In those companies, the inward focus required to integrate a large acquisition diverted management's attention from the need for continual product innovation. Only the programmatic acquirers tended to outperform across most industries. The results are also consistent with 2017 research by Fich, Nguyen, and Officer, who found that large companies acquiring small companies tend to create more value than when they buy large companies.[10]

The news is not all bad for large acquisitions. Researchers have identified specific factors that differentiate successful deals from unsuccessful ones, based on returns to the acquirer's shareholders. This research points to four important characteristics:

1. *Strong operators are more successful.* According to empirical research, acquirers whose earnings and share price grew at a rate above the industry average for three years before the acquisition earn statistically significant positive returns on announcement.[11] Another study found similar results using the market-to-book ratio as a measure of corporate performance.[12]

2. *Low transaction premiums are better.* Researchers have found that acquirers paying a high premium earn negative returns on announcement.[13]

3. *Being the sole bidder helps.* Several studies have found that acquirer stock returns are negatively correlated with the number of bidders; the more companies attempting to buy the target, the higher the price.[14]

4. *Private deals perform better.* Acquisitions of private companies and subsidiaries of large companies have higher excess returns than acquisitions of public companies.[15]

---

[10] Eliezer M. Fich, Tu Nguyen, and Micah S. Officer, "Large Wealth Creation in Mergers and Acquisitions" (paper presented at American Finance Association 2013 annual meeting, San Diego, CA, January 4–6, 2013, revised November 8, 2017), available at http://dx.doi.org/10.2139/ssrn.2020507.

[11] R. Morck, A. Shleifer, and R. Vishny, "Do Managerial Objectives Drive Bad Acquisitions?" *Journal of Finance* 45 (1990): 31–48.

[12] H. Servaes, "Tobin's q and the Gains from Takeovers," *Journal of Finance* 46 (1991): 409–419; and Fich et al., "Large Wealth Creation in Mergers and Acquisitions."

[13] M. L. Sirower, *The Synergy Trap* (New York: Free Press, 1997); and N. G. Travlos, "Corporate Takeover Bids, Methods of Payment, and Bidding Firms' Stock Return," *Journal of Finance* 42 (1987): 943–963. The result was statistically significant in Sirower but not significant in Travlos.

[14] Morck et al., "Do Managerial Objectives Drive Bad Acquisitions?"; and D. K. Datta, V. K. Narayanan, and G. E. Pinches, "Factors Influencing Wealth Creation from Mergers and Acquisitions: A Meta-Analysis," *Strategic Management Journal* 13 (1992): 67–84.

[15] See, for example, L. Capron and J. Shen, "Acquisitions of Private versus Public Firms: Private Information, Target Selection and Acquirer Returns" (INSEAD Working Paper Series, 2005); and P. Draper and K. Paudyal, "Acquisitions: Public versus Private," *European Financial Management* 12, no. 1 (2006): 57–80.

Perhaps it is just as important to identify the characteristics that don't matter. There is no evidence that the following acquisition dimensions indicate either value creation or value destruction:

- Whether the transaction increases or dilutes earnings per share
- The price-to-earnings ratio (P/E) of the acquirer relative to the target's P/E
- The degree to which the acquirer and the target are related, based on Standard Industrial Classification (SIC) codes
- Whether deals are made when the economy is strong or weak[16]

This empirical evidence is important because it shows that there is no magic formula to make an acquisition successful. Like any other business strategy, acquisitions are not inherently good or bad, just as marketing or research and development (R&D) are not inherently good or bad. Each deal must have its own strategic logic, and the company must have the relevant skills to execute deals or deal programs. In our experience, acquirers in the most successful deals have well-articulated, specific value creation ideas going into each deal. The strategic rationales for less successful deals tend to be vague, such as to pursue international scale, fill in portfolio gaps, or build a third leg of the portfolio.

ARCHETYPES FOR VALUE-CREATING ACQUISITIONS

The empirical analysis is limited in its ability to identify specific acquisition strategies that create value. This is because acquisitions come in a wide variety of shapes and sizes and also because there is no objective way to classify acquisitions by strategy. Furthermore, the stated strategy may not be the real strategy. Companies typically talk up all kinds of strategic benefits from acquisitions that are really all about cutting costs.

In the absence of empirical research, our suggestions for strategies that create value are based on our acquisitions work with companies. In our experience, the strategic rationale for an acquisition that creates value for acquirers typically fits one of the following six archetypes:

1. Improve the performance of the target company.
2. Consolidate to remove excess capacity from an industry.
3. Create market access for the target's (or, in some cases, the buyer's) products.

---

[16] Fich et al., "Large Wealth Creation in Mergers and Acquisitions."

4. Acquire skills or technologies more quickly or at lower cost than they could be built in-house.

5. Exploit a business's industry-specific scalability.

6. Pick winners early and help them develop their businesses.

If an acquisition does not fit one or more of these archetypes, it's unlikely to create value.

The strategic rationale for an acquisition should be a specific articulation of one of these archetypes, not a vague concept like growth or strategic positioning. While growth and strategic positioning may be important, they need to be translated into something tangible. Furthermore, even if your acquisition conforms to one of these archetypes, it still won't create value if you overpay.

Improve Target Company's Performance

One of the most common value-creating acquisition strategies is improving the performance of the target company. Put simply, you buy a company and radically reduce costs to improve margins and cash flows. In some cases, the acquirer may also take steps to accelerate revenue growth.

Pursuing this strategy is what the best private-equity firms do. Acharya, Hahn, and Kehoe studied successful private-equity acquisitions where the target company was bought, improved, and sold with no additional acquisitions along the way.[17] They found that the operating profit margins of the acquired businesses increased by an average of about 2.5 percentage points more than at peer companies during the private-equity firm's ownership. That means many of the transactions increased operating profit margins even more.

Keep in mind that it is easier to improve the performance of a company with low margins and low return on invested capital (ROIC) than that of a high-margin, high-ROIC company. Consider the case of buying a company with a 6 percent operating profit margin. Reducing costs by three percentage points from 94 percent of revenues to 91 percent of revenues increases the margin to 9 percent and could lead to a 50 percent increase in the value of the company. In contrast, if the company's operating profit margin is 30 percent, increasing the company's value by 50 percent requires increasing the margin to 45 percent. Costs would need to decline from 70 percent of revenues to 55 percent, a 21 percent reduction in the cost base. That expectation might be unreasonable.

Consolidate to Remove Excess Capacity

As industries mature, they typically develop excess capacity. For example, in chemicals, companies are constantly looking for ways to get more production

---

[17] V. V. Acharya, M. Hahn, and C. Kehoe, "Corporate Governance and Value Creation: Evidence from Private Equity" (working paper, Social Science Research Network, February 17, 2010).

out of their plants at the same time as new competitors (for example, Saudi Arabia in petrochemicals) continue to enter the industry. The combination of higher production from existing capacity and new capacity from new entrants often leads to more supply than demand. However, it is in no single competitor's interest to shut a plant. Companies often find it easier to shut plants across the larger combined entity resulting from an acquisition than absent an acquisition, to shut their least productive plants and end up with a smaller company.

Reducing excess capacity is not limited to shutting factories but can extend to less tangible forms of capacity. For example, consolidation in the pharmaceutical industry has significantly reduced sales force capacity as merged companies' portfolios of products have changed and they have rethought how to interact with doctors. The larger pharmaceutical companies have also significantly reduced their research and development capacity as they have found more productive ways to conduct research and pruned their portfolios of development projects.

While there is substantial value to be created from removing excess capacity, the bulk of the value nevertheless often accrues to the seller's shareholders, not the buyer's. In addition, all the other competitors in the industry may benefit from the capacity reduction without having to take any action of their own (the free-rider problem).

Accelerate Market Access for Products

Often, relatively small companies with innovative products have difficulty accessing the entire potential market for their products. For instance, small pharmaceutical companies typically lack the large sales forces required to access the many doctors they need to see in order to promote their products. Larger pharmaceutical companies sometimes purchase these smaller companies and use their own large-scale sales forces to accelerate the sales growth of the smaller companies' products.

IBM has pursued this strategy in its software and services businesses. Between 2010 and 2013, IBM acquired 43 companies for an average of $350 million each. By pushing the products of these companies through IBM's global sales force, IBM estimated that it was able to substantially accelerate the acquired companies' revenues, sometimes by over 40 percent in the first two years after each acquisition.[18]

In some cases, the target can also help accelerate the acquirer's revenue growth. In Procter & Gamble's acquisition of Gillette, the combined company benefited because P&G had stronger sales in some emerging markets while Gillette had a bigger share of others. Working together, they were able to introduce their products into new markets much more quickly.

---

[18] IBM Investor Briefing website, 2014.

Acquire Skills or Technologies Faster or at Lower Cost

Many technology-based companies buy other companies whose technologies the acquirers need to enhance their own products. They do this because they can acquire the technology more quickly than developing it themselves, avoid royalty payments on patented technologies, and keep the technology away from competitors. For example, Apple bought Siri (the automated personal assistant) in 2010 to enhance its iPhones. In 2014, Apple purchased Novauris Technologies, a speech recognition technology company, to further enhance Siri's capabilities. During the same year, Apple also purchased Beats Electronics, which had recently launched a music-streaming service. One reason for the acquisition was that Apple could quickly offer its customers a music-streaming service as the market was moving away from its iTunes business model of purchasing and downloading music.

Cisco Systems, the network product and services company (with $49 billion in revenue in 2018), used acquisitions of key technologies to assemble a broad line of network solution products during the frenzied Internet growth period. From 1993 to 2001, Cisco acquired 71 companies at an average price of approximately $350 million each, helping it to increase revenues from $650 million in 1993 to $22 billion in 2001, with nearly 40 percent of its 2001 revenues coming directly from these acquisitions.

Exploit a Business's Industry-Specific Scalability

Economies of scale are often cited as a key source of value creation in M&A. While they can be, you have to be very careful in justifying an acquisition by economies of scale, especially for large acquisitions. That's because large companies often are already operating at scale, in which case combining them will not likely lead to lower unit costs. Take big package-delivery companies, for example. They already have some of the largest airline fleets in the world and operate them very efficiently. If they were to combine, it's unlikely that there would be substantial savings in their flight operations.

Economies of scale can be important sources of value in acquisitions when the unit of incremental capacity is large or when a larger company buys a subscale company. For example, the cost to develop a new car platform is enormous, so auto companies try to minimize the number of platforms they need. The combination of Audi, Porsche, and VW allows the three companies to share some platforms. For example, the Audi Q7, Porsche Cayenne, and VW Touareg are all based on the same underlying platform.

Companies also find economies of scale in the purchasing function, but such benefits often come with nuances. For example, when health insurance companies combine, they can negotiate better rates with hospital systems—savings they can pass to their customers. However, merging health insurers typically derive these savings only in cities where both insurers are already present. That's because most hospital systems are local, so insurers are competitors only if they serve the same local market. For insurers that operate in different cities, combining therefore does not put them in a stronger position to gain purchasing benefits from these local hospitals.

While economies of scale can be a significant source of acquisition value creation, rarely are generic economies of scale, like back-office savings, significant enough to justify an acquisition. Economies of scale must be unique to be large enough to justify an acquisition.

Pick Winners Early and Help Develop Their Businesses

The final winning acquisition strategy involves making acquisitions early in the life cycle of a new product area or industry line, long before most others recognize that the industry will grow. Typical examples come from the medical-device business, where larger companies buy young, innovative companies, help them refine their technology, and accelerate and turbocharge their product launches. It's not unusual in these cases, though, for a payoff to take five or more years.

This strategy can involve a high level of risk. Consider the example of cannabis in the United States. At the time of this writing, several state governments have legalized the recreational sale of cannabis, which remains illegal to possess or sell under federal law. Some major consumer-goods companies have purchased cannabis companies in anticipation of high growth, despite uncertainty about how the industry will develop and fit their business model. We won't know for a while how this will play out.

This acquisition strategy requires managers to take a disciplined approach in three dimensions. First, you need to be willing to make investments early, long before your competitors and the market see the industry's or company's potential. Second, you need to make multiple bets and expect some to fail. Third, you need to have the skills and patience to nurture the acquired businesses.

LONGER-ODDS STRATEGIES FOR CREATING VALUE FROM ACQUISITIONS

Beyond the six main acquisition archetypes just described, a handful of other acquisition strategies can create value. However, these are more difficult to execute successfully.

Rolling Up

Roll-up strategies are used to consolidate highly fragmented markets, where the current competitors are too small to achieve scale economies. An example is Service Corporation International's roll-up of the U.S. funeral business.

Beginning in the 1960s, Service Corporation grew from one funeral home in Houston, Texas, to almost 2,000 funeral homes and cemeteries in 2018. The strategy works when the businesses as a group can realize substantial cost savings or achieve higher revenues than the individual businesses. For example, Service Corporation's funeral homes in a single city can share vehicles, purchasing, and back-office operations. They can also coordinate advertising across a city to reduce costs and realize higher revenues.

Size per se is not what creates a successful roll-up. What matters is the right kind of size. For Service Corporation, having multiple locations in the same city has been more important than simply having many branches spread over many cities, because the cost savings, such as sharing vehicles, can be realized only if the branches are near one another.

Because roll-up strategies are hard to disguise, they invite copycats. As others tried to copy Service Corporation's strategy, prices for some funeral homes were eventually bid up to levels that made additional acquisitions uneconomic.

Consolidate to Improve Competitive Behavior

Many executives in highly competitive industries hope consolidation will lead competitors to focus less on price competition, thereby improving the industry's ROIC. However, the evidence shows that unless an industry consolidates down to just three or four competitors and can keep entrants out, competitor pricing behavior does not change: there's often an incentive for smaller companies or new entrants to gain share through price competition. So in an industry with ten competitors, lots of deals must be completed before the basis of competition changes.

Enter into a Transformational Merger

A commonly mentioned reason for an acquisition or merger is to transform one or both companies. Transformational mergers are rare, however, because the circumstances must be just right, and the management team needs to execute the strategy well. The best way to describe a transformational merger is by example. One of the world's leading pharmaceutical companies, Novartis of Switzerland, was formed by the $30 billion merger of Sandoz and Ciba-Geigy, announced in 1996. But this merger was much more than a simple combination of businesses. Under the leadership of the new CEO, Daniel Vasella, Sandoz and Ciba-Geigy were transformed into an entirely new company. Using the merger as a catalyst for change, Vasella and his management team not only captured $1.4 billion in cost synergies but also redefined the company's mission and strategy, portfolio and organization, and all key processes from research to sales. In all areas, there was no automatic choice for either the Ciba or the Sandoz way of doing things; instead, a systematic effort was made to find the *best* way of doing things.

Novartis shifted its strategic focus to innovation in its life sciences business (pharmaceuticals, nutrition, and agricultural) and spun off the $7 billion Ciba Specialty Chemicals business in 1997. Organizational changes included reorganizing research and development worldwide by therapeutic rather than geographic area, enabling Novartis to build up a world-leading oncology franchise. Across all departments and management layers, Novartis created a strong performance-oriented culture, supported by a change from a seniority-based to a performance-based compensation system for its managers.

Buy Cheap

The final way to create value from an acquisition is to buy cheap—in other words, at a price below the target's intrinsic value. In our experience, however, opportunities to create value in this way are rare and relatively small.

Although market values revert to intrinsic values over longer periods, there can be brief moments when the two fall out of alignment. Markets sometimes overreact to negative news, such as the criminal investigation of an executive or the failure of a single product in a portfolio of many strong products. Such moments are less rare in cyclical industries, where assets are often undervalued at the bottom of the cycle. Comparing actual market valuations with intrinsic values based on a "perfect foresight" model, we found that companies in cyclical industries could more than double shareholder returns (relative to actual returns) if they acquired assets at the bottom of a cycle and sold at the top.[19]

However, while markets do provide occasional opportunities for companies to buy below intrinsic value, we haven't seen many cases. To gain control of the target, the acquirer must pay the target's shareholders a premium over the current market value. Although premiums can vary widely, the average premiums for corporate control have been fairly stable, near 30 percent of the preannouncement price of the target's equity.

For targets pursued by multiple acquirers, the premium rises dramatically, creating the so-called winner's curse. If several companies evaluate a given target and all identify roughly the same synergies, the one who overestimates potential synergies the most will offer the highest price. Since the offer price is based on an overestimate of value to be created, the supposed winner overpays—and is ultimately a loser.[20] A related problem is hubris, or the tendency of the acquirer's management to overstate its ability to capture performance improvements from the acquisition.[21]

Since market values can sometimes deviate from intrinsic values, management must also be wary of the possibility that markets may be overvaluing a

[19] T. Koller and M. de Heer, "Valuing Cyclical Companies," *McKinsey Quarterly*, no. 2 (2000): 62–69.
[20] K. Rock, "Why New Issues Are Underpriced," *Journal of Financial Economics* 15 (1986): 187–212.
[21] R. Roll, "The Hubris Hypothesis of Corporate Takeovers," *Journal of Business* 59 (1986): 197–216.

potential acquisition. Consider the stock market bubble during the late 1990s. Companies that merged with or acquired technology, media, and telecommunications companies saw their share prices plummet when the market reverted to earlier levels. Overpaying when the market is inflated is a serious concern, because M&A activity seems to rise following periods of strong market performance. If (and when) prices are artificially high, large improvements are necessary to justify an acquisition, even when the target can be purchased at no premium to market value.

ESTIMATING OPERATING IMPROVEMENTS

As we've been discussing, the main sources of value created through M&A are the cost, capital, and revenue improvements, often referred to as synergies, that the combined company makes. Rarely does a cheap purchase price make the same sort of difference. So estimating the potential improvements is one of the most important success factors for M&A—along with executing on those improvements once the deal is completed.

Before getting into the estimation, it's worth emphasizing that estimating improvements from combining corporate entities is not a one-time event. It's done multiple times: first, before negotiations even begin; second, during negotiations, as the acquirer gets more information; and finally, after the deal closes. Some companies give short shrift to the last step, but it is critical. Some of our colleagues found that almost 50 percent of the time, pre-closing estimates failed to provide an adequate road map for fully identifying improvement opportunities.[22]

We find that companies do a much better job of realizing cost savings than revenue improvements. McKinsey's Merger Management Practice analyzed 90 acquisitions and found that 86 percent of the acquirers were able to capture at least 70 percent of the estimated cost savings.[23] In contrast, almost half of the acquirers realized *less* than 70 percent of the targeted revenue improvements, and in almost one-quarter of the observed acquisitions, the acquirer realized less than 30 percent of the targeted revenue improvements.

Estimating Cost and Capital Savings

Too often, managers estimate cost savings simply by calculating the difference in financial performance between the bidder and the target. Having an earnings before interest, taxes, and amortization (EBITA) margin 200 basis

---

[22] O. Engert and R. Rosiello, "Opening the Aperture 1: A McKinsey Perspective on Value Creation and Synergies" (working paper, McKinsey & Company, June 2010), www.mckinsey.com.
[23] S. A. Christofferson, R. S. McNish, and D. L. Sias, "Where Mergers Go Wrong," *McKinsey Quarterly*, no. 2 (2004): 93–99.

EXHIBIT 31.6 **Sample Framework for Estimating Cost Savings**

Function	Example Savings
Research and development	• Stopping redundant projects • Eliminating overlap in research personnel • Developing new products through transferred technology
Procurement	• Pooled purchasing • Standardizing products
Manufacturing	• Eliminating overcapacity • Transferring best operating practices
Sales and marketing	• Cross-selling products • Using common channels • Transferring best practices • Lowering combined marketing budget
Distribution	• Consolidating warehouses and truck routes
Administration	• Exploiting economies of scale in finance/accounting and other back-office functions • Consolidating strategy and leadership functions

points higher than the target, however, will not necessarily translate into better performance for the target. There are no easy rules of thumb in estimating cost and capital savings. The best estimates are based on detailed analysis. Cost and capital reduction should follow a systematic process: estimating a baseline, estimating savings for each category, and testing the results against benchmarks.

Begin with a detailed baseline for cost and capital as if the two companies remained independent across the different parts of the companies' cost structures. The purpose of the baseline is to ensure that all costs of both the acquirer and target are accounted for and that you don't run the risk of double-counting when you estimate savings. Make sure the baseline costs and capital requirements are consistent with the intrinsic valuations.

Now you can systematically estimate the potential cost and capital savings for each cost category of both the acquirer and the target. While there are some typical types of savings, as Exhibit 31.6 shows, you should ensure that the cost categories and savings ideas are tailored to the company and industry. For an accurate estimate of potential savings, tie the savings explicitly to operational activities in the business. For example, what is the equivalent head count reduction responsible for the cost savings in selling, general, and administrative (SG&A) expense? What is the resulting revenue per head count? How much will distribution costs fall when trucks are fully loaded, rather than partially loaded? Are revenues sufficient to guarantee fully loaded trucks?

When tying savings to operational drivers, involve experienced line managers in the process. An integrated team that includes both financial analysts and experienced line managers is more likely to be accurate than a pure finance team is. In addition, experienced line managers often will already know details about the target. If so, you will generate insights on capacity, quality issues, and unit sales not easily found in the public domain.

EXHIBIT 31.7 **Automotive Merger: Estimated Cost Savings**

% of original costs

Overhead	24
Sales, distribution	3
Marketing	0
Manufacturing	14
Procurement	5
Research and development	33

Consider an acquisition where the head of operations took the lead in estimating the savings from rationalizing manufacturing capacity, distribution networks, and suppliers.[24] His in-depth knowledge about the unusual manufacturing requirements for a key product line and looming investment needs at the target's main plant substantially improved savings estimates. In addition, this manager conducted a due-diligence interview with the target's head of operations, learning that the target did not have an enterprise resource planning (ERP) system. Each of these facts improved negotiations and deal structuring, for example, by permitting management to promise that the target's main European location would be retained while maintaining flexibility about the target's main U.S. facility. Moreover, the involvement of the operations manager ensured that the company was prepared to act quickly and decisively to capture savings following the deal's closure.

After you complete the assessment, always compare the aggregate results for the combined companies with industry benchmarks for operating margins and capital efficiency. Ask whether the resulting ROIC and growth projections make sense, given the overall expected economics of the industry. Only a fully developed integrated income statement and balance sheet will ensure that savings estimates are in line with economic reality. In particular, ensure that the ROIC for the new combination lands at the right level for the continuing value and is in line with the underlying competitive structure of the industry. The more difficult it is to sustain a competitive advantage, the more you need to scale down the performance improvements over the longer term.

You'll also find that the potential cost savings vary widely by cost category. Exhibit 31.7 presents the cost savings by category for an automotive-industry acquisition. While the overall estimated cost savings for the automotive acquisition were about 10 percent of total combined costs, the savings varied considerably across category. For example, although procurement costs are the single largest cost category for automotive manufacturers, most companies already have the necessary scale to negotiate favorable contracts. Therefore, savings from procurement were estimated at only 5 percent. In contrast,

[24] This and other examples can be found in Christofferson et al., "Where Mergers Go Wrong."

research and development reductions were estimated at 33 percent, as the two companies consolidated new-product development, paring down the number of expected offerings. This reduction also had a follow-on effect in manufacturing, as product designs would move toward a common platform, lowering overall manufacturing costs. Finally, while sales and distribution expenses could be lowered, management decided to preserve the combined company's marketing budget.

Estimating Revenue Improvements

Although it is tempting to assume that revenues for the newly combined company will equal stand-alone sales plus new cross-selling, the reality is often quite different. First, the merger often disrupts existing customer relationships, leading to a loss of business. Also, smart competitors use mergers as a prime opportunity to recruit star salespeople and product specialists. Some customers may have used the acquirer and target as dual sources, so they will move part of their business to another company to maintain a minimum of two suppliers. Finally, customers who decide to stay during the merger will not be shy in asking for price and other concessions that salespeople will be eager to offer, for fear of losing the business.

Make sure to develop estimates of pricing power and market share that are consistent with market growth and competitive reality. As in the process for estimating cost savings, calibrate the pro forma assumptions against the realities of the marketplace. One global financial company estimated that an acquisition would net €1 billion in sales improvements within the next five years, including double-digit profit growth in the first year. However, overall market growth was limited, so the only way to achieve these sales goals was to lower prices. Actual profit growth was a mere 2 percent.

When estimating revenue improvements, be explicit about where any growth in revenues beyond base case assessments is expected to originate. Revenue improvements will typically come from one or more of four sources:

1. Increasing each product's peak sales level
2. Reaching the increased peak sales faster
3. Extending each product's life
4. Adding new products (or features) that could not have been developed if the two companies had remained independent

Alternatively, revenue increases could come from higher prices, achievable because the acquisition reduces competition. However, antitrust regulations are in place precisely to prevent companies from using this lever, which would transfer value from customers to shareholders. Instead, any increase in price must be directly attributable to an increase in value to the customer and not to reduced choice.

604 MERGERS AND ACQUISITIONS

We also suggest you project revenue improvements in absolute amounts per year or as a percentage of stand-alone revenues, rather than as an increase in the revenue growth rate. With the growth rate approach, you can easily overestimate the true impact of revenue improvements.

Implementation Costs, Requirements, and Timing

Although performance improvements often result from doing more with less, making a change or combining systems always involves some costs. Some are obvious, such as the costs to decommission a plant and the severance that must be paid to employees being let go. Others are more subtle, such as rebranding campaigns when the name of the target is changed, integration costs for different information technology (IT) systems, and the retraining of employees. But these costs, often forgotten, must also be identified and estimated. It is not unusual for total implementation costs to be equivalent to a full year of cost savings or more.

Bear in mind that acquirers often make overly optimistic assumptions about how long it will take to capture improvements. Reality intervenes in many ways: ensuring stable supplies to customers while closing a plant can be more complicated than the acquirer expects, disparate customer lists from multiple sources can be tricky to integrate, and examining thousands of line items in the purchasing database almost always takes more hours than estimated, just to name a few possibilities.

Moreover, timing problems can affect whether the improvements are captured at all. Our experience suggests that improvements not captured within the first full budget year after consolidation may never be captured, as the drive to capture them is overtaken by subsequent events. Persistent management attention matters.

Neglecting the "use by" date of certain savings can be equally problematic. Many potential savings do not stay on the table forever. For example, one source of cost savings is eliminating cyclical excess capacity in a growing industry. But in these circumstances, the excess capacity will eventually be eliminated through natural growth. Thus, reducing capacity can achieve *incremental* savings only if the reduction comes during the expected duration of any capacity overhang.

HOW TO PAY: WITH CASH OR STOCK?

Should the acquiring company pay in cash or in shares? Research shows that, on average, an acquirer's stock returns surrounding the acquisition announcement are higher when the acquirer offers cash than when it offers shares. We hesitate, however, to draw a conclusion based solely on aggregate statistics; after all, even companies that offer cash can pay too much.

EXHIBIT 31.8 **Paying with Cash vs. Stock: Impact on Value**

Value to shareholders after transaction, $ million

Market value before deal

Acquirer	1,000
Target	500
Price paid (30% premium)	650
Ownership ratio (stock deal)	39.4%/60.6%

	Downside scenario (Synergies = 100)	Upside scenario (Synergies = 200)
Consideration in cash		
Combined value	1,600	1,700
Price paid	(650)	(650)
Value of acquirer postdeal	950	1,050
Target value created (destroyed)	150	150
Value of acquirer predeal	(1,000)	(1,000)
Acquirer value created (destroyed)	(50)	50
Consideration in stock		
Combined value	1,600	1,700
Target's share (39.4%)	(630)	(670)
Value of acquirer postdeal	970	1,020
Target value created (destroyed)	130	170
Value of acquirer predeal	(1,000)	(1,000)
Acquirer value created (destroyed)	(30)	30

Assuming that the acquirer is not capital constrained, the real issue is whether the risks and rewards of the deal should be shared with the target's shareholders. When the acquiring company pays in cash, its shareholders carry the entire risk of capturing synergies and paying too much. If the companies exchange shares, the target's shareholders assume a portion of the risk.

To show the impact on value of paying in cash rather than shares, Exhibit 31.8 outlines a hypothetical transaction. Assume that the acquirer and the target have a market capitalization of $1 billion and $500 million, respectively. The acquirer pays a total price of $650 million, including a premium of 30 percent. We calculate the estimated discounted-cash-flow (DCF) values after the transaction under two scenarios: (1) a downside scenario in which the value of operating improvements is $50 million lower than the premium paid, and (2) an upside scenario in which the value of these improvements is $50 million higher than the premium. (To simplify, we assume that market value equals intrinsic value for both the target and the acquirer.)

If the payment is entirely in cash, the target's shareholders get $650 million, regardless of whether the improvements are high enough to justify the premium. These shareholders do not share in the implementation risk. The acquirer's shareholders see the value of their stake increase by $50 million in the upside case and decrease by the same amount in the downside case. They carry the full risk.

Next, consider the same transaction paid for in shares. The target's shareholders participate in the implementation risk by virtue of being shareholders in the new combined entity.[25] In the upside case, their payout from the acquisition increases as improvements increase: they receive $670 million in value, as opposed to $650 million. Effectively, even more value has been transferred from the acquirer's shareholders to the target's shareholders. The acquirer's shareholders are willing to allow this form of payment, however, because they are protected if implementation goes poorly. If the deal destroys value, the target's shareholders now get less than before, but still a nice premium, since their portion of the combined company is worth $630 million, compared with the $500 million market value before the deal.

From this perspective, two key issues should influence your choice of payment. First, do you think the target, and/or your company, is overvalued or undervalued? During a bubble, you will be more inclined to pay in shares, as everybody will then share the burden of the market correction. In such a scenario, develop a perspective on relative overvaluation of the two businesses. If you believe your shares are more overvalued than the target's, they are valuable in their own right as transaction currency.[26] Second, how confident are you in the ability of the deal to create value overall? The more confident you are, the more you should be inclined to pay in cash.

When weighing whether to pay in cash or in shares, you should also consider what your optimal capital structure will be. Can your company raise enough cash through a debt offering to pay for the target entirely in cash? Overextending credit lines to acquire a company can devastate the borrower. One company, an automotive supplier, borrowed cash to pay for a string of acquisitions. Operating improvements did not materialize as originally expected (partly because execution of the post-merger plan was not rigorous), and the company ended up with a debt burden that it could not bear, leading to bankruptcy.

If the capital structure of the combined entity cannot accommodate any extra debt incurred by paying cash for the acquisition, then you need to consider paying partially or fully in shares, regardless of any desire to share risk among the shareholders of the new entity.

FOCUS ON VALUE CREATION, NOT ACCOUNTING

Many managers focus on the accretion and dilution of earnings brought about by an acquisition, rather than the value it could create. They do so despite numerous studies showing that stock markets pay no attention to the effects of

---

[25] Target shareholders with small stakes can sell their shares in the public market to avoid implementation risk. Influential shareholders with large stakes, such as company founders and senior executives, will often agree not to sell shares for a specified period. In this case, they share the risk of implementation.

[26] The signaling effect of share consideration is similar to that of share issuance. The capital markets will use this new information (that the shares might be overvalued) when pricing the shares.

EXHIBIT 31.9 **EPS Accretion with Value Destruction**

Assumptions	Acquirer	Target
Net income, $ million	80.0	30.0
Shares outstanding, million	40.0	10.0
EPS, $	2.0	3.0
Preannouncement share price, $	40.0	40.0
Price-to-earnings ratio	20.0	13.3
Market value, $ million	1,600.0	400.0
Price paid, $ million	–	500.0

Impact on EPS	Cash deal	Stock deal
Net income, $ million		
Net income from acquirer	80.0	80.0
Net income from target	30.0	30.0
Additional interest[1]	(19.5)	–
Net income after acquisition	90.5	110.0
Number of shares, million		
Original shares	40.0	40.0
New shares	–	12.5
Number of shares	40.0	52.5
Earnings per share, $		
EPS before acquisition	2.00	2.00
EPS accretion	0.26	0.10
EPS after acquisition	2.26	2.10

[1] Pretax cost of debt at 6%, tax rate of 35%.

an acquisition on accounting numbers but react only to the value that the deal is estimated to create. Focusing on accounting measures is therefore dangerous and can easily lead to poor decisions.

For example, in 2005, both International Financial Reporting Standards (IFRS) and U.S. Generally Accepted Accounting Principles (GAAP) eliminated amortization of goodwill. Overnight, most acquisitions that would have been dilutive to earnings per share (EPS) were now accretive. In cash deals, the only dilution is from additional interest expense, which after taxes is typically less than 4 percent of the deal value. In the case of share deals, the deal is accretive if the acquirer's P/E is higher than the target's.

But changing accounting doesn't change the economics of the deals. Many acquisitions are earnings accretive but destroy value. Consider the hypothetical deal in Exhibit 31.9. You are deciding whether to purchase a company currently priced in the market at $400 million for $500 million in cash. Your company, the acquirer, is worth $1.6 billion and has a net income of $80 million. For simplicity, assume there are no operating improvements to come from the deal. You decide to finance this deal by raising debt at a pretax interest rate of 6 percent. This deal destroys value: you overpay by $100 million (remember, no improvements). Even so, next year's earnings and earnings per share actually increase because the after-tax earnings from the acquired company ($30 million) exceed the after-tax interest required for the new debt ($19.5 million).

How can a deal increase earnings yet destroy value? The acquirer is borrowing 100 percent of the deal value based on the combined cash flows of both companies. But the acquired business could not sustain this level of debt on its own. Since the acquirer puts an increased debt burden on the existing shareholders without properly compensating them for the additional risk, it is destroying value. Only when the ROIC (calculated as target profits plus improvements

EXHIBIT 31.10 **Market Reaction to EPS Impact of Acquisitions**

EPS impact in year 2	Proportion of acquirers with positive market reactions, %		Number of transactions[1]
	1 month after announcement	1 year after announcement	
Accretive	41	52	63
Neutral	40	43	23
Dilutive	42	54	31
	Average = 41	Average = 50	

Note: The difference in returns between accretive and dilutive is not statistically significant. Returns were risk-adjusted using the capital asset pricing model (CAPM).
[1] The sample set included 117 transactions greater than $3 billion by U.S. companies between January 1999 and December 2000.
Source: Thomson, analyst reports, Compustat.

divided by the total purchase price) is greater than the weighted average cost of capital are shareholders appropriately compensated. In our hypothetical deal, the investment is $500 million, and the after-tax profit is $30 million—a mere 6 percent return on invested capital. While this is above the 3.9 percent after-tax cost of financing the debt, it is below the weighted average cost of capital.

Now suppose the same target is acquired through an exchange of shares. The acquirer would need to issue 12.5 million new shares to provide the 25 percent acquisition premium that the target company's shareholders demand.[27] After the deal, the combined company would have 52.5 million shares outstanding and earnings of $110 million. The earnings per share for the new company rise to $2.10, so the deal is again accretive without having created any underlying value. The increase is a result of mathematics rather than value created by the deal.

Conversely, companies sometimes pass up acquisitions that can create value just because they are earnings dilutive in the first several years. Suppose you spend $100 million to buy a fast-growing company in an attractive market, with a P/E of 30 times. Before performance improvements, the earnings from the acquisition will be $3.3 million. If you borrow at 4 percent after taxes, interest expense will be $4.0 million, leading to earnings dilution of $0.7 million. However, if you are able to accelerate the target's growth rate to 20 percent for the next five years and the target earns a 25 percent return on capital, it will probably create value for shareholders, even though the earnings and ROIC will be depressed for a couple of years.

Financial markets understand the difference between creating real value and increasing EPS. In a study of 117 U.S. transactions larger than $3 billion, our colleagues found that earnings accretion or dilution resulting from the deals was not a factor in the market's reaction to the deals (see Exhibit 31.10).

[27] The exchange ratio in this hypothetical deal is 1.25 shares of the acquiring company for each share of the target company. We assume that the capital market does not penalize the acquirer and that the exchange ratio can be set in relation to the preannouncement share price plus the 25 percent acquisition premium.

Regardless of whether the expected EPS was greater, smaller, or the same two years after the deal, the market's reaction was similar (within the bounds of statistical significance) at one month after the announcement and one year after the announcement.

CHARACTERISTICS OF BETTER ACQUIRERS

This chapter ends with some observations about the characteristics of companies that are better acquirers. Companies are more successful at M&A when they apply the same focus, consistency, and professionalism to it as they do to other critical disciplines.[28] This requires building four often-neglected institutional capabilities: engaging in M&A thematically, managing their reputation as an acquirer, confirming their strategic vision, and managing performance improvement targets across the M&A life cycle.

Engaging in M&A Thematically

Successful companies develop a pipeline of potential acquisitions around two or three explicit M&A themes that support the corporate strategy. These themes are effectively business plans that utilize both M&A and organic investments to meet a specific objective while explicitly considering an organization's capabilities and its characteristics as the best owner of a business. Priority themes are those where the company needs M&A to deliver its strategy and to have the ability to add value to targets. They are also highly detailed, and their effect is measurable in market share, customer segment, or product development goals.

Consider, for example, a global retail company's M&A theme: to grow through entry into two emerging markets by acquiring only local companies that are unprofitable yet in the top three of their market. That's a level of specificity few companies approach. To get there, managers started with the company's strategic goal: to become the third-largest player in its sector within five years, something it could achieve only by aggressively entering emerging markets. A less disciplined company might have accepted the strategic goal as its M&A objective and moved on to a broad scan for targets. But managers at the retail company refined their M&A goals further. They concluded that trying to enter too many markets at once was impractical, due to constraints on management time and the complexities of entering new geographies, so they limited their search to the two most promising regions. They also knew their lean operations would offer cost performance improvements in companies with bloated operations—especially given the

---

[28] Adapted from C. Ferrer, R. Uhlaner, and A. West, "M&A as a Competitive Advantage," *McKinsey on Finance*, no. 47 (Summer 2013): 2–5.

importance of economies of scale in the industry—and that local branding and catering to local preferences were critical. With their M&A theme defined so precisely, managers were able to narrow the list of potential candidates to a handful of companies.

Managing Reputation as an Acquirer

Few companies consider how they are perceived by targets or how their value proposition as an acquirer compares with that of their competitors. Many are too slow and reactive at identifying potential acquisition targets, too timid in courting and building relationships with them, or too tactical when initiating conversations. They may have such broad goals that they can't proactively approach a list of potential targets.

In our observation, companies that invest in their reputation as acquirers are perceived as bold, focused on collaboration, and able to provide real mentorship and distinctive capabilities for the target. Even some of the largest and most complex organizations can be perceived as attractive buyers by small and nimble targets, largely due to the way they present themselves and manage M&A. The best among them tend to lead with deep industry insight and a business case that is practical and focused on winning in a marketplace, rather than via synergies or deal value. They let target-company managers see how they can be successful in the new organization, typically by enabling the aggressive growth vision of the smaller company. They also have scalable functions and a predictable, transparent M&A process that targets can easily navigate. As a result, they can use their position in the market to succeed in dimensions that go beyond price—and are often approached by targets that aren't even yet for sale. This is a real competitive advantage, as the best assets migrate to the companies they perceive will add value, and this decreases search time, complexity of integration, and the chances of a bidding war.

At one high-tech company, for example, these concepts came together around the theme of enabling innovation. The company's investment in its reputation as an acquirer started with an external marketing campaign but quickly made its way deep into the M&A process. In discussions at conferences and in engineering communities, managers used testimonials from acquired employees to underscore their track record at buying companies and providing them with the expertise and resources they need to accelerate their product pipelines. They developed useful personal relationships with target-company executives by discussing ways to work together even beyond the context of a deal (or instead of a deal). And when it came time to present integration plans and future investment models to targets, managers made sure the proposals were consistent with the acquiring company's reputation.

Confirming the Strategic Vision

For many companies, the link between strategy and a transaction breaks down during due diligence. By focusing strictly on financial, legal, tax, and operations issues, the typical due diligence fails to bring in data critical to testing whether the strategic vision for the deal is valid.

To underpin the strategic impulse behind the deal, companies should bolster the usual financial due diligence with strategic due diligence. This entails testing the value creation rationale for a deal against the more detailed information available to them after signing the letter of intent, as well as seeing whether their vision of the future operating model is actually achievable. A strategic due diligence should explicitly confirm the assets, capabilities, and relationships that make a buyer the best owner of a specific target company. It should bolster an executive team's confidence that they are truly an advantaged buyer of an asset.

It is critical for executives to be honest and thorough when assessing their advantages. Ideally, they develop a fact-based point of view on their beliefs—testing them with anyone responsible for delivering value from the deal, including salespeople, R&D engineers, and their human resources and finance departments. Such an approach would have helped a large financial company whose due diligence for the deal focused on auditing existing operations rather than testing the viability of the future operating models. The advantaged-buyer criteria assumed by the company focused on being one of the most effective operators in the industry, supported by strong IT systems and processes. Executives proceeded with the deal without ever learning that the IT team had a different picture of the eventual end state, and they learned only after close that the two companies' IT systems could not be integrated.

Reassessing Performance Improvement Targets

One of the most common but avoidable pitfalls in any transaction is failing to update expectations on performance improvements as the buyer learns more about the target during integration. Companies that treat M&A as a project typically build and secure approval for a company's valuation only once, during due diligence, and then build these targets into operating budgets. This forces the organization's aspirations down to the lowest common denominator by freezing expectations at a time when information is uncertain and rarely correlated with the real potential of a deal.

Managing this challenge can be complex but worthwhile. One consumer packaged-goods company boosted run-rate synergies by 75 percent after managers recognized that the target's superior approach to in-store promotions could be used to improve its base business. A pharmaceutical company raised its synergies by over 40 percent in a very large transaction by actively revisiting estimates immediately after the deal closed, creating a risk-free environment for managers to come up with new ideas. A few years later, it had captured those higher synergies.

Companies can employ various tactics to build a real capability at realizing synergies. They might, for example, bring stakeholders together in so-called value creation summits that mimic the intensity and focus of a due-diligence effort but change the incentives to focus on the upside. And we've seen experienced acquirers take a blank-sheet approach to foster creativity, rather than anchor the exercise in a financial due-diligence model, which often leads to incremental synergies. These and similar activities allow companies to reinforce the idea that due-diligence estimates of performance improvements are the lowest acceptable performance, and they get managers used to setting their sights higher.

CLOSING THOUGHTS

Acquisitions are good for the economy when they allocate resources more efficiently between owners. However, most acquisitions create more value for the shareholders of the target company than for those of the buyer, and many destroy value for the buyer's shareholders. This is perhaps not surprising when we recall that acquisitions can create value for acquirers only if the target company's performance improves by more than the value of the premium over the target's intrinsic value that the acquirer had to offer for the target in order to persuade its shareholders to part with it.

Managers can help to ensure that their acquisitions are among those that create value for their shareholders by choosing one of the limited number of acquisition archetypes that have created value for acquirers in the past. Success also depends critically on making realistic estimates of the cost and revenue improvements that the target company can realize under new ownership, taking into account the often-substantial cost of implementing those improvements.

Managers should bear in mind that stock markets are interested only in the impact of acquisitions on the intrinsic value of the combined company. Whether an acquisition will increase or decrease earnings per share in the short term has no effect on the direction and extent of movements in the buyer's share price following the acquisition announcement.

Finally, the best acquirers build systematic institutional skills in defining their M&A strategy, managing their reputation as an acquirer, and consistently looking for performance improvement opportunities beyond those estimated before the deal was complete.

32

Divestitures[*]

Divestitures, like mergers and acquisitions, tend to occur in waves, as Exhibit 32.1 shows. In the decade following the conglomerate excesses of the 1960s and 1970s, many companies refocused their portfolios. These divestitures were generally sales to other companies or private buyout firms. By the 1990s, divestiture activity included more public-ownership transactions—spin-offs, carve-outs, and tracking stocks. Such public-ownership transactions have since become an established divestment approach, although most divestitures still take the form of deals between companies.

As Chapter 28's discussion of corporate portfolio management indicates, any program to create value should include systematically reviewing your portfolio of businesses. In our analyses of the largest global exchange-listed companies, those that endure at the top ranks combine their mergers and acquisitions (M&A) programs with selected divestitures, including shedding businesses performing well that could do better under different ownership. Evidence shows that divestitures lead to higher shareholder returns in the short term around their announcement, as well as in the years following the divestiture, especially for companies employing such a balanced portfolio approach.

Still, many executives shy away from actively pursuing divestitures as part of a value creation program. Moreover, many divestitures still occur not as an expression of a strategic plan but in reaction to pressure from outside the corporation. For example, in 2017, AkzoNobel announced the divestiture of its specialty chemicals business when faced with an activist-investor campaign and a takeover attempt by competitor PPG.

*Special thanks to André Annema for coauthoring this chapter.

EXHIBIT 32.1 **Divestitures Volume vs. M&A Volume**

$ billion[1]

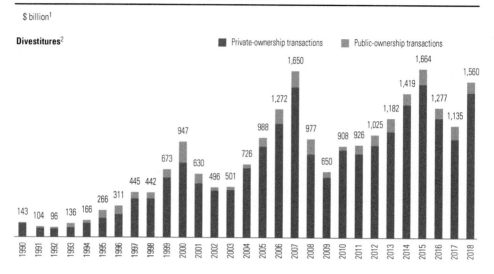

Divestitures[2]

■ Private-ownership transactions ■ Public-ownership transactions

Mergers and acquisitions

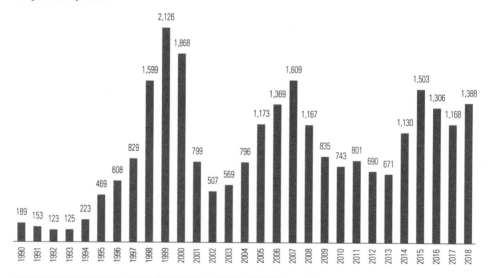

[1] Transactions with deal value above $50 million. Deals involving U.S. or European target and/or acquirer.

[2] Divestitures include sales of equity stakes >50%, business unit sales, asset sales, and public-ownership transactions (spin-offs, carve-outs, split-offs).

Source: Securities Data Company; Dealogic; Corporate Performance Analysis by McKinsey.

This chapter first presents the evidence that divestitures create value and the factors that go into creating that value. Then it discusses why, despite this evidence, executives often shy away from proactively pursuing divestitures. The next section shows how to assess a divestiture's value creation potential. The final section provides some guidance on how to choose the specific type of transaction for a divestiture.

EXHIBIT 32.2 **Market-Adjusted Announcement Returns of Divestitures**

	Cumulative abnormal returns (CAR),[1] %	Number of empirical studies	Number of transactions[2]	Time frame[3]
	Lowest CAR Sample-size-weighted CAR Highest CAR			
Spin-offs	1.7 3.3 5.6	24	2,957	1962–2007
Carve-outs	0.5 1.8 2.7	10	1,251	1965–2007
Asset sales	0.3 1.2 3.4	25	7,544	1963–2005

[1] CAR measured from 1 day before to 1 day after announcement and shown as highest, lowest, and sample-size-weighted value across the individual empirical studies.

[2] Sum of the sample sizes of all individual empirical studies.

[3] Years for which at least 1 of the empirical studies included a transaction.

Source: B. Eckbo and K. Thornburn, "Corporate Restructuring," *Foundations and Trends in Finance* 7 (2012): 159–288.

VALUE CREATION FROM DIVESTITURES

Academic research provides abundant evidence of divestitures' potential to create value.[1] A 2012 survey of the empirical results of more than 10,000 private and public transactions found significant positive excess returns associated with the announcement of different types of divestitures.[2] Exhibit 32.2 summarizes the results. Actual excess returns are probably higher because many companies disclose their intentions to divest well before the transaction is announced.[3]

[1] See, for example, J. Mulherin and A. Boone, "Comparing Acquisitions and Divestitures," *Journal of Corporate Finance* 6 (2000): 117–139; J. Miles and J. Rosenfeld, "The Effect of Voluntary Spin-Off Announcements on Shareholder Wealth," *Journal of Finance* 38 (1983): 1597–1606; K. Schipper and A. Smith, "A Comparison of Equity Carve-Outs and Seasoned Equity Offerings: Share Price Effects and Corporate Restructuring," *Journal of Financial Economics* 15 (1986): 153–186; K. Schipper and A. Smith, "Effects of Recontracting on Shareholder Wealth: The Case of Voluntary Spin-Offs," *Journal of Financial Economics* 12 (1983): 437–468; J. Allen and J. McConnell, "Equity Carve-Outs and Managerial Discretion," *Journal of Finance* 53 (1998): 163–186; and R. Michaely and W. Shaw, "The Choice of Going Public: Spin-Offs vs. Carve-Outs," *Financial Management* 24 (1995): 5–21.

[2] B. Eckbo and K. Thornburn, "Corporate Restructuring," *Foundations and Trends in Finance* 7 (2012): 159–288.

[3] See P. Ghazizadeh, A. de Jong, and F. Schlingemann, "Voluntary Disclosures of Asset Sales," working paper, 2018. Around 40 percent of the companies analyzed disclosed their intention to divest some six months before the announcement of the divestment transaction itself. When the excess returns associated with that disclosure were considered, they added around 2.4 percent to the overall results estimated for divestiture announcements.

The excess returns on announcement reflect the market's expectation that performance will improve at both the parent company and the business to be divested. Such expectations are justified. For example, operating margins of parent and spun-off businesses significantly improve during the five years after completing the transaction, and the growth rate of spun-off businesses nearly doubles.[4] Academic research confirms the improvements in operating performance, with larger improvements for the subsidiary than for the parent company.[5] As in acquisitions, experience pays off: companies that divest more often also generate more value from a divestiture.[6]

That said, value creation from divestitures is far from guaranteed. A McKinsey study of large U.S. spin-offs found that the best divestors indeed outperform the market as a whole, but that those at the bottom fall even further behind.[7] It underlines that large divestitures carry significant risks for a company and require thoughtful preparation and execution. Not surprisingly, speed matters. For large U.S. divestitures completed within 12 months, excess returns were around 6 percent, compared with –11 percent returns for those completed in 13 to 24 months.[8] Lengthy divestiture trajectories are often an indication of poor preparation and execution. Lack of speed also increases the risk of business erosion (for example, the loss of key employees, managers, and customers in the business to be divested). Success is not only determined by divestiture preparation and execution, but also by a company's portfolio strategy. A McKinsey study of 200 large U.S. companies over a ten-year period showed that companies with a passive portfolio approach—those that did not sell businesses or only sold poor businesses under pressure—underperformed companies with an active portfolio approach over those years.[9] The best performers systematically divested companies as well as acquired them.

An example of a company with a systematic approach is Germany-based Siemens, which for many years has pursued a theme of profitable growth, including a complete portfolio restructuring via targeted acquisitions and a series of major divestitures. Siemens put its telecommunication carrier business into a 50–50 joint venture with Nokia in 2006 and sold its joint venture stake to Nokia in 2013. In 2007, it sold its Siemens VDO business (supplying parts and

---

[4] See B. Huyett and T. Koller, "Finding the Courage to Shrink," *McKinsey on Finance*, no. 41 (Autumn 2011): 2–6.

[5] P. Cusatis, J. Miles, and J. Woolridge, "Some New Evidence That Spinoffs Create Value," *Journal of Applied Corporate Finance* 7 (1994): 100–107.

[6] M. Humphery-Jenner, R. Powell, and E. Jincheng Zhang, "Practice Makes Progress: Evidence from Divestitures," *Journal of Banking and Finance* 105 (2019): 1–19.

[7] The range between highest- and lowest-quartile shareholder returns over one, two, and three years after spin-off was significantly higher for divestors than for the market as a whole in a sample of 132 large U.S. spin-offs between 1992 and 2013. See S. O'Connell and J. Thomsen, "Divestitures: How to Invest for Success," *McKinsey on Finance* (Summer 2015): 2–6.

[8] O. Ezekoye and J. Thomsen, "Going, Going, Gone," *McKinsey on Finance* (August 2018): 2–6.

[9] J. Brandimarte, W. Fallon, and R. McNish, "Trading the Corporate Portfolio," *McKinsey on Finance* (Fall 2001): 1–5.

components, as well as software, to carmakers) to Continental. In 2013, it spun off its OSRAM lighting division. Siemens merged its wind-power business with Spain's Gamesa in 2017, creating a new industry leader. The health-care business was carved out in 2018 as Siemens Healthineers in a minority initial public offering (IPO), one of the largest public offerings in German history. In May 2019, Siemens announced plans to spin off its gas and power division by 2020 as an independent company with about €30 billion in revenues. After 2020, Siemens's core businesses will be Digital Industries (industrial software and automation) and Smart Infrastructure (systems for safety and security, grid control, and energy storage). The series of transactions radically oriented the group's portfolio toward the business areas that the company considers more attractive in the long term.[10] Siemens demonstrated that it earmarks for divestment not only underperforming businesses (such as gas and power) but also other businesses (such as health care) that no longer fit well with its corporate strategy.

The process of systematic divestment is natural and ongoing, as the Siemens example highlights. A divested unit may pursue further separations later in its lifetime, especially in dynamic industries undergoing rapid growth and technological change. For example, in 2007, Tyco International split itself into three independent listed businesses: Tyco Healthcare (Covidien), Tyco Electronics (TE Connectivity), and Tyco International. In 2012, Tyco International split itself again into three independent businesses: Tyco (commercial security and fire protection), Pentair (flow-control products), and ADT (residential security). The process did not stop there. TE Connectivity sold its BroadBand Network Solutions business to Commscope in 2015. Covidien, which primarily focused on medical devices, spun off Mallinckrodt, its pharmaceutical division, in 2013. ADT merged with home-security company Protection 1 in 2016.

Divesting a business unit creates value when other owners can extract more value from it than the current owners can. This is the "best owner" principle described in Chapter 28. Value creation occurs because a new owner can realize superior synergies, but also because the divestiture eliminates some unique costs of the business unit itself and/or its current owner. An active portfolio management approach creates value by avoiding, eliminating, or at least minimizing these costs.

The Costs of Holding On

For underperforming businesses, the clear benefit from divesting lies in avoiding the direct costs of bearing deteriorating results. Companies that hold on to underperforming businesses too long risk bringing down the value of the

---

[10] The portfolio change included many other divestments (and acquisitions), such as the sale of, for example, the audiology business and the household appliance business.

entire corporation. By the time the company is forced to conduct a fire sale of the assets, it has already destroyed substantial value and generally will receive limited proceeds from the divestiture. Managers should be in a better position than outsiders to determine a business's performance prospects. Research has shown that as a business becomes more mature and competitive challenges increase, it loses the potential for ongoing value creation, and its total shareholder returns start to decline, relative to the business's industry sector.[11] An opportune moment to divest the business is therefore shortly before market valuations begin to reflect its lower performance expectations.

For profitable and/or growing businesses, divesting can benefit both the parent and the business unit. Well-established, mature businesses provide a company with stability and cash flows, but holding on too long to this can also lead to what we would call *corporate inertia*. For example, relatively large and stable units may dampen the impetus to innovate—a critical driver of success for smaller businesses in the portfolio. In addition, such large units often absorb a significant share of scarce management time that might be better spent on identifying growth opportunities. For example, under Bristol-Myers Squibb's ownership, the orthopedic-devices business Zimmer relied on pricing to grow its revenues. After its spin-off in 2001, it was able to boost growth by investing more aggressively in new technologies, introducing new products, and expanding to new markets.

Other costs include the distortion of economic incentives as a result of *cross-subsidization* between business units. This can lead to inferior decision making, as well as conflicts of interest between business units. For example, during the early 1990s, Lucent—at that time a business unit of AT&T and a successful maker of telecom equipment—was selling its products to many of AT&T's competitors. To avoid conflict and to ease possible customer concerns, AT&T arranged to spin off Lucent in 1996. Conflicts of interest between business units can also arise from capital structure decisions, which was a key reason for Tyco International's 2006 health-care divestiture announcement. As Tyco CFO Chris Coughlin explains, "We were driving the capital structure of all of Tyco on the basis of what a company in the healthcare industry needed, but healthcare was only a quarter of our revenues. The other businesses clearly did not require that kind of a capital structure."[12] In these situations, a divestiture may create value because the subsidiary can become more competitive as a result of greater freedom to tailor financing and investment decisions, improved management incentives, or better focus.

A lack of *parent company capabilities* can hamper a business unit's performance. All businesses evolve through a life cycle, from start-up through

---

[11] R. Foster and S. Kaplan, *Creative Destruction* (New York: Doubleday, 2001).
[12] L. Corb and T. Koller, "When to Break Up a Conglomerate: An Interview with Tyco International's CFO," *McKinsey on Finance* (Autumn 2007): 12–18.

expansion to maturity. Different skills and capabilities are needed to manage the business well at different moments in its life cycle: from a focus on innovation in the start-up phase, when a viable business idea and platform are created, to cost management skills at maturity, when efficiency is the key driver of success. Many corporations lack the full breadth and depth of skills. Typically, they excel in only a few capabilities, which also tend to be fairly static over time. Businesses ripe for divestiture could be at any stage in their life cycle and might well include a profitable, cash-generating business or a business with relatively high growth potential.

A common misperception about divestments is that they are an easy solution for undervaluation in the stock market. Some managers interpret the positive excess returns to divestment announcements as a confirmation that the divestment exposes value the market had overlooked. That interpretation is wrong. It is often based on a misleading "sum of the parts" analysis, showing that the current market value of the company is smaller than the sum of the values of its individual business. Unfortunately, the analyses often rely on valuation multiples of industry peers with higher performance or from different sectors than the company's businesses. When the analysis uses true peers, the conglomerate discount typically disappears (see Chapter 19).

WHY EXECUTIVES SHY AWAY FROM DIVESTITURES

Although an active portfolio approach recognizes the value to be created from divestitures, most executives seem to shy away from initiating them. Looking at the 690 companies that remained in the global top 1,000 during the period from 2000 until 2013, almost 60 percent did not execute in any single year divestitures that exceeded 5 percent of their market value. About 20 percent of the companies had only one year out of the 14 in which divestments amounted to at least 5 percent of their value. The previously mentioned McKinsey study of 200 U.S. companies found that at least 75 percent of the transactions were made in reaction to some form of pressure, such as underperformance of the corporate parent, the business unit, or both.

When underperformance eventually becomes transparent to the market, investors exert continuous pressure on the corporation to divest. Academic research finds that companies that decided to sell assets tended to be poor performers and highly leveraged, suggesting that most voluntary asset sales are reactive rather than part of a proactive divestiture program.[13] Several publications have confirmed that parent companies tend to hold on to

---

[13] L. Lang, A. Poulsen, and R. Stulz, "Asset Sales, Firm Performance, and the Agency Costs of Managerial Discretion," *Journal of Financial Economics* 37 (1994): 3–37.

EXHIBIT 32.3 **Earnings Dilution through Divestitures**

$ million

	Company	Divested business unit	Use of proceeds Hold cash	Debt repayment	Share buyback
Value of operations	2,800	450	2,350	2,350	2,350
Cash	–	–	550	–	–
Enterprise value	2,800	–	2,900	2,350	2,350
Debt	(600)	–	(600)	(50)	(600)
Market value of equity	2,200	–	2,300	2,300	1,750
Shares outstanding	100.0	–	100.0	100.0	76.1
Share price	22.0	–	23.0	23.0	23.0
Invested capital	1,800	150	1,650	1,650	1,650
EBIT	236.0	50.0	186.0	186.0	186.0
Interest income (2%)	–	–	11.0	–	–
Interest expense (6%)	(36.0)	–	(36.0)	(3.0)	(36.0)
Pretax income	200.0	50.0	161.0	183.0	150.0
Taxes (25%)	(50.0)	(12.5)	(40.3)	(45.8)	(37.5)
Net income	150.0	37.5	120.8	137.3	112.5
Earnings per share, $	1.50	–	1.21	1.37	1.48
P/E	14.7	14.7	19.0	16.8	15.6
Earnings yield, %	6.8	6.8	5.3	6.0	6.4
Pretax ROIC, %	13	33.3	11.3	11.3	11.3
Operating value/EBIT	11.9	9.0	15.6	12.6	12.6

underperforming businesses too long, waiting until they have to respond to economic, technological, or regulatory shocks.[14]

In our experience, many managers dislike divestitures because these transactions could reduce the company's earnings per share, price-to-earnings ratio (P/E), or other performance indicators. However, if the business is worth more to an outsider or as an independent company, the divestiture will create value and should be pursued. The example in Exhibit 32.3 illustrates this.

The company described in the left side of the exhibit can raise $550 million in cash from a divestment of a mature business unit. This unit has a relatively high return on invested capital (ROIC) but limited growth potential. The value of the business to the company is estimated at $450 million, so that selling it at $550 million clearly creates value for the company. Any resulting changes in

[14] See, for example, Mulherin and Boone, "Comparing Acquisitions and Divestitures"; D. Ravenscraft and F. Scherer, *Mergers, Sell-Offs, and Economic Efficiency* (Washington, DC: Brookings Institution, 1987), 167; and M. Cho and M. Cohen, "The Economic Causes and Consequences of Corporate Divestiture," *Managerial and Decision Economics* 18 (1997): 367–374.

earnings multiples (whether P/E or enterprise value to EBIT) or earnings per share for the company after the transaction are irrelevant. Because divested units are typically the more mature businesses in a company's portfolio (with lower earnings multiples), divestitures often lead to increases in earnings multiples and decreases in earnings per share. But this does not indicate anything about value creation. For example, this particular divestment would increase the company's earnings multiple even when carried out at a price below $450 million (which would clearly destroy value).

In addition, changes in earnings per share and the earnings multiple depend on how the company decides to use the cash proceeds from the divestment:

- *Holding cash.* If the parent holds on to the proceeds, it will dilute its earnings per share. The reason is straightforward: the interest rate earned on the cash (1.5 percent, calculated as 2 percent less taxes at 25 percent) is lower than the so-called earnings yield (earnings relative to the value of sales proceeds, 6.8 percent after taxes) of the divested business unit. This is just simple mathematics. However, the equity value increases because the divestiture creates value, and the company's P/E is higher than before.

- *Repaying debt.* If the parent uses the proceeds to repay debt, earnings per share will still be diluted; the interest rate on the debt, at 4.5 percent after taxes (calculated as 6 percent less taxes at 25 percent), is also lower than the earnings yield of the divested business. Dilution is less than in the scenario where the parent holds the cash, because the interest rate on debt is higher than on cash. Again, the company's P/E goes up as earnings per share go down, but less so than in the prior scenario.

- *Buying back shares.* If the parent uses the proceeds to buy back shares, earnings per share will be diluted because the earnings yield of the remaining business (the inverse of the P/E, 6.4 percent) is lower than the earnings yield of the divested business unit (6.8 percent), but the dilution is less than in the other scenarios. The P/E increases but ends up below the P/E in the other two scenarios. In the example shown, the sale proceeds and the amount used for buybacks would have to increase to above $583 million in order for the divestment to become earnings accretive.

Even though the divestment causes the size of the company to be smaller (in terms of revenues and market capitalization) and its earnings per share to be lower, shareholders still benefit from this divestment. What matters is that the company generates more value from selling this business than from running it. Shareholders care about value, not size.

ASSESSING POTENTIAL VALUE FROM DIVESTITURES

A value-creating approach to divestitures can result in divesting good and bad businesses at any stage of their life cycle. Clearly, divesting a good business is often not an intuitive choice and may be hard for managers. It therefore makes sense to enforce some discipline in active portfolio management—for example, by holding regular, dedicated business exit review meetings, to ensure that the topic remains on the executive agenda, and by assigning units a "date stamp," or estimated time of exit. This practice has the advantage of obliging executives to evaluate all businesses as their sell-by date approaches, although executives may decide to retain businesses after that date. Other approaches to promote discipline include setting a limit on the number of businesses in the corporate portfolio or aiming for a target balance in acquisitions and divestitures. Such practices help transform divestitures from evidence of failure into shrewd strategies for building value.

The value created in a divestment for a parent company equals the price received minus the value forgone minus separation costs incurred by the parent:

$$\text{Value Created} = \text{Price Received} - \text{Value Forgone}$$
$$- \text{Costs of Separation}$$

The value forgone equals the stand-alone value of the divested business as run by the current management team, plus any synergies with the rest of the parent's businesses. It represents the cash flows that the parent company has given up by selling the business. The costs of separation include the costs that the parent incurs to disentangle the business from its other businesses, plus the so-called stranded costs of any assets or activities that have become redundant after the divestment—costs that, as we will see, can often be substantially mitigated by restructuring central and shared services in the parent company. With this further breakdown, we have the following expression for value created:

$$\text{Value Created} = \text{Price Received}$$
$$- \text{Stand-Alone Value of Divested Business}$$
$$- \text{Lost Synergies}$$
$$- \text{Disentanglement Costs}$$
$$- \text{Stranded Costs}$$

This section discusses these synergies and costs. Also, it examines practical challenges around legal and regulatory issues, as well as pricing and liquidity of the businesses.

Lost Synergies

When a company divests a business unit, it may lose with it certain synergy benefits of having that business in its portfolio, even if the company isn't the best owner of the business. For example, a business unit may give cross-selling opportunities to other units. Likewise, a corporation may bundle its procurement for various businesses globally so that it enjoys significant discounts. Thus, divestment can result in lower discounts and higher costs for the remaining businesses, as well as for the divested business unit itself, when volumes decrease.

Divestments could also lead to the loss of nonoperating synergies related to taxes and financing, although these tend to be relatively small. For example, an integrated electricity player that divests its (regulated) transmission and/or distribution network business and keeps a portfolio of generation and supply units will have a higher risk profile after the divestiture and, consequently, a lower debt capacity and corresponding value from tax shields.

Disentanglement Costs

Depending on the extent to which a business unit is integrated within an organization and its operations, disentangling it can incur substantial expenses. Examples of such expenses include legal and advisory fees, information technology (IT) system replacement or reconfiguration costs, relocation costs, and retention bonuses. Disentanglements can be more complex than the integration processes of large M&A deals.

Taxes triggered by the divestment depend on the details of a proposed deal structure, but they too can have real impact on post-deal economics. Differences in fiscal regimes also play a role. In many European countries, profit (including capital gains) distributions from subsidiaries to parents are to some extent exempt from corporate income and withholding taxes. In the United States, corporations do not enjoy this so-called participation exemption for capital gains on divested subsidiaries. Depending on the fiscal regime, executives may therefore prefer different types of transactions (see discussion later in the chapter).

Stranded Costs

Stranded costs can be real but are easily overestimated. These are (corporate) costs for assets and activities associated with the business unit but ultimately not transferred with it. Stranded costs can relate to shared services, such as procurement, marketing, and investor relations. They can also refer to IT infrastructure and shared production assets—for example, when a single manufacturing facility consists of production lines of products from different business units. And they can relate to general overhead costs that are allocated to businesses, such as costs for the board of directors, legal counsel, and corporate compliance.

In our experience, divestments often bring to light excessive corporate overhead that cannot be transferred to the divested business unit and is subsumed under stranded costs. Large companies tend to have many layers of management and communication. This easily leads to redundancy and unnecessary costs. For example, sizable business units often have managers in human resources, strategic planning, or financial controlling functions whose primary job is to coordinate and communicate with their counterparts in the corporate headquarters. After a divestiture, such intercompany transaction costs can be largely eliminated in both the parent company and the divested businesses. In fact, successful sellers often use divestitures as a catalyst to reduce overhead and improve efficiency in the remaining business.

Real stranded costs from divestitures take considerable time and effort to unwind. Some stranded costs are fixed and difficult to reduce, as in the case of shared IT systems. Others can be more readily managed over time—for example, by head-count reductions in shared service centers. McKinsey research has found that it often takes up to three years for the parent company to recover from stranded costs, leaving it with substantially lower profit margins during this period.[15] A seller could therefore consider including transitional service agreements for the divested business. This could help cover the costs for central and shared support services, at least in the near term. But sellers should be careful that the transitional agreements do not diminish the pressure on the organization to reduce the stranded costs in the longer term. How to handle stranded costs will vary with the type of buyer. A strategic buyer may be able to absorb the divested business unit without all the corporate support services or even production facilities; a financial buyer may be more interested in acquiring the business with these services and facilities included.

Legal and Regulatory Barriers

The divestment process may be complicated by legal or regulatory issues. These are typically not large enough to distort the value creation potential, but they can seriously slow down the process and add to the amount of work to be done, thereby increasing the time and resources required to come to closure. For example, pharmaceutical companies are required to have a so-called marketing authorization to sell an individual product in a specific market, typically a single country. If a pharmaceutical company decides to sell a particular product portfolio (e.g., oncology, respiratory, vaccines) to another

---

[15] D. Fubini, M. Park, and K. Thomas, "Profitably Parting Ways: Getting More Value from Divestitures," *McKinsey on Finance* (Winter 2013): 14–21.

pharmaceutical company, it needs to apply for a transfer of the marketing authorization for each individual product in each specific market. This is a time-consuming process that requires additional expenses. Asset transactions can be especially complex, because they require extensive documentation and contracts with respect to all the different categories of assets involved.

Contractual issues often come as unpleasant surprises that typically surface after companies have started the divestiture process. Procurement contracts, long-term contracts with customers, and loan agreements, for example, often require the creation of transitional service agreements between buyer and seller to guarantee continuity of the business unit. Or they may include change-of-ownership clauses activated upon divestiture that render the existing contract or agreement invalid when ownership in the business transfers.

Pricing and Liquidity

As discussed in Chapter 7, market valuation levels are generally in line with intrinsic value potential in the long term but can deviate in the short term. A near-term divestiture would seem to be a good idea if the market would price a business above management's estimate of its intrinsic value. The reverse holds as well: Siemens, for example, abandoned the initial public offering (IPO) of its lighting business OSRAM several times due to adverse market conditions.

Although external market factors may lower potential proceeds from a divestiture, management should balance this against the (hidden) costs of continuing with the status quo. Alternatively, management could look into transaction types that do not generate cash proceeds and thereby do not lock in an exit price for the company's shareholders. For example, as the credit crunch unfolded in 2008, Cadbury decided against a planned trade sale (in cash) of its American beverages business. Instead, it opted for a noncash demerger of the corporate group into two listed entities. This left Cadbury shareholders with the option to hold the shares of the American business and sell at some later stage, when prices might be higher.

Even when market valuation levels seem to be free of distortions and a seller could reasonably expect a value-creating offer, a lack of competing buyers may make the seller reluctant to pursue the transaction. An academic study concluded that companies are less likely to pursue divestitures of particular assets when the markets for these assets are less liquid in terms of the volume of transactions.[16] The more liquid a market for particular assets, the better the price setting is expected to be.

---

[16] F. Schlingemann, R. Stulz, and R. Walkling, "Divestitures and the Liquidity of the Market for Corporate Assets," *Journal of Financial Economics* 64 (2002): 117–144.

DECIDING ON TRANSACTION TYPE

Once a corporation has identified businesses for divestiture, it must decide what transaction structure to use. Its choices will depend on the availability of strategic or financial buyers, the need to raise cash, the benefits of retaining some level of control during the first phase of the separation, and fiscal implications for the company and/or its shareholders.

The remainder of this chapter provides a brief overview of different transaction types and discusses the trade-offs among alternative forms of public-ownership transactions, their impact on long-term performance, and the dynamics of ownership structures over time. Executives can choose from many types of structures for private and public transactions:

Private transactions

- *Trade sale:* sale of part or all of a business to a strategic or financial investor
- *Joint venture:* a combination of part or all of a business with other industry players, other companies in the value chain, or venture capitalists

Public transactions

- *Initial public offering (IPO):* sale of all shares of a subsidiary to new shareholders in the stock market
- *Carve-out (IPO of a minority stake):* sale of part of the shares in a subsidiary to new shareholders in the stock market
- *Spin-off (or demerger):* distribution of all shares in a subsidiary to existing shareholders of the parent company
- *Split-off:* an offer to existing shareholders of the parent company to exchange their shares in the parent company for shares in the subsidiary
- *Tracking stock:* a separate class of parent shares that is distributed to existing shareholders of the parent company through a spin-off or sold to new shareholders through a carve-out

Private Transactions

Private transactions typically create the most value if other parties are judged to be better owners of the business. Private transactions allow the company to sell the business unit at a premium and capture value immediately. In most situations, the counterparties will be strategic buyers (that is, other industry players), but potential financial buyers also should be considered.

However, an outright sale may result in taxable gains that will put this alternative at a disadvantage. In the United States, for example, a company must pay income tax on gains from a business sale. Businesses with relatively high ROIC or low capital intensity may therefore be less attractive candidates for an outright sale unless the premium offered justifies the capital gains tax. In many European countries, the so-called participation exemption makes the sale of the parent's shares in a subsidiary exempt from taxes.

Public Transactions

If the company cannot identify another company as a better owner, it can consider public restructuring alternatives. All the public transactions in the preceding list involve the creation of a new public security, but not all of them actually result in cash proceeds. Full IPOs and carve-outs result in cash proceeds as securities are sold to new shareholders. In spin-off and split-off transactions, new securities are offered to existing shareholders, sometimes in exchange for other existing shares (split-offs).

In public transactions, shareholders do not earn a premium from the divestiture itself, but significant value may be created for shareholders in the future. For example, if industry consolidation is expected, a public transaction may be more beneficial for the shareholders in the long term if the newly floated business unit would drive the consolidation or would be a takeover candidate.

Spin-Offs The most common form of public-ownership transaction is a spin-off. In the case of a spin-off, the parent company gives up control over the business unit by distributing the subsidiary shares to the parent's shareholders. This full separation maximizes the strategic flexibility of the subsidiary, provides the greatest freedom to improve operations by sourcing from more competitive companies (instead of the former parent), and avoids conflicts of interest between the parent company and the business unit. Spin-offs are usually carried out to improve operating performance of the business units.

Depending on the jurisdiction, spin-offs can also offer tax benefits over alternatives such as trade sales and IPOs. In the United States, United Kingdom, and several countries of continental Europe, spin-offs can be structured as tax-free transactions. Such benefits can make a spin-off more value-creating for shareholders than a trade sale at a sizable premium in countries such as the United States, where gains from a trade sale are taxed. Consider a hypothetical example in which a business with a tax book value of $200 million can be sold for $1.2 billion or spun off at an expected market capitalization of $1 billion. At a tax rate of 25 percent, the sale would leave the parent company with after-tax proceeds of $950 million that it could return to its shareholders. In a spin-off, the parent company would distribute shares in the business with an expected value of $1 billion to its shareholders.

Sometimes spin-offs are executed in two steps: a minority IPO (carve-out) followed by a full spin-off relatively shortly thereafter. Some advocates claim that a two-step spin-off has benefits: the initial minority listing establishes

EXHIBIT 32.4 **Long-Term Market Performance of Spin-Offs**

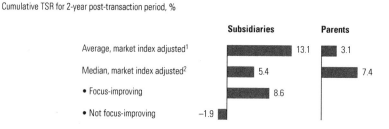

Cumulative TSR for 2-year post-transaction period, %

	Subsidiaries	Parents
Average, market index adjusted[1]	13.1	3.1
Median, market index adjusted[2]	5.4	7.4
• Focus-improving	8.6	
• Not focus-improving	−1.9	

[1] Adjusted for either U.S. or European market index.
[2] Adjusted for median return of index constituents over similar measurement period.
Source: Datastream; Compustat.

dedicated equity coverage, creates market making in the shares, and may reduce the risk of price pressure from flow-back by developing an interested investor base.[17] However, in most situations, these potential issues are rarely material and can be well managed in a one-step spin-off. For example, when Siemens spun off its OSRAM lighting business in 2013, some analysts and investors were concerned about flow-back because they considered OSRAM as one of Siemens's least attractive businesses. But the flow-back was effectively handled in a so-called balancing book that was used to match supply and demand for the OSRAM shares. No price pressure occurred. A one-step spin-off has the benefit of being less complex and does not depend on market circumstances, as no shares need to be sold to investors.

The evidence shows that spin-offs typically lead to significant improvements in operating margins for both parents and spun-off businesses during the five years after the transaction's completion. For the spun-off businesses studied, growth rates nearly doubled in this time span.[18] Academic research confirms the improvements in operating performance, with larger improvements for the subsidiary than for the parent company.[19] Some research concludes that operating improvements were significant only for focus-improving spin-offs—that is, transactions where the business spun off was different from the parent's core line of business.[20]

Post-transaction total shareholder returns (TSR) for spin-off parents and subsidiaries are consistent with the results on operating improvements (see Exhibit 32.4). Academic research also shows that focus-improving spin-offs drive the subsidiaries' positive performance. Transactions that did not improve focus had mostly negative post-transaction returns.[21]

---

[17] In a spin-off, all parent shareholders receive shares of the spun-off subsidiary. When parent shareholders subsequently sell these shares in the stock market, this gives rise to flow-back.
[18] See Huyett and Koller, "Finding the Courage to Shrink."
[19] Cusatis, Miles, and Woolridge, "Some New Evidence."
[20] L. Daley, V. Mehrotra, and R. Sivakumar, "Corporate Focus and Value Creation: Evidence from Spin-offs," *Journal of Financial Economics* 45 (1997): 257–281.
[21] Cusatis, Miles, and Woolridge, in "Some New Evidence," find similar shareholder returns for parents and subsidiaries.

EXHIBIT 32.5 **Typical Carve-Out Trajectories**

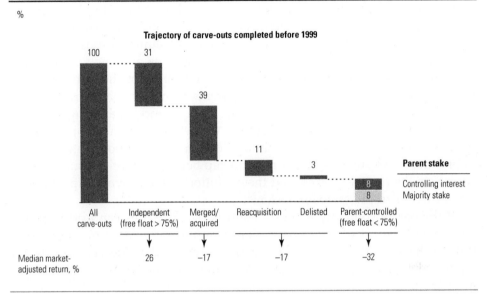

%

Trajectory of carve-outs completed before 1999

	All carve-outs	Independent (free float > 75%)	Merged/ acquired	Reacquisition	Delisted	Parent-controlled (free float < 75%)
	100	31	39	11	3	8 / 8

Parent stake
Controlling interest
Majority stake

| Median market-adjusted return, % | | 26 | −17 | | −17 | | −32 |

Source: Datastream; Factiva.

Carve-Outs   If parent companies do not want to give up control over a business unit immediately, they can consider carving out a minority ownership stake through an IPO. Another reason to consider a carve-out is that the parent needs cash for an acquisition or recapitalization. Carve-outs were popular in the late 1990s during the boom in the telecom, media, and technology (TMT) sector. Since then the allure of carve-outs has faded, with the need for cash propelling most decisions to pursue one. In the United States, the number of carve-outs has averaged about three to four per year since 2001, compared with about 15 to 20 per year during the TMT boom.

When thinking about partially separating ownership of a business unit through a carve-out, executives should plan for full separation and independence. The separated businesses should be able to attract new equity financing to fund their growth or perhaps pursuit of acquisitions, both of which will most likely dilute the parent's stake, ultimately leading to loss of control. Carve-outs produce real benefits only if they achieve real independence from the parent company. The arc toward independence should be clear from the start. For example, Philips publicly committed to gradually selling down its remaining stake in its lighting business (Signify) after the IPO of that business in 2016. In September 2019, Philips sold its last remaining shares in Signify.

In our research on more than 200 transactions completed in the carve-out boom of the 1990s, the majority of the carve-out entities did not last.[22] As shown in Exhibit 32.5, only 8 percent of the carve-out subsidiaries analyzed

[22] A. Annema, W. Fallon, and M. Goedhart, "Do Carve-Outs Make Sense?," *McKinsey on Finance* (Fall 2001): 6–10.

remained majority-controlled by the parent. Only the carve-outs that gained independence from the parent delivered positive returns to shareholders. Those that were reacquired or remained parent-controlled showed negative shareholder returns. Academic research has found similar results.[23] The market-adjusted long-term performance for carve-outs on average was negative, but different types of carve-outs differed significantly in their performance. Carve-outs from financially distressed parents showed negative returns and continue to have relatively low operating performance, indicating that they were partly contributing to the distress. Market performance appears to be better for carve-out transactions that improve the focus of both entities. Some publications also suggest a clear relationship between carve-out subsidiaries' success in the capital markets and the evolution of their ownership structure, similar to our results in Exhibit 32.5.[24]

If the parent company retains a controlling stake, this can lead to governance conflicts in the longer term. For example, enforcing a minimum controlling stake may restrict (acquisition) growth and value creation by the separated business, which would destroy the benefits that the carve-out was intended to deliver.

Tracking Stock An alternative form of public ownership restructuring is the issuance of tracking stock. Tracking stock offers a parent the advantage of maintaining control over a separated subsidiary, but it often complicates corporate governance. Because there is no formal, legal separation between the subsidiary and the parent, a single board of directors needs to decide on potentially competing needs of common and tracking stock shareholders.

In addition to producing competing needs, tracking stocks also result in both entities being liable for each other's debt, which precludes flexible capital raising. Although there may be specific tax or legal barriers in the way of separation that would favor the use of a tracking stock alternative, the evidence for tracking stock is far from convincing. In an analysis of tracking stocks, this kind of transaction appeared to destroy value in the long term.[25] On the elimination of tracking stock, the announcement effect for the parent was positive, reflecting the market's relief that the structure had been discontinued.

[23] See, for example, J. Madura and T. Nixon, "The Long-Term Performance of Parent and Units Following Equity Carve-Outs," *Applied Financial Economics* 12 (2002): 171–181; and A. Vijh, "Long-Term Returns from Equity Carveouts," *Journal of Financial Economics* 51 (1999): 273–308.
[24] A. Klein, J. Rosenfeld, and W. Beranek, "The Two Stages of an Equity Carve-Out and the Price Response of Parent and Subsidiary Stock," *Managerial and Decision Economics* 12 (1991): 449–460; K. Gleason, J. Madura, and A. K. Pennathur, "Valuation and Performance of Reacquisitions Following Equity Carve-Outs," *Financial Review* 41 (2006): 229–246; and M. Otsubo, "Gains from Equity Carve-Outs and Subsequent Events," *Journal of Business Research* 62 (2008): 1207–1213.
[25] M. Billett and A. Vijh, "The Wealth Effects of Tracking Stock Restructurings," *Journal of Financial Research* 27 (2004): 559–583.

As we write this, no major U.S. or European company has tracking stock outstanding, underlining the point that this form of ownership restructuring fails to bring the benefits executives are looking for.

SUMMARY

As businesses develop through their life cycles, they pose new challenges to the parent company. Parent companies therefore should continually reevaluate which businesses to keep and which to divest. However, most corporations divest businesses only after resisting shareholder pressure. In delaying, they risk forgoing potentially significant value.

Senior executives should prepare the organization for this cultural shift to a more active approach. They should deliver the message that their new approach will entail divesting good businesses, and such divestitures should not be considered failures. Because managers may find it difficult to divest good businesses, corporations should build forcing mechanisms into their divestiture programs.

There is no guarantee that divestitures will create value. The best divestitures indeed outperform the market, but those at the bottom fall even further behind. To increase the chances of a successful divestiture, executives should thoroughly identify the implications for the economics of the remaining businesses and consider these implications when structuring the divestiture agreement. Executives should also take care not to underestimate the time and effort required to complete a divestiture.

33

Capital Structure, Dividends, and Share Repurchases

Shaping a modern corporation's financial profile might appear to be an infinitely complex task. But in practice, it typically boils down to just three decisions: how much to invest, how much debt to carry, and how much cash to return to shareholders. In this book, we devote most of our attention to exploring the first of these topics, but the others are also important. It's not so much that making the right decisions about capital structure will create a great deal of value; it's that making the wrong calls can destroy tremendous amounts of it. For example, during the high-tech bubble of the late 1990s, many European telecommunication companies accumulated unprecedented levels of debt on their balance sheets to fund investments in digital mobile networks, expecting to issue equity at a later stage to repay the borrowing. But before they could, the bursting of the high-tech bubble in 2000 drove down the earnings outlook for mobile services and the share prices for telecom players. Providers had to recapitalize their balance sheets at great pain and cost, losing billions of shareholder value.

The primary objective of a company's decisions to structure its capital, pay dividends, and repurchase shares should be to ensure that the company has enough capital to pursue its strategic objectives and to weather any cash shortfalls along the way. If a company doesn't have enough capital, it will either pass up opportunities or, worse, fall into financial distress or even bankruptcy. When a company holds too much capital, the remedy is much easier: it can always increase its cash distributions to shareholders.

This chapter explores the options managers have for choosing an appropriate capital structure for their company and how they should develop a supporting policy for returning cash to shareholders or raising new capital. In the first two sections, we discuss some practical guidelines and a four-step approach to deciding a company's capital structure, payout, and financing. The remainder of the chapter discusses key theoretical and empirical findings on capital structure and payout that form the basis for our guidelines and approach.

PRACTICAL GUIDELINES

Finance theory has much to say about capital structure and payout—for example, about the costs and benefits of leverage, the way markets react to shareholder payouts, and the ability of managers to time their buying back of shares.[1] But it does not tell us how to set an effective capital structure and payout policy for a given company. Building on insights from finance theory (explored later in this chapter), we offer the following practical guidelines to help executives make the right choices on capital structure and payout:

- *Decisions about capital structure, dividends, and share repurchases should be an integral part of overall cash deployment.* This matches investment needs across businesses with funding opportunities and payouts to shareholders to best support the company's strategy and risk preferences. When deciding to deploy cash (for example, by using it for share repurchases), companies should consider all alternative uses of cash and set priorities for the uses according to their potential to create value, as laid out in Exhibit 33.1. The greatest opportunity to create value comes from investing cash in business operations (organic growth) and acquisitions at returns above the cost of capital.[2] The returns are typically higher for organic growth, making it the first choice for deploying cash. One level below is using cash for growth by acquisitions, where returns on capital tend be somewhat lower because acquiring assets usually requires paying a premium.[3] Financing—that is, using (or raising) cash to adjust a company's capital structure—should assume a lower priority. This does not mean that capital structure decisions are unimportant; rather, they are a necessary means of ensuring that sufficient funding is available to capture attractive investment opportunities and withstand cash shortfalls. At the bottom of the list of cash alternatives are payout decisions. These don't drive value directly but should aim to return cash to shareholders when a company has insufficient opportunities to reinvest at returns above the cost of capital.

---

[1] For an overview of the literature, see M. Barclay and C. Smith, "The Capital Structure Puzzle: The Evidence Revisited," *Journal of Applied Corporate Finance* 17, no. 1 (2005): 8–17.

[2] Following the conservation of value principle in Chapter 4, this is the primary source of value creation for companies.

[3] See M. Goedhart and T. Koller, "The Value Premium of Organic Growth," *McKinsey on Finance*, no. 61 (2017): 14–15.

- *For their capital structure, large companies should target investment-grade credit ratings between A+ and BBB– to maintain adequate flexibility for difficult times.* Most large exchange-listed companies worldwide have capital structures in this range of credit ratings. Lower ratings typically lead to a significant loss of flexibility, due to restrictive covenants built into loan agreements for sub-investment-grade companies. Higher credit ratings offer little or no additional benefits, as a company typically has enough flexibility to pursue investment opportunities once it reaches a solid investment-grade rating.

- *Payout decisions should consider their short-term impact on stock prices.* Dividends and share repurchases are value neutral over the long term but can lead to earlier recognition of value creation in a company's share price. Although long-term value creation comes from business operations and investments that generate returns above the cost of capital, not from a company's payouts to shareholders, short-term price increases can result from increased payouts that signal management discipline in the use of capital and confidence in the company's outlook. In applying this guideline, keep in mind that such increases in share price reflect higher expectations of future value creation. If the company fails to meet these expectations, the price will drop again.

- *Dividends should be set at a level that a company can sustain under plausible adverse conditions—for example, during the bottom of the earnings cycle.* Most shareholders expect that regular dividends (or dividend payout ratios) will be cut from customary levels only in cases of severe setbacks.[4] Investors almost always perceive the cutting of regular dividends as a signal of significantly lower future value creation, so these cuts generally lead to sharp declines in share price and increases in share price volatility.

- *Share repurchases should be used to return excess cash over and above dividend levels to shareholders.* Investors do not consider share buybacks to be the same long-term commitment as regular dividends. As a result, repurchases are a flexible way to pay out cash amounts that vary from year to year. Unlike dividends, share repurchases typically increase a company's earnings per share, but that does not mean share repurchases create value. Keep in mind that repurchasing shares, like paying regular dividends, is value neutral. In fact, both types of payouts could even indirectly destroy value if they come at the expense of attractive investments; that is why these decisions need to be part of planning a company's broader cash deployment.

---

[4] A small number of companies have a variable dividend policy that targets a fixed payout ratio (or range) of dividends relative to earnings.

Figure 33.1 **Cash Deployment: Value Creation Hierarchy**

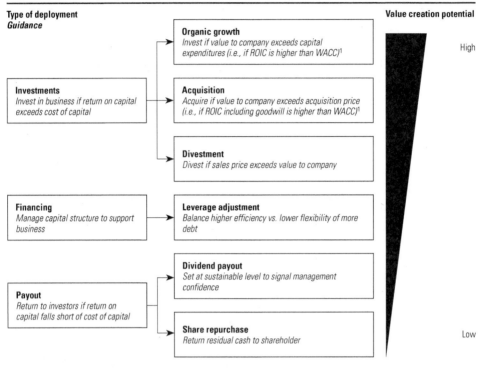

¹ ROIC is return on invested capital; WACC is weighted average cost of capital.

A FOUR-STEP APPROACH

With these guidelines in mind, we recommend a sequential approach to establishing capital structure and payout policies. With a clearly defined corporate strategy in place, the approach itself consists of four stages:

1. Project and stress-test the operating cash flows.
2. Develop a capital structure target based on the company's risk profile and risk appetite.
3. Estimate the surplus or deficit cash flow to shareholders by combining the operating cash flow and the capital structure target.
4. Decide on the payout of cash flow surplus and financing of cash flow deficit, including tactical measures, such as share repurchases, dividend payouts, share issuances, and measures to adjust the company's debt to the specified target levels.

To illustrate the approach, we can apply it to a hypothetical company in international branded consumer products. In the past, the company, which we call MaxNV, has generated annual operating earnings before interest, taxes, depreciation, and amortization (EBITDA) of around $1 billion, with some fluctuations resulting from movements in raw-materials prices and currency rates. MaxNV has held little debt, but acquisitions have driven up its ratio of net debt to EBITDA from 1.5 in 2015 to 2.8 at the beginning of 2020 (calculated as net debt at beginning of year over expected EBITDA for the year, which for 2020 would equal $2.8 billion divided by $1.0 billion).

Step 1: Project and Stress-Test Operating Cash Flows

MaxNV's strategic plan under a base-case scenario foresees annual EBITDA growth of 5 percent, from $1.0 billion in 2020 to $1.2 billion in 2024 (see Exhibit 33.2). Growth derives in part from planned bolt-on acquisitions of around $0.2 billion per year, with some revenue lost to minor divestments. In the base case, MaxNV generates around $3.0 billion in free cash flow from operations over the next five years.

We tested some of the most important business risks for MaxNV's key market and product segments by developing two downside scenarios. In a competitive-disruption scenario, new entrants with direct-to-customer sales will be more successful than anticipated. Beyond 2021, this will start to depress price and volume levels and require MaxNV to accelerate acquisitions

EXHIBIT 33.2 **MaxNV: Projections of Operating Cash Flows**

$ million

		Projections					Cumulative, 2020–2024
		2020	2021	2022	2023	2024	
EBITDA[1]	Base	1,000	1,050	1,103	1,158	1,216	5,526
	Competitive-disruption impact	–	–	(100)	(200)	(200)	(500)
	Economic-downturn impact	–	(100)	(150)	(100)	(100)	(450)
Capital expenditures	Base	(100)	(105)	(110)	(116)	(122)	(553)
	Competitive-disruption impact	–	(50)	(50)	(50)	(50)	(200)
Acquisitions	Base	(200)	(200)	(200)	(200)	(200)	(1,000)
	Competitive-disruption impact	–	–	(500)	–	–	(500)
Divestments	Base	–	25	50	–	–	75
	Competitive-disruption impact	–	–	–	25	25	50
Operating taxes	Base	(188)	(197)	(207)	(217)	(228)	(1,036)
	Competitive-disruption impact	–	–	25	50	50	125
FCF[2] **from operations**	Base	513	573	636	625	666	3,012
	Competitive-disruption impact	–	(50)	(625)	(175)	(175)	(1,025)
	Economic-downturn impact	–	(100)	(150)	(100)	(100)	(450)

[1] Earnings before interest, taxes, depreciation, and amortization.
[2] Future cash flows.

and investments in its own direct-to-customer channels. Compared with the base case, annual EBITDA will be around $200 million lower and capital expenditures around $50 million higher by 2024. Including an additional $500 million spent on acquisitions, MaxNV will generate about $1.0 billion less in after-tax cash flow from operations than in the base case. The second downside scenario sees this competitive disruption aggravated by a major economic downturn, depressing revenues and earnings across the sector. EBITDA will now be $300 million lower in 2024 compared with the base case.

For companies in industries where price and volume risks are greater, such as commodities, you might replace the use of scenarios with a more sophisticated approach: modeling future cash flows by using stochastic simulation techniques to estimate the probability of financial distress at the various debt levels.

Step 2: Develop a Capital Structure Target

Next, we set a target credit rating and estimated the corresponding coverage ratios to develop a capital structure target. Although MaxNV's operating performance is normally stable (as it is with most branded-consumer-goods players), we targeted the high end of a BBB credit rating because of the company's currency risk as an exporter. We translated the target credit rating to a target net-debt-to-EBITDA coverage ratio of 2.5 times.[5] This coverage ratio was applied in all scenarios.

Step 3: Estimate Surplus or Deficit

Based on the target coverage ratio and projections of operating cash flows, we estimated MaxNV's target capital structure and cash surpluses (or deficits) for each of the next five years. The detailed calculations are shown in Exhibit 33.3. For example, in the base case scenario, $1.0 billion of EBITDA in 2020 and a target coverage ratio of 2.5 times result in a target debt level of $2.5 billion for the end of the year. Starting with $2.8 billion of debt at the beginning of 2020, deducting $513 million of free cash flow from operations and adding $105 million of after-tax interest expenses leave MaxNV with surplus cash of $108 million that could be distributed to shareholders in 2020. With the same calculation through the remaining years of the forecast, the cumulative cash surplus for distribution amounts to around $2.7 billion over the five-year period. Exhibit 33.3 also shows the cumulative surplus for the competitive-disruption scenario ($1.2 billion) and the economic-downturn scenario ($552 million).

---

[5] As discussed later in this chapter, empirical analysis shows that approximate credit ratings can be estimated well with three factors: industry, size, and interest coverage.

EXHIBIT 33.3 **MaxNV: Estimates of Cash Surplus and Deficit**

$ million

Base case scenario	2020	2021	2022	2023	2024	Cumulative, 2020–2024
			Projections			
EBITDA[1]	1,000	1,050	1,103	1,158	1,216	5,526
Net debt, beginning of year	(2,800)	(2,500)	(2,625)	(2,756)	(2,894)	(2,800)
FCF[2] from operations	513	573	636	625	666	3,012
Interest, after-tax	(105)	(94)	(98)	(103)	(109)	(509)
Add: Target net debt, end of year @ 2.5× EBITDA[1]	2,500	2,625	2,756	2,894	3,039	3,039
Cash surplus paid out to equity (cash deficit funded with debt)	108	604	668	659	702	2,742
Target net debt EOY @ 2.5× EBITDA	(2,500)	(2,625)	(2,756)	(2,894)	(3,039)	
Excess debt	–	–	–	–	–	
Cash deficit funded with debt	(2,500)	(2,625)	(2,756)	(2,894)	(3,039)	
Competitive-disruption scenario						
EBITDA[1]	1,000	1,050	1,003	958	1,016	5,026
Net debt, beginning of year	(2,800)	(2,500)	(2,625)	(2,713)	(2,394)	(2,800)
FCF[2] from operations	513	523	11	450	491	1,987
Interest, after-tax	(105)	(94)	(98)	(102)	(90)	(489)
Add: Target net debt, end of year @ 2.5× EBITDA[2]	2,500	2,625	2,506	2,394	2,539	2,539
Cash surplus paid out to equity (cash deficit funded with debt)	108	554	(207)	29	546	1,237
Target net debt, end of year	(2,500)	(2,625)	(2,506)	(2,394)	(2,539)	
Excess debt	–	–	(207)	–	–	
Net debt, end of year	(2,500)	(2,625)	(2,713)	(2,394)	(2,539)	
Economic-downturn scenario						
EBITDA[1]	1,000	950	853	858	916	4,576
Net debt, beginning of year	(2,800)	(2,500)	(2,375)	(2,604)	(2,351)	(2,800)
FCF[2] from operations	513	423	(139)	350	391	1,537
Interest, after-tax	(105)	(94)	(89)	(98)	(88)	(474)
Add: Target net debt, end of year @ 2.5× EBITDA[2]	2,500	2,375	2,131	2,144	2,289	2,289
Cash surplus paid out to equity (cash deficit funded with debt)	108	204	(472)	(207)	240	552
Target net debt, end of year	(2,500)	(2,375)	(2,131)	(2,144)	(2,289)	
Excess debt	–	–	(472)	(207)	–	
Net debt, end of year	(2,500)	(2,375)	(2,604)	(2,351)	(2,289)	

[1] Earnings before interest, taxes, depreciation, and amortization.

[2] Future cash flows.

For both downside scenarios, a cash deficit occurs in some individual years. For these years, MaxNV could decide to simply exceed target debt levels and return to target levels later. Alternatively, it could build up excess debt capacity in prior years to ensure target debt levels are met in each year. Of course, if a cumulative deficit occurred for the entire planning horizon, MaxNV would need to consider issuing equity or find other financing opportunities, such as additional divestitures or cost savings.

Step 4: Decide on a Surplus Payout and Deficit Financing

The final step is to decide what payout and financing over the ensuing years will move the company to its target capital structure. Consider Exhibit 33.4, which summarizes the cumulative cash flows associated with the four steps for each of the three scenarios. Over the next five years under all scenarios, MaxNV can easily return $450 million ($90 million per year) in the form of regular dividends. Taking a less conservative stance, MaxNV could even consider a dividend payout of about $1 billion ($200 million per year), which it would need to cut back in the case of a downturn scenario. If the new dividend payout represents an increase from current levels, its announcement would send a strong signal to the stock market that MaxNV is confident about its business outlook and its ability to sustain this dividend level.

EXHIBIT 33.4 **MaxNV: Deciding on Payout**

$ million

| | Cumulative cash flows, 2020–2024 | | | | |
| | Base case | Competitive disruption | | Economic downturn | |
	Scenario	Disruption impact	Scenario	Downturn impact	Scenario
Step 1					
Project operational cash flows					
EBITDA[1]	5,526	(500)	5,026	(450)	4,576
Capital expenditures	(553)	(200)	(753)		(753)
Acquisitions	(1,000)	(500)	(1,500)		(1,500)
Divestments	75	50	125		125
Operating taxes	(1,036)	125	(911)		(911)
Future cash flow from operations	3,012	(1,025)	1,987	(450)	1,537
Step 2					
Develop capital structure target					
Net debt/EBITDA target	2.5		2.5		2.5
Step 3					
Estimate surplus (deficit)					
Net debt, beginning of year 2020	(2,800)		(2,800)		(2,800)
Future cash flow from operations	3,012		1,987		1,537
Interest, after taxes	(509)		(489)		(474)
Add: Target net debt, end of year 2024 @ 2.5× EBITDA	3,039		2,539		2,289
Cash surplus paid out to equity	2,742		1,237		552
Step 4					
Decide on payout (financing)					
Dividend payout	450		450		450
Share buybacks	2,292		787		102
Cash surplus paid out to equity	2,742		1,237		552
Dividend per year, average	90		90		90
Buyback per year, average	458		157		20

[1] Earnings before interest, taxes, depreciation, and amortization.

Any remaining cash for each of the scenarios could be returned to share-holders over the next several years through share repurchases or extraordinary dividends. The amount based on a conservative $450 million dividend payout would be almost $2.3 billion under the base case, about $800 million under the disruption scenario, and about $100 million under the downturn scenario. Like a dividend increase, share repurchases and extraordinary dividends signal confidence, but they have the advantage that investors won't see them as a commitment to additional payouts in future years. This gives MaxNV valuable flexibility to change the amount of cash paid out over the next years in accordance with business results and market developments. It might increase its payout, for example, as management becomes more certain that the company will achieve the base-case projection, or it could withhold most of the cash as long as it considers a downturn scenario more likely.

SETTING A TARGET CAPITAL STRUCTURE

Financing instruments vary widely, offering many options, from traditional common equity and straight debt to more exotic instruments, among them convertible preferred equity and convertible and commodity-linked debt. But the essential choice remains between straight debt and common equity. In this balancing act, tilting toward equity gives managers more flexibility to work through unexpected downturns or take advantage of unforeseen opportunities, such as acquisitions. Taking on more debt delivers higher efficiency from tax benefits and enhances management discipline over investment spending.

Empirical research shows that companies actively manage their capital structure around certain leverage boundaries.[6] They make adjustments to regain their target capital structure after they have missed it for one or two years, rather than immediately after each change in leverage. Continual adjustment would be impractical and costly, due to share price volatility and transaction costs.[7]

Fundamental Debt/Equity Trade-Offs

For decades, academic researchers have sought to learn which debt-to-equity ratio represents the best trade-off between flexibility and efficiency and maximizes value for shareholders. Unfortunately, a clear model remains elusive.[8]

---

[6] P. Marsh, "The Choice between Equity and Debt: An Empirical Study," *Journal of Finance* 37, no. 1 (1982): 121–144.
[7] See, for example, M. Leary and M. Roberts, "Do Firms Rebalance Their Capital Structures?" *Journal of Finance* 60, no. 6 (2005): 2575–2619.
[8] For an overview, see Barclay and Smith, "The Capital Structure Puzzle."

The most obvious benefit of debt over equity is a reduction in taxes. Interest charges for debt are typically tax deductible; payments to shareholders as dividends and share repurchases are not.[9] Reducing taxes by replacing equity with debt increases a company's aggregate cash flow and its value.[10] That said, this advantage does not necessarily make 100 percent debt funding the most tax-efficient approach. More debt funding may reduce corporate taxes but could actually lead to higher taxes for investors. In many countries, investors pay higher taxes on interest income than on capital gains from equity holdings. Under these circumstances equity funding could prove more attractive than debt, depending on the relevant tax rates for corporations and investors.[11]

Private-equity firms have known for decades that debt can also impose investment discipline on managers, according to the free-cash-flow hypothesis.[12] Especially in companies with strong cash flows and few growth opportunities, managers may be tempted to increase corporate spending on perks or investment projects and acquisitions that will boost growth at the expense of value. If share ownership is widely dispersed, it is difficult and costly for shareholders to assess when managers are engaging in such overinvestment. Debt restrains such behavior by forcing the company to pay out free cash flow according to scheduled interest and principal obligations before managers can make any additional investments.

However, higher levels of debt reduce financial flexibility for companies. This can give rise to costs from business erosion and investor conflicts.[13] Highly leveraged companies have less flexibility to pursue investment opportunities or free up budgets for research and development (R&D), since they need cash available to repay debts on time. These companies typically face covenants in loan agreements that limit their freedom of action. When credit is tight, they may also have limited access to new borrowing, especially if their debt is not investment grade. This was the case during the 2008 financial crisis.

As a result, these companies may miss significant opportunities to create value. They are also more likely to lose customers, employees, and suppliers because of their greater risk of financial distress. For example, suppliers to highly indebted retailers typically demand up-front payment, sometimes

---

[9] Interest charges are not always deductible in full. Many countries have "thin capitalization rules" that limit interest deductibility for taxes. For example, as of 2018, corporations in the United States can deduct interest charges only up to 30 percent of EBITDA.

[10] For an overview, see M. Grinblatt and S. Titman, *Financial Markets and Corporate Strategy*, 2nd ed. (New York: McGraw-Hill, 2002), chap. 14; and R. Brealey, S. Myers, and F. Allen, *Principles of Corporate Finance*, 13th ed. (New York: McGraw-Hill, 2019), chap. 18.

[11] M. Miller, "Debt and Taxes," *Journal of Finance* 32, no. 2 (1977): 261–275.

[12] M. Jensen, "Agency Costs of Free Cash Flow, Corporate Finance and Takeovers," *American Economic Review* 76, no. 2 (1986): 323–339.

[13] We prefer the term *business erosion* to the more often used *financial distress* because the associated costs arise very gradually and long before there may be an actual distress event, such as nonperformance on debt.

creating a negative cycle of lower inventories that lead to lower sales, which then leads to more difficulty in meeting debt schedules, and so on. The risk of losing customers is particularly high when the products require long-term service and maintenance. For example, Chrysler and General Motors lost considerable market share to Japanese and European competitors as they faced financial distress during the 2008 credit crisis. Ultimately, such business erosion can even lead to bankruptcy.

Higher leverage may cause additional value destruction as a result of conflicts of interest among debt holders, shareholders, and managers. For example, when companies come close to defaulting on their debt, shareholders will prefer to take out cash or invest it in high-risk opportunities, at debt holders' expense.[14] Of course, debt holders anticipate such conflicts and try to protect themselves with restrictive covenants and other costly measures.

Evidence on Debt/Equity Trade-Offs

Although finance theory is clear about the sources of costs and benefits of leverage, it does not tell us specifically how to measure the best capital structure for a given company. Fortunately, it turns out that capital structure has less impact on value than many practitioners think. In addition, evidence from academic research provides some guidance on leverage profiles for companies, depending on their characteristics, as one would expect from fundamental debt/equity trade-offs.[15]

Leverage should be higher for companies with higher returns, lower growth and risk, or larger and more fungible assets. Indeed, the most highly leveraged industries are typically mature and asset intensive (think cement, packaged consumer goods, and utilities). Their stable profits enable high tax savings from interest deductibility, and their low growth calls for strong management discipline, given the likelihood of overinvesting. Because such companies have assets that can serve as collateral and be redeployed after bankruptcy, their expected costs of business erosion are lower. This also explains why airlines can sustain high leverage: in spite of their low returns and high risk, airplanes are easily deployed for use by other airline companies in the event of a bankruptcy.[16] Note that direct bankruptcy costs are relatively small, around 3 percent of a company's market value, before the company becomes distressed.[17]

---

[14] In finance theory, these effects from high leverage are called corporate underinvestment (taking out cash rather than investing at low risk) and asset substitution (exchanging lower-risk assets for higher-risk assets). See, for example, S. Ross, R. Westerfield, J. Jaffe, and B. Jordan, *Corporate Finance*, 12th ed. (New York: McGraw-Hill, 2019), chap. 17.

[15] R. Rajan and L. Zingales, "What Do We Know about Capital Structure? Some Evidence from International Data," *Journal of Finance* 50, no. 5 (1995): 1421–1460.

[16] Specifically, leverage is high when the operating leases of aircraft are taken into account.

[17] See, for example, L. Weiss, "Bankruptcy Resolution: Direct Costs and Violation of Priority of Claims," *Journal of Financial Economics* 27, no. 2 (1990): 285–314.

Leverage should be lower for companies with lower returns, higher growth potential and risk, or highly specific assets and capabilities. This is the case in sectors such as software, biotechnology, and high-tech start-ups. Potential tax savings are small, because their taxable profits are low in the near term. Management needs more financial freedom, because investments are essential to capture future growth. In contrast, the costs of business erosion are high, because these companies would quickly lose valuable growth opportunities, and any remaining assets have very little value to third parties. For the same reasons, companies with more volatile earnings and higher advertising and R&D costs are generally financed with less debt.[18] Leverage also tends to be low for companies producing durable goods, such as machinery and equipment, requiring long-term maintenance and support. The highly specific capabilities of these companies make financial distress costly for their customers.[19]

Although some finance textbooks show a high potential tax benefit from higher leverage, the benefit is usually limited for large, investment-grade companies. To illustrate, consider a simple example. Exhibit 33.5 shows how the multiple of enterprise value over earnings before interest, taxes, and amortization (EBITA) for an average company in the S&P 500 would change along with the amount of the company's debt financing, as measured by the EBITA-to-interest coverage ratio. The EBITA multiple is estimated using the basic value driver formula, presented in Chapter 3, and applied using an adjusted-present-value (APV) methodology.[20] We assume a long-term ROIC of 14 percent and an unlevered cost of capital of 9 percent—typical scores for a middle-of-the-road S&P 500 company. As the exhibit shows, tax-related benefits from debt do not change enterprise value dramatically, except at very low levels

---

[18] M. Bradley, G. Jarell, and E. Kim, "On the Existence of an Optimal Capital Structure: Theory and Evidence," *Journal of Finance* 39, no. 3 (1984): 857–878; and M. Long and I. Malitz, "The Investment-Financing Nexus: Some Empirical Evidence," *Midland Corporate Finance Journal* 3, no. 3 (1985): 53–59.

[19] See Barclay and Smith, "The Capital Structure Puzzle"; and S. Titman and R. Wessels, "The Determinants of Capital Structure Choice," *Journal of Finance* 43, no. 1 (1988): 1–19.

[20] Applying the APV methodology to the value driver formula and discounting the tax shield on interest at the unlevered cost of equity results in the following formula:

$$\text{Value} = \text{NOPAT} \left(\frac{1 - \dfrac{g}{\text{ROIC}}}{k_u - g} \right) + \sum_{t=1}^{\infty} \frac{k_D \times T \times D_t}{(1 + k_u)^t}$$

where k_u is the unlevered cost of equity, D_t is the debt in year t, k_D is the cost of debt, T is the tax rate, and all other symbols are as defined in Chapter 3.

If we make the additional assumption that companies finance with debt while maintaining a stable interest coverage ratio, the formula can be simplified as follows:

$$\text{Value} = \text{NOPAT} \left(\frac{1 - \dfrac{g}{\text{ROIC}} + \dfrac{T}{1-T} \left[\dfrac{\text{Interest}}{\text{EBITA}} \right]}{k_u - g} \right)$$

where EBITA/Interest is the target coverage ratio.

EXHIBIT 33.5 **Capital Structure's Limited Impact on Enterprise Value**

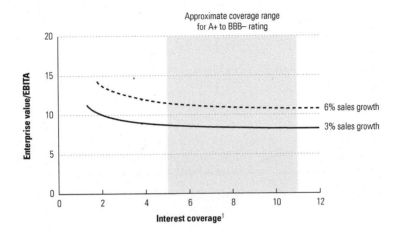

[1] EBITA/interest.

of interest coverage (below 2) rarely seen for large, investment-grade companies.[21] Compare that with the much bigger impact on shareholder value of key value drivers such as return on invested capital (ROIC) and growth.

In contrast, losses in flexibility from higher leverage do translate to significant value destruction. John Graham and others examined listed U.S. companies over a period of more than 25 years and analyzed the loss in a company's value due to deviations of its leverage from what was estimated as its theoretical optimum.[22] The analysis offers two key insights, illustrated in Exhibit 33.6. First, it confirms our analysis that value at stake is limited to no more than a couple of percentage points for a fairly wide range of leverage around the theoretical optimum. Second, it shows that there is a lot more downside from having too much debt than from having too little. In other words, the losses due to diminished flexibility tend to outweigh the gains from tax benefits and management discipline.

Credit Ratings and Target Capital Structure

Difficult as it may be to determine an *optimal* capital structure, it is much easier to find an *effective* structure—that is, one that cannot clearly be improved upon in terms of shareholder value creation because it is somewhere in the relatively flat range of the valuation curves of Exhibits 33.5 and 33.6.

[21] Note that at such low levels of coverage, the expected value of any tax savings will itself decline because of the growing probability that the company will not capture these savings in the first place. As a result, the true curve would be even flatter than shown here.
[22] See, for example, J. Van Binsbergen, J. Graham, and J. Yang, "The Cost of Debt," *Journal of Finance* 65, no. 6 (2010): 2089–2136.

EXHIBIT 33.6 **More to Lose Than to Gain from Capital Structure Management**

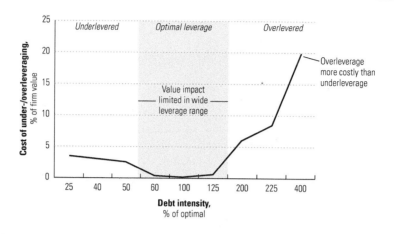

Source: J. Van Binsbergen, J. Graham, and J. Yang, "The Cost of Debt," *Journal of Finance* 65, no. 6 (2010).

Exhibit 33.7 shows the distribution of credit ratings and the associated average probability of default for all private and public companies worldwide with revenues in 2018 over €1 billion, according to Standard & Poor's. The ratings, which serve as indicators of a company's credit quality, range between AAA (highest quality) and D (defaulted). Ratings of BBB– and higher indicate so-called investment-grade quality. A majority (60 percent) of the companies in Exhibit 33.7 are in the rating categories of A+ to BBB–; an even larger share (71 percent) fall in this range when we consider only companies with a market capitalization over €5 billion. This is apparently an effective rating level: credit ratings are fairly stable over time, so most companies probably do not move in and out of this range. Few companies are at rating levels of AA– and higher, because too little leverage would leave too much value on the table in the form of tax savings and management discipline. At the other extreme, below the rating level of BBB–, the costs of business erosion and investor conflicts associated with high leverage become too onerous. At these ratings, the opportunities for debt funding are also much smaller, because many investors are barred from investing in sub-investment-grade debt.

Over the past decade, credit ratings for these large companies have declined on average, shifting the distribution in Exhibit 33.7 to the right.[23] In the United States, some experts and policy makers have expressed concerns about rising levels of corporate debt and deteriorating credit ratings.[24] However,

---

[23] See for example: "Carry the Weight: Should the World Worry about America's Corporate-Debt Mountain?" *The Economist*, March 14, 2019, www.economist.com.

[24] See for example, J. Cox, "Yellen and the Fed Are Afraid of a Corporate Debt Bubble, but Investors Still Aren't," CNBC, December 11, 2018, www.cnbc.com; N. Timiraos and A. Ackerman, "Fed Chairman Powell Warns of Economic Risks from Rising Business Debt," *Wall Street Journal*, May 20, 2019, www.wsj.com.

EXHIBIT 33.7 **Credit Ratings for Large Companies: Mostly between A+ and BBB–**

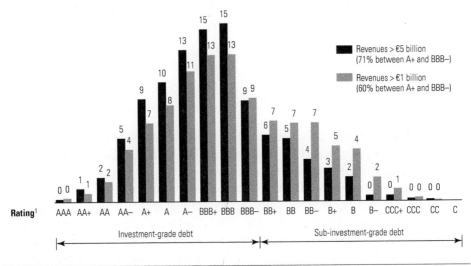

% of companies sampled, by company size (revenues)

Legend:
■ Revenues > €5 billion (71% between A+ and BBB–)
■ Revenues > €1 billion (60% between A+ and BBB–)

Ratings from left to right (Revenues > €5 billion, Revenues > €1 billion):
AAA: 0, 0
AA+: 1, 1
AA: 2, 2
AA–: 5, 4
A+: 9, 7
A: 10, 8
A–: 13, 11
BBB+: 15, 13
BBB: 15, 13
BBB–: 9, 9
BB+: 6, 7
BB: 5, 7
BB–: 4, 7
B+: 3, 5
B: 2, 4
B–: 0, 2
CCC+: 0, 1
CCC: 0, 0
CC: 0, 0
C: 0, 0

Rating[1]

Investment-grade debt ◄─────────────────► Sub-investment-grade debt

[1] Standard & Poor's credit ratings for all private and public companies with 2018 revenues exceeding €1 billion.

Source: S&P Capital IQ; Corporate Performance Analytics by McKinsey.

these trends do not necessarily mean that companies have taken on too much debt. The fraction of sub-investment-grade companies did indeed increase from 2008 to 2018, but this was driven not so much by downgrades of corporations as it was by newly rated corporations that probably entered debt markets to benefit from historically low interest rates. And while it is true that between 2008 and 2018, corporate debt in the United States grew from $2.3 trillion to $5.2 trillion, key credit ratios are still similar to those of the prior ten-year period.[25] (Authors' note: As this book went to press in March 2020, companies and governments were just beginning to assess and respond to the economic effects of the global COVID-19 pandemic.)

To translate an investment-grade (AAA to BBB–) rating into a capital structure target for a company, you must understand what a company's credit rating represents and what goes into determining it. Empirical evidence shows that credit ratings are primarily related to two financial indicators.[26] The first indicator is *size* in terms of sales or market capitalization. However, this indicator makes a difference only for very large or very small companies. For example, as of 2019, all industrial companies with AAA ratings, such as Microsoft and Johnson & Johnson, have market capitalizations

[25] See T. Khurana, W. Rehm, and A. Srivastava, "Is a Leverage Reckoning Coming?" *McKinsey on Finance*, no. 70 (May 2019): 1–6.

[26] For an overview, see R. Cantor, "An Introduction to Recent Research on Credit Ratings," *Journal of Banking and Finance* 28, no. 11 (2004): 2565–2573; E. Altman, "Financial Ratios, Discriminant Analysis, and the Prediction of Corporate Bankruptcy," *Journal of Finance* 23, no. 4 (1968): 589–609; and J. Pettit, C. Fitt, S. Orlov, and A. Kalsekar, "The New World of Credit Ratings," UBS research report (September 2004).

above $350 billion. One possible explanation: larger companies are more likely to diversify their risk.

The second indicator is *coverage* in terms of EBITA or EBITDA relative to interest expense or debt, defined as follows:

$$\text{Debt Coverage} = \frac{\text{Net Debt}}{\text{EBITA}} \text{ or } \frac{\text{Net Debt}}{\text{EBITDA}}$$

$$\text{Interest Coverage} = \frac{\text{EBITA}}{\text{Interest}} \text{ or } \frac{\text{EBITDA}}{\text{Interest}}$$

A similar indicator that is widely used by credit analysts is based on so-called free flow from operations (FFO) instead of EBITA or EBITDA. FFO is defined as EBITDA minus interest and tax charges.

Coverage is more relevant than size when you are setting a capital structure target. Basically, it represents a company's ability to comply with its debt service obligations. For example, EBITA interest coverage measures how many times a company could pay its interest commitments out of its pretax operational cash flow if it invested only an amount equal to its annual depreciation charges to keep the business running (or, for EBITDA coverage, if it invested nothing at all). In today's low-interest-rate environment, however, debt coverage is a better measure of a company's long-term ability to service its debt. Interest coverage ratios might appear strong today for some companies simply because they attracted debt at low interest rates over the past few years. When these companies need to re-fund the debt at higher rates in the future, their interest coverage will plummet.

Exhibit 33.8 shows how interest coverage and debt coverage explain rating differences for a sample of large U.S. companies rated by Standard & Poor's (excluding financial institutions). Obviously, we could further refine the analysis by including more explanatory ratios, such as free flow from operations (FFO) to interest, solvency, and more. However, these ratios are often highly correlated, so calculating them does not always produce a clearer explanation.

For a given credit rating, the coverage will typically differ by industry (see Exhibit 33.9). This is because of differences in underlying business risk. Companies in industries with more volatile earnings need higher coverage to attain a given credit rating, because their cash flow is more likely to fall short of their interest commitments.[27] For example, companies in basic materials—say, steel companies—will need higher levels of interest coverage than food and beverage companies to attain the same credit rating. By taking into account these differences in coverage requirements across industries, we can translate a company's targeted credit rating into a target coverage ratio. Based on the company's estimated future operating profit (and interest rate), we can derive

---

[27] Earnings volatility is measured here as the average standard deviation of relative annual changes in EBITDA for companies in each sector.

EXHIBIT 33.8 **Credit Rating vs. Interest and Debt Coverage**

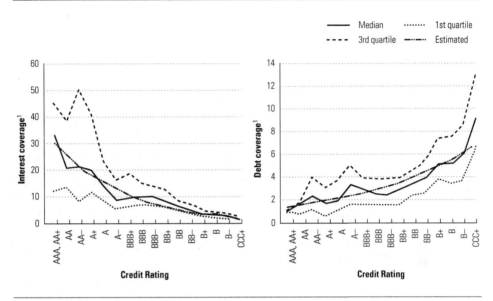

[1] EBITDA/interest. EBITDA is earnings before interest, taxes, depreciation, and amortization.

[2] Net debt/EBITDA.

Source: S&P Capital IQ; Corporate Performance Analytics by McKinsey.

its maximum debt capacity for the chosen credit rating and, thereby, its target capital structure. For example, companies aiming for an investment-grade rating in the food and beverage sector would typically need to have an EBITDA-to-interest ratio of around 5 or better. Given projections of near-term EBITDA and interest rates, you can derive a first estimate of the target amount of net debt for such a company to reach an investment-grade rating. A definitive rating estimate would require more in-depth analysis of specific financial and business risks that the company is facing. A place to start is, for example, with the websites for Standard & Poor's (www.spratings.com) or Moody's (www.moodys.com).

It is important to compare a target capital structure for a company against that of its industry peer group. The key determinants of value trade-offs in designing capital structure—growth, return, and asset specificity—are largely industry specific, so any large differences in capital structure would require further investigation. It also makes sense from a competitive perspective: as long as your capital structure is not too different, you have at least not given away any competitive advantage derived from capital structure (nor have you gained any).[28] Since the 1960s, a body of evidence has built up showing

[28] For example, there is academic evidence that high-leverage companies sometimes fall victim to price wars started by financially stronger competitors. See P. Bolton and D. Scharfstein, "A Theory of Predation Based on Agency Problems in Financial Contracting," *American Economic Review* 80, no. 1 (1990): 93–106.

EXHIBIT 33.9 **Interest Coverage and Credit Rating for Selected Industry Sectors**

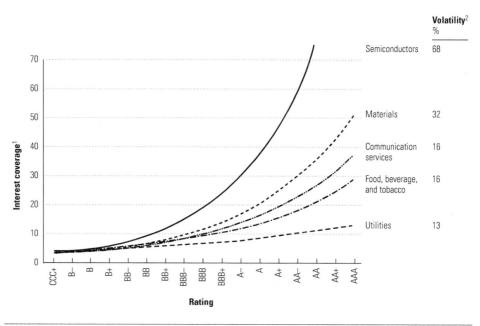

[1] EBITDA/interest. EBITDA is earnings before interest, taxes, depreciation, and amortization.

[2] Median volatility of EBITDA over the prior 5 years in each sector.

Source: S&P Capital IQ; Corporate Performance Analytics by McKinsey.

company credit ratios clustered around industry-specific averages, further indicating that each industry has its own effective capital structure.[29]

From a company's credit rating, you can also estimate the interest rate payable on its debt funding. The difference between the yields on corporate bonds and risk-free bonds—the credit spread—is greater for companies with lower credit ratings, because their probability of default is higher. Exhibit 33.10 plots cumulative default probabilities against the credit ratings over five and ten years and the average credit spread for each rating. The credit spread reflects the increasing default probability almost proportionally, but for ratings below the investment-grade benchmark of BBB, it increases more sharply. One explanation is that some institutional investors cannot invest in debt that is below investment grade (BBB−), so the debt market is considerably smaller for below-investment-grade debt, and interest rates correspondingly higher.

[29] E. Schwarz and R. Aronson, "Some Surrogate Evidence in Support of the Concept of Optimal Financial Structure," *Journal of Finance* 22, no. 1 (1967): 10–18.

EXHIBIT 33.10 **Default Probability and Credit Spread**

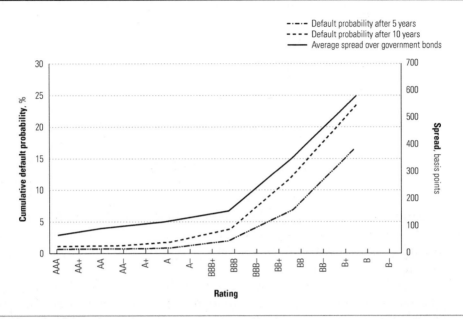

Source: S&P Capital IQ; Corporate Performance Analytics by McKinsey.

PAYOUTS TO SHAREHOLDERS

Most successful companies, at some point, find it virtually impossible to reinvest all the cash they generate. In that case, there is little alternative but to return surplus cash to shareholders. Although some executives might consider that a failure to find value-creating investments, it is actually an inevitable consequence for maturing companies with high returns on capital and moderate growth. For example, a company with $1 billion of net operating profit after taxes (NOPAT), a return on invested capital of 25 percent, and annual revenue growth of 5 percent needs net investments of only $200 million per year to continue its growth at that rate. That leaves $800 million of surplus cash flow for additional investments or payouts to shareholders (see Exhibit 33.11). Finding $800 million of new investment opportunities at attractive returns in every year is a challenge in many industries. Reinvesting all its surplus cash flow in new opportunities at its current return on capital of 25 percent would imply that the company grows revenues by 20 percent each year.

The payout levels for different combinations of return and growth in Exhibit 33.11 indicate that for most successful companies, even those with double-digit growth rates, the implications will eventually be similar: there is no choice but to return substantial amounts of cash to shareholders. Between 2002 and 2014, Procter & Gamble returned $113 billion in dividends and share repurchases to its shareholders, representing more than 90 percent of

EXHIBIT 33.11 **Surplus Cash Flow, Given Earnings of $1 Billion**

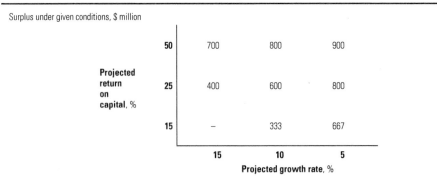

Surplus under given conditions, $ million

		700	800	900
Projected return on capital, %	**50**			
	25	400	600	800
	15	–	333	667
		15	**10**	**5**

Projected growth rate, %

its net earnings over these years. Even for a company like Procter & Gamble, it would have been close to impossible to reinvest that amount of cash, given that it had already spent some $2 billion per year on R&D and $8 billion on advertising.

Companies with cash surpluses have three basic alternatives for paying out the surpluses to shareholders: dividend increases, share repurchases, and extraordinary dividends. All three provide a positive signal to the capital market about a company's prospects. The potential negative signal that a cash payout could send is that the company has run out of investment opportunities. This assumes that investors did not already know that the company was generating more cash flow than it could reinvest. However, such cases are extremely rare; investors typically anticipate payouts long before managers make that decision, as illustrated by the simple math in our example in Exhibit 33.11.[30]

Dividends

Companies that increase their dividends receive positive market reactions averaging around 2 percent on the day of announcement.[31] For companies that initiate dividend payments, the impact is even greater.[32] In general, investors interpret dividend increases as good news about the company's long-term

---

[30] One such rare example is that of Merck, one of the largest pharmaceutical companies worldwide. In 2000, it announced a $10 billion share repurchase, which led to a 15 percent fall in its share price in the next four weeks (although the initial price reaction was favorable). This would have happened if investors assumed that Merck had been unable to find interesting R&D opportunities and could no longer maintain its long-term earnings growth target of 20 percent. See J. Pettit, "Is a Share Buyback Right for Your Company?" *Harvard Business Review* 79, no. 4 (2001): 141–147.

[31] See, for example, S. Benartzi, R. Michaely, and R. Thaler, "Do Changes in Dividends Signal the Future or the Past?" *Journal of Finance* 52, no. 3 (1997): 1007–1034; and J. Aharony and I. Swarey, "Quarterly Dividends and Earnings Announcements and Stockholders," *Journal of Finance* 35, no. 1 (1980): 1–12.

[32] P. Healey and K. Palepu, "Earnings Information Conveyed by Dividend Initiations and Omissions," *Journal of Financial Economics* 21, no. 2 (1988): 149–175.

outlook for future earnings and cash flows. On average, they are right, according to the evidence. Most companies that increase their dividend payout usually do so after strong earnings growth and when they are able to maintain such high levels of earnings in the year following the dividend increase. Companies that start paying dividends for the first time typically continue to experience high rates of earnings growth.

The drawback of increasing dividends is that investors interpret this action as a long-term commitment to higher payouts. Companies, especially in the United States, have created expectations among shareholders that dividends will be cut only in case of severe setbacks. The stock market greatly penalizes companies for cutting dividends from customary long-term levels. Between 1994 and 2008, only 5 percent of U.S. listed companies with revenues greater than $500 million cut their dividends, and in almost every case, the company faced a severe financial crisis.

A few companies do not commit to dividends or dividend growth rates that are supposed to be upheld even in the face of adverse events or declining business conditions. Instead, they have variable dividend policies and try to manage investor expectations of future payouts by explicitly relating the dividend payouts to business results. For example, in 2016 Anglo-Australian resources companies BHP and Rio Tinto adopted a dividend payout policy in which dividends are more closely related to underlying business results. BHP switched to a minimum dividend payout ratio equal to 50 percent of underlying profit, with additional payouts made in the form of special dividends or share repurchases if and when the company's financial position allowed (for example, to pay out divestment proceeds).[33] From a value creation perspective, a variable dividend policy is not better or worse than a fixed (or progressive) dividend policy. But it does create more financial flexibility, saving managers from feeling compelled to uphold dividends even if that means forgoing attractive investment opportunities or divesting assets.

Managers considering increases in dividend commitments—whether in the form of fixed dividends or a payout ratio for variable dividends—should be confident that future cash flows from operations will be sufficient to pay for capital expenditures as well as higher dividends. Furthermore, a higher dividend payout could lead to higher taxable income for shareholders, depending on the jurisdiction and their individual tax position. Such shareholders could suffer a tax loss if a company would make unexpected, significant changes to the dividend payout ratio. In other words, dividend increases are useful to handle structural cash surpluses over time but much less suitable for a one-time surplus payout.

---

[33] BHP's new dividend policy was announced in the release of the second half-year results for 2015 on February 23, 2016. Rio Tinto's dividend policy states that it expects to pay out dividends in a range of 40 to 60 percent of aggregate underlying profit through the cycle (https://www.riotinto.com/investors-87.aspx).

Share Repurchases

In the early 1980s, share repurchases represented less than 10 percent of cash payouts to shareholders. Since then, they have gained notable importance as an alternative way to distribute cash to shareholders, mainly because key regulatory limits for corporations to purchase their own shares were removed in the United States in 1982.[34] By 1999, for example, share repurchases totaled $181 billion, close to the $216 billion in regular dividend payments for companies listed on the New York Stock Exchange.[35] Even in the wake of the stock market downturn in 2000, major companies in different sectors have continued to repurchase shares on a large scale; examples include ExxonMobil, IBM, Marks & Spencer, Shell, Unilever, and Viacom. In 2018, about 60 percent of cash distributions to shareholders in the United States were share repurchases.

Investors typically interpret share repurchases positively, for several reasons. First, a share buyback shows that managers are confident that future cash flows are strong enough to support future investments and debt commitments. Second, it signals that the company will not spend its excess cash on value-destroying investments. Third, buying back shares indicates to investors that management believes the company's shares are undervalued. If management itself buys back shares, this effect is reinforced. Research shows that because of this signaling, share prices historically increased 2 to 3 percent on average on the day of announcement for smaller repurchase programs (in which less than 10 percent of shares outstanding were acquired through open-market transactions).[36] However, these results were mostly driven by share price increases for smaller companies. In addition, repurchases have become a regular payout instrument, so that their signaling effect has declined over the years.

These signaling effects should not be confused with value creation for shareholders, as they only reflect higher market expectations of future performance. If the company does not deliver against these higher expectations, the share price will come down again. As is the case for all cash payouts to shareholders, repurchases do not create value for shareholders, because they do not increase the company's cash flows from operations. This is confirmed by empirical evidence that earnings multiples are not related to the amount or the form of the cash returns, whether in dividends or via share buybacks (see Exhibit 33.12).[37]

---

[34] Following Rule 10b-18 of the U.S. Securities and Exchange Commission.

[35] See Pettit, "Is a Share Buyback Right for Your Company?"

[36] In smaller programs, companies typically buy their own shares at no premium or a limited premium in so-called open-market purchases. Larger programs are often organized in the form of tender offers in which companies announce that they will repurchase a particular number of shares at a significant premium. See, for example, R. Comment and J. Jarrell, "The Relative Signaling Power of Dutch-Auction and Fixed Price Self-Tender Offers and Open-Market Repurchases," *Journal of Finance* 46, no. 4 (1991): 1243–1272; and T. Vermaelen, "Common Stock Repurchases and Market Signaling: An Empirical Study," *Journal of Financial Economics* 9, no. 2 (1981): 138–183.

[37] See B. Jiang and T. Koller, "Paying Back Your Shareholders," *McKinsey on Finance*, no. 39 (2011): 2–7.

EXHIBIT 33.12 **Valuation Unrelated to Payout Level or Payout Mix**

Median enterprise-value-to-EBITDA multiple,[1] end of year 2007

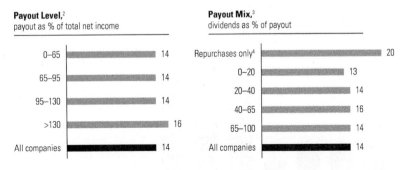

Payout Level,[2] payout as % of total net income		Payout Mix,[3] dividends as % of payout	
0–65	14	Repurchases only[4]	20
65–95	14	0–20	13
95–130	14	20–40	14
>130	16	40–65	16
All companies	14	65–100	14
		All companies	14

[1] Median multiple of nonfinancial companies in S&P 500 index.

[2] Payout defined as dividends paid plus share repurchases, 2002–2007.

[3] Average proportional share of dividends in total payout, 2002–2007.

[4] This category's higher level results from a higher proportion of fast-growing companies relative to other categories.

Source: Corporate Performance Analytics by McKinsey.

Nevertheless, two myths about share repurchases seem to persist among analysts and managers. The first is that managers can create value by repurchasing shares when they are undervalued.[38] Managers have inside information and could be in a better position than investors to assess when the company's shares are undervalued in the stock market and to buy these at the right time. Buying the undervalued shares would create value for those shareholders who hold on to them. However, the empirical evidence shows that companies rarely pick the right time to buy back shares.[39] For 2001 through 2010, a majority of the S&P 500 companies bought back shares when prices were high, and few bought shares when prices were low. In fact, the timing of share repurchases by more than three-quarters of S&P 500 companies resulted in lower shareholder returns than a simple strategy of equally distributed repurchases over time would have generated (see Exhibit 33.13).

The second myth is that repurchases create value simply because they increase earnings per share (EPS). The implicit assumption is that the price-to-earnings ratio (P/E) remains constant. As explained in Chapter 3, the logic is flawed: when share repurchases are financed with excess cash or new debt, a company's EPS indeed goes up, simply because the P/E for cash or debt is higher than for the company's equity.[40] However, after the repurchase, the

[38] See B. Jiang and T. Koller, "The Savvy Executive's Guide to Buying Back Shares," *McKinsey on Finance*, no. 41 (2011): 14–17.

[39] Some academic studies have concluded that companies do, in fact, time their repurchases well. Those findings, however, are driven primarily by smaller companies that make a one-time decision to repurchase shares. Once those smaller companies are excluded, the smart-timing effect disappears.

[40] We define the P/E here in general terms as the market value of an asset or liability divided by its after-tax earnings contribution. The P/Es for cash and debt are the inverse of their after-tax interest rates and are typically higher than for the company's equity.

EXHIBIT 33.13 **Relative Performance of Timing Share Repurchases**

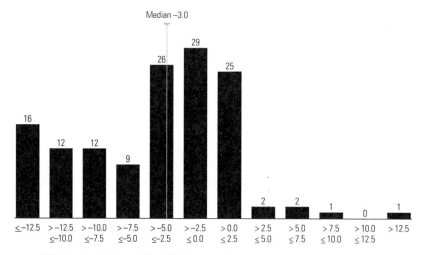

Number of companies per TSR cohort,[1] 2004–2010

TSR cohorts based on 3-year TSR vs. TSR if shares purchased evenly across periods, percentage points

[1] Based on 135 S&P 500 companies that repurchased shares from 2004 to 2010. TSR is total shareholder returns.
Source: Corporate Performance Analytics by McKinsey.

equity P/E will be lower because the company's leverage has increased.[41] The increase in EPS does not lead to value creation for shareholders, because it is exactly offset by the decline in P/E. Of course, in a large sample of companies and over long periods of time, there is always an apparent correlation between EPS growth and total shareholder returns (TSR), but that is entirely attributable to revenue growth and return on capital. After controlling for these value drivers, there is no correlation between a company's share repurchase intensity and its shareholder returns.[42]

The real value creation from share repurchases can only be assessed in comparison with alternative cash deployments, such as business investments, debt repayments, cash holdings, or dividend payments. Contrary to common beliefs, EPS and P/Es provide no guidance in making the assessment. Alternative deployments of cash have a mechanical impact on these metrics that does not necessarily correlate with value creation. This is illustrated in Exhibit 33.14 with a hypothetical company that generates net operating profit after

[41] There are two ways to explain the P/E decline. The first considers the P/E for a company's equity as a weighted average of the P/Es for its operations, cash, and debt. Paying out cash reduces the weight of the relatively high P/E for cash and therefore lowers the P/E for a company's equity. Attracting debt increases the negative weight of its relatively high P/E and lowers the equity P/E as well. The second explanation says that with higher leverage, shareholder risk has increased. This drives up the cost of equity and leads to a lower P/E multiple.

[42] See O. Ezekoye, T. Koller, and A. Mittal, "How Share Repurchases Boost Earnings without Improving Returns," *McKinsey on Finance*, no. 58 (2016): 15–24.

taxes (NOPAT) of $100, which translates to an enterprise value of $1,500 (at an enterprise-value-to-NOPAT multiple of 15 times). The company has an excess-cash position of $100, no debt, and 100 shares outstanding. It can decide to hold on to the cash or use it to repurchase shares, pay dividends, or invest in operations. Shareholder value increases for the investment alternative because the return on capital exceeds the cost of capital. But it remains unchanged for the other three alternatives, even though the associated changes in EPS or P/E appear to indicate otherwise. The exhibit compares all four alternative cash deployments in detail:

1. *Hold cash.* In this case, the company keeps the excess cash, and net income for the upcoming year is $102 (assuming the after-tax interest rate on the $100 cash is 2 percent). The company's value per share is $16, EPS is $1.02, and the P/E is 15.7.

2. *Repurchase shares.* The company uses its $100 in cash to buy back 6.25 units of its own shares (equal to $100 divided by a share price of $16). The value per share is unchanged at $16 (the remaining equity value of $1,500 divided by 93.75 remaining shares). But the EPS increases to $1.07, even though no value is created. This is simply due to the fact that the P/E for cash is higher than for shares.[43] After the share buyback, the company's equity has a lower P/E because leverage is now higher. The decline in P/E cancels out the increase in EPS, keeping shareholder value unchanged.

3. *Pay dividends.* The company pays a $1 dividend on each of its 100 shares outstanding. Although the value per share declines from $16 to $15, each shareholder still ends up with a total value including dividends of $16 per share. Again, there is no value creation, but now the EPS declines to $1.00 because the interest-generating cash has been paid out to the shareholders. The P/E for the company's equity also declines, because leverage increases due to the cash payout. The lower EPS and P/E tie with the decline in value per share of $1, which is exactly equal to the dividend paid per share.

4. *Invest.* The value for shareholders does change when the company can invest the $100 in the business at an after-tax return (ROIC) of 15 percent. At a constant enterprise-value multiple of 15 times, the enterprise and equity value will increase to $1.725 (as NOPAT increases to $115 from $100). Because of the high return on investment, the EPS increases to $1.15, clearly above any other scenario. The value per share is now $17.25, higher than in all other scenarios, because the business investment creates $125 additional value for shareholders ($1.25 per share).

---

[43] The P/E for cash in this example is 50 times (equal to the inverse of the after-tax interest rate of 2 percent).

The erratic pattern of EPS changes across the alternative allocations demonstrates that it does not move in line with value creation. Even though it is highest for the alternative with the highest value creation, this does not mean EPS is a reliable indicator of value creation. For example, assume that the investment would not produce operating earnings in the upcoming year, but only after several years. Of course, the investment would still create value.[44] But now the EPS would not increase to $1.15; it would instead decline to $1.00. Also, changes in the P/E would send the wrong signal. Delayed earnings would further increase the P/E for the investment alternative, not because value creation is higher, but simply because the company's earnings for the upcoming year would be lower. Exhibit 33.14 also shows that share repurchases can destroy value if they prevent the company from pursuing attractive investment opportunities. This underlines that payout decisions, whether repurchases or dividends, always need to be considered as part of a company's overall cash deployment.

EXHIBIT 33.14 **Value Creation from Share Repurchases vs. Alternatives for Cash Deployment**

$

	Hold cash	Repurchase shares	Pay dividends	Invest
Earnings per share				
NOPAT[1]	100.0	100.0	100.0	115.0
After-tax interest income (expense)[2]	2.0	–	–	–
Net income	102.0	100.0	100.0	115.0
Number of shares	100.00	93.75	100.00	100.00
Earnings per share	1.02	1.07	1.00	1.15
Enterprise and equity value				
Enterprise value/NOPAT	15	15	15	15
Enterprise value	1,500.0	1,500.0	1,500.0	1,725.0
Cash	100.0	–	–	–
Equity value	1,600.0	1,500.0	1,500.0	1,725.0
Pay out: Dividends			100.0	
Pay out: Share repurchases		100.0		
Equity value including payouts	1,600.0	1,600.0	1,600.0	1,725.0
Value per share				
Value per share	16.00	16.00	15.00	17.25
Dividend per share	–	–	1.00	–
Value per share including dividends	16.00	16.00	16.00	17.25
Price/earnings	15.7	15.0	15.0	15.0

[1] Net operating profit after taxes.

[2] After-tax interest rate on cash is assumed to be 2% per year.

[44] Assuming the same 15 percent ROIC and 15 times enterprise value multiple.

When a company then decides to pay out cash to shareholders, there are some good reasons to use share repurchases. In contrast to dividend increases, repurchases offer companies more flexibility in adapting their payouts to unexpected investment needs in a volatile economy. Share buyback programs are not seen as long-term commitments and can be adjusted without influencing investor expectations as much as adjustments to regular dividends would. In addition, they offer investors the flexibility to participate or not. For institutional investors, this means they can choose to uphold the amount invested in a stock—for example, because of a client mandate or because they are tracking an index—without having to reinvest dividends and incur any transaction costs. Finally, share buybacks can result in lower taxes than dividend payments for investors in countries where capital gains are taxed at lower rates. In some countries, individuals have the option to defer taxes on any capital gains and realize such gains in a more tax-efficient manner, potentially years later. Because of their flexibility, share repurchases are a very effective way to pay out any cash surpluses that exceed the level of regular dividends.

Extraordinary Dividends

As an alternative to share repurchases, a company could declare an extraordinary dividend payout, as Microsoft did in 2004 as part of its $75 billion, four-year cash return program. Microsoft paid out a significant portion in the form of an extraordinary dividend because of its concern that the share repurchase was so massive that it would swamp the liquidity in the market for Microsoft stock. The drawback of extraordinary dividends, compared with share repurchases, is that they offer no flexibility to shareholders and force the cash payout on all of them, regardless of their preferences for capital gains or dividends.

EQUITY FINANCING

If a company is facing a cash deficit and has already reached its long-term leverage target, it has little choice (other than selling noncore businesses, as discussed later in this chapter) but to raise equity or cut its dividends. As with all payout and financing decisions, this does not create or destroy value in itself. But raising equity and—especially—cutting dividends will send negative signals to investors.

As noted, companies are extremely reluctant to cut dividends to free up funds for new investments, because the stock market typically interprets such reductions as a strong signal of lower future cash flows. Share prices on average decline around 9 percent on the day a company announces dividend cuts or omissions.[45] Furthermore, some investor groups count on dividends being

[45] Healey and Palepu, "Earnings Information Conveyed by Dividend Initiations and Omissions."

paid out every year. Skipping these dividends will force these investors to liquidate parts of their portfolios, leading to unnecessary transaction costs. Only very compelling growth opportunities might somewhat mitigate the negative price reactions.[46] Finally, the amount of funds freed up by cutting dividends is often limited, so dividend cuts alone are unlikely to resolve more substantial funding shortages.

Issuing equity is also likely to lead to a short-term drop in share prices. Typically, share prices decline by around 3 percent on announcements of so-called seasoned equity offerings.[47] Because investors assume that managers have superior insights into the company's true business and financial outlook, they believe managers will issue equity only if a company's shares are overvalued in the stock market. Therefore, the share price will likely decrease in the short term on the announcement of an equity issuance, even if it is not actually overvalued. A similar price reaction can be expected for various equity-like instruments, such as preferred stock, convertibles, warrants, and more exotic hybrid forms of capital.

DEBT FINANCING

In principle, the amount of debt that needs to be issued or redeemed follows from a company's actual and targeted capital structure. In contrast to equity financing, issuing or redeeming debt typically does not send strong signals to investors about the company's future cash flows.

When issuing debt, companies commit to fixed future interest payments that can be withheld only at considerable cost. Investors also know that debt is more likely to be issued when management perceives a company's share price to be undervalued. As a result, the issuance of debt typically meets with more favorable share price reactions than the issuance of new equity. Empirical evidence shows that the price reaction is typically flat.[48]

Redeeming debt does not meet with significant stock market reactions, either, unless the company is in financial distress. In that case, buying back bonds can send a positive signal to the equity markets. For distressed companies, bond prices go up and down with the enterprise value, just as share prices do. A bond buyback could therefore be a credible signal that management

---

[46] L. Lang and R. Litzenberger, "Dividend Announcements: Cash Flow Signaling versus Free Cash Flow Hypothesis," *Journal of Financial Economics* 24, no. 1 (1989): 181–192.

[47] See, for example, B. Eckbo and R. Masulis, "Seasoned Equity Offerings: A Survey," in *Handbooks in Operations Research and Management Science* 9, ed. R. Jarrow, V. Maksimovic, and W. Ziemba (Amsterdam: Elsevier, 1995); and C. Smith, "Investment Banking and the Capital Acquisition Process," *Journal of Financial Economics* 15, nos. 1/2 (1986): 3–29.

[48] See, for example, W. Mikkelson and M. Partch, "Valuation Effects of Security Offerings and the Issuance Process," *Journal of Financial Economics* 15, nos. 1/2 (1986): 31–60; and Smith, "Investment Banking and the Capital Acquisition Process."

believes the bonds are undervalued (and because in this case bonds are similar to equity, this must also mean that shares are undervalued). For example, when the Swiss-Swedish engineering company ABB announced a €775 million bond buyback in July 2004, its share price increased 4 percent on the day of the announcement. The stock market apparently saw the buyback as further evidence that the company was on a trajectory to recover from an earlier financial crisis.

DIVESTITURES OF NONCORE BUSINESSES

As discussed in Chapter 28, companies should regularly monitor whether there are businesses in their portfolio for which they are no longer the best owner. Such businesses could generate more value in the hands of new owners—for example, because of a buyer's distinctive skills, better governance, superior insight and foresight, or strong synergies with their existing businesses. Ideally, portfolio monitoring should form an integral part of a cash deployment process where companies match investment needs across business with funding opportunities from debt, equity financing, and divestitures, also keeping in mind payouts to shareholders.

In recent years, BP, General Electric, and other companies have divested more than $40 billion in noncore assets, restructuring their corporate portfolios as well as strengthening their balance sheets. Similarly, Royal Philips divested significant parts of its portfolio, such as its lighting business, freeing up cash for investments in organic growth and acquisitions in its core healthcare businesses. Such examples underline the importance of always considering divestitures in cash deployment because they form an important source of funds as well as value creation.

CREATING VALUE FROM FINANCIAL ENGINEERING

Managing a company's capital structure with financial instruments beyond straight debt and equity—our definition of financial engineering—typically involves complex and sometimes even exotic instruments such as synthetic leasing, mezzanine finance, securitization, commodity-linked debt, commodity and currency derivatives, and balance sheet insurance. In general, capital markets do a good job of pricing even complex financial instruments, and companies will have difficulty boosting their share prices by accessing so-called cheap funding, no matter how complex the funding structures are. Nevertheless, financial engineering can create shareholder value under specific conditions, both directly (through tax savings or lower costs of funding) and indirectly (for example, by increasing a company's debt capacity so it can raise funds to capture more value-creating investment opportunities). However, such benefits need to outweigh any potential unintended consequences that inevitably arise with the complexity of financial engineering.

This section considers three of the more common tools of financial engineering: derivative instruments that transfer company risks to third parties, off-balance-sheet financing that detaches funding from the company's credit risk, and hybrid financing that offers new risk/return financing combinations.

Derivative Instruments

With derivative instruments, such as forwards, swaps, and options, a company can transfer particular risks to third parties that can carry these risks at a lower cost. For example, many airlines hedge their fuel costs with derivatives to be less exposed to sudden changes in oil prices. Of course, this does not make airlines immune to prolonged periods of high oil prices, because the derivative positions must be renewed at some point. But derivatives at least give the airlines some time to prepare business measures such as cost cuts or price increases.

Derivatives are not relevant to all companies, and there are many examples where the complexity around the use of derivatives has been badly managed.[49] In general, derivatives are useful tools for financial managers when risks are clearly identified, derivative contracts are available at reasonable prices because of liquid markets, and the total risk exposures are so large that they could seriously harm a corporation's health.

Off-Balance-Sheet Financing

A wide range of instruments fall under the umbrella of off-balance-sheet financing. These include, for example, real estate investment trusts (REITs), securitization, project finance, synthetic leases, and operating leases. Although the variety of these instruments is huge, they have a common element: companies effectively raise debt funding without carrying all the debt on their own balance sheets. Although they are still referred to as off-balance-sheet financing, new standards for U.S. Generally Accepted Accounting Principles (U.S. GAAP) and International Financial Reporting Standards (IFRS) require that most of these instruments be recognized in the balance sheet, as is also the case since 2019 for operating leases and rentals.

In most cases, off-balance-sheet financing is used to capture tax advantages. For example, many of the largest hotel companies in the United States don't own most of the hotels they operate. Instead, the hotels themselves are owned by other companies, often structured as partnerships or REITs. Unlike corporations, partnerships and REITs don't pay U.S. income taxes; taxes are

---

[49] In the 1990s, some high-profile scandals—for example, at Metallgesellschaft and Orange County, California—underlined the need for such caution.

paid only by their owners. Therefore, in the United States, placing hotels in partnerships and REITs eliminates an entire layer of taxation. With ownership and operations separated in this manner, total income taxes are lower, so investors in the ownership and operating companies are better off as a group because their aggregate cash flows are higher.

However, these deals are very complex, because they need to ensure that the interests of the owner and management company are aligned. For example, the deals need to define in advance how the REITs and the hotel companies will make decisions about renovating the hotels, terminating the leases, and other situations where the interests of both parties could conflict. Unfortunately, such potential conflicts are sometimes overlooked or are simply too complex to cover in advance. The owners of Mervyn's (a clothing retail chain in the United States) attempted something similar in 2004 but failed to align the interests of the real estate company and the operating company.[50] While Mervyn's had plenty of other problems, this structure exacerbated the difficulty of improving the company's performance. Mervyn's filed for bankruptcy in 2008. All its stores were closed and its assets liquidated in 2009.

In other cases, off-balance-sheet financing aims primarily at enabling a company to attract debt funding on terms that would have been impossible to realize for traditional forms of debt. A well-known example is the large-scale securitization of customer receivables undertaken by several auto companies. These companies sold large sums of their receivables to fully owned but legally separate entities.[51] Because the receivables represented relatively sound collateral, these entities had better credit ratings and credit terms than their parent companies. This effectively enabled the companies to tap large sums of debt for investments that otherwise would have been difficult to obtain at similar terms—although one can question whether the investments they made resulted in any value creation, as the securitization structures fell apart in the 2008 credit crisis.

Other successful examples include the use of project financing for building and running large infrastructure projects such as gas pipelines, toll bridges, and tunnels. Companies (or sometimes governments) in emerging markets and with low credit ratings may have difficulty attracting large sums of debt. But they can use project financing to raise cash for the initial investments; once the infrastructure asset is operational, the interest and principal on the debt are paid to the lender directly from the cash flows from the asset's revenues. In this way, the debt service is assured, even if the company itself goes bankrupt.

Some managers find off-balance-sheet financing more attractive because it reduces the amount of assets shown on the balance sheet and increases the

---

[50] Emily Thornton, "What Have You Done to My Company?" *BusinessWeek*, December 8, 2008, pp. 40–44.

[51] These represent examples of a so-called special-purpose entity, or—as referred to under U.S. Generally Accepted Accounting Principles—a variable-interest entity.

reported return on assets. That is not a good reason to do it. Investors will see through accounting representations, as discussed in Chapter 7. Furthermore, as already mentioned, following the latest U.S. and international accounting standards, operating leases and special-purpose entities for off-balance-sheet financing need to be fully recognized on the balance sheet.

Hybrid Financing

Hybrid financing involves forms of funding that share some elements of both equity and debt. Examples are convertible debt, convertible preferred stock, and callable perpetual debt. In particular, issuance of convertible debt has seen strong growth over the past decades, and the amount of convertible debt outstanding surpassed €400 billion in 2014.[52]

Convertible debt, or debt that may be exchanged for common stock in a given proportion within or after a specified period, is an efficient form of debt financing when investors or lenders differ from managers in their assessment of the company's credit risk.[53] When the discrepancy is great, it may become difficult or even impossible to achieve agreement on the terms of credit. But a company's credit risk has less impact on credit terms if the debt is convertible. The key reason is that higher credit risk makes the straight-debt component of the convertible less attractive and the warrant component more attractive, so the two components balance each other to an extent. Overall, convertible debt is less sensitive to differences in credit risk assessment and may therefore facilitate agreement on credit terms that are attractive to both parties. This also explains why high-growth companies use this instrument much more than other companies; they usually face more uncertainty about their future credit risk. In 2018, high-tech companies in the United States issued record levels of convertibles, often with so-called call spread overlays that raise the conversion price at which the bond can be exchanged for common equity shares (see Chapter 16 for an example).

Do not issue convertible debt just because it has a low coupon. The coupon is low because the debt also includes a conversion option. It is a fallacy to think that convertible debt is cheap funding. This holds regardless of whether it is straight convertible debt, mandatory convertible debt, convertible debt with or without call spread overlays, or any other of the many variations possible. Also avoid issuing convertible debt simply because it is a way to issue equity against the current share price at some point in the future when share prices will be much higher. That future value is already priced into the conversion options. Furthermore, if the company's share price does not increase sufficiently, the convertible debt will not be converted to equity, and the company will end up with interest-bearing debt instead.

---

[52] Bank for International Settlements, *BIS Quarterly Review*, September 2014.
[53] See M. Brennan and E. Schwartz, "The Case for Convertibles," *Journal of Applied Corporate Finance* 1, no. 2 (1988): 55–64.

SUMMARY

Although a poorly managed capital structure can lead to financial distress and value destruction, capital structure is not a key value driver. For companies whose leverage is already at reasonable levels, the potential to add value is limited, especially relative to the impact of improvements in returns on invested capital and growth. Managers should refrain from fine-tuning for the optimal capital structure and from simply giving in to any shareholder demands for higher payouts. Instead, they should make sure capital structure and payout decisions are integral parts of a cash deployment that ensures the company has enough financial flexibility to support its strategy while at the same time minimizing the risk of financial distress.

34

Investor Communications*

The value of investor communications is a subject of considerable controversy. Some executives, practitioners, and academics argue that actively handling relations with investors is a waste of management time and has no effect on a company's share price. Others have unrealistic expectations, assuming that you can talk up your company's stock and, if your investor relations staff is really sharp, it can tell you why the share price went down by 1.2 percent yesterday.

We fall somewhere in between. It's virtually impossible to interpret short-term price movements with any useful insights. And even if you could talk up your share price beyond its intrinsic value, you probably shouldn't. Nevertheless, good investor communications can ensure that your share price doesn't get out of line with its intrinsic value, can build a base of loyal investors, and can ensure that executives don't make poor strategic decisions based on misunderstanding what investors are saying to them. Too often, however, executives don't know how to interpret what they are hearing from investors, because they are listening to the wrong investors.

The point of good investor communications is to build relationships with the right kinds of investors and communicate with them at their level. It also entails being selective about which sell-side analysts to focus on, not being overly concerned with investors who have a short-term orientation, and not being overly occupied with media coverage of your company. Finally, it's as much about executives listening to the right investors as it is about delivering the company's message to investors.

This chapter also deals with two questions linked to investor communications. First, should companies provide earnings guidance? There is no evidence that companies benefit from the practice. Similarly, should companies

---

*This chapter draws heavily on research by Robert Palter and Werner Rehm and their article with Jonathan Shih, "Communicating with the Right Investors," *McKinsey on Finance* (Spring 2008): 1–4.

be concerned about meeting or beating consensus earnings forecasts? Again, the evidence shows that performance—return on invested capital (ROIC) and growth—is more important than whether a company meets the consensus earnings forecast.

OBJECTIVES OF INVESTOR COMMUNICATIONS

Good investor communications must be founded on the right objectives. Achieving the highest-possible share price is not one of them. Instead, the overriding objective of investor communications should be to align a company's share price with management's perspective on the intrinsic value of the company.

When a gap forms between a company's market value and its intrinsic value, all the company's stakeholders are put at a disadvantage. If the share price rises too high and exceeds the company's intrinsic value, the company's real performance will eventually become evident to the market, and the price will fall. When that decline occurs, employee morale will suffer, and management will have to face a concerned board of directors who may not understand why the price is falling so far and so fast. A share price that's too high may also encourage managers to keep it high by adopting short-term tactics, such as deferring investments or maintenance costs, which will hamper value creation in the long run. Conversely, a share price that is too low has additional drawbacks, especially the threat of takeover or attack by an activist investor. Furthermore, an undervalued stock makes paying for acquisitions with shares an unattractive option and may demoralize managers and employees.

A second objective of investor communications is to develop support from a group of sophisticated intrinsic investors who thoroughly understand the company's strategies, strengths, and weaknesses—and who can better distinguish between the shorter and longer term. These investors will also be likely to purchase shares on short-term dips in the share price.

A final objective is to learn what your investors like and don't like about your company as an investment. Here it is important to focus on the sophisticated longer-term investors who own your shares or investors who follow you but don't own your shares. Investors have many different investing strategies. Some will be focused on the short term. It is important to separate the concerns of the shorter-term investors from those of the long-term investors. You probably can't please them all, so priority should be given to the views of longer-term investors. These investors can also be a source of intelligence about your customers, competitors, and suppliers. The best investors will be talking regularly with these groups and may give senior management information that is more objective than the results of the company's own research efforts.

INTRINSIC VALUE vs. MARKET VALUE

Senior executives often claim that the stock market undervalues or "doesn't appreciate" their company. They say this not just in public, where you would expect them to, but also in private. They truly believe that if only they had different investors, or if only the investors or analysts understood their company better, the company's share price would be higher. Yet often these senior executives have not performed an objective outside-in valuation of their company, viewing it through the lens of a sophisticated investor. Their optimistic belief is based on a superficial comparison of price-to-earnings ratios (P/Es) or a stray comment by an analyst that the shares are undervalued.

Any good strategy must begin with an honest assessment of the situation, and a plan for investor communications is no different. It should start with an estimate of the size of the gap, if any, between management's view of the company's intrinsic value and the stock market value. In practice, we typically find that no significant gap exists or that any gap can be explained by the company's historical performance relative to peers or by the way the market is valuing the entire industry. Let's illustrate with a disguised example.

A large apparel manufacturer we'll call Fashion Co. earns a return on invested capital (ROIC) of about 20 percent, but its product lines are in slow-growth segments, so its revenue growth has been low. Fashion Co. recently adopted a strategy to buy small companies in faster-growing areas of the industry with higher ROIC, intending to apply its manufacturing and distribution skills to improve the performance of the acquired companies. Currently, 18 months since the company made its first acquisitions under this strategy, Fashion Co. derives 5 percent of its revenues from the fast-growth segments.

Fashion Co.'s managers were concerned that the company's P/E trailed the P/Es of many companies with which it compared itself. They wondered whether the low value resulted from such factors as the company's old-fashioned name or the small number of analysts covering the industry.

We began analyzing the apparent discrepancy by assessing Fashion Co.'s value relative to companies it considered peers. Some of the supposed peers were 100 percent involved in the fast-growth segments, far exceeding Fashion Co.'s 5 percent revenue stream from them. When we segmented Fashion Co.'s peers by growth rates, we found that its earnings multiple—enterprise value divided by earnings before interest, taxes, and amortization (EBITA)—was in line with those of its close peers but behind those of the companies in the fast-growing segment (see Exhibit 34.1). Fashion Co. and its closest peers also had lower ROIC than the fast-growth companies. A third set of companies, also shown in Exhibit 34.1, had high multiples because of current low earnings due to restructuring. So based on recent performance, Fashion Co.'s value was aligned with its performance relative to its closest peers.

EXHIBIT 34.1 **Fashion Co.: Valuation in Line with Close Peers**

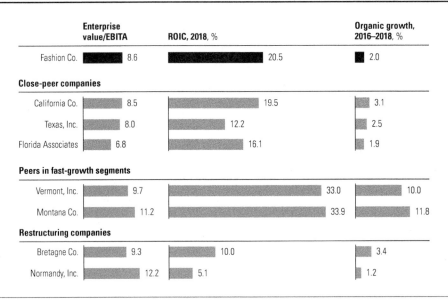

	Enterprise value/EBITA	ROIC, 2018, %	Organic growth, 2016–2018, %
Fashion Co.	8.6	20.5	2.0
Close-peer companies			
California Co.	8.5	19.5	3.1
Texas, Inc.	8.0	12.2	2.5
Florida Associates	6.8	16.1	1.9
Peers in fast-growth segments			
Vermont, Inc.	9.7	33.0	10.0
Montana Co.	11.2	33.9	11.8
Restructuring companies			
Bretagne Co.	9.3	10.0	3.4
Normandy, Inc.	12.2	5.1	1.2

Next, we reverse engineered the share price of Fashion Co. and its peers by building a discounted-cash-flow (DCF) model for each company and estimating what levels of future performance would be consistent with the current share price. We found that if Fashion Co. increased its revenues at 2 percent per year and maintained its most recent level of margins and capital turnover, its DCF value would equal its current share price. This growth rate was in line with the implicit growth of its closest peers and lower than the companies in the fast-growing segment.

WHICH INVESTORS MATTER?

Does it matter who your investors are? It is not clear whether one investor base is better than another in the sense of helping to align the share price with a company's intrinsic value. But understanding a company's investor base can give managers insights that might help them anticipate how the market will react to important events and strategic actions, as well as help managers improve the effectiveness and efficiency of their investor relations activities.

One way to begin seeking an answer to this question is by acknowledging that retail investors do not qualify for consideration in our examination. The reason is that they rarely matter when it comes to influencing a company's share price. Despite collectively holding around 30 to 40 percent of U.S. equity, they do not move prices, because they do not trade very much. The real drivers of share prices are institutional investors, who manage hedge funds, mutual funds, or pension funds and can hold significant positions in individual companies.

That said, we do not get much help from the common approaches to understanding institutional investors. For example, sometimes investors are labeled as growth or value investors, depending on the type of stocks or indexes they invest in. Most growth and value indexes, like that of Standard & Poor's, use price-to-earnings (P/E) or market-to-book ratios to categorize companies as either value or growth: companies with high P/E and market-to-book ratios are labeled growth companies, and those with low P/E and market-to-book ratios are value companies. However, growth is only one factor driving differences in P/E and market-to-book ratios. In fact, as we discuss in more detail in Chapter 7, we have found no difference in the distribution of growth rates between so-called value and growth stocks.[1] As you might expect, differences in market-to-book ratios derive mainly from differences in return on capital. The median return on capital for so-called value companies was 15 percent, compared with 35 percent for the growth companies. So the companies whose shares were classified as growth stocks did not grow faster, but they did have higher returns on capital. That's why a modestly growing company, like the high-ROIC consumer packaged-goods company Clorox, ends up on the growth-stock list.

Many executives mistakenly believe they can increase their share price (and valuation multiple) by better marketing their shares to growth investors, because growth investors tend to own shares with higher valuation multiples. But the causality runs in reverse: in our analysis of companies whose stock prices have recently increased enough to shift them from the value classification to the growth classification, what precipitated the rise in their market value was clearly not an influx of growth investors. Rather, growth investors responded to higher multiples, moving into the stock only after the share price had already risen.

Investor Segmentation by Strategy

A more useful way to categorize and understand investors is to classify them by their investment strategy. Do they develop a view on the value of a company, or do they look for short-term price movements? Do they conduct extensive research and make a few big bets, or do they make lots of small bets with less information? Do they build their portfolios from the bottom up, or do they mirror an index?

Using this approach, we classify institutional investors into four types: intrinsic investors, traders, mechanical investors, and closet indexers.[2] These groups differ in their investment objectives and the way they build their portfolios. As a result, their portfolios vary along several important dimensions, including turnover rate, positions held, and the number of positions held per investment professional (see Exhibit 34.2).

[1] See T. Koller and B. Jiang, "The Truth about Growth and Value Stocks," *McKinsey on Finance*, no. 22 (Winter 2007): 12–15.
[2] Palter et al., "Communicating with the Right Investors."

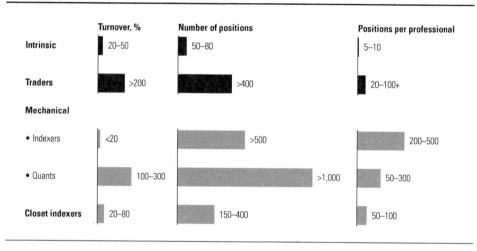

EXHIBIT 34.2 **Investors Segmented by Investment Strategies**

Intrinsic investors take positions only after undertaking rigorous due diligence of a company's inherent ability to create long-term value. This scrutiny typically takes more than a month. The depth of the intrinsic investor's research is evidenced by the fact that such investors typically hold fewer than 80 stocks at any time, and their investment professionals manage only a few positions each, usually between five and ten. Portfolio turnover is low, as intrinsic investors typically accept that price-to-value discrepancies may persist for up to three or four years before disappearing. We estimate that these investors hold around 20 to 25 percent of institutional U.S. equity and contribute 10 percent of the trading volume in the U.S. stock market.

Examples of intrinsic investors include the William Blair Growth Fund. In June 2019, it held shares in 57 companies and had a turnover rate of 38 percent. From the hedge fund world, Pzena and Hermes Capital are good examples of intrinsic investors. One prominent hedge fund manager, Lee Ainslie of Maverick Capital, is proud that Maverick holds only five positions per investment professional, and many of his staff members have followed a single industry for ten years or more.[3]

Traders seek profits by betting on short-term movements in share prices, typically based on announcements about the company or technical factors, like the momentum of the company's share price. The typical investment professional in this segment has 20 or more positions to follow and trades in and out of them quickly to capture small gains over short periods—as short as a few days or even hours. We estimate that traders own about 35 to 40 percent of institutional equity holdings in the United States.

[3] R. Dobbs and T. Koller, "Inside a Hedge Fund: An Interview with the Managing Partner of Maverick Capital," *McKinsey on Finance*, no. 19 (Spring 2006): 6–11.

Traders don't need to develop a point of view on a company's intrinsic value, just on whether its shares will go up or down in the very short term. For example, traders may develop a view that a drug company is about to announce good news about a product trial that will boost the company's share price. The trader would buy the shares, wait for the announcement and the subsequent rise in the share price, and then immediately unwind the position. Some traders are in and out of the same stock many times during the year. This does not mean that traders don't understand the companies or industries they invest in; on the contrary, they follow the news about these companies closely and often approach companies directly, seeking nuances or insights that could matter greatly in the short term. However, they don't take a view on companies' long-term strategies and business performance.

Mechanical investors control about 25 to 30 percent of institutional equity in the United States. They make decisions based on strict criteria or rules. Index funds are the prototypical mechanical investor, merely building their portfolios by matching the composition of an index such as the S&P 500. Another group of mechanical investors are the so-called quantitative investors, who use mathematical models to build their portfolios and make no qualitative judgments on a company's intrinsic value.

Finally, *closet indexers*, although they are promoted as active managers, have portfolios that look like an index. Basing their portfolio on an index and making some adjustments, they hold a great many stocks and don't have the time and resources to do in-depth research on them.[4] By contrast, intrinsic investors know every company in their portfolios in depth and build their portfolios from scratch, without taking their cue from any index.

The extent to which an investment fund might be considered a closet indexer is now measured, and often published, using a metric called active share. Active share is a measure of how much an investment portfolio differs from its benchmark index, based on a scale of 0 percent (complete overlap with the index) to 100 percent (no overlap). An index fund would have an active share of 0 percent. Funds with active shares below 60 percent are often considered closet indexers. For example, while the William Blair Growth Fund, mentioned earlier as an intrinsic investor, typically has an active share above 70 percent, Putnam Investors Fund typically has an active share of about 40 percent. Antti Petajisto, a researcher and fund manager who taught at the Yale School of Management, has estimated that the percentage of funds that might be considered closet indexers increased from 1 percent in 1980 to almost 30 percent in 2009.[5]

---

[4] For more on closet index funds, see M. Cremers and A. Petajisto, "How Active Is Your Fund Manager? A New Measure That Predicts Performance" (paper presented at American Finance Association 2007 Chicago Meetings, January 15, 2007); and E. Khusainova and J. Mier, *Taking a Closer Look at Active Share*, Lazard Asset Management, September 2017, www.lazardassetmanagement.com.

[5] A. Petajisto, "Active Share and Mutual Fund Performance," December 2010, available at SSRN: http://ssrn.com/abstract=1685942 or http://dx.doi.org/10.2139/ssrn.1685942.

Targeting Communications by Segment

Which of these investors matter most for the stock price? Analyzing the trading behavior of all four investor groups in more detail, we find support for the idea that intrinsic investors are the ultimate drivers of share prices over the long term.

Exhibit 34.3 helps make the case, setting aside the inherently short-term-focused mechanical investors and closet indexers. At face value, traders might seem to be the most likely candidates for influencing share price in the market. They own 35 to 40 percent of the institutional U.S. equity base, and as the first two columns show, they trade much more than intrinsic investors. Their overall transaction volume is made up of many more trades—of which many are trades in the same stock within relatively short time periods. The average trader fund bought and sold over $80 billion worth of shares in 2006, more than 12 times the amount traded by the typical intrinsic investor. Similarly, as shown in the third column, the typical trader also buys or sells around $277 million in each equity stock he or she holds—far more per stock than the average intrinsic investor.

But the last column in the exhibit, which shows the value of effective daily trading per investment on the days that an investor traded at all, is the figure that discloses the real impact of each investor group on share prices in the market. Effective daily trading is higher by far among intrinsic investors: *when intrinsic investors trade, they buy or sell in much larger quantities than traders do.* Although they trade much less frequently than the traders group, they hold much larger percentages of the companies in their portfolios, so when they do trade, they can move the prices of these companies' shares. Ultimately, therefore, intrinsic investors are the most important investor group for setting prices in the market over the longer term.

As a result, companies should focus their investor communications effort on intrinsic investors. If intrinsic investors' view of the value of your company is consistent with your own view, the market as a whole is likely to value

EXHIBIT 34.3 **Intrinsic Investors Have Greatest Impact on Share Price**

	Total trading per year			Effective trading per day[1]
	Per segment, $ trillion	Per investor,[2] $ billion	Per investment,[3] $ million	Per investment,[3] $ million
Intrinsic	3	6	72	7–30
Trader	11	88	277	1

[1] Trading activity in segment per day that trade is made.

[2] Per investor in segment.

[3] Per investor in segment per investment.

Source: R. Palter, W. Rehm, and J. Shih, "Communicating with the Right Investors," *McKinsey on Finance*, no. 27 (Spring 2008): 1–5.

your company as you do, because of the role intrinsic investors play in driving share prices. Their understanding of long-term value creation also means they're more likely than other investors to hold on to a stock, supporting the management team through periods of short-term volatility (so long as they believe these periods do not reflect a material change in the underlying value of the company). These are the investors to whom you should listen when you want to understand what the market thinks of your company.

A conundrum for companies is how to treat closet indexers, because they may be some of a company's largest investors. Remember, a closet indexer is likely to have more than 200 different companies in his or her portfolio, and most of this investor's holdings are in proportion to the company's size in an index such as the S&P 500. Our first step is to examine whether the closet indexer is significantly over- or underweight in any company or industry. If the answer is yes, we move them to the intrinsic category with respect to that company or industry. If not, we keep the investor categorized with the closet indexers.

CEOs and CFOs have substantial demands on their time, and investors worry when they spend too much time with investors instead of running the company. Just as a CEO must decide which customers to spend time with, CEOs and CFOs must proactively decide which investors will get their time. Our investor segmentation makes it clear that CEOs and CFOs should focus their time on a small set of intrinsic investors, and delegate interactions with trading investors and closet indexers to their investor relations executives. In fact, one of the key roles of the investor relations department should be to determine analytically which investors CEOs and CFOs should develop relationships with, facilitate those relationships, and be the gatekeeper who handles low-priority investors on behalf of the CEO or CFO. The gatekeeper role may not be popular with investors, but it's essential.

Of course, CEOs and CFOs can't ignore the sell-side analysts, whose role has changed over time. Their job is to support their clients, and their most important clients are those who generate the most trading commissions—the trading-oriented investors. Many sophisticated trading (and intrinsic) investors are less concerned about whether the analyst has issued a buy or a hold on a stock (sell recommendations are almost nonexistent), preferring up-to-date news about the company. Hence, sell-side analysts tend to focus on short-term events and near-term earnings so they can be first to pass the news to their clients.

This said, there are often one to three sell-side analysts with deep understanding of the industry dynamics and the company's strategies, opportunities, and risks. These sell-side analysts resemble intrinsic investors in their approach. The logical way to treat sell-side analysts is to segment them into those whose interests and approach tend to mimic trading investors and those whose approach mimics intrinsic investors, and then to pay more attention to the latter segment.

COMMUNICATING WITH INTRINSIC INVESTORS

Intrinsic investors are sophisticated and have spent considerable effort to understand your business. They want transparency about results, management's candid assessment of the company's performance, and insightful guidance about the company's targets and strategies. Their role in determining stock prices makes it worth management's time to address intrinsic investors' desire for clear, well-informed communication.

What Investors Want

In 2015, McKinsey and the Aspen Institute Business and Society Program surveyed and interviewed intrinsic investors to find out what was important to them.[6] One highlight from the survey was intrinsic investors' overwhelming support of companies' efforts to pursue long-term value, even at the expense of short-term earnings. A second highlight was that intrinsic investors expressed a desire for managers to provide what the investors called education about companies' strategies and the dynamics of their industries.

Intrinsic investors overwhelmingly favor decisions that lead to long-term value creation even at the expense of short-term earnings shortfalls. The McKinsey–Aspen survey presented an investment scenario in which a U.S.-based company that earns 70 percent of its revenues and profits abroad experienced a major decline in short-term profits because of a large shift in foreign-exchange rates. Respondents answered questions about their support for a range of potential management decisions. Out of 24 intrinsic investors, 19 said they would be neutral if the company took no action and simply reported lower profits, while nearly two-thirds said they would take a negative view of an order for across-the-board cost reductions. Intrinsic investors realize that companies can't control or predict exchange rates, and they don't want companies to cut costs arbitrarily to meet current earnings expectations if it might hurt the business later. Twenty-one out of 23 intrinsic investors negatively viewed accelerating cost cutting in the following year to keep earnings rising (assuming exchange rates stayed the same), if long-term revenues could be negatively affected. In subsequent interviews, some investors noted that this could lead to a downward spiral of shrinking investments and revenue growth. In another scenario, a new CEO decides to continue operating a legacy unit even though it is a money loser with no expectation of turning profitable. Seventeen out of 24 investors had a negative view of sustaining the unit to avoid recognizing the shutdown costs, while 20 were neutral or positive about the company shutting it down despite the one-time hit to earnings. Most favored an attempt to divest the unit in the CEO's first year on the job; the only dissenter worried that year 1 might be too soon.

---

[6] This section is from R. Darr and T. Koller, "How to Build an Alliance against Corporate Short-Termism," *McKinsey on Finance*, no. 61 (2017): 2–9.

These investors said they favor companies with executive teams that are confident about telling their companies' stories in the way the teams see them, proactively choosing how, what, and when to communicate. Many of our survey panelists considered this approach the opposite of what many companies do today. To paraphrase one investor, "An exceptional CEO knows what I need to know and tries to persuade me of that. He or she doesn't try to guess what I want to hear."

Intrinsic investors expressed this as a desire for what they called education. One investor told us, "I just need to be educated. Help me understand your business and strategy. If I disagree, I don't have to invest." They want to know what a company's competitive advantages are and how its strategy builds on those advantages. They want to know what external and competitive forces a company faces. And they want to know what concrete actions, including talent management, the company is taking to realize its aspirations. They don't want sugarcoating, opacity, or "selling." They interpret overly elaborate presentations as suggesting a potential lack of substance.

Investors also said they want to learn how CEOs make decisions, whether a company's approach is aligned with long-term value creation, and whether the whole management team is singing from the same song sheet. This is not surprising, given that 23 out of 24 long-term investors taking the survey identified management credibility as one of the most important factors to consider in making investments. Management credibility includes both clarity of decision making and openness when not everything goes well. One investor put it this way: "There are always bumps in the road. You earn trust and respect by not trying to sugarcoat. That doesn't mean the stock price won't go down. But it will mean the recovery will be better because investors will have more confidence in managers who are level-headed and matter-of-fact." Said another investor, "I get them to talk about something other than what's in their pitch book. I want to know how they think. For example, what's their rationale for a particular decision that will increase value?" Another common theme, which is supported by research in behavioral psychology, is that managers would do well to ensure that the long term and its context are part of every investor engagement, especially when talking about short-term results. This approach starts with the long term as the wide lens on a business and then zooms in on the details as needed. As one investor said, "It's all about the horizon. Long-term investors don't need a lot of detailed guidance about quarterly numbers. They need clarity, consistency, and transparency from managers in communicating strategic priorities and their long-term expectations."

Benefits of Transparency

Many companies are reluctant to provide a detailed discussion of results, issues, and opportunities. Their rationale is that this kind of disclosure reduces their flexibility to manage reported profits or will reveal sensitive information to competitors. In our experience, however, a company's competitors, customers, and suppliers already know more about any business than its managers might expect. For example, there's a cottage industry of photographers dedicated to searching for and publicizing new car models that automotive manufacturers have not yet formally acknowledged. In addition, a company's competitors will be talking regularly to the company's customers and suppliers, who won't hesitate to share information about the company whenever that's in their interest. Therefore, revealing details about yourself is unlikely to affect your company as adversely as you might expect. Managers should keep that in mind as they assess the competitive costs and benefits of greater transparency.

In some situations, companies might even be able to gain an advantage over their competitors by being more transparent. Suppose a company has developed a new technology, product, or manufacturing process that management feels sure will give the company a lead over competitors. Furthermore, managers believe competitors will be unable to copy the innovation. At a strategic level, disclosing the innovation might discourage competitors from even trying to compete, if they believe the company has too great a lead. From an investor's perspective, disclosure of the innovation could increase the company's share price relative to its competitors, thus making it more attractive to potential partners and key employees, as well as reducing the price of stock-based acquisitions.

Sophisticated investors build up their view of a company's overall value by summing the values of its discrete businesses. They're not much concerned with aggregate results: these are simply averages, providing little insight into how the company's individual businesses might be positioned for future growth and returns on invested capital. At many companies, management teams that desire a closer match between their company's market value and their own assessment might achieve this by disclosing more about the performances of their individual businesses.

Ideally, companies should provide an income statement for each business unit, down to the level of EBITA at least. They should also provide all operating items in the balance sheet—such as property, plant, and equipment (PP&E) and working capital—reconciled with the consolidated reported numbers. Even companies with a single line of business can improve their disclosures without giving away strategically sensitive information. In the period when it was growing quickly and before it was acquired by Amazon in 2017, Whole Foods Market, a U.S. natural-foods supermarket chain, provided investors with its ROIC numbers by age of store, as well as a detailed table explaining how it calculated its returns. Such openness gives investors deeper insights into the company's economic life cycle.

Concerning operational data, what to disclose depends on the key value drivers of a business or business unit. Ideally, these should be the metrics that management uses to make strategic or operational decisions. For example, each quarter, the leading research and advisory firm Gartner discloses a narrow but highly relevant set of metrics for each of its three business units. As Gartner's CFO explains, the firm publishes only the most important of the metrics that management uses to examine the performance of the business. Similarly, companies in some industries, such as steel and airlines, regularly disclose volumes and average prices, as well as the use and cost of energy, which are the key drivers of value in these sectors. Home improvement retailer Lowe's provides helpful information about key value drivers such as the number of transactions and the average ticket size, as shown in Exhibit 34.4.

Choosing transparency can be difficult. Some companies that have preferred greater discretion hesitate to increase openness. These are often strong performers with good track records. Over many years, that performance record (frequently in the form of steady earnings increases) has provided leverage to rebuff investors' demands for more transparency. But it is the nature of every business's life cycle that growth will slow even after years of success as the business matures or markets become more competitive. At that juncture, the company needs new strategies to keep creating value for shareholders, and these changes should be communicated to investors; doing so ensures that the market share price continues to reflect the company's true worth.

In one situation, a large company didn't disclose that most of its profits came from aging, low-growth products with a large installed base, while its newer high-growth products were far less profitable due to competition and new technologies. In another case, a consumer products company kept its earnings growing by selectively reducing investments in advertising and promotion. Because both companies had long histories of success, any sudden disclosure of these changes would surely cause their stock prices to decline sharply; academic research suggests that when companies in these circumstances fall, they fall hard.[7]

EXHIBIT 34.4 **Lowe's: Operating Statistics and ROIC**

	2016	2017	2018
Comparable sales increase, %	4.2	4.0	2.4
Customer transactions, millions	945	953	941
Average ticket, $	68.83	72.00	75.79
Number of stores	2,129	2,152	2,015
Sales floor square feet, millions	213	215	209
Average store size, selling square feet, thousands	100	100	104
Return on invested capital, %	15.8	18.8	12.8

Source: Company SEC filings.

[7] D. J. Skinner and R. G. Sloan, "Earnings Surprises, Growth Expectations, and Stock Returns, or Don't Let an Earnings Torpedo Sink Your Portfolio," *Review of Accounting Studies* 7 (2002): 289–312. See also J. N. Myers, L. A. Myers, and D. J. Skinner, "Earnings Momentum and Earnings Management" (working paper, August 2006), available at http://ssrn.com/abstract=741244.

Executives at such companies need to decide whether their current predicament will be short-lived or if the days of strong growth and high returns are, in fact, over. If the latter, the executives clearly need a quick transition plan. If the former, they need to assess whether they should practice greater transparency and accept the likely price volatility it will cause until they've returned to their growth path.

Legislation and accounting rules have been requiring ever-greater transparency. Even so, results that are transparent enough to meet today's regulatory requirements may fail to meet the standard of transparency that satisfies intrinsic investors. Companies within an industry typically start to disclose information more useful to such investors in response to the investors' explicit demands or the leadership of one or more industry pioneers. For example, the petroleum industry has for many years published detailed fact books that describe oil production and reserves by geography—key parameters that investors want to know when valuing petroleum companies. In pharmaceuticals, companies provide detailed information about their product pipelines at every stage of research and development. In these industries, any company that failed to disclose what others disclose would likely lose the market's trust.

In most industries, however, the level of disclosure and transparency has been less standardized, so management must choose how transparent it wants to be. In these cases, managers are too often cowed by fears that a detailed discussion of the issues and opportunities facing their company will reveal sensitive information to competitors or make it harder to put the best gloss on their results. One large global electronics company, for example, reports gross margins for both its product and services businesses. But nowhere does it provide operating margins for the different units—information that is crucial to helping investors value businesses with differing levels of expenditure on R&D and selling, general, and administrative costs. In another case, a U.S. media conglomerate provides detailed information by business unit on the income statement but leaves it to investors to sort out the balance sheet by business unit. Failing to report such information often gives investors the impression that management is trying to obscure some underlying performance issues.

LISTENING TO INVESTORS

The final element of effective investor communications is listening to investors. Listening to gain competitive intelligence is, of course, a no-lose proposition. But to what extent should executives be influenced by investors' opinions about what strategies the company should pursue (expressed either as opinions or by the nature of the questions the investors ask), particularly when those opinions run counter to what the senior executives believe is the best strategy for creating long-term value?

The answer lies again in the segmentation of the investors and the interpretation of investor input in light of the investors' own strategies. For example, trading investors, who tend to be the most vocal and frequent voices, base their trading strategies on *events*. So they prefer frequent announcements and short-term actions to create trading opportunities. Intrinsic investors, in contrast, are more concerned with longer-term strategic initiatives and the broader forces driving the company and industry. Segmenting investor input helps executives sort through the competing views. We typically find that when executives segment the input they receive from investors, the input from the intrinsic investors is most helpful.

In the end, though, executives have more information than investors about their company, its capabilities, opportunities, and threats. They need to be confident about their strategic choices and convey that confidence to investors. You can't expect to please all investors. You must do what's right for long-term value creation.

EARNINGS GUIDANCE

Many executives view the ritual of issuing guidance on their likely earnings per share (EPS) in the next quarter or year as a necessary, if sometimes onerous, part of communicating with financial markets. In a survey, we found that they saw three primary benefits of issuing earnings guidance: higher valuations, lower share price volatility, and improved liquidity. Yet several analyses found no evidence that those expected benefits materialize.[8] Therefore, instead of EPS guidance, we believe executives should provide investors with the broader operational measures shaping company performance, such as volume targets, revenue targets, and initiatives to reduce costs.

No Payoff for Earnings Guidance

It's a myth that quarterly EPS guidance is necessary and that almost everyone does it. In 2002, Coca-Cola became one of the earliest large companies to stop issuing guidance. Its executives had concluded that providing short-term guidance prevented management from concentrating on strategic initiatives to build its businesses over the long term. Gary Fayard, CFO at that time, believed that, rather than indicating weak earnings, the move signaled a renewed focus on long-term goals. The market seemed to agree and did not react negatively: Coke's share price held steady.[9] Since then, many other companies

---

[8] P. Hsieh, T. Koller, and S. Rajan, "The Misguided Practice of Earnings Guidance," *McKinsey on Finance* (Spring 2006): 1–5; and A. Babcock and S. Williamson, *Moving beyond Quarterly Guidance: A Relic of the Past*, FCLTGlobal, October 2017, www.fcltglobal.org.

[9] D. M. Katz, "Nothing but the Real Thing," *CFO*, March 2003, cfo.com.

have stopped providing guidance entirely or have shifted the focus of their guidance away from EPS and toward broader indicators of performance. In fact, in 2016, only 28 percent of S&P 500 companies provided quarterly EPS guidance, while 31 percent gave only annual guidance. Forty-one percent gave no EPS guidance.[10] In Europe, the share of companies providing EPS guidance is much lower: only 4 percent of the Eurostoxx 300.

To test whether companies providing EPS guidance are rewarded with higher valuations, we compared the earnings multiples of companies that provided guidance with the multiples of those that did not, industry by industry. For most industries, the underlying distributions of the two sets of companies were statistically indistinguishable. Similar results were found by researchers at the Harvard Business School and KKS Advisors.[11]

Companies that decide to begin offering guidance may hope the effort will boost total shareholder returns (TSR). Yet in the year companies begin to offer guidance, their TSR on average is no different from that of companies not offering guidance at all. Returns to shareholders are just as likely to be above the market as below the market in the year a company starts providing guidance.

On the issue of share price volatility, we found that when a company begins to issue earnings guidance, the likelihood of volatility in its share price increasing or decreasing is the same as it is for companies that don't issue guidance. Finally, we found that when companies begin issuing earnings guidance, they do indeed experience an increase in trading volumes relative to companies that don't provide it, as their management anticipates. However, the effect wears off the next year. The same results were found by the Harvard Business School researchers and KKS Advisors.[12]

When we asked executives about ceasing earnings guidance, many feared that their share price would decline and its volatility would increase. But when we analyzed 126 companies that had discontinued issuing guidance, we found they were just about as likely as the rest of the market to see higher or lower shareholder returns. Of the 126 companies, 58 had higher returns than the overall market in the year they stopped issuing guidance, and 68 had lower returns. Furthermore, our analysis showed that the lower-than-market returns of companies that discontinued guidance resulted from poor underlying performance, not from the act of ending guidance. For example, two-thirds of the companies that halted guidance and experienced lower returns on capital saw lower TSR than the market. For companies that increased ROIC, only about one-third had delivered lower TSR than the market.

Our conclusion was that issuing guidance offers companies and investors no real benefits. On the contrary, it can trigger real costs and unfortunate unintended consequences. The difficulty of predicting earnings accurately, for

---

[10] Babcock and Williamson, *Moving beyond Quarterly Guidance.*
[11] Babcock and Williamson, *Moving beyond Quarterly Guidance.*
[12] Babcock and Williamson, *Moving beyond Quarterly Guidance.*

example, frequently causes management teams to endure the painful experience of missing quarterly forecasts. That, in turn, can be a powerful incentive for management to focus excessive attention on the short term, at the expense of longer-term investments, and to manage earnings inappropriately from quarter to quarter to create the illusion of stability. Moreover, our research with intrinsic investors indicates that they realize that earnings are inherently unpredictable. Consequently, they prefer that companies not issue quarterly EPS guidance. Only 20 percent of intrinsic investors surveyed by McKinsey and the Aspen Institute said they would see a company's announced intention to discontinue earnings guidance one year from the announcement as a "yellow flag."[13] In a survey by the Rivel Research Group's Intelligence Council, just 7 percent of investors said that they want companies to offer guidance on any metrics at all (financial and operational) for periods less than one year.[14]

An Alternative to Earnings Guidance

As an alternative, we believe executives will gain advantages from providing guidance on the real short-, medium-, and long-term value drivers of their businesses, providing ranges rather than point estimates. For example, some companies provide target ranges for returns on capital. Other companies provide a range of possibilities for revenue growth under a variety of assumptions about inflation, and they discuss the growth of individual business units when that matters. Some companies also provide information on value drivers that can help investors assess the sustainability of growth. Humana, for example, provides guidance on estimated membership in its health plans, including plans whose membership the company expects will decline.

The value drivers a business chooses to publicize will depend on the unique characteristics of the business. For example, a leading project-based company provides details on the performance of individual current projects, plus the timing and expected returns of potential projects. One European company provides investors with a tax estimation tool, which uses the investors' assessments of regional growth rates to provide a best guess on the tax rates the company will face.

Ideally, a company would provide the kind of information that would help investors make their own projections of the company's performance based on their assessment of external factors. For example, in resource industries, prices are volatile for extracted commodities such as gold, copper, or oil. For such companies, a management team's view on future prices is not necessarily better than that of their investors. Investors would therefore find production targets more useful than revenue targets in these industries. Similarly, exchange

---

[13] Darr and Koller, "How to Build an Alliance."
[14] "Evolving Guidance Preferences: Attitudes and Practices of the Global Buy Side," Intelligence Council, Rivel Research Group, September 2017.

rates are unpredictable, yet they can affect the profits of multinationals by 5 percent or more in a given year. Companies should therefore avoid predicting exchange rates and locking them into EPS targets. Rather, they should discuss their targets at constant currency rates. This would give investors a much clearer picture of expected performance.

MEETING CONSENSUS EARNINGS FORECASTS

Whether or not a company provides guidance, there will be an analyst consensus earnings forecast to meet or beat.[15] The conventional wisdom, mistaken though it is, is that missing the consensus earnings forecast, even by a small amount, means that your share price will drop. A striking example: in early 2005, when eBay reported that it had missed the fourth-quarter 2004 consensus estimate by just one penny, its share price plunged 22 percent. Conversely, many executives believe that consistently beating the consensus leads to a premium share price. Thus, a common reason given for choosing to provide earnings guidance is to influence the consensus.

Besides trying to influence the consensus, executives often go to some lengths to meet or beat consensus estimates—even acting in ways that could damage the longer-term health of the business. It's not uncommon, for example, for companies to offer customers steep discounts in the final days of a reporting period in order to stoke sales numbers, in effect borrowing from the next quarter's sales. As other researchers have shown, executives may forgo value-creating investments in favor of short-term results,[16] or they might manage earnings inappropriately to create the illusion of stability.

Yet our analysis of large U.S. companies shows that these fears are unfounded.[17] In the near term, falling short of consensus earnings estimates is seldom catastrophic. Even consistently beating or meeting consensus estimates over several years does not matter, once differences in companies' growth and operating performance are considered. In fact, a company's performance relative to consensus earnings seems to matter only when the company consistently misses earnings estimates over several years.

This doesn't mean that companies should ignore consensus estimates, which can hint at what is on investors' minds and why. For example, how does the industry growth outlook of investors compare with that of executives? The consensus can also be used to assess how well analysts and

---

[15] The section is adapted from T. Koller, R. Raj, and A. Saxena, "Avoiding the Consensus Earnings Trap," *McKinsey on Finance*, no. 45 (Winter 2013).

[16] J. R. Graham, C. Harvey, and S. Rajgopal, "Value Destruction and Financial Reporting Decisions," *Financial Analysts Journal* 62 (2006): 27–39, which found that a majority of CFOs would "avoid initiating a positive NPV project if it meant falling short of the current quarter's consensus earnings."

[17] This conclusion is based on analysis of the largest U.S.-based nonfinancial companies with a December 31 fiscal year-end, a sample of 266 companies.

investors understand the drivers of a company's performance. Our findings demonstrate that when investors are valuing a company, they consider more indicators of financial health than just whether the company meets its consensus earnings estimates. Thus, companies need not go to extremes to meet or beat analysts' expectations if it means damaging the long-term prospects of the company.

When Companies Fall Short

Most executives haven't personally experienced many catastrophic drops in share price after minor earnings misses, so they conclude that such misses are rare. The mechanics of earnings estimates lend some support to that perception. After all, analysts' estimates typically are overly optimistic at the beginning of the financial year, but by the third quarter, it's reasonable to expect them to fall roughly in line with the eventual reported earnings—a pattern borne out by previous research.[18] According to standard practice, a company has beaten the consensus estimate if its actual earnings are greater than the last available estimate for the year (almost always projected after the year is over). Consequently, one would expect analyst estimates at that stage to be accurate. Moreover, executives tend to focus on dramatic press accounts of earnings mishaps that are among the most extreme outliers, as in the eBay example where barely missing the consensus forecast led to a sharp drop in share prices.

In fact, falling short is common, and the effect is benign. More than 40 percent of companies generate earnings below consensus estimates, whether those estimates are compiled an entire year or just three days before an earnings announcement. Although some academics have documented a correlation between the change in a company's share price before and after the announcement of earnings and the degree to which it meets the consensus earnings estimate, the size of the effect is small. Indeed, our analysis suggests that missing the consensus by 1 percent would lead to a share price decrease of only 0.2 percent in the five days after the announcement. In other words, missing the consensus estimate by a penny or so usually doesn't matter (despite the unusual case of eBay).

Executives concerned about their company's performance relative to consensus estimates should also consider that 40 percent of companies that saw their earnings miss the consensus estimate also saw their share price, adjusted for the market, move in the opposite direction. For example, when PPG Industries, a global supplier of paints, coatings, and chemicals, announced earnings for 2010 that were 4 percent below the consensus, the market reacted positively with an excess return of 7 percent. Why? On digging deeper, investors

[18] M. Goedhart, B. Russell, and Z. Williams, "Prophets and Profits" *McKinsey on Finance*, no. 2 (Autumn 2001): 11–14.

saw that the long-term outlook had improved. Sales were stronger than expected in nearly all business segments. The CEO also announced some investment initiatives that investors viewed as having the potential to create value in the longer term.

When Companies Meet or Beat the Consensus Forecast

Similarly, meeting or exceeding the consensus estimate is less important than how the earnings were reached. That's because investors are continually assessing other news, such as whether the company met the consensus estimate for revenues as well as earnings. When North American brewing company Molson Coors beat the consensus estimate by 2 percent in 2010, the market nevertheless reacted negatively, with an excess return of –7 percent. Investors saw that the company's sales volume had declined by 2 percent and that margins also were down; the company beat the consensus only because of a lower-than-expected tax rate. The market reacted to the fundamental drivers of performance—volume and margin—rather than EPS itself.

Investors are also able to see through cases where one-off items are responsible for meeting the consensus estimate. Meanwhile, earnings announcements themselves often include information that helps investors reassess a company's long-term performance outlook. Our research has shown that the market reaction at the time of an earnings announcement is influenced more by changes in analysts' expectations for longer-term earnings than by whether the most recent results met the consensus estimate. A company might fall short of current-year earnings estimates and still see its share price increase if analysts revised their earnings estimates upward for the next two years (see Exhibit 34.5).

EXHIBIT 34.5 **Impact of EPS vs. Earnings Surprise**

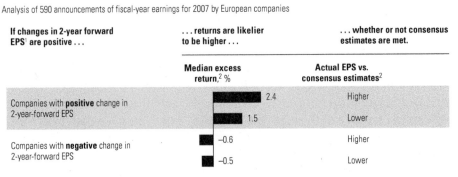

Analysis of 590 announcements of fiscal-year earnings for 2007 by European companies

If changes in 2-year forward EPS[1] are positive . . .	. . . returns are likelier to be higher . . .	. . . whether or not consensus estimates are met.
	Median excess return,[2] %	Actual EPS vs. consensus estimates[2]
Companies with **positive** change in 2-year-forward EPS	2.4	Higher
	1.5	Lower
Companies with **negative** change in 2-year-forward EPS	–0.6	Higher
	–0.5	Lower

[1] Earnings per share.

[2] Excess return over market return.

[3] Sample size: posititve and lower = 127, positive and higher = 203, negative and lower =118, negative and higher = 142.

EXHIBIT 34.6 **Fundamentals vs. Consensus Estimates**

Median excess return vs. sector return,[1] 2005–2011, %

	High growth + high ROIC[3]	High growth + low ROIC[3]	Low growth + high ROIC[3]	Low growth + low ROIC[3]
Consistently beating[2]	4	3	0	–2
Inconsistent[2]	2	0	0	–3
Consistently missing[2]	0	–5	–5	–6

[1] Company's total shareholder returns (TSR) minus median TSR of the sector. Sample size is 243 nonfinancial S&P 500 companies with December fiscal year-end.

[2] Difference between actual earnings per share and consensus estimate 30 days prior to earnings announcement. "Consistently beating" defined as beating expectations by >2% at least 4 out of 7 years, 2005–2011. "Consistently missing" defined as missing expectations by >2% at least 4 out of 7 years. Companies consistently meeting expectations (by +/– 2% at least 4 out of 7 years) are not shown due to small sample size.

[3] ROIC = return on invested capital (2005–2011); growth = compound annual growth rate of revenue (2004–2011). Companies categorized as high ROIC or high growth exceeded the absolute reference points of 15% for ROIC and 7% for growth or the median of the respective sector in the sample.

Source: Standard & Poor's Capital IQ.

Just as critical, the notion that markets reward companies with higher share prices when they consistently beat the earnings consensus turns out to be wrong. Here again, while some researchers have found this to be true, their analysis doesn't take into consideration the underlying performance of companies as measured by revenue growth and return on capital.[19] Once adjusted for performance, the apparent effect of beating the consensus consistently (which we define as four or more years out of seven) disappears. Companies with strong growth or ROIC had high shareholder returns regardless of whether they consistently beat the consensus. Only the companies that missed it consistently—again, in four years out of seven—showed a statistically significant negative effect from doing so (see Exhibit 34.6).

SUMMARY

The issues surrounding investor communications will remain unresolved for some time. Traditionally, there have been two camps: those who believe you can talk up your share price and those who believe companies shouldn't

[19] See, for example, R. Kasznik and M. McNichols, "Does Meeting Earnings Expectations Matter? Evidence from Analyst Forecast Revisions and Share Prices," *Journal of Accounting Research* 40, no. 3 (June 2002): 727–759.

spend much time or effort on investor communications at all, because it won't make any difference to their market value. Our view is, first, that investors can more accurately value a company if they have the right information and, second, that a market value aligned with the true value of your company is the best outcome of your investor communications strategy. Moreover, even if you do manage to talk up the stock in the short term, this is unlikely to be the best thing for the company in the long run.

You can better align your company's stock market value with its intrinsic value by applying some of the systematic approaches described in this chapter for identifying value, understanding your current and potential investors, and communicating with the sophisticated investors who ultimately drive a company's share price. These principles also can help managers use their scarce time for investor communications more efficiently and effectively.

Moreover, rather than providing precise earnings guidance or taking actions to achieve consensus earnings forecasts, managers should focus on driving return on invested capital (ROIC) and growth to create maximum value for shareholders. Managers should not be distracted from their efforts to drive ROIC and growth by any short-term price volatility—that is, any temporary deviation in their share price from its intrinsic value—because such deviations are likely to occur from time to time, even in the most efficient stock market.

Part Five

Special Situations

35

Emerging Markets*

The world's emerging economies, home of 86 percent of the population, accounted for about 59 percent of global GDP in 2017 and are growing faster than the developed economies.[1] As emerging markets become more important to the global economy and to investors, sound methods are needed for analyzing and valuing companies and business units in these markets.

Chapters 26 and 27 discussed general issues related to forecasting cash flows, estimating the cost of capital in a foreign currency, and incorporating high inflation rates into cash flow projections. This chapter focuses on additional issues that arise in emerging markets, such as the potential for extreme economic contractions or unexpected government actions like asset appropriation. It is impossible to generalize about these risks, as they differ by country and may affect businesses in different ways. Academics, investment bankers, and industry practitioners subscribe to different methods and often make arbitrary adjustments based on intuition and limited empirical evidence.

For accurate valuation of companies in emerging markets, we recommend using a scenario discounted-cash-flow (DCF) approach as described in Chapter 16 to prepare multiple cash flow scenarios reflecting the outcomes of different risks that a company could face. These scenarios are each discounted and then weighted by probabilities assigned to each. You can supplement this method by comparing the results with two secondary approaches: a DCF valuation with a country risk premium built into the cost of capital and a valuation based on the multiples of comparable companies.

* The authors would like thank Andre Gaeta, Daniel Guzman, Paulo Guimaraes, Joao Lopes Sousa, and Barbara Castro for their contributions to this chapter.
[1] China's and India's shares of global GDP, at purchasing parity prices (PPP), were 19 and 8 percent, respectively, and 19 and 18 percent of population, respectively. International Monetary Fund, "GDP Based on PPP, Share of World," IMF DataMapper, imf.org.

WHY SCENARIO DCF IS MORE ACCURATE THAN RISK PREMIUMS

The most vigorously debated issue about valuing companies in emerging markets is whether to incorporate a country risk premium in the cost of capital. A common practice has been to add a country risk premium to the discount rate to account for the higher risks of operating in emerging markets.[2] Often, the premium is based on the government's borrowing rate relative to a benchmark, such as the borrowing rates for the U.S. government.

A major problem with this approach is that the riskiness of lending to a government may have little to do with the risk of investing in a business. It is possible for a company to have a cost of equity that is lower than the interest rate on the government debt in the country. This seems counterintuitive, but compare the riskiness of a consumer packaged-goods (CPG) producer in an emerging market versus the government debt of that country. The CPG producer may experience a large drop in earnings during an economic crisis, but it typically springs back relatively quickly. And in contrast to the political environment facing banks and mining or energy companies, CPG businesses face little risk of appropriation by the government. With regard to government debt, however, it's not unusual for governments to default. Since 1990, Russia and Argentina have each defaulted, and oil-rich Nigeria has defaulted three times. Even Greece required bailout loans from the International Monetary Fund and European Central bank in 2010, 2012, and 2015. It's also possible that the cost of debt for some companies is lower than that of their government, as is the case in Brazil, where a number of companies' debt is rated investment grade while the government's is not.

Furthermore, it's illogical to apply the same risk premium across all industries. CPG producers generally survive economic disruptions, while banks may go bankrupt. For example, over the period 2013–2018, Brazilian ten-year government bonds were more volatile than beverage company Ambev and less volatile than the major Brazilian banks. Some companies (raw-materials exporters) might benefit from a currency devaluation, while others (raw-materials importers) will be damaged.

We've also found that the country risk premiums used in practice are too high and lead to overcompensation in the company's projected performance. Analysts using high premiums frequently compensate by making aggressive forecasts for growth and return on invested capital (ROIC). An example is the valuation we undertook of a large Brazilian chemicals company. Using a local weighted average cost of capital (WACC) of 10 percent, we reached an enterprise value of 4.0 to 4.5 times earnings before interest, taxes, depreciation, and amortization (EBITDA). A second adviser was asked to value the company

---

[2] T. Keck, E. Levengood, and A. Longfield, "Using Discounted Cash Flow Analysis in an International Setting: A Survey of Issues in Modeling the Cost of Capital," *Journal of Applied Corporate Finance* 11, no. 3 (1998): 82–99.

and came to a similar valuation—an EBITDA multiple of around 4.5—despite using a very high country risk premium of 11 percent on top of the WACC. The result was similar because the second adviser made performance assumptions that were far too aggressive: real sales growth of almost 10 percent per year and a ROIC increasing to 46 percent in the long term. Such long-term performance assumptions are unrealistic for a commodity-based, competitive industry such as chemicals. In another, broader set of analyst forecasts from 2015 to 2018, 30 percent of industries were expected to achieve growth rates more than 20 percent, while in the United States, only 5 percent were expected to achieve similar results. It's hard to imagine 30 percent of industries growing more than 20 percent per year.

These are among the reasons we favor a scenario DCF approach to valuing emerging-markets companies. It allows you to focus on company-specific risks, not generic risks.

Our empirical research also shows that there isn't much of a country risk premium built into the valuation of stocks in some emerging markets. If there were a substantial country risk premium, we'd expect price-to-earnings ratios (P/Es) to be much smaller than they are.

Consider Brazil. Over the past decade, many valuations we've seen have incorporated country risk premiums of 3 to 5 percent, plus an inflation differential versus U.S. companies of about 2 to 3 percent. That leads to a cost of equity of 15 to 18 percent. From 2015 to 2018, the P/E for the major Brazilian market index has been in the range of 10 to 17 times. Going back to the value driver formula derived in Chapter 3, we can solve for the expected growth in earnings, given estimates for the other values:

$$\frac{P}{E} = \left(1 - \frac{g}{\text{ROE}}\right) / (k_e - g)$$

where g is the growth rate of earnings, ROE is return on equity, and k_e is the cost of equity.

If we assume a P/E of 12 times, a cost of equity of 15 percent, and a marginal return on equity of 20 percent (above historical averages), the implied growth rate of earnings in perpetuity would have to be about 11.5 percent nominal, or about 7.5 percent in real terms (assuming 4 percent inflation, based on 2 percent in the United States and two percentage points higher inflation in Brazil). But 7.5 percent real growth in perpetuity is clearly unrealistic.

Looked at another way, if we assume 3.5 percent real growth in earnings in perpetuity (an optimistic view), the implied P/E at a 15 percent cost of equity is 8.3 times, which is about 30 percent lower than current P/Es. It's impossible to come up with a consistent set of assumptions that ties together a P/E of 12 and 15 percent cost of equity.

If we eliminate the country risk premium, our results work mathematically and economically. We'll use 2016 as an example and solve for the implied cost of equity. The P/E was about 13 times. Assuming 3.5 percent long-term real growth plus 4 percent inflation and a 14 percent ROE, we calculate a nominal cost of equity of about 11 percent. Subtracting inflation at 4 percent gives us a 7 percent real cost of equity, not very different from the real cost of equity of the United States (see Chapter 15).

Of course, these results are highly sensitive to small changes in some of the assumptions. The key point is that it is very difficult to reconcile current P/Es with a country risk premium of 3 percent or more. Exhibit 35.1 shows a time series of implied costs of equity for the Brazilian index over the ten years from 2009 to 2018. The nominal cost of equity stays within a range of 10 to 12 percent, or about 6 to 8 percent real. An implied country risk premium for Brazil is more likely to be closer to 1 percent than 3 to 5 percent.

One reason country risk premiums should be lower than levels used by many is that many country risks, including expropriation, devaluation, and war, are largely diversifiable. Consider the international consumer-goods player illustrated in Exhibit 35.2. Its returns on invested capital were highly volatile for individual emerging markets. Taken together, however, these markets were hardly more volatile than developed markets; the corporate portfolio diversified away most of the risks. Finance theory clearly indicates that the cost of capital should not reflect risk that can be diversified. This does not mean that diversifiable risk is irrelevant for a valuation: the possibility of adverse future events will affect the level of expected cash flows. But once this has been incorporated into the forecast for cash flows, there is no need for an additional markup of the cost of capital if the risk is diversifiable.

EXHIBIT 35.1 **Low Variability in Implied Cost of Equity**

Brazilian implied cost of equity, nominal[1]
%

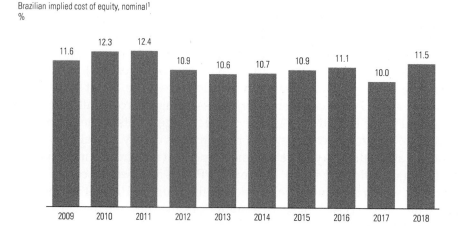

[1] Assuming average prior 10-year ROE, 4.0% long-term inflation, 3.5% long-term real profit growth.
Source: Capital IQ.

EXHIBIT 35.2 **Returns on a Diverse Emerging-Market Portfolio**

Select individual emerging-market returns on capital[1]

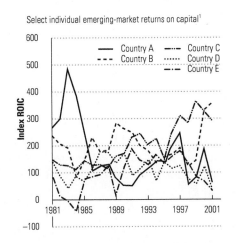

Combined portfolio returns on capital[2]

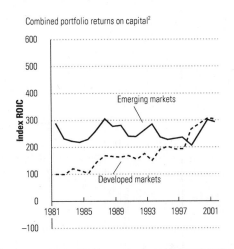

[1] In stable currency and adjusted for local accounting differences.

[2] Combined portfolio included additional countries not reflected here.

Source: Company information.

Finally, most of us underestimate the impact that even a small country risk premium has on valuations, as we will show in the next section.

APPLYING THE SCENARIO DCF APPROACH

The preceding analysis of the Brazilian cost of equity masks a wide variation in P/Es across the economy. That's where the scenario DCF approach proves its advantages; it allows you to assess the risk of each company based on company-specific risk factors. At a minimum, model two scenarios. The first should assume that cash flow develops according to conditions reflecting business as usual (i.e., without major economic distress). The second should reflect cash flows assuming that one or more emerging-market risks materialize.

Exhibit 35.3 compares the valuation of a company with a European factory and an emerging-market factory with a similar outlook except for the emerging-market risk. In the example, the cash flows for the European factory grow steadily at 3 percent per year into perpetuity. For the factory in the emerging market, the cash flow growth is the same under a business-as-usual scenario, but there is a 25 percent probability of economic distress resulting in a cash flow that is 55 percent lower into perpetuity. The emerging-market risk is taken into account, not in the cost of capital but in the lower expected value of future cash flows from weighting both scenarios by the assumed probabilities. The resulting value of the emerging-market factory (€1,917) is clearly below the value of its European sister factory (€2,222), using a WACC of 7.5 percent.

EXHIBIT 35.3 **Scenario DCF vs. Country Risk Premium DCF**

€

Net present value for identical facilities in . . .

. . . a European market

Scenario approach

Cash flows in perpetuity[1]

	Probability	Year 1	2	3	4	...
"As usual"	100%	100	103	106	109	...
"Distressed"	0%					

Expected cash flows

		100	103	106	109	

Cost of capital 7.5%
Net present value 2,222

Country risk premium approach

Cash flows in perpetuity[1]

	Year 1	2	3	4	...
"As usual"	100	103	106	109	...

Cost of capital 7.5%
Net present value 2,222

. . . an emerging market

Scenario approach

Cash flows in perpetuity[2]

	Probability	Year 1	2	3	4	...
"As usual"	75%	100	103	106	109	...
"Distressed"	25%	45	46	48	49	

Expected cash flows

		86	89	92	94	

Cost of capital 7.5%
Net present value 1,917 → 86% of European NPV

Country risk premium approach

Cash flows in perpetuity[2]

	Year 1	2	3	4	...
"As usual"	100	103	106	109	...

Cost of capital 7.5%
Country risk premium 0.7%
Adjusted cost of capital 8.2%
Net present value 1,917 → 86% of European NPV

[1] Assuming perpetuity cash flow growth of 3%.
[2] Assuming perpetuity cash flow growth of 3% and recovery under distress of 45% of cash flows "as usual."

We assumed for simplicity that if adverse economic conditions develop in the emerging market, they will do so in the first year of the plant's operation. In reality, of course, the investment will face a probability of domestic economic distress in each year of its lifetime. Modeling risk over time would require more complex calculations yet would not change the basic results. We also assumed that the emerging-market business would face significantly lower cash flows in a local crisis but not wind up entirely worthless.

We can also see from Exhibit 35.3 how easy it is to overestimate the country risk premium. As you can see, despite the 25 percent chance that the cash flows would be 55 percent lower than the base case, the equivalent country risk premium is only 0.7 percent (estimated by reverse engineering the valuation and solving for the discount rate based on the base-case cash flows). If we had used a country risk premium of 3 percent, the implied probability of economic distress would be 70 percent, versus 25 percent in the example.

Exhibit 35.4 gives an indication of the premium required for different combinations of the probability and size of an investment's permanent cash flow reduction. The premium is easily overestimated. For example, if there is a probability of 50 percent that future cash flows will be permanently lower by 40 percent, the risk premium should be just 1.5 percent. Actual premiums will also vary, depending on the underlying cash flow profile and cost of capital.[3] Nevertheless, the table allows for some calibration of premiums and risks.

While estimating probabilities of economic distress for the base case and downside scenarios is ultimately a matter of management judgment, there are indicators to suggest reasonable probabilities. Historical data on previous crises can give some indication of the frequency and severity of country

EXHIBIT 35.4 **Probability of Economic Distress Given Small Variations in Risk Premium**

Risk premium that reflects given conditions, %

		Size of cash-flow reduction, %				
		20	40	60	80	100
Probability of lower cash flow, %	10	0.1	0.2	0.4	0.5	0.7
	20	0.2	0.5	0.8	1.1	1.5
	30	0.4	0.8	1.3	1.9	2.6
	40	0.5	1.1	1.9	2.8	4.0
	50	0.7	**1.5**	2.6	4.0	**6.0**

A 1.5% risk premium is assuming even odds that an investment will lose 40% of its value.

A 6% risk premium is assuming even odds it will lose all its value.

Note: Chart assumes a smooth cash-flow profile, 8% weighted average cost of capital, 2% terminal growth, binomial outcome.

Source: R. Davis, M. Goedhart, and T. Koller, "Avoiding a Risk Premium That Unnecessarily Kills Your Project," *McKinsey Quarterly* (August 2012).

[3] The higher the cash flow's growth rate, the stronger is the impact of a risk premium on the DCF value.

risk and the time required for recovery. We analyzed the changes in GDP of 20 emerging economies since 1985 and found that they had experienced economic distress, defined as a real-terms GDP decline of more than 5 percent, about once every five years. This would suggest a 20 percent probability for a downside scenario.

Another source of information for estimating probabilities is prospective data from current government bond prices.[4] Academic research suggests that government default probabilities in emerging markets such as Argentina five years into the future were around 30 percent in nondistress years.[5]

In our example, we could simply reverse engineer the country risk premium, because the true value of the plant was already known from the scenario approach. But for practical purposes, there is no agreed-upon approach to estimate the premium. Estimates from different analysts usually fall into a wide range because of the different methods used. The country risk premium is sometimes set at the so-called sovereign risk premium: the spread of the local government bond yield denominated in U.S. dollars and a U.S. government bond of similar maturity. However, that is reasonable only if the returns on local government debt are highly correlated with returns on corporate investments. In our experience, this is rarely the case.

From an operational viewpoint, using scenarios forces managers to discuss emerging-market risks and their effect on cash flows, thereby gaining more insights than they would secure from an arbitrary addition to the discount rate. By identifying specific factors with a large impact on value, managers can plan to mitigate these risks.

ESTIMATING COST OF CAPITAL IN EMERGING MARKETS

Calculating the cost of capital in any country can be challenging, but for emerging markets, the challenge is an order of magnitude greater. This section provides our fundamental assumptions, background on the important issues, and a practical way to estimate the components of the cost of capital.

General Guidelines

Our analysis adopts the perspective of a global investor—either a multinational company or a global investor with a diversified portfolio. Of course, some emerging markets are not yet well integrated with the global market. In China, for example, local investors may face barriers to investing outside

---

[4] See, for example, D. Duffie and K. Singleton, "Modeling Term Structures of Defaultable Bonds," *Review of Financial Studies* 12 (1999): 687–720; and R. Merton, "On the Pricing of Corporate Debt: The Risk Structure of Interest Rates," *Journal of Finance* 29, no. 2 (1974): 449–470.

[5] See J. Merrick, "Crisis Dynamics of Implied Default Recovery Ratios: Evidence from Russia and Argentina," *Journal of Banking and Finance* 25, no. 10 (2001): 1921–1939.

their home market. As a result, local investors in such markets cannot always hold well-diversified portfolios, and their cost of capital may be considerably different from that of a global investor. Unfortunately, there is no established framework for estimating the capital cost for local investors. However, if the local stock market is fully integrated into the global markets (investors both in and out of the country can freely trade both locally and internationally), local prices will more likely be linked to an international cost of capital.

Another assumption is that, from the perspective of the global investor, most country risks are diversifiable. We therefore need no additional risk premiums in the cost of capital for the risks encountered in emerging markets when discounting expected cash flows in the scenario DCF approach. Of course, if you choose to discount the promised cash flow from the business-as-usual scenario only, you should add a separate country risk premium, as discussed earlier.

Given these assumptions, the cost of capital in emerging markets should generally be close to a global cost of capital adjusted for local inflation and capital structure. It is also useful to keep some general guidelines in mind:

- *Use the capital asset pricing model (CAPM) to estimate the cost of equity in emerging markets.* The CAPM may be a less robust model for the less integrated emerging markets, but there is no better alternative model today.

- *There is no one right answer, so be pragmatic.* In emerging markets, there are often significant gaps in information and data (for example, in estimating betas). Be flexible as you assemble the available information piece by piece to build the cost of capital.

- *Be sure monetary assumptions are consistent.* Ground your model in a common set of monetary assumptions to ensure that the cash flow forecasts and discount rate are consistent. If you are using local nominal cash flows, the cost of capital must reflect the local inflation rate embedded in the cash flow projections. For real-terms cash flows, subtract inflation from the nominal cost of capital.

- *Allow for changes in cost of capital.* The cost of capital in an emerging-market valuation may change, based on evolving inflation expectations, changes in a company's capital structure and cost of debt, or foreseeable reforms in the tax system. For example, in Argentina during the economic and monetary crisis of 2002, the short-term inflation rate was 30 percent. This could not have been a reasonable rate for a long-term cost of capital estimate, because such a crisis could not be expected to last forever.[6] In such cases, estimate the cost of capital on a year-by-year basis, following the underlying set of basic monetary assumptions.

---

[6] Annual consumer price inflation came down to around 5 percent in Argentina in 2004.

- *Don't mix approaches.* Use the cost of capital to discount the cash flows in a scenario DCF approach. Do not add any risk premium, because you would then be double-counting risk. If you are discounting only future cash flows in a business-as-usual scenario, add a risk premium to the discount rate.

Estimating the Cost of Equity

To estimate the components of the cost of equity, use the approach described in Chapter 15, with the following considerations for the risk-free rate, market risk premium, and beta.

In emerging markets, it is harder than in developed markets to estimate the risk-free rate from government bonds. Three main problems arise. First, most of the government debt in emerging markets is not, in fact, risk free: the ratings on much of this debt are often well below investment grade. Second, it is difficult to find long-term government bonds that are actively traded with sufficient liquidity. Finally, the long-term debt that is traded is often in U.S. dollars or the euro, so it is not appropriate for discounting local nominal cash flows.

We recommend a straightforward approach. Start with a risk-free rate based on the ten-year U.S. government bond yield, as in developed markets. Add to this the projected difference over time between U.S. and local inflation, to arrive at a nominal risk-free rate in local currency.[7] For emerging-market bonds with relatively low risk, you can derive this inflation differential from the spread between local bond yields denominated in local currency and those denominated in U.S. dollars.

Sometimes practitioners calculate beta relative to the local market index. This is not only inconsistent from the perspective of a global investor, but also potentially distorted by the fact that the index in an emerging market will rarely be representative of a diversified economy. Instead, estimate industry betas relative to a well-diversified or global market index, as recommended in Chapter 15.

Excess returns of local equity markets over local bond returns are not a good proxy for the market risk premium. This holds even more so for emerging markets, given the lack of diversification in the local equity market. Furthermore, the quality and the length of available data on equity and bond market returns usually make such data unsuitable for long-term estimates. To use a market risk premium that is consistent with the perspective of a global investor, use a global estimate (as discussed in Chapter 15) of 4.5 to 5.5 percent.

---

[7] Technically, we should also model the U.S. term structure of interest rates, but it will not make a large difference in the valuation.

Estimating the After-Tax Cost of Debt

In most emerging economies, there are no liquid markets for corporate bonds, so little or no market information is available to estimate the cost of debt. However, from a global investor's perspective, the cost of debt in local currency should simply equal the sum of the dollar (or euro) risk-free rate, the systematic part of the credit spread (which depends on the debt's beta; see the section titled "Estimating the After-Tax Cost of Debt in Chapter 15), and the inflation differential between local currency and dollars (or euros). Most of the country risk can be diversified away in a global bond portfolio. Therefore, the systematic part of the default risk is probably no larger than that of companies in international markets, and the cost of debt should not include a separate country risk premium.[8] Furthermore, companies in countries like Brazil often hold large amounts of cash to provide liquidity and minimize their net debt.

The marginal tax rate in emerging markets can be very different from the effective tax rate, which often includes investment tax credits, export tax credits, taxes, equity or dividend credits, and operating loss credits. Few of these arrangements provide a tax shield on interest expense, and only those few should be incorporated in the after-tax-cost-of-debt component of the WACC. Other taxes or credits should be modeled directly in the cash flows.

Estimating Capital Structure and WACC

Having estimated the cost of equity and after-tax cost of debt, we need debt and equity weights to derive an estimate of the weighted average cost of capital. In emerging markets, many companies have unusual capital structures compared with their international peers. One reason is, of course, the country risk: the possibility of macroeconomic distress makes companies more conservative in setting their leverage. Another reason could be anomalies in the local debt or equity markets. In the long run, when the anomalies are corrected, the companies should expect to develop a capital structure similar to that of their global competitors. You could forecast explicitly how the company evolves to a capital structure that is more like global standards. In that case, you should consider using the adjusted-present-value (APV) approach, discussed in Chapter 10.

OTHER COMPLICATIONS IN VALUING EMERGING-MARKETS COMPANIES

Other complications that should be considered in valuing emerging-markets companies include consistent macroeconomic parameters, accounting differences, nonoperating assets, and inefficient capital markets.

---

[8] This explains why multinationals with extensive emerging-market portfolios—companies such as Coca-Cola and Colgate-Palmolive—have a cost of debt that is no higher than that of their mainly U.S.-focused competitors.

Every forecast of a company's financial performance is based on assumptions about real GDP growth, inflation rates, interest and exchange rates, and whatever other parameters, such as energy prices, are relevant. In emerging markets, these parameters can fluctuate wildly from year to year. It becomes all the more important that forecasts be based on an integrated set of economic and monetary assumptions of future inflation, interest rates, exchange rates, and cost of capital (see Chapters 26 and 27 for more details). For instance, make sure that the same inflation rates underlie the financial projections and cost of capital estimates for the company.

One parameter deserves special attention: exchange rates. Although exchange rates converge to purchasing power parity (PPP) in the long run,[9] short-term deviations can be sizable and last for several years—especially in the case of emerging markets. In Chapter 27, Exhibit 27.3 shows how even on an inflation-adjusted basis, the exchange rate of Brazil's currency, the real (plural: reais), has fluctuated strongly over the past 50 years versus the U.S. dollar. If the long-term average real exchange rate is indicative of PPP,[10] the Brazilian currency could have been overvalued versus the U.S. dollar and other currencies by as much as 20 to 35 percent in 2008. Any exchange rate convergence to PPP would not be likely to affect the cash flows and value generated by a retailer, as its revenues and costs are mainly determined in Brazilian reais. But an exchange rate change would affect its cash flow and value measured in foreign currency. Because predicting exchange rates is virtually impossible,[11] a range estimate of the impact on a company's value measured in foreign currency is more meaningful. For primarily local companies, like retailers, it would therefore be best to perform the DCF valuation in Brazilian reais and—if needed—translate the result at both the actual and the PPP exchange rates to obtain a value range in foreign currency.

Fortunately, many of the complications arising from different accounting standards have been resolved over the past decades. Almost all countries outside the United States have adopted IFRS accounting standards, with the notable exceptions of China and India. This has reduced the complexity of adjusting their financial statements for valuation purposes. Even in China and India, the vast majority of accounting standards have been converging with IFRS and are now substantially the same.

Nonoperating assets remain a challenge, however. Companies in emerging markets—which are often conglomerates with a wide range of businesses—frequently have a large amount of nonoperating assets, including unconsolidated equity investments and real estate. For example, Reliance Industries,

---

[9] For an overview, see A. M. Taylor and M. P. Taylor, "The Purchasing Power Parity Debate," *Journal of Economic Perspectives* 18, no. 4 (Fall 2004): 135–158.

[10] See Chapter 27 for more details on PPP and exchange rates.

[11] As Exhibit 27.3 also shows, the Brazilian real further strengthened against the U.S. dollar and other currencies in real terms after 2008, before showing some correction in 2013.

one of India's largest companies, with 2018 revenues of $60 billion, has operations in oil refining and marketing, petrochemicals, oil and gas exploration and production, retail, digital services, and media and entertainment. Its balance sheet also includes $11 billion book value of investments that need to be valued separately (relative to a market capitalization of about $105 billion).

The capital markets in which emerging-markets companies trade may have inefficiencies. In many cases, these companies may have limited float because controlling shareholders may hold large stakes. The presence of controlling shareholders (often founding families) may also raise concerns about governance and whether there are potential conflicts between the interests of public shareholders and the controlling shareholders. This could lead to a lower share price than otherwise warranted. Some countries (particularly China and India) also have restrictions on investors, or the governments actively intervene in the markets, causing deviations in share prices from intrinsic values. For example, in China, Chinese citizens are not allowed to invest in shares outside the country, so the share prices of mainland Chinese companies can be disconnected from intrinsic value and the value of similar companies outside China. This could be caused by an imbalance of supply and demand for shares that cannot be corrected by arbitrage with other equity markets. Unlike most markets, the Chinese traded market is also dominated by retail investors (75 percent of holdings), roughly the reverse of the U.S. market, where institutional investors own most shares. Retail investors aren't as sophisticated and don't do as much research as institutional investors. They also tend to move in the same direction, leading to large swings in prices. Such market inefficiencies can make it difficult to reconcile DCF values with market values. Finally, companies in emerging markets often have complex corporate structures with voting and nonvoting shares. This often leads to a small group of investors controlling the company even though they own less than 50 percent. In some countries with weak governance, public market investors will discount the value of these companies if they don't believe the controlling shareholders make decisions in the interests of all shareholders.

TRIANGULATING VALUATION

We recommend triangulating the results of the scenario DCF approach with a comparable multiples approach and DCF using a country risk premium. We'll illustrate with the example of a Brazilian retail company we'll call ConsuCo.

We constructed two scenarios, a business-as-usual case (the base case) and a downside case reflecting performance under adverse economic conditions. Exhibit 35.5 shows the ROIC projections. Brazil has experienced several severe economic and monetary downturns, including an inflation rate that topped 2,000 percent in 1993. Judging by its key financial indicators, such as EBITDA to sales and real-terms sales growth, the impact on ConsuCo's business performance had been significant. ConsuCo's cash operating margin had been negative for four years, at around –10 to –5 percent, before recovering to its normal levels. In the same period, sales in real terms declined by 10 to 15 percent per year but grew sharply after the crisis. For the downside scenario projections, we assumed similar negative cash margins and a decline in sales, in real terms, for up to five years, followed by a gradual return to the long-term margins and growth assumed under the business-as-usual scenario.

EXHIBIT 35.5 **ConsuCo: ROIC and Financials, Base Case vs. Downside Scenario**

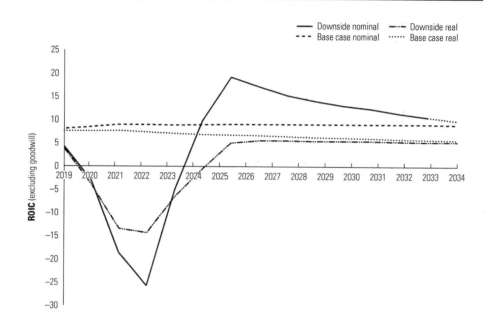

Financials, %	2019	2020	2021	2022	2023	2024
Nominal indicators: Base case						
Sales growth	15.3	14.5	13.6	12.6	11.7	10.8
Adjusted EBITA/sales	6.1	6.2	6.4	6.4	6.4	6.4
NOPAT/sales	4.4	4.5	4.6	4.5	4.4	4.4
Invested capital (excluding goodwill)/sales	54	53	51	51	50	49
Invested capital (including goodwill)/sales	62	59	57	56	55	54
ROIC (excluding goodwill)	8.1	8.5	9.0	9.0	8.9	9.0
Free cash flow, reais million	(63)	(136)	(94)	(91)	(85)	113
Nominal indicators: Downside scenario						
Sales growth	10.0	25.0	66.3	66.3	25.0	11.3
Adjusted EBITA/sales	3.1	(2.2)	(8.0)	(7.6)	(1.1)	3.3
NOPAT/sales	2.3	(1.5)	(5.8)	(5.8)	(1.1)	2.2
Invested capital (excluding goodwill)/sales	55	47	31	22	21	22
Invested capital (including goodwill)/sales	63	54	35	25	23	24
ROIC (excluding goodwill)	4.2	(3.2)	(18.6)	(25.7)	(5.0)	9.9
Free cash flow, reais million	(149)	(777)	(2,533)	(4,504)	(2,677)	(558)

We discounted the free cash flows for ConsuCo under the base case and the downside scenario. The resulting present values of operations are shown in Exhibit 35.6. Note that we conducted the analysis in both nominal and real cash flows to show that the results were identical. We then weighted the valuation results by the scenario probabilities to derive the present value of operations. Finally, we added the market value of the nonoperating assets and subtracted the financial claims to arrive at the estimated equity value. The estimated equity value obtained for ConsuCo was about 32 reais per share, given a 30 percent probability of economic distress. This was somewhat lower than ConsuCo's share price in the stock market of around 37 reais at the time of valuation.

To triangulate with multiples, we apply Chapter 18's guidance on how to perform a best-practice multiples analysis to check valuation results. For the ConsuCo example, we compared the implied multiple of enterprise value over EBITDA with those of peer companies. All multiples were forward-looking

EXHIBIT 35.6 **ConsuCo: Scenario DCF Valuation**

reais, million

			2019	2020	2021	2022	2023	2024	...	2029	...	2034
		Base case										
		Nominal projections										
		Free cash flow	(63)	(136)	(94)	(91)	(85)	113	...	301	...	516
		WACC, %	11.1	9.5	9.3	9.2	9.1	9.0	...	9.0	...	9.0
		Real projections										
		Free cash flow	(60)	(125)	(83)	(77)	(68)	87	...	187	...	257
		WACC, %	6.0	5.1	4.9	4.7	4.5	4.4	...	4.4	...	4.4
		DCF value	14,451									
		Nonoperating assets	1,139									
Probability		Debt and debt equivalents	(5,605)									
70%		Equity value	9,985									
		Value per share	42.4									
		Downside scenario										
		Nominal projections										
Value	32	Free cash flow	(149)	(777)	(2,533)	(4,504)	(2,677)	(558)	...	250	...	834
per share		WACC, %	11.1	29.4	76.7	76.4	28.7	9.5	...	9.0	...	9.0
		Real projections										
		Free cash flow	(142)	(593)	(1,105)	(1,123)	(534)	(106)	...	38	...	102
		WACC, %	6.0	3.5	1.0	0.8	2.9	4.3	...	4.4	...	4.4
		DCF value	6,313									
		Nonoperating assets	1,139									
Probability		Debt and debt equivalents	(5,605)									
30%		Equity value	1,847									
		Value per share	7.9									

multiples over EBITDA. As Exhibit 35.7 illustrates, the implied multiple from our ConsuCo valuation was significantly higher than for U.S. and European peers, which was not surprising, given its higher growth outlook in the Brazilian market compared with that of large established chains in the U.S. and European markets. ConsuCo's valuation was at the low end of the range for Latin American peers, which also was not unreasonable. Relative to regional peers, ConsuCo could have been expected to have fewer growth opportunities, as it was already very well established and geographically widespread. It also had somewhat more exposure than listed peers had to the lower-growth food segment.

The last part of the triangulation consisted of valuing ConsuCo using a country risk premium approach. Using Exhibit 35.4, we estimated a country risk premium for ConsuCo. We observed from history that the probability of country crises appears to be around 20 to 30 percent and that for consumer goods businesses, it rarely leads to a loss of all cash flows. Taking that into account, a country risk premium for a Brazilian retailer like ConsuCo was likely in the range of 1 to 2 percent, rather than 3 to 5 percent or higher, as analysts often estimate.

Discounting the business-as-usual scenario at the cost of capital plus a country risk premium in this range led to a value per share below 20 reais, far lower than the 32-reais result obtained in the scenario DCF approach. The

EXHIBIT 35.7 **ConsuCo: Multiples Analysis vs. Peers**

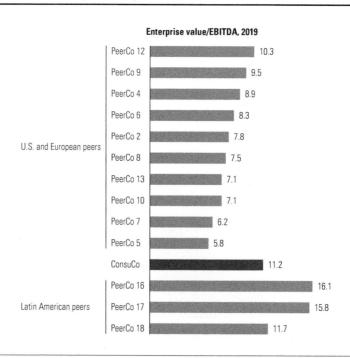

reason for this gap lies in ConsuCo's cash flow profile, and it highlights why a scenario approach is preferable to using a discount rate reflecting a country risk premium. Due to ConsuCo's high anticipated growth and corresponding investments, its free cash flows were forecast to be negative for the first five years, pushing value creation forward in time. But the further ahead a company's positive cash flows lie, the more those cash flows are penalized by the country risk premium approach, because a markup in WACC accumulates over time. This does not happen in a scenario approach, because the scenario probabilities affect all future cash flows equally.

If ConsuCo had had a lower-growth outlook, the country risk premium approach would have produced a valuation much closer to the valuation from the scenario approach. Note that irrespective of ConsuCo's cash flow profile, a risk premium of 3 to 5 percent (as is typically used in emerging markets) would have either resulted in unrealistically low valuations relative to current share price and peer group multiples or else required an unrealistically bullish forecast of future performance.

SUMMARY

To value companies in emerging markets, we use concepts similar to the ones applied to developed markets. However, it's necessary to incorporate into valuations the unique risks of emerging markets, such as macroeconomic or political crises, by following the scenario DCF approach. This approach develops alternative scenarios for future cash flows, discounts the cash flows at the cost of capital without a country risk premium, and then weights the DCF values by the scenario probabilities. The cost of capital estimates for emerging markets build on the assumption of a global risk-free rate, market risk premium, and beta, following guidelines similar to those used for developed markets. Since company values in emerging markets are often more volatile than values in developed markets, we recommend triangulating the scenario DCF results with two other valuations: one that is based on discounting cash flows developed in a business-as-usual projection but using a cost of capital that includes a country risk premium, and another that is based on multiples.

36

High-Growth Companies

Valuing high-growth companies is a challenge; some practitioners even describe it as hopeless. Yet we've found that the valuation principles in this book work well for coping with the great uncertainty that accompanies these rapid growers.[1] The best way to value such companies is to start with a discounted-cash-flow (DCF) valuation and buttress it with economic fundamentals and probability-weighted scenarios.

Although DCF may sound suspiciously retro, it works where other methods fail, since the core principles of economics and finance apply even in uncharted territory. Alternatives, such as enterprise value multiples, generate imprecise results when earnings are highly volatile, cannot be used when earnings are negative, and provide little insight into what drives the company's valuation. More important, shorthand methods cannot account for the unique characteristics of each company in a fast-changing environment. Another alternative, real options, requires estimates of the long-term revenue growth rate, long-term volatility of revenue growth, and profit margins—the same requirements as for discounted cash flow.[2]

This chapter details the differences in the order and emphasis of DCF valuation in the case of high-growth, rather than established, companies. Instead of starting with an analysis of the company's and its industry's past performance, the valuation process begins with an estimation of what the future economics of the company and industry might become. Since these long-term projections are highly uncertain, create multiple scenarios, each with its own value. If you need a single-point estimate, weight the scenario values by their probability of occurrence. In our practice, we avoid using single-point

---

[1] We define high-growth companies as those whose organic revenue growth exceeds 15 percent annually.

[2] In Chapter 39, we demonstrate how real options can lead to a more theoretically robust valuation than scenario analysis. But unlike scenario analysis, real-options models are complex and obscure the competitive dynamics driving a company's value.

estimates, because this approach implies precision that doesn't exist and obscures the key uncertainties that could improve decision making.

Keep in mind that while scenario-based DCF techniques can help bound and quantify uncertainty, they will not make it disappear. High-growth companies have volatile stock prices for sound reasons.

A VALUATION PROCESS FOR HIGH-GROWTH COMPANIES

When valuing an established company, the first step is to analyze historical performance. But in the case of a high-growth company, historical financial results provide limited clues about future prospects. Therefore, begin with the future, not with the past. Focus on sizing the potential market, estimating the share of the market the company will capture, predicting the level of sustainable operating margin, and approximating the investments necessary to achieve scale. To make these estimates, choose a point well into the future at a time when the company's financial performance is likely to stabilize, and begin forecasting.

Once you have developed a long-term future view, work backward to link the future to current performance. Current performance measured using accounting statements will mix together investments and expenses. When possible, capitalize hidden investments, even those expensed under traditional accounting rules.[3] This is challenging, as the distinction between investment and expense is often unobservable and subjective.

Given the uncertainty associated with high-growth companies, do not rely on a single long-term forecast. Describe the market's development in terms of multiple scenarios, including total size, likely competitive structure, and so on. When you build a comprehensive scenario, be sure all forecasts, including revenue growth, profitability margins, and required investment, are consistent with the underlying assumptions of the particular scenario. Apply probabilistic weights to each scenario, using weights that are consistent with long-term historical evidence on corporate growth. As we saw during the dot-com bubble of the late 1990s, valuations that rely on unrealistic assessments can lead to overestimates of value, poor investment returns, and strategic errors.

Start from the Future

Begin by thinking about what the industry and company might look like as the company evolves from its current high-growth, uncertain condition to a

---

[3] Chapter 24 presents a methodology for capitalizing intangible expenses, such as research and development.

state of sustainable, moderate growth in the future. Then interpolate back to current performance. The future state should be defined and bounded by measures of operating performance, such as customer penetration rates, average revenue per customer, and sustainable margins. Next, determine how long growth will continue at an elevated rate before it stabilizes to normal levels. Since most high-growth companies are start-ups, stable economics probably lie at least 10 to 15 years in the future.

To demonstrate the valuation process for high-growth companies, we examine Farfetch, a popular online marketplace for luxury goods. Founded in 2007 by José Neves, Farfetch was conceived in response to the founder's own struggles to transition from an in-store boutique to a web-based e-tailer. Neves believed that local boutiques lacked the skills and scale to successfully migrate the transition to digital on their own. Farfetch would fill this gap.

The company launched its website in 2008, selling luxury products from 25 boutiques in five countries. Over the next decade, the company raised nearly $700 million in private capital, growing revenue to more than $600 million by 2018. As Exhibit 36.1 demonstrates, the company has grown at more than 50 percent in each of the last three years. This level of growth significantly outpaces the growth at more established technology-enabled marketplaces.

To estimate the size of a potential market, start by assessing how the company fulfills a customer need. Then determine how the company generates

EXHIBIT 36.1 **Farfetch: Revenues, 2015–2018**

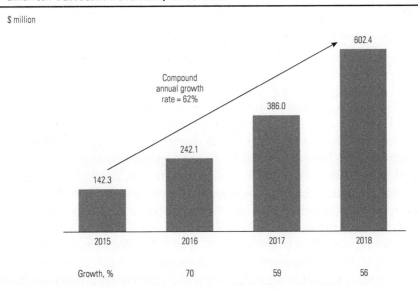

EXHIBIT 36.2 **Farfetch: Revenue by Product Type and Geography**

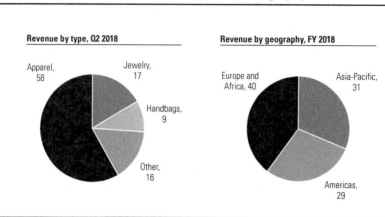

Source: Farfetch F-1 filing and 2018 20-F filing; Deutsche Bank estimates.

(or plans to generate) revenues. Understanding how a start-up makes money is critical. Technology start-ups rely on many revenue streams, including advertising, product sales, subscriptions, and commissions, among others. Many young companies build a product or service that meets the customer's need, but too many can't identify how to monetize the value they provide.

Understanding a company's growth potential requires identifying which product categories are part of its current and future portfolio. To this end, the left side of Exhibit 36.2 presents Farfetch revenue by product type. While high-end fashion apparel accounts for the majority of its sales, the company also sells high-end jewelry, handbags, and shoes.

In the case of luxury goods, it is important to assess where the company sells its products, since the luxury-goods market varies dramatically across regions. Understanding the geographic presence will help with sizing future markets and assessing the impact of potential competition. The right side of Exhibit 36.2 presents Farfetch's revenue by geography. Although Farfetch launched in Europe, it now has a significant presence in the Americas and Asia.

Across these product lines and regions, Farfetch generates revenue from multiple activities. Whenever possible, try to separate sources of revenue, as each will have its own dynamics concerning growth, profitability, and required investment. Farfetch's primary source of revenue is from its third-party (3P) marketplace. As in other popular marketplaces, a consumer purchases a product from a company other than Farfetch, and Farfetch facilitates the transaction, taking a portion of the revenue. In a technology-enabled marketplace, the level of the commission is known as the "take rate," and it varies substantially across product categories. For Farfetch, the take rate hovers around 30 percent, higher than most technology marketplaces. As part of the transaction,

EXHIBIT 36.3 **Farfetch: Revenue Model, 2018**

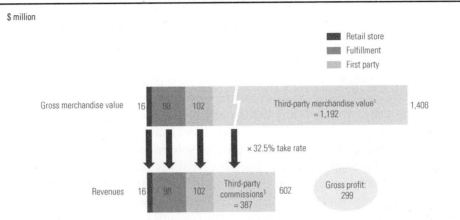

$ million

Legend:
- Retail store
- Fulfillment
- First party

Gross merchandise value: 16 | 98 | 102 | Third-party merchandise value[1] = 1,192 | 1,408

× 32.5% take rate

Revenues: 16 | 98 | 102 | Third-party commissions[1] = 387 | 602 | Gross profit: 299

[1] Includes Black & White outsourcing revenue, estimated net of returns.

Source: Farfetch F-1 filing and 2018 20-F filing, Cowen and Company estimates.

Farfetch will also charge for shipping, customs, and taxes. While these fees are bundled together from the customer's perspective, Farfetch separates fulfillment-related charges from other revenues.

In addition to the marketplace, Farfetch generates revenue from three other sources. The company sells luxury goods direct to consumers through its platform (first-party sales, or 1P) and through two London-based retail stores, known as Browns. Through a business unit it calls Black & White (now known as Farfetch Platform Solutions), Farfetch also works directly with luxury brands to operate their e-commerce sites.

Since a company's take rate varies over time and across businesses, do not start your valuation with company revenue, but rather with gross merchandise value (GMV). Exhibit 36.3 presents Farfetch's GMV and resulting revenue by operating segment. GMV represents the value of goods sold on the platform, net of returns—$1.4 billion in 2018. Since Farfetch keeps only a portion of the gross merchandise value traded, revenue is limited to the portion retained. This is not unique to Farfetch. Many technology companies report both gross and net sales. For instance, ride-sharing companies report their gross bookings but net out driver payments before reporting revenue. Assess the market power of various stakeholders, like luxury boutiques or global luxury brands, to determine the future direction of take rates.

For in-store sales, first-party sales, and platform fulfillment, revenue equals the gross merchandise value. Since direct sales and the third-party marketplace have different levels of profitability and capital needs, always analyze them separately. In this chapter we examine only the third-party marketplace in detail, though we estimated the other revenue sources using a similar methodology.

Sizing the Market   For many young, high-growth companies, it's challenging to estimate the size of the potential market. You must be creative and clever about what data to collect to bound your forecasts. In the case of the ride-share market, for example, you can start with global taxi revenue. But you must also consider how many new rides will occur because of the ease of access, as well as how many riders are likely to replace their cars altogether.

Compared with other nascent technology companies, Farfetch's product markets are easier to size. Many investment banks and consulting firms study the global luxury market in depth. Information is available on the number of products and the total value of merchandise sold in stores and online.

Exhibit 36.4 presents revenue for the global luxury market between 2010 and 2018, with analyst forecasts extending through 2025. Bolstered by strong growth in Asia, the luxury market is expected to grow between 4 and 5 percent annually, reaching $450 billion by 2025. Growth looks to be uneven across channels, however. Expectations are that over the next decade, in-store sales of luxury products will remain flat, while online sales will increase from 10 percent to 25 percent of the total market.

The online migration of luxury goods is far from certain, however. No one really knows if these high-end products will migrate as much or as quickly as have media, electronics, and other items. Later in the chapter we develop multiple scenarios, with each scenario based on a different level of online penetration.

EXHIBIT 36.4 **Global Luxury Market: Offline vs. Online Sales, 2010–2025E**

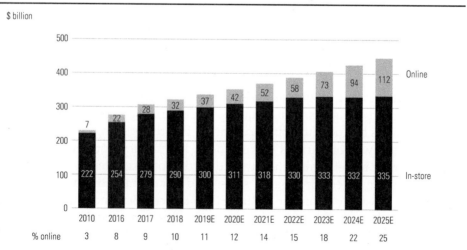

Source: Farfetch Investor Presentation, December 4, 2019, Bain & Company.

EXHIBIT 36.5 **Farfetch: Revenue Model for Third-Party Marketplace, 2017–2028E**

$ million, except where noted

	2017	2018	2019E	2020E	2021E	2022E	...	2028E
Third-party revenue model								
Unique customers, thousands	936	1,353	1,787	2,293	2,897	3,603	...	9,911
× Orders per customer	2.01	2.15	2.31	2.33	2.35	2.38	...	2.52
Number of orders, thousands	1,881	2,913	4,121	5,342	6,817	8,563	...	25,005
× Average order value, $	620	618	605	637	650	659	...	700
Gross transaction value[1]	1,166	1,801	2,493	3,402	4,428	5,645	...	17,500
Net of returns	(290)	(439)	(577)	(782)	(1,018)	(1,411)	...	(4,375)
Net of fulfillment revenue	(74)	(98)	(138)	(197)	(256)	(318)	...	(984)
GMV, net of fulfillment revenue[2]	802	1,265	1,777	2,423	3,154	3,917	...	12,140
× Portion generated by third party	95.0%	91.9%	91.5%	92.2%	92.8%	93.3%	...	93.3%
× Take rate	32.8%	32.5%	30.9%	30.9%	30.6%	30.3%	...	29.4%
Third-party revenue	250	377	503	691	896	1,108	...	3,331
Other Revenue								
Platform fulfillment revenue	74	98	138	197	256	318	...	984
First-party revenue	40	102	152	189	228	261	...	815
Black & White segment	6	10	16	23	30	37		135
Browns' in-store revenue	15	16	18	20	22	23	...	30
Farfetch revenue	386	602	827	1,119	1,430	1,746	...	5,296

[1] Excluding Black & White's outsourcing revenue and Browns' in-store revenue.

[2] Gross merchandise value, net of fulfillment revenue.

Source: Farfetch F-1 filing and 2018 20-F filing; Cowen and Company estimates.

Modeling Revenues   A robust revenue model, especially for nascent companies, will incorporate operational data mirroring the company's economics. In the case of consumer companies, these include the number of customers, transactions per customer, average transaction size, and other items. Exhibit 36.5 presents a revenue model for Farfetch's third-party marketplace, based on forecasts by the research team at Cowen and Company.[4] These particular estimates underpin one of our four scenarios presented later in the chapter.

The revenue model in Exhibit 36.5 starts with the number of customers, which in 2018 was approximately 1.4 million. Since the typical customer makes a purchase just over twice a year, the company generated just under 3 million transactions that year. The size of the average order was about $600, leading to an estimated $1.8 billion in gross transaction value. Since some transactions will

---

[4] To create one of our scenarios, we used data from John Blackledge et al., "FTCH 2Q Preview: Order Growth Momentum in Focus when FTCH Reports 8/8" (unpublished manuscript, Cowen and Company, August 5, 2019), available from Bloomberg. We thank the team at Cowen and Company for providing data used throughout the chapter.

be returned, they are netted from the original order count. We also net out process fulfillment costs, leading to GMV, net of fulfillment revenue of $1.3 billion—just under 4 percent of the online luxury market, estimated at $32 billion.

We assume that 2028 is the year that Farfetch matures into a profitable, stable company, so we create our projections for this scenario around estimates for that year's results. We project 9.9 million unique customers and 2.5 transactions per customer to arrive at 25 million transactions at an average of $700 per transaction. That leads to gross transaction value near $17.5 billion. After returns and adjustment for fulfillment costs, revenues from Farfetch's digital platform would be $12.1 billion.

With 93.3 percent of revenue generated from third-party sales and a 29.4 percent take rate, third-party revenues equal $3.3 billion. First-party revenues equal $815 million (that is, 6.7 percent of $12.1 billion). Other revenues, primarily from process fulfillment, outsourcing, and in-store sales, are $1.1 billion, for total revenues of $5.3 billion.

We also looked at this revenue estimate from the perspective of the total market and Farfetch's share. The total luxury-goods market, growing modestly, reaches about $500 billion in 2028. Assuming 30 percent online penetration and Farfetch achieving an 8 percent market share (with adjustments for first-party versus third-party sales and in-store sales) brings us to a scenario in which Farfetch achieves 2028 revenue of $5.3 billion.

One of the key uncertainties for estimating Farfetch's revenues is online penetration of the luxury-goods market. For this scenario, our projected 30 percent penetration is based on a comparison with other product categories. Exhibit 36.6

EXHIBIT 36.6 **U.S. E-Commerce Penetration by Vertical, 2000–2023E**

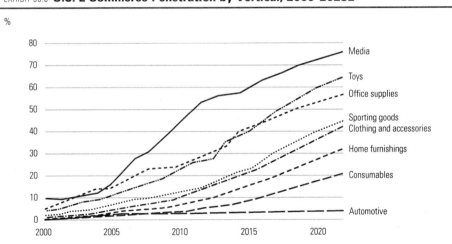

Source: U.S. Census Bureau; Cowen and Company estimates.

presents e-commerce penetration in the United States across various product categories. Most sales of media and toy products now take place online. In contrast, luxury goods lag most product categories. One product category that analysts point to as a useful comparable is clothing and accessories, projected to reach 42 percent by 2023. Luxury-goods customers like to feel and touch their purchases, so for this scenario, we've kept penetration at 30 percent. In the most optimistic scenario we'll use for our valuation, we'll bring penetration to 40 percent.

Estimating Operating Margin, Capital Intensity, and ROIC   With a revenue forecast in hand, next forecast long-term operating margins, required capital investments, and ROIC. To estimate operating margin, triangulate between expected price versus cost to serve and operating margins for established players. Refer to Chapter 8 for the range of ROIC for different industries and a discussion of the drivers of ROIC. Chapter 6 discusses the types of business conditions that lead to high levels of ROIC from network effects.

Because the underlying economics of Farfetch's business segments differ so much, it is important to evaluate each segment separately. Regarding the company's third-party marketplace, Farfetch neither manufactures nor holds inventory, but only facilitates transactions between other parties. Therefore, the segment has a low cost of sales, requires little capital, and is highly scalable. To project steady-state margins and capital intensity, we look to established players that operate technology marketplaces that earned margins exceeding 20 percent. While these competitors can provide some insight on the evolution of margins and capital intensity, differences in each competitor's business mix may hamper direct comparison. Therefore, substantial judgment is required.

In the case of first-party sales directly to the consumer, margins will more closely resemble those of an online e-tailer (for sales conducted online) or a luxury-goods retailer (for sales conducted in their stores). In contrast to the third-party marketplace, growth will require purchasing more goods, holding more inventory, and perhaps someday capital investment in warehouses and stores. These margins are much lower than for technology marketplaces, often far less than 10 percent.

Exhibit 36.7 presents one research analyst's forecast of how Farfetch's margins might evolve over time. Although gross profits were positive in 2018, the company was losing money, as marketing and other support expenses exceeded the gross profits from product sales. Technology costs and general expenses are expected to rise as the company grows, though at a slower rate than revenue. As a consequence, these expenses will drop as a percentage of sales, and operating margins will increase. This is not the case for every expense. Some accounts, such as cost of sales, will remain a relatively constant

EXHIBIT 36.7 **Farfetch: Current and Forecast Margins, 2017–2028E**

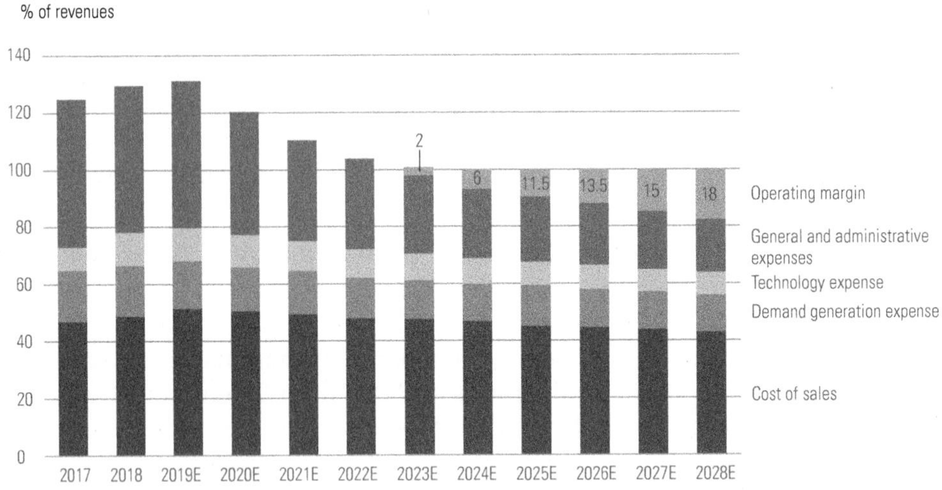

% of revenues

Source: Farfetch F-1 filing and 2018 20-F filing; Cowen and Company estimates.

proportion of sales. This is because the company will need to purchase additional products to support higher sales.

For 2028, the exhibit shows a forecast operating profit margin of 18 percent, which we'll use in our scenario B. Later, we'll show a range of margin forecasts. We've also assumed that Farfetch's capital productivity is a hybrid of a marketplace and e-tailer in proportion to Farfetch's relative third-party versus first-party sales.

Work Backward to Current Performance

After completing a forecast for total market size, market share, operating margin, and capital intensity, reconnect the long-term forecast to current performance. To do this, you must assess the speed of transition from current performance to future long-term performance. Estimates must be consistent with economic principles and industry characteristics. For instance, from the perspective of operating margin, how long will fixed costs dominate variable costs, resulting in low margins? Concerning capital turnover, what scale is required before revenues rise faster than capital? As scale is reached, will competition drive down prices? Often the questions outnumber the answers.

To determine the speed of transition from current performance to target performance, examine the historical progression for similar companies. Unfortunately, analyzing historical financial performance for high-growth companies is often misleading, because long-term investments for high-growth companies tend to be intangible. Under current accounting rules, these investments must be expensed. Therefore, both early accounting profits and invested capital will be understated. With so little formal capital, many companies have unreasonably high ROICs as soon as they become profitable.

Develop Scenarios

A simple and straightforward way to deal with uncertainty associated with high-growth companies is to use probability-weighted scenarios. Developing even a few scenarios makes the critical assumptions and interactions more transparent than you will achieve with other modeling approaches, such as real options and Monte Carlo simulation.

To develop probability-weighted scenarios, estimate financial performance for a full range of outcomes, some optimistic and some pessimistic. For Farfetch, we have developed four future scenarios for 2028, summarized in Exhibit 36.8.

In scenario A, we forecast that Farfetch benefits from favorable market conditions and delayed competitive entry. While the aggregate luxury-goods market continues to grow at a steady pace, online penetration in the space accelerates beyond analyst expectations as brands and consumers quickly embrace electronic channels. Online adoption in the luxury-goods market mimics the pattern of the clothing market, peaking at 40 percent penetration. Farfetch achieves 12 percent market share, leading to $11.4 billion in revenue in 2028. Competitive entry is forestalled, and operating margins approach those of best-in-class technology marketplaces at 22 percent. Scenario A represents an

EXHIBIT 36.8 **Farfetch: Key Drivers by Scenario, 2028 Forecast**

	Online penetration of luxury, %	Farfetch market share,[1] %	Total revenues, $ million	Operating margin, %	Description
Scenario A	40	12	11.4	22	Online penetration of the luxury market accelerates, following the path of clothing and accessories; margins are strong as the company leads the category.
Scenario B	30	8	5.3	18	Online penetration follows historical progression; margins match analyst expecations.
Scenario C	30	5	3.3	14	Online penetration follows historical progression; margins fail to materialize as larger competitors enter the category.
Scenario D	15	4	1.2	6	Online penetration fails to meet expectations; margin pressure intensifies due to large-scale entrants and increased omnichannel presence from traditional retailers.

[1] Measured as gross merchandise value to online purchases.

optimistic forecast, but structural similarities between the online luxury and clothing markets make this scenario entirely plausible.

Scenarios B through D follow a similar construct but vary key assumptions. In scenarios B and C, penetration rates reach only 30 percent, reflecting the desire among luxury goods buyers for a greater physical shopping experience than with other categories. Farfetch's market share reaches a healthy, but not overly aggressive, 8 percent and 5 percent, respectively. Margins are somewhat lower than the best e-tailers because of stronger supplier market power, in the range of 14 to 18 percent. Scenario D is characterized by sluggish growth in online penetration that more closely mirrors the home furnishings industry, a segment that is less conducive to electronic retail. In scenario D, by 2028, online penetration is 15 percent, and Farfetch achieves revenues of just $1.2 billion. Increased pressure from new entrants and more widespread omnichannel adoption by individual brands result in more moderate margin expansion, reaching only 6 percent, comparable to discount retailers.

Weight Scenarios

To derive current equity value for Farfetch, weight the intrinsic equity valuation from each scenario by its estimated likelihood of occurrence, and sum across the weighted scenarios. Exhibit 36.9 lists the intrinsic equity valuations and the probability of occurrence for each scenario. At a 10 percent probability for scenario A, 30 percent for scenario B, 35 percent for scenario C, and 25 percent for scenario D, Farfetch's equity value equals $6.1 billion and value per share at $20, matching its 2018 IPO price. Whether this price is appropriate depends on your belief in the forecasts and their respective probabilities. Were they too optimistic, too pessimistic, or just right?

EXHIBIT 36.9 **Farfetch: Probability-Weighted Expected Value**

Scenario	Intrinsic equity valuation, $ billion	×	Probability, %	=	Contribution to equity valuation, $ billion
Scenario A	19.6		10		2.0
Scenario B	8.2		30		2.5
Scenario C	4.1		35		1.4
Scenario D	1.0		25		0.2
			100		6.1
		Shares outstanding, millions			300.0
		Value per share, $			20

UNCERTAINTY IS HERE TO STAY

By adapting the DCF approach, it is possible to generate reasonable valuations for dramatically changing businesses. But investors and companies entering fast-growth markets like those related to new technologies and complex business ecosystems still face huge uncertainties. To see why, look at what could happen under our four scenarios to an investor who holds a share of Farfetch stock for five years after buying it in 2018 for $20. To facilitate the calculation, we assume the investor gradually learns about the most likely scenario.

If scenario A plays out, the investor will earn a 39 percent annual return, and as of 2018, the market will seem to have drastically undervalued Farfetch. If scenario C plays out, the investment will make just 2 percent annually, failing to earn its cost of capital. If scenario D plays out, the investment will lose 23 percent a year, and it will appear that the company was significantly overvalued in 2018. Going forward, these high or low potential returns should not be interpreted as implying that the current share price was irrational; they merely reflect uncertainty about the future.

Accurately predicting which scenario will occur is a laudable goal, but unlikely to happen. Investors struggle to incorporate new information every day, and this leads to high volatility in the share prices of young companies. Farfetch, for instance, saw its price rise 50 percent on the day of its initial public offering (IPO). Then its shares dropped 40 percent in August 2019, when

EXHIBIT 36.10 **Farfetch: Share Price, 2018–2019**

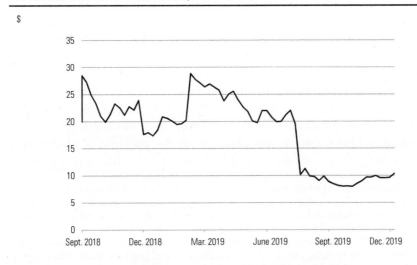

EXHIBIT 36.11 **Distribution of Annualized Total Shareholder Returns for U.S. IPOs**

Number of companies

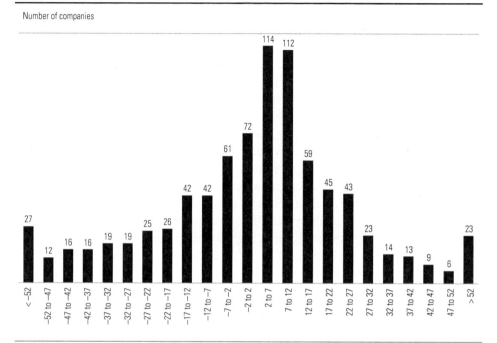

Note: Total shareholder returns for 838 initial public offerings (IPOs) between 2010 and 2017. Returns are measured from the first day of trading through December 31, 2019.

estimates on transaction counts were revised downward (see Exhibit 36.10).[5] The company had five times the volatility of the S&P 500 during its first two years of trading.

As Farfetch's prospects begin to stabilize, however, it should be possible to tighten the range of potential outcomes. These gains in precision should be reflected in a decrease in the stock's volatility.

The challenge of accurate valuation is not limited to Farfetch. We examined the total shareholder returns for more than 800 initial public offerings since 2010. Only 112 of the 838 IPOs earned between 7 and 12 percent, a range many consider the fair rate of return for investing in equities. Instead, investors either made or lost much more than anticipated. In fact, nearly 10 percent of IPOs either generated or lost 50 percent of their value since going public.[6]

A great deal of uncertainty is associated with the problem of identifying the eventual winner in a competitive field. History shows that a few players

[5] In August 2019, Farfetch announced the acquisition of New Guards Group, an Italian brand platform that operates a portfolio of luxury fashion labels. The company purchased New Guards to further differentiate its product portfolio and capture a greater share of the online market, but some analysts expressed concern about a potential shift away from the company's asset-light third-party model. At the same time, Farfetch lowered near-term GMV forecasts to reflect a decrease in promotional spending. We believe that our four scenarios, modeled earlier in the year, still ring true, albeit with a greater probability for the less favorable scenarios than when originally created.

[6] The results come from Corporate Performance Analytics by McKinsey, which relies on financial data provided by Standard & Poor's Compustat and Capital IQ.

will win big, while the vast majority will toil away in obscurity. It is difficult to predict which companies will prosper and which will not. Neither investors nor companies can eliminate this uncertainty; that is why advisers tell investors to diversify their portfolios, and why companies do not pay cash when acquiring young, high-growth firms.

SUMMARY

The emergence of Internet, mobile, and other technology companies has created impressive value for some high-growth enterprises. It has also raised questions about the sanity of a stock market that at times has appeared to assign higher value to companies the more their losses mounted. But as this chapter demonstrates, the DCF approach remains an essential tool for understanding the value of high-growth companies. You must adapt your approach when valuing these companies: start from the future rather than the present when making your forecast, think in terms of scenarios, and compare the economics of the business model with peers. Though you cannot reduce the volatility of these companies, you can at least understand it.

37

Cyclical Companies

A cyclical company is one whose earnings demonstrate a repeating pattern of significant increases and decreases. The earnings of cyclical companies, including those in the steel, airline, paper, and chemical industries, fluctuate because the prices of their products change dramatically as demand and/or supply varies. The companies themselves often create too much capacity. Volatile earnings within the cycle introduce additional complexity into the valuation of these cyclical companies. For example, historical performance must be assessed in the context of the cycle. A decline in recent performance does not necessarily indicate a long-term negative trend, but rather may signal a shift to a different part of the cycle.

This chapter explores the valuation issues particular to cyclical companies. It starts with an examination of how the share prices of cyclical companies behave. This leads to a suggested approach for valuing these companies, as well as possible implications for managers.

SHARE PRICE BEHAVIOR

Suppose you were using the discounted-cash-flow (DCF) approach to value a cyclical company and had perfect foresight about the industry cycle. Would the company's value and earnings behave similarly? No. A succession of DCF values would exhibit much lower volatility than the earnings or cash flows. DCF reduces future expected cash flows to a single value. As a result, any single year is unimportant. For a cyclical company, the high cash flows cancel out the low cash flows. Only the long-term trend really matters.

To illustrate, suppose that the business cycle of Company A is ten years. Exhibit 37.1, part 1, shows the company's hypothetical cash flow pattern. It is highly volatile, containing both positive and negative cash flows. Discounting the future free cash flows at 10 percent produces the succession of DCF values in part 2 of the exhibit. Part 3 compares the cash flows and the perfect-foresight

EXHIBIT 37.1 **The Long-Term View: Free Cash Flow and DCF Volatility**

Free cash flow pattern, Company A, $ million

1

	Period, years										
	0	1	2	3	4	5	6	7	8	9	10
After-tax operating profit	10	9	6	3	–	(2)	3	18	7	6	10
Net investment	(3)	(3)	(2)	(2)	(1)	(3)	(5)	(3)	(3)	(3)	(3)
Free cash flow	7	6	4	1	(1)	(5)	(3)	15	4	3	7

Cash flows valued from any 1 year forward

2 DCF value

	34	33	27	28	30	35	40	33	33	34	31

3 Free cash flow and DCF value patterns

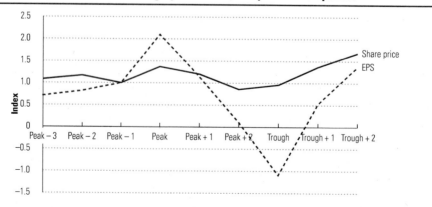

DCF values (the values are indexed for comparability). It shows that the DCF value is far less volatile than the underlying cash flow, because no single year's performance has a significant impact on the value of the company.

In the real world, the share prices of cyclical companies are less stable than the example in Exhibit 37.1. Exhibit 37.2 shows the earnings per share (EPS)

EXHIBIT 37.2 **Share Prices and Earnings per Share: 15 Cyclical Companies**

EXHIBIT 37.3 **Actual EPS and Consensus EPS Forecasts: 15 Cyclical Companies**

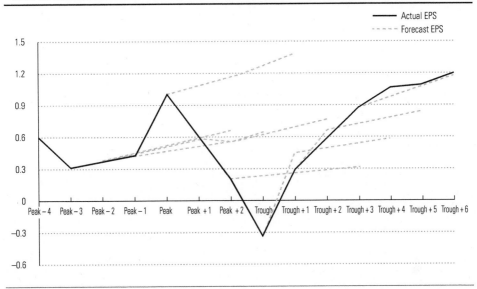

and share prices, both indexed, for 15 companies with a four-year cycle. The share prices are more volatile than the DCF approach would predict, which suggests that market prices exhibit the bias of anchoring on current earnings.

How can this apparent anomaly be explained? We examined equity analysts' consensus earnings forecasts for cyclical companies to look for clues to these companies' volatile stock prices. Consensus earnings forecasts for cyclical companies appeared to ignore cyclicality entirely. The forecasts invariably showed an upward-sloping trend, whether the companies were at the peak or trough of the cycle.

What became apparent was not that the DCF model was inconsistent with the facts, but that the market's projections of earnings and cash flow (assuming the market followed the analysts' consensus) were to blame. This conclusion was based on an analysis of 36 U.S. cyclical companies during 1985 to 1997. We divided them into groups with similar cycles (e.g., three, four, or five years from peak to trough) and calculated scaled average earnings and earnings forecasts. We then compared actual earnings with consensus earnings forecasts over the cycle.[1]

Exhibit 37.3 plots the actual earnings and consensus earnings forecasts for the set of 15 companies with four-year cycles in primary metals and manufacturing transportation equipment. The consensus forecasts do not predict the earnings cycle at all. In fact, except for the next-year forecasts in the years following the trough, the earnings per share are forecast to follow an upward-sloping path with no future variation.[2]

---

[1] Note that we have already adjusted downward the normal positive bias of analyst forecasts to focus on just the cyclicality issue. V. K. Chopra, "Why So Much Error in Analysts' Earnings Forecasts?" *Financial Analysts Journal* (November/December 1998): 35–42.

[2] Similar results were found for companies with three- and five-year cycles.

EXHIBIT 37.4 **When the Cycle Changes**

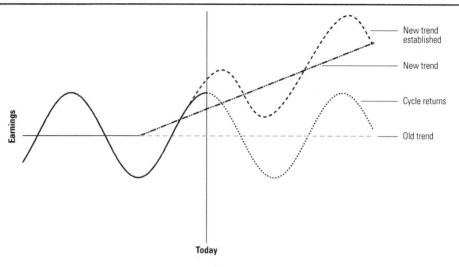

One explanation could be that equity analysts have incentives to avoid predicting the earnings cycle, particularly the down part. Academic research has shown that earnings forecasts have a positive bias that is sometimes attributed to the incentives facing equity analysts at investment banks.[3] Pessimistic earnings forecasts may damage relations between an analyst's employer—an investment bank—and a particular company. In addition, companies that are the target of negative commentary might cut off an analyst's access to management. From this evidence, we could conclude that analysts as a group are unable or unwilling to predict the cycles for these companies. If the market followed analyst forecasts, that behavior could account for the high volatility of cyclical companies' share prices.

We know that it is difficult to predict cycles, particularly their inflection points. So it is unsurprising that the market does not get it exactly right. However, we would be surprised if the stock market entirely missed the cycle, as the analysis of consensus forecasts suggests. To address this issue, we returned to the question of how the market should behave. Should it be able to predict the cycle and therefore exhibit little share price volatility? That would probably be asking too much. At any point, the company or industry could break out of its cycle and move to one that is higher or lower, as illustrated in Exhibit 37.4.

[3] The following articles discuss this hypothesis: M. R. Clayman and R. A. Schwartz, "Falling in Love Again: Analysts' Estimates and Reality," *Financial Analysts Journal* (September/October 1994): 66–68; J. Francis and D. Philbrick, "Analysts' Decisions as Products of a Multi-Task Environment," *Journal of Accounting Research* 31, no. 2 (Autumn 1993): 216–230; K. Schipper, "Commentary on Analysts' Forecasts," *Accounting Horizons* (December 1991): 105–121; B. Trueman, "On the Incentives for Security Analysts to Revise Their Earnings Forecasts," *Contemporary Accounting Research* 7, no. 1 (1990): 203–222.

Suppose you are valuing a company that seems to be at a peak in its earnings cycle. You will never have perfect foresight of the market cycle. Based on past cycles, you expect the industry to turn down soon. However, there are signs that the industry is about to break out of the old cycle. A reasonable valuation approach, therefore, would be to build two scenarios and weight their values. Suppose you assumed, with a 50 percent probability, that the cycle will follow the past and that the industry will turn down in the next year or so. The second scenario, also with 50 percent probability, would be that the industry will break out of the cycle and follow a new long-term trend based on current improved performance. The value of the company would then be the weighted average of these two values.

We found evidence that this is, in fact, the way the market behaves. We valued the four-year cyclical companies three ways:

1. With perfect foresight about the upcoming cycle
2. With zero foresight, assuming that current performance represents a point on a new long-term trend (essentially the consensus earnings forecast)
3. With a 50/50 forecast: 50 percent perfect foresight and 50 percent zero foresight

Exhibit 37.5 summarizes the results, comparing them with actual share prices. As shown, the market does not follow either the perfect-foresight or the zero-foresight path; it follows a blended path, much closer to the 50/50 path. So the

EXHIBIT 37.5 **Market Values of Cyclical Companies: Forecasts with Three Levels of Foresight**

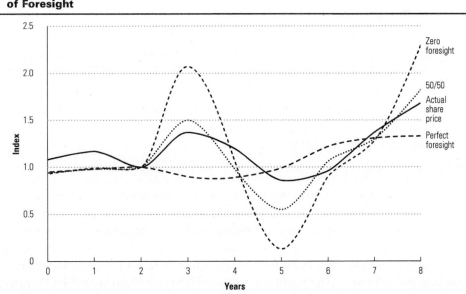

market has neither perfect foresight nor zero foresight. One could argue that this 50/50 valuation is the right place for the market to be.

AN APPROACH TO VALUING CYCLICAL COMPANIES

No one can precisely predict the earnings cycle for an industry, and any single forecast of performance must be wrong. Managers and investors can benefit from following explicitly the multiple-scenario probabilistic approach to valuing cyclical companies, similar to the approach used in Chapter 16 and the high-growth-company valuation in Chapter 36. The probabilistic approach avoids the traps of a single forecast and allows exploration of a wider range of outcomes and their implications.

Here is a two-scenario approach for valuing cyclical companies in four steps (of course, you could always have more than two scenarios):

1. Construct and value the normal cycle scenario, using information about past cycles. Pay particular attention to the long-term trend lines of operating profits, cash flow, and return on invested capital (ROIC), because they will have the largest impact on the valuation. Make sure the continuing value is based on a normalized level of profits (i.e., a point on the company's long-term cash flow trend line), not a peak or trough.

2. Construct and value a new trend line scenario based on the company's recent performance. Once again, focus primarily on the long-term trend line, because it will have the largest impact on value. Do not worry too much about modeling future cyclicality (although future cyclicality will be important for financial solvency).

3. Develop the economic rationale for each of the two scenarios, considering factors such as demand growth, companies entering or exiting the industry, and technology changes that will affect the balance of supply and demand.

4. Assign probabilities to the scenarios and calculate their weighted values. Use the economic rationale and its likelihood to estimate the weights assigned to each scenario.

This approach provides an estimate of the value as well as scenarios that put boundaries on the valuation. Managers can use these boundaries to improve their strategy and respond to signals about which scenario is likely to occur.

Another consideration when valuing cyclical companies in commodity-linked industries is that starting with revenues may not be the best way to model performance. Consider a polyethylene manufacturer, which processes natural gas into polyethylene. The traditional approach to valuation would be to model sales volumes and polyethylene prices to estimate revenues, from which you

EXHIBIT 37.6 **ROIC and Investment Rate: Commodity Chemicals, 1980–2013**

Median of North American companies, %

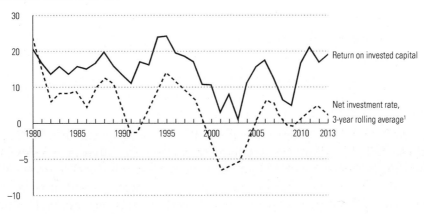

¹ Change in net property, plant, and equipment adjusted for inflation.

would subtract the cost of purchasing natural gas (volume times natural-gas prices) and operating costs to estimate operating profits. It may be simpler, however, to model only volumes and the "crack spread"—the difference between polyethylene prices and the cost of natural gas—and then subtract operating costs. What ultimately matters is the crack spread, not the revenues. The crack spread will often be set by the demand–supply balance for polyethylene, not the level of natural-gas prices. For example, during a decline in natural-gas prices, the crack spread might remain constant as producers pass on the lower natural-gas prices to customers by lowering polyethylene prices. If volumes were stable, so would be operating profits, despite a decline in revenues.[4]

IMPLICATIONS FOR MANAGING CYCLICAL COMPANIES

Is there anything managers can do to reduce or take advantage of the cyclicality of their industry? Evidence suggests that, in many cyclical industries, the companies themselves are what drive cyclicality. Exhibit 37.6 shows the ROIC and net investment in commodity chemicals from 1980 to 2013. The chart shows that, collectively, commodity chemical companies invest large amounts when prices and returns are high. But since capacity comes on line in very large chunks, utilization plunges, and this places downward pressure on price and ROIC. The cyclical investment in capacity is the driver of the cyclical profitability. Fluctuations in demand from customers do not cause cyclicality in profits. Producer supply does.

Managers who have detailed information about their product markets should be able to do a better job than the financial market in figuring out the

[4] The analysis is more complicated than this example suggests, because some polyethylene producers use naphtha rather than natural gas as their raw material.

EXHIBIT 37.7 **Relative Returns from Capital Expenditure Timing**

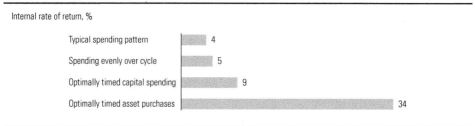

Internal rate of return, %

Typical spending pattern	4
Spending evenly over cycle	5
Optimally timed capital spending	9
Optimally timed asset purchases	34

cycle and then take appropriate actions. We can only speculate why they do not do so. Still, based on conversations with these executives, we believe that the herding behavior is caused by three factors: First, it is easier to invest when prices are high, because that is when cash is available. Second, it is easier to get approval from boards of directors to invest when profits are high. Finally, executives are concerned about their rivals growing faster than themselves (investments are a way to maintain market share).

This behavior also sends confusing signals to the stock market. Expanding when prices are high tells the financial market that the future looks great (often just before the cycle turns down). Signaling pessimism just before an upturn also confuses the market. Perhaps it should be no surprise that the stock market has difficulty valuing cyclical companies.

How could managers exploit their superior knowledge of the cycle? The most obvious action would be to improve the timing of capital spending. Companies could also pursue financial strategies, such as issuing shares at the peak of the cycle or repurchasing shares at the cycle's trough. The most aggressive managers could take this one step further by adopting a trading approach, making acquisitions at the bottom of the cycle and selling assets at the top. Exhibit 37.7 shows the results of a simulation of optimal cycle timing. The typical company's returns on investment could increase substantially.

Can companies really behave this way and invest against the cycle? It is actually very difficult for a company to take the contrarian view. The CEO must convince the board and the company's bankers to expand when the industry outlook is gloomy and competitors are retrenching. In addition, the CEO has to hold back while competitors build at the top of the cycle. Breaking out of the cycle may be possible, but it is the rare CEO who can do it.

SUMMARY

At first glance, the share prices of cyclical companies appear too volatile to be consistent with the DCF valuation approach. This chapter shows, however, that share price volatility can be explained by the uncertainty surrounding the industry cycle. Using scenarios and probabilities, managers and investors can take a systematic DCF approach to valuing and analyzing cyclical companies.

38

Banks

Banks are among the most complex businesses to value, especially from the outside in. Published accounts give an overview of a bank's financial performance but often lack vital information about its underlying economics, such as the extent of its credit losses or any mismatch between its assets and liabilities. Moreover, banks are highly levered, making bank valuations even more contingent on changing economic circumstances than are valuations in other sectors. Finally, most banks are in fact multibusiness companies, requiring separate analysis and valuation of their key business segments. So-called universal banks today engage in a wide range of businesses, including retail and wholesale banking, investment banking, and asset management.

In the view of some academics, managers, and regulators, the size, complexity, and lack of transparency of universal banks in the United States and Europe has led to undesirable systemic risks, among them that some banks have become "too big to fail."[1] During the 2008 credit crisis, the threat of collapse by some large universal banks led governments to bail out these institutions, triggering an ongoing debate about whether such institutions should be split into smaller and separate investment and commercial banks.[2]

This chapter provides a general overview of how to value banks and highlights some of the most common valuation challenges peculiar to the sector. First, it discusses the economic fundamentals of banking and trends in performance and growth, and then it describes how to use the equity cash flow approach for valuing banks, using a hypothetical, simplified example. It concludes by offering some practical recommendations for valuing universal banks in all their real-world complexity.

---

[1] See M. Egan, "Too-Big-to-Fail Banks Keep Getting Bigger," *CNNMoney*, November 21, 2017, money .cnn.com. Also see "Universal Banking: Together, Forever?" *The Economist*, August 12, 2012, www .economist.com.
[2] For analyses of the costs and benefits of large universal banks, see *Global Financial Stability Report 2014*, International Monetary Fund, April 2014, www.imf.org; and *Large Bank Holding Companies: Expectations of Government Support*, GAO-14-621, U.S. Government Accountability Office, July 2014, www.gao.gov.

ECONOMICS OF BANKING

After years of strong profitability and growth in the U.S. and European banking sectors, the crisis in the mortgage-backed securities market in 2007 sent many large banks spiraling into financial distress. Many large institutions on either side of the Atlantic went bankrupt or were kept afloat with costly government bailouts. The fallout in the real economy from what was originally a crisis in the banking sector ultimately curtailed growth in almost all sectors around the globe, bringing economic growth to a halt worldwide in 2008.

Since then, the sector has gone through years of restructuring, involving mergers, government bailouts, nationalizations, and bankruptcies. Regulation has intensified, leading to stricter capital requirements, restrictions on trading operations, and—in some European countries—caps on bonus payments for bank employees and executives. By 2018, banks in the United States had ridden stronger domestic economic growth, rebounding loan demand, and a reduction in bad debts to regain and even surpass their pre-crisis profit levels. In contrast, European banks were still below their pre-crisis profit levels, mainly due to lower economic growth across the European Union and the 2010 euro sovereign-debt crisis.

The credit crisis demonstrates the extent to which the banking industry is both a critical and a vulnerable component of modern economies. Banks are vulnerable because they are highly leveraged and their funding depends on investor and customer confidence. This can disappear overnight, sending a bank plummeting into failure. As a result, more uncertainty surrounds the valuation of banks than the valuation of most industrial companies. Therefore, it is all the more important for anyone valuing a bank to understand the business activities undertaken by banks, the ways in which banks create value, and the drivers of that value creation.

Universal banks may engage in any or all of a wide variety of business activities, including lending and borrowing, underwriting and placement of securities, payment services, asset management, proprietary trading, and brokerage. For the purpose of financial analysis and valuation, we group these activities according to the three types of income they generate for a bank: net interest income, fee and commission income, and trading income. "Other income" forms a fourth and generally smaller residual category of income from activities unrelated to the main banking businesses.

Net Interest Income

In their traditional role, banks act as intermediaries between parties with funding surpluses and those with deficits. They attract funds in the form of customer deposits and debt to provide funds to customers in the form of loans such as mortgages, credit card loans, and corporate loans. The difference between the interest income a bank earns from lending and the interest expense it pays to borrow funds is its net interest income. For the regional retail banks in the United States and retail-focused universal banks such as Banco Santander and ING Group, net interest income is typically the biggest component of total net revenues.

As we discuss later in this chapter, it is important to understand that not all of a bank's net interest income creates value. Most banks have a maturity mismatch as a result of using short-term deposits as funding to back long-term loans and mortgages. In this case, the bank earns income from holding positions on different parts of the yield curve. Typically, deposits are a low-cost and predictable form of funding, so that borrowing for the short term costs a bank less than what it can earn from long-term lending. Yet it is unclear whether all of this income represents value creation. For example, the true value created from lending is measured by the difference between the rate that banks receive on their outstanding loans and their returns in the financial markets on loans with the same maturity (see the section on economic-spread analysis later in this chapter).

Fee and Commission Income

For services such as transaction advisory, underwriting and placement of securities, managing investment assets, securities brokerage, and many others, banks typically charge their customers a fee or commission. For investment banks (like Morgan Stanley and Goldman Sachs), such commissions and fees typically make up around half of total net revenues and around one-third or more for universal banks with large investment-banking activities (among them HSBC and Bank of America). Fee income is usually easier to understand than net interest income, as it is independent of financing. However, some forms of fee income are highly cyclical; examples include fees from underwriting and transaction advisory services.

Trading Income

Over the past 30 years, proprietary trading emerged as a third main category of income for the banking sector as a whole. This can involve not only a wide variety of instruments traded on exchanges and over the counter, such as equity stocks, bonds, and foreign exchange, but also more exotic products, such as credit default swaps and asset-backed debt obligations, traded mostly over the counter.

Trading profits tend to be highly volatile: gains made over several years may be wiped out by large losses in a single year, as the credit crisis painfully illustrated. These activities have also attracted considerable attention in the wake of the crisis. In 2010, the United States adopted legislation preventing

EXHIBIT 38.1 **Income Sources for European Banks, 1988–2018**

Income streams/total net revenues,[1] %

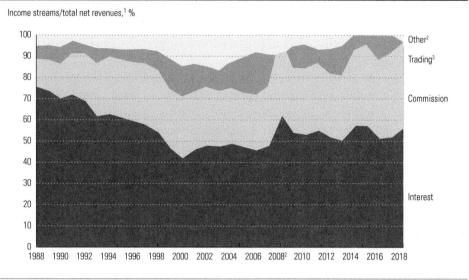

[1] For 1988–2007, based on a sample of 113 EU banks, of which 109 were active in 2007. For 2008–2013, based on a sample of 211 EU banks active in 2013.
  For 2014–2018, based on a sample of largest 80 EU banks in 2014.

[2] Other income was negative from 2014 to 2017.

[3] Trading income was –9% in 2008.

Source: Bloomberg, Compustat, Datastream, CapitalIQ.

banks from engaging in proprietary trading for their own profit.[3] This resulted in steeply lower overall trading income, as the law permits only trading related to serving the bank's customers. In Europe, restrictions on trading activities also were adopted—for example, through the 2017 Markets in Financial Instruments Directive II (MiFID II). Trading income for European banks has sharply declined since 2008.

Other Income

Some banks also generate income from a range of nonbanking activities, including real estate development, minority investments in industrial companies, and distribution of investment, insurance, and pension products and services for third parties. Typically, these activities make only small contributions to overall income and are unrelated to the bank's main banking activities.

As Exhibit 38.1 shows for the European banking sector, the relative importance of these four income sources has changed radically over past decades. European banks shifted away during the 1990s from interest income toward

---

[3] The 2010 Dodd-Frank Wall Street Reform and Consumer Protection Act aimed to improve the stability of the U.S. financial system through increased regulation and supervision. For example, it established restrictions on proprietary trading by banks through the so-called Volcker Rule and new government agencies such as the Financial Stability Oversight Council.

commission and trading income. However, trading income collapsed during the credit crisis. Despite recovering somewhat since then, it has not regained pre-crisis levels.

As the banks have shifted their sources of income, the cyclicality of their profitability and market valuations has increased. This is measured by their return on equity and their market-to-book ratios (see Exhibit 38.2). These measures for the sector in both the United States and Europe rose sharply after 1995 to reach historic peaks in 2006. But they fell sharply during the credit crisis, with European banks suffering a second decline during the 2010 euro bond crisis. In 2018, profitability and valuation levels remained well below their peak levels on both sides of the Atlantic, though American banks were much more successful than their European counterparts in regaining some ground.

EXHIBIT 38.2 **Increased Cyclicality in Banking**

Market value of equity/book value of equity

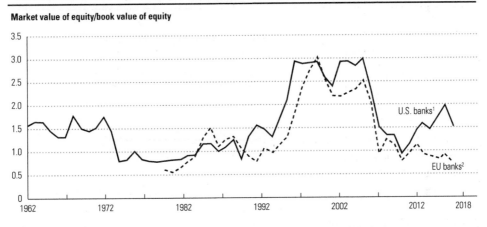

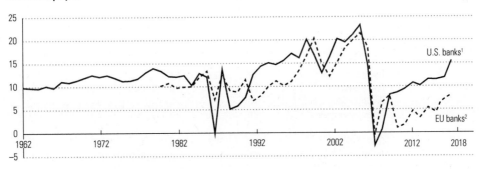

¹ U.S. banks: For 1962–2007, based on aggregate financials and valuation of 957 U.S. banks, of which 346 were active in 2007. For 2008–2013, based on a sample of 509 U.S. banks active in 2013. For 2014–2018, based on a sample of largest 156 US banks active in 2014. Book value excludes goodwill.

² EU banks: For 1980–2007, based on aggregate financials and valuation of 113 EU banks, of which 109 were active in 2007. For 2008–2013, based on a sample of 211 EU banks active in 2013. For 2014–2018, based on a sample of largest 80 EU banks active in 2014. Book value excludes goodwill.

Source: Bloomberg, Compustat, Datastream, CapitalIQ.

PRINCIPLES OF BANK VALUATION

Throughout most of this book, we apply the enterprise discounted-cash-flow (DCF) approach to valuation. Discounting free cash flows is the appropriate approach for nonfinancial companies, where operating decisions and financing decisions are separate. For banks, however, we cannot value operations separately from interest income and expense, since these are the main categories of a bank's core operations. It is necessary to value the cash flow to equity, which includes both the operational and financial cash flows. For valuation of banks, we therefore recommend the equity DCF method.[4] To understand the principles of the equity DCF method, let's explore a stylized example of a retail bank. ABC Bank attracts customer deposits to provide funds for loans and mortgages to other customers. ABC's historical balance sheet, income statement, and key financial indicators are shown in Exhibit 38.3.

EXHIBIT 38.3 **ABC Bank: Historical Financial Statements**

$ million

	2015	2016	2017	2018	2019
Balance sheet[1]					
Loans	1,030.0	1,063.5	1,097.5	1,133.7	1,173.4
Total assets	1,030.0	1,063.5	1,097.5	1,133.7	1,173.4
Deposits	988.8	999.7	1,009.7	1,043.0	1,079.5
Equity	41.2	63.8	87.8	90.7	93.9
Total liabilities	1,030.0	1,063.5	1,097.5	1,133.7	1,173.4
Income statement					
Interest income	70.0	72.1	74.4	71.3	73.7
Interest expense	(48.0)	(47.5)	(47.0)	(45.4)	(44.9)
Net interest income	22.0	24.6	27.5	25.9	28.8
Operating expenses	(11.2)	(13.1)	(14.3)	(12.2)	(13.0)
Operating profit before taxes	10.8	11.6	13.2	13.7	15.9
Income taxes	(3.2)	(3.5)	(4.0)	(4.1)	(4.8)
Net income	7.5	8.1	9.2	9.6	11.1
Key ratios, %					
Loan growth	3.0	3.3	3.2	3.3	3.5
Loan interest rate	7.0	7.0	7.0	6.5	6.5
Deposit growth	3.0	1.1	1.0	3.3	3.5
Deposit interest rate	5.0	4.8	4.7	4.5	4.3
Cost/income	51.0	53.0	52.0	47.0	45.0
Tax rate	30.0	30.0	30.0	30.0	30.0
Equity/total assets	4.0	6.0	8.0	8.0	8.0
Return on equity[2]	18.9	19.7	14.5	10.9	12.2

[1] Book value per end of year.
[2] Return on beginning-of-year equity.

[4] See Chapter 10 for a comparison of the enterprise and equity DCF methods.

At of the end of 2018, the bank has $1.134 billion of loans outstanding with customers, generating 6.5 percent interest income. To meet regulatory requirements, ABC must maintain an 8 percent ratio of Tier 1 equity capital to loan assets, which we define for this example as the ratio of equity divided by total assets. This means that 8 percent, or $91 million, of its loans are funded by equity capital, and the rest of the loans are funded by $1.043 billion of deposits. The deposits carry 4.3 percent interest, generating total interest expenses of $45 million.

Net interest income for ABC amounted to $29 million in 2019, thanks to the higher rates received on loans than paid on deposits. All capital gains or losses on loans and deposits are included in interest income and expenses. Operating expenses such as labor and rental costs are $13 million, which brings ABC's cost-to-income ratio to 45 percent of net interest income. After subtracting taxes at 30 percent, net income equals $11 million, which translates into a return on equity of 12.2 percent.

As discussed in Chapter 10, the equity value of a company equals the present value of its future cash flow to equity (CFE), discounted at the cost of equity, k_e:

$$V_e = \sum_{t=1}^{\infty} \frac{CFE_t}{(1+k_e)^t}$$

We can derive equity cash flow from two starting points. First, equity cash flow equals net income minus the earnings retained in the business:

$$CFE_t = NI_t - \Delta E_t + OCI_t$$

where CFE is equity cash flow, NI is net income, ΔE is the increase in the book value of equity, and OCI is noncash other comprehensive income.

Net income represents the earnings theoretically available to shareholders after payment of all expenses, including those to depositors and debt holders. However, net income by itself is not cash flow. As a bank grows, it will need to increase its equity; otherwise, its ratio of debt plus deposits over equity would rise, which might cause regulators and customers to worry about the bank's solvency. Increases in equity reduce equity cash flow, because they mean the bank is issuing more shares or setting aside earnings that could otherwise be paid out to shareholders. The last step in calculating equity cash flow is to add noncash other comprehensive income, such as net unrealized gains and losses on certain equity and debt investments, hedging activities, adjustments to the minimum pension liability, and foreign-currency translation items. This cancels out any noncash adjustment to equity.[5]

Exhibit 38.4 shows the equity cash flow calculation for ABC Bank. Note that in 2015, ABC's other comprehensive income included a translation gain on its overseas loan business, which was discontinued in the same year. ABC's cash flow to equity was negative in 2016 and 2017 because it raised new equity to lift its Tier 1 ratio from 4 percent to 8 percent.

---

[5] Of course, you can also calculate equity cash flow from the changes in all the balance sheet accounts. For example, equity cash flow for a bank equals net income plus the increase in deposits and reserves, less the increase in loans and investments, and so on.

EXHIBIT 38.4 **ABC Bank: Historical Cash Flow to Equity**

$ million

	2015	2016	2017	2018	2019
Cash flow statement					
Net income	7.5	8.1	9.2	9.6	11.1
(Increase) decrease in equity	(1.2)	(22.6)	(24.0)	(2.9)	(3.2)
Other comprehensive income (loss)	0.2	–	–	–	–
Cash flow to equity	6.5	(14.5)	(14.8)	6.7	7.9

Another way to calculate equity cash flow is to sum all cash paid to or received from shareholders, including cash changing hands as dividends, through share repurchases, and through new share issuances. Both calculations arrive at the same result. Note that equity cash flow is not the same as dividends paid out to shareholders, because share buybacks and issuance can also form a significant part of cash flow to and from equity.

Analyzing and Forecasting Equity Cash Flows

The generic value driver tree for a retail bank, shown in Exhibit 38.5, is conceptually the same as one for an industrial company. Following the tree's branches, we analyze ABC's historical performance as laid out in Exhibit 38.3.

EXHIBIT 38.5 **Generic Value Driver Tree for Retail Banking: Equity DCF Version**

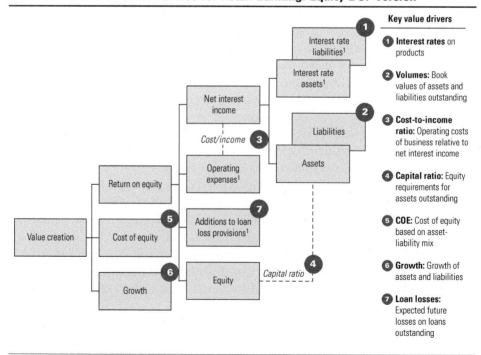

[1] After taxes.

Over the five years analyzed, ABC's loan portfolio has grown by around 3.0 to 3.5 percent annually. Since 2015, ABC's interest rates on loans have been declining from 7.0 percent to 6.5 percent in 2019, but this was offset by an even stronger decrease in rates on deposits from 5.0 percent to 4.3 percent over the same period. Combined with the growth in its loan portfolio, this lifted ABC's net interest income from $22 million in 2015 to $29 million in 2019. The bank also managed to improve its cost-to-income ratio significantly from a peak level of 53 percent in 2016 to 45 percent in 2019.

Higher regulatory requirements for equity risk capital forced ABC to double its Tier 1 ratio (equity to total assets) from 4 percent to 8 percent over the period. The combination of loan portfolio growth and stricter regulatory requirements has forced ABC to increase its equity capital by some $50 million since 2015. As a result, ABC's return on equity declined significantly in 2019 to 12 percent, from nearly 20 percent in 2016.

Exhibit 38.6 shows the financial forecasts for ABC Bank, assuming its loan portfolio growth rate increases to 4.5 percent in the short term and settles at 3.5 percent in perpetuity. Interest rates on loans and deposits are expected to decrease to 6.1 and 3.9 percent, respectively. Operating expenses will decline to 43 percent of net interest income. As a result, ABC's return on equity increases somewhat to 12.8 percent in 2021 and stays at that level in perpetuity. Note that a mere one-percentage-point increase in interest rates on loans would translate into a change in return on equity of around 12 percentage points, a function of ABC's high leverage (equity capital at 8 percent of total assets).

Discounting Equity Cash Flows

To estimate the cost of equity, k_e, for ABC Bank, we use a beta of 1.1 (based on the average beta for its banking peers), a long-term risk-free interest rate of 4.5 percent, and a market risk premium of 5 percent:[6]

$$k_e = r_f + \beta \times \text{MRP} = 4.5\% + 1.1 \times 5.0\% = 10.0\%$$

where r_f is the risk-free rate, β is the equity beta, and MRP is the market risk premium. (There is no need to adjust any estimates of equity betas of banking peers for leverage when deriving ABC's equity beta, assuming that banking peers have similar capital coverage ratios.)

In the equity DCF approach, we use an adapted version of the value driver formula presented in Chapter 3, replacing return on invested capital (ROIC) and return on new invested capital (RONIC) with return on equity (ROE) and

[6] See Chapter 15 for more details on estimating the cost of capital.

EXHIBIT 38.6 **ABC Bank: Financial Forecasts**

$ million

	2020	2021	2022	2023	2024	2025
Balance sheet[1]						
Loans	1,226.2	1,281.4	1,332.6	1,379.3	1,427.6	1,477.5
Total assets	1,226.2	1,281.4	1,332.6	1,379.3	1,427.6	1,477.5
Deposits	1,128.1	1,178.9	1,226.0	1,268.9	1,313.4	1,359.3
Equity	98.1	102.5	106.6	110.3	114.2	118.2
Total liabilities	1,226.2	1,281.4	1,332.6	1,379.3	1,427.6	1,477.5
Income statement						
Interest income	71.6	74.8	78.2	81.3	84.1	87.1
Interest expense	(41.6)	(43.4)	(45.4)	(47.2)	(48.9)	(50.6)
Net interest income	30.0	31.4	32.8	34.1	35.3	36.5
Operating expense	(13.5)	(13.5)	(14.1)	(14.7)	(15.2)	(15.7)
Operating profit before tax	16.5	17.9	18.7	19.4	20.1	20.8
Income taxes	(5.0)	(5.4)	(5.6)	(5.8)	(6.0)	(6.2)
Net income	11.6	12.5	13.1	13.6	14.1	14.6
Cash flow statement						
Net income	11.6	12.5	13.1	13.6	14.1	14.6
(Increase) decrease in equity	(4.2)	(4.4)	(4.1)	(3.7)	(3.9)	(4.0)
Other comprehensive (income) loss	–	–	–	–	–	–
Cash flow to equity	7.3	8.1	9.0	9.9	10.2	10.6
Key ratios, %						
Loan growth	4.5	4.5	4.0	3.5	3.5	3.5
Loan interest rate	6.1	6.1	6.1	6.1	6.1	6.1
Deposit growth	4.5	4.5	4.0	3.5	3.5	3.5
Deposit interest rate	3.9	3.9	3.9	3.9	3.9	3.9
Cost/income	45.0	43.0	43.0	43.0	43.0	43.0
Tax rate	30.0	30.0	30.0	30.0	30.0	30.0
Equity/total assets	8.0	8.0	8.0	8.0	8.0	8.0
Return on equity[2]	12.3	12.8	12.8	12.8	12.8	12.8

[1] Book value per end of year.

[2] Return on beginning-of-year equity.

return on new equity investments (RONE), and replacing net operating profit after taxes (NOPAT) with net income:

$$CV_t = \frac{NI_{t+1}\left(1 - \dfrac{g}{RONE}\right)}{k_e - g}$$

where CV_t is the continuing value as of year t, NI_{t+1} is the net income in year $t + 1$, g equals growth, and k_e is the cost of equity.

EXHIBIT 38.7 **ABC Bank: Valuation**

$ million

	Cash flow to equity (CFE)	Discount factor	Present value of CFE
2020	7.3	0.909	6.7
2021	8.1	0.826	6.7
2022	9.0	0.751	6.7
2023	9.9	0.683	6.7
2024	10.2	0.621	6.3
2025	10.6	0.564	6.0
Continuing value	168.4	0.564	95.0
Value of equity			134.2
Market-to-book ratio			1.4
P/E ratio[1]			11.6

[1] Forward price-to-earnings ratio on 2020 net income.

Assuming that ABC Bank continues to generate a 12.8 percent ROE on its new business investments in perpetuity while growing at 3.5 percent per year,[7] its continuing value as of 2025 is as follows:

$$CV = \frac{\$15.1 \text{ million}\left(1 - \dfrac{3.5\%}{12.8\%}\right)}{10.0\% - 3.5\%} = \$168.4 \text{ million}$$

The calculation of the discounted value of ABC's cash flow to equity is presented in Exhibit 38.7. The present value of ABC's equity amounts to $134.2 million, which implies a market-to-book ratio for its equity of 1.4 and a price-to-earnings (P/E) ratio of 11.6. As for industrial companies, whenever possible you should triangulate your results with an analysis based on multiples (see Chapter 18). Note that the market-to-book ratio indicates that ABC is creating value over its book value of equity, which is consistent with a long-term return on equity of 12.8 percent (which is above the cost of equity of 10.0 percent).

Pitfalls of Equity DCF Valuation

The equity DCF approach as illustrated here is straightforward and theoretically correct. However, the approach involves some potential pitfalls. These concern the sources of value creation, the impact of leverage and business risk on the cost of equity, and the tax penalty on holding equity risk capital.

---

[7] If the return on new equity investments (RONE) equals the return on equity (ROE), the formula can be simplified as follows:

$$CV_t = \frac{NI_{t+1}\left(1 - \dfrac{g}{ROE}\right)}{k_e - g} = E_t\left(\frac{ROE - g}{k_e - g}\right)$$

where E is the book value of equity.

Sources of Value Creation   The equity DCF approach does not tell us how and where ABC Bank creates value in its operations. Is ABC creating or destroying value when receiving 6.5 percent interest on its loans or when paying 4.3 percent on deposits? To what extent does ABC's net income reflect intrinsic value creation?

You can overcome this pitfall by undertaking economic-spread analysis, described in the next section. As that section will show, ABC is creating value in its lending business but much less so in deposits, which were not creating any value before 2019 in this particular example. A significant part of ABC's net interest income in 2019 is, in fact, driven by the mismatch in maturities of its short-term borrowing and long-term lending. The mismatch in itself does not necessarily create any value for shareholders, because they could set up a similar position in the bond market. The key question is whether ABC Bank can attract deposits and provide loans at better-than-market interest rates—and this is addressed by economic-spread analysis.

Impact of Leverage and Business Risk on Cost of Equity   As for industrial companies, the cost of equity for a bank such as ABC should reflect its business risk and leverage. Its equity beta is a weighted average of the betas of all its loan and deposit businesses. So when you project significant changes in a bank's asset or liability composition or equity capital ratios, you cannot leave the cost of equity unchanged.

For instance, if ABC were to decrease its equity capital ratio, its expected return on equity would go up. But in the absence of taxes, this by itself should not increase the intrinsic equity value, because ABC's cost of equity would also rise, as its cash flows would now be riskier. It will increase ABC's value only to the extent that the bank is creating value on the deposit business that it is growing as a result of the leverage increase (see next section, on economic-spread analysis).[8]

The same line of reasoning holds for changes in the asset or liability mix. Assume ABC raises an additional $50 million in equity and invests this in government bonds at the risk-free rate of 4.5 percent, reducing future returns on equity. If you left ABC's cost of equity unchanged at 10.0 percent, the estimated equity value per share would decline. But in the absence of taxation, the risk-free investment cannot be value-destroying, because its expected return exactly equals the cost of capital for risk-free assets. There is no impact on value creation if we assume that the bank has no competitive (dis)advantage in investing in government bonds. The assumption seems reasonable, as it implies that the bank does not obtain the government bonds at a premium or

---

[8] Note that leverage has a different impact on the value of banks than on the value of industrial companies. An industrial company's value is not affected by leverage in the absence of corporate income taxes, because it is assumed that there is no value creation in the issuance of corporate debt raised at market rates (see Chapter 10).

discount to their fair market value. As a result, if you accounted properly for the impact of the change in its asset mix on the cost of equity and the resulting reduction in the beta of its business, ABC's equity value would remain unchanged.

Tax Penalty on Holding Equity Risk Capital   Holding equity risk capital represents a cost for banks, and it is important to understand what drives this cost. Consider again the example of ABC Bank issuing new equity and investing in risk-free assets, thereby increasing its equity risk capital. In the absence of taxation, this extra layer of risk capital would have no impact on value, and there would be no cost to holding it. But interest income *is* taxed, and that is what makes holding equity risk capital costly; equity, unlike debt or deposits, provides no tax shield. In this example, ABC will pay taxes on the risk-free interest income from the $50 million of risk-free bonds that cannot be offset by tax shields on interest charges on deposits or debt, because the investment was funded with equity, for which there are no tax-deductible interest charges.

The true cost of holding equity capital is this so-called tax penalty, whose present value equals the equity capital times the tax rate. If ABC Bank were to increase its equity capital by $50 million to invest in risk-free bonds, holding everything else constant, this would entail destroying $15 million of present value (30 percent times $50 million) because of the tax penalty. As long as the cost of equity reflects the bank's leverage and business risk, the tax penalty is implicitly included in the equity DCF. However, in the economic-spread analysis discussed next, we explicitly include the tax penalty as a cost of the bank's lending business.

Economic-Spread Analysis

The equity DCF approach does not reveal the sources of value creation in a bank. To understand how much value ABC Bank is creating in its different product lines, we can analyze them by their economic spread.[9] We define the pretax economic spread on ABC's loan business in 2019 as the interest rate on loans minus the matched-opportunity rate (MOR) for loans, multiplied by the amount of loans outstanding at the beginning of the year:

$$S_{BT} = L(r_L - k_L) = 1,133.7\,(6.5\% - 5.1\%) = 15.9$$

where S_{BT} is the pretax spread in millions of dollars, L is the amount of the loans (also in millions of dollars), r_L is the interest rate on the loans, and k_L is the MOR for the loans.

---

[9] The approach is similar to those described by J. Dermine, *Bank Valuation and Value-Based Management* (New York: McGraw-Hill, 2009).

The matched-opportunity rate is the cost of capital for the loans—that is, the return the bank could have captured for investments in the financial market with similar duration and risk as the loans. Note that the actual interest rate a bank is paying for deposit or debt funding is not necessarily relevant, because the maturity and risk of its loans and mortgages often do not match those of its deposits and debt. For example, the MOR for high-quality four-year loans should be close to the yield on investment-grade corporate bonds with four years to maturity that are traded in the market. Banks create value on their loan business if the loan interest rate is above the matched-opportunity rate.

To obtain the economic spread after taxes (S_{AT}), it is necessary to deduct the taxes on the spread itself, a tax penalty on the equity required for the loan business (TPE), and the tax on any maturity mismatch in the funding of the loans (TMM):

$$S_{AT} = L(r_L - k_L)(1 - T) - \text{TPE} - \text{TMM}$$

The tax penalty on equity occurs because, in contrast to deposit and debt funding, equity provides no tax shield, as dividend payments are not tax deductible.[10] Thus, the more a bank relies on equity funding instead of deposits or debt, the less value it creates, everything else being equal. Of course, banks have to fund their operations at least partly with equity. One reason is that regulators in most countries have established solvency restrictions that require banks to hold on to certain minimum equity levels relative to their asset bases. In addition, banks with little or no equity funding would not be able to attract deposits from customers or debt, because their default risk would be too high. For ABC's loan business, this tax penalty in 2019 is calculated as follows:[11]

$$\text{TPE} = T \times L \times e_L \times k_D$$
$$= 30\%(1,133.7)(8.0\%)(4.6\%) = 1.3$$

where e_L is the required equity capital divided by the amount of loans outstanding and k_D is the MOR for deposits.

In addition, the tax on a maturity mismatch (TMM) needs to be included if the maturity of the loans does not correspond to that of the bank's deposits. Typically, the maturity of a bank's loans is longer than that of the deposits by which it funds its operations, and a difference arises in the matched-opportunity rates. For example, in the case of ABC Bank, the loans have a longer maturity than the deposits. As a result, the MOR for loans (5.1 percent) is above the MOR for deposits (4.6 percent). The maturity difference in itself does not create or destroy any value, as it does not affect the economic spread

---

[10] Debt funding provides a tax shield, whereas equity funding generates a tax penalty. See also Dermine, *Bank Valuation*, 77.

[11] In case of multiple loan products, you can allocate the tax penalty to the individual product lines according to their equity capital requirements.

EXHIBIT 38.8 ABC Bank: Historical Economic Spread by Product Line

$ million

	2015	2016	2017	2018	2019
Loans interest rate, %	7.0	7.0	7.0	6.5	6.5
Matched-opportunity rate (MOR), %	5.5	5.5	5.5	5.5	5.1
Loans relative economic spread, %	1.5	1.5	1.5	1.0	1.4
Loans book value[1]	1,000.0	1,030.0	1,063.5	1,097.5	1,133.7
Loans economic spread before taxes	15.0	15.5	16.0	11.0	15.9
Taxes on economic spread	(4.5)	(4.6)	(4.8)	(3.3)	(4.8)
Tax penalty on equity and maturity mismatch	(2.1)	(3.1)	(3.8)	(4.5)	(3.0)
Loans economic spread[2]	8.4	7.8	7.4	3.2	8.2
Deposits interest rate, %	5.0	4.8	4.7	4.5	4.3
Matched-opportunity rate (MOR), %	5.0	4.7	4.6	4.5	4.6
Deposits spread, %	–	–0.1	–0.1	–	0.3
Deposits book value[1]	960.0	988.8	999.7	1,009.7	1,043.0
Deposits economic spread[2]	–	(0.7)	(0.7)	–	2.2

[1] Beginning of year.
[2] After taxes.

on deposits or loans. But the taxation of the interest income that the mismatch generates has an impact on value, which should be included in the economic spread on loans. Note that the tax result on the maturity mismatch could be positive in the (unlikely) case that a bank's loans have a shorter maturity than its deposits. The TMM (in millions of dollars) for ABC Bank's loans in 2019 is calculated as follows:

$$TMM = T \times L(k_L - k_D)$$
$$= 30\%(1,133.7)(5.1\% - 4.6\%) = 1.7$$

The after-tax economic spread on loans is then derived as:

$$S_{AT} = 15.9(1 - 30\%) - 1.3 - 1.7 = 8.2$$

This number represents the dollar amount of value (in millions) created by ABC's loan business. Along the same lines, we can define the economic spread for ABC Bank's deposit products as well (see Exhibit 38.8). Our analysis explicitly includes the spread on deposits because banks (in contrast to industrial companies) aim to create value in their funding operations. For example, ABC Bank created value for its shareholders in its deposit business in 2019 because it attracted deposits at a 4.3 percent interest rate, below the 4.6 percent rate for traded bonds with the same high credit rating as ABC had.[12]

[12] Note that the spread for deposits does not include a tax charge for maturity mismatch and equity risk capital; these are included in the spread for loans.

Figure 38.9 **Generic Value Driver Tree for Retail Banking: Economic Spread**

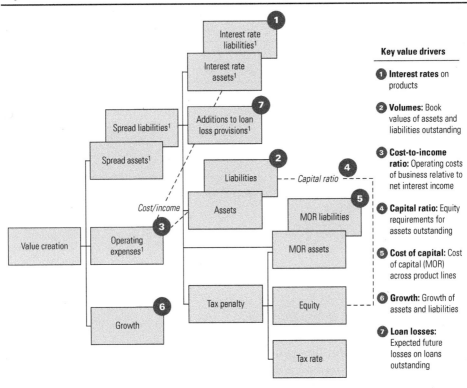

¹ After taxes.

When comparing the spread across ABC product lines over the past few years, we can immediately see that most of the value created comes from its lending business. In fact, ABC was not making any money on its deposit funding from 2015 to 2019, as shown by the zero or negative spreads in those years.

From our calculations of the economic spreads of the two businesses, it is possible to rearrange the value driver tree from the equity DCF approach shown previously in Exhibit 38.5. In the revised value driver tree shown in Exhibit 38.9, the key drivers are virtually identical but highlight some important messages about value creation for banks:

- Interest income on assets creates value only if the interest rate exceeds the cost of capital for those assets (i.e., the matched-opportunity rate) by more than the taxes on any maturity mismatch.

- Changes in the capital ratio affect value creation only through the tax penalty on equity.

- Growth adds value only if the economic spread from the additional product sold is positive and sufficient to cover any operating expenses.

EXHIBIT 38.10 **ABC Bank: Net Interest Income and Value Creation**

$ million

	2019	Description
Net interest income (after tax)	20.2	$(1 - T)(L \times r_L - D \times r_D)$
Matched-capital charge	4.2	$(L - D) k_D = (L \times e_L \times k_D)$
Mismatched-capital charge	5.7	$L \times (k_L - k_D)$
Economic spread (after tax)	10.3	$= (1 - T) L (r_L - k_L) - T \times L \times e_L \times k_D - T \times L (k_L - k_D) + (1 - T) D (r_D - k_D)$

$$S_{BT} = 11.2 \qquad TPE = -1.3 \qquad TMM = -1.7 \qquad S_{BT} = 2.2$$

For loans: 8.2   For deposits: 2.2

Note that we could further refine the tree by allocating the operating expenses to the product lines, represented by the different asset and liability categories. This is worth doing if there is enough information on the operating costs incurred by each product line and the equity capital required for each.

Economic Spread vs. Net Interest Income

The spread analysis helps to show why a bank's reported net interest income does not reveal the value created by the bank and should be interpreted with care. For example, out of ABC Bank's 2019 net interest income after taxes of $20.2 million, only $10.3 million represents true value created (the economic spread of $8.2 million on loans plus $2.2 million on deposits minus a rounding difference, as shown in Exhibit 38.10). The remaining $9.9 million is income but not value, because it is offset by the following two charges shown in the exhibit:

1. The matched-capital charge, amounting to $4.2 million for ABC in 2019, is the income that would be required on assets and liabilities if there were no maturity mismatch and no economic spread. In that case, all assets and liabilities would have identical duration (and risk) to deposits, so that their return would equal k_D (the MOR on deposits) and net interest income would equal equity times k_D. This component of net interest income does not represent value; it only provides shareholders the required return on their equity investment in a perfectly matched bank.[13]

---

[13] The cost of capital for the bank's equity would then also equal k_D, because it is the value-weighted average of the cost of capital of all assets and liabilities.

2. The mismatched-capital charge, amounting to $5.7 million of ABC's net interest income, arises from the difference in the duration of ABC's assets and deposits. To illustrate, when a bank borrows at short maturity and invests at long maturity, it creates income. The income does not represent value when the risks of taking positions on the yield curve are taken into account. The mismatched-capital charge represents the component of net interest income required to compensate shareholders for that risk.[14]

COMPLICATIONS IN BANK VALUATIONS

When you value banks, significant challenges arise in addition to those discussed in the hypothetical ABC Bank example. In reality, banks have many interest-generating business lines, including credit card loans, mortgage loans, and corporate loans, all involving loans of varying maturities. On the liability side, banks could carry a variety of customer deposits as well as different forms of straight and hybrid debt. Banks need to invest in working capital and in property, plant, and equipment, although the amounts are typically small fractions of total assets. Obviously, this variety makes the analysis of real-world banks more complex, but the principles laid out in the ABC example remain generally applicable. This section discusses some practical challenges in the analysis and valuation of banks.

Convergence of Forward Interest Rates

For ABC Bank, we assumed a perpetual difference in short-term and long-term interest rates. As a result, ABC generates a permanent, positive net interest income from a maturity mismatch: using short-term customer deposits as funding for investments in long-term loans. However, following the expectations theory of interest rates, long-term rates move higher when short-term rates are expected to increase, and vice versa. Following this theory, it is necessary to ensure that our expectations for interest rates in future years are consistent with the current yield curve.

Exhibit 38.11 shows an example of a set of future one-, three-, five-, and ten-year interest rates that are consistent with a hypothetical yield curve as of 2019. The forecasts for a bank's interest income and expenses should be based on these forward rates, which constitute the matched-opportunity rates for the different product lines. For example, if the bank's deposits have a three-year maturity on average, you should use the interest rates from the forward three-year interest rate curve minus an expected spread for the bank to forecast the expected interest rates on deposits in your DCF

---

[14] Note that the taxes on the matched capital and the maturity mismatch are included as charges in the economic spread.

EXHIBIT 38.11 **Yield Curve and Future Interest Rates**

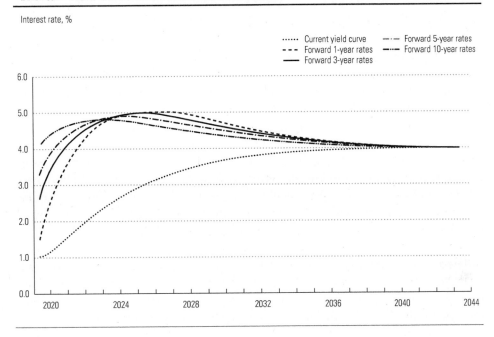

Interest rate, %

Legend:
...... Current yield curve
- - - Forward 1-year rates
—— Forward 3-year rates
—·— Forward 5-year rates
—··— Forward 10-year rates

model. The rates are all derived from the current yield curve. To illustrate, the expected three-year interest rate in 2021 follows from the current three- and six-year yields:

$$r_{2021-2024} = \left[\frac{(1+Y_{2024})^6}{(1+Y_{2021})^3} - 1 \right]^{\frac{1}{3}} = \left[\frac{(1+2.82\%)^6}{(1+1.66\%)^3} - 1 \right]^{\frac{1}{3}} = 4.0\%$$

where $r_{2021-2024}$ is the expected three-year interest rate as of 2021, Y_{2021} is the current three-year interest rate, and Y_{2024} is the current six-year interest rate.

In practice, forward rate curves derived from the yield curve will rarely follow the smooth patterns of Exhibit 38.11. Small irregularities in the current yield curve can lead to large spikes and dents in the forward rate curves, which would produce large fluctuations in net interest income forecasts. As a practical solution, use the following procedure. First, obtain the forward one-year interest rates from the current yield curve. Then smooth these forward one-year rates to even out the spikes and dents arising from irregularities in the yield curve. Finally, derive the two-year and longer-maturity forward rates from the smoothed forward one-year interest rates. As the exhibit shows, all interest rates should converge toward the current yield curve in the long term. As a result, the bank's income contribution from any maturity difference in deposits and loans disappears in the long term as well.

Loan Loss Provisions

For our ABC Bank valuation, we did not model any losses from defaults on loans outstanding to customers. In real life, your analysis and valuation have to include loan loss forecasts, because loan losses are among the most important factors determining the value of retail and wholesale banking activities. For estimating expected loan losses from defaults across different loan categories, a useful first indicator would be a bank's historical additions to loan loss provisions or sector-wide estimates of loan losses (see Exhibit 38.12). As the exhibit shows, these losses increased sharply during the 2008 credit crisis but recovered to pre-crisis levels by 2013. Credit cards typically have the highest losses, and mortgages the lowest, with business loans somewhere in between. All default losses are strongly correlated with overall economic growth, so use through-the-economic-cycle estimates of additions to arrive at future annual loan loss rates to apply to your forecasts of equity cash flows.

To project the future interest income from a bank's loans, deduct the estimated future loan loss rates from the future interest rates on loans for each year. You should also review the quality of the bank's current loan portfolio to assess whether it is under- or overprovisioned for loan losses. Any required increase in the loan loss provision translates into less equity value.

EXHIBIT 38.12 **Annual Losses for U.S. Banks by Loan Category**

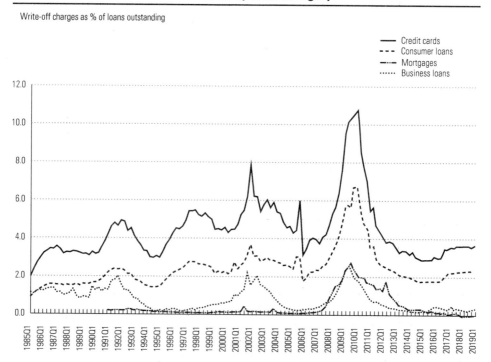

Write-off charges as % of loans outstanding

Source: Federal Reserve, "Charge-Off and Delinquency Rates on Loans and Leases at Commercial Banks," www.federalreserve.gov.

Risk-Weighted Assets and Equity Risk Capital

Banks are required to hold a minimum level of equity capital that can absorb potential losses to safeguard the bank's obligations to its customers and financiers. In December 2010, new regulatory requirements for capital adequacy were specified in the Basel III guidelines, replacing the 2007 Basel II accords, which were no longer considered adequate in the wake of the 2008 and 2010 financial crises.[15] The new guidelines are being gradually implemented by banks across the world between 2013 and 2022.

Basel III specifies rules for banks regarding how much equity capital they must hold based on the bank's so-called risk-weighted assets (RWA).[16] The level of RWA is driven by the riskiness of a bank's asset portfolio and its trading book. Banks have some flexibility to choose either internal risk models or standardized Basel approaches to estimate their RWA. All such models rest on the general principle that the total RWA is the sum of separate RWA estimates for credit risk, market risk, and operational risk. However, banks do not publish the risk models they use. If you are conducting an outside-in valuation, you need an approximation of a bank's future equity risk capital needs. Because banks typically provide information on total RWA but not on the risk weighting for its asset groups, trading book, and operations, you have to make an approximation of the key categories' contribution to total RWA for the bank in order to project RWA and risk capital for future years.[17]

Exhibit 38.13 shows such an outside-in approximation of RWA for a large European bank. The bank separately reports the total RWA for credit risk, market risk, and operational risk.

- To approximate the RWA for *credit risk*, you can use the risk weights from the Basel II Standardized Approach (see Exhibit 38.14) and information on the credit quality of the bank's loans. Estimate the risk weighting and RWA for each of the loan categories in such a way that your estimate fits the reported RWA for all loans (€202 billion in this example).

- *Market risk* is a bank's exposure to changes in interest rates, stock prices, currency rates, and commodity prices. It is typically related to its value at risk (VaR), which is the maximum loss for the bank under a worst-case scenario of a given probability for these market prices. For an approximation, use the reported VaR over several years to estimate the bank's RWA as a percentage of VaR (242 percent in the example).

[15] The Basel accords are recommendations on laws and regulations for banking and are issued by the Basel Committee on Banking Supervision (BCBS).
[16] In addition, Basel III sets requirements for liquidity and restrictions on leverage in the form of a minimum liquidity coverage ratio (LCR) and net stable funding ratio (NSFR) and a threshold leverage ratio (LR). We focus here on capital adequacy, as that is typically the most critical requirement to take into account when valuing a bank.
[17] Without RWA estimates by business line, you could only project the bank's risk capital for a scenario in which all business lines grow at the same rate.

EXHIBIT 38.13 **Estimating Risk-Weighted Assets (RWA) for a Large European Bank**

€ billion

		Reported RWA				Estimated RWA parameters			
	Year	Asset category	Loans outstanding	RWA		Standardized RWA/loans, %	Standardized RWA	Allocated RWA	Estimated RWA/ loans, %
Credit risk	2013	Loans to countries	16,228			10	1,623	2,220	14
		Loans to banks	25,100			35	8,785	12,016	48
		Loans to corporations	147,242			35	51,535	70,486	48
		Residential mortgages	148,076		→	35	51,827	70,885	48
		Other consumer loans	45,440			75	34,080	46,613	103
		Overall	382,086	202,219			147,489	202,219	53

	Year		VaR trading book	RWA		Estimated RWA/ VaR	
Market risk	2013		19,564	47,259	├→	242%	

	Year		Revenues	RWA		Estimated RWA/ revenues	
Operational risk	2013		32,826	50,891	├→	155%	

- *Operational risk* is all risk that is neither market nor credit risk. It is usually related to a bank's net revenues (net interest income plus net other income). Use the bank's average revenues over the previous year(s) to estimate RWA per unit of revenue (155 percent in the example).

Based on your forecasts for growth across different loan categories, VaR requirements for trading activities, and a bank's net revenues, you can estimate the total RWA in each future year.

Basel III establishes stricter rules for banks regarding how much capital they must hold based on their level of RWA. Requirements are defined for the bank's so-called common-equity Tier 1 (CET1), additional Tier 1, and Tier 2 capital levels, relative to RWA. Of these capital ratios, CET1 to RWA is typically the most stringent. The total minimum CET1 requirements for a

EXHIBIT 38.14 **Risk Weights in Basel II Standardized Approach**

%

	Asset category						
Credit risk	AAA to AA–	A+ to A–	BBB+ to BBB–	BB+ to BB–	B+ to B–	Below B–	Unrated
Loans to countries	–	20	50	100	100	150	100
Loans to banks	20	50	50	100	100	150	50
Loans to corporations	20	50	100	100	150	150	100

Residential mortgages	Local regulator flexibility: Mortgages with low loan-to-value ratio, 35%; otherwise, 100%
Other consumer loans	Risk weighting of 75%

bank consist of different layers that add up to a total of 8.0 to 10.5 percent of RWA:

Basel III CET1 capital requirements

% of risk-weighted assets	
Legal minimum	4.5
Capital conservation buffer	2.5
G-SIB countercyclical buffer	1.0–3.5
Total	8.0–10.5

The first 4.5 percent is the so-called legal minimum that applies to any bank in any given year. The second layer of 2.5 percent is the capital conservation buffer, which can be drawn down in years of losses and then rebuilt in profitable years. The third, or countercyclical, layer can be up to 3.5 percent of RWA but applies only to so-called global systemically important banks (G-SIBs). These banks are identified by the Financial Stability Board (FSB) as sources of systemic risk to the international financial system because of their size and complexity.[18] In November of each year, the FSB publishes the additional capital charge for each G-SIB, which depends on the FSB's assessment of the risk that the bank represents. Among these largest global banks, JPMorgan Chase faced a surcharge of 2.5 percent in 2018, with Citigroup, Deutsche Bank, and HSBC in the next-lower bucket of 2.0 percent. For the smaller G-SIBs, such as Santander, ING Bank, Agricultural Bank of China, and Morgan Stanley, the surcharge amounted to 1.0 percent.

Many of the larger banks nowadays already target CET1 at around 13 percent of RWA or higher, reflecting not only stricter regulations but also increased investor requirements. According to the Bank for International Settlements (BIS), the worldwide average CET1 for large international banks was at 12.9 percent of RWA in 2018, well above the 2013 level of 9.5 percent.[19]

Using your RWA forecasts and the targeted CET1 ratio, you can estimate the required Tier 1 capital in each future year. From the projected CET1 capital requirements, you can estimate the implied shareholders' equity requirements by applying an average historical ratio of CET1 capital to shareholders' equity excluding goodwill and deferred-tax assets. Historical Tier 1 capital is reported separately in the notes to the bank's financial statements and is typically close to straightforward shareholders' equity excluding goodwill and deferred-tax assets.

Value Drivers for Different Banking Activities

Given that many banks have portfolios of different business activities, sometimes as distinct as consumer credit card loans and proprietary trading, their

[18] The FSB is an international body monitoring the stability of the international financial system and was established by the G20 Leaders' Summit of April 2009.
[19] *Basel III Monitoring Report*, Bank for International Settlements, March 2019, p. 2 (available at www .bis.org).

businesses can have very distinct risks and returns, making the bank's consolidated financial results difficult to interpret, let alone forecast. The businesses are best valued separately, as in the case of multibusiness companies, discussed in Chapter 19. Unfortunately, financial statements for multibusiness banks often lack separately reported income statements and balance sheets for different business activities. In that case, you have to construct separate statements following the guidelines described in Chapter 19.

Interest-Generating Activities   Retail banking, credit card services, and wholesale lending generate interest income from large asset positions and risk capital. These interest-generating activities can be analyzed using the economic-spread approach and valued using the equity DCF model, as discussed for ABC Bank in the previous section.

Trading Activities   Like a bank's interest-generating activities, its trading activities also generate income from large asset positions and significant risk capital. However, trading incomes tend to be far more volatile than interest incomes. Although peak income can be very high, the average trading income across the cycle generally turns out to be limited. The key value drivers are shown in Exhibit 38.15, a simplified value driver tree for trading activities.

EXHIBIT 38.15 **Value Drivers: Trading Activities (Simplified)**

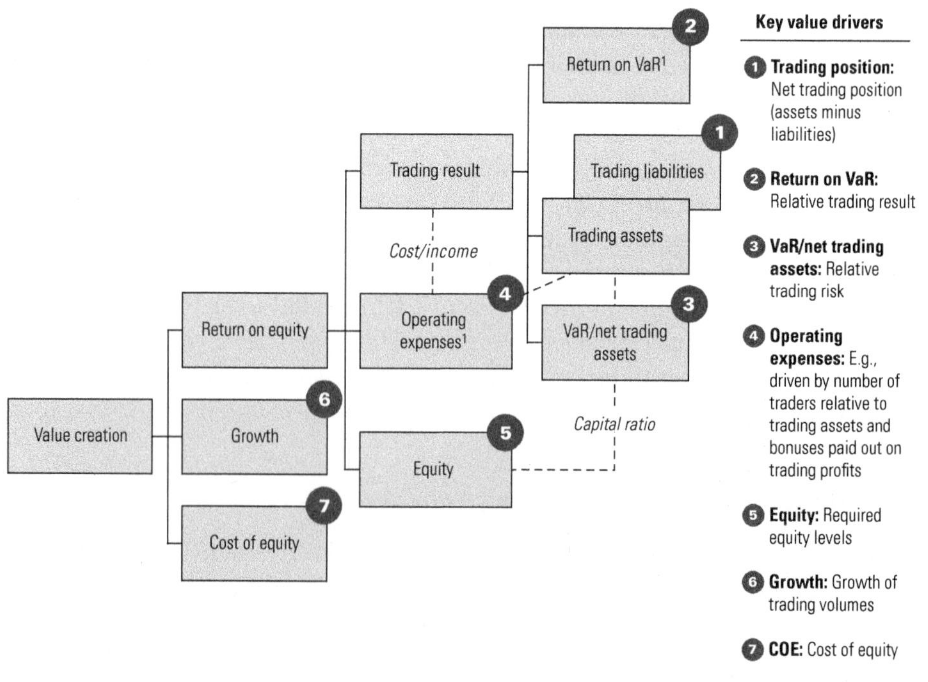

[1] After taxes.

You can think of a bank's trading results as driven by the size of its trading positions, the risk taken in trading (as measured by the total VaR), and the trading result per unit of risk (measured by return on VaR). The ratio of VaR to net trading position is an indication of the relative risk taking in trading. The more risk a bank takes in trading, the higher the expected trading return should be, as well as the required risk capital. The required equity risk capital for the trading activities follows from the VaR (and RWA), as discussed earlier in the chapter. Operating expenses, which include information technology (IT) infrastructure, back-office costs, and employee compensation, are partly related to the size of positions (or number of transactions) and partly related to trading results (for example, employee bonuses).

Fee- and Commission-Generating Activities   A bank's fee- and commission-generating activities, such as brokerage, transaction advisory, and asset management services, have different economics, based on limited asset positions and minimal risk capital. The value drivers in asset management, for example, are very different from those in the interest-generating businesses, as the generic example in Exhibit 38.16 shows. Key drivers are the growth of assets under management and the fees earned on those assets, such as management fees related to the amount of assets under management and performance fees related to the returns achieved on those assets.

EXHIBIT 38.16 **Value Drivers: Asset Management (Simplified)**

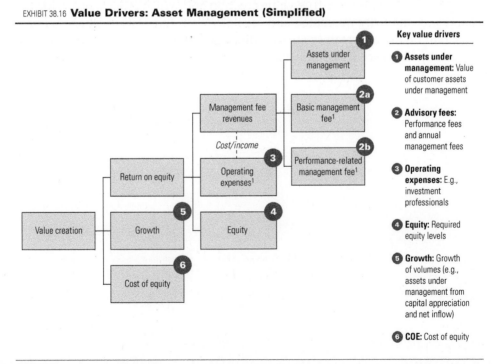

[1] After taxes.

Along with these variables in activities, remember that banks are highly leveraged and that many of their businesses are cyclical. When performing a bank valuation, you should not rely on point estimates but should use scenarios for future financial performance to understand the range of possible outcomes and the key underlying value drivers.

SUMMARY

The fundamentals of the discounted-cash-flow (DCF) approach laid out in this book apply equally to banks. The equity cash flow version of the DCF approach is most appropriate for valuing banks, because the operational and financial cash flows of these organizations cannot be separated, given that banks are expected to create value from funding as well as lending operations.

Valuing banks remains a delicate task because of the diversity of the business portfolio, the cyclicality of many bank businesses (especially trading and fee-based business), and high leverage. Because of the difference in underlying value drivers, it is best to value a bank by its key parts according to the source of income: interest-generating business, fee and commission business, and trading. To understand the sources of value creation in a bank's interest-generating business, supplement the equity DCF approach with an economic-spread analysis. This analysis reveals which part of a bank's net interest income represents true value creation and which reflects not value but charges for maturity mismatch and capital. When forecasting a bank's financials, handle the uncertainty surrounding the bank's future performance and growth by using scenarios that capture the cyclicality of its key businesses.

39

Flexibility

Properly managing a modern business is about making choices to create value. Valuation provides important insights for executives faced with making decisions on corporate strategy, acquisitions and divestments, capital structure, and other management actions. All these decisions take place against a backdrop of uncertainty about the outcomes of alternative courses of action.[1] However, in some cases, you can face decisions where not only is uncertainty present, but so is flexibility.

Managerial flexibility and uncertainty are not the same. In cases of uncertainty, the future of a company or a project may be extremely difficult to predict and depends on a single management decision—for example, to launch a new product line or to invest in a new production facility. Flexibility, in contrast, refers to choices managers may make between alternative plans in response to events. This is especially true when you are conducting valuations of investment projects.

The difference is important in deciding your approach to valuation. Whatever the degree of uncertainty, it is possible to value the asset in question by using a *standard* discounted-cash-flow (DCF) approach combined with either different scenarios or a stochastic simulation (see, for example, Chapter 17). But suppose management has planned to stage its investments in a business start-up. In that case, the managers may decide at each stage whether to proceed, depending on information arising from the previous stage. Where managers expect to respond flexibly to events, they need so-called *contingent valuation* approaches. These forecast, implicitly or explicitly, the future free cash flows, depending on the future states of the world and management decisions, and then discount these to today's value. For such decisions, alternative approaches provide more accurate valuation results and, perhaps even more important, deeper insights into what creates value.

Flexibility comes in many forms and can substantially alter the value of a business or project. But the business or project can have value only if

---

[1] See Chapters 4 and 13 for ideas on handling uncertainty, for example, with scenario-based approaches.

executives actively manage it to make better decisions. This chapter concentrates on the basic concepts of valuing managerial flexibility and real options in businesses and projects. It focuses on the following topics:

- Fundamental concepts behind uncertainty, flexibility, and value (when and why flexibility has value)
- Managing flexibility in terms of real options to defer investments; making follow-on investments; and expanding, changing, or abandoning production
- Comparison of decision tree analysis (DTA) and real-option valuation (ROV) to valuing flexibility, including situations in which each approach is more appropriate
- A four-step approach to analyzing and valuing real options, illustrated with numerical examples using ROV and DTA

A HIERARCHY OF APPROACHES

It is possible to illustrate a hierarchy of standard and contingent approaches to valuation under situations of uncertainty and flexibility and suggest when it is best to apply each (Exhibit 39.1). When a flexible response is neither expected

EXHIBIT 39.1 **Valuation under Uncertainty: Approaches**

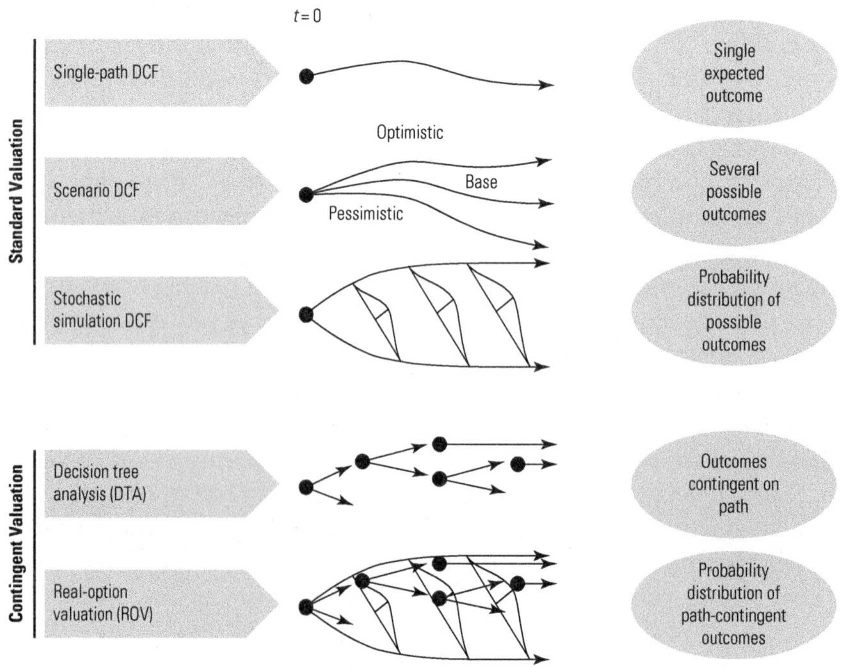

nor required, you can choose from the following three variations of a standard DCF approach, depending on the level of uncertainty:

1. *Single-path DCF valuation.* When little uncertainty exists about future outcomes or when uncertainty is evenly spread around the expected outcomes, use a standard, single-path DCF analysis based on point estimates of future cash flows.

2. *Scenario-based DCF.* When significant uncertainty exists, especially when there is a possibility of much more upside than downside (or vice versa) in future cash flows, it is best to model future outcomes in two or more scenarios that capture the variation in the paths of future cash flow. This approach is easy to apply in, for example, valuing corporate or business strategies.

3. *Stochastic simulation DCF.* If you have reliable estimates about the underlying probability distributions of cash flows into the future, such as mean, standard deviation, and possibly skewness, it may be worthwhile to use a stochastic simulation DCF approach. In this approach, future cash flow paths are explicitly modeled and valued in a stochastic simulation. Because this approach is complex and requires voluminous data, applications are mostly restricted to specific industries, such as the valuation of insurance companies, and commodity-based businesses.

When managerial flexibility is called for, you need one of the following contingent valuation approaches, selected according to the amount of information available:

- *Decision tree analysis (DTA).* If there is limited information about the distribution of future cash flow paths and the decisions that management can take depending on these cash flows, use a decision tree analysis. As the following sections discuss, it builds on scenario DCF valuation and is straightforward and transparent. DTA is especially effective for valuing flexibility related to technological risks that are not priced in the market, such as investments in research and development (R&D) projects, product launches, and plant-decommissioning decisions.

- *Real-option valuation (ROV).* If you have reliable information about the underlying probability distributions of future cash flow paths, like those required for stochastic simulation, ROV could provide better results and insights. However, it requires sophisticated, formal option-pricing models that are harder for managers to decipher than DTA. The ROV approach is best suited to decisions in commodity-based businesses, such as investments in oil and gas fields, refining facilities, chemical plants, and power generators, because the underlying commodity risk is priced in the market.[2]

---

[2] See, for example, E. S. Schwartz and L. Trigeorgis, eds., *Real Options and Investment under Uncertainty: Classical Readings and Recent Contributions* (Cambridge, MA: MIT Press, 2001); T. Copeland and V. Antikarov, *Real Options: A Practitioner's Guide* (New York: Texere, 2003); or L. Trigeorgis, *Real Options: Managerial Flexibility and Strategy in Resource Allocation* (Cambridge, MA: MIT Press, 1996).

There are advantages to using either ROV or DTA, depending on the types of risks involved. In theory, ROV is more accurate. But it is not the right approach in every case. It cannot replace traditional discounted cash flow, because valuing an option using ROV still depends on knowing the value of the underlying assets. Unless the assets have an observable market price, you will have to estimate that value using traditional DCF.

Company-wide valuation models rarely take flexibility into account. To analyze and model flexibility accurately, you must be able to describe the set of specific decisions managers could make in response to future events and include the cash flow implications of those decisions. In valuing a company, flexibility therefore becomes relevant only in cases where management responds to specific events that may change the course of the whole company. For example, to value internet or biotech companies with a handful of promising new products in development, you could project sales, profit, and investments for the company as a whole that are conditional on the success of product development.[3] Another example is a company that has built its strategy around buying up smaller players and integrating them into a bigger entity, capturing synergies along the way. The first acquisitions may not create value in their own right but may open opportunities for value creation through further acquisitions.

Flexibility is typically more relevant in the valuation of individual businesses and projects, as it mostly concerns detailed decisions related to production, capacity investment, marketing, research and development, and other factors.

UNCERTAINTY, FLEXIBILITY, AND VALUE

To appreciate the value of flexibility and its key value drivers, consider a simple example.[4] Suppose you are deciding whether to invest $6,000 one year from now to produce and distribute a new pharmaceutical drug already under development. In the upcoming final development stage, the product will undergo clinical tests on patients for one year, for which all investments have already been made. These tests involve no future cash flows. The trials could have one of two possible outcomes. If the drug proves to be highly effective, it will generate an annual net cash inflow of $500 into perpetuity. If it is only somewhat effective, the annual net cash inflow will be $100 into perpetuity. These outcomes are equally probable.

Based on this information, the expected future net cash flow is $300, the probability-weighted average of the risky outcomes ($500 and $100). To keep it simple, we assume that success in developing the new product and the value

---

[3] See, for example, E. S. Schwartz and M. Moon, "Rational Pricing of Internet Companies," *Financial Analysts Journal* 56, no. 3 (2000): 62–75; and D. Kellogg and J. Charnes, "Real-Options Valuation for a Biotechnology Company," *Financial Analysts Journal* 56, no. 3 (2000): 76–84.

[4] The example is inspired by A. Dixit and R. Pindyck, *Investment under Uncertainty* (Princeton, NJ: Princeton University Press, 1994), 26.

of the new product are unrelated to what happens in the overall economy, so this risk is fully diversifiable by the company's investors. Therefore, the beta for this product is zero, and the cost of capital equals the risk-free rate—say, 5 percent. Assuming that the company will realize its first year's product sales immediately upon completing the trials and at the end of each year thereafter, the net present value (NPV) of the investment is estimated as follows:

$$NPV = \frac{-\$6,000}{1.05} + \sum_{t=1}^{\infty} \frac{\$300}{(1.05)^t} = \$286$$

To apply the NPV approach, we discount the incremental expected project cash flows at the cost of capital. Any prior development expenses are irrelevant, because they are sunk costs. Alternatively, if the project is canceled, the NPV equals $0. Therefore, management should approve the incremental investment of $6,000.

In this example of the NPV decision rule, undertaking development creates value. But there are more alternatives than deciding *today* whether to invest. Using an approach like the scenario approach described in Chapter 17, we can rewrite the previous NPV calculation in terms of the probability-weighted values of the drug, discounted to today:

$$NPV = 0.5\left[\frac{-\$6,000}{1.05} + \sum_{t=1}^{\infty} \frac{\$500}{(1.05)^t}\right] + 0.5\left[\frac{-\$6,000}{1.05} + \sum_{t=1}^{\infty} \frac{\$100}{(1.05)^t}\right]$$
$$= 0.5(\$4,286) + 0.5(-\$3,714)$$
$$= \$286$$

Here, the NPV is shown as the weighted average of two distinct results: a positive NPV of $4,286 following a favorable trial outcome and a negative NPV of –$3,714 for an unfavorable outcome. If the decision to invest can be deferred until trial results are known, the project becomes much more attractive. Specifically, if the drug proves to be less effective, the project can be halted, avoiding the negative NPV. You invest only if the drug is highly effective, and the annual cash flow of $500 more than compensates for the investment required. In practice, there would likely be an upfront investment need for the trial, regardless of its outcome, but we have abstracted from such costs to keep the example simple.

This flexibility is an option to defer the investment decision. To value the option, a contingent NPV approach can be used, working from right to left in the payoff tree shown in Exhibit 39.2.

$$NPV = 0.5 \times \text{Max}\left[\left(\frac{-\$6,000}{1.05} + \sum_{t=1}^{\infty} \frac{\$500}{(1.05)^t}\right), 0\right]$$
$$+ 0.5 \times \text{Max}\left[\left(\frac{-\$6,000}{1.05} + \sum_{t=1}^{\infty} \frac{\$100}{(1.05)^t}\right), 0\right]$$
$$= 0.5(\$4,286) + 0.5(0) = \$2,143$$

EXHIBIT 39.2 **Value of Flexibility to Defer Investment**

$					$t=1$	$t=2$	...	?
$t=0$								
			Successful product	Cash flow	500	500	...	500
	$p=$		50%	Investment	(6,000)	–	...	–
Contingent NPV = 2,143								
	$1-p=$		50%	Cash flow	100	100	...	100
Cost of capital = 5%			*Unsuccessful product*	Investment	(6,000)	–	...	–

Note: t = time, in years
      p = probability

The contingent NPV of $2,143 is considerably higher than the $286 NPV of committing today. Therefore, the best alternative is to defer a decision until the trial outcomes are known. The value of the option to defer investment is the difference between the value of the project with flexibility and its value without flexibility: $2,143 – $286 = $1,857.

Based on this example, it is possible to summarize the distinction between the standard and contingent NPVs. The standard NPV is the maximum, decided today, of the expected discounted cash flows or zero:

$$\text{Standard NPV} = \underset{t=0}{\text{Max}} \left(\frac{\text{Expected (Cash Flows)}}{\text{Cost of Capital}}, 0 \right)$$

The contingent NPV is the expected value of the maximums, decided when information arrives, of the discounted cash flows in each future state or zero:

$$\text{Contingent NPV} = \text{Expected}_{t=0}$$
$$\times \left[\text{Max} \left(\frac{\text{Cash Flows Contingent on Information}}{\text{Cost of Capital}}, 0 \right) \right]$$

These two NPV approaches use information quite differently. Standard NPV forces a decision based on today's expectation of future information, whereas contingent NPV permits the flexibility of making decisions after the information arrives. Unlike standard NPV, it captures the value of flexibility. A project's contingent NPV will always be greater than or equal to its standard NPV.

The value of flexibility is related to the degree of uncertainty and the room for managerial reaction (see Exhibit 39.3). It is greatest when uncertainty is high and managers can react to new information. In contrast, if there is little uncertainty, managers are unlikely to receive new information that would alter future decisions, so flexibility has little value. Similarly, if managers cannot act on new information that becomes available, the value of flexibility is low.

Including flexibility in a project valuation is most important when the project's standard NPV is close to zero—that is, when the decision whether to go ahead with the project is a close call. Sometimes senior management intuitively overrules standard NPV results and accepts an investment project for strategic reasons, for example, because the project creates an initial market position that can be expanded at a later stage if and when the company has

EXHIBIT 39.3 **When Is Flexibility Valuable?**

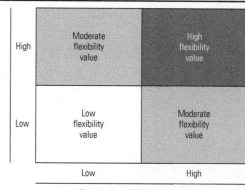

the competitive products or services to offer. In these cases, the flexibility recognized in contingent valuation fits better with strategic intuition than do the rigid assumptions of standard NPV approaches.

What Creates Flexibility Value

To identify and value flexibility, you must understand where its value comes from. Consider what happens if the range of possible annual cash flow outcomes (originally $500 versus $100 per year) increases to $600 versus $0. Since expected cash flows and cost of capital remain unchanged, the standard NPV is the same ($286).[5] However, the contingent NPV increases from its prior level of $2,143:

$$
\begin{aligned}
\text{NPV} &= 0.5 \times \text{Max}\left[\left(\frac{-\$6,000}{1.05} + \sum_{t=1}^{\infty}\frac{\$600}{(1.05)^t}\right), 0\right] \\
&\quad + 0.5 \times \text{Max}\left[\left(\frac{-\$6,000}{1.05} + \sum_{t=1}^{\infty}\frac{\$0}{(1.05)^t}\right), 0\right] \\
&= 0.5(\$6,286) + 0.5(0) \\
&= \$3,143
\end{aligned}
$$

The contingent NPV of $3,143 is almost 50 percent greater at this higher level of uncertainty. Why? As in the original case, only the cash flows from the favorable outcome affect the contingent valuation. Since these cash flow projections have increased by 20 percent and the required investment has not changed, the contingent NPV increases substantially. The value of the deferral option rises from $1,857 to $2,857 (computed as $3,143 – $286).

---

[5] We assume that the trial outcome risk is uncorrelated with the overall economy.

EXHIBIT 39.4 **Drivers of Flexibility Value**

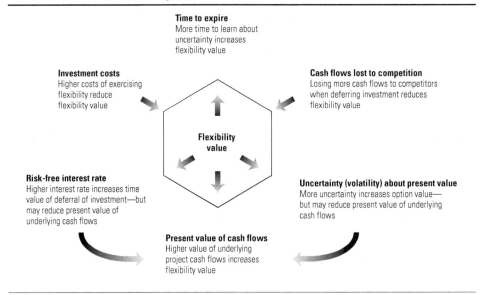

Time to expire
More time to learn about
uncertainty increases
flexibility value

Investment costs
Higher costs of exercising
flexibility reduce
flexibility value

Cash flows lost to competition
Losing more cash flows to competitors
when deferring investment reduces
flexibility value

**Flexibility
value**

Risk-free interest rate
Higher interest rate increases time
value of deferral of investment—but
may reduce present value of
underlying cash flows

Uncertainty (volatility) about present value
More uncertainty increases option value—
but may reduce present value of underlying
cash flows

Present value of cash flows
Higher value of underlying
project cash flows increases
flexibility value

We can formally derive the key value drivers of real options from the pricing theory of financial options such as, for example, call and put options on equity shares. In our original example, the deferral option is identical to a call option with an exercise price of $6,000 and a one-year maturity on an underlying risky asset that has a current value of $6,000 and a variance determined by the cash flow spread of $400 across outcomes.[6] As with financial options, the value of a real option depends on six drivers, summarized in Exhibit 39.4.

These drivers of option value show how allowing for flexibility affects the valuation of a particular investment project. Holding other drivers constant, option value decreases with higher investment costs and more cash flows lost while holding the option. Option value increases with higher value of the underlying asset's cash flows, greater uncertainty, higher risk-free interest rates, and a longer lifetime of the option. With higher option values, a standard DCF calculation that ignores flexibility will more seriously underestimate the true value of an investment project.

Be careful how you interpret the impact of value drivers when designing investment strategies to exploit flexibility. The impact of any individual driver described in Exhibit 39.4 holds only when all other value drivers remain constant. In practice, changes in uncertainty and interest rates not only affect the value of the option but usually change the value of the underlying

---

[6] The current value of the underlying risky asset is the present value of expected annual cash flows of $300 into perpetuity, discounted at a 5 percent cost of capital.

asset as well. When you assess the impact of these drivers, you should assess all their effects on the option's value, both direct and indirect. Take the case of higher uncertainty. In our example, we increased the uncertainty of future cash flows by widening the gap between future cash flows in the favorable and unfavorable scenarios from $400 to $600. But we kept the expected value of the future cash flows unchanged at $300 so that their present value remained constant. However, if greater uncertainty lowers the expected level of cash flows or raises the cost of capital, the value of the underlying asset declines so that the impact on the value of the option could be negative. The same holds for the impact of an increase in the risk-free interest rate. Higher interest rates reduce the present value of the required investment, thereby increasing the option value—if the value of the underlying asset is assumed constant. But if higher interest rates lead to an increase in the cost of capital, the present value of cash flows on the underlying asset would decrease, which could lower the option's value.

MANAGING FLEXIBILITY

Contingent valuation is an important tool for managers trying to make the right decisions to maximize shareholder value when faced with strategic or operating flexibility. In actual practice, however, flexibility is never as well defined and straightforward as in the preceding examples. Much depends on management's ability to recognize, structure, and manage opportunities to create value from operating and strategic flexibility. A detailed discussion is beyond the scope of this book,[7] but we provide some basic guidelines here.

To *recognize* opportunities for creating value from flexibility when assessing investment projects or strategies, managers should try to be as explicit as possible about the following details:

- *Events.* What are the key sources of uncertainty? Which events will bring new information and when? A source of uncertainty is important only if relevant new information about it is likely to trigger a decision change. For example, investing in a pilot project for a product launch makes sense only if there is a chance that the pilot outcome would actually change the launch decision. Similarly, options to switch inputs for manufacturing processes are valuable only if the input prices can be expected to diverge significantly.
- *Decisions.* What decisions can management make in response to events? It is important that managers have some discretion to react to a relevant event. For example, intense competition among smartphone

---

[7] For a more in-depth discussion, see, for example, Copeland and Antikarov, *Real Options*, or Trigeorgis, *Real Options*.

manufacturers makes it unattractive for managers to defer a decision to launch new product versions with innovative features such as voice-control or foldable-screen technology until there is more information about potential demand for such features.

- *Payoffs.* What payoffs are linked to these decisions? Bear in mind that there should be a positive NPV to be captured in some realistic future state of the world. This NPV should be derived from sustainable competitive advantages. For example, some investors attribute high value to certain e-commerce start-ups as "options for future growth," often based on multiples of enterprise value over unique website visitors per month. But website visits alone do not create value. Moreover, the value of e-commerce start-ups depends upon their future cash flows. Start-ups can represent valuable options only if they build sustainable, competitive business models in some plausible future scenarios. Valuing start-ups as options requires articulating what the scenarios are, as well as predicting their likelihood of success and associated businesses cash flows.

With regard to *structuring* flexibility, some projects or strategies have predefined, built-in flexibility. Take, for example, research and development (R&D) investments in pharmaceutical products where the outcomes of clinical or patient trials provide natural moments to decide whether to stop or proceed with investments. But in many other cases, flexibility can be incorporated into a project to create maximum value. One example would be redesigning infrastructure investments in ports or airfields in stages such that future expansion takes place only if and when needed. Another would be reshaping a growth strategy in such a way that it explicitly includes options to redirect resources as more information becomes available.

In the end, flexibility has value only if managers actually *manage* it—that is, use new information to make appropriate changes to their decisions. Therefore, companies should ensure that their managers face proper incentives to capture potential value from flexibility. For example, the option to pull out of a staged-investment project when intermediate results are disappointing has no value if managers do not act on the information. As is sometimes the case, managers will point to nothing more than large sunk costs as the rationale for their inaction. But they forget that value is determined only by future cash flows, so that sunk costs are always irrelevant. In the case where a company bases its strategy on creating growth options through a string of acquisitions, those options generate maximum value only if the company delays further acquisitions until new, positive information about their potential arrives. The company leaves the option value on the table if it proceeds with additional acquisitions in the dark.

EXHIBIT 39.5 **Classification of Real Options**

Option type	Financial equivalent	Definitions	Example(s)
Option to defer investment	Call option	The option to defer an investment until the present value of an asset rises above the development costs	The ability of a leaseholder of an undeveloped oil reserve to defer development and investment until oil prices have elevated the value of the reserves above their development costs
Abandonment option	Put option	The option to abandon a project if its present value falls below its liquidation value	Long-term rental leases of airplanes that give the lessee the flexibility to prematurely dissolve the contract and return the plane to the lessor at a prespecified termination fee
Follow-on (compound) option	Series of options on options	The option to invest in stages, contingent on performance	A factory, R&D program, new-product launch, or oil field built so that management can continue the project at each stage by investing additional funds (an exercise price) or abandon it for whatever they can fetch
Option to expand or contract	Call or put option	The option to resize an investment depending on performance	A production facility built so that it can be easily expanded or contracted if a product is more or less successful than anticipated
Option to extend or shorten	Call or put option	The option to shorten or extend the life of an asset or contract	Real estate leases with clauses that allow lessors to extend or shorten the term of the lease
Option to increase scope	Call option	The ability to increase or decrease the number of activities in the future	A hotel designed so that the owner can easily diversify beyond lodging services, such as by adding conference facilities
Switching options	Portfolio of call and put options	The ability to switch the operation of a project on and off—or to switch operations between two distinct locations	A flexible manufacturing system that can produce two or more different products, peak-load power generation, or the ability to exit and reenter an industry

To help managers recognize, structure, and manage opportunities for capturing value from flexibility, we segment options into the categories described in Exhibit 39.5 and provide some examples.

METHODS FOR VALUING FLEXIBILITY

As mentioned earlier in this chapter, the two methods for contingent valuation are decision tree analysis (DTA) and real-option valuation (ROV) using formal option-pricing models. We will illustrate each method with a simple example: the opportunity to invest $105 at the end of one year in a mining project that has an equal chance of returning either $150 or $50 in cash flow, depending on the mineral price. The risk-free rate, r_f, is 5 percent, and the weighted average cost of capital (WACC) for the project is 10 percent. The present value (PV) of the cash flows today is:

$$PV = \frac{0.5(\$150) + 0.5(\$50)}{1.10} = \$90.9$$

EXHIBIT 39.6 **Contingent Payoffs for Investment Project, Twin Security, and Risk-Free Bond**

$

t = 0			t = 1				
				Project without flexibility	Project with flexibility	Twin security	Risk-free bond
	Successful project		Cash flow	150	150		
	p =	50%	Investment	(105)	(105)		
			Net cash flow	**45**	**45**	**50**	**1.05**
NPV = ?							
	1 – p =	50%	Cash flow	50	50		
	Unsuccessful project		Investment	(105)	(105)		
Risk-free rate = 5%			**Net cash flow**	**(55)**	**–**	**16.7**	**1.05**
WACC = 10%							

Note: t = time, in years
   p = probability

If an investment decision were required immediately, the project would be declined. The standard NPV of the mining project equals the discounted expected cash flow of $90.90 minus the present value of the investment outlay of $105 next year. Since the level of investment is certain, it should be discounted at the risk-free rate of 5 percent:

$$\text{Standard NPV} = \$90.9 - \frac{\$105}{1.05} = \$90.9 - \$100 = -\$9.1$$

The answer changes if management has flexibility to defer the investment decision for one year, allowing it to make the decision after observing next year's mineral price and the associated cash flow outcome (see Exhibit 39.6). The net cash flows in the favorable state are $150 – $105 = $45. In the unfavorable state, management would decline to invest, accepting net cash flows of $0.

To value this flexibility, we first use an ROV approach and then repeat the valuation with the DTA approach.

Real-Option Valuation

Option-pricing models use a *replicating portfolio* to value the project. The basic idea of a replicating portfolio is straightforward: if you can construct a portfolio of priced securities that has the same payouts as an option, the portfolio and option should have the same price. If the securities and the option are traded in an open market, this identity is required; otherwise arbitrage profits are possible. The interesting implication is that the ROV approach lets you correctly value complex, contingent cash flow patterns.

Returning to our $105 investment project, assume there exists a perfectly correlated security (or commodity, in this example) that trades in the market for $30.30

per share (or unit).[8] Its payouts ($50 and $16.70) equal one-third of the payouts of the project, and its expected return equals the underlying project's cost of capital.

This twin security can be used to value the project, including the option to defer, by forming a replicating portfolio.[9] Consider a portfolio consisting of N shares of the twin security and B risk-free bonds with a face value of $1. In the favorable state, the twin security pays $50 for each of the N shares, and each bond pays its face value plus interest, or $(1 + r_f)$. Together, these payouts must equal $45. Applying a similar construction to the unfavorable state, we can write two equations with two unknowns:

$$\$50.0N + \$1.05B = \$45$$
$$\$16.7N + \$1.05B = 0$$

The solution is $N = 1.35$ and $B = -21.43$. Thus, to build a replicating portfolio, buy 1.35 shares and short 21.43 bonds (shorting a bond is common language for selling a bond, or borrowing money).

This position produces the same cash flow as the investment project under both states. Therefore, the value of the project, including the ability to defer, should equal the value of the replicating portfolio:

$$\text{Contingent NPV} = N(\text{Price of Twin Security}) - B(\$1)$$
$$= 1.35(\$30.3) - 21.43(\$1)$$
$$= \$19.5$$

The value of the deferral option is the difference between the total contingent NPV of the project and its standard NPV without flexibility: $19.50 - (-$9.10) = $28.60 (remember, the standard NPV was negative).

Contingent NPV can also be determined with an alternative ROV approach called *risk-neutral valuation*. The name is somewhat misleading because a risk-neutral valuation does adjust for risk, but as part of the scenario probabilities rather than the discount rate. To value an option, weight the future cash flows by risk-adjusted (or so-called risk-neutral) probabilities instead of the actual scenario probabilities. Then discount the probability-weighted average cash flow by the risk-free rate to determine current value. The risk-neutral probability of the favorable state, $p*$, is defined as follows:[10]

$$p* = \frac{1 + r_f - d}{u - d} = 0.45$$

---

[8] You could also use this twin security to value the investment project without flexibility by means of a replicating portfolio. Because the twin security's cash flows are always exactly one-third of the project cash flows, the project without flexibility should be worth three times as much as the twin security, or $90.90 (= 3 × $30.30). The twin security is a basic concept that is implicitly used in standard DCF as well; you derive the beta of a project by identifying a highly correlated traded security and use that security's beta as input for the cost of capital in the DCF valuation.

[9] If the project itself were traded, you would not need a twin security but would construct a replicating portfolio with the traded value of the project itself, as in the case of financial options on traded stocks.

[10] See, for example, Trigeorgis, *Real Options*, 75–76.

where

$$u = \frac{\text{FV(Favorable State)}}{\text{PV}} = \frac{\$50.0}{\$30.3} = 1.65$$

$$d = \frac{\text{FV(Unfavorable State)}}{\text{PV}} = \frac{\$16.7}{\$30.3} = 0.55$$

Solve by substituting:

$$p^* = 0.45$$

$$1 - p^* = 0.55$$

These probabilities implicitly capture the risk premium for investments perfectly correlated with the twin security. We discount the future cash flows weighted by the risk-neutral probabilities at the risk-free rate of 5 percent, arriving at exactly the same value determined using the replicating portfolio:

$$\text{Contingent NPV} = \frac{0.45(\$45) + 0.55(0)}{1.05} = \$19.5$$

It is no coincidence that the replicating portfolio and risk-neutral valuation lead to the same result. They are mathematically equivalent, and both rely on the price of the twin security to derive the value of an investment project with an option to defer.

Valuation Based on Decision Tree Analysis

A second method for valuing a project with flexibility is to use DTA. This leads to the right answer in principle, but only if we apply the correct cost of capital for a project's contingent cash flows.

One DTA approach is to discount the project's contingent payoffs net of the investment requirements. Unfortunately, we can only derive the correct cost of capital for these cash flows from the ROV results. Given the project's contingent NPV of $19.50 with equal chances of paying off $45 or $0, the implied discount rate from the ROV analysis is 15.5 percent.[11] This is significantly above the underlying asset's 10 percent cost of capital, because the contingent cash flows are riskier. The contingent NPV has an equal chance of increasing by 131 percent or decreasing by 100 percent. The value of the underlying asset ($90.90) has a 50–50 chance of going up 65 percent (to $150) or down 45 percent (to $50). If the underlying asset's cost of capital of 10 percent were used, the DTA results would therefore be too high relative to the correct ROV result:

$$\text{Contingent NPV} = \frac{0.5(\$45) + 0.5(0)}{1.10} = \$20.5$$

---

[11] In this simplified example, there is one value for the cost of capital. In general, the cost of capital for the contingent cash flows is not constant. It changes with the risk of the option across time and states of the world.

A better DTA approach separately discounts the two components of the contingent cash flows. The contingent payoffs from the underlying asset are discounted at the cost of capital of the underlying asset. The investment requirements are discounted at the risk-free rate:

$$\text{Contingent NPV} = 0.5\left(\frac{\$150}{1.10} - \frac{\$105}{1.05}\right) + 0.5(0) = \$18.2$$

For longer-term contingent payoffs, this DTA approach generates results that are closer to the correct ROV value. The next section discusses how this second DTA approach can lead to the exact ROV outcome if the underlying risk is either diversifiable or nondiversifiable but is too small to influence the future investment decision (that is, if the project value would exceed the investment requirements even in the unfavorable state).

Comparing ROV and DTA Approaches

As summarized in Exhibit 39.7, the standard NPV approach undervalues our mining project at –$9.10. The ROV approach generates a correct value (NPV = $19.50) because it captures the value of flexibility by using a replicating portfolio or risk-neutral valuation. The DTA approach at $18.20 is quite close in this example, capturing almost the entire gap between the standard NPV valuation and the more granular ROV result. But the DTA results might

EXHIBIT 39.7 **Valuation Result: Standard vs. Contingent NPV**

$

Standard NPV

		Cash flow	150
	$p=$ 50%	Investment	(105)
NPV (9.1)		Net cash flow	45
	$1-p=$ 50%	Cash flow	50
		Investment	(105)
Risk-free rate = 5%		Net cash flow	(55)
WACC = 10%			

Contingent NPV

Decision tree analysis[1]

	$p=$ 50%	Cash flow	150
		Investment	(105)
NPV 18.2		Net cash flow	45
	$1-p=$ 50%	Cash flow	50
		Investment	(105)
		Net cash flow	–

Real-option valuation[2]

	p^* 45%	Cash flow	150
		Investment	(105)
NPV 19.5		Net cash flow	45
	$1-p^*$ 55%	Cash flow	50
		Investment	(105)
		Net cash flow	–

Note: t = time, in years; p = probability; p^* = binomial (risk-neutral) probability.

[1] Discounting cash flows at the project's cost of capital of 10% and investments at the risk-free rate of 5%.

[2] Using risk-neutral valuation.

EXHIBIT 39.8 **Application Opportunities for Real-Option Valuation vs. Decision Tree Analysis**

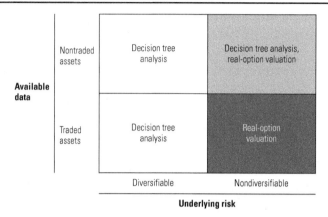

be further off or closer to the ROV mark, depending on the project's payoffs and risks.

This example does not mean that ROV is always the best approach to valuing managerial flexibility. The stylized example did not take into account two important aspects of real-life investment decisions: the type of prevailing risk and the availability of data on the value and variance of cash flows from the underlying asset. Exhibit 39.8 identifies when each method is most suitable. As we explain next, the more straightforward DTA is often the better approach because in practice (most of) the underlying risk is diversifiable or because only rough estimates are available for required inputs such as the underlying asset value and variance. In addition, DTA is easier to use and understand. ROV works best only when the future cash flows are closely linked to traded commodities, securities, or currencies. Not surprisingly, real-option valuations are most often used for commodity-linked investments, such as in the mining and oil industries.

Prevailing Risk: Diversifiable and Nondiversifiable   Investment projects can be exposed to a wide range of risks, such as product price and demand risk, interest and currency risks, technological risk, and political risk. The question is which particular risk (or group of risks) is *prevailing*—in other words, which risk could affect a project's cash flow to such an extent that it would change management's future decisions. The following examples of prevailing risks describe whether the risks are diversifiable and how this affects the choice of a valuation tool:

- If commodity prices (as in mining, the oil industry, or power generation) or currency and interest rates are keys to future investment decisions, the prevailing risk *is not diversifiable,* and only ROV leads to the theoretically correct valuation. This was illustrated in the previous example in this chapter, where the difference in mining payoffs stemmed from changes in the mineral price. The DTA approach could not provide a correct value, although it was quite close in that particular case.

- If technological risks (such as customer preferences, technological innovations, drug trial outcomes, or geological survey results) are critical to future investment decisions, the prevailing risk *is diversifiable*, and both ROV and DTA are effective tools for valuing flexibility. In our experience, this is the more common case for prevailing risk. Applying DTA, it is possible to discount the project's payoffs in each scenario at the cost of capital of the underlying asset and discount the investment requirements at the risk-free rate (see Equation 39.1 in the example of the pharmaceutical drug company presented near the beginning of the chapter).[12]

Let's illustrate how you can apply ROV and DTA, depending on which group of risks dominates in a more complex version of the mining example from the previous section. In addition to price risk, there is now also uncertainty about the size of the reserves found (see Exhibit 39.9, Example 1). The mine is either very large, with reserves at 2.50 times the expected level, or very small, at 0.26 times the expected level. The probability of very large mining reserves is 33 percent, versus a probability of 67 percent for very small reserves. This implies that there are not just two but four possible outcomes to the initial investment, with cash flows ranging from $375 in the large-mine and high-mineral-price scenario ($150 × 2.50) to $13 in the small-mine and low-price scenario ($50 × 0.26). As the conditional payoffs in the exhibit reflect, the rational decision is to start production only if the mine turns out to be large, regardless of the commodity price. For a small mine, even the high-price scenario does not justify production, as the investment requirements ($105) exceed the cash flow ($39 = $150 × 0.26).

To use the ROV approach to derive the valuation results, multiply the conditional payoffs by the risk-neutral (pseudo-)probabilities for the price scenarios and the normal probabilities for the quantity scenarios, and then discount at the risk-free rate.[13] For example, for the large-mine, high-price scenario:

$$\frac{0.45 \times 0.33 \times \$270}{1 + 5\%} = \$38.6$$

---

[12] To value the drug development project with an ROV approach, we build a replicating portfolio. Assume a twin security exists whose payoffs are perfectly correlated with the outcome of the drug trial, generating $52.50 when the outcome is favorable and $10.50 when it is unfavorable. Because its cash flows are driven by technological risk only, the security's market beta is zero, and its present value must be $30. A replicating portfolio consists of a long position of 107.1 of these securities and a short position of $1,071.40 in risk-free bonds. The ROV is therefore 107.1($30) − $1,071.4(1) = $2,143. See also Dixit and Pindyck, *Investment under Uncertainty*, 30–32, for a similar proof.

[13] We can use the risk-neutral probabilities from the original example because the mineral price risk has not changed. For the quantity risk, no risk adjustment to the probabilities is needed because it is diversifiable. We used the risk-neutral probability approach for the ROV valuation because it is more straightforward to apply here; of course, the replicating portfolio approach leads to an identical value.

EXHIBIT 39.9 **Valuation Result for Mixed Price and Quantity Risk**

● Price risk event
■ Quantity risk event

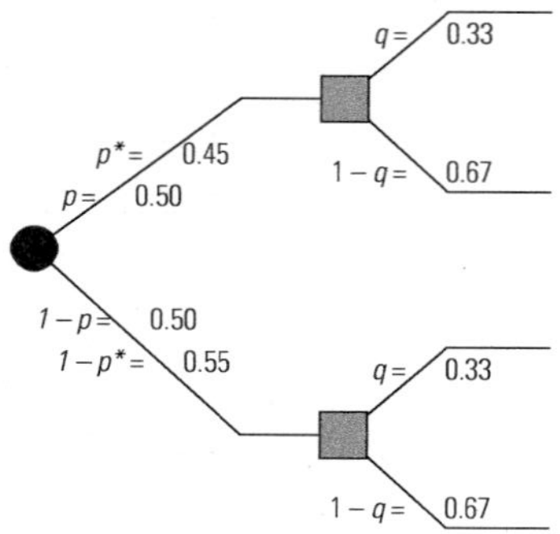

Example 1: High technology risk

Price	Size	Cash flow	Investment	Net cash flow	ROV	DTA
150	2.50	375	(105)	270	38.6	39.8
150	0.26	39	(105)	–	–	–
50	2.50	125	(105)	20	3.4	2.3
50	0.26	13	(105)	–	–	–
				Value	42.0	42.0

Example 2: Low technology risk

Price	Size	Cash flow	Investment	Net cash flow	ROV	DTA
150	1.50	225	(105)	120	17.1	17.3
150	0.75	113	(105)	8	2.3	0.9
50	1.50	75	(105)	–	–	–
50	0.75	38	(105)	–	–	–
				Value	19.5	18.2

Decision tree:

- $p^* = 0.45$, $p = 0.50$ (upper branch from price risk event)
  - $q = 0.33$
  - $1 - q = 0.67$
- $1 - p = 0.50$, $1 - p^* = 0.55$ (lower branch from price risk event)
  - $q = 0.33$
  - $1 - q = 0.67$

Note. p = probability of mineral price being high
p^* = binomial (risk-neutral) probability
q = probability of mine size being large

Summing these values over all possible scenarios leads to an ROV of $42.[14]

Taking a DTA approach instead, we would multiply the conditional payoffs by the normal probabilities for price and quantity scenarios and then separately discount the cash inflows at the mine's cost of capital and the investment cash flow at the risk-free rate. For the large-mine, high-price scenario, for example:

$$0.50 \times 0.33 \times \left(\frac{\$375}{1+10\%} - \frac{\$105}{1+5\%} \right) = \$39.8$$

Similarly, summing the results over all scenarios, we obtain a DTA value of $42, which is exactly equal to the ROV result. The reason is that the decision is driven entirely by the diversifiable, technological risk related to the size of mine. The nondiversifiable price risk leads to different cash flows but does not matter for the investment decision.[15]

The DTA and ROV approaches both provide the theoretically correct answer when the contingent decisions are (predominantly) driven by diversifiable underlying risk. Examples are geological risks, such as the size of an undeveloped oil field, and even some forms of marketing risk, such as consumer acceptance of a new product. As in the numerical illustration, these risks often have more impact on value than nondiversifiable risks. For example, the driver of the decision to invest in drug development is whether the drug passes the trials, not whether the drug—once successfully developed—is worth more or less, depending on general economic conditions.

In contrast, only the ROV approach is theoretically correct if the contingent decision is affected by nondiversifiable risk; the DTA result would lead to an approximate result. For the same numerical illustration as before, the nondiversifiable price risk does affect the investment decision if the quantity risk is smaller (see Exhibit 39.9, Example 2). As shown in the exhibit, the variation in price becomes the prevailing risk that drives the decision to start production in the case of lower variation in potential mine size outcomes. For example, if the price turns out to be high, production is started whether the mine size ends up at the higher or lower end of its range. As a result, the DTA approach now only provides an approximation ($18.20) of the correct ROV value ($19.50).[16] Similarly, for some real-world investments, the nondiversifiable risks outweigh any technological, regulatory, or other diversifiable risks. For example, decisions to invest in the expansion of a power plant are typically driven by the difference between fuel and power prices and by overall demand for power.

---

[14] Note that this value is higher than in the original example, because we now develop the mine only if the reserves are large; we have introduced additional flexibility.

[15] If the probability distribution of the commodity price was continuous rather than discrete as in this example, there would always be some price outcome overturning the production decision. But the point remains that if the probability of reaching such price levels is small, the difference between the ROV and DTA outcome would be small, too.

[16] For the ROV result, the present value of the large-mine and high-price scenario would now be (0.45 × 0.33 × $120)/(1 + 5%) = $17.1. Adding this to the present value for the small-mine and high-price scenario, or (0.45 × 0.67 × $7.5)/(1 + 5%) = $2.3, leads to total ROV of $19.5 when rounded.

Data Availability: Traded vs. Untraded Assets   The results of any contingent valuation critically depend on well-grounded estimates for the value and the variance of cash flows from the underlying asset.

If the estimate for the *underlying asset value* is inaccurate, the flexibility value also will be inaccurate. Returning to our first example, if we estimate incorrectly the future cash flows generated by a highly effective drug, the value of the option to defer will be inaccurate. In practice, you would have to estimate the value with a full-fledged DCF model projecting sales growth, operating margins, capital turnovers, and so on. All ROV (and DTA) approaches build on this valuation of the underlying asset.

A similar argument holds for estimates of the variance of the underlying asset's cash flows (called *volatility* in the option-pricing literature). Volatility can have a great impact on value, because real options typically have long lifetimes and are often at-the-money or close to it,[17] meaning the decision of whether to undertake the project is a close call.[18] Still, for many managers and practitioners, volatility remains an abstract concept: how do you reasonably estimate the range of cash flow outcomes from the sale of a product that has yet to be released?[19]

Sometimes the underlying asset value and variance can be derived from traded assets. Examples include options to shut down gas-fueled power generation, abandon a copper mine, or defer production of an oil field. In such cases, because you can estimate the key inputs with reasonable accuracy, ROV should be more accurate than DTA. When estimates for the underlying asset valuation and variance (volatility) cannot be derived from traded assets and are largely judgmental, a DTA approach is more appropriate. It is more straightforward and transparent to decision makers than the ROV approach. Transparency is especially important when critical valuation assumptions require the decision maker's judgment. DTA captures the essence of flexibility value, and the theoretical advantage of ROV is less important if required inputs are unavailable.

FOUR STEPS TO VALUING FLEXIBILITY

To value flexibility, use the four-step process illustrated in Exhibit 39.10. In step 1, conduct a valuation of the investment project without flexibility, using a traditional discounted-cash-flow model. In step 2, expand the DCF model into an event tree, mapping how the value of the project evolves over time, using (unadjusted) probabilities and the weighted average cost of capital. At this stage, the model does not include flexibility, so the present value of the

---

[17] It follows from option-pricing theory that the sensitivity of option value to changes in variance (referred to as vega) increases as the option's lifetime increases and as the option is closer to the money. An option is at-the-money if its exercise price equals the value of the underlying asset.
[18] If the investment decision were a clear go or no-go, there would be little value in flexibility in the first place, and no need to consider the option value.
[19] The range needs to include the associated probabilities to provide a variance estimate.

EXHIBIT 39.10 **Four-Step Process for Valuing Flexibility**

	Estimate NPV without flexibility	Model uncertainty in event tree	Model flexibility in decision tree	Estimate contingent NPV
Objectives	Compute base-case present value without flexibility	Understand how present value develops with respect to changing uncertainty	Analyze event tree to identify and incorporate managerial flexibility to respond to new information	Value total project using DTA or ROV approach
Comments	Standard NPV approach is used for valuation of underlying asset.	No flexibility modeled; valuation following event tree should equal standard NPV	Flexibility is incorporated into event tree, transforming it into decision tree	Under high uncertainty and managerial flexibility, contingent NPV will be significantly higher than standard NPV

project, based on discounting the cash flows in the event tree, should still equal the standard DCF value from the first step.

In step 3, turn the event tree into a decision tree by identifying the types of managerial flexibility that are available. Build the flexibility into the nodes of the tree. Multiple sources of flexibility are possible at a single decision node, such as the option to abandon or expand, but it is important to have clear priorities among them. Be careful in establishing the sequence of decisions regarding flexibility, especially when the decision tree has compound options.

Finally, step 4 entails recognizing how the exercise of flexibility alters the project's risk characteristics. If the prevailing risk affecting the contingent cash flows is fully diversifiable, you need no special modeling; you can use DTA, discounting investment cash flows at the risk-free rate and the underlying project's cash flows at the weighted average cost of capital, as in the pharmaceutical example in the upcoming section on ROV and DTA. If the prevailing risk is nondiversifiable and priced in the market, the appropriate risk-adjusted discount rate for the project's cash flows is no longer the weighted average cost of capital used in step 1. In that case, apply an ROV approach for the project with flexibility, using risk-neutral valuation or a replicating portfolio.

Real-Option Valuation: A Numerical Example

Using the four-step process, we illustrate the ROV approach with a straightforward binomial lattice for valuing flexibility that is assumed to be driven by nondiversifiable risk. The results are identical to alternative option-pricing models that use more complicated mathematics such as stochastic calculus or Monte Carlo simulation.

Step 1: Estimate Net Present Value without Flexibility   Assume that an investment in a project to build a factory generates cash flows whose present value (PV) equals $100, and its expected rate of return and cost of capital (k) equal

EXHIBIT 39.11 **Event Tree: Factory without Flexibility**

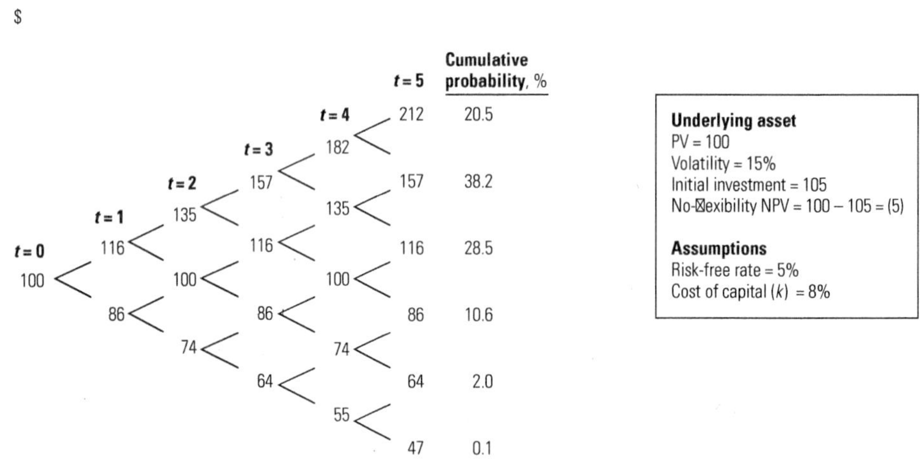

$

| | | Cumulative |
| | $t=5$ | probability, % |

	$t=4$	212	20.5
$t=3$	182		
$t=2$	157	157	38.2
$t=1$	135	135	
$t=0$	116	116	116	28.5
100	100	100		
86	86	86	10.6
74	74		
64	64	2.0
55		
47	0.1

Underlying asset
PV = 100
Volatility = 15%
Initial investment = 105
No-flexibility NPV = 100 − 105 = (5)

Assumptions
Risk-free rate = 5%
Cost of capital (*k*) = 8%

Note: *t* = time, in years

8 percent. The risk-free rate is 5 percent per year, and the cash outflow necessary to undertake the project, if we invest in it immediately, is $105. Thus, the standard NPV is –$5, equal to the expected present value of $100 less the investment of $105, and we would not undertake the project if we had to commit today.

Step 2: Model Uncertainty Using Event Tree   The lattice that models the potential values of the underlying risky asset is called an event tree. It contains no decision nodes and simply models the evolution of the underlying asset. Exhibit 39.11 illustrates potential values the factory might take for each of next five years, assuming a volatility of 15 percent per year.[20] Defining T as the number of years per upward movement and σ as the annualized volatility of the underlying factory value, determine the up-and-down movements by using the following formulas:[21]

$$\text{Up Movement} = u = e^{\sigma\sqrt{T}}$$

$$\text{Down Movement} = d = \frac{1}{u}$$

Substitute numerical values into these formulas:

$$u = e^{0.15\sqrt{1}} = 1.1618$$

$$d = \frac{1}{1.1618} = 0.8607$$

[20] The standard deviation of the rate of change of the factory value.
[21] J. Cox, M. Rubinstein, and S. Ross, "Option Pricing: A Simplified Approach," *Journal of Financial Economics* 7, no. 3 (1979): 229–263. As T becomes smaller, the binomial lattice results converge to the true value of the option. In this example, we have chosen $T = 1$ for ease of illustration.

EXHIBIT 39.12 **Decision Tree: Option to Expand Factory**

$

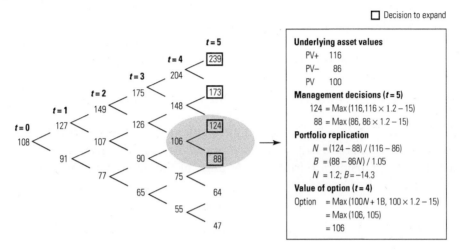

☐ Decision to expand

Underlying asset values

Underlying asset values
PV+   116
PV−   86
PV   100
Management decisions ($t = 5$)
   124 = Max (116,116 × 1.2 − 15)
   88 = Max (86, 86 × 1.2 − 15)
Portfolio replication
   N = (124 − 88) / (116 − 86)
   B = (88 − 86N) / 1.05
   N = 1.2; B = −14.3
Value of option ($t = 4$)
   Option   = Max (100N + 1B, 100 × 1.2 − 15)
      = Max (106, 105)
      = 106

Note: t = time, in years
   PV = present value
   N = number of replicating securities
   B = number of risk-free bonds
   Incremental investment: $15
   Incremental payoff: 20%

Based on traditional DCF using an 8 percent cost of capital, the probability of an up movement is 72.82 percent, and the probability of a down movement is 27.18 percent.[22] As can be verified, the present value of any branch in the event tree equals the expected payout discounted at the 8 percent cost of capital. For example, take the uppermost branch in the fifth time period. Its present value is:

$$PV_{t=4} = \frac{E(PV_{t=5})}{(1+k)} = \frac{0.7282(\$211.7)+0.2718(\$156.8)}{1.08} = \$182.2$$

A similar calculation will produce any of the values in the event tree, resulting in a PV of the project of $100 at $t = 0$. That present value equals the result in step 1, so we know the tree is correct.

Step 3: Model Flexibility Using a Decision Tree   When you add decision points to an event tree, it becomes a decision tree. Suppose the factory can be expanded for an additional $15. The expansion increases the factory's value at that node by 20 percent. The option can be exercised at any time during the next five years—but only once.

Exhibit 39.12 shows the resulting decision tree. To find the payouts at a given point on the tree, start with the final branches. Consider the uppermost

[22] See the previous note for the derivation of the formula for estimating the upward probability:

$$\frac{(1+k)^T - d}{u - d} = \frac{(1+8\%) - 0.8607}{1.1618 - 0.8607} = 0.7282$$

branch in period 5. On the upward limb, the payout absent expansion would be $211.70, as Exhibit 39.11 shows. But with expansion, it is $1.20 \times \$211.70 - \$15 = \$239.00$. Since the value with expansion is higher, we would decide to expand. On the lower limb of that same node, the payout with expansion is $1.20 \times \$156.80 - \$15 = \$173.20$, versus $156.80 without expansion, so again we would expand. In this way, complete the payoff estimates for all final branches.

Step 4: Estimate Contingent Net Present Value   To determine the value of the project with the flexibility to expand, work backward through the decision tree, using the replicating-portfolio method at each node. For the node highlighted in Exhibit 39.12, you can replicate the payoffs from the option to expand in $t = 5$, using a portfolio of N units of the underlying project and B units of $1 risk-free bonds:[23]

$$\$116.2N + \$1.05B = \$124.4$$
$$\$86.1N + \$1.05B = \$88.3$$

Solving the equations, we find that $N = 1.2$, and $B = -14.3$. Therefore, a replicating portfolio consists of 1.2 units of the project without flexibility (at that node, valued at $100 in the event tree of Exhibit 39.11), plus a short position of 14.3 bonds worth $1. As shown in the calculations in Exhibit 39.12, the value of the option in the node at $t = 4$ is then:

$$PV = \$100N + \$1B = \$105.7$$

Work backward from right to left, node by node, to obtain a present value of $108.40 for a project that has an option to expand. As a result, the net present value of the project increases from –$5.00 to $3.40, so the option itself is worth $8.40. Note that the analysis also provides the value-maximizing decision strategy: management should expand the factory only after five years and only if the factory is worth $75 or more as indicated by the boxed nodes in Exhibit 39.12.[24]

If, instead, management had the option to abandon the factory at any node for a fixed liquidation value of $100, the valuation would be as shown in Exhibit 39.13. Determine the contingent payoffs for final branches. Then work again from right to left through the decision tree. For the highlighted node at $t = 4$, the value of the underlying factory is $116.20 in the upward branch and $86.10 in the downward branch (see in the event tree of Exhibit 39.11). Given the ability to do so, the company would abandon the project for $100

---

[23] If the project itself is not traded but a traded twin security exists, we can construct the portfolio in a similar way with units of the twin security and risk-free bonds.

[24] This is analogous to a call option on a stock that does not pay dividends: it is never exercised prematurely. For example, in the node highlighted in Exhibit 39.12, the value in year 4 of deferring the expansion of the factory to year 5 is $105.70, as calculated in the preceding equation. The value of expanding in year 4 is $100 \times 1.20 - \$15 = \$105$. It is therefore optimal to defer expansion, as is the case for all nodes before year 5.

EXHIBIT 39.13 **Decision Tree: Option to Abandon Factory**

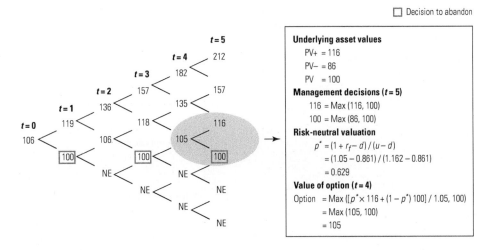

$

☐ Decision to abandon

Underlying asset values
  PV+ = 116
  PV− = 86
  PV = 100
Management decisions (*t* = 5)
  116 = Max (116, 100)
  100 = Max (86, 100)
Risk-neutral valuation
  $p^* = (1 + r_f - d) / (u - d)$
    $= (1.05 - 0.861) / (1.162 - 0.861)$
    $= 0.629$
Value of option (*t* = 4)
  Option = Max ([p^* × 116 + (1 − p^*) 100] / 1.05, 100)
    = Max (105, 100)
    = 105

Note: *t* = time, in years
  NE = nonexisting state
  PV = present value
  *p** = binomial (risk-neutral) probability
  r$_f$ = risk-free rate
  d = downward movement of value
  u = upward movement of value
    Liquidation value: $100

in the downward branch, so the payoffs in the decision tree are $116.20 in the upward branch and $100 in the downward branch. Using risk-neutral valuation this time, the abandonment option can be valued in the node at *t* = 4 at $104.90, as shown in Exhibit 39.13 (the same result a replicating portfolio would have generated). Working backward through time, the value for a factory with the ability to abandon is $106.40, so that the abandonment option is worth $6.40. Now the value-maximizing decision strategy is to abandon the factory immediately in any year in which its value drops below $100.

Multiple sources of flexibility can be combined within a single decision tree, as illustrated in Exhibit 39.14, using risk-neutral valuation. The value of the project, including the options to abandon and expand, would be $113.50 rather than $100, its stand-alone value without flexibility. With these options, the correct decision would be to accept the project. Note that the value of the combined expansion-abandonment flexibility, $13.50, is less than the sum of the individual flexibility values ($8.40 + $6.40 = $14.80) but greater than either of them individually. The values of both options are not additive, because they interact in complex ways (for example, you cannot expand the factory once you have abandoned it). As indicated in Exhibit 39.14, the best decision strategy is to abandon the factory whenever its value[25] drops below $100 and to expand only in year 5 if its value exceeds $75.

[25] Note that this is the value of the factory including the option to expand. Therefore, abandonment occurs only in more unfavorable states of the world than in Exhibit 39.13.

EXHIBIT 39.14 **Decision Tree: Option to Expand or Abandon Factory**

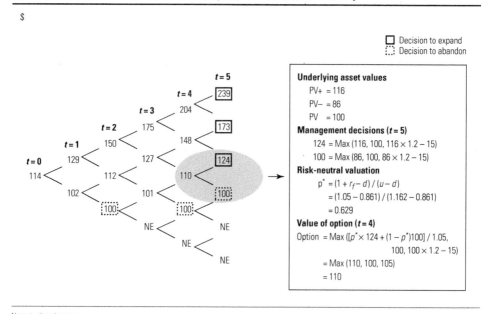

Note: *t* = time, in years
    NE = nonexisting state
    PV = present value
    p* = binomial (risk-neutral) probability
    r_f = risk-free rate
    d = downward movement of value
    u = upward movement of value
      Liquidation value: $100
      Incremental investment: $15
      Incremental payoff: 20%

REAL-OPTION VALUATION AND DECISION TREE ANALYSIS: A NUMERICAL EXAMPLE

Our next example applies both the DTA and the ROV approaches in the valuation of a research and development project. Assume a company needs to decide whether to develop a new pharmaceutical drug. In our simplified example,[26] the first step in development is a research phase of three years, in which the most promising chemical compounds are selected. The probability of success in the research phase is estimated at 15 percent. This is followed by a three-year testing phase, during which the compounds are tested in laboratory and clinical settings. The chance of successfully completing the testing phase is 40 percent. If there are successful results, the drug can be released in the market. On failure in any phase, the company terminates development, and the product dies worthless.

---

[26] Pharmaceutical R&D is much more complex and consists of more phases than shown in this example. For a more extensive example of valuing flexibility in pharmaceutical research and development, see Kellogg and Charnes, "Real-Options Valuation for a Biotechnology Company."

DTA Approach: Technological Risk

The DTA approach presented next follows the four steps for the valuation of flexibility as described in the previous section. In the DTA valuation of the research and development project, we consider only the prevailing technological risk relating to the research and testing outcomes. The commercial risk concerning the future profitability of the drug and the technological risk are taken into account jointly in the ROV approach discussed in the next section.

Step 1: Estimate Present Value without Flexibility   If the development process succeeds, the drug will deliver substantial value in six years' time. Margins in the pharmaceutical industry are high because patents protect drugs against competition. A successful drug is expected to generate annual sales of $2,925 million and 45 percent earnings before interest, taxes, depreciation, and amortization (EBITDA) margin on sales until its patent expires, ten years after its market launch. (Because prices decline drastically after a patent expires, we do not count cash flows beyond that time.) Assuming a 30 percent tax rate and a 7 percent cost of capital, a marketable drug's present value at the launch date would therefore be $6,475 million. Unfortunately, the odds of successful development are small. The cumulative probability of success over the research and testing phase is only 6 percent (0.15 for research $\times$ 0.40 for testing). In addition, the investments needed to develop, test, and market a drug are high: $100 million in the research phase, $250 million in the testing phase, and $150 million in marketing.

   If we had to commit to all three investments today, we should not proceed, because the NPV would be negative:

$$\text{Standard NPV}_0 = \text{PV}_0(\text{Expected Cash Flows}) - \text{PV}_0(\text{Investments})$$

$$= 0.06\left[\frac{\$6,475}{(1.07)^6}\right] - \$100 - \frac{\$250}{(1.05)^3} - \frac{\$150}{(1.05)^6}$$

$$= -\$169$$

However, if we take into account management's ability to abandon the project before completion, the value is significantly higher.

Step 2: Model Uncertainty Using an Event Tree   For this development project, you can model the prevailing technological risk using a straightforward event tree (see Exhibit 39.15). The expected value of a marketable drug after successful development is shown at its DCF value of $6,475 million as of $t = 6$.

Step 3: Model Flexibility Using a Decision Tree   Next, include decision flexibility in the tree, working from right to left. At the end of the testing phase, we have the option to invest $150 million in marketing to launch the product.

EXHIBIT 39.15 **Event Tree: R&D Option with Technological Risk**

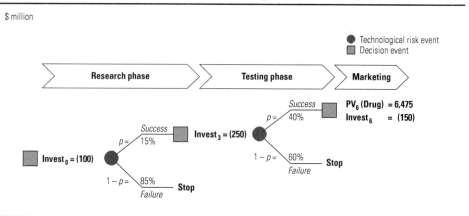

Note: PV$_t$ = present value of marketable drug as of year t
      p = probability of technological success

We should invest only if testing has produced a marketable product. At the end of the research phase, we have the option to proceed with the testing phase. We proceed to testing only if the payoffs justify the incremental investment of $250 million.

Step 4: Estimate Value of Flexibility Because the technological risk is fully diversifiable, apply a straightforward DTA approach for the valuation of flexibility. Again, work from right to left in the tree (see Exhibit 39.16). After six years, at the end of the testing phase, we proceed with launching the product only if there is a marketable product. The value in millions at this point in time is therefore $NPV_6 = Max[(\$6{,}475 - \$150), 0] = \$6{,}325$. At the end of the research

EXHIBIT 39.16 **Decision Tree: R&D Option with Technological Risk**

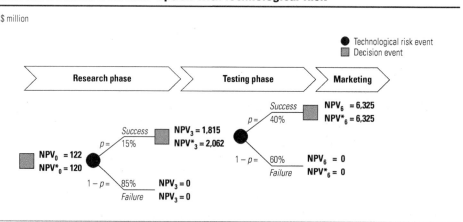

Note: NPV$_t$ = net present value as of year t
      NPV* = contingent NPV
      p = probability of technological success

phase, we continue to the testing phase if the future payoffs outweigh the required investments. The value of the project at this point, after three years is:

$$NPV_3 \text{ (Option)} = \text{Max } [PV_3 \text{(Testing)} - Inv_3 \text{(Testing)}, 0]$$

In this equation, PV_3(Testing) equals the probability-weighted future payoffs discounted by three years at the cost of capital of 7 percent:

$$PV_3 \text{(Testing)} = 0.40 \left[\frac{\$6,475 - \$150}{(1.07)^3} \right] + 0.60(0) = \$2,065$$

With Inv_3(Testing) equal to the $250 million investment requirement for the testing phase, the project value prior to the testing phase amounts to:

$$NPV_3 \text{ (Option)} = \text{Max } [(\$2,065 - \$250), 0] = \$1,815$$

Working further from right to left in the tree, we find the contingent NPV for the entire project prior to the research phase:

$$NPV_0 \text{ (Option)} = \text{Max } [PV_0 \text{(Research)} - Inv_0 \text{(Research)}, 0]$$

$$= \text{Max } \left[0.15 \left(\frac{\$1,815}{(1.07)^3} \right) + 0.85(0) - \$100, 0 \right]$$

$$= \$122$$

This value including flexibility is significantly higher than the standard NPV of −$169 million. Note that we discounted all contingent payoffs at the underlying asset's cost of capital, so the $122 million only approximates the true contingent value. But the result is close, as we show in the calculations immediately following, and this approach is straightforward to apply and easy to explain.

The true contingent value turns out to be $120 million and follows from a refined DTA approach that separately discounts the asset cash flows at the cost of capital of 7 percent and the investment cash flows at the risk-free rate of 5 percent.[27] The value of proceeding with testing now becomes:[28]

$$PV_3^* \text{(Testing)} = 0.40 \left(\frac{\$6,475}{(1.07)^3} - \frac{\$150}{(1.05)^3} \right) + 0.60(0) = \$2,114 - \$52 = \$2,062$$

The value of the option to proceed with the testing phase is then:

$$NPV_3^* \text{(Option)} = \text{Max } [(\$2,144 - \$52) - \$250, 0] = \$2,144 - \$302 = \$1,812$$

---

[27] See the example in Exhibit 39.7. The assumption to discount investment outlays at the risk-free rate is also implicitly made in ROV approaches.

[28] In prior editions of this book, we adopted an alternative but equivalent decision tree where all values of asset and investment cash flows were discounted to $t = 0$ before deriving the contingent value by working from right to left in the tree. The contingent NPV results are identical.

Working from right to left but now separately discounting asset and investment cash flows in each step, we obtain the contingent NPV* per $t = 0$:

$$\text{NPV}_0^*(\text{Option}) = \text{Max}\,[\text{PV}_0^*(\text{Research}) - \text{Inv}_0(\text{Research}), 0]$$

$$= \text{Max}\left[0.15\left(\frac{\$2,114}{(1.07)^3} - \frac{\$302}{(1.05)^3}\right) + 0.85(0) - \$100, 0\right]$$

$$= \$120$$

To illustrate, we obtain the same value of $120 million with yet another approach: the ROV method. In this approach, project the future value of the underlying asset under "risk-neutral" return assumptions, and then discount all contingent payoffs at the risk-free rate. The risk-neutral future value of a successfully developed drug is its value as of today, compounded at the risk-free rate for six years:

$$\text{PV}_6^{**}(\text{Drug}) = \$4,314(1.05)^6 = \$5,781$$

This means that the risk-neutral value of proceeding with testing is:

$$\text{PV}_3^{**}(\text{Testing}) = 0.40\left(\frac{\$5,781 - \$150}{(1.05)^3}\right) + 0.60(0) = \$1,946$$

The risk-neutral value of the option to proceed with testing as of $t = 3$ is:

$$\text{NPV}_3^{**}(\text{Option}) = \text{Max}[\$1,946 - \$250, 0] = \$1,696$$

Working from right to left while discounting all cash flows at the risk-free rate gives us the contingent NPV at $t = 0$, which is $120 million:

$$\text{NPV}_0^{**}(\text{Option}) = \text{Max}[\text{PV}_0^{**}(\text{Research}) - \text{Inv}_0(\text{Research}), 0]$$

$$= \text{Max}\left[0.15\left(\frac{\$1,696}{(1.05)^3}\right) + 0.85(0) - \$100, 0\right]$$

$$= \$120$$

ROV Approach: Technological and Commercial Risk

Our analysis thus far did not include the other source of uncertainty in the development project: the commercial risk concerning the future cash flow potential of the successfully developed and marketed drug. ROV is necessary to handle both technological and commercial risk.

Step 1: Estimate Present Value without Flexibility   The first step, estimating present value without flexibility, is identical for the DTA and ROV approaches.

EXHIBIT 39.17 **Event Tree: R&D Option with Technological and Commercial Risk**

$ million

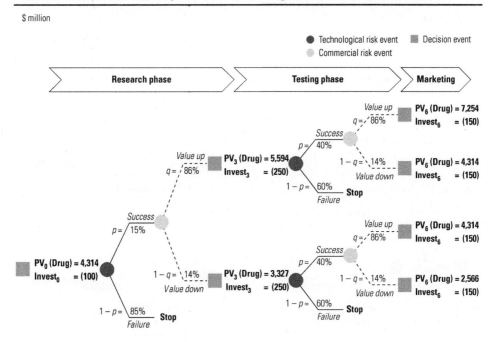

● Technological risk event   ◼ Decision event
◌ Commercial risk event

Research phase | Testing phase | Marketing

PV₀ (Drug) = 4,314
Invest₀ = (100)

$$PV_0 \text{ (Drug)} = 4,314$$
$$\text{Invest}_0 = (100)$$

Note: PV_t (Drug) = present value of marketable drug as of year t
        Invest_t = investment as of year t
        p = probability of technological success
        q = probability of drug value increase

Step 2: Model Uncertainty Using an Event Tree

Both risks can be modeled in a combined event tree (see Exhibit 39.17). For simplicity, we have chosen a one-step binomial lattice to describe the evolution of the drug value over each three-year period.[29] Assuming an annual volatility of 15 percent, we can derive the upward and downward movements, u and d, as follows:

$$u = e^{\sigma\sqrt{T}} = e^{0.15\sqrt{3}} = 1.30$$

$$d = \frac{1}{u} = \frac{1}{1.30} = 0.77$$

The probability of an upward movement is 86 percent, and the probability of a downward movement is 14 percent.[30] The value of a marketable drug

[29] With more nodes, the tree quickly becomes too complex to show in an exhibit, because it does not converge in the technological risk. We carried out the analysis with ten nodes and found that doing so did not affect the results for this particular example.

[30] The formula for estimating the upward probability is:

$$\frac{(1+k)^T - d}{u - d} = \frac{1.07^3 - 0.77}{1.30 - 0.77} = 0.86$$

where k is the expected return on the asset.

EXHIBIT 39.18 **Decision Tree: R&D Option with Technological and Commercial Risk**

$ million

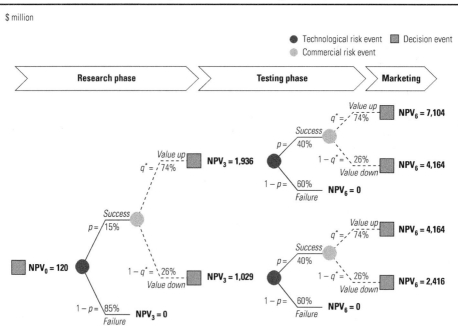

Note: NPV$_t$ = net present value of project as of year t
      q^* = binomial (risk-neutral) probability of an increase in marketable drug value
      p = probability of technological success

at the start of the research phase is $4,314 million. At the end of the research phase, there are three possible outcomes: success combined with an increase in the value of a marketable drug to $5,594 million, success combined with a decrease in the value of a marketable drug to $3,327 million, and failure leading to a drug value of $0. Following the same logic, there are six possible outcomes after the testing phase.

Step 3: Model Flexibility Using a Decision Tree   The logic underlying the decision tree including commercial risk (see Exhibit 39.18) is the same as under the DTA approach. For example, the payoff at the end of the testing phase in the top branch equals Max[($7,254 – $150), 0] = $7,104. The primary difference is that the ROV version of the tree recognizes the ability to abandon development if the value of a marketable drug drops too much.

Step 4: Estimate Contingent NPV   The commercial risk regarding the drug's future cash flows is not diversifiable,[31] so you need to use an ROV approach to include it in your valuation. This example uses risk-neutral valuation.

---

[31] Recall that we assumed the cost of capital for a marketed drug is 7 percent. Given our assumption for a risk-free rate of 5 percent, its beta must be different from zero.

Therefore, risk-adjust all probabilities of the upward and downward movements for the drug's value:

$$p^* = \frac{(1+r_f)^T - d}{u - d} = \frac{1.05^3 - 0.77}{1.30 - 0.77} = 0.74$$

Having applied the risk-neutral probabilities, discount all contingent payoffs at the risk-free rate, working from right to left in the tree. Because the technological risk is fully diversifiable, there is no need to adjust the probabilities for success and failure in research or testing.

For example, from Exhibit 39.18, the value of the option at the end of the research phase showing a drop in the value of the drug is expressed as follows:

$$NPV_3(\text{Option}) = \text{Max}[PV_3(\text{Testing}) - \text{Inv}_3(\text{Testing}), 0]$$

In this equation, PV_3(Testing) represents the value of proceeding with testing at this node. It equals the value of the future payoffs weighted by risk-neutral probabilities and discounted at the risk-free rate:

$$PV_3(\text{Testing}) = \frac{0.40[0.74(\$4,164) + 0.26(\$2,416)] + 0.60(0)}{(1.05)^3} = \$1,279$$

Inv_3(Testing) equals \$250 million, so the value of the development project at this node is as follows:

$$NPV_3(\text{Option}) = \text{Max}[(\$1,279 - \$250), 0] = \$1,029$$

Solve for the other nodes in the same way. Working backward through the tree gives us an estimate of the contingent NPV: \$120 million, the same result as obtained in the DTA approach without commercial risk.

This is not surprising. A closer look at the decision tree reveals that uncertainty about the future value of the drug if it is marketable is not significant enough to influence any of the decisions in the development process. In this example, the commercial risk makes no difference, even if we assume volatility as high as 50 percent (an amount that exceeds the volatility of many high-tech stocks). As noted earlier, when nondiversifiable risk (the drug's commercial risk as measured by its beta) does not influence investment decisions, the DTA and ROV results are equivalent.

Moreover, in real situations, the prevailing uncertainty in drug development is whether the drug proves to be an effective disease treatment without serious side effects. The commercial risk is far less relevant, because a truly effective drug almost always generates attractive margins. The example illustrates how in such cases it is more practical to focus on the technological risk entirely, using a DTA approach. Explicitly modeling the nondiversifiable (e.g., commercial) risk requires an ROV approach that is more complex and may not even affect the valuation results.

In general, when faced with multiple sources of underlying risk, carefully assess whether all of these possible risks are important or whether one prevails. Sometimes you can focus the valuation approach on just one or two sources of uncertainty and greatly simplify the analysis.

SUMMARY

Managerial flexibility lets executives defer or change investment decisions as a business or project develops. It can substantially alter the value of a business or project. Rigidly applying standard DCF analysis fails to account for the impact that exercising flexibility can have on present value.

Flexibility takes many forms, such as the option to defer, expand, contract, or abandon projects, or to switch them on and off. This chapter has illustrated only a few applications. Contingent NPV analysis, in the form of decision tree analysis (DTA) or real-option valuation (ROV) models, correctly captures flexibility's impact on value. The ROV approach is theoretically superior to DTA, but applying it is more complicated. So ROV is often limited to valuing flexibility in commodity-based industries where prices are measurable, making its application more straightforward. In most other cases, a careful DTA approach delivers results that are reasonably solid and can provide more valuable insights.

Discounted Economic Profit Equals Discounted Free Cash Flow

This appendix demonstrates algebraically the equivalence between discounted cash flow and discounted economic profit. In the first section, we convert the key value driver formula presented in Chapter 3 into a value driver formula based on economic profit. This formula is used in Chapter 10 to estimate continuing value in the economic-profit valuation. The second section of this appendix generalizes the proof to any set of cash flows.

PROOF USING PERPETUITIES

To convert the key value driver formula into an economic-profit-based formula, start with the growing cash flow perpetuity:

$$V = \frac{\text{FCF}_{t=1}}{\text{WACC} - g}$$

where V = value of operations

    $\text{FCF}_{t=1}$ = free cash flow in year 1

    WACC = weighted average cost of capital

    g = growth in NOPAT

In Chapter 3, we convert the growing perpetuity into the key value driver formula:

$$V = \frac{\text{NOPAT}_{t=1}\left(1 - \dfrac{g}{\text{RONIC}}\right)}{\text{WACC} - g}$$

where $\text{NOPAT}_{t=1}$ = net operating profit after taxes

RONIC = return on new invested capital

The key value driver formula can be rearranged further into a formula based on economic profit. We do this to demonstrate that discounted cash flow is equivalent to the book value of invested capital plus the present value of future economic profit.

To begin, start with the key value driver formula, and replace NOPAT with invested capital times return on invested capital (ROIC):

$$V = \frac{\text{Invested Capital}_0 \times \text{ROIC} \times \left(1 - \dfrac{g}{\text{RONIC}}\right)}{\text{WACC} - g}$$

If we assume that the return on new invested capital (RONIC) equals the return on existing invested capital (ROIC), it is possible to simplify the preceding equation by distributing ROIC in the numerator:[1]

$$V = \text{Invested Capital}_0 \left(\frac{\text{ROIC} - g}{\text{WACC} - g}\right)$$

To complete the transformation to economic profit, add and subtract WACC in the numerator:

$$V = \text{Invested Capital}_0 \left(\frac{\text{ROIC} - \text{WACC} + \text{WACC} - g}{\text{WACC} - g}\right)$$

Separate the fraction into two components, and then simplify:

$$V = \text{Invested Capital}_0 \left(\frac{\text{ROIC} - \text{WACC}}{\text{WACC} - g}\right) + \text{Invested Capital}_0 \left(\frac{\text{WACC} - g}{\text{WACC} - g}\right)$$

$$= \text{Invested Capital}_0 + \text{Invested Capital}_0 \left(\frac{\text{ROIC} - \text{WACC}}{\text{WACC} - g}\right)$$

[1] This equation highlights two requirements for using the key value driver formula: both WACC and ROIC must be greater than the rate of growth in cash flows. If WACC is less than the cash flow growth rate, cash flows grow faster than they can be discounted, and value approaches infinity. (Perpetuity-based formulas should never be used to value cash flows whose growth rates exceed WACC.) If ROIC is lower than the growth rate, cash flows are negative, producing a negative value. In actuality, this situation is unlikely; investors would not finance a company that is never expected to generate or enable positive cash flow.

Economic profit is defined as invested capital times the difference of ROIC minus WACC. Substituting this definition into the previous equation leads to our final equation:

$$V = \text{Invested Capital}_0 + \frac{\text{Economic Profit}_1}{\text{WACC} - g}$$

According to this formula, a company's operating value equals the book value of its invested capital plus the present value of all future economic profits. (The final term is a growing perpetuity of economic profits.) If future economic profits are expected to be zero, the intrinsic value of a company equals its book value. In addition, if future economic profits are expected to be less than zero, then enterprise value should trade at less than the book value of invested capital—an occurrence observed in practice.

GENERALIZED PROOF

The previous section limited our proof to a set of cash flows growing at a constant rate. This section generalizes the proof to any set of cash flows. To demonstrate equivalence, start by computing the present value of a periodic stream of cash flows:

$$V = \sum_{t=1}^{\infty} \frac{\text{FCF}_t}{(1 + \text{WACC})^t}$$

where
V = value of operations
FCF_t = free cash flow in year t
WACC = weighted average cost of capital

To this value, add and subtract the cumulative sum of all current and future amounts of invested capital (IC):

$$V = \sum_{t=0}^{\infty} \frac{\text{IC}_t}{(1 + \text{WACC})^t} - \sum_{t=0}^{\infty} \frac{\text{IC}_t}{(1 + \text{WACC})^t} + \sum_{t=1}^{\infty} \frac{\text{FCF}_t}{(1 + \text{WACC})^t}$$

where IC_t = invested capital for year t.

Next, adjust the preceding equation slightly to restate the same value using terms that can be canceled later. First, strip invested capital at time zero from the first cumulative sum. Then modify the second cumulative sum to $t = 1$ to infinity, by changing each t inside the second cumulative sum to $t - 1$. This new representation is identical to the original representation but will allow us to cancel terms later. The new representation is as follows:

$$V = IC_0 + \sum_{t=1}^{\infty} \frac{IC_t}{(1+WACC)^t} - \sum_{t=1}^{\infty} \frac{IC_{t-1}}{(1+WACC)^{t-1}} + \sum_{t=1}^{\infty} \frac{FCF_t}{(1+WACC)^t}$$

Multiply the second cumulative sum by $(1 + WACC)/(1 + WACC)$. This action converts the exponent $t - 1$ in the denominator of the cumulative sum to t. Also substitute for free cash flow in the third cumulative sum, using its definition, NOPAT less the increase in invested capital:

$$V = IC_0 + \sum_{t=1}^{\infty} \frac{IC_t}{(1+WACC)^t} - \sum_{t=1}^{\infty} \frac{(1+WACC)IC_{t-1}}{(1+WACC)^t} + \sum_{t=1}^{\infty} \frac{NOPAT_t - (IC_t - IC_{t-1})}{(1+WACC)^t}$$

Because there is now a consistent denominator across all three cumulative sums, combine them into a single cumulative sum:

$$V = IC_0 + \sum_{t=1}^{\infty} \frac{IC_t - (1+WACC)IC_{t-1} + NOPAT_t - IC_t + IC_{t-1}}{(1+WACC)^t}$$

In the second term of the numerator, distribute $(1 + WACC)IC_{t-1}$ into its two components, IC_{t-1} and $WACC(IC_{t-1})$:

$$V = IC_0 + \sum_{t=1}^{\infty} \frac{IC_t - IC_{t-1} - WACC(IC_{t-1}) + NOPAT_t - IC_t + IC_{t-1}}{(1+WACC)^t}$$

Simplify by collecting terms:

$$V = IC_0 + \sum_{t=1}^{\infty} \frac{NOPAT_t - WACC(IC_{t-1})}{(1+WACC)^t}$$

The numerator is the definition of economic profit, so the result is a valuation based on economic profit:

$$V = IC_0 + \sum_{t=1}^{\infty} \frac{\text{Economic Profit}_t}{(1+WACC)^t}$$

The enterprise value of a company equals the book value of its invested capital plus the present value of all future economic profits. To calculate the value correctly, you must calculate economic profit using last year's (i.e., beginning-of-year) invested capital—a subtle but important distinction.

The interdependence of invested capital, economic profit, and free cash flow is not surprising. Think of discounted cash flow this way: a portion of future cash flows is required to cover the required return for the investor's capital. The remaining cash flow is either used to grow invested capital (to generate additional future cash flows) or returned to investors as an extra bonus. This bonus is valuable, so investors are willing to pay a premium for cash flows above the amount required. Subsequently, companies with positive economic profits will trade at a premium to the book value of invested capital.

Derivation of Free Cash Flow, Weighted Average Cost of Capital, and Adjusted Present Value

Chapter 10 demonstrated numerically the equivalence of enterprise discounted cash flow (DCF), adjusted present value (APV), and the cash-flow-to-equity valuation when leverage (as measured by the market-based debt-to-equity ratio) is constant. This appendix derives the key terms in each model—namely, free cash flow (FCF) and the weighted average cost of capital (WACC)—and demonstrates their equivalence algebraically.

To simplify the analysis, we assume cash flows to equity are growing at a constant rate, g. This way we can use growth perpetuities to analyze the relationship between methods.[1]

ENTERPRISE DISCOUNTED CASH FLOW

By definition, enterprise value (V) equals the market value of debt (D) plus the market value of equity (E):

$$V = D + E$$

---

[1] For an analysis that applies to more complex situations (i.e., when cash flows can follow any pattern), see J. A. Miles and J. R. Ezzell, "The Weighted Average Cost of Capital, Perfect Capital Markets, and Project Life: A Clarification," *Journal of Financial and Quantitative Analysis* 15 (1980): 719–730 (for a discussion of enterprise DCF and WACC); and S. C. Myers, "Interactions of Corporate Financing and Investment Decisions: Implications for Capital Budgeting," *Journal of Finance* 29 (1974): 1–25 (for a discussion of adjusted present value).

To examine the components of enterprise value, multiply the right side of the equation by a complex fraction equivalent to 1 (the numerator equals the denominator, an algebraic trick we will use many times):

$$V = (D+E)\left(\frac{D(1-T_m)k_d + CF_e - D(g)}{D(1-T_m)k_d + CF_e - D(g)} \right) \tag{B.1}$$

where T_m = marginal tax rate

k_d = cost of debt

CF_e = cash flow to equity holders

g = growth in cash flow to equity holders

Over the next few steps, the fraction's numerator will be converted to free cash flow (FCF). We will show later that the denominator equals the weighted average cost of capital. Start by defining the numerator as FCF:

$$FCF = D(1-T_m)k_d + CF_e - D(g)$$

If the market value of debt equals the face value of debt, the cost of debt will equal the coupon rate, and D times k_d will equal the company's interest expense. Therefore,

$$FCF = \text{Interest}(1-T_m) + CF_e - D(g)$$

By definition, cash flow to equity (CF_e) equals earnings before interest and taxes (EBIT) minus interest, taxes, and net investment, plus the increase in debt. Assuming the ratio of debt to equity is constant, the annual increase in debt will equal $D(g)$. Why? Since cash flows to equity are growing at g, the value of equity also grows at g. Since the ratio of debt to equity remains constant (a key assumption), the value of debt must also grow at g. Substitute the definition of cash flow to equity into the preceding equation:

$$FCF = \text{Interest}(1-T_m) + EBIT - \text{Interest} - \text{Taxes} - \text{Net Investment} + D(g) - D(g)$$

Next, distribute the after-tax interest expression into its two components, and cancel $D(g)$:

$$FCF = \text{Interest} - T_m(\text{Interest}) + EBIT - \text{Interest} - \text{Taxes} - \text{Net Investment}$$

Simplify by canceling the interest terms and rearranging the remaining terms:

$$FCF = EBIT - \left[\text{Taxes} + T_m(\text{Interest}) \right] - \text{Net Investment}$$

Chapter 11 defines operating taxes as the taxes a company would pay if the company were financed entirely with equity. Operating taxes therefore equal reported taxes plus the interest tax shield (as interest is eliminated, taxes would rise by the interest tax shield). This leads to the definition of free cash flow we use throughout the book:

$$FCF = EBIT - Operating\ Taxes - Net\ Investment$$

Next, we focus on the denominator. To derive the weighted average cost of capital (WACC), start with Equation B.1, and multiply CF_e by 1, denoted as $(k_e - g)/(k_e - g)$:

$$V = (D+E)\left(\frac{FCF}{D(1-T_m)k_d + \dfrac{CF_e}{k_e - g}(k_e - g) - D(g)} \right)$$

where k_e = cost of equity.

If equity cash flows are growing at a constant rate, the value of equity equals CF_e divided by $(k_e - g)$. Therefore, the growing perpetuity in the denominator can be replaced by the value of equity (E) and distributed:

$$V = (D+E)\left(\frac{FCF}{D(1-T_m)k_d + E(k_e) - E(g) - D(g)} \right)$$

In the denominator, collapse $E(g)$ and $D(g)$ into a single term:

$$V = (D+E)\left(\frac{FCF}{D(1-T_m)k_d + E(k_e) - (D+E)g} \right)$$

To complete the derivation of WACC in the denominator, divide the numerator and denominator by $(D + E)$. This will eliminate the $(D + E)$ expression on the left and place it in the denominator as a divisor. Distributing the term across the denominator, the result is the following equation:

$$V = \frac{FCF}{\dfrac{D}{D+E}(k_d)(1-T_m) + \dfrac{E}{D+E}(k_e) - \dfrac{D+E}{D+E}(g)}$$

The expression in the denominator is the weighted average cost of capital (WACC) minus the growth in cash flow (g). Therefore, Equation B.1 can be rewritten as:

$$V = \frac{FCF}{WACC - g}$$

such that:

$$
\text{WACC} = \frac{D}{D+E}(k_d)(1-T_m) + \frac{E}{D+E}(k_e)
$$

Note how the after-tax cost of debt and the cost of equity are weighted by each security's *market-based* weight to enterprise value. This is why you should use market-based values, and not book values, to build the cost of capital. This is also why you should discount free cash flow at the weighted average cost of capital to determine enterprise value. Remember, however, that you can only use a constant WACC when leverage is expected to remain constant (i.e., debt grows as the business grows).[2]

ADJUSTED PRESENT VALUE

To determine enterprise value using adjusted present value, once again start with $V = D + E$ and multiply by a fraction equal to 1. This time, however, do not include the marginal tax rate in the fraction:

$$
V = (D+E)\left(\frac{D(k_d)+\text{CF}_e - D(g)}{D(k_d)+\text{CF}_e - D(g)}\right)
$$

Following the same process as before, convert each cash flow in the denominator to its present value times its expected return, and divide the fraction by $(D+E)/(D+E)$:

$$
V = \frac{D(k_d)+\text{CF}_e - D(g)}{\dfrac{D}{D+E}(k_d) + \dfrac{E}{D+E}(k_e) - g}
$$

Appendix C shows that if the company's interest tax shields have the same risk as the company's operating assets (as one would expect when the company maintains a constant capital structure), the fraction's denominator equals k_u, the unlevered cost of equity, minus the growth in cash flow (g). Make this substitution into the previous equation:

$$
V = \frac{D(k_d)+\text{CF}_e - D(g)}{k_u - g}
$$

[2] To see this restriction applied in a more general setting, see Miles and Ezzell, "Weighted Average Cost of Capital."

Next, focus on the numerator. Substitute the definitions of cash flow to debt and cash flow to equity, as we did earlier in this appendix:

$$V = \frac{\text{Interest} + \text{EBIT} - \text{Interest} - \text{Taxes} - \text{Net Investment} + D(g) - D(g)}{k_u - g}$$

In this equation, the two interest terms cancel and the two $D(g)$ terms cancel, so simplify by canceling these terms. Also insert $T_m(\text{Interest}) - T_m(\text{Interest})$ into the numerator of the expression:

$$V = \frac{\text{EBIT} - \text{Taxes} + T_m(\text{Interest}) - T_m(\text{Interest}) - \text{Net Investment}}{k_u - g}$$

Aggregate reported taxes and the negative expression for $T_m(\text{Interest})$ into all-equity taxes. Move the positive expression for $T_m(\text{Interest})$ into a separate fraction:

$$V = \frac{\text{EBIT} - \left[\text{Taxes} + T_m(\text{Interest})\right] - \text{Net Investment}}{k_u - g} + \frac{T_m(\text{Interest})}{k_u - g}$$

At this point, we once again have free cash flow in the numerator of the first fraction. The second fraction equals the present value of the interest tax shield. Thus, enterprise value equals free cash flow discounted by the unlevered cost of equity plus the present value of the interest tax shield:

$$V = \frac{\text{FCF}}{k_u - g} + \text{PV}(\text{Interest Tax Shield})$$

This expression is commonly referred to as adjusted present value.

In this simple proof, we assumed tax shields should be discounted at the unlevered cost of equity. This need not be the case. Some financial analysts discount expected interest tax shields at the cost of debt. If you do this, however, free cash flow discounted at the traditional WACC (defined earlier) and adjusted present value will lead to different valuations. In this case, WACC must be adjusted to reflect the alternative assumption concerning the risk of tax shields.

APPENDIX C

Levering and Unlevering
the Cost of Equity

This appendix derives various formulas that can be used to compute unlevered beta and the unlevered cost of equity under different assumptions. Unlevered betas are required to estimate an industry beta, as detailed in Chapter 15. We prefer using an industry beta rather than a company beta to determine the cost of capital because company betas cannot be estimated accurately. As discussed in Chapter 10, the unlevered cost of equity is used to discount free cash flow to compute adjusted present value. For companies with substantial postretirement obligations, the appendix concludes by incorporating pensions and other postretirement benefits into the unlevering process.

UNLEVERED COST OF EQUITY

Franco Modigliani and Merton Miller postulated that the market value of a company's economic assets, such as operating assets (V_u) and tax shields (V_{txa}), should equal the market value of its financial claims, such as debt (D) and equity (E):

$$V_u + V_{txa} = \text{Enterprise Value} = D + E \tag{C.1}$$

A second result of Modigliani and Miller's work is that the total risk of the company's economic assets, operating and financial, must equal the total risk of the financial claims against those assets:

$$\frac{V_u}{V_u + V_{txa}}(k_u) + \frac{V_{txa}}{V_u + V_{txa}}(k_{txa}) = \frac{D}{D+E}(k_d) + \frac{E}{D+E}(k_e) \tag{C.2}$$

where k_u = unlevered cost of equity

k_{txa} = cost of capital for the company's interest tax shields

k_d = cost of debt

k_e = cost of equity

The four terms in this equation represent the proportional risk of operating assets, tax assets, debt, and equity, respectively.

Since the cost of operating assets (k_u) is unobservable, it is necessary to solve for it using the equation's other inputs. The required return on tax shields (k_{txa}) also is unobservable. With two unknowns and only one equation, it is therefore necessary to impose additional restrictions to solve for k_u. If debt is a constant proportion of enterprise value (i.e., debt grows as the business grows), k_{txa} equals k_u. Imposing this restriction leads to the following equation:

$$\frac{V_u}{V_u+V_{txa}}(k_u)+\frac{V_{txa}}{V_u+V_{txa}}(k_u)=\frac{D}{D+E}(k_d)+\frac{E}{D+E}(k_e)$$

Combining terms on the left side generates an equation for the unlevered cost of equity when debt is a constant proportion of enterprise value:

$$k_u = \frac{D}{D+E}(k_d)+\frac{E}{D+E}(k_e) \tag{C.3}$$

Since most companies manage their debt-to-value ratio to stay within a particular range, we believe this formula and its resulting derivations are the most appropriate for standard valuation.

Unlevered Cost of Equity When k_{txa} Equals k_d

Some financial analysts set the required return on interest tax shields equal to the cost of debt. In this case, Equation C.2 can be expressed as follows:

$$\frac{V_u}{V_u+V_{txa}}(k_u)+\frac{V_{txa}}{V_u+V_{txa}}(k_d)=\frac{D}{D+E}(k_d)+\frac{E}{D+E}(k_e)$$

To solve for k_u, multiply both sides by enterprise value:

$$V_u(k_u)+V_{txa}(k_d)=D(k_d)+E(k_e)$$

and move $V_{txa}(k_d)$ to the right side of the equation:

$$V_u(k_u)=(D-V_{txa})k_d+E(k_e)$$

EXHIBIT C.1 **Unlevered Cost of Equity**

	Dollar level of debt fluctuates	Dollar level of debt is constant
Tax shields have same risk as operating assets $k_{txa} = k_u$	$k_u = \dfrac{D}{D+E} k_d + \dfrac{E}{D+E} k_e$	$k_u = \dfrac{D}{D+E} k_d + \dfrac{E}{D+E} k_e$
Tax shields have same risk as debt $k_{txa} = k_d$	$k_u = \dfrac{D - V_{txa}}{D - V_{txa} + E} k_d + \dfrac{E}{D - V_{txa} + E} k_e$	$k_u = \dfrac{D(1 - T_m)}{D(1 - T_m) + E} k_d + \dfrac{E}{D(1 - T_m) + E} k_e$

Note: k_e = cost of equity
 k_d = cost of debt
 k_u = unlevered cost of equity
 k_{txa} = cost of capital for tax shields
 T_m = marginal tax rate
 D = debt
 E = equity
 V_{txa} = present value of tax shields

To eliminate V_u from the left side of the equation, rearrange Equation C.1 to $V_u = D - V_{txa} + E$, and divide both sides by this value:

$$k_u = \frac{D - V_{txa}}{D - V_{txa} + E}(k_d) + \frac{E}{D - V_{txa} + E}(k_e) \tag{C.4}$$

Equation C.4 mirrors Equation C.2 closely. It differs from Equation C.2 only in that the market value of debt is reduced by the present value of expected tax shields.

Unlevered Cost of Equity When Debt Is Constant

Exhibit C.1 summarizes three methods to estimate the unlevered cost of equity. The two formulas in the top row assume that the risk associated with interest tax shields (k_{txa}) equals the risk of operations (k_u). When this is true, whether debt is constant or expected to change, the formula remains the same.

The bottom-row formulas assume that the risk of interest tax shields equals the risk of debt. On the left, future debt can take on any value. On the right, an additional restriction is imposed that debt remains constant—in absolute terms, not as a percentage of enterprise value. In this case, the annual interest payment equals $D(k_d)$, and the annual tax shield equals $D(k_d)(T_m)$. Since tax shields are constant, they can be valued using a constant perpetuity:

$$PV(\text{Tax Shields}) = \frac{D(k_d)(T_m)}{k_d} = D(T_m)$$

Consequently, V_{txa} in the formula in the bottom left corner is replaced with $D(T_m)$. The equation is simplified by converting $D - D(T_m)$ into $D(1 - T_m)$. The resulting equation is presented in the bottom right corner.

LEVERED COST OF EQUITY

In certain situations, you will have already estimated the unlevered cost of equity and need to relever the cost of equity to a new target structure. In this case, use Equation C.2 to solve for the levered cost of equity, k_e:

$$\frac{V_u}{V_u + V_{txa}}(k_u) + \frac{V_{txa}}{V_u + V_{txa}}(k_{txa}) = \frac{D}{D+E}(k_d) + \frac{E}{D+E}(k_e)$$

Multiply both sides by enterprise value:

$$V_u(k_u) + V_{txa}(k_{txa}) = D(k_d) + E(k_e)$$

Next, subtract $D(k_d)$ from both sides of the equation:

$$V_u(k_u) - D(k_d) + V_{txa}(k_{txa}) = E(k_e)$$

and divide the entire equation by the market value of equity, E:

$$k_e = \frac{V_u}{E}(k_u) - \frac{D}{E}(k_d) + \frac{V_{txa}}{E}(k_{txa})$$

To eliminate V_u from the right side of the equation, rearrange Equation C.1 to $V_u = D - V_{txa} + E$, and use this identity to replace V_u:

$$k_e = \frac{D - V_{txa} + E}{E}(k_u) - \frac{D}{E}(k_d) + \frac{V_{txa}}{E}(k_{txa})$$

Distribute the first fraction into its component parts:

$$k_e = \frac{D}{E}(k_u) - \frac{V_{txa}}{E}(k_u) + k_u - \frac{D}{E}(k_d) + \frac{V_{txa}}{E}(k_{txa}) \tag{C.5}$$

Consolidating terms and rearranging leads to the general equation for the cost of equity:

$$k_e = k_u + \frac{D}{E}(k_u - k_d) - \frac{V_{txa}}{E}(k_u - k_{txa}) \tag{C.6}$$

If debt is a constant proportion of enterprise value (i.e., debt grows as the business grows), k_u will equal k_{txa}. Consequently, the final term drops out:

$$k_e = k_u + \frac{D}{E}(k_u - k_d)$$

We believe this equation best represents the relationship between the levered cost of equity and the unlevered cost of equity.

The same analysis can be repeated under the assumption that the risk of interest tax shields equals the risk of debt. Rather than repeat the first few steps, we start with Equation C.5:

$$k_e = \frac{D}{E}(k_u) - \frac{V_{txa}}{E}(k_u) + k_u - \frac{D}{E}(k_d) + \frac{V_{txa}}{E}(k_{txa})$$

To solve for k_e, replace k_{txa} with k_d:

$$k_e = \frac{D}{E}(k_u) - \frac{V_{txa}}{E}(k_u) + k_u - \frac{D}{E}(k_d) + \frac{V_{txa}}{E}(k_d)$$

Consolidate like terms and reorder:

$$k_e = k_u + \frac{D - V_{txa}}{E}(k_u) - \frac{D - V_{txa}}{E}(k_d)$$

Finally, further simplify the equation by once again combining like terms:

$$k_e = k_u + \frac{D - V_{txa}}{E}(k_u - k_d)$$

The resulting equation is the levered cost of equity for a company whose debt can take any value but whose interest tax shields have the same risk as the company's debt.

Exhibit C.2 summarizes the formulas that can be used to estimate the levered cost of equity. The top row in the exhibit contains formulas that assume k_{txa} equals k_u. The bottom row contains formulas that assume k_{txa} equals k_d. The formulas on the left side are flexible enough to handle any future capital structure but require valuing the tax shields separately. The formulas on the right side assume the dollar level of debt is fixed over time.

EXHIBIT C.2 **Levered Cost of Equity**

	Dollar level of debt fluctuates	Dollar level of debt is constant
Tax shields have same risk as operating assets $k_{txa} = k_u$	$k_e = k_u + \dfrac{D}{E}\left(k_u - k_d\right)$	$k_e = k_u + \dfrac{D}{E}\left(k_u - k_d\right)$
Tax shields have same risk as debt $k_{txa} = k_d$	$k_e = k_u + \dfrac{D - V_{txa}}{E}\left(k_u - k_d\right)$	$k_e = k_u + \left(1 - T_m\right)\dfrac{D}{E}\left(k_u - k_d\right)$

Note: k_e = cost of equity
k_d = cost of debt
k_u = unlevered cost of equity
k_{txa} = cost of capital for tax shields
T_m = marginal tax rate
D = debt
E = equity
V_{txa} = present value of tax shields

LEVERED BETA

Similar to the cost of capital, the weighted average beta of a company's assets, both operating and financial, must equal the weighted average beta of its financial claims:

$$\frac{V_u}{V_u + V_{txa}}(\beta_u) + \frac{V_{txa}}{V_u + V_{txa}}(\beta_{txa}) = \frac{D}{D+E}(\beta_d) + \frac{E}{D+E}(\beta_e)$$

Since the form of this equation is identical to the cost of capital, it is possible to rearrange the formula using the same process as previously described. Rather than repeat the analysis, we provide a summary of levered beta in Exhibit C.3. As expected, the first two columns are identical in form to Exhibit C.2, except that the beta (β) replaces the cost of capital (k).

By using beta, it is possible to make one additional simplification. If debt is risk free, the beta of debt is 0, and β_d drops out. This allows us to convert the following general equation (when β_{txa} equals β_u):

$$\beta_e = \beta_u + \frac{D}{E}(\beta_u - \beta_d)$$

into the following:

$$\beta_e = \left(1 + \frac{D}{E}\right)\beta_u$$

EXHIBIT C.3 **Levered Beta**

	Dollar level of debt fluctuates	Dollar level of debt is constant and debt is risky	Debt is risk free
Tax shields have same risk as operating assets $\beta_{txa} = \beta_u$	$\beta_e = \beta_u + \frac{D}{E}(\beta_u - \beta_d)$	$\beta_e = \beta_u + \frac{D}{E}(\beta_u - \beta_d)$	$\beta_e = \left(1 + \frac{D}{E}\right)\beta_u$
Tax shields have same risk as debt $\beta_{txa} = \beta_d$	$\beta_e = \beta_u + \frac{D - V_{txa}}{E}(\beta_u - \beta_d)$	$\beta_e = \beta_u + (1 - T_m)\frac{D}{E}(\beta_u - \beta_d)$	$\beta_e = \left[1 + (1 - T_m)\frac{D}{E}\right]\beta_u$

Note: β_e = beta of equity
β_d = beta of debt
β_u = unlevered beta of equity
β_{txa} = beta of capital for tax shields
T_m = marginal tax rate
D = debt
E = equity
V_{txa} = present value of tax shields

This last equation is an often-applied formula for levering (and unlevering) beta when the risk of interest tax shields (β_{txa}) equals the risk of operating assets (β_u) *and* the company's debt is risk free. For investment-grade companies, debt is nearly risk free, so any errors using this formula will be small. If the company is highly leveraged, however, errors can be large. In this situation, estimate the beta of debt, and use the more general version of the formula.

UNLEVERED BETA AND PENSIONS

Since stockholders are responsible for future pension payments and other retirement obligations, the risks associated with these employee benefits can affect a company's beta. If a company has significant pensions, especially unfunded pensions, make sure to include them in the unlevering process.

If you believe the risk of pension assets matches the risk of future obligations, only the unfunded portion of benefit obligations affects the equity beta. In this case, use the unlevering equations in the preceding sections, but treat any unfunded benefit obligations identically to debt.

If you believe the risk of pension assets does not match the risk of future obligations, the unlevering formulas can be reworked such that the risk of pension assets and risk of benefit obligations are evaluated separately. To do this, start with the portfolio equation for beta:

$$\frac{V_u}{V}\beta_u + \frac{V_{pa}}{V}\beta_{pa} = \frac{V_{pbo}}{V}\beta_{pbo} + \frac{D}{V}\beta_d + \frac{E}{V}\beta_e$$

where V_{pa} = value of pension assets

V_{pbo} = present value of pension benefit obligations

β_{pa} = beta of pension assets

β_{pbo} = beta of pension benefit obligations

V = sum of debt, equity, and benefit obligations

Next, multiply both sides by V:

$$V_u\,\beta_u + V_{pa}\,\beta_{pa} = V_{pbo}\,\beta_{pbo} + D\beta_d + E\beta_e$$

Subtract the term related to pension assets from both sides of the equation:

$$V_u\,\beta_u = V_{pbo}\,\beta_{pbo} + D\beta_d + E\beta_e - V_{pa}\,\beta_{pa}$$

To isolate β_u, divide both sides by V_u. This leads to the general equation for estimating unlevered beta, inclusive of pensions:

$$\beta_u = \frac{V_{pbo}}{V_u}\beta_{pbo} + \frac{V_d}{V_u}\beta_d + \frac{V_e}{V_u}\beta_e - \frac{V_{pa}}{V_u}\beta_{pa}$$

If debt and pension liabilities have the same beta, simplify the last equation by combining terms:

$$\beta_u = \frac{D + V_{pbo}}{V_u}\beta_d + \frac{E}{V_u}\beta_e - \frac{V_{pa}}{V_u}\beta_{pa}$$

Chapter 23 discusses how to incorporate pensions into a valuation. In Exhibit 23.5, we use the equation above to unlever beta for a set of food manufacturers. Given the small size of each company's pension relative to the respective company's market value of equity, the difference in unlevered beta with and without the pension adjustment is minor. We therefore recommend adjusting beta for pensions only when pension assets and liabilities are substantial. In most situations, the unlevering equations that classify the unfunded portion of pensions as debt will suffice.

Leverage and the Price-to-Earnings Multiple

This appendix demonstrates that the price-to-earnings (P/E) multiple of a levered company depends on its unlevered (all-equity) P/E, its cost of debt, and its debt-to-value ratio. When the unlevered P/E is less than $1/k_d$ (where k_d equals the cost of debt), the P/E falls as leverage rises. Conversely, when the unlevered P/E is greater than $1/k_d$, the P/E rises with increased leverage.

In this proof, we assume the company faces no taxes and no distress costs. We do this to avoid modeling the complex relationship between capital structure and enterprise value. Instead, our goal is to show that there is a systematic relationship between the debt-to-value ratio and the P/E.

STEP 1: DEFINING UNLEVERED P/E

To determine the relationship between P/E and leverage, start by defining the unlevered P/E (PE_u). When a company is entirely financed with equity, its enterprise value equals its equity value, and its net operating profit after taxes (NOPAT) equals its net income:

$$PE_u = \frac{V_{ENT}}{NOPAT_{t+1}}$$

where V_{ENT} = enterprise value

$NOPAT_{t+1}$ = net operating profit after taxes in year $t+1$

This equation can be rearranged to solve for the enterprise value, which we will use in the next step:

$$V_{ENT} = NOPAT_{t+1}(PE_u)$$

(D.1)

STEP 2: LINKING NET INCOME TO NOPAT

For a company partially financed with debt, net income (NI) equals NOPAT less after-tax interest payments. Assuming the value of debt equals its face value, the company's interest expense will equal the cost of debt times the value of debt, which can be defined by multiplying enterprise value by the debt-to-value ratio:

$$NI_{t+1} = NOPAT_{t+1} - V_{ENT}\left(\frac{D}{V}\right)k_d$$

Substitute Equation D.1 for the enterprise value:

$$NI_{t+1} = NOPAT_{t+1} - NOPAT_{t+1}(PE_u)\left(\frac{D}{V}\right)k_d$$

Factor NOPAT into a single term:

$$NI_{t+1} = NOPAT_{t+1}\left[1 - PE_u\left(\frac{D}{V}\right)k_d\right]$$

(D.2)

STEP 3: DERIVING LEVERED P/E

At this point, we are ready to solve for the company's price-to-earnings ratio. Since P/E is based on equity values, first convert enterprise value to equity value. To do this, once again start with Equation D.1:

$$V_{ENT} = NOPAT_{t+1}(PE_u)$$

To convert enterprise value into equity value, multiply both sides by 1 minus the debt-to-value ratio:

$$V_{ENT}\left(1 - \frac{D}{V_{ENT}}\right) = NOPAT_{t+1}(PE_u)\left(1 - \frac{D}{V_{ENT}}\right)$$

Distribute V_{ENT} into the parentheses:

$$V_{ENT} - D = NOPAT_{t+1}(PE_u)\left(1 - \frac{D}{V_{ENT}}\right)$$

Replace enterprise value (V_{ENT}) minus debt (D) with equity value (E):

$$E = \text{NOPAT}_{t+1} \left(\text{PE}_u \right) \left(1 - \frac{D}{V_{\text{ENT}}} \right)$$

Next, use Equation D.2 to eliminate NOPAT_{t+1}:

$$E = \frac{\text{NI}_{t+1} \left(\text{PE}_u \right) \left(1 - \dfrac{D}{V} \right)}{1 - \text{PE}_u \left(\dfrac{D}{V} \right) k_d}$$

Divide both sides by net income to find the levered P/E:

$$\frac{E}{\text{NI}_{t+1}} = \frac{\text{PE}_u - \text{PE}_u \left(\dfrac{D}{V} \right)}{1 - \text{PE}_u \left(\dfrac{D}{V} \right) k_d}$$

At this point, we have a relationship between equity value and net income, which depends on the unlevered P/E, the debt-to-value ratio, and the cost of debt. Debt-to-value, however, is in both the numerator and the denominator, so it is difficult to distinguish how leverage affects the levered P/E. To eliminate the debt-to-value ratio in the numerator, use a few algebraic tricks. First, multiply both the numerator and denominator by k_d:

$$\frac{E}{\text{NI}_{t+1}} = \frac{\text{PE}_u \left(k_d \right) - \text{PE}_u \left(\dfrac{D}{V} \right) \left(k_d \right)}{k_d \left[1 - \text{PE}_u \left(\dfrac{D}{V} \right) \left(k_d \right) \right]}$$

Next, subtract and add 1 (a net difference of 0) in the numerator:

$$\frac{E}{\text{NI}_{t+1}} = \frac{\left[\text{PE}_u \left(k_d \right) - 1 \right] + \left[1 - \text{PE}_u \left(\dfrac{D}{V} \right) \left(k_d \right) \right]}{k_d \left[1 - \text{PE}_u \left(\dfrac{D}{V} \right) \left(k_d \right) \right]}$$

After separating the numerator into two distinct terms, you can eliminate the components of the right-hand term by canceling them with the denominator. This allows you to remove debt-to-value from the numerator:

$$\frac{E}{\text{NI}_{t+1}} = \frac{\text{PE}_u \left(k_d \right) - 1}{k_d \left[1 - \text{PE}_u \left(\dfrac{D}{V} \right) \left(k_d \right) \right]} + \frac{1}{k_d}$$

To simplify the expression further, divide both the numerator and denominator of the complex fraction by k_d:

$$\frac{E}{NI_{t+1}} = \frac{1}{k_d} + \frac{PE_u - \dfrac{1}{k_d}}{1 - PE_u\left(\dfrac{D}{V}\right)(k_d)}$$

Finally, multiply the numerator and denominator of the second term by -1:

$$\frac{E}{NI_{t+1}} = \frac{1}{k_d} + \frac{\dfrac{1}{k_d} - PE_u}{\left(\dfrac{D}{V}\right)k_d(PE_u) - 1}$$

As this final equation shows, a company's P/E is a function of its unlevered P/E, its cost of debt, and its debt-to-value ratio. When the unlevered P/E equals the reciprocal of the cost of debt, the numerator of the second fraction equals zero, and leverage has no effect on the P/E. For companies with large unlevered P/Es, P/E systematically increases with leverage. Conversely, companies with small unlevered P/Es would exhibit a drop in P/E as leverage rises.

Other Capital Structure Issues

This appendix discusses alternative models of capital structure and credit rating estimations. These models offer some interesting insights but tend to be less useful in practice for designing a company's capital structure. Finally, the appendix shows the similarities and differences between widely used credit ratios such as leverage, coverage, and solvency.

PECKING-ORDER THEORY

An alternative to the view that there are trade-offs between equity and debt is a school of thought in finance theory that sees a pecking order in financing.[1] According to this theory, companies meet their investment needs first by using internal funds (from retained earnings), then by issuing debt, and finally by issuing equity. One of the causes of this pecking order is that investors interpret financing decisions by managers as signals of a company's financial prospects. For example, investors will interpret an equity issue as a signal that management believes shares are overvalued. Anticipating this interpretation, rational managers will turn to equity funding only as a last resort, because it could cause the share price to fall. An analogous argument holds for debt issues, although the overvaluation signal is much smaller because the value of debt is much less sensitive to a company's financial success.[2]

---

[1] See G. Donaldson, "Corporate Debt Capacity: A Study of Corporate Debt Policy and the Determination of Corporate Debt Capacity" (Harvard Graduate School of Business, 1961); and S. Myers, "The Capital Structure Puzzle," *Journal of Finance* 39, no. 3 (1974): 575–592.
[2] An exception is, of course, the value of debt in a financially distressed company.

According to the theory, companies will have lower leverage when they are more mature and profitable, simply because they can fund internally and do not need any debt or equity funding. However, evidence for the theory is not conclusive. For example, mature companies generating strong cash flows are among the most highly leveraged, whereas the pecking-order theory would predict them to have the lowest leverage. High-tech start-up companies are among the least leveraged, rather than debt loaded, as the theory would predict.[3] Empirical research shows how the signaling hypotheses underlying the pecking-order theory are more relevant to financial managers in selecting and timing specific funding alternatives than for setting long-term capital structure targets.[4] Surveys among financial executives confirm these findings.[5]

MARKET-BASED RATING APPROACH

Alternative metrics to credit ratings have been developed based on the notion that equity can be modeled as a call option on the company's enterprise value, with the debt obligations as the exercise price.[6] Using option valuation models and market data on price and volatility of the shares, these approaches estimate the future probability of default—that is, the probability that enterprise value will be below the value of debt obligations.[7] The advantage is that all information captured by the equity markets is directly translated into the default estimates. Traditional credit ratings tend to lag changes in a company's performance and outlook because they aim to measure credit quality "through the cycle"[8] and are less sensitive to short-term fluctuations in quality.

The disadvantage of market-based ratings is that no fundamental analysis is performed on the company's underlying business and financial health. If

[3] See M. Barclay and C. Smith, "The Capital Structure Puzzle: The Evidence Revisited," *Journal of Applied Corporate Finance* 17, no. 1 (2005): 8–17; and M. Baker and J. Wurgler, "Market Timing and Capital Structure," *Journal of Finance* 52, no. 1 (2002): 1–32.

[4] See also A. Hovakimian, T. Opler, and S. Titman, "The Debt-Equity Choice," *Journal of Financial and Quantitative Analysis* 36, no. 1 (2001): 1–24, for evidence that the pecking-order theory predicts short-term movements in corporate debt levels but that long-term changes are more in line with the trade-offs discussed earlier in this section.

[5] J. Graham and H. Campbell, "How Do CFOs Make Capital Budgeting and Capital Structure Decisions?" *Journal of Applied Corporate Finance* 15, no. 1 (2002): 8–23.

[6] This is because equity is a residual claim on the enterprise value after payment of principal and interest for debt. It has value only to the extent that enterprise value exceeds debt commitments. See R. Merton, "On the Pricing of Corporate Debt: The Risk Structure of Interest Rates," *Journal of Finance* 29 (1974): 449–470; or for an introduction, R. Brealey, S. Myers and F. Allen, *Principles of Corporate Finance*, 13th ed. (New York: McGraw-Hill, 2020), chap. 23.

[7] See P. Crosbie and J. Bohn, "Modeling Default Risk" (Moody's KMV White Paper, December 2003).

[8] See E. Altman and H. Rijken, "How Rating Agencies Achieve Rating Stability," *Journal of Banking and Finance* 28, no. 11 (2004): 2679–2714.

equity markets have missed some critical information, the resulting estimates of default probability do not reflect their omission. As discussed in Chapter 7, markets reflect company fundamentals most of the time, but not always. When they do not, the market-based rating approaches would incorrectly estimate default risk as well.[9]

LEVERAGE, COVERAGE, AND SOLVENCY

The leverage measure used in the academic literature is typically defined as the market value of debt (D) over the market value of debt plus equity (E):

$$\text{Leverage} = \frac{D}{D+E}$$

This ratio measures how much of the company's enterprise value is claimed by debt holders and is an important concept for estimating the benefits of tax shields arising from debt financing. It is therefore also a crucial input in calculating the weighted average cost of capital (WACC; see Chapter 15 on capital structure weights).

Compared with coverage ratios such as earnings before interest, taxes, and amortization (EBITA) to interest, leverage ratios suffer from several drawbacks as a way to measure and target a company's capital structure. First, companies could have very low leverage in terms of market value but still be at a high risk of financial distress if their short-term cash flow is low relative to interest payments. High-growth companies usually have very low levels of leverage, but this does not mean their debt is low-risk. A second drawback is that market value can change radically (especially for high-growth, high-multiple companies), making leverage a fast-moving indicator. For example, during the stock market boom of the late 1990s, several European telecom companies had what appeared to be reasonable levels of debt financing in terms of leverage. Credit providers appeared willing to provide credit even though the underlying near-term cash flows were not very high relative to debt service obligations. But when the companies' market values plummeted in 2001, leverage for these companies shot up, and financial distress loomed. Thus, it is risky to base a capital structure target on a market-value-based measure.

This does not mean that leverage and coverage are fundamentally divergent measures. Far from it: they actually measure the same thing but over different time horizons. For ease of explanation, consider a company that has

[9] See Crosbie and Bohn, "Modeling Default Risk," 23.

no growth in revenues, profit, or cash flows. For this company, it is possible to express the leverage and coverage as follows:[10]

$$\text{Leverage} = \frac{D}{D+E}$$

$$= \frac{\text{Interest}_1 + \text{PV}(\text{Interest}_2) + ... + \text{PV}(\text{Interest}_\infty)}{\text{NOPAT}_1 + \text{PV}(\text{NOPAT}_2) + ... + \text{PV}(\text{NOPAT}_\infty)}$$

$$\text{Coverage} = \frac{\text{EBITA}}{\text{Interest}} = \frac{1}{(1-T)} \times \frac{\text{NOPAT}}{\text{Interest}}$$

where
D = market value of debt
E = market value of equity
NOPAT_t = net operating profit after taxes in year t
Interest_t = interest expenses in year t
T = tax rate

The market value of debt captures the present value of all future interest payments, assuming perpetual rollover of debt financing. The enterprise value $(E + D)$ is equal to the present value of future NOPAT, because depreciation equals capital expenditures for a zero-growth company. A leverage ratio therefore measures the company's ability to cover its interest payments over a very long term. The problem is that short-term interest obligations are what mainly get a company into financial distress. Coverage, in contrast, focuses on the short-term part of the leverage definition, keeping in mind that NOPAT roughly equals EBITA $\times (1 - T)$. It indicates how easily a company can service its debt in the near term.

Both measures are meaningful, and they are complementary. For example, if market leverage were very high in combination with strong current interest coverage, this could indicate the possibility of future difficulties in sustaining current debt levels in, for example, a single-product company faced with rapidly eroding margins and cash flows because the product is approaching the end of its life cycle. Despite very high interest coverage today, such a company might not be given a high credit rating, and its capacity to borrow could be limited.

Solvency measures of debt over book value of total assets or equity are seldom as meaningful as coverage or leverage. The key reason is that these book value ratios fail to capture the company's ability to comply with debt service requirements in either the short term or the long term. Market-to-book ratios

---

[10] The simplifying no-growth assumption is for illustration purposes only. For a growing company, the same point holds.

can vary significantly across sectors and over time, making solvency a poor proxy for long-term ability to service debt.

Solvency becomes more relevant in times of financial distress, when a company's creditors use it as a rough measure of the available collateral. Higher levels of solvency usually indicate that debt holders stand better chances of recovering their principal and interest due—assuming that asset book values are reasonable approximations of asset liquidation values. However, in a going concern, solvency is much less relevant for deciding capital structure than coverage and leverage measures.

Technical Issues in Estimating the Market Risk Premium

In its simplest form, the historical market risk premium can be measured by subtracting the return on government bonds from the return (total return to shareholders) on a large sample of companies over some time frame. But this requires many choices that will affect the results. For the best measurement of the risk premium using historical data, follow the guidelines presented in this appendix.

CALCULATE PREMIUM RELATIVE TO LONG-TERM GOVERNMENT BONDS

When calculating the market risk premium, compare historical market returns with the return on ten-year government bonds. Long-term government bonds match the duration of a company's cash flows better than short-term bonds.

USE THE LONGEST PERIOD POSSIBLE

How far back should you look when using historical observations to predict future results? If the market risk premium is stable, a longer history will reduce estimation error. Alternatively, if the premium changes and estimation error is small, a shorter period is better. To determine the appropriate historical period, consider any trends in the market risk premium compared with the imprecision associated with short-term estimates.

To test for the presence of a long-term trend, we regress the U.S. market risk premium against time. Over the past 119 years, no statistically significant trend is observable.[1] Based on regression results, the average excess return has fallen by two basis points a year, but this result cannot be statistically distinguished from zero. Premiums calculated over shorter periods are too volatile to be meaningful. For instance, U.S. stocks outperformed bonds by 18 percent in the 1950s but offered no premium in the 1970s. Given the lack of any discernible trend and the significant volatility of shorter periods, use the longest time series possible.

USE AN ARITHMETIC AVERAGE OF LONGER-DATED (E.G., TEN-YEAR) INTERVALS

When reporting market risk premiums, most data providers report an annual number, such as 6.3 percent per year. But how do they convert a century of data into an annual number? And is the annualized number even relevant?

Annual returns can be calculated using either an arithmetic average or a geometric average. An arithmetic (simple) average sums each year's observed premium and divides by the number of observations:

$$\text{Arithmetic Average} = \frac{1}{T}\sum_{t=1}^{T}\frac{1+R_m(t)}{1+r_f(t)} - 1$$

where T = number of observations
   $R_m(t)$ = market return in year t
   $r_f(t)$ = risk-free rate in year t

A geometric average compounds each year's excess return and takes the root of the resulting product:

$$\text{Geometric Average} = \left(\prod_{t=1}^{T}\frac{1+R_m(t)}{1+r_f(t)}\right)^{1/T} - 1$$

The choice of averaging methodology will affect the results. For instance, between 1900 and 2019, U.S. stocks outperformed long-term government bonds by 6.3 percent per year when averaged arithmetically. Using a

---

[1] Some authors, such as Jonathan Lewellen, argue that the market risk premium does change over time—and can be measured using financial ratios, such as the dividend yield. We address these models separately. J. Lewellen, "Predicting Returns with Financial Ratios," *Journal of Financial Economics*, 74, no. 2 (2004): 209–235.

geometric average, the outperformance drops to 4.2 percent. This difference is not random; arithmetic averages always exceed geometric averages when returns are volatile.

So which averaging method on historical data best estimates the *expected* rate of return? Well-accepted statistical principles dictate that the best unbiased estimator of the mean (expectation) for any random variable is the arithmetic average. Therefore, to determine a security's expected return for *one period*, the best unbiased predictor is the arithmetic average of many one-period returns. A one-period risk premium, however, can't value a company with many years of cash flow. Instead, long-dated cash flows must be discounted using a compounded rate of return. But when compounded, the arithmetic average will generate a discount factor that is biased upward (too high).

The cause of the bias is quite technical, so we provide only a summary here. There are two reasons why compounding the historical arithmetic average leads to a biased discount factor. First, the arithmetic average is measured with error. Although this estimation error will not affect a one-period forecast (the error has an expectation of zero), squaring the estimate (as you do in compounding) in effect squares the measurement error, causing the error to be positive. This positive error leads to a multiyear expected return that is too high. Second, a number of researchers have argued that stock market returns are negatively autocorrelated over time. If positive returns are typically followed by negative returns (and vice versa), then squaring the average will lead to a discount factor that overestimates the actual two-period return, again causing an upward bias.

We have two choices to correct for the bias caused by estimation error and negative autocorrelation in returns. First, we can calculate multiyear returns directly from the data, rather than compound single-year averages. Using this method, a cash flow received in ten years will be discounted by the average ten-year market risk premium, not by the annual market risk premium compounded ten times.[2] From 1900 through 2019, the average one-year excess return equaled 6.3 percent. The average ten-year cumulative excess return equaled 71.3 percent.[3] This translates to an annual rate of 5.5 percent. Alternatively, researchers have used simulation to show that an estimator proposed

[2] Jay Ritter writes, "There is no theoretical reason why one year is the appropriate holding period. People are used to thinking of interest rates as a rate per year, so reporting annualized numbers makes it easy for people to focus on the numbers. But I can think of no reason other than convenience for the use of annual returns." J. Ritter, "The Biggest Mistakes We Teach," *Journal of Financial Research* 25 (2002): 159–168.

[3] To compute the average ten-year cumulative return, we use overlapping ten-year periods. To avoid underweighting early and late observations (for instance, the first observation would be included only once, whereas a middle observation would be included in ten separate samples), we create a synthetic ten-year period by combining the most recent observations with the oldest observations. Nonoverlapping windows lead to similar results but are highly dependent on the starting year.

by Marshall Blume best adjusts for problems caused by estimation error and autocorrelation of returns:[4]

$$R = \left(\frac{T-N}{T-1}\right)R_A + \left(\frac{N-1}{T-1}\right)R_G$$

where T = number of historical observations in sample
N = forecast period being discounted
R_A = arithmetic average of historical sample
R_G = geometric average of historical sample

Blume's estimator depends on the length of time for which you plan to discount. The first year's cash flow should be discounted using the arithmetic average ($T = 119$, $N = 1$), whereas the tenth year's cash flow should be discounted based on a return constructed with a 92.4 percent weighting on the arithmetic average and an 8.3 percent weighting on the long-term geometric average ($T = 119$, $N = 10$). The resulting estimator for the ten-year cash flow equals 6.2 percent.

Even with the best statistical techniques, however, these estimates are probably too high, because our sample includes only U.S. data, representing the best-performing market over the past century. Since it is unlikely that the U.S. stock market will replicate its performance over the next century, we adjust downward the historical market risk premium. Research shows that the U.S. arithmetic annual return exceeded a 17-country composite return by 0.8 percent in real terms.[5] If we subtract an 0.8 percent survivorship premium from the values presented above, this leads to an expected return of between 5.0 percent and 5.5 percent.

---

[4] D. C. Indro and W. Y. Lee, "Biases in Arithmetic and Geometric Averages as Estimates of Long-Run Expected Returns and Risk Premia," *Financial Management* 26, no. 4 (Winter 1997): 81–90; and M. E. Blume, "Unbiased Estimators of Long-Run Expected Rates of Return," *Journal of the American Statistical Association* 69, no. 347 (September 1974): 634–638.

[5] E. Dimson, P. Marsh, and M. Staunton, "The Worldwide Equity Premium: A Smaller Puzzle," in *Handbook of Investments: Equity Risk Premium*, ed. R. Mehra (Amsterdam: Elsevier Science, 2007).

APPENDIX G

Global, International, and Local CAPM

The standard capital asset pricing model (CAPM), introduced in Chapter 15, for estimating the cost of capital, does not explicitly account for foreign assets, foreign investors, or currencies. This raises the question whether such a model can provide the right cost of capital for investments in foreign currencies. If foreign-currency rates are changing, the same investment will generate different returns to investors from different countries. Take the case of a German government bond denominated in euros. From the perspective of a German or Dutch investor, this bond generates a risk-free return (assuming there is no inflation), because the euro is also the investor's domestic currency. But the bond's return is not risk free for investors in the United States, because the return measured in U.S. dollars will vary with the dollar-to-euro exchange rate.

As a general rule, investors from countries with different currencies are likely to disagree about an asset's expected return and risk. In theory, this means that the standard CAPM no longer holds, and a more complex, international CAPM is required. In practice, however, we find that the CAPM-based approach as laid out in Chapter 15 is still valid for estimating the cost of capital for cross-border investments. This appendix provides further background for our recommendations and practical guidelines for estimating the cost of capital in foreign currency.

GLOBAL CAPM

Investors' disagreement about the return and risk of international investments disappears if purchasing power parity (PPP) holds across all currencies. In that case, changes in exchange rates perfectly match differences in inflation between currencies:[1]

$$X_t = X_{t-1} \left(\frac{1 + i_A}{1 + i_B} \right)$$

where X_t = exchange rate of currency B expressed in units of currency A at time t

i_A, i_B = inflation rate for currency A, B

As a result, the expected return and risk in real terms for any asset will be the same for all investors, regardless of their domestic currency. In the German bond example, any appreciation of the U.S. dollar relative to the euro would make the nominal bond return for U.S. investors lower. But if PPP holds, the inflation rate in the United States would be lower by exactly the same amount, so the payoff in real terms for U.S. and German investors would be equal. In real terms, there is no currency risk for investors. They will all hold the same global market portfolio of risky assets and face the same real risk-free rate as if there were only a single currency.

The resulting so-called global CAPM is in fact the standard CAPM with a global market portfolio. It expresses the expected real return for an asset j as follows:

$$E(r_j) = r_f + \beta_{j,G} \left[E(r_G) - r_f \right]$$

where r_j = return for asset j

r_f = risk-free rate

$\beta_{j,G}$ = beta of asset j versus global market portfolio G

r_G = return for global market portfolio G

According to the global CAPM, the cost of capital for domestic as well as foreign assets follows from the asset's beta relative to the global market portfolio and the market risk premium of that market portfolio relative to the risk-free rate.

Technically, the global CAPM is valid only if PPP holds. Evidence on PPP has been mixed, but academic research appears to conclude that deviations

---

[1] Technically, this is so-called relative purchasing power parity, referring to changes in prices and exchange rates. Absolute purchasing power parity requires that prices be the same across currencies; see, for example, R. Brealey, S. Myers, and F. Allen, *Principles of Corporate Finance*, 13th ed. (New York: McGraw-Hill, 2020), chap. 27.

from PPP between currencies are typically reduced to half their value within three to five years.[2] In other words, exchange rates do adjust for differences in inflation between countries, although not immediately and perfectly.

For investors and companies able to invest outside their home markets without restrictions, we recommend using the global CAPM to estimate the cost of capital for foreign as well as domestic investments. Effectively, this means applying the approach described in Chapter 15. Although the alternative, international CAPM (discussed next), may be theoretically superior, it is far more complex and does not lead to materially different results in practice.

INTERNATIONAL CAPM

If PPP does not hold, real returns from foreign assets are no longer free from currency risk, because changes in exchange rates are not offset by differences in inflation. The greater the correlation between the return on a foreign asset and the relevant currency rate, the higher the risk for an investor. Take, for example, a Dutch company whose stock returns, measured in euros, tend to be higher when the euro appreciates against the U.S. dollar and vice versa (for instance, because the company imports components from the United States and sells end products in Europe). The stock's returns will be riskier for an American investor than for a European investor, because the exchange rate tends to amplify the returns when translated into U.S. dollars. The absence of PPP means that disparities between dollar and euro inflation will not offset this difference in returns when measured in real terms.

To hold foreign assets, rational investors will require some compensation in the form of a higher expected return for an asset, depending on its exposure to currency risk. As a result, what matters for an asset's expected return is no longer only the asset's beta versus the global market portfolio (as in case of the global CAPM). The international CAPM captures the additional return requirements by also including asset betas versus currency exchange rates. For example, in a world consisting of three countries, each with its own currency, the international CAPM would define the expected return on asset j in a given home currency as follows:[3]

$$E(r_j) = r_f + \beta_{j,G}\left[E(r_G) - r_f\right] + \beta_{j,A}\text{CRP}_A + \beta_{j,B}\text{CRP}_B \tag{G.1}$$

---

[2] For an overview, see A. M. Taylor and M. P. Taylor, "The Purchasing Power Parity Debate," *Journal of Economic Perspectives* 18, no. 4 (Fall 2004): 135–158.

[3] This is a simplified version of the Solnik-Sercu international CAPM; see, for example, P. Sercu, *International Finance* (Princeton, NJ: Princeton University Press, 2009), chap. 19; and S. Armitage, *The Cost of Capital* (Cambridge: Cambridge University Press, 2005), chap. 11.

where
$$r_j = \text{return for asset } j$$
$$r_f = \text{risk-free rate}$$
$$\beta_{j,G} = \text{beta of asset } j \text{ versus global market portfolio } G$$
$$\beta_{j,A}, \beta_{j,B} = \text{beta of asset } j \text{ versus currency rate } X_A, X_B$$
$$CRP_A, CRP_B = \text{risk premium for currency } A, B$$

The currency risk premiums are defined as follows:

$$CRP_n = \frac{E(X_{n1}) - F_{n1}}{X_{n0}} \tag{G.2}$$

where $X_{nt} = $ exchange rate of home currency expressed in units of currency n at time t where $n = A, B$

$F_{n1} = $ forward rate for $t = 1$ of home currency expressed in units of currency n

Although theoretically correct, the international CAPM is probably too cumbersome for practical use. In particular, it is not clear how many of the world's currencies to include in estimating the cost of capital. Even taking only a handful of leading global currencies would require that you estimate as many currency risk premiums. Further, in addition to an asset's market beta, you would need to estimate its beta versus each of these currencies.

Another reason not to use the international CAPM is that empirical research has shown that the currency risk premiums are typically too small to matter when estimating a cost of capital.[4] According to recent research that compared cost of capital estimates from a global and an international CAPM for large U.S. companies, differences are probably less than half a percentage point.[5] As we can see from Equations G.1 and G.2, the international CAPM simplifies to the global CAPM when currency risk premiums are negligible. In other words, PPP apparently holds sufficiently well for the global CAPM to lead to the same cost of capital as the international CAPM. Expressed either way, this evidence reinforces our recommendation to use the global CAPM.

[4] Sercu, *International Finance*, chap. 19.
[5] See W. Dolde, C. Giaccotto, D. Mishra, and T. O'Brien, "Should Managers Estimate Cost of Equity Using a Two-Factor International CAPM?" *Managerial Finance* 38, no. 8 (2012): 708–728; and D. Mishra and T. O'Brien, "A Comparison of Cost of Equity Estimates of Local and Global CAPMs," *Financial Review* 36, no. 4 (2001): 27–48.

LOCAL CAPM

Some practitioners and academic researchers propose estimating the cost of capital for an investment opportunity in a particular country by using a local CAPM. The investment's beta is then estimated versus the market portfolio of the country, and the market risk premium follows from the excess return of that same market portfolio over the local risk-free rate. The approach is theoretically correct if stocks are correlated to the global market portfolio only through the local market:[6]

$$\beta_{j,G} = \beta_{j,L} \times \beta_{L,G} \tag{G.3}$$

where $\beta_{j,G}$ = beta of asset j versus global market portfolio G

$\beta_{j,L}$ = beta of asset j versus local market portfolio L

$\beta_{L,G}$ = beta of local market portfolio L versus global market portfolio G

This implies that any international risk factors influencing the returns of companies in a given country are fully captured by the local market portfolio of that country. You can then indirectly estimate any asset's global beta by multiplying its local beta by the global beta of the local market. If the local stock market is fully integrated and correctly priced in the global market, its expected return is:

$$E(r_L) = r_f + \beta_{L,G}[E(r_G) - r_f] \tag{G.4}$$

where r_L = expected return for local market portfolio L

r_f = risk-free rate

r_G = return for global market portfolio G

Combining Equations G.3 and G.4 shows that the expected return for a stock j estimated via the local and global CAPM should be equal as well. Following the global CAPM, this return is given by:

$$E(r_j) = r_f + \beta_{j,G}[E(r_G) - r_f]$$

Substituting the asset's global beta by the indirect beta defined previously in Equation G.3 leads to:

$$E(r_j) = r_f + \beta_{j,L} \times \beta_{L,G}[E(r_G) - r_f]$$

---

[6] See R. Stulz, "The Cost of Capital in Internationally Integrated Markets: The Case of Nestlé," *European Financial Management* 1, no. 1 (1995): 11–22.

This can be rearranged to show equivalence with the local CAPM:

$$E(r_j) = r_f + \beta_{j,L}[E(r_L) - r_f]$$

Although the assumptions may not seem very realistic at face value, there is evidence that the local and global CAPM generate similar results. Empirical research finds that the cost of capital estimated for U.S. companies with a local CAPM is very close to the estimate based on a global CAPM.[7] For U.S. stocks, this may not be surprising, as the U.S. market portfolio is well diversified and highly correlated with the global market portfolio. But supporting evidence also comes from nine developed economies, including not only the United States but also the United Kingdom, Germany, France, and smaller economies such as the Netherlands and Switzerland. An analysis of beta estimates for companies versus a local and global market portfolio has shown that for these countries, the betas are typically related, as indicated by Equation G.3.[8]

However, the local CAPM approach, when compared with the global CAPM, has some practical drawbacks. First is that when you apply the local CAPM to investments in different countries, you should estimate the local market risk premium and beta for each of these countries, instead of only the global market risk premium, as you would do when applying the global CAPM. Also, with a local CAPM, you cannot make a straightforward estimate of a company's beta based on the average of the estimated betas for a sample of industry peers (which Chapter 15 recommends to reduce the standard error of the company's beta). The reason is that if the peers are in different countries, their local betas are not directly comparable. Finally, local risk premiums are typically less stable over time than their aggregate, the global risk premium. For example, Exhibit G.1 compares the realized premiums on local stock market indexes with government bond returns for several countries and a globally diversified portfolio, using data from Dimson, Marsh, and Staunton's analysis of long-term average returns on equities and corporate and government bonds.[9] The individual countries' risk premiums vary considerably, depending on the time period over which they are measured, while the global premium remains almost unchanged.

Note that the risk premium differences shown in Exhibit G.1 do not mean that the price for risk varies across these countries. These differences are driven by several factors. First, levels of economic development and, therefore, profit

---

[7] R. Harris, F. Marston, D. Mishra, and T. O'Brien, "Ex-Ante Cost of Equity Estimates of S&P 500 Firms: The Choice between Domestic and Global CAPM," *Financial Management* 32, no. 3 (2003): 51–66.

[8] See C. Koedijk, C. Kool, P. Schotman, and M. van Dijk, "The Cost of Capital in International Financial Markets: Local or Global?," *Journal of International Money and Finance* 21, no. 6 (2002): 905–929.

[9] E. Dimson, P. Marsh, and M. Staunton, *Triumph of the Optimists: 101 Years of Global Investment Returns* (Princeton, NJ: Princeton University Press, 2002); and E. Dimson, P. Marsh, M. Staunton, and J. Wilmot, *Credit Suisse Global Investment Returns Yearbook 2016* (London: Credit Suisse Research Institute, 2016).

EXHIBIT G.1 **Comparing Risk Premiums across Countries and over Time**

Annualized market risk premium over 1-year Treasury bills, %

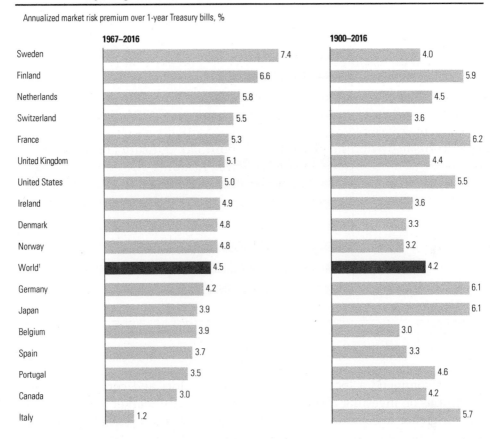

Source: E. Dimson, P. Marsh, and M. Staunton, *Triumph of the Optimists: 101 Years of Global Investment Returns* (Princeton, NJ: Princeton University Press, 2002); E. Dimson, P. Marsh, M. Staunton, and J. Wilmot, *Credit Suisse Global Investment Yearbook 2016* (London: Credit Suisse Research Institute, February 2016).

[1] Globally diversified portfolio.

growth have varied over the past century among the countries. Second, capital markets were less integrated in the past, so prices across countries may not have been equalized. The main reason, though, is that many of the stock market indexes used had different levels of diversification and beta. Therefore, their performance was skewed by different industry concentrations. In most European countries, the key stock market indexes, which account for the majority of their stock markets' total capitalization, typically include only 25 to 40 companies, often from a limited range of industries. Indeed, research has shown that a large fraction of the variation in returns on European market indexes could be explained by their industry composition (see Exhibit G.2).[10]

[10] R. Roll, "Industrial Structure and the Comparative Behavior of International Stock Market Indexes," *Journal of Finance* 47, no. 1 (1992): 3–42.

EXHIBIT G.2 **Share of Equity Returns Explained by Industry Composition of Index**

Adjusted R^2, %

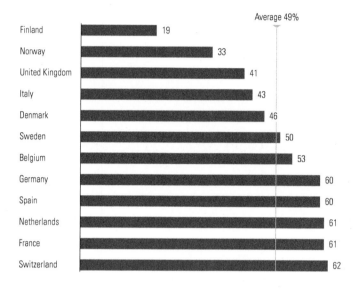

Source: R. Roll, "Industrial Structure and the Comparative Behaviour of International Stock Market Indexes," *Journal of Finance* 47, no. 1 (1992): 3–42.

We recommend a local CAPM only for investors and companies facing restrictions on investing abroad. In that case, the local market portfolio is the right reference to estimate the cost of capital. As a result, valuations in such restricted markets can be out of line with those in global markets—which is what we have encountered in the past for valuations in, for example, Asian stock markets.

APPENDIX H

A Valuation of Costco Wholesale

This appendix shows a typical outside-in valuation model, using Costco Wholesale as an example. Our historical analysis is based on Costco's published income statements and balance sheets from its 2015 to 2019 annual reports. Companies rarely restate balance sheets more than one or two years back in time, so we use original data to avoid confusion. The line item names and references to footnotes are worded according to the conventions of the 2019 annual report.

The valuation process we apply here is detailed in Part Two. The following commentary provides an informal guide to each of the exhibits, including clarification of items that may not be apparent. We hope our references to specific chapters will help readers connect the exhibits to general principles explored in the book.

MODELING THE FINANCIAL STATEMENTS

The valuation process begins by modeling the financial statements in a spreadsheet, including the income statement, the balance sheet, the statement of shareholders' equity, and the tax reconciliation table. The first three statements for Costco are presented in the annual report following the auditor's letter. The company's tax reconciliation table is found in the notes to the financial statements.

Exhibit H.1: Income Statement. We present the income statement as reported by the company, with two exceptions. First, the exhibit separates depreciation from selling, general, and administrative expenses. Costco reports depreciation in its statement of cash flows. Second, we separate interest income from other income. We do this to enable the modeling of income generated from future balances of excess cash. Costco provides details on interest and other income in the section on management's discussion and analysis.

For each of the financial statements, we provide the historical values reported by the company as well as our forecasts of future performance. The final year is denoted by CV, which represents the base year used in continuing value. We discuss continuing value later in this appendix.

Exhibit H.2: Balance Sheet. We present the balance sheet as reported by the company, with three exceptions. First, we aggregate cash and short-term investments into a single account.

Second, we separate deferred taxes from other current assets, other assets, and other liabilities. This allows us to estimate cash taxes, identify tax loss carryforwards, and reclassify remaining amounts as equity equivalents during reorganization. Costco reports deferred taxes and their location on the balance sheet in Note 8, Taxes.

Third, because capital leases are a form of debt financing, we separate them from other current liabilities and other liabilities. In our experience, most companies embed capital leases within debt, but this is not the case for Costco. The company reports capital leases and their location on the balance sheet in Note 5, Leases.

Exhibit H.3: Statement of Shareholders' Equity. The statement of shareholders' equity explains the change in equity from one year to the next. The statement includes the translation adjustment for foreign operations, stock-based compensation, repurchases of common stock, and dividends. These accounts are required for reconciling free cash flow to cash flow available to investors. For some accounts, like dividends, the account appears directly in the reconciliation of cash flow. In other cases, it is used to eliminate a noncash change in a balance sheet account, such as the foreign-currency translation adjustment.

Exhibit H.4: Tax Reconciliation Table. The tax reconciliation table is required to estimate operating taxes and reconcile net operating profit after taxes (NOPAT) to net income. Costco reports the tax reconciliation table in Note 8, Taxes. While most companies report the table in either their home currency or percentages, Costco reports both versions.

REORGANIZING THE FINANCIAL STATEMENTS

With financial statements in hand, we next reorganize them into NOPAT, operating taxes, invested capital, and total funds invested. Here we briefly describe the reorganization; Chapter 11 presents a full description of how to reorganize the financial statements.

Exhibit H.5: NOPAT. This exhibit reorganizes the income statement into NOPAT and reconciles NOPAT to net income. In the case of Costco, unadjusted EBITA matches operating profit as reported on the company's income statement. This is not always the case. As we discuss in Chapter 21, many companies include nonrecurring items such as restructuring costs as part of operating profit. Only ongoing operating expenses should be deducted from revenue to estimate EBITA.

As we prescribed in Chapter 11, we remove operating lease interest from operating profit and treat it as a financial expense. The lease interest is calculated by multiplying the cost of debt by capitalized operating leases in the previous year, which can be found in Exhibit H.8. Do not add back interest expense related to capital leases. This item is already incorporated into interest expense.

Exhibit H.6: Taxes. To calculate NOPAT and its reconciliation to net income, it is necessary to disaggregate taxes into operating taxes, taxes on nonoperating accounts, and other nonoperating taxes. Exhibit H.6 estimates operating cash taxes, using the three-step method introduced in Chapter 11 and discussed in detail in Chapter 20. First, multiply EBITA by the statutory tax rate presented in Exhibit H.4. The statutory tax rate equals the sum of the federal income and state income tax rates.

Next, adjust statutory taxes on EBITA by ongoing, operating-related adjustments. Use judgment to identify which adjustments are ongoing and operating related. For Costco, we adjust statutory taxes on EBITA by two items: the foreign tax differential and tax related to the employee stock ownership plan. Finally, to convert operating taxes into operating cash taxes, subtract the increase in operating-related deferred-tax liabilities, net of deferred-tax assets. An increase in deferred tax liabilities means the company paid less in taxes than reported on its income statement.

Exhibit H.7: Deferred Taxes. To create the inputs needed for the cash tax rate, reorganize the deferred-tax table into tax loss carryforwards; operating deferred-tax assets, net of liabilities; and nonoperating deferred-tax assets, net of liabilities. As with the tax reconciliation table, classification of an account as operating or nonoperating requires judgment. Ask yourself which accounts are operating related and likely to scale with revenue. To calculate the amount of operating taxes that are deferred, add (subtract) the increase (decrease) in the operating deferred account to (from) operating taxes.

For more on the concepts underpinning the operating tax rate and the treatment of deferred taxes, see Chapter 20.

Exhibit H.8: Invested Capital and Total Funds Invested. To estimate invested capital, pull each account directly from the balance sheet, except two: operating cash and capitalized operating leases. Operating cash is estimated at 2 percent of revenues. Cash in excess of 2 percent of revenues is classified as excess cash.

Starting with fiscal years that end in December 2019, new accounting standards require companies to capitalize operating leases onto their balance sheet. Costco uses an August 31 year-end, so its 2019 financial statements are reported under the previous standards, whereby the value of the leases is not capitalized. Given this circumstance, we add the capitalized value of leases to invested capital and the reconciliation of total funds invested. Going forward, this step will no longer be necessary. Chapter 22 explains how to adjust for operating leases under the new standards. Exhibit 22.10 demonstrates how to value operating leases for 2019, the last year of our Costco historical data, by using the present value of rental commitments.

Exhibit H.9: Reconciliation of Total Funds Invested. To better understand how the business is financed and to assure accuracy through a second set of calculations, recalculate total funds invested, but this time using sources of capital. Exhibit H.9 calculates debt and debt equivalents, which include capitalized operating leases. Equity includes common stock and retained earnings. Equity equivalents include deferred-tax accounts, except for tax loss carryforwards. For Costco, the deferred-tax accounts are negative in some years and act as an offset to equity because deferred-tax assets are larger than the corresponding liabilities.

Costco's total funds invested are financed mostly by equity. For more on how to evaluate and create an appropriate capital structure to support the operations of a business, see Chapter 33.

FORECASTING THE FINANCIALS

For each financial statement, we present a ten-year forecast. Chapter 13 demonstrates how to create a set of forecasts, link your forecasts to the financial statements, and avoid common pitfalls.

Exhibit H.10: Income Statement Forecast Ratios. To estimate revenue growth and cost of sales for Costco, we rely on analyst reports from September 2019. One such report is detailed in Exhibit 13.3. We forecast the remaining accounts using financial ratios from either the last fiscal year or an average of the last five fiscal years, depending on the account's stability.

To forecast the interest expense on debt, we estimate interest expense as a percentage of prior-year debt. Since we value operations using free cash flow, our forecast of interest expense will not affect the value of operations. We create a forecast solely for the purpose of cash flow planning and to create an integrated set of financial statements. Integrated financials reduce the likelihood of modeling errors.

Exhibit H.11: Balance Sheet Forecast Ratios. For the balance sheet, we organize the forecast ratios into working capital, long-term assets, debt, and equity. Most working-capital items are forecast using days in revenues. The exceptions are merchandise inventories and accounts payable, which are linked to merchandise cost. Long-term assets and liabilities are estimated at a constant percent of revenues.

To estimate leverage, we assume Costco will maintain its current debt-to-value ratio. We then split total leverage across short-term debt, long-term debt, and capital leases based on the five-year averages. Stock-based compensation is forecast as a percent of revenues. Dividends are forecast as a percent of net income. Excess cash is paid out over five years, and cash flows not required for investment, payments to debt holders, or dividends are used to repurchase shares. (Share repurchases become a plug in this model to balance the cash flows after all other items are accounted for.)

While the forecasts related to debt and share repurchases affect the income statement and balance sheet, they will have no effect on value in an enterprise DCF. Capital structure affects valuation only through the weighted average cost of capital (WACC).

Exhibit H.12: Free Cash Flow and Cash Flow to Investors. Exhibit H.12 shows how free cash flow is estimated. Most accounts, such as operating working capital, equal the change in the corresponding invested-capital account. Capital expenditures are reported on the statement of cash flows. Because of currency translations, capital expenditures do not equal the change in net property, plant, and equipment plus depreciation. The link between capital expenditures and the change in net property, plant, and equipment (PP&E) is detailed in Exhibit 11.14. Unexplained currency translations are treated as a nonoperating cash flow.[1]

Exhibit H.13: Reconciliation of Cash Flow to Investors. To reconcile cash flow to investors, we accumulate the changes in debt and equity accounts. Debt includes traditional debt, capital leases, and capitalized operating leases. Equity includes stock-based compensation, repurchases of common stock, dividends, and payments to noncontrolling interests.

ESTIMATING CONTINUING VALUE

Next, use a continuing-value formula to estimate the value of cash flows beyond the explicit forecast period. Start using the continuing-value formula only at the point when the company has reached a steady state.

Exhibit H.14: Continuing Value. We use the key value driver formula to estimate continuing value. The formula requires a forecast of NOPAT in 2030 (known as the continuing-value year, abbreviated as CV in Exhibits H.1, H.5, H.6, H.10, and H.17) to determine the continuing value as of 2029. We do not generate forecasts for continuing value for invested capital or free cash flow in the continuing-value year; they are unnecessary for the calculation.

One critical forecast in the continuing value is long-run revenue growth. Given the historical strength of Costco's ability to grow, we use a growth rate

---

[1] If the data are available. Currency translations should be netted against their corresponding account. This will bring the change in the account closer to the true cash inflow or outflow.

of 4 percent to estimate the long-run growth rate. For a comprehensive discussion of how to estimate continuing value, see Chapter 14.

ESTIMATING THE WEIGHTED AVERAGE COST OF CAPITAL

To value operations, discount cash flow at the weighted average cost of capital. The WACC incorporates the required return from all sources of capital into a single number.

Exhibit H.15: Weighted Average Cost of Capital. Net of excess cash, Costco uses less debt than any of its industry peers. With this in mind, we assume that Costco will disgorge excess cash and set their target debt-to-value ratio to their current debt-to-value as measured on a gross basis.

Likewise, when we estimate the cost of debt and cost of equity, we use the same debt-to-value ratio. For a comprehensive discussion of the cost of capital, see Chapter 15.

VALUING THE ENTERPRISE AND CONVERTING TO EQUITY

To value Costco, we use both enterprise DCF and discounted economic profit. Free cash flow (FCF) models measure how cash flows in and out of the company, regardless of accounting. Economic profit links better to value creation. Implemented correctly, both models will lead to the same valuation result.

Exhibit H.16: Enterprise DCF Valuation. To arrive at the present value of cash flow, we sum each year's discounted FCF with the discounted value of continuing value. Then we adjust the resulting value by half a year to estimate the value of operations, reflecting that cash flows are generated throughout the year. To the value of operations, we add any nonoperating assets that are excluded from free cash flow—in this case, excess cash and the value of tax loss carryforwards. For simplicity, we value tax loss carryforwards at book value less the valuation allowance.

Do not add other deferred-tax assets, such as those related to equity compensation or deferred membership fees, to the value of operations. The value of these tax assets is already incorporated into NOPAT using cash-based taxes. Consequently, they are classified as an equity equivalent and ignored.

To estimate intrinsic equity value, subtract debt and debt equivalents from enterprise value. This includes all debt, capitalized operating leases, and noncontrolling interests. While we use the book values for ease of exposition, use the market value of each account when available. Dividing equity value by the number of shares leads to a value of almost $220 per share, which matches the share price in early 2019. For more on converting enterprise value into equity value by adding nonoperating assets and subtracting debt equivalents, see Chapter 16.

Exhibit H.17: ROIC and Economic Profit. A robust valuation will focus not only on the resulting share price, but also on the critical value drivers that result from the model. Exhibit H.17 presents ROIC and economic profit by year. When benchmarking across companies or over time, we usually calculate ROIC using a two-year average of invested capital. In this situation, we calculate ROIC using invested capital from the beginning of the year, in order to create an economic-profit valuation that matches the results from enterprise DCF. In this exhibit, we present only a high-level analysis of performance. For more on how to disaggregate and assess ROIC in depth, see Chapter 12.

Exhibit H.18: Valuation Using Economic Profit. To determine the value of operations, add discounted economic profit to invested capital. As expected, an economic-profit-based valuation leads to the same value of operations as an enterprise DCF valuation.

PUTTING THE MODEL TO WORK

While the valuation model is complete, a good financial analyst or investor will now put it to work. Ask yourself several questions: Which variables are the most critical to value? What is the value if performance remains unchanged? How does this value differ from one based on other forecasts? What is the value with proposed improvements? Are there scenarios that may provide additional insights on various strategies?

A model is more than its resulting valuation. As we discuss in Chapter 17, the most important insights are the ones you develop by testing alternatives and creating scenarios.

EXHIBIT H.1 **Costco: Income Statement**

$ million

| | Historical | | | | | Forecast | | | | | | | | | | |
	2015	2016	2017	2018	2019	2020	2021	2022	2023	2024	2025	2026	2027	2028	2029	CV[2]
Merchandise sales	113,666	116,073	126,172	138,434	149,351	163,570	174,630	185,926	197,112	208,140	218,970	229,565	239,896	249,937	259,934	270,331
Membership fees	2,533	2,646	2,853	3,142	3,352	3,671	3,919	4,173	4,424	4,671	4,915	5,152	5,384	5,610	5,834	6,067
Revenues	116,199	118,719	129,025	141,576	152,703	167,241	178,549	190,099	201,536	212,811	223,884	234,718	245,281	255,546	265,768	276,399
Merchandise costs	(101,065)	(102,901)	(111,882)	(123,152)	(132,886)	(145,370)	(155,021)	(164,859)	(174,777)	(184,555)	(194,158)	(203,553)	(212,713)	(221,616)	(230,481)	(239,700)
Selling and general	(10,318)	(10,813)	(11,580)	(12,439)	(13,502)	(14,787)	(15,787)	(16,809)	(17,820)	(18,817)	(19,796)	(20,754)	(21,688)	(22,595)	(23,499)	(24,439)
Depreciation[1]	(1,127)	(1,255)	(1,370)	(1,437)	(1,492)	(1,584)	(1,734)	(1,852)	(1,971)	(2,090)	(2,207)	(2,322)	(2,434)	(2,544)	(2,650)	(2,756)
Preopening expenses	(65)	(78)	(82)	(68)	(86)	(94)	(101)	(107)	(114)	(120)	(126)	(132)	(138)	(144)	(150)	(156)
Operating income	3,624	3,672	4,111	4,480	4,737	5,406	5,906	6,473	6,854	7,229	7,597	7,957	8,307	8,647	8,988	9,348
Interest expense	(124)	(133)	(134)	(159)	(150)	(277)	(302)	(315)	(327)	(340)	(354)	(368)	(382)	(397)	(413)	(429)
Interest income	50	41	50	75	126	64	51	38	26	13	—	—	—	—	—	—
Other income	54	39	12	46	52	—	—	—	—	—	—	—	—	—	—	—
Earnings before taxes	3,604	3,619	4,039	4,442	4,765	5,192	5,655	6,197	6,552	6,902	7,244	7,589	7,925	8,250	8,575	8,918
Provision for income taxes	(1,195)	(1,243)	(1,325)	(1,263)	(1,061)	(1,255)	(1,369)	(1,503)	(1,590)	(1,676)	(1,760)	(1,845)	(1,928)	(2,008)	(2,088)	(2,172)
Net income, consolidated	2,409	2,376	2,714	3,179	3,704	3,937	4,286	4,694	4,962	5,226	5,484	5,744	5,997	6,242	6,488	6,746
Noncontrolling interests	(32)	(26)	(35)	(45)	(45)	(49)	(53)	(56)	(59)	(63)	(66)	(69)	(72)	(75)	(78)	(81)
Net income, Costco	2,377	2,350	2,679	3,134	3,659	3,888	4,233	4,638	4,903	5,163	5,418	5,675	5,925	6,167	6,409	6,665

[1] Aggregated in selling, general, and administrative expenses in original filings.
[2] Continuing-value forecast.

EXHIBIT H.2 **Costco: Balance Sheet**

$ million

	Historical					Forecast									
	2015	2016	2017	2018	2019	2020	2021	2022	2023	2024	2025	2026	2027	2028	2029
Assets															
Cash and cash equivalents[1]	6,419	4,729	5,779	7,259	9,444	8,457	7,405	6,358	5,309	4,256	4,478	4,694	4,906	5,111	5,315
Receivables, net	1,224	1,252	1,432	1,669	1,535	1,681	1,795	1,911	2,026	2,139	2,251	2,359	2,466	2,569	2,672
Merchandise inventories	8,908	8,969	9,834	11,040	11,395	12,466	13,293	14,137	14,987	15,826	16,649	17,455	18,240	19,004	19,764
Deferred income taxes[2]	521	–	–	–	–	–	–	–	–	–	–	–	–	–	–
Other current assets	227	268	272	321	1,111	1,217	1,299	1,383	1,466	1,548	1,629	1,708	1,785	1,859	1,934
Total current assets	17,299	15,218	17,317	20,289	23,485	23,820	23,792	23,789	23,788	23,769	25,006	26,216	27,396	28,543	29,684
Property, plant, and equipment	15,401	17,043	18,161	19,681	20,890	22,879	24,426	26,006	27,570	29,113	30,628	32,110	33,555	34,959	36,357
Deferred income taxes[2]	109	202	254	316	398	513	640	797	868	1,002	1,241	1,410	1,587	1,770	1,956
Other assets	631	700	615	544	627	687	733	781	828	874	919	964	1,007	1,049	1,091
Total assets	33,440	33,163	36,347	40,830	45,400	47,899	49,591	51,372	53,053	54,758	57,794	60,700	63,544	66,321	69,089
Liabilities and shareholders' equity															
Accounts payable	9,011	7,612	9,608	11,237	11,679	12,776	13,624	14,489	15,361	16,220	17,064	17,890	18,695	19,477	20,256
Accrued salaries and benefits	2,468	2,629	2,703	2,994	3,176	3,478	3,714	3,954	4,192	4,426	4,656	4,882	5,101	5,315	5,528
Accrued member rewards	813	869	961	1,057	1,180	1,292	1,380	1,469	1,557	1,644	1,730	1,814	1,895	1,975	2,054
Deferred membership fees	1,269	1,362	1,498	1,624	1,711	1,874	2,001	2,130	2,258	2,384	2,509	2,630	2,748	2,863	2,978
Current portion of long-term debt	1,283	1,100	86	90	1,699	1,038	1,082	1,028	953	1,137	1,357	1,256	1,296	1,335	1,395
Current portion of capital leases[3]	10	10	7	7	26	14	15	16	18	20	19	20	21	22	23
Other current liabilities	1,686	1,993	2,632	2,917	3,766	4,125	4,403	4,688	4,970	5,248	5,521	5,789	6,049	6,302	6,554
Total current liabilities	16,540	15,575	17,495	19,926	23,237	24,597	26,218	27,774	29,309	31,081	32,857	34,279	35,805	37,290	38,788
Long-term debt	4,864	4,061	6,573	6,487	5,124	6,408	6,661	7,038	7,430	7,576	7,697	8,154	8,488	8,837	9,185
Capital leases[3]	286	364	373	390	395	432	467	470	493	511	532	555	574	598	622
Deferred income taxes[2]	462	297	312	317	543	700	873	1,087	1,184	1,367	1,693	1,924	2,165	2,415	2,669
Other liabilities	445	534	515	607	517	566	605	644	682	721	758	795	830	865	900
Total liabilities	22,597	20,831	25,268	27,727	29,816	32,704	34,824	37,013	39,098	41,256	43,537	45,706	47,863	50,005	52,163
Costco shareholders' equity	10,617	12,079	10,778	12,799	15,243	14,854	14,425	14,018	13,615	13,161	13,916	14,652	15,340	15,975	16,585
Noncontrolling interests	226	253	301	304	341	341	341	341	341	341	341	341	341	341	341
Total shareholders' equity	10,843	12,332	11,079	13,103	15,584	15,195	14,766	14,359	13,956	13,502	14,257	14,993	15,681	16,316	16,926
Liabilities and shareholders' equity	33,440	33,163	36,347	40,830	45,400	47,899	49,591	51,372	53,053	54,758	57,794	60,700	63,544	66,321	69,089

[1] Includes short-term investments.

[2] Deferred taxes are aggregated in other current assets, other assets, and other liabilities in original filings.

[3] Capital leases are aggregated in other current liabilities and other liabilities in original filings.

EXHIBIT H.3 **Costco: Statement of Shareholders' Equity**

$ million

	Historical									Forecast					
	2015	2016	2017	2018	2019	2020	2021	2022	2023	2024	2025	2026	2027	2028	2029
Equity, beginning of year	12,303	10,617	12,079	10,778	12,799	15,243	14,854	14,425	14,018	13,615	13,161	13,916	14,652	15,340	15,975
Net income	2,377	2,350	2,679	3,134	3,659	3,888	4,233	4,638	4,903	5,163	5,418	5,675	5,925	6,167	6,409
Foreign-currency translation adjustment	(1,045)	22	85	(185)	(237)	—	—	—	—	—	—	—	—	—	—
Comprehensive income	1,332	2,372	2,764	2,949	3,422	3,888	4,233	4,638	4,903	5,163	5,418	5,675	5,925	6,167	6,409
Stock-based compensation	394	459	518	547	598	655	699	744	789	833	877	919	961	1,001	1,041
Stock options exercised	69	—	—	—	—	—	—	—	—	—	—	—	—	—	—
Release of vested restricted stock units	(122)	(146)	(165)	(217)	(272)	(298)	(318)	(339)	(359)	(379)	(399)	(418)	(437)	(455)	(473)
Repurchases of common stock	(494)	(477)	(473)	(322)	(247)	(2,128)	(2,315)	(2,463)	(2,577)	(2,744)	(1,649)	(1,782)	(1,942)	(2,104)	(2,236)
Cash dividends declared	(2,865)	(746)	(3,945)	(936)	(1,057)	(2,505)	(2,728)	(2,989)	(3,160)	(3,327)	(3,491)	(3,657)	(3,818)	(3,974)	(4,130)
Equity, end of year	10,617	12,079	10,778	12,799	15,243	14,854	14,425	14,018	13,615	13,161	13,916	14,652	15,340	15,975	16,585

EXHIBIT H.4 **Costco: Tax Reconciliation Table**

$ million

	2015	2016	2017	2018	2019
Federal taxes at statutory rate	1,262	1,267	1,414	1,136	1,001
State taxes, net	85	91	116	154	171
Foreign taxes, net	(125)	(21)	(64)	32	(1)
Employee stock ownership plan (ESOP)	(66)	(17)	(104)	(14)	(18)
2017 Tax Act	—	—	—	19	(123)
Other	39	(77)	(37)	(64)	31
U.S. and foreign tax expense (benefit)	1,195	1,243	1,325	1,263	1,061
Tax rates[1]					
Federal income tax rate, %	35.0	35.0	35.0	25.6	21.0
State income tax rate, %	2.4	2.5	2.9	3.5	3.6
Statutory tax rate, %	37.4	37.5	37.9	29.0	24.6

[1] To determine each tax rate, divide each tax amount by earnings before taxes. Earnings before taxes are reported in Exhibit H.1.

Source: Reported in Costco's annual report, note 8: Income Taxes.

EXHIBIT H.5 **Costco: NOPAT and Its Reconciliation to Net Income**

$ million

	Historical					Forecast										CV
	2015	2016	2017	2018	2019	2020	2021	2022	2023	2024	2025	2026	2027	2028	2029	
Revenues	116,199	118,719	129,025	141,576	152,703	167,241	178,549	190,099	201,536	212,811	223,884	234,718	245,281	255,546	265,768	276,399
Merchandise costs	(101,065)	(102,901)	(111,882)	(123,152)	(132,886)	(145,370)	(155,021)	(164,859)	(174,777)	(184,555)	(194,158)	(203,553)	(212,713)	(221,616)	(230,481)	(239,700)
Selling and general	(10,318)	(10,813)	(11,580)	(12,439)	(13,502)	(14,787)	(15,787)	(16,809)	(17,820)	(18,817)	(19,796)	(20,754)	(21,688)	(22,595)	(23,499)	(24,439)
Depreciation	(1,127)	(1,255)	(1,370)	(1,437)	(1,492)	(1,584)	(1,734)	(1,852)	(1,971)	(2,090)	(2,207)	(2,322)	(2,434)	(2,544)	(2,650)	(2,756)
Preopening expenses	(65)	(78)	(82)	(68)	(86)	(94)	(101)	(107)	(114)	(120)	(126)	(132)	(138)	(144)	(150)	(156)
EBITA, unadjusted[1]	3,624	3,672	4,111	4,480	4,737	5,406	5,906	6,473	6,854	7,229	7,597	7,957	8,307	8,647	8,988	9,348
Operating lease interest[2]	73	75	57	74	91	88	96	103	109	116	122	129	135	141	147	153
EBITA, adjusted	3,697	3,747	4,168	4,554	4,828	5,493	6,002	6,576	6,963	7,345	7,719	8,085	8,442	8,788	9,135	9,500
Operating cash taxes[3]	(1,184)	(1,149)	(1,493)	(1,455)	(1,009)	(1,287)	(1,409)	(1,538)	(1,665)	(1,736)	(1,790)	(1,905)	(1,990)	(2,073)	(2,157)	(2,239)
NOPAT	2,513	2,598	2,675	3,098	3,818	4,206	4,593	5,037	5,298	5,609	5,929	6,180	6,451	6,715	6,978	7,262
Reconciliation to net income																
Net income, consolidated	2,409	2,376	2,714	3,179	3,704	3,937	4,286	4,694	4,962	5,226	5,484	5,744	5,997	6,242	6,488	6,746
Operating taxes deferred[3]	7	219	(82)	(115)	159	42	46	57	26	49	87	62	64	67	68	76
Adjusted net income	2,416	2,595	2,632	3,064	3,863	3,979	4,332	4,751	4,988	5,275	5,570	5,806	6,062	6,309	6,556	6,823
Interest expense	124	133	134	159	150	277	302	315	327	340	354	368	382	397	413	429
Operating lease interest[2]	73	75	57	74	91	88	96	103	109	116	122	129	135	141	147	153
Interest income	(50)	(41)	(50)	(75)	(126)	(64)	(51)	(38)	(26)	(13)	—	—	—	—	—	—
Other income[4]	(54)	(39)	(12)	(46)	(52)	—	—	—	—	—	—	—	—	—	—	—
Taxes related to nonoperating accounts[5]	(35)	(48)	(49)	(32)	(15)	(74)	(85)	(93)	(101)	(109)	(117)	(122)	(127)	(132)	(138)	(143)
Other nonoperating taxes[3]	39	(77)	(37)	(45)	(92)	—	0	0	(0)	(0)	(0)	(0)	—	—	—	—
NOPAT	2,513	2,598	2,675	3,098	3,818	4,206	4,593	5,037	5,298	5,609	5,929	6,180	6,451	6,715	6,978	7,262

[1] Earnings before interest, taxes, and amortization.
[2] Estimated by multiplying beginning-of-year capitalized operating leases by the interest rate on 10-year AA-rated debt. Capitalized operating leases are reported in Exhibit H.8. Interest rates are reported in Exhibit H.10.
[3] Operating cash taxes and other nonoperating taxes are detailed in Exhibit H.6.
[4] Other income consists primarily of foreign-currency transaction gains and is treated as nonoperating for simplicity of exposition.
[5] Estimated by multiplying the statutory tax rate by the sum of interest and operating lease interest expense, less the sum of interest and other income. The statutory tax rate is reported in Exhibit H.6.

EXHIBIT H.6 **Costco: Taxes**

$ million

	Historical					Forecast										
	2015	2016	2017	2018	2019	2020	2021	2022	2023	2024	2025	2026	2027	2028	2029	CV
EBITA	3,697	3,747	4,168	4,554	4,828	5,493	6,002	6,576	6,963	7,345	7,719	8,085	8,442	8,788	9,135	9,500
× Statutory tax rate[1]	37.4%	37.5%	37.9%	29.0%	24.6%	24.6%	24.6%	24.6%	24.6%	24.6%	24.6%	24.6%	24.6%	24.6%	24.6%	24.6%
Statutory taxes on EBITA	1,382	1,406	1,579	1,322	1,187	1,351	1,476	1,617	1,713	1,807	1,899	1,989	2,076	2,161	2,247	2,337
Foreign taxes, net[2]	(125)	(21)	(64)	32	(1)	(1)	(1)	(1)	(1)	(1)	(1)	(1)	(1)	(1)	(1)	(1)
Employee stock ownership plan (ESOP)[2]	(66)	(17)	(104)	(14)	(18)	(20)	(20)	(20)	(20)	(20)	(20)	(20)	(20)	(20)	(20)	(20)
Operating taxes	1,191	1,368	1,411	1,340	1,168	1,330	1,455	1,596	1,691	1,785	1,877	1,967	2,055	2,140	2,225	2,315
Operating taxes deferred[3]	(7)	(219)	82	115	(159)	(42)	(46)	(57)	(26)	(49)	(87)	(62)	(64)	(67)	(68)	(76)
Operating cash taxes	1,184	1,149	1,493	1,455	1,009	1,287	1,409	1,538	1,665	1,736	1,790	1,905	1,990	2,073	2,157	2,239
Tax rates, % of EBITA																
Statutory tax rate[1]	37.4	37.5	37.9	29.0	24.6	24.6	24.6	24.6	24.6	24.6	24.6	24.6	24.6	24.6	24.6	24.6
Other operating taxes	(5.2)	(1.0)	(4.0)	0.4	(0.4)	(0.4)	(0.4)	(0.4)	(0.4)	(0.4)	(0.4)	(0.4)	(0.4)	(0.4)	(0.4)	(0.4)
Operating tax rate	32.2	36.5	33.8	29.4	24.2	24.2	24.2	24.2	24.2	24.2	24.2	24.2	24.2	24.2	24.2	24.2
% deferred	0.6	16.0	(5.8)	(8.6)	13.6	3.2	3.2	3.6	1.5	2.7	4.6	3.1	3.1	3.1	3.0	3.3
Operating cash tax rate[4]	32.0	30.7	35.8	32.0	20.9	23.4	23.5	23.4	23.9	23.6	23.2	23.6	23.6	23.6	23.6	23.6

[1] Estimated by dividing federal plus state income taxes by earnings before taxes.
[2] Reported in the tax reconciliation table presented in Exhibit H.4.
[3] Computed as the decrease (increase) in operating deferred taxes, as reported in Exhibit H.9.
[4] The operating cash tax rate equals the operating tax rate times one minus the percent of operating taxes deferred.

EXHIBIT H.7 **Costco: Reorganized Deferred Taxes**

$ million

	As reported			Reorganized		
	2017	2018	2019	2017	2018	2019
Deferred-tax assets						
Equity compensation	109	72	74			
Deferred income/membership fees	167	136	180			
Foreign tax credit carryforward	—	—	65			
Accrued liabilities and reserves	647	484	566			
Other	18	—	—			
Total deferred-tax assets	941	692	885			
Valuation allowance	—	—	(76)			
Total net deferred-tax assets	941	692	809			
Deferred-tax liabilities						
Property and equipment	(747)	(478)	(677)			
Merchandise inventories	(252)	(175)	(187)			
Foreign-branch deferreds	—	—	(69)			
Other	—	(40)	(21)			
Total deferred-tax liabilities	(999)	(693)	(954)			
Operating deferred-tax assets, net of liabilities						
Equity compensation				109	72	74
Deferred income/membership fees				167	136	180
Accrued liabilities and reserves				647	484	566
Property and equipment				(747)	(478)	(677)
Merchandise inventories				(252)	(175)	(187)
Valuation allowance				(76)	—	(76)
Operating deferred-tax assets, net of liabilities				(76)	39	(120)
Nonoperating deferred-tax assets, net of liabilities						
Other assets				18	—	—
Foreign-branch deferreds				—	—	(69)
Other liabilities				—	(40)	(21)
Nonoperating deferred-tax assets, net of liabilities				18	(40)	(90)
Tax loss carryforwards						
Foreign tax credit carryforward				—	—	65
Deferred-tax assets, net of liabilities	(58)	(1)	(145)	(58)	(1)	(145)

EXHIBIT H.8 **Costco: Invested Capital and Total Funds Invested**

$ million

	Historical					Forecast									
	2015	2016	2017	2018	2019	2020	2021	2022	2023	2024	2025	2026	2027	2028	2029
Operating cash[1]	2,324	2,374	2,581	2,832	3,054	3,345	3,571	3,802	4,031	4,256	4,478	4,694	4,906	5,111	5,315
Receivables, net	1,224	1,252	1,432	1,669	1,535	1,681	1,795	1,911	2,026	2,139	2,251	2,359	2,466	2,569	2,672
Merchandise inventories	8,908	8,969	9,834	11,040	11,395	12,466	13,293	14,137	14,987	15,826	16,649	17,455	18,240	19,004	19,764
Other current assets	227	268	272	321	1,111	1,217	1,299	1,383	1,466	1,548	1,629	1,708	1,785	1,859	1,934
Operating current assets	12,683	12,863	14,119	15,862	17,095	18,708	19,958	21,233	22,510	23,769	25,006	26,216	27,396	28,543	29,684
Accounts payable	(9,011)	(7,612)	(9,608)	(11,237)	(11,679)	(12,776)	(13,624)	(14,489)	(15,361)	(16,220)	(17,064)	(17,890)	(18,695)	(19,477)	(20,256)
Accrued salaries and benefits	(2,468)	(2,629)	(2,703)	(2,994)	(3,176)	(3,478)	(3,714)	(3,954)	(4,192)	(4,426)	(4,656)	(4,882)	(5,101)	(5,315)	(5,528)
Accrued member rewards	(813)	(869)	(961)	(1,057)	(1,180)	(1,292)	(1,380)	(1,469)	(1,557)	(1,644)	(1,730)	(1,814)	(1,895)	(1,975)	(2,054)
Deferred membership fees	(1,269)	(1,362)	(1,498)	(1,624)	(1,711)	(1,874)	(2,001)	(2,130)	(2,258)	(2,384)	(2,509)	(2,630)	(2,748)	(2,863)	(2,978)
Other current liabilities	(1,686)	(1,993)	(2,632)	(2,917)	(3,766)	(4,125)	(4,403)	(4,688)	(4,970)	(5,248)	(5,521)	(5,789)	(6,049)	(6,302)	(6,554)
Operating current liabilities	(15,247)	(14,465)	(17,402)	(19,829)	(21,512)	(23,545)	(25,122)	(26,730)	(28,338)	(29,924)	(31,481)	(33,004)	(34,489)	(35,933)	(37,370)
Operating working capital	(2,564)	(1,602)	(3,284)	(3,967)	(4,417)	(4,837)	(5,164)	(5,497)	(5,828)	(6,154)	(6,474)	(6,788)	(7,093)	(7,390)	(7,686)
Property, plant, and equipment	15,401	17,043	18,161	19,681	20,890	22,879	24,426	26,006	27,570	29,113	30,628	32,110	33,555	34,959	36,357
Capitalized operating leases[2]	2,230	2,320	2,528	2,500	2,414	2,644	2,823	3,005	3,186	3,364	3,539	3,711	3,878	4,040	4,202
Other assets[3]	631	700	615	544	627	687	733	781	828	874	919	964	1,007	1,049	1,091
Other liabilities[3]	(445)	(534)	(515)	(607)	(517)	(566)	(605)	(644)	(682)	(721)	(758)	(795)	(830)	(865)	(900)
Invested capital	15,253	17,928	17,506	18,151	18,997	20,806	22,213	23,651	25,073	26,476	27,854	29,202	30,516	31,793	33,065
Excess cash[1]	4,095	2,355	3,199	4,427	6,390	5,112	3,834	2,556	1,278	—	—	—	—	—	—
Foreign tax credit carryforward[4]	—	—	—	—	65	65	65	65	65	65	65	65	65	65	65
Total funds invested	19,348	20,282	20,704	22,578	25,452	25,983	26,112	26,272	26,416	26,541	27,919	29,267	30,581	31,858	33,130

[1] Operating cash is estimated at 2% of revenues. Remaining cash is treated as excess cash.
[2] Capitalized operating leases are estimated for 2019 in Exhibit 22.10.
[3] Other assets and liabilities are classified as operating because no description is provided by the company.
[4] Foreign tax credit carryforward is reported in Exhibit H.7.

EXHIBIT H.9 **Costco: Reconciliation of Total Funds Invested**

$ million

	Historical					Forecast									
	2015	2016	2017	2018	2019	2020	2021	2022	2023	2024	2025	2026	2027	2028	2029
Long-term debt and capital leases[1]	6,443	5,535	7,039	6,974	7,244	7,892	8,225	8,552	8,894	9,245	9,606	9,984	10,379	10,792	11,224
Capitalized operating leases[2]	2,230	2,320	2,528	2,500	2,414	2,644	2,823	3,005	3,186	3,364	3,539	3,711	3,878	4,040	4,202
Debt and debt equivalents	8,673	7,855	9,567	9,474	9,658	10,536	11,048	11,558	12,080	12,609	13,145	13,695	14,257	14,832	15,426
Deferred income taxes, operating[3]	(61)	158	76	(39)	120	162	208	265	291	340	427	489	553	620	688
Deferred income taxes, nonoperating[3]	(107)	(63)	(18)	40	90	90	90	90	90	90	90	90	90	90	90
Noncontrolling interests	226	253	301	304	341	341	341	341	341	341	341	341	341	341	341
Costco shareholders' equity	10,617	12,079	10,778	12,799	15,243	14,854	14,425	14,018	13,615	13,161	13,916	14,652	15,340	15,975	16,585
Equity and equity equivalents	10,675	12,427	11,137	13,104	15,794	15,447	15,065	14,714	14,337	13,932	14,774	15,572	16,324	17,026	17,704
Total funds invested	19,348	20,282	20,704	22,578	25,452	25,983	26,112	26,272	26,416	26,541	27,919	29,267	30,581	31,858	33,130

[1] Including current portion.

[2] Capitalized operating leases are estimated for 2019 in Exhibit 22.10.

[3] Deferred-tax liabilities, net of assets. Deferred taxes are detailed in Exhibit H.7.

%

EXHIBIT H.10 **Costco: Income Statement Forecast Ratios**

	Historical					Forecast										CV	Forecast ratio
	2015	2016	2017	2018	2019	2020	2021	2022	2023	2024	2025	2026	2027	2028	2029		
Revenue growth	3.2	2.2	8.7	9.7	7.9	9.5	6.8	6.5	6.0	5.6	5.2	4.8	4.5	4.2	4.0	4.0	% of prior-year revenues
Revenue split																	
Merchandise sales	97.8	97.8	97.8	97.8	97.8	97.8	97.8	97.8	97.8	97.8	97.8	97.8	97.8	97.8	97.8	97.8	% of revenues
Membership fees	2.2	2.2	2.2	2.2	2.2	2.2	2.2	2.2	2.2	2.2	2.2	2.2	2.2	2.2	2.2	2.2	% of revenues
Revenues	100.0	100.0	100.0	100.0	100.0	100.0	100.0	100.0	100.0	100.0	100.0	100.0	100.0	100.0	100.0	100.0	
Operating expenses																	
Merchandise costs[1]	87.0	86.7	86.7	87.0	87.0	86.9	86.8	86.7	86.7	86.7	86.7	86.7	86.7	86.7	86.7	86.7	% of revenues
Selling, general, and administrative	8.9	9.1	9.0	8.8	8.8	8.8	8.8	8.8	8.8	8.8	8.8	8.8	8.8	8.8	8.8	8.8	% of revenues
Depreciation	7.6	8.1	8.0	7.9	7.6	7.6	7.6	7.6	7.6	7.6	7.6	7.6	7.6	7.6	7.6	7.6	% of net PP&E
Preopening expenses	<0.1	<0.1	<0.1	<0.1	<0.1	<0.1	<0.1	<0.1	<0.1	<0.1	<0.1	<0.1	<0.1	<0.1	<0.1	<0.1	% of revenues
Nonoperating items																	
Interest rate on debt[2]	3.5	3.6	2.6	3.1	3.8	3.8	3.8	3.8	3.8	3.8	3.8	3.8	3.8	3.8	3.8	3.8	% of total debt
Interest rate on leases	3.2	3.4	2.4	2.9	3.6	3.6	3.6	3.6	3.6	3.6	3.6	3.6	3.6	3.6	3.6	3.6	% of leases
Interest rate on excess cash	1.0	1.0	2.1	2.3	2.8	1.0	1.0	1.0	1.0	1.0	1.0	1.0	1.0	1.0	1.0	1.0	% of excess cash
Other income[3]	<0.1	<0.1	<0.1	<0.1	<0.1	—	—	—	—	—	—	—	—	—	—	—	% of revenues

[1] Estimated as a percentage of total revenues to better understand components of operating margin. To compare with companies that do not charge for membership, exclude fees.

[2] Interest expense forecast based on 10-year A-rated debt. The cost of debt is used to estimate cost of capital is based on the average long-run real rate plus expected inflation. For more on the cost of capital, see Chapter 15.

[3] Other income consists primarily of foreign-currency transaction gains and set to 0 in forecast.

EXHIBIT H.11 **Costco: Balance Sheet Forecast Ratios**

Working capital in days; all other accounts in %

	Historical					Forecast										Forecast Ratio
	2015	2016	2017	2018	2019	2020	2021	2022	2023	2024	2025	2026	2027	2028	2029	
Working capital																
Operating cash	20.2	14.5	16.3	18.7	22.6	7.3	7.3	7.3	7.3	7.3	7.3	7.3	7.3	7.3	7.3	Days in revenues
Receivables, net	3.8	3.8	4.1	4.3	3.7	3.7	3.7	3.7	3.7	3.7	3.7	3.7	3.7	3.7	3.7	Days in merchandise cost
Merchandise inventories	32.2	31.8	32.1	32.7	31.3	31.3	31.3	31.3	31.3	31.3	31.3	31.3	31.3	31.3	31.3	Days in revenues
Other current assets	0.7	0.8	0.8	0.8	2.7	2.7	2.7	2.7	2.7	2.7	2.7	2.7	2.7	2.7	2.7	Days in revenues
Accounts payable	32.5	27.0	31.3	33.3	32.1	32.1	32.1	32.1	32.1	32.1	32.1	32.1	32.1	32.1	32.1	Days in merchandise cost
Accrued salaries and benefits	7.8	8.1	7.6	7.7	7.6	7.6	7.6	7.6	7.6	7.6	7.6	7.6	7.6	7.6	7.6	Days in revenues
Accrued member rewards	2.6	2.7	2.7	2.7	2.8	2.8	2.8	2.8	2.8	2.8	2.8	2.8	2.8	2.8	2.8	Days in revenues
Deferred membership fees	4.0	4.2	4.2	4.2	4.1	4.1	4.1	4.1	4.1	4.1	4.1	4.1	4.1	4.1	4.1	Days in revenues
Other current liabilities	5.3	6.1	7.4	7.5	9.0	9.0	9.0	9.0	9.0	9.0	9.0	9.0	9.0	9.0	9.0	Days in revenues
Long-term assets and liabilities																
Property, plant, and equipment	13.3	14.4	14.1	13.9	13.7	13.7	13.7	13.7	13.7	13.7	13.7	13.7	13.7	13.7	13.7	% of revenues
Capitalized operating leases	1.9	2.0	2.0	1.8	1.6	1.6	1.6	1.6	1.6	1.6	1.6	1.6	1.6	1.6	1.6	% of revenues
Other assets	0.5	0.6	0.5	0.4	0.4	0.4	0.4	0.4	0.4	0.4	0.4	0.4	0.4	0.4	0.4	% of revenues
Other liabilities	0.4	0.4	0.4	0.4	0.3	0.3	0.3	0.3	0.3	0.3	0.3	0.3	0.3	0.3	0.3	% of revenues
Debt and capital leases[1]																
Current portion of long-term debt	19.9	19.9	1.2	1.3	23.5	13.2	13.2	12.0	10.7	12.3	14.1	12.6	12.5	12.4	12.4	% of total debt
Current portion of capital leases	0.2	0.2	0.1	0.1	0.4	0.2	0.2	0.2	0.2	0.2	0.2	0.2	0.2	0.2	0.2	% of total debt
Long-term debt	75.5	73.4	93.4	93.0	70.7	81.2	81.0	82.3	83.5	82.0	80.1	81.7	81.8	81.9	81.8	% of total debt
Capital leases	4.4	6.6	5.3	5.6	5.5	5.5	5.7	5.5	5.5	5.5	5.5	5.6	5.5	5.5	5.5	% of total debt
Debt and capital leases	100.0	100.0	100.0	100.0	100.0	100.0	100.0	100.0	100.0	100.0	100.0	100.0	100.0	100.0	100.0	
Equity accounts[2]																
Stock-based compensation	0.3	0.4	0.4	0.4	0.4	0.4	0.4	0.4	0.4	0.4	0.4	0.4	0.4	0.4	0.4	% of revenues
Stock options exercised	0.1	—	—	—	—	—	—	—	—	—	—	—	—	—	—	% of revenues
Release of vested restricted stock units	0.1	0.1	0.1	0.2	0.2	0.2	0.2	0.2	0.2	0.2	0.2	0.2	0.2	0.2	0.2	% of revenues
Dividends	120.5	31.7	147.3	29.9	28.9	64.4	64.4	64.4	64.4	64.4	64.4	64.4	64.4	64.4	64.4	% of net income

[1] The sum of debt and debt equivalents, inclusive of leases, is forecast as a fixed percentage of projected enterprise value, using a target debt-to-value ratio. Total debt is split between debt and capital leases and between current and long-term, based on a 5-year historical average.

[2] Excess cash is paid out over 5 years. Remaining cash flow is used to repurchase shares.

852

EXHIBIT H.12 **Costco: Free Cash Flow and Cash Flow to Investors**

$ million

	Historical				Forecast									
	2016	2017	2018	2019	2020	2021	2022	2023	2024	2025	2026	2027	2028	2029
NOPAT	2,598	2,675	3,098	3,818	4,206	4,593	5,037	5,298	5,609	5,929	6,180	6,451	6,715	6,978
Depreciation	1,255	1,370	1,437	1,492	1,584	1,734	1,852	1,971	2,090	2,207	2,322	2,434	2,544	2,650
Gross cash flow	3,853	4,045	4,535	5,310	5,790	6,328	6,889	7,269	7,699	8,136	8,502	8,886	9,259	9,628
Decrease (increase) in working capital	(962)	1,682	684	449	420	327	334	331	326	320	313	305	297	296
Less: Capital expenditures[1]	(2,649)	(2,502)	(2,969)	(2,998)	(3,573)	(3,281)	(3,432)	(3,536)	(3,633)	(3,722)	(3,804)	(3,879)	(3,948)	(4,049)
Decrease (increase) in capitalized operating leases	(91)	(208)	28	86	(230)	(179)	(183)	(181)	(178)	(175)	(171)	(167)	(162)	(162)
Decrease (increase) in other assets, net of liabilities	20	66	163	(173)	(10)	(8)	(8)	(8)	(8)	(8)	(8)	(8)	(7)	(7)
Free cash flow	**171**	**3,083**	**2,441**	**2,675**	**2,397**	**3,186**	**3,600**	**3,875**	**4,206**	**4,552**	**4,832**	**5,137**	**5,438**	**5,706**
Interest income	41	50	75	126	64	51	38	26	13	—	—	—	—	—
Other income	39	12	46	52	—	—	—	—	—	—	—	—	—	—
Taxes related to nonoperating accounts	48	49	32	15	74	85	93	101	109	117	122	127	132	138
Other nonoperating taxes	77	37	45	92	—	—	—	—	—	—	—	—	—	—
Decrease (increase) in excess cash	1,740	(844)	(1,229)	(1,962)	1,278	1,278	1,278	1,278	1,278	—	—	—	—	—
Decrease (Increase) in tax credit carryforward	0	—	—	(65)	—	—	—	—	—	—	—	—	—	—
Unexplained foreign-currency translation[2]	(226)	99	(173)	60	—	—	—	—	—	—	—	—	—	—
Cash flow to investors	1,890	2,486	1,238	993	3,813	4,601	5,009	5,280	5,606	4,669	4,954	5,264	5,570	5,844

[1] Capital expenditures are reported on the statement of cash flows.

[2] Foreign-currency translation adjustment, less the portion estimated in the change of property, plant, and equipment, detailed in Exhibit 11.14.

EXHIBIT H.13 **Costco: Reconciliation of Cash Flow to Investors**

$ million

	Historical				Forecast									
	2016	2017	2018	2019	2020	2021	2022	2023	2024	2025	2026	2027	2028	2029
Interest expense	133	134	159	150	277	302	315	327	340	354	368	382	397	413
Operating lease interest	75	57	74	91	88	96	103	109	116	122	129	135	141	147
Decrease (increase) in long-term debt	908	(1,504)	65	(270)	(648)	(333)	(327)	(341)	(351)	(361)	(378)	(395)	(413)	(432)
Decrease (increase) in capitalized operating leases	(91)	(208)	28	86	(230)	(179)	(183)	(181)	(178)	(175)	(171)	(167)	(162)	(162)
Cash flow to debt and debt equivalents	1,025	(1,521)	326	57	(513)	(114)	(93)	(86)	(73)	(60)	(54)	(45)	(38)	(34)
Nonoperating deferred income taxes	(44)	(45)	(58)	(50)	—	—	—	—	—	—	—	—	—	—
Shares issued for stock-based compensation, net[1]	(313)	(353)	(330)	(326)	(357)	(381)	(406)	(430)	(454)	(478)	(501)	(524)	(546)	(567)
Repurchases of common stock	477	473	322	247	2,128	2,315	2,463	2,577	2,744	1,649	1,782	1,942	2,104	2,236
Dividends	746	3,945	936	1,057	2,505	2,728	2,989	3,160	3,327	3,491	3,657	3,818	3,974	4,130
Payments to (investments in) noncontrolling interests[2]	(1)	(13)	42	8	49	53	56	59	63	66	69	72	75	78
Cash flow to equity and equity equivalents	865	4,007	912	936	4,326	4,715	5,102	5,365	5,679	4,729	5,008	5,309	5,608	5,878
Cash flow to investors	1,890	2,486	1,238	993	3,813	4,601	5,009	5,280	5,606	4,669	4,954	5,264	5,570	5,844

[1] Includes stock-based compensation, stock options exercised, net of the release of vested restricted stock units.
[2] Equals net income to nonconsolidated interests minus (plus) the increase (decrease) in noncontrolling interests.

EXHIBIT H.14 **Costco: Continuing Value**

$ million

Key inputs

Projected NOPAT in final forecast year	7,261.7
NOPAT growth rate in perpetuity (g)	4.0%
Return on new invested capital (RONIC)	22.0%
Weighted average cost of capital (WACC)	8.0%

$$\text{Continuing Value}_t = \frac{\text{NOPAT}_{t+1}\left(1-\dfrac{g}{\text{RONIC}}\right)}{\text{WACC}-g}$$

$$= 148{,}301.9$$

Note: Continuing value of $148,301.9 million is calculated from unrounded data. Rounded inputs calculate to $148,534.8 million.

EXHIBIT H.15 **Costco: Weighted Average Cost of Capital**

%

Source of capital	Target proportion of total capital	Cost of capital	Marginal tax rate	After-tax cost of capital	Contribution to weighted average
Debt	10.4	4.9	24.6	3.7	0.4
Equity	89.6	8.5		8.5	7.6
WACC	100.0				8.0

EXHIBIT H.16 **Costco: Enterprise DCF Valuation**

$ million, except where noted

Forecast year	Free cash flow (FCF)	Discount factor at 8.0%	Present value of FCF
2020	2,397	0.926	2,219
2021	3,186	0.857	2,731
2022	3,600	0.794	2,857
2023	3,875	0.735	2,848
2024	4,206	0.680	2,862
2025	4,552	0.630	2,868
2026	4,832	0.583	2,819
2027	5,137	0.540	2,775
2028	5,438	0.500	2,719
2029	5,706	0.463	2,642
Continuing value	148,302	0.463	68,662
Present value of cash flow			96,002
Midyear adjustment factor			1.039
Value of operations			99,770
Value of excess cash			6,390
Value of foreign tax credit carryforward			65
Enterprise value			106,225
Less: Value of debt and capital leases			(7,244)
Less: Value of capitalized operating leases			(2,414)
Less: Value of noncontrolling interests			(341)
Equity value			96,226
Shares outstanding, millions			440
Equity value			218.80

EXHIBIT H.17 **Costco: ROIC and Economic Profit**

$ million, except where noted

	Historical					Forecast										CV
	2015	2016	2017	2018	2019	2020	2021	2022	2023	2024	2025	2026	2027	2028	2029	
Method 1																
Return on invested capital,[1] %	16.8	17.0	14.9	17.7	21.0	22.1	22.1	22.7	22.4	22.4	22.4	22.2	22.1	22.0	21.9	22.0
Weighted average cost of capital, %	(6.5)	(6.3)	(5.5)	(6.4)	(7.0)	(8.0)	(8.0)	(8.0)	(8.0)	(8.0)	(8.0)	(8.0)	(8.0)	(8.0)	(8.0)	(8.0)
Economic spread, %	10.4	10.7	9.4	11.3	14.0	14.1	14.1	14.7	14.4	14.4	14.4	14.2	14.1	14.0	13.9	14.0
× Invested capital[1]	14,941	15,253	17,928	17,506	18,151	18,997	20,806	22,213	23,651	25,073	26,476	27,854	29,202	30,516	31,793	33,065
Economic profit	1,549	1,639	1,682	1,978	2,541	2,685	2,928	3,259	3,405	3,602	3,810	3,950	4,114	4,272	4,433	4,615
Method 2																
Invested capital[1]	14,941	15,253	17,928	17,506	18,151	18,997	20,806	22,213	23,651	25,073	26,476	27,854	29,202	30,516	31,793	33,065
× Weighted average cost of capital, %	6.5%	6.3%	5.5%	6.4%	7.0%	8.0%	8.0%	8.0%	8.0%	8.0%	8.0%	8.0%	8.0%	8.0%	8.0%	8.0%
Capital charge	964	959	993	1,120	1,277	1,521	1,665	1,778	1,893	2,007	2,119	2,230	2,338	2,443	2,545	2,647
NOPAT	2,513	2,598	2,675	3,098	3,818	4,206	4,593	5,037	5,298	5,609	5,929	6,180	6,451	6,715	6,978	7,262
Capital charge	(964)	(959)	(993)	(1,120)	(1,277)	(1,521)	(1,665)	(1,778)	(1,893)	(2,007)	(2,119)	(2,230)	(2,338)	(2,443)	(2,545)	(2,647)
Economic profit	1,549	1,639	1,682	1,978	2,541	2,685	2,928	3,259	3,405	3,602	3,810	3,950	4,114	4,272	4,433	4,615

[1] Invested capital measured at the beginning of the year.

EXHIBIT H.18 **Costco: Valuation Using Economic Profit**

$ million, except where noted

Forecast year	Invested capital[1]	ROIC,[1] %	WACC, %	Economic profit	Discount factor at 8.0%	Present value of economic profit
2020	18,997	22.1	8.0	2,685	0.926	2,486
2021	20,806	22.1	8.0	2,928	0.857	2,510
2022	22,213	22.7	8.0	3,259	0.794	2,587
2023	23,651	22.4	8.0	3,405	0.735	2,502
2024	25,073	22.4	8.0	3,602	0.680	2,451
2025	26,476	22.4	8.0	3,810	0.630	2,400
2026	27,854	22.2	8.0	3,950	0.583	2,304
2027	29,202	22.1	8.0	4,114	0.540	2,222
2028	30,516	22.0	8.0	4,272	0.500	2,136
2029	31,793	21.9	8.0	4,433	0.463	2,052
Continuing value				115,237	0.463	53,354
Present value of economic profit						77,005
Invested capital in 2019						18,997
Invested capital and economic profit						96,002
Midyear adjustment factor						1.039
Value of operations						99,770
Value of excess cash						6,390
Value of foreign tax credit carryforward						65
Enterprise value						106,225
Less: Value of debt and capital leases						(7,244)
Less: Value of capitalized operating leases						(2,414)
Less: Value of noncontrolling interests						(341)
Equity value						96,226

[1] Invested capital measured at the beginning of the year.

Two-Stage Formula for Continuing Value

In certain situations, you may want to break up the continuing-value (CV) period into two periods with different assumptions for growth and return on invested capital (ROIC). In a situation such as this, you can use a two-stage variation of the value driver formula for discounted cash flow (DCF) valuations. The first stage is based on a limited-life annuity formula, and the second stage is based on a perpetuity:

$$CV = \text{Annuity Stage} + \text{Perpetuity Stage}$$

such that

$$\text{Annuity Stage} = \left[\frac{\text{NOPAT}_{t+1}\left(1 - \dfrac{g_A}{\text{RONIC}_A}\right)}{\text{WACC} - g_A} \right]\left[1 - \left(\frac{1+g_A}{1+\text{WACC}}\right)^N\right]$$

$$\text{Perpetuity Stage} = \frac{1}{(1+\text{WACC})^N} \times \frac{\text{NOPAT}_{t+1}(1+g_A)^N\left(1 - \dfrac{g_B}{\text{RONIC}_B}\right)}{(\text{WACC} - g_B)}$$

where NOPAT = net operating profit after taxes
g_A = expected growth rate in the first stage of the CV period
RONIC_A = expected return on new invested capital during the first stage of the CV period
WACC = weighted average cost of capital
N = number of years in the first stage of the CV period
g_B = expected growth rate in the second stage of the CV period
RONIC_B = expected return on new invested capital during the second stage of the CV period

Note that g_A can take any value; it does not have to be less than the weighted average cost of capital. Conversely, g_B must be less than WACC for this perpetuity formula to be valid. Otherwise the formula goes to infinity, and the company eventually overtakes the world economy.

A two-stage variation can also be used for the economic-profit continuing-value formula:[1]

$$CV = \frac{\text{Economic Profit}_{t+1}}{\text{WACC}}$$

$$+ \left[\frac{\text{NOPAT}_{t+1} \left(\dfrac{g_A}{\text{RONIC}_A} \right) (\text{RONIC}_A - \text{WACC})}{\text{WACC}(\text{WACC} - g_A)} \right] \left[1 - \left(\frac{1 + g_A}{1 + \text{WACC}} \right)^N \right]$$

$$+ \frac{\text{NOPAT}(1 + g_A)^N \left(\dfrac{g_B}{\text{RONIC}_B} \right) (\text{RONIC}_B - \text{WACC})}{\text{WACC}(\text{WACC} - g_B)(1 + \text{WACC})^N}$$

These formulas assume that the return on the base level of capital remains constant. If you want to model a decline in ROIC for all capital, including the base level of capital, it is best to model this into the explicit forecast.

It is difficult to model changes in average ROIC with formulas, because the growth rate in revenues and NOPAT will not equal the growth rate in free cash flow (FCF), and there are multiple ways for the ROIC to decline. You could model declining ROIC by setting the growth rate for capital and reducing NOPAT over time (in which case NOPAT will grow much more slowly than capital). Or you could set the growth rate for NOPAT and adjust FCF each period (so FCF growth again will be slower than NOPAT growth). The dynamics of these relationships are complex, and we do not recommend embedding the dynamics in continuing-value formulas, especially if the key value drivers become less transparent.

---

[1] Thanks to Pieter de Wit and David Krieger for deriving this formula.

Index

Risk:
 cash flow risk, 63–66
 diversifiable vs. nondiversifiable, 774–777
 exposure level, 63–66
 hedging, 66–67
 price of, 57–59
Risk-free rate, 312–314, 700
Risk-neutral valuation, 771–772
Risk-weighted assets (RWA), 753–755
Robotic process automation (RBA), 91, 94
Rockwell Automation, 35
ROIC. *See* Return on invested capital (ROIC)
Roll-up strategies, 597–598
RONIC (return on new invested capital), 288, 289, 294, 298
Rossi, Stefano, 590
RSC, 46
Ruback, Richard, 199
Ryanair, 131

Sale-leaseback transactions, 48–49, 237
Sales productivity, 556
Sanofi Aventis, 536
Scalability of products/processes, 137–138
Scenario analysis, 60–61, 357, 362–366
Scenario DCF approach, 692–698, 709–710, 761
Scenario development, 719–720
Scenario weighting, 720
Scholes, Myron, 203
Securities and Exchange Commission, 69
Securitized receivables, 443
Sell-side analysts, 675
Sensitivity analysis, 357, 360–362
Service Corporation International, 597–598
Shareholder capitalism, 3, 9–11
Shareholder payouts, 651–658
Shareholder returns. *See* Total shareholder returns (TSR)
Shareholder value creation, 5–6

Share repurchases, 44–46, 233, 633, 635, 654–659
 EPS growth, 111
Shiller, Robert, 99
Short-termism, 6–9
Siemens, 217, 616–617, 625, 628
Simplified intermediate forecast, 260
Single-path DCF, 761
Social responsibility, 11–12
Sodexo, 12, 248–249, 251
Solvency, 820–821
Spin-offs, 626, 627–628
Split-offs, 626, 627
Stability bias, 576
Stafford, Erik, 589–590
Stakeholder interests, 11–14
Statement on the Purpose of a Corporation (Business Roundtable), 4, 12, 85
Staunton, Mike, 311, 312, 832
Stochastic simulation DCF, 761
Stock market, 99–126
 bubbles, 103 (*see also* Financial crises)
 cross-listings, 121–122
 diversification, 118–119
 earnings (*see* Earnings per share (EPS))
 fundamentals of, 100–109
 index membership impact on company, 120–121
 informed investors vs. noise investors, 100–101
 market mechanics, 120
 relationship of company size to value, 119–120
 stock splits, 123–124
 total returns to shareholders (*see* Total shareholder returns (TSR))
 understanding expectations, 80–81
Stock splits, 123–124
Stranded costs, 623–624
Strategic health, 558
Strategic management
 analytics, 547–569
  adopting granular perspective, 548–550
  monitoring results, 567–569